DICTIONARY OF
CLASSICAL
MYTHOLOGY

11/11/88

COLLINS
REFERENCE

DICTIONARY OF
CLASSICAL
MYTHOLOGY

EDWARD TRIPP

COLLINS
London and Glasgow

Published in hardback as *Crowell's Handbook of Classical Mythology* in
the United States of America by Harper and Row Publishers, Inc.,
and in Canada by Fitzhenry and Whiteside, Toronto.

Copyright © 1970 by Edward Tripp

This edition first published 1988 by Collins Publishers, London and
Glasgow

ISBN 0 00 434380 8

British Library Cataloguing in Publication Data
Tripp, Edward
  [Crowell's Handbook of classical mythology]
  Collins dictionary of classical mythology.
  1. Classical myths — Encyclopaedias
  I. [Crowell's handbook of classical mythology]
  II. Title 292′.13′0321

Printed in Great Britain by Collins, Glasgow

For Rhoda

Preface

This book is a collection of stories. It is intended not to expound the myths of Greece and Rome, but to tell them in a readable and convenient form. It is not concerned with cult; and it ventures into interpretation of the myths only where description of the gods' functions makes interpretation unavoidable. I hope, however, that it will prove useful to readers of western literatures from Classical times to the present, since these literatures abound in allusions to mythology. I hope, too, that the stories will be enjoyed for their own sake.

For the most part, the myths have been drawn from those Classical works most likely to be read by the layman, and from the principal ancient collections of mythology. The more obscure sources, and those that contain little myth, did not add much to Classical mythology and hardly influenced the versions found in later writings, so I have not often consulted them. I have turned to reference books only in search of clues to points that I might otherwise have missed.

Sources include the epics of Homer, Vergil, and Apollonius Rhodius; all of Greek tragic drama; the poems of Hesiod; the Homeric Hymns; Pindar's odes; Ovid's *Metamorphoses;* and three of Plutarch's *Parallel Lives.* The *Library* of Apollodorus and Pausanias' *Description of Greece* were especially valuable sources. I turned to Herodotus for traditions of the origins of nations and cautiously consulted Diodorus Siculus where he seemed not to have tampered much with a myth. A few glancing references to myths came from Vergil's minor poems. Hyginus' *Fabulae* and *Poetica Astronomica,* for all their author's carelessness, helped to supply details not to be found elsewhere. Finally, I disregarded my own rule of avoiding obscure works whenever interesting bits of information turned up in fragmentary works of comparatively early date, such as those from the Epic Cycle.

An alphabetical arrangement seemed desirable for reference purposes. The alphabet is, however, a mixed blessing when one deals with a subject so tortuously interconnected as mythology. The writer is faced with a choice of producing a few long articles and a vast number of cross references (thereby defeating the purpose of the alphabetical arrangement) or allowing a great deal of information to be repeated in two or more entries, which considerably increases the size of his book. I have chosen a middle course. With some exceptions, each major myth is told once in full, in an entry on one of its principal characters. Details about lesser characters that are peripheral to the main story are related in separate entries on those characters.

Cross references are fairly plentiful, but it should be noted that they are used only when the entry to which the reader is referred contains additional information about the entry in which the reference is made. It can generally be assumed that, if a character mentioned in an entry sounds interesting enough to warrant pursuing him further, he will have an entry of his own.

If there is relatively little Roman mythology in this book, it is because there is little of it to record. As H. J. Rose has written in his *Handbook of Greek Mythology*, "Italian gods were vague personalities, with definite and limited functions, and are not thought of as marrying, having children, forming connexions of love or friendship with mortals, or doing any of the things which Greek imagination ascribed to the Olympians." Something is known of Roman cult, but that does not fall within the scope of this book. Little is left but Roman traditions of their origin as a people, as recorded by, among others, the poets Vergil and Ovid and the historians Livy and Plutarch. Rose warns that "the overwhelming majority of [the traditions] are not genuine popular native traditions at all, but comparatively late, artificial tales, put together either by Greeks or under Greek influence." Nevertheless I have included many of these legends, up to that of the expulsion of the Tarquins, for their intrinsic interest.

A major problem in retelling myths is that of synthesis. Many of the stories are found in bits and pieces in a variety of sources written over a period of centuries. When these sources disagree, it is necessary in a serious reference work to give all significant versions, rather than discard those that cannot be tailored to a neatly plausible continuity. The resulting prevalence of phrases such as "some say" and "others say" does not enhance the elegance of the narrative, but that is a small enough price to pay for completeness and fidelity. I have ignored variant accounts only when the differences seemed inconsequential or the result of simple mistakes in recording the statements of earlier writers, as is often the case in Hyginus' two books.

A subtler difficulty arises when accounts do not actually contradict one another but may be suspected of arising from different traditions, or when one seems transparently "literary." The comprehensive European dictionaries of mythology solve this problem by fragmenting the myths according to incident and source. This approach is desirable in works intended for the use of scholars, but it is disastrous to readability.

Since the process of accretion through which the myths developed will be of only passing interest to most readers of this handbook, I have combined disparate, though not contradictory, elements into single narratives. In the longer stories, I have generally indicated major breaks in the tradition (as, for instance, in the case of Odysseus' career after the point at which Homer leaves him at the end of the *Odyssey*), and I have used various means to separate incidents that seem to me uneasy companions. Such decisions are, however, highly subjective.

Because this book is designed as a companion to reading, I have usually placed the principal emphasis in my retellings on those versions of myths that are best known to modern readers of the Classics. The tragic fate of Oedipus, for example, is most familiar to us from the plays of Sophocles, though Homer's references to him give evidence of a very different and presumably earlier tradition. Where stories are unlikely to be known to many readers in any form, I have generally chosen to emphasize the earlier versions that seem to reflect popular myth rather than literary invention. I have, however, sometimes deviated from both of these practices in favor of basing an entry mainly on the work of some Classical mythographer such as Apollodorus, when he had dealt with it in a particularly thorough and continuous narrative.

Rather than interrupt the flow of the stories with citations of sources, I have placed them at the ends of entries or, in the case of long entries on the sagas, at the ends of sections. Citations are not intended to be complete. I have seldom referred to sources that merely corroborate statements made in better-known or fuller sources, or that deal with inconsequential details, unless they seemed for some reason more than usually interesting. All citations refer to editions included in the Loeb Classical Library, except for the works of Hyginus, which are available in English only in a 1960 translation by Mary Grant.

The time would seem to be long overdue in which we can spell Greek names in direct transliteration instead of in latinized form. Because, however, this book will generally be turned to from books that use the old-fashioned traditional spellings, I have regretfully bowed to the convention and used them myself throughout the text. The pronouncing index gives the Greek spellings as well as the Latin.

I am indebted for various kinds of aid and encouragement to Professors Konrad Gries and Lillian Feder, both of Queens College of the City University of New York, and to Professor Cedric H. Whitman of Harvard University. I owe them equally my gratitude and acknowledgment of the fact that they are in no way responsible for any deficiencies this book may have. My editors at the Thomas Y. Crowell Company, Miss Joan Cenedella and Mrs. Carol B. Cutler, devoted many hours of patient and diligent work to the improvement of the manuscript, and I thank them for their collaboration.

Contents

ATLANTIC OCEAN

Rhine R.

ALPS

Rhone R.

Po River

LIGURIA

ETRURIA

Adria

CORSICA

Rome

LATIUM

Nap

SARDINIA

Mt.Vesuv

Guadalquivir R.

Tartessus

Gadeira (Erytheia)

PILLARS OF HERCULES

MEDITER

Str.of Messi

Mt.Aetna

SICILY

Syra

Carthage

R

A

ATLAS MTS.

N

L. Tritonis

Syrtis Minor

Libyan

LIBYA

0   250   500 kil.

0   250   500 m.

D. deFontaine

THE MEDITERRANEAN WORLD

Tanais R. (Don)

SAUROMATIANS ~ SCYTHIANS

TAURIANS

CAUCASUS MTS.

Danube (Ister)

HAEMUS MTS.

COLCHIS

Black Sea

Phasis R.

PAEONIA RHODOPE MTS.

Salmydessus

Sinope

THRACE

Sea of Marmara

BITHYNIA

Ancyra

Themiscyra

MACEDONIA

Troy MYSIA

Sangarius

Halys River

EPEIRUS

Mt.Ida

Pergamon

Mt.Dindymus

PHRYGIA

Gordium

A N A T O L I A

Aegean Sea

LYDIA

Mt.Sipylus

Sardis

Pessinus

Thebes

Athens

Ephesus

Celaenae

CARIA

Maeander

Sparta

SOLYMI

LYCIA

CILICIA

Mallus

SYRIA

Cnossus

CRETE

CYPRUS

Byblus

Sidon

Tyre

E A N   S E A

Joppa

Cyrene

Ascalon

PHAROS

Canobus

Memphis

Cairo

ARABIA

E G Y P T

Nile River

Red Sea

ETHIOPIA

Chemmis

ATTICA

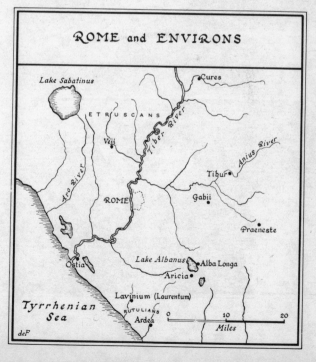

ROME and ENVIRONS

A

Abantes. A Euboean tribe. The Abantes were named for Abas, about whom little is known. Under Abas' son Chalcodon, they engaged in an unsuccessful struggle for power with Thebes. Chalcodon's son, Elephenor, later gave sanctuary in Euboea to the two sons of Theseus, king of Athens. Still later, he led the Euboean forces to the Trojan War. Large numbers of Abantes were among the Greek migrants who colonized various cities of Ionia, in Asia Minor.

Abas (1). A king of Argos. Abas, a son of Lynceus and Hypermnestra, was a great warrior and succeeded his father on the throne. He married Aglaea, a daughter of Mantineus, who bore him twin sons, Acrisius and Proëtus, and a daughter, Idomene. Abas also had a bastard son, Lyrcus. Hyginus [*Fabulae* 244] mentions that Abas avenged Lynceus by killing Megapenthes, but nothing more is known of the incident. Abae, in Phocis, is said to have been named for Abas. [Apollodorus 2.2.1–2.]

Abas (2). A son of Melampus and Lysippe. Abas was the father of Coeranus and of Lysimache, who married Talaüs.

Abas (3). The eponym of the Abantes tribe of Euboea. Little is known of Abas except that he was the father of Chalcodon, the Euboean hero.

Abdera. A Thracian city near the mouth of the Nestos River (now the Mesta) opposite the island of Thasus. Abdera was founded by Heracles in honor of Abderus.

Abderus. A son of Hermes from Opus, in Locris. Abderus is generally said to have been a young lover of Heracles. Heracles left him to guard the notorious man-eating mares of the Bistonian king Diomedes and returned to find that the youth had been eaten. He built the city of Abdera in Abderus' memory.

Absyrtus. See APSYRTUS.

Abydus. A city on the Asian side of the Hellespont. Abydus, like many other cities on either side of the Hellespont, was allied with Troy in the Trojan War. It is better remembered, however, as the home of Leander, in the Hellenistic romance of Hero and Leander, than as the site of events in mythology.

Acacallis or **Acalle.** A daughter of Minos and Pasiphaë. Acacallis became pregnant by Apollo and was banished by her father to Libya. There she bore Amphithemis, who is also called Garamas. The Cretans claimed that she was also the mother, by Hermes, of Cydon, eponym of the Cretan city of Cydonia, although the Arcadians say that Cydon was a son of Tegeates and migrated to Crete. Some say that Acacallis also had a son, Miletus, by Apollo. [Pausanias 8.53.4; Apollonius Rhodius 4.1489–1494.]

Acamas. A son of Theseus and Phaedra. When Theseus was exiled from Athens, Acamas and his brother Demophon were sent for safety to King Elephenor in Euboea. They grew up there and accompanied Elephenor to the Trojan War, where they were able to rescue their grandmother, Aethra, from Helen. On the return voyage Acamas stopped in Thrace and married Phyllis, daughter of the Bisaltian king. He declined the kingdom, which was offered as a dowry, and, leaving Phyllis behind, sailed away, promising to return at a specified time. As he left, Phyllis gave him a box which, she said, contained an object sacred to the goddess Rhea. She warned him never to open it unless he had given up the intention of returning. Acamas sailed to Cyprus and, finding it pleasant, settled there. When he did not return at the appointed time, Phyllis cursed him and hanged herself. Eventually Acamas opened the box and, terrified by its contents, galloped wildly away on his horse until he was thrown and died by falling on his own sword. According to another version of the tale, Acamas returned to Thrace. When he embraced the bare almond tree that grew on Phyllis' grave, it burst into leaf.

The same story is told of Demophon in some sources [Apollodorus "Epitome" 6.16–17; Hyginus, *Fabulae*, 59, 243], but it conflicts in that case with the usual tradition that Demophon ruled Athens after Menestheus and also with the fact that a promontory in Cyprus was named for Acamas. On the other hand, Acamas was named by the Athenians among the eponyms of the ten tribes. [Apollodorus "Epitome" 1.18, 1.23, 5.22.]

Acarnan. A son of ALCMEON and Callirrhoë. After avenging their father's death, Acarnan and Amphoterus settled Acarnania with colonists from Epeirus.

Acarnania. That part of the Greek coastal territory on the Ionian Sea opposite the islands of Cephallenia and Leucas. Acarnania was traditionally settled by the sons of Alcmeon with colonists from Epeirus, to the north.

Acastus. A king of Iolcus. Acastus was the only son of Pelias, king of Iolcus. His mother was either Anaxibia, daughter of Bias, or Phylomache, daughter of Amphion. In defiance of his father's orders, Acastus sailed with the Argonauts under Pelias' enemy Jason. Some say that, on their return, Jason, after taking Iolcus, generously turned it over to Acastus. The more usual story is that Acastus and the Iolcans expelled Jason and his wife, Medea, for their treacherous murder of Pelias. In any case, Acastus' first act as king was to hold funeral games for his father, which were attended by all the Argonauts. Later, he went on the Calydonian boar hunt.

Acastus married Astydameia or else Hippolyte, daughter of Cretheus, and had three daughters—Laodameia, Sterope, and Sthenele—and sons whose names are unknown. PELEUS [A, C], Acastus' fellow Argonaut, came to Iolcus after murdering Phocus or accidentally killing Eurytion, and Acastus purified him. When the guest spurned the advances of Acastus' wife, she told Acastus that he had tried to violate her. Acastus would not kill a man whom he had purified, but, as they were hunting on Mount Pelion, he stole Peleus' sword, hoping that the centaurs would kill him. The Centaur Cheiron saved Peleus, however, and he returned. With the aid of Jason and the Dioscuri, he destroyed Iolcus and killed Acastus' wife. Some say that he killed Acastus as well, but others claim that Acastus, or his sons, later exiled Peleus from his kingdom of Phthia. Acastus was still alive when LAODAMEIA's husband, Protesilaüs, was killed in the Trojan War. [Apollodorus 1.9.10, 1.9.16, 1.9.27, 3.13.2–3, "Epitome" 6.7; Pindar, *Nemean Odes*, 4.]

Acca Larentia. See LARENTIA.

Acestes. A king of Eryx, in western Sicily. Acestes, the son of a Trojan mother and the river-god Crinisus, was descended from Eryx, the eponym of his land. He entertained AENEAS [B] and his followers on their way to Italy. The less vigorous members of Aeneas' company remained in Eryx and founded a town that they named Acesta in the king's honor.

Achaea. A region of the Peloponnesus on the Gulf of Corinth between Elis and Sicyonia and north of Arcadia. Achaea was originally named Aegialus, perhaps for Aegialeus, an early king of Sicyonia. When the Thessalian Xuthus was banished from Athens, he settled in Aegialus with his sons, Achaeüs and Ion, and died there. Achaeüs went to Thessaly and succeeded, with the aid of Aegialian and Athenian allies, in recovering the throne that his father had lost. He named that part of Thessaly Achaea, for himself. Ion, meanwhile, began gathering forces to seize power in Aegialus, but King Selinus forestalled this move by marrying his only daughter, Helice, to Ion and adopting him as heir to the throne. Upon Selinus' death, Ion became king and renamed the land Ionia.

The sons of Achaeüs, Archander and Architeles, went to Argos and married Scaea and Automate, daughters of King Danaüs. The brothers became so influential there that the Argives were called Achaeans. Much later, at the return of the Heraclids, these Achaeans were driven from the region about Argos. They moved northward, under the leadership of Tisamenus, and offered to settle peaceably in Ionia. But the Ionians, fearing that Tisamenus' prestige would soon make him dominant in the state, refused his request. The Achaeans then invaded the land and drove out the Ionians, who took refuge in Attica. Tisamenus died in the fighting; his sons survived and renamed the land Achaea. They shared the rule with two Spartans of ancient lineage, Preugenes and his son Patreus; the latter founded Patrae. (See also ACHAEANS.)

Achaea. A region in southern Thessaly. According to Homer [*Iliad* 2.681–685], this Achaea was near Phthia and Pelasgian Argos. These three territories participated in the Trojan War under Achilles' leadership. Achaea was named for Achaeüs, son of Xuthus, who had been expelled from Thessaly by his brothers. When Xuthus died, Achaeüs returned to Thessaly and, on the death of

Aeolus, regained his father's lost throne and renamed the territory for himself.

Achaeans. The inhabitants of either of the two Greek regions known as Achaea. Homer, however, regularly applied the name Achaeans (Achaioi) to all the Greek forces in the Trojan War; but he also said [*Iliad* 2.681–685] that the name was particularly used for a people of southern Thessaly who, together with two other local tribes, the Myrmidons and the Hellenes, were led to the Trojan War by Achilles. It is not known how common was Homer's broader use of the name. In spite of the respect generally shown to Homeric traditions, later writers generally used the name Hellenes to distinguish Greeks from foreigners. Many modern scholars assign arbitrary meanings to the two words, calling "Hellenes" all the Indo-European tribes that are believed to have invaded Greece from the north over a period of many centuries and reserving the term "Achaeans" for a particular wave in the tide of emigration. Just when the Achaeans arrived, to what degree they differed from earlier or later Hellenic groups, and what happened to them are questions that remain to be answered.

Greek traditions traced the Achaeans to the same source as the other main branches of the Hellenes: the family of Aeolus, king of Thessaly. Aeolus, a son of Hellen, gave his name to the Aeolians; the Dorians were named after his brother Dorus; Aeolus' nephews Ion and Achaeüs were eponyms of the Ionians and the Achaeans. According to Pausanias, writing a thousand years after the *Iliad* was written, Achaeüs ruled the Thessalian Achaea known to Homer. His sons emigrated to Argos and became so prominent there that they were able to rename the Argives Achaeans in honor of their father. The Greek troops at Troy were presumably called Achaeans because they were dominated by Argive leaders. At the time of the Dorian invasion, the Argive Achaeans were driven to the northern part of the Peloponnesus, known as Aegialus, and conquered it. They expelled the IONIANS and gave the region the name of Achaea, which it retained under the Romans.

Although it is hard to see why there is no mention of local Achaeans in the many myths of the southern Peloponnesus, the broad outlines of this tradition lend some support to the historical view that the people whom scholars call the Achaeans were a group of Hellenic tribes that entered Greece through Thessaly after the Ionian invasion and before that of the Dorians. During the last few centuries of the Mycenaean era, probably the fourteenth through the twelfth centuries B.C., they formed the ruling classes of many regions of Greece and, perhaps, of certain coastal areas of Asia Minor, where they came into contact with the Hittite Empire. They were the leaders of the Greeks who attacked Troy. The DORIAN invasion drove a considerable group of them to their last stronghold in the northern Peloponnesus, to which they bequeathed their name. Traditions recorded by Pausanias of relations between the rulers of Peloponnesian cities and the Dorian invaders suggest that, in many regions, the Achaean population, doubtless combined with many survivors from earlier inhabitant groups, remained where it was and accommodated to the Dorian new-comers.

Achaeüs. The eponym of the Achaeans. Achaeüs and Ion, eponym of the Ionians, were sons of the Thessalian XUTHUS. They went to Aegialus, in the Peloponnesus, with their father. Ion eventually became king of the land. Achaeüs gathered allies from both Athens and Aegialus and recovered the Thessalian throne of which their father had been deprived long before. This region, or a part of it, came to be called Achaea. Achaeüs' sons, Archander and Architeles, migrated to Argos, where they married daughters of Danaüs and rose to such prominence that the Argives too came to be called Achaeans, after their father. [Pausanias 7.1.2–3, 7.1.6.]

Achates. A friend of Aeneas. Achates is Aeneas' loyal companion through-out Vergil's *Aeneïd.*

Acheloüs. The principal river of the southwestern mainland area of Greece, and its god. The Acheloüs flows southward, dividing Acarnania from Aetolia, to empty into the Ionian Sea near the entrance to the series of gulfs that separate the Peloponnesus from the mainland to the north. It was noted in Classical times for the rapidity with which silt carried downstream was ex-tending the land of the delta to include some of the Echinadian Islands. This phenomenon, mentioned by Herodotus, had been considerably reduced a half century later because the near depopulation of Aetolia by wars had prevented cultivation of the area. The rapid spread of the alluvial deposits lent plausibil-ity to the myth of Alcmeon, who found refuge from the Erinyes of his mother on this new land because it had not existed when she cursed the earth that might shelter him after he killed her.

Acheloüs, god of one of the most turbulent of Greek rivers, played a role in several myths. When five local nymphs failed to honor him sufficiently, he swept them away, and they became the Echinadian Islands. He fell in love with Perimele and seduced her. Her father flung her from a cliff, but Acheloüs persuaded Poseidon to transform her into an island. The river-god himself had the power to change his shape, but it did not help him when he wrestled HERACLES [M] for the hand of Deïaneira. After several changes, he became a bull. Heracles not only vanquished him but broke off one of his horns. Achel-oüs was the father of Alcmeon's second wife, Callirrhoë; of Peirene, nymph of the famous spring at Corinth; of Castalia, nymph of the even more famous spring at Delphi; and of the Sirens. Acheloüs was frequently represented in art, often in the form of a bull with the horned head of a man.

There were two other rivers named Acheloüs, one in Lydia, the other a small stream in Arcadia. [Ovid, *Metamorphoses,* 8.547–9.88; Pausanias 2.2.3, 8.24.9–11, 8.38.9–10, 9.34.3, 10.8.9.]

Acheron. A river of the Underworld. The Acheron, rather than the Styx, was sometimes said to be the boundary of Hades across which souls were fer-ried by Charon. It was sometimes conceived of as a swampy lake, such as the

Acherusian Lake near Cumae. Acheron was often used, by extension, as a name for Hades itself. Several actual rivers bore the name. The Acheron was, like other rivers, sometimes personified. As a god, Acheron was the father of Ascalaphus by either Orphne or Gorgyra.

Achilles. The son of Peleus, king of Phthia, and Thetis.

A. Peleus' marriage to a sea-goddess, after a wedding that had been arranged and attended by the gods, was a happy one until the birth of their first child, Ligyron. Thetis, wishing to make her son immortal like herself, anointed him with ambrosia during the day and laid him in the embers of the fire by night. When her husband saw her one evening placing their baby in the fireplace, he cried out in alarm. Thetis, annoyed, left both husband and child and went back to her home in the sea. (According to a much later version of the story, Thetis dipped the baby in the waters of the river Styx, making his body invulnerable except for the heel by which she held him.)

Peleus turned the child over to the wise Centaur Cheiron, who gave him a new name: Achilles. Cheiron taught him manly arts and instilled courage in him by feeding him on the entrails of wild animals. Achilles became so swift that he could overtake a deer. He was still living with Cheiron on Mount Pelion while Helen's suitors were making the rash promise to Tyndareüs that was to send so many Greeks to their deaths in Troy. While still quite young, he returned to his father's court and was placed under the tutelage of Phoenix, a suppliant from Ormenium whom Peleus had made king of the Dolopians. At about the same time, Menoetius also came as a suppliant to Phthia with his young son, Patroclus, who had accidentally killed a playmate in Opus. Peleus made Patroclus a squire to Achilles, who was several years younger. The two youths became constant companions and, in time, devoted lovers.

According to an alternative tradition, which was never reconciled with that of Achilles' training under Cheiron and Phoenix, Thetis knew that her son was fated to die if he went to Troy. She sent him to the court of Lycomedes on the Aegean island of Scyrus, east of Euboea. He was only nine years old when Calchas, the seer attached to the Greek forces, announced that Troy could not be taken without the boy's aid. At Thetis' insistence, Lycomedes dressed Achilles as a girl and reared him under the name of Pyrrha along with his own daughters. The girls must have been in on the secret, for Lycomedes' daughter Deïdameia later bore Achilles a son, who was named Neoptolemus or Pyrrhus.

Thetis' precautions were of no use, for Achilles' disguise was penetrated by Odysseus, who came with a recruiting expedition to Scyrus in search of him. Lycomedes denied that the boy was there, and allowed the ambassadors to see for themselves by searching the palace. Odysseus wasted no time in this pursuit. He placed on the porch of the palace various feminine trinkets, together with a spear and a shield. While the girls were examining the baubles, he had a trumpet blown at a distance, as if in warning that the island was being invaded. Achilles instantly stripped off his girl's clothing and snatched up the spear and shield. Once discovered, Achilles paid no further attention to his mother's fears but volunteered eagerly for the war, even though, not having wooed Helen, he had not taken the vow to defend her husband that bound most of the other Greek leaders. At the age of fifteen Achilles was made admiral of the Greek fleet.

B. When Agamemnon was forced to sacrifice his daughter Iphigeneia in order to insure favorable winds for sailing, he lured her to the port of Aulis with a promise of marriage to Achilles. According to Euripides, the young man was unaware of this ruse and defied the entire Greek army in an attempt to save the girl's life, but Iphigeneia finally offered herself for the sacrifice. The Greeks were able to sail, but not to find Troy. Landing by mistake in Mysia, they were met by a force led by Telephus, king of Teuthrania (later named Pergamon). Telephus, a son of Heracles, quickly drove the Greeks, except for Achilles, back to their ships. Achilles stood his ground and wounded Telephus in the thigh. The Greeks returned to their homes or to Argos, the kingdom of their commander-in-chief. Telephus meanwhile consulted an oracle about his wound and was told that only the inflictor could cure it. Dressed in rags, the Teuthranian king journeyed to Argos as a suppliant and begged Achilles to heal him. Achilles, who knew nothing of medicine, was willing but puzzled, until Odysseus pointed out that the true "inflictor" of the wound was the spear. Achilles scraped rust from the weapon into the wound and Telephus quickly recovered. In return for this favor, he guided the Greeks to Troy ten years, according to some accounts, after their first embarkation.

Thetis had warned her son that he was fated to spend either a long, comfortable life at home in Phthia or a short, glorious one in the Trojan War. Achilles chose glory. Thetis also warned him that he must not kill Tenes, king of the island of Tenedos, for the young man's father, Apollo, would be sure to avenge him. The Greeks landed on the island, which was just off the coast of the Troad, and Achilles killed Tenes almost immediately, perhaps because he did not recognize him. He listened more carefully to his mother's next warning: that he must not be the first to land at Troy. Protesilaüs disembarked first, and was the first Greek to be killed. In this opening battle Achilles was pitted against Cycnus, king of Colonae. Discovering that this son of Poseidon was invulnerable to weapons, Achilles strangled him with the thongs of his own helmet. Not long after arriving at Troy, Achilles conceived a desire to see Helen, who was the ostensible cause of the war. Since he obviously could not say much of this wish to the other Greek leaders, Thetis and Aphrodite somehow arranged for him to meet the former Spartan queen. In spite of these excellent auspices, however, nothing seems to have come of this historic encounter.

The city of Troy seemed impregnable within its great walls, so the Greeks set about systematically reducing the surrounding towns, whose rulers were vassals of Priam, the Trojan king. This operation, which took nine years, seems to have been under the command of Achilles. The young man proved to be as ruthless as he was powerful. He sacked twelve cities by sea, including several islands, and eleven more by land. Among these were Lyrnessus and Hypoplacian Thebes. The latter city was ruled by Eëtion, the father-in-law of Hector, commander of the Trojan forces. Achilles killed the king and his seven sons in one day and held the queen for ransom. Out of respect for Eëtion's prowess, however, he did not plunder the corpse but buried the king in his armor. According to Homer [Iliad 9.666–668], Scyrus was one of these captured Trojan cities—not the place of Achilles' upbringing; and its king was not Lycomedes but Enyeus. Achilles drove Aeneas from his home on Mount Ida and killed Priam's son Troïlus. Later, he captured another of Priam's sons, Lycaon, while he worked in an orchard, and sold him and his brothers Isus and Antiphus for ransom, only to kill thém all later in battle.

C. During his attack on Lyrnessus, Achilles had killed Mynes and Epistrophus, sons of King Evenus, and had carried off a beautiful Lyrnessan woman named Briseïs as his concubine. Some time later Agamemnon was forced by the insistence of Achilles and the other leaders to give up his own concubine, Chryseïs, to save the Greeks from a plague. Enraged, he took Briseïs from Achilles. Achilles surrendered her but refused to fight any longer or to allow his troops to do so. His mother appealed to Zeus to give the Trojans victory so that the Greeks should be forced to heap honors on Achilles in order to win his help. Zeus consented. As a result, the Greeks were gradually beaten back to their ships in an assault led by Hector. Agamemnon sent old Phoenix, together with Odysseus and Ajax, to offer not only Briseïs but a great deal of treasure as well if Achilles would rejoin the fighting. Achilles refused, and kept Phoenix with him. Shortly thereafter Patroclus, seeing the Trojans threatening to burn the Greek ships, begged to be allowed to wear Achilles' armor into battle. Achilles consented. Patroclus, after distinguishing himself in a spectacular manner, was killed by Hector.

Filled with grief and rage, Achilles turned back the Trojans with a shout and rejoined the fighting. Insatiably eager for revenge, he killed dozens of Trojans and even fought the river Scamander when the river-god, finding his waters choked with Achilles' victims, rose against him. Achilles would have been drowned had not Hephaestus dried up the river. Undaunted, Achilles continued his onslaught until the Trojans were driven back within their walls. Hector alone turned to meet Achilles before the gates. Achilles, aided by Athena, killed him and, stripping him of his armor, dragged his body behind his chariot to the ships. Some say that he first pulled it three times around the city. He then further defiled the corpse and refused to give it up for burial. Achilles slaughtered twelve Trojan youths on Patroclus' pyre and held elaborate funeral games in his honor. At last, when Priam came to him alone at night and pleaded to be allowed to ransom Hector's corpse, Achilles consented, heeding the advice of Thetis.

D. Not long after Hector's death, the Amazon queen Penthesileia came to Troy as an ally of Priam. She killed many Greeks and gained a great reputation by her prowess. Achilles killed her but fell in love with her corpse. When the sharp-tongued Thersites taunted him for this, Achilles killed him. Although Thersites had been unpopular, Achilles nevertheless had to sail to Lesbos, sacrifice to Leto, Apollo, and Artemis, and be purified of murder by Odysseus before he could rejoin the Greek host.

In one of his last single combats, Achilles killed Memnon, an Ethiopian or Assyrian ally of the Trojans. He was himself killed by Paris, who shot him with an arrow from the safety of the Trojan walls. Paris' hand was guided by Apollo, either because Achilles had killed his son Tenes, or at the request of Poseidon, father of Achilles' victim Cycnus, or merely because Apollo had sided with the Trojans from the first. There was a terrible struggle over the corpse. Ajax finally carried it from the field, while Odysseus defended his rear. Achilles' ashes were buried in a golden urn, mixed with those of Patroclus, and a great barrow was raised over them by the sea.

Ajax and Odysseus vied for Achilles' armor, which Hephaestus had made for him. When the other Greek leaders awarded it to Odysseus, Ajax went mad and killed himself. The captured Trojan prophet Helenus predicted that Troy would fall only if Achilles' son, Neoptolemus, fought with the Greeks. Odysseus and Phoenix went to Scyrus to ask his aid, and Odysseus gave him his father's armor. After the fall of Troy, when the Greeks were preparing to sail for home, the ghost of Achilles appeared to them to demand that they sacrifice Priam's daughter Polyxena on his tomb. Late Classical writers invented a reason for this: Achilles had been in love with the girl. He had, in fact, gone to her home to sue for her hand, but her brothers Paris and Deïphobus had ambushed and killed him. When Odysseus visited the Underworld, he met Achilles' ghost there and cheered him somewhat with news of the prowess of his son. According to a later tradition, Achilles lived forever, together with Patroclus, both Ajaxes, and Antilochus, on the White Island, in the western Black Sea. Some say, surprisingly, that he was married there to Medea.

E. Achilles is the principal hero of Homer's *Iliad* and appears after death in his *Odyssey* [11.465–540, 24.15–97]. He is an important character in Euripides' *Iphigeneia in Aulis*. Many of his adventures are summarized by Apollodorus [3.13.6; 3.13.8; "Epitome" 3.16–17, 3.20, 3.26, 3.29–33, 4.6–5.7, 5.23]. Details of his discovery on Scyrus and of his love for Polyxena are given by Hyginus [*Fabulae* 96, 101].

Acis. See POLYPHEMUS (1).

Acoetes. A Tyrrhenian sailor. When Acoetes' fellow seamen kidnapped DIONYSUS [B], Acoetes tried to defend him and was saved by the god from the fate of the rest of the crew, who were changed into dolphins. Acoetes became a follower of the god and may have been the leader of his maenads when Pentheus, king of Thebes, unsuccessfully tried to imprison them.

Acrisius. A king of Argos. Descended from Danaüs, Acrisius was a son of Abas and Aglaea. His early life was occupied from the womb with quarrels with his twin brother, Proëtus, whom he drove from Argos. Later he was forced to divide Argolis with Proëtus, who thereafter ruled in Tiryns.

Acrisius married Eurydice, a daughter of Lacedaemon, and she bore him a single daughter, Danaë. When he inquired of an oracle how he might have sons, he was told merely that a son of Danaë would one day kill him. To prevent this, Acrisius built either a tower or an underground chamber of brass and imprisoned his daughter in it. But Zeus, in the form of a shower of gold, poured through the roof into her lap and Danaë bore a child, whom she named PERSEUS [A, E]. There were rumors that not Zeus but Proëtus had found his way into her cell and taken revenge on his brother. Acrisius punished Danaë by shutting her and the child in a chest and throwing it into the sea.

The king heard no more of them for many years. Meanwhile the god Dionysus came to Argos with his wild band of satyrs and bacchants, and Acrisius barred the gates against them. Although he is said to have regretted the act later, there is no record that he was severely punished for his defiance.

In time Acrisius learned of Perseus' survival and his heroic exploits. Hearing that the youth was returning to Argos, he fled to Larisa in Thessaly. Ovid says that he had been driven from his throne by Proëtus and that Perseus avenged him. Hyginus tells a different story, claiming that Acrisius pursued Perseus to Seriphus, but was there reconciled with him. All versions agree, however, that the king was accidentally killed by a discus thrown by Perseus, and the oracle was thus fulfilled. [Apollodorus 2.2.4; Pausanias 2.16.1–3; Hyginus, *Fabulae*, 63, 64.]

acropolis. The highest part of a Greek city; literally, "highest city." Many ancient cities were built on hills for defensive purposes. As they grew larger, the cities spread outward on the plains, but the original fortified hilltop was retained as a citadel. Examples of such citadels were the Cadmeia of Thebes, the Acrocorinth of Corinth, and the Larisa of Argos. The word *pergamon* (Latin, *pergamum*), which had much the same meaning as *akropolis,* was used for the citadel at Troy and for the entire city of Pergamon, the site of which was a steep mountainside. In common parlance today, the word Acropolis refers to the old citadel of Athens. In Mycenaean times this steep, rocky, and well-fortified hill was the site of the king's palace. Later it became the principal religious center of the city, on which were built the Parthenon, the Erechtheüm, and many other temples.

Actaeon. The son of Aristaeüs and Autonoë. Actaeon was taught the art of hunting. Several explanations are offered of how he fatally offended the goddess Artemis. Some say that he claimed to be a better hunter, others that he offered to violate Artemis in her temple, still others that she destroyed him at Zeus's bidding because he wanted to marry his aunt Semele, whom Zeus was currently courting. According to the most usual account, Actaeon's crime was the accident of coming upon the goddess as she was bathing with her nymphs on Mount Cithaeron. To prevent him from telling others of the indignity that she had suffered, Artemis changed him into a stag, or else threw a deerskin around him, and he was torn to pieces by his own hounds. The hounds, who could not now find their master, howled in grief until the Centaur Cheiron took pity on them and made a statue of Actaeon to soothe them. [Apollodorus 3.4.4; Ovid, *Metamorphoses*, 3.138–252; Hyginus, *Fabulae*, 180, 181.]

Actaeüs. An early king of Attica. Attica was originally called Acte or Actaea, after Actaeüs. Cecrops married Actaeüs' daughter Agraulus and, on succeeding to the rule, renamed the region Cecropia. According to some accounts Attica took its final name directly from Actaeüs, instead of from Atthis, daughter of Cecrops' successor, Cranaüs. [Apollodorus 3.14.2; Pausanias 1.2.6.]

Acte or **Actaea.** See ACTAEÜS.

Actor (1). A son of Deïon and Diomede, daughter of Xuthus. Actor was the father, by Aegina, of the Argonaut Menoetius, father of Patroclus. [Apollodorus 1.9.4, 1.9.16.]

Actor (2). A son of Phorbas and Hyrmina, and brother of Augeias. An Eleian, Actor is known mainly as the father, by Molione, of the twins Cteatus and Eurytus, called the Moliones or Molionides. Tradition denied him even this distinction by making Poseidon their true father. [Apollodorus 2.7.2; Pausanias 5.1.10.]

Actor (3). An Argonaut. Apollodorus [1.9.16] identified this Actor merely as a son of Hippasus, but did not specify to which of many mythical characters named Hippasus he was referring.

Actor (4). A king of Phthia. Actor was a son of Myrmidon and Peisidice, daughter of Aeolus. According to some accounts, it was he who welcomed Peleus to Phthia. Dying childless, he left the rule to Peleus. More usually, Actor is said to have had a son, Eurytion, who befriended Peleus. [Apollodorus 1.7.3, 1.8.2; Diodorus Siculus 4.72.6.]

Admetus. A king of Pherae. Admetus was the elder son of Pheres—founder and king of Pherae, a city in Thessaly—and Periclymene, a daughter of Minyas. When Jason, son of Pheres' brother Aeson, came to nearby Iolcus to claim his father's throne from the usurper Pelias, Admetus went with Pheres to support Jason at the confrontation. He joined Jason's crew of Argonauts in search of the golden fleece, and the cousins both took part in the Calydonian boar hunt. According to Diodorus Siculus [4.53.2, 6.7.8], it was Jason who gave Pelias' daughter Alcestis to Admetus as his bride, but the usual story is quite different.

Pheres resigned his throne to his son while Admetus was still young. The new king gained a reputation for piety that made the gods regard him favorably. When Zeus condemned Apollo to spend a year in servitude to a mortal, it was to Admetus' court that the god came. The king treated him with such kindness and respect that Apollo made all his cows bear twins, and remained eternally grateful. He had an opportunity to show his gratitude again when Admetus determined to win the hand of Alcestis. This young woman, the eldest, most beautiful, and most pious of Pelias' daughters, had so many suitors that her father set an almost impossible test for her hand: the man who would win her must first yoke two wild beasts to a chariot. Admetus asked Apollo for help, and the god quickly harnessed a lion and a boar for him. Admetus took them to Pelias and brought Alcestis home to Pherae. During the marriage rites he forgot to pay the proper honors to Artemis. That night he was dismayed to find the bridal room filled with snakes. Apollo explained his mistake and Admetus hastily appeased the goddess with sacrifices.

Alcestis bore a son, Eumelus, and a daughter, and seemed the model of a proper wife. It was not until later, however, that Admetus realized the extent of her wifely piety. While still in the prime of life, he fell ill and was about to die. Apollo once more came to his aid. Either by persuading Artemis or by tricking the Fates, after first inducing them to drink too much wine, he won a special dispensation for Admetus: the king need not die if someone else would consent to die in his place. Admetus appealed first to his aged parents, but they were unwilling to give up the few years left to them. Alcestis, though still young, agreed to die for her husband and accompanied Thanatos, the implacable god of death, when he came to escort her to the Underworld. Admetus, though plunged into grief, did not refuse his wife's self-sacrifice. She was saved from her fate either because Heracles wrestled with Thanatos and brought her back or because Persephone, queen of the Underworld, sent her up again to the world of the living.

Admetus and Alcestis are principal characters in Euripides' play *Alcestis*, which tells of her death and resurrection. The other most extended account of Admetus' life is given by Apollodorus [1.9.14–16, 3.10.4].

Adonis. A Greek hero of Asiatic origin. Adonis was said in the *Catalogues of Women* [21] to be the son of Phoenix and Alphesiboea; Apollodorus calls him a son of Cinyras, king of Paphos, in Cyprus, by his wife, Metharme, daughter of Pygmalion. A more usual tradition makes him the son of an incestuous union of Cinyras or Theias, king of Assyria, with his daughter, named MYRRHA or Smyrna. For not giving due honor to Aphrodite, the girl was punished by the goddess with an uncontrollable love for her father. Myrrha satisfied her desire with the help of her nurse and became pregnant. When the father learned what had happened, he pursued the girl with a sword. The gods changed her into a myrrh tree, which split open in due course, revealing the infant Adonis inside.

According to one version of the story, Aphrodite, on seeing that the child was beautiful, put him secretly into a chest and entrusted him to Persephone's keeping. Persephone looked into the chest and, finding the boy as attractive as Aphrodite did, refused to give him up. Aphrodite referred her case to Zeus, who decreed that Adonis should spend a third of the year with each goddess and have the remaining third for himself. He chose to spend his free time with Aphrodite. Some say, however, that Zeus shrewdly avoided judging the case himself and appointed the Muse Calliope as arbitress, and that she assigned half of the young man's time to each goddess. Aphrodite, infuriated, caused the death of Calliope's son Orpheus. Aphrodite had little joy of Adonis, however, for he was killed at an early age by a boar.

According to a different version of Adonis' story, Aphrodite saw Adonis for the first time when he was already a handsome youth. She fell in love with him and spent much of her time with him. Adonis, however, loved the hunt and paid little attention to the goddess' anxious pleas that he confine his activities to the pursuit of small game. Aphrodite's fears were well grounded. While still a stripling, Adonis was killed by a boar. Aphrodite grieved for him inconsolably and caused the blood-red anemone to sprout from his blood.

Followers of Adonis' cult, which moved from Asia to Greece and Rome, mourned his death in part by planting "gardens of Adonis"—green plants seeded in shallow soil, which sprang up quickly and as quickly withered. Adonis was often identified with the ancient Near Eastern deity Tammuz, or Dumuzi, a consort of the Great Goddess, of whom Aphrodite, herself Asiatic, was a type. [Apollodorus 3.14.3–4; Ovid, *Metamorphoses*, 10.519–559, 10.708–739; Hyginus, *Fabulae*, 58, 248, 251, and *Poetica Astronomica*, 2.7.]

Adrasteia. A nymph of the Cretan Mount Ida. Adrasteia, a daughter of Melisseus, received the infant Zeus from his mother, Rhea, and fed him on the milk of the goat Amaltheia (and perhaps on honey as well, to judge from the fact that her father's name means "Bee-Man"). The nymph Idaea and the Curetes aided her in her task. She gave the baby a beautiful ball, with which Aphrodite later tried to bribe her son Eros. [Apollodorus 1.1.6–7; Apollonius Rhodius 3.132–134.]

Adrastus (1). A king of Argos and leader of the SEVEN AGAINST THEBES. Adrastus was a son of Talaüs and Lysimache. By his niece Amphithea he had two sons, Aegialeus and Cyanippus (unless this was Aegialeus' son), and three daughters, Argeia, Deïpyle, and Aegialeia (unless she was Aegialeus' daughter). He was driven from his throne in a feud with the seer Amphiaraüs and took refuge in Sicyon, where, after the death of the childless king Polybus, he became king. While there, he founded the Sicyonian games.

In time Adrastus and his brothers patched up their quarrel with Amphiaraüs, and the seer married their sister Eriphyle. Again on the Argive throne, Adrastus was visited by Polyneices and Tydeus. Because of an oracle, he married them to his daughters and, in spite of Amphiaraüs' warnings of disaster, raised a force from among his Argive kinsmen—seven champions and their followers—to restore Polyneices to power in Thebes.

The expedition began with the ominous death of the infant Opheltes at

Nemea; in his honor Adrastus instituted the Nemean games. At Thebes, the rash courage of the seven Argive champions could not prevent their rout and death. Adrastus was saved only by the swiftness of his fabulous horse, Arion. He was forced to go as a suppliant to Theseus at Thebes before he could even bury his dead.

When they reached manhood, the sons of the Seven, called the EPIGONI, marched against Thebes under Alcmeon to avenge their fathers. Adrastus accompanied them. This campaign succeeded, but, as Adrastus alone had survived the first war, his son Aegialeus was the only Argive leader to die in the second. Adrastus died of grief and old age at Megara on his way home with the victors. Hyginus [*Fabulae* 242] claims, however, that Adrastus and a son named Hipponoüs threw themselves into a fire because of an oracle from Apollo. [Pindar, *Nemean Odes*, 9.9; Apollodorus 3.6.1–3.7.2; Euripides, *The Suppliants*.]

Adrastus (2). A son of Polyneices and Argeia. This Adrastus is mentioned by Pausanias [2.20.5] as one of the EPIGONI.

Adriatic Sea. The sea that divides Italy from Yugoslavia (ancient Illyria).

Aea. See COLCHIS.

Aeacus. The first king of Aegina. Aeacus was the son of Zeus and Aegina, daughter of the Sicyonian river-god Asopus. Zeus carried Aegina off to Oenone or Oenopia, an island lying off the coast of Argolis in the Saronic Gulf. What happened to her after this is not clear. As a young man Aeacus lived alone on an otherwise uninhabited island. He prayed to his father for companions, and the ants on the island were transformed into men and women. Aeacus called them Myrmidons, from *myrmex* ("ant"). Some say, however, that the Myrmidons appeared only after a plague had decimated the population of Oenone. Others claim that the people sprang from the earth itself. Aeacus renamed the island Aegina, for his mother, and became its king.

Aeacus soon gained a widespread reputation for piety and respect for justice. When Nisus and Sceiron were disputing each other's claims to the rule of Megara, Aeacus was asked to decided between them. He pronounced Nisus king, Sceiron minister of war. Sceiron evidently believed that Aeacus had acted fairly, for he gave him his daughter, Endeïs, for his wife. Later all or many Greek lands were struck with a terrible drought, the result of Pelops' murder of Stymphalus, Aegeus' treachery toward Androgeus, or some other cause. The cities sent envoys to Delphi and were told by the oracle that only the prayers of Aeacus could help them. Aeacus consented to do what he could. He prayed to Zeus, and fertility returned to the earth, or else to all of it but Attica, where only Aegeus' capitulation to his enemy Minos lifted the plague.

When Apollo and Poseidon were building the walls of Troy, they called on Aeacus for help. The walls were scarcely erected when three snakes attacked them. Two fell dead, but the third, which had assaulted the part that

Aeacus had built, was able to enter. Apollo correctly interpreted this omen to mean that the descendants of Aeacus would bring destruction on Troy during three generations.

Endeïs bore two sons, Peleus and Telamon. Aeacus had a third son, Phocus, by the nereïd Psamathe. Phocus grew up to excel his half-brothers in athletic prowess and they killed him. When Aeacus learned of the murder he exiled both sons. Since Phocus' sons also emigrated, Aeacus was left to a lonely rule. After his death he became either a gatekeeper or a judge in Hades. [Apollodorus 3.12.6; Hesiod, *Theogony*, 1003–1005; *Catalogues of Women* 53; Pindar, *Olympian Odes*, 8.30–46; Ovid, *Metamorphoses*, 7.517–660; Pausanias 1.39.6, 2.29.7–10.]

Aeaea. The island home of Circe. Homer did not locate this island, but later writers placed it off the western coast of Italy or identified it with Cape Circeo, south of Rome, which was said to have once been an island.

Aeëtes. A king of Colchis. Aeëtes, a son of Helius, the sun-god, and Perse or Perseïs, a daughter of Oceanus, was the brother of Circe and Pasiphaë. He was a ruthless king of a barbarian race, the Colchians, who lived at the eastern end of the Black Sea. His palace, in his capital of Aea, had been built for him by Hephaestus. Aeëtes married Eidyia, a daughter of Oceanus. She bore him a son, Apsyrtus, and two daughters, Medea, a sorceress, and Chalciope or Iophossa. Some call Apsyrtus the son of Asterodeia, a Caucasian nymph. Aeëtes welcomed Phrixus, at the command of Zeus, when the boy arrived on the back of a flying ram. After the ram's golden fleece was nailed to a tree in Ares' grove, the king gave Phrixus his daughter Chalciope in marriage. Hyginus [*Fabulae* 3, 21] says that Aeëtes later killed Phrixus because an oracle warned that the king would die at the hands of an Aeolid. This oracle, or another, also said that he would die when the fleece was stolen. Therefore the king distrusted the Argonauts when they appeared in Colchis.

According to the more usual story, Aeëtes' treatment of the ARGONAUTS [L–N] was due largely to normal Colchian hostility toward strangers. This feeling was aggravated by the fact that Chalciope's four sons by Phrixus had allied themselves with the Argonauts. Aeëtes, because of an oracle, feared treachery from within his own family. When Jason demanded the golden fleece, the king set for him the seemingly impossible task (though one that Aeëtes himself regularly performed) of harnessing fire-breathing bulls to a plow, sowing a field with dragon's teeth, and killing the armed men that would spring up from this seed. With the aid of Medea's sorcery, Jason succeeded and, moreover, made off with both the fleece and Medea. Aeëtes either pursued the Argonauts himself or sent Apsyrtus in charge of the fleet. Apsyrtus was treacherously killed by Medea and Jason, and the *Argo* escaped. (Diodorus Siculus [4.45.1–4.48.4] says in his long and totally different account of Aeëtes' family that the Argonaut Meleager killed Aeëtes in his palace during a violent battle.)

At some time after the visit of the Argonauts, Aeëtes was deposed by his brother Perses, king of the Taurians, but Medea eventually returned to Colchis, killed Perses, and restored Aeëtes to his throne. In another story, Perses was killed at Medea's instigation by her son Medeiüs or Medus, who took the throne himself, his grandfather apparently having died earlier. [Apollonius Rhodius 2.1140–4.241; Apollodorus 1.9.23–24.]

Aegae. A coastal city in the Peloponnesian Achaea. Since most of the northern coast of the Peloponnesus seems to have been sacred to Poseidon, this city may well have been the Aegae where his sea palace was said by Homer and others to be located, although there were other cities of the same name.

Aegaeon. See BRIAREÜS.

Aegean Sea. The sea that divides Greece from Asia Minor. The Aegean contains many islands, large and small, among them the Cyclades and the Sporades, which include the Dodecanese.

Aegeus. A king of Athens.

A. Aegeus was the eldest son of Pandion, a deposed king of Athens, and Pylia, a daughter of Pylas, whom Pandion had succeeded as king of Megara. This, at least, was the official report. It was widely believed that Aegeus was actually a son of Scyrius, eponym of the island of Scyrus, and had been adopted by Pandion. On Pandion's death, his four sons agreed that Nisus should rule Megara, while Aegeus, Pallas, and Lycus divided the rule of Attica. Aegeus' brothers helped him to expel from Athens the sons of Metion, who had usurped Pandion's throne. Aegeus alone, however, became king of Athens. He married first Meta, daughter of Hoples, then Chalciope, daughter of Rhexenor, but neither marriage produced children. Aegeus went to Delphi to inquire of the oracle how he might continue his line. He was told that he should not loosen the foot (that is, the spout) of the wineskin until he reached Athens. A literal-minded man, Aegeus did not grasp the meaning of this advice. He decided to return home by way of Troezen, hoping that his friend King Pittheus, one of the wisest of Greeks, could solve the mystery for him. On his way he passed through Corinth. Medea, about to be exiled by King Creon, promised to use her sorcery to help Aegeus have children if he would give her asylum at Athens. This the naïve king vowed to do, and went on his way.

On arriving at Troezen, Aegeus told Pittheus what the oracle had said. Pittheus, whose reputation for shrewdness was well deserved, at once recognized the meaning of the words, but kept it to himself. Plying his guest with wine, he managed to have him lie with his daughter, Aethra. This event occurred on the island of Sphaeria, where Aethra had gone to bear libations to the tomb of Sphaerus, a charioteer of her grandfather Pelops. (As it happened, Poseidon chose the same night to visit the island, with the result that Aethra could never be sure who was the father of the child that she bore some months later.) Aegeus, doubtless unaware of the competition, placed a sword and a pair of sandals under a huge stone. He told Aethra that, when the son whom she hoped to bear reached manhood, she was to show him these tokens. If he could lift the stone, she should send him with sword and sandals to Aegeus, who would thus recognize his son. Having delivered these admonitions, Aegeus left for Athens.

B. The king had hardly reached home when Medea arrived in her chariot drawn by winged dragons. Aegeus not only welcomed the sorceress to Athens but, in his eagerness to have children, married her. According to some accounts, she did, in fact, bear a son, Medus. This son may well have been the cause of her hostility toward a young man who, much later, came to Athens from Troezen. Though only sixteen years old, this youth, who was named Theseus, had already made a reputation for himself by clearing the Isthmus of Corinth of the dangerous outlaws who had infested it. Medea persuaded Aegeus that Theseus would be likely to side with the king's brother Pallas, who, with his fifty sons, had long been rebelling against the king's rule.

Aegeus therefore sent Theseus out to fight the wild bull from Marathon that had recently disposed of Androgeüs, son of Minos, king of Crete. Aegeus was chagrined when Theseus brought the bull back captive, but Medea was ready with another scheme. Mixing aconite in a cup of wine, she induced Aegeus to offer it to Theseus. Just as the unsuspecting youth was about to drink it, Aegeus caught sight of a sword slung at Theseus' side. He dashed the cup from the boy's hand and embraced him, for the sword was the one that he had left beneath the stone at Troezen. Medea had recognized Theseus at once as her husband's son and, fearing that Medus would be disinherited, had tried to dispose of his rival. For her treachery Aegeus banished mother and son from Athens.

The king publicly acknowledged Theseus as his son amid great rejoicing. Theseus took up his father's struggle with the sons of Pallas, who, finding that their hope of ruling after Aegeus' death was now vain, broke into open mutiny. Theseus and Aegeus put down the rebellion and drove the Pallantids from Athens. Aegeus' brother Lycus, who apparently had sided with Pallas, was also banished. Some say that it was now, rather than earlier, that Theseus captured the Marathonian bull, which he sacrificed to Delphinian Apollo.

C. For the first time Aegeus sat confidently upon his throne. But not for long. Early in his reign he had incurred the enmity of Minos, the powerful king of Crete, by his implication in the death of Androgeüs. Many say that this prince, who had grown up at Athens, was treacherously killed, probably at Aegeus' instigation, as he journeyed to Laïus' funeral games at Thebes and not by the bull of Marathon. Aegeus had continued to defy Minos even after the fall of Megara, ruled by Aegeus' brother and ally Nisus. When, however, a plague struck Athens and even the sacrifice of the four daughters of Hyacinth did not bring relief, Aegeus had no choice but to follow the advice of the

Delphic oracle that he accede to whatever demands Minos might make. The Cretan king's determination was that Athens should be left its autonomy, as long as it provided a tribute every nine years of seven youths and seven girls to be fed to the Minotaur, a monster with a bull's head that Minos kept hidden in the Labyrinth at Cnossus. (Some say, however, that the young Athenians were merely enslaved by the Cretans, not destroyed.)

Not long after Theseus' arrival in Athens, Minos' heralds appeared for the third time to collect this tribute. Strong resentment arose against Aegeus among the Athenians, who had to offer their children to be chosen by lot for the tribute, while the king's son, both a stranger and a bastard, was exempt. Theseus therefore volunteered to go to Crete as one of the fourteen, and Aegeus' entreaties could not dissuade him. The ship sailed, bearing a black sail as a symbol of its mournful mission, but Aegeus made his son promise that, if he were able to destroy the Minotaur, as the young man confidently expected, he would raise a white or scarlet sail as a sign of triumph on the return voyage. Much later the old king saw the ship approaching under the black sail. Broken with grief, he flung himself from the Acropolis near the shrine of Athena Nike, or else into the sea, which thus received the name Aegean. He died unaware that Theseus had in fact been successful and ended the tribute forever, but had forgotten to change the sails. Aegeus was forever honored at a hero shrine beneath the walls from which he had leaped. His son succeeded him and became the most famous of all the legendary kings of Athens.

D. It is widely believed by scholars that Aegeus was originally a form of Poseidon, the god of the Aegean Sea. As his divine functions were taken over by Poseidon, Aegeus was demoted to mortal rank, and many elements of folktale became attached to his myth. [Plutarch, *Parallel Lives*, "Theseus"; Apollodorus 1.9.28, 3.15.5–3.16.1, "Epitome" 1.5–11; Hyginus, *Fabulae*, 37, 43; Ovid, *Metamorphoses*, 7.402–458.]

Aegialeia. A daughter of Adrastus and Amphithea. Aegialeia married Diomedes, but Nauplius induced her to commit adultery with Cometes, son of Diomedes' friend Sthenelus. [Apollodorus 1.9.13, "Epitome" 6.9.]

Aegialeia. An ancient name of the city Sicyon; it was also sometimes used for the region, Sicyonia.

Aegialeus (1). A son of Inachus, the Argive river-god, and Melia. A large part of the Peloponnesus was named Aegialus in his honor, but he died childless and Apis, the son of his brother, Phoroneus, soon renamed it Apia for himself. The Sicyonians claimed that Aegialeus founded their city, which was first named Aegialeia, and that he had descendants who ruled in the region for many generations, beginning with his son Europs. [Apollodorus 2.1.1; Pausanias 2.5.6.]

Aegialeus (2). The eldest son of Adrastus and Amphithea. Aegialeus, the only leader of the Epigoni to die in taking Thebes, was killed by Laodamas at Glisas. He was buried at Pagae. When Adrastus died of grief, Aegialeus' son or younger brother, Cyanippus, succeeded to the throne of Argos. [Pausanias 1.44.4, 9.5.13.]

Aegialus. An early name for a somewhat vague region of the Peloponnesus. Aegialus was that part of the peninsula from which the IONIANS were driven by the Achaeans. The northern coastal section of the Peloponnesus inherited the invaders' name and was primarily thought of as Achaea in Classical times, long after the supposed expulsion had taken place. The Sicyonians, however, insisted that Sicyon had first been called Aegialeia in honor of Aegialeus, eponym of Aegialus, and the Argives claimed that Aegialeus was a son of their own river-god Inachus. They claimed, moreover, that Aegialus was renamed Apia, which in turn was named once again by Pelops after himself. Together with the tradition that both Epidaurus and Troezen had been Ionian and the fact that the west coast of the entire peninsula was washed, then as now, by the Ionian Sea, these claims suggest that the greater part, if not all, of the Peloponnesus was the Ionian territory known as Aegialus.

Aegimius. A king of the Dorians. When Aegimius' lands of Doris and Hestiaeotis were threatened by the Lapiths under Coronus, he called on Heracles for help, promising him a third of his kingdom. Heracles led the Dorians in defeating the Lapiths and killed Coronus, but either refused payment or else instructed Aegimius to hold the land in trust for his (Heracles') descendants, the Heraclids. After Heracles' death and the defeat of his son Hyllus, the Heraclids lived for a time on this land in Doris. The Dorians became their allies in their successful invasion of the Peloponnesus. Aegimius' sons, Pamphylus and Dymas, were killed, but were thereafter greatly honored by the Dorians, who named the three main divisions of their people for them and for Hyllus. [Apollodorus 2.7.7, 2.8.3; Diodorus Siculus 4.37.3, 4.58.6.]

Aegimius. A lost poem once attributed to Hesiod, among other poets. The very few surviving fragments of this poem include a few interesting details about Thetis and Io. They are available in the volume of Hesiod's works in the Loeb Classical Library.

Aegina. A daughter of the Sicyonian river-god Asopus. Aegina was seduced by Zeus, possibly in the form of a flame, and carried off by him to the island of Oenone or Oenopia, where she bore a son, Aeacus. Asopus bribed Sisyphus, king of Corinth, to tell him who had stolen his daughter, and pursued Zeus until he was turned back with thunderbolts. Hyginus [*Fabulae* 52] says that Hera, out of jealousy, dropped a snake into the island's water source and thereby poisoned it. The implication seems to be that Aegina died as a result, leaving Aeacus unprotected. According to Pindar [*Olympian Odes* 9.69–70], she was also the mother of Menoetius by Actor. Aeacus renamed the island of Oenone Aegina in his mother's honor. [Pausanias 2.5.1–2; Apollodorus 1.9.3, 3.12.6.]

Aegina. An island in the Saronic Gulf off the coast of Argolis. This island was named by Aeacus, its first king, for his mother, Aegina, whom Zeus had abducted from her father Asopus and brought to the uninhabited island, at that time called Oenone or Oenopia. Answering the prayers of his son Aeacus, who grew up alone on the island, Zeus peopled the place by changing the ants to men and women, whom Aeacus called Myrmidons. Aeacus gained a reputation for piety and just dealings and enjoyed a long and peaceful reign. Because he exiled Telamon and Peleus, his two sons by Endeïs, for killing Phocus, his son by Psamathe, Aeacus had no heirs and the island fell under the domination of Argos. When the Heraclids took Epidaurus, Aegina became Dorian territory.

Aegipan. A Pan-like mythological personage whose name means "Goat-Pan." Classical writers could not decide whether Aegipan was only another name of Pan or whether he was a different character entirely. Hyginus, quoting earlier writers, called him a son of Zeus by the nymph Aex or by the goat Boetis. Aex was said to be a daughter of Helius or of Pan, but some writers seem to have regarded her as a goat (as her name implies)—indeed, as the particular goat whose skin became Zeus's aegis. Aegipan and Hermes recovered Zeus's stolen sinews, which Typhöeus had severed and hidden with the monster Delphyne. Later Aegipan recommended that the gods change their shapes to escape Typhöeus in Egypt. He himself became a goat with the lower body of a fish, and was commemorated in this form by Zeus in one or the other of two constellations, Capricorn and Capra. [Hyginus, *Fabulae*, 196, and *Poetica Astronomica*, 2.13, 2.28; Apollodorus 1.6.3.]

aegis. The shield of Zeus. This awesome piece of armor, when used by Zeus, paralyzed his enemies with terror. Zeus lent it often to Athena, less frequently to Apollo. Some scholars have argued that the aegis was the private thundercloud of the sky-god, whose unfailing weapon was lightning. Others say that it was merely an Olympian version of a primitive Hellenic shield made from the hide (*aigis*) of a goat.

Aegisthus. The son of Thyestes by his daughter, Pelopia. Exposed by his mother and suckled by a goat (*aix, aigos*), from which he took his name, Aegisthus was reared by ATREUS [C, D], who had married Pelopia. Learning his true identity, the youth killed Atreus. When Atreus' son AGAMEMNON [A, C], king of Mycenae, left for Troy, Aegisthus ignored a warning from Hermes and seduced Clytemnestra, Agamemnon's wife. The lovers killed Agamemnon on his return, together with Cassandra, and Aegisthus ruled Mycenae for seven years. By Clytemnestra he had a daughter, Erigone, and, some say, a son, Aletes. Agamemnon's son ORESTES [A] returned from exile and avenged his father by killing both Aegisthus and his own mother, Clytemnestra.

Aegisthus is a principal character in Aeschylus' *Oresteia* trilogy, in Sophocles' *Electra*, and in Seneca's *Agamemnon*. See also Homer, *Odyssey*, 1.29–43, 3.249–275, 4.524–537; Hyginus, *Fabulae*, 87, 88, 119.

Aegium. A seaport of Achaea on the Gulf of Corinth. Aegium claimed the honor of having been the city at which Agamemnon called together for a council of war the Greek leaders who were to accompany him to Troy. [Pausanias 7.24.2.]

Aegle. See THESEUS [E].

Aegyptus. A king of Egypt. Aegyptus and DANAÜS [A] were twin sons of Belus and Anchinoë. Their quarrel led to Danaüs' flight to Argos and his daughters' murder of Aegyptus' sons. [Apollodorus 2.1.4–5.]

Aeneas. A Trojan leader and ancestor of the first emperors of Rome.

A. Aeneas was the son of Aphrodite by ANCHISES, a member of the royal line of Dardania. Born on Mount Ida, he was reared by nymphs and brought to Anchises when he was five years old. Anchises was maimed by Zeus for revealing the name of the child's mother. Aeneas grew up to be the leader of the Dardanian troops, which were under the high command of Hector, son of Priam. Aeneas resented his subordinate position, and perhaps the domination of Ilium over his native city, which was older. Nevertheless, after being driven from Mount Ida by Achilles, he fought bravely in defense of Ilium in the Trojan War. Seriously wounded, he was spirited from the field by his mother and Apollo and was healed by Artemis and Leto. Later Apollo urged him to challenge Achilles, but Poseidon removed him from the battle, explaining to the other gods that Aeneas and his descendants were destined to rule Troy.

If this was the tradition in Homer's day, it was later altered to assign Aeneas an even greater destiny: that of founding Rome. (According to the *Little Iliad* [14], Aeneas was captured and given as a slave to Neoptolemus; in the *Sack of Ilium* [1], he deserted Troy and returned to Mount Ida in fear of the omen of Laocoön's death.) By far the most prominent tradition is the Roman one detailed by Vergil in his *Aeneïd*. At the fall of Troy, Aeneas left the burning city when he could no longer defend it. He carried the aged Anchises on his back and took with him the household gods (penates) of the Trojans. During their escape Aeneas' wife, Creüsa, became separated from him and died, but their son, Iülus, remained with his father until they reached Ida. (According to Apollodorus, the Greeks allowed Aeneas to leave out of respect for his filial piety.)

With the coming of summer, Aeneas sailed away with twenty shiploads of his followers. They intended to found a city in Thrace, but were warned away by the ghost of Priam's son Polydorus, who had been treacherously murdered there. Stopping with Anchises' old friend Anius, king of Delos, they were advised to seek their "ancient mother," which Anchises took to mean Crete, home of their ancestor Teucer. They reached that island only to be met with famine and told by their penates that Italy, homeland of Dardanus, was to be their home. Driven by a storm to the Strophades Islands, they were plundered by the Harpies and warned of many perils to come before they could found their new city. The Trojans' discouragement was somewhat lessened when they reached Buthrotum and found ruling there Priam's prophetic son Helenus. Thanks to Helenus' directions, Aeneas' ships safely reached Drepanum, in the region of Eryx in western Sicily. There Anchises died and was buried with great honor.

B. As the Trojans left Sicily to sail northward, Juno (Hera) commanded Aeolus, keeper of the winds, to destroy the Trojan fleet. The goddess had not forgotten her anger at Venus (Aphrodite) for winning the golden apple, and at the Trojans for awarding it and for their descent from Electra, one of Zeus's mistresses. Moreover, she knew that the Trojans' descendants, the Romans, were destined one day to destroy Carthage, her favorite city. Juno's evil designs on the Trojan fleet were foiled, however, by Neptune (Poseidon), who calmed the sea.

Aeneas reached Carthage in safety. Venus sent her son Cupid (Eros), disguised as Aeneas' son Ascanius (another name for Iülus), to cause Dido, the Carthaginian queen, to fall in love with Aeneas. Dido's husband, Sychaeüs, had been murdered by her brother Pygmalion in their native Tyre, and she herself had not long been in Carthage. She warmly welcomed the Trojans, whose story she knew. Her love for Aeneas was returned so eagerly that the Trojan forgot his destiny in Italy and had to be twice reminded of it by Mercury (Hermes). Finally he sailed away. The inconsolable queen killed herself, lamented by her sister, Anna.

Landing again in Sicily, where they were entertained by a kinsman, Acestes, Aeneas held funeral games in Anchises' honor. The Trojan mothers, instigated by Juno and wearied by seven years of voyaging, burned some of the ships in the hope that they might remain in the friendly land of Eryx with Acestes. Aeneas allowed the oldest and most discouraged members of his company to remain and found the city of Acesta, while he and his more vigorous followers pressed on to Italy.

On reaching Cumae, near Naples, Aeneas visited the prophetic Sibyl and asked her to guide him to the Underworld to consult Anchises, whose ghost had commanded him to undertake that journey. The Sibyl consented to do so after Aeneas had plucked a magical golden bough in a nearby wood. On the shore of the river Styx they encountered the souls of the unburied dead whom the ferryman, Charon, would not allow to cross into Hades. Among these was Palinurus, one of Aeneas' steersmen, who had been washed overboard during the northward journey. Aeneas promised to bury him. Charon, on seeing the golden bough, ferried Aeneas and the Sibyl across the Styx.

Among the souls in Hades, Aeneas met that of Dido, who, reunited with the soul of her husband, would not recognize him. In the Elysian Fields he found Anchises, who showed his son various souls waiting to be reborn at some future time. Anchises then predicted the founding of Rome by Aeneas' descendants, and, reassured, Aeneas returned to the upper world and sailed with his followers for their destined home. They anchored in the Tiber River, in the land called Latium. The king of this region was the aged Latinus, son of Faunus, and a direct descendant of Saturn (Cronus). The neighboring Rutulians were ruled by young Turnus, a descendant of the Argive princess Danaë, who had founded the city of Ardea after her adventures with her son Perseus. Turnus had long courted Latinus' daughter Lavinia, whose mother, Amata, had encouraged him. Latinus, however, knew from oracles that his daughter must marry a foreigner. He therefore welcomed Aeneas' ambassadors and hinted that Aeneas was to become his son-in-law.

C. Before the two kings could meet, the implacable Juno stepped in. Fetching the Fury Alecto from Hades, she had her stir up both Amata and Turnus against the strangers, then cause a needless quarrel between Latins and Trojans. Refusing to declare war, Latinus abdicated and Juno herself opened the gates of the temple of Janus, the signal of war. Turnus took as his allies Aventinus, a son of Heracles; Camilla, the Amazon-like leader of the Volscians; and Mezentius, an exiled Etruscan king. Turnus failed, however, to enlist the aid of the Greek Diomedes, who was having too many troubles of his own in his recently founded city of Argyripa. Aeneas found a friend in the Arcadian Evander, who ruled Pallanteum, on the site of the later city of Rome. Himself too old for war, Evander sent his son Pallas with the Arcadian troops. The Etruscans, too, aided Aeneas, out of hatred for the cruel Mezentius.

A bloody war ensued. Turnus' men fired Aeneas' ships, only to see them change into sea-nymphs and swim away—a miracle caused by the Phrygian goddess Cybele. Turnus killed Pallas and wore his belt as a prize of war. Aeneas killed Mezentius and his son, Lausus. During a truce many of Turnus' allies turned against him, but rallied to the cause again when the Trojans attacked. Camilla was killed in battle and her troops were routed. Turnus and Aeneas agreed to settle the outcome of the war by single combat, but the Latins broke the truce at Juno's instigation. Aeneas was wounded, but was cured by Venus. The Trojans again besieged the Latins' city, and Amata, thinking Turnus dead, killed herself. Again Turnus suggested single combat. Aeneas consented and sorely wounded Turnus. About to grant his adversary's request to be carried to his aged father Daunus to die, Aeneas caught sight of Pallas' belt vauntingly displayed on Turnus' armor. He killed Turnus, thus ending the war.

Aeneas now made peace with the Latins and married Lavinia. The Trojans gave up their name and language, while the Latins agreed to worship the penates of the foreigners. As Anchises' shade had predicted, Silvius, Aeneas' son by Lavinia, founded the city of Alba Longa, which was to remain the capital of the Latins until the founding of Rome by Aeneas' descendant Romulus, many generations later. Iülus, moreover, would give his name to the Julian house, which boasted the caesars Julius and Augustus among its distinguished members.

D. Aeneas figured prominently in Homer's *Iliad* and, apparently, in several works of the Epic Cycle, now mostly lost. His adventures beginning with the fall of Troy were the subject of Vergil's *Aeneïd*. Ovid sketched Aeneas' tale in the *Metamorphoses* [13.623–726, 14.72–157, 14.441–622], with many interruptions but with only minor variations from Vergil's version. Other references to Aeneas are found in Apollodorus "Epitome" 3.32, 3.34, 4.2, 5.21; *Homeric Hymn to Aphrodite* 5; *Cypria* 1; Pausanias 2.23.5, 3.22.11, 8.12.8, 10.17.6.

Aeneïd. See VERGIL.

Aeolia. The island kingdom of Aeolus, keeper of the winds. Homer did not locate this island in the *Odyssey*, but later writers identified it as one or another of the islands north of eastern Sicily that are still called the Aeolian Islands (Isole Eolie), as well as the Lipari Islands, their more modern name.

Aeolus (1). The eponym of the Aeolians. Aeolus was a son of Hellen and the nymph Orseïs. When Hellen divided the Greek lands between Aeolus and his brothers, Dorus and Xuthus, Aeolus received Thessaly. He named the people Aeolians, for himself. His sons by Enarete, daughter of Deïmachus, included several of the most powerful rulers of their time: Cretheus, Athamas, Sisyphus, Salmoneus, and Perieres. Other sons, according to some writers, were Magnes, Deïon, Macar or Macareus, and Aëthlius, though the last is generally called a son of Zeus. Aeolus' daughters were Canace, Alcyone, Peisidice, Calyce, Perimele, Tanagra, and Arne. Aeolus killed Canace for committing incest with Macareus, who then killed himself. This Aeolus was regarded by many late authors as the same as Aeolus the guardian of the winds. [Apollodorus 1.7.3.]

Aeolus (2). The keeper of the winds. Aeolus, a son of Hippotas, was king of the island of Aeolia, which came to be identified with one or another of the Aeolian Islands, including Lipara, Hiera, and Stromboli, that lie north of eastern Sicily. For some reason Zeus gave Aeolus charge of the winds, which he kept confined in a cave but could release at will. He lived an easy life with his wife and their six sons and six daughters, who were married to one another. Aeolus often either freed or penned up the winds at the bidding of some deity. Hera, for example, requested him to still the winds, except for a gentle west wind, in order to insure an easy homeward passage of the *Argo*. Later she commanded him to destroy the ships of Aeneas, but Poseidon, jealous of his authority over the sea, interfered and quieted the storm.

Aeolus hospitably entertained ODYSSEUS [F] and his shipmates after their misadventure in Polyphemus' cave. He gave Odysseus all the winds, except the west wind, tied in a bag of oxhide. The ships came within sight of Ithaca, but Odysseus' men secretly opened the bag and the ships were driven back to Aeolus' island. Fearing to aid anyone who was so obviously hated by the gods, Aeolus this time drove them away.

Late Classical writers came to regard Aeolus as a god, rather than a mere mortal whom Zeus had honored. They also often confused him with Hellen's son Aeolus, eponym of the Aeolians. [Homer, *Odyssey*, 10.1–77; Vergil, *Aeneïd*, 1.50–86, 8.416; Apollonius Rhodius 4.818–822.]

Aepytus. A king of Messenia. The youngest son of Cresphontes, the first

Heraclid king of Messenia, and Merope, Aepytus was reared by his maternal grandfather, Cypselus, king of Arcadia, and thus escaped the fate of his two elder brothers and his father, who were killed by Polyphontes. This usurper forced Merope to marry him. When Aepytus grew to manhood, he returned to Messenia, supported by Cypselus and the Heraclid kings of Argos and Sparta. He killed Polyphontes and his followers and recovered the throne. According to Hyginus [*Fabulae* 137], Merope had hidden the infant Aepytus (whom Hyginus calls Telephon) and spirited him away to the home of an ally in Aetolia. Polyphontes offered a reward to anyone who would find and kill the boy, but Aepytus grew to manhood determined to avenge his father and rescue his mother from her enforced marriage.

In time he returned, unrecognized, to Polyphontes' court and claimed to have killed Aepytus. Merope would have killed him while he slept, but an old man recognized him in time. Together the mother and son plotted Polyphontes' death. The king offered a sacrifice of triumph for Aepytus' death and invited the supposed murderer to assist him in the rite. The youth raised the ax ostensibly to kill the sacrificial victim, but brought it down on Polyphontes instead. As ruler of Messenia, Aepytus was both just and shrewd. He won over the wealthy with deference, the poor with gifts. He gained such honor that his descendants were no longer called Heraclidae but Aepytidae. His son Glaucus followed his example of rule and reestablished certain religious rites that had been observed by the Messenians before the Heraclid invasion. [Pausanias 4.3.6–9.]

Aërope. A daughter of Catreus, king of Crete. Having learned from an oracle that one of his own children would kill him, Aërope's father gave her and her sister Clymene to Nauplius, king of Nauplia, to be sold abroad. (Sophocles [*Ajax* 1295–1297] says that Catreus threw Aërope into the sea for taking a foreign slave as her lover.) ATREUS married her, but her adultery with his brother Thyestes led to the bloody feud between the brothers. According to Hesiod and Aeschylus, Aërope was the mother of Pleisthenes; the more usual story is that she was the mother of Agamemnon and Menelaüs. [Apollodorus 3.2.1–2, "Epitome" 2.10.]

Aërope. See ARES.

Aesacus. The son of Priam by his first wife, Arisbe, daughter of Merops, or by the nymph Alexiroë, daughter of the river-god Granicus. Aesacus learned the art of prophecy from Merops. Some say that it was Aesacus, rather than Cassandra, who interpreted Hecuba's dream and warned that the infant Paris should be killed. Aesacus married Asterope, daughter of the river-god Cebren. When she died he mourned for her and was transformed into a bird. Some say, however, that Aesacus loved Cebren's daughter Hesperia and pursued her through the woods, until she was bitten by a snake and died. In remorse, Aesacus leaped into the sea, but the goddess Tethys changed him into the diver bird. [Ovid, *Metamorphoses*, 11.749–795; Apollodorus 3.12.5.]

Aeschylus (525 or 524 to 456 or 455 B.C.). A Greek tragic dramatist. The six of Aeschylus' surviving plays that are concerned with mythological subjects deal with the tragedy of the house of Atreus, the punishment of Prometheus, the arrival of Danaüs and his daughters at Argos, and the war of the Seven against Thebes.

Aesculapius. The Roman name of ASCLEPIUS.

Aeson. A son of Cretheus, king of Iolcus, and Tyro. As the king's eldest son, Aeson should have inherited the throne, but his half-brother PELIAS seized the power. Aeson's wife—variously said to be Alcimede, daughter of Phylacus; Polymede, daughter of Autolycus; or someone else—gave birth to a boy. For fear of Pelias, they let it be known that the child was born dead and secretly sent him to Cheiron the Centaur. Twenty years later the boy, JASON, reappeared and led the expedition of the Argonauts. It is generally said that during his absence Pelias forced Aeson to commit suicide. There is also a tradition that Aeson was restored to youth by Medea, but nothing is said of his life after this event.

Aethalia. See ELBA.

Aethalides. The herald of the Argonauts. Aethalides was a son of Hermes, the god of heralds, by Eupolemeia, daughter of Myrmidon. He came from Phthia to join the crew of the *Argo*. His only deed during this adventure was to persuade the Lemnian women to permit the Argonauts to stay the night—a task that required no great eloquence. Hermes had endowed his son with a memory so unfailing that it did not desert him even in Hades. Aethalides spent only a part of his time after death in the Underworld, for his soul inhabited a new body from time to time. It turned up eventually in the philosopher Pythagoras, still able to recall its successive incarnations. [Apollonius Rhodius 1.51–55, 1.640–652; Diogenes Laertius 8.4.]

Aether. The upper air or sky. Aether, apparently a personification of the upper sky as distinguished from the air (*aer*) that immediately surrounds the earth, was said by Hesiod to be, with his sister Hemera (Day), the offspring of Erebus (Darkness) and Nyx (Night). He was called by some the father of Uranus, another, somewhat less vaguely personified, god of the sky. [Hesiod, *Theogony*, 124–125; *Titanomachia* 2.]

Aethiopis. See EPIC CYCLE.

Aëthlius. A son of Zeus or Aeolus and Protogeneia, daughter of Deucalion. Some call Endymion, Aëthlius' son by Calyce, the founder of Elis; others give that honor to Aëthlius himself. [Apollodorus 1.7, 2.5; Pausanias 5.1.3.]

Aethra. A daughter of Pittheus, king of Troezen. Bellerophon—son of Glaucus, king of Corinth—went to Troezen to ask Pittheus for Aethra's hand in marriage. Before the wedding could take place, however, the young man was banished from his city for murder. While Pittheus was casting about for a suitable match for his daughter, he was visited by the childless AEGEUS, king of Athens. Pittheus arranged that Aethra should lie with their guest on the little island of Sphaeria, where she had gone with libations for the hero Sphaerus. Only Aethra knew that she lay with Poseidon in the same night.

The next morning Aegeus placed a sword and sandals under a heavy stone and gave Aethra directions that, if she bore a son who on reaching manhood was strong enough to lift the stone, she should send him with the tokens to Aegeus at Athens. Her son, Theseus, proved more than equal to this task and succeeded Aegeus as king of Athens. He sent for Aethra, but, during his later absence from Attica, she was carried off from the town of Aphidnae by the Dioscuri, who gave her as a slave to their sister Helen. Helen took Aethra with her to Troy. When the city was destroyed, the old woman escaped to the Greek camp. Theseus' sons asked Agamemnon to be allowed to take her with them. With Helen's permission, he consented. [Hyginus, *Fabulae*, 37; Pausanias 1.41.4, 2.31.9, 2.33.1.]

Aetna, Mount. A mountain near the eastern coast of Sicily. Aetna, about 11,000 feet in height, is Europe's highest volcano. The Greeks explained its activity by the myth that Zeus or Athena imprisoned either the monster Typhöeus or the Giant Enceladus under the mountain or beneath the island of Sicily. Roman writers claimed that Aetna was the smithy of Vulcan (Hephaestus), which was manned by the Cyclopes.

Aetolia. A large area of the mainland of Greece north of the Gulf of Patrae and between the river Acheloüs on the west and Mount Parnassus in the east. The eponym of Aetolia was Aetolus, an Eleian, and Aetolia seems to have maintained connections with Elis throughout its history. The aboriginal inhabitants of Aetolia were the Curetes, and they seem to have been at odds with the ruling house at Calydon, the principal city of the region, during most of Aetolian legendary history. Pleuron, the second city of Aetolia, may have remained a stronghold of the Curetes. The only famous king of Aetolia was Oeneus. Two of his sons, Meleager and Tydeus, were well known for their prowess, but one died young and the other was exiled. The dynasty of Oeneus seems to have lasted no more than two generations after his death. Wars and invasions are known to have largely depopulated the region before the Classical period.

Aetolus. The eponym of Aetolia. Aetolus was a son of Endymion, king of Elis, by a woman who is variously identified. He succeeded his brother Epeius to the Eleian rule. At funeral games held in honor of Azan, an Arcadian, Aetolus accidentally killed Apis, an Argive or Arcadian, by running him down with his chariot. He fled or was exiled and went to the land of the Curetes, on the river Acheloüs. After killing Dorus, Laodocus, and Polypoetes, sons of Apollo by Phthia, he conquered the Curetes and named the land Aetolia, for himself. He married Pronoë, daughter of Phorbus, who bore Pleuron and Calydon, eponyms of two principal cities of Aetolia. [Apollodorus 1.7.6; Pausanias 5.1.4–5, 5.1.8.]

Agamedes. See STYMPHALUS; TROPHONIUS.

Agamemnon. A king of Mycenae.

A. Agamemnon and Menelaüs were known as the Atreidae—that is, sons of ATREUS [A, D]—though some say that they were actually sons of Atreus' son Pleisthenes. According to one story, they were mere boys at the time of Aegisthus' murder of Atreus and were saved from Thyestes' vengeance by being reared at the courts of Sicyon and Calydon. On reaching manhood, they returned, with the help of Tyndareüs, king of Sparta, and overthrew Thyestes. The more usual tale has it that they were grown men long before Atreus' death and acted as his agent in his long quarrel with Thyestes. In either case, Agamemnon took his father's throne at Mycenae, or at Argos or at Amyclae, as some writers say. He soon dominated all of Argolis.

One of his first acts was to kill Tantalus, a son of Thyestes who had married Tyndareüs' daughter Clytemnestra. Snatching their baby from her breast, he dashed out its brains and presently made its mother his wife. Clytemnestra bore Agamemnon four children; Iphigeneia, Electra, Chrysothemis, and Orestes. (Homer calls the first two Iphianassa and Laodice.) Pausanias says, however, that the Argives, as well as the poet Stesichorus, claimed that Iphigeneia was actually the daughter of Helen and Theseus, and was reared by Clytemnestra.

Agamemnon, having inherited the most powerful kingdom in the Peloponnesus, set about to consolidate his strength. He marched on Sicyon and made it subject to Mycenae. When most of the princes of Greek cities were suing for the hand of Clytemnestra's sister Helen, Agamemnon used his influence as Tyndareüs' son-in-law to urge Menelaüs' claim. The wily old King Tyndareüs left the choice to his daughter, and Helen, no doubt aware of the immense wealth of the brothers from Mycenae, chose Menelaüs.

B. This triumph proved a short-lived one for both the Atreidae. When Helen was abducted by the Trojan prince Paris, Menelaüs called on Agamemnon to use his great prestige in raising a Greek force to win her back. Agreeing, Agamemnon soon had to pay a heavy price for the honor. While the fleet was drawn up at Aulis, ready to sail against Troy, he carelessly compared his skill at hunting to that of Artemis. This so enraged the goddess that she becalmed the ships, or else sent violent storms that prevented their departure. The seer Calchas predicted that only the sacrifice of Agamemnon's eldest daughter, Iphigeneia, would appease Artemis and bring sailing weather. Pressed by the other generals, Agamemnon had to place his duty as commander-in-chief above his feelings as a father. He sent Odysseus and Diomedes to Mycenae with a false message for Clytemnestra, directing her to send Iphigeneia with them to be married to Achilles at Aulis. When the girl arrived, Agamemnon prepared her for the sacrifice. At the last moment, Artemis substituted a stag on the altar and carried Iphigeneia away to be her priestess among the Taurians. The witnesses could only report to Clytemnestra that her daughter had miraculously vanished—a tale that she refused to believe. Agamemnon both lost a daughter and gained the implacable hatred of his wife.

C. The Greek forces were, however, able to sail for Troy, and Agamemnon's role in that bitter struggle belongs to the story of the TROJAN WAR. In the meantime, Thyestes' son Aegisthus, ignoring a warning from Hermes, killed the minstrel that Agamemnon had left to guard his wife, seduced Clytemnestra, and made himself ruler of Argolis. (Hyginus [*Fabulae* 117] claims that Clytemnestra was unfaithful less because of Iphigeneia's death than from anger at Oeax' advance report that her husband was bringing home Priam's daughter Cassandra as his concubine. Oeax thus avenged Agamemnon's condemnation of his innocent brother PALAMEDES at Troy. Others say that Palamedes' father, Nauplius, avenged his son by causing Aegisthus' seduction of Clytemnestra.) For a full year before Agamemnon's return, the lovers kept watchmen on the roads to warn them of his approach. Aeschylus says that beacon fires on mountaintops all the way from Trojan Ida signaled his coming. His wife and her paramour were ready.

Accounts differ as to how the returning king was greeted. According to Homer [*Odyssey* 4.519–537], Aegisthus invited him to a feast, then set upon him and his followers with twenty armed men. The dramatists say that while the king was bathing, his wife and her lover trapped him in a net or a voluminous robe and killed him with an ax. Clytemnestra herself killed Cassandra. Together the lovers killed Cassandra's children by Agamemnon, Teledamus and Pelops. They would no doubt have killed Orestes as well, but his sister Electra or some loyal retainer sent him away secretly to the court of Strophius, king of Phocis, where he grew to manhood. The vengeance of brother and sister on the murderers of their father belongs to the story of ORESTES [A].

Agamemnon's murder is the subject of tragedies, bearing his name, by Aeschylus and Seneca. The sacrifice of his daughter was related by Euripides in his *Iphigeneia in Aulis*. Agamemnon is a principal character in the *Iliad*, and his death is related in the *Odyssey* by Menelaüs [Book 4] and by his own ghost [Book 11].

Agapenor. A king of Tegea in Arcadia. A son of Ancaeüs, Agapenor succeeded Echemus on the throne. The sons of the Psophian king Phegeus sold their sister Arsinoë to him as a slave. The sons of her husband, Alcmeon, later encountered Phegeus' sons at Agapenor's house and killed them. Agapenor led the Arcadian forces to the Trojan War in ships borrowed from Agamemnon. Driven by a storm to Cyprus during the return voyage, he remained there with his followers and founded the city of Paphos. [Homer, *Iliad*, 2.603–614; Apollodorus 3.7.5–6; Pausanias 8.5.2.]

Agasthenes. A king of Elis. Agasthenes inherited the Eleian throne from Augeias, as his elder brother Phyleus preferred to rule in Dulichium. His son Polyxeinus was a leader of Eleian forces at Troy.

Agave. A daughter of Cadmus, king of Thebes, and Harmonia. Agave married Echion, one of the Sparti, and bore a son, PENTHEUS. Together with her sisters Autonoë and Ino, she maligned their sister Semele, who had died pregnant by Zeus with Dionysus. According to some writers, it was for this calumny that Agave was punished with madness, in which she tore Pentheus to pieces. Exiled from Thebes, Agave went to Illyria and married King Lycotherses, then killed him in order that Cadmus might have his throne.

Agave is a character in Euripides' tragedy *The Bacchants*. See also Hyginus [*Fabulae* 184, 240, 254].

Agdistis. See CYBELE.

Agenor (1). A king of Tyre or Sidon, in Phoenicia. Agenor and his twin brother, Belus, were sons of Poseidon and the Egyptian goddess Libya. Agenor migrated to Phoenicia, leaving his brother to rule Egypt. He married Telephassa or Argiope, who bore Europa and several sons, Cadmus, Phoenix, Cilix, Phineus, and Thasus. (Several of these children are credited by various writers to other fathers, but all seem to be descended from Agenor.) According to the *Catalogues of Women* [22], Agenor also had a daughter Demodoce. Europa was kidnapped by Zeus. Agenor, not knowing what had happened to her, ordered his sons to find her or else not to return. None of them returned, nor did Telephassa, who sailed with them and died in Thrace. The others all founded colonies in lands bordering the Aegean. [Apollodorus 2.1.4, 3.1.1.]

Agenor (2). A king of Argos. By one account, Agenor was the son of Ecbasus and father of Argus Panoptes. By another, he and Iasus were sons of Triopas. Agenor was the great-grandfather of Gelanor, who was ruling Argos when Danaüs arrived. [Apollodorus 2.1.2; Pausanias 2.16.1.]

Agenor (3). The name given by Hyginus [*Fabulae* 64] to Andromeda's betrothed, who was killed by PERSEUS [D]. In other versions of the myth, Perseus' rival is called Phineus.

Agenor (4). A son of Pleuron and Xanthippe, daughter of Dorus. Agenor married Epicaste, daughter of Calydon. She bore him Porthaon and Demonice, and perhaps Thestius as well. [Apollodorus 1.7.7; Pausanias 3.13.8.]

Agenor (5). A son of Antenor. One of the bravest of the Trojan soldiers, Agenor dared to challenge Achilles in order to permit the fleeing Trojans to escape into their city. When he was wounded, Apollo spirited him away and, assuming his form, lured Achilles from the gates until the Trojans were safe. [Homer, *Iliad*, 11.56–60, 21.544–611.]

ages of man. See RACES OF MAN.

Aglaea. A daughter of Mantineus, and mother by Abas of the twins Acrisius and Proëtus. [Apollodorus 2.2.1.]

Aglaea. See GRACES.

Agraulus or **Aglaurus** (1). A daughter of Actaeüs. Agraulus, who is generally called merely a daughter of Actaeüs and not named, married Cecrops and bore Erysichthon, Agraulus, Herse, and Pandrosus. [Apollodorus 3.14.2.]

Agraulus or **Aglaurus** (2). A daughter of Cecrops and Agraulus. Agraulus had a daughter, Alcippe, by Ares and, according to the Cerycians, was the mother of their eponym, Ceryx. Together with her sister Herse, Agraulus betrayed Athena's trust in spying on ERICHTHONIUS (1). In most accounts, the guilty pair went mad and committed suicide, but Ovid [*Metamorphoses* 2.552–562, 2.708–832] claims that they survived. Later Hermes fell in love with Herse. Agraulus, filled with envy, barred the god's way to Herse's chamber and was turned to stone. [Apollodorus 3.14.2, 3.14.6; Pausanias 1.18.2–3.]

Agrius (1). A king of Calydon. Agrius was a son of Porthaon and Euryte. When his brother Oeneus, king of Calydon, was left undefended by the death of his son Meleager, Agrius' sons drove Oeneus from the throne and gave the rule to their father. Some say that they first rid the area of Oeneus' other famous son, Tydeus, by insisting on his exile for the killing of one or more relatives, who are variously identified. Later Tydeus' son, Diomedes, avenged his grandfather by killing some or all of Agrius' sons. If Agrius was not killed with his sons, he committed suicide. [Apollodorus 1.7.10, 1.8.5–6; Hyginus, *Fabulae*, 175.]

Agrius (2). One of the GIANTS. In the war between Giants and gods, the Fates killed Agrius and his brother Thoas with brazen clubs. [Apollodorus 1.6.2.]

Agyïeus or **Aguïeus**. A title of Apollo. This epithet, meaning "He of the Ways," referred to the god's patronage of doors, roads, and public places. Apollo was represented in this aspect of his divinity by a conical, possibly phallic, pillar, which was set up in private courtyards and in marketplaces.

Aïdoneus. See HADES.

Ajax (1). The son of Telamon and Periboea or Eëriboea. When Heracles prayed to Zeus to send a brave son to his friend Telamon, an eagle (*aietos*) appeared, signaling the god's assent; the son who was born was named Ajax (Aias) for the eagle. Ajax made his great reputation—and lost it—at the Trojan War, to which he led twelve ships from his father's island kingdom of Salamis. Taller by a head than the other Greeks and, next to Achilles, the handsomest of them, he was a bulwark on the field of battle. He fought most often side by side with Ajax of Locris, but his half-brother, Teucer, occasionally used his huge shield as a haven from behind which he could shoot arrows in safety. Ajax met Hector in single combat and they fought until the heralds parted them; afterward they exchanged gifts, Hector giving Ajax a sword in return for his belt. Ajax was the strongest defender of the Greek ships when they were threatened by a Trojan advance. He was a member of the embassy sent to plead with Achilles to rejoin the fighting, but, being a better soldier than speaker, he left most of the persuasion to Odysseus and Phoenix. He defended the corpse of Patroclus and, later, carried the dead Achilles from the field while Odysseus held back the Trojans.

Ajax and Odysseus contested the right to be awarded Achilles' arms in recognition of their services to the Greek cause. Either with the aid of Athena or through some collusion with the judges, the eloquent Odysseus won the arms. Ajax was so distressed by this blow to his honor that he went mad and slaughtered the herds of the Greek forces, imagining them to be the leaders who had injured him. On recovering his senses, Ajax was overcome with shame and committed suicide with the sword that Hector had given him. Agamemnon and Menelaüs would not at first allow his body to be buried, but finally relented at the request of Odysseus. It is said that a flower sprang up from Ajax' blood, bearing on its petals the letters *AI*, which were both a part of Ajax' Greek name and an exclamation of grief. Ajax was seen by Odysseus in the Underworld, according to Homer [*Odyssey* 11.543–567]. Later traditions made him, like Achilles, immortal, and placed him on the White Island in the western Black Sea.

Ajax was survived by a son, Eurysaces, and by the boy's mother, Tecmessa, whom Ajax had taken while sacking the city of the Phrygian king Teleutas. After the death of Telamon, who had unjustly exiled Teucer for not preventing Ajax' death, Eurysaces became king of Salamis. He gave over the rule of the island to nearby Athens, which in turn named Ajax one of the *eponymoi,* or purported founders, of its ten tribes. According to Herodotus [6.39], it was another son, Philaeüs, who went to Athens. Ajax was honored as a hero at Athens, Salamis, and many other places in Greece.

Ajax was the principal character of Sophocles' tragedy *Ajax,* which deals with his suicide and burial. He appears throughout Homer's *Iliad.* The main events of his life were summarized by Apollodorus [3.10.8; 3.12.7; "Epitome" 5.4, 5.6–7]. Ovid recounted the contest for Achilles' arms [*Metamorphoses* 12.624–13.398], and Pindar explained the origin of his name [*Isthmian Odes* 6.41–54].

Ajax (2). The son of Oïleus, a Locrian king, by his wife, Eriopis, or by a nymph, Rhene. Born in the Locrian town of Naryx, Ajax led forty Locrian ships to the Trojan War. There he became inseparable from Ajax of Salamis, a man of huge stature, and the two fought side by side. The "lesser" Ajax was a fine spearman, and the fastest runner of the Greeks except for Achilles. He was particularly successful at the capture of fleeing enemies. Ajax became one of the most respected of Greek warriors, but brought disaster on the whole force after the fall of Troy by alienating their chief patroness, Athena. This he did by dragging Cassandra from Athena's shrine in order to rape her. Some say that the goddess' statue was knocked down, others that its eyes thereafter looked up to heaven in horror.

Odysseus wanted Ajax stoned for thus angering the gods, but the Greeks did not dare to touch him, for he clung as a suppliant to the image which he had just desecrated. Athena enlisted the aid of Zeus and Poseidon to avenge the outrage. Together they caused the Greek fleet to be wrecked off Cape Caphareus, in southern Euboea. Some say that Athena struck Ajax dead with a thunderbolt, others that Poseidon let him swim in safety to a huge rock called Gyrae. There the rash man boasted that he had saved himself in spite of any god. Poseidon thereupon split the rock with a thunderbolt, and Ajax was drowned.

Ajax appears repeatedly throughout Homer's *Iliad*, usually with the other Ajax; they are often referred to as the Aiantes (Ajaxes). See also the *Odyssey* [4.499–511], Euripides [*Trojan Women* 48–97], Vergil [*Aeneïd* 1.39–45, 2.403–406], and Apollodorus ["Epitome" 5.22–23, 6.6].

Alalcomenae. A town on the shores of Lake Copaïs, in Boeotia. Alalcomenae's only claim to fame was its insistence that Athena had been born, not beside the great Libyan lake Tritonis, but by a local stream of no importance called Triton, and had received from it her well-known title Tritogeneia. Alalcomeneus, the city's eponym, was said to have reared her there.

Alba Longa. The second capital of the people later called Romans. Ascanius (Iülus), the son of Aeneas, moved the capital of the Trojan conquerors of Latium from Lavinium to Alba Longa. Alba Longa remained the capital, through the reigns of ten or twelve kings, until Romulus founded Rome. The ruins of the undoubtedly ancient city of Alba Longa are found southeast of Rome, not far from Velletri.

Albula River. The original name of the river that flows through Rome. When King Tiberinus drowned in the Albula, it was renamed the Tiber.

Albunea. An obscure goddess worshipped at Tibur (now Tivoli), in Italy. Albunea was listed by Varro as one of the Sibyls, but was more likely a local goddess.

Alcaeüs (1). A son of Perseus and Andromeda. Alcaeüs was the father of Amphitryon and Anaxo by Astydameia, daughter of Pelops, or by Laonome, daughter of Guneus, or by Hipponome, daughter of Menoeceus. [Apollodorus 2.4.5.]

Alcaeüs (2) and **Sthenelus.** Sons of Androgeüs. When Heracles sacked the island of Paros on his way to the Amazon campaign, he took these two young men as hostages. On the return voyage he conquered the island of Thasus, off the coast of Thrace, and left them to rule it. [Apollodorus 2.5.9.]

Alcaeüs (3). The name given at birth to HERACLES. This name commemorated Amphitryon's father, Alcaeüs.

Alcathoüs (1). A king of Megara. A son of Pelops and Hippodameia, Alcathoüs came to Megara and, for killing the Cithaeronian lion, was awarded the kingdom and the hand of Euaechme, daughter of the former king, Megareus. Alcathoüs rebuilt the city walls, which had been destroyed by the armies of Minos during the reign of Nisus. Alcathoüs had two sons, Ischepolis and Callipolis, and three daughters, Periboea, Automedusa, and Iphinoë. When Ischepolis was killed during the Calydonian boar hunt, Callipolis rushed to where his father was sacrificing to Apollo and interrupted the rite. Alcathoüs killed him on the spot for his impiety, learning its cause too late. The famous seer Polyeidus came to Megara to purify Alcathoüs for this killing. Alcathoüs left his throne to his famous grandson Ajax, son of Periboea, who had married Telamon. [Pausanias 1.41.3–6, 1.42.1–6.]

Alcathoüs (2). A son of Porthaon and Euryte. Alcathoüs' only claim to distinction is that he was killed by his nephew Tydeus, or else by Oenomaüs, when he (Alcathoüs) became one of many suitors for the hand of Hippodameia. [Apollodorus 1.7.10, 1.8.5; *Great Eoiae* 10.]

Alcestis. The eldest daughter of Pelias, king of Iolcus. Because of her piety, Alcestis could not bring herself to take part with her sisters in their fatal attempt to rejuvenate their father. She was therefore spared the ruin brought upon the royal house through the plot of Medea and JASON [D, E]. Alcestis married the equally pious ADMETUS, king of Pherae, who had Apollo's help in performing the feat required by her father of the many suitors who were attracted by Alcestis' beauty. She bore a son, Eumelus, and a daughter, whose name is not recorded. Later she gave her own life as a substitute for her husband's, but was returned to the land of the living by Persephone or Heracles. Alcestis is the heroine of the play by Euripides that bears her name.

Alcidice. A daughter of Aleüs. Alcidice married Salmoneus, king of Salmonia, in Elis, and bore him a beautiful daughter, Tyro. After Alcidice's death, Salmoneus married Sidero.

Alcimede. A daughter of Phylacus, king of Phylace, and Clymene. Alcimede married Aeson and bore JASON [A, C] and, much later, Promachus. When Pelias, king of Iolcus, killed Promachus and forced her husband to commit suicide, Alcimede cursed him and killed herself with a sword. Many writers say, however, that Aeson's wife was Polymede, daughter of Autolycus, or some other woman.

Alcinoüs. A king of the Phaeacians. Alcinoüs was a son of Nausithoüs, who had led the Phaeacians from Hypereia to the island of Scherië, or Drepane. He married Arete, daughter of his deceased brother, Rhexenor, and she bore five sons and a daughter, Nausicaä. Alcinoüs was a wise and also a generous man. Even though he had been warned that he would one day bring down on his people the calamitous anger of Poseidon because he saved so many shipwrecked sailors, he continued his kindly services. At the urging of Arete, Alcinoüs protected Jason and Medea against the Colchian fleet that had pursued the Argonauts to Drepane. A generation later he entertained the shipwrecked Odysseus and sent him home in a Phaeacian ship. [Homer, *Odyssey*, Books 6, 7, 8, 13; Apollonius Rhodius 4.982–1222.]

Alcippe. See HALIRRHOTHIUS.

Alcmene. The daughter of Electryon and Anaxo. Although the poet Asius claimed that Alcmene's parents were Amphiaraüs and Eriphyle, the prevailing tradition named Electryon, Perseus' son and successor as king of Tiryns and Mycenae, as her father. Alcmene married her cousin Amphitryon, but refused to lie with him until he avenged the murder of her brothers by Taphians during a cattle raid. Amphitryon recovered the cattle for his father-in-law, but killed him, accidentally or otherwise, while delivering them. He was exiled for this deed by Electryon's brother Sthenelus, who usurped Electryon's kingdom. Alcmene fled with her husband and her half-brother, Licymnius, to Thebes, where they were welcomed by King Creon and his wife, Eniocha. Amphitryon raised an army, which he led in a successful expedition against the Taphians. Returning to Thebes and his wife's bed, he found that someone had got there before him. The seer Teiresias explained that it had been Zeus and that Alcmene had been tricked by the god. AMPHITRYON [B], relieved at her innocence, also spent a night with her.

In due course Alcmene gave birth to twins, but not without complications caused by Hera's jealousy over her husband's escapade with Alcmene. Zeus announced one day on Olympus that a son of his lineage was about to be born and was fated to become lord of his people. This meant, as Hera knew, that if Zeus's son by Alcmene were to be born at the proper time, he would succeed to the rule of Tiryns that his grandfather had held. She therefore tricked her unwary husband into decreeing that whatever descendant of his was born that day would rule. As soon as he had pronounced the words, Hera dispatched their daughter Eileithyia, a goddess of childbirth, to Thebes to retard the delivery of Alcmene's child. She herself hurried to Tiryns, where she brought about the premature birth of Eurystheus, son of Sthenelus and grandson of Zeus's son Perseus. Thus Eurystheus, rather than the rightful descendant of Electryon, was fated to rule in Mycenae and Tiryns.

In Thebes, meanwhile, Alcmene had been seven days in labor. Some believe that Hera, not content with depriving her child of his throne, wanted to kill him, and his mother as well. Eileithyia was preventing the birth by sitting on her altar by the door of the bedroom with legs and fingers tightly crossed. Alcmene's Theban attendants had almost given up hope for her life when one of them—a woman named Galanthis, or a daughter of Teiresias named Historis —thought of a way to break the spell. She cried out happily that the baby was born. The astonished Eileithyia leaped to her feet, uncrossing her legs and fingers. In the moment before the goddess discovered the deception, twins were born to Alcmene. The frustrated Eileithyia punished Galanthis by changing her into a weasel. Pausanias [9.11.3] told a somewhat different version of this event, in which some witches took the role of Eileithyia.

Alcmene and Amphitryon named their children Heracles and Iphicles. (Some say that Heracles was originally called Alcaeüs.) It soon became clear that one of the twins was the son of Zeus, the other of Amphitryon. At the age of eight or ten months Heracles strangled two snakes that Hera sent to the twins' crib to kill him. He continued to grow so strong and bold that, even as a youth, he became famous throughout the Greek lands. He remained, however, subject to the tyrannical Eurystheus. He died when still young and was deified.

Alcmene survived her son, but the accounts of her death are confused.

Some writers say that after Amphitryon's death she married the Cretan law-giver Rhadamanthys, who had fled in exile to Boeotia. There they both died and were buried near Haliartus. According to a better-known version of Alcmene's late years, she and her grandchildren took refuge at Marathon from Eurystheus, who was trying to capture them. Heracles' son Hyllus or his nephew, Iolaüs, supported by the Athenians, routed the Tirynthian invaders and disposed of Eurystheus. Alcmene insisted on his execution, or else she gouged the eyes from his severed head when Hyllus sent it to her. She died either at Thebes or at Megara.

Alcmene is a principal character in Euripides' tragedy *The Children of Heracles*, which tells of Eurystheus' invasion of Attica, and in Plautus' comedy *Amphitryon*, the story of her night with Zeus. Homer [*Iliad* 19.96-133] told of the trick that Hera played on Zeus, and Ovid [*Metamorphoses* 9.280-323] related the events of Heracles' birth.

Alcmeon or **Alcmaeon.** A son of the seer Amphiaraüs and Eriphyle.

A. While only boys, Alcmeon and his younger brother, Amphilochus, were commanded by their father to kill their mother. Bribed by Polyneices with the necklace given his ancestress Harmonia at her wedding to Cadmus, Eriphyle had forced Amphiaraüs to march with the SEVEN AGAINST THEBES. Although he knew that he would die there, Amphiaraüs was bound by a pact to do Eriphyle's bidding in the matter. Her sons did not move to punish her until Polyneices' son bribed her a second time (this time with Harmonia's wedding robe) and she urged Alcmeon to lead the sons of the Seven, the EPIGONI, in an expedition to avenge their fathers. Alcmeon and Amphilochus went to Thebes, where some say Alcmeon killed King Laodamas. Dedicating some of the spoils at Delphi, he consulted the oracle and was again ordered to kill Eriphyle. This he did, possibly with his brother's aid, and the Erinyes of his mother drove him mad. In this state he wandered first to the Arcadian court of his grandfather Oïcles, then to that of Phegeus at Psophis, in Phegia. Phegeus purified him and gave him his daughter (Arsinoë or Alphesiboea) as his wife. Alcmeon presented her with Harmonia's necklace and robe, with which his mother had twice been bribed. Arsinoë bore him a son, Clytius.

Alcmeon's madness did not improve and Phegia became barren because of the presence of a matricide. Again Alcmeon went to Delphi. This time the oracle suggested that he go to the newly silted delta of the river Acheloüs, explaining that Eriphyle's Erinyes could not harm him on land that had not existed at the time of the murder. On his way Alcmeon was entertained by King Oeneus at Calydon, but expelled by the Thesprotians from their country.

Reaching the delta, Alcmeon was purified of the matricide by the river-god, Acheloüs, and the madness left him at last. He settled down by the river's mouth and married Acheloüs' daughter, Callirrhoë, who bore him Acarnan and Amphoterus. Alcmeon might have lived out his life there in peace had his wife not heard of the fabulous necklace and robe and demanded them for herself.

Reluctantly Alcmeon left his haven and returned to Psophis. He told Phegeus that an oracle had said that he would be free of madness if he would dedicate the necklace and the robe at Delphi. Phegeus believed him and gave them to him, but as Alcmeon was about to leave, one of his servants blurted out the truth. Enraged, Phegeus ordered his sons, Pronoüs and Agenor (or Temenus and Axion), to kill Alcmeon. They did so from ambush and buried him in a cypress grove. When Arsinoë protested her husband's murder, her brothers put her in a chest and sold her as a slave to Agapenor, king of Tegea, telling him that it was she who had killed Alcmeon.

B. Callirrhoë had meanwhile been seduced by Zeus. Learning of her husband's death, she asked the god to grant that her sons grow to manhood overnight in order to avenge their father. Zeus granted her request and Acarnan and Amphoterus, fully grown, started at once for Psophis. Stopping by chance at Agapenor's palace, they met the murderers, who were on their way to dedicate the necklace and robe at Delphi, or had just done so. Alcmeon's sons not only killed the sons of Phegeus but went on to Psophis and killed Phegeus and his wife as well, after which they took the fatal gifts to Delphi. Returning to their homeland, Acarnan and his brother settled the land north of the Acheloüs along the coast and called it Acarnania.

Euripides is said to have claimed in a play, now lost, that during Alcmeon's wanderings he had two children by Teiresias' daughter, Manto, whom he and the other Epigoni had dedicated to Apollo among the spoils of war. Alcmeon gave the children, Amphilochus and Tisiphone, to King Creon of Corinth to rear. Later, when Creon's wife saw how beautiful Tisiphone was growing, she sold her as a slave. By an extraordinary coincidence, Alcmeon bought her, not knowing at first who she was. In time he also took Amphilochus back from Creon. This boy later colonized Amphilochian Argos in Aetolia.

At some point in his career, Alcmeon is said to have aided Diomedes in his vengeance on the sons of Agrius in Calydon. Others say, however, that it was Diomedes' companion Sthenelus who did this. [Apollodorus 3.6.2, 3.7.2–7.]

Alcyone (1). A daughter of Aeolus and Enarete or Aegiale. Alcyone married Ceÿx, king of Trachis. When Ceÿx was shipwrecked and drowned on his way to Delphi, Alcyone grieved for him so deeply that husband and wife were turned into kingfishers (halcyons), which were said to nest on the sea for seven days every winter, during which the waters remain calm. Sailors call this time "halcyon days." According to another story, husband and wife were transformed by Zeus as a punishment for calling each other Zeus and Hera. Alcyone became a kingfisher, Ceÿx a gannet or sea gull (ceÿx). [Ovid, *Metamorphoses*, 11.410–748; Apollodorus 1.7.3–4.]

Alcyone (2). A daughter of Atlas and the Oceanid Pleïone. One of the PLEIADES, Alcyone was seduced by Poseidon and bore two sons, Hyreius and Hyperenor, and a daughter, Aethusa. The Troezenians claimed that she was also the mother of Hyperes and Anthas, two early kings of their city. [Apollo-dorus 3.10.1; Pausanias 2.6.8.]

Alcyone. See STHENELUS (1).

Alcyoneus. One of the GIANTS. Alcyoneus and his brother Porphyrion were the strongest of the Giants. Alcyoneus was, moreover, invulnerable as long as he remained within the boundaries of his homeland, the Thracian peninsula of Pallene. He drove away Helius' cattle from the island of Erytheia. Later, in the war between the gods and the Giants, he was shot by Heracles, who dragged him outside Pallene. There, no longer invulnerable, he died. Some say that Telamon aided Heracles in this adventure. [Apollodorus 1.6.1; Pindar, *Nemean Odes*, 4.27–30, and *Isthmian Odes*, 6.32–35.]

Alcyonian Lake. A reputedly bottomless lake at Lerna. This swampy lake was claimed locally to be the entrance to Hades used by Dionysus to bring up his mother, Semele, and by Heracles to bring up Cerberus. The emperor Nero had the lake plumbed, but no bottom could be found.

Alecto or **Allecto.** See ERINYES.

Alector. A king of Argos. A son of Anaxagoras, Alector was the father of Iphis and, according to some, of Capaneus. [Pausanias 2.18.5.]

Aletes. See ORESTES [D].

Aleüs. A king of Arcadia. Aleüs succeeded his father, Apheidas, as king of Tegea and became king of all Arcadia, ruling from Tegea, when Aepytus died. He married Neaera, daughter of his brother Pereus, and they had four children: a daughter, Auge, and three sons, Lycurgus, Amphidamas, and Cepheus. Aleüs extended the city of Tegea and founded another city in northeastern Arcadia, which he named Alea, after himself. He is best known for his attempt to dispose of AUGE after her seduction by Heracles. Fond of his grandson Ancaeüs, Aleüs tried vainly to prevent his sailing with the Argonauts by hiding his armor. [Apollodorus 2.7.4, 3.9.1; Apollonius Rhodius 1.165–171; Pausanias 8.4.4–10, 8.48.7.]

Alexander or **Alexandrus.** See PARIS.

Almus. A son of Sisyphus. Almus migrated from Corinth to Boeotia, where Eteocles, king of Orchomenus, gave him land. The village that he founded was called Almones, but later the name was corrupted to Olmones. Almus had two daughters, Chryse and Chrysogeneia, both of whom had sons who reigned in Orchomenus. [Pausanias 2.4.3, 9.34.10, 9.36.1–4.]

Aloadae. See OTUS.

Alöeus (1). A son of Poseidon and Canace, daughter of Aeolus. Alöeus married Iphimedeia, daughter of his brother Triops, but she fell in love with Poseidon and had by him two sons, Otus and Ephialtes. This remarkable pair of giants were, nevertheless, called the Aloadae, for their supposed father, Alöeus. Alöeus at some point took a second wife, Eëriboea, who reported to Hermes her stepsons' mistreatment of Ares. Alöeus seems to have been often confused with the Sicyonian king of the same name, or else was the same personage. The first is called a brother of Epopeus, king of Sicyon, the other his father. [Homer, *Odyssey*, 11.305–310; Apollodorus 1.7.4.]

Alöeus (2). A king of Asopia. Alöeus received Asopia (Sicyonia) from his father, Helius, and bequeathed it to his son, Epopeus. (See also ALÖEUS, 1.) [Pausanias 2.1.1, 2.3.10.]

Alope. A daughter of Cercyon, king of Eleusis. Seduced by Poseidon, Alope bore a son, Hippothoön or Hippothoüs, but exposed him for fear of her father's anger. The child was suckled by mares. Shepherds who found him fell to arguing over the fine clothing the child wore and took their dispute to the king. Cercyon, recognizing the clothing as his daughter's work, killed Alope and had the child exposed a second time. Again Hippothoön was fed by mares. When he grew to manhood, he went to Theseus, king of Athens, and asked to be made ruler of Eleusis. Theseus had earlier killed Cercyon in self-defense, but he granted the young man's request because Hippothoön was, like himself, a son of Poseidon. Hippothoön was listed as the eponym of one of the ten tribes of Athens. [Hyginus, *Fabulae*, 187; Pausanias 1.5.1–2, 1.39.3.]

Alpheius. The principal river of Elis, rising in Arcadia; also, the god of this river. Alpheius was a son of Oceanus and Tethys. He fell in love with the nymph Arethusa when she bathed in his waters. Taking human form, he pursued her. She fled as far as the island of Ortygia, off the Sicilian coast, and there became a spring. Some say that the transformation, arranged by Artemis at Arethusa's request, took place in Greece and that the spring was somehow transported to Italy. Alpheius, not to be frustrated, flowed under the sea all the way from the Peloponnesian coast to Ortygia, where, rising to the surface, he mingled his waters with the spring. As a river he played a less romantic role when Heracles turned him through the cattle yards of Augeias to flush them of dung. Many say, however, that some other river was used for this purpose, for Elis is a long way from the course of the Alpheius. Alpheius was the father of Ortilochus. [Pausanias 5.6.2–3; Ovid, *Metamorphoses*, 5.572–641.]

Alphesiboea. See ADONIS; ARSINOË (2); BIAS.

Althaea. A daughter of Thestius and Eurythemis. Althaea married her uncle Oeneus, king of Calydon, and bore two daughters, Gorge and Deïaneira, and several sons, the most famous of whom was MELEAGER. Some say, however, that Deïaneira was Dionysus' daughter and Meleager a son of Ares. Others claim that Althaea had a son by Poseidon. In a quarrel that arose during the CALYDONIAN BOAR HUNT, Meleager killed some or all of his mother's brothers. Althaea either cursed him or caused his death by burning a magical charred brand, knowing that her son would die when it was consumed. Stricken with guilt, she hanged or stabbed herself. [Homer, *Iliad*, 9.543–599; Apollodorus 1.7.10–1.8.3.]

Althaemenes. The son of Catreus, king of Crete. Catreus was told by an oracle that one of his four children would kill him. He kept the warning secret, but Althaemenes somehow learned of it and emigrated to avoid the risk of patricide, taking his sister Apemosyne with him. In Rhodes he founded the city of Cretinia and also the shrine of Atabyrian Zeus on the summit of Mount Ata-byrius, from which, on a clear day, he could see his homeland. Apemosyne was one day discovered to be pregnant. She claimed that Hermes had raped her, but Athaemenes disbelieved her and kicked her to death. Some time later the aged Catreus sailed for Rhodes, wishing to fetch his son home in order that he might bequeath to him the kingdom. When he and his crew landed on a Rhodian beach, they were mistaken by the islanders for pirates and attacked. Althaemenes hurried into the fight and killed Catreus. When he recognized his father's body, he either died of grief or prayed to the gods and was swallowed up by the earth. [Apollodorus 3.2.1–2.]

Amarynceus. An Eleian leader. A son of Pyttius, a Thessalian immigrant to Elis, Amarynceus was given a share in the government by King Augeias, who needed allies against Heracles. Amarynceus had two sons, Diores and Hippo-stratus. Funeral games were held for Amarynceus at Buprasium. [Pausanias 5.1.10.]

Amata. See AENEAS [B, C]; LATINUS.

Amazons. A tribe of warrior women. Perhaps the first Greek to encounter the Amazons was Io, the Argive heifer-woman, as she was wandering through the regions surrounding the Black Sea. She found them living at Themiscyra (now Termeh), on the Thermodon River, which emptied into the Black Sea along its southern shore about two-thirds of the way from the Bosporus to the eastern end of the sea. At some earlier time, according to Aeschylus, they had lived in the Caucasus Mountains. Several generations later Bellerophon fought the Amazons while staying with Iobates, king of Lycia. Still later Heracles defeated them and killed their queen. Theseus either accompanied Heracles on this campaign or engaged in one of his own soon after it. He abducted An-tiope (or Hippolyte), who was either the Amazon queen or her sister, and took her to Athens, where she bore a son, Hippolytus. The Amazons came all the way to Attica in pursuit and, entrenching themselves on the Areopagus, made formidable attacks on the Athenians. At last Theseus either defeated them or battled to a draw and made a treaty with them.

Shortly before or after their expedition against Attica, the Amazons fought the Mygdonians and other Phrygian tribes, who were aided by the Trojans under the young Priam. Perhaps because the Amazons hated the Greeks more than they did the Trojans, their queen, Penthesileia, came to the aid of Priam late in the Trojan War. She was killed by Achilles, but only after inflicting much damage on the Greeks.

Many attempts have been made to identify the Amazons with historical tribes, though even some Classical writers doubted their existence. Descrip-tions of their way of life accounted for the perpetuation of their female culture by saying that they copulated at intervals with men of neighboring tribes, but reared only their girls. The male children either were sent to the fathers' tribes or were mutilated and enslaved. The name Amazon was usually interpreted by the Greeks as "Breastless." It was explained that the women seared off one of each girl child's breasts so that it would not interfere with her use of the javelin or the bow and arrow. Herodotus [4.110–117] believed that a planned intermarriage between Amazons and Scythians resulted in the tribe known as the Sauromatians (perhaps the same as the Sarmatians), who eventually supplanted the Scythians north of the Black Sea. Diodorus Siculus went into some detail not only about the Asiatic Amazons, but about a powerful tribe of the same name said to have ruled Libya in an earlier period. As Greek acquaintance with geography increased, mythological accounts placed the Amazons farther and farther from the known world.

It is now generally agreed that the Amazons were wholly mythical, though it is not unlikely that rumors of seemingly masculine customs among the women of barbarian tribes of Asia Minor and Scythia colored the legend. No satisfactory explanation has been found of the myth of the Amazon invasion of Attica. "Amazon" monuments, mainly tombs, were found in Classical times not only at Athens and Megara but at several points along the supposed route of the invasion from Thessaly southward. [Homer, *Iliad*, 3.184–190, 6.186; Aeschylus, *Eumenides*, 685–690, and *Prometheus Bound*, 723; Vergil, *Aeneïd*, 11.648–663; Apollodorus 2.3.2, 2.5.9, "Epitome" 1.16–17; *Aethiopis* 1, 2; Pausanias 1.2.1, 1.41.7, 2.32.9, 7.2.7–8.]

Amber Islands. A group of islands at the mouth of the Eridanus River. When the HELIADES were transformed into poplars, they wept drops of amber into the sands of the Eridanus River, and it is presumably to the Amber Islands that the drops were carried. The Argonauts stopped twice at the Amber Islands on their homeward journey. (See also PHAËTHON, 1.)

Ambracia. A city and region of southern Epeirus. Ambracia was said to be the homeland of Geryon before he was relocated in Erytheia.

Amisodarus. A Lycian chieftain. Amisodarus reared the Chimaera, a monster. His sons, Maris and Atymnius, died in the Trojan War. [Homer, *Iliad*, 16.327–329.]

Amor. A Roman name for the Greek god EROS. Amor (like CUPID, another Roman form of Eros) was borrowed from the Greeks. He had, however, few of the dignified characteristics of Eros, but was regarded merely as a mischievous boy-god.

Amphianax. See PROËTUS [A].

Amphiaraüs. An Argive warrior and seer. Amphiaraüs, a son of Oïcles and Hypermnestra and a descendant of Melampus, was the great diviner of his day. Loved by both Zeus and Apollo, he received his second sight from Zeus. Amphiaraüs hunted the Calydonian boar and, some say, was second only after Atalanta in shooting it. He drove Adrastus from the Argive throne, but the quarrel was patched up. He married Adrastus' sister Eriphyle and agreed that she should thereafter act as arbiter between himself and Adrastus, each agreeing to abide by her decisions.

When Oedipus died, Amphiaraüs helped to officiate at his funeral and was much admired by the Theban women. Later, knowing that only Adrastus would survive the campaign of the SEVEN AGAINST THEBES, he at first refused to join it, but Eriphyle, bribed by Polyneices, forced him to go. Amphiaraüs made his sons, ALCMEON and Amphilochus, vow to avenge him.

On the way to Thebes, Amphiaraüs repeatedly warned of impending disaster, blaming Tydeus for fomenting the war. Nevertheless he was second only to Adrastus as a leader and may have surpassed him. He avenged himself on Tydeus by preventing his immortalization by Athena. Zeus saved the seer from the shame of being speared in the back by Periclymenus by splitting the earth with a thunderbolt. Amphiaraüs, together with his chariot, charioteer, and horses, vanished forever.

Amphiaraüs was avenged on the Thebans and Eriphyle by Alcmeon. His daughter Demonassa married Thersander. If not deified, as some claim, Amphiaraüs was greatly honored at his oracular shrine. According to Herodotus [1.46–52], Croesus found his oracle as reliable as that at Delphi. [Apollodorus 1.8.2 passim; Pindar, Nemean Odes, 9.13–27.]

Amphictyon. A king of Athens. A son of Deucalion and Pyrrha, or else born from the earth in Attica, Amphictyon deposed his father-in-law, Cranaüs. He ruled for twelve years and was deposed in turn by Erichthonius. [Apollodorus 3.14.6; Pausanias 1.2.6.]

Amphidamas (1). A king of Tegea. Amphidamas, a son of Aleüs, sailed with the Argonauts together with his brother Cepheus, and later seems to have shared the rule of Tegea with Cepheus and their elder brother, Lycurgus. [Apollonius Rhodius 1.161–163, 2.1046–1068.]

Amphidamas (2). A son of Lycurgus. Amphidamas was the father of Melanion and of Antimache, who married Eurystheus. He may be the same as Amphidamas (1). [Apollodorus 3.9.2.]

Amphilochian Argos. A city on the Ambracian Gulf, in southern Epeirus. This city was traditionally founded by Epeirot colonists led by the Argive Amphilochus, son of Amphiaraüs, or by his nephew of the same name.

Amphilochus (1). The younger son of Amphiaraüs and Eriphyle. With his brother, Alcmeon, Amphilochus was commanded by his father to avenge him on the Thebans and on Eriphyle. He marched with the EPIGONI, but apparently did not abet Alcmeon in killing their mother. Later Amphilochus became one of the suitors of Helen. Ancient writers disagree as to whether it was this Amphilochus or his nephew who fought at Troy and afterward founded Amphilochian Mallus or Poseideion in Cilicia. This colonist either was killed by Apollo at Soli or fought a single combat with the seer Mopsus in which both were killed but later shared an infallible oracle at Mallus. [Apollodorus 3.6.2, 3.10.8.]

Amphilochus (2). A son of Alcmeon and Manto, daughter of Teiresias. Amphilochus was reared by Creon, king of Corinth, during his father's madness, but later ALCMEON [B] took him back. Either Amphilochus or his uncle of the same name colonized Amphilochian Argos in Epeirus. Although not mentioned by Homer, Amphilochus is said to have fought at the Trojan War and to have journeyed afterward with several other leaders, including the seer Calchas, to Colophon. There they encountered Mopsus, who defeated Calchas in a contest of divination. Amphilochus joined forces with Mopsus, who, also a son of Manto, was his half-brother, and they went to Cilicia. There they founded the city of Mallus. Some time thereafter they quarreled and killed one another in single combat. This did not prevent them from sharing an oracle that enjoyed a high reputation until at least the second century A.D. [Apollodorus 3.7.7, "Epitome" 6.2, 6.19; Pausanias 1.34.3.]

Amphimachus. A son of Cteatus and Theronice. One of Helen's suitors, Amphimachus led some of the Eleian forces to Troy, where he was killed by Hector. [Homer, *Iliad*, 2.615–624, 13.184–196.]

Amphinomus. The leader of Penelope's suitors from Dulichium. Amphinomus was pious enough to dissuade the other suitors from murdering Telemachus on his return from Pylus unless the gods gave a sign of their approval. Nevertheless he was killed by Telemachus along with the other suitors. He appears frequently in the Ithacan books of Homer's *Odyssey*.

Amphion (1) and **Zethus.** Co-kings of Thebes. When pregnant by Zeus, ANTIOPE fled from the anger of her father, Nycteus, the Theban regent, to the court of Epopeus, king of Sicyon. In his shame Nycteus appointed his brother, Lycus, regent and killed himself. Lycus pursued Antiope and dragged her back to prison. On the way she gave birth to twin sons in the village of Eleutherae, on Mount Cithaeron. Lycus had the babies, Amphion and Zethus, exposed, but they were discovered and reared by herdsmen in their hut on the mountain. The boys grew to manhood unaware of their parentage. Antiope at last escaped the cruel treatment to which Lycus and his wife, Dirce, had subjected her and made herself known to her sons. They tied Dirce to an untamed bull and let her be dragged to death. Next they either killed Lycus or drove him from the throne. The child Laïus, for whom Lycus had been acting as regent, fled to the Peloponnesus.

Amphion and Zethus, unlike most joint kings, shared the rule of Thebes amicably, though they were very different in temperament. Zethus was mainly interested in such practical pursuits as cattle breeding, but Amphion devoted his time to music, Hermes having given him a lyre and taught him to play it. Amphion married Niobe, daughter of the Lydian king Tantalus. Through this connection he learned the Lydian mode and also added three strings to the four that the lyre had previously had. Zethus used to scoff at Amphion's fondness for music, but he learned to respect it when the brothers undertook to build walls around the lower city that had grown up on the hill that bore Cadmus' ancient citadel. While Zethus staggered under the weight of great stones, Amphion played his lyre. His share of the stones, charmed by the music, lumbered after him and fell into place of their own accord. When the brothers had finished their task they changed the name of the city from Cadmeia to Thebes, in honor of Thebe, Zethus' wife. The citadel, however, was still called Cadmeia, after its founder.

The joint reign that began so promisingly ended in tragedy. Niobe bore her husband many sons and daughters, but grew so proud of this accomplishment that she spoke disparagingly of Leto, who had only two. The goddess, offended, called on her son and daughter, Apollo and Artemis, for vengeance. Apollo killed Niobe's sons, Artemis her daughters, though some writers say that one of each, Amyclas and Chloris, survived. Niobe went home to Lydia and was turned to stone on Mount Sipylus. Amphion, if he was not killed along with his sons, stabbed himself in grief, or else went mad and, while attacking Apollo's temple, was shot to death by the god.

Zethus had only one son, but, because of some unrecorded mistake of Thebe's, the boy died, and his father succumbed to a broken heart. According to Homer [*Odyssey* 19.518–523], Zethus' wife was a daughter of Pandareüs, who, after accidentally killing her own son, Itylus, was transformed into a nightingale. Laïus returned from the Peloponnesus to take the throne, and no descendants of Amphion or Zethus ever ruled Thebes. Amphion's surviving daughter, Chloris, married Neleus, king of Messenia, and some say that his daughter Phylomache became the wife of Pelias. According to Homer [*Odyssey* 11.281–284], Amphion, the father of Chloris, was a son of an unidentified Iasus and ruled Orchomenus. This may have been an early tradition about the man usually called a king of Thebes. [Apollodorus 3.5.5–6; Hyginus, *Fabulae*, 7, 8, 9, 11; Pausanias 9.5.6–9; Ovid, *Metamorphoses*, 6.146–312.]

Amphion (2). An Argonaut. Amphion, a son of Hyperasius or Hippasus, came from Pellene, in the Peloponnesian Achaea. He and his brother, Asterius, sailed in the *Argo*. [Apollonius Rhodius 1.176–178.]

Amphithea. A daughter of Pronax. Amphithea married her uncle Adrastus and became the mother of Aegialeus, perhaps of Cyanippus, and of Argeia, Deïpyle, and Aegialeia.

Amphithea. See LYCURGUS (3).

Amphithemis. A Libyan chieftain, also called Garamas. Under the latter name, he was presumably the eponym of the Garamantian tribe in Libya. Amphithemis was a son of Apollo and Acacallis, whose father, King Minos of Crete, had banished her to Libya on finding her pregnant. Amphithemis married Tritonis, the nymph of the lake of that name. She bore him two sons, Nasamon and Caphaurus or Cephalion. Caphaurus was killed by the Argonauts for his sheep. [Apollonius Rhodius 4.1489–1501.]

Amphitrite. A sea-goddess. Amphitrite was a daughter of Nereus and Doris or of Oceanus and Tethys. Poseidon wanted to marry her, but Amphitrite fled to the protection of the Titan Atlas. Poseidon sent messengers throughout the world to find her. One of them, Delphin, discovered her hiding place and persuaded her to marry the sea-god, who gratefully placed the dolphin in the stars in his honor. Amphitrite bore Triton, Rhode, and Benthesicyme. She is said to have given Theseus a golden crown with which to prove his kinship to Poseidon. Except in this tale, however, the goddess seldom appears in myth as anything but a personification of the sea. [Hesiod, *Theogony*, 243, 254; Apollodorus 1.2.2, 1.2.7, 1.4.5, 3.13.4; Hyginus, *Poetica Astronomica*, 2.17; Pausanias 1.17.3.]

Amphitryon. The son of Alcaeüs, son of Perseus.

A. Amphitryon's mother may have been Astydameia or Lysidice, both of whom were daughters of Pelops; Laonome, daughter of Guneus; or Hipponome, daughter of Menoeceus. After the death of Perseus, king of Tiryns and Mycenae, Alcaeüs' brother Electryon became king. Amphitryon married his uncle Electryon's daughter, Alcmene, but Electryon stipulated that she remain a virgin until he returned from a punitive expedition against the Taphians, or Teleboans, who had killed his sons in a cattle raid. Amphitryon was to rule in Electryon's absence. First, however, the king sent Amphitryon to Elis to ransom his stolen cattle from King Polyxenus, in whose care the Taphians had left them.

On his return, Amphitryon turned over the cattle to his father-in-law. Unfortunately, in throwing a club at one of them, he accidentally hit Electryon, who died instantly. Electryon's brother Sthenelus took this opportunity to seize the throne, exiling Amphitryon on the grounds that he had murdered Electryon for the cattle—which, according to the *Shield of Heracles* [78–87], was in fact the case. Amphitryon, Alcmene, and Licymnius, Amphitryon's half-brother, fled as suppliants to Creon, king of Thebes, who, with his wife, Eniocha, received them kindly. (If Amphitryon's mother was Hipponome, he would have been Creon's nephew.)

Alcmene must have believed her husband innocent of Electryon's murder, for she left her homeland to go with him. However, she was equally faithful to the memory of her father and brothers. She refused to lie with Amphitryon until he had avenged Electryon's sons on the Taphians. Amphitryon tried to persuade Creon to accompany him on the campaign. Creon agreed on the condition that Amphitryon rid Thebes of the vixen which, for unexplained reasons, had been sent by Hera or Dionysus to ravage the area around Teumessus. Amphitryon consented. His first move was to enlist the aid of Cephalus, whose hound, Laelaps, was destined by Zeus to catch whatever prey it pursued. In return for a promised share of the spoils from the Taphian raid, Cephalus set the hound after the fox. Since the vixen had been destined by Hera never to be caught, the chase might never have ended had not Zeus avoided an embarrassing situation by turning both animals to stone. Amphitryon, at least indirectly, could take credit for saving Thebes from the fox.

B. At last the Taphian campaign, planned long before by Electryon, got under way. Creon honored his promise to join it, Cephalus went along to protect his own interests, and Amphitryon found other allies in his uncle Heleius, Panopeus of Phocis, and a small force from Locris. The company sailed against the Taphian Islands, off the coast of Acarnania, where King Pterelaüs ruled the Taphians. The siege seemed doomed to failure, for Pterelaüs possessed a single golden hair that made him immortal. But the king's daughter, Comaetho, unexpectedly fell in love with Amphitryon and plucked her father's magic hair. Pterelaüs died instantly. Indignant at this treachery, Amphitryon executed the girl, but did not hesitate to take advantage of her deed. He conquered the islands, gave Cephallenia to Cephalus and the other islands to Heleius, and returned to Thebes loaded with spoils.

Although Amphitryon had been married for a year or more, he had yet to lie with his wife. Now that he had successfully carried out the task that Alcmene had set for him, he naturally expected to receive a warm welcome at home. Instead, Alcmene did not even come out to greet him. When he expressed disappointment at this, his wife was more astonished than he. He had arrived the day before, she said. He had told her of all his adventures and they had spent a delightful night in bed.

Amphitryon was chagrined, but, realizing that Alcmene was genuinely surprised, he hurried off to ask the famous seer Teiresias for an explanation. The old man told him not to worry. It was Zeus who had taken his place the night before. In fact, he had prolonged the darkness for the length of three normal nights. Amphitryon, relieved that Alcmene had not knowingly betrayed him, at long last spent a night with her himself. Some say, however, that Alcmene entertained both Zeus and her husband in a single night.

In due course twin sons were born. It soon became clear that one was far stronger than the other: at the age of eight or ten months he strangled two snakes that Hera, jealous of her husband's night with Alcmene, had sent to the crib. (According to Pherecydes, Amphitryon himself had placed the snakes in the crib, for he felt a nagging desire to know which child was his.) In any case, it was now obvious that Iphicles was the mortal son, Heracles the god's offspring.

C. Amphitryon remained at Thebes for the rest of his life, enjoying the reflected glory of the great Heracles' exploits and a considerable reputation of his own. At some point he is said to have killed Chalcodon, leader of the Euboean forces in a war between Euboea and Thebes. This was perhaps the invasion in which Lycus murdered Creon and made himself tyrant of Thebes. Lycus would have executed Heracles' wife, his children, and Amphitryon had not Heracles returned from an expedition in time to prevent the slaughter by killing Lycus. There ensued, however, a greater tragedy, which saddened Amphitryon's old age. Driven mad by Hera, Heracles himself murdered the wife and children whom he had just saved from Lycus. The Thebans claimed that

Heracles would have killed Amphitryon as well if Athena had not stunned him with a stone. Amphitryon is said to have died fighting, together with Heracles, against the Minyans. He was buried at Thebes.

Amphitryon is a leading character in Plautus' comedy that bears his name and in Euripides' tragedy *Heracles*. The first deals with the famous events in Alcmene's bedchamber, the second with the death of Lycus and Heracles' subsequent madness. Apollodorus [2.4.5–11] gives the most connected account of Amphitryon's adventures.

Amphoterus. See ALCMEON.

Ampycus or **Ampyx.** A Thessalian seer. Ampycus was a son of Elatus, Titaron, or Ares. He is scarcely known except as the father, by Chloris, of the more famous seer Mopsus.

Amulius. A king of Alba Longa. Amulius drove his brother, Numitor, from power and killed his sons. Numitor's grandsons, ROMULUS AND REMUS [A], later killed Amulius and restored Numitor to the throne.

Amyclae. A city near Sparta, in Laconia. Amyclae was founded by Amyclas, a son of Lacedaemon, the founder of Sparta. Amyclae was a small but important city, partly because of its highly regarded cult of Apollo and Hyacinth, which is thought to have been pre-Hellenic in origin. There was also a shrine of Alexandra, who was identified as Cassandra. Agamemnon and Clytemnestra were also said to be buried at Amyclae. The city was reduced to a village during the Dorian invasion and never recovered its earlier importance.

Amyclas. A king of Sparta and eponym of Amyclae, near Sparta. Amyclas was the son of Lacedaemon and Sparta. He married Diomede, daughter of Lapithes, who bore him Hyacinth, Argalus, Cynortas, and Leaneira. [Apollodorus 1.9.5, 3.9.1, 3.10.3; Pausanias 3.1.3.]

Amycus. A king of the Bebryces. Amycus was a son of Poseidon and Melië, one of the ash-nymphs. He engaged in battle with Dascylus (or his son Lycus), king of the Mariandyni, a Mysian tribe who disputed the Bebrycian claim to certain iron-bearing lands. With Heracles' aid Dascylus won the battle and annexed some Bebrycian territory. Amycus, who had lost his brother Mygdon in the war, nevertheless continued the feud and won back much of the land. A barbarous man, he cared nothing for the laws of hospitality, and forced all newcomers to his territory to meet him in boxing. He was a man of great strength and killed many opponents. When the ARGONAUTS [G] landed on his shores, however, he met his match in Polydeuces, who killed him with a blow on the ear, or else the elbow. [Apollonius Rhodius 2.1–97, 2.754–795; Apollodorus 2.5.9.]

Amymone. A daughter of DANAÜS. Shortly after his arrival in the arid land of Argos, Danaüs sent his daughters to find water. Amymone, growing bored with this chore, began to chase a deer. The javelin that she flung at it struck a sleeping satyr, who leaped up and began to chase Amymone. Poseidon appeared, frightened the lustful satyr away with a cast of his trident, and turned

47

his own attention to Amymone, who, finding him less unattractive than the satyr, lay with him. Later Amymone remembered her errand. Poseidon, by now in a benevolent mood, tore his trident from the rock where it had stuck. Out flowed a triple stream of water, which was named the river Amymone, but later called the spring of Lerna. In due course Amymone bore a son, Nauplius, who became a famous seaman. [Apollodorus 2.1.4; Hyginus, *Fabulae*, 149A.]

Amyntor. A king of Eleon or of Ormenium, at the foot of Mount Pelion, in Pelasgiotis. Amyntor, a son of Ormenus, went in his youth on the Calydonian boar hunt. Autolycus once broke into his house and stole a helmet, which found its way through a series of hands back to Autolycus' grandson, Odysseus. According to Ovid [*Metamorphoses* 12.361–368], Amyntor was defeated in war by Peleus and gave up as a pledge of peace his son Crantor, who was later killed fighting beside Peleus in the battle between the Lapiths and the Centaurs. Amyntor's wife, becoming violently jealous when he took a concubine, persuaded her son Phoenix to dishonor the woman by seducing or raping her. For this crime Amyntor asked the Erinyes to deny Phoenix children. Phoenix was so enraged at this curse that he nearly killed his father, but went instead to Peleus, in Phthia, and became king there of the Dolopians. According to another version of this story, Phoenix was unjustly accused by the concubine, but Amyntor believed her story and blinded his son. Phoenix was later cured by Cheiron the Centaur. When Heracles wanted to pass through Ormenian territory, Amyntor refused him permission and was killed. Some say that Heracles had asked to marry Amyntor's daughter, Deïdameia. In any case, she later bore him a son, Ctessipus. [Homer, *Iliad*, 9.447–480, 10.260–271; Apollodorus 2.7.7–8, 3.13.8.]

Amythaon. A son of Cretheus and Tyro. With his wife, Idomene, daughter of Pheres, and their sons, Melampus and Bias, Amythaon migrated from Thessaly to Messene, where he settled at the court of Neleus, his half-brother. Amythaon also had a daughter, Aeolia, who married Calydon. He is said to have held the Olympic games after the sons of Pelops left Elis. When his nephew Jason appeared at the court of Pelias at Iolcus, Amythaon journeyed there to greet him. [Homer, *Odyssey*, 11.258; Pindar, *Pythian Odes*, 4.124; Apollodorus 1.9.11; Pausanias 5.8.2.]

Anactoria. An ancient name for the city of Miletus, in Asia Minor.

Anaphe. A small island north of Crete and a little east of Thera. When the homeward-bound Argonauts were lost in darkness, Apollo shot a flaming arrow into the sea and revealed the island to them. The Greeks thus explained the origin of the island's name, interpreting Anaphe to mean "Revelation." A local custom of accompanying the rites of Apollo with ribald joking between the sexes was also said to date from the Argonauts' visit.

Anatolia. Asia Minor. Anatolia (meaning "the East" in Greek) is the great peninsula bordered by the Black, Aegean, and Mediterranean seas that now comprises the greater part of Turkey.

Anaurus River. A stream near Iolcus, in southeastern Thessaly. It was in the Anaurus that Jason lost his sandal while carrying the disguised Hera across the river.

Anaxagoras. A king of Argos. Anaxagoras was a son of Megapenthes, or of his son Argeius. Some writers claim that he, and not his grandfather Proëtus, bargained with MELAMPUS [C] for the cure of the maddened Argive women. Anaxagoras was the father of Alector. [Pausanias 2.18.4.]

Anaxibia (1). A daughter of Bias. Anaxibia married Pelias, king of Iolcus, and bore a son, Acastus, and several daughters. According to some accounts, however, Pelias' wife was Phylomache, daughter of Amphion.

Anaxibia (2). A daughter of Pleisthenes and Cleolla. A sister of Agamemnon and Menelaüs, Anaxibia became the mother of Pylades by Strophius. [*Catalogues of Women* 69; Pausanias 2.29.4.]

Anaxo. A daughter of Alcaeüs and Astydameia. Anaxo married her uncle Electryon and they had a daughter, Alcmene, and many sons.

Ancaeüs (1). A son of Lycurgus, king of Arcadia, by Cleophyle or Eurynome. Lycurgus sent Ancaeüs on the voyage of the Argonauts, accompanied by Amphidamas and Cepheus, Lycurgus' brothers. Ancaeüs' doting grandfather Aleüs hid the boy's armor in an attempt to prevent his going, but he went off wearing a bearskin and carrying an ax. Because of his youthful strength, Ancaeüs was chosen to row beside Heracles. After the return of the *Argo*, he took part in the Calydonian boar hunt, where his foolhardy courage and, perhaps, a slighting remark that he made about Artemis led to his fatal goring by the boar. Ancaeüs' son, Agapenor, led the Arcadian forces to Troy. [Apollonius Rhodius 1.161–171; Ovid, *Metamorphoses*, 8.315–407.]

Ancaeüs (2). A Lelegian king of Samos. Ancaeüs was a son of Phoenix' daughter Astypalaea by Poseidon. One of the Argonauts, he became pilot of the *Argo* on the death of Tiphys. Ancaeüs married Samia, daughter of the Maeander River. She bore him four sons of no great prominence and a daughter, Parthenope.

Ancient writers often confused this Ancaeüs with Ancaeüs of Arcadia. Both were Argonauts and both were killed by wild boars. Apollodorus makes Arcadian Ancaeüs steersman of the *Argo*—an implausible occupation for a native of a landlocked country. Since Samos was famous for its wine, it is likely, too, to have been Lelegian Ancaeüs who was told by a seer that he would not live to taste the wine of the grapes he had planted. When they were pressed, Ancaeüs boldly lifted a cup of the wine. "There is many a slip 'twixt the cup and the lip," the seer muttered darkly. At that moment Ancaeüs heard that a wild boar was ravaging his vineyard. Putting down his cup untasted, he went out to drive away the boar and was, of course, killed. The seer's saying became proverbial. [Apollonius Rhodius 1.185–189, 2.864–898; Pausanias 7.4.1.]

Anchialus. A Taphian chief. A friend of Laërtes, king of Ithaca, Anchialus gave Odysseus arrow poison after Ilus, king of Ephyra, had refused it to him. [Homer, *Odyssey*, 1.180–181, 1.260–264.]

Anchises. A king of Dardania. Anchises was the son of Capys and Themiste, descended through both parents from Tros, the eponym of Troy. Though Laomedon, king of Troy, was his mother's brother, Anchises stole some of his famous horses as studs for his mares.

Anchises was a handsome youth and Aphrodite fell in love with him. This affair was brought about by Zeus, who was tired of hearing the goddess mock the numerous other gods and goddesses whom she had caused to fall in love with mortals. Aphrodite appeared to Anchises while he was tending his cattle on Mount Ida. She pretended to be a mortal, the daughter of the Phrygian king Otreus, and the young man happily lay with her. He became distressed, however, when she revealed her true identity, for he knew that mortals who won the love of gods seldom fared well thereafter. The goddess reassured him, saying that she would bear a son on the mountain and that the nymphs would rear him. She herself would bring the boy to his father in his fifth year. He was to be named Aeneas. All would be well as long as Anchises did not reveal the boy's true mother, but pretended that he was a nymph's child.

These things happened as the goddess had predicted. Some say that Aphrodite also bore a second son, Lyrus, of whom nothing more is known. One day, however, Anchises drank too much and blurted out his secret. Zeus struck him with a thunderbolt for embarrassing the goddess and left him crippled for life. Anchises later had several daughters, presumably by a mortal wife. Aeneas became the leader of the Dardanians, who were allies of the Trojans in the war with the Greeks. When the city fell, he carried his old father on his back to safety. Anchises sailed with Aeneas and the Trojan survivors as far as Sicily, where he died and was buried. The Arcadians, however, claimed, implausibly, that he was buried at the foot of their Mount Anchisia, which they said was named for him. [*Homeric Hymn to Aphrodite* 5; Vergil, *Aeneïd*, 2.647–649, 2.707–789; Homer, *Iliad*, 5.268–272, 13.428–431; Hyginus, *Fabulae*, 94; Pausanias 8.12.8–9.]

Ancient Latins. See LATINS.

Ancus Marcius. The fourth king of Rome. A grandson of the great Sabine king of Rome, Numa Pompilius, Ancus was elected after the death of Tullus Hostilius. During the twenty-four years of his reign, he tried to combine the peaceful virtues of Numa with the warlike ones of Romulus. He conquered several Latin towns and founded the city of Ostia at the mouth of the Tiber River to serve as a port for Rome. [Livy 1.32.1–35.1.]

Ancyra. An ancient city in Asia Minor. Ancyra was founded by Midas, son of Gordius. His city was identified as that Ancyra which became Ankara, the present capital of Turkey.

Andania. An ancient inland city in Messenia. Andania, which may first have been named Messene, was founded by Polycaon and Messene, the first rulers of Messenia. When Perieres was invited from Thessaly to become king, he moved the capital to Arene, but Andania remained the center of certain ancient cults, particularly that of Demeter and Persephone.

Andraemon. A king of Calydon. Andraemon married Gorge, daughter of Oeneus, king of Calydon; they had a son, Thoas. When Diomedes killed Agrius' sons, who had usurped the rule from Oeneus, he gave the throne to Andraemon, since Oeneus was too old to rule. [Homer, *Iliad*, 2.638–640; Apollodorus 1.8.1, 1.8.6.]

Andreïs. See ANDREUS.

Andreus. The first king of the region of Boeotian Orchomenus. Andreus, a son of the Thessalian river-god Peneius, settled in northern Boeotia and called the land Andreïs. He divided this territory willingly on the arrival of Athamas and married Euippe, the daughter of Athamas' son Leucon. Some say that they became the parents of the succeeding ruler, Eteocles; others call Eteocles a son of the river-god Cephissus. [Pausanias 9.34.6–10.]

Androgeüs or **Androgeus.** A son of Minos, king of Crete, and Pasiphaë. For some reason Androgeüs grew up at Athens, where he won all the events at the Panathenaic games. He met his death as a young man while fighting the Marathonian bull, or from ambush as he traveled to Thebes. Minos, rightfully suspecting that Aegeus, king of Athens, had played a part in Androgeüs' death, declared war on Athens, which led to the circumstance of young Athenians being periodically fed to the Minotaur, until Theseus ended this tribute. Androgeüs was honored at Athens with games, under the name of Eurygyes. He was survived by his two sons, Alcaeüs and Sthenelus. [Apollodorus 3.15.7; *Catalogues of Women* 75; Pausanias 1.27.9–10.]

Andromache. A daughter of Eëtion, king of Thebes, a city at the foot of Mount Placus in the Troad. In the early years of the Trojan War, Andromache's father was killed and his city sacked by Achilles. Andromache had married the chief Trojan leader, Hector, son of Priam and Hecuba. She bore him a son, Astyanax, whom his father called Scamandrius. After Hector's death and the fall of Troy she was awarded as a slave and concubine to Achilles' son, NEOPTOLEMUS. Either Neoptolemus or Odysseus murdered Astyanax before leaving Troy. Andromache's new master seems to have treated her well enough. She bore him three sons, Molossus, Pielus, and Pergamus. Later, however, he took a wife, Hermione, daughter of Menelaüs and Helen. According to Euripides, this woman, who had no children, envied and hated Andromache and treated her cruelly during Neoptolemus' absence at Delphi. Peleus, Neoptolemus' aged grandfather, protected her and Molossus from death.

In another version of the story, which places the action in Epeirus, rather than in Achilles' capital of Phthia, Neoptolemus, on marrying Hermione, turned Andromache over to Hector's brother Helenus, who had become Neoptolemus' ally. Helenus acted as guardian of Andromache's children and she bore a son, Cestrinus, by him. Later she went to Mysia with Pergamus, who captured Teuthrania and renamed it Pergamon. Andromache's descendants ruled Epeirus for many generations. She herself had a shrine at Pergamon.

Andromache is a leading character in Euripides' tragedy that bears her name, and plays a smaller role in his *Trojan Women*. See also Homer, *Iliad*, 6.390–502, 24.723–745; Vergil, *Aeneïd*, 3.294–348; Pausanias 1.11.1–2.

Andromeda. The daughter of CEPHEUS (1), king of Ethiopia, and CASSIOPEIA. Cepheus chained Andromeda to a rock in order to placate a sea-monster, but PERSEUS rescued her and took her home with him to Argolis, where she bore him many children. At her death she was placed by Athena among the stars. [Apollodorus 2.4.3–5; Ovid, *Metamorphoses*, 4.670 ff; Hyginus, *Fabulae*, 64, and *Poetica Astronomica*, 2.11.]

Anius. A king of Delos and priest of Apollo. Anius is said by some to have been a son of Apollo by Rhoeo, daughter of Staphylus and Chrysothemis. On discovering that his daughter was pregnant, Staphylus placed her in a chest and threw it into the sea. It came ashore on the island of Delos. There Rhoeo bore a son and, placing the baby on Apollo's altar, challenged him to care for it, if it was his. The god hid the child for a time, then taught him the art of prophecy and heaped various honors on him. Anius, as he was named, became king of Delos and Apollo's priest there as well. He had a son and three daughters. The son became king of Andros.

The daughters were apparently devotees of Dionysus, for the god gave them the extraordinary ability to produce oil, corn, and wine from the ground or, some say, merely by touch. The young women were appropriately named Elaïs (Olive), Spermo (Seed), and Oino (Wine); together they were called the "Winegrowers." Their gift proved their downfall. Agamemnon and the Greeks learned of it on their way to the Trojan War and kidnaped the girls in order that they might feed the Greek army. The captives escaped, but their brother gave them up again to the Greeks. As they were about to be bound, they prayed to Dionysus. He transformed them into white doves. Later Anius, an old friend of Anchises, entertained him, his son Aeneas, and their company as they were escaping the ruins of Troy. [Ovid, *Metamorphoses*, 13.628–704; Vergil, *Aeneïd*, 3.80–83; Apollodorus, "Epitome" 3.10.]

Anna. The sister of DIDO. Anna encouraged her sister's love for Aeneas and, later, unknowingly helped her to prepare for her death.

Antaeüs. A Libyan giant. Antaeüs was a son of Poseidon and Ge. According to late Classical authors, he derived his prodigious strength from contact with his mother, the earth. When strangers came to Antaeüs' kingdom in western Libya, it was his custom to require them to wrestle with him. Since, on the infrequent occasions when he was thrown, his strength was immediately renewed by the earth, he invariably won these contests. He would celebrate his victory by piously using the victim's skull as roofing material for his father's temple. Antaeüs finally met his match in Heracles, who was shrewd as well as strong. On discovering that Antaeüs only grew stronger each time that he was thrown, Heracles lifted him from the earth in a great hug and squeezed until the giant's body was broken and he died. [Apollodorus 2.5.11; Pindar, *Isthmian Odes*, 4.52–55.]

Anteia. See STHENEBOEA.

Antenor. A Trojan elder. Antenor, a Dardanian, was one of the most conservative and respected of Priam's council of elders. When Odysseus and Menelaüs came to Troy as envoys before the war to request the return of Helen, Antenor entertained them courteously and intervened to save their lives from rasher Trojans who wanted to kill them. At the height of the war, he advocated that Helen be returned to the Greeks, but this time Priam supported Paris' refusal. By his wife, Theano, Antenor had many sons, including Archeloüs and Acamas, who shared leadership of the Dardanian forces with Aeneas.

During the sack of Troy, Antenor, Theano, and their few surviving children were protected by Odysseus and Menelaüs, who were grateful for Antenor's earlier kindnesses. They placed a leopard skin over Antenor's door as a warning to the Greek soldiers to harm no one within. The two Greek leaders saved the life of Antenor's son Glaucus, and Odysseus carried another son, the wounded Helicaon, from the battle on his back. There are various traditions as to Antenor's life after Troy's fall. Two of them make him the founder of Cyrene, in Libya, or of Patavi (Padua), in Italy. Late Roman writers presented Antenor as a virtual traitor to Troy. [Homer, *Iliad*, 3.203–224, 7.344–353; Pausanias 10.26.7–8, 10.27.3–4; Pindar, *Pythian Odes*, 5.80–87; Vergil, *Aeneïd*, 1.242–249.]

Anthedon. A city of Boeotia, opposite Euboea. Anthedon was known mainly as the home of the sea-god Glaucus before his transformation.

Anthemoëssa. The island of the Sirens. The name Anthemoëssa (Flowery) is said to have been given to this island by Hesiod. The tradition is perpetuated by Apollonius Rhodius in his *Argonautica*.

Anticleia. A daughter of Autolycus. In order to avenge Autolycus' theft of his cattle, Sisyphus seduced Anticleia. Autolycus married the pregnant girl to Laërtes, and she bore Odysseus. Many say, however, that Odysseus was, in fact, Laërtes' son. Anticleia died of grief while Odysseus was fighting at Troy, or else she killed herself on hearing a false report of his death. Her shade was among those which hovered about Odysseus' sacrifice when he consulted Teiresias. [Hyginus, *Fabulae*, 201, 243; Homer, *Odyssey*, 11.84–89.]

Antigone. A daughter of Oedipus, king of Thebes, by Jocasta or Euryganeia. Antigone was betrothed to Haemon, a son of her uncle, Creon. When the self-blinded OEDIPUS was sent into exile by Creon (or by his own sons), Antigone acted as his guide until his death at Colonus. Shortly before that event, Creon kidnaped her in the hope of capturing Oedipus, but she was rescued by Theseus. Antigone's brothers, Eteocles and Polyneices, killed each other in the war of the SEVEN AGAINST THEBES, in which the banished Polyneices tried to regain his right to the throne. Creon decreed, perhaps on Eteocles' dying orders, that no one should bury the bodies of the invaders. Antigone defied this order and gave at least token funeral rites to Polyneices. (Some say that, aided by Polyneices' Argive wife, Argeia, she dragged the corpse onto Eteocles' pyre.) Although Haemon pleaded for her, she was imprisoned in a cave or entombed alive in Polyneices' grave. She committed suicide and Haemon, on finding her body, did the same; or else they were entombed together and killed themselves. According to another story, Antigone refused to marry Haemon because of Creon's decree concerning Polyneices' body, and went into voluntary exile with her father.

In Hyginus' very different version [*Fabulae* 72], thought by some to have been based on Euripides' lost play *Antigone*, Creon turned Antigone over to Haemon for punishment. Instead of killing her, he gave her to shepherds to smuggle away. She bore Haemon a son, who later came to Thebes, where Creon recognized him by a mark on his body that was common to all descendants of the Sparti. Creon would not forgive his disobedient son, even though Heracles pleaded for him. Haemon thereupon killed both Antigone and himself. The fate of their son is not recorded.

Antigone's story is known almost exclusively from the works of the three Greek tragic playwrights and those writers who followed their accounts. She appears in Aeschylus' *Seven Against Thebes* (the ending of which was probably altered because of the popularity of Sophocles' *Antigone*); in Sophocles' *Oedipus at Colonus* and *Antigone*, and in a mute role in his *Oedipus the King*; and in Euripides' *Phoenician Women*.

Antigone. See PELEUS [A].

Antilochus. A son of Nestor and Anaxibia or Eurydice. Antilochus was one of the suitors of Helen. He went with his father and his brother Thrasymedes to the Trojan War, leaving behind a son, Paeon. At Troy he was one of the youngest and bravest of the Greek leaders. Youthful enthusiasm and his father's advice caused Antilochus to resort to trickery in order to win second place from Menelaüs in the chariot race at Patroclus' funeral games, but he apologized to Menelaüs and offered to return the prize. According to Pindar [*Pythian Odes* 6], Antilochus died while defending Nestor from an attack by the Ethiopian general Memnon. After death he was transported, with the ghosts of Achilles and Ajax, to the White Island. [Homer, *Iliad*, 5.565–589, 13.545–566, 15.568–591, 23.301 ff.]

Antimachus. A Trojan elder. A greedy warmonger, Antimachus vehemently opposed giving up Helen when Menelaüs and Odysseus came as ambassadors to Priam to demand her return. He was so eager for rewards from

Paris that he recommended that the envoys be murdered. Menelaüs and Aga-memnon recalled this event when Menelaüs captured two of Antimachus' sons, Peisander and Hippolochus. Scorning offers of ransom, the two Greeks slaugh-tered their captives. Antimachus' third son, Hippomachus, was killed by Leon-teus. [Homer, *Iliad*, 11.122–147, 12.188–189.]

Antinoüs. A young Ithacan noble. A son of EUPEITHES, Antinoüs was the most insolent of Penelope's suitors and the first to be killed by Odysseus on his return to Ithaca. Antinoüs appears throughout the Ithacan books of Homer's *Odyssey*.

Antion. The father of Ixion. Antion, the eldest son of Periphas and Astyagyïa, lay with Amythaon's daughter Perimela. She bore him Ixion. Some writers, however, call Ixion a son of Phlegyas. [Diodorus Siculus 4.69.3.]

Antiope (1). A daughter of Nycteus, regent of Thebes, and Polyxo, or of the Boeotian river-god Asopus. Antiope, who was very beautiful, caught the eye of Zeus and he lay with her in the guise of a satyr. When she became pregnant she fled from Thebes, out of fear of her father's anger. She came to Sicyon, where King Epopeus married her. Some writers take the view that Epopeus had, in fact, kidnaped her from her father's palace and that she was pregnant by him, rather than by a god. Some say that Nycteus pursued Antiope to Sicyon, but returned, dying, to Thebes after exchanging wounds with Epo-peus; others claim that Nycteus killed himself from shame. In either case, he enjoined his brother, Lycus, to avenge him on Epopeus and to punish Antiope. Lycus marched on Sicyon and killed Epopeus, or else found him already dead from his wound and was given Antiope by the new king. Lycus took her back to Thebes. When they came to the village of Eleutherae, on Mount Cithaeron, Antiope gave birth to twins, but Lycus immediately had them exposed on the mountain.

In Thebes, Lycus imprisoned Antiope, but left further punishment in the hands of his wife, Dirce. For some reason Dirce felt an implacable hatred for the girl and abused her cruelly. (Hyginus explains this by making Antiope Lycus' first wife.) After many years Antiope was miraculously freed and es-caped to Mount Cithaeron, where she took refuge in a herdsman's hut. Here she found two young men named Amphion and Zethus. On learning from the herdsman that Antiope was their mother, they went to Thebes and killed Lycus, or at least drove him from the throne. They tied Dirce to a bull, which dragged her to death.

In Euripides' tragedy *Antiope*, known only from a doubtful summary by Hyginus and from a few fragments, Antiope was refused a haven on first meet-ing Zethus, who thought her merely a runaway. She was captured by Dirce, who was reveling as a bacchant on Mount Cithaeron, and was about to be tied by the hair to an untamed bull. The herdsman, meanwhile, returned to his hut and told the young men, whom he had reared, that the woman they had refused to help was their mother. In the nick of time they saved Antiope from Dirce and subjected the queen to the punishment that she had intended for her hated victim.

Because Dirce had been a votary of Dionysus, the god punished Antiope by driving her mad. She wandered about Greece until she encountered Phocus, son of Ornytion. Phocus cured her and they were married. At their deaths they were buried in a common grave at Tithorea, in Phocis. [Apollodorus 3.5.5; Hyginus, *Fabulae*, 7, 8; Pausanias 2.6.1–4, 9.17.6.]

Antiope (2). An Amazon queen. Antiope is the name most often given to the leader of the Amazons whom THESEUS [F] abducted and took to Athens with him. She was called Hippolyte by several writers, Melanippe or Glauce by others. Hippolyte is sometimes said to have been Antiope's sister, who led a punitive force of Amazons to Athens and died, after her defeat, at Megara. Whatever the name of Theseus' Amazon wife, she bore him a son, Hippolytus (and possibly Demophon, as well), and seems to have died shortly thereafter in Athens. Some say that she was killed when she and her followers appeared at Theseus' wedding to Phaedra and threatened to kill all the guests, others that Theseus killed her in battle, still others that she was accidentally shot by an ally, Penthesileia. This Hippolyte is sometimes identified with Hippolyte (1). [Apollodorus, "Epitome" 1.16–17 and 5.1–2.]

Antiphates. A son of Melampus and Lysippe. Antiphates' son Oïcles became the father of Amphiaraüs.

Antiphates. See LAESTRYGONIANS.

Antiphus. A son of Priam and Hecuba. Antiphus and his brother Isus were captured by Achilles as they tended sheep on Mount Ida. Priam ransomed them, but Agamemnon later killed both in battle. [Homer, *Iliad*, 11.101–121.]

Aonians or **Aones.** A Boeotian tribe. When Cadmus and his Phoenician followers conquered the region of Thebes, the Aonians sued for peace and were permitted to remain, living in villages in the hills. Their eponym was Aon, who is not otherwise known. The epithet Aonian was often applied by poets to Boeotia.

Apemosyne. See ALTHAEMENES.

Aphaea. See BRITOMARTIS.

Aphareus. A king of Messenia. A son of Perieres and Gorgophone, Aphareus and his less influential brother, Leucippus, inherited the rule of Messenia at their father's death. Aphareus married Arene, his mother's daughter by her second husband, Oebalus. She bore him Idas, Lynceus, and Peisus, though some call Idas a son of Poseidon. Aphareus founded the city named for his wife. A hospitable ruler, he welcomed to his land two exiled princes—his cousin Neleus, son of Cretheus; and Lycus, son of Pandion, who had been banished from Athens by Aegeus. To Neleus, Aphareus gave much of the land along the shore of Messenia, with several cities including Pylus. Having outlived his sons, Aphareus left the rule to Neleus, or to Neleus' son Nestor. [Pausanias 4.2.4–7.]

Aphidnae or **Aphidna.** A town in Attica northwest of Marathon. When Theseus abducted Helen from Sparta, he hid her at Aphidnae. Her brothers, the Dioscuri, recovered her by force.

Aphrodite. A goddess of erotic love, identified by the Romans with Venus.

A. There are two principal accounts of Aphrodite's birth. According to Homer, she was a daughter of Zeus and Dione, but Hesiod declared that she had sprung from the foam that gathered about the severed genitals of Uranus as they floated through the sea to the island of Cyprus. The Greeks associated Aphrodite's name with *aphros* ("sea-foam") and often called her Cypris, for the place where she was said to have come ashore after her birth in the sea. (They also called her Cythereia, for, in some stories, she came ashore at Cythera, an island off the southern shore of the Peloponnesus.) Although later legends made Eros Aphrodite's son, Hesiod claimed that he was on hand to greet her when she came out of the sea. The early Lycian poet Olen made both Aphrodite and Eros children of Eileithyia, the goddess of childbirth, who, Olen said, was older than Cronus.

Aphrodite married the lame fire-god Hephaestus but, as might be expected of so amorous a goddess, she did not long remain faithful to her unromantic husband. She carried on a protracted affair with Ares [A], who visited her in Hephaestus' bed whenever that god left Olympus. Hephaestus, warned by Helius, trapped the lovers naked in bed at one point and subjected them to the ridicule of the other gods. Ares and Aphrodite had several children: Eros, Deimus (Fear), Phobus (Panic), and Harmonia. Aphrodite had brief affairs with two or three other gods. In one of these the love-goddess was a surprisingly reluctant partner. She repulsed the advances of Hermes until Zeus took pity on him and sent an eagle to snatch her sandal and carry it to him. The goddess had to submit to him in order to recover it. She bore Hermaphroditus, whose name was compounded of the names of his parents. The amorous god Priapus was reputed to be a son of Aphrodite by Dionysus, but nothing is known of the circumstances leading to their match. Poseidon was said by some to be the father of Aphrodite's son Eryx, king of the region of western Sicily that was named for him, but others say that Butes was the father.

The goddess did not, however, confine her attentions to gods. The best known of her many love affairs with mortals began on her favorite island of Cyprus. Somehow, the daughters of King Cinyras incurred her displeasure. She caused three of them, Orsedice, Laogore, and Braesia, to lie with strangers, and they ended their days far away in Egypt. The goddess punished the fourth, Myrrha or Smyrna, more severely than her sisters because Myrrha's mother rashly boasted that the girl was more beautiful than Aphrodite. Myrrha was suddenly smitten with love for her own father and managed to lie with him. The result of this union was Adonis. Aphrodite loved the beautiful infant. Placing him in a chest, she gave him to Persephone for safekeeping. Persephone, herself enamored of the boy, refused to return him, until Zeus submitted the quarrel to the Muse Calliope for arbitration. Calliope decreed that Adonis, now a handsome youth, should spend a part of the year with each goddess. Aphrodite punished Calliope's fair-mindedness by causing the death of her son Orpheus, but she could not alter the judgment. She later lost Adonis altogether when he was killed by a boar. To commemorate him she caused the blood-red anemone to grow from his blood.

Aphrodite had another famous mortal lover, Anchises, of the royal line of Dardania. Their love was brought about by Zeus as a countermeasure to the goddess' habit of making the other gods fall in love with mortals, then laughing at their embarrassment. Aphrodite saw Anchises as he tended his herds on Mount Ida and fell madly in love with him. When she appeared to him and invited him to lie with her, he was at first afraid that intercourse with a goddess might deprive him of his manly vigor, so Aphrodite pretended to be a mortal, the daughter of King Otreus. Anchises consented, and learned too late that his fears had been well founded. The goddess bore a son, Aeneas, who was reared by the Idaean nymphs. Anchises, contrary to the goddess' command, later revealed the child's true parentage and was maimed by Zeus with a thunderbolt. Aphrodite never lost her interest in her son, defending him as best she could during both the Trojan War and his subsequent voyage to a new home in Italy.

B. Aphrodite also favored another Trojan, Paris—with disastrous results for Troy. When she engaged in a contest with Hera and Athena for the beauty prize of the golden apple, Paris, acting as judge, awarded it to her. She paid him the bribe that she had promised in return for this decision: the hand of Helen, queen of Sparta. During the war that followed Paris' abduction of Helen, Aphrodite saved Paris from death until the end. She fought on the side of the Trojans in this conflict, but was ingloriously wounded by the mortal Diomedes while saving Aeneas and was later knocked down by Athena while aiding her lover Ares. In spite of her preference for the Trojan cause, she lent Hera her magic belt, when that goddess wanted to lure Zeus from the fray with her charms for the sake of the Greeks. Aphrodite even seems to have forgotten Paris for a time if, as the *Cypria* [1] claimed, she and Thetis arranged a meeting between Achilles and Helen. Nothing seems to have come of this rendezvous, however.

The love-goddess never tired of aiding young lovers. It was she who gave Melanion (or Hippomenes) the golden apples with which he won Atalanta. Later, however, she indirectly caused their transformation into lions because Melanion forgot to thank her. At the request of Jason's divine patronesses, Hera and Athena, Aphrodite persuaded Eros to make Medea love Jason. She transformed Selemnus into an Achaean river when he died for love. Even Zeus turned to the goddess for help when Nemesis avoided him. When he became a swan, Aphrodite pursued him in the shape of an eagle so that he might plausibly take refuge in Nemesis' lap.

Like other Olympian deities, Aphrodite was often harsh toward those who defied her, usually by refusing the pleasures of love. Her best-known victim was Hippolytus, son of Theseus. Aphrodite caused his stepmother, Phaedra, to fall in love with him. This domestic tragedy ended with the deaths of both Hippolytus and Phaedra. When Tyndareüs, king of Argos, failed to honor Aphrodite to her satisfaction, she arranged that his three daughters, Helen, Clytemnestra, and Timandra, should all betray their husbands. For a similar reason she made the Cretan queen Pasiphaë love a bull. She cruelly punished the Lemnian women for ignoring her worship by giving them a bad odor. Their husbands thereupon took foreign wives and the Lemnian women killed all the men on the island. After several lonely years, they learned to regret this rash act. To please her husband, Hephaestus, divine patron of Lemnos, Aphrodite relented and caused the women to fall in love with the Argonauts, thus repeopling the island.

Mortals were not alone in suffering Aphrodite's anger. The Muse Cleio was punished by her (though less severely than her sister Calliope) by falling in love with the mortal Pierus. Aphrodite paid back Eos for lying with Ares by afflicting her with incessant infatuation with one mortal or another. The goddess later carried off Phaëthon, Eos' son by Cephalus, to be the night warder of her shrine. She punished Helius, for tattling on her and Ares, by making him love Leucothoë, which led to the innocent woman's death.

The goddess is said by some to have concerned herself with love among animals as well as gods and men. When Glaucus refused to allow his notorious herd of mares to breed, she made them avenge their frustration by eating their master alive.

Aphrodite could on occasion be benevolent in matters that had no apparent connection with erotic love. She adopted the orphaned daughters of Pandareüs and even went to Olympus to arrange good marriages for them. Unfortunately they were snatched away by the Harpies during her absence.

Aphrodite rescued Aeneas' first wife, Creüsa, from slavery among the Greeks. She rescued the Argonaut Butes as he was swimming toward the Sirens' island and carried him off to Lilybaeüm, in Eryx, a part of Sicily that was under the goddess' protection. (Some say that she had a son, Eryx, by Butes.) Aphrodite also took pity on Ino when she jumped into the sea with her infant son Melicertes in her arms. It was she who persuaded Poseidon to immortalize the pair as the sea-deities Leucothea and Palaemon.

C. When the gods fled to Egypt to escape the monster Typhöeus and transformed themselves into animals, Aphrodite became a fish. Hyginus said, however, that this happened at the Euphrates River, in Syria, where Aphrodite was known as the Syrian Goddess. Hyginus added that the Syrians ate neither fish nor doves because of their version of the circumstances of the goddess' birth: a huge egg had fallen into the Euphrates; fish had rolled it ashore and doves had hatched it; out had stepped the goddess. The fish were placed in the stars and the doves were universally held sacred to the goddess, both as the Syrian Goddess and as Aphrodite.

The Greeks had always known that Aphrodite was an Asiatic goddess. Herodotus stated that the oldest shrine of Aphrodite Urania (Heavenly Aphrodite) was in the Phoenician city of Ascalon and that her worship had spread from there to Cyprus and to Cythera. He further reported that the goddess was widely worshiped in Asian lands, where she was called Mylitta by the Assyrians, Alilat by the Arabians, Mitra by the Persians, and Argimpasa by the Scythians.

There is little doubt that Aphrodite, like Artemis, was originally a mother-goddess, of a type almost universally worshiped in the Near East and perhaps best known under the name of Ishtar or Astarte. This goddess had a male cult partner of less importance than herself. In Aphrodite's case this role was played by Adonis, by Anchises, and, in Sicily, perhaps by Butes. The Near Eastern goddess was often a goddess of war as well as of love. Aphrodite had both these functions in warlike Sparta. She was, moreover, often worshiped together with Ares and was the mother by him of Deimus and Phobus (Fear and Panic), his constant companions in battle.

According to Herodotus, Mylitta's worship in Babylon required every woman at some point in her life to offer herself to a stranger in the goddess' temple. Any man could enter the shrine, throw money into the woman's lap, and say, "I demand you in Mylitta's name." Regardless of the amount of money, she had to consent. The difficulty was that an ugly woman might have to remain in the temple for three or four years before receiving an offer at any price. Similar customs existed, the historian added, at Paphos, the goddess' chief center in Cyprus. This account is borne out in myth with Ovid's mention of Aphrodite in connection with the Propoetides of Cyprus, whom he called the first prostitutes; with Apollodorus' report that the goddess made Cinyras' daughters lie with strangers; and possibly with the statement in the *Catalogues of Women* [67] that she made Tyndareüs' daughters unfaithful to their husbands. Pindar mentioned that Aphrodite's temple at Corinth also had a corps of prostitutes. This temple stood on the Acrocorinth, which, according to Pausanias, had once been ceded to the goddess by Helius. Hints of Aphrodite's Asiatic character as an all-knowing queen of heaven are found in remarks by Pausanias that Aphrodite Urania was called, at her shrine at Athens, the eldest of the Fates, and in Hyginus' statement that she taught the workings of the planets to Hermes.

Aphrodite, like the foreign deities Artemis and Ares, was early added to the Olympian pantheon of the Greeks. In Homer's *Iliad* all three appear in a somewhat ridiculous light, and Aphrodite is portrayed as distinctly subordinate to Hera, and even to Athena, in so late a work as the *Argonautica* of Apollonius Rhodius. The Greeks perhaps never wholly esteemed this rather disturbing goddess. The Romans, however, took her seriously, partly no doubt because the powerful Julian clan (which included Julius Caesar and Augustus) claimed her as their ancestor, through Iülus, son of Aeneas. The Romans identified her with their own Venus, originally a minor fertility-goddess.

D. Aphrodite appears in a not very sympathetic role at the beginning of Euripides' tragedy *Hippolytus*. Her affair with Anchises is related at length in the *Homeric Hymn to Aphrodite* [5]. Ovid tells of her connections with the Cyprian family of Pygmalion down to his descendant Adonis in the *Metamorphoses* [10.519–739]. Apollonius Rhodius describes in charming detail her relations with Hera and Athena and her problems as the somewhat ineffectual mother of the unruly Eros in the *Argonautica* [2.25–155]. Her poor record in war is revealed in the *Iliad* [5.311–430, 21.416–433]. Homer also tells of her embarrassment by Hephaestus in the *Odyssey* [8.266–366]. As Venus, she appears importantly in Vergil's *Aeneïd*. Other references to the goddess are numerous, but briefer. They include the following: Homer, *Iliad*, 3.373–425, 14.187–221, 23.185–187, and *Odyssey*, 4.259–264, 20.67–78; Hesiod, *Theogony*, 188–206, 975, 986–991; Pindar, *Pythian Odes*, 4.213–219, and *Fragments*, 122; Ovid, *Metamorphoses*, 4.169–192, 4.285–388, 4.531–538, 5.331, 10.639–707, 14.484–511; Apollodorus 1.3.3, 1.4.4, 1.9.17, 3.4.2, 3.14.3–4, "Epitome" 3.2; Vergil, *Georgics*, 3.267–268; Hyginus, *Fabulae*, 14–15, 40, 58, 92, 94, 147–148, 185, and *Poetica Astronomica*, 2.7, 2.16, 2.30, 2.43; Pausanias 1.3.1, 1.19.2, 2.4.6, 5.11.8, 7.23.2, 9.27.2, 9.31.2, 10.26.1, 10.30. 1–2. Herodotus' reports on Aphrodite's Asian counterparts are found at 1.105, 1.131, 1.199, 3.8, 4.59, and 4.67.

Apia. An ancient name for the Peloponnesus or that part of it south of the Isthmus of Corinth. Apia was supposedly named for an early king, Apis. [Aeschylus, *Agamemnon*, 256, and *Suppliant Women*, 128 *passim*, 260; Pausanias 2.5.6.]

Apis. A son of Phoroneus and the nymph Teledice. Apis named the Peloponnesus or a part of it Apia, for himself, but ruled it so tyrannically that he was deposed by Thelxion and Telchis. He was later avenged by Argus Panoptes. Apis was killed by Aetolus, son of Endymion. Dying childless, he was succeeded by another Argus, the son of his sister Niobe by Zeus. Aeschylus, however, calls Apis a son of Apollo, saying that he was a seer and physician from Naupactus who drove monsters, snakes, and plagues out of Argos. [Aeschylus, *Suppliant Women*, 262–269; Apollodorus 2.1.1, 2.1.2.]

Apollo. A god of youth, music, prophecy, archery, and healing.

A. Apollo was the son of Zeus and the Titaness LETO. After many hardships brought upon her through the jealousy of Hera, Leto bore Apollo and his sister, Artemis, on the island of Delos, one of the Cyclades. Themis nourished the boy on nectar and ambrosia. At an early age (only four days, according to Hyginus) Apollo traveled to Delphi and there killed a huge serpent. Accounts of this event differ. In some, the snake is a she-dragon that has long harassed the country. In others, it is the guardian snake of the ancient oracle, which it defends against the invader Apollo. In still others, it is an oracular serpent that has tried to kill Leto, knowing that it was fated to die at the hands of any offspring she might have. The later versions call the snake Python. Apollo (and Artemis, in accounts in which she helps her brother) had to be purified after this murder. Some say that this ceremony was performed by a Cretan king named Carmanor.

Afterward Apollo returned to Delphi to take over the oracle. This oracle had originally belonged to Ge, or to Ge and Poseidon. More recently it had been in the hands of another earth-goddess, Themis, who, some say, willingly turned it over to Apollo. He established his own cult there, giving to Poseidon in exchange for his share the island of Calaureia, off Troezen.

On his way to Delphi, Apollo had looked for other likely spots to establish his oracle. One of these had been at the spring Telphusa, but the nymph of this spring, jealous of her territorial rights, had given him plausible reasons why he should go to Delphi instead. Now, belatedly recognizing the nymph's motive, Apollo returned to Telphusa and dried up the spring. Next he set out to find men to carry on the business of his oracle. Meeting a Cretan ship in the Mediterranean, he leaped on board in the form of a giant dolphin and caused the ship and its astounded crew to make for the port nearest Delphi. There the god revealed himself to them, commanded them to establish a shrine of Apollo Delphinius (He of the Dolphin), and appointed them keepers of his oracle. He is said to have made a woman named Phenomoë the first Pythia, or prophetess who delivered his oracles.

Apollo and Artemis together shot the giant Tityus, who had tried to violate their mother before their birth. Tityus was condemned to be further punished in Hades. The brother and sister avenged another affront to Leto—Niobe's boast that she had borne more and better children—by shooting all or nearly all the Theban queen's many offspring. Apollo and Artemis, or Apollo alone, also shot down the young giants Otus and Ephialtes, who had violently courted Hera and Artemis.

B. Apollo was so universally known as a god of prophecy—though some hint that he learned the art from Pan—that most seers were said to have learned their art from him, if not to have been his sons. Similarly, Apollo was recognized as the god of music and was often represented as playing the lyre and leading the Muses in song, either on Mount Parnassus or in heaven. Far from inventing the lyre, however, he bought it from his baby brother HERMES [A], who had made it out of an empty tortoise shell. In return, he gave Hermes the caduceus, a minor oracle, some advice, and a promise to forget that the child had stolen his cattle. Some writers claim that Apollo later invented the cithara, or lute.

Apollo became extremely proficient on the lyre. When the Phrygian satyr Marsyas challenged him to a musical contest, flute against lyre, Apollo was not content merely to win; he flayed his opponent alive. He engaged in a similar contest, also in Phrygia, with Pan and again won. The victim this time was King Midas, who received ass's ears for mentioning that he had personally preferred Pan's pipe music. It was a long time before Apollo would consent to hear a flute under any circumstances, but he finally allowed one to be played at Delphi on special occasions to celebrate his defeat of the dragon. Three of Apollo's sons were famous for their minstrelsy: Orpheus, Linus, and Philammon. (Orpheus, however, was generally regarded as Oeagrus' son by Calliope.) Famous bards were sooner or later rumored to be sons of Apollo, much as famous seers were reputed to have learned their art from the god. Even the Corybantes were said by some to be Apollo's sons by the Muse Thaleia.

Apollo was also knowledgeable in medicine, and came to be identified at times with PAEËON, the Olympian healer. One of the most famous of his sons was Asclepius, the divine physician, born to Coronis. Apollo courted Coronis, daughter of King Phlegyas, for some time, but she was unfaithful to him with Ischys, son of Elatus. The flouted lover either killed Coronis himself or sent Artemis to do so, then turned to black the originally white crow that had tattled on her. Too late he regretted his harshness toward Coronis and snatched from her body his infant son. (Some claim, however, that Asclepius' mother was Arsinoë, a daughter of Leucippus.)

This boy grew to manhood and became a great physician. When he went so far as to restore a dead man to life, Zeus blasted him with a thunderbolt for his presumption. Apollo was so furious over this act that he killed the Cyclopes, who furnished Zeus with his thunderbolts. Zeus would have flung him into Tartarus, if Leto had not intervened. In a calmer mood, Zeus commanded Apollo to work for one year as a mortal's hireling. Apollo chose to serve the pious Admetus, king of Pherae, in Thessaly. He received such good treatment that he repaid Admetus by making his cows drop twins, by winning Pelias' daughter Alcestis as a bride for him, and by tricking the Fates into allowing Admetus to find a substitute when he was faced with death.

Apollo's other well-known experience with a human employer was less successful. For some reason Apollo and Poseidon hired themselves out to Laomedon, king of Troy, to build the walls of the city, or of its citadel, the Pergamum. When Laomedon refused them their wages, Apollo visited the city with a plague and Poseidon sent a sea-monster, which Heracles later killed. On another occasion, Apollo volunteered to assist Alcathoüs in building the walls of Megara. He also is said to have ordered Amphion to construct the outer walls of Thebes.

C. Apollo had many loves, male and female, but his record of success was not impressive, at least not in the better-known affairs. He and Poseidon both courted his aunt Hestia, but she was determined to remain a virgin, and did so. He gave Priam's daughter CASSANDRA prophetic gifts to buy her favors. When she still refused, he condemned her always to go unheeded. In a similar case, he granted the Cumaean Sibyl's rash wish for as many years as there were grains in a pile of sand. He then offered to grant her youth, without which the first gift would be merely an affliction, if she would accept him as a lover. She proudly refused, and lived to be a decrepit thousand years old. Apollo pursued the nymph DAPHNE, but she became a laurel bush rather than submit to him. He had to content himself with killing Leucippus, a young rival, and making the laurel his sacred plant.

Apollo fell in love with Marpessa, daughter of the river-god Evenus, but IDAS carried her off. Apollo followed him to Messene and would have taken the girl by force, but Zeus intervened and allowed Marpessa to make her own choice of a husband. She chose Idas, believing that Apollo would grow weary of her as she aged. The god's love for the nymph Sinope also went unrewarded. Before yielding to his advances, she insisted that he grant her a boon. Apollo agreed, whereupon Sinope asked to remain a virgin all her life. The frustrated lover had to console himself with the knowledge that Zeus had been tricked in the same way.

Apollo's two well-known affairs with young men both ended in tragedy. He loved HYACINTH, a beautiful youth of Amyclae, but accidentally killed him with a discus. As a memorial, he caused a flower to grow from the young man's blood. In Ceüs the god fell in love with a lovely lad named Cyparissus. A promising friendship was cut short when the boy accidentally killed a pet stag. Apollo found that his love could not assuage Cyparissus' grief. Chagrined, he finally consented to change the boy into a cypress tree.

Not all Apollo's loves led to disaster. Erechtheus' daughter Creüsa bore him Ion, eponym of the Ionians. He was the father of Eleuther by Poseidon's daughter Aethusa. He transported the nymph Cyrene from the banks of the Thessalian river Peneius to Libya. There she bore Aristaeüs and had a great city named for her. The bard Philammon was Apollo's son by Chione, daughter of Daedalion. When Artemis killed the girl because of an arrogant remark that she made, Daedalion grieved so inconsolably that Apollo changed him into a hawk. Apollo was also claimed as the father, by various women and nymphs, of many other persons of modest fame.

D. When Heracles went to Delphi to ask how he might be cured of the disease that had resulted from his murder of Iphitus, the Pythia refused to give an answer. Heracles thereupon snatched the sacred tripod and threatened to set up an oracle of his own. Apollo appeared to rescue his property, and a fatal brawl might have ensued if Zeus had not thrown a thunderbolt between his sons. Apollo then gave Heracles the advice that he sought. His initial reluctance to aid the suppliant is hard to explain, in view of the fact that Apollo had himself killed Iphitus' father, Eurytus, for daring to challenge him to a contest in archery.

Apollo was intimately involved in two major conflicts, the Trojan War and the struggle for power in Argos that followed the murder of Agamemnon. The god fully supported the Trojan cause. He was said by some writers to be the father by Hecuba of Troïlus and by Procleia of Tenes, king of Tenedos. Early in the conflict, he afflicted the Greeks with a plague in punishment for Agamemnon's refusal to accept ransom from Chryses, a priest of the god, for his daughter Chryseïs. Apollo frequently aided the Trojans in battle and guided the hand of Paris when he shot Achilles. Some say that this was his vengeance on the Greek champion for killing Tenes. Inadvertently Apollo became responsible for the fall of Troy. Angry at his priest Laocoön for having married against his will, he sent two sea serpents to kill him and his sons. The Trojans misinterpreted this omen to mean that they should admit the WOODEN HORSE to Troy, and the city fell to the Greeks.

When ORESTES, the exiled son of Agamemnon, went to Delphi to inquire what he should do about his faithless mother, who had married his father's murderer, he was told by the god's oracle that he must kill both Clytemnestra and Aegisthus. He did so, whereupon the god seemed to abandon him to his enemies and to the Erinyes, who drove him mad. At last Apollo came to Orestes' aid, successfully defending him against the accusing Erinyes on the Areopagus.

E. The origins and even the name of Apollo have long been subjects of speculation. Although the god seems the mythical embodiment of the "Hellenic spirit"—at least in its Apollonian aspects—it is generally agreed that he was not at first a god either of the Hellenes or of the pre-Hellenic inhabitants of Greece. A prolonged controversy over whether his provenance was northern or eastern is still far from settled. The Greeks of the Classical era believed that the name of the Hyperboreans, a legendary people with whom Apollo was said to spend his winters, referred to their residence "beyond the north wind." Modern scholars reject this etymology and many believe that the scanty accounts [see, for example, Herodotus 4.13, 4.32–36] indicate a central Asian home for the Hyperboreans.

Although it is not unlikely that the myths of Apollo included elements from northern Europe, the evidence now seems to weigh in favor of an eastern origin for the god. His familiar epithet Lyceius may have meant simply Lycian, rather than "Wolf-God" or "Light-God," as has often been suggested. In the *Iliad*, Apollo often seems essentially a local deity who spent much of his time watching the progress of the war from the Trojan citadel. His mother, Leto, and his sister, Artemis, were certainly Asiatic goddesses, though probably not originally connected with Apollo's cult. It is known that Apollo was worshiped deep in Anatolia, beyond the coastal sphere of strong Greek influence. Some scholars have traced his name to Apulunas, a Hittite god.

If Apollo was a healer, it was possibly because, as a god who brought disease and sudden death, he was also entreated to avert them. His arrows, like those of Artemis, were held responsible for deaths not caused by violence. In much of Homer, being shot by either of these deities is merely a metaphor for death from plague or some unexplained cause. Similarly, Apollo was on occasion a god both of flocks and of the wolves that are their enemies. He was also, as Apollo Agyïeus (He of the Ways), a protector of the entrances to dwellings and streets. The Argonauts prayed to him as a god of shores and of embarkations.

Some fairly early writers identified Phoebus Apollo with Helius, the ancient sun-god, and transferred to him certain of the latter's myths. The well-known tale of Helius' son Phaëthon, for example, was told by Ovid [*Metamorphoses* 1.750–2.400] of Apollo.

In several parts of Asia Minor, Apollo was worshiped under the name Smintheus. This epithet is generally believed to refer to his functions as a god of mice, though some prefer to believe that it is merely his name as god of the city of Sminthe, in the Troad. If the first view is correct, the connection of the god with mice may lie in the fact that mice were regarded in some places as prophetic animals, or Apollo may have caused (and protected his worshipers from) plagues of mice, as he did other plagues.

F. Apollo figures prominently in Homer's *Iliad* and appears in person in Aeschylus' *Eumenides* and Euripides' *Orestes*. The god's justice is subjected to some question in the latter play; in two other of Euripides' plays about O-restes, *Electra* and *Iphigeneia among the Taurians;* and in his *Ion*—or at least so it seems to many modern readers. The *Homeric Hymn to Apollo* [3] recounts in detail the story of his birth at Delos and his subsequent acquisition of the oracle at Delphi. Hermes' theft of Apollo's cattle and the brothers' reconciliation are the subject of the *Homeric Hymn to Hermes* [4]. Many of the tales of Apollo's loves were recounted with romantic detail by Ovid in his *Metamorphoses*: Daphne [1.438–567], Coronis [2.535–632], Chione [11.303–345], the Cumaean Sibyl [14.129–153], Hyacinth [10.162–219], and Cyparissus [10.106–142].

Among innumerable other references to the god's myths are the following: Homer, *Odyssey*, 8.226–228, 15.243–253; Hesiod, *Theogony*, 94–95, 346–348; *Catalogues of Women* 63–64, 83, 88–93, 98; *Shield of Heracles* 68–69, 477–480; Aeschylus, *Agamemnon*, 1202–1212; Pindar, *Pythian Odes*, 3.1–67, 9.1–70; Apollodorus 1.3.2–4, 1.4.1–2, 1.7.8–9, 1.9.15, 2.5.9, 2.6.2, 3.10. 1–4, 3.12.5, "Epitome" 3.23–26 and 5.3; Ovid, *Metamorphoses*, 6.204–266, 6.382–400, 11.153–171; Apollonius Rhodius 2.500–520, 2.946–953, 4.611–618; Hyginus, *Fabulae*, 9–10, 28, 32, 49–51, 107, 135, 140, 165, 191, 200; Pausanias 1.30.3, 1.42.2, 1.43.7–8, 2.30.3, 2.33.2, 5.14.8, 8.30.3–4, 9.10.5–6, 10.5.6.

Apollodorus. A Greek mythographer. Nothing is known of Apollodorus' life, but it is conjectured that he lived in the first or second century A.D. He wrote a prose account of the origin of the universe and the adventures of the Greek gods and heroes. This work, known as *The Library*, is, in the words of one of its finest translators, James G. Frazer, "a history of the world as it was conceived by the Greeks." Apollodorus drew largely on works now lost that dated as far back as the fifth century B.C., and his scrupulous faithfulness in recording the statements of extant works suggests that all his sources are reliably represented. The first two books of *The Library* and a part of the third survive almost intact; the remainder is summarized in an "epitome," perhaps the work of the twelfth-century Greek writer Johannes Tzetzes. Well organized on a genealogical basis, *The Library* is one of the most convenient and readable ancient works on Greek mythology. Frazer's translation, with copious notes, is found in the Loeb Classical Library.

Apollonius Rhodius. A Greek poet who wrote in Alexandria and Rhodes during the third century B.C. Apollonius is known only for his long poem *Argonautica*, which tells in great detail the story of the voyage of the *Argo*.

Apsyrtides. Islands at the mouth of the supposed branch of the Danube River down which the Argonauts sailed into the Adriatic Sea. No such branch exists, but it was apparently thought to empty into the northeastern Adriatic near Istria. These islands were settled by some of the Argonauts' Colchian pursuers after the death of their leader, Apsyrtus. The two Brygeian Islands, a part of this group, were sacred to Artemis.

Apsyrtus or **Absyrtus.** The son of Aeëtes, king of Colchis. Apsyrtus' mother was either Asterodeia, a Caucasian nymph, or Aeëtes' wife, Eidyia, daughter of Oceanus and Tethys. Because he outshone all other Colchian youths in prowess, Apsyrtus was called Phaëthon (Shining One). According to Apollonius Rhodius, Apsyrtus led the Colchian pursuit of the ARGONAUTS [N] as they sailed away with his sister Medea and the golden fleece. In the delta of the Danube, Medea lured him to a meeting with her at which Jason ambushed and killed him. Apollodorus makes Apsyrtus a mere child, whom Medea dismembered and strewed on the water. Aeëtes abandoned pursuit in order to collect the pieces and bury them at Tomi, on the western coast of the Black Sea. In either case, Zeus's anger at this outrage resulted in a violent storm, or in the entire succession of hardships that the Argonauts faced on their homeward voyage. They were purified of murder by Circe, Apsyrtus' aunt. Hyginus [*Fabulae* 23] says that Jason fairly killed Apsyrtus when the Colchians pursued him even after the Phaeacian king Alcinoüs had arbitrated their dispute in Jason's favor. According to this story, Medea buried her brother at Absoros. Later, when the city was infested with snakes, she confined them by enchantment in his tomb. [Apollonius Rhodius 4.303–481; Apollodorus 1.9.24.]

Apulia. That part of the Adriatic coast of Italy immediately north of the "heel." King Daunus welcomed Diomedes to Apulia. The Argive founded there the town of Argyripa (later Arpi) but did not prosper.

Aquarius (The Water-Carrier). A constellation. This group of stars is usually said to represent Ganymede, Zeus's cupbearer. Some say, however, that he is Deucalion or Cecrops. [Hyginus, *Poetica Astronomica*, 2.29.]

Aquila (The Eagle). A constellation. These stars represent the eagle that carried Ganymede up to heaven, or the one that carried Aphrodite's slipper to Hermes, or the bird that appeared as a favorable omen to Zeus when he was deciding whether to go to war with the Titans. Or they may be Meropes, king of Cos, whom Hera changed into an eagle when he was grief-stricken over his wife's death. [Hyginus, *Poetica Astronomica*, 2.16.]

Aquilo. The Latin name for the north wind. When personified as a god by the Romans, this wind was often called by his Greek name, Boreas.

Arabus. A son of Hermaon and Thronia, daughter of Belus. Arabus was presumably the eponym of Arabia. [*Catalogues of Women* 15.]

Arachne. A young Lydian woman adept at weaving. Arachne, daughter of Idmon of Colophon, became famous throughout Lydia for her skill at the loom. She boasted that she would not hesitate to pit her art against that of Athena, the goddess of crafts. Athena visited the girl in the form of an old woman and warned her of the dangers of presumption. When Arachne scorned this advice, the goddess revealed herself and a contest began. The goddess wove legends of human beings who had been punished by the gods for arrogance. Arachne countered by flawlessly depicting a few Olympian scandals. Athena had been merely annoyed by the girl's boasts. When she perceived that Arachne's skill was in fact equal to her own, she flew into a rage, tore the girl's tapestry to shreds, and began beating her with her shuttle. Arachne, unable to bear the punishment, hanged herself. The goddess completed her vengeance by changing her rival into a spider, but Arachne's talent for spinning survived unimpaired. [Ovid, *Metamorphoses*, 6.1–145.]

Araethyrea. The eponym of the country of that name. Araethyrea was a daughter of Aras, the founder of Arantia (Phliasia). She ruled jointly with her brother Aoris, who renamed the land for her after her death. (See also PHLIUS.) [Pausanias 2.12.4.]

Arantia. The earliest name of PHLIUS and Phliasia.

Aras. The founder of Phlius and Phliasia, both of which he called Arantia. The Phliasians claimed that this autochthonous inhabitant of their land lived in the days of Prometheus. They did not explain how Aras survived the flood in the time of Deucalion, Prometheus' son. Aras was succeeded by his son and daughter, Aoris and Araethyrea. [Pausanias 2.12.4.]

Arcadia. The mountainous interior region of the Peloponnesus. The first ruler of Arcadia was Pelasgus, who was either born from the earth there or an immigrant from Argos. He taught the naked, root-eating aborigines, then called Pelasgians, the rudiments of shelter, clothing, and diet. Lycaon, Pelasgus' son by the nymph Cyllene or the Oceanid Meliboea, succeeded him. Either Lycaon's own savagery or the impiety of his fifty sons brought upon them the anger of Zeus, who turned Lycaon into a wolf and destroyed all the sons except Nyctimus, who became king. Nyctimus apparently did not rule for long. He was succeeded by his nephew Arcas, Zeus's son by Lycaon's daughter, Callisto. Arcas lent the area his name and continued the civilizing work of

Pelasgus, teaching his still-primitive people the arts of cultivation, bread-making, and weaving. He also fortified the city of Trapezus. Arcas divided the kingdom by lot among his three sons: Azania went to Azan, Tegea to Apheidas, and Mount Cyllene to Elatus.

Of the sons of Elatus, Stymphalus ruled in the north in a city that he named for himself. He successfully defended his kingdom against the Phrygian invader Pelops until he was treacherously murdered. Lycurgus, son of Apheidas' son Aleüs, ruled into extreme old age at Tegea, outliving his sons, Epochus and Ancaeüs. Ancaeüs' son, Agapenor, led Arcadian forces to the Trojan War, borrowing ships from Mycenae, since landlocked Arcadia had none of its own. Instead of returning to Arcadia at the close of the war, Agapenor settled in Cyprus. Echemus, a great-grandson of Aleüs, became king and successfully resisted the first attempt of the Heraclids to invade the Peloponnesus, killing Hyllus in single combat. Three generations later King Cypselus, a descendant of Stymphalus, saw that the Dorian invasion could no longer be prevented and shrewdly married his daughter, Merope, to Cresphontes, the Heraclid king of neighboring Messenia. As a result of this move, the line of Cypselus reigned in Arcadia for many generations.

In ancient Greece, Arcadia was regarded, with some justice, as a primitive region where rude, even barbarous, customs and rites persisted. The view of Arcadia as an idyllic land inhabited by nymphs and shepherds was conceived much later by writers whose romantic imaginations were not inhibited by firsthand knowledge of the country.

Arcas. The king and eponym of Arcadia. Son of Zeus and CALLISTO, Arcas was saved by Hermes from his dead mother's womb and reared by Maia in Arcadia, or else brought to the court of his grandfather King Lycaon after Callisto's transformation into a bear. Lycaon cut him into pieces and served him in a stew to Zeus, but the god reassembled his son and restored him to life. Arcas succeeded his uncle Nyctimus on the throne and introduced to the primitive Arcadians—thitherto called Pelasgians—the arts of weaving and bread-making and the cultivation of crops, which he had learned from Triptolemus. Arcas had three sons, Azan, Apheidas, and Elatus, by a wife who is variously identified, and also an illegitimate son, Autolaüs. The legitimate sons drew lots for shares in their father's kingdom and received, respectively, Azania, Tegea, and Mount Cyllene. At the instigation of the Delphic oracle, the Mantineians later brought the bones of Arcas to their city from the ruins of Maenalus. Arcas was commonly supposed, however, to have been transported to the heavens by his father, Zeus, as the constellation Arctophylax, guardian of the Great Bear, his mother. [*Astronomy* 4; Hyginus, *Poetica Astronomica*, 2.4; Pausanias 8.4.1–8.]

Arceisius. A son of Zeus or of Cephalus and Procris. Arceisius was the father of Laërtes and grandfather of Odysseus. [Homer, *Odyssey*, 16.118; Ovid, *Metamorphoses*, 13.143–145; Hyginus, *Fabulae*, 189.]

Arcesilaüs. See BATTUS [B].

Archemorus. See OPHELTES.

Archer, The. See SAGITTARIUS.

Arctophylax. See URSA MAJOR.

Arctos. See URSA MAJOR.

Ardea. A coastal city south of Rome. Ardea, said to have been founded by Danaë, was the capital of the Rutulians, the principal Latin tribe defeated by Aeneas and the Trojans.

Areius. An Argonaut. Areius, a son of Bias and Pero, sailed in the *Argo* with his brothers Talaüs and Leodocus, but none of the three distinguished himself during the voyage. [Apollonius Rhodius 1.118–121.]

Arene. A city in Messenia. Perieres made Arene his capital when he came from Thessaly, but, on the death of APHAREUS, the rule passed to Neleus at Pylus.

Areopagus. A rocky hill near the Acropolis at Athens. The name Areopagus was generally interpreted by the Athenians of the Classical era as "Hill of Ares," which the Romans translated as "Mars's Hill." Some modern scholars are more inclined to believe that the word actually meant "Hill of Curses," a name reflecting the fact that the chief shrine of the Semnai (August Goddesses) was located there. Aeschylus identified these deities as the Erinyes, who were probably associated with the working-out of curses. In a myth intended to explain the name, Ares was said to have been the first person to be tried there for murder. In the *Eumenides* of Aeschylus, the Areopagus is the scene of Orestes' trial for the murder of his mother. The Areopagus was the seat of the early Athenian council of elders (*boule*), the chief administrative and judicial body of its time. The powers of this aristocratic council were reduced to those of a homicide court, but were largely restored in the Roman era.

Ares. The god of war, identified by the Romans with MARS.

A. Ares was the only son of Zeus and Hera. He did not marry, but had many children by a variety of liaisons with goddesses and mortal women. Demonice, daughter of the Calydonian lord Agenor, bore him four sons, Evenus, Thestius, and the more obscure Pylus and Molus. Also from Aetolia was Ares' son Dryas, an Argonaut. Even Meleager was said by some to have been fathered by Ares rather than Oeneus. Two other Argonauts, Ialmenus and Ascalaphus, who later led the Minyan forces from Orchomenus to Troy, were sons of Ares by Astyoche. Phlegyas, another king of Orchomenus, was his son by Dotis or Chryse. Cyrene gave birth to the notorious Thracian king Diomedes by the god; Pyrene or Pelopia was the mother of his son Cycnus. Some say that the Arcadian leader Parthenopaeüs was a child of Ares by Atalanta. The Amazon queen Penthesileia was his daughter by Otrere. Tereus, another notorious Thracian, was Ares' son.

The Eleians claimed that their famous king Oenomaüs was the offspring of Ares by the Pleiad Asterope or by Harpina. Their later king Oxylus was also a son of Ares, his mother being Protogeneia, daughter of Calydon. Aërope, daughter of the Arcadian Cepheus, bore the god a son, Aëropus. When Aërope died in childbirth, Ares enabled the child to survive by sucking at its dead mother's breast. Ares seduced Erechtheus' daughter Agraulus, who bore a daughter, Alcippe. When Poseidon's son Halirrhothius raped Alcippe, Ares killed him and became the first being, mortal or divine, to be tried for murder. The god was acquitted and the hill at Athens where the event occurred was thereafter called the Areopagus, after him. The goddess Eos also had an affair with Ares, but no children resulted. Aphrodite was so angry that she punished Eos by causing her to be perpetually in love.

The reason for Aphrodite's annoyance was that Ares was her lover as well, although she was married to Hephaestus. Their affair lasted long enough to produce three sons, Eros (Love), Deimus (Fear), and Phobus (Panic), and a daughter, Harmonia. Deimus and Phobus drove their father's chariot in battle. Harmonia, who came from Samothrace, married Cadmus. The liaison of Ares and Aphrodite ended ignominiously when Helius betrayed them to Hephaestus. The artisan-god constructed a marvelous net, which he hid above the bed before pretending to leave for Lemnos. As so many times before, Ares took advantage of this opportunity to join Aphrodite in the absent husband's bed. No sooner had they got into it together than the net fell over them, holding them motionless. Hephaestus then called the other Olympian gods to view the guilty lovers naked and helpless on the bed. After the gods had enjoyed a hearty laugh at their expense, Poseidon persuaded Hephaestus to accept reparations from Ares, and himself went bond for the evidently unreliable god. The injured husband released the pair and they slunk away, Aphrodite to her island of Cyprus, Ares to his home in Thrace.

B. In spite of being a war-god, Ares seems to have been none too successful in battle. Otus and Ephialtes once bound him, stuffed him into a bronze jar, and left him there for thirteen months. The god (though supposedly immortal) would have died if Eëriboea, the stepmother of the young giants, had not told Hermes of Ares' plight. Hermes rescued him in the nick of time. Heracles is said to have felled Ares four times in the battle for the city of Pylus. Zeus flung a thunderbolt between the two to prevent a battle on a later occasion after Heracles had killed Ares' son Cycnus. During the Trojan War, Diomedes, urged on by Athena, wounded Ares severely. The god, yelling mightily in pain, fled to Olympus and complained to Zeus. Far from cheering him up, Zeus told him that the other gods detested him. Later Ares foolishly took on Athena as an opponent and was flattened with a huge stone. Aphrodite hastened to his aid, only to be laid out beside him with a cuff from Athena. Ares acquitted himself better in the war between the gods and the Giants, killing the Giant Mimas.

Most of the principal sites of Ares' worship were outside the boundaries of Greece. As well as in Thrace, he was worshiped in Scythia, where men and animals were sacrificed before a sword that represented the god. In Colchis he had a sacred grove, where the golden fleece was guarded by a dragon. The field that Jason plowed with the fire-breathing bulls was also named for the god. The Amazons claimed to be descended from Ares and a nymph of the Acmonian Wood named Harmonia. They worshiped him in the form of a black stone (probably a meteorite) on the island of Dia, where they sacrificed horses to him. The famous belt that Heracles took from Queen Hippolyte had been a token from Ares. Some say that the Areopagus was named by the Amazons, who sacrificed to the god there during their invasion of Athens.

Ares did have, at least in early times, one important cult center in a Greek city. The dragon that guarded the spring of Dirce at Thebes was sacred to him, if it was not, in fact, his offspring. When Cadmus killed it he had to serve Ares for eight years, after which he married the god's daughter Harmonia. Cadmus and Harmonia were transformed into snakes by the god at their deaths. Later, during the assault by the Seven against Thebes, Menoeceus sacrificed himself to Ares in order to save the city from destruction.

C. The Greeks evidently had mixed feelings about Ares. On the one hand, they often engaged in war and appreciated the need for courage and prowess. On the other hand, they were deeply suspicious of the bloodlust and the mindless spirit of destruction that Ares represented, ever accompanied as he was by Fear and Panic. It is no accident that, as early as Homer, who extolled the ways of a time when courage in battle gained a man his highest glory, Ares was regularly defeated by the equally warlike but disciplined and clearheaded Athena. Ares was relatively little worshiped by the Greeks and may have had a foreign origin, though he was already one of the Olympian gods at an early period.

There are a few indications that he, or perhaps local gods who came to be identified with him, had some functions connected with fertility: for example, his miraculous saving of the infant Aëropus at Tegea, where he was worshiped as Aphneius (Bountiful). The *Homeric Hymn to Ares* [8], moreover, prays to the god for courage in war, but also for courage to observe the rule of law and keep the peace. This aspect of Ares' nature is much more striking in the god Mars, whom the Romans identified with Ares. Mars seems to have been primarily an agricultural deity who assumed more warlike functions as the early Romans became increasingly powerful and aggressive.

D. Ares figures prominently in Homer's *Iliad* and, as Mars, in Vergil's *Aeneïd*. The story of his embarrassment in Aphrodite's bed is first told in the *Odyssey* [8.266–366]. See also Hesiod's *Theogony* [921–923, 934–937], *Shield of Heracles*, *Telegony* [1], Aeschylus' *Eumenides* [685–690], Euripides' *Electra* [1258–1262], Apollodorus' *Library* [1.4.4, 1.7.7, 1.8.2, 1.9.16, 2.5.8–9, 3.4.1–2, 3.5.5, 3.9.2, 3.14.8, "Epitome" 2.5 and 5.1], Apollonius Rhodius' *Argonautica* [2.404–406, 2.989–992, 2.1169–1176, 3.409–413, 3.1227], Ovid's *Metamorphoses* [15.862–863], Hyginus' *Fabulae* [159], and Pausanias' *Description of Greece* [5.7.10, 5.22.6, 8.44.7–8, 9.36.1, 9.37.7].

Arete. A queen of the Phaeacians. A daughter of Rhexenor, Arete married her uncle, Alcinoüs, king of the Phaeacians. She bore five sons and a daughter, Nausicaä. Alcinoüs respected his wife's judgment and she influenced him on many occasions. When Jason and Medea came to Drepane, Arete persuaded Alcinoüs to vow to protect them against the pursuing Colchians if the pair's marriage had been consummated. She then secretly arranged for their wedding night in the cave of Macris. On the advice of Nausicaä, the shipwrecked Odysseus knelt as a suppliant first to Arete, rather than to her husband. [Homer, *Odyssey*, 7.53–338, 8.423–445, 13.56–69; Apollonius Rhodius 4.982–1222.]

Arethusa. See ALPHEIUS.

Argeia (1). A daughter of Adrastus and Amphithea. Argeia married Polyneices and was the mother of Thersander. According to the *Catalogues of Women* [24, 99A], she attended the funeral of her father-in-law, Oedipus. Hyginus [*Fabulae* 72] claims that she helped Antigone to lift Polyneices' unburied body onto Eteocles' funeral pyre. (See also SEVEN AGAINST THEBES, A.)

Argeia (2). A daughter of Autesion. Argeia married the Heraclid leader Aristodemus and bore him twin sons, Procles and Eurysthenes. When Aristodemus was killed, Argeia's brother Theras became their guardian. [Pausanias 3.1.7.]

Argeius. A son of Licymnius. Argeius and his brother Melas were killed fighting with their cousin HERACLES [N] against Eurytus, king of Oechalia. [Apollodorus 2.7.7.]

Argiope. See TELEPHASSA; THAMYRIS.

Argives. The citizens of Argos and, by extension, the inhabitants of Argolis. Homer used the name Argives, as well as Danaäns, to designate all the Greeks who fought at Troy under the leadership of Agamemnon, king of Mycenae or Argos.

Argolis. The region at the head of the Gulf of Argolis in the Peloponnesus. Often called Argos, after its principal city, it included Mycenae, Tiryns, Nemea, Midea, Epidaurus, Nauplia, and several smaller cities.

Argolis, Gulf of. A deeply indented bay in the eastern Peloponnesus. The Gulf of Argolis was the closest connection with the Mediterranean Sea for all the major cities of Argolis except Epidaurus and Troezen. Mycenae, Tiryns, and Nauplia, as well as Argos, were in the valley that spread northward from this gulf.

Argonautica. See APOLLONIUS RHODIUS.

Argonauts. A company of adventurous Greeks who sailed with Jason in quest of the golden fleece.

A. When Jason demanded from the usurper Pelias the throne of Iolcus, which rightfully belonged to his father, Aeson, he was tricked by the wily king into promising to bring the golden fleece home to Thessaly. This fleece had belonged to a miraculous ram which, a generation earlier, had rescued the youth PHRIXUS from death and borne him through the air to Aea, the capital of Colchis, a land at the farthest end of the Black Sea. Phrixus had sacrificed the ram and nailed its fleece to a tree in a grove sacred to Ares, where it had since been guarded by an unsleeping dragon. Aeëtes, king of Colchis, would never willingly allow the fleece to be removed, either because of his traditional Colchian hostility toward strangers or because he had learned from an oracle that he would rule only as long as the fleece remained in the grove. Pelias knew, therefore, that even if Jason were to survive the perilous voyage to Aea, it was extremely unlikely that he would ever return.

Jason went to Delphi to inquire of the oracle what were his chances of carrying out his rash promise. The reply is not recorded, but it must have been encouraging, for Jason enlisted the aid of Argus, an expert boat builder, in building the largest and most elaborate ship that had yet been designed. Argus (variously called a son of Argeia by Arestor or Phrixus or Danaüs or Polybus) turned to Athena for advice. She gave it freely, and herself fitted a miraculous speaking beam from the oaks of Dodona into the prow. The huge craft, the marvel of all who saw it, was christened *Argo*, for its builder.

Jason now sent out heralds to announce his intentions in all the Greek lands. Hardly an able-bodied nobleman who heard of the projected voyage was able to withstand the lure of winning glory for himself as a member of the crew. From as far away as Pylus, on the western coast of the Peloponnesus, they began arriving at Iolcus. Rosters of this illustrious company have been drawn up by several writers. These disagree at many points, but certain names appear on every list: Heracles, Orpheus, the Dioscuri, Zetes and Calaïs, Telamon and Peleus, Idas and Lynceus, Admetus, Periclymenus, Augeias, Argus, Tiphys. Several other personages are not everywhere mentioned, but play important roles in one or two accounts. Notable among these are Meleager and the two seers Idmon and Mopsus. Theseus and Atalanta appear in some rolls, but Apollonius specifically states in his *Argonautica* that Theseus was detained in Hades at the time and that Atalanta, although she volunteered for the voyage, was politely refused by Jason, who rightly believed that there would be enough causes for dissension in the *Argo* without having a woman on board.

B. When the men were assembled, Jason asked them to elect a leader for the expedition. They unanimously chose Heracles, who had already won a great reputation for himself and was by far the strongest of the crew. Heracles not only declined the honor but declared that he would let no one accept it but Jason. The others agreed and set about launching the ship under the direction of Tiphys, son of Hagnias, who was to be the pilot. At nearly the last moment Argus and Acastus came hurrying down to the *Argo*. Argus wanted to accompany the ship he had built in order to keep it in good repair. Acastus, the only son of Pelias, was defying his father's wishes, either out of sympathy for Jason or from simple desire for the glory to be gained in the venture.

The Argonauts' last act before setting sail was to make a sacrifice to Apollo, god of embarkations. The seer Idmon, reading the future in the coils of smoke rising from the altar, predicted that the others would reach home again bearing the fleece. He had long known that he was himself fated to die along the way, but had undertaken the voyage nonetheless rather than be thought fearful of his fate.

As the Argonauts pushed off at dawn, the speaking beam in the *Argo*'s prow cried out, eager to be under way. The ship quickly slipped out of the Gulf of Pagasae and rounded the Magnesian Peninsula, and the sailors headed northward along the western coast of the Aegean Sea. In several days of rowing they saw Mount Ossa, then Mount Olympus on their left, and shortly afterward struck eastward across the sea, making for the island of Lemnos. [Apollonius Rhodius 1.1–608.]

C. Lemnos lies in the northern Aegean, midway between Thrace and the Troad. At the time of the *Argo*'s arrival it was inhabited entirely by women. The Lemnians were thrown into a panic at the sight of a ship approaching from the direction of Thrace. They had reason to dread a Thracian invasion, or indeed any visitors at all. Some years before, the goddess Aphrodite, angry because the Lemnian women had neglected to honor her, had punished them by causing them to give off an unpleasant smell, which quickly caused their husbands to seek other companionship. The men, who were given to raiding the Thracian mainland, now began taking their female captives into their homes and having children by them instead of by their wives. One day the jealous wives rose up in a body and killed both the Thracian women and their own husbands. In order to avoid retribution, they then had to finish the work by killing all other males on the island: their own fathers and sons, as well as the sons of the Thracians. Ever since this outrage they had lived in fear that a punitive expedition would be sent from Thrace to avenge the slaughtered women.

When the *Argo* reached the shore, its crew saw a wild and disorganized band of women pouring from the gates of the city. Their queen, Hypsipyle, was wearing the armor of her father, Thoas, the former king, whose life she had secretly saved. Jason sent the Argonauts' herald, Aethalides—a son of the patron of heralds, Hermes—to greet the queen and request that the men be permitted to spend the night on shore. Aethalides' courteous words calmed the women somewhat and Hypsipyle summoned them to a council in the marketplace. There she advised them to conciliate the newcomers by providing them with ample supplies, in the hope that they would be encouraged to sail away in the morning without entering the city. Her shrewd old nurse, Polyxo, offered a counterproposal. Reminding the women that when they grew old there would be no one to defend them against Thracian attack or even to yoke the oxen and plow the fields, she advised them to invite the men not only into the city, but into their homes as well. In spite of their fears, the women were not displeased with this suggestion. Hypsipyle agreed to it and sent one of the women down to the beach to extend the invitation officially.

Jason and most of his men hastily got ready to visit the city. Heracles, who had brought his pretty young friend Hylas with him on the voyage, preferred to remain on board, as did two or three of the others. Jason, a tall and handsome young man, dressed himself in his finest cloak, a gift from Athena, and made his way to the palace. Hypsipyle cautiously told him a false tale of how she and her women, dishonored by their husbands with the Thracian women, had finally locked them out of the city, upon which the men had gone to live in Thrace. She went on to invite the Argonauts to settle among them, and even indicated that Jason would doubtless become the Lemnian king.

Jason displayed the irresistible way with women that was more than once to prove his chief contribution to the success of the voyage. In a brief but gracious speech he accepted the Lemnian hospitality for himself and his men, but made it clear that they must soon be on their way again. Just how long the Argonauts remained on Lemnos is in dispute, but most writers say that it was only a few days. Heracles, growing restive on the *Argo*, sent ashore an ironic message about his shipmates' methods of winning glory, and they shamefacedly returned to the ship. Though the Lemnian women were sad for a time, Polyxo's recommended strategy accomplished its purpose. At a reasonable interval after the departure of the visitors, a new crop of Lemnians, male and female, sprang up to take the place of those who had been cut down. Hypsipyle became the mother of two sons by Jason: Euneüs and Nebrophonus or Deïpylus. She did not, however, follow their father's advice that she send them to Aeson at Iolcus. This may have been because the Lemnian women, on learning that their queen had earlier saved Thoas' life in defiance of their decision to kill all the men, sold her into slavery. Whatever the reason, Euneüs remained on Lemnos and was its king at the time of the Trojan War. [Apollonius Rhodius 1.609–909; Apollodorus 3.6.4; Hyginus, *Fabulae*, 15, 74, 254; Homer, *Iliad*, 7.469.]

D. On leaving Lemnos the Argonauts followed the advice of Orpheus and, instead of sailing due east toward the Hellespont, headed northward for Samothrace. Here they were initiated into the Samothracian mysteries, in the hope that they would gain additional protection for their dangerous voyage. From Samothrace they sailed without incident through the Hellespont into the Sea of Marmara and put in at a harbor called Fair, on the western side of a hilly island, known as Bear Mountain, that was connected by a narrow isthmus to the mainland. The Doliones, who inhabited the mainland, greeted the Argonauts with openhanded friendliness. Their king, Cyzicus, was a youth no older than Jason. A son of Aeneus and Aenete, daughter of Eusorus, he had recently married Cleite, daughter of the soothsayer Merops, king of Rhindacus, but they had as yet no children. Cyzicus had learned from an oracle that he should offer hospitality to just such a band of voyagers as the Argonauts. He invited them, therefore, to row a little farther and beach the *Argo* at the Dolionian harbor in the bay of Chytus. When the Argonauts had done so, Cyzicus gave them ample provisions for their journey. In the morning the Argonauts climbed Mount Dindymus, which offered a view east in the direction that they would take. Cyzicus told them of the tribes on the shores of the Sea of Marmara, but he was ignorant of what lay beyond.

Apparently the king neglected to mention the earthborn giants who inhabited Bear Mountain. These six-armed monsters did not dare to attack the Doliones because they were protected by the god Poseidon, from whom they were descended. But the *Argo*, with the few men left to guard it, seemed an easy prey to the monsters. They did not reckon with Heracles, who was one of the guards. At the monsters' first charge he brought down several with his arrows. The other crewmen, returning suddenly from the mountain, did not take long to dispose of the last of the giants.

E. Leaving the dead monsters heaped on the beach, the Argonauts put out to sea. It took much of the day to skirt the rugged coast of Bear Mountain; then the *Argo* headed eastward. Toward evening the wind turned against the ship and it was driven back into a bay, where the crew managed to land. In the growing darkness, not even the expert pilot Tiphys realized that they had landed on the isthmus of Bear Mountain, only a short distance from where they had pushed off that very morning. The Doliones, too, were confused in the poor light and thought that they were being attacked by the Pelasgian raiders who often harassed their shore. They dashed down to the sea to repulse the enemy. A desperate battle ensued, from which the Doliones at last fled back to their city, after suffering heavy casualties. The Argonauts rested watchfully on the beach, fearing another attack. They did not know what they had done until dawn showed them the faces of the dead. First among the corpses they found that of Cyzicus, his breast torn open by Jason's spear.

Both the Argonauts and the Doliones were struck with horror at their mistake. Together they buried Cyzicus with great honor and celebrated funeral games. The grief of Cleite, Cyzicus' young bride, was so great that she hanged herself. She is remembered in the name of a spring, Cleite, which is said to have been formed of the tears of the wood-nymphs who mourned her death. Long after the Doliones had ceased to exist as a separate tribe, Cyzicus was annually honored in the city that bears his name, even by the Ionian settlers who came to govern the land.

After the funeral, storms arose that kept the *Argo* in the harbor for twelve days, showing no sign of abating. At last the seer Mopsus, interpreting the cries of a kingfisher, explained that the Argonauts must propitiate the Mother of the Gods, the Phrygian goddess Cybele, in her ancient shrine on Mount Dindymus. They danced there in full armor about a crude statue of the goddess, clashing their shields and spears to drown out the noise of the Doliones' mourning. (Some say that this was the origin of the noisy dance that accompanied Cybele's rites, but it is generally believed that the Corybantes were the first to perform it.) Fruit, flowers, and springs of water sprang up on the mountain. By the time the ritual feast was eaten, the stormy winds had fallen.

The *Argo* was again on its way at dawn. (It should perhaps be pointed out that the geography of this incident is confused. Dindymus is far inland in Asia Minor.) [Apollonius Rhodius 1.910–1152.]

F. During the next, hard day of rowing along the Mysian coast, Heracles broke his oar. His weary companions were well content to go ashore at dusk at a village on the Cius River at the head of the Cianian Bay. They were welcomed by the hospitable Mysian inhabitants, who gave them ample provisions for the next lap of their journey. Heracles went into the woods to cut himself a new oar. His squire, Hylas, went to a spring called Pegae to draw water. This young man had been kidnaped by Heracles, who had killed his father, Theiodamas, king of the Dryopes. The youthful beauty that had so attracted Heracles proved to be a curse to Hylas, for the nymph of the spring saw him in the moonlight and was so infatuated that she dragged him down into the depths of the water. From some distance away Polyphemus, one of the older Argonauts, heard the boy's cry and rushed to his aid. Finding no trace of him, Polyphemus assumed that the youth had been carried off by robbers or wild animals and ran to find Heracles.

Heracles was wild with grief at the loss of his young lover. Forgetting everything else, he went raging through the woods, shouting for Hylas. Morning came and the Argonauts, eager to take advantage of a favorable wind, put out to sea without noticing that three of their company were missing. They soon realized their mistake and, after a fierce quarrel, would have turned back, if Calaïs and Zetes had not insisted that they go on. Their minds were put at ease by the sea-god Glaucus, who arose from the water to tell them that it had not been the will of Zeus that Heracles go to Colchis, for he still had several labors to complete for Eurystheus. Hylas, Glaucus added, was now married to the nymph of the spring, who had presumably taught him to live under water.

Heracles finally gave up hope of finding Hylas. Nevertheless he threatened to ravage all Mysia if the Mysians did not continue the search after his departure. To insure that they would do so, he took with him the sons of the noblest families as hostages. The Mysians, true to their promise, continued for many centuries to search for Hylas once every year, wandering about the countryside and calling his name. One reason for their loyalty to Heracles may be the fact that Polyphemus founded the city of Cius in the seaside village where the *Argo* had landed. Heracles settled the Mysian hostages in Trachis, and this city and Cius thereafter maintained close relations.

Heracles went on about his labors, but he did not forget that the Argonauts had abandoned him. After the return of the *Argo* to Iolcus he learned that it was Zetes and Calaïs who had persuaded the crew not to go back for him. He met them as they were coming from the funeral games held for Pelias and killed them both. According to both the ancient mythographer Pherecydes and Herodotus [7.193], Heracles was abandoned before the *Argo* had even left the Gulf of Pagasae. He had gone ashore to draw water, but no reason is given for his abandonment. Other writers claimed that Heracles reached Colchis on foot from Mysia; that he sailed there; and even that he, not Jason, was the leader of the Argonauts. [Apollonius Rhodius 1.1153–1362; Apollodorus 1.9.19.]

G. From the Cianian Bay the Argonauts sailed on for a day and a night before beaching the *Argo* for a rest. They had scarcely landed before a fierce-looking band of men confronted them. These were the Bebryces, whose king was the notorious bully Amycus, a son of Poseidon and an ash-nymph, Melia. Amycus arrogantly announced that it was the rule in his land that newcomers must box with him willingly or be forced to do so. He might have added that he had already disposed of a number of his neighbors through this hospitable custom. Instead of being cowed at the sight of this monstrously ugly brute, the Argonauts were infuriated by his barbaric manners. Polydeuces, a son of Zeus and Leda, and the best boxer in the company, immediately accepted the challenge, though he was weary after a day and night of rowing. His brother, Castor, and the Argive Talaüs bound the gloves on his hands. Polydeuces and Amycus fought until both had to retire momentarily from exhaustion, then they rushed together again. Amycus had the greater weight, but Polydeuces was nimbler and made up in craft what he lacked in brute strength. At last, sidestepping a killing blow from the Bebrycian, he darted in and delivered a blow that crushed the bones behind Amycus' ear. The man crumpled to his knees and died. (Some insist, implausibly, that Amycus died of a blow on the elbow.)

The Bebryces now rushed at the winner with spears and clubs, but his fellow Argonauts defended him. Although Talaüs and Iphitus were slightly wounded in the fierce fight that followed, the companions soon routed the Bebryces, who retreated inland. The Argonauts helped themselves to as many Bebrycian sheep as they could use. At the same moment the Mariandyni, enemies of the Bebryces on the northeast who had long disputed with them a territory rich in iron, took advantage of their confusion to raid their cattle. The Argonauts spent the day and night in this place, resting and feasting. [Apollonius Rhodius 2.1–163; Apollodorus 2.5.9.]

H. In the morning the Argonauts pushed off again and headed for the Bosporus, which was not far away. The *Argo* was nearly overwhelmed in the narrow strait by a huge wave, but the expert seamanship of Tiphys saved the ship from harm. After an otherwise uneventful voyage the company landed at Salmydessus, capital of Thynia, a Thracian land near the northern end of the Bosporus. Its ruler was Phineus, whose first wife, Cleopatra, daughter of Boreas, was a sister of Zetes and Calaïs.

There are two entirely different versions of what happened to the Argonauts in Salmydessus. According to one, they discovered that Phineus had taken a second wife, Idaea, daughter of the Scythian king Dardanus. Hating her two stepsons, this woman falsely told Phineus that they had violated her.

He believed her and either blinded his sons, allowed Idaea to blind them, or imprisoned them in a tomb, where they were continually whipped. The Argonauts found the young men and when Phineus refused to release them, they blinded or killed him. (According to this tale, Boreas, who was traveling with the Argonauts, helped with the punishment.) The Argonauts then turned the kingdom over to the sons, who in turn gave it to Cleopatra in order that they might accompany the *Argo* to Colchis.

The second of the two main versions of the Argonauts' visit to Phineus bears no resemblance to the first. According to this more familiar and cheerful story, the crew of the *Argo* arrived to find the old king already blind and harried by the Harpies as punishment for having revealed, through his powers of prophecy, too much of Zeus's plan for the human race. He was so nearly starved that he could no longer care for himself. Every time food was set before him the Harpies would sweep down from the sky and snatch it away, befouling whatever remained so that it gave off a vile stench. The old man's skin was caked with grime and he had hardly the strength to move. Yet, when he heard the Argonauts approaching, he knew that they were destined to relieve him of his suffering, for the powers of prophecy given him by Apollo had not deserted him. Telling them that an oracle had predicted that two sons of the North Wind who were brothers of his wife, Cleopatra, would at last drive away the Harpies, Phineus implored them to save him.

The Argonauts took pity on the once-great king. They prepared a meal and, when the lightning-swift Harpies flew off with it over the sea, Zetes and Calaïs, who bore wings on their backs or ankles, leaped into the sky and sped after them. While waiting for the brothers' return, the other Argonauts bathed Phineus and prepared a feast, the first that the old man had been able to eat in a very long time. In gratitude he told them what their voyage held for them, taking care to omit some details, for his sufferings had taught him that Zeus did not intend that human beings should grasp the whole of his design.

Most useful to the sailors was Phineus' advice on how to pass through the Clashing Rocks, at the northern end of the Bosporus. This obstacle had so far prevented mariners from sailing between the Aegean and Black seas. The old seer also described their entire course along the southern shore of the Black Sea as far as Colchis. Of their return journey he would say nothing except that they would have many guides and that, above all else, they should rely on the favor of the goddess Aphrodite.

The seer had scarcely ended his prediction when Boreas' twin sons flew in, flushed with success. They reported that they had chased the two birdlike monsters until they overtook them above the Floating Islands, or Echinades, off the coast of Acarnania. There they would have killed them if Iris had not flown quickly down from Olympus with a message from Zeus. She had ordered the brothers to spare the Harpies, for they served as the "hounds of Zeus." In return for this clemency she swore by the river Styx that they would never again trouble Phineus. Zetes and Calaïs obeyed the command and turned back. The Floating Islands were thereafter called the Strophades, or "Islands of Turning." As for the Harpies, they limped on to their den on the island of Crete.

Some say, however, that the sons of Boreas lost their lives on this mission. The Harpies were too swift for them, and the brothers were fated to die if they failed to overtake anything they pursued. According to this version of the story, the Harpies died too, as a result of sheer exhaustion. One fell to earth on the Strophades, the other into the Peloponnesian river Tigres, which was renamed Harpys as a consequence.

After the joyful return of the Boreades, the Argonauts left the happy Phineus in the charge of his old friend Paraebius and other loyal subjects who had taken care of him in his misery. When still a powerful king, Phineus had showed equal concern for the welfare of rich and poor, and they had not forgotten him. The Argonauts left Phineus looking forward contentedly to death, for he knew that he was fated to enjoy perpetual happiness in the Underworld. [Apollonius Rhodius 2.164–499; Apollodorus 1.9.21, 3.15.2; Diodorus Siculus 4.43.3–4.44.7; Sophocles, *Antigone*, 968–987.]

I. As they rowed northward through the narrowing Bosporus between rugged cliffs, the Argonauts prepared to meet the greatest test of their seamanship. Ahead they could hear the thunderous roar with which the Clashing Rocks—floating islands at either side of the northern entrance to the Bosporus —rushed together at irregular intervals, driven by the wind. Phineus had told the company what precautions to take, but he had not promised that they would be successful. Following the seer's advice, Euphemus took a dove that he had brought aboard and climbed with it into the *Argo*'s prow. (This seaman, a son of Tityus' daughter Europa by Poseidon, was no doubt chosen for this risky job because, as one of the swiftest men in the world, he could, if need be, run across the surface of the sea without wetting his feet in the waves.)

As soon as the ship rounded a bend in the tortuous channel and the rocks came into view, he flung the bird into the air. It flew straight ahead between the rocks. The Argonauts watched anxiously, for Phineus had warned them that if the dove failed to pass through the Clashing Rocks, it would be useless for them to try and the entire expedition would have to be abandoned. As the bird flew on, the rocks rushed together once more with lightning speed. The men shouted with triumph, for they saw that the dove had escaped, leaving only the tips of her tailfeathers in the grip of the rocky jaws.

As soon as the rocks parted again, the seamen put their backs into their rowing and, aided by the backwash filling the channel, were soon between the rocks. Now, however, a great wave threatened to swamp the *Argo*. No matter how hard the oarsmen pulled, they could make no headway, but remained at exactly the point where in a moment the rocks would crash together with shattering force. The Argonautic expedition would have ended in a cloud of spray if Athena had not intervened in the nick of time. Having supervised the building of the *Argo*, the goddess was perhaps as much concerned with the fate of the ship as with that of its crew. In any case, she had hurried down from Olympus when she saw the Argonauts approaching the Clashing Rocks. Now, as the rocks shuddered before beginning their rush together, Athena held one of them with her left hand and pushed the *Argo* with her right. The ship shot out into the open water of the Black Sea. The rocks claimed only a bit of the stern ornament as they met. Falling open again, they became rooted forever to their places, for the gods had decreed that once a ship passed safely between them the Clashing Rocks would clash no more. [Apollonius Rhodius 2.317–340, 2.549–610.]

J. The Argonauts—except for Jason, who was subject to fits of depression—were overjoyed at their success, for Phineus had predicted that if they safely passed the Clashing Rocks they would encounter no more insuperable obstacles. Following Phineus' advice, they rowed all day and night along the northern coast of Bithynia and reached the desert island of Thynias. As they went ashore exhausted, they had a vision of Apollo passing through the sky on his way from Lycia to the land of the Hyperboreans. They offered sacrifices to him and Orpheus led them in a hymn that had originated with the Corycian nymphs. After another day of travel they beached the *Argo* in the shelter of Cape Acherusias, near where the river Acheron empties into the Black Sea. The Mariandynian inhabitants of this region, led by Lycus, their king, ran down to the sea to greet them, for word had already come to them of the strangers' victory over the Bebryces, who had been enemies of the Mariandyni for many years. Polydeuces, in particular, was hailed as a god.

Lycus entertained the Argonauts royally, but was grieved to hear that Heracles had been left behind. Lycus had been a boy when Heracles, returning from his battle with the Amazons, had aided Dascylus, Lycus' father, in conquering his enemies on all sides—Mysians, Phrygians, Bithynians, Paphlagonians. After Heracles' departure, however, the Bebryces had won back much territory, so the Mariandyni were grateful that the Argonauts had disposed of the brutal Amycus. Lycus not only heaped gifts on the Greeks, but sent his own son Dascylus to be a member of the crew.

This addition was fortunate, for among the Mariandyni the *Argo* lost two members of its crew, the first of the Argonauts to die. The seer Idmon, who had known that he would not return to Greece, was killed by a wild boar. No sooner had his companions observed funeral rites for him than Tiphys, the steersman who had so often guided the *Argo* through dangerous seas, fell sick and died. This disaster plunged the company into gloom, but Ancaeüs, a son of Poseidon and Astypalaea from the island of Samos and an experienced seaman, modestly offered to take the helm. As usual at moments of crisis, Jason could see no hope, but his companions quickly elected Ancaeüs pilot and the *Argo* was soon under way again. [Apollonius Rhodius 2.611–898.]

K. Continuing eastward along the coast, the *Argo* stopped briefly near the Assyrian port of Sinope, at the mouth of the Halys River. Here they discovered Deïleon, Autolycus, and Phlogius, sons of Deïmachus, of the Thessalian city of Tricca. These three brothers had joined Heracles in his war with the Amazons, but had somehow become separated from him and had settled at Sinope. Although the Thessalians appear to have prospered in this region, they were delighted to join with fellow Greeks on another expedition, and the *Argo* sailed on with nearly a full crew.

The next stop would have been Themiscyra, at the mouth of the Thermodon, where Hippolyte and her Amazons were already preparing for battle with the strangers, had not Zeus sent a northwest wind that enabled the Argonauts to sail past this inhospitable shore. After passing the lands of the Chalybes, the Tibareni, and the Mossynoeci, the *Argo* reached a barren island sacred to Ares. Phineus had advised the crew to put in at this lonely shore, where, he had promised mysteriously, a boon would come to them out of the sea. He had also warned them that trouble would come to them out of the sky, for this island was haunted by great numbers of unfriendly birds that attacked strangers with showers of arrowlike feathers, which they shook from their wings. No sooner had the Argonauts come in sight of the island than one of these birds flew over their heads and a feather buried itself in the shoulder of Oïleus. Clytius, son of Eurytus, managed to kill a second bird, but it was evident that arrows would avail little against the huge flock of these birds on the island.

Fortunately Amphidamas, who had come from Arcadia with his brother, Cepheus, to join the crew, recalled what Heracles had done to drive away the plague of birds that lived on Lake Stymphalus. Following Amphidamas' advice, half of the Argonauts roofed over the *Argo* with their shields. The other half rowed for the island, while the feathery darts pattered harmlessly on the shields. As soon as the men could beach the ship, they leaped out and began to make a tremendous din by shouting and beating their swords on their shields. Thousands of birds rose up in dismay and, after milling about in confusion, flew off toward the mainland.

Looking about the desert island, the Argonauts saw four men approaching, naked and scarcely able to stand. One of them, though obviously dazed, managed to ask for assistance. Jason, suspecting that these men had something to do with the boon promised by Phineus, questioned their leader closely. His name was Argus, he said. With his three brothers—Cytissorus, Phrontis, and Melas—he had been cast away the previous day on this island after many hours of clinging to a beam of their wrecked ship. Obeying their father's deathbed command, they had been on their way to Orchomenus to claim his inheritance. Astounded, the Argonauts realized that they were talking to the sons of Phrixus, who had long ago flown from Orchomenus to Colchis on the back of the very ram whose golden fleece the *Argo* had set sail to fetch. Aeëtes had welcomed Phrixus and given him his daughter Chalciope as his bride. She had borne Argus and his brothers. Jason and Admetus, both grandsons of

Phrixus' uncle Cretheus, were glad to aid their cousins. But they and their companions also had in mind that these unexpected allies might in turn be of great help in carrying out the theft of the fleece.

When Jason proposed to the brothers that they return to Colchis in the *Argo*, they were far from enthusiastic over the prospect. Argus pointed out that Aeëtes was a powerful and ruthless king who would be very unlikely to allow the Greeks to carry away the fleece. Even if he could be persuaded, the dragon that guarded it—the offspring of Ge by the blood of Typhaon—could not be. The Argonauts, themselves somewhat daunted by Argus' warning, nevertheless prevailed on the brothers to accompany them to Aea, if only because this was their only chance of escape from the isle of Ares. [Apollonius Rhodius 2.899–1230; Hyginus, *Fabulae*, 20, 21.]

L. The *Argo* set sail at dawn. Passing the island of Philyra it moved eastward along the coast where lived the Macrones, the Becheiri, the Sapeires, and, beyond them, the Byzeres. At last the great Caucasus Range, which lay beyond Colchis, came into view. By night the new crew member Argus piloted them into the mouth of the river Phasis, on the banks of which stood Aea. Here they cast their anchor and, with libations of honey and wine, begged Mother Earth and the gods and heroes of the land to look favorably upon their coming.

In his *Argonautica*, Apollonius Rhodius goes into some detail about how the goddess Hera went about achieving the purpose for which she had sent Jason to Colchis: to bring the sorceress Medea to Iolcus to destroy Pelias. Hera, together with Athena, who also had an interest in the *Argo*'s voyage, saw the ship lying in a quiet backwater near the mouth of the Phasis and retired to their private chambers on Mount Olympus to plan a campaign by which the Argonauts might complete their mission. Aeëtes, a son of Helius, was such a formidable ruler that even the two goddesses could find no way by which the Greeks could challenge him openly and escape with their lives. Hera suggested, therefore, that they find a subtler approach to the problem.

Paying a visit to Aphrodite, she and Athena asked her to persuade her son Eros to wound Medea with one of his arrows and make her love Jason so madly that she would be eager to aid him even against her father, Aeëtes. Aphrodite was flattered that these two great goddesses had come to ask a favor of her. She promised to do what she could to help, though she was not at all sure that her willful boy would do what she asked. She persuaded him with a bribe, a lovely golden ball. Delighted with his prize, Eros went flying down from Olympus, bow in hand, in search of Medea.

The Argonauts, meanwhile, were holding a council aboard the *Argo*. They agreed with Jason's suggestion that they should first see what persuasion might accomplish with the king of Aea. Accordingly Jason, Telamon, and Augeias set out for the city, guided by the sons of Phrixus. To help them reach the palace unchallenged, Hera enveloped the countryside in a mist. The strangers were awed when the mist lifted to reveal the fabulous palace constructed for Aeëtes by Hephaestus. Hera saw to it that the first Colchian to see the Greeks was Medea. At that moment Eros wounded her in the heart with one of his arrows. Medea's sister Chalciope was delighted to see her sons again, but their reunion was interrupted by the appearance of the king with his wife, Eidyia, the youngest daughter of Tethys and Oceanus.

Even the cold-hearted Aeëtes knew the laws of hospitality. He greeted the strangers civilly and invited them to a banquet. When they had eaten, Argus rose and introduced Jason and his companions. He made much of their relationship to Phrixus or their descent from gods, for Telamon was a grandson of Zeus, and Augeias, like Aeëtes himself, claimed Helius for a father. Aeëtes did not believe a word of Argus' story. He accused the visitors and his grandsons alike of plotting to seize his throne. Jason assured him in a conciliatory manner that all the Argonauts wanted was the fleece. In return for it, he said, they would gladly go to war with Aeëtes' perennial enemies the Sauromatians.

Aeëtes was totally unmoved, but he did not wish to destroy the Greeks outright. Barbarian though he was, he doubtless knew that Zeus protected wanderers in foreign lands. After a moment's thought he announced his decision. He promised that he would freely give the fleece to Jason provided that the young man was able to pass a certain test of strength: Jason must yoke fire-breathing bulls to a plow, plow a field with them and sow it with dragon's teeth, then kill the armed men who would quickly spring up from the newly seeded ground. If Jason failed, the king indicated, he and his companions would be treated in a manner that would make them examples to other unwelcome adventurers. Jason accepted the challenge—but only because there was nothing else to do. He and his companions left the hall with little confidence that they would ever again see Greece. Argus accompanied them to the *Argo,* where they were to await the ordeal, but left his brothers behind with their mother. [Apollonius Rhodius 2.1231–3.470; Apollodorus 1.9.23; Pindar, *Pythian Odes,* 4.208–211.]

M. At first the other Argonauts were stunned to learn of the seemingly impossible tasks set for Jason. They soon recovered their courage, however, and several of them, led by Peleus, even offered to take Jason's place. Still, except for the blustering Idas, they were ready enough to follow the advice of Argus, who offered to return to Aea and try to enlist the help of Medea and her powerful sorcery.

Even as Argus set out, the treacherous Aeëtes was whipping his people into a frenzy of suspicion and hatred of the Greek visitors, who, he was sure, were no better than pirates. The king ordered that, as soon as Jason was destroyed by the bulls, the *Argo* be burned with every man aboard. Aeëtes reminded the Aeans that it was not the Colchian custom to welcome strangers. He declared that he had treated Phrixus hospitably only because Zeus himself had commanded it. The king further revealed that his father, Helius, had long ago warned him to beware of treachery from his own family. He was confident of the loyalty of his son, Apsyrtus, and of his two daughters, so the betrayers could only be Chalciope's half-Greek sons. Some say that Aeëtes had, moreover, been told by an oracle that he would die when strangers tried to carry off the golden fleece, and that he planned to offer the Argonauts as a sacrifice in order to confirm the Colchian reputation for cruelty and thus frighten away other adventurers who might cast an acquisitive eye toward the wealthy city of Aea.

While Aeëtes and the Aeans were plotting to destroy the Argonauts, including Chalciope's sons, Argus reached his mother's rooms in the palace and asked her help. She had already thought of appealing to her sister to save her sons. Medea needed no urging, for, thanks to Eros' arrow, she was already madly in love with Jason. Argus returned to the Argo and the next day at dawn led Jason, accompanied by Mopsus, to the shrine of Hecate, outside the city. The two companions remained outside and Jason entered the shrine to meet the goddess' priestess, Medea, alone for the first time. When he appeared, the young woman's twelve maiden attendants discreetly disappeared, leaving the two together.

Phineus had been right in advising that the Argonauts should put their trust in Aphrodite. Jason was, as usual, at his best in making himself charming to a woman, and Medea found him even more irresistible than she had at her first glimpse of him. She gave him a magic drug, made from a plant that had grown from the blood of Prometheus as it dripped from the eagle's talons, and told him how to use it and how to enlist the aid of Hecate. In return, Jason first promised that Medea's name would be honored in his homeland, then found himself vowing to take her there himself in the Argo. After a long talk, Jason returned with his companions to the ship and Medea went back to the palace. [Apollonius Rhodius 3.471–1172; Apollodorus 1.9.23; Pindar, Pythian Odes, 4.220-223; Ovid, Metamorphoses, 7.75–99.]

N. The next morning Jason, accompanied this time by Telamon and Aethalides, son of Hermes, went to Aeëtes' palace. The king gave them the seed for the next day's planting: half of the teeth of the serpent sacred to Ares that Cadmus had killed at Thebes. Athena had saved them and given them to the king. Jason returned to the Argo and waited until night, after the constellation of the Bear had declined. Then, putting on dark clothes suitable for a sacrifice to Hecate, a goddess of the Underworld, he went out alone to a clearing near the Phasis. He bathed himself thoroughly in the sacred river, dug a pit, and, after burning a ewe in it, called on Hecate by the name of Brimo. The fearful goddess rose from below, amid the flicker of torches and the barking of hell-hounds, to accept the offering, but Jason, following Medea's admonitions, walked away without looking back. At dawn he anointed his body and his weapons with the drug that Medea had given him and was suddenly flooded with strength and confidence. Together with his companions, he rowed the Argo upstream to the plain of Ares, the place appointed for the test.

There the Greeks found the Colchians assembled. Aeëtes, driving about in his chariot, was wearing a golden helmet and a cuirass that Ares had given him. Jason stepped from the ship and strode boldly to the plow. Almost at once two brazen-footed bulls rushed at him from a cave. Pindar [*Pythian Odes* 4.220–229] claims that Aeëtes yoked the team and plowed the first furrow, but it is usually said that Jason accomplished this by himself. He warded off the bulls' charge with his shield. They enveloped his body in the flames that spurted from their nostrils, but Medea's magical drug kept him unhurt. He forced the bulls to their knees, yoked them to the plow, and, as it tore the earth, sowed the dragon's teeth behind him. By midafternoon Jason had plowed the entire field of four acres and buried the last of the seed. Now the earthborn men began to shoot up from the furrows, fully armed. Following Medea's advice, Jason hurled a boulder among them and they began fighting among themselves. He rushed into their midst and hacked about him with his sword until the last of them lay dead in his own blood. As the sun sank from the sky Jason had completed his task.

Instead of turning over the golden fleece to Jason, as he had promised, Aeëtes and the Colchians returned without a word to the city. There the king and his nobles spent the night plotting treachery against the Greeks. Medea was fearful, for herself as well as for the Argonauts, for she realized that her father would know that Jason could not have achieved his success without her help. In the dead of night she stole out of the palace and made her way to the river, where, on the far bank, the Greeks were celebrating Jason's victory. Jason and her nephews welcomed her. Before all his companions, their leader called on Hera, goddess of marriage, to hear his promise to wed his benefactress when they reached Greece.

Medea then led them to the sacred wood of Ares, where the dragon guarded the golden fleece. With incantations and a magical herb, she put the snake to sleep and Jason tore the fleece from the great oak to which Phrixus had nailed it long before. Hurrying back to the *Argo* with Medea and their prize, he told his companions to row as fast as possible for the river's mouth, for he feared that the Colchians would try to cut off their escape. His foresight caught the Colchians unawares and the *Argo* safely reached the sea. Nevertheless Aeëtes' soldiers, driven by threats from their furious king, took only a few hours to ready a whole fleet of ships. They were soon streaming down the Phasis in pursuit.

According to some unusual accounts, Aeëtes fought the Greeks in Colchis. He killed Iphitus, brother of Eurystheus, and Clytius, son of Eurytus, but was himself killed by Meleager. [Apollonius Rhodius 3.1172–4.240; Apollodorus 1.9.23.]

O. Aided by winds sent by Hera, the Argonauts made rapid headway. After three days they stopped, at Medea's urging, at the mouth of the Halys and sacrificed to Hecate. The goddess showed them the way by placing a light in the western sky. Argus, too, helped them with his knowledge of the ancient geographical lore of the Egyptian founders of Aea. He told them to make for the Danube (then called the Ister), at the farthest end of the Black Sea. This they did, stopping again only to leave their young ally Dascylus on the shore of his father's Mariandynian kingdom.

The Colchian pursuers also knew that the Danube offered a second means of exit from the Black Sea, and they had a force large enough to cover all escape routes. While half of their fleet sailed through the Bosporus, the other half, commanded by Aeëtes' son, Apsyrtus, made directly for the mouths of the Danube and reached one of its two main outlets, Fair Mouth, before the *Argo*. None of the natives of this land had ever before seen ships and they were terrified by the appearance of the seeming monsters from the sea. A little later the Argonauts entered the Narex, or northern mouth of the Danube, and sailed up the river to the rock of Cauliacus and down the branch flowing into the Adriatic Sea (see DANUBE). Apsyrtus had reached the sea before them and the Colchians were guarding every mouth of the river by which they might escape. The Argonauts found a momentary haven on one of the two Brygeian islands, where the Colchians did not dare to land because it was sacred to Artemis. The two leaders now held a parley. Apsyrtus, a more scrupulous man than his father, agreed to honor Aeëtes' promise to give the fleece to the Argonauts if Jason would leave Medea on Artemis' island until some disinterested king of the region could decide whom she should belong to.

This bargain infuriated Medea, who upbraided Jason for breaking his vows to her. Jason tried to pacify her by claiming that he had only been trying to gain time so that he might in some way entrap Apsyrtus. At once Medea promised to lure her brother into Jason's hands, if Jason had the stomach to kill him. Jason, who was slightly less awed by the Colchian horde than he was by the angry sorceress, agreed to this plan. Pretending to have been kidnaped by the Argonauts, Medea tricked Apsyrtus into coming alone to Artemis' island, and there Jason cut down the defenseless Aean. He cut the fingers and toes from the corpse, and three times sucked and spat out the blood, as killers did in the hope of expiating murder by treachery. The other Argonauts then killed the entire crew of Apsyrtus' ship, and they fled down the Adriatic. The Colchians would have pursued the Greeks, but Hera sent a terrible thunderstorm to deter them. At last, discouraged from the chase, but afraid to return to Aeëtes' kingdom, they split into small groups and settled along the shores of the Adriatic, particularly on the islands surrounding the site of their leader's death. These they named the Apsyrtides and founded there a town, which they called Absoros.

According to another version of the Argonauts' escape, Apsyrtus was a mere child who, for some reason, sailed from Colchis on the *Argo* with Medea. When Aeëtes followed with his fleet, Medea cut her brother into pieces and threw them into the sea. Aeëtes stopped to pick up these pieces for burial and gave up the pursuit, though he sent many of his people after the Argonauts.

Others say that Medea killed Apsyrtus in the palace before the *Argo* left Aea. Still others claim that Medea's brother overtook the Argonauts much later, when they had reached the island of the Phaeacians. Instead of abiding by the judgment of the Phaeacian king, Alcinoüs, that Medea should go with the Argonauts, her brother followed them to the island of Athena (near Pola, in Istria), found Jason sacrificing to the goddess, and was killed by him. In this version, the Colchians settled in the vicinity and founded a town that they called Absoros, in their dead leader's honor. [Apollonius Rhodius 4.241–521; Apollodorus 1.9.24; Hyginus, *Fabulae*, 23.]

P. After the murder the Argonauts crossed the northern end of the Adriatic to the Amber Islands that cluster about the mouth of the ERIDANUS River and remained hidden there until they felt safe from further Colchian pursuit. Unable to proceed southward along the Italian coast because of the multitude of small islands, they sailed back across the Adriatic to the land of the Hylleans, named for Heracles' son Hyllus, who had been their king until his death. From here the Argonauts sailed southward halfway down the Adriatic coast past Black Corcyra and Melite. Suddenly, however, they encountered a strong headwind that drove the *Argo* all the way back to the Amber Islands. The companions were devastated by this reverse when they had been so near to familiar lands, but their momentary misfortune was, in fact, sent by Hera to save them from a worse fate. Zeus, outraged at the treacherous murder of Apsyrtus, had sworn that the Argonauts should not reach home until they had been purified of their victim's blood by Circe, Aeëtes' sorceress sister. Even then they must suffer great hardships before they saw Iolcus again.

As the Argo was being driven northward by the gale, its speaking beam warned the crew of the fate in store for them and counseled that the sons of Zeus should pray to the gods to let them enter the Italian Sea, where lay the island of Aeaea, Circe's home. Polydeuces and Castor offered such a prayer and the *Argo* found its way without difficulty up the Eridanus. Accounts vary as to how the ship got from there to Aeaea. Apollonius believed that the Argonauts were able to proceed directly from the Eridanus to the Rhone. After being saved by Hera from a dangerous digression northward, apparently down the Rhine, they sailed by way of the Rhone into the Mediterranean Sea. Stopping briefly at the Stoëchades Islands, they traveled eastward, then southward along the coast of Etruria. They paused again at Elba and soon afterward came to the island of Aeaea.

The Argonauts found Circe at the seashore. Bidding the men remain with the ship, Jason and Medea silently followed the sorceress to her house. There she purified them of murder with the blood of a pig and offered sacrifices to Zeus and to the Erinyes. Only when the rites were completed did she ask who her visitors might be. Medea, speaking in the Colchian language, told her aunt the entire story, except for the murder of her brother. Circe was shocked at Medea's account of her conduct toward her father and ordered her to leave.

89

Chastened, Medea and Jason returned to their companions on the shore. [Apollonius Rhodius 4.522–752.]

Q. Now that Zeus's condition was fulfilled, Hera set about putting an end to the delays that had slowed the *Argo*'s return to Iolcus. She sent Iris with an order to Aeolus for favorable winds, a request to Hephaestus that he shut down operations in his smithy under Mount Aetna while the *Argo* was passing, and a summons for the sea-goddess Thetis. The two gods agreed at once to Hera's request. Thetis, when she learned Hera's wishes, consented to forget her anger at the Argonaut Peleus, her former husband, and to help guide the *Argo* safely between Scylla and Charybdis and through the Wandering Rocks. Hera's prophecy that Achilles, Thetis' son by Peleus, would one day marry Medea in the Elysian Fields gave Thetis an additional reason for aiding the Argonauts.

As soon as Hera had made her request, the sea-goddess plunged down to enlist the aid of her fellow Nereïds in the depths of the sea. She then hurried to the beach at Aeaea, where the Argonauts were resting from their arduous voyage. Appearing to Peleus, she told him to urge his companions to be on their way, since the Nereïds were waiting to help them. Peleus told the others what Thetis had said and they made preparations to leave at dawn.

Sailing southward again along the Italian coast, the *Argo* soon came to the lovely island of Anthemoëssa, the home of the Sirens, whose songs lured sailors to their destruction. Like many others before them, the Argonauts would have forgotten everything else and anchored the *Argo* forever on the beach, content to die of starvation while they listened to the seductive voices of the bird-women, had not Orpheus had the presence of mind to strike up a tune, loud and fast, on his lyre. The resulting confusion of sounds diminished the allure of the Sirens' singing enough that the Argonauts—all but one—could sail safely past. Butes, son of Teleon, who was either more amorous or sharper-eared than his friends, dived into the sea and made for the island. There he would have died if Aphrodite had not saved him by transporting him to Lilybaeüm, on the west coast of Sicily.

Before long the Argonauts sighted Scylla's cliff on their left and, on their right, the whirlpool where the monster Charybdis waited to swallow the *Argo* whole. The company sailed bravely ahead, though they knew that disaster awaited them on either side of the narrow strait. At this moment the Nereïds appeared, swimming on either side of the ship. Thetis, unknown to the Argonauts, guided the steering oar. The *Argo* glided swiftly down the middle of the Strait of Messina.

The Nereïds stayed with the *Argo* as it began to toss in the steaming waters that churned about the Wandering Rocks. These rocks lay almost under the shadow of Aetna, where Hephaestus had banked his fires. The sea-nymphs ran beside the ship and kept it skimming over the tops of the waves, so that the treacherous currents could not carry it against the rocks. In a short while the Argonauts were safely past the danger. The Nereïds dived beneath the waters, their mission completed.

The *Argo* continued under full sail down the eastern coast of Thrinacië, the island where Helius' daughters herded his great flocks of sheep and cattle, the latter pure white with golden horns. Turning eastward, the ship crossed the vast breadth of the Ionian Sea until it reached Drepane (Corcyra), home of the Phaeacians. There the weary sailors were greeted with openhanded hospitality by King Alcinoüs and his people. But they had hardly arrived when they were endangered by several Colchian ships, the contingent that had sailed in pursuit of the Argonauts through the southerly exit from the Black Sea. The Colchians demanded the immediate return of Medea.

Medea appealed for protection to the Argonauts, then, unconvinced by their ready protestations of support, turned to Queen Arete. The queen responded sympathetically and that night extracted a promise from her judicious husband that, if the marriage of Jason and Medea had already been consummated, he would not allow the Colchians to take the young woman from her husband. Then, when Alcinoüs was asleep, Arete sent word to Jason of the king's decision. The Argonauts hastily performed the marriage rites for their leader and the Colchian girl. That night the couple slept together in a sacred cave that had once been the home of Macris, the nurse of Dionysus. (After this wedding night the place became known as Medea's Cave.) The next morning Alcinoüs told the Colchians of his decision. When it became known that Jason and Medea were man and wife, the Colchians dared neither to challenge the king's judgment nor to return home emptyhanded. They therefore asked, and received, permission to settle in Drepane. The friendly Phaeacians then loaded the *Argo* with gifts and Queen Arete gave Medea twelve serving-girls to go with her to Greece. [Apollonius Rhodius 4.753–1219; Apollodorus 1.9.25.]

R. From Drepane the *Argo* sailed rapidly southward and came within sight of the Peloponnesus. But the weary seamen were still not destined to reach their homes. A sudden and prolonged gale drove them southwestward across the Mediterranean Sea and deep into the Gulf of Syrtis Minor, at the western end of the Libyan Sea. There the *Argo* was carried far inland by a wave and left stranded on the sands. Even if the Argonauts had been able to carry the ship back to the gulf, the innumerable shoals and the tangled seaweed that grew there would have prevented them from ever reaching open water. The Argonauts, who had survived so many hardships, were completely demoralized by this disaster. Each sat down alone, wrapped in his cloak, and prepared to die helplessly in the desert. They would no doubt have done so if the three guardian nymphs of the land had not taken pity on them. Appearing to Jason in their goatskin cloaks, they cryptically directed that when Amphitrite unyoked the horses of her husband, Poseidon, from his chariot, the Argonauts should repay their mother for the long time that she had borne them in her womb. The goddesses vanished. Jason, after thanking them for the prophecy, of which he had understood hardly a word, rushed off to tell his companions the news. As he was recounting his experience, an enormous horse suddenly came splashing up out of the sea and galloped away across the desert. Peleus realized that this must be one of Poseidon's horses. Moreover, he recognized that the "mother" of the company could only be the *Argo*, which had so long carried them inside her body. Given strength by the divine promise of success if they did not falter, they repaid the huge ship by carrying her on their shoulders for nine days, until they came to the brackish Lake Tritonis.

The Argonauts arrived burning with thirst after the arduous portage. Their search for fresh water led them to a grove that turned out to be the garden of Atlas, whose apple trees were tended by the Hesperides, daughters of Oceanus. Ladon, the great snake that had so long guarded the fruit, lay dead on the ground. The Hesperides were gathered about him wailing, but they vanished the moment that the strangers appeared. Nonetheless Orpheus prayed to them to show him and his companions where they might find water. The nymphs forgot their grief long enough to take pity on the parched company. Reappearing in the forms of three varieties of tree, the sisters—Hespere, Erytheïs, and Aegale—told them that the ugly brute who had only yesterday killed the snake and stolen the apples had been as thirsty as they. He had kicked at a rock near the lake and water had gushed out at its base. On hearing this the Argonauts rushed off, not only to slake their thirst, but to look for Heracles, for they were sure from the nymphs' description that the apple thief could have only been he.

Calaïs and Zetes, Euphemus the swift runner, and Lynceus of the marvelous vision set out to find their former companion. Canthus, a Euboean, went too, eager for news of his old friend Polyphemus, who had been left behind with Heracles in Mysia. The first four returned safely. Lynceus had spied Heracles, but at much too great a distance for his friends to overtake him. When Canthus failed to return, the Argonauts went in search of him. They found him dead. Caphaurus, a Libyan native of distinguished lineage, was tending a flock of sheep near by. He had killed Canthus when the Greek tried to drive off some of the sheep for his companions. The Argonauts killed Caphaurus and took the corpse of Canthus, together with the sheep, back to their ship.

Canthus was hardly buried when the seer Mopsus was killed by a snake—one of a deadly species, the seps, that had sprung from the bloody drops that had fallen from the head of Medusa as Perseus flew with it over Libya. The Argonauts buried their second comrade and hurriedly set out in the *Argo* on Lake Tritonis before any further disasters could befall them in this desolate land.

Unfortunately they had no idea how to get from the lake to the sea. When they had spent a whole day vainly searching for an outlet, Orpheus suggested that Jason offer the gods of the region a bronze tripod that had been given him by Apollo, perhaps during his visit to Delphi before the voyage began. Jason agreed. They had scarcely begun the appropriate rites when a handsome young man appeared, introducing himself as Eurypylus, a son of Poseidon and king of the surrounding territory. He handed them in welcome a clod of earth. Euphemus courteously accepted the token and asked the way to the sea. The young man gave them explicit directions and wished them a good voyage. The Argonauts shoved off hopefully, leaving the tripod behind in gratitude. Looking back, they were startled to see Eurypylus pick up the tripod and walk straight into the lake.

The Greeks realized that they had been aided by a god. They sacrificed a sheep and flung it into the water. Immediately the god reappeared in his own form. Down to the hips he was a powerfully built man, but in lieu of legs he had two fishlike tails. Seizing the stern of the *Argo* he pushed it through a difficult and tortuous route all the way to the open sea, then disappeared beneath the waves. The grateful Argonauts spent the next day on the shore setting up altars to the god—it was Triton—and to his father, Poseidon. After a night's sleep they followed the directions that Triton had given them, sailing eastward, then northward, keeping the Libyan coast always on their right. When the land fell away to the east, they steered out to sea on a direct line for Crete.

Some time later Euphemus had a dream about the clod that Triton had given him. He was holding it to his breast and suckling it. It turned into a young woman and he lay with her. Afterward he felt guilty at having done this, but she consoled him with the assurance that she was a daughter of Triton and Libya and would nurse Euphemus' children if he would give her a home in the sea. Jason explained that this meant that the clod would become an island that would give a home to Euphemus' descendants. Euphemus therefore threw the clod into the sea north of Crete, and out of it in time grew the island of Calliste. Generations later Theras led descendants of Euphemus in colonizing this island and renamed it THERA. Still later one of Theras' descendants, Battus, went to Libya and founded the city of Cyrene. Some say that the clod was swept out of the *Argo* by the sea spray, but followed the ship until it washed up on the island of Thera. [Apollonius Rhodius 4.1219–1637; Pindar, *Pythian Odes*, 4.1–63.]

S. Nearing Crete, the Argonauts wished to land, but were kept away by Talus, who hurled huge rocks at the *Argo*. This bronze giant was the last living member of the ancient brazen race. Zeus had made a present of him to Europa to guard her island, or else Hephaestus had fashioned him for King Minos. Every day he ran around the circumference of Crete three times. Talus' brazen body was invulnerable except for a single vein that lay just below the surface at his ankle. The Argonauts hastily got the ship out of range of Talus' missiles, and Medea tried what her sorcery could do against the giant. Invoking the malevolent strength of the death-spirits, she fixed him with the evil eye. The spell worked. Seemingly by accident Talus struck his vulnerable ankle on a sharp stone, and the vital fluid that filled his veins drained out. After a few moments he toppled forward and the bronze body crashed down from the cliff into the sea.

According to some accounts, Medea destroyed Talus through the use of drugs, or else promised to make him immortal, then drew out the bronze nail that closed the end of his single vein. Others say that the Argonaut Poeas shot him dead with an arrow in his ankle. Still others claim that Talus was not a man at all, but a bull.

The Argonauts were now able to land and draw the water that they desperately needed after their long voyage from Libya. While they were ashore, they dedicated a shrine to Minoan Athena. Proceeding northward through the Cretan Sea, they were enveloped at night in darkness so impenetrable that they thought that it must have risen from the Underworld. Not a star could be seen to steer by and the *Argo* drifted helplessly through the blackness. Jason prayed to Apollo for help, not failing to mention that if they reached home safely they would bring many rich offerings to the god's most famous shrines. Apollo heard the prayer and shot a flaming bolt from his bow into the sea. By its light the Argonauts were able to see an island close at hand. Landing on it they built a shrine to Apollo, god of light, and named the island Anaphe, or "Revelation." Because the men had no wine and only poor fare to sacrifice to the god, Medea's serving-girls ridiculed them in a friendly way. The Argonauts responded in kind, and the custom of ribald joking at the rites of Apollo was afterward carried on by the women of the island. Some say, however, that the *Argo* came to Anaphe while on its way from Drepane to Crete.

From Anaphe the Argonauts sailed to the island of Aegina, in the Saronic Gulf. There the weary men, relieved to be on Greek soil once again, amused themselves with seeing who could reach the ship first with a jar of water on his shoulder. Ever since, the Aeginetans have celebrated the event with a foot-race of youths bearing water jars. No further obstacles stood in the way of the adventurers. They rounded Attica, sailed northward between Euboea and the mainland, passed Locris, and finally came once more to the Gulf of Pagasae, from which they had sailed so long before.

Many alternate routes have been suggested for the *Argo*'s homeward voyage. According to Pindar [*Pythian Odes* 4.251–252], it reached the river Ocean (perhaps by sailing up the Phasis) and returned to the Mediterranean through the Red Sea. From there, apparently, it made for Libya, and thence homeward. Diodorus Siculus [4.56.3–67] quotes the Sicilian historian Ti-maeüs as saying that the Argonauts sailed up the river Don (Tanaïs), instead of the Danube, as far as its source. A portage brought them to another river that flowed, apparently, into the Baltic Sea. From there they sailed through the North Sea and down the west coast of Europe to reenter the Mediterranean Sea through the Pillars of Hercules. [Apollonius Rhodius 4.1638–1781; Apollodorus 1.9.26.]

T. Jason and the Argonauts had attained their objective. So had Hera. She had arranged the entire expedition in order to get Medea to Iolcus to dispose of PELIAS. There are several versions of the Argonauts' return to the city, but Pelias was the victim in all of them, murdered by his well-intentioned daughters as the result of an elaborate magical trick of Medea's. As a part of this trick the sorceress rejuvenated her father-in-law, Aeson. (Some say that she did the same for Aeëtes many years later.) Most of the Argonauts took part in the funeral games that were held in honor of the dead king of Iolcus. The great adventure of the voyage gained fame for Jason, but little else. He was exiled with Medea from Iolcus for their treacherous murder of Pelias. The king's son, Acastus, inherited the throne that had rightfully belonged to Jason's father, and for which Jason had made his great voyage.

The most important single account of the Argonauts' voyage is the *Argonautica* of Apollonius Rhodius, written in the third century B.C. The only surviving earlier account of any length is the fourth Pythian Ode of Pindar. In the first century A.D., Valerius Flaccus closely followed Apollonius in the *Argonautica* that is either partly lost or was never finished. A short *Argonautica* by an unknown late Classical author was attributed to Orpheus. Diodorus Siculus told some of the Argonauts' story and the subsequent adventures of Jason and Medea, making his usual attempt to replace the mythological elements with equally absurd "history." The sketchy accounts of Apollodorus and Hyginus in general followed that of Apollonius. The tale of the *Argo*'s voyage is, however, a very old one that had long been famous in Homer's day.

Argos. A city in the eastern Peloponnesus. Argos lay in a valley called Argolis on the Gulf of Argolis. Though periodically troubled with drought, it was one of the most fertile regions in Greece. The city was on the Inachus River, but, since this stream was often dry, it obtained much of its water from springs at nearby Lerna. The citadel, situated on a conical hill, was called the Larisa. A modern town still called Argos lies at the foot of this hill.

Argos seems to have dominated Argolis until the rise of Mycenae. Even after that time the names of Argos and the Argives, its inhabitants, were often used to designate the entire region and its people. In Aeschylus' *Oresteia* trilogy, for example, Agamemnon is called king of Argos, rather than of Mycenae, and many supposedly contemporary rulers in the region from the time of Proëtus to the Epigoni are referred to by other writers as kings of Argos. From Homer's time, moreover, the names "Argives" and "Danaäns" (after the legendary Argive ruler Danaüs) were often applied to the Greeks as a whole.

Argolis has a full and ancient mythology, some of which seems to have belonged to the pre-Greek inhabitants. Except for the famous story of Io, the early mythical figures are shadowy. The first inhabitant was Inachus, the river-god, who introduced the worship of Hera, known from archaeological remains to be very ancient in Argolis. Along with two other local river-gods who judged a contest for patronship of the land, he awarded it to the goddess. His

Descendants of Danaüs Ruling in Argolis

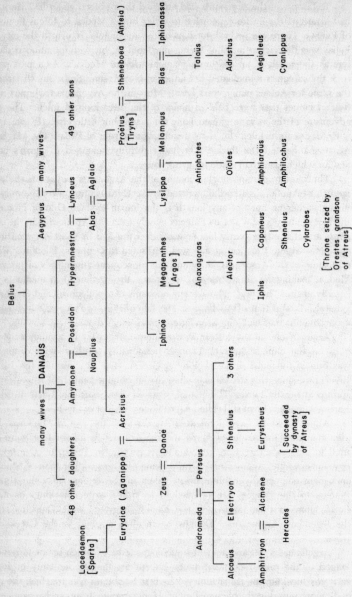

Belus

├─ many wives ═ **DANAÜS** ═ many wives
│   ├─ 48 other daughters
│   ├─ Amymone ═ Poseidon
│   │   └─ Nauplius
│   └─ Hypermnestra ═ Lynceus
│
└─ Aegyptus ═ many wives
    ├─ Lynceus
    └─ 49 other sons

Eurydice (Aganippe) ═ Acrisius

Lacedaemon [Sparta]

Abas ═ Aglaia

Proëtus [Tiryns] ═ Stheneboea (Anteia)

Zeus ═ Danaë

Megapenthes [Argos]

Lysippe ═ Melampus

Bias ═ Iphianassa

Andromeda ═ Perseus

Iphinoë

Anaxagoras

Antiphates

Talaüs

Alcaeus

Electryon

Sthenelus

Alector

Oicles

Adrastus

Amphitryon ═ Alcmene

Eurystheus [Succeeded by dynasty of Atreus]

Iphis   Capaneus

Amphiaraüs

Aegialeus

Heracles

3 others

Shenelus

Amphilochus

Cyanippus

Cylarabes [Throne seized by Orestes, grandson of Atreus]

son Phoroneus founded the city of Phoronea, later renamed Argos; he was honored in Argos even in Pausanias' day (second century A.D.). Inachus' daughter, Io, fled Argos in the form of a cow and reached Egypt, where she gave birth to a son by Zeus. She was to become the ancestress of the ruling houses of Thebes and Crete, as well as of Argos.

Meanwhile Phoroneus' son Apis named the Peloponnesus Apia, but died without children. He was succeeded by Argus, the son of Apis' sister Niobe, the first mortal woman to be seduced by Zeus. Argus renamed the city Argos, for himself. Pelasgus (who may have been Argus' brother, though he is generally said to have been born of the soil) ruled at this time in Arcadia and civilized the people, called after him Pelasgians. (This name was given by the Greeks to those tribes that had inhabited Greece before their arrival.) The next several generations of Inachus' dynasty have contradictory accounts that are filled with the names of eponymous heroes like Epidaurus and Tiryns, who are known for nothing except giving their names to cities.

The detailed history of Argos begins with the arrival of Danaüs, a descendant of Io and also of Zeus and Poseidon. Although for three generations the ancestors of Danaüs and his followers had been born in Egypt—Herodotus believed that they were, in fact, Egyptians—they claimed a right to Argos. They were either welcomed by Pelasgus or opposed by King Gelanor, who was also directly descended from Inachus. (For the story of Danaüs' rule and the strange marriage night of his daughters, see DANAÜS.) Danaüs was succeeded by his son-in-law and nephew, Lynceus, whose son Abas, a great warrior, was the father of the contentious twins Acrisius and Proëtus. Proëtus became king of Tiryns. During his reign Melampus and Bias, brothers from Messene, acquired kingdoms in Argolis.

Acrisius' grandson, Perseus, having accidentally killed his grandfather, traded the throne of Argos for that of Tiryns, which was occupied by Proëtus' son, Megapenthes. Perseus founded Mycenae and fortified the nearby town of Midea. Four of his sons ruled in Argolis—Electryon, Alcaeüs, Sthenelus, and Mestor; his daughter, Gorgophone, became the mother of the Spartan king Tyndareüs. Three of Perseus' sons married daughters of the powerful Pisan king Pelops, an immigrant from Phrygia who had given his name to the entire Peloponnesus. As a result, the throne of Mycenae fell, on the death of Sthenelus' son Eurystheus, to Pelops' son Atreus. However, the rightful ruler of Mycenae was not Eurystheus but Heracles, whose mother, Alcmene, Electryon's daughter, was married to Amphitryon, Alcaeüs' son. Heracles had been deprived of the throne through the enmity of Hera.

Atreus' sons, Agamemnon and Menelaüs, became rulers, respectively, of Mycenae and Sparta and were leaders in the Trojan War, which resulted from the abduction of Menelaüs' wife, Helen. On his return from the war, Agamemnon was murdered by his wife and his cousin, Aegisthus, but was avenged on both by Orestes, his son. Orestes, who, according to some accounts, later became king of Sparta, was the last major figure in the legendary history of Argos.

There is, however, another important series of events in that history which cannot be reconciled with that of the houses of Perseus and of Atreus, though they must have occurred in the same period. The wars with Thebes, told in the myths of the Seven against Thebes and of the Epigoni, antedated the Trojan War by one or two generations; the sons of some of the Epigoni took part in that war. Most of the principal figures in those conflicts are said to have been descended from Proëtus, Melampus, or Bias. Of these three dynasties, two or three sons of the Epigoni were the last figures of any significance in myth.

Argus (1). A son of Zeus and Niobe, daughter of Phoroneus. The first offspring of Zeus and a mortal woman, Argus succeeded Niobe's brother Apis as king of Phoronea and renamed it Argos, in his own honor. He married Evadne, daughter of Strymon and Neaera, and she bore him Ecbasus, Peiras, Epidaurus, and Criasus. Another account does not name Argus' wife, but makes him father of Peiras, Phorbas, and Tiryns. Of all these children hardly anything is known but their names and their position in the royal genealogy of Argos, which is disputed. Epidaurus and Tiryns founded the cities that bear their names. [Apollodorus 2.1.1–2; Pausanias 2.16.1, 2.22.5.]

Argus (2). The builder of the *Argo*. Argus' parentage is variously reported, as is the country of his birth. He is well known solely for having built, at Jason's request and under the direction of Athena, the fifty-oared ship in which the ARGONAUTS [A] made their famous voyage and which, according to some writers, they named for him. Argus sailed with the crew, but nothing is known of his part in the subsequent adventures. [Apollodorus 1.9.16; Apollonius Rhodius 1.18–19, 1.321–326.]

Argus (3). The eldest son of Phrixus by Chalciope (or Iophossa), daughter of Aeëtes, or by Perimele, daughter of Admetus. Argus and his brothers, Phrontis, Melas, and Cytissorus, left their homeland of Colchis to claim their dead father's hereditary rights in Orchomenus, but got only as far as the uninhabited island of Ares in the eastern part of the Black Sea, where they were shipwrecked. They were rescued by the ARGONAUTS [H–N] and returned with them to Colchis. Argus spoke in favor of the strangers' cause to King Aeëtes and later importuned his mother to enlist the aid of his aunt, the sorceress Medea. The four brothers all escaped in the *Argo* and sailed to Greece. Argus became, according to the *Great Eoiae* [15, 16], the father of Magnes, who is usually said to have been one of the sons of Aeolus.

Argus Panoptes (All-Seeing). A man with many eyes. The earliest mention of Argus gave him only four eyes; later he was said to have one hundred, placed all over his body. His parentage was a matter of dispute. Apollodorus mentions five versions of it: he was the son of Agenor, of Arestor, of Inachus, or of Argus and Ismene, or he was born of the soil. Some say that he married Ismene, Asopus' daughter, and she bore him Iasus. In various adventures he is said to have killed and dressed in the hide of a bull that was ravaging his Arcadian homeland, to have killed a satyr that was stealing cattle, to have killed the monster Echidna while she slept because she had carried off passersby, and to have avenged the murder of Apis.

Only the story of Argus' death, however, seems to have been universally known. Hera, who had given him untiring strength, set him to watch the cow Io [A], but Hermes, sent by Zeus, killed him. Hera placed his eyes in the tail of her bird, the peacock, for which it was called the Argus-pheasant. In Aeschylus' *Prometheus Bound* [566], Argus' ghost pursues Io and drives her into a frenzy. [Apollodorus 2.2.2–3; Ovid, *Metamorphoses*, 1.622–723.]

Argyripa. A city in Apulia. Argyripa (later Arpi) was founded by Diomedes, who was welcomed to Italy by Daunus, the Apulian king.

Ariadne. A daughter of Minos, king of Crete. When THESEUS [E] came to Crete with the other intended victims of the Minotaur, Ariadne fell in love with him and helped him to escape from the Labyrinth after he had killed the monster. As he had sworn to do, Theseus took her with him, but left her on the island of Dia (Naxos). His reason for this act is much disputed. He may simply have deserted her, or Dionysus may have kidnaped her or taken her by force of arms. If she was abandoned, she either committed suicide from grief or was found and married by Dionysus, although some say that she married the god's priest Oenarus. The Cypriots say, however, that Theseus brought Ariadne, pregnant, to Cyprus and was carried away from the island in his ship by storms. Ariadne died of grief and was worshiped in a grove sacred to Aphrodite Ariadne. According to the earliest story of all, Ariadne was killed at Dia by Artemis because of something that Dionysus told the goddess.

Ariadne is said by various writers to have borne several children by Dionysus: Staphylus, Phanus, Oenopion, Thoas, Peparethus, and Ceramus. Most of these sons may have been born on the island of Lemnos, where Thoas later ruled. The Argives claimed to possess Ariadne's tomb at Argos. After her death Dionysus honored her by placing in the sky, as the constellation Corona Borealis, the crown that he had given her at their wedding. Some claim, however, that this gift was made by Theseus, and that he was the father of Staphylus and Oenopion.

Most modern authorities believe that Ariadne was not merely a mortal character of mythology but a Cretan goddess. She was worshiped in several widely scattered parts of the ancient world. To judge from the Cypriot cult of Aphrodite Ariadne, the two goddesses were similar in nature and were identified with each other in some places. [Homer, *Odyssey*, 11.321–325, and *Iliad*, 18.590–592; Hesiod, *Theogony*, 947–949; *Catalogues of Women* 76; Plutarch, *Parallel Lives*, "Theseus"; Apollodorus 3.1.2, "Epitome" 1.8–10; Pausanias 2.23.8, 10.29.3–4.]

Aricia. An ancient town southeast of Rome. Aricia was famous as a center of Diana's cult. Her grove there was the home of the minor god Virbius.

Aries (The Ram). A constellation. The ram represented by these stars is generally said to have been the one with the golden fleece that carried PHRIXUS to Colchis. Some writers say, however, that it was an animal that appeared unexpectedly to Dionysus in the Libyan Desert and showed him the way to water. [Hyginus, *Poetica Astronomica*, 2.20.]

Arimaspians or **Arimaspi**. A fabulous one-eyed people. According to Herodotus, as well as later writers, the Arimaspians lived beyond the Issedones, who lived beyond the Scythians. Their country, said Aeschylus [*Prometheus Bound* 804–807], was on a gold-bearing river, but most accounts have it that the gold was in the keeping of griffins, who lived beyond the Arimaspians, next to the Hyperboreans. The Arimaspians were perpetually at war with the griffins and stole their gold at every opportunity. Herodotus was careful to point out that his information was derived from a poem called *Arimaspeia*, which was attributed to a certain Aristeas, a poet who lived at least as early as Homer on the island of Proconnesus (now Marmara) in the Sea of Marmara. This Aristeas had a career as fabulous as the subject of his epic, living at least three lives over a period of several centuries, and Herodotus was clearly skeptical of his qualifications as a historian. He believed that the reports of the Arimaspians had been spread by the Scythians, who had heard them from the Issedones, and that their name was a Scythian word for "One-Eyed." If there are any historical elements in this legend, the Arimaspians, the Issedones, and even the griffins may have been among the many tribes that moved westward in successive waves from eastern and central Asia. They may at one time have lived in the gold-bearing Altai Mountains of central Asia. [Herodotus 3.116, 4.13, 4.27.]

Arion. A Greek poet and bard who flourished about A.D. 700. Arion, a native of the Lesbian city of Methymna, spent much of his life at the court of Periander, tyrant of Corinth. He was credited with the invention of the dithyramb, but is best remembered for a legend told of his escape from the sea. Having acquired a reputation as the world's greatest singer, he made a profitable tour of Sicily. The crew of the vessel bearing him on his return journey from Tarentum to Corinth determined to kill him for his wealth and refused to accept gold in return for his life. They did, however, grant the bard's request that he be allowed to sing once more before dying. Arion put on his full minstrel's regalia and began to sing a hymn to Apollo. Seeing that many dolphins, attracted by his song, were playing about the ship, he leaped into the sea. One of the dolphins took him on its back and carried him to the shore at Taenarum.

Arion then proceeded to Corinth, where he told the story to Periander. The king did not believe him until the ship arrived in port and the villainous crew reported that Arion had remained in Sicily. Arion suddenly appeared wearing the robes in which the sailors had last seen him. The terrified crew admitted their guilt and were crucified by Periander. A bronze statue of a man on a dolphin commemorated the event at Taenarum for many centuries.

Apollo, moreover, placed both Arion and the dolphin in the stars. [Herodotus 1.23–24; Hyginus, *Fabulae*, 194, and *Poetica Astronomica*, 2.17.]

Arion or **Areion**. A divine horse. While Demeter was seeking Persephone, Poseidon pursued her. To escape his advances she became a mare among the herds of Oncius in Arcadia, but the horse-god became a stallion and mounted her. Two offspring resulted from this union: a daughter, Despoina, whose name was known only to initiates in the goddess' mysteries, and a horse, Arion. (Some, however, called him the offspring of Ge.) Fabulously swift, Arion ran with Oncius' herds until Heracles begged for him. Later Heracles gave Arion to Adrastus. The horse saved his master's life during the war of the SEVEN AGAINST THEBES. His harness mate was Caerus. [Pausanias 8.25.7–10.]

Arisbe. A daughter of Merops, king of Percote. Arisbe married Priam and bore a son, Aesacus. For some reason Priam turned Arisbe over to Hyrtacus and married Hecuba. She was the eponym of the town of Arisbe in the Troad. [Apollodorus 3.12.5.]

Aristaeüs. A minor deity of various rustic pursuits. Like Dionysus and Heracles, Aristaeüs was originally a mortal, though of divine parentage. His father, Apollo, one day saw the huntress-nymph Cyrene wrestling a lion on the slopes of Mount Pelion. Calling the wise Centaur Cheiron from his cave near by, the god asked him about the girl's parentage. The Centaur, divining that Apollo's interest was more than genealogical, did not bother to tell him that she was a daughter of the Lapith king Hypseus, but predicted that the god would carry her off to Libya and make her queen of a city named for her. Apollo wasted no time in making the prophecy come true. In due course Cyrene bore a son, Aristaeüs. The father, or Hermes as his agent, immediately took the child from his mother and gave him either to Cheiron, to Ge and the Seasons, or to certain nymphs to rear. Apollo compensated Cyrene by granting her a long life.

From his various nurses and tutors or from the Muses, Aristaeüs learned the arts of healing, prophecy, and hunting, and especially the agricultural practices of beekeeping, olive-growing, and cheese-making. The Muses found a bride for him and he lived happily for a time as shepherd of their flocks in the Thessalian valley of Tempe, beside the Peneius River—the god of which was Aristaeüs' great-grandfather. One day the young man caught sight of a beautiful dryad and chased her. In her eagerness to escape, she stepped on a snake and died almost at once of its poison.

Some time later, Aristaeüs' bees began to sicken and die and all his knowledge could not save them. Going to the spring at the source of the Peneius, he called on his mother, who was living there under the water. Cyrene advised her son to capture the old seal-shepherd Proteus and ask his advice. She showed him Proteus' lair in Thessaly, and Aristaeüs caught and bound him. After changing his shape several times without escaping, the wily and prophetic sea-god told the youth what he wanted to know. The dryad whose death he had caused had been Eurydice. Her lover, Orpheus, had died too, as a result of the tragedy. The other dryads had caused Aristaeüs' bees to die in revenge for their sister's death. Aristaeüs, carefully following Proteus' further advice, sacrificed bulls in a grove to the dryads and to Orpheus. Returning to the scene in nine days, he was astonished to see bees swarming in the rotting carcasses of the bulls.

Aristaeüs apparently abandoned his Thessalian bride, for he married Autonoë, daughter of Cadmus, king of Thebes. She bore him a son, Actaeon, who became a great hunter, like his father and grandmother. When Actaeon died, Aristaeüs was so grief-stricken that he left the mainland of Greece forever. A delegation from the Minoan Islands, knowing of his agricultural accomplishments, asked him to do something about the parching heat in their lands, which had begun at the rising of Sirius, the dog star. On Apollo's orders, Aristaeüs emigrated with some Parrhasian colonists to the island of Ceüs, where he was at once made king. He sacrificed to Sirius and especially to Zeus, praying that he would grant relief from the scorching heat. Zeus sent the cooling etesian winds, which ever afterward blew each year for forty days to alleviate the heat that regularly accompanies the dog star's rising. Later Aristaeüs went to Sardinia, perhaps by way of Libya, and cultivated the island. Some add that he performed the same service for Sicily.

Wherever Aristaeüs went he taught the inhabitants the agricultural arts. In some parts he was called by the epithets Agreus and Nomius—respectively, "Hunter" and "Shepherd." His benefits to many regions of the Mediterranean world were, like those of Dionysus, so great that he was worshiped as a god. Some say that at last he went to join Dionysus in Thrace and, after living for a time near Mount Haemus, disappeared from the sight of men. His daughter, Macris, was Dionysus' nurse. [Pindar, *Pythian Odes*, 9; Vergil, *Georgics*, 4.315–558; Apollonius Rhodius 2.500–527; Diodorus Siculus 4.81–82.]

Aristeas. See ARIMASPIANS.

Aristodemus. One of the Heraclids, son of Aristomachus. While preparing to sail from Naupactus with his brothers, Temenus and Cresphontes, against the Peloponnesus, Aristodemus died. He is variously said to have been killed by a thunderbolt, by an arrow of Apollo, or by the sons of Pylades and Electra, whose cousin Tisamenus ruled Argos, the first target of the invasion. Procles and Eurysthenes, Aristomachus' twin sons by Argeia, daughter of Autesion, sailed in his place. [Pausanias 2.1.5–6, 2.18.7.]

Aristomachus (1). One of the HERACLIDS and son of Cleodaeüs. Failing to understand the oracle that had also misled his grandfather Hyllus, Aristomachus was killed in an abortive attempt to conquer the Peloponnesus. His sons Temenus and Cresphontes succeeded where he had failed; a third son, Aristodemus, died before the invasion. [Apollodorus 2.8.2; Pausanias 2.7.6, 2.18.7.]

Aristomachus (2). A son of Talaüs and Lysimache. He was either the father or the brother of Hippomedon. [Apollodorus 1.9.13, 3.6.3.]

Aroë. See PATRAE.

Arrow, The. See SAGITTA.

Arsinoë (1). A daughter of Leucippus. The Messenians claimed that Arsinoë was the mother of Asclepius and Eriopis by Apollo, but others said that Coronis bore Asclepius. [Pausanias 2.26.7.]

Arsinoë (2). A daughter·of Phegeus, king of Psophis. Arsinoë married ALCMEON [A] and bore him a son, Clytius. Alcmeon deserted her in his madness. When her brothers later murdered him, she protested and they sold her as a slave to Agapenor. Though it is unrecorded, her stepsons may have freed her when they killed her brothers in Agapenor's house. Pausanias calls Phegeus' daughter Alphesiboea.

Artemis. A virgin goddess of childbirth and of wild animals.

A. Artemis, whom the Romans identified with their goddess DIANA, was the daughter of Zeus and LETO and the sister of Apollo. According to some accounts, brother and sister were both born on the island of Delos. According to others, Artemis was born on the neighboring island of Ortygia and, shortly thereafter, assisted her mother in giving birth to Apollo on Delos. The brother and sister avenged their mother not long afterward by shooting Tityus, the giant who had tried to rape Leto before their birth. Later they shot all or nearly all the children of Niobe because the Theban queen had boasted of her superiority to Leto, who had only two children.

Artemis and Apollo remained close friends, often hunting together. Artemis, in fact, spent most of her time in hunting, in the company of various nymphs whom she required to remain virgins like herself. She was not always successful in holding her followers to this strict rule. For example, one of her favorite companions, Callisto, was raped by Zeus. When Artemis discovered her pregnancy she drove the girl away, or shot her, or transformed her into a bear. This transformation was, however, usually attributed to Zeus or to the jealous Hera, who afterward induced Artemis to shoot the bear. In Crete, Artemis would not allow PROCRIS to hunt with her because she was married, but, taking pity on her for her marital troubles, she gave her a hound, Laelaps, that was destined always to catch its prey; a spear that never missed its mark; and some advice that led to reconciliation with her husband, Cephalus.

Artemis' virginity was endangered on numerous occasions. Nearly always she defended it with disastrous results for her wooers. She shot Buphagus, son of Iapetus and Thornax, when he tried to rape her on Mount Pholoë, in Arcadia. On another occasion she was assaulted by the boisterous young giant Otus, while his brother, Ephialtes, pursued Hera. Apollo came to his sister's rescue by sending a deer between the brothers. Flinging their spears at·it, they killed each other instead. Some claim that this deer was Artemis herself.

Orion, too, tried to violate Artemis, according to some accounts, and was killed by her. A more usual version of the tale has it that Artemis and Leto persuaded Zeus to immortalize Orion, their former companion on the hunt, as a constellation after Ge had sent a scorpion to kill him because of a boast that had offended her. Other accounts say that Artemis killed Orion because he challenged her to a game of quoits, or because he raped Opis, or because he lay with Eos.

According to one version of Orion's death, the giant hunter had won the goddess' confidence and she seriously considered marrying him. This prospect so disturbed Apollo that he found a way of disposing of the suitor. One day as he and his sister were hunting near the shore, he noticed Orion swimming far out at sea. Pointing to the black object, which Artemis had not recognized, he wagered with her that she could not hit it with an arrow. She won the bet by piercing her lover's head. When Orion's body washed ashore, the goddess was horrified at what she had done and made amends by placing him in the sky as the constellation.

Apollo had disposed of his sister's lover, ostensibly out of concern for her honor. Artemis returned the compliment by killing his mistress Coronis for lying with a mortal while she was carrying the god's child. Only Hermes' quick action saved the child, Asclepius. Some say that Apollo sent Artemis to punish Coronis. In any case, her enthusiasm for the project led her to kill several innocent persons as well.

B. Artemis was remarkably jealous of her honors, even for an Olympian deity. When Admetus inadvertently failed to include her among those to whom he sacrificed at his wedding, he led his bride to their bedchamber only to find it filled with snakes. Oeneus, king of Calydon, once neglected to dedicate the firstfruits of the year's harvest to her and was punished when his entire land was ravaged by a monstrous boar. Agamemnon received even more severe treatment for idly boasting that he could hunt as well as Artemis. The goddess sent unfavorable winds to keep the entire Greek fleet, which Agamemnon commanded, at Aulis. She then demanded—if the priest Calchas was to be believed—the sacrifice of Agamemnon's fairest daughter. Some say that when the sacrifice was carried out, she substituted a deer on the altar and spirited Iphigeneia away to the land of the barbaric Taurians to be her priestess there. Some accounts claim that the original cause of Artemis' enmity toward Agamemnon was no act of his but rather the failure, long before, of his father, Atreus, to sacrifice the best lamb of his flock to the goddess. He had promised it to her, but when it was born with a golden fleece, he hid it instead of sacrificing it.

Artemis shot Chione for a rash boast; Ethemea, daughter of Meropes, and Melanippe, daughter of Cheiron, for ceasing to worship her. When Actaeon happened on the spring where she was bathing, she feared that he would report the incident. Therefore she splashed water in his face and transformed him into a deer, with the result that his own hounds tore him to pieces. The goddess could, however, be kind to her loyal worshipers. For example, after

Hippolytus was brought back to life by Asclepius, Artemis transported him to Italy as the minor deity Virbius.

C. In spite of Artemis' familiar reputation in both art and literature as a chaste huntress, most scholars are agreed that she was originally far from a virginal goddess; moreover, she was certainly not Greek. In cult she was a patroness of all young living things, animal or human. At Ephesus, where her great temple was one of the "seven wonders of the world," she (or a goddess early identified with her) was depicted grotesquely with many breasts, an obvious symbol of motherhood. It is generally believed that Artemis was originally a mother-goddess similar to the Minoan "Lady of the Wild Things" and the Phrygian Cybele. At Brauron, her chief cult center in Attica, her priestesses were probably dressed as bears, and the bear Callisto may have been a local form of Artemis herself. Among the Greeks she became, paradoxically, a virgin goddess of childbirth.

As a guardian of wild animals Artemis was invoked by hunters. Several of her companion nymphs or priestesses seem to have been either versions of Artemis herself or similar local goddesses who were assimilated to her worship. Iphigeneia was almost certainly a form of Artemis. The goddess' association with the moon was a widespread, but late, development, as was her name Phoebe. Britomartis and Dictynna were Cretan goddesses who were identified with Artemis, as was Hecate on occasion. Diana, a Roman goddess of fertility, was sufficiently like Artemis to make their identification considerably more plausible than in the cases of several other major deities.

D. Accounts of the myths concerning Artemis are scattered throughout Greek and Roman literature. Homer told of her punishment of Oeneus and Niobe and of her ignominious defeat in the war of the gods in the *Iliad* [9.533–536, 20.30–39, 20.70–71, 21.468–513, 24.605–607]. His other references to Artemis follow an apparent convention of ascribing to her arrows all swift, but not violent, deaths of women. Euripides' *Iphigeneia in Aulis* deals with Agamemnon's sacrifice of his daughter; the ending of the play, though spurious, records a standard version of Iphigeneia's fate. Artemis appears as *dea ex machina* at the end of Euripides' *Hippolytus*. Differing versions of the deaths of Orion and of Otus and Ephialtes are found in Homer [*Odyssey* 5.121–124], Apollodorus [1.4.3–5, 1.7.4], and Hyginus [*Fabulae*, 28, 195, and *Poetica Astronomica*, 2.26, 2.34]. The transformations of Actaeon and Callisto are recounted by Ovid [*Metamorphoses* 3.138–252, 2.401–530], Apollodorus [3.4.4, 3.8.2], Hyginus [*Poetica Astronomica* 2.1], and Pausanias [8.3.6, 9.2.3]. Other references to Artemis include passages in Apollodorus [1.4.1, 1.8.2, 1.9.15, 2.5.3, 3.5.6, 3.14.4, "Epitome" 2.2, 2.10, 3.21–22], *Homeric Hymn to Apollo* [3.15–16], Hyginus [*Fabulae*, 9, 53, 98, 122, 150, 189, 200, and *Poetica Astronomica*, 2.7, 2.16, 2.18], Ovid [*Metamorphoses* 5.330, 6.204–312, 8.271–283, 11.321–327, 12.27–38, 15.487–551],

Pausanias [2.7.7–8, 2.26.6, 3.18.15, 8.27.17, 8.53.1–3, 9.19.1, 9.19.7], and Pindar [*Olympian Odes*, 3.25–30, and *Pythian Odes*, 3.31–37, 4.90–92].

Ascalabus. A rude boy who laughed at Demeter. When DEMETER [C], weary from her long search for her daughter Persephone, was offered barley water by Ascalabus' mother, he ridiculed her greedy drinking. The offended goddess turned him into a lizard (*askalabos*) that bore spots formed by the barley meal in the drink. [Ovid, *Metamorphoses*, 5.446–461.]

Ascalaphus (1). A son of the river-god Acheron by Orphne or Gorgyra. When Persephone ate pomegranate seeds in the Underworld, Ascalaphus told Hades. Persephone changed him into an owl by flinging water from the Underworld river Phlegethon in his face. According to another tradition, Persephone's mother, DEMETER [D], punished Ascalaphus by placing a heavy stone on him in Hades. Heracles rolled this stone away during his visit to the Underworld, but Demeter immediately transformed her rescued victim into an owl. [Ovid, *Metamorphoses*, 5.533–550; Apollodorus 1.5.3, 2.5.12.]

Ascalaphus (2). A son of Ares; his mother was Astyoche, although which of many women so named is not known. Ascalaphus and his brother, Ialmenus, were co-kings of the Minyan city Orchomenus, in Boeotia. Both were Argonauts and suitors of Helen. Together they led thirty ships to the Trojan War, where Ascalaphus was killed by Deïphobus. In one reference to Ascalaphus and Ialmenus, Hyginus [*Fabulae* 97] calls them sons of Lycus and Pernis and says that each led thirty ships to Troy. This may be merely an error, however, for elsewhere the writer calls them sons of Ares. [Homer, *Iliad*, 2.511–516, 13.518–528; Apollodorus 1.9.16, 3.10.8.]

Ascanius. See IÜLUS.

Asclepius. A god of healing. Asclepius, a mortal who, like Heracles, was deified, was a son of Apollo. His mother may have been Arsinoë, daughter of Leucippus, as the Messenians claimed; certainly Machaon and Podaleirius, whom Homer [*Iliad* 2.729–733] calls his sons, came from Messenia. But the citizens of Epidaurus, the chief center of Asclepius' cult, called him the son of Coronis, daughter of King Phlegyas. They say that Coronis bore the child while on a visit with her father to Epidaurus and, to avoid detection, exposed him on Mount Myrtium. There he was suckled by goats, guarded by their watchdog, and eventually discovered by the goatherd, Aresthanes—who, however, went away and left him when he saw lightning shooting from the child's body. This official Epidaurian version omits any mention of the scandal that is prominent in the more usual story, which claims that Coronis, while pregnant with Apollo's child, lay with a young Thessalian or Arcadian, Ischys, son of Elatus. For this insult to her divine lover, she was shot to death by Artemis, or by Apollo himself. Apollo also killed Ischys and turned the crow that had tattled on Coronis from its former white to black. Apollo or Hermes rescued Coronis' unborn child from the funeral pyre and gave him to Cheiron to rear. The wise Centaur taught the boy the art of healing.

This art, which Asclepius brought to perfection, was a great boon to mankind, but the undoing of Asclepius himself. Not content with healing living men, he undertook to revive the dead. Athena had given him two vials of Gorgon's blood: one, containing blood from the veins on the right side, revived; the other, containing blood from the left side, destroyed life. Just what person was resurrected by Asclepius has been much disputed. It may have been Capaneus, Lycurgus, Tyndareüs, Hymenaeüs, or Minos' son Glaucus, though Glaucus' cure is generally attributed to Polyeidus. It is perhaps most often said, however, that Asclepius raised from death Hippolytus, who was then spirited away by Artemis to become the Roman god Virbius. In any case, Zeus regarded the raising of dead mortals as a dangerous precedent and killed the wonder-worker with a thunderbolt. Apollo, furious but unable to avenge himself on Zeus, killed instead the Cyclopes, who had forged the thunderbolt. For this act he was punished by having to serve a mortal for the space of a year. Some say that Zeus placed Asclepius among the stars as Ophiuchus, the Serpent-Holder, because he was a god's son and deserved honor for his healing gifts. Asclepius left two sons, by Xanthe or Epione: Machaon and Podaleirius.

It is uncertain when Asclepius came to be worshiped as a god; some say that he was always one. During a disastrous plague the Romans brought the god in the form of a huge snake from Epidaurus to Rome, where he promptly cured the sickness. He was widely worshiped there as Aesculapius. The snake was regularly associated with the god's cult. [Apollodorus 3.10.3–4; Pausanias 2.26.3–10, 8.25.11; Hyginus, *Poetica Astronomica*, 2.14; Ovid, *Metamorphoses*, 15.533–546, 15.626–744.]

Asellus Borealis (The Asses). A constellation. The two stars in this group represent either the ass killed by PRIAPUS and immortalized by Dionysus, or the asses whose braying caused panic among the Giants in their war with the gods. [Hyginus, *Poetica Astronomica*, 2.23.]

Asia. A daughter of Oceanus and Tethys. Asia was the mother by the Titan Iapetus of Atlas, Prometheus, Epimetheus, and Menoetius. According to some accounts, however, their mother was Clymene. [Apollodorus 1.2.3.]

Asius (1). A Trojan ally. Asius was a young brother of Hecuba and son of Dymas, king of a Phrygian tribe who lived on the Sangarius River. He led that nation's forces in the Trojan War. [Homer, *Iliad*, 16.715–725.]

Asius (2). A son of Hyrtacus, king of Arisbe. Asius led allies from Percote, Sestus, Abydus, and other cities on the Hellespont, as well as Arisbe, to the aid of Troy. A rash man, he charged the Greek wall in a chariot against Hector's orders, but was held off by the Lapith defenders. Shortly afterward Asius was killed by Idomeneus. [Homer, *Iliad*, 12.108–174, 13.383–393.]

Asopia. An early name for Sicyonia. The region was so called from the Asopus River, which flowed through it. (See SICYON.)

Asopus. The name of two important Greek rivers and their gods. One of these rivers rose in Phliasia and flowed through Sicyonia (formerly called Asopia) into the Gulf of Corinth. The other flowed eastward through southern Boeotia into the gulf that separates that land from southern Euboea. The gods of both these rivers were generally said to be sons of Oceanus and Tethys, but alternative parentages (Zeus and Eurynome, or Poseidon and either Pero or Celusa) were sometimes assigned to the Sicyonian god. One or both of the river-gods were said to have married Metope, daughter of the river-god Ladon. Metope bore two sons, Ismenus and Pelagon, and many daughters, among them Aegina, Salamis, Thebe, Ismene, and Corcyra.

The nymph Aegina disappeared one day. The distracted father inquired of Sisyphus, king of Corinth, and learned that Zeus had carried the girl off to the island of Oenone (later renamed Aegina). Asopus pursued the pair but was driven back by Zeus's thunderbolts. He retired to his bed, in which live coals were found for centuries after his chastening. As for Sisyphus, Zeus condemned the informer to eternal torment in Hades.

Most of the children of the Asopuses were claimed by both Thebans and Sicyonians. Since the justice of these claims cannot be sorted out with certainty, it is convenient to credit the children to the river nearest the regions of which the children were eponyms. The Boeotian Asopus may be regarded as the father of Thebe, and also of Ismenus and Ismene, for whom a stream near Thebes was named. To the Sicyonian river-god may be awarded Aegina and Salamis, nymphs of neighboring islands in the Saronic Gulf, and Corcyra, who was claimed as the eponym of both Corcyra and Black Corcyra, to one of which islands she was abducted by Poseidon.

asphodel. The plant that covered the Plain of Asphodel, the dwelling of most of the shades in Hades. In spite of its romantic-sounding name, which has inspired poets to charming fancies, asphodel (*Asphodelus ramosus*) is, in fact, a singularly unattractive weed. It was no doubt chosen by the Greeks as appropriate to an Underworld existence because it is a ghostly gray and as incapable of giving pleasure as was the life of the shades.

Assaracus. A Trojan leader. Assaracus was a son of Tros and Callirrhoë, daughter of the river-god Scamander. He is referred to by Vergil as the progenitor of the Romans because Rome's founder, Aeneas, was descended from Capys, Assaracus' son by Hieromneme, daughter of the river-god Simöeis. Priam and his enormous family were descendants of Assaracus' brother, Ilus. [Homer, *Iliad*, 20.231–240; Apollodorus 3.12.2.]

Asses, The. See ASELLUS BOREALIS.

Astacus, sons of. Astacus, a Theban, is known mainly as the father of Ismarus, Leades, Amphidocus (or Asphodicus), and Melanippus, who were leading defenders of Thebes in the war of the Seven against Thebes. The first three killed, respectively, Hippomedon, Eteoclus, and Parthenopaeüs (though the last Argive is often called the victim of Periclymenus). Melanippus wounded Tydeus mortally, but was himself killed by Amphiaraüs or Tydeus, who ate his brains. [Apollodorus 3.6.8.]

Asteria. A daughter of the Titans Phoebe and Coeüs. Asteria married Perses, also an offspring of Titans, and bore the goddess Hecate. Later, pursued by the amorous Zeus, she leaped into the sea, or was flung into it by her frustrated lover, and became a quail (*ortyx*). An island grew up on that spot and was named Asteria or Ortygia. Later the island offered a haven to Asteria's sister, Leto. It was renamed Delos or else was near Delos. [Hesiod, *Theogony*, 404–412; Apollodorus 1.4.1; Hyginus, *Fabulae*, 53; Ovid, *Metamorphoses*, 6.108.]

Asterion. An Argonaut; also called Asterius. Asterion was a son of Cometes and Antigone, daughter of Pheres, and came from Peiresiae, near Mount Phylleius, in Thessaly. [Apollonius Rhodius 1.35–39.]

Asterion. A small river in the region of Argolis, and its god. Asterion helped Inachus and Cephissus judge the contest between Poseidon and Hera for recognition as the patron deity of Argos.

Asterius (1). A king of Crete; also called Asterion. Asterius was the son of Tectamus by a daughter of Cretheus. Tectamus had invaded Crete with a force of Aeolians and Pelasgians. Asterius succeeded to the rule. After Europa had borne three sons—Minos, Rhadamanthys, and Sarpedon—of Zeus, the god married her to Asterius. He adopted the children, since she bore him only a daughter, Crete. Minos became king at Asterius' death. Asterius was also the name of the MINOTAUR. [Diodorus Siculus 4.60.2–3.]

Asterius (2). An Argonaut. A son of Hyperasius or Hippasus, Asterius came with his brother Amphion from Pellene, in the Peloponnesian Achaea, to join the crew of the *Argo*. [Apollonius Rhodius 1.176–178.]

Asterius. See ASTERION.

Asterope. A daughter of Atlas and the Oceanid Pleïone. One of the PLEIADES, Asterope was either the mother of Oenomaüs, by Ares, or the wife of that king of Elis. She was sometimes called Sterope. [Apollodorus 3.10.1; Hyginus, *Poetica Astronomica*, 2.21.]

Astraeüs. A son of the Titans Crius and Eurybia. Astraeüs, whose name means "Starry," was the father by Eos of the winds Boreas, Zephyrus, and Notus, and of the stars. [Hesiod, *Theogony*, 375–382.]

Astronomy. A lost Greek work on the constellations. Of this poem, once attributed to Hesiod, only brief fragments remain. These deal with the Pleiades and the Hyades, Ursa Major, and Orion. The fragments are available in the volume of Hesiod's works in the Loeb Classical Library.

Astyagyïa. A daughter of the early Thessalian king Hypseus. Astyagyïa married Periphas, son of Lapithes, and bore him eight sons. The eldest of these, Antion, was the father of Ixion. [Diodorus Siculus 4.69.3.]

Astyanax. The son of Hector and Andromache. Astyanax was called Scamandrius by his father. After the sack of Troy the child was flung to his death from the city walls because Odysseus warned the Greeks not to allow any descendant of Priam to survive. According to the lost *Little Iliad* [14], Neoptolemus tore the child from his mother's arms on his own impulse and hurled him down. Astyanax appears as a mute character in Euripides' tragedy *The Trojan Women*.

Astydameia. The wife of Acastus, king of Iolcus. Astydameia was presumably the mother of Acastus' three daughters, Laodameia, Sthenele, and Sterope, and his unnamed sons. She fell in love with Peleus and, when he spurned her, falsely accused him of trying to violate her. Believing her, Acastus plotted Peleus' death. Peleus, after escaping, returned to Iolcus with an army, killed Astydameia, cut up her body, and marched his men between the pieces into the city. Pindar and others said that Acastus' wife was Cretheus' daughter Hippolyte, about whom they told the same story. [Apollodorus 3.13.2–3, 3.13.7.]

Astypalaea. A daughter of Phoenix and Perimede, daughter of Oeneus. Astypalaea was the mother by Poseidon of Ancaeüs and Eurypylus. She was the eponym of an island in the southeastern Cyclades. [Pausanias 7.4.1; Apollodorus 2.7.1.]

Atalanta or **Atalante.** A virgin huntress.

A. Whether there were two persons named Atalanta—one Arcadian, the other Boeotian—or only one who was claimed as a heroine in two regions, is not certain. If there were two, their stories were so thoroughly confused even by early writers that it is more convenient to assume, for the sake of the narrative, that there was a single Atalanta. She was the daughter of Iasus, king of either Tegea or Maenalus, by Clymene, daughter of Minyas; or else her father was Schoeneus, a son of Athamas. (Euripides called her father Maenalus.) Wanting only sons, Atalanta's father exposed his infant daughter in a forest, but she was suckled by a bear and eventually found by hunters, who brought her up. Atalanta grew to adulthood loving the hunt above all other things and wished to remain a virgin in order that she might continue to enjoy the sport. Some say that she received, moreover, an oracle to the effect that disaster would result if she married. Therefore she associated with men only as occasional companions on some great adventure. When the centaurs Rhoecus and Hylaeüs attempted to rape her, she shot and killed them with her arrows.

Some writers claim that Atalanta sailed with the Argonauts, but Apollonius Rhodius, in his *Argonautica* [1.769–773], says that Jason regretfully declined her request to accompany him because he feared that dissension would arise if there were a woman aboard the *Argo*.

Later, during the CALYDONIAN BOAR HUNT, Jason's qualms were shown to have been well founded. Atalanta's participation in this event, together with some of the most famous young men of the age, led to the death of the sons of Thestius, and perhaps also of Meleager, who had fallen in love with Atalanta.

B. After this episode Atalanta's fame spread widely, and her identity somehow became known to her father, who now generously welcomed home the child whom he had once tried to dispose of. This proved a mixed blessing for

Atalanta, for the king, in belatedly undertaking his fatherly duties, proposed to find a husband for her. Declaring that she preferred to remain unattached, Atalanta devised a plan for achieving this purpose without publicly refusing to marry, which might have aroused dangerous resentment—the same dilemma that later taxed the ingenuity of Penelope. Atalanta, or perhaps her father, who apparently acquiesced in the scheme, entertained bids from suitors, turning no one away. The king did not even demand a bride-price for his daughter. Only one requirement was made of the young candidate: he must run a footrace with his prospective bride. If he won, Atalanta would be his. If he did not, however, he would be instantly killed and his head would adorn one of the poles set up about the stadium.

The suitors were given every chance. They ran naked, whereas Atalanta was encumbered with armor and, according to some accounts, ran twice as far. Some say that she carried a sword, with which she personally dispatched her opponents when she caught up with them. And Atalanta always did catch up with them, for, with the possible exceptions of Iphiclus of Phylace and Euphemus, she was the fleetest-footed mortal alive. She was also one of the most beautiful. So, in spite of the discouraging terms of the contest, there was never a lack of hopeful young men to enter it, and severed heads proliferated around the racecourse.

Yet Atalanta was not fated to remain forever a maiden. One of her suitors was the Arcadian Melanion, son of Amphidamas, or else the Boeotian Hippomenes, son of Megareus, of Onchestus. This young man—whichever he was—had the foresight to pray to Aphrodite, who customarily looked with disfavor on resolute virgins of either sex. The goddess readily came to his aid, giving him three golden apples plucked either in the garden of the Hesperides or in Aphrodite's grove at Tamasus, in Cyprus. Melanion (or Hippomenes) used these beautiful objects according to the goddess' instructions. Atalanta easily passed him as they raced along the track, but, just as she did so, the young man dropped one of the apples. Her curiosity piqued, Atalanta paused to pick up the apple. She quickly overtook her rival, but he dropped another. As she caught up with him a third time, near the end of the course, the youth flung the last apple far to one side. Whether Atalanta overestimated her own powers, was overweeningly greedy, or (as the romantic Ovid insists) wanted her handsome suitor to win can only be conjectured. Whatever her reasons, she retrieved the apple and Hippomenes (or Melanion) won the race.

C. Apparently the huntress was not displeased at her loss of freedom, but she was not to enjoy happiness for long; the warning of the oracle had not been false. Atalanta's young lover, filled with delight in his triumph and his prize, forgot that he owed both to Aphrodite and did not pay her suitable honors. Not without a sense of irony, the angry goddess punished her ungrateful client by gratifying the very emotion that had made him neglect her—his impatience for the delights of love. On his way home, stopping in the sacred precinct of Zeus Victor on Parnassus, or of Cybele near Onchestus, Hippomenes was overcome with passion and lay with his wife at the shrine. For this sacrilege the pair were instantly changed by the insulted god or goddess into tawny lions. In this way Aphrodite enjoyed a delicious revenge, for lions, it was said, do not mate with one another, but only with leopards.

In spite of the brevity of her marriage and her reputed contempt for intercourse with men, Atalanta gave birth at some point to a child. Whether the father was Melanion or Meleager or the god Ares is disputed. The embarrassed young woman exposed the child on Mount Parthenius, eager at all costs to preserve her reputation as a virgin. It was discovered by shepherds at the same time as Auge's child, Telephus, and was named Parthenopaeüs for the mountain. The two foundlings became allies. [Apollodorus 1.8.2–3, 3.9.2; Ovid, *Metamorphoses*, 10.560–704; Hyginus, *Fabulae*, 99, 174, 185.]

Ate. The personification of moral blindness. Homer called her the eldest daughter of Zeus but added that Zeus flung her from Olympus when she helped Hera to trick him into the vow that led to Eurystheus' birth before that of Heracles. Ate fell, it was later said, on the hill of Phrygian Ate, near Troy. Hesiod called Ate a child of Eris (Strife). [Homer, *Iliad*, 9.502–512, 19.91–136; Apollodorus 3.12.3.]

Athamantia or **Athamania.** A region named for ATHAMAS [D]. Athamantia is generally said to have been in southern Thessaly. Athamas settled there and married Themisto.

Athamas. A king of Orchomenus.

A. A son of the powerful Thessalian king Aeolus, Athamas migrated southward into northern Boeotia, where he became king. His capital is generally said to have been the wealthy city of Orchomenus, on the western shore of Lake Copaïs. For all his prestige, Athamas was one of the most unlucky men who ever lived. His troubles began with his decision to take a second wife while his first, Nephele, still lived. Athamas brought Ino, one of Cadmus' daughters, from Thebes and installed her in his palace. She bore him two sons, Learchus and Melicertes, but could not rest content while Nephele's children, Phrixus and Helle, lived, presumably because Phrixus might be expected to succeed his father as king. Ino did not dare to oppose Nephele's children openly, so she devised an elaborate plot that would result in Phrixus' destruction without implicating herself.

On some pretext Ino persuaded the Boeotian women secretly to parch the seed grain set aside for the next sowing. As a result, the next season's crop failed and disaster threatened. Athamas sent messengers to consult the Delphic oracle, precisely as Ino had anticipated. The ambitious woman was now ready to tighten the snare that she had laid for her children's rival. She bribed the messengers as they returned from Delphi, and they reported to the king a false oracle: if famine were to be averted, Phrixus must be sacrificed. The unhappy king at first refused to commit such an act, but either he was forced by his people to agree to it or else Phrixus volunteered to die. Athamas led his son to the altar—apparently that of Laphystian Zeus—and prepared him for the sacrifice. At the last moment, however, a miraculous ram appeared from nowhere. Phrixus and his sister Helle climbed onto its back. It rose with them into the air and flew off toward the northeast, never again to be seen by the Boeotians.

This ram was an extraordinary creature. Its fleece was of a golden shade, and it not only could fly but could talk as well. It is said by some to have been an offspring of Poseidon and Theophane, but whether it was sent to the children's rescue by Zeus or by their mother after she had acquired it from Hermes is disputed. For further episodes in its history, see PHRIXUS.

B. Hyginus [*Fabulae* 2, 4] told contradictory versions of the events surrounding Phrixus' near-sacrifice. A servant who knew of Ino's plot revealed it to the king. Athamas condemned her and her younger son, Melicertes, to death, but Dionysus wrapped them in a cloud and saved them for the moment. Further, the god drove Phrixus and Helle mad and they wandered in a forest. It was there that Nephele brought the ram to their aid. Another version gives an entirely different reason for the sacrifice. Athamas' brother Cretheus, king of Iolcus, was married to Demodice or Biadice. This woman, attracted by the handsome Phrixus, tried to seduce him, but he would have none of her. She therefore told her husband that Phrixus had tried to violate her. Cretheus reported this to Athamas, who felt that honor required that he execute his son for the outrage. Phrixus was not only rescued by the ram but was later brought back by Hermes and shown to his father as proof that the youth had been innocent of Cretheus' charge.

C. Athamas had now lost two of his children through the envy of his wife. He was soon to lose the remaining two through the jealousy of Zeus's wife. Many years earlier Zeus had fallen in love with Ino's sister Semele, but Hera's wiles had brought about her death. Zeus had rescued the unborn Dionysus from her womb and later had sent Hermes with the infant to the home of Ino and Athamas. They acceded to his request that they hide the child from Hera by rearing him in girl's clothing. Ino became his nurse. Through their kindness they brought the goddess' enmity upon their own heads.

Not long after the disappearance of Nephele's children, Hera's anger caught up with Athamas and Ino. With the aid of the Erinyes she drove them both mad. Athamas, under the delusion that his son Learchus was either a deer or a lion's whelp, shot him with an arrow. Ino snatched up Melicertes and, running with him to the Molurian Rocks on the Isthmus of Corinth, leaped with him into the Saronic Gulf. Some say that she first flung the child into a boiling cauldron. Athamas' brother Sisyphus, king of Corinth, later found Melicertes' body, which a dolphin had carried to the beach, and founded the Isthmian games in his honor. Mother and child, under the names of Leucothea and Palaemon, became sea-deities who aided sailors in distress. (See also INO.)

D. Athamas, bereft of all his children, was now exiled from his kingdom for the murder of Learchus. He inquired of the Delphic oracle where he might live and was told to go where wild beasts would entertain him. After long wandering, the homeless king came upon a pack of wolves ravaging a flock of sheep. They ran off, leaving their half-eaten prey to Athamas. Realizing that the oracle was fulfilled, he settled in this region and called it Athamantia or Athamania. The location of the place is uncertain, but it is usually said to have been in Thessaly. There Athamas married a third time. His wife, Themisto, daughter of the Lapith king Hypseus, bore him four sons: Leucon, Erythrius, Schoeneus, and Ptoüs.

Of this marriage Hyginus [*Fabulae* 4] has a very different version, which he ascribes to Euripides' play *Ino,* now lost. According to this story, Ino disappeared leaving her children behind. Athamas, believing her dead, married Themisto. She bore two sons, Sphincius and Orchomenus. Athamas later discovered that Ino was, in fact, reveling as a bacchant on Mount Parnassus. (It was perhaps during her mad wanderings that Ino and her sisters destroyed PENTHEUS at Thebes.) He sent for her secretly and, on her return, kept her identity hidden from Themisto. Themisto learned somehow that her rival had returned, but did not know who she was. Determining to kill Ino's children, she confided in their nurse, a woman who had recently been brought into the palace. The nurse was instructed to cover Ino's children that night with black cloth, Themisto's with white. The nurse—who was, of course, Ino herself—did exactly the opposite. Themisto, stealing into the bedroom in near-darkness, murdered her own children. In another version of Athamas' story, one son by Themisto, Leucon, survived. On learning what she had done, she killed herself. Ino's triumph was short-lived, however, for this story ends, like the others, with her and Athamas destroying *their* children in a fit of madness.

E. Herodotus [7.197] related that Athamas was himself nearly sacrificed late in life to Laphystian Zeus by the people of Thessalian Achaea, an oracle having named him a scapegoat for the land. Covering him with garlands, they led him in procession to the altar. He was saved by the unexpected appearance of Cytissorus, a son of Phrixus, who had returned with the Argonauts from Colchis, where Phrixus, unknown to the Boeotians, had found a haven. But in saving his grandfather, Cytissorus brought trouble on his own descendants. It was decreed that the eldest in each generation of Phrixus' line would be forbidden to enter the town hall of the Achaeans. If he did so he would suffer the fate that Athamas had narrowly escaped.

According to Pausanias [9.34.5–9], Athamas returned in his old age to Orchomenus and was welcomed by King Andreüs, son of the river-god Peneius (for whom the land was at this time named Andreïs). Andreüs gave the region about Mount Laphystius to Athamas. The old king believed that all his children were dead, Leucon, his son by Themisto, having died of an illness. He therefore sent to Corinth for Coronus and Haliartus, grandsons of his brother Sisyphus, and adopted them as his heirs. Later Phrixus, or Presbon, Phrixus' son, returned from Colchis. The Corinthian brothers gracefully resigned their claims to the throne in favor of Athamas' grandson (or son) and founded the nearby cities of Coroneia and Haliartus. Andreüs had married Leucon's daughter Euippe. Their son Eteocles succeeded to the rule of Orchomenus. Thus Athamas' life, which had been filled with disasters, ended in peace and his descendants reigned in the city that had been his.

F. Although Athamas' story was well known to ancient writers and was the background for the saga of the ARGONAUTS, no play or epic on the subject survives. The tale is told in part by Apollodorus [1.9.1–2, 3.4.2–3], in the first four *Fabulae* of Hyginus, in Ovid's *Metamorphoses* [4.416–542], and by Pausanias [1.44.7–8, 9.23.6, 9.34.5–9].

Athena or **Athene.** The virgin goddess of arts, crafts, and war, and the patroness of Athens, identified by the Romans with Minerva.

A. The first wife of Zeus was the wise Oceanid Metis. When she was pregnant, Zeus was warned by Ge and Uranus that if she bore a second child it was destined to be a son who would rule heaven. Zeus, who had overthrown his own father and did not wish to suffer a similar fate, circumvented this catastrophe by swallowing Metis. Only later, when it was time for Metis' daughter to be born, did it occur to him that he might have acted hastily. He called on either the Titan Prometheus or the craftsman-god Hephaestus to extricate him from his predicament. One or the other solved the problem in a forthright manner by splitting open Zeus's head with an ax. Out leaped the goddess Athena, wearing full armor. The gods were profoundly alarmed at this prodigy until the goddess removed the armor and revealed herself in a less formidable aspect.

A seemingly unrelated tradition has it that Athena was born beside a river named Triton or Tritonis. Small towns in both Arcadia and Boeotia had streams of that name and claimed to be the goddess' birthplace. The Lybians insisted that Athena was the daughter of Poseidon and Tritonis, nymph of the large lake that bore her name. Some say that Athena was reared by nymphs near this lake, others that the sea-god Triton brought her up. The citizens of the town of Alalcomenae, near the Boeotian Tritonis, claimed that their eponym, Alalcomeneus, reared the goddess.

Athena admired courage and ingenuity and aided many young men in the performance of difficult tasks. She helped her half-brother PERSEUS to kill Medusa, though this act may have been inspired as much by enmity toward the Gorgon as by friendly feelings toward Perseus. Athena had been outraged when the beautiful Medusa was seduced by Poseidon in her shrine, and had turned the woman's hair to snakes. Perseus, after killing Medusa, gave the head to Athena, who thereafter wore it in the center of her shield. Some say that she killed the Gorgon herself. Listening to the weird dirge of Medusa's Gorgon sisters, she made it into a flute tune. She also saved some of Medusa's blood, giving a little of it to her foster son, Erichthonius, and the rest to Asclepius, who used it among his medicines.

Athena aided HERACLES on many occasions and gave BELLEROPHON the magic bridle with which he tamed Pegasus. (Earlier she had taught Bellerophon's mother, Eurynome, to be as wise as the gods.) She told Cadmus, who worshiped her under the Canaanite name of Onca or Onga, to sow half the teeth of the dragon that he had slain, and later saw to it that he gained the Theban throne. For some reason, she gave the other half of the dragon's teeth to Aeëtes, king of Colchis. Athena would have saved the life of the wounded Tydeus in the Argive war with Thebes, but when she saw him eating the brains of a slain enemy, she was so disgusted that she withheld the medicine that she had begged from Zeus for him.

As a goddess of crafts, both of men and women, Athena often aided clever artisans. She taught Danaüs to build the first two-prowed ship and Argus to build the *Argo*, in which she installed a speaking beam made from one of the oracular oaks of Dodona. She helped Epeius with construction of the wooden horse. When Perdix, Daedalus' inventive nephew, was thrown from the Acropolis by his jealous uncle, the goddess changed the young man into a partridge. Her interest in the Argonauts continued throughout their journey, and it was she, rather than Jason's patroness, Hera, who got them safely through the Clashing Rocks.

Athena was concerned with all the household arts practiced by women, but her specialty seems to have been weaving. She was piqued when ARACHNE boasted that she was at least as expert at the loom, and furious when the girl proved her claim. After causing Arachne to hang herself, she changed her into a spider. Athena's interest in music led her to invent the double flute. Ridiculed by Aphrodite and Hera because playing the instrument distorted her face, she flung it away and beat the satyr Marsyas for picking it up.

B. Athena's home, when she was not on Olympus, was on the Acropolis of Athens, where she shared a shrine with Erechtheus and had one of her own. Her interest in this city went back to its earliest days, when she vied with Poseidon for recognition as its patron deity. Poseidon produced a salt spring on the Acropolis in support of his claim, but Athena caused the olive tree to spring up near by. The arbiters—the gods, or one or another of the Athenian kings—decided that this was the more useful gift and awarded the city to Athena. Poseidon angrily flooded a part of Attica, but later relented and was worshiped side by side with Athena in Athens. According to the Troezenians, a dispute between the same deities over their city was summarily ended by Zeus, who ordered them to share equally in local honors.

During the reign of the Athenian king Cecrops, Hephaestus took a strong fancy to the virgin goddess and tried to violate her when she did not respond to his courtship. During the ensuing struggle, the god's semen fell on the ground of the Acropolis and an infant, ERICHTHONIUS (1), was born. Athena placed him in a chest and gave it to Cecrops' three daughters for safekeeping. Two of them peeked into the box and, driven mad by what they saw, leaped from the Acropolis. The goddess reared the child in her shrine and he later became a king of Athens.

It was on the Athenian Areopagus that Athena presided over the trial of Orestes for the murder of his mother. She cast a deciding vote in favor of his acquittal, but also arranged that his bitter accusers, the Erinyes, should be thereafter worshiped at Athens as the Semnai Theai, or Eumenides. She later saved Orestes and his sister Iphigeneia from death at the hands of the barbaric Taurians.

Athena did not lose the warlike characteristics with which she was born. Her prowess was an important factor in the success of the gods in their war with the GIANTS. She killed the Giant Pallas, flayed him, and used his skin as a shield. Some say that she, rather than Zeus, flung Sicily on top of Enceladus. On frequent occasions Athena borrowed her father's aegis and, more rarely, even his thunderbolts. She had only contempt, however, for the mindless lust for killing that was characteristic of her half-brother Ares, and she usually defeated him in their encounters.

The goddess was also connected with another Pallas, a daughter of Triton, according to those who say that the sea-god reared her. The two girls were close friends and used to practice warlike games together. Once they lost their tempers and Zeus, seeing Pallas about to strike his daughter, distracted her with his aegis. She dropped her guard and Athena killed her. Grief-stricken, she made a wooden image of Pallas, wrapped it in the aegis, and set it up on Olympus. Zeus later threw it out of heaven and it was placed on the Trojan citadel as the Palladium. Another display of the goddess' temper led to the blinding of TEIRESIAS, the son of her favorite nymph, Chariclo. Athena again regretted her act and consoled Charicolo by giving Teiresias a knowledge of prophecy.

Athena and Hera, angered when the Trojan prince PARIS awarded the golden apple to Aphrodite, strongly supported the Greeks in the Trojan War. Athena was particularly helpful to the wily ODYSSEUS and the courageous Diomedes. After the war, however, she turned violently against the Greeks when Ajax raped Cassandra at her shrine. She and Poseidon arranged the destruction of much of the Greek fleet. She did not, however, desert Odysseus, and managed, in spite of Poseidon's enmity toward the wanderer, to bring him safely back to his home.

C. Athena is widely believed to have been a pre-Hellenic goddess, perhaps of the "mountain-mother" type represented by Cybele, who was the patroness of the royal house of Athens. The original meaning of her probably non-Greek epithet "Tritogeneia" is not understood. The myths of her birth beside some body of water called Trito or Tritonis were apparently invented to explain it. Her title Pallas, perhaps a Greek word meaning "Girl," is thought

117

by some scholars to have been the name of a rather Amazonian virgin goddess of the Hellenes whom they identified with the locally established deity. As goddess of the king's household that in Mycenaean times occupied a palace on the Acropolis, Athena was concerned with those activities of both men and women that furthered the interests of the city. Hence, as indicated by her epithets Promachus (Champion) and Ergane (Worker), among others, she led the people both in war and in their daily tasks.

In late Classical times, Athena came to be regarded as a goddess of wisdom in an abstract sense. In earlier ages, however, this virtue, if it was recognized at all, was not highly valued. The "wisdom" that Athena encouraged was the practical sense and cunning of an Odysseus or the technical skill of an Argus or an Epeius.

The goddess was regularly represented in art, even from early times, as a tall, stately woman wearing a crested helmet and often carrying spear and shield. Her bird was the owl and she was sometimes depicted—for example, in the huge statue of Athena Promachus that stood on the Acropolis—accompanied by a snake.

D. Athena appears in Aeschylus' *Eumenides*, in Sophocles' *Ajax*, and in several plays of Euripides: *The Suppliants, Ion, Rhesus, Trojan Women*, and *Iphigeneia among the Taurians*. She figures prominently throughout Homer's *Iliad* and *Odyssey* and plays a significant role in the *Argonautica* of Apollonius Rhodius. Among innumerable other references to the goddess are the following: Hesiod, *Theogony*, 886–900, 924–929†; *Catalogues of Women* 7, 10; *Shield of Heracles* 325–344, 443–471; *Homeric Hymn to Aphrodite* 5.8–15; *Cypria* 1; *Little Iliad* 1; *Telegony* 1; Pindar, *Olympian Odes*, 13.63–82, and *Pythian Odes*, 12.6–27; Apollodorus 1.3.6, 1.4.2, 1.6.1–2, 2.1.4–5, 2.4.1–3, 2.5.6, 3.4.1–2, 3.6.7–8, 3.12.3, 3.14.1, 3.14.6, "Epitome" 5.22.–6.6, 6.20–22; Herodotus 4.180; Hyginus, *Fabulae*, 142, 165, 168; Ovid, *Metamorphoses*, 4.790–803, 6.1–145, 8.251–253; Pausanias 1.24.1–7, 2.30.6, 8.26.6, 9.11.2, 9.33.7.

Athens. The principal city of Attica. The early history of Attica and Athens is confused. Cecrops is often called the first king, but some writers say that he succeeded Actaeüs, whose daughter he had married. Pausanias mentions the names of at least two kings who ruled before Actaeüs, but adds that the land may, in fact, have been desolate from the days of the ancient king Ogygus to Cecrops' time. Cecrops, an earthborn creature who was half snake, ruled at the time when Athena and Poseidon vied for the name of patron of Athens. With a blow of his trident Poseidon produced a sea (or at least a saltwater well) on the Acropolis in order to demonstrate his power. Athena gave the olive tree. Cecrops, some other king, or the gods ruled that the goddess had made the more useful gift. In a rage, Poseidon flooded Attica.

On Cecrops' death, Cranaüs became king, but was deposed by his son-in-law Amphictyon. After twelve years Amphictyon was in turn deposed by Erichthonius. This king, a son of Hephaestus and Ge, was reared by Athena in her precinct after Cecrops' daughters had failed to guard the chest in which he had been entrusted to them as an infant. Erichthonius, like Cecrops, was at least partly a snake. He is said to have instituted the Panathenaic festival. His son Pandion succeeded to the rule. In a boundary war with the Theban king Labdacus, Pandion allied himself with Tereus, a barbaric king from Thrace or Phocis. Pandion's son Erechtheus (who is often thought to have been the same man as his grandfather Erichthonius, in this confused genealogy) succeeded him. Erechtheus waged a successful war with Eleusis, which resulted in that city's falling under the dominance of Athens, but Erechtheus was killed. His son Cecrops came to power and was followed in turn by his son Pandion, who was expelled by the rebellious sons of his uncle Metion.

Pandion married the daughter of the king of Megara and soon succeeded to the rule of that Isthmian city. His four sons returned to Athens and expelled the Metionids; Aegeus, the eldest, regained the power that his father had lost. Aegeus was rumored to be only an adopted son of Pandion and was troubled throughout his reign by his rebellious brother Pallas and his fifty sons, who used doubts of Aegeus' paternity as an excuse to foment violence. An even more serious situation in the city was a war with Crete in which Athens, defeated, was forced to send fourteen young citizens to Crete every nine years to be eaten by the Minotaur.

The threat to Aegeus' throne and the tribute to Crete ended with the arrival of Theseus, Aegeus' son by Aethra, daughter of King Pittheus of Troezen. Leading an expedition to Crete as one of the intended victims, he slew the Minotaur, thus ending the tribute forever. He returned to find Aegeus dead. Theseus became king and secured his rule by destroying the mutinous Pallantids. According to tradition, it was Theseus who combined the demes (townships) of Attica into an Athenian commonwealth and formalized the city's dominance over Eleusis and Megara. He is even credited with taking the first steps toward democratic government by relinquishing some of his own powers to the people. In his old age Theseus, who had unnecessarily invited war with Sparta by kidnaping Helen, was overthrown by Menestheus, a descendant of Erechtheus. Theseus died or was murdered on the island of Scyrus. Menestheus was killed in the Trojan War and Theseus' son Demophon ruled for a time.

As a result of the Dorian invasion of the Peloponnesus, a large number of Messenian refugees, under Melanthus, invaded Attica. They deposed Thymoetes, the last Theseïd to rule Athens, and Melanthus became king. He welcomed to Attica a second wave of refugees, the Ionians driven from the northern Peloponnesus by the Achaeans. The ostensible reason for Melanthus' generosity was the fact that Ion, eponym of the Ionians, had had Athenian connections, but the shrewd king also hoped to gain more allies in case of a Dorian invasion of Attica. That invasion came in the reign of Codrus, Melanthus' son by an Athenian woman. Codrus repelled it through the voluntary sacrifice of his own life. On their way home the Peloponnesians annexed Megara to Corinth, but the rest of Attica was saved.

Codrus' many sons quarreled over the throne. When the Delphic oracle awarded it to Medon, his brothers gathered about them the Ionians, together with dissident groups and refugees from many Greek cities. With this motley company they emigrated to Asia Minor, where they colonized most of the cities later called Ionian. For unrecorded reasons, the Athenians reduced Medon's powers as king. This was the first of a series of limitations on the monarchy that led, within a relatively short time, to the institution of the archonship at Athens.

Atlantis. A legendary island. Larger than Asia and Libya together, this island lay beyond the Pillars of Hercules in the Atlantic Ocean. Its earthborn first inhabitant, Evenor, married Leucippe and they had a daughter, Cleito. Poseidon, the patron god of the island, became Cleito's lover and she bore five pairs of twin sons. Poseidon divided the island and its people among these sons, making Atlas, the eldest, high king. Atlas lived in a palace on an acropolis at the very center of the island. Poseidon had surrounded this hill with concentric belts of water and land for the protection of Cleito. The industrious Atlantians connected it with the rest of the island and the sea by means of bridges, canals, and tunnels.

The Atlantians became prosperous and extremely powerful, extending their dominion through Europe as far as northern Italy, and through Libya as far as Egypt. The descendants of Poseidon ruled benevolently for many generations, but, as their divine blood became increasingly diluted with mortality, they grew overbearing and tyrannical and undertook to conquer the remaining nations of the world. After a prolonged war they were defeated by these nations under the leadership of Athens. Later Atlantis was destroyed in a cataclysmic earthquake. The island sank into the sea. The earthquake and the accompanying floods swept away most of the peoples of the known world, including the Athenians.

The legend of Atlantis is known only from two connected dialogues of Plato, the *Timaeüs* [24E–25D] and the incomplete *Critias* [108E–109A, 113B to end]. It is purported to have been recounted to Solon by Egyptians; the events are said to have occurred about 9500 B.C. No recollections of Atlantis are reflected in Greek mythology, however, and since Plato told the story to illustrate a thesis in political philosophy, he may well have invented it for that purpose. Nevertheless, innumerable theories have been put forward as to the location and fate of "Lost Atlantis." The most recent one hinges on the catastrophic explosions that destroyed much of the island of Thera on more than one occasion.

Atlas. A Titan. Atlas was a son of the Titan Iapetus by the Oceanid Clymene or by Asia. He was the father, by the Oceanid Pleïone, of the goddess

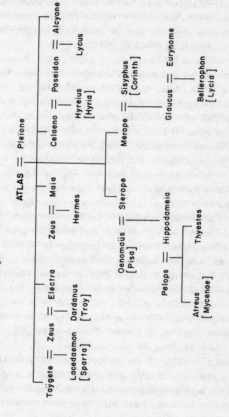

The Descendants of Atlas

ATLAS = Pleïone

Taÿgete = Zeus   Electra = Zeus   Maia = Zeus   Sterope   Merope =   Celaeno = Poseidon   Alcyone

Lacedaemon   Dardanus   Hermes   Hyreius   Lycus
[Sparta]   [Troy]   [Hyria]

Oenomaüs = Sterope   Sisyphus   Glaucus   Eurynome
[Pisa]   [Corinth]

Pelops = Hippodameia   Bellerophon
                                 [Lycia]

Atreus   Thyestes
[Mycenae]

Calypso, of the Pleiades, and, some say, of the Hyades. Atlas, whose name may be derived from a word meaning "to bear," was best known as the half-divine giant who upheld the sky, keeping it separate from the earth. He held the sky on his shoulders or head, or else steadied the pillars that supported it. Atlas stood at one of the far ends of the earth. He was most often said to be in northwestern Africa, where a great range of mountains bears his name today. In some accounts he seems to be no more than a personification of the mountains, but various myths were told to explain how he came to be assigned his arduous task. It was generally said to have been his punishment for siding with his brother Titans in their war against Zeus.

According to Ovid [*Metamorphoses* 4.628–662], Perseus flew to Atlas' western kingdom on his way home after killing the Gorgon Medusa and asked lodging for the night. Atlas rudely refused this request, for he had been warned long before by Themis that a son of Zeus (which Perseus claimed to be) would one day rob him of the golden apples that grew in his garden, where they were guarded by the serpent Ladon and tended by the nymphs called Hesperides. Angered at the Titan's inhospitable threats, Perseus showed him Medusa's head and transformed him into a mountain.

This tale is self-contradictory, however, for, by the same account, Atlas still had his human form when two generations later he encountered the thief of whom he had been warned. Heracles, sent by Eurystheus for the golden apples, took the grateful advice of Atlas' brother Prometheus (whom Heracles had just rescued from his long torment) and asked the giant to pluck the apples for him. When Heracles offered to hold the sky while Atlas went on the errand, the Titan, who was none too intelligent, consented. He soon returned with the apples, but offered to deliver them in person to Eurystheus, intending never to return. Heracles shrewdly agreed, but asked Atlas to hold the sky again for a moment while he placed a pad on his head. Once free of the burden, Heracles strode away with the apples, leaving Atlas worse off than before. [Homer, *Odyssey*, 1.51, 7.245; Hesiod, *Theogony*, 507, 744, 938; Apollodorus 1.2.3, 2.5.11, 3.10.1; Hyginus, *Fabulae*, 150, 192.]

Atlas, Mount. A range of mountains in northwestern Africa. The mountains called by this name in ancient times are those in western and southern Morocco that are now designated as the Grand Atlas Range. They were associated in mythology with the Titan Atlas, who bore the heavens on his shoulders.

Atreidae. The sons of Atreus (or of his son Pleisthenes) by Aërope, that is, Agamemnon and Menelaüs.

Atreus. A king of Mycenae.

A. A son of Pelops and Hippodameia, Atreus, together with his brother Thyestes, killed Pelops' bastard son, Chrysippus, to please their mother. For this crime the brothers were banished from Pisa, but their brother-in-law Sthenelus, king of Mycenae, invited them to rule the city of Midea. Atreus bought and married AËROPE, a daughter of the Cretan king Catreus, who had sent her to Nauplius, king of Nauplia, to be sold. Aërope bore two sons, Agamemnon and Menelaüs. (Greek mythographers knew of an alternative genealogy at least as old as Hesiod: Atreus was the father not of these famous brothers but of Pleisthenes, who became, by Cleolla, the father of Agamemnon, Menelaüs, and Anaxibia. Because Pleisthenes died young, the boys were reared by their grandfather and became known as the Atreidae, or sons of Atreus.)

Aërope loved Thyestes, rather than her husband, and she betrayed to him one of Atreus' darkest secrets: Atreus had once vowed to sacrifice to Artemis the finest of his flocks, but, when a lamb with a golden fleece was born, he killed it and hid the fleece in a box instead of burning it on the goddess' altar. Aërope gave this box to her lover. Not long afterward, both Sthenelus and his son, Eurystheus, having died, the Mycenaeans consulted an oracle and were told to elect as their new king one of the rulers of Midea. When they could not choose between the two brothers, Thyestes suggested that the throne be given to the one who could produce a fleece of gold. Atreus confidently agreed to this bargain, not knowing that his hoard was gone. Thyestes brought forth the fleece and was made king.

Atreus claimed that his rights had been usurped, but could offer no proof. At this point Zeus, who for some reason favored Atreus, sent Hermes to advise him to propose that the kingdom should belong to the man who could produce an even greater marvel: a reversal of the sun's flight and a change in the Pleiades' course. Thyestes, perhaps thinking that his brother had gone mad, readily agreed to this further test. To his astonishment the seemingly impossible events occurred. The Mycenaeans accepted this as proof of Atreus' claim and awarded him the throne. His first official act was to banish Thyestes.

B. Atreus soon learned how Thyestes had come by the fleece and regretted having exiled him out of reach of vengeance. He therefore pretended to make peace with his brother and invited him to a banquet. (Some say that Thyestes returned voluntarily as a suppliant.) Atreus then secretly killed Thyestes' sons, even though they clung to the altar of Zeus. These children were Aglaüs, Callileon, and Orchomenus, Thyestes' children by a naïad, or else they were Tantalus and Pleisthenes. (According to some versions of the tale, this Tantalus lived to marry Clytemnestra and was killed by Agamemnon.) Cutting them into pieces, Atreus served them to Thyestes at the feast, much as their grandfather Tantalus had once served up his son Pelops to the gods. At the end of the meal Atreus showed his brother the heads and hands of his children and once more drove him from Mycenae. Hyginus [*Fabulae* 86] claims that Pleisthenes was not Thyestes' son, but Atreus', Thyestes having reared him. If this was the case, Atreus killed his own child along with a child of Thyestes.

C. Thyestes consulted an oracle as to how he might avenge himself on his brother. He was advised to have a child by his own daughter, Pelopia, and did

123

as he was told. Hyginus, who tells the story in detail [*Fabulae* 88], says that this event happened by chance. By this account, Thyestes went, after his banishment, first to Thesprotia, where Pelopia lived, then to Sicyon, where she was staying. There he stopped at a stream near where some young women were performing a dance sacred to Athena. The leader of the dance soon came down to the stream to wash the blood of some animal from her tunic. Not recognizing his daughter, Pelopia, Thyestes leaped from hiding and raped her. The next day he asked the Sicyonian king to send him to Lydia, where he would be safe from the enmity of Atreus. Pelopia, who had taken Thyestes' sword as he lay with her, hid it under the pedestal of Athena's statue.

Atreus, meanwhile, had consulted an oracle about how to end a famine that had resulted from his murder of the children. He was told to bring Thyestes back to Mycenae. Searching for him, Atreus came to King Thesprotus. He saw the lovely Pelopia, who had returned to Thesprotia, and, thinking that she was the king's daughter, asked for her hand. Thesprotus agreed, afraid either to explain that she was really Thyestes' daughter or to mention that she was pregnant by a stranger. Atreus returned with her to Mycenae. When her child was born, Pelopia exposed it, but some shepherds rescued it and gave it to a goat to suckle. Later Atreus learned of the child and reared him as his own son. The boy was named Aegisthus, for the goat (*aix, aigos*).

D. Atreus now sent his sons by Aërope—Agamemnon and Menelaüs—to Delphi to inquire of the oracle where Thyestes could be found. By chance Thyestes came there at the same time, still seeking a means of vengeance on his brother. His nephews seized him and took him back to Mycenae, where Atreus flung him into prison and sent Aegisthus to kill him. When the youth appeared in the cell with a drawn sword, Thyestes recognized it as his own lost weapon. Astonished, Aegisthus confided that his mother had given it to him and Thyestes begged to see her. Pelopia came to his cell, told the story of the sword, and, on learning that its owner was her father, killed herself with it. Aegisthus refused to murder the man who had turned out to be his father. Instead he took the bloody sword to Atreus as evidence that Thyestes was dead. Overjoyed that his hated brother was dead at last, the king went down to the shore to offer sacrifices in gratitude to the gods. There Aegisthus killed him.

Thyestes once again sat on the throne of Mycenae, but not for long. Atreus' sons had long before taken refuge with Polypheides, king of Sicyon, and later with Oeneus, king of Aetolia. In time the Spartan king Tyndareüs brought them back to Mycenae. They drove out Thyestes and forced him to take refuge in Cytheria. Agamemnon made himself king and Thyestes never returned to Mycenae. Many years later he was avenged on Agamemnon by Aegisthus, who was killed in turn by Agamemnon's son, Orestes.

These successive horrors were attributed by ancient writers to the working-out of Thyestes' curse on Atreus for the murder of his children, or of Myrtilus' earlier curse on his murderer, Pelops. The feud between the brother enemies is related in Seneca's tragedy *Thyestes* and forms the background for Aeschylus' *Agamemnon*. [Apollodorus 2.4.6, "Epitome" 2.10–15; *Catalogues of Women* 69.]

Atropos. See FATES.

Attica. The most southeasterly part of the Greek mainland. The peninsular region bounded on the north by Mount Cithaeron and lying between the Saronic Gulf and the Aegean Sea was known in ancient times, as it is today, as Attica. The most important city in this region has since prehistoric times been Athens. After conquering Eleusis, Athens had no further rivals for the domination of the peninsula. It was Theseus who, according to tradition, completed the federation of the demes, or townships, of Attica. He included the city of Megara, thereby extending Athenian domination along the isthmus as far as the boundaries of Corinth.

The origin of the name of Attica was disputed. Some claimed that it was named for an ancient king, Actaeüs. According to others, the region, although first called Acte or Actaea for this king, was renamed Cecropia by his son-in-law Cecrops and received its present name in honor of Atthis, a daughter of Cecrops' successor, Cranaüs.

Attis or **Atys.** The young consort of the Phrygian goddess CYBELE. Attis was a son of Nana, a daughter of the river-god Sangarius who had been impregnated by an almond fallen from a tree that had sprung from the severed male genitals of Agdistis (Cybele). Suckled by a he-goat, he grew to handsome manhood and was loved from afar by Cybele, who jealously drove him mad when he planned marriage. He castrated himself and died; according to some, he was then changed by the goddess into a pine tree.

Atymnius. A son of Zeus and Cassiopeia. According to some writers, it was a quarrel with Minos over the love of the boy Atymnius (rather than Miletus) that caused Rhadamanthys and Sarpedon to leave Crete. [Apollodorus 3.1.1.]

Atys. See ATTIS.

Auge. The daughter of Aleüs, king of Arcadia, and his niece Neaera. Auge was a priestess of Athena at Tegea. When Heracles stopped at that city on his way to Elis to make war on King Augeias, he was hospitably entertained by King Aleüs. During his brief stay Heracles found time to seduce the beautiful priestess, whom he may or may not have known to be his host's daughter. There are several versions of the ensuing events. According to one, Auge bore a son secretly and hid him in the precinct of Athena. Aleüs, subsequently inquiring of the Delphic oracle the reason that the land had grown barren, learned that the shrine had been polluted. He found the child and exposed him on Mount Parthenius. He then turned Auge over to Nauplius with instructions to drown her or to sell her abroad. In other versions, Auge herself exposed the child in order to hide her shame, or gave birth on Parthenius as she was being taken away by Nauplius. In any case, Auge's life was saved by Nauplius' desire for gain, for he sold her into slavery instead of killing her. Either by Nauplius or by some Carian sailors to whom he had sold her, Auge was sold to Teuthras, king of Teuthrania, in Mysia. The king fell in love with her and married her.

Some writers say that Nauplius sold Auge's infant son to Teuthras along with Auge herself; others, that mother and child arrived in Mysia in a chest in which Aleüs had set them afloat, as Acrisius had done with Danaë and Perseus. The most usual version, however, has it that the child was suckled by a doe on Mount Parthenius and found by the shepherds of King Corythus, who named him Telephus, for the doe (*elaphos*). On reaching manhood, the youth went to the Delphic oracle to inquire where he might find his parents. With unusual straightforwardness, the oracle directed him to Mysia, where he not only found his mother but was adopted by Teuthras, who married Telephus to Argiope, his daughter (perhaps by an earlier marriage).

Hyginus [*Fabulae* 99, 100] tells a more complicated story. At the same time that Auge was exposing her child on Mount Parthenius, Atalanta was doing the same with Parthenopaeüs, her child by Meleager. Shepherds found both children and reared them together. The youths became close friends and Parthenopaeüs accompanied Telephus to Mysia, where Telephus was seeking his parents on the oracle's advice. There Telephus found that Teuthras had adopted Auge as his daughter (not married her, as in other versions), but the young man did not, of course, recognize her. Teuthras, threatened by war with Idas, offered to give his supposed daughter to Telephus in return for the young man's help in the conflict. Telephus and Parthenopaeüs defeated Idas, and Telephus claimed his bride. Auge, perhaps out of fidelity to Heracles, wanted nothing further to do with men. On her wedding night she attempted to kill her young husband with a sword, but a huge snake suddenly appeared and crawled between them. Terrified, Auge confessed her intention, and Telephus prepared to kill her for her treachery. Auge, however, cried out for protection to Heracles and Telephus discovered her identity. He then returned with her to Arcadia. Auge's tomb, however, was shown to visitors at Pergamon, in Mysia. [Apollodorus 2.7.4, 3.9.1; Pausanias 8.4.8–9, 8.48.7.]

Augeias or **Augeas.** A king of Elis. Although Augeias was perhaps the best known of Eleian kings, his parentage was in doubt. He was called a son of Phorbas, of Poseidon, and of Helius. Pausanias [5.8.3] suggested that this last claim resulted merely from a misunderstanding of the name of Augeias' true father, Eleius, a grandson of Endymion. Augeias sailed with the Argonauts and he sent a punitive expedition against Pylus during Neleus' reign, but his only claim to fame seems to have been his war with Heracles. The source of Augeias' considerable wealth was his huge herds of cattle and goats. These left much of the land too deeply covered in dung to be cultivated. The king's cattle yards and stables were so filthy that cleaning them seemed a hopeless task. No doubt for this reason Eurystheus assigned the labor to HERACLES [F], adding that it must be completed in a single day. Without mentioning this order to Augeias, Heracles made a bargain with him, in the presence of the king's eldest son, Phyleus, to do the job for pay. Augeias, who believed it impossible, readily agreed, but when Heracles, after flushing out the yard with one or two rivers, came to collect his wages, Augeias repudiated the bargain. The honest Phyleus protested, and was driven from Elis along with Heracles. Phyleus took refuge in Dulichium; Heracles went on about his labors, but he did not forget Augeias' duplicity.

Augeias realized that he had made a dangerous enemy. He therefore made allies of the three most formidable men in Elis—his twin nephews, the Moliones, and Amarynceus, son of a Thessalian immigrant—by offering them shares in the government. When Heracles returned with a Tirynthian army, as Augeias had anticipated, Augeias' powerful allies defeated the invaders and forced them to retreat. Heracles resorted to treachery, killing the Moliones from ambush during a truce, then descended on Elis with another army and sacked the city. Some say that he killed Augeias, others that he released him and the other prisoners out of respect for Phyleus, whom he made king of Elis. After a time Phyleus returned to Dulichium, and Augeias, dying at an advanced age, left the Eleian throne to a younger son, Agasthenes, and to the two sons of the Moliones. Augeias was paid hero's honors in Elis for centuries after his death. [Apollodorus 2.5.5., 2.7.2; Pausanias 5.1.9–5.3.3.]

Aulis. A Boeotian city on the Euripus, the strait separating Euboea from the mainland. The Greeks were becalmed here before sailing against Troy, and Agamemnon was forced by his troops to sacrifice his daughter Iphigeneia in order to appease Artemis. By Pausanias' day (second century A.D.) the city was no more than a village of potters.

Auriga (The Charioteer). A constellation. Although it was generally agreed in Classical times that this group of stars represented the driver of a four-horse chariot, he was variously identified as Erichthonius, king of Athens, or an Argive named Orsilochus, or Myrtilus, the famous charioteer of Oenomaüs. [Hyginus, *Poetica Astronomica*, 2.9.]

Aurora. The Roman name for the goddess of the dawn, called Eos by the Greeks.

Ausonia. The land of the Ausonii or Ausonidae, an ancient tribe who inhabited southern Italy. By extension, the name came to be applied poetically to all Italy. The Ausonian Sea was an early name for the Ligurian Sea.

Autesion. A Theban king. Autesion, son of Thersander's son Tisamenus, was hounded by the Erinyes of his ancestors Laïus and Oedipus. On the advice of an oracle, he left the throne of Thebes to Damasichthon and joined the Dorians, who were soon to invade the Peloponnesus with the Heraclids. His daughter, Argeia, married Aristodemus, one of the Heraclid leaders. When Aristodemus was killed, Autesion's son, Theras, became the guardian of his nephews, Eurysthenes and Procles, who eventually ruled Sparta. [Herodotus 4.147; Pausanias 9.5.15–16.]

autochthon. One of the original inhabitants of a region. The word implies a person literally sprung up out of the earth like the Sparti of Thebes. Many peoples of Greece, among them the Athenians, claimed to be indigenous (autochthonous) to their country. Such a claim had obvious political value in a land repeatedly disrupted by migrations and invasions.

Autolycus (1). A mythical thief. Autolycus is generally called a son of Hermes, the god of thieves, and Chione, but his father is sometimes said to have been Apollo or Daedalion. Autolycus was able to escape with anything that he got his hands on and, if need be, to make it change its color or form. It was he who stole the cattle of Eurytus, who blamed the deed on Heracles. Autolycus also stole from Amyntor's armory at Eleon a helmet that ultimately was given to Odysseus by Meriones.

Autolycus met his match in Sisyphus, king of Corinth, who was as great a rogue as the thief himself. Autolycus repeatedly stole Sisyphus' cattle. The king noticed that his herd was unaccountably diminishing, while that of Autolycus kept increasing. He could prove nothing, however, presumably because Autolycus changed the cattle's appearance. Finally Sisyphus hit upon the scheme of marking the hooves of his herd. After a few more such losses he went to Autolycus and, pointing to the marks, accused him of thievery. Sisyphus not only took back his cattle but punished the thief by seducing Anticleia, Autolycus' daughter by Neaera, daughter of Pereus, or by Erysichthon's daughter. Soon afterward Anticleia married Laërtes and had a son, but it was widely suspected that the child—Odysseus—was the son of the wily Sisyphus.

Not long after the boy's birth Autolycus paid a visit to his daughter in Ithaca and was asked by her to name the child. He called him Odysseus (from *odyssomai,* "to be angry at") because he (Autolycus) had been angry at so many men. He told Anticleia to send the boy to him when he was grown to receive appropriate gifts. As a youth, Odysseus accordingly visited his grandfather at his home on Mount Parnassus. There he received a tusk wound in his thigh while hunting boar with Autolycus' sons. These sons are unidentified. Apollodorus said that Autolycus taught Heracles to wrestle. He also named him among the Argonauts, but he may have confused the famous thief with the Thessalian Autolycus, who joined the expedition in Sinope. In Apollodorus' account, Autolycus is said to have been the father of Jason's mother, Polymede, as well as of Anticleia. [Homer, *Iliad,* 10.266–271, and *Odyssey,* 19.392–466; Hyginus, *Fabulae,* 201; Apollodorus 1.9.16, 2.4.9, 2.6.2.]

Autolycus (2). A son of Deïmachus of Tricca, in Thessaly. With his brothers, Phlogius and Deïleon, Autolycus joined Heracles' expedition against the Amazons, but they became separated from their leader and settled in Sinope, which Autolycus was often said to have founded. The brothers later joined the Argonauts when the *Argo* stopped at Sinope. Hyginus, confusing them with the sons of Phrixus, called Deïleon Demoleon and added a fourth brother, Phronius. [Apollonius Rhodius 2.955–961; Hyginus, *Fabulae,* 14.]

Automedon. The charioteer of Achilles. Automedon, a son of Diores, accompanied Achilles from Scyrus to the Trojan War, or else brought ten ships of his own. He drove Achilles' immortal horses for Patroclus, as well as for their master. A brave fighter in his own right, he killed the Trojan Aretus to avenge Patroclus' death. After Achilles' death he fought beside the dead hero's son, Neoptolemus. [Homer, *Iliad*, 16.472–476, 16.864–867, 17.426–542, 19.392–399; Vergil, *Aeneïd*, 2.476–478; Hyginus, *Fabulae*, 97.]

Autonoë. A daughter of Cadmus, king of Thebes, and Harmonia. Autonoë married Aristaeüs and bore a son, Actaeon. Macris may have been their daughter. Autonoë and two of her sisters maligned a fourth sister, Semele, and were punished by her son, Dionysus, by being driven, in a Bacchic frenzy, to dismember King Pentheus. When Actaeon was eaten by his hounds, his grief-stricken parents separately left Thebes. Autonoë went to the village of Ereneia, near Megara, and eventually died there. [Apollodorus 3.4.2; Euripides, *The Bacchants*, 1130; Pausanias 1.44.5.]

Aventinus. A Latin leader in the war against the Trojans. Aventinus, born on the Aventine Hill of Rome, was a son of Heracles by a priestess of Rhea. He was an ally of Turnus against Aeneas' forces. [Vergil, *Aeneïd*, 7.655–669.]

Avernus. A lake near Naples, still called Lago d'Averno. Avernus, near Cumae, was regarded by the Romans—or at least by their poets—as an entrance to the Underworld. Not far away were Hecate's grove and the cave of the Cumaean Sibyl.

Axion. See ALCMEON.

Azania. A region of Arcadia. Azania was presumably in the southeastern part of Arcadia, since its eponym, Azan, a son of Arcas, was said to have lived in Lycosura.

B

bacchants or **bacchanals.** See MAENADS.

Bacchus. An alternative Greek name for DIONYSUS. The Romans used this name for the god as well as identifying him with their own god Liber.

Balius. See XANTHUS.

Bateia. A daughter of Teucer, king of the region later known as Troy. Dardanus, an immigrant from Samothrace, was welcomed by Teucer and married Bateia, who bore two sons, Ilus and Erichthonius. Since the first died childless, Erichthonius succeeded to his father's kingdom of Dardania; his son Tros became king and eponym of Troy. Bateia thus became the mother of the Trojan race. A town near Troy was named for her. [Apollodorus 3.12.1–2.]

Baton. The charioteer of Amphiaraüs. Baton, whom some call Elato, vanished with his kinsman Amphiaraüs when their chariot was engulfed.

Battus. The founder of Cyrene.

A. Battus, one of the most celebrated colonizers in Greek legend, was also one of the most reluctant. He was a son of a Theraean nobleman, Polymnestus, and a direct descendant, in the seventeenth generation, of the Argonaut EUPHEMUS, whose Minyan descendants had colonized the island of Thera together with a company of Spartans under THERAS. According to Cyrenaean tradition, Battus' mother was Phronime, daughter of Etearchus, king of the Cretan city of Oaxus. When Phronime's mother died, Etearchus took a second wife, who mistreated the girl and finally persuaded the king that she was unchaste. Etearchus, not wishing to kill his daughter himself, made friends with a Theraean trader, Themison, and heaped him with favors until the man one day vowed to do in return whatever the king might ask. Etearchus promptly demanded that Themison take away his daughter and throw her into the sea. The outraged trader broke off relations with the king, but was still bound by his vow. This he neatly circumvented by binding Phronime and tossing her into the sea, then immediately pulling her up again. He took her home with him to Thera, where she became the concubine of Polymnestus. She bore him a son, whom they named Aristoteles.

This boy was afflicted with a severe speech impediment, which some believe was the origin of the name Battus (from *battarizo*, "stammer"), by which he came to be known. When he was grown he went to Delphi to inquire of the oracle how to overcome this defect. He was told to found a colony in

Libya. (Some say that this command was given to Grinnus, the Theraean king, whom Battus had accompanied to Delphi, but Grinnus complained that he was too old and asked that the injunction be transferred to Battus.) Battus protested, since he had no way of raising a force of colonists and, in any case, neither he nor any other Theraean even knew where Libya was. The Pythia said no more, and Battus and Grinnus went home to Thera and did nothing about the oracle for seven years.

During this period no rain fell on Thera. The Theraeans sent again to Delphi, this time to inquire what was wrong. They were reminded of the command to·Battus and were advised to help him found the colony. Since there was nothing else to do, they sent a party to Crete to find someone who could guide them to Libya. They eventually found a fisherman named Corobius, who had once been driven off course to Libya while fishing for the murex, a mollusk that was a source of Tyrian purple. Although he did not know the mainland, he knew of an island called Platea that lay off the coast. The Theraeans sailed to Platea, left Corobius there with a few of their own men and provisions for several months, and returned to Thera to recruit more settlers.

B. This task did not prove easy. The Theraeans were not eager to leave their homes to found a city in an unknown land. But the drought continued and it was decreed that one of each pair of brothers in the seven divisions of the island should be chosen to go under the leadership of Battus, who so far had made no move to carry out the command of Apollo. Corobius, meanwhile, would have starved to death with his companions had not a Samian vessel stopped at Platea on its way to open the Iberian port of Tartessus to Greek trade. The Samians generously left a year's provisions for the stranded colonists, a deed that in later years led to friendly relations among the three nations of Samos, Thera, and Cyrene.

At last Battus set sail with his reluctant crew in two fifty-oared ships. After one glimpse of the inhospitable land of Libya, they sailed back to Thera. The Theraeans, whose lives depended on satisfying Apollo by obeying his oracle, greeted their former countrymen with flights of arrows. The ships hurriedly pulled away and headed a second time for Libya. For two years they remained on Platea, but things went from bad to worse. They sent a third time to Delphi, where the Pythia coldly reminded them that they had not yet colonized Libya, but only an island.

The discouraged Theraeans left Platea and settled at a pleasant spot on the coast near the island of Aziris. Apparently this colony was only moderately successful for, after seven years, the numerous tribes of the region were able to persuade the Theraeans to move to a supposedly more desirable spot, which they promised to show them. The natives led the settlers westward, carefully arranging the marches so that they should pass the pleasantest regions at night. Finally they reached the site of Cyrene, where, sixteen years after receiving the first oracle, Battus and the Theraeans planted a permanent colony on the coast of Libya. Thus Battus fulfilled the destiny implied by the sea-god Triton when, seventeen generations earlier, he had given a clod of Libyan soil to Battus' ancestor Euphemus.

The Theraeans' helpful Libyan neighbors in the region of Aziris had doubtless led them to the new site merely in an attempt to get the interlopers out of their own territory. Nevertheless the new land proved to be well supplied with rain and the Theraean colony at last prospered. According to one tradition, the region had been occupied by descendants of the Trojan survivor Antenor. They welcomed Battus' settlers. The newcomers must have soon dominated, for Battus ruled in peace for forty years. Indeed, some believe that his name is only a Libyan word for "king." Not long after reaching the new region he was cured of his stammer when, venturing into the desert that surrounded his city, he encountered a lion. He let out a yell of terror (which in turn frightened away the lion) and thereafter had no trouble in speaking.

Battus was succeeded by his son, Arcesilaüs, who ruled for sixteen years. These two kings were followed by six more generations of their line, which alternated the names Battus and Arcesilaüs. Battus II, anticipating trouble from Egypt, invited more colonists to come to Cyrene, offering them plots of land. Encouraged by the Delphic oracle, hordes migrated to the region, particularly from the Peloponnesus and Crete, and displaced some of the neighboring tribes. These, led by King Adicran, appealed to the Egyptian pharaoh Apries, but the Greeks were strong enough to repel the Egyptian army that marched against them.

C. The story of Battus and the Theraean colonization of Cyrene was told at length by Herodotus [4.150–167] and some of it, particularly of the later generations, is largely historical. Pindar addressed his fourth and fifth Pythian odes to Arcesilaüs IV, the last Cyrenaean king of Battus' line. Pausanias told a more realistic version [10.15.6–7] of Battus' recovery from stammering than Pindar's account.

Battus. See HERMES [A].

Baucis and **Philemon.** Elderly peasants of Bithynia. When Zeus and Hermes were wandering through Phrygia disguised as mortals, they were refused hospitality in a thousand homes. On the hillside above a particularly unfriendly town they at last came to the poor hut of Philemon and Baucis. The old couple entertained them with great kindness. During the meal the hosts noticed that the wine bowl miraculously kept refilling itself and realized that their guests were more than human. The two gods revealed their identity and led the old couple to the top of the hill. When they turned back they saw that the inhospitable town in the valley below had become a lake. Their own hut was now a temple. Zeus offered to grant any boon that the pair might ask. Philemon wished only that they might spend the rest of their lives as priestly keepers of the temple and that, at the end, neither should outlive the other. The wish was granted. Baucis and Philemon tended the temple for the rest of their days and, in the moment of dying, were changed one to an oak, the other to a linden, that grew side by side. [Ovid, *Metamorphoses.* 8.618–724.]

Bear Mountain. A mountainous peninsula on the Mysian coast of the Sea of Marmara. Bear Mountain, now called Kapidagi, was the haunt of six-armed, earthborn monsters. These attacked the *Argo* and were killed by Heracles and the Argonauts.

Bebryces. A warlike Mysian tribe. The Bebryces lived near the eastern end of the Sea of Marmara and feuded with the Mariandyni over certain territories lying between their lands. Heracles aided the latter tribe for a time, but, after his departure, Amycus, the Bebrycian king, won back much of the land that he had lost. Amycus was killed in a boxing match with Polydeuces during the visit of the ARGONAUTS [G].

Bellerophon or **Bellerophontes.** The son of Glaucus, king of Ephyra (Corinth), and Eurynome or Eurymede.

A. Having accidentally killed his brother or someone else, Bellerophon was exiled from Ephyra. (Some say that the victim was a Corinthian named Bellerus, and that Bellerophon, whose real name was Hipponoüs, received his familiar epithet, meaning "Bellerus-Killer," from this deed.) He came to the court of PROËTUS, king of Tiryns, who purified him. Proëtus' wife, whom Homer calls Anteia but whom other writers call Stheneboea, found the young man attractive and tried to seduce him, but Bellerophon remained unimpressed. Enraged, the queen told her husband that the youth had tried to violate her, and demanded justice. Proëtus, who had scruples against killing a guest and suppliant, sent Bellerophon to Lycia with a sealed letter to King Iobates, Stheneboea's father. Bellerophon willingly undertook the errand, unaware that the message requested Iobates to dispose of his daughter's attempted seducer.

The outcome of this trick was not what Proëtus intended. Escorted by the gods, Bellerophon made the journey easily and was warmly entertained by Iobates for nine days before he asked to see the message. Reading it, Iobates was faced with the same problem as Proëtus: how to dispose of a guest—whose life was sacred—without offending the gods. He remembered the CHIMAERA, a monster that had been ravaging the Lycian countryside, and asked Bellerophon to kill it. Bellerophon readily agreed, and Iobates was certain that he would be killed. He failed to reckon with the interest that the gods took in this young man, who, some say, was not Glaucus' son at all but Poseidon's, the god having visited Eurynome in Glaucus' house.

B. The gods helped Bellerophon win the help of a semidivine companion, the winged horse Pegasus. As a youth in Ephyra, Bellerophon had yearned to capture this fabulous creature, an offspring of Poseidon and Medusa who roamed the sky and land and would let no man come near. After many vain attempts to approach him, Bellerophon went to Polyeidus for help. At the seer's bidding he spent the night on Athena's altar and was rewarded with a dream in which the goddess offered him a magical golden bridle. The youth awoke with the bridle in his hand. After sacrificing to Athena and Poseidon, he rushed to the spring Peirene, where the horse calmly allowed him to place the bridle about its head. Some say, however, that either Athena or Poseidon presented the horse to Bellerophon. The Troezenians added that soon after this event Bellerophon rode his winged steed to Troezen to ask King Pittheus for his daughter Aethra. Before the marriage could take place, Bellerophon was banished from his homeland.

C. Pegasus and the favor of the gods now enabled Bellerophon to carry out Iobates' order safely. The Chimaera was a fire-breathing monster that was part goat, part lion, and part snake, but Bellerophon, on Pegasus' back, had little trouble in shooting it down with his arrows. Homer, however, does not mention Pegasus, implying that Bellerophon relied simply on his own courage.

Iobates was glad to be rid of the Chimaera, but determined to be rid of his guest as well. He sent him against the Solymi, a neighboring tribe who had long been enemies of the Lycians. They put up a fierce fight, but, mounted on Pegasus, Bellerophon managed to rout them. Returning from this campaign, he was sent to fight the Amazons. They, too, were soon defeated. Desperate, Iobates set the pick of his Lycian soldiers in ambush with orders to destroy Bellerophon at all costs. Instead, Bellerophon killed them to a man.

When the seemingly invincible young man returned once more, the king belatedly realized that he was dealing with one who was favored by the gods. The amends that he made were handsome. He offered half of his kingdom to Bellerophon, and his daughter Philonoë (or Anticleia or Casandra) as well. The grateful Lycians, moreover, gave him the finest farmland in the region. Accepting these tokens, Bellerophon remained in Lycia, though Euripides claimed in a play, now lost, that the young man avenged himself on Stheneboea by inviting her to ride on Pegasus and pushing her off at a great height. According to Hyginus, she killed herself from chagrin over learning that the youth had married her sister.

Philonoë bore two sons, Isander and Hippolochus, and two daughters, Laodameia and Deïdameia. Adored by the Lycians, Bellerophon now seemed at the height of his glory. But not content with merely mortal honors, he envied the gods who had so befriended him. One day he leaped onto Pegasus' back and flew steadily upward, intending to reach heaven itself. Angered by this presumption, Zeus sent a gadfly, which stung Pegasus and caused him to fling his master from his back. Bellerophon fell to earth. Alive but lamed, he wandered across the earth alone, for no man dared befriend one who had been spurned by the gods. No one marked the time or place of his death. [Homer, *Iliad*, 6.154; Apollodorus 2.3; Pindar, *Olympian Odes.* 13, 60–91.]

Bellona. A Roman goddess of war. Bellona was sometimes identified with the Greek goddess Enyo but had a far more important cult. Like Enyo, however, she had little or no mythology, beyond being symbolically called the wife, sister, or companion of Mars or Quirinus, Roman war-gods.

Belus. A king of Egypt. A son of Poseidon and Libya, Belus was a brother of Agenor, his twin, and Lelex. Agenor migrated to Canaan, leaving Belus to rule Egypt. Belus married Anchinoë, daughter of the god Nile. She bore him a daughter, Thronia; twin sons, Aegyptus and Danaüs; and, some add, Cepheus and Phineus. Belus gave Libya to Danaüs, Arabia to Aegyptus. He was said to have been the ancestor of the Persian kings and of Dido, queen of Carthage. His name is probably a Greek form of the Phoenician Baal (Lord), an epithet applied to many local gods in the Near East. [Apollodorus 2.1.4.]

Benthesicyme. See EUMOLPUS.

Beroë. See SEMELE.

Bia. A personification of force and violence. Bia, called a son of Styx and the Titan Pallas, was used, together with his brother Cratus (Strength), as a symbol of Zeus's absolute power in Aeschylus' *Prometheus Bound* [1–87], where the two help Hephaestus to nail Prometheus to a cliff. With their brother and sister, Zelus (Emulation) and Nike (Victory), they were always at Zeus's side. [Hesiod, *Theogony*, 383–388.]

Bias. A son of Amythaon and Idomene. Bias and his brother, MELAMPUS, emigrated with their father to Messenia. Melampus, a seer, won for Bias first the price of his bride, Pero, daughter of Neleus, and later a kingdom in Argolis. Pero bore Talaüs, and possibly also Areius, Leodocus, Perialces, Aretus, and Alphesiboea. Bias also had a daughter, Anaxibia, who married Pelias, king of Iolcus. Her mother was perhaps Bias' second wife, Proëtus' daughter Iphianassa. Bias was succeeded on his throne by Talaüs.

Bistonians or **Bistones.** A Thracian tribe. Some Roman writers place the Bistonians in 'the Thracian Chersonese and say that Polymestor was one of their kings. Earlier writers, including Herodotus, locate them on the south shore of Thrace east of the Nestos River, where Lake Bistonis bore their name. The city of Abdera, in this region, was founded by Heracles after his battle with the notorious Bistonian king Diomedes, who kept man-eating mares.

Bithynia. The most northwesterly part of Asia Minor, bordering the Black Sea and the Sea of Marmara. Bithynia was the home of Baucis and Philemon.

Black Corcyra. The island now called Korčula, off the Yugoslav coast. This island, one of the group of large islands south of Split, was named for Corcyra, daughter of the Phliasian river-god Asopus. It shares this distinction with Corcyra (Corfu).

Black Sea. The large inland sea north of Asia Minor. The northern coast of Asia Minor was the home of the Amazons, as well as of many historical tribes that figure in myths. Colchis lay at the eastern end of the Black Sea, and the Crimean Peninsula in the north was the land of the Taurians. The Argonauts, having entered the sea through the Bosporus, in the southwest, escaped from it by sailing up the Ister (Danube) in the west. Near the mouth of this river was White Island, one of the Islands of the Blessed. The sea was called by the ancients the Euxine.

Boeotia. The region of Greece lying to the north and west of Attica. Bounded by the range of the Cithaeron Mountains on the south and by Phocis and Locris to the northwest, Boeotia lies between the Euboean Sea and the Gulf of Corinth. Its two major, and rival, cities were Thebes, in the southeastern part, and Orchomenus, in the northwest on the shores of Lake Copaïs. The Helicon Range lay in the west. Boeotia was in both a strategic and a vulnerable position, since all land routes to Attica and the Peloponnesus ran through Boeotian territory.

Bona Dea. An ancient and obscure Roman goddess. The real name of the Bona Dea (which is a title meaning merely "the Good Goddess") was Fauna. The god Faunus was said to be either married or otherwise related to her. The Bona Dea, exclusively a goddess of women, seems to have been a deity connected with fertility.

Boötes. See Ursa Major.

Boreades. Sons of Boreas (North Wind). Zetes and Calaïs are often referred to by this epithet.

Boreas. The north wind and the god of that wind. Boreas, a son of Eos and Astraeüs, lived in Thrace, which lay to the north of Greece. He and Zephyrus, the west wind, were more often personified than were the other two winds. Boreas was sometimes represented in art with snake tails in place of feet. Boreas' best-known deed was to court Oreithyia, a daughter of Erechtheus, king of Athens. The Athenians, who hated all Thracians after their experience with Tereus, disapproved of the match. Boreas therefore swooped down on Oreithyia as she played by the Ilissus River and carried her off to his home in Thrace. There she bore him two winged sons, Zetes and Calaïs, and two daughters, Cleopatra and Chione. The god is said to have had two other sons, Lycurgus and Butes, by different women. Boreas must have settled his quarrel with the Athenians for, centuries later, the god saved them from invasion by destroying Persian ships. He also saved the inhabitants of Megalopolis, in Arcadia, from a Spartan attack, and was thereafter worshiped in that city above all other gods.

Zetes and Calaïs incurred the enmity of Heracles as they sailed together with the Argonauts. He later killed them on the island of Tenos and set up two pillars over their graves. One of these swayed whenever Boreas blew on it. Although Boreas seems to have been on the whole a faithful husband, it was reported that he fathered twelve stallions on some mares belonging to the Trojan king Erichthonius. As might have been expected, these horses could run like the wind. [Apollodorus 3.15.1–4; Apollonius Rhodius 1.211–223, 1.1302–1308; Ovid, *Metamorphoses*, 6.682–722; Hesiod, *Theogony*, 378–380; Homer, *Iliad*, 20.221–229; Pausanias 1.19.5, 5.19.1, 8.27.14, 8.36.6.]

Borus. A son of Perieres. He married Peleus' daughter Polydora. [Pausanias 3.13.1.]

Bosporus. The name of two straits leading to the Black Sea. The Thracian

Bosporus, dividing Asian from European Turkey today, connects the Sea of Marmara with the Black Sea. The Cimmerian Bosporus (the modern Kerch Strait) connects the Sea of Azov, formerly called Lake Maeotis, with the Black Sea. This passage, once also known as the Strait of Maeotis, was called the Bosporus (Cow's Ford) after the cow-woman Io had crossed it during her wanderings.

Bowl, The. See CROW; MASTUSIUS.

Brasiae. A town on the coast of northern Laconia. Brasiae is known solely for its unique version of the infancy of DIONYSUS [A].

Brauron. A town in eastern Attica. Brauron was known primarily as the cult center of Brauronian Artemis. The natives claimed that their ancient statue of the goddess was the one stolen from the Taurians by Orestes and Iphigeneia.

Briareüs, Obriareüs, or **Aegaeon.** One of the HUNDRED-HANDED. When the other gods revolted against Zeus, Thetis summoned Briareüs (whom men called Aegaeon) to his aid. The monster, a son of Poseidon or of Ge and Uranus, quickly put down the rebellion and was rewarded with Zeus's daughter Cymopola. Although Briareüs' regular duty was, with his brothers, Gyes and Cottus, to guard the Titans in Tartarus, he was called in to arbitrate a dispute over the patronship of Corinth between Helius and Poseidon. He awarded the citadel of Acrocorinth to the sun-god, the isthmus to the sea-god. [Homer, *Iliad*, 1.401–406; Hesiod, *Theogony*, 817; *Titanomachia* 3; Pausanias 2.1.6, 2.4.6.]

Briseïs. Achilles' concubine. Achilles carried off Briseïs from the city of Lyrnessus after killing her husband, parents, and three brothers during his sack of their city. When Agamemnon was forced to give up his own concubine, Chryseïs, he took Briseïs. Achilles thereupon refused to fight with the Greeks and did not relent until after the death of Patroclus. At this time Briseïs was returned to Achilles. [Homer, *Iliad*, 1.181–187, 1.318–348, 19.246–302.]

Britomartis. A Cretan goddess. Britomartis was the daughter of Zeus and Carme, daughter of Eubulus. She loved the hunt and was a favorite of Artemis. Minos, king of Crete, pursued the young woman amorously until, in desperation, she leaped into the sea. She fell into the nets of some fisherman and, according to some versions of her story, was thus saved. In the more usual (and probably the original) version, she became immortal at the moment of her supposed death, as did Ino under similar circumstances. Her title as a goddess was Dictynna, which the Greeks translated as "Lady of the Nets." This title was also given by some late Classical writers to Artemis, whose cult absorbed some of the features of the Cretan goddess' cult. Britomartis was worshiped on the island of Aegina under the name of Aphaea. She had shrines at Sparta as well. [Pausanias 2.30.2–3; Diodorus Siculus 5.76.3–4.]

Bromios. An epithet (meaning "Thunderer") of DIONYSUS [H].

Broteas. A son of the Phrygian king Tantalus. Broteas was credited with carving the oldest image of Cybele on a rock named Coddinus, north of Mount Sipylus. Later Broteas incurred the anger of Artemis by refusing to honor her. The goddess drove him mad and, believing himself immune to flames, he threw himself into a fire and died. Some say that Broteas was the father of Tantalus, the first husband of Clytemnestra. [Apollodorus "Epitome" 2.2; Pausanias 3.22.4.]

Brygeian Islands. See APSYRTIDES.

Brygeians or **Brygi.** A tribe in Epeirus. Odysseus led the Thesprotians against the Brygeians, but the latter, supported by Ares, defeated him. [*Telegony* 1.]

Bull, The. See TAURUS.

bull of Minos. See MINOTAUR.

Bunus. A king of Corinth. When Aeëtes, the first king of Ephyra (Corinth), departed for Colchis, he left the kingdom to Bunus, a son of Hermes and Alcidamea. [Pausanias 2.3.10.]

Busiris. An Egyptian king. A son of Poseidon and Epaphus' daughter Lysianassa, Busiris ruled Egypt. During a prolonged drought he took the advice of a Cypriot seer and sacrificed to Zeus strangers to his land. HERACLES [H] defeated and killed him. [Apollodorus 2.5.11; Hyginus, *Fabulae*, 31, 51.]

Butes (1). An Argonaut. Butes was a son of Teleon or Poseidon and Zeuxippe, daughter of the Athenian river-god Eridanus. He joined the crew of the *Argo*, but jumped overboard on the homeward journey and swam toward the Sirens, who were singing on their island of Anthemoëssa. Aphrodite took pity on him and transported him to Lilybaeüm, in Sicily, where she bore his son, Eryx. Butes was also the father of Polycaon. (See also BUTES, 2.) [Apollonius Rhodius 1.95–96, 4.912–921.]

Butes (2). Son of Pandion, king of Athens, and Zeuxippe. This Butes, who may be the same as the Argonaut Butes, was a twin brother of Erechtheus. He married his brother's daughter, Chthonia. On the death of Pandion, Erechtheus received the rule, Butes the priesthood of Athena and of Poseidon Erechtheus. After his death he was himself honored with sacrifices in the Erechtheüm. [Apollodorus 3.14.8–3.15.1.]

Butes (3). A son of Boreas. Butes plotted against his half-brother Lycurgus, king of Thrace, and was exiled. He and his followers took the island of Strongyle (later called Naxos) and became pirates. Repulsed in a raid on Euboea, they went to Drius in Phthiotis and tried to carry off a group of bacchants. Butes made the mistake of raping one, named Coronis. She complained to Dionysus. The god drove Butes mad and he jumped into a well and drowned. [Diodorus Siculus 5.50.1–5.]

Buthrotum. A port in Epeirus opposite the island of Corcyra. Buthrotum was founded by the Trojan Helenus, who had been brought there by Neoptolemus after the fall of Troy.

Byblis and **Caunus.** Twin children of Miletus and Cyaneë, daughter of the river-god Maeander. Byblis fell in love with her brother. When, after much anguish, she confessed her passion to him, Caunus was horrified. The girl soon became so importunate that Caunus left his native city of Miletus forever and founded a new city in southern Caria, which he named for himself. Byblis went mad and wandered everywhere in search of her brother. Finally, inconsolable in her grief, she was transformed into a spring. She was said by some to be the eponym of the Phoenician city of Byblus.

Byblus. An ancient Phoenician city, now the village of Jubayl on the Lebanese coast. Io found her son Epaphus being cared for by the queen of Byblus after his abduction by the Curetes. Some say that the city was named for the Miletian girl Byblis.

C

Cabeiri. Obscure divinities of Phrygia and certain islands of the northern Aegean Sea. The Cabeiri were prominently worshiped on the three large islands clustered near the Aegean end of the Hellespont—Samothrace, Lemnos, and Imbros—and also had a cult near Thebes, but their worship is thought to have originated on the mainland in Phrygia. They were honored in the Samothracian mysteries, which were second in importance only to the Eleusinian mysteries. They shared these rites with the Great Gods of Samothrace, who were often identified by late Classical writers as Demeter or Rhea, Hermes, and other Olympian divinities.

For two thousand years writers have speculated about the identity and nature of the Cabeiri. It is now generally believed that they were originally fertility-spirits whose reputation for bringing safety and good fortune, as well as good crops, spread widely. In time the local rites grew into a popular mystery cult that eventually attracted even so prominent an initiate as Alexander the Great. It is not clear whether the Cabeiri were regarded as attendants of the variously identified "Great Gods" or whether that epithet was their own. The Argonauts are said to have followed the advice of Orpheus and paused at Samothrace in order to be initiated into the mysteries and thereby gain added protection on their voyage.

Cacus. A son of Vulcan. A fire-breathing giant, Cacus stole cattle of Geryon that HERACLES [H] was leading home through Italy. He dragged them by the tails to his cave at Rome so that their owner could not follow their trail. Heracles would not have found the missing cattle if one of them had not lowed from Cacus' cave as Heracles' herd was passing by. Heracles killed the giant and was thereafter honored as a hero by the people of the region. [Vergil, *Aeneïd*, 8.193–270.]

Cadmeia. A city founded by Cadmus. Cadmeia, atop a hill north of the Boeotian river Asopus, was the nucleus of the great city of THEBES that grew up about the foot of the hill. After the name was changed, the old citadel was still called Cadmeia, which remained also a standard poetic name for Thebes.

Cadmus. The founder and king of Cadmeia, later called Thebes.

A. Cadmus was a son of Agenor, king of Tyre or Sidon, and Telephassa or Argiope. When his sister, Europa, was kidnaped by Zeus, Cadmus and his brothers were ordered by their father to find her or never to return home. Tele-

140

phassa sailed with them on their mission. The brothers seem to have had little hope of success, for they took with them enough followers to found colonies in several lands. Phoenix settled in Phoenicia (the land from which the expedition had started), Cilix in Cilicia, Thasus on the island off Thrace that bears his name. Cadmus left a small party under his kinsman Membliarus on the island of Calliste (later Thera) and still had a considerable company with him when, after a long time, he came to Boeotia.

His brothers having dropped off at their respective new homes, Cadmus reached Thrace with his mother. They were welcomed there and stayed until Telephassa died. Then Cadmus moved on with his followers to Delphi, in order to ask the oracle's advice. He was told to give up the search for Europa and settle where a cow would lie down. Following the oracle's advice, Cadmus found a cow, or bought one from King Pelagon, that had markings like full moons on its sides. He drove the indefatigable animal all the way from Phocis to southern Boeotia. There, on one of three hills near the Asopus River, it at last sank to the earth.

On this spot Cadmus built a town that he called Cadmeia. His first move, however, was to sacrifice to his patroness, the Phoenician goddess Onca, whom the Greeks identified with Athena. He sent several of his men to fetch water for the rite from a nearby spring. When they did not return, he went to investigate and found a dragon feasting on their bodies. Cadmus killed the snake with a stone, unaware that it was the guardian of a spring sacred to Ares, the chief god of the region. Athena appeared and directed Cadmus to draw the dragon's teeth and sow half of them. (Athena reserved the other half, which she later gave to Aeëtes, king of Colchis.)

Cadmus had no sooner plowed the teeth under than armed men began springing up from the ground. They immediately began to fight one another, perhaps because Cadmus flung a stone among them which they thought was thrown by one of their own company. The ensuing battle claimed the lives of all but five of the Sparti, or Sown-men. These five brothers—Echion, Udaeüs, Chthonius, Hyperenor, and Pelorus—made peace with one another and with Cadmus. To atone for killing the dragon, Cadmus had to serve Ares for a "great year" or "eternal year," a period of eight ordinary years. At the end of this time Athena made him king of the new city that he built on the hill.

According to a less picturesque story, Cadmus and his Phoenician invaders merely conquered the Hyantes and Aones, the two Boeotian tribes that occupied the region. The Hyantes they drove out of the land, but the Aones, who sued for peace, were allowed to remain.

B. Cadmus was honored by Zeus with the gift of Harmonia, daughter of Ares and Aphrodite (or of Zeus and Electra), as his bride. The gods attended the wedding, a compliment that they were to pay no other mortal but Peleus, when he married Thetis. The occasion was as elegant as might have been expected. Music was provided by Apollo and the Muses, and the immortal guests brought splendid gifts. Hermes presented a lyre, Athena (or Hephaestus, Aphrodite, Europa, or Cadmus) gave Harmonia a necklace made by Hephaestus and a beautiful robe, Demeter made a gift of corn. Only one incident marred the wedding. Demeter, becoming infatuated with Harmonia's handsome brother, Iasion, consented to lie with him in a thrice-plowed field. Zeus killed the young man with a thunderbolt for his presumption. Harmonia's necklace and robe were to bring disaster upon their later owners (see ALCMEON, A, B), but she herself was untouched by the curse that seems to have attached itself to the objects.

It was a different curse that ruined Cadmus' married life, which had begun so auspiciously. Ares, though he presumably consented to having Cadmus for a son-in-law, never forgave him for killing the sacred snake. Only one of Cadmus' children—his son, Polydorus—did not come to grief. Harmonia bore Cadmus four daughters—Autonoë, Semele, Ino, and Agave—as well as the son. Autonoë married Aristaeüs. Their only son, Actaeon, was torn apart by his own hounds. Semele was visited by Zeus and became by him the mother of Dionysus, but was destroyed by lightning when she insisted on seeing her lover in his true form. Ino and her husband, Athamas, incurred Hera's anger by protecting Semele's infant son. The goddess brought a fit of madness upon them and, in a frenzy, Athamas killed one of their two sons and Ino leaped into the sea with the other. When Dionysus returned to Cadmeia as a god, accompanied by his disorderly band of bacchants, Agave (and Cadmus) joined them. Pentheus, Agave's straitlaced son by Echion, leader of the Sparti, tried vainly to imprison the god. While spying on the bacchants on Mount Cithaeron, Pentheus was torn to pieces by his own mother and her sisters (Ino being still in Thebes, in some versions). In their Dionysian madness, they mistook him for a lion's whelp.

Bowed by grief, Cadmus and Harmonia emigrated in their old age to Illyria. According to a myth mentioned by Hyginus [Fabulae 240, 254], Agave married the Illyrian king Lycotherses, but killed him in order to give his throne to her father. The more familiar story is that Cadmus and his wife, on the advice of an oracle, went to the land of the Encheleans, an obscure, barbarian tribe of Illyria. Riding in an oxcart they led the tribe to repeated victories in various wars. When the Encheleans began rifling the shrines of Apollo they were routed, but Ares saved Cadmus and Harmonia. Transforming them into snakes, he sent them to live in the Elysian Fields. Some Classical writers regarded this as a final punishment for the killing of Ares' sacred snake. More probably it was a sign of perpetual honor, for the spirit of a dead hero was widely believed to return in the form of a benevolent snake.

The Thebans honored Cadmus as the founder of their city. They called their citadel Cadmeia and were often themselves referred to as Cadmeians. They claimed descent from the Sparti, born of the dragon's teeth. For some reason Cadmus also had a hero shrine at Sparta. The people of Brasiae, on the

Laconian coast, claimed that Cadmus, when Semele's son was born, had flung mother and baby into the sea in a chest, which came ashore at Brasiae. This tale, known only in Brasiae, was no doubt intended to lend dignity to the history of an insignificant town. The inhabitants of the port of Lindus, in Rhodes, claimed that Cadmus, when buffeted by the winds during his voyage in search of Europa, had promised to dedicate a cauldron to Poseidon if he survived, and did so at Lindus. Herodotus believed that Cadmus taught Dionysus' rites to Melampus, who taught them to the Greeks. Perhaps Cadmus' most important act was to introduce the Phoenician alphabet to Greece, a deed with which he was widely credited.

Cadmus was known to all Greek writers and parts of his story were often referred to. The fullest narrative is that of Apollodorus [3.4.1–2, 3.5.2, 3.5.4]. Cadmus appears prominently in Euripides' *Bacchants*, the story of Pentheus, and is frequently alluded to in his *Phoenician Women*. Interesting details are added by Herodotus [2.49, 4.147], Diodorus Siculus [5.58.2], and Pausanias [3.24.3, 9.5.1–3, 9.12.1–3.]

caduceus. A wand borne by HERMES [A]. The caduceus, or *kerykeion*, is a rod entwined by snakes and sometimes furnished with small wings near the tip. It was the badge of Hermes' office as herald of the gods and as guide of the dead, though in the latter capacity he is occasionally shown carrying merely a forked stick. Some scholars believe that the caduceus was originally decorated with ribbons rather than snakes.

Caeculus. A Latin leader in the war against the Trojans. Caeculus, having been conceived when a spark from a hearthfire flew into his mother's lap, was regarded as a son of the fire-god Vulcan. He was born among herds in the country, exposed by his mother, and found near the hearth at Jupiter's shrine. He founded the city of Praeneste. Later he fought as an ally of Turnus against Aeneas' forces. [Vergil, *Aeneïd*, 7.678–690.]

Caeneus. A Lapith chieftain. Caeneus was born a girl, Caenis, daughter of the Thessalian king Elatus. She was very beautiful, but refused to take a husband. Poseidon saw her one day on the seashore and violated her. Afterward, when he offered to grant whatever boon she might choose, she asked him to make her a man so that such an indignity might never happen to her again. Poseidon not only kept his promise, but made Caenis—now Caeneus—invulnerable to weapons as well. Caeneus became one of the leaders of the Lapiths. During the famous battle between the Lapiths and Centaurs at Peirithoüs' wedding, Caeneus killed several Centaurs. They were unable to harm his body with spears or swords, but they finally beat him on the head with fir trees, or else heaped a great weight of them on him, until he was driven into the ground. According to Ovid [*Metamorphoses* 12.169–209, 12.459–535], Caeneus was changed into a bird. Caeneus had one son, Coronus.

Caenis. See CAENEUS.

Calaïs. See ZETES.

Calaureia. An island (now called Poros) in the Saronic Gulf off the Argolid coast near Troezen. Calaureia, the site of an ancient oracle of Apollo, was traded by that god to Poseidon in return for the sea-god's relinquishment of his claims to Delphi.

Calchas. A seer attached to the Greek forces during the Trojan War. Calchas, a son of Thestor, enjoyed such a reputation before the war broke out that Agamemnon came in person to his home in Megara to persuade him to accompany the army. While there the commander-in-chief built a temple to Artemis, perhaps to please Calchas, who may have been her priest. The seer is said to have predicted when Achilles was only nine years old that Troy could not be taken without his aid. When the Greek fleet was assembled at Aulis to prepare for the voyage to Troy, and the leaders were sacrificing hecatombs to the gods beside a spring, a snake with a blood-red back glided from beneath the altar, climbed a plane tree that overhung the spring, and devoured a sparrow with her eight babies. Thereupon Zeus turned the snake to stone. Calchas interpreted this omen to mean that the Greeks would fight at Troy for nine years and would take the city in the tenth.

The ships were becalmed, however, and it seemed that they would never leave Aulis. Calchas now divined that Agamemnon had offended Artemis with a careless boast. He announced that the goddess would send favorable winds only if Agamemnon were to sacrifice to her his daughter Iphigeneia. At Troy, Calchas again made a pronouncement unfavorable to the commander-in-chief: Agamemnon's capture of Chryseïs had led to Apollo's punishment of the Greek forces with a pestilence. In the last year of the war a seer described the steps necessary to the capture of Troy. Some say that this service was somewhat belatedly rendered by Calchas, but it is more often attributed to the captured Trojan Helenus.

Calchas' art seems to have been susceptible to outside influences, especially when they were reinforced with gold. He is said to have been deeply involved in the treacherous plot that led to the death of Palamedes. Considering that Calchas had so often held the fate of the entire Greek army in his hands, the manner of his death was somewhat anticlimactic. He had learned early in his career that he was fated to die when he met a diviner better than himself. This event occurred not long after the fall of Troy. Perhaps because he knew that Athena's anger at the Greeks on account of Cassandra's rape by Ajax would result in the destruction of the fleet, he did not return to Greece but went overland to Colophon, in Asia Minor, accompanied by several of the Greek leaders. There he encountered the diviner Mopsus, a grandson of Teiresias.

Calchas seems to have conceived an instant dislike for this potential rival, for his first move was to ask him what he doubtless imagined to be an unanswerable question: the number of figs on a particularly prolific wild fig tree. Mopsus, without a moment's hesitation, replied, "Ten thousand, one bushel, and a fig left over." Someone evidently took the trouble to count the figs, for

Mopsus' prediction turned out to be correct down to the last fig. Mopsus then asked Calchas how many pigs a certain pregnant sow was carrying. Calchas hazarded a guess that there were eight. "Wrong!" Mopsus corrected him. "There are nine, they are all male, and they will be born tomorrow at the sixth hour." When it came about precisely as Mopsus had foretold, Calchas' chagrin was unbounded. He went into a decline and soon died of a broken heart, or else of sheer envy of his rival's powers. He was buried at Notium by his Greek companions. According to the *Cypria* [1], Calchas had gone to Colophon to bury Teiresias, but this story differs so much from the usual tradition of Teiresias' death that it may result from confusion with the tale of Calchas' own death in Colophon. [Homer, *Iliad*, 1.68–100, 2.299–332; Aeschylus, *Agamemnon*, 104–216; Apollodorus 3.13.8, "Epitome" 3.15, 3.20–21, 5.8–9, 5.23–6.4.]

Callidice. A queen of Thesprotia. During his inland journey after killing Penelope's suitors in Ithaca, Odysseus came to Thesprotia. Queen Callidice married him and bore a son, Polypoetes. Odysseus led her people against the Brygeians, but was defeated. When Callidice died Odysseus left the rule to Polypoetes and returned to Penelope in Ithaca. [*Telegony* 1; Apollodorus "Epitome" 7.35.]

Calliope. One of the nine MUSES. Calliope, a daughter of Zeus and Mnemosyne, is sometimes said to have been the chief of the Muses. She was the mother of Orpheus and Linus by the Thracian king Oeagrus, or else by Apollo. Some say that she was also the mother of the Thracian king Rhesus by the river-god Strymon. Hyginus [*Poetica Astronomica* 2.7] explained Orpheus' death as the result of Aphrodite's revenge on Calliope, who, when asked by Zeus to arbitrate between Aphrodite and Persephone in their feud over Adonis, had awarded him for half a year to each. [Hesiod, *Theogony*, 53–80; Apollodorus 1.3.1–4.]

Callirrhoë or **Callirhoë** (1). A daughter of Acheloüs. Callirrhoë married ALCMEON, but unwittingly sent him to his death in search of a bride gift. Their two sons, Acarnan and Amphoterus, grew miraculously to manhood overnight and avenged Alcmeon, as Callirrhoë requested in a prayer to her lover, Zeus.

Callirrhoë (2). A daughter of Oceanus. Callirrhoë had a son, the three-headed cowherd Geryon, by Chrysaor, an offspring of Medusa. [Hesiod, *Theogony*, 287–288.]

Callirrhoë (3). A daughter of the Trojan river-god Scamander. Callirrhoë married Tros, the eponym of Troy, and bore three sons—Ilus, eponym of Ilium; Assaracus; and Ganymede—and a daughter, Cleopatra. [Apollodorus 3.12.3.]

Calliste. See THERA.

Callisto. An Arcadian favorite of Artemis. Callisto was variously called a nymph or a daughter of Lycaon, Nycteus, or Ceteus. The details of her fate, too, have many versions, but the principal events are the same. Callisto spent her time in the Arcadian Mountains as a favorite hunting companion of Artemis. Some say that, like many other of Artemis' attendants, she had taken a vow of chastity. Zeus saw her one day as she was resting alone in the woods. Disguising himself as Apollo, or as Artemis, he gained the innocent girl's confidence and promptly abused it. As a result, Callisto became a bear. Some say that Zeus transformed her in order to cover his embarrassment when Hera spied on them; others blame the jealous Hera for the transformation; still others cite Artemis' anger over the girl's breaking of her vow.

There are many versions, too, of Callisto's end. One is that Artemis shot her while hunting, Hera having kindly pointed out the bear to her. Hermes, sent by Zeus, rescued Zeus's baby, Arcas, from Callisto's womb and gave it to his mother, Maia, to bring up. According to another story, Arcas, when grown to manhood, saw the bear in the woods and shot at it. Another tale has it that the bear, which had been brought to Lycaon as a gift by some goatherds, wandered into the forbidden shrine of Zeus Lycaeüs and was about to be shot by Arcas and the other Arcadians for this sacrilege. In all these versions, Zeus immortalized Callisto by transporting her to the stars as the constellation Arctos, the Great Bear. Either then or later Arcas became the nearby constellation Arctophylax, which appears to be guarding the Bear. The relentless Hera was further offended by this glorification of her rival and extracted a promise from her old nurse, the sea-goddess Tethys, and her venerable husband, Oceanus, that they would never permit Callisto to enter their realm, as the other constellations do when they set. The Great Bear, therefore, is doomed to revolve ceaselessly about the North Star. [Apollodorus 3.8.2–3.9.1; *Astronomy* 4; Ovid, *Metamorphoses*, 2.409–531; Hyginus, *Fabulae*, 176–177, and *Poetica Astronomica*, 2.1.]

Calyce. A daughter of Aeolus and Enarete. Calyce married Aëthlius and became the mother of Endymion either by her husband or by Zeus. [Apollodorus 1.7.3, 1.7.5.]

Calydon. The eponym of the Aetolian city of Calydon. Son of Aetolus and Pronoë, Calydon married Aeolia, who bore Epicasta and Protogeneia. [Apollodorus 1.7.7.]

Calydon. The principal city of Aetolia. Calydon and Pleuron were reputed to have been founded by the two sons of Aetolus from whom they take their names. Calydon appears to have been the main seat of the Eleian invaders who ruled much of Aetolia down to the time of Oeneus, and perhaps beyond. The struggle between these conquerors and the natives whom Homer called Curetes continued through six generations to Meleager's day. Several marriages of Oeneus' shadowy forebears may have represented shaky alliances between the two groups. If this is the case, the quarrel between Calydonians and Curetes and that between Meleager and the sons of Thestius may be the same conflict. In any case, the first name in the Calydonian dynasty to be associated with mythological events of any consequence was Oeneus; the last names were those of several of his children. Calydon seems to have come suddenly into prominence with Oeneus, who played host to at least one god, Dionysus, and to famous visitors from Thebes, Corinth, and Argos—namely, Heracles, Bellerophon, Alcmeon, Agamemnon, and Menelaüs.

The well-known Calydonian boar hunt drew many Greek leaders to Calydon and Oeneus' son Meleager, though short-lived, became one of the most admired of Greek heroes. Another of Oeneus' sons, Tydeus, became known for his prowess only after he was banished. This exile seems to have been engineered by Oeneus' brothers. His brother Agrius and Agrius' sons overthrew and imprisoned the old king himself as soon as Tydeus was out of the way. Oeneus was rescued by his grandson Diomedes, who turned over the rule to Oeneus' son-in-law Andraemon. Andraemon's son, Thoas, led forty Aetolian ships to Troy. He returned to Aetolia, but little is heard of Calydon after this time.

Calydonian boar hunt. Oeneus, king of Calydon, regularly sacrificed the firstfruits of each harvest to the gods. One year he forgot to include Artemis in the rites. The goddess repaid Oeneus for this insult by sending a gigantic boar to ravage the land. It destroyed the crops, killed men and cattle, and so terrified the Calydonians that they did not dare to venture out to the fields when it was time for sowing. Oeneus asked other Greek cities for help, offering the boar's skin as a prize for the man who drew first blood. The cities sent many of their best men in response. Even the Calydonians' often hostile neighbors the Curetes joined in the hunt. Among the assembled company was the Arcadian huntress Atalanta. Her fellow Arcadians Ancaeüs and Cepheus and a few others at first refused to hunt with a woman. Meleager, Oeneus' son, who happened to be in love with Atalanta, forced them to remain in the hunt, perhaps reminding them that they had enjoyed his father's hospitality for nine days.

The hunt began. Ancaeüs and two or three other hunters were killed by the boar; Eurytion by his friend Peleus, through some accident. Atalanta is said by many to have shot the boar with an arrow, after which Amphiaraüs drew second blood. All accounts agree that it was Meleager who killed the beast and was awarded its skin. Homer [*Iliad* 9.543–599] says that a quarrel broke out between the Curetes and the Calydonians over the prize and war ensued. Many later writers say that the quarrel was between Meleager and his mother's brothers, the sons of Thestius, who were angered by their nephew's gift of the hide to Atalanta. For the fatal results, in either event, of the quarrel, see MELEAGER.

Although the Calydonian boar hunt is the subject of no surviving epic, it was often represented in Greek art and was well known to all writers. Ovid's account [*Metamorphoses* 8.268–546], in verse, and that of Apollodorus [1.8. 2–3], in prose, are the fullest.

Calypso. A daughter of Atlas. Calypso was a goddess or nymph who, like Circe, was associated with a particular locality—the island of Ogygia—where she lived alone. She was unknown to mythology except in connection with ODYSSEUS [J], who was washed ashore on her island after being shipwrecked. She fell in love with him and kept him with her for seven years, but Odysseus, yearning for his home and wife, spurned her offer to make him ageless and immortal if he would remain in Ogygia. At last Zeus sent Hermes to command Calypso to let Odysseus go. She did so and provided well for his voyage. She was said by some writers to have been the mother of Nausinoüs and Nausithoüs or of Teledamus, or Telegonus, by Odysseus. Telegonus is usually called Odysseus' son by Circe. [Homer, *Odyssey*, 1.13–15, 1.48–50, 1.84–87, 5.55–268, 7.244–269.]

Cameirus. One of the earliest cities on the island of Rhodes. Some say that Cameirus was the scene of the tragic death of Catreus at the hands of his son, Althaemenes. The eponym of this city, Cameirus, was a grandson of Helius and Rhode.

Camenae. Roman goddesses or nymphs identified with the Muses. The Camenae were worshiped from early times in Italy and had a sacred grove at Rome, but their functions are obscure.

Camilla. A Volscian queen. Camilla was the daughter of Metabus and Casmilla. When Metabus was driven from the rule of Privernum, he took with him his infant daughter, feeding her with mare's milk. She grew up a warrior, devoted to Diana. She led the Volscians to war against AENEAS [C] as allies of Turnus and was killed from ambush by Arruns. [Vergil, *Aeneïd*, Book 12.]

Canace. A daughter of Aeolus. There are two accounts of Canace's life which appear to be unrelated, although they are not necessarily so. According to one, she had several children (Hopleus, Nireus, Epopeus, Aloeüs, and Triopas) by Poseidon, who came to her in the form of a bull. According to another, she committed incest with her brother Macareus and either killed herself in shame or was destroyed by her father. Macareus committed suicide. [Apollodorus 1.7.3–4; Hyginus, *Fabulae*, 238, 242.]

Cancer. See CRAB.

Canens. See PICUS.

Canicula. See CANIS MAJOR.

Canis Major (The Dog) and **Canis Minor (The Lesser Dog).** Two constellations. The dog represented in the larger of these groups of stars is said to have been Orion's hound, Icarius' dog Maera, or Laelaps, the hound that pursued the Teumessian fox. Canis Minor, rather than Canis Major, was sometimes identified as Maera. Canis Minor was called Canicula by the Romans, and Procyon by the Greeks. Procyon was also the name of the single star in the dog's tongue, as it is today. Both the Lesser Dog and the bright star Sirius (the dog star), in the head of Canis Major, were thought to bring disastrous droughts when they rose.

Canobus or **Canopus.** An ancient Egyptian city near Alexandria. It was at either Canobus or Memphis that the heifer-woman Io ended her long wanderings and bore her son Epaphus beside the Nile.

Canthus. An Argonaut from Euboea. A son of Canethus, son of Abas, Canthus willingly joined the Argonauts at his father's bidding. Little is known of him except that he was a friend of Polyphemus, whom his companions left behind with Heracles in Mysia. It was to get news of Polyphemus that Canthus joined four other ARGONAUTS [R] in a vain search for Heracles in the Libyan Desert. Coming across the flock of Caphaurus or Cephalion, a Libyan, he started to drive the sheep to the *Argo*, but was killed by their owner. Some say that Eribotes was killed with him. [Apollonius Rhodius 4.1464–1501.]

Capaneus. One of the SEVEN AGAINST THEBES. Capaneus was a son of Hipponoüs and Astynome, a sister of Adrastus. His wife, Evadne, bore him Sthenelus. Scaling the walls during the Argive siege of Thebes, he boasted that he would fire the city even if Zeus himself opposed it. He was killed with a thunderbolt for his presumption. Evadne leaped onto the pyre on which he was cremated. Stesichorus claimed that Capaneus was resurrected by the healer Asclepius. [Apollodorus 3.6.3, 3.6.7, 3.7.1, 3.10.3.]

Caphareus, Cape. A rocky promontory at the southeastern tip of Euboea. This notoriously dangerous spot was the scene of the destruction of most of the Greek fleet as it returned from the Trojan War. Nauplius was said to have lighted false beacons here to lead the ships onto the rocks.

Caphaurus or **Cephalion.** A wellborn Libyan shepherd. Amphithemis or Garamas, Caphaurus' father by a Tritonian nymph, was a son of Apollo and Acacallis, daughter of Minos. Caphaurus killed Canthus and Eribotes, both ARGONAUTS [R], in order to protect his sheep, but the thieves' companions killed him in turn and took the sheep. [Apollonius Rhodius 4.1485–1501.]

Capra (The Goat). A constellation. The goat represented in this star cluster is either Amaltheia, who gave milk for the infant Zeus, or merely a goat placed in the sky by Zeus to commemorate the services of Aegipan (Goat-Pan). (Since Capricorn is said to be Aegipan, the latter explanation seems unlikely.) Two nearby stars are known as the Kids. These are either the twin offspring of Amaltheia or Aex and Helice, daughters of an obscure Olenus, who were also Zeus's nurses, though Aex was perhaps a goat. Hyginus [*Poetica Astronomica* 2.9] says of this second identification that father and daughters were the eponyms of widely scattered cities in the Peloponnesus, Boeotia, and Haemonia. It would seem more likely that all three, if they were originally connected at all, belonged to some myth, now lost, of Peloponnesian Achaea. In this region were cities named Olenus, Helice, Aegae, and Aegium. Either of the last two might have claimed Aex as an eponym.

Capricorn. A constellation. This group of stars, in the form of a goat with the lower half of a fish, represents AEGIPAN, who was immortalized by Zeus for several favors to him and the other Olympians. [Hyginus, *Poetica Astronomica*, 2.28]

Capys. A Trojan ruler. A son of Assaracus, Capys became the father of Anchises by Hieromneme, daughter of the river-god Simöeis. [Homer, *Iliad*, 20.239; Apollodorus 3.12.2.]

Car. A son of Phoroneus, perhaps by his wife, Cerdo. Car became king of Megara, naming the citadel Caria for himself and instituting the worship of Demeter there. [Pausanias 1.39.5–6, 1.40.6.]

Caria. The southwestern part of Asia Minor. Caria was the home in historical times of the Carians; of the Caunians, an obscure and backward tribe believed by Herodotus to be aboriginal; and of Dorian and Ionian invaders who had colonized the coastal regions.

Caria. The citadel of Megara. It was said to have been named by Car, a son of Phoroneus who became king of Megara.

Carians. An ancient people, distinct from the Pelasgians, who were among the earliest inhabitants of Greece. The Carians were closely related to the Lelegians. Herodotus said, in fact, that they had been known as Lelegians when they occupied the Aegean islands. Although under Cretan domination, they were among the most important peoples of their age. Later, when they were driven from the islands to the mainland of southwestern Asia Minor by Ionians and Dorians, they called themselves Carians. (This region was still occupied by Carians in historical times, but most of them had been subjugated, particularly along the coast, by successive waves of invasion by Ionian and Dorian settlers.) Homer listed Carians, Lelegians, and Pelasgians as important allies of the Trojans in the war with the Greeks. Pausanias located a group of the Carians in Megara, where their eponym, an ancient Argive named Car, gave his name to the citadel, the Caria.

The Carians must have been widely dispersed during the centuries after the disintegration of Minoan power, for they were reported as mercenaries in the armies of many nations, including Egypt. The Greeks were unable to understand the Carian tongue, which is now believed not to have been Indo-European. If there is any truth in the legend that the Boeotian oracle of Ptoan Apollo spoke in Carian to an envoy of the Persian Mardonius, then small groups of Semitic-speaking people may have long remained in the region of Thebes, which traditionally was founded by a Phoenician, Cadmus. It is more likely, however, that the tale was invented to enhance the prestige of the oracle.

Carme. A daughter of Eubulus or Phoenix. Carme is scarcely known except as the mother by Zeus of the Cretan goddess Britomartis. According to Vergil's poem *Ciris*, in which she appears, she was later carried as a captive to Megara, where she became nursemaid to King Nisus' daughter, Scylla.

Carmenta or **Carmentis.** An obscure Roman goddess. Carmenta's original attributes and functions are not clearly known. She was said by Plutarch [*Parallel Lives*, "Romulus," 21.1–2] to have been worshiped by mothers as the Fate who presided over birth. She was also said to have adapted the Greek alphabet to the Latin language. As her cult diminished in importance, she was converted, at least in literature, into a mortal, the wife or mother of the Arcadian immigrant Evander. She was a prophetess, in whose honor an annual festival, the Carmentalia, was held.

Carnabon. A king of the Getae of Thrace. When Triptolemus appeared in his winged chariot drawn by snakes, Carnabon welcomed him. He soon grew envious, however, of the benefits the young man was bringing to his people. He seized Triptolemus and killed one of his miraculous snakes in order to prevent his escape. Demeter brought another snake to rescue her son and Triptolemus flew away in his chariot. The goddess placed the wicked king in the sky as the constellation Serpent-Holder, presumably as a warning to evildoers. [Hyginus, *Poetica Astronomica*, 2.14.]

Carpathus. An island lying midway between Rhodes and Crete. Carpathus was said by some writers to have been the location of the cave of Proteus, the seal-herder.

Carthage. A coastal city of North Africa, near modern Tunis. Carthage was traditionally founded by Dido, who sailed with colonists from Tyre. The earliest city was called Byrsa, a Phoenician word for "citadel" that the Greeks mistook for their similar word meaning "bull's-hide." When the city expanded, it was renamed Carthage, but the citadel kept the old name. Aeneas' fleet put in at Carthage, and the Trojan warrior fell in love with Dido. When he deserted the queen to pursue his destiny in Italy, she committed suicide. In historical times Carthage became the formidable enemy of Rome in the Punic Wars.

Cassandra. A Trojan prophetess. Cassandra was a daughter of Priam and Hecuba. As a young woman she caught the eye of Apollo, whose priestess she was. The god, hoping to win her favors, taught her the art of prophecy. Cassandra let him hope, but remained chaste. The frustrated god condemned her to the worst fate that can befall a seer: not to be taken seriously. Cassandra's first recorded prophecy was, according to some reports, believed, at least for a time. Before the birth of Paris she warned that the child would bring destruction on Troy. Since Cassandra was younger than Paris, this story is, to say the least, implausible, and the warning is often attributed to Aesacus. In any case, the parents exposed the infant. He was rescued and reared by shepherds. Later, when Cassandra recognized him, his family welcomed him home.

After this exceptional, and improbable, first instance, no one paid attention to Cassandra's frequent predictions of disaster. Some writers explain that Apollo had driven her mad, but it was traditional for the god's Sibyls to deliver oracles while in a state of mantic frenzy. Cassandra foretold that Paris' projected voyage to Sparta would bring calamity on Troy, but Priam let him go. At the end of the resulting war, she warned that the wooden horse was filled with Greek soldiers, but the Trojans dragged it inside their gates.

Being ignored was only one of Cassandra's misfortunes. Coroebus, son of the Phrygian king Mygdon, and Othryoneus of Cabesus both became Trojan allies in the hope of winning the hand of the mad but beautiful prophetess. The first was killed by either Diomedes or Neoptolemus, the second by Idomeneus. When Troy fell, the Locrian Ajax raped Cassandra at Athena's altar, overturning in his haste the goddess' statue. For this insult to herself, Athena destroyed many of the homeward-bound Greek ships. She did nothing, however, for the pious Cassandra, who was carried off as a slave and concubine by Agamemnon. Cassandra is said to have borne two sons, Teledamus and Pelops, by the Greek. On reaching Mycenae, she and the sons were murdered, together with her new master, by Clytemnestra and Aegisthus. She was buried near Amyclae, where she had a shrine under the name Alexandra.

Cassandra appears prominently in two Greek tragedies: Aeschylus' *Agamemnon*, in which, just before her death, she prophesies the bloody future of the house of Atreus; and Euripides' *Trojan Women*. See also Euripides, *Andromache*, 293–300; Homer, *Iliad*, 13.361–382, and *Odyssey*, 11.421–423; Apollodorus 3.12.5, "Epitome" 5.17, 5.22–23; *Cypria* 1; *Sack of Ilium* 1; Pausanias 2.16.6–7, 3.19.6, 3.26.5, 10.27.1.

Cassiopeia. The wife of Cepheus, king of Ethiopia. Because Cassiopeia claimed that she, or her daughter, Andromeda, was more beautiful than the Nereïds, Poseidon or Ammon sent a sea-monster to ravage the land. Cepheus prepared to sacrifice Andromeda, but PERSEUS [D] rescued her. At Cassiopeia's death Poseidon placed her among the stars in a chair—but on her back with her feet in the air, as further punishment for her pride. [Apollodorus 2.4.3; Hyginus, *Fabulae*, 64, and *Poetica Astronomica*, 10, 11.]

Castor. See DIOSCURI.

Catalogues of Women or **Eoiae.** A fragmentary catalogue of Greek mythological heroines. What little is left of this long series of sketches of women has been, for the most part, pieced together from brief passages quoted or summarized by ancient writers. There remain no extended narratives, but the fragments are a rich source of mythological details. The *Catalogues* were generally ascribed in Classical times to Hesiod. They are available in the volume of his works in the Loeb Classical Library.

Catamitus. See GANYMEDE.

Catreus. A son of Minos and Pasiphaë. Catreus ruled some part of Crete—no doubt the city named for him. He had a son, Althaemenes, and three daughters, Aërope, Clymene, and Apemosyne. An oracle warned him that one of these children would kill him. Althaemenes emigrated to Rhodes with Apemosyne in order to avoid this fate. Catreus gave his two remaining daughters to Nauplius to sell abroad. Nauplius, however, sold Aërope to Atreus (or Pleisthenes) as a wife and married Clymene himself. Growing old, the lonely Catreus wanted to leave his kingdom to his son. He therefore sailed for Rhodes. On landing, he and his crew were mistaken for pirates and Althaemenes killed Catreus. It was in order to preside at Catreus' funeral that Aërope's son Menelaüs sailed for Crete, leaving a treacherous guest, Paris, to be entertained at his Spartan palace by his fickle wife, Helen. [Apollodorus 3.1.2, 3.2.1–2, "Epitome" 3.3.]

Caunus. See BYBLIS.

Cebren. A river in the region of Troy; also, its god. The god was the father of Oenone, Paris' first wife, and of Hesperia (or Asterope), whom Aesacus loved.

Cebriones. A half-brother of Hector. Cebriones, one of Priam's innumerable bastard sons, was a brave warrior and often drove Hector's chariot or fought beside him on foot. In the Trojan War, Patroclus killed him and the Greeks stripped his corpse in spite of Hector's attempts to defend it. [Homer, *Iliad*, 8.318, 11.521–537, 12.88–92, 16.726–782.]

Cecropia. An ancient name of Attica.

Cecrops (1). A king of Attica. Cecrops, who was born from the earth, had a man's body ending in a snake's tail. He married Agraulus, daughter of Actaeüs, king of Acte. She bore a son, Erysichthon, and three daughters, Pandrosus, Agraulus, and Herse. Succeeding to the rule on Actaeüs' death, Cecrops renamed the region (later called Attica) Cecropia. Cecrops, often called the first king of Attica, was appointed by Zeus as arbiter in the contest between Athena and Poseidon for recognition as the patron deity of Athens. He ruled in favor of Athena. (This decision is sometimes said to have been made by his son, Erysichthon; by his successor, Cranaüs; or by the Olympian gods.) Cecrops is also credited with having first acknowledged Zeus as the supreme god and with having ended the practice of sacrificing human beings. Since Erechtheus, a later king of Athens, is known to have sacrificed his own daughter, this last claim is not very convincing. Cecrops' son did not survive him and the rule fell to Cranaüs. [Apollodorus 3.14.1–2, 3.14.5; Pausanias 1.2.6, 8.2.2–3.]

Cecrops (2). A king of Athens. Cecrops was the eldest son of Erechtheus and Praxithea. On the death of Erechtheus, Cecrops' brother-in-law, Xuthus, was asked to choose a successor from among Erechtheus' sons. Xuthus chose Cecrops and was banished from Athens by the rival brothers, Pandorus and Metion. Cecrops married Metiadusa, daughter of Eupalamus, and she bore a son, Pandion. Pandion succeeded to the rule when Cecrops died or migrated to Euboea.

This Cecrops is thought by many scholars to be (like Pandion II) a mere name invented to fill a gap in the confused succession of early Athenian kings. Yet another Cecrops, called a son of one of the Pandions, was worshiped as a hero at Haliartus, in Boeotia. [Apollodorus 3.15.1, 3.15.5; Pausanias 1.5.3, 7.1.2, 9.33.1.]

Cedalion. See ORION.

Ceisus. A son of Temenus, king of Argos. Ceisus and his younger brothers deposed their father, and Ceisus seized the throne of Argos. He exiled his brother-in-law, Deïphontes, of whom he was envious. His son Medon succeeded to the throne, but his power was curtailed by the people. Ceisus' later descendants ruled in name only for ten generations, after which Meltas, the last of the line to rule, was finally deposed. [Pausanias 2.19.1–2, 2.28.1–7.]

Celaeno. A daughter of Atlas and the Oceanid Pleïone. One of the

PLEIADES, Celaeno bore by Poseidon a son named Lycus, whom his father transported, for unrecorded reasons, to the Islands of the Blessed. Some say that Celaeno and Poseidon were the parents of the brothers Lycus and Nycteus, who usurped the rule of Thebes. These brothers are usually said, however, to be sons of Celaeno's sister Alcyone and the god Hyreius. [Apollodorus 3.10.1; Hyginus, *Poetica Astronomica*, 2.21.]

Celaeno. See HARPIES.

Celeüs. A king of Eleusis. Celeüs and his wife, Metaneira, had four daughters and a son, Demophoön. Some say that Triptolemus was also their son. They welcomed DEMETER to Eleusis and the goddess taught her rites, which became the Eleusinian mysteries, to Celeüs, Eumolpus, and their allies. [*Homeric Hymn to Demeter* 2.]

centaur. A creature half horse and half man. The centaurs, sometimes called hippocentaurs, were descended from Centaurus, a son of Apollo and Stilbe or of Ixion and the cloud that Zeus substituted for Hera in Ixion's bed. The centaurs were probably bred out of Magnesian mares by Centaurus. They are generally shown in art as horses whose shoulders merge into the upper bodies of men instead of into normal horses' heads. Although the centaurs came to be thought of as monsters, they seem originally to have been an uncivilized tribe living in the mountains of Magnesia, and this is the role they play in Greek mythology.

The tribe of Centaurs are principally known for their famous battle with the Lapiths, another Thessalian mountain tribe. This event was depicted in many works of art, most prominently on a pediment of the temple of Zeus at Olympia. The conflict began when Peirithoüs, a Lapith king, inherited the rule of a part of Thessaly from his father, Ixion. The Centaurs, who were also Ixion's sons (or grandsons), claimed a share in the rule. War ensued, but a peace was arranged. Later Peirithoüs invited the Centaurs to his wedding. Unused to wine, they became violent and, led by Eurytion, tried to carry off the Lapith women. The result was a bloody battle, which ended with the Centaurs being driven out of the region by the Lapiths.

Although the Centaurs are usually said to have taken refuge on Mount Malea, in the southern Peloponnesus, Heracles encountered them in western Arcadia. He was being entertained by Pholus, a civilized member of the tribe, when the other Centaurs, aroused by the odor of wine, broke up the feast. Heracles killed many of them and drove away the others, most of whom fled either to Malea, to Mount Pholoë (named for Pholus), or to Eleusis, where Poseidon hid them in a mountain. NESSUS, however, went to Aetolia, where he ultimately took a terrible revenge on Heracles, and Eurytion was killed by Heracles when he tried to carry off the daughter of Dexamenus, king of Olenus. An innocent victim of Heracles' war with the Centaurs was Pholus, who dropped one of his guest's poisoned arrows on his foot. Heracles also inadvertently caused the death of the wise Centaur CHEIRON, who had reared

Jason and Achilles. Cheiron is often said to have been the king of the Centaurs. The constellation Centaurus represents either Cheiron or Pholus.

Centaurus. A forebear of the CENTAURS. Centaurus was the son either of Apollo and Stilbe, daughter of the river-god Peneius, or of IXION and the cloud that Zeus substituted for Hera in Ixion's bed. He was, according to Pindar [*Pythian Odes* 2.42–48], in disrepute with both gods and men. Centaurus mounted Magnesian mares and they gave birth to the race of centaurs. [Diodorus Siculus 4.69.1.]

Cephalion. See CAPHAURUS.

Cephallenia. A large island in the Ionian Sea off the coast of Acarnania. Cephallenia was named for Cephalus, who was awarded the island by Amphitryon for his aid in a campaign against the Taphians. Later Cephallenia seems to have come under the domination of the smaller island of Ithaca, just to the east. Some say that Neoptolemus, while reigning in Epeirus, ruled against his former friend Odysseus in an arbitration, in order to gain control of Cephallenia.

Cephalus (1). A son of Deïon, king of Phocis, and Diomede, daughter of Xuthus. Cephalus came to Athens and married Procris, daughter of Erechtheus. According to some writers, she was a faithless wife, who, having been seduced by Pteleon, fled to Crete. There she was seduced by King Minos and, fearing his wife's anger more than her own husband's, hastened home. Two gifts that Minos had given her helped to bring about a reconciliation. The first was a hound, Laelaps, that could not fail to catch its prey; the second a javelin that could not miss its mark. Cephalus took his wife back and they lived happily until tragedy overtook them. Hyginus [*Fabulae* 189] claimed that they had a son, Laërtes, who became Odysseus' father.

According to other writers, Procris was a model of faithfulness, but was deeply wounded by Cephalus' suspicion of her, which caused him to test her fidelity by courting her disguised as a stranger. Somewhat later the tables were turned when a busybody told Procris that her husband had been overheard, during the hunt, calling the name Aura. Not realizing that Cephalus, when weary from the hunt, was given to calling on a breeze (*aura*) to cool his brow, Procris hid in a thicket to spy on him. Cephalus saw the bushes moving and, imagining that an animal was hidden there, flung the infallible spear. A few moments later his beloved wife died in his arms. Cephalus was tried for murder on the Areopagus and banished.

After this sad event Cephalus was called to Thebes, where Amphitryon offered him a large reward for the loan of Laelaps. Amphitryon wanted to use the dog to catch the vixen of Teumessus, which Hera had sent to ravage Theban territory. The goddess had decreed that the fox could never be captured. Zeus, faced with the dilemma of an inescapable hound chasing an uncatchable fox, solved it in typically Olympian fashion by turning them both to stone. The payment that Amphitryon had promised Cephalus was a share in the spoils of a war that was not yet fought. Cephalus decided to accompany him on his long-intended raid against the Teleboans. Amphitryon was successful and generously rewarded Cephalus with a large island, which Cephalus named Cephallenia. Some say that Cephalus married Clymene, daughter of Minyas, and became by her the father of Iphiclus.

Cephalus, a Phocian by birth and grandson of the Thessalian king Aeolus, was nevertheless identified by late Classical writers with the Athenian Cephalus, a son of Hermes and Erechtheus' daughter Herse. Ovid ingeniously combined the story of Eos' abduction of the latter Cephalus with the former's trial of his wife's fidelity. In view of the Athenian connections of the Phocian Cephalus—Hyginus [*Fabulae* 48] even lists him among the kings of Athens—it is possible that there was originally only one Cephalus and that the varying traditions concerning him became separated. [Ovid, *Metamorphoses*, 7.668–862; Apollodorus 1.9.4, 2.4.7, 3.15.1; *Epic Cycle* 2; Pausanias 1.37.6, 10.29.6.]

Cephalus (2). A son of Herse, daughter of Erechtheus, by Hermes. In spite of the attempts of Agraulus to bar his way, Hermes visited her sister Herse in her father's palace. She subsequently bore a son, Cephalus. This young man was so handsome that the amorous goddess Eos carried him off to Syria, or else up to heaven. There she became by him the mother of Phaëthon. Some say, however, that Eos bore Tithonus (who is usually called her consort) rather than Phaëthon; that it was not Eos (Dawn) but Hemera (Day) who abducted Cephalus; and that he was a son of Creüsa rather than Herse, or Pandion rather than Hermes. This confusion is compounded by the fact that Cephalus' story is often combined with that of Phocian Cephalus. [Hesiod, *Theogony*, 986–987; Euripides, *Hippolytus*, 454; Apollodorus 3.14.3; Pausanias 1.3.1.]

Cepheus (1). A king of Ethiopia. According to Apollodorus, Euripides called Cepheus a son of Belus, but that would make his daughter Andromeda older by four generations than her husband, PERSEUS [D]. Cepheus married Cassiopeia, who bore him Andromeda. He later offered his daughter to a sea-monster, but she was saved by Perseus in return for her hand. Perseus was attacked for this by Cepheus' brother Phineus or by Agenor. Ovid says that Cepheus upbraided Phineus, but Hyginus claims that he plotted with Agenor against Perseus and that he tried to dissuade Andromeda from leaving with Perseus. Since Cepheus had no sons, Andromeda's son Perses succeeded him on the throne. At their deaths Cepheus and Cassiopeia were placed by Poseidon among the stars. [Apollodorus, 2.1.4, 2.4.3; Ovid, *Metamorphoses*, 4.668–5.45; Hyginus, *Fabulae*, 64, and *Poetica Astronomica*, 10, 11.]

Cepheus (2). A king of Tegea. Cepheus was a son of Aleüs and Neaera. As a youth, he, his brother Amphidamas, and their nephew Ancaeüs sailed with the Argonauts; Cepheus and Ancaeüs also hunted the Calydonian boar. Later Cepheus refused to join his former shipmate Heracles on his expedition against

Sparta, fearing that Argive enemies would attack Tegea in his absence. Heracles gave to Cepheus' daughter Sterope a lock of Medusa's hair with the promise that it would repel any enemy if she merely held it up three times on the city walls. Reassured, Cepheus marched with Heracles. Tegea did indeed remain safe, but Cepheus and all his sons except Echemus were killed in the war. Echemus became king of Arcadia after the death of Cepheus' elder brother, Lycurgus. Another daughter of Cepheus, Aërope, died in bearing a child by Ares. Ares caused the child to survive by sucking at its dead mother's breast. [Apollodorus 2.7.3; Apollonius Rhodius 1.161–163; Pausanias 8.44.7–8, 8.47.5.]

Cephissus or **Cephisus River.** A river of Attica. The Cephissus flows into the Saronic Gulf near Athens. (See INACHUS.)

Ceraunian Sea. See IONIAN SEA.

Cerberus. The watchdog of Hades. Cerberus was one of the monstrous brood of Typhon and Echidna, which included the Hydra and the Chimaera. According to Hesiod, Cerberus had fifty heads, but most writers were content to give him only three, along with a snake's tail and snake heads sprouting from his back. Cerberus fawned on spirits entering Hades, but ate those who tried to leave. Orpheus, however, managed to charm the hound with his singing, and HERACLES [1] carried him by main force to the upper world, showed him to Eurystheus, and returned him to his home. During this foray an unidentified man was turned to stone at the mere sight of the monster. From the foam that dripped from the hound's jaws, there sprang up the poisonous plant aconite, which Medea used in her unsuccessful attempt to poison Theseus. [Homer, *Iliad*, 8.366–368; Hesiod, *Theogony*, 310–312, 769–774; Apollodorus 2.5.12; Ovid, *Metamorphoses*, 7.408–419, 10.65–67.]

Cercopes. Thievish and dwarfish creatures who inhabited Lydia. The Cercopes were among the predatory ruffians killed or captured by Heracles, either while he worked as a slave of Omphale, a Lydian queen, or during his travels in southern Thessaly. Some say that there were two Cercopes—Passalus and Acmon—who were sons of Oceanus and Theia (either the Titaness or a daughter of Memnon); other writers claim that there was an entire tribe of Cercopes. The two Cercopes had been warned by their mother not to fall into the hands of Blackbottom. When Heracles tied their feet to a pole and carried them off, head down, over his shoulder, they realized that it was Heracles about whom Theia had admonished them. However, their jokes about their captor's hairiness so amused Heracles that he let them go. Unchastened, the Cercopes continued their careers of knavery until Zeus put a stop to them by turning them to stone, or else transforming them into monkeys. The Romans claimed that the Pithecusae (Monkey Islands), near the Bay of Naples, were named for the Cercopes.

Although a brief fragment remains of a fairly early comic epic, *Cercopes*, and a Thessalian site connected with their capture by Heracles was mentioned by Herodotus [7.216], most references to the Cercopes are tantalizingly short and by late Classical authors. It has been suggested that their tales grew out of confused reports of actual pygmies, or out of attempts to explain the man-like appearance of apes when these animals first were brought to the Greek world.

Cercopes. A lost burlesque epic poem. The single surviving fragment of this poem is published in the volume of Hesiod's works in the Loeb Classical Library.

Cerdo. The wife of Phoroneus, king of Argos. Though Cerdo's tomb was shown near that of her husband at Argos, little else is known of her. She was not the mother of his children Apis and Niobe, but may have borne him Car. [Pausanias 2.21.1.]

Cerynitian hind. A golden-horned deer sacred to Artemis. This deer, which is sometimes said to have been a stag, roamed through the region about Oenoë, in Argolis. HERACLES [E] captured it alive as his third labor and brought it back to Eurystheus after Artemis withdrew her objections.

Cestrinus. The eponym of Cestrine, in Epeirus. Cestrinus was the son of Helenus and Andromache. Since his half-brother Molossus succeeded his father on the throne of Buthrotum, Cestrinus led colonists to a region north of the Thyamis River and named it Cestrine. [Pausanias 1.11.1–2, 2.23.6.]

Ceto. The sea-monster daughter of Pontus and Ge. Ceto, whose name means any large denizen of the sea, was said to have borne, by her brother, the ancient sea-god Phorcys, the Gorgons, the Graeae, Echidna, and Ladon. [Hesiod, *Theogony*, 237–336.]

Cetus (The Sea-Monster or **The Whale).** A constellation. This group of stars represents the monster sent by Poseidon to devour Andromeda in order to punish her boastful mother, Cassiopeia. It was killed by Perseus. The entire cast of characters of this familiar tale appears in the sky: Perseus, Andromeda, Cassiopeia, and her husband, Cepheus, as well as the Sea-Monster.

Ceüs. An island off the southern tip of Attica. When Ceüs was scorched by drought during the rising of Sirius, the dog star, the islanders called on Aristaeüs for help. He sacrificed to Zeus, who sent the cooling etesian winds to relieve the island for forty days at this time every year. Ceüs was also the scene of Apollo's sad affair with Cyparissus.

Ceÿx. A king of Trachis. Ceÿx was a son of Eosphorus, the morning star. A hospitable man, he welcomed Peleus when he was banished from Aegina, and Heracles when he fled Eurystheus. Heracles aided him by driving the hostile Dryopes from the region. After Heracles' death Ceÿx sent the hero's children to Theseus for protection, for he was not himself powerful enough to oppose Eurystheus. Ceÿx was drowned on a sea voyage to Delphi. His wife, Alcyone, was grief-stricken, and husband and wife were transformed into king-fishers, apparently through the pity of a god. Apollodorus [1.7.4] says, however, that their transformation was a punishment for their having called each other Zeus and Hera. He claims that Ceÿx became a gull or gannet, which is what his name means. [Ovid, *Metamorphoses*, 11.268–748; Pausanias 1.32.6.]

Chalciope. A daughter of Aeëtes, king of Colchis, and Eidyia, daughter of Oceanus. Aeëtes married Chalciope to Phrixus and she bore him four sons, Argus, Phrontis, Melas, and Cytissorus. Later she begged her sister, Medea, to help Jason in order that her sons might escape Aeëtes' anger at their friendship with the ARGONAUTS [M]. Hesiod [*Great Eoiae* 15] calls Chalciope Iophossa. [Apollonius Rhodius 3.609–743.]

Chalcodon. A Euboean king. Chalcodon, a son of Abas, led his people, the Abantes, in an attack on Thebes, where he was killed by Amphitryon. He was buried near Teumessus on the road from Thebes to Chalcis, Chalcodon's city. Oddly, the Arcadian city of Pheneus also claimed his grave. His son, Eleᵃ phenor, led forty shiploads of Abantes to the Trojan War. [Homer, *Iliad*, 2.536–545; Pausanias 8.15.6, 9.17.3, 9.19.3.]

Chalybes. A tribe inhabiting a part of the southern coast of the Black Sea. The Chalybes, who were thought by the Greeks to be hostile, naked savages, were famous as workers in iron. Apollonius Rhodius [2.1000–1008] speaks of their existence, devoted solely to mining and smelting, as a miserable one. Their reputation for savagery seems to have derived, at least in part, from the martial uses to which their iron was put by their customers. The Chalybes were said by Herodotus to have been subdued by Croesus, king of Sardis.

Chaos. The void that was the first thing to appear at the creation of the universe. It is not clear how the Greeks conceived Chaos, which was not in existence from the first, but came into being. Out of Chaos, or together with it, came Ge (Earth), Tartarus, and Eros (Love), who appears as the son of Aphrodite only in later works. Chaos bore Erebus (Darkness) and Nyx (Night). At times Chaos was thought of as a part of the Underworld. [Hesiod, *Theogony*, 116–123, 814.]

Charioteer, The. See AURIGA.

Charon. The ferryman of Hades. Charon ferried the souls of the dead who had been properly buried across the river Styx (or Acheron) into Hades. For this service he charged a fee of one obol, and the dead were consequently buried with the required fare in their mouths. Charon was represented in Euripides' *Alcestis* [252–259] and in Aristophanes' *Frogs* [138–140, 180–269] merely as an aged and rather grumpy boatman. Later authors, notably Vergil [*Aeneid* 6.295–330, 6.384–416], portrayed him as a squalid and malign minor god of the Underworld.

Charybdis. A whirlpool on the western side of the northern entrance to the Strait of Messina. This whirlpool was imagined as a female monster that three times daily sucked down the waters in the area and later belched them forth again. This made her a terror of sailors. In avoiding Charybdis, they fell prey to the monster Scylla, who inhabited a cave in the cliff opposite the whirlpool. The *Argo*, guided by Thetis and the other Nereïds, avoided both monsters, but ODYSSEUS [H, I], in steering clear of Charybdis, lost six seamen to Scylla. Later his ship was driven back to Charybdis and destroyed. Odysseus was saved by clinging to a fig tree that grew over the whirlpool. [Homer, *Odyssey*, 12.101–110, 12.234–244; Apollonius Rhodius 4.825–826.]

Cheiron. A Centaur. Unlike the other Centaurs, which were descended from Ixion or Centaurus, Cheiron was the son of the Titan Cronus and Philyra, and was immortal. He differed from other Centaurs in his nature as well, for, whereas they were barbaric and unrestrained in their habits, Cheiron was one of the wisest and most learned of living beings. As a result, several of the greatest of the Greeks were sent as children to his cave on Mount Pelion to be reared by him. Among these pupils were Jason, Asclepius, Actaeon, and Achilles.

Cheiron also befriended Peleus (whose mother, Endeïs, was said in some accounts to be Cheiron's daughter, rather than Sceiron's) when he was deserted without weapons on Mount Pelion by Acastus. Cheiron saved Peleus from an attack by hostile Centaurs and found for him the sword that Acastus had hidden. Later he told Peleus how to win the love of Thetis. Cheiron was noted for his knowledge of medicine, which he taught to Asclepius, and he was a competent sculptor as well. When, after Actaeon's death, his dogs howled in loneliness, the Centaur comforted them by making a statue of their master.

Cheiron is sometimes said to have been king of the Centaurs. With them he was driven from Pelion by the Lapiths, after a protracted war between the two tribes. The Centaurs took refuge at Mount Malea in the southern Peloponnesus, but were encountered by Heracles in Arcadia when he hunted the Erymanthian boar. When they attacked the friendly Centaur Pholus, Heracles killed many and drove the others from the land. During these hostilities Cheiron was accidentally shot by Heracles, or else dropped one of Heracles' poisoned arrows on his foot, as did Pholus. Cheiron could not die, but the pain of the wound, and perhaps the fate of his people, made him regret his immortality. Some say that the Titan Prometheus agreed to take on Cheiron's immortality and that the Centaur thus happily died. This is implausible, however, since as a Titan Prometheus must already have been immortal. According to other writers Cheiron achieved another kind of immortality by being placed among the stars as the constellation Centaurus. [Apollodorus 1.2.4, 2.5.4, 3.4.4, 3.13.3–5; Hyginus, *Poetica Astronomica*, 2.38.]

Chemmis. An Egyptian city near Thebes. According to Herodotus, Chemmis was the home of Danaüs and Lynceus. Perseus stopped there on his travels and was thereafter worshiped by the Chemmites. [Herodotus 2.91.]

Chimaera. A Lycian monster. The Chimaera was one of a grim brood spawned by Typhaon and Echidna that included the Hydra, Cerberus, and the hound Orthus. She has been variously described as having either three heads —those of a lion, of a goat, and of a snake—or the front parts of a lion, the middle of a goat, and a snake's tail; or all these peculiarities at once. All accounts agree that she breathed fire. Reared, according to Homer, by Amisodarus, she ravaged the land of Lycia, destroying cattle and setting fires, until she was killed by BELLEROPHON [A, C]. [Homer, *Iliad*, 6.178–183; Hesiod, *Theogony*, 319–325.]

Chione (1). A daughter of Daedalion. On reaching the marriageable age of fourteen, the lovely Chione had innumerable suitors. One day Hermes and Apollo spied her and both were enchanted. Apollo waited until nightfall before approaching her, but Hermes put her to sleep at once and violated her. In due course the girl bore two sons in one day: Autolycus to Hermes, Philammon to Apollo. This unusual distinction so turned Chione's head that she began to boast that she was more beautiful than Artemis. The goddess avenged the insult by shooting and killing the girl with an arrow. Chione's father was so grief-stricken that he flung himself from a peak of Parnassus and was changed by Apollo into a hawk. [Ovid, *Metamorphoses*, 11.291–345.]

Chione (2). A daughter of Boreas and Oreithyia. Chione was seduced by Poseidon. Ashamed, she flung her child, Eumolpus, into the sea, but his father rescued him. [Apollodorus 3.15.2, 4.]

Chios. A large Aegean island off the coast of Ionia in Asia Minor. Chios was colonized by the Cretan Oenopion, son of Dionysus and Ariadne. Chios was the scene of King Oenopion's blinding of Orion.

Chiron. See CHEIRON.

Chloris. A daughter of Amphion and Niobe. When Apollo and Artemis slaughtered Niobe's children, only a daughter, Meliboea or Chloris, and a son, Amyclas, survived, they having prayed to Leto. Pausanias claims that Chloris (Pale) was merely the name given to Meliboea when she turned pale from fright. Neleus, king of Messenia, found her so beautiful that he journeyed to Boeotian Orchomenus to make her his bride. She bore him a daughter, Pero, and twelve sons. Chloris is said to have been one of the winners of the Heraean games. [Pausanias 2.21.9.]

Chromius. See NELEUS.

Chrysaor. An offspring of Poseidon and MEDUSA. Poseidon lay with Medusa in a flowery field. When she was later decapitated by Perseus, Chrysaor and Pegasus sprang from the wound. Chrysaor fathered the three-headed monster Geryon on Callirrhoë, a daughter of Oceanus. Except that Chrysaor's name means "Golden Sword" and that he is called "stouthearted" by Hesiod, nothing is known of his nature. His mother, brother, and son were all monsters, however, and it seems likely that Chrysaor, too, was conceived of as in some way monstrous—at best a giant. [Hesiod, *Theogony*, 278–288, 979–983.]

Chryse. A daughter of Almus, king of Almones, near Boeotian Orchomenus. By Ares, Chryse became the mother of Phlegyas. [Pausanias 9.36.1.]

Chryse. An island near Troy and its nymph patroness. This island was the home of Chryses, a priest of Apollo Smintheus, and of the priest's daughter, Chryseïs, who was abducted by Agamemnon. Chryse was also the place where Philoctetes was bitten by a snake while sacrificing at the nymph's shrine. This island, which is probably the one that Hyginus calls Zminthe, was said by Pausanias to have sunk into the sea.

Chryseïs. The daughter of Chryses, a priest of Apollo Smintheus on the island of Chryse, not far from Troy. Chryseïs was carried off by Agamemnon during the Trojan War. He preferred her charms to those of his wife and refused to give her up to her father for ransom. Chryses prayed to Apollo and the god punished the Greeks with a pestilence. Pressure from the other Greek leaders forced Agamemnon to surrender Chryseïs. His insistence on seizing Achilles' concubine, Briseïs, as compensation led to Achilles' disastrous withdrawal from the war. According to an elaborate tale told only by Hyginus [*Fabulae* 120–121], Chryseïs was pregnant when Agamemnon returned her to Chryses, but she insisted to her father that she had conceived not by her captor but by Apollo. When the baby, whom she called Chryses, had grown to young manhood, Orestes, Pylades, and Iphigeneia landed on the island of Zminthe (perhaps another name for Chryse), fleeing from Thoas, king of the Taurians, from whom they had stolen a statue of Artemis. The pious younger Chryses was about to return them to Thoas as prisoners when his grandfather revealed that, since Orestes and Iphigeneia were children of Agamemnon, the younger Chryses was their half-brother. Placing the ties of blood above religion, the young man not only released the Greeks but helped Orestes to kill Thoas. [Homer, *Iliad*, 1.8–474.]

Chryses. A king of Phlegyantis. Chryses, a son of Poseidon and Chrysogeneia, daughter of Almus, succeeded the childless Phlegyas to the rule of the Boeotian region later called Orchomenus. He was succeeded in turn by his son Minyas. [Pausanias 9.36.4.]

Chryses. See CHRYSEÏS.

Chrysippus. An illegitimate son of Pelops by the nymph Axioche or Astyoche, a daughter of Danaüs. Chrysippus, because of his beauty, was carried off to Thebes by LAÏUS, who had been living at Pelops' court in Pisa. The boy either killed himself or was murdered by his half-brothers, Atreus and Thyestes, because of the jealousy of their mother, Hippodameia, who feared that Pelops might bequeath the throne to Chrysippus instead of his legitimate sons. Some say that the boy's death occurred after his rescue by Pelops, who marched against Thebes with an army. Hyginus' statement that Chrysippus was kidnaped by Theseus was apparently a mistake, for the writer elsewhere records the usual story. [Apollodorus 3.5.5; Hyginus, *Fabulae*, 85, 271.]

Chrysothemis. A daughter of Agamemnon and Clytemnestra. In Sophocles' *Electra*, Chrysothemis is sympathetic with Electra's loyalty to her father, but counsels against defying her mother and Aegisthus.

Chthon. The earth. An occasionally used alternative name for GE or Gaea, which have the same meaning.

chthonian deities. Spirits of the earth or Underworld. This term is used of deities, spirits (*daimones*), and heroes who were thought to live in or beneath the earth and whose concern was with the dead or with the fertility of the earth. Many chthonian divinities combined these two functions. Some scholars believe that they were originally differentiated; but spirits who lived in the earth, where the dead were buried and from which the crops arose each year, almost inevitably came to be associated with both events. The chief chthonian gods (*chthonioi*) were Hades and Persephone; Hecate was also prominent among them. The Erinyes and Keres were chthonian spirits, as were many local spirits or divinities of the earth, such as the Eumenides and the Semnai Theai, both of which were identified with the Erinyes by Aeschylus. Human beings who died and became heroes (see HERO) also were worshiped as chthonian *daimones*.

The adjective "chthonian" is often applied to gods of the earth or the Underworld in distinction to the Ouranioi, the "heavenly" or Olympian gods. Some of the Olympians, however, had certain chthonian characteristics. Hermes, for example, guided the dead to the Underworld. Demeter was often worshiped with typically chthonian rites, which were appropriate to an earth-goddess and the mother of Persephone. Even Zeus, under his epithets of Mei-lichios and Ktesios, was worshiped as a sacred snake, a common form taken by chthonian spirits. This character, however, had originally nothing to do with the Olympian Zeus as conceived by Homer; local worship of certain chthonian spirits called Meilichios (He Who Is Easily Placated) and Ktesios (He of the Storeroom) was assimilated by the Hellenic sky-god as his influence spread through the Greek states.

Chthonius. One of the Sparti of Thebes. Chthonius was said by some writers to have been the father of Lycus and Nycteus.

Chthonophyle. A daughter of Sicyon. Chthonophyle bore Polybus by Hermes, but later married Phlias, by whom she had a son, Androdamas. [Pausanias 2.6.6.]

Ciconians or **Cicones.** A tribe of the southwestern coast of Thrace. The Ciconians were raided by ODYSSEUS [D] on his way home from Troy, and only Maron and his wife were spared. The survivors summoned more belligerent neighboring tribes to their aid. Odysseus retreated after losing six men from each of his ships. [Homer, *Odyssey*, 9.39–66, 9.196–211.]

Cilicia. The southeasternmost coastal region of Asia Minor, north of Cyprus. The eponym of Cilicia was Cilix, one of the sons of the Phoenician king Agenor. The monster Typhöeus and the dragon Delphyne occupied the Corycian Cave in Cilicia. Cinyras, king of Cyprus, is said to have emigrated to that island from Celenderis, in Cilicia. After the Trojan War the Colophonian seer

Mopsus, together with his partner, Amphilocus, founded the Cilician city of Mallus. Cilicia is often said to have been the site of Hypoplacian Thebes, the homeland of Andromache.

Cilix. The eponym of Cilicia. Cilix was one of the sons of Agenor, king of Tyre or Sidon, who were sent by their father to find their kidnaped sister, Europa, or face exile. Cilix settled on the southeastern shore of the great peninsula in Asia Minor that is now occupied by Turkey. There the Hypachaei, among whom he lived, renamed themselves Cilicians in his honor. Some say that Thasus was a son of Cilix, rather than a brother. [Apollodorus 3.1.1; Herodotus 7.91.]

Cinyras. A king of Cyrus. Homer [*Iliad* 11.19–28], who speaks of Cinyras only as a wealthy Cypriot king, says that, on hearing of the Greek expedition assembling to sail against Troy, he sent Agamemnon a magnificent breastplate. A later tradition put his eager generosity in an ironic light: Menelaüs, Odysseus, and Talthybius came to Paphos, the city that Cinyras had founded, in order to enlist him in the Greek forces. Cinyras promised to send fifty ships. He kept this promise in a novel way. The flagship commanded by Cinyras' son Mygdalion was followed to sea by forty-nine toy ships made of clay and manned by clay sailors. Nearly all the Cypriot fleet melted beneath the waves shortly after its launching.

Hyginus calls Cinyras an Assyrian; Ovid makes him a son of Paphos, Pygmalion's daughter by the famous statue. Most writers, including the Roman historian Tacitus, agree that he was a Cilician who migrated to Cyprus. Apollodorus says that he was a son of Sandocus, a Syrian descendant of Eos and Tithonus, and Pharnace, daughter of Megassares, king of Hyria. Cinyras was born after Sandocus had migrated to Cilicia and founded the city of Celenderis. He migrated in turn to Cyprus, founded Paphos, and married Metharme, daughter of the Cypriot king PYGMALION. Metharme bore several children, including Adonis.

Other writers record the more usual tradition that Adonis was the son of Cinyras, or some other king, by his own daughter. A priest of Aphrodite (according to Pindar) as well as king, Cinyras was nevertheless punished for the blasphemy of Cenchreïs, his wife in Ovid's account. Cenchreïs boasted that her daughter Myrrha or Smyrna was lovelier than the goddess. Aphrodite caused the girl to fall in love with her father and, aided by her nurse, to conceive a child (Adonis) by him while he was intoxicated. When Cinyras learned the truth he killed himself. He was honored in Cyprus as a hero. [Apollodorus 3.9.1, 3.14.3, "Epitome" 3.9; Ovid, *Metamorphoses,* 10.298–518; Hyginus, *Fabulae,* 58, 242; Pindar, *Pythian Odes,* 2.15–17.]

Circe. A sorceress. Circe was a daughter of Helius and Perse (or Perseïs), daughter of Oceanus. She lived on the island of Aeaea, which late Classical writers said was off the western coast of Italy, or identified specifically with

Cape Circeo, south of Rome, which is said to have once been an island. Circe came there in her father's chariot from Colchis, a land ruled by her brother, Aeëtes. Circe is sometimes called a goddess, sometimes a nymph. Her principal activity seems to have been transforming men and women into beasts. Picus, son of Saturn, was seen and loved by her. When he repulsed her advances, for love of his betrothed, the nymph Canens, Circe turned him into a woodpecker.

The amorous witch behaved in much the same way toward the young sea-god Glaucus when he came to her to beg for a love potion that might influence Scylla. Circe wooed him herself, but he had eyes for no one but Scylla. The angry sorceress, unable to harm the god, gave him a potion which, instead of making Scylla love him, changed her into a hideous monster. Jason and Medea, fleeing Aeëtes after their treacherous murder of Apsyrtus, traveled to Aeaea at Zeus's command in order to be purified. Circe performed the rite, but, on learning what crime they had committed, drove them from her island.

Much later ODYSSEUS [F] came to Aeaea in his last remaining ship. Circe transformed half of his men to stone, but Hermes gave him the herb moly as an antidote against her drugs. When she tried to transform Odysseus as well, he forced her at swordpoint to vow not to harm him. Falling in love with him, she changed his men back to their original form. Odysseus remained with her a year, after which she sent him on his way with good advice for his homeward voyage. Some say that she bore sons by Odysseus: Nausithoüs, or Telegonus, or Agrius and Latinus.

According to Hyginus [*Fabulae* 125, 127], Circe sent Telegonus to find his father. On reaching Ithaca he killed Odysseus unawares, but brought his body back to Aeaea for burial. Penelope and Telemachus, Odysseus' wife and son, accompanied him. Circe made them immortal and married Telemachus, while Telegonus married Penelope. Their sons, respectively, were Latinus and Italus. [Homer, *Odyssey*, 10.133–574, 12.8–150; Hesiod, *Theogony*, 956–957, 1011–1014; Apollonius Rhodius 4.559–591, 4.659–752; Ovid, *Metamorphoses*, 13.966–14.71, 14.248–440; *Telegony* 1.]

Cithaeron, Mount. A range of mountains separating Attica and Boeotia. The small cities of Plataea and Eleutherae were in these mountains. Their northern slopes, not far from Thebes, were the site of many legendary events: the death of Actaeon and the blinding of Teiresias for happening on goddesses bathing; the dismembering of Pentheus during bacchanalian revels; the birth of Amphion and Zethus; the exposure of Oedipus. The mountains were sacred to Cithaeronian Zeus. Mount Cithaeron was said to have been named for Cithaeron, an early king of Plataea.

Cius. A port on the Mysian coast of the Sea of Marmara. Cius, now the Turkish city of Gemlik, was founded by Polyphemus, son of Eilatus, who was abandoned there by the Argonauts, together with Heracles and Hylas. The city was on the site of a Mysian village where the river Cius emptied into the

Cianian Bay. Cius had close relations with the Thessalian city of Trachis, because Heracles had settled Cian hostages there. He had taken them as pledges that the Cians would annually search for Hylas, who had disappeared at Cius.

Clashing Rocks. Two rocks on either side of the northern entrance of the Bosporus. The Clashing Rocks (Symplegades), which were also called the Cyanean (Dark Blue) Rocks, were said to have clashed together with tremendous force when driven by the wind. These jaws of the Bosporus had prevented ships from entering the Black Sea until the Argonauts, aided by Athena, made the passage successfully. Thereafter the rocks remained stationary. Their behavior, though not their location, was almost identical with that of the WANDERING ROCKS.

Cleio or **Clio.** One of the nine Muses. Cleio, a daughter of Zeus and Mnemosyne, laughed at Aphrodite for her infatuation with the mortal Adonis. The goddess had her revenge by making Cleio fall in love with Pierus, son of Magnes, by whom she bore a son, Hyacinth. [Apollodorus 1.3.1–3.]

Cleite. A daughter of Merops, king of Percote, on the Hellespont. Cleite married Cyzicus, the young king of the Doliones, in Mysia. Before they could have children, he was accidentally killed by the ARGONAUTS [D, E]. Cleite killed herself in grief. The wood-nymphs mourned her and their tears formed a spring that was named for her. [Apollonius Rhodius 1.974–977, 1.1063–1069.]

Cleitus. A son of Mantius. Because of his beauty, Eos carried Cleitus off to live with the gods. [Homer, *Odyssey*, 15.249.]

Cleodaeüs. A Heraclid. A son of Hyllus, Cleodaeüs was the father of Aristomachus, whose sons led the return of the Heraclids to the Peloponnesus.

Cleopatra (1). A daughter of Idas and Marpessa. Cleopatra married Meleager. According to Homer [*Iliad* 9.553–596], it was she who persuaded Meleager to save Aetolia from the avenging Curetes when anger at his mother made him refuse to fight. Cleopatra bore a daughter, Polydora, who married Protesilaüs. [Pausanias 4.2.7.]

Cleopatra (2). A daughter of Boreas and Oreithyia, daughter of Erechtheus. Cleopatra married Phineus, king of Salmydessus, and bore him two sons, who are variously named. When these sons were grown, Phineus took a second wife, Idaea, whose enmity toward her stepsons led Phineus to blind them or otherwise torture them. They were rescued by the ARGONAUTS [H].

Clotho. See FATES.

Clymene (1). A daughter of Minyas. Clymene, of whom nothing personal is known, formed a link in several genealogies, perhaps indicating that Minyan ancestry was claimed by the families involved. She is said to have been the mother of Iphiclus by Phylacus or by his brother Cephalus; of Atalanta by the Arcadian king Iasus; and of Alcimede, the mother of Jason.

Clymene (2). A daughter of Catreus, king of Crete. Because of an oracle that one of his children would kill him, Catreus gave his daughters Clymene and Aërope to the Argive sailor Nauplius to sell as slaves. Instead Nauplius gave Aërope to Atreus for a wife and married Clymene himself. She bore Palamedes, Oeax, and Nausimedon. [Apollodorus 2.1.5, 3.2.1.]

Clymene (3). A daughter of Oceanus and Tethys. Clymene was said by Hesiod [*Theogony* 507–514] to be the mother of Atlas, Menoetius, Prometheus, and Epimetheus. According to Ovid [*Metamorphoses* 1.750–2.366], she was the mother of Phaëthon by Helius (Phoebus Apollo), though married to Merops, king of Egypt. The Heliades were presumably her children.

Clymenus (1). A king of Arcadia. Clymenus raped his daughter Harpalyce. She contained her anger and shame until a child was born to her, then took her revenge. Cutting up the newborn child, she served it to Clymenus at a banquet. On discovering what he had eaten, Clymenus killed his daughter, then himself. [Hyginus, *Fabulae*, 206, 242, 246, 255.]

Clymenus (2). A king of Boeotian Orchomenus. A son of Presbon, son of Phrixus, Clymenus came to power on the death of Orchomenus. He had five sons, of whom only Erginus and Azeus were of any importance. Taking part in a feast of Poseidon at nearby Onchestus, Clymenus was killed with a stone in an altercation with some Thebans over some trivial matter. The murderer was Perieres, charioteer of one or the other of the Thebans named Menoeceus. Carried dying back to Orchomenus, Clymenus made Erginus vow to avenge his death on the Thebans. Hyginus [*Fabulae* 14] calls Clymenus Periclymenus. [Apollodorus 2.4.11; Pausanias 9.36.1–2.]

Clymenus (3). An early king of Olympia. A Cretan from Cydonia, Clymenus was the son of Cardys. He came to Olympia fifty years after Deucalion's Flood and held games in honor of his ancestor Heracles the Dactyl, who had originated them. Clymenus was overthrown by Endymion. [Pausanias 6.21.6.]

Clymenus (4). The father of Nestor's wife, Eurydice. Homer [*Odyssey* 3.452] does not further identify this man; he may be Orchomenian Clymenus.

Clytemnestra. A daughter of Tyndareüs, king of Sparta, and Leda. Tyndareüs married Clytemnestra to Tantalus, son of Thyestes (or Broteas). AGAMEMNON, king of Mycenae, killed her husband and her baby, whereupon Tyndareüs gave her to him in marriage. She bore several children to Agamemnon: Iphigeneia (Iphianassa), Electra (Laodice), Chrysothemis, and Orestes. Agamemnon deceived her into sending Iphigeneia to Aulis, on the pretext of marrying her to Achilles; in reality he was preparing to sacrifice her to Artemis. When Clytemnestra discovered this treachery she conceived a great hatred for her husband and plotted with her lover, Aegisthus, to kill him on his return from the Trojan War. This they did, Clytemnestra herself killing Agamemnon's concubine Cassandra. Aegisthus and Clytemnestra had two children, Erigone and Aletes. ORESTES [A], who escaped to Phocis at his father's death, returned and killed his mother and Aegisthus, with the help of Electra. For this crime Clytemnestra's Erinyes drove him mad.

Clytemnestra is a principal character in Aeschylus' *Oresteia* trilogy, Sophocles' *Electra*, Euripides' *Electra* and *Iphigeneia in Aulis*, and Seneca's *Agamemnon*. See also Homer, *Odyssey*, 3.262–272, 11.404–454; Hyginus, *Fabulae*, 77–78, 117, 119.

Clytië. A nymph. Clytië, spurned by her former lover HELIUS [B], tattled on him to the father of his new mistress. The resulting disaster caused Helius to hate Clytië, and she wasted away until she was transformed into a heliotrope—a flower whose head turns to follow the sun's course through the sky each day.

Clytius (1). A son of Eurytus, king of Oechalia, and Antiope. Clytius and his brother, Iphitus, sailed with the Argonauts. Clytius distinguished himself in several encounters on the outward voyage, but was killed by Aeëtes in Colchis. [Apollonius Rhodius 1.86–89; Hyginus, *Fabulae*, 14.]

Clytius (2). A Trojan elder. Clytius, son of Laomedon and Strymo, Leucippe, or Placia, and a brother of Priam, was the father of Caletor, who was killed in the Trojan War. [Homer, *Iliad*, 3.146–151, 15.319, 20.236–239; Apollodorus 3.12.3.]

Clytius (3). One of the GIANTS. In the war between gods and Giants, Hecate killed Clytius with her torches. [Apollodorus 1.6.2.]

Cnossus. The principal city of Crete. Cnossus was the capital of the Minoan Empire. Although there were several other important Cretan cities, Cnossus was the site of most of the familiar myths concerning Crete.

Cocalus. See DAEDALUS [B].

Cocytus River. An Underworld river. The Cocytus (Wailing) River formed one of the boundaries of Hades.

Codrus. A legendary king of Athens. Codrus was a son of Melanthus, leader of the Messenian refugees who had invaded Athens after the Dorian invasion. Codrus married an Athenian woman, thus making himself more acceptable to the people of Athens. According to legend, Dorians from the Peloponnesus made a rather desultory attack on Attica, but were careful not to injure the king, having learned from an oracle that they could not take Athens if they did. Codrus, too, learned of this oracle and, disguising himself, picked a quarrel with the invaders, so that they killed him. On discovering what they had done, the Peloponnesians marched home again, convinced that they would be defeated if they continued their attack. Codrus was succeeded by his son Medon. His other sons led an expedition composed of Ionians and many other groups to Asia Minor, where they conquered or founded most of the cities of Ionia.

Coeüs. A Titan, son of Ge and Uranus. Coeüs was the father, by his sister Titan Phoebe, of Leto and Asteria. [Hesiod, *Theogony*, 134, 409–410.]

Colchis. A land at the eastern end of the Black Sea. Aea, the capital of Colchis, was built near the mouth of the river Phasis. Although the name of Colchis was well known in Classical times, its history was obscure. Herodotus [2.104–105] was convinced that Colchis had been colonized by a part of the army of the Egyptian pharaoh Sesostris (Ramses II). The myth that the Colchian king Aeëtes was a brother of Pasiphaë suggests also a tradition of Cretan connections. Like most nations of the Near East, Colchis paid tribute to Persia during the reign of Darius and there were Colchian contingents in Xerxes' army. In mythology, Colchis is known primarily as the realm of Aeëtes, putative son of Helius, to which Jason sailed with the Argonauts, carrying off both the golden fleece and Aeëtes' daughter Medea. Later the king was deposed by his brother, Perses, but restored by Medea or her son Medus. In its hostility to strangers, Colchis resembles the Crimean kingdom of the Taurians, and some say that Perses was king of that land.

Collatinus, Lucius Tarquinius. One of the first two Roman praetors. The rape of Collatinus' chaste wife, LUCRETIA, by Sextus Tarquinius led to Collatinus' involvement in the overthrow of Sextus' father, Lucius Tarquinius Superbus, the last Roman king. Collatinus and Lucius Junius Brutus were declared praetors of the new Roman republic. Popular suspicion of the Tarquinii, however, soon forced Collatinus to resign and go into exile in Lavinium. [Livy 1.57.6–1.60.4, 2.2.3–2.2.10.]

Comaetho. A priestess of Artemis Triclaria at Patrae. According to local legend, Comaetho and Melanippus were deeply in love, but their parents prevented their marriage. Recklessly, the pair slept together in the goddess' shrine, and this sacrilege brought famine on the land. Inquiring of the Delphic oracle, the people of Patrae discovered the cause and sacrificed Comaetho and her lover to Artemis. Thereafter for many generations the fairest youth and maiden of Patrae were periodically sacrificed at the shrine, until the practice was ended by EURYPYLUS (1). [Pausanias 7.19.2–4.]

Comaetho. See PTERELAÜS.

Consus. An obscure Roman god. Consus, whose altar was said to have been discovered underground by Romulus, was probably one of the CHTHONIAN DEITIES. He seems to have had a connection with horses and mules. He and Ops, the Roman goddess of plenty, were often worshiped together.

Copreus. The herald of Eurystheus. A son of Pelops, Copreus killed someone called Iphitus and fled from Elis. He came to Mycenae, was purified by his nephew, King Eurystheus, and was thereafter employed by him to bear his orders concerning the twelve labors to Heracles. Copreus is presented in Euripides' tragedy *The Children of Heracles* as a contemptible bully. His son Periphetes died in the Trojan War. [Homer, *Iliad*, 15.638–643; Apollodorus 2.5.1.]

Corcyra. A daughter of the Phliasian river-god Asopus. Poseidon fell in love with Corcyra and carried her off either to the island of Corcyra (Corfu) or to Black Corcyra, the island now called Korčula, off the Yugoslav coast. These islands were named for her. [Apollonius Rhodius 4.566–571; Pausanias 2.5.2, 5.22.6.]

Corcyra or **Kerkyra**. An island, now often called Corfu, off the coast of Epeirus. Corcyra, named for a daughter of the Sicyonian river-god Asopus, was early identified with the legendary island of Scherië, or Drepane, home of the Phaeacians. They were visited there by the Argonauts and by Odysseus.

cordax. A lascivious choral dance. The cordax was danced in Greek comedy, but, at least in Classical times, was regarded as too indecent for performance on any other occasion. According to Pausanias [6.22.1], the dance was Phrygian in origin and was first danced in Greece by the followers of Pelops while celebrating their conquest of Pisa.

Core. See KORE.

Coresus. A priest of Dionysus at Calydon. Coresus loved Callirrhoë, but she detested him. When he prayed to Dionysus for help, the god caused the Calydonians to go mad. They applied to the oracle of Dodona and were told to sacrifice Callirrhoë to Dionysus, unless she could persuade someone to die in her place. Callirrhoë found many well-wishers but no substitutes. She was dragged to the altar, where Coresus stood waiting, knife in hand. At the last moment the young priest discovered that he loved Callirrhoë better than his revenge, but, having enlisted divine aid, he had no hope of finding a rational human solution to the dilemma. Coresus took the only course left to him: plunging the knife into his own breast, he became the proxy victim. Seeing the young man dead at her feet, Callirrhoë was suddenly seized with remorse for her hardheartedness and killed herself as well—thereby making her lover's self-sacrifice redundant. [Pausanias 7.21.1–5.]

Corinth. A city at the western end of the isthmus that joins the Peloponnesus to Boeotia. Corinth was originally called Ephyra, for a daughter of Oceanus; the region around it was called Ephyraea. This land and Asopia, the adjoining region on the Gulf of Corinth, were given by Helius to his sons Aeëtes and Aloeüs, respectively. Aeëtes went to Colchis, leaving the rule of Ephyraea in the hands of Bunus, son of Hermes and Alcidamia. Upon Bunus' death, Epopeus, son of Aloeüs, added Ephyraea to Asopia, but his son Marathon later redivided them between his own sons, giving Ephyraea to Corinthus, Asopia to Sicyon. (Some, however, call Sicyon a son of Erechtheus or of Pelops.) These kings renamed the two principal cities in their own honor. When Corinthus died childless, the Corinthians sent to Colchis for Aeëtes' daughter Medea to rule them. This she did, making her husband, Jason, her consort on the throne; when he deserted her, Medea left the city to Sisyphus, an immigrant from Thessaly. According to another version of the tale, Creon was king of Corinth at this time and Jason repudiated Medea in order to marry the king's daughter, Glauce or Creüsa.

Sisyphus, often called the founder of Corinth, was certainly its most notorious ruler, though few of the tales of his frauds and trickery involve his rule. As king he established the Isthmian games in honor of Melicertes. He married the Pleiad Merope. Of their four sons, Ornytion succeeded to the throne, his brother Glaucus, father of Bellerophon, having been eaten by his own horses; and the other two sons, Almus and Thersander, took up residence in Orchomenus. Ornytion's younger son, Thoas, succeeded him because his elder brother, Phocus, had emigrated to the land later named Phocis in his honor. Thoas' great-grandsons prudently turned over the throne to the Heraclid Aletes in return for their continued residence in the city; their Corinthian subjects were expelled. About ten generations later the rule of kings was discontinued in favor of government by *prytanes* (presidents).

According to tradition, Helius and Poseidon had early quarreled about who should be patron of Corinth and the isthmus. Briareüs, called in to arbitrate, gave the isthmus to the sea-god and awarded the sun-god the Acrocorinth, the mountain that looms steeply over the city. This height Helius later turned over to Aphrodite.

Corinth, Gulf of. The body of water that separates the northeastern Peloponnesus from the Greek mainland.

Corinth, Isthmus of. The narrow strip of land by which the Peloponnesus is attached to mainland Greece. The isthmus, a region of strategic importance as a land route to the Peloponnesus, was controlled by the city of Megara. This city was, however, dominated during Minos' reign by Crete, in Theseus' time by Athens, and later by Corinth. The principal myths of the region are those concerned with MEGARA or with THESEUS' exploits in clearing the isthmus of outlaws. The western part of the isthmus seems to have been sacred to Poseidon. It was the site of the Isthmian games.

Corinthus. The eponym of Corinth. Corinthus renamed the city of Ephyra and the surrounding region, Ephyraea, for himself on receiving them from his father, Marathon. Corinthus had a daughter, Sylea, the mother of Sinis, but no sons. The rule passed at his death to Medea, daughter of the first king, Aeëtes. [Pausanias 2.1.1; Apollodorus 3.16.2.]

Coroebus. See CASSANDRA.

Corona Borealis (The Crown). A constellation. The crown that was preserved in these stars was said to have been a wedding gift to Ariadne, either from Theseus, who had received it from Thetis, or from Dionysus, who had been given it by Aphrodite. In either case, Dionysus placed it in the stars after Ariadne's death. [Hyginus, *Poetica Astronomica*, 2.5.]

Coronis. See ASCLEPIUS.

Coronus (1). A leader of the Lapiths. Coronus, a son of Caeneus, left his home in Gyrton in his youth to sail with the Argonauts. Later he and his people became involved in border disputes with the Dorians. HERACLES [M], coming to the aid of the Dorian king Aegimius, killed Coronus. Some accounts say that a son of Coronus named Caeneus sailed with the Argonauts, but this statement appears to be the result of confused genealogy. Coronus' son Leonteus fought in the Trojan War. [Homer, *Iliad*, 2.745–747; Apollonius Rhodius 1.57–58.]

Coronus (2). A king of Sicyon. Coronus, a son of Apollo and Chrysorthe, had two sons, Corax and Lamedon. During Lamedon's reign the Thessalian Epopeus seized the throne. [Pausanias 2.5.8–2.6.1.]

Coronus (3). A son of Thersander, son of Sisyphus. Coronus and his brother Haliartus migrated from Corinth to Orchomenus, where King Athamas adopted them, believing that all his own descendants were dead. When Athamas' son Phrixus (or his grandson Presbon) appeared from Colchis, the brothers willingly relinquished their claims to the throne and founded Coroneia and Haliartus on land given them by Athamas. [Pausanias 9.34.7–8.]

Corvus (The Crow). A constellation. For explanations of why the crow was placed in the stars, see CROW.

Corybantes. Male attendants of CYBELE. Like the Cretan CURETES (1), with whom the Greeks regularly identified them, the Corybantes celebrated the goddess' rites with armed dances during which they clashed spears and shields. Cybele's human worshipers imitated this ritual by dancing to the noise of flutes, drums, and cymbals. The Corybantes' frenzied rites had much in common with the dancing and music of the SATYRS who attended Dionysus.

Corynetes. See PERIPHETES.

Cos. One of the Dodecanese Islands off the southwestern coast of Asia Minor; also, its principal city. During the battle between the gods and the Giants, Poseidon chased Polybotes to Cos, broke off a promontory, and crushed the Giant beneath it. This rock is now the sizable island of Nisyrus, south of Cos. The Coans were originally called Meropes, after an early king, Merops or Meropes, whom Hera commemorated as Aquila, the constellation of the Eagle. The goddess later sent storms to drive her enemy Heracles to the island, where the islanders, thinking his men pirates, nearly killed him. Heracles was saved by Zeus, who severely punished Hera.

Cottus. See HUNDRED-HANDED.

crab. An ally of the Hydra. This animal aided the Hydra in her fight with HERACLES [D] by biting his foot. For this service the crab was immortalized by Hera as the constellation Cancer. [Hyginus, *Poetica Astronomica*, 2.23.]

Cranaüs. An early king of Athens. Cranaüs succeeded Cecrops to the rule of Cecropia. His wife, Pedias, was a Spartan. On the death of their daughter the virgin Atthis, Cranaüs renamed the region Attica in her honor. Deucalion's Flood is said to have occurred during Cranaüs' reign. He was deposed by Amphictyon, the husband of his daughter Cranaë. [Apollodorus 3.14.5–6.]

Crataeïs or **Crataiïs.** A nymph known only as the mother of Scylla. Apollonius Rhodius [4.825–832] says that Crataeïs is merely an epithet for Hecate, who was the mother of Scylla by Phorcys. Hyginus [*Fabulae* 199] calls Crateïs a river, and presumably conceived of her as a male deity, like most other river-gods.

Crater (The Bowl). For two explanations of the presence of a drinking or mixing bowl among the stars, see CROW and MASTUSIUS.

Cratus. See BIA.

creation myths. According to the mythical explanation of the creation of the universe that was most widely accepted by the ancient Greeks, Chaos existed before anything else, though not necessarily from the beginning of time. Out of Chaos (which means "Gulf" and was presumably conceived of as a mass of nothingness) came Ge (Earth), Tartarus, and Eros. Eros, not yet the handsome young god of later myth, probably represented the sexual force that would permit the work of creation to continue from its rather unpromising beginning. It was no doubt the presence of Eros that enabled the next two beings emerging from Chaos, Erebus (Darkness) and Nyx (Night), to unite and bring forth Aether (Upper Air) and Hemera (Day). Ge too began to produce offspring: Uranus (sky), Ourea (Mountains), and Pontus (Sea). Ge then lay with her son Uranus and bore the Titans.

These earliest beings, most of whom seem to have been scarcely personified natural phenomena, gave birth in turn to other rather abstract figures and to personages such as Nereus and Phorcys, who may have been ancient gods. Many of the nymphs, river-gods, and other spirits that peopled the earth and sea were descendants of these figures or of the Titans Oceanus and Tethys. The other Titans, a few of whom were more clearly personified, brought into being more Titans and the first generation of Olympian gods.

The earliest extant account of these primal events is Hesiod's *Theogony*. Parts of Hesiod's view of the origins of the universe and the gods—particularly the succession of ruling gods, each overthrowing his predecessor—were borrowed from myths of Anatolia. A very different concept of creation was expressed in the myths of the Greek cult of Orphism. Ancient references to these accounts are too fragmentary to permit reconstruction. Much of the Orphic story was probably artificial, but it may well have contained elements from ancient myths that are now lost.

Creon (1). A ruler of Thebes. Creon and his sister, Jocasta or Epicasta, were children of Menoeceus and descendants through Pentheus of both Cadmus and the Sparti. When Jocasta's husband, King Laïus, left Thebes on a journey to Delphi, he entrusted the rule to Creon during his absence. Shortly thereafter Thebes was ravaged by the Sphinx, who killed Creon's son Haemon, among other Theban youths. Laïus failed to return, and news came of his death. Creon offered Jocasta's hand, together with a share in the rule, to any man who could save the city from the Sphinx. Oedipus, a stranger from Corinth, defeated the monster and received the promised rewards. Much later he was discovered to be both the son and the unwitting murderer of Laïus, who had had Oedipus exposed as an infant. Oedipus was exiled by either Creon or his own sons, Eteocles and Polyneices.

The brothers, perhaps after a period during which Creon again acted as regent, agreed to share the rule equally. They quarreled, however, and Eteocles banished his brother. Polyneices gained the support of an Argive army and attacked Thebes (see SEVEN AGAINST THEBES). During this war Creon lost a second son, Menoeceus, who sacrificed himself for the city in obedience to an oracle. The Thebans repulsed the Argives, but both brothers were killed.

Creon again assumed the rule, this time as regent for Eteocles' young son, Laodamas. His first act was to deny burial to Polyneices and the Argive dead. Antigone, Oedipus' daughter, who was betrothed to Creon's third son, also named Haemon, defied the edict and was entombed alive. Relenting too late, Creon found that Haemon had killed himself together with Antigone. Creon's wife, Eurydice (or Eniocha), hanged herself from grief. An Athenian army under Theseus forced Creon to allow the burial of the Argives.

When Amphitryon was banished from Argos, Creon and his wife welcomed him and his wife Alcmene. Their daughter Megara later married Heracles, Alcmene's son by Zeus. In Creon's old age Thebes was invaded by Lycus, a descendant of the earlier Theban king named Lycus. This man, a Euboean, killed Creon and usurped the rule, but was killed by Heracles. The throne now reverted to Laodamas, who was king when Thebes was destroyed by the Epigoni. Creon is said to have had yet another son, Lycomedes, who fought with the Greek forces at Troy, and two more daughters, of whom nothing is known but their names, Henioche and Pyrrha.

Creon appeared prominently in all three of Sophocles' Theban plays—*Oedipus. the King, Oedipus at Colonus,* and *Antigone*—and in Euripides' *Phoenician Women.*

Creon (2). A king of Corinth. Alcmeon had a son and a daughter, Amphilochus and Tisiphone, by Manto, daughter of Teiresias. For some reason he brought them as infants to Creon, who agreed to rear them. When Tisiphone grew up she was so lovely that Creon's wife feared that he would discard her and marry the girl. She therefore sold her into slavery. Not knowing his daughter, Alcmeon bought her. On learning her identity, he recovered his son from Creon.

Creon welcomed Jason to Corinth and betrothed to him his daughter, Glauce or Creüsa. Jason divorced his Colchian wife, Medea, in order to advance his prospects in Corinth. (This act is the more ironic if, as some say, Medea's father, Aeëtes, had once been king of Corinth.) Fearing Medea's sorcery, Creon banished her from the city, but was persuaded to allow her a day to provide for her two children by Jason. Instead she sent a poisoned robe and crown to Glauce, and both the girl and her father died in the flames that burst from the gifts. According to the lost epic *The Taking of Oechalia* [4], Medea poisoned Creon and, leaving her sons in sanctuary at the altar of Hera Acraea, escaped to Athens. Creon's relatives killed the children, but pretended that Medea had herself done away with them.

Creon appears in Euripides' tragedy *Medea.* The story of his rearing of Alcmeon's children is also attributed by Apollodorus [3.7.7] to Euripides.

Cresphontes. A king of Messenia. Cresphontes, his brother Temenus, and

Procles and Eurysthenes, the sons of their dead brother Aristodemus, were chief among the Heraclids in the third generation after Heracles. Having seized the Peloponnesus, they determined to divide among themselves the three chief regions by drawing lots of baked clay marked with their names from a pitcher of water. According to one version of the story, Argos, Sparta, and Messenia would be awarded in that order as the names were drawn. Since Cresphontes wanted the last choice, he dropped into the pitcher an unfired sherd, which dissolved, leaving the other lots to be withdrawn first. In another version, Argos had already been assigned to Temenus and the winner of the drawing was to receive Messenia. Cresphontes ·persuaded Temenus, the referee, to aid him by throwing in a piece of sun-dried clay for the sons of Aristodemus; this dissolved, and Cresphontes' fired-clay potsherd was drawn.

Cresphontes did not live to enjoy his success for long. He was accepted by the Messenians as their ruler and established his capital at Stenyclerus, but his rule so favored the common people that the wealthy grew resentful and killed him, together with his two older sons. His successor, Polyphontes, also a Heraclid, forced Merope, Cresphontes' widow, to marry him; but her youngest son, Aepytus, who had been reared by her father, Cypselus, king of Arcadia, avenged Cresphontes on reaching manhood and recovered the throne. [Pausanias 4.3.3–8; Apollodorus 2.8.4–5.]

Cretan bull. A bull sacred to Poseidon. When Minos [A] claimed the rule of Crete by divine right, he prayed to Poseidon for confirmation of this claim. The god sent a bull up from the sea, with orders that Minos sacrifice the bull to him. The miracle silenced Minos' rivals, but the king sacrificed a less handsome bull. In revenge Poseidon caused Minos' wife, Pasiphaë, to have a monstrous offspring, the Minotaur, by the bull. Thereafter the bull roamed Crete. Eurystheus ordered Heracles [F] to bring the animal alive to Tiryns as his seventh labor. With or without Minos' help Heracles did so, then released it. It wandered through Sparta and Arcadia and came finally to Marathon, near Athens, where it caused havoc. According to some accounts, Aegeus [B], king of Athens, sent Minos' son Androgeüs out to capture the bull, and the young man was killed, as the king had hoped. Later, instigated by Medea, Aegeus ordered Theseus to capture the bull. Theseus brought it back to Athens, where either he or Aegeus sacrificed it.

Crete. A daughter of Asterius, king of Crete. According to Asclepiades, Crete married her foster brother Minos and, presumably, bore his children. Pasiphaë, rather than Crete, is generally said to have been Minos' queen. Crete was no doubt considered the eponym of the island. [Apollodorus 3.1.2.]

Crete. A large island in the Mediterranean Sea, southeast of Greece. Crete was the center of the Minoan civilization that dominated the eastern Mediterranean area until the fall of Cnossus about 1400 B.C. According to legend, Crete was settled by Tectamus, son of Dorus, and a force of Aeolians and Pelasgians. A generation later Zeus abducted Europa from Phoenicia and carried her to Crete, where she bore three sons, Minos, Rhadamanthys, and Sarpedon. Zeus then married her to Asterius, who had succeeded his father Tectamus as king. Asterius, whose daughter Crete was the eponym of the island, adopted his wife's sons and bequeathed his throne to Minos. A quarrel among the brothers led to the departure of Sarpedon for Lycia and Rhadamanthys for some other part of Asia Minor or for Boeotia.

Minos (or a dynasty of kings bearing that name) ruled for several generations. Under his just reign, his maritime nation and its allies, the Carians and Lelegians, held sway over most of the Aegean islands and many parts of the mainland. Minos conquered Megara, on the Isthmus of Corinth, and forced Athens to pay tribute to Crete. After the famous episode of Theseus and the Minotaur, Minos lost control of the mainland. According to tradition, he was killed in Sicily. His son Deucalion became king and evidently established friendly relations with Athens, for Theseus married Deucalion's sister Phaedra. Deucalion's son Idomeneus succeeded him and led a Cretan force to the Trojan War. On his return, however, he was deposed by the treacherous Leucus and emigrated to Italy. Nothing further of consequence is known of events in Crete.

A tradition of close connections between Crete and Phoenicia, hinted at in the myth of Europa's abduction from Tyre or Sidon, is borne out by a wide variety of archaeological evidence.

Cretheus. The founder and first king of Iolcus. Cretheus was one of the famous sons of Aeolus and Enarete. He married Tyro, the beautiful daughter of his brother Salmoneus. Some say that she had been his ward from childhood, presumably because her father had emigrated to Elis. It is not certain whether the marriage took place before or after Tyro bore two children by Poseidon, but she seems to have been a dutiful wife. Cretheus and Tyro had three sons, Aeson, Pheres, and Amythaon. According to Pindar [*Nemean Odes* 5.25–26], Acastus' treacherous wife, Hippolyte, was Cretheus' daughter. [Homer, *Odyssey*, 11.235–237, 11.258–259; Apollodorus 1.7.3, 1.9.8, 1.9.11.]

Creüsa (1). The youngest daughter of Erechtheus, king of Athens, and Praxithea. Creüsa married her father's Aeolid ally XUTHUS. According to Euripides' *Ion*, in which she is a principal character, she was raped by Apollo in a cave under the Acropolis and exposed her child there, but was later reunited with him at Delphi. The child, ION, is generally called Creüsa's son by Xuthus, as is his brother, Achaeüs. Euripides claims that Creüsa was also the mother of Dorus.

Creüsa (2). A daughter of Priam and Hecuba. Creüsa married Aeneas, leader of the Dardanian allies of the Trojans, and bore Ascanius (Iülus). She was captured by the Greeks, but saved by Cybele and Aphrodite. Later she disappeared as her family was escaping from the burning Troy, and was presumed dead. [Vergil, *Aeneïd*, 2.596–598, 2.673–674, 2.736–795; Pausanias 10.26.1.]

Creüsa. See GLAUCE.

Crisus or **Crissus.** A son of Phocus and eponym of a Phocian town, Crisa. When Phocus was murdered in Aegina, Crisus and his brother Panopeus emigrated to Phocis. Crisus' son Strophius, king of Phocis, was Agamemnon's son-in-law and ally and the father of Pylades. [Pausanias 2.29.4.]

Crius. A Titan. A son of Ge and Uranus, Crius was the father by his sister Titan, Eurybia, of Astraeüs, Pallas, and Perses. [Hesiod, *Theogony*, 134, 375-377.]

Crommyonian sow. A wild pig named Phaea. This beast, which some call an offspring of Echidna and Typhon, ravaged the town of Crommyon, on the Isthmus of Corinth, until it was killed by THESEUS [B]. It was called Phaea for the woman who bred it.

Cronian Sea. See ADRIATIC SEA.

Cronus. The ruler of the Titans. Cronus (whom the Romans identified with their god Saturn) and the other Titans were children of Ge (Earth) and Uranus (Sky). Ge complained bitterly to her children that her husband was mistreating her by imprisoning his children the Hundred-handed and the Cyclopes within her body. She made a sickle of flint and gave it to Cronus, the boldest and craftiest of her sons. He waited until his father next lay with Ge and castrated him. Some say that the other Titans aided him, others that Cronus acted alone. In any case, Uranus withdrew and Cronus ruled over his brothers and sisters. He soon proved to be as tyrannical as his father. He released the Hundred-handed and the Cyclopes only to imprison them again. Having been warned by his parents that he was destined to be deposed in turn by one of his children, he swallowed the offspring of Rhea, his sister and wife, as they were born. These children were Hestia, Demeter, Hera, Hades, and Poseidon.

When Rhea's last child, Zeus, was born, she gave it secretly to Ge in Crete and presented her husband instead with a stone wrapped in swaddling clothes, which he swallowed. (Some say that Rhea had also tricked Cronus after the birth of Poseidon, hiding the infant among lambs and giving her husband in its place a foal, which she claimed that she had just borne. The Titan was perhaps not greatly surprised, for he had earlier fathered the Centaur Cheiron on PHILYRA, taking a horse's form to hide from Rhea.) Zeus was thus reared in Crete. On reaching maturity he married the wise Oceanid Metis. She found a pretext to offer an emetic to Cronus, who vomited up his other children. They immediately joined with Zeus in a war on Cronus and some of his brother Titans. Zeus released the Hundred-handed and the Cyclopes, who aided the gods in the ten-year-long conflict. Cronus and the other Titans were flung into Tartarus, where the Hundred-handed became their jailers.

A very different tradition existed side by side with that of the Titans' imprisonment. According to this view, Cronus' rule was a golden age in which men lived like gods and death was no more than a sleep. When Cronus no longer ruled in Olympus, he became king of the Islands of the Blessed, where men favored by the gods went at their deaths. The Romans claimed that Cronus (Saturn) was the first king of Latium and, through his son Picus, ancestor of the Roman kings. A still different, and very obscure, tradition held that Cronus and Rhea deposed from Olympus not Uranus but Ophion and Eurynome, whom they flung into Oceanus.

It is generally believed that Cronus was a deity of the fertility of the earth, and that the sickle that he carries in his representations in art referred to that function, rather than to his mutilation of Uranus. [Homer, *Iliad*, 8.478–481, 14.203–204; Hesiod, *Theogony*, 137–138, 168–182, and *Works and Days*, 109–120, 169–169a; Apollodorus 1.1.3–1.2.1; Pausanias 1.7.6–10, 8.8.2, 8.36.2–3, 10.24.6.]

crow. There are many myths about this bird, all of them to its discredit. According to one, the crow was originally a daughter of Coroneus, a Phocian king. Pursued by Poseidon, the girl prayed to Athena, who transformed her into a crow and made a companion of her. The bird tattled when Cecrops' daughters disobeyed the goddess, and Athena rejected her in favor of the owl.

The crow (or raven) is usually said, however, to have been Apollo's bird. The tale of its transformation from white to black after informing on Coronis (see ASCLEPIUS) is well known, and many believe that the crow was placed in the sky as the constellation Corvus to serve as a caution to tattlers. Some writers, however, tell a different story about this same crow. Apollo sent it to a spring to fill his drinking bowl with water. Near the spring the crow noticed some promising, though still green, figs on a tree. The greedy bird forgot its instructions and perched on the tree to wait for the fruit to ripen. Several days later, after gorging itself on figs, the crow recalled its master's command and hurried back to Apollo with a bowlful of water. The god punished the dilatory bird by making it unable to drink during the season when figs are ripening. As a warning, Apollo placed the crow in the stars, with the bowl at its head and a water snake at its feet to frighten it away from the water. Alternative explanations are given, however, for the constellations of the Bowl (see MASTUSIUS) and HYDRA. [Ovid, *Metamorphoses*, 2.534–632; Hyginus, *Poetica Astronomica*, 2.40.]

Crown, The. See CORONA BOREALIS.

Cteatus. See MOLIONES.

Cupid. A Roman name for the Greek god EROS. (See also AMOR.)

Cures. A Sabine city northeast of Rome. Cures was ruled by Numa Pompilius at the time that he was chosen to be the second king of Rome. Some commentators traced the name of the god Quirinus to the name of this city.

Curetes (1). Cretan *daimones*, or spirits. When Rhea or Ge hid the baby ZEUS [A] from Cronus in a Cretan cave, the Curetes danced about, clashing their spears and shields in order to drown his cries. According to Hesiod [*Fragments* 6], the Curetes, the mountain-nymphs, and the satyrs were offspring of the daughters of Hecaterus, whoever he may have been. The Curetes were said to have stolen the infant Epaphus from Io to please Hera. For this offense they were killed by Zeus. The Curetes were evidently diviners, for Minos consulted them as to how he might recover his lost son Glaucus. Greek writers early recognized the similarity of behavior between the Curetes, attendants of Rhea, and the CORYBANTES, attendants of the Phrygian goddess Cybele, who was often identified with Rhea.

The name Curetes is probably derived from *kouros* ("youth"). They are generally believed to have been semidivine counterparts of young Cretans who performed armed dances in honor of the boy god the Cretan Zeus. References to them in Greek and Roman works are numerous, but all three principal events of their myth are found in Apollodorus [1.1.6–7, 2.1.3, 3.3.1].

Curetes (2). Early inhabitants of Aetolia. When Aetolus came from Elis to the land drained by the Acheloüs River, he found the Curetes living there. He killed three sons of Apollo and Phthia—Dorus, Laodocus, and Polypoetes— before making himself ruler of the land and naming it for himself. Presumably these were leaders of the Curetes. The Curetes continued opposing the invaders for several generations and early overran Calydon in the reign of Oeneus. After this time nothing is heard of them.

It is possible that several marriages of the mythical line that descended from Aetolus through Oeneus represent an unesasy truce between a ruling dynasty of Eleian conquerors and a more numerous native population. If, for example, Thestius was a leader of the Curetes, then the quarrel between his sons and Meleager, and Althaea's anger at her son would both be a part of the trouble between Curetes and Calydonians that grew out of the Calydonian boar hunt, rather than different versions of Meleager's death.

Cyanean Rocks. See CLASHING ROCKS.

Cybele or **Cybebe**. A Phrygian mother-goddess. Cybele was often referred to as the Mother of the Gods. She was also called Dindymene or the Dindymenian Mother because of her association with Mount Dindymus, in Asia Minor. The Greeks identified Cybele with RHEA, the mother of Zeus. According to a Phrygian myth recounted by Pausanias [7.17.9–12], Zeus once ejaculated on the ground while sleeping on Mount Dindymus. There grew up on this spot a strange creature with both male and female organs. The other gods, alarmed at the thought of what such an offspring of Zeus might do on reaching full size, cut off the male genitals. The castrated creature grew to be the goddess Agdistis, or Cybele.

From the severed genitals an almond tree grew. One day Nana, daughter of the river-god Sangarius, placed one of the fruits of this tree in her lap. It vanished and Nana found herself pregnant. In time she gave birth to a boy, whom she exposed. This child, Attis, was somehow suckled by a he-goat and grew up to be a handsome young man. Agdistis saw him one day and fell in love with him, but the youth, apparently unaware of this fact, prepared to marry a daughter of the king of Pessinus, a city at the foot of Dindymus. Madly jealous, Agdistis drove both Attis and the king mad. They castrated themselves in their frenzy and Attis died. Agdistis, regretting her fury too late, asked Zeus to grant that Attis' corpse never decay. He was buried at Pessinus, below Agdus, the rocky outcropping of Dindymus that gave Agdistis her name. Some say that Attis was transformed into the evergreen pine; this tree was at least sacred to him.

Cybele does not often appear in Greek literature, except as she is identified with Rhea, the mother of most of the Olympian gods. In this guise she is said to have purified the young Dionysus and taught him his rites at Cybela, in Phrygia. She also taught prophecy to Oenone. As the mother-goddess of Mount Tmolus, she was the mother by Gordius of Midas. Because Aeneas' ships were made of her sacred pine trees on Mount Ida, Cybele is said to have prevented them from being burned by Turnus 'and to have changed them into sea-nymphs.

Cybele was represented in art wearing a crown shaped like a turreted city wall and riding in a chariot drawn by lions. She was attended by maenads like those of Dionysus and, more particularly, by the Corybantes. These were young male divinities who danced in armor, clashing their shields and spears. The Greeks identified the Corybantes with the Curetes, who behaved similarly while attending the child Zeus in Crete. Cybele's male worshipers accompanied their own dancing with the music of shrill flutes, drums, rattles, and cymbals. Her priests castrated themselves in honor of Attis.

Although a foreign goddess with no place in the Greek pantheon, Cybele had shrines in many parts of Greece. She was perhaps the leading representative known to the Greeks of the Classical Age of a universal type of mother-goddess that had been worshiped in the Mediterranean region since prehistoric times. Such a goddess personified the regenerative forces of nature, of animals as well as vegetation. She usually had as a consort a younger god, such as Attis, who was subordinate to her. [Apollodorus 3.12.6; Apollonius Rhodius 1.1092–1152; Ovid, *Metamorphoses*, 10.102–105, 10.686–704, 14.535–555; *Homeric Hymn to the Mother of the Gods* 14; Hyginus, *Fabulae*, 191; Vergil, *Ciris*, 163–167.]

Cychreus. The first king of Salamis, which island he named for his mother. Cychreus welcomed Telamon when he was exiled from Aegina and, dying childless, left the kingdom to him. According to the early mythographer Pherecydes, Telamon was, in fact, a son of Cychreus' daughter, Glauce, and Actaeüs. Cychreus was associated in every story with a snake. Some say that he was given the rule of Salamis for killing a dangerous snake. Others claim that he bred the snake, which, when it was driven from Salamis by Eurylochus, went to the nearby mainland at Eleusis and was taken by the goddess Demeter as her attendant. Cychreus is said to have appeared to the Greek fleet during the battle of Salamis as a snake. It is likely that Cychreus, like many another hero, was honored in the form of a snake. [Apollodorus 3.12.6–7; *Catalogues of Women* 77; Pausanias 1.35.2, 1.36.1.]

Cyclopes. Monsters, each with one eye in the center of his forehead. The three original Cyclopes—Arges, Brontes, and Steropes or Pyracmon—were born to Uranus and Ge after the Titans. Uranus imprisoned the Cyclopes, along with the three Hundred-handed, in Tartarus. They were released by the Titans, but Cronus once again imprisoned them. Zeus, in his war with the Titans, again released the Cyclopes and they forged his thunderbolts for him. They continued to perform this service until Apollo killed them in order to avenge himself on Zeus for killing his son Ascelpius.

The relationship between these semidivine figures and the uncivilized shepherds encountered by Odysseus is not clear. Polyphemus and his numerous fellows were also one-eyed giants called Cyclopes. But although they were said to be close to the gods, they behaved like savages, with little regard for either men or gods. Late Classical writers tried to reconcile the two kinds of Cyclopes. Vergil, for example, located their thunderbolt forge in Vulcan's smithy in a cave of Mount Aetna, on the island of Sicily, which had early been identified as the home of Odysseus' shepherd giants. Many monumental works of craft from past ages, such as the walls of Tiryns and Mycenae, were attributed by Greeks of the Classical Age to the Cyclopes because they seemed too difficult for mere human beings to have accomplished. The Cyclopes had a shrine on the Isthmus of Corinth where sacrifices were offered to them. [Homer, *Odyssey*, Book 9; Hesiod, *Theogony*, 139–146; Euripides, *Alcestis*, 3; Vergil, *Aeneïd*, 8.439–453; Apollodorus 1.1.2, 1.1.4–5, 1.2.1; Pausanias 2.2.1, 2.25.8, 7.25.6.]

Cycnus (1). A son of Ares by Pelopia or Pyrene. Cycnus challenged HERA-CLES [M] to single combat when Heracles was passing near Itonus, in Phthiotis. He was aided in the ensuing battle by his father, but Heracles killed him nevertheless, and also wounded the god. On the advice of Athena, Heracles did not pursue Ares, or else was prevented from doing so when Zeus flung a thunderbolt between the two. Apollodorus, who is one of many writers to tell this tale, tells an almost identical one that he places in Macedonia, on the river Echedorus. This appears to be accidental repetition. [Apollodorus 2.5.11, 2.7.7; *Shield of Heracles* 57–480.]

Cycnus (2). A musician king of the Ligurians. A son of an unidentified Sthenelus, Cycnus was a relation and devoted friend of Phaëthon. When Phaëthon fell from the sky into the Eridanus River and his weeping sisters were turned into poplars beside this stream, Cycnus wandered grieving through the grove until, by Apollo's will, he became a swan and, according to some writers, was transported to the stars as the constellation Cygnus. Swans, it is said, have ever afterward sung sad songs when they are about to die. [Ovid, *Metamorphoses*, 2.367–380; Vergil, *Aeneïd*, 189–193.]

Cycnus (3). A king of Colonae, near Troy. Cycnus was a son of Poseidon by Calyce, daughter of Hecato. His first wife, Procleia, daughter of Laomedon or Clytius, bore a son and daughter, Tenes and Hemithea. The lying accusations against Tenes by Cycnus' second wife, Philonome, daughter of Cragasus, led the king to set both his children afloat in a chest. Later, on discovering the truth, Cycnus killed Philonome and tried vainly to win his son's forgiveness.

Cycnus joined the Trojans in an attempt to repulse the Greeks in their first landing. Poseidon having made him invulnerable to weapons, he was a formidable opponent, but Achilles finally strangled him with his own helmet thongs. According to Ovid [*Metamorphoses* 12.71–145, 12.580–606], his body was transformed by his divine father into a swan, which is the meaning of his name. [Apollodorus "Epitome" 3.23–25; Pausanias 10.14.1–4; *Cypria* 1.]

Cygnus (The Swan). A constellation. The Swan was placed in the sky by Zeus to commemorate the form that he had assumed to seduce Leda or Nemesis, whichever was the mother of Helen. This constellation is also said by various writers to represent one or another of the several mythical personages named Cycnus. [Hyginus, *Poetica Astronomica*, 2.8.]

Cyllene. See PELASGUS.

Cynortas or **Cynortes.** A king of Sparta. A son of Amyclas and Diomede, Cynortas became king at the death of his elder brother Argalus. He left the throne to his son Perieres or Oebalus. [Apollodorus 3.10.3; Pausanias 3.1.3.]

Cynthia. An epithet given by Roman poets to Diana (Artemis) in reference to the hill of Cynthus on the island of Delos, her birthplace.

Cyparissus. A beautiful Cean boy loved by Apollo. Cyparissus accidentally killed a pet stag that he loved very much. Grief-stricken, he asked Apollo to let him mourn forever. At last Apollo, unable to assuage the boy's sorrow, agreed and transformed him into a cypress tree, which is the meaning of his name. [Ovid, *Metamorphoses*, 10.106–142.]

Cypria. See EPIC CYCLE.

Cypris. A title of APHRODITE. The island of Cyprus was one of the chief centers of the goddess' cult; hence her title Cypris, meaning "the Cypriot."

Cyprus. An island in the northeastern end of the Mediterranean Sea. Cyprus was the principal cult center of the goddess Aphrodite, who figures in many of the myths of the place. Notable among these is the story of Adonis, a son of the Cypriot king Cinyras by his own daughter. Pygmalion was another well-known king of Cyprus. Several Greeks are said to have founded cities there. The Arcadian leader at Troy, Agapenor, was one of many supposed founders of Paphos, which existed, in fact, much earlier than the Trojan War. Teucer, exiled from his homeland of Salamis by his father, founded a new city named Salamis in Cyprus, where he was welcomed by Cinyras. According to another tradition, Teucer was given Cyprus by the Phoenician king Belus, who had conquered it. The Cypriot kings for many generations traced their ancestry to Teucer. Theseus' son Acamas also settled in Cyprus, where a promontory was named for him.

Cypselus. A king of Arcadia. Cypselus, a descendant of Stymphalus, was reigning when the Heraclids and Dorians successfully invaded the Peloponnesus. Seeing kingdoms falling to the Dorians on all sides of Arcadia, he realized that resistance would be futile. He therefore married his daughter, Merope, to Cresphontes, the Heraclid king of Messenia, and established an alliance that guaranteed autonomy to Arcadia for many generations. When Polyphontes seized power in Messenia, forcing Merope to marry him, Cypselus reared Aepytus, Merope's son by Cresphontes, at his court. When the youth was old enough, Cypselus joined with Heraclid rulers of other states to restore Aepytus to the Messenian throne. The Arcadian bond with Messenia was to serve Arcadia well in generations of wars with Sparta.

Cyrene. A nymph, the daughter of Hypseus, king of the Lapiths, or of the river-god Peneius. A huntress on Mount Pelion, Cyrene was seen by Apollo and carried to Libya, where a city was founded in her honor. She bore ARISTAEÜS, who became an agricultural god, and the seer Idmon.

Cyrene. A city on the northern coast of Africa just east of the Libyan Sea. According to Greek tradition, Cyrene was founded by descendants of the Trojan Antenor. They later welcomed settlers from the island of Thera, led by Battus. This band of unwilling pioneers settled first on the island of Platea. After two years of misfortune they moved to a pleasant part of the mainland near the island of Aziris. Seven years later they let themselves be lured westward by the Libyan natives with promises of a more desirable site. Although the tribesmen doubtless merely wanted to rid their land of the Greeks, the new land, which they named Cyrene, turned out to be well situated. Battus and his descendants ruled for eight generations, successive kings alternately bearing the names Battus and Arcesilaüs. In the reign of Battus II many new colonists arrived, chiefly from Crete and the Peloponnesus. They were attracted by offers of free land and reassured by the encouragement of the Delphic oracle. The colony, thus strengthened, was able to withstand an attack by the forces of the Egyptian pharaoh Apries. Cyrene prospered, though its subsequent history, recorded at length by Herodotus, was troubled both by struggles with Libyan tribes and by internal dissension.

Cythera. An island off the southern coast of the Peloponnesus. This island is known principally as a cult center of Aphrodite, who is often called Cythereia. Herodotus said that the Phoenicians founded her shrine there.

Cytissorus or **Cytisorus.** One of the four sons of Phrixus. With his brothers, Cytissorus helped the ARGONAUTS [K–N] to capture the golden fleece and escape from Colchis. When his grandfather Athamas was declared a scapegoat for the Thessalian Achaeans, Cytissorus saved him from sacrifice, but thus brought the anger of Laphystian Zeus down on his own posterity. Hyginus [*Fabulae* 3, 21] calls Cytissorus Cylindrus. [Herodotus 7.197.]

Cyzicus. A king of the Doliones, a Mysian tribe. Cyzicus was the son of Aeneus and Aenete, daughter of Eusorus. He married Cleite, daughter of Merops, but both died too young to have children. Cyzicus entertained the ARGONAUTS [D, E] hospitably, but was killed by Jason in a nocturnal battle between Argonauts and Doliones in which neither group recognized the other. Cleite committed suicide from grief. Cyzicus' city was renamed for him and his memory was honored for centuries at his burial mound. [Apollonius Rhodius 1.936–1077.]

Cyzicus. A city on the Mysian coast of the Sea of Marmara. Cyzicus was named for the young king of the Doliones who was killed in error by the Argonauts.

ⅅ

Dactyls. Obscure Cretan *daimones*, or spirits. The Dactyls (Fingers), who were also called Idaeans because of their birth on Mount Ida in Crete, were said to be sons of the nymph Anchiale. Having some association with Rhea in Crete, they came to be connected with her Phrygian counterpart, Cybele, and, according to Apollonius Rhodius [1.1125–1131], two of them, Titias and Cyllenus, were Cybele's "dispensers of doom and assessors." Diodorus Siculus [5.64.3–7] recorded that the Cretan gods called Dactyls were magicians and smiths who worked in Phrygia. They were sometimes thought to have come from the Asian Mount Ida. Some writers claimed that there were a hundred Dactyls, but Pausanias [5.7.6–5.8.1] mentioned only five—Heracles, Paeonaeüs, Epimedes, Iasius, and Idas—whom he identified with the Curetes that saved the infant Zeus from Cronus. Heracles, the eldest, led his brothers to Olympia, where he founded the Olympic games.

Daedalion. See CHIONE (1).

Daedalus. An Athenian master craftsman and inventor.

A. Daedalus and his sister, Perdix, were children of either Metion or Eupalamus, and directly descended from Erechtheus, king of Athens. Daedalus early acquired an enviable reputation as a sculptor and inventor. He accepted his nephew Perdix (or Talus or Calus) as a pupil, but, when the young man showed signs of surpassing his teacher as an inventor, Daedalus killed him. His crime was discovered and Daedalus was tried on the Areopagus and exiled, or else fled the city. He took refuge in Crete, where King Minos welcomed him and kept him busy with various projects. Daedalus' strangest commission, however, was given him not by Minos but, secretly, by the king's wife, Pasiphaë. This lady, who was in love with a handsome bull, induced the inventor to construct a hollow, wooden cow, covered with hides. The cow was wheeled into the pasture and Pasiphaë hid inside it. The false cow was so lifelike that even the bull was deceived, with the result that, in due course, the queen gave birth to the Minotaur, a monster with a man's body and the head of a bull.

This triumph led to another commission for Daedalus: the construction of the Labyrinth, as a prison in which the king might hide the Minotaur, evidence of his wife's shame. The passageways of this building were so intricate that anyone who entered without knowing its secret would never find his way out. Into it were sent every nine years a group of Athenian youths and girls to provide food for the captive monster. When the Athenian prince Theseus came voluntarily as one of these victims, Minos' daughter Ariadne fell in love with him and begged Daedalus to help her rescue him. At Daedalus' suggestion she gave Theseus a ball of thread, which he was to unwind as he penetrated the Labyrinth so that he could later retrace his steps. He was thus able to escape from the Labyrinth after killing the Minotaur.

Perhaps because Minos knew that Daedalus must have had a hand in this plot, he jailed the inventor and his son, Icarus, in the Labyrinth. Some say that Daedalus was released by Pasiphaë and, inventing the first sail, escaped in a boat with Icarus. According to a much better-known tale, the two flew away from the island on wings made by Daedalus of wax and feathers. The inventor warned his son not to fly too low, where the sea spray might wet his wings, or too high, where the sun might melt them. As they were flying over the eastern Aegean Icarus forgot this warning and soared too near the sun. The wings lost their feathers and the rash youth plummeted into the sea that separates the Sporades from the Asian mainland. From this event the sea is called Icarian, and the island on which the body washed ashore Icaria.

B. Icarus must have flown considerably off course, as well as too high, for Daedalus was making for Sicily. He reached it at last and took refuge with Cocalus, king of Camicus. Minos, meanwhile, had been looking everywhere for the missing inventor. Sailing from port to port, the Cretan king, whose power had long dominated the seas, demanded of each local ruler that he thread a spiral seashell. None of the kings could accomplish this seemingly impossible trick until Minos reached Sicily. Presented with the same demand, Cocalus returned the shell to Minos the next day completely threaded. The shrewd Minos knew that Daedalus must have found a haven here, for no one else in the world was clever enough to solve the problem. He was right. Cocalus had given the shell to Daedalus. The inventor, no doubt recalling Theseus' escape from the Labyrinth, had tied one end of the thread to an ant, and the ant, for obscure reasons of its own, had made its way through the tortuous windings of the shell.

Having discovered the whereabouts of the culprit, Minos demanded that Cocalus surrender him. To his astonishment, the Sicilian king dared to refuse. Daedalus had already executed some projects for Cocalus and, moreover, his daughters had grown devoted to the clever man. According to some writers Minos made war on Cocalus and was killed in the fighting. A more colorful version of the event has it that Cocalus promised to return the inventor after a feast. As the royal guest was having a bath, attended by Cocalus' daughters, they poured boiling water over him. Daedalus remained in Sicily for a considerable time and left many works there. Later he is said to have gone to Sardinia, either with the colony led by Iolaüs or with Aristaeüs. While there he built many unspecified works called Daedaleia.

Scores of statues and buildings, from Egypt through Crete and mainland

Greece to Sicily and Sardinia, were attributed to Daedalus. His mythical career seems to record the spread of an advanced material culture, perhaps from Crete, westward and northward through the Mediterranean area. The Sardinian Daedaleia were probably the numerous conical towers of the Bronze Age known locally as *nuraghi*. Particular mention was made by late writers of Daedalus' improvements in the lifelike qualities of sculpture. When the extraordinary buildings, art works, and religious beliefs of Egypt became known to Greek writers they often attempted to connect them with works and myths of their own land. Diodorus Siculus [1.61.1–2, 1.97.5–6], for example, claims that Daedalus built the great temple of Hephaestus (Ptah) at Memphis and was honored with a shrine of his own. He adds that the Labyrinth in Crete was inspired by one built by a pharaoh named Mendes or Marrus. Since the most specific parts of Daedalus' mythical career are associated with Crete, it may be that his legend arose with the spread of Minoan culture and, during the decline of Cretan power, was taken over by the Mycenaean culture of the mainland, particularly in Attica. [Apollodorus 3.1.4, 3.15.8, "Epitome" 1.8–15; Ovid, *Metamorphoses*, 8.183–262.]

daimon or **daemon.** A spirit. *Daimon* is a term often used to designate any of a large class of supernatural beings that may or may not be personified and that are both less individualized than most gods and more confined in function. Among the many divinities that can be described as *daimones* are nymphs, satyrs, river-gods, penates, and genii. *Daimones* generally resided in a particular object, place, or natural phenomenon. Although there are exceptions to this rule, nymphs were usually restricted to a single tree, spring, mountain, or the like; satyrs to a single wooded area; penates to family storerooms; Nereïds to the waves of the sea; and harpies (originally, at least) to gusts of wind. Nymphs were often freed from these limitations and individualized by the fancy of poets—or else mortal characters were awarded the rank and romantic aura of nymphs. Satyrs might wander far from their native woods in the train of Dionysus, but they, like their companion bacchants, functioned more as idealized representations of the god's mortal worshipers and lost some of their character of woodland spirits. River-*daimones* somehow acquired the nominal status of gods, but, in spite of the prominence that some of them gained in myth, they remained confined to their beds and most references to them scarcely distinguish the spirits from the streams they inhabit.

Mortals often approached *daimones* in the hope of winning their favor. Thus the Romans honored the penates who controlled their stores of food. Even an offended nymph was sometimes appeased with offerings. Local heroes often functioned as *daimones* and were induced with special sacrifices to favor their countrymen in some fashion. Many scholars believe that *daimones* were the raw material out of which gods were made.

Damastes. See PROCRUSTES.

Danaë. The daughter of ACRISIUS, king of Argos, and Eurydice. Although imprisoned by her father, Danaë bore a son, PERSEUS [A, E], by Zeus. Acrisius set mother and child adrift in a chest, but they reached the island of Seriphus. There King Polydectes tried to force her to marry him, but Perseus eventually rescued her and took her home to Argos. According to Vergil [*Aeneïd* 7.371–372, 7.406–413], Danaë emigrated for some reason to Italy and founded Ardea, the capital city of her descendant Turnus, king of the Rutulians. [Apollodorus 2.2–4; Hyginus, *Fabulae*, 63.]

Danaïdes. The daughters of Danaüs.

Danaüs. A king of Argos.

A. Danaüs and Aegyptus were twin sons of Belus, who ruled the vast territory under the domination of the kingdom on the Nile. The brothers each had fifty children by many wives, but Aegyptus' offspring were all sons, whereas Danaüs had only daughters. Belus gave Libya to Danaüs, Arabia to Aegyptus. Aegyptus promptly conquered the Melampodes and named their land Egypt after himself. When he asked for his nieces as brides for his sons, Danaüs rightly suspected that his brother was plotting to kill him in order to win all Belus' lands for himself. With the aid of Athena, Danaüs constructed a large boat, perhaps the first two-prowed vessel, and set sail with his daughters for Argos, the homeland of his ancestress Io. On the voyage they put in briefly at Lindos, on the island of Rhodes, and there dedicated a famous statue of Athena in gratitude for her help.

Landing at last at Apobathmi, near Lerna, Danaüs and his daughters advanced to the borders of Argos. There are, however, two very different accounts of what happened next. According to Pausanias, Danaüs laid claim to the throne on the basis of his descent from Io, an Argive princess. Since Gelanor, who presently occupied the throne, was descended from the same line, Danaüs might have received little support from the Argive assembly, except for a disturbing incident that occurred on the night before it was to judge between the claimants. A ferocious wolf descended upon the herds and killed the lead bull. The Argives took this as an omen that Danaüs, who, like the wolf, had lived alone on the borders of the community, might take similar vengeance if frustrated. Prudently they made him king. Danaüs piously dedicated a temple to Apollo Lyceius, god of wolves. By the time Aegyptus' sons arrived to claim his daughters once more, Danaüs was well established in Argos.

B. In his play *The Suppliants*, Aeschylus told a very different story. Arriving at Argos, Danaüs and his daughters begged protection from King Pelasgus and the Argives against the sons of Aegyptus, who were in hot pursuit, under orders from their father (Hyginus adds) not to return while Danaüs lived. The Argives agreed and prepared to battle the arrogant Egyptian invaders. Since the remaining plays of Aeschylus' trilogy are lost, the ensuing events are unclear.

The outcome of the conflict is well known, however, from many other accounts. Danaüs was either forced or persuaded to agree to his daughters' marriage with their cousins. (Apollodorus and Hyginus both give lists, though not the same lists, of the couples.) On the wedding night Danaüs secretly issued daggers to the brides and commanded them to kill their husbands. All but one of them obeyed, and dawn revealed forty-nine corpses in the Egyptians' beds. Hypermnestra, the eldest girl, was touched by the fact that her husband, Lynceus, had spared her virginity. She helped him to escape to the nearby village of Lyrceia. There he lighted a signal fire to let her know that he was safe and Hypermnestra answered with another on the Larisa, the Argive citadel. Danaüs punished her disobedience with imprisonment and later brought her to trial, but the Argives acquitted her. In time Danaüs was reconciled to both Hypermnestra and Lynceus.

C. Meanwhile, the other Danaïdes had lopped off their husbands' heads and brought them to their father as proof of their dutifulness. They buried the heads on the Larisa and the headless trunks at Lerna, or the other way around. Before long, word got around of the bridegrooms' fate. When Danaüs decided that it was time to find new husbands for his daughters, he encountered considerable reluctance on the part of the young men of Argos, in spite of his wealth and influence. Danaüs finally succeeded by offering the young widows as prizes in a footrace, but felt it necessary to throw in some handsome shields as an additional inducement.

If the young women got off rather easily while they remained on earth, they fared less well in the Underworld. There, according to some late accounts, they were required ceaselessly to draw water, but in leaky jars that had to be forever refilled. For this task they had gained a good deal of experience in life, for they had found Argos a dry region, as the result of Poseidon's punishment of Inachus long before. Danaüs was later recalled as the man who first watered the land, presumably by sinking wells. His daughter AMYMONE helped by winning the favor of Poseidon, who showed her the springs at Lerna. When he died Danaüs was buried with great honor near the temple of Apollo Lyceius. He was succeeded on the throne by Lynceus. [Apollodorus 2.1.4–2.2.1; Pausanias 2.19.3.]

Danube River. A river rising in Germany and flowing southeastward into the Black Sea. Classical writers called the Danube the Ister. Escaping from the Colchians, the Argonauts sailed up it and down a branch that led into the Adriatic Sea. No such branch exists, but ancient writers may have believed that the Save, a tributary of the Danube rising near the Adriatic, actually flowed into that sea.

Daphne. A nymph. Daphne, whose name means "Laurel," was either an Arcadian girl or a daughter of the Thessalian river-god Peneius. In the former version, she loved to hunt with other girls along the banks of the Ladon River. Leucippus, son of Oenomaüs, king of Elis, fell in love with her, but she would have nothing to do with men. Since Leucippus was already growing his hair long in honor of the river Alpheius, he decided to dress as a girl. Pretending to be a daughter of Oenomaüs named Oeno, he asked to be allowed to hunt with Daphne and she agreed. Her new friend's prowess at the hunt won her admiration and the two became boon companions. One day Daphne and some other girls wished to swim in the Ladon. Leucippus refused on some pretext, but the others playfully stripped him. On discovering his sex, they indignantly killed him with their spears. Some say that Apollo had caused this to happen because he wanted Daphne for himself.

The better-known version does not include this episode. Both end, however, with Daphne paying dearly for her avoidance of men. Eros, angry at Apollo for saying that the boy should leave archery to men, shot the god with one of his gold-tipped arrows. When Apollo fell madly in love with Daphne, Eros shot her with a leaden point, which caused her to reject male advances. She persuaded her father to let her remain a virgin forever. Apollo, however, would not be denied. He pursued Daphne through the woods until, seeing that she could not escape, she prayed to Ge for help. The goddess transformed her into a laurel tree. The frustrated god had to content himself with breaking off a branch to wear on his head. Thereafter the laurel was sacred to Apollo. [Pausanias 10.7.8; Ovid, *Metamorphoses*, 1.452–567; Hyginus, *Fabulae*, 203.]

Daphne. See MANTO.

Dardania. The region near, or including, Troy. This land, first ruled by the indigenous king Teucer, fell to his son-in-law, Dardanus, who named it Dardania. Although this name is often used as a synonym for Ilium (Troy), the Dardanians were actually neighbors and allies of the Trojans. Dardanus or Dardania, their capital, was on the slopes of Mount Ida, whereas Troy was on the plain not far from the sea. The Dardanian line descended from Assaracus, a great-grandson of Dardanus; the Trojan line, from his brother Ilus.

Dardanus is said to have given the name Dardania as well to the island where he was born or spent some years. This island was later renamed Samothrace by settlers from Samos.

Dardanus (1). The son of Zeus and Electra, daughter of Atlas. According to the Greeks, Dardanus was born in the region later called Troy, or came there from Samothrace or Crete. The Romans claimed that he was born in Italy and reached Troy by way of Samothrace. Whatever his origin, he was welcomed to the land by Teucer, its first king. Teucer gave him land and the hand of his daughter, Bateia. Dardanus founded a city, Dardania, and, on succeeding to Teucer's rule at the king's death, extended the name to the entire region. He was regarded as the first ancestor of the Trojans. Homer claimed that he was Zeus's favorite of all his sons by mortal women. He was the father by Bateia of Ilus and Erichthonius. [Homer, *Iliad*, 20.215–222, 20.302–305; Apollodorus 3.12.1–2, 3.15.3; Vergil, *Aeneïd*, 7.205–208, 8.134–137.]

Dardanus (2). A king of the Scythians. Dardanus was the father of Idaea, second wife of Phineus, king of Salmydessus. He condemned her to death for her crimes against her stepsons.

Dascylus (1). A king of the Mariandynians. Dascylus was helped by Heracles to put down his Phrygian, Mystian, Paphlagonian, and Bithynian enemies. He was succeeded by his son Lycus. [Apollonius Rhodius 2.774–791.]

Dascylus (2). A son of Lycus, king of the Mariandynians. Dascylus was sent by his father with the Argonauts to insure them a friendly welcome among his allies as far as the Thermodon. [Apollonius Rhodius 2.802–805.]

dawn. Eos was the Greek goddess of the dawn, Aurora the Roman.

Death. See THANATOS.

Deïaneira. A daughter of Oeneus, king of Calydon, and Althaea. Deïaneira was courted by both the river-god Acheloüs and HERACLES [M, N]. Heracles won the resulting contest of strength and married Deïaneira. When he exiled himself from Calydon after an accidental killing, she accompanied him to Trachis. On the way the Centaur Nessus tried to rape her. As he was dying at Heracles' hands he gave Deïaneira a mixture of his blood and semen, claiming that the potion would insure Heracles' love for her. Later, Deïaneira learned that Heracles had taken Iole as a concubine. She spread the potion on a tunic and sent it to him, unaware that the Centaur's blood contained deadly Hydra venom. When she learned that it had caused her husband's death, she killed herself. She had borne several children by Heracles, including Hyllus.

Deïaneira is a leading character in Sophocles' play *Women of Trachis*. See also Apollodorus 2.7.5–8.

Deïmachus. See AEOLUS (1); AUTOLYCUS (2).

Deimus. See PHOBUS.

Deïon. A king of Phocis. Deïon, a son of Aeolus and Enarete, married Diomede, daughter of Xuthus. She bore him a daughter, Asterodia, and four sons; Aenetus, Actor, Phylacus, and Cephalus. [Apollodorus 1.9.4, 3.15.1.]

Deïphobus. A son of Priam and Hecuba. After Paris' death, Deïphobus and his brother Helenus both claimed the right to marry the widowed Helen. She was awarded to Deïphobus. When the Greeks took Troy, Menelaüs and Odysseus went to Deïphobus' house to take Helen, and, in the ensuing fight, Menelaüs killed him. Some say that Helen betrayed Deïphobus to the Greeks. [Homer, *Iliad*, 13.402–539, and *Odyssey*, 4.274–276, 8.516–520; Vergil, *Aeneïd*, 6.494–547; Apollodorus "Epitome" 5.9, 5.22; Hyginus, *Fabulae*, 91, 110.]

Deïphontes. A son of Antimachus, a Heraclid. Temenus, a leader of the Heraclids and king of Argos, regarded Deïphontes so highly that he gave him his daughter Hyrnetho for his wife and made him his chief adviser. Temenus' sons, fearing that they would lose the succession, overthrew Temenus, and Deïphontes withdrew to Epidaurus, which King Pityreus turned over to him. Ceisus, Temenus' eldest son, who had seized the Argive throne, sent his brothers Cerynes and Phalces to persuade their sister to leave her husband. Hyrnetho, pregnant with Deïphontes' fifth child, refused and they kidnaped her. Deïphontes killed Cerynes, but Phalces, in his eagerness to escape, handled

Hyrnetho so roughly that she died. Deïphontes buried her in an olive grove in which she was later honored as a heroine. Before her death she had borne him three sons and a daughter. [Apollodorus 2.8.5; Pausanias 2.19.1, 2.26.1–2, 2.28.1–7.]

Deïpyle. A daughter of Adrastus and Amphithea. Deïpyle married Tydeus and was the mother of Diomedes. (See SEVEN AGAINST THEBES, A.)

Delia. An occasional epithet of Diana, arising from Delos, the island of her birth.

Delos. A small island in the Cyclades. Delos was most famous as the birthplace of Apollo and, in some traditions, of Artemis. This reputation made the island one of the most sacred and prosperous places in Greece. Delos was said by some writers to have once been called Asteria or Ortygia, though others said that these were names of a nearby island. Artemis took her late but wellknown epithet Cynthia from Cynthus, a hill in Delos. Apart from the island's association with the births of two important deities, Delos is known only as the home of Anius, its priest-king. Anius' daughters, votaries of Dionysus, were given the gift of turning everything that they touched to food, a boon which led, however, to their destruction. Aeneas stopped at Delos on his trip to Italy and was entertained there by Anius.

Delphi. A city in Phocis. The city of Delphi, the principal religious center common to all Greeks, clung to the dizzyingly steep slopes of Mount Parnassus, with forbidding cliffs above it and a gulf beneath. Accounts of the founding of Delphi are contradictory, but most Greeks agreed in general on the history of the oracle that made the city famous. This oracle originally belonged to Ge (Earth), though some say that she shared it with Poseidon, who spoke through a prophet named Pyrcon. Ge turned over the oracle, or her share of it, to Themis, also an earth-goddess. Aeschylus claimed that Themis gave up her rights to the Titaness Phoebe, who in turn relinquished them to Apollo. Other versions have it that Themis turned over the oracle directly to Apollo or that he took it by force. Some add that he exchanged the island of Calaureia for Poseidon's interest in the oracle.

Although long before Classical times Apollo had been the unquestioned patron of the Delphic oracle, it was universally agreed that he had not instituted it and that, moreover, he had had to kill a dragon in order to establish his claim. This monster, often called PYTHON, had probably been an oracular snake connected with the earth's shrine. Its name survived in Delphi's alternate name, Pytho, and in the title of Apollo's prophetess there, the Pythia. It was believed that the exact center or navel (*omphalos*) of the earth was at Delphi, and it was shown there in the form of a beehive-shaped stone. Two eagles (or swans, or crows) flying from the ends of the earth were said to have met at this point.

Near the *omphalos*, which was Apollo's seat, the Pythia sat on a tripod and uttered her oracles. An old woman, except in very early times, she gave these prophecies while in a state of trance. She was believed to be possessed by the god, much as a modern medium is thought by believers to be possessed by the spirit of a dead person. Some Classical writers tried to explain the trance by saying that the Pythia was affected by vapor issuing from a cleft under the tripod, but extensive investigation at Delphi has showed no such cleft. There is, moreover, no medical basis for the theory sometimes advanced that the Pythia's custom of chewing leaves of the laurel or bay, sacred to Apollo, contributed to her trance. The mutterings of the prophetess were interpreted and set down in verse by priests connected with the shrine of Apollo.

The Delphic oracle's reputation for reliability extended throughout the Mediterranean world in quite early times. To judge from the prophecies recorded by tradition, this reputation may have been preserved through the cleverly ambiguous wording devised by the priests. According to Herodotus, the famous Lydian monarch Croesus consulted the oracle as to whether he should attack the Persians, who were then threatening his kingdom. He was told that if he did he would destroy a great empire. Taking this to mean the Persian empire, Croesus attacked, was defeated, and saw the destruction of Lydia, which had also been a great empire.

The Delphic oracle figured prominently in innumerable myths. In some of these, the answers given to suppliants were cryptic, as in the case of Aegeus; clear but misleading, as in the warning given to Oedipus; equally clear, but of doubtful wisdom, as in Apollo's command to Orestes.

Delphinius. An epithet (He of the Dolphin) of Apollo. APOLLO [A] had a shrine at Delphi under the name Delphinius. This fact was accounted for either by his having killed the dragon Delphyne or by the legend that the god assumed a dolphin's form to lead Cretan sailors to Delphi, where they established his shrine. The latter explanation—together with the fact that other prominent shrines of Delphinius existed in Crete and in cities with strong Cretan connections, such as Athens and Didyma, in Caria—suggests either that Apollo's worship in the Minoan territories was associated with dolphins or that a dolphin-god became identified with Apollo. Whether the epithet had a connection with the place-name Delphi is not clear.

Delphinus (The Dolphin). A constellation. The dolphin immortalized in these stars may be the one that persuaded Amphitrite to marry Poseidon or perhaps the one that carried Arion to safety. Then again, he may be one of the dolphins into which Dionysus changed the Tyrrhenian pirates. [Hyginus, *Poetica Astronomica*, 2.1.]

Delphyne. A dragon-woman. When Typhöeus severed Zeus's sinews during his assault on the gods, he hid them in the Corycian Cave, in Cilicia, in Delphyne's keeping. The monster, half serpent and half woman, made a poor watchdog. Hermes and Aegipan stole the sinews and restored them to Zeus. Delphyne was later killed at Parnassus by Apollo. This story of her death may, however, result from confusion with the snake Python, compounded by the fact that there were Corycian caves both in Cilicia and at Delphi. [Apollodorus 1.6.3; Apollonius Rhodius 2.705–707.]

Deluge. See DEUCALION (1).

Demeter. An ancient goddess of corn or of the earth and its fertility in general. Demeter was also known to the Greeks as Deo; the Romans called her CERES.

A. Demeter was one of the children of Cronus and Rhea who were swallowed by their father. Rescued when their brother Zeus induced Metis to feed an emetic to Cronus, she joined her brothers and sisters on Mount Olympus. At a banquet given by the Phrygian king Tantalus for the gods, Demeter ate the shoulder or arm of Tantalus' son, Pelops, whom Tantalus had served in a stew to test the wisdom of the gods. She made up for this faux pas by providing the boy with a new arm of ivory when he was restored to life and one piece by the gods.

At the marriage of Cadmus and Harmonia, Demeter was seduced by Iasion, brother of the Samothracian bride. The lovers lay together in a thrice-plowed field in Crete. Zeus indignantly killed Iasion with a thunderbolt for his presumption. Some say, however, that Iasion lived to old age in the goddess' company and that she would have had him rejuvenated if Hebe, the goddess of youth, had been willing. In any case, Demeter bore two sons by Iasion: Plutus and Philomelus. Plutus became a god of the wealth of the earth. His brother, a poor farmer, delighted Demeter by inventing the wagon. She rewarded him by placing him in the stars at his death as the constellation Boötes.

Demeter's true concerns were not on Olympus, but on the earth. She presided over the crops, and over the grains in particular. For some reason she held the bean in contempt as impure. She was fond of the nymph Macris, who lived in a cave on the island of Drepane, or Scherië. For love of her the goddess taught the Titans to sow corn there. The island is named, in fact, for Demeter's sickle (*drepane*).

B. By Zeus, Demeter had a daughter, Persephone (though some say that Styx was the mother). One day Hades, the brother of Zeus who ruled in the Underworld, saw Persephone and fell in love with her. Zeus readily agreed to the marriage, but warned Hades that Demeter probably would not approve of her daughter's leaving for a sunless home in the bowels of the earth. He suggested, therefore, that Hades carry the girl off. Zeus assisted him by inducing Ge to send up, near where Persephone lived, hosts of lovely flowers, among them a narcissus with a hundred blooms. While the girl was gathering these flowers in the company of several goddesses, or of some Oceanids and the daughters of Melpomene and Acheloüs, Hades suddenly appeared in his four-horse chariot, snatched up the girl, and drove quickly back to the Underworld. There is much disputing about where this happened, but one widespread view places the event near the city of Henna.

Persephone must have wandered away from her companions before Hades appeared, for none of them could say what had happened to her when her mother inquired of them. Some say that Demeter changed Melpomene's daughters into Sirens for their unwillingness to join in the search, but others suggest that the girls themselves asked to be granted wings in order to seek their former companion more effectively. Only the nymph Arethusa, the sungod, Helius, and Hecate, who lived near by in a cave, had heard the girl's cries or witnessed her abduction—or, if others knew the truth, they would not tell it. For nine days and nights Demeter wandered over the earth with torches, searching everywhere for her daughter, without stopping either to bathe or to eat. On the tenth day Hecate met her and told her that Persephone had been carried off, though she could not say by whom. Both goddesses then hurried to visit Helius to find out what he might have seen. He told them what had happened, but tried to persuade Demeter that Hades, brother of Zeus and ruler of a third part of the universe, was not an unfit husband for Persephone. (Some say that it was Arethusa, or an Argive woman or nymph named Chrysanthis, or the people of Hermion who betrayed Hades.)

Far from being comforted, Demeter was so enraged that she refused to return to Olympus. She wandered over the earth in human form, caring nothing for her appearance. While she was passing through Arcadia, Poseidon tried to rape her. The goddess changed herself into a mare in order to avoid his attentions and grazed with the mares in the herds of Oncius, at Thelpusa. Not fooled, Poseidon became a stallion and mounted Demeter. She bore Arion, the remarkable horse, and a goddess whom the Arcadians call merely the Mistress (Despoina), her name being a secret revealed only at her mysteries. Furious at Zeus, Poseidon, and the world in general, Demeter shut herself in a cave on Mount Elaeüs, near Phigalia. Pan eventually found her there and told Zeus. The worried god sent the Fates to talk with Demeter. They were able to persuade her to calm her anger and grief and to accept the marriage of Persephone and Hades as inevitable. Thereafter the people of this part of Arcadia worshiped both a mare-headed Demeter and Poseidon the Horse.

C. According to a more widespread tradition, Demeter visited the cities of men during the time of her grief, appearing as an old woman. Where she was welcomed, she taught the cultivation of corn, and perhaps other agricultural pursuits. Where she was shown no honor, or too little, she punished the culprits severely. Somewhere, for example, she asked a woman for a drink and received a cup of *kykeon*, water mixed with meal and pennyroyal. The weary goddess drank it so greedily that she was ridiculed by the woman's rude boy, Ascalabus. Demeter flung the dregs in his face. Instantly he was changed into a spotted lizard (*askalabos*).

Many cities claim that Demeter came to them, but best known are her deeds in the town of Eleusis, near Athens. There are varying versions of this tale, but they agree on the essential points. Coming to the town, the goddess sat down on a rock near a well. When the four daughters of King Celeüs, son of Eleusis, came to the well to draw water, they greeted the old woman courteously and invited her to return with them to the palace. Demeter, introducing herself as Doso, a Cretan woman carried off by pirates, agreed and offered to work at any of the many tasks appropriate to old women. Metaneira, Celeüs' wife, welcomed her, but at first the goddess sat in a corner immersed in her grief until a waiting woman named Iambe induced her to smile at her quips. She then accepted a cup of *kykeon*. Metaneira made Doso the nurse of her son Demophon.

The goddess was as solicitous for her foster child as she had been for her own daughter. In her eagerness to make him immortal and ageless, she anointed him daily with ambrosia and at night laid him to sleep in the embers of the fire. All would have gone well had not Metaneira, or a woman named Praxithea, spied on the nurse at night. Horrified at what she saw, she cried out in alarm. Angrily the strange nurse flung the baby onto the floor and, returning to her own majestic form, revealed herself to be a goddess. (Some say that she allowed Demophon to burn to death. The Eleusinians deny this, and add that he grew up to be one of their great leaders.) Relenting somewhat, Demeter taught Celeüs and his people the rites in her honor that were to be celebrated for many centuries as the Eleusinian mysteries.

D. Demeter had not forgotten her daughter. In spite of her kindness to the Eleusinians, she brought famine on the earth for an entire year, and it seemed that the race of men would soon starve to death. Zeus, realizing that such a tragedy would mean an end of sacrifices to the gods, sent Iris to summon Demeter to Olympus. She refused to go. Now the other gods were growing alarmed. They went in a body to implore Demeter to forget her anger and return to Olympus so that the crops might grow again. The goddess would not budge from her new temple at Eleusis. Defeated, the king of the gods sent Hermes down to Hades to fetch Persephone. Hades blandly consented to her leaving him and kindly offered her a pomegranate seed to eat.

Hermes brought the girl to Eleusis. A joyful reunion followed, but the mother's first question to her daughter was, "Did you taste any food in the Underworld?" Persephone admitted that she had. Demeter at once realized that she had been tricked, for anyone who tasted the food of Hades had to spend at least the third part of every year in the Underworld. Some claim, however, that Persephone had been so hungry that she ate seven of the seeds secretly, of her own accord. Ascalaphus, a son of the Underworld river-god Acheron by Orphne or Gorgyra, spied on her and told Hades. Persephone turned Ascalaphus into an owl by splashing him with water from the river Phlegethon, or else Demeter punished him by pinning him beneath a great rock. Heracles later rolled this rock away, but Demeter at once changed Ascalaphus into an owl.

Zeus, hoping to avert further famine, sent Rhea—the mother of Demeter, of Hades, and of Zeus himself—to reason with her daughter. Demeter, knowing that she would have Persephone with her for two-thirds of each year, relented and agreed to allow the grain to grow once again. With her daughter she at last returned to Olympus.

Before leaving Eleusis the goddess lent her dragon-drawn, winged chariot to TRIPTOLEMUS. This young Eleusinian may have been an elder son of Celeüs, but there are many other versions of his parentage. In the chariot he flew through the air sowing corn, or else teaching the people of many lands how to cultivate grains. On two or three occasions Demeter came to his aid when he was threatened with harm by unfriendly kings. Also at or near Eleusis the goddess gave a gift of the fig tree to a man named Phytalus, who had been gracious to her during her stay.

According to one account, the king of Eleusis during Demeter's visit was Eleusinus, eponym of the city. His wife was Cothonea and his son Triptolemus was the boy whom the goddess nursed. When Eleusinus protested on finding his son in the fire, the goddess struck the king dead. Later Triptolemus returned from his journeys promoting the use of grain. For some reason Celeüs, the new king, planned to execute the young man for his activities. Demeter forced him instead to turn over the kingdom to Triptolemus, who established Demeter's festival called the Thesmophoria.

E. It is generally agreed that Demeter was a pre-Hellenic goddess of a type familiar as the "earth-mother"—which may, in fact, be the meaning of Demeter's name. At least by Classical times, her functions were confined to presiding over agriculture, and particularly over the cultivation of various grains. The annual return to earth of her daughter was, of course, an allegory of the sprouting of the seed that had lain dormant in the soil during the winter months. Persephone was also, however, an Underworld goddess, and Demeter herself had some chthonian aspects. Her worship was widespread and her rites were celebrated in many places. Because of the power of Athens, which had early incorporated the town of Eleusis within its boundaries, the Eleusinian mysteries became the best known and most influential of all the religious mysteries of the Greeks. The Thesmophoria, also an important festival, was celebrated yearly by Athenian women.

F. The ancient *Homeric Hymn to Demeter* [2] told in detail the story of the rape of Persephone and of Demeter's activities at Eleusis. These events were also described by Apollodorus [1.5.1–3, 2.5.12] and Hyginus [*Fabulae* 141, 146, 147]; Ovid [*Metamorphoses* 5.341–571] told Persephone's story alone, as did Euripides [*Helen* 1301–1368] in a song that attributes many elements of the cult of Cybele to Demeter. Pausanias [8.15.1–4, 8.25.2–7, 8.37.6, 8.42.1–13] gave much information on Demeter's myths and rites in Arcadia. Aristophanes dealt irreverently with the Athenian festival in his *Women Celebrating the Thesmophoria*. Other references to Demeter's story are to be found in Hesiod, *Theogony*, 453–506, 912–914, 969–974; Homer,

Odyssey, 5.125–128; Apollonius Rhodius 4.986–990; Hyginus, *Fabulae*, 83, and *Poetica Astronomica*, 2.4, 2.25; Apollodorus 1.1.5–1.2.1, 3.6.8, 3.12.1, 3.14.7; Ovid, *Metamorphoses*, 5.642–661, 6.118–119, 8.738–878, 9.422–423; Pausanias 1.14.1–3, 1.37.2, 2.5.8.

Demodice. See ATHAMAS [B].

Demonassa. A daughter of Amphiaraüs. Demonassa married Thersander and bore him Tisamenus. [Pausanias 9.5.15.]

Demonice or **Demodoce.** A daughter of Agenor and Epicasta. Demonice was the mother by Ares of Evenus, Molus, Pylus, and Thestius. [Apollodorus 1.7.7.]

Demophon or **Demophoön** (1). A son of Theseus and Phaedra or Antiope. Although Pindar called Demophon a son of Theseus' mistress, the Amazon queen Antiope, he and his brother, Acamas, were usually considered to be the sons of Theseus' wife, Phaedra. The boys were sent to Euboea to be protected by Elephenor when Theseus was exiled from Athens. When the brothers grew up they went with Elephenor to the Trojan War and there rescued their grandmother Aethra, who had been abducted from Aphidnae long before to be Helen's nurse.

Although the story of ACAMAS' desertion of Phyllis and his death on the island of Cyprus is told as well of Demophon [Apollodorus "Epitome" 1.16–17; Hyginus, *Fabulae*, 59, 263], it is generally believed that he returned to Athens, where, the usurper Menestheus having died at Troy, he was given the rule. Demophon appears in Euripides' *Children of Heracles* as a defender of Heracles' family against Eurystheus.

Demophon or **Demophoön** (2). A son of Celeüs, king of Eleusis, and Metaneira. Demophon was nursed by DEMETER [C], who nightly placed him in a fire in order to immortalize him. When his mother showed her horror at this treatment, the goddess, according to some accounts, indignantly let the child burn. [*Homeric Hymn to Demeter* 2; Apollodorus 1.5.1.]

Dendrites. An epithet (meaning He of the Trees) of DIONYSUS [H].

Deo. A name of DEMETER.

Despoina. The daughter of Demeter and Horse Poseidon. While Demeter was wandering through the world in search of her daughter, Persephone, whom Hades had carried off, Poseidon pursued her. She changed herself into a mare and grazed with the herds of Oncius near Thelpusa, in Arcadia. Poseidon became a stallion and mounted the goddess. According to one tradition, Demeter gave birth to the horse Arion, but the Phigalians claimed that she bore Despoina, who was their chief goddess.

Despoina, which means Mistress, was merely her cult title. Her name was never mentioned except during her secret rites, and the secret was so well kept that it is unknown today. Pausanias implies that Despoina was not identical with Kore (Maid), the cult name of PERSEPHONE at Eleusis, but similarities between their cults and the fact that the pomegranate alone of all fruits was not offered to the Arcadian goddess make the resemblance striking. A male figure named Anytus, said to be a Titan and represented as armed, was honored together with Despoina and her mother. [Pausanias 8.37.1–10, 8.42.1.]

Deucalion (1). The son of Prometheus and Pronoea. Deucalion ruled Phthia and was married to Pyrrha, daughter of Epimetheus and Pandora. When Zeus determined to destroy the human race with a great flood, Prometheus advised his son to build a boat and stock it with provisions. Deucalion did so, and he and Pyrrha floated about in the boat for nine days and nights before running aground on Mount Parnassus. There they sacrificed to the Corycian nymphs, to the mountain-nymphs, and to Themis, who in those early days had charge of the Delphic oracle. Some say that they first sacrificed to Zeus.

Deucalion and his wife were safe but lonely. Faced with spending the rest of their lives alone on earth, they appealed to Themis' oracle and were told to throw over their shoulders the bones of their mother. The literal-minded Pyrrha refused to commit such an outrage, but Deucalion guessed the key to the oracle: stones were the bones of their mother Earth. According to a different story, Deucalion prayed to Zeus either to repeople the earth or to destroy him and Pyrrha as well. Zeus gave the same instructions as Themis, but without disguising his meaning. Not without some doubts, the lonely couple picked up stones and threw them behind them. Those that Deucalion threw became men; Pyrrha's stones became women. These were the Lelegians. After this momentous event, Deucalion settled in the Locrian city of Opus or in Athens. Pyrrha bore him five children: Hellen, Amphictyon, Protogeneia, Pandora, and Thyia.

Zeus is generally said to have destroyed the human race except for Deucalion and Pyrrha. Many claim, however, that the Deluge was far from efficient. Megarus, a son of Zeus by a Sithnid nymph, swam in the darkness that accompanied the rains toward the cries of cranes and found a haven on the peak of a mountain on the Isthmus of Corinth, which was thereafter called Mount Geranium (Crane Mountain). One Cerambus is said to have been saved by nymphs, who bore him up on wings. And some of the inhabitants of Delphi followed the howling of wolves to one of the peaks of Parnassus, where later they built the town of Lycoreia (Place of the Mountain Wolves). Moreover, when Deucalion's grandsons set out to occupy the lands of Greece, which their father had allotted them, they found them well populated. [Apollodorus 1.7.1–2; Ovid, *Metamorphoses*, 1.318–415.]

Deucalion (2). An Argonaut. Deucalion was one of the sons of Minos and Pasiphaë. Hyginus [*Fabulae* 14] lists him among the Argonauts. He was the father of Idomeneus, Crete, and a bastard son, Molus. [Apollodorus 3.1.2, 3.3.1.]

Dexamenus. A king of Olenus. Dexamenus entertained Heracles at his court and his guest saved the king's daughter Mnesimache from forced marriage with the Centaur Eurytion. Dexamenus' twin daughters, Theronice and

Theraephone, married Heracles' enemies the Moliones. He also had a son, Eurypylus.

Dia. A daughter of Eioneus or Deïoneus. Dia was the mother, either by her husband, Ixion, or by Zeus, of Peirithoüs.

Dia. The name of two islands. Dia was an early name of Naxos and also the name of the island of Ares, in the Black Sea, where the Argonauts were attacked by brazen-feathered birds.

Diana. An ancient Italic goddess. Diana, originally a deity of the Latins or Sabines, was a patroness of wild things and of birth, both human and animal. Apparently a fertility goddess of the "mountain-mother" type, she was easily identified with the Greek ARTEMIS. Diana was the patron goddess of the Roman plebeians, most of whom were of Latin or Sabine origin. She was associated with an obscure deity named VIRBIUS, who may have corresponded to the Attis-Adonis type of consort who usually attended a mountain-mother goddess.

Dicte, Mount. A mountain somewhat east of central Crete. A cave in this mountain was the haven of the infant Zeus, although the same honor was later claimed for another Cretan mountain, Ida. The obscure Cretan goddess Dictynna was probably worshiped chiefly on this mountain. Dicte was also said by some to be the home of the Harpies.

Dictynna. An epithet interpreted by Classical writers as "Lady of the Nets." This title originally belonged to the Cretan goddess BRITOMARTIS, but was later often given to Artemis. The true meaning of the word was probably "She of Mount Dicte."

Dictys. A fisherman of Seriphus. Dictys protected PERSEUS [A, E] and Danaë from his brother, POLYDECTES, and became king of Seriphus.

Dido. The founder and first queen of Carthage. Dido, or Elissa, as she was also called, was a daughter of Belus, Agenor, or some other Tyrian king. Her brother, Pygmalion, succeeded to the rule and Dido married their uncle Sychaeüs. Pygmalion, discovering that Sychaeüs had much hidden wealth, treacherously murdered him for it. Dido learned of the murder from her husband's ghost, which warned her to leave Tyre. Keeping her preparations secret, she gathered together provisions and a company of Tyrians who were disaffected with Pygmalion's rule. She sailed to Cyprus, and from there to the Libyan coast, where she bought from the natives as much land as could be encompassed by a bull's hide. Dido had a hide cut into exceedingly thin strips, which, when tied end to end, enclosed enough land for the citadel of a town. This town was called by a Phoenician word meaning citadel, which sounded to the Greeks like *byrsa*, a hide.

The new city prospered quickly, attracting many people from surrounding regions. According to early Roman accounts, the Libyan king Iarbas (or Hiarbal) grew alarmed and forced the Phoenician nobles to urge Dido to marry him. Knowing that he would overrun Carthage if she refused, she consented, but asked time to prepare for the nuptials. Secretly she ordered a funeral pyre to be built and killed herself upon it.

Vergil, perhaps taking a cue from an earlier Roman author, introduced AENEAS [B] into Dido's story. The queen welcomed Aeneas to Carthage and the two fell in love with one another. Dido's infatuation led her to neglect affairs of state, but Aeneas, twice reminded by Mercury of his destined future in Italy, regretfully sailed away. Distraught, Dido committed suicide.

Since Dido's other name, Elissa, and those of her husband and her sister, Anna, seem to be versions of Semitic names, it is likely that the story contains genuine elements of some Phoenician myth. It is believed by many scholars that Dido, and perhaps other characters in the story, were Phoenician divinities, but little more can be gleaned from existing evidence.

Dido is a famous tragic heroine almost exclusively as a result of her sympathetic treatment by Vergil in the *Aeneïd* [1.335–756, 4.1–705, 6.450–476].

Dike. See SEASONS.

Dindymene. See CYBELE.

Dindymus, Mount. A mountain near the Sangarius River and the ancient city of Gordium, not far from modern Ankara. Mount Dindymus was a favorite haunt of the Phrygian goddess Cybele, the Great Mother of the Gods, who was often called Dindymene for this reason. The Argonauts sacrificed to Cybele on the mountain.

Diodorus Siculus. A Greek historian born in Sicily in the first century B.C. The considerable surviving parts of Diodorus' long history of the world are useful sources of myth. Diodorus was given to inventing rational explanations of myths that were often as preposterous as the originals, but those stories that he did not tamper with contain many details not found elsewhere. Diodorus' history is published in the Loeb Classical Library.

Diomedes (1). An Argive leader. Diomedes was the son of Tydeus and Deïpyle, daughter of Adrastus. Tydeus had joined the expedition of the Seven against Thebes, led by Adrastus, and was killed before that city. Diomedes, on reaching manhood, married Aegialeia, daughter of Adrastus or Aegialeus. Together with the other sons of the Seven, called the Epigoni, he marched against Thebes. They razed it in vengeance for their fathers' deaths. After their return to Argos, Diomedes went with Alcmeon, leader of the Epigoni, to Calydon to avenge Tydeus' father, Oeneus, on the sons of his brother Agrius, who had usurped the throne. They expelled Agrius, killed most of his sons, and restored Oeneus to power. According to some writers, however, Oeneus was now too old to rule, so Diomedes turned the government over to Oeneus' son-in-law Andraemon and took the old man home with him to Argos. Oeneus died there of old age and was buried in Oenoë, the town named for him. Some say that two of Agrius' sons, Onchestus and Thersites, had escaped death and killed Oeneus as he and Diomedes were passing through Arcadia. Having been a suitor of Helen, presumably before his marriage, Diomedes was required by his oath to Tyndareüs to join the Trojan War. Aided by two other Epigoni, Sthenelus and Euryalus, who were subordinate to him, he led eighty ships from Argos and allied cities, including Tiryns, Epidaurus, and Troezen.

Though still very young, Diomedes was one of the bravest of the Greek leaders. In one day of triumph, supported by Athena, he killed Pandarus, seriously wounded Aeneas, and wounded even Aphrodite, sending her fleeing to Olympus for comfort. He met the Lycian leader Glaucus on the battlefield and was about to fight him to the death when he discovered that Glaucus' grandfather Bellerophon had been a guest-friend of Oeneus. At this revelation the two exchanged armor instead of fighting. Diomedes was the only Greek to come to Nestor's aid when the old man's horses were killed on the field. Together the two pursued Hector and might have killed him had not Zeus stopped them by flinging a thunderbolt. Later Diomedes volunteered to join Odysseus in a nocturnal spying excursion. They captured and killed the Trojan spy Dolon and killed the sleeping Thracian king Rhesus, together with twelve of his men. Diomedes was Odysseus' companion on more than one occasion. Earlier the two are said by some writers to have lured Iphigeneia to Aulis and to have joined in the treacherous murder of Palamedes. Near the end of the war Diomedes (or Neoptolemus) went with Odysseus to Lesbos to bring Philoctetes to Troy. The same pair slipped into Troy at night and stole the Palladium.

Diomedes was one of the few Greek leaders at Troy to return safely and promptly to his home. What happened to him after he got there is not clear. Although Diomedes was Adrastus' son-in-law, he had less claim to the throne, according to the Argive laws of his day, then did the boy Cyanippus, son of Adrastus' son Aegialeus, who had been killed at Thebes in the campaign of the Epigoni. Diomedes and Cyanippus' cousin Euryalus acted as the boy's guardians. When the boy died childless, the throne reverted to Cylarabes, son of Sthenelus, for Sthenelus, though only Diomedes' squire at Troy, came of an ancient Argive family with a better claim to the throne than even that of Adrastus, whose ancestors were Messenian.

It was perhaps at this time that Diomedes, whose wife had earlier been seduced by Sthenelus' son Cometes at the instigation of NAUPLIUS (1), was exiled from Argos. With his followers he emigrated to Italy. There he married the daughter of Daunus, king of Apulia, and founded the city of Argyripa (Arpi). Aphrodite had never forgiven him for the wound that he had given her at Troy. Thanks to her enmity he was so beset with problems that, in later years, he was unable to offer aid to Turnus against the Trojan invader Aeneas. [Homer, *Iliad*, 2.559–568, 5.1–444, 6.119–236, 8.78–171, 10.219–579, 14.109–134, 14.109–132; Apollodorus 1.8.5–6; Hyginus, *Fabulae*, 98, 102, 108, 175; Pausanias 2.25.2, 2.30.10; *Little Iliad* 1; *Cypria* 19; Vergil, *Aeneïd*, 8.9–17, 9.225–295; Ovid, *Metamorphoses*, 14.457–513.]

Diomedes (2). A king of the Bistones, of Thrace. Diomedes, a son of Ares by Cyrene or Asterië, daughter of Atlas, owned four mares which he valued so highly that he fed them on human flesh. As his eighth labor HERACLES [G] killed Diomedes, subdued the horses (perhaps by feeding their master to them), and brought them to Tiryns. After showing them to Eurystheus he freed them. They were later eaten by wild animals on Mount Olympus, where they had presumably gone while wandering back to Thrace.

Dione. A Titan or Oceanid. Dione is an obscure deity in extant writings, but two facts suggest to some scholars that she may once have been important: she is called by Homer, among others, the mother of Aphrodite, who is Zeus's daughter; and her name is a feminine form of Zeus's own. [Homer, *Iliad*, 5.370–416; Euripides, *Helen*, 1098; Hesiod, *Theogony*, 353; Apollodorus 1.1.3, 1.3.1.]

Dionysus. A Greek god of wine, and of vegetation in general. Dionysus was also known to the Greeks as Bacchus (Bakchos). This name was also used by the Romans, but they often identified Dionysus with their own god Father Liber and called him by this name as well.

A. There are many versions of Dionysus' birth. According to the Orphic account, known only from late Classical writers, Zeus lay with Persephone in the form of a snake. The result of this union was the child Zagreus, who was often identified with Dionysus. Zeus's jealous wife, Hera, persuaded the Titans to tear the child to bits and eat him. Athena saved his heart, however, and brought it to Zeus, who swallowed it. He then fathered the child a second time by seducing Semele, a daughter of Cadmus, king of Thebes. In a variation of this story, Zeus fed the pieces of Dionysus' heart to Semele in a drink and she conceived. The god's second birth at Thebes (which in this tale accounts for his common epithet "Twice-born") corresponds fairly closely to the more usual version of the myth.

The generally accepted account begins with Zeus's seduction of Semele. (Many places other than Thebes claim credit for Dionysus' birth, among them Dracanum, Naxos, Icarus, and Mount Nysa.) When Hera discovered that Semele was pregnant by Zeus, she disguised herself as the girl's old nurse, Beroë. Without much difficulty she persuaded Semele to insist that her divine lover appear to her in his full majesty, as he did to his wife. The rash girl made Zeus promise to grant whatever boon she asked, then demanded what Hera had suggested. Unable to dissuade Semele, Zeus reluctantly agreed and visited her as a thunderbolt, or else in a chariot amid thunder and lightning. Semele was blasted or died of fright. Zeus snatched the unborn child from her womb and the flames of the burning chamber and sewed it into his own thigh. In due course he opened the stitches and removed the infant, thus providing another reason to call Dionysus the twice-born god. Hermes took the baby to Ino, Semele's sister (or to certain nymphs on Mount Nysa, or to Macris in Euboea).

Ino and her sisters, Agave and Autonoë, had spread a rumor after Semele's death that her story of being seduced by a god was a lie. Nevertheless, Ino accepted the child from Hermes and, with the approval of her husband, ATHAMAS [C], acted for a time as his nurse, agreeing to rear him as a girl, as Hermes requested, presumably in the vain hope of deceiving Hera. Hera hated the child and punished one or both of its foster parents with madness for succoring it. When Dionysus grew up, after many further vicissitudes, he remained grateful to his former nurse, though he could not save her from the troubles that Hera brought on her. At some point the god, presumably to please Ino, drove to madness Phrixus and Helle, Athamas' children by his first wife. At another time he wrapped Ino in a mist in order to save her from being executed for her machinations against these same children. When Dionysus returned in triumph to Thebes, Ino was there to revel on Mount Cithaeron in his orgiastic rites with her sisters. Finally the mad Ino leaped into the sea with her son Melicertes. Dionysus immortalized this pair as the minor sea deities Leucothea and Palaemon.

Pausanias [3.24.3–4] reported an entirely different tradition of Dionysus' birth, one which he said was known only to the inhabitants of Brasiae, a coastal town in Laconia. According to their story, Semele lived to bear her baby at Thebes, but King Cadmus did not believe her tale about being seduced by Zeus. He locked mother and child in a chest and flung it into the sea. It eventually washed ashore at Brasiae. Semele was dead, but the baby was saved. At this point Ino arrived at Brasiae in the course of her mad wanderings and nursed Dionysus in a cave. Although this myth contradicts the usual story, it is one of a number of indications in art and minor myths that Dionysus had strong connections with the sea.

B. After Ino had nursed the child (or before, in some accounts), Zeus transformed him into a kid in order to hide him from the jealous Hera. Hermes then carried him to the nymphs of Nysa, a mountain that different writers have located in Thrace, Asia, and Africa. Some accounts identify these nymphs as the HYADES, formerly called the Dodonidae, and add that Dionysus later placed them in the stars out of gratitude. Whoever they were, the Nysaean nymphs reared the goat-child in a cave on the mountain. Later, when Dionysus had returned to human form, they became his followers, the maenads, and shared much of the persecution to which the god was subjected. When they grew old, Dionysus persuaded Medea to rejuvenate them, no doubt by boiling them with herbs in her ever-handy cauldron. Some say that Dionysus' principal nurse was the Euboean nymph Macris.

For some reason the "nurses" (as his female votaries seem to have been called) were not at hand on the day that Dionysus was kidnaped from the island of Icaria by piratical Tyrrhenian sailors. (This event, like many other trials of Dionysus, has been blamed on Hera.) Some say that the nurses were waiting for him on the island of Naxos, or that he had other reasons for wanting to go there. In any case, although he was a mere boy, he asked the sailors for passage to the island. They agreed and took him aboard, for they believed him to be the son of some wealthy family who would pay them well. Greed overcame them and they steered the ship off course, planning to hold the lad for ransom. Some add that he was so handsome that they also tried to rape him. The helmsman, Acoetes, did his best to save the passenger, for he sensed that he was more than an ordinary mortal, but the other sailors threatened or manhandled him for interfering.

Suddenly, in spite of a stiff breeze in its sails, the ship stood still. A sound of flutes was heard. Ivy and grapevines twined themselves about the oars and masts, or the oars turned to snakes. The astonishment of the sailors turned to terror as wild beasts—panthers, lions, and bears—appeared on the deck. Some say that the captain was eaten by a lion, others that he ordered Acoetes to turn back to the proper course, but it was too late. In a frenzy of fear the sailors leaped into the sea, where they were changed into dolphins. Acoetes would have followed, but Dionysus restrained him, assuring him that he had won his favor by his attempts to save him. As for the dolphins, having once been human themselves, they ever afterward remained friendly to human beings. Dionysus placed one of them among the stars to commemorate his triumph and, no doubt, as a warning to pirates.

In a variant of this tale, Dionysus and some of his followers sailed together in the pirate ship. When he was bound by the sailors he told his friends to sing. They did so, and the sailors began a wild dance. It was so wild, in fact, that they danced off the boat into the sea, leaving the god and his company in full command.

C. The vengeance of Hera caught up with Dionysus during his youth and he went mad. He ran away from his nurses and wandered through Egypt, Syria, and other lands. Some say that he went to Dodona in order to consult the oracle there, and perhaps also because, according to this tale, his nurses had originally come from there. Two asses who carried the god across the river were rewarded by being placed in the stars. To one of them the god gave a human voice, which may later have led to his death at the hands of Dionysus' son Priapus.

At length Dionysus came to Phrygia. There Cybele, whom the Greeks identified with Rhea, purified him and presumably cured him of his madness. It was while he was in Phrygia that he adopted the oriental costume that he and his followers affected; there also he instituted many of his own rites, some of which resemble those of Cybele.

Precisely at what point the mortal-born Dionysus became a full-fledged god is not certain. Unlike Heracles, another mortal who achieved divine status, he did not wait for death to receive it. When Dionysus left Phrygia to establish his own worship in much of the region of the eastern Mediterranean, there is no doubt that he was already a god. Wherever people honored him and observed his rites he rewarded them with many blessings, particularly the knowledge of the cultivation of the grape and the pleasures of wine. Where he encountered opposition, he brought terrible destruction on those who defied him.

Dionysus traveled with a strange company of MAENADS, SATYRS, and seileni (see SEILENUS). Male as well as female votaries dressed in flowing garments that seemed effeminate to the Greeks. During their revels they wore animal skins and carried *thyrsi*, poles twined with ivy and grapevines and often surmounted with pine cones. They worshiped the god, or achieved communion with him, in orgiastic, often nocturnal, rites on the mountains. When these revels reached their peak, under the influence of religious frenzy (and probably of wine, as well), the revelers often had visions of their god, who might appear in the form of a bull or a goat. The women suckled kids or fawns, and sometimes tore them apart with their bare hands and ritually ate them. To judge from characteristic representations of satyrs in art, sexual license may also have been a part of the rites.

Dionysus first met violent opposition at the hands of Lycurgus, son of Dryas. Lycurgus was king of the Edonians, who lived on the river Strymon, in Thrace. He drove away the god and his "nurses" with an ox-goad. The terrified Dionysus, and perhaps all but one of his nurses as well, took refuge in the depths of the sea with Thetis. According to Homer [*Iliad* 6.119–143], Lycurgus' behavior angered the other gods. Zeus blinded him and he did not live long thereafter. Later writers report the king's punishment in more detail, and in a variety of ways. In all of the accounts Dionysus used against the king his infallible weapon: madness. Some say that he imprisoned Lycurgus in a cave until he came to his senses. Others claim that, while mad or drunk, the king tried to destroy with an ax the vines that the god had taught his people to plant. Instead, he hacked to death his son, Dryas, or his wife and son, and cut off his own or his son's feet. Lycurgus recovered his senses, but the land produced no crops. Through his oracle, Dionysus declared that it would remain barren as long as the king lived. The Edonians thereupon bound Lycurgus on Mount Pangaeüs and caused him to be killed by horses, or else the god threw him to his panthers on Mount Rhodope.

D. Dionysus next came to his birthplace, Thebes. Because his mother's sisters had refused to acknowledge his divinity after Semele's death, he drove them and all the women of Thebes mad. (This harshness toward all three sisters seems to conflict with Dionysus' gratitude, in other accounts, toward Ino for having nursed him.) They deserted their homes and rushed off to the slopes of Mount Cithaeron to join his maenads in their wild rites. Old King Cadmus, who had abdicated the throne in favor of his grandson, Pentheus, accepted the god, as did the seer Teiresias. The young Pentheus, however, was outraged by what seemed to him the excesses of the god's strange band of votaries, and by their unsettling influence on the local women. He had the maenads imprisoned, together with a young priest, their leader. (Some say that this young man was Acoetes, the Tyrrhenian sailor who had become a convert to the god's cult, but he was generally thought to be Dionysus himself in disguise.)

Jails and chains could not confine the prisoners. The leader, working his influence on the king himself, persuaded him to accompany him, dressed as a maenad, to spy on the women at their revels. Pentheus climbed a pine tree on the mountain to watch them as they danced and tore animals limb from limb. They soon discovered him and uprooted the tree. Believing him in their frenzy to be a lion, they tore him into pieces, which they scattered about the mountainside. Agave, Pentheus' mother, triumphantly returned to Thebes with her son's head impaled on her thyrsus. Only then did she come to her senses and realize what she had done. Dionysus exiled Agave and both her parents from Thebes because of their long reluctance to acknowledge him. Cadmus and Harmonia also were exiled. In the land of the Encheleans they were changed into serpents by Dionysus or Ares and eventually went to the Elysian Fields.

Thebes became the principal Greek center of the god's cult. Pentheus was succeeded by his uncle, Polydorus. It was perhaps this king who officially instituted the god's rites at Thebes. It is recorded that he enshrined a log that had mysteriously fallen from heaven at the time that Semele was blasted by the thunderbolt. Polydorus had the log ornamented with bronze and it was thereafter honored as Dionysus Cadmus.

The daughters of Minyas, king of nearby Orchomenus, were no more willing to accept Dionysus than Cadmus' daughters had been. Denying that he was a god, they remained in the palace and busied themselves with what had always been regarded as the proper tasks of women, rather than dressing in animal skins and dancing in the woods. Dionysus punished them in his usual way. In their madness they tore to pieces the infant son of one of the sisters, after choosing the victim by lot. Dionysus changed them into bats.

E. The god next came to Argos, where either Proëtus or Anaxagoras was king. Proëtus (in that version of the tale) had three daughters, Lysippe, Iphinoë, and Iphianassa. Like the three daughters of Cadmus, and of Minyas, they refused to worship the new god. In the protracted fit of madness with which he afflicted them, they roamed the mountains in a disheveled state, imagined themselves to be cows, and ate the children that they suckled at their breasts. Some say that this disease affected all the Argive women, or that it was sent by Hera, not Dionysus. In any case, the Argive men called in the seer MELAMPUS [C] from Pylus to cure the women. He did so for a fee that amounted to a sizable share of the kingdom.

According to an entirely different tradition, Dionysus came to Argos in company with a band of women from the Aegean islands, whom the Argives dubbed Haliae (Sea-women). Perseus, king of Mycenae, went to war with them and killed many, burying them in a mass grave at Argos. (Some very late

Classical writers say that he killed Dionysus himself.) The Argives of Pausanias' day claimed, on the other hand, that Perseus and the god were reconciled and that the latter was worshiped at Argos as the Cretan Dionysus. There was a tomb of Dionysus' wife Ariadne at Argos.

During the reign of Pandion, Dionysus came to Attica. Instead of seeking a direct confrontation with the king, however, he chose to teach the culture of the vine to a man named ICARIUS (2) and his daughter, Erigone. Icarius was delighted with this boon to mankind, but when he gave some wine to the local peasants they thought themselves poisoned and killed Icarius. Erigone hanged herself. Dionysus drove the women of Attica mad and they too began hanging themselves. Their husbands, after consulting an oracle, punished Icarius' murderers and instituted an annual "swinging festival" in Erigone's honor. Dionysus relented and the women of Attica regained their sanity. He placed Icarius, Erigone, and even their dog, Maeara, in the stars as the constellations Boötes, Virgo, and Canicula or Procyon.

When the god went to Aetolia he met with a hospitable welcome from King Oeneus. Not only did he entertain Dionysus, but, on realizing that his guest wanted to sleep with his wife, Althaea, he found a pretext to leave town for a discreet interval. When he returned, Althaea was pregnant (and later gave birth to a daughter, Deïaneira). Dionysus rewarded Oeneus' generosity, or prudence, with the gift of the vine and went on his way.

F. Dionysus' triumphant travels carried him to many parts of the world. He is said, for example, to have routed the Amazons before Heracles made his famous expedition to their country. The god also led his followers (whom late Classical writers often conceived of as an army) into Egypt. There they were lost for a time in the desert without water. Either the god or some of the army spied a stray ram and followed it. It vanished, but on the spot where it was last seen they discovered a spring. To commemorate this event, Dionysus established a shrine of the ram-headed god Ammon. Furthermore, he placed the ram in the stars as the constellation Aries.

Dionysus' most distant expedition led him as far as the Ganges River, in India. In order to cross the Euphrates River, he constructed a bridge with cables plaited of ivy and vine strands. Seilenus, his old companion, disappeared one day as Dionysus' army was crossing Phrygia, or possibly Macedonia. He reappeared some days later with an honor guard sent along by Midas, king of the Mygdonians. The king, or some of his peasants, had easily captured the ever-thirsty old man by setting out bowls of wine. Midas had entertained him with splendid hospitality, and Dionysus rewarded him by offering to grant any boon that he asked. Midas foolishly requested that everything he touched should turn to gold. The god reluctantly consented, but was not surprised when Midas, starving because he could not eat gold, returned to ask that the gift be withdrawn. Even a god cannot rescind his own vows, but Dionysus told Midas how to wash away his "golden touch" by bathing in the river Pactolus.

Before going to India Dionysus had left Nysus in charge of Thebes. Nysus (who, according to this rather obscure tale, had been the god's nurse on Mount Nysa) refused to turn over the rule again on Dionysus' return. The god was unusually patient with him. After waiting three years he ostensibly made up their quarrel and received permission to celebrate his rites at Thebes. He then dressed his soldiers as maenads and seized the throne in a coup.

At some point during his travels Dionysus came to the island of Dia, later called Naxos, and there found Ariadne, daughter of the Cretan king Minos, who had been abandoned by her lover, Theseus. According to most traditions Dionysus married her, though the circumstances vary considerably. Some say, for example, that he took Ariadne from Theseus by force of arms; others that, while visiting Minos, he bribed Ariadne with a crown to let him sleep with her. The Lemnians claimed that Dionysus brought his bride to their island and that she bore four sons: Thoas, Staphylus, Oenopion, and Peparethus. The Argives, however, said that Ariadne died in their city. Homer's statement that Artemis shot Ariadne at Dionysus' instigation seems at odds with all other accounts.

Ariadne was not the only mortal woman whom the god loved. In addition to Deïaneira, his daughter by Althaea, he had a son, Phlias, by Araethyrea, at Phlius; a son, Phanus, perhaps by Ariadne; and another, Narcaeüs, by Physcoa, an Eleian woman. Since the god is said to have deceived Erigone with a false bunch of grapes, it may be that his generosity to Icarius was motivated by the same kind of gratitude that he felt toward Oeneus.

G. When Dionysus had firmly established his worship throughout the lands of the eastern Mediterranean and as far east as India, he withdrew from earth and took his place with the other gods on Mount Olympus. First, however, he descended into Hades to bring up his mother. Several Greek cities later claimed that this memorable event had occurred in their territory. Instead of going by a land route, Dionysus apparently dived into the water, either the bottomless Alcyonian Lake, at Lerna, or the bay of Troezen. He was shown this route by a native guide named Prosymnus, Polymnus, or Hypolipnus. On meeting the handsome young god, the guide demanded that he lie with him. Dionysus, unwilling to delay his rescue of his mother, vowed to pay Prosymnus on his return. When the time came, Prosymnus was dead. The god discharged his debt by whittling out of fig-wood an image of the organ that the guide had admired, and leaving it at the tomb. Semele he took with him up to Olympus, where she assumed the name Thyone and lived among the gods. Nothing further was heard of her, however.

Dionysus soon found himself involved in the war between the gods and the GIANTS. Although he was not warlike by nature, he managed to dispatch the Giant Eurytus with his thyrsus. Some say that the Giants were routed in terror by the braying of the asses on which Dionysus, with his satyrs and seileni, rode into the battle, accompanied by Hephaestus. Later Dionysus and many of the other gods ignominiously fled to Egypt before the onslaught of the monster Typhöeus. There they disguised themselves as various animals, Dionysus taking the form of a goat. They returned to Olympus after Zeus had disposed of the monster.

Dionysus forgot the enmity that Hera had borne him and helped to extricate her from an embarrassing predicament. Hephaestus, resentful of being thrown out of heaven by his mother, trapped her in a golden chair from which she could not escape. Dionysus, who had evidently struck up a friendship with the divine artisan, made him drunk and lured him back to Olympus, where he was persuaded to release Hera.

Although Dionysus was often harsh in punishing his enemies, he showed unusual concern for the welfare of his loyal worshipers. To the daughters of ANIUS, king of Delos, he gave the power to turn everything that they touched into wine, corn, or oil. When Amphion and Zethus killed Dirce for her cruelty to their mother, ANTIOPE, the god punished Antiope with madness because Dirce had been his votary. He also caused a spring to appear at Thebes at the spot where Dirce had died. Dionysus came to the rescue of the women of Tanagra when they were attacked by a TRITON while celebrating his rites. He also punished BUTES (3) for his attack on a group of Thessalian maenads. On the other hand, some say that he changed some of his own Thracian bacchants into oak trees for killing his priest ORPHEUS. This is uncertain, however, for, although Orpheus is widely credited with having taught, or even invented, the mysteries of Dionysus, he is also said by some writers to have been punished with death for neglecting the god's worship.

H. Although there are confusing elements in the myths of Dionysus and the accounts of his worship, the general outlines are fairly clearly recognized by scholars. Dionysus was an example of a type of fertility god that was worshiped throughout the Mediterranean world by the agricultural populations. His rites involved a mystical communion in which, during moments of religious frenzy induced with the aid of wine, music, and dancing, his worshipers became identified with the god and were called by his name, Bacchus. Dionysus was almost certainly native to Thrace and Phrygia, where he was known as Diounsis, his mother as Zemelo. Not only was Dionysus not native to the Greek states, but his orgiastic rites in celebration of the earth's fertility and the whole idea of mortals achieving oneness with a god were foreign to the Greek ruling classes. Originally a nomadic people with little direct concern for the yearly rebirth of vegetation, they subscribed to the austere religion of the Homeric heroes, to whom the gulf between gods and men was unbridgeable. The Dionysiac cult underwent, therefore, considerable modification during the period, many centuries before Christ, when it was becoming prevalent in Greece.

The many mythical conflicts between the god and local kings may reflect to some extent the historical resistance to the spread of the cult. On the other hand, symbolic or actual death and dismemberment were a regular part of the god's rituals, so conflicts leading to such an end would be expected to appear in the aetiological myths that were told to explain the origins of those rituals.

Elements of the myth and ritual of Dionysus have much in common with those of the Cretan ZEUS [E] and of ZAGREUS. The obscure god Iacchus, who was celebrated in the Eleusinian mysteries, was often identified with Dionysus, but this may be only because the names Iacchus and Bacchus were confused. Dionysus had many names and epithets, among them Bromios (Thunderer), Lenaeüs (He of the Wine-press), Lyaeüs (He Who Frees), and Dendrites (He of the Trees).

I. The most extended single account of Dionysus' adventures on earth is given by Apollodorus in Book III [4.2–5.3] of his *Library*, with further references at 1.3.2, 1.6.2, 1.9.12, 1.9.16, 2.2.2, 3.14.7, and "Epitome" 1.9 and 3.10. Homer's only references to the god are at 6.119–143 and 14.323–325 in the *Iliad* and 11.324–325 in the *Odyssey*. Dionysus' triumph over Pentheus is the subject of Euripides' tragedy *The Bacchants* and of a passage of Ovid's *Metamorphoses* [3.513–4.41, 4.389–419], which includes an account of the fate of Minyas' daughters. The god appears as a comic figure in Aristophanes' *Frogs*. His encounter with the pirates is related in the *Homeric Hymn to Dionysus* [7], by Hyginus [*Fabulae* 134 and *Poetica Astronomica* 2.17], and by Ovid in the passage mentioned above. Among innumerable other references to Dionysus in Classical writings are the following: Hesiod, *Theogony*, 940–942, 947–949; *Catalogues of Women* 18, 86; *Homeric Hymns to Dionysus* 1, 26; Sophocles, *Antigone*, 955–963; Herodotus 2.48–49; Hyginus, *Fabulae*, 1–4, 7, 43, 129–134, 166–167, 169, 184, 191–192, and *Poetica Astronomica*, 2.4–7, 2.21, 2.23; and Ovid, *Metamorphoses*, 3.259–315, 5.329, 7.294–296, 8.176–182, 11.67–84, 11.89–145, 13.650–674. References by Pausanias are too numerous to cite.

Diores. A son of Amarynceus. Although Diores' rank is uncertain, he led some of the Eleian forces to Troy, where he was killed by the Thracian leader Pieros. [Homer, *Iliad*, 2.615–624, 4.517–526.]

Dioscuri. Castor and Polydeuces (or Pollux).

A. To Homer, these two brothers were merely sons of Tyndareüs, king of Sparta, and his wife, Leda, daughter of Thestius, though he knew that they were honored as gods after their deaths and were, in a unique way, immortal. Later writers call them Dioscuri, "sons of Zeus," though Castor is usually said to be Tyndareüs' child and mortal, like his sister Clytemnestra, while Polydeuces and Helen are considered his mother's children by Zeus and immortal.

When they were quite young, the Dioscuri sailed with the ARGONAUTS. Castor, famous as a tamer of horses, did not have much opportunity to practice his specialty along the way, but his brother's prowess as a boxer stood the company in good stead when they were challenged to box by Amycus, the brutal Bebrycian king. After their return from the voyage they joined Jason in helping their fellow Argonaut Peleus to destroy Iolcus. Ovid [*Metamorphoses* 8.301–302, 372–375] adds the Dioscuri to the roster of those who hunted the Calydonian boar.

Theseus and his friend Peirithoüs, eager to marry daughters of Zeus, carried off Helen to the city of Aphidnae, in Attica, to become Theseus' bride. The Dioscuri waited until Theseus was away on another adventure, then captured Aphidnae, and perhaps Athens as well, with the aid of Spartan and Arcadian armies. They rescued Helen, carried off Theseus' mother, Aethra, and Peirithoüs' sister, Phisadië, and placed Theseus' rival Menestheus on the Athenian throne.

B. Castor and Polydeuces also were interested in acquiring wives. Leucippus, a brother of Tyndareüs who lived in Messenia, had two beautiful daughters, Phoebe and Hiläeira. The Dioscuri, ignoring the fact that these girls were betrothed to their cousins Lynceus and Idas, carried them off to Sparta. Hiläeira bore Anaxis or Anogon by Castor; Phoebe bore Mnasinoüs or Mnesileüs by Polydeuces.

Some say that it was this abduction which led to a fatal quarrel between the brothers and their brother cousins, but the trouble is generally thought to have arisen after a joint raid that they made on some Arcadian cattle. According to one version of the story, the division of the spoils was left to Idas. He cut a horse into four pieces and suddenly announced that half of the cattle would go to the man who ate his quarter first, the other half to the one who finished second. The Dioscuri, taken off guard by this decision, were outpaced by their Messenian cousins and watched helplessly as Lynceus and Idas went off toward Messenia driving the entire herd. When they realized that they had been tricked, they determined to retaliate. They marched on Messenia, recovered the cattle, and started for Sparta. Lynceus and Idas pursued them. Lynceus, who had fabulous powers of vision, stood on Mount Taÿgetus and spied the twins far away hiding inside a hollow oak tree, either for shelter or because they planned to ambush their pursuers.

The order of events in the ensuing fight has been variously reported. It is usually said that Idas killed Castor with a spear. Polydeuces then chased his cousins as far as the tomb of their father, Aphareus, and killed Lynceus. Idas tried to push or throw the heavy tombstone at Polydeuces, but Zeus came to his son's rescue and killed Idas with a thunderbolt. Castor would have gone down to Hades with other mortal shades, but Polydeuces, who loved his brother more than his life, prayed to his father that he might share his own immortality with Castor. Zeus granted his request, with the result that the brothers spent alternate days on Olympus and in Hades. They were, moreover, transported to the sky as stars and became guardians of mariners endangered by storms, to whom they often appeared as St. Elmo's fire. According to Pliny

[*Natural History* 2.101], one ball of this mysterious fire was the sign of their sister Helen, and a bad omen; two balls revealed the kindly presence of the Dioscuri. Late writers identified the twins with the constellation Gemini. They were widely worshiped in most regions of Greece, especially in their native Sparta.

The Dioscuri do not figure actively in any major literary work except the *Argonautica* of Apollonius Rhodius, but they are repeatedly mentioned elsewhere both as gods and heroes. They appear as gods at the ends of two plays of Euripides, *Electra* and *Helen*. [See also Apollodorus 3.11.2; Apollonius Rhodius 2.1–97; Pindar, *Nemean Odes*, 10.]

Diounsis. See DIONYSUS [H].

Dirce. The wife of Lycus, king of Thebes. Dirce hated her husband's niece ANTIOPE and treated her cruelly. Antiope's sons, Amphion and Zethus, avenged their mother by tying Dirce to a bull, which killed her. Because Dirce had been a devoted bacchant, Dionysus caused a spring to burst out of the place on Mount Cithaeron or at Thebes where her body was flung to the ground by the bull.

Dis. An alternative Roman name for Pluto, god of the Underworld. In addition to borrowing the Greek name Pluto (from *ploutos*, "wealth"), the Romans translated it literally as Dives, which they contracted to Dis. Like Pluto, this name was a euphemism used by those who felt it risky to mention the god by name (Hades).

Dius. A king of Elis. Although Pausanias says that Eleius, a son of Polyxeinus, ruled Elis at the time of the Heraclid invasion, it was Dius who resisted Oxylus' Aetolian usurpation but agreed to let the matter be settled in single combat. When the Aetolian champion won, Oxylus nevertheless gave Dius privileges in Elis. [Pausanias 5.4.1–2.]

Dodona. A city in Epeirus. Dodona, although it does not figure prominently in myth, was reputed to be one of the most ancient centers of the worship of Zeus. It was famous for its oracles, interpreted from rustlings of old oak trees and other natural sounds. At Dodona, Zeus was worshiped together with Dione, who is thought by some scholars to have antedated Hera as his consort. The *Argo*'s speaking beam was made by Athena from one of the oaks at Dodona.

Dog, The. See CANIS MAJOR.

Doliche. See ICARIA.

Doliones. A Mysian tribe. The Doliones hospitably welcomed the ARGONAUTS [D, E], but were later attacked by them in error, and their young king, Cyzicus, was killed. The Dolionian capital was renamed Cyzicus in his memory.

Dolius. An old servant of Odysseus. Dolius and six of his sons remained faithful to their master's interests during his long absence from Ithaca and helped to defend him against the Ithacan relatives of the suitors. Dolius' seventh son, Melantheus, and his daughter, Melantho, attached themselves to the suitors and were killed on Odysseus' return. [Homer, *Odyssey*, 24.386–411, 24.492–501.]

Dolon. A Trojan spy. Dolon was the only son of Eumedes or Eumelus, a Trojan herald. He was ugly, rich, and greedy. He offered to spy by night on the Greek camp, not for glory or from patriotism, but for the reward of Achilles' horses and chariot. Although Dolon was quick on his feet, he was an incompetent spy and was captured almost at once by Odysseus and Diomedes. Terrified, he offered them a great ransom to let him go and willingly revealed the layout of the Trojan camp, with the positions of the Trojan allies. He even hinted that the camp of the newly arrived Thracian king Rhesus would offer rich rewards if Odysseus and Diomedes were to investigate it. After contemptuously killing Dolon, the two Greeks took his advice. Eumedes, a grandson of Dolon, later accompanied Aeneas to Italy. Dolon appears in Euripides' *Rhesus* as a braver man than he seems in the famous passage in Homer's *Iliad* [10.299–464], and it is Athena, not Dolon, who betrays Rhesus to his killers in Vergil's *Aeneïd* [12.346–352.]

Dolphin, The. See DELPHINUS.

Dorians. One of the main branches of the Hellenes. According to legend, the Dorians were descended from Dorus, one of the three sons of Hellen. He was allotted the region about Mount Parnassus. Dorus' brother Aeolus and his nephews Ion and Achaeüs founded the other Hellenic groups. According to Herodotus [1.56], the Dorians came from Phthia, in southern Thessaly, and moved to several parts of northern Greece before invading the Peloponnesus. Herodotus, however, used the name Dorian to mean all the Hellenes; he believed the Ionians to be Pelasgians, pre-Hellenic inhabitants of Greece. The actual origin of the Dorians is uncertain, but the principal event in their legendary history, their invasion of the Peloponnesus, seems to be based in fact. The Dorian alliance with the Heraclids was accounted for by the legend of Heracles' aid to the Dorian king Aegimius in his war with the Lapiths. Together, these two peoples invaded the Peloponnesus from Aetolia and quickly conquered Argolis, Sparta, and Messenia. Later they brought Megara and Corinth under their domination. Thucydides dated the invasion at eighty years after the fall of Troy.

Doris. A sea-goddess. Doris is usually called a daughter of Oceanus and Tethys and mother by the old sea-god Nereus of fifty daughters, the Nereïds. Like Poseidon's wife, Amphitrite, Doris is often merely a personification of the sea. [Hesiod, *Theogony*, 240–264, 350.]

Dorus (1). The eponym of the Dorians. Dorus was a son of Hellen and the nymph Orseïs. (In his *Ion* [1589–1590], Euripides calls Dorus a son of Erechtheus' daughter Creüsa (1) and Xuthus, but the playwright was no doubt tampering with the tradition in order to give the Athenians a more impressive genealogy than that of their Dorian enemies.) Hellen, dividing the Greek lands among his three sons—Dorus, Aeolus, and Xuthus—gave Dorus the region about Parnassus. Dorus named the people Dorians for himself. [Apollodorus 1.7.3.]

Dorus (2). A son of Apollo and Phthia. Dorus and his brothers, Laodocus and Polypoetes, leaders of the Curetes, were killed by Aetolus when he invaded the land later called Aetolia. Aetolus' son Pleuron married Dorus' daughter, Xanthippe, and they had several children, including Agenor, grandfather of Oeneus. It is possible that, in one tradition, this Dorus was regarded as the eponym of the Dorians, who invaded the Peloponnesus from Aetolia. See DORUS (1).

Doso. The name by which DEMETER [C] called herself when she came to Eleusis.

Draco (The Serpent). A constellation. Draco is generally said to represent Ladon, the dragon that guarded the garden of the Hesperides. Some astronomers claimed, however, that it was a snake that the Giants had flung at Athena during the war between gods and Giants. Athena tossed it into the sky. [Hyginus, *Poetica Astronomica*, 2.3.]

Drepane. The island home of the Phaeacians. This island is called Scherië by Homer, Corcyra by Apollodorus. Apollonius Rhodius, who names it Drepane (Sickle), explains that it took its name either from the sickle with which Cronos castrated his father, Uranus, or from that of the corn-goddess Demeter, who had once lived on the island and there taught the Titans to plant corn. She did this out of fondness for Macris, daughter of Aristaeüs, who also lived on the island. According to some, Macris had nursed the infant Dionysus with honey at her home in Euboea. Driven from there by the angry Hera, she took refuge in a cave on Drepane and caused abundant crops to grow on the island. This sacred cave later became the scene of Medea's marriage to Jason and was renamed Medea's Cave.

dryad. See NYMPH.

Dryas. See LYCURGUS (1).

Dryope. A daughter of EURYTUS (1), king of Oechalia, by his first wife. Dryope was seduced by Apollo. Marrying Andraemon, she bore a son to the god whom her father christened Amphissus. Dryope once plucked the flowers of the lotus tree and was transformed into such a tree herself. [Ovid, *Metamorphoses*, 9.324–393.]

Dryopians or **Dryopes.** A people living originally in the valley of the Spercheius River and southward through Doris to Mount Parnassus. The eponym of the Dryopians was Dryops, a son of either Apollo or the river-god Spercheius. Driven from their homeland by HERACLES [M], who was an ally of either Aegimius or Ceÿx, some Dryopes emigrated to Asine, southeast of Nauplia. Later they were driven out by the Argives and founded a new Asine in southeastern Messenia. Other Dryopians went from Doris to Euboea, where they settled in Styra and no longer called themselves Dryopians.

Ɛ

Eagle, The. See AQUILA.

Earthborn Monsters or **Gegeneës.** A tribe of six-armed giants. These monsters inhabited Bear Mountain, on the Mysian coast. They attacked the ARGONAUTS [D] and were destroyed by them.

Echemus. A king of Arcadia. A son of Aëropus, Echemus succeeded the aged Lycurgus on the throne at Tegea. He won the wrestling match at the Olympic games held by Heracles. Later, offering himself as champion of the Arcadian forces defending the Peloponnesus against the Heraclids, he killed Heracles' son Hyllus in a duel. Echemus married Tyndareüs' daughter Timandra, but she deserted him for Phyleus after bearing Echemus a son, Laodocus. [Pausanias 1.41.2, 8.5.1–2; Pindar, *Olympian Odes*, 10.]

Echetus. A king of Epeirus. Echetus was proverbial for his cruelty, having blinded his own daughter, thrust her into a dungeon, and forced her to grind grains of bronze. His name inspired such terror that the suitors of Penelope used it to threaten beggars. [Apollonius Rhodius 4.1092–1095; Homer, *Odyssey*, 18.83–87.]

Echidna. A monster. Described by Hesiod as half nymph, half speckled snake, Echidna lived in a cave, from which she sallied to snatch and eat passersby. She was one of the monstrous brood of Ceto and Phorcys, or Ge and Tartarus, or, some say, of Styx and Peiras. Her own children by Typhaon were hardly more attractive: the Chimaera, the Hydra, and the hounds Cerberus and Orthus; by Orthus (or Typhon) she later bore the Sphinx, the Nemean lion, and the Crommyonian sow; Vergil [*Ciris* 67] suggests that she may also have spawned Scylla. Although Echidna never grew old, she was not immortal; Argus Panoptes ended her depredations in Arcadia by killing her one day while she slept. [Hesiod, *Theogony*, 295–332.]

Echinadian Islands or **Echinades.** See STROPHADES.

Echion (1). One of the SPARTI. Echion was the most prominent of the five survivors of the crop of armed men who sprang up when CADMUS [A] sowed the teeth of Ares' sacred dragon at Thebes. He married Cadmus' daughter Agave and became by her the father of Pentheus, who succeeded Cadmus on the throne of Cadmeia, later called Thebes. [Apollodorus 3.4.2; Euripides, *The Bacchants*, 537.]

Echion (2). An Argonaut. Echion and his brother, Erytus or Eurytus, were sons of Hermes by Antianeira, daughter of Menetes. They came from the Thessalian city of Alope to join the *Argo*'s crew. Echion also threw the first spear in the Calydonian boar hunt. Apollonius' epithet for him, "guileful," suggests that, in the longer, original version of his *Argonautica*, Echion acted as a spy for the company, as he did in the Orphic *Argonautica*. [Apollonius Rhodius 1.57–58; Homer, *Iliad*, 2.745–747.]

Echo. A nymph of Mount Helicon. Echo, an attendant of Hera, would keep her mistress entertained with endless chatter while Zeus dallied with the other nymphs. Catching onto this ruse, the angry goddess punished her with a curious speech impediment: Echo could begin no conversation, but only repeat the words of others. While under this handicap, the nymph became one of the innumerable lovers of the beautiful, but cold, youth Narcissus. He spurned her advances, and she faded away, sick with love, until only her voice remained to haunt the mountain. [Ovid, *Metamorphoses*, 3.356–410.]

Ectenes. An aboriginal tribe of the region of Thebes. Their king was Ogygus. The entire tribe was destroyed by plague. [Pausanias 9.5.1.]

Edonians or **Edoni.** A Thracian tribe living about Mount Pangaeüs. The Edonians were best known in myth for the persecution of Dionysus and his followers by their king Lycurgus. On learning from an oracle that a severe drought had been inflicted on the country as punishment for Lycurgus' crimes, the Edonians had him torn apart by horses on Pangaeüs, or else some other terrible fate overtook him.

Eëriboea. See Otus.

Eëtion. A king of Hypoplacian Thebes, in the Troad. Eëtion, Andromache's father, was an ally of the Trojans. He and his seven sons were killed in one day by Achilles. [Homer, *Iliad*, 6.395–397, 6.414–428.]

Egeria. An obscure Roman goddess or nymph. According to Vergil [*Aeneïd* 7.761–777] Egeria was the nymph of Diana's grove at Aricia, the home of Virbius. Numa Pompilius, the second Roman king, claimed that Egeria was his mistress and adviser, whom he met for consultations in the grove of the Camenae, at Rome. She was said by Ovid [*Metamorphoses* 15.482–551] to have fled to Aricia at Numa's death and to have been converted into a spring.

Egypt. The country about the Nile River. Egypt, named for Aegyptus, a son of King Belus, was the scene of many Greek myths: the last travels of Io, who became identified with the Egyptian goddess Isis; the youth of Phaëthon; the rivalry between Aegyptus and Danaüs; the oracles of the old seal herder Proteus, who lived on the island of Pharos; Heracles' encounter with Busiris; and the unorthodox legend of Helen's stay in Egypt during the Trojan War. In several of these myths, however, there seems to have been confusion in the minds of Greek writers between Egypt and the Near East. (Similar confusion existed over the whereabouts of Ethiopia.) One example is a version of the story of Belus, in which he is said to have remained in Egypt as king while his brother Agenor emigrated to Phoenicia. But Belus is also said to have been a king of Tyre, the father of Dido, and an ancestor of Persian kings. It is believed by most scholars, moreover, that Belus' name is a Greek form of the common Canaanite title *ba'al* (lord, or possessor).

Eidothea. See PROTEUS (2).

Eidyia or **Idyia.** A daughter of Oceanus and Tethys. Eidyia married Aeëtes, king of Colchis, and bore him Medea and Chalciope, and, according to some accounts, also Apsyrtus. [Hesiod, *Theogony,* 346–352, 958–962.]

Eileithyia. A goddess of childbirth. Homer [*Iliad* 11.269–272, 19.103–119] speaks of Eileithyiae, in the plural, saying that Hera would not allow these divine midwives, her daughters, to attend Alcmene when she was in labor with Heracles. Hesiod [*Theogony* 921–923] mentions Eileithyia only once and identifies her as a daughter of Zeus and Hera. In his account, Hera kept Eileithyia on Olympus on another occasion, hoping that she would not hear of Leto's sufferings in childbirth on Delos. The other goddesses managed to lure Eileithyia to the island to assist at Apollo's birth. Some say that she came to Delos from the land of the Hyperboreans and that her widespread cult traveled from there to other Greek lands. The Cretans also claimed her, pointing out a sacred cave at Amnisus where she was born. She was worshiped at Elis as the mother of the local god Sosipolis. The Lycian poet Olen said that Eileithyia was older than Cronus and called her the mother of Eros. The Romans knew her as Lucina, who was often identified with Juno. Juno and Hera both functioned at times as goddesses of childbirth. [Pausanias 1.18.5, 2.22.6, 6.20.2–6, 8.21.3, 9.27.2; *Homeric Hymn to Apollo* 3.97–116.]

Eioneus. See IXION.

Eirene. See SEASONS.

Elatus (1). A king of Arcadia. One of the three sons of Arcas, Elatus received Mount Cyllene as his portion of his father's kingdom. He married Laodice, daughter of Cinyras, who bore Stymphalus and several other sons. Elatus left Arcadia for Phocis, where he aided the natives against the Phlegyans and founded the city of Elateia. He is often called the father of Ischys, the mortal lover of Coronis, but this may result from confusion with another Elatus, a Lapith. [Pausanias 8.4.2–6.]

Elatus (2). A Lapith chieftain. Elatus was the father of Caenis (who became Caeneus) and Polyphemus. He was also probably the father of Ischys, the mortal lover of Coronis, though the Arcadian Elatus is sometimes called Ischys' father.

Elba. An island off the western coast of Italy. Elba was known in Classical times as Aethalia or Ilva. The Argonauts stopped there on their homeward voyage.

Electra (1). A daughter of Agamemnon and Clytemnestra. When her father was murdered by her mother and her mother's lover, Aegisthus, it was Electra, some say, who saved her young brother, ORESTES [A, B], by sending him to Phocis. Aegisthus kept her imprisoned in the palace, or else married her to a commoner to prevent her from bearing noble sons capable of challenging him. Eagerly she hoped for Orestes' return to avenge their father. When he appeared, she helped him and Pylades to kill Aegisthus and Clytemnestra. According to Euripides' *Orestes*, she also abetted the young men in their attacks on Helen and Hermione. Electra married Pylades and bore two sons, Medon and Strophius. Hyginus [*Fabulae* 122] relates that Electra nearly blinded her sister Iphigeneia at Delphi with a firebrand because a messenger had falsely told her that Iphigeneia (whom she did not recognize) had sacrificed Orestes to Artemis. Orestes intervened in time to prevent this catastrophe.

Electra is a principal character in five Classical tragedies: Aeschylus' *Libation Bearers*, Sophocles' *Electra*, Euripides' *Electra* and *Orestes*, and Seneca's *Agamemnon*.

Electra (2). A daughter of Oceanus and Tethys. By the Titan Thaumas, Electra was the mother of Iris and the Harpies. [Hesiod, *Theogony*, 265–269.]

Electra (3). A daughter of Atlas and the Oceanid Pleïone. One of the PLEIADES, Electra lived on the island of Samothrace. Zeus fell in love with her and carried her off to Olympus. She clung for refuge to the Palladium, but Zeus, forgetting in his eagerness that he was a god of suppliants, flung the sacred image out of heaven. Electra returned to her island and bore Dardanus and Iasion. Some say that the dim or invisible star among the Pleiades is Electra, who retired to the Arctic Circle in grief at the death of Dardanus or the sack of Troy. [Apollodorus 3.10.1, 3.12.1, 3.12.3; Hyginus, *Poetica Astronomica*, 2.21.]

Electryon. A son of Perseus and Andromeda. Electryon inherited the throne of Mycenae from his father. By his wife, Anaxo, he had a daughter, Alcmene, and many sons. A Phrygian woman named Midea also bore him a son, Licymnius. One day, as the young men were tending their father's cattle, they were attacked by a raiding party of Taphians, or Teleboans, sons of Pterelaüs, a descendant of Electryon's brother Mestor. The only survivors of the ensuing battle were Licymnius, who was too young to join in, and Everes, who guarded the Taphian ships. Electryon was himself killed in a quarrel over cattle with his son-in-law, AMPHITRYON, though Apollodorus calls it an accident. Sthenelus seized the throne and banished Amphitryon, who nevertheless avenged Electryon's sons on the Taphians. [Apollodorus 2.4.5–6.]

Eleius. A king of Elis and the city's eponym. A son of Poseidon by Eurycyda, daughter of Endymion, Eleius succeeded to the throne when his uncle Aetolus went into exile. Until his accession the Eleians had been called Epeians. [Pausanias 5.1.8–9.]

Elephenor. A king of the Abantes, of Euboea. Elephenor was a son of Chalcodon and Alcyone or Imenarete. He gave Theseus' sons, Demophon and Acamas, refuge when they fled to Euboea in fear of Menestheus, the usurping king of Athens. He led forty Euboean ships to Troy, where he was killed by Agenor. On their way home, his men were shipwrecked in Epeirus, where they founded Apollonia. [Homer, *Iliad*, 2.536–545, 4.463–472; Pausanias 1.17.6; Apollodorus, "Epitome" 6.15b.]

Eleusis or **Eleusinus.** The eponym of Eleusis, a city in Attica. Eleusis was said by some to be a son of Ogygus, an ancient king of the region around Thebes. Some add that he was the father of Triptolemus by his wife Cothonea. Hyginus [*Fabulae* 147] attributes to Eleusis the role usually played by CE-LEÜS in the story of Demeter's stay at Eleusis as nurse of the king's son. In this version the king (Eleusis), rather than his wife, sees his son being roasted in the fire. He is killed by the goddess when he interferes, but the child (Triptolemus instead of Demophoön) survives and is honored. [Apollodorus 1.5.2; Pausanias 1.38.7.]

Eleusis. A city of Attica on the Saronic Gulf near the Isthmus of Corinth. The city's eponym was Eleusis or Eleusinus, who came from southern Boeotia. Under King Celeüs, Eleusis became the chief of several cult centers of Demeter. During the reign of the early Athenian king Erechtheus, war broke out between the neighboring cities. In spite of help from the Thracian Eumolpus, Eleusis was defeated and fell under the domination of Athens. Theseus, who in his youth had killed the Eleusinian king Cercyon, later united the city with Athens, though allowing it considerable autonomy. It was famous throughout the ancient world as the site of the Eleusinian mysteries.

Eleutherae. A town in the Cithaeron range between Attica and Boeotia. Eleutherae was the site of the birth of Amphion and Zethus. The Argive common soldiers who died in the war of the Seven against Thebes were buried at Eleutherae.

Elicius. An epithet (from *elicio,* "I call forth") of Jupiter as a god of lightning and thunder. This god was successfully evoked by the wise Numa Pompilius, the second Roman king, but the attempts of his superstitious successor, Tullus Hostilius, to do the same only brought down the lightning on his own head.

Elis. A fertile region in the northwestern Peloponnesus and the principal city of that area. Elis was founded either by Aëthlius, a son by Zeus or Aeolus of Deucalion's daughter Protogeneia, or by Endymion, Aëthlius' son by Calyce, daughter of Aeolus. In either case the first settlers were colonists from Thessaly. Endymion drove King Clymenus, a Cretan, from Olympia and annexed that city. The neighboring town of Pisa, too, was a part of Elis. Before retiring to Caria for his perpetual sleep, Endymion held a footrace at Olympia for his three sons, Epeius, Aetolus, and Paeon, with succession to the throne as the prize. When Epeius won, Paeon exiled himself, but Aetolus remained. During Epeius' rule, Pelops, a Phrygian, killed Oenomaüs, king of Pisa, and made that city independent of Eleian domination. When Epeius died without sons, Aetolus came to the throne, but he was banished for an accidental killing and fled across the Gulf of Corinth to a land he named Aetolia. He was succeeded in Elis by Eleius, son of his sister, Eurycyda. Eleius may have given the country its name of Elis. The next king was Augeias, a son of Eleius or of Phorbas, a Thessalian, though he is often called a son of Poseidon or Helius.

Augeias became wealthy as a cattle raiser, but incurred the enmity of Heracles by refusing him his wages for cleaning the royal cattle-yard. Too busy at the time to avenge this act, Heracles returned later with an army, which was defeated largely through the efforts of the twin Moliones and of Amarynceus, whose aid Augeias had won by offering them shares in the kingdom. Heracles later treacherously killed the Moliones at Cleonae and, on his second attempt, sacked Elis. He placed Augeias' eldest son, Phyleus, on the throne, but Phyleus, preferring to rule in Dulichium, left the kingship of Elis to be inherited on Augeias' death by a younger son, Agasthenes. By the time of the Trojan War, in the next generation, various parts of the region known as Elis were ruled by descendants of Augeias, the Moliones, and Amarynceus.

In the following generation, or perhaps later, the invasion of the Heraclids placed an Aetolian, Oxylus, on the throne. A shrewd king who made himself accepted by the Eleians, Oxylus was succeeded by his son Laïas, but the line ended with him. Elis was noted for many centuries for its control of the Olympic games, which the Eleians claimed to have exercised as early as the days of Endymion. It is more likely, however, that management of the games originally belonged to Pisa, a city which Elis, with the aid of Sparta, destroyed in the late sixth century B.C.

Elissa. See DIDO.

Elpenor. The youngest member of Odysseus' crew. On the hot summer night before ODYSSEUS [F, G] left Circe's island of Aeaea on his voyage to Hades, Elpenor slept on the roof of Circe's house to keep cool. Odysseus roused his men early in the morning with news of their immediate departure. Elpenor, still groggy from the wine that he had drunk the night before, and none too bright a man even when sober, descended from the roof without remembering to use the ladder. Shortly afterward, when Odysseus visited Hades, Elpenor's ghost reminded him that he had not received a proper funeral. Odysseus dutifully sailed back to Aeaea to correct this oversight. He and his crew burned Elpenor's corpse and erected his oar on the mound that they heaped over his ashes. [Homer, *Odyssey*, 10.551–560, 11.51–83.]

Elysium or **Elysian Fields.** The dwelling place of mortals made immortal through the favor of the gods. In Menelaüs' encounter with Proteus in Homer's *Odyssey* [4.561–569], he learned that he was destined, as a son-in-law of Zeus, to live forever in Elysium, instead of descending at his death to Hades. This happy land, ruled by Rhadamanthys, lay somewhere near the river Oceanus. Hesiod [*Works and Days* 167–173] described a similar place, under Cronus' rule, which he called the Islands of the Blessed. Pindar [*Olympian Odes* 2.61–84 and *Dirges* 129–130 (95)] described these islands in more detail as a place where the virtuous dead, retaining their faculties, unlike the shades in Hades, enjoyed lives free of care or work and engaged in the same activities, such as sports, music, or feasting, that gave them pleasure in life. Pindar numbered among these immortals Peleus and Cadmus. Although these heroes were, like Menelaüs, related to the gods, Pindar may have been speaking for a growing belief that men were rewarded after their deaths for their virtues, and not merely through Olympian favoritism.

Later writers often described Elysium as a section of Hades isolated from the home of the ordinary shades. The Islands of the Blessed, however, were occasionally localized on earth. According to Pausanias [3.19.11–13], Leonymus, a general of Crotona, was commanded by the Delphic oracle to sail to the White Island, near the mouths of the Danube, in the Black Sea, if he wished to be cured of a wound. There he found, living in eternal bliss, Achilles, Patroclus, Antilochus, Helen, and the two Ajaxes. Presumably the White Island had gained its reputation as a home of the immortals at a time when it was far more remote from the routes of Greek travelers than it was by Pausanias' day. How it had managed to retain this reputation down to the second century A.D. is hard to explain. See also METEMPSYCHOSIS.

Enceladus. A giant. In the war between gods and GIANTS, Enceladus fought against Athena. After fleeing to Sicily, he was struck down and either Zeus or Athena piled Mount Aetna, or perhaps the entire island, on his body. He still breathed flames through the volcano. A similar story is told of Typhöeus. [Apollodorus 1.6.2; Vergil, *Aeneïd*, 3.578–582.]

Endeïs. A daughter of Sceiron and the daughter of Pandion. Endeïs, whom some call a daughter of Cheiron, married Aeacus and bore Telamon and Peleus. Her hatred of Phocus, her husband's son by Psamathe, led to his murder by her sons and their resulting exile. [Pausanias 1.39.6, 2.29.9–10.]

Endymion. A king of Elis. Endymion was a son of Aëthlius and Calyce, daughter of Aeolus. Either Endymion or his father founded Elis. The name of Endymion's wife is variously given by Pausanias; whoever she was, she bore him Paeon, Epeius, and Aetolus, and a daughter, Eurycyda. Endymion overthrew Clymenus, the Cretan king of Olympia, and added that city to his own kingdom. Later, he held a footrace there in order to choose a successor to the throne from among his three sons. Epeius won. Amorous Selene, the moon, fell in love with the handsome Endymion and, according to one story, bore him fifty daughters. Zeus gave him the unique opportunity of choosing his own fate. Endymion chose to sleep forever, never growing old. It is said that he retired to Mount Latmus, near Heracleia in Caria, for his final sleep. According to the *Great Eoiae* [11], however, Endymion suffered the fate of Ixion: taken to heaven by Zeus, he fell in love with Hera and was flung into Hades for his temerity. [Apollodorus 1.7.5–6; Pausanias 5.1.3–5, 5.8.1.]

Enna. See HENNA.

Enyalius. A god of war. Enyalius, at least as used by Homer, seems to be simply an epithet of Ares. Spartan youths sacrificed puppies to him, but he has no myth. If he had an existence apart from Ares, it was hardly more than as a personification of war. [Homer, *Iliad*, 13.518–522, 20.69; Pausanias 3.14.9–10, 5.18.5.]

Enyo. A goddess of war. Enyo accompanied Ares into battle. She seems to have been little more than a personification of war. The Romans identified her with their war-goddess Bellona. [Homer, *Iliad*, 5.333, 5.590–593; Pausanias 1.8.4.]

Eoiae. See CATALOGUES OF WOMEN.

Eos. The goddess of the dawn, called Aurora by the Romans. Eos, with her brother and sister, Helius (Sun) and Selene (Moon), was a child of the Titans Hyperion or Pallas and Theia or Euryphaëssa. She seems to have personified not merely the early light of morning, but the light of day as well. She, rather than Hemera (Day), was often thought to accompany Helius on his journey through the sky. By Astraeüs, who, as a fellow Titan, was perhaps her original consort, Eos bore several offspring: the north, south, and west winds (Boreas, Notus, and Zephyrus) and the stars, notably Eosphorus (Dawnbringer), the morning star. Eos was an amorous goddess, given to carrying off beautiful young men. Some say that she was afflicted with this propensity by Aphrodite, who was angry at her for having an affair with Aphrodite's lover Ares.

One of Eos' lovers was Cephalus. He was happily married to Procris when Eos carried him away, and the goddess allowed him to return to his wife after she had borne by him a son, Phaëthon. Another lover was Orion, whom Eos transported to Ortygia (Delos), but the gods were displeased with this union and Artemis shot Orion. Least known of Eos' young consorts was Cleitus, a descendant of Melampus, whom she carried off to live with the gods.

Perhaps the most famous of her love affairs was that with Tithonus, a young son or brother of the Trojan king Laomedon. Eos took him to live in her palace in the East, from which she arose every day to announce the coming of the sun. She received from Zeus the gift of immortality for Tithonus, but forgot to ask that he remain ageless as well. She bore Tithonus two sons, Memnon and Emathion, and they lived happily together, but in due course the beautiful youth turned into a shriveled, croaking old man. Eos locked him in a room where, though he was nearly paralyzed, he babbled incessantly. Some say that the goddess eventually transformed him into a cicada. Eos' son Emathion became king of Arabia and was killed by Heracles. His brother, Memnon, leader of the Ethiopian forces in the Trojan War, died in single combat with Achilles. At Eos' plea, Zeus granted special honors to his corpse. [Homer, *Odyssey*, 5.121–124, 15.249–251; Hesiod, *Theogony*, 371–382, 984–991; *Homeric Hymn to Aphrodite* 5.218–238; *Homeric Hymn to Helius* 31.1–7; *Aethiopis* 1; Ovid, *Metamorphoses*, 9.421–422, 13.576–622; Hyginus, *Fabulae*, 189; Apollodorus 1.4.5, 3.12.4, 3.14.3.]

Eosphorus. The morning star. Eosphorus, whose name means Dawnbringer (as the name of his Roman equivalent, Lucifer, means Lightbringer), was, like the other stars, a child of Eos (Dawn) by the Titan Astraeüs (Starry). He was the father of Ceÿx, king of Trachis, and Leuconoë. [Hesiod, *Theogony*, 381–382; Apollodorus 1.7.4.]

Epaphus. A king of Egypt. Named for the touch (*ephapsis*) of Zeus, by which his mother, the cow-maiden Io [B], conceived him, Epaphus was born at Memphis or Canobus, on the Nile. He was stolen as a child on Hera's orders, but recovered by Io. He ruled Egypt, founding many cities, and married Memphis, daughter of the god Nile. She bore him Libya. His descendants colonized Thebes, Crete, and Argos. Hyginus says that Hera caused Epaphus to be killed while hunting. Herodotus identified Epaphus (whom Aeschylus calls "the calf born of Zeus") with the Egyptian bull-god Apis. [Apollodorus 2.1.3–4; Herodotus 3.27; Aeschylus, *Prometheus Bound*, 850, and *Suppliants*, 48; Hyginus, *Fabulae*, 145, 149, 150.]

Epeirus. The Adriatic coastal region of Greece from the Ambracian Gulf to the area that is now southern Albania. This region, which extended far inland, was regarded by the Greeks as somewhat barbaric. The southern part of Epeirus, called Thesprotia, was the scene of some little-known adventures of Odysseus, and Heracles conquered its principal city, Ephyra. Neoptolemus ruled in Ephyra after the Trojan War, and his Trojan captive Helenus founded Buthrotum. Although a few Greek myths involve Epeirus (one Epeirot city, Dodona, was highly respected by the Greeks for its ancient oracle of Zeus), no Epeirots have important myths of their own.

Epeius (1). A son of Panopeus. Epeius, one of the Phocian leaders in the Trojan War, was the ingenious artisan who built the WOODEN HORSE, with the aid of Athena. According to Homer [*Iliad* 23.664–699], he was a powerful boxer and a brave soldier, and Vergil lists him among the Greeks in the horse. Late Classical traditions made him, for some reason, a notorious coward.

Epeius (2). A king of Elis. Endymion held a footrace at Olympia in which his three sons—Epeius, Aetolus, and Paeon—vied for succession to his throne. Epeius won and, on becoming king, named the people Epeians after himself. It was during his reign that Pelops, a Phrygian, wrested the rule of Pisa from Oenomaüs and made it independent of the domination of Elis. Epeius married Anaxiroë, daughter of Coronus, who bore him a daughter, Hyrmina, but no sons. On his death he was succeeded by Aetolus. [Pausanias 5.1.8–9.]

Ephialtes. One of the Giants. In the war between the gods and the GIANTS, Apollo shot Ephialtes in his left eye. Heracles then killed him with an arrow in his right eye. [Apollodorus 1.6.2.]

Ephialtes. See OTUS.

Ephyra. A daughter of Oceanus. Ephyra was the first inhabitant and eponym of Ephyra and of Ephyraea, the region surrounding it.

Ephyra or **Ephyre.** An early name of CORINTH, or of an earlier city that was later incorporated into Corinth.

Ephyra or **Ephyre.** A city in Thesprotia. Ephyra, ruled by King Phylas, was often at war with Calydon. When Heracles led a Calydonian army against it, the city was destroyed, Phylas killed, and his daughter Astyoche carried off by Heracles as his concubine. She bore Tlepolemus by her abductor. At some point Ilus, a descendant of Medea and Jason, was king of Ephyra and the city became known as a source of poisons. Ilus was a pious king, however, and refused to sell arrow poison to the young Odysseus. According to some accounts Neoptolemus conquered Ephyra after the Trojan War and became its king.

Epicasta. A daughter of Calydon and Aeolia, daughter of Amythaon. Epicasta married Agenor, son of Pleuron, and bore a son and a daughter, Porthaon and Demonice or Demodoce. [Apollodorus 1.7.7.]

Epicasta. See JOCASTA.

Epic Cycle. A group of fairly early Greek epic poems in imitation of Homer. The term "Epic Cycle" was loosely applied by some ancient writers to a considerable number of epic poems, some of which were already lost before the Hellenistic era. The authors, too, were mostly forgotten, and many of the poems were variously attributed. Most of those of which fragments survive deal with incidents in the Trojan War and the lives of the returning Greek warriors, or in the history of Thebes. In the former case, they complete the Trojan saga by filling in events not narrated in the *Iliad* or the *Odyssey*.

Among the Theban epics were the *Oedipodeia,* concerned with the history of Oedipus; the *Thebaïd,* a detailed account of the war between Thebes and Argos; and the *Epigoni,* the story of the avenging of the Argive champions by their sons. The Trojan poems included the *Cypria,* which dealt with events of the Trojan War that preceded the incidents which open the *Iliad.* The account in Homer's poem of Achilles' life was followed in the *Aethiopis* with the tale of his last deeds and of his death and burial. Two other epics that related events following those of the *Iliad* were the *Little Iliad* and *The Sack of Troy.* The story in the *Odyssey* of the voyages and homecoming of Odysseus was paralleled for other Greek heroes in the *Returns (Nostoi).* The *Telegony* continued the adventures of Odysseus. The extant fragments of these poems, which are the source of many details in the heroic sagas, are published in the volume of works of Hesiod in the Loeb Classical Library.

Epidaurus. The founder and eponym of the city of that name. The Argives called Epidaurus a son of Argus and Evadne; the Eleians, a son of Pelops; the Epidaurians, a son of Apollo. [Apollodorus, 2.1.2; Pausanias, 2.26.1–2.]

Epidaurus. A city on the Saronic coast of Argolis. The mythical history of this city begins with an eponymous founder who was a son of Argus, Pelops, or Apollo. Little else is told of the region before it became Dorian territory. This fact, together with the legend that it was the home of Periphetes, the brutal bandit killed by Theseus, suggests that Epidaurus was not one of the oldest centers of culture. It became prominent, however, as the birthplace and cult center of the god Asclepius. When Deïphontes, the able general of the

Heraclid leader Temenus, left Argos because of a quarrel with Temenus' sons, he settled in Epidaurus. King Pityreus ceded the rule to him without a struggle and migrated with his people to Attica. Under Deïphontes the city became independent of Argos, perhaps for the first time in its history.

Epigoni. Sons of the SEVEN AGAINST THEBES.

A. After the disastrous expedition against Thebes, only Adrastus of the Argive chieftains remained alive. All but Eteoclus, however, left sons to avenge them. Adrastus had two, Aegialeus and Cyanippus (who may have been his grandson); Amphiaraüs also had two, Alcmeon and Amphilochus; the other leaders—Capaneus, Hippomedon, Mecisteus, and Parthenopaeüs, and the foreigners, Polyneices and Tydeus—each had one son. These were, respectively, Sthenelus, Polydorus, Euryalus, Promachus or Tlesimenes, Thersander, and Diomedes. Pausanias mentions also two brothers of Thersander, Adrastus and Timeas. These sons, some of whom were eager to avenge their fathers, became known to legend as the Epigoni, because they were "born later" (than the Seven). The Delphic oracle assured them that they would succeed in destroying Thebes if Alcmeon led them. Amphiaraüs had bidden his sons to avenge him on both the Thebans and their mother, Eriphyle, who had been bribed by Polyneices to send her husband to his death. So far the young men had made no move to carry out either command, though Alcmeon claimed that he was reluctant to leave for Thebes until he had punished his mother. Eriphyle began urging her sons to go to war, and at last they agreed.

B. Under Alcmeon's leadership, then, the Epigoni marched on Thebes. The Thebans, led by Eteocles' son Laodamas, met them at a town called Glisas. A terrible battle ensued in which Laodamas killed Aegialeus and, according to Apollodorus, was himself killed by Alcmeon. Although the grave of Promachus was later shown at nearby Teumessus, most accounts agree that Aegialeus was the only one of the Epigoni to die at Thebes, as his father, Adrastus, had been the only one of the seven champions to survive the earlier war. The Thebans now took shelter within the walls and consulted the seer Teiresias as to what they should do. Foreseeing that it was useless to resist further, he advised them to send a herald to discuss surrender. Meanwhile, the Thebans prepared to escape under cover of night. Most of them stole away in carts and went northward to Illyria, where their ancestor Cadmus had gone long before. Some say that Laodamas had not died, but led this expedition. Near Haliartus, not far from Thebes, they stopped at the spring called Telphusa and there Teiresias, after drinking, died. He had lived for seven generations.

When the Argives discovered that the Thebans were gone, they razed the city and turned what remained of it over to Thersander, who thus made good his father's claim to the throne. A part of the spoils, among them Manto, Teiresias' daughter, were sent to Delphi and dedicated to Apollo; some say that it was on his way there as a prisoner that Teiresias himself died. Some Thebans had gone to Thessaly in preference to Illyria, and these Thersander invited to return to Thebes. The rest of the Epigoni went home to Argos, but Adrastus, who had accompanied them, died on the way out of grief for Aegialeus. Cyanippus, the young son of either Adrastus or Aegialeus, inherited the throne, Diomedes and Euryalus acting as regents. When Cyanippus died childless, Sthenelus became king of Argos. As for ALCMEON, the leader of the Epigoni, he at last killed Eriphyle and wandered the earth a maddened exile. Most of his former companions eventually distinguished themselves fighting with the Greeks at Troy under Diomedes' leadership. [Apollodorus 3.7.2–4.]

Epigoni. See EPIC CYCLE.

Epimetheus. A son of the Titan Iapetus and the Oceanid Clymene or Asia. Epimetheus (Afterthought) ignored the warning of his brother Prometheus (Forethought) to accept no gifts from the gods. He took from Hermes the first woman, PANDORA (1), together with her jar full of evils. He married her, she opened the jar, and man's troubles began. Pyrrha, Epimetheus' daughter by Pandora, was the first woman born of a mortal. [Hesiod, *Theogony*, 507–514, and *Works and Days*, 47–105; Apollodorus 1.2.3, 1.7.2.]

eponym. A legendary figure from whom a people or a place is said to have taken its name. Only a few of these eponymous ancestors play significant roles in myth. Most are no more than names inserted into the accepted genealogies of great heroes in order that clans or cities might win luster or political advantage by claiming descent from those heroes. Pausanias records that Epidaurus, the supposed founder of the city of that name, was said by the Argives to be a son of their own eponym, Argos, whereas the inhabitants of Elis insisted that their famous hero Pelops was Epidaurus' father. It seems likely that both of these Peloponnesian cities nurtured political claims in Epidaurus. The Epidaurians, however, apparently preferred independence; they boasted that their founder was a son of Apollo.

For whatever reasons they may have been originally invented, dozens of names like Mycene, Thebe, and Tiryns (eponyms respectively of Mycenae, Thebes, and Tiryns) have been duly recorded by Greek and Roman mythographers and historians. Plutarch begins his life of Romulus by listing seven other persons, called either Romus or Roma, for whom the city of Rome was said to have been named. Pausanias reports seeing in the Athenian market place statues erected in honor of the eponyms of the ten tribes of Athens.

Epopeus. A king of Sicyon. There are two very different versions of Epopeus' parentage. According to one, he inherited the throne of Asopia (Sicyonia) from his father, Alöeus (whom some call his brother), and annexed the neighboring land of Ephyraea (Corinth) on the death of Bunus, who had succeeded Epopeus' uncle Aeëtes as king. Epopeus' son, Marathon, emigrated to Attica to escape his father's violent behavior. When Epopeus died, Marathon gave Asopia and Ephyraea respectively to his sons Sicyon and Corinthus, who renamed them after themselves. The second version of Epopeus' origin names Asopia Aegialeia and makes Epopeus a Thessalian who, for some reason, took the throne on the death without issue of the previous ruler, Corax. In this version, Epopeus himself died without sons and the throne fell to Lamedon, Corax' younger brother.

Both versions agree on the event for which Epopeus is famous: his marriage to Antiope. Some say that he carried her off from the palace of her father, Nycteus, king of Thebes. Others claim that he received her at Sicyon as she fled from her father. In the ensuing battle with Nycteus, both kings were wounded and Nycteus soon died. His brother, Lycus, marched on Sicyon, but Epopeus died of his neglected wound before he could defend the city. His successor, Lamedon, gave up Antiope and averted a war. [Apollodorus 3.5.5; Pausanias 2.1.1, 2.3.10, 2.6.1–3.]

Erato. See MUSES.

Erebus. The darkness of the Underworld. Erebus and his sister, Nyx (Night), were born of Chaos. He later fathered Aether (Upper Air) and Hemera (Day) on Nyx. Apart from this quasi-philosophical genealogy in Hesiod's *Theogony* [123–125], Erebus is generally no more than a synonym for Hades, the Underworld.

Erechtheus. A king of Athens. The earliest reference to Erechtheus [Homer, *Iliad*, 2.544–551] calls him "earth-born" and says that he was reared by Athena, as was his grandfather Erichthonius, with whom he was sometimes identified. Later traditions make him a son of Pandion and Zeuxippe. Erechtheus married Praxithea, daughter of Phrasimus and Diogeneia. She bore three sons—Cecrops, Pandorus, and Metion—and many daughters, among them Procris, Oreithyia, and Creüsa. Some say that Erechtheus was also the father of Sicyon, Thespius, Eupalamus, and Orneus. During his reign, war broke out with neighboring Eleusis. The Eleusinians called on the Thracian Eumolpus for help. (The chronology here is rather odd, since Eumolpus was a grandson of Oreithyia.)

Erechtheus learned from an oracle that only the sacrifice of one of his daughters would help his cause. He killed the youngest and a number of the others committed suicide, some say because of a pact that they had made to die together. Several daughters escaped this fate, however: Oreithyia had been carried off by Boreas, Procris was married to Cephalus, and Creüsa was a mere infant. Erechtheus was now victorious and killed either Eumolpus or his son. Poseidon, Eumolpus' father, avenged his son by killing Erechtheus with his trident or inducing Zeus to do so with a thunderbolt. Xuthus, a Thessalian ally and son-in-law of Erechtheus, was called upon to choose a successor from among his sons. He chose Cecrops.

The rites with which Erechtheus was honored on the Acropolis were closely identified with those of Poseidon. This fact, and others, have suggested to scholars that Erechtheus was originally a local deity, rather than merely a legendary king. His attributes, similar to those of Poseidon, were to only a partial degree taken over by that god. In the Erechtheüm, a temple on the Acropolis second in importance only to the Parthenon, Erechtheus and his twin brother Butes received sacrifices side by side with Poseidon and Hephaestus. [Euripides, *Ion*, 275–282; Apollodorus 3.15.4–5.]

Erginus (1). A king of Boeotian Orchomenus. Erginus, a son of Clymenus, promised his dying father to avenge his murder at the hands of Thebans. He led troops to Thebes, then apparently under the rule of Creon; conquered the city; and took away with him all the men's armor, after forcing the Thebans to promise an annual payment of one hundred oxen for the next twenty years. When HERACLES [C] grew to manhood he mutilated the Orchomenian heralds sent to exact the tribute and, when Erginus came with an army to avenge this insult, he (Heracles) defeated them, killed Erginus, and destroyed much of Orchomenus. According to Pausanias [9.37.3–4], Erginus was not killed, but was forced to devote most of the rest of his life to recovering his prosperity. In old age, wifeless and childless, he went to Delphi to inquire of the oracle whether life had passed him by. He was advised to fix a new tip to his plow. He therefore married a young wife and became the father of Trophonius and Agamedes (though Trophonius later acquired the reputation of being a son of Apollo).

At some point when he was no longer young, Erginus amused the women of Lemnos by challenging Zetes and Calaïs to an armed footrace. Their amusement changed to admiration when he won the race. Since the Argonaut Erginus (2) would have visited Lemnos on the outward voyage it is possible that the two Erginuses were originally the same, though later writers made the Argonaut a Miletian and a son of Poseidon. [Pindar, *Olympian Odes*, 4.19–28; Apollodorus 2.4.11; Pausanias 9.37.1–2; Diodorus Siculus 4.10.3–5.]

Erginus (2). An Argonaut. Erginus, a native of Miletus, was usually called a son of Poseidon, but his father was also identified as Clymenus or as Periclymenus of Orchomenus. Since he was the son of a sea-god and volunteered to steer the *Argo* after the death of Tiphys, he was doubtless an excellent seaman. [Apollonius Rhodius 1.185–189.]

Eribotes or **Eurybates**. An Argonaut. Eribotes is known only as the son of Teleon, who is not known at all. According to Hyginus [*Fabulae* 14], Eribotes was killed along with Canthus, another of the ARGONAUTS [R], as they were trying to steal the sheep of the Libyan shepherd Caphaurus.

Erichthonius (1). An early king of Athens. Erichthonius was said by some writers to be a son of Hephaestus and Atthis, daughter of Cranaüs. The more usual tradition was that Hephaestus tried to rape Athena, but the goddess defended herself and Hephaestus' semen spilled on the earth (Ge), which later gave birth to Erichthonius. Athena put the infant into a chest and gave it to the three daughters of Cecrops, king of Athens, with strict orders not to lift the lid. Pandrosus obeyed her, but Agraulus and Herse, overcome by curiosity, peeked. In the chest they saw either a snake, a child with a snake's tail in place of legs, or a child coiled about by a snake. Some say that the snake destroyed the guilty sisters. It is more commonly believed that they were driven mad by the sight, or by Athena, who learned of their disobedience from a spying crow. In either case they jumped from the walls of the Acropolis and were killed. (Both of them, however, were honored with shrines on the Acropolis.) Athena brought up the infant on the Acropolis.

Erichthonius, on reaching manhood, drove out King Amphictyon, who had usurped the throne twelve years earlier from Cranaüs. His deeds as king are not spectacular: he instituted the Panathenaic festival and set up a wooden statue of Athena on the Acropolis. On his death he was succeeded by Pandion, his son by the Naïad nymph Praxithea. Erichthonius was often identified by ancient writers with his descendant Erechtheus, who was also said by many to have been born from the earth. Erichthonius was represented in the famous statue of Athena in the Parthenon as a snake partly hidden behind her shield. Like Cecrops, he may have been worshiped in the form of a sacred serpent. Oddly enough, he was said by some to have been transported to the stars as the constellation Auriga (the Charioteer). [Apollodorus 3.14.6; Euripides, *Ion*, 20–24, 260–274; Hyginus, *Fabulae*, 166, and *Poetica Astronomica*, 2.13; Pausanias 1.24.7]

Erichthonius (2). A king of Dardania. A son of Dardanus and Bateia, daughter of Teucer, Erichthonius succeeded to the rule at his father's death, his elder brother, Ilus, having died childless. Erichthonius became the world's richest man, the owner of three thousand horses. The mares of this herd were so splendid looking that Boreas took the form of a stallion for the pleasure of mounting them. The king married Astyoche, daughter of the river-god Simöeis, and became the father of Tros, eponym of Troy. [Homer, *Iliad*, 30.219–230; Apollodorus 3.12.1–2.]

Eridanus. A mythical European river and its god. Eridanus was, like most river-gods, a son of Oceanus and Tethys. The river itself, however, was harder to identify. Herodotus [3.115] doubted that it existed. Most writers thought that it was an ancient name for the Po, but this identification does not fit the requirements of legend that it empty into the northern sea or into Oceanus, and that its sands bear amber, a precious substance that came from much farther north. According to mythology, Phaëthon fell from the sky into the Eridanus, where his body was still sending up noxious vapors when the Argonauts came by much later. Phaëthon's sisters wept bitterly by the banks of the Eridanus. Changed into poplars, they continued to drop tears, now pure amber, into its sands.

The Eridanus was also the route by which the Argonauts [P] sailed from the Adriatic Sea to the Rhone—an impossibility if it was the Po. It has been suggested that Eridanus was a name given by the Greeks to one or more of the great northward-flowing European rivers that they had vaguely heard of from Celtic traders in tin and amber from the north. A tiny tributary of the Athenian river Ilissus was also called Eridanus.

The mythical Eridanus still flows in starry form through the sky, though some claim that this constellation actually represents either the river Oceanus or the Nile.

Erigone. The daughter of Aegisthus and Clytemnestra. Apart from Erigone's parentage, the details of her story are sketchy and somewhat contradictory. Hyginus [*Fabulae* 122] says that Orestes would have killed her together with her brother, Aletes, but Diana rescued her and made her her priestess in Attica. Apollodorus ["Epitome" 6.25 and 28] refers to unnamed sources which claimed that, on the one hand, Erigone brought Orestes to trial for matricide and that, on the other hand, she married him and bore his son and heir, Tisamenus. She was certainly the mother of his son Penthilus.

Erigone. See ICARIUS (2).

Erinyes. Female spirits who punished offenders against blood kin. The Erinyes, whom the Romans called Furies, were born, together with the Giants and the Meliae, from the earth when it was fertilized by drops of blood from the castrated Uranus. Some writers identify three of them, whom they name Alecto, Tisiphone, and Megaera, but they are usually neither named nor counted. They were described by Aeschylus as frighteningly hideous, but were seldom shown so in art. Their principal function was to avenge fathers or, more often, mothers, upon their undutiful children; they also took the part of elder children against younger. In the famous cases of Orestes and Alcmeon, the Erinyes hounded both young men into insanity for murdering their mothers. Althaea called on them to punish her son Meleager for killing her brothers. When a man failed to avenge the murder of a member of his family, the Erinyes avenged the death on him. (This fact left Orestes in an insoluble dilemma: since his mother had killed his father, he would have been punished by the Erinyes if he killed her or if he did not.) The Erinyes were said by some writers to inflict in Hades the tortures prescribed by the gods for such rogues as Sisyphus and Tantalus.

The Erinyes were often invoked in curses, the aggrieved party pounding on the ground, apparently to catch their attention. Some scholars believe, in fact, that the Erinyes were originally personified curses. Whatever their precise origin, they reflect a very ancient Greek belief in a divine mechanism of retributive justice. NEMESIS grew out of this same conviction, and her functions often overlapped those of the Erinyes. Cruel and blood-thirsty though the Erinyes seemed, they were not regarded, at least in primitive times, as unjust or even malign. Their work of retribution protected those whom human law failed to protect, usually those injured by members of their own families. This function was necessary to the orderly operation of society. In some places the grim Erinyes were closely associated in cult with the benevolent Graces. According to Aeschylus, they were themselves known at Athens as the Eumenides (Kindly Ones) and the Semnai Theai (Venerable Goddesses), both of which were local goddesses of the fertility of the earth. This combination of the terrible and the benign was frequently found in the character of CHTHONIAN DEITIES, a notable example being Persephone.

Aeschylus' tragedy *Eumenides* recounts the manner in which Athena forced the Erinyes to cease persecuting Orestes and persuaded them to give up their primitive functions as bringer of retribution in favor of new roles as the gracious Eumenides. Their maddening of Orestes is demonstrated (without their appearing) in many plays and other accounts concerned with Orestes. Their hounding of Alcmeon for the same crime, matricide, is told of by Apollodorus [3.7.5]. Ovid [*Metamorphoses* 4.451–511] vividly describes the Furies as Hera summons them from Hades to punish Athamas. Other references to the Erinyes by Greek and Roman authors are innumerable.

Eriopis. See ARSINOË (1); JASON [F].

Eriphyle. A daughter of Talaüs and Lysimache. Eriphyle married Amphiaraüs and became arbiter between him and her brother Adrastus. Polyneices bribed her to send her husband to his death with the SEVEN AGAINST THEBES [B]. Similarly persuaded by Thersander, she later urged her sons, ALCMEON and Amphilochus, to lead the EPIGONI against Thebes. On his return Alcmeon killed her, but her Erinyes drove him mad. Eriphyle had two daughters, Demonassa and Eurydice. [Apollodorus 3.6.2, 3.7.2–5.]

Eris. The goddess of discord. Eris is little more than a personification of strife, except in the familiar tale of the golden apple. Because of her disagreeable nature she was the only one of the gods not to receive an invitation to the wedding of Peleus and Thetis. She came anyway and was refused admittance. Furious, she threw a golden apple, inscribed "For the fairest," among the guests. Three goddesses claimed it and Paris was asked to judge among them. The ultimate result was the Trojan War. Eris' activities in that conflict are described by Homer [*Iliad* 4.439–445, 11.3–14]. Hesiod calls Eris the mother of a long list of personified abstractions as disagreeable as herself. [Hesiod, *Works and Days*, 11–19, and *Theogony*, 225–232.]

Eros. A god of love, called Amor or Cupid by the Romans. According to Hesiod's *Theogony* [120–122, 201], Eros existed almost from the beginning of time, being born, together with Ge (Earth) and Tartarus, out of, or at the same time as, Chaos. Far from being Aphrodite's roguish little boy, as he appears in the works of later writers, Eros was on hand to greet that goddess at her birth. The ancient poet Olen is said to have called Eros a son of Eileithyia, the goddess of birth. Shown in Greek art as a beautiful youth, he seems to have been worshiped, particularly at the Boeotian city of Thespiae, as a god of love and loyalty between young men. When Prometheus was creating men and showing them to Zeus for his approval, Eros revealed that Prometheus had avoided displaying his most beautiful creation, a youth called Phaënon.

Later writers depict Eros, or his more frivolous Roman counterparts, Amor and Cupid, as the youngest of the gods, an archer whose gold-tipped arrows could make even gods fall in love. According to Ovid [*Metamorphoses* 1.452–473, 5.362–384], it was he who made the cold-hearted god Hades love Persephone. On another occasion, annoyed because Apollo had advised him to leave archery to men, he shot the god, making him fall in love with Daphne. At the same time, he shot the nymph with one of the lead-tipped arrows that he also carried, causing her to be immune to Apollo's pleas. Apollonius Rhodius [3.119–166, 3.275–298] details Aphrodite's efforts to persuade Eros to make Medea fall in love with Jason. The best known myth of Eros, that of his love for PSYCHE, was told only by Apuleius and was perhaps a literary creation built of familiar elements from folklore. Eros sometimes is spoken of in the plural (Erotes). In art these "Loves" are generally shown as small, winged spirits such as might have escaped from Pandora's jar. [Hyginus, *Poetica Astronomica*, 2.30, 2.42; Vergil, *Aeneïd*, 667–722; Pausanias 5.11.8, 9.27.1–4, 9.31.3.]

Erymanthian boar. A giant boar that lived on Mount Erymanthus, in northwestern Arcadia. HERACLES [E] was required, as his fourth labor, to bring this animal back alive to Tiryns. He did so after trapping it in deep snow.

Erymanthus. A mountain in the extreme northwest of Arcadia on the borders of Achaea and Elis. Erymanthus was the home of the Erymanthian boar, caught by Heracles. A river Erymanthus flowed south from the mountain to join the Alpheius. Erymanthus was also the earliest name of the Arcadian city of Psophis.

Erysichthon (1). A son of Cecrops and Agraulus. Nothing is known of Erysichthon except that he died childless before his father, perhaps while bringing a statue of the goddess Eileithyia home to Athens from Delos. [Apollodorus 3.14.1–2; Pausanias 1.18.5, 1.31.2.]

Erysichthon (2). A son of Triopas. Erysichthon was a ruthless man who scorned the gods. One day he cut down an oak tree that grew in a grove sacred to Demeter, ignoring the groans of the dryad nymph whose blood flowed from the wounds made by the ax. The other dryads of the grove prayed to Demeter to punish the culprit for the sacrilege and avenge their sister. At once Erysichthon was afflicted with an insatiable hunger. Having eaten all his food, he sold his daughter, Mestra, to buy more. She, however, was given the power to change her shape, a gift from Poseidon, who had once been her lover. In various forms she was able not only to avoid the chains of successive purchasers, but to forage for food for her father. Her extraordinary display of filial piety was of no use, however. Unable to quiet the pangs of hunger, Erysichthon eventually fell to gnawing his own flesh and died. The same story is told in brief of Erysichthon's father, who is said by Hyginus [*Poetica Astronomica* 2.14] to be commemorated in the constellation Serpent-Holder. [Ovid, *Metamorphoses*, 8.738–878.]

Erytheia. The island home of Geryon. Erytheia (Red Island) was located in the far west in the river Oceanus. At one time it was said to be in Ambracia, in western Greece, but it was moved farther west to the Spanish coast near Gadeira (Cadiz) as Greek knowledge of the Mediterranean world increased. Helius pastured his cattle there until they were stolen by the Giant Alcyoneus. Later Geryon's cattle were similarly stolen by Heracles.

Erythras. The eponym of Erythrae, in southern Boeotia. A son of Athamas' son Leucon, Erythras was one of Hippodameia's suitors killed by her father, Oenomaüs. [Pausanias 6.21.11.]

Erythrius. A son of Athamas and Themisto. Erythrius, like Erythras, son of Athamas' son Leucon, may have been regarded as the eponym of Erythrae, in southern Boeotia.

Erytus or **Eurytus.** An Argonaut. Erytus and his brother, Echion, were sons of Hermes by Antianeira, daughter of Menetes. They lived in the Thessalian city of Alope. Erytus, whose name is often spelled Eurytus, may also be the Eurytion mentioned together with Echion by Ovid as present at the Calydonian boar hunt. [Apollonius Rhodius 1.51–56; Ovid, *Metamorphoses*, 8.311.]

Eryx. An early king of northwestern Sicily. A son of Aphrodite by Poseidon or the Argonaut Butes, Eryx named a city and a mountain for himself. When a bull from the herd of HERACLES [H] wandered into his territory, he challenged the stranger to box or wrestle, staking his kingdom against Heracles' herd. Heracles killed him in the ensuing match. AENEAS [B] later visited with Eryx' descendant Acestes and sacrificed to Eryx as a hero. The Romans claimed that Eryx was of Phrygian descent; since Butes was said to be his father it is likely that the Greeks also claimed him. [Apollodorus 2.5.10; Pausanias 3.16.4–5; Diodorus Siculus 4.23.2–3; Vergil, *Aeneïd*, 5.400–419, 5.772–773.]

Eryx. A mountain near the western end of Sicily and the surrounding region. This land was named by Eryx, who founded a city that bears his name (Erice) even today. This entire region, including Lilybaeüm (now Marsala), was a famous cult center of Eryx' mother, Aphrodite.

Etearchus. A king of Oaxus, in Crete. Persuaded by his second wife that his first wife's daughter, Phronime, was unchaste, Etearchus befriended a Theraean trader, Themison, and tricked him into vowing to throw the girl into the sea. Themison did so, but rescued her and took her to Thera, where she became the mother of BATTUS [A] by Polymnestus.

Eteocles (1). A son of Oedipus, king of Thebes, and Jocasta or Euryganeia. After Oedipus' disgrace, Eteocles and his brother, POLYNEICES, agreed to rule Thebes jointly, but Eteocles did not honor the bargain and banished his brother. This quarrel, the result of Oedipus' curse on his sons, resulted in the war of the SEVEN AGAINST THEBES and the death of the brothers at each other's hands. Eteocles was succeeded on the throne by his son Laodamas, or by Creon, who was perhaps acting as regent for the boy.

Eteocles is a leading character in Aeschylus' *Seven Against Thebes* and Euripides' *Phoenician Women*. See also Apollodorus [3.6.5–6] and Pausanias [9.5.11–13.]

Eteocles (2). A king of Boeotian Orchomenus. Eteocles was a son of Andreus and Euippe, daughter of Athamas' son Leucon. Some, however, call him a son of the river-god Cephisus. He succeeded Andreus as king of Andreïs, the region about Orchomenus, and, on dying childless, left the rule to Almus. Eteocles was known less as a king than as the first man to name three Graces and sacrifice to them. [Pausanias 9.34.9–9.35.1, 9.36.1.]

Eteoclus. One of the SEVEN AGAINST THEBES. Eteoclus was the son of Iphis. Though poor, he was honored at Argos for his integrity. He was killed at Thebes by Leades or Megareus.

etesian winds. See ARISTAEÜS.

Ethiopia. A land south of Egypt. The Greek historians and geographers knew Ethiopia (Aithiopia) as a land extending southward from Egypt (from an east-west line at about the first cataract of the Nile, near the present city of Aswan) along the Red Sea and beyond. The Ethiopia of mythology, however, seems to have little to do with any actual land. Homer located the Ethiopians on the banks of Oceanus, at both the eastern and western extremities of the earth. He made them a fabulous people whose feasts were attended by the gods. The Ethiopian king Memnon, a son of Eos (Dawn), was doubtless believed to live near where the sun rose and, in fact, was sometimes called an Assyrian. The story of Perseus and Andromeda, set in a land called Ethiopia, is said by some writers to have taken place at Joppa, on the Syrian coast. Andromeda's father, Cepheus, though called Ethiopian, was said by some to be a son of Phoenix, the eponym of Phoenicia. The fight of an air-borne hero with a sea monster is, moreover, reminiscent of Canaanite myths of the storm-god Baal. Ethiopia, in short, must be thought of in many myths as lying at the ends of the earth, in others as somewhere in the Near East.

Etna, Mount. See Mount AETNA.

Etruscans. A group of tribes who inhabited Etruria, the coastal regions of Italy north of Rome. Called Tyrrhenians or Tyrsenians by the Greeks, the Etruscans gave their name to the Tyrrhenian Sea. They reached a period of great prosperity and power in the sixth century B.C., during which they ruled Rome as well as their own numerous cities. The most prominent Etrurian city was Tarquinia. According to legend, the first Etruscan king of Rome was Lucius Tarquinius Priscus, a man of Greek ancestry who had ingratiated himself with his Roman predecessor, King Ancus Marcius. The next two kings belonged to the Etruscan dynasty, though Tarquinius' successor, Servius Tullius, is said by some to have been a Latin. Servius was murdered by Tarquinius' son Lucius Tarquinius Superbus. This Tarquin was expelled from Rome after twenty-five years of brutally tyrannical rule, and the kingship was replaced by a republican government. In fact, Rome lost by this act the prosperity that it had enjoyed under the Etruscans and devoted much of its energies for a long time thereafter to quelling various Etruscan attempts to regain the rule.

Euboea. A long, narrow island off the eastern coast of Boeotia and Locris. Euboea was the home of the Abantes, whose most prominent leaders were Chalcodon and his son Elephenor. Elephenor led Euboean forces to the Trojan War. Over a period of many years, the Euboeans, whose principal city was Chalcis, were often in conflict with Thebes, the nearest major city on the mainland. They seem to have had friendly relations with Athens, however, for Theseus' sons took refuge with Elephenor when their father was embattled in Athens. Euboea was a principal cult center of Hera and, like many other places, claimed to have been her birthplace.

Euchenor. A son or grandson of Polyeidus the seer. Euchenor, a wealthy Corinthian, was told by Polyeidus that he was fated either to die at home of disease or be killed in the Trojan War. He chose to win glory at Troy and, in doing so, avoid both the disease and the fine that would have been imposed on him if he had refused to go. Paris shot and killed him. [Homer, *Iliad*, 13.660–672.]

Euippe. See ATHAMAS [E]; PIERUS.

Eumaeüs. Chief swineherd of Laërtes, king of Ithaca, and later of Laërtes' son, Odysseus. Eumaeüs' father was Ctesius, son of Ormenus, king of the island of Syria. When Eumaeüs was a child he was lured away by his Phoenician nurse to the ship of some Phoenician merchants, who sold him as a slave to Laërtes. When Laërtes later abdicated in favor of his son, Eumaeüs served Odysseus' family and remained loyal to his interests during his long absence, refusing to have anything to do with Penelope's greedy suitors. He stayed in his own hut in the countryside with the younger herdsmen. When ODYSSEUS [L–N] returned, disguised as a beggar, Eumaeüs generously entertained him. It was in Eumaeüs' hut that Odysseus revealed himself secretly to his son, Telemachus. The swineherd later aided his masters in disposing of the suitors. [Homer, *Odyssey*, 14–24.]

Eumelus (1). A son of Admetus and Alcestis. Eumelus married Penelope's sister Iphthime. He led eleven ships from Pherae to the Trojan War. With them went the mares that Apollo had reared while working for Admetus. They would have brought him to victory in the chariot race at Patroclus' funeral games if Athena had not broken their yoke to spite Apollo. Eumelus was more fortunate at Achilles' funeral games, where he won first prize. [Homer, *Iliad*, 2.711–715, 2.763–767, 23.288–565, and *Odyssey*, 4.795–798; Apollodorus "Epitome" 5.5.]

Eumelus (2). Aboriginal king of the region of Patrae, in Achaea. Eumelus learned from Triptolemus how to cultivate corn. He founded the city of Aroë on the shores of the gulf of Patrae. Later he and Triptolemus founded another city, Antheia, in memory of Eumelus' son, Antheias, who had been killed in a rash attempt to ride in Triptolemus' winged, dragon-drawn chariot while the god was sleeping. Aroë was later incorporated within the walls of Patrae. [Pausanias 7.18.2–3.]

Eumenides. Goddesses worshiped at various Greek cities. The Eumenides (Kindly Ones) were characteristic of many CHTHONIAN goddesses who insured the fertility of the earth and were worshiped under various titles at different localities, for example, as the Semnai Theai, at Athens. Aeschylus, in his play named for them, identified them with the ERINYES, but it is not certain that they were generally regarded as having the harsh side of the Erinyes.

Eumolpus. A Thracian ally of the Eleusinians. Eumolpus was a son of Chione by Poseidon. Fearing the anger of her father, Boreas, Chione threw her newborn infant into the sea. Poseidon caught him and took him to his daughter Benthesicyme, who was married to an Ethiopian king. When the boy, Eumolpus, grew up the king gave him one of his two daughters as a bride. She bore a son, Ismarus or Immaradus. Eumolpus, however, preferred his sister-in-law to his wife and tried to rape her. Banished with his son, he went to the court of Tegyrius, a Thracian king, who married his daughter to Eumolpus' son. Eumolpus again ruined his chances for advancement, this time by plotting against Tegyrius. Banished for a second time, he took refuge in Eleusis. On the death of his son, who had apparently not been implicated in the plot against Tegyrius, Eumolpus was recalled to Thrace and was made king when Tegyrius died. When war broke out between Athens and Eleusis, the Eleusinians called on Eumolpus for help and he responded with a large Thracian army. He, or his son (who in some versions was still living), was killed in this war.

The early career of Eumolpus was recounted only by the mythographer Apollodorus [3.15.4–5]. Early works, such as the *Homeric Hymn to Demeter*, mention him merely as an Eleusinian leader, though his Thracian origins seem to have been a strong tradition. Together with Celeüs, king of Eleusis, Eumolpus was a founder of the Eleusinian mysteries. It was he who initiated Heracles into these mysteries, after purifying him of his murder of the Centaurs. Poseidon's destruction of the Athenian king Erechtheus may have been vengeance for Eumolpus' death in the war. According to some writers Eumolpus was the father of Ceryx, eponym of the Cerycians.

Euneüs. A king of Lemnos. Euneüs was a son by Jason of Hypsipyle, queen of Lemnos. He evidently succeeded his mother on the throne at some time after her expulsion by the Lemnian women. At the time of the Trojan War Euneüs' ships provided the Greek forces with wine. He may, however, have remained neutral in the struggle, for he gave an antique Phoenician silver bowl to ransom Priam's son Lycaon from Patroclus. (Elsewhere, however,

Homer says that Euneüs bought Lycaon and Eëtion of Imbros ransomed him.) [Homer, *Iliad*, 7.467–471, 23.746–747.]

Eunomia. See SEASONS.

Eunomus. A cupbearer and relative of Oeneus. Eunomus, a son of Architeles, annoyed HERACLES [M] while pouring wine or water for him. Heracles accidentally killed him with a rap of his knuckles. Eunomus is sometimes called Cyathus or Eurynomus.

Eupeithes. An Ithacan noble. As a young man Eupeithes had joined Taphian pirates in a raid on the Thesprotians, with whom the Ithacans were at peace. Odysseus saved his life from the angry Ithacans. Eupeithes forgot this favor in later years, permitting his son, Antinoüs, to become the most insolent of Penelope's suitors during Odysseus' long absence. Odysseus returned and killed all the suitors. Eupeithes led their relatives in an insurrection against Odysseus, but was killed by Odysseus' aged father, Laërtes. [Homer, *Odyssey*, 16.424–432, 24.421–471, 24.520–525.]

Euphemus. A fleet-footed Argonaut. Euphemus was a son of Poseidon by Europa, daughter of Tityus, or by Mecionice, a native of Hyria. He was so swift that he could run across waves without wetting his feet. His home was at Taenarum, the southernmost tip of the Peloponnesus, where there was an entrance to the Underworld. Euphemus joined the ARGONAUTS [I, R], and his fleet-footedness may, in a lost version of the story, have played an important part in one of their adventures. As the *Argo* approached the Clashing Rocks, it was Euphemus who released the dove, then ran back and forth urging his comrades to row faster. It is possible that originally he ran before or beside the ship, perhaps pulling it ahead, as the Nereïds and Thetis did later when it reached the Wandering Rocks.

Euphemus was the divinely appointed ancestor of the Greek colonists who founded the north African seaport of Cyrene. When the Argonauts were stranded in Libya, the sea-god Triton appeared to them in the guise of a young king, Eurypylus. As a gesture of welcome, he offered them a clod of earth, which Euphemus accepted and saved. Later he dreamed that he suckled it at his breast and it turned into a beautiful young woman, whom he lay with. Afterward he felt remorseful, but she assured him that she was an immortal daughter of Triton. She promised that if he would give her a home near the island of Anaphe she would reappear from the sea one day to nurse his descendants as Euphemus had nursed her. Euphemus awoke and, on telling Jason the dream, was advised to throw the clod into the sea. In later years, as Jason predicted, an island (called Calliste) grew up where the clod had sunk.

According to Pindar, the clod had fallen from the *Argo* and washed up on the shore of Calliste. Pindar claimed that, if Euphemus had taken it home to the gate of Hades at Taenarum, the Greeks would eventually have ruled all of Africa. He gave no mythological source for this statement, which was probably intended to flatter the ambitions of the Cyrenian nobles whom he was addressing.

While the island was growing, Euphemus' descendants were growing up on the island of Lemnos, where the Argonauts had visited. Driven out by the Tyrrhenians, they went to Sparta. Later, many generations after Euphemus' death, they were led by Theras to colonize Calliste, which they renamed Thera. Still later, Greeks from Thera, led by BATTUS, a descendant of Euphemus, founded a new city in Libya—Cyrene, in the general area where Euphemus had received the clod. [Apollonius Rhodius 1.179–184, 2.531–590, 4.1464–1484, 4.1731–1764; Pindar, *Pythian Odes*, 4.]

Euripides (c. 485–c. 407 B.C.). A Greek tragic dramatist. The nineteen surviving plays of Euripides include two that are concerned with Heracles and his family, four that recount episodes from the Trojan War and its immediate aftermath, two that do the same for the war of the Seven against Thebes, and four that deal with Orestes and his sisters. The subjects of other dramas are episodes in the lives of Hippolytus, Alcestis, Ion, Dionysus at Thebes, and Helen in Egypt.

Euripus. The strait separating Euboea from the mainland of Greece. The Euripus was notorious for its dangerous currents.

Europa. The daughter of Agenor, king of Tyre or Sidon, and Telephassa or Argiope. (Some say that Europa was the daughter of Agenor's son Phoenix, also king of Tyre or Sidon, by Perimede.) Zeus fell in love with Europa. Taking the form of a beautiful white bull, he wandered among the herds that Hermes had driven down to the seashore where Europa was playing. He looked so gentle munching a crocus that the girl felt quite safe with him and eventually climbed onto his back. Before she knew what was happening, the bull was swimming toward Crete. (Some say that the bull was not Zeus himself, but was merely sent by the god to lure the girl away from her father's watchful eyes.) Arriving in Crete, Europa became Zeus's mistress. In order to guard her from harm—or perhaps to guard her—he gave her Laelaps, the watchdog that Minos later gave to Procris. Another present was Talus, the bronze giant. Zeus had three sons by Europa: Minos, Rhadamanthys, and Sarpedon. Eventually Zeus married Europa to Asterius, king of Crete, and she bore a daughter, Crete. Asterius, having no sons of his own, adopted the three boys. [Apollodorus 3.1.1–2; Homer, *Iliad*, 14.321–322; Ovid, *Metamorphoses*, 2.836–875.]

Europa. See EUPHEMUS.

Eurotas. An early king of Laconia. Eurotas was said to be the son of Lelex, by the naïad nymph Cleocharia, or of Lelex' son Myles. His chief contribution to his country was to build a canal to carry off stagnant water from the Laconian plain. He gave his name to the principal river of this region. Another river, the Tiasa, took its name from one of his daughters. Sparta, Eurotas' other daughter, was the eponym of the great city founded by her husband, Lacedaemon. It is likely that Eurotas was originally a river-god who, like the Argive Inachus, was later rationalized into an early king. [Apollodorus 3.10.3; Pausanias 3.1.1–2, 3.18.6.]

Euryalus. The son of Mecisteus. Euryalus marched with the EPIGONI. With Diomedes he became guardian of Cyanippus, son or grandson of Adrastus. He sailed with the Argonauts and later went to Troy with Diomedes and Sthenelus.

Eurybates. An Ithacan herald who served both Agamemnon and Odysseus during the Trojan War. When Agamemnon decided to take Achilles' concubine, Briseïs, Eurybates reluctantly went with Talthybius to fetch her from Achilles' camp. Later, with Odius, he accompanied the embassy sent by Agamemnon in a vain attempt to appease Achilles. Eurybates, though round-shouldered, swarthy, and curly-haired, was valued by Odysseus for his quick wit. [Homer, *Iliad*, 1.318–348, 9.170, and *Odyssey*, 19.244–248.]

Eurybates. See ERIBOTES.

Eurybia. A daughter of Pontus and Ge. Described by Hesiod for no apparent reason as "flint-hearted," Eurybia bore Astraeüs, Pallas, and Perses by the Titan Crius. [Hesiod, *Theogony*, 239, 375–377.]

Eurycleia. The nurse of Odysseus. A daughter of Ops, Eurycleia was bought by Laërtes, king of Ithaca, for twenty oxen. He treated her as a member of the family, but never lay with her for fear of the anger of his wife, Anticleia. Eurycleia recognized the disguised Odysseus on his return to Ithaca by a scar on his thigh. She aided him in his battle with his wife's suitors and informed him which of his womenservants had been disloyal to him. Eurycleia appears often in the Ithacan books of the *Odyssey* of Homer.

Eurycyda. A daughter of Endymion. At the exile from Elis of Eurycyda's brother Aetolus, Eleius, her son by Poseidon, became king. [Pausanias 5.1.8–9.]

Eurydamas. An Argonaut. Eurydamas was a son of Ctimenus, from Dolopia. Hyginus [*Fabulae* 14] seems to have confused him with the Argonaut Eurytion, son of Irus and Demonassa. [Apollonius Rhodius 1.65.8.]

Eurydice (1). A Thracian nymph. Eurydice married ORPHEUS, but died of a snakebite. Orpheus was allowed to bring her back from Hades, provided that he did not look at her on the way. Unable to bear the strain, he turned to look and Eurydice was lost to him forever.

Eurydice (2). A daughter of Lacedaemon. She married ACRISIUS and bore him Danaë.

Eurydice (3). The wife of Creon, king of Thebes. Eurydice killed herself in grief after the suicide of her son HAEMON (2). She appears briefly in Sophocles' tragedy *Antigone* [1183–1243].

Eurydice (4). A daughter of a king, probably Trojan, named Adrastus. Eurydice married Ilus and became the mother of Laomedon. [Apollodorus 3.12.3.]

Eurydice. See NESTOR; OPHELTES.

Euryganeia. See OEDIPUS [A].

Eurygyes. See ANDROGEÜS.

Eurylochus. The most aggressive member of Odysseus' crew. Eurylochus was leader of the scouting party that explored Circe's island and was turned into swine. Eurylochus, too cautious to enter the sorceress' house, escaped and took the news to ODYSSEUS [F, I]. At first he refused to return to the house when Odysseus had subdued the sorceress, but finally did so because he feared his captain more than Circe. It was Eurylochus who forced Odysseus to land on Thrinacia by arousing the weary crew's resentment against him. He later induced his shipmates to kill some of Helius' cattle and thus brought down Zeus's anger on them all, resulting in the deaths of all but Odysseus. [Homer, *Odyssey*, 10.203–272, 10.429–448, 12.276–352.]

Eurymachus. An Ithacan noble. A son of Polybus, Eurymachus was the most favored of the suitors of Penelope. He was the second to be killed by Odysseus on his return. He appears throughout the Ithacan books of Homer's *Odyssey*.

Eurymede. See EURYNOME (1).

Eurynome (1). A daughter of Nisus. Athena taught Eurynome wit and wisdom until she was as wise as the gods. Glaucus (1), Sisyphus' son, won her, but Poseidon lay with her and she bore Bellerophon. Apollodorus calls Glaucus' wife Eurymede. [*Catalogues of Women*, 7.]

Eurynome (2). An Oceanid. Eurynome, a daughter of Oceanus and Tethys, bore the Graces, and perhaps the river Asopus, by Zeus. According to an obscure tradition mentioned by Apollonius Rhodius [1.503–506], Eurynome was the most ancient of the goddesses, ruling Olympus with Ophion until they were supplanted by Cronus and Rhea and fell into Oceanus. Eurynome is said to have had a shrine at Phigalia, in Arcadia, where she was shown in mermaid's form. [Hesiod, *Theogony*, 358, 907–911; Apollodorus 3.12.6; Pausanias 8.41.4–6.]

Eurynome. See LYCURGUS (2); TALAÜS.

Euryphaëssa. A Titaness. According to the *Homeric Hymn to Helius* [31], Euryphaëssa was the mother by the Titan Hyperion of Helius, Selene, and Eos. Her name, which means "Wide-shining," may be merely an alternate title of Theia, who is usually said to have been Hyperion's consort.

Eurypylus (1). A son of Euaemon and Opis. Eurypylus led forty Thessalian ships to the Trojan War from Ormenius. He killed Priam's son Axion, but was wounded by Axion's brother Paris. Patroclus tended his wound. During the fall of the city, Eurypylus found an elaborate chest that had either been left behind by Aeneas or thrown out by Cassandra to become a curse to a Greek finder. It contained an image of Dionysus that Hephaestus had made and Dardanus had received from Zeus. When Eurypylus opened the chest and saw the image he went mad. Going to Delphi, he was told by the oracle that he would be cured if he settled in a spot where people made a strange sacrifice. The winds carried his ship to Aroë. There he found a youth and a young woman about to be sacrificed to Artemis Triclaria. The people held up the rite when Eurypylus showed them the statue of Dionysus, for they recalled an oracle directing them to end this annual ritual when a strange king appeared with a strange god. Eurypylus was cured of his madness and no doubt instituted, in place of the bloody rite, the pleasanter worship of Dionysus. [Homer, *Iliad*, 2.734–737, 11.806–848, 15.390–404; Pausanias 7.19.6–10.]

Eurypylus (2). Son of Telephus, king of Pergamon, and Astyoche or Laodice. Eurypylus' mother tried to dissuade him from risking his life fighting the Greeks at Troy until Priam's gift of a golden vine induced her to withdraw her objections. Eurypylus led a large Mysian force to Troy. He distinguished himself there by killing Machaon and Peneleüs, but was himself killed by Neoptolemus. [Homer, *Odyssey*, 11.519–521; *Little Iliad* 1, 8; Pausanias 9.5.15.]

Eurysaces. See AJAX (1).

Eurysthenes. See PROCLES.

Eurystheus. A king of Mycenae and Tiryns. Eurystheus is remembered not for his own accomplishments, but for his lifelong persecution of HERACLES. He was a son of Perseus' son Sthenelus and of Nicippe, a daughter of Pelops. Sthenelus had usurped the rule of Mycenae on the death of his brother Electryon. Heracles, as a son of Electryon's daughter, Alcmene, should have inherited the throne, but Hera, hating the offspring of one of her husband's illicit affairs, arranged that Eurystheus should be born first and thus receive the rule. When Heracles killed his wife and children in a fit of madness, the Delphic oracle required him to serve Eurystheus for twelve years and perform ten or, according to most writers, twelve labors that Eurystheus might demand of him. Eurystheus, eager to dispose of this powerful vassal, imposed on him a series of difficult and usually dangerous labors. When Heracles brought back the skin of the Nemean lion, Eurystheus was so terrified that he hid in a bronze jar buried in the ground. He decreed that Heracles should never again enter the gates of Mycenae, and thereafter Eurystheus' uncle Copreus, who served as his herald, carried the king's messages to Heracles.

Heracles completed the labors and eventually achieved immortality. After the hero's disappearance from the earth, Eurystheus felt no more secure than before, for Heracles had left behind him innumerable children. Many of Heracles' descendants, the HERACLIDS, begged the protection of Ceÿx, king of Trachis. When Ceÿx regretfully declared his city too weak to withstand a possible Mycenaean invasion, the Heraclids, together with Heracles' aged parents, found a haven at Marathon. The king of Athens, either Theseus or his son Demophon, undertook to defend them and defeated Eurystheus' Argive forces that moved against them. What happened to Eurystheus in this conflict is disputed. Some say that he fled the battle in a chariot, but was killed by Heracles' son Hyllus at the Sceironian Rocks on the Isthmus of Corinth. Hyllus brought his head to Alcmene, who gouged out the eyes. Other writers claim that Eurystheus was captured alive and brought to Alcmene. In spite of the protests of the humane Athenians, the vindictive woman ordered his execution.

Eurystheus appears as a cruel but not cowardly character in Euripides' *Children of Heracles*. He is frequently mentioned in many other Classical works, but the most connected account of his long persecution of Heracles is found in Apollodorus [2.4.12–2.5.12, 2.8.1].

Euryte. A daughter of Hippodamas. Euryte married Porthaon, king of Calydon, and was the mother of Oeneus, Agrius, Melas, and several other children, who are given various names. [Apollodorus 1.7.10.]

Eurytion (1). A king of Phthia. Eurytion was a son of Actor or of Irus and Demonassa (in which case he was Actor's grandson). Peleus, fleeing Aegina after murdering his brother, came to Eurytion's court. The king purified him and gave him his daughter Antigone and a third of his kingdom. He and Peleus sailed with the Argonauts and later went together to the Calydonian boar hunt. There Eurytion was accidentally killed by Peleus with a wild throw of his spear. [Apollodorus 3.13.1–2; Apollonius Rhodius 1.71–74.]

Eurytion (2). A Centaur; also called Eurytus. At the wedding of PEIRITHOÜS and Hippodameia, it was Eurytion who led his companions in a drunken attempt to carry off the bride and other Lapith women. He was either killed or mutilated and the Centaurs were driven from their home on Mount Pelion. It may have been this same Centaur whom HERACLES [E] drove from the region of Mount Pholoë. Later Eurytion forced a marriage with Mnesimache, daughter of King Dexamenus of Olenus, but when he came to collect his bride he was killed by Heracles, who happened to be the king's guest.

Eurytion (3). A herdsman of Geryon, king of Erytheia. Eurytion and his dog, Orthus, were killed by HERACLES [H] when he stole Geryon's cattle as his tenth labor. [Apollodorus 2.5.10.]

Eurytus (1). A king of Oechalia. Eurytus is said by some writers to have trained HERACLES [B, J, N] in the use of the bow. If so, he must have regretted this kindness many times. At about the time that Heracles finished his twelve labors, Eurytus held a contest, offering as a prize the hand of his daughter, Iole, to anyone who could defeat him and his sons in archery. Heracles won the contest, but Eurytus, recalling that Heracles had killed his children by his first wife, refused him Iole. Heracles left Oechalia in anger. At the same time Eurytus' mares vanished. His son Iphitus, who had tried to persuade his father to honor his promise to Heracles, refused to believe that Heracles was the thief—and indeed it may have been Autolycus. Iphitus went to Tiryns and asked Heracles to help him find the mares. Either on purpose or in a fit of madness, Heracles killed him. Much later he avenged himself on Eurytus by murdering him and his surviving sons and abducting Iole. This act indirectly brought about Heracles' death through the resulting jealousy of his wife, Deïaneira. According to Homer [*Odyssey* 8.223–228, 21.11–33], Eurytus had died young, before Iphitus began his search for the mares, killed by Apollo for daring to challenge him to a contest of archery. He left his great bow to Iphitus, who gave it to his friend Odysseus. Odysseus later used it to kill his wife's suitors. Eurytus had a daughter, Dryope, by his first wife.

Eurytus (2). One of the GIANTS. In the war between gods and Giants Dionysus killed Eurytus with his thyrsus. [Apollodorus 1.6.2.]

Eurytus. See ERYTUS; EURYTION (2); MOLIONES.

Euterpe. One of the nine Muses. Either Euterpe or her sister Calliope was the mother of the Thracian king Rhesus by the river-god Strymon. [Apollodorus 1.3.1–4.]

Euthymus. A son of Astycles or the river-god Caecinus. Euthymus, who came from Locri, in Italy, won several boxing contests in the Olympic games. On returning to Italy and settling in the town of Temesa, he found that the inhabitants annually sacrificed a young woman to the Hero, the ghost of one of Odysseus' sailors, Lycas or Polites, whom their ancestors had stoned to death for raping a local girl. The ghost had killed a number of Temesians before, on the advice of the Delphic oracle, they instituted the sacrifice. Determining to end the tyranny of the Hero, Euthymus put on his armor and fought the ghost, which finally sank into the sea. [Pausanias 6.6.4–11.]

Euxine Sea. An ancient name for the BLACK SEA.

Evadne (1). A daughter of Strymon and Neaera. Evadne married Argus, king of Argos, and bore him Ecbasus, Peiras, Epidaurus, and Criasus. [Apollodorus 2.1.2.]

Evadne (2). The daughter of Iphis. When her husband, CAPANEUS, was cremated after the siege of Thebes, Evadne flung herself on his pyre. [Euripides, *The Suppliants*, 990–1071.]

Evadne (3). A daughter of Poseidon by the Laconian nymph Pitane. Pitane kept her pregnancy secret and, after the birth, sent the child to Aepytus, son of Eilatus, king of the Arcadians of Phaesane. Evadne, as the girl was called, grew to be a beautiful woman and caught Apollo's eye. He seduced her and she became pregnant. On discovering her situation, Aepytus went to Delphi for advice. The oracle told him that Apollo was the father and Aepytus was content. On his return, however, he could find no one who knew of the child. Evadne had borne a son in the fields, with the help of Eileithyia and the Fates, whom Apollo had sent to aid her. Not daring to take the child home, Evadne had left it in a thicket. Two snakes had fed it with honey. When the boy, whose name was Iamus, grew up, he went to Olympia. There his father gave him the gift of prophecy—if he had not already received it from the snakes. [Pindar, *Olympian Odes*, 6.27–70.]

Evander. An Arcadian settler in Italy. Evander, a son of Hermes and an Arcadian nymph, founded a city on the banks of the Tiber and named it for his Arcadian home town, Pallantium. An old man when Aeneas came to Italy, Evander sent his son Pallas to fight with Aeneas against the Latins. Pallas was killed. The local Roman place names Palatium and Palatine Hill were said to be derived from the name of Evander's city. [Vergil, *Aeneïd*, 8.51–369; Pausanias 8.43.2, 8.44.5.]

Evenus. A son of Ares and Demonice. When Idas carried off Evenus' daughter, Marpessa, Evenus pursued Idas' winged chariot as far as the Aetolian river Lycormas. Unable to go farther, he killed his horses and drowned himself from rage or grief. The river was thereupon renamed for him. [Apollodorus 1.7.7–8.]

F

Fates. Divine beings who determined the course of events in human lives. The Fates were called Moerae by the Greeks, Fata or Parcae by the Romans. In part personifications of the idea of implacable destiny, they were differently conceived by different writers. Their number varied from one to three. In some cases they seem merely to carry out the will of the gods, in others even Zeus bows to their will. In the *Theogony*, the earliest extant work to name them individually, Hesiod identifies them first as three daughters of Nyx (Night): Clotho, Lachesis, and Atropos. Later in the same work he calls them daughters of Zeus and Themis and sisters of the Seasons. The first passage [217–222] associates, if not identifies, them with the Keres, grim spirits who carried the dead to Hades. (In the *Shield of Heracles* they rule over the Keres; often they are connected with the Erinyes.) The later passage [901–906] treats them, like their sisters, the Seasons, as abstractions of aspects of the orderly working of the universe. As such they were appropriately daughters of the all-powerful sky-god and of Themis, an ancient, all-wise earth-goddess who had come to stand for order in the communal affairs of men.

As often as the Fates were associated with the end of life, they were active at its beginning. They appeared, for example, to Althaea seven days after the birth of MELEAGER and, in the manner of birth spirits, predicted his future. Their name Parcae (Bringers Forth) refers to this function. Moerae, meaning "Parts" or allotted portions, identifies them merely as men's lots in life, and Lachesis' name (Apportioner of Lots) reinforces this concept. The metaphor of spinning used repeatedly by Homer in speaking of the gods allotting destinies to men seems to have given rise to Clotho's name (Spinner) and to many later representations of the three women spinning, measuring, and cutting the thread of life. Clotho is sometimes called the principal Fate; sometimes it is Atropos, who is described in the *Shield of Heracles* as the eldest and best of the sisters—and, for some reason, the shortest. The earliest writers seem to have conceived of the Fates as carrying out the will of the gods, particularly of Zeus. Aeschylus, however, in his *Prometheus Bound* [515–518] represented even Zeus as bound by their decisions.

The Fates generally remained personally remote from the affairs of gods and men. On two occasions, however, they took part in the battles of the gods. In the war with the Giants they sided with the gods, killing Agrius and Thoas with bronze clubs. Later they came to the aid of Zeus by inducing his formidable enemy Typhöeus to taste human food. It proved a debilitating diet for him and led to his downfall. On very rare occasions the Fates might even be influenced in the usually relentless performance of their functions. To please Apollo, for example, they permitted Admetus to seek a substitute to die in his place when his allotted life span came to an end. To win his way, however, the god had to cheat the Fates, or else to make them drunk.

The Fates were worshiped in many parts of Greece. At Sicyon, at least, they received sacrifices similar to those usually dedicated to the Erinyes. An inscription on a herm-like image of Aphrodite Urania (Heavenly) called this goddess the oldest of the Fates, but nothing further is known of such an identification. [Aeschylus, *Eumenides*, 334–335, 956–967; Apollodorus 1.4.2, 1.6.3, 1.8.2; Ovid, *Metamorphoses*, 8.451–456, 15.807–815; Hyginus, *Fabulae*, 171, and *Poetica Astronomica*, 2.15; Pausanias 1.19.2, 2.11.4, 8.42.3, 10.24.4.]

Fauna. See BONA DEA.

fauns or **fauni.** See SATYRS.

Faunus. A Roman god, somewhat like Pan. Faunus, who was sometimes conceived of in the plural as the satyrlike Fauni, was a sylvan deity with prophetic powers and influence over the fertility of both flocks and crops. Like many Roman deities, including his father, Picus, and his grandfather Saturn, Faunus came to be regarded as an early Italian king. He was said to have been the father of Latinus, king of Latium, by a water-nymph named Marica. He was worshiped together with Fauna, a goddess known as the Bona Dea. [Vergil, *Aeneïd*, 7.45–103.]

Faustulus. See ROMULUS AND REMUS [A].

Fishes, The. See PISCES.

Floating Islands. See STROPHADES.

Flood. See DEUCALION (1).

Flora. A Roman goddess of flowering plants. An ancient goddess, Flora was worshiped during a spring festival with rites that emphasized her character as a goddess of fertility.

Fortuna. A Roman goddess. Although Fortuna was thought to bring her worshipers good luck, she was also regarded as a goddess of fortune in its broader sense. Originally, no doubt, she was credited with the prosperity that comes from the fertility of the earth.

Furies. See ERINYES.

G

Gabii. A Latin town east of Rome. Lucius Tarquinius Superbus conquered Gabii without a battle as a result of the treacherous activities there of his son Sextus.

Gaea. A common variant of the name GE.

Galanthis. A Theban attendant of ALCMENE at the birth of Heracles. Galanthis tricked the goddess Eileithyia into abandoning her charms that were preventing the delivery. Eileithyia turned her into a weasel.

Galatea. See POLYPHEMUS (1).

Ganymede or **Ganymedes.** A beautiful youth of the Trojan royal line. Ganymede has been identified as a son of almost every king of Troy, most often of Tros or Laomedon. According to Homer [*Iliad* 20.231–235], Ganymede, because of his beauty, was carried to heaven by the gods to be Zeus's cupbearer. Most later accounts say that Zeus himself abducted him for this purpose and (usually) to be his lover as well. There are several versions of the abduction. In some, Ganymede is carried off by a whirlwind; in others, he is snatched up by an eagle, which may have been Zeus himself. Zeus sent Hermes to console the boy's father with news of Ganymede's new honor, and to recompense him for his loss with a pair of fine mares or a golden grapevine, made by Hephaestus. In Rome, Ganymede's name was often corrupted to Catamitus, which gave origin to the word "catamite." Ganymede was immortalized as the constellation Aquarius, the eagle as Aquila. [Apollodorus 2.5.9, 3.12.2; *Homeric Hymn to Aphrodite* 5.202–217; *Little Iliad* 7; Hyginus, *Poetica Astronomica*, 2.16, 2.29.]

Ge or **Gaea.** The earth, and the goddess of the earth. Ge was known to the Romans as Terra or Tellus. According to Hesiod's account of the CREATION of the universe, Ge, together with Tartarus and Eros, was born from Chaos, or at the same time. Without a mate she bore Uranus (Sky), Ourea (Mountains), and Pontus (Sea). Then, marrying Uranus, she bore the Titans, the Cyclopes, and the Hundred-handed. Uranus hated the last two, either for their strength or for their monstrous appearance, and hid them within Ge's body (that is, in the earth), causing her great pain. Ge resented this tyranny. Making a sickle of flint, she urged her sons to punish their father with it. Only the bold and wily Titan Cronus dared to do so. Ge gave him the sickle and, after telling him what to do, hid him. That night, when Uranus lay with his wife, Cronus castrated him. From the drops of his blood falling upon the earth Ge bore the Erinyes, the Giants, and the Meliae, or ash-nymphs. Finally, by Pontus she bore Nereus, Thaumas, Phorcys, Ceto, and Eurybia.

Cronus, who now reigned over his brother and sister Titans, proved to be as great a tyrant as his father had been. He did not release the Cyclopes or the Hundred-handed from Tartarus, or else he reimprisoned them. When Ge and Uranus (who seems to have withdrawn to some remote part of the sky) warned him that a son of his would one day overthrow him, he ate, one by one, the children whom his sister-wife, Rhea, had borne him. Ge helped her daughter to hide her youngest child, Zeus, and gave Cronus a stone to swallow instead. Zeus grew to maturity and overthrew Cronus and the other Titans, rescuing his brothers and sisters whom Cronus had swallowed. Although Ge advised her grandchildren to make Zeus their king, she came to resent his high-handed ways. She bore by Tartarus the monster Typhöeus, who became Zeus's most formidable enemy. Moreover, Ge encouraged the Giants (whom some call her sons by Uranus) to storm Olympus. She searched for a drug to make them immortal, but Zeus, commanding Eos, Helius, and Selene not to shine, found the drug himself. Ge warned Zeus that his first wife, the Oceanid Metis, would, after bearing him a daughter, have a son who would rule heaven. Zeus therefore swallowed his wife.

Ge bore other offspring, many of them monstrous. She was either the mother or the nurse of Tityus; some call her the mother of the horse Arion and the snake that guarded the golden fleece; she bore Echidna to Tartarus; Antaeüs may have been her son; and Hephaestus accidentally fathered Erichthonius on her. Some say that Triptolemus was Ge's son by Oceanus. Although most myths in which Ge participates tell of the eons in which a struggle for power was going on in heaven, she occasionally concerned herself in later times with less world-shaking matters. Some say, for example, that she intervened to save Nyctimus when Zeus had killed all the other sons of Lycaon, and that she turned Daphne into a laurel when the nymph was trying to escape Apollo's unwelcome attentions. Ge and the Seasons nursed the infant Aristaeüs when he was brought to her by Hermes. To protect the animals of the earth from Orion, who had boasted that he could kill them all, she sent a scorpion to kill the giant hunter.

Like many other earth-goddesses, Ge was infinitely wise, and she had more than one oracle. She was the first of a series of deities to prophesy through the oracle at Delphi, her pronouncements being spoken by Daphnis, a mountain-nymph. Later, Ge turned the oracle over to either the Titaness Themis or the snake Python. Some say that she shared the oracle with Poseidon and spoke the prophecies herself. Ge was worshiped at shrines in many parts of Greece.

Ge's activities as a major force in the universe are detailed by Hesiod in his *Theogony* [116–187, 233–239, 459–497, 820–822, 881–885]. Much of the story is repeated, with some variations, by Apollodorus [1.1.1–5, 1.2.1, 1.2.6, 1.3.6, 1.5.2, 1.6.1–3, 2.1.2, 2.5.11, 3.8.1]. See also Homer's *Odyssey* [11.576], Pindar's *Pythian Odes* [9.59–65], Hyginus' *Fabulae* [203], and many passages of Pausanias [1.2.6, 1.14.3, 5.14.10, 7.25.13, 8.25.8–10, 10.5.6, 10.6.6].

Gebeleïzis. See SALMOXIS.

Gegeneës. See EARTHBORN MONSTERS.

Gelanor. See DANAÜS [A].

Gemini (The Twins). A constellation. These two stars are generally said to immortalize the Dioscuri, Castor and Polydeuces. Some say, however, that they are Apollo and Heracles or Triptolemus and Iasion. [Hyginus, *Poetica Astronomica*, 2.21.]

genius. In Roman religion, the spirit believed to inhabit a person or thing. These spirits are thought to have been confined originally to personifications of the reproductive powers of the male and female heads of a household, on whom the family's future depended. Eventually, however, the idea of a genius or divine counterpart of the personality was extended to all individuals. A genius functioned as a kind of guardian spirit. Ultimately groups of persons, including the state, and even places came to be thought to have genii. A building or monument, for example, had its *genius loci*.

Gerenia. A city in Messenia or Laconia. Gerenia was located on the eastern shore of the large bay on the southern coast of Messenia. The Gerenians were famous as horse breeders. For some reason, Nestor, youngest son of Neleus, king of Pylus, was reared among them and thus escaped the fate of his eleven brothers at the hands of Heracles. When Sparta extended her territory west of the Taÿgetus Range, Gerenia was included within her boundaries.

Geryon or **Geryones.** A king of Erytheia or Erythrea, now Cadiz. Geryon, son of the Oceanid Callirrhoë and Chrysaor, son of the Gorgon Medusa, had three heads, or else the body of three men from the waist down. He owned a large herd of cattle, which he entrusted to Eurytion and his two-headed dog, Orthus. HERACLES [H] killed both herdsman and hound and drove off the cattle. Following him, Geryon was killed at the river Anthemus. [Apollodorus 2.5.10.]

Giants. Monstrous offspring of Ge and Uranus.

A. There were many giants in Greek mythology, but the creatures called simply by this name (Gigantes) were born, together with the Erinyes and the Meliae, to Ge (Earth) when she was impregnated by the blood of the castrated Uranus (Sky). Some say that she bore them out of rage at Zeus's destruction of the Titans. The Giants are variously described, but are most often shown with legs ending in the tails of snakes. The Giants and, before them, their half-brothers the Titans warred with the gods of Olympus. These two conflicts are often confused—as is the Gigantomachy (War of the Giants) with the later siege of Olympus by Otus and Ephialtes. The Giants lived in the vicinity of Phlegra, which, although it was said by many writers to be near Mount Vesuvius, in Italy, seems to have been originally located in Thrace. Urged on by their mother, the Giants, under the leadership of Eurymedon, flung huge rocks and burning oaks at the sky. Ge searched for a plant that would make her monstrous brood, like the gods, immortal, but Zeus forbade Eos, Helius, and Selene to give light and, by finding it himself in the darkness, kept it from the Giants.

Although the gods seemed to have the advantage, they learned from an oracle that they could never defeat the Giants without the aid of a mortal. Athena therefore enlisted Heracles in their ranks. The strongest of the Giants were Alcyoneus and Porphyrion. Alcyoneus was immortal only within the confines of his native land of Pallene, one of the three peninsulas jutting into the Aegean Sea from Chalcidice. Heracles shot him, then dragged him outside the boundaries of Pallene, where he died. Porphyrion attacked Heracles and Hera. He would have raped the goddess, but Zeus struck him with a thunderbolt and Heracles finished him with an arrow. Ephialtes was similarly disposed of in a joint venture, Apollo shooting him in the left eye, Heracles in the right. Dionysus somehow managed to kill Eurytus with his thyrsus; Hecate burned Clytius to death with her torches; and Hephaestus flung red-hot metal with deadly aim at Mimas. Enceladus fled westward, but Athena crushed him by flinging the island of Sicily on top of him. She then killed and flayed Pallas and used his skin as a shield. Poseidon chased Polybotes through the Aegean to Cos and threw Nisyrus, a piece of the island, on top of him. Hermes, invisible in the cap of darkness borrowed from Hades, killed Hippolytus. Artemis shot Gration. The Fates killed Agrius and Thoas with clubs of bronze. The rest of the Giants were dealt with as was Porphyrion, felled with Zeus's thunderbolts and killed by Heracles with his arrows. Thus the gods, with a mortal's aid, defeated their enemies the Giants. Ge, angrier than ever, gave birth to Typhöeus, who was far more formidable than any of the Giants.

B. Some ancient writers, apparently refusing to take the War of the Giants seriously, claimed that the monsters were routed not by force of arms but by the unfamiliar noise of Triton blowing through his conch shell or the raucous braying of asses ridden into the fray by Hephaestus, the Satyrs, and the Seileni. According to the Arcadians, who claimed that the war took place in their own land, near Trapezus, a small group of giants led by Hopladamus had earlier helped to protect Rhea, at her request, against the danger of ill treatment by Cronus while she gave birth to Zeus. Since the usual story has it that Ge did not bear the Giants until Zeus had defeated the Titans, Hopladamus' giants must have belonged to an entirely different breed. Perhaps they were merely an Arcadian substitute for the Curetes, who were usually said to have protected the infant Zeus from harm. Yet another group of giants, called by Apollonius Rhodius the Gegeneës (Earthborn), were killed by Heracles and the ARGONAUTS [D] in Mysia on their voyage to Colchis, but they seem to have little connection with the Giants who fought the gods.

The War of the Giants was described in greatest detail by Apollodorus [1.6.1–3]. See also Homer, *Odyssey*, 7.58–60, 7.204–206; Hyginus, *Poetica Astronomica*, 2.3, 2.23; Pausanias 1.25.2, 8.29.1–4, 8.32.5, 8.36.2.

Glauce. The daughter of Creon, king of Corinth. At her wedding with JASON [F] Glauce was killed, together with her father, while trying on a poisoned robe sent her by Jason's divorced wife Medea. She is sometimes called Creüsa.

Glaucus (1). A king of Ephyra (Corinth). A son of Sisyphus and Merope, Atlas' daughter, Glaucus succeeded his father on the throne, though some say that he lived, or pastured his horses, at Potniae, near Thebes. With the aid of Athena he won Eurynome or Eurymede, daughter of Nisus, who, thanks to Athena's teaching, was as wise as the gods. Zeus, who had reason to hate Sisyphus, had sworn that Sisyphus' son would father the children of others but never his own. So it happened that Glaucus proudly reared Bellerophon in his palace, unaware that Poseidon had visited Eurynome and begotten the child. Later, at the funeral games held at Iolcus in honor of Pelias, Glaucus lost the chariot race to Iolaüs and his maddened mares ate him. Many reasons were given for this accident by late commentators on mythology, the most gruesome being that Glaucus had fed them on human flesh. In any case, his ghost scared horses on the Isthmus of Corinth for generations thereafter. [*Catalogues of Women* 7; Hyginus, *Fabulae*, 273.]

Glaucus (2). A minor sea-god. Glaucus was originally a fisherman who lived at Anthedon, a town on the Euripus. One day he ate an unfamiliar herb and was transformed. Diving into the sea, he found that his legs became a fish's tail. The other sea-gods accepted him as one of themselves and he acquired the prophetic knowledge that they possessed. Glaucus fell in love with the beautiful virgin Scylla. When she repulsed him he went to Circe for advice, only to be ardently wooed by her. He repulsed Circe in turn, caring for no one but Scylla. Angered, the sorceress poisoned the waters where Scylla often swam with the sea-nymphs. When next the girl waded there she was transformed into a horrible monster.

Glaucus became a favorite patron of sailors. He gave news and good advice to the ARGONAUTS [F] and, according to Euripides' play *Orestes* [362–367], to Menelaüs, though Proteus was said by Homer to have been Menelaüs' informant. Euripides called Glaucus a son of Nereus. [Ovid, *Metamorphoses*, 13.898–14.69; Apollonius Rhodius 1.1310–1328.]

Glaucus (3). A son of Minos. As a child, Glaucus drowned in a storage jug of honey while playing. He was found and revived by the seer POLYEIDUS. Polyeidus taught the boy the art of divining, but later caused him to forget his learning. Some accounts say that it was Asclepius who revived Glaucus. [Apollodorus 3.3.1–2.]

Glaucus (4). The co-captain, with Sarpedon, of Lycian forces at Troy. Glaucus, a son of Hippolochus, was one of the bravest of the Trojan allies. He met his death at the hands of the Salaminian Ajax while fighting for the corpse of Achilles. He is best remembered, however, for his encounter with the Greek general Diomedes, as recounted by Homer [*Iliad* 6.119–236]. Preparing to fight to the death, the two warriors exchanged accounts of their respective lineages. On discovering that Diomedes' grandfather Oeneus had once entertained Glaucus' grandfather Bellerophon, thus binding the two families in ties of guest-friendship, the two not only refrained from fighting but exchanged armor, Glaucus giving up his rich golden armor for Diomedes' bronze armor.

Glaucus. See AEPYTUS.

Goat, The. See CAPRA.

golden apple. A beauty prize awarded by Paris. When Peleus was married to the sea-goddess Thetis, her fellow gods attended the wedding, but no invitation was offered to the disagreeable goddess Eris (Strife). She came anyway, but was denied admittance, whereupon she angrily produced a golden apple and threw it among the group. It was found to be inscribed with the words "For the fairest." Three goddesses, Hera, Athena, and Aphrodite, each assumed that it was meant for her. As Eris had intended, strife immediately broke out among the contenders and their supporters. Zeus, not wanting the party ruined, commanded Hermes to take the three goddesses and their quarrel to PARIS [B], son of Priam, who was keeping flocks on Mount Ida, near Troy. Paris' judgment, and the bribe that he accepted to award the apple to Aphrodite, led to the disastrous Trojan War.

golden bough. A magical bough that grew on a tree near Cumae. On the advice of the Cumaean Sibyl, Aeneas plucked this bough as a sign to Charon and a gift for Proserpina when he descended into the Underworld. Without it, he would not have gained access there. The golden bough, familiar from Vergil's *Aeneïd*, won new literary prominence when Sir James Frazer chose it as a peg to hang his own *Golden Bough* on. This thirteen-volume work proved a monumental contribution to the study of comparative religion.

golden fleece. The fleece of the ram that rescued PHRIXUS from being sacrificed by his father, Athamas. The offspring of Poseidon and Theophane, this ram could fly and speak. After its sacrifice by Phrixus, its golden fleece became the object of the ARGONAUTS' voyage. The ram was placed among the stars as the constellation Aries.

Gorge. A daughter of Oeneus and Althaea. Gorge married Andraemon and became the mother of Thoas, who led the Aetolian troops to Troy. Some claim that she, not Periboea, was the mother by Oeneus of Tydeus, because Zeus, for some unexplained reason, had willed that Oeneus should fall in love with his own daughter. [Apollodorus 1.8.1, 1.8.5.]

Gorgons. Three snaky-haired monsters, named Stheno, Euryale, and Medusa. In his *Ion*, Euripides says that Ge brought forth "the Gorgon" to aid her children, the Giants, in their war with the gods. Others claim that the Gorgons were among the brood that sprang from the union of the ancient sea-god Phorcys and his sea-monster sister, Ceto; these offspring included Echidna, Ladon, and the Graeae. The Gorgons had brazen hands and wings of gold; red tongues lolled from their mouths between tusks like those of swine; and serpents writhed about their heads. Their faces were so hideous that a glimpse of them would turn man or beast to stone. Of the three, only Medusa was mortal. She was killed by Perseus. [Hesiod, *Theogony*, 270–283. See also references under PERSEUS.]

Gorgophone. The only daughter of Perseus and Andromeda. The genealogies of Gorgophone's husbands are hopelessly confused. According to one of the clearer versions, she first married PERIERES, a son of Aeolus, and bore him Aphareus and Leucippus, who became prominent in Messenia. At Perieres' death she married OEBALUS, king of Sparta, thus becoming the first widow to remarry. By Oebalus she had three sons, Tyndareüs, Hippocoön, and Icarius, and two daughters, Arene and Peirene. Through Tyndareüs and Aphareus, Gorgophone was the grandmother of Helen, the Dioscuri, Clytemnestra, Lynceus, and Idas.

Graces. Personifications of beauty and grace. The Graces (Charites to the Greeks, Gratiae to the Romans) varied in name, number, and parentage from one account to another. One of them, called simply Charis (Grace) by Homer in the *Iliad* and named Aglaea by Hesiod, was said by these early poets to be the wife of Hephaestus. (According to later poets and to Homer's *Odyssey*, the god was married to Aphrodite.) The youngest Grace, Pasithea, was promised by Hera to Hypnos as a bride. Apart from these minor roles, however, the Graces play little part in myth except as abstractions. They are generally described as attending Aphrodite or some other goddess, giving beauty to young girls, and otherwise dispensing gentle and lovely qualities on appropriate occasions. The Graces, who were usually three after Hesiod's account, were favorite subjects in art, often being shown nude and dancing in a circle. Pausanias gave a detailed report on the spread of their worship in Greek lands. Most remarkably, they were worshiped at Boeotian Orchomenus in the form of stones that were evidently meteorites. [Homer, *Iliad*, 14.267–269, 14.275–276, 18.382–383; Hesiod, *Theogony*, 64–65, 945–946; Pausanias 6.24.6–7, 9.35.1–7.]

Gradivus. See MARS.

Graeae. Two ancient hags, named Enyo and Pemphredo or Pephredo; occasionally writers mentioned a third, called Deino. The Graeae (Gray Women), gray-haired from birth, were daughters of Phorcys and Ceto, and sisters of the Gorgons, as well as of Echidna and Ladon. In his *Prometheus Bound* [794–795], Aeschylus says that they were shaped like swans. They had only one eye and one tooth between them, and these were stolen by PERSEUS [B]. [Hesiod, *Theogony*, 270–283; Apollodorus 2.4.1–2.]

Great Eoiae. A lost poem similar in form to the series of sketches called *Catalogues of Women*. This poem, like the *Catalogues*, was once attributed to

Hesiod. The few fragments that remain can be found in the volume of that author's works in the Loeb Classical Library.

Great Goddess. A title of DEMETER.

Great Gods of Samothrace. See CABEIRI.

Great Mother of the Gods. See CYBELE.

griffin. A fabulous beast with the head and wings of an eagle and the body of a lion. The legend of the griffins is Asiatic in origin. It became widely known in Greece through Aristeas of Proconnesus, who claimed that griffins guarded hoards of gold from their warlike and greedy neighbors, the Arimaspians. Herodotus suggested that word of these creatures reached Greece through the Scythians, and griffins are known to have been one of the stylized animal forms popular in Scythian art. It is possible that the "gold-guarding griffins" were once an Asiatic tribe to which popular imagination assigned fabulous characteristics—much as in the case of the Greek centaurs, believed by many scholars to have been a wild tribe of Magnesia.

Guneus. A king of Cyphus, near Dodona, in Epeirus. A son of Ocytus, Guneus led twenty-two ships to the Trojan War. From Troy he went to Libya and founded a settlement on the Cinyps River. [Homer, *Iliad*, 2.748–755; Apollodorus "Epitome" 3.14–15a.]

Guneus. See ALCAEÜS (1).

Gyes. See HUNDRED-HANDED.

H

Hades. The god of the Underworld. Hades' name, which sometimes appeared in an extended form, Aïdoneus, probably meant "Unseen One." Even though this was less a name than a title, the Greeks were hesitant about using it in speech, apparently out of fear of attracting the attention of the awesome lord of the dead. Therefore they generally referred to the god as Pluto (Plouton). This name, a form of *ploutos* ("wealth"), was a reference to the god's rule beneath the earth, from which sprang the wealth of the crops. The Romans borrowed this name and added two of their own: Dis (which was similar in meaning to Pluto) and, less often, Orcus. The Greek Underworld, which Homer called "the House of Hades," came to be referred to simply as Hades.

Hades, a son of Cronus and Rhea, was swallowed by his father, together with his brother Poseidon and his sisters. The youngest brother, Zeus, escaped this fate and forced Cronus to vomit up his children. Although most other accounts imply that Zeus was then chosen by his brothers and sisters to rule the universe, Homer [15.187–193] said that the three brothers divided it among themselves by casting lots. Hades received the Underworld, Poseidon the sea, Zeus the sky. Olympus and the earth were the joint domain of all three. Hades preferred, however, to spend his time in his own dark domain, leaving it perhaps only once. A remark of Homer's—that Heracles had shot Hades with an arrow in Pylus—was interpreted to mean that the god had emerged to defend the city of Pylus against Heracles' invasion, and it was added that when wounded he went up to Olympus for aid. What Homer probably meant was that Heracles shot Hades (who was often referred to as the gatekeeper of his own realm) at the gate (*pylos*) of the Underworld.

This leaves only one other significant instance in which Hades left the Underworld. He fell in love with Persephone, daughter of Zeus and Demeter, and dutifully asked her father's permission to marry her. Zeus approved the match, but rightly guessed that Demeter would never allow her daughter to live in the dank halls of Hades' palace. He therefore advised his brother to carry off the girl by force. Hades, emerging from the earth in his four-horse chariot, snatched Persephone up as she was picking flowers and carried her down to his home. Eventually Demeter forced Zeus to order his brother to bring back his stolen bride. Hades did so, but first induced or forced the girl to eat a pomegranate seed. Having eaten the food of Hades, she had to return to him each year to spend four to six months with him. In spite of her origins, Persephone was evidently soon acclimated to her new home and came to be known as a ruler of the dead no less inexorable than her husband.

Hades' power was so nearly absolute in his own realm that he was often referred to as "the Zeus of the Underworld" (Zeus Katachthonios). He was a grim god but not a malign one, having nothing in common with the Devil of the Christians. With the aid of his three-headed watchdog, Cerberus, he saw to it that none of the dead escaped his domain, which he kept locked. He also supervised the punishments of malefactors, such as Tityus and Sisyphus, who had been consigned to eternal torment by other gods. There were few of these, however, and the actual tortures were said by some to be carried out by the ERINYES.

In one instance—the attempt by PEIRITHOÜS and Theseus to carry off Persephone—Hades understandably took a personal interest in individual punishment. One late Classical writer claims that he had the two culprits stretched out and tortured for a long time by the Erinyes, but in most accounts he confined himself to trapping them in the Chair of Forgetfulness—though he eventually released Theseus at the request of HERACLES [I]. As for Heracles himself, he either forced or persuaded the god to permit him to carry off Cerberus, whom he promptly returned to his post after showing the beast to Eurystheus. In spite of Hades' reputation for having a cold heart, he permitted Eurydice to leave his domain, though under a condition that her husband, ORPHEUS, proved unable to meet.

Hades, like his brother Poseidon, had some connection with horses. He also owned a herd of cattle, which were tended, either in the Underworld or on the island of Erytheia, by a herdsman named Menoetes. Hades' epithet Pluto strongly suggests that, like the god Plutus and his own wife (both of whom were children of Demeter, goddess of the crops), Hades was associated with the fertility of the earth. This was a common function of CHTHONIAN DEITIES, and seems to have been associated at times with the dead by their human relatives. For the most part, however, Hades was merely the keeper of the place to which men went when they died. His character was scarcely individualized beyond personification of the fear and awe that this inevitable fate aroused in men's minds. He was very little worshiped by the Greeks.

Hades appeared as little in art as he did in myth. The main sources for his rape of Persephone are the *Homeric Hymn to Demeter* [2] and Ovid's *Metamorphoses* [5.359–424]. See also Hesiod, *Theogony*, 453–506, 850; Apollodorus 1.1.5–1.2.1, 1.3.2, 1.5.1–1.5.3, 2.5.12; Homer, *Iliad*, 5.844–845, 9.568–570; Hyginus, *Fabulae*, 79, 146.

Hades. The abode of the dead. Hades, originally called "the House of Hades," took its name from its ruler, the keeper of the dead. It seems to have been early located somewhere in the western reaches of the Greek world, but it may also have been conceived of from the first as underground, where it was regularly placed by writers later than Homer. Many localities claimed entrances to Hades, notably Taenarum, in the southern Peloponnesus; the Alcyonian Lake at Lerna, in Argolis; and Lake Avernus, near Naples. In works later than Homer's *Odyssey*, in which Odysseus crossed the river Oceanus to reach Hades, the boundary is usually the Styx, although sometimes it is Acheron, a swampy river or lake. Other rivers of Hades were the flaming Phlegethon or Pyriphlegethon, Cocytus, and Lethe, the river of forgetting.

The dead descended to Hades as shades, or phantoms (*eidola kamonton*) —mere semblances of their living selves, deprived of bodies and consciousness. If they had received proper funeral rites, they were ferried across the Styx or the Acheron by old Charon, who exacted an obol as fare. The three-headed watchdog Cerberus readily allowed them to enter the gates of Hades but not to leave again. According to late Classical writers, the dead lost their memories of their lives on earth when they drank the water of Lethe. Most shades remained forever on the Plain of Asphodel, sometimes going through the motions of their former lives, but without pleasure or pain. So flavorless was this existence that the shade of Achilles declared to Odysseus that he would rather be a poor man's slave than rule in Hades [Homer, *Odyssey*, 11.489–491].

The souls of the dead were judged by one or more of three judges: Minos, his brother Rhadamanthys, and Aeacus. It is not clear, however, what effect their decisions had on the fates of these shades, for the few souls who suffered eternal punishment in Hades had already been condemned by the gods. Notable among these unfortunates were Tantalus, Sisyphus, Tityus, Ixion, the Danaïdes, and Ocnus. Peirithoüs and, for a time at least, Theseus were confined in Hades for having attempted to abduct Persephone. Salmoneus was said by some late Classical writers to have also been punished there. The usual agents of these tortures were the Erinyes. In spite of these special cases, however, Hades was in no way regarded as a place of torment comparable to the Christian hell.

A select few mortals, through the favor of the gods, escaped the loss of their faculties as shades and resided, not on the Plain of Asphodel, but in ELYSIUM or on the Islands of the Blessed. These places were variously located, sometimes in remote parts of the earth, sometimes in regions of Hades separate from the dwelling of the shades. Another separate part of Hades was TARTARUS. In this dank place of eternal blackness the Titans were confined, guarded by the Hundred-handed. Tartarus was also the scene, in some accounts, of the torments of the damned. CHAOS was occasionally conceived of as yet another part of Hades, though this was neither its original nor its usual meaning.

Haemon (1). A son of Creon, ruler of Thebes. Haemon, a boy noted for his beauty, was killed by the Sphinx when he could not answer her riddle. [Apollodorus 3.5.8.]

Haemon (2). The youngest son of Creon, ruler of Thebes, and Eurydice. Haemon was betrothed to ANTIGONE and died with her in defiance of his father. He is a leading character in Sophocles' *Antigone*. The stories of this youth and of Creon's other son of the same name may represent separate traditions about a single personage. One of the Haemons was said to be the father of Maeon.

Haemus, Mount. The range of mountains in Thrace that are now called the Balkans. The Greeks derived the name Haemus from *haima* ("blood"), explaining that Typhöeus had lost a great deal of blood there when Zeus pelted him with thunderbolts. Aristaeüs is said to have lived near Mount Haemus for a while before vanishing from the earth.

Haliartus. See CORONUS (3).

Haliartus. A town south of Lake Copaïs, in Boeotia. The town was founded by and named for a grandson of Sisyphus, Haliartus, who was welcomed to the region of Orchomenus by Athamas. Near the town was the oracular spring Telphusa, where Teiresias died, having lived through seven generations.

Halirrhothius. A son of Poseidon by the nymph Euryte. Halirrhothius achieved distinction only by his death. He raped Alcippe, daughter of Ares by Agraulus, near the Acropolis. Ares killed him for this deed. Poseidon brought charges against Ares on the Areopagus for murder, but Ares was acquitted at the trial. This was said to be the first murder trial and the origin of the name Areopagus (Hill of Ares). [Euripides, *Electra*, 1258–1261; Apollodorus 3.14.2.]

Halitherses. An Ithacan seer. An old friend of Odysseus, Halitherses predicted the wanderer's return to his homeland. He was unable to dissuade the relatives of Penelope's dead suitors from trying to avenge them on Odysseus. [Homer, *Odyssey*, 2.146–176, 24.451–462.]

Halys River. A large river of northeastern Asia Minor, now called Kizil Irmak. The Halys flows west, then north to empty into the Black Sea east of Sinope.

hamadryad. See NYMPH.

Hare, The. See LEPUS.

Harmonia. The wife of CADMUS [B], king of Thebes. Harmonia is generally called the daughter of Ares and Aphrodite, but her parents are occasionally said to have been Zeus and Electra, a daughter of Atlas. She was given to Cadmus as a bride by Zeus and their wedding was attended by the gods. Among her wedding presents were a necklace made by Hephaestus and a robe. These gifts were to bring disaster upon their later owners. (See ALC-MEON, A, B.)

Harmonia and Cadmus had a son, Polydorus, and four daughters: Ino, Autonoë, Semele, and Agave. When Cadmus, grief-stricken at the tragedies that had befallen each of his daughters, emigrated to the Encheleans in Illyria, Harmonia went with him. Both were changed into snakes by Ares and went to live in the Elysian Fields.

Harpies. Birdlike female monsters. According to Hesiod [*Theogony*

265–269], there were two Harpies, Aëllo and Ocypetes, daughters of Thaumas and the Oceanid Electra. Late Classical writers described the two (or three) Harpies as either birds with faces of women or women with the wings, heads, and talons of birds. Homer describes them merely as "snatchers" (the meaning of their name) who were responsible for sudden disappearances that could not otherwise be explained. Telemachus says that his father has been snatched away by the Harpies [Homer, *Odyssey*, 1.241], and Penelope asks Artemis [*Odyssey* 20.61–78] to carry her out of the world as the Harpies did the daughters of Pandareus, giving them to the Erinyes. Homer and Hesiod seem to have envisioned these creatures as personifications of storm winds, and the swiftness and suddenness of winds always remained one of their chief characteristics. Nearly all the various names that are given to them refer to their fleetness. Podarge (Fleetfoot), the only Harpy named by Homer [*Iliad* 16.148–151], gave birth to Achilles' horses, Xanthus and Balius, after being impregnated by the west wind beside the river Oceanus. Some scholars believe, however, that the Harpies, as well as various other birdlike female creatures, were also ghosts, who might snatch away living beings. Their connection with the Erinyes in Vergil [*Aeneïd* 3.209–257], as well as in Homer, may support this view.

The Harpies are best known as the "hounds of Zeus," sent by that god to punish the Thracian king Phineus by continually snatching away his food. With their beaks or droppings they left such a stench behind that the remaining food was made inedible. When the ARGONAUTS [H] visited Phineus, Zetes and Calaïs pursued the Harpies through the sky. These winged sons of the North Wind proved to be as swift as their prey. According to one story, they failed to overtake the Harpies, but all died of starvation. One Harpy fell into the Tigres River in the Peloponnesus, which was thereafter called the Harpys; the other reached the Strophades Islands, in the Ionian Sea off the coast of Acarnania. It is more commonly said that Zetes and Calaïs overtook the Harpies over the Strophades, but Iris or Hermes appeared and commanded the brothers to spare their lives, promising that they would leave Phineus in peace. The Harpies retired to their cave on the side of Mount Dicte, in Crete.

Aeneas and the Trojans encountered the Harpies on the Strophades on their way to Italy. In Vergil's account, their metallic feathers were impervious to the Trojans' swords and they twice escaped unharmed with a feast. Their vindictive leader, Celaeno, perched on a rock long enough to gloat over the fact that the Trojans would be hungrier yet before they reached their destination. In this speech she referred to herself as "the eldest of the Furies." Terrified, the Trojans took to their ships. [Apollonius Rhodius 2.234–434.]

Harpina. The mother, according to some, of Oenomaüs, king of Pisa. The Eleians said that Oenomaüs named the city of Harpina for his mother. Asterope is also called Oenomaüs' mother. [Pausanias 6.21.8.]

Hebe. A personification of the beauty of youth. Hebe, a daughter of Zeus and Hera, or of Hera alone, was the official cupbearer of the gods. When Heracles achieved immortality and went to live on Mount Olympus with the gods, Hebe became his wife and bore him two sons, Alexiares and Anicetus, of whom nothing further is known. At her husband's request Hebe restored the youth of IOLAÜS as he rode into battle to defend Heracles' mortal children. Hebe and Heracles are said to have appeared as two stars at Iolaüs' chariot yoke as he pursued Eurystheus. Hebe, whose name means "Youth," was known to the Romans as Juventas. [Homer, *Iliad*, 4.2–3, 5.719–723, and *Odyssey*, 11.602–604; Ovid, *Metamorphoses*, 9.397–401, 9.416–417; Euripides, *Children of Heracles*, 847–858.]

Hebrus River. A principal river of Thrace, now the boundary between Greece and Turkey. When Orpheus was killed and dismembered by the Ciconian women, his head and his lyre floated down the Hebrus and across the Aegean Sea to Lemnos.

Hecate. An Underworld goddess. Hecate was the daughter of Perses or Persaeüs and Asteria. According to Hesiod [*Theogony* 409–452], she was a Titan who retained all her honors after the degradation by Zeus of most of the other Titans and was, in fact, honored by Zeus above all other deities. Hesiod credited her with power in heaven, earth, and sea, bringing wealth and victory to her worshipers, whether they were farmers, soldiers, fishermen, or athletes. Zeus made her nurse of the young. Her attributes as a goddess of fertility caused her to be closely associated in ritual with Demeter. She was occasionally called Demeter's daughter, but more often was said merely to have aided her in her search for her lost daughter, Persephone.

Hecate, like Persephone, was also associated with the dead in the Underworld, who were often thought to send up the wealth of the earth—the crops—to the living. Among later writers, few of whom shared Hesiod's enthusiasm for the goddess, the darker aspects of Hecate's character were emphasized. She became the patroness of such sorceresses as Medea, appearing as a terrible goddess at night, accompanied by hellhounds. Crossroads were her particular province. Late writers often identified her with Artemis—even calling her, like Artemis, a daughter of Leto—and connected both with the moon. Hecate was also identified with Iphigeneia, as was Artemis. As a nocturnal goddess, Hecate regularly carried torches, with which she is said to have killed Clytius, one of the GIANTS [A] who were warring with the gods.

The rites of Hecate were described at length by Apollonius Rhodius [3.477–478, 3.528–530, 3.1035–1041, 3.1207–1224, 4.827–829]. See also Euripides' *Phoenician Women* [109–110] and *Ion* [1049]; *Homeric Hymn to Demeter* [2.25–62, 2.438–440]; Apollodorus [1.6.2]; Pausanias [1.43.1, 2.30.2]; and Vergil's *Aeneïd* [4.511, 4.609–610, 6.247].

Hecatoncheires. See HUNDRED-HANDED.

Hector. The leader of the Trojan forces in the Trojan War. Hector was the eldest son of Priam, king of Troy, and Hecuba. He married Andromache, daughter of Eëtion, king of the nearby city of Thebes, situated at the foot of Mount Placus. Hector, though a blunt and overbold man who was often impatient of prudent advice, was represented by Homer in the *Iliad* as possessing compassion, as well as nobility. He deplored Paris' irresponsible act that plunged Troy into a protracted war. Nevertheless it was Hector who killed Protesilaüs, the first Greek to step ashore at Troy, and he remained the bulwark of the Trojan army until his death in the tenth year of the war. He proposed that Paris and Menelaüs decide the outcome in single combat, and later fought Ajax to a draw. Still later he led the Trojans in an advance that nearly succeeded in burning the Greek ships.

When Achilles rejoined the battle after a long period of resentful withdrawal, Hector refused at first to let the Trojans take refuge within their city. Achilles trapped him outside the walls and, aided by Athena, killed him. Realizing that he was about to die, Hector had predicted Achilles' imminent death. Achilles dragged Hector's body behind his chariot to the ships, or three times around the walls of Troy. He refused to give up the corpse for burial until his mother, Thetis, urged him to. (Aphrodite, however, had embalmed it with ambrosia to keep it from harm.) Finally Achilles permitted Priam to ransom Hector's body and the Greeks allowed the Trojans an eleven-day truce for mourning. According to a Theban tradition recorded by Pausanias [9.18.5], Hector's bones were brought to Thebes in obedience to an oracle advising the Thebans to worship him as a hero if they wanted wealth.

Hector is one of the most prominent figures in the *Iliad*. He appears briefly in Euripides' play *Rhesus*. Few other references to Hector deviate from the Homeric story.

Hecuba or **Hecabe**. A daughter of Dymas, of Cisseus, or of the river-god Sangarius and Metope. Whatever Hecuba's parentage, she came from a tribe that lived on the Sangarius, which flows into the Black Sea east of the Bosporus. The Trojan king Priam divorced his first wife, Arisbe, and married Hecuba. She bore many children, among them Hector, Paris, Helenus, Deïphobus, Troïlus, Polydorus, Cassandra, Polyxena, Creüsa, and Laodice. She is said by some to have borne Troïlus by Apollo rather than her husband. When Hecuba was about to bear her second child, Paris, she dreamed that she gave birth to a firebrand or a monster, which destroyed the city. Either Aesacus or Cassandra predicted that the child would be Troy's doom and advised that he be killed, but he was saved from exposure and later received into the royal family.

At Troy's fall Hecuba was awarded as a slave to Odysseus. He stopped, on his homeward voyage, on the shores of the Thracian Chersonese, ruled by King Polymestor, a former Trojan ally. Hecuba discovered that Polymestor had treacherously murdered her son POLYDORUS for his gold. She lured the king to her tent and blinded him, after killing his infant sons. Shortly thereafter Hecuba was transformed into a fiery-eyed dog. The dog's grave became well known to sailors as Cynossema or Cyneus. According to the lost epic *Sack of Ilium*, Apollo brought Hecuba at last to Lycia.

In Euripides' tragedy *The Trojan Women*, Hecuba laments the murders of her daughter Polyxena and her grandson Astyanax and the other misfortunes of her family and city. The same playwright's *Hecuba* tells of her vengeance on Polymestor and her strange end. The tale of her transformation is thought by some scholars to have grown out of the identification of Hecuba, or at least of her Greek name, Hecabe, with the goddess Hecate, who was regularly attended by dogs with flaming eyes. See also Ovid, *Metamorphoses*, 13.536–575; Pindar, *Paeans*, 8; Apollodorus "Epitome" 5.23; Hyginus, *Fabulae*, 91, 111; Pausanias 10.27.2.

Heleius or **Helius**. A son of Perseus and Andromeda. Heleius founded the city of Helos, in Argolis. When his nephew Amphitryon raided the Taphian Islands, Heleius and Cephalus were given rule over them. [Apollodorus 2.4.5, 2.4.7.]

Helen. A queen of Sparta.

A. Helen was universally admitted to be a daughter of Zeus, but her mother was variously reported to have been Leda, Nemesis, or a daughter of Oceanus. According to one version of Helen's birth, Zeus fell in love with Nemesis, but she fled from him, taking the form of a goose. Zeus quickly changed himself into a swan and caught up with her. As a result, she laid an egg in a grove near Sparta. Shepherds found the egg and took it to Leda, wife of King Tyndareüs. In time Helen was hatched from it and Leda reared her as her own daughter. Many claim, however, that Leda herself was wooed by the swan. Others say that in one night she gave birth to Helen and Polydeuces (or Pollux), who were Zeus's children and immortal, and to Clytemnestra and Castor, her husband's mortal offspring.

B. Helen was so extraordinarily beautiful that, when the time came for her to marry, most of the princes of Greek cities vied for her hand. She was twice abducted—though the first time this happened she was only twelve years old and her lineage, rather than her beauty, was the cause. Theseus, king of Athens, and his friend the Lapith Peirithoüs had determined that they would marry daughters of Zeus. (Some say that Theseus wanted to be related to the Dioscuri, Helen's brothers.) Together they kidnaped Helen while she was sacrificing to Artemis and took her to Aphidnae, in Attica. They then descended to Hades with the bold scheme of bringing back Persephone, another of Zeus's daughters, as a bride for Peirithoüs. While they were away, the Dioscuri, leading an army of Spartans and Arcadians, took Aphidnae, and perhaps sacked Athens as well. They rescued Helen and carried off Theseus' mother, Aethra, and Peirithoüs' sister, Phisadië, to be Helen's handmaidens.

C. It was not long after this that Tyndareüs decided to seek a husband for his supposed daughter. Since by now her beauty was famous far and wide, he had no difficulty in finding candidates. Greek nobles from nearly all the great cities sent spokesmen with rich gifts to plead their causes. Idomeneus came in person all the way from Crete. Only Odysseus sent no gifts. Perhaps because he knew Helen's nature, he was sure that he stood no chance of success beside the wealthy Menelaüs, whose brother, king of powerful Mycenae, was already married to Clytemnestra. Besides, Odysseus was interested in marrying Helen's cousin Penelope. Tyndareüs was afraid of trouble from the disappointed suitors once a husband had been chosen. He therefore followed Odysseus' shrewd advice and made them swear to abide by his decision and to defend Helen and her chosen mate, whoever he might be, from harm. Little knowing the disaster this oath would lead them into, the suitors willingly took the vow, standing on pieces of a horse in order to make it more solemn. Some say that Tyndareüs was still afraid to make a choice and left it up to his daughter. As Odysseus had anticipated, she chose Menelaüs.

D. For a time Helen seemed a model wife. She bore a daughter, Hermione, and perhaps a son, Nicostratus. (On the authority of Stesichorus, among others, Pausanias [2.22.6–7] said that Iphigeneia was Helen's daughter by Theseus; she gave the baby to Clytemnestra to rear as her own child.) Meanwhile a young Trojan prince named Paris had judged a beauty contest among three goddesses, and Helen had, without knowing it, been offered as a bribe to the judge by the winner, Aphrodite (see PARIS, B). It was (or so Helen later claimed) this powerful but unscrupulous goddess who caused her to lose her head when the handsome young man appeared at Sparta. Menelaüs entertained him royally for a time, and all might have gone well had not the king's grandfather Catreus died in Crete. Menelaüs sailed for Crete to officiate at the funeral, leaving his wife to make the guest feel welcome. This she did so well that Paris sailed away one night with Helen and a large amount of Menelaüs' property in his ship.

The lovers made for Troy. According to the lost epic *Cypria*, they reached the distant city in only three days, but it is usually said that they were first driven by storms to the Syrian port of Sidon. These storms were sent by Hera, who, as goddess of marriage, disapproved of the lovers' behavior. After a time the weather calmed and Helen and Paris sailed along the coast to Troy.

E. The steps that Menelaüs took to win back his wife belong to the story of the Trojan War. In this expedition he was joined by the disappointed suitors, true to their oaths to defend Helen and her husband. Near the end of the war Paris was killed by Philoctetes and Helen married his brother Deïphobus. At moments Helen felt pangs of loyalty to the Greeks. When Odysseus entered Troy disguised as a beggar, she did not betray him; some say that she even helped him to steal the Palladium. Yet, later, she tried to trick the leaders in the wooden horse into revealing their presence to the Trojans. Walking around the horse with Deïphobus she called the name of each leader, cleverly imitating the voice of his wife. Only the shrewdness of Odysseus prevented the men from answering. The horse was admitted to Troy and the city fell. Menelaüs killed Deïphobus, with Helen's aid, and threatened to kill Helen as well, a deed which would have met with approval from Greeks and Trojans alike. But Helen, though no longer young, was still beautiful and seductive. Menelaüs contented himself with taking her to his ship, claiming the intention of killing her when they reached Sparta. By the time they arrived, seven years later, he had entirely forgiven his wife for her unfaithfulness.

During their long and devious journey Menelaüs amassed great wealth. They spent considerable time in Egypt, where Helen learned the lore of healing herbs from Polydamna, the wife of Thon or Thonis, warden of the mouth of the Nile. Menelaüs was told by Proteus, the Old Man of the Sea, that his brother Agamemnon, on reaching home, had been killed by his wife and her lover. Proteus warned him that before he reached Sparta Orestes might already have taken vengeance on his father's killers. In fact, on the very day of Menelaüs' return, Orestes was condemned to death for the murder of his mother, Clytemnestra, and Aegisthus. According to Euripides' *Orestes*, Menelaüs refused to defend his nephew against the sentence. The desperate young man, aided by his friend Pylades, seized Helen and would have killed her, but she vanished into the sky, where, like her brothers, she became a guardian of sailors.

F. This version of Helen's fate is not generally accepted. Homer, in the *Odyssey* [Book 4], shows Helen helping her husband to entertain Telemachus at Sparta some time after their return. Pausanias says that the Rhodians claimed that Helen survived Menelaüs, but was driven from Sparta by Nicostratus and Megapenthes, Menelaüs' sons by slave women. She took refuge with Polyxo, the widow of Tlepolemus, king of Rhodes, who had died in the Trojan War. This Polyxo, an Argive woman who formerly had been a friend of Helen's, pretended to welcome her. Secretly, however, she determined to avenge on Helen the death of Tlepolemus at Troy. At her orders her maids dressed themselves as Erinyes and hanged Helen to a tree. Thereafter she was worshiped in Rhodes as Helen of the Tree.

The people of Crotona and Himera told a different version of Helen's end. A Crotonan general, Leonymus, inquired of the Delphic oracle how he might be healed of a wound. He was told to visit White Island, in the Euxine (Black) Sea near the mouths of the Ister (Danube), where the long-dead hero Ajax of Locris would cure him. On his return from this islet, thitherto unknown to the Greeks, Leonymus claimed that there he saw not only his healer but several other heroes of the war with Troy: Ajax of Salamis, Patroclus, Antilochus, and Achilles, who was married to Helen. Helen directed Leonymus to tell the Himerian poet Stesichorus that his blindness was due to her anger at some unkind remarks that he had made about her in a poem. Leonymus delivered this message and the poet composed his *Palinodia* or *Recantation*, which so appeased Helen that Stesichorus recovered his sight.

G. So far as is known, Stesichorus' new version of Helen's story was his own invention, but it became widely familiar and formed the basis of Euripides' romantic comedy *Helen*. According to this extraordinary tale, Helen never went to Troy at all. In *Helen* [31–48], the heroine explains that Hera, angry at Paris for judging in favor of Aphrodite, gave him a phantom Helen made of cloud, while Zeus arranged that Hermes should transport the real Helen to Egypt. There King Proteus took charge of her. In his *Electra* [1280–1283], Euripides lays the blame for creating the phantom Helen on Zeus, who sent her to Troy solely for the purpose of provoking war. Herodotus tells an Egyptian version in which Paris stopped at Egypt on his way to Troy with Helen. Proteus, indignant at the abduction, which some of Paris' sailors reported to him, kept Helen and sent Paris on his way. The Greeks arrived at Troy and refused to believe the Trojan protestations that Helen was not there. Only after destroying the city and most of its inhabitants did they discover that the Trojans had been telling the truth. In every version of the story of Helen in Egypt, Menelaüs eventually discovered her there and returned with her to Sparta. At their deaths Helen and Menelaüs were buried at Therapne, near Sparta. Menelaüs was made immortal by Hera, and husband and wife went to the Elysian Fields.

Although Helen is the heroine of Euripides' *Helen* and is exonerated of guilt for the Trojan War in his *Electra*, she plays her more familiar role of a vain and heartless woman in his tragedy *The Trojan Women*. She has only a minor part in his *Orestes*. Helen appears in both the *Iliad* [Book 3] and the *Odyssey* [Books 4 and 15]. See also *Catalogues of Women* 65–68; *Cypria* 1, 8–11; Apollodorus 3.10.7–3.11.1, "Epitome" 1.23, 6.29; Pausanias 2.22.-6–7, 3.19.9–3.20.1 (and many other references); Herodotus 2.112–120.

Helenus. A Trojan seer. Helenus was a son of Priam and Hecuba. He fought bravely with the Trojans against the Greeks, but he was most useful as an augur who could accurately foretell the future. He is said to have vainly warned Paris of disaster if he sailed to Sparta. Later he was captured by Odysseus and the same talents were equally useful to the Greeks. His apparent willingness to cooperate with his captors may have been due in part to disgruntlement. He and his brother Deïphobus had quarreled over the right to marry Helen after Paris' death, and she had been awarded to Deïphobus. Helenus had angrily withdrawn from Troy to Mount Ida. No great force seems to have been required to persuade him to reveal to the Greeks the oracles, known only to himself, about his city's fate. Troy would be taken, he said, if the Palladium were stolen from the city; if Pelops' bones were brought to Troy; and if both Neoptolemus (Achilles' son) and Philoctetes, the latter with Heracles' bow and arrows, were persuaded to fight with the Greeks.

All of these conditions were met and Troy fell. Helenus traveled thereafter with Neoptolemus, but more as a vassal than a slave. According to some accounts, Neoptolemus, on Helenus' advice, took an overland route which saved him from the shipwrecks that destroyed so many of his former companions on their homeward journeys. He went to Epeirus and there permitted Helenus to found the city of Buthrotum. When Neoptolemus left Epeirus he turned his concubine, Andromache, over to Helenus, who was her brother-in-law. She bore him a son, Cestrinus. Helenus acted as guardian for her children by Neoptolemus. Some say, however, that he married Neoptolemus' mother, Deïdameia, rather than Andromache. When Aeneas and his Trojan followers stopped at Buthrotum, Helenus foretold Aeneas' founding of Rome. [Homer, *Iliad*, 6.72–101, 7.44–53, 13.576–600; Ovid, *Metamorphoses*, 15.437–452; Sophocles, *Philoctetes*, 604–613, 1337–1342; Vergil, *Aeneïd*, 3.294–491; *Cypria* 1; Pausanias 1.11.1–2; Apollodorus "Epitome" 5.9–10, 5.23, 6.12–13.]

Heliades. Daughters of Helius, the sun-god. Circe and Pasiphaë were his daughters by Perseïs. Phaëthusa and Lampetië, his daughters (or Hyperion's) by Neaera, tended the god's cattle and sheep on the island of Thrinacia. The name Heliades, however, seems to have been arbitrarily restricted to references to Helius' daughters by Clymene. After the death of their beloved brother Phaëthon, they were transformed into poplars beside the Eridanus River and mourned him with amber tears.

Helicaon. A son of ANTENOR and Theano. Wounded in the night battle when the Greeks entered Troy, Helicaon was carried to safety by Odysseus, who owed a debt of friendship to Antenor.

Helice. A daughter of Selinus, king of Aegialus. Helice's father married her to Ion to forestall his attempt to seize the power. Her husband founded a seaport on the Gulf of Corinth and named it for her.

Helice. A seaport of Achaea on the Gulf of Corinth. Ion founded the city, naming it for his wife, Helice. It was a leading seaport in the days when the Ionians occupied the region; they took refuge there when besieged by their Achaean conquerors. The city was famous for a shrine of Heliconian Poseidon. The Achaeans desecrated this shrine by removing and killing certain suppliants who had taken sanctuary there. The god punished this outrage by first leveling Helice with an earthquake, then sending a tidal wave that swallowed it up. [Pausanias 7.24.5–7.25.4.]

Helicon, Mount. A range of mountains in western Boeotia. Helicon was early claimed as the favorite haunt of the Muses, but it was rivaled for this honor by both Olympus and Parnassus.

Helius. The sun, and the god of the sun.

A. Helius, called Sol by the Romans, was a son of the Titans Hyperion and Theia, who is sometimes called Euryphaëssa. Selene (Moon) and Eos (Dawn) were his sisters. Helius, who is occasionally called merely Titan, was often confused with his father, who was also a sun-god; Homer called the son Helius Hyperion. He was conceived of as driving his four-horse chariot through the sky during the day, heralded and accompanied by Eos. At night he returned, from west to east, riding the river Oceanus in an enormous golden cup. On his daily round Helius had an opportunity to observe everything that happened on, and perhaps under, the earth. It was he who reported to Demeter what had happened to her daughter, Persephone, and he also revealed Aphrodite's affair with Ares to her husband, Hephaestus. As an all-seeing god he was regularly invoked as a witness to oaths. For example, the Greek and Trojan leaders swore by Helius and Ge to abide by the results of the single combat between Paris and Menelaüs.

Because Helius was away on his regular business when the earth was divided among the gods, he got no share. Zeus was reluctant to draw lots over again, so, when Helius spied a large island rising from the eastern Aegean Sea and asked for it, Zeus readily gave it to him. This island, Rhodes, became sacred to Helius, and he remained its patron god down to Classical times. The famous Colossus of Rhodes was a statue of him which stood near the harbor. Helius disputed the region of Corinth with Poseidon. Briareüs, called in as arbiter, awarded the heights of the Acrocorinth to Helius, the isthmus to Poseidon. Helius gave the territory to his son Aeëtes, but it soon passed out of his hands. Helius later ceded his rights as patron to Aphrodite, but retained an altar on the Acrocorinth.

B. Helius was married to Perseïs, or Perse, a daughter of Oceanus and Tethys, who bore him several notorious offspring: Aeëtes, the barbarous king of Colchis; Circe, the Aeaean sorceress; and Pasiphaë, Minos' queen, who is best remembered for her affair with a bull. Perses, who some say was a king of the Taurians, was also a son of Helius, and even more cruel than his Colchian brother. Augeias, king of Elis, claimed Helius for his father, but some writers say that this was mere boasting. Helius himself displayed none of the unpleasant traits of his children, but he remained loyal to them. Both Aeëtes and Circe rode with him occasionally in his chariot, and he lent a chariot drawn by winged dragons to his granddaughter Medea.

Helius had children also by several mistresses. Rhode, a daughter of Poseidon, and the eponymous nymph of the island of Rhodes, bore him seven sons. One of these sons became the father of Cameirus, Ialysus, and Lindus, who divided the island between them and gave their names to its principal cities. According to the fifth-century poet Onomacritus, Helius was the father of the Graces by Aegle.

Aphrodite, angry at Helius for reporting to her husband her affair with Ares, caused him to fall in love with Leucothoë, daughter of the Persian king Orchamus. The girl must have been well protected, for the god found it necessary to disguise himself as her mother in order to gain access to her bedroom. Once inside, he returned to his own form and seduced her. The nymph Clytië, an old flame, was consumed with jealousy and reported the incident to Orchamus, who buried his daughter alive as a punishment. The grief-stricken Helius transformed Leucothoë into a shrub that gives frankincense. Clytië, whose spite had alienated her former lover completely, wasted away. In dying, she became the heliotrope, the flower whose head turns to follow the course of the sun across the sky each day.

C. Helius' best-known child was PHAËTHON (1), his son by the Oceanid Clymene. (Some say that Phaëthon was actually Helius' grandson, a son of Clymenus, whose mother was the Oceanid Merope.) Phaëthon demanded, as proof that the god was his father, the right to drive the sun chariot through the sky for one day. Helius, having vowed to grant whatever boon the boy asked, could not refuse. Unable to control the horses, Phaëthon was flung from the chariot into the river Eridanus. His sisters, usually called the Heliades, wept so profusely over him that they were changed into poplars.

Lampetië and Phaëthusa, Helius' daughters by Neaera, tended the huge herds of cattle and sheep that Helius pastured on the island of Thrinacia, which came to be identified with Sicily. When the sailors of ODYSSEUS [I] slaughtered some of the cattle, Helius demanded that they be punished, even threatening to go and shine in Hades if his wish were not honored. Zeus agreed and destroyed the entire crew, except for Odysseus.

Helius was more friendly toward another mortal who was also making a famous journey. When HERACLES [H] was traveling through northern Africa on his way to seize Geryon's cattle in Erytheia, he grew so angry at the burning heat that he drew his bow at the sun. Instead of taking offense, Helius was delighted with Heracles' boldness and lent him his golden cup for the sea journey to Erytheia, off the coast of Spain. He lent it to him again during his search for the garden of the Hesperides. Helius may conceivably have had some personal interest in Heracles' quarrel with Geryon, for he himself had once pastured cattle on Erytheia. They were carried off by the Giant Alcyoneus, who was later killed by Heracles and Zeus. Helius performed a service on another occasion for the giant hunter ORION by healing him of blindness. The god was credited by the inhabitants of India with having created the first men by warming the earth when it was still wet in the days of creation, but this was not a Greek myth.

The myths concerning Helius are to be found scattered through the works of many writers. Homer dealt in the *Odyssey* [1.8–9, 8.270–271, 8.302, 11.104–115, 12.260–419] with his enmity toward Odysseus' men and his trouble with Aphrodite. Hesiod gave his family connections in the *Theogony* [371–374, 956–962]. The *Homeric Hymn to Demeter* [2.26–27, 2.62–89] told of his aid to that goddess. Ovid, in his *Metamorphoses*, recounted at length the stories of Phaëthon [1.750–2.400] and Clytië [4.169–270]. (In the former tale, he substituted Phoebus Apollo for Helius.) Other significant references are to be found in Pindar [*Olympian Odes* 7.54–76], Hyginus [*Fabulae* 154], Apollonius Rhodius [4.964–974], Apollodorus [1.6.1, 2.5.10–11, "Epitome" 2.12], and Pausanias [2.1.6, 2.3.10, 2.4.6, 8.29.4, 9.25.5].

Helle. The daughter of Athamas and Nephele. When, as a result of a plot by her stepmother Ino, Helle's brother, Phrixus, was about to be sacrificed by their father, a miraculous ram appeared. The two children climbed onto its back and it flew off with them. Helle lost her hold as they crossed the strait between Europe and Asia and fell into the waters. The strait was thereafter named Hellespont—"Sea of Helle." According to Hyginus [*Poetica Astronomica* 2.20], Helle did not die. Poseidon lay with her and she gave birth to either Paeon or Edonus.

Hellen. The eponym of the HELLENES. Hellen was the eldest son of Deucalion and Pyrrha, though some call him a son of Zeus. He was the father, by the nymph Orseïs, of Dorus, eponym of the Dorians; Aeolus, eponym of the Aeolians; and Xuthus, whose sons, Achaeüs and Ion, were eponyms, respectively, of the Achaeans and the Ionians.

Hellenes. The Greeks; specifically, all who shared the Greek language and culture. Homer [*Iliad* 681–685] knew the Hellenes only as a tribe living in Hellas, in southern Thessaly. They sent ships to Troy under the leadership of Achilles, ruler of the neighboring state of Phthia. Homer's name for the Greeks as a whole, "Achaeans," may have been archaic in his own day. "Hellas" early came to be applied to all Greece, and "Hellenes" distinguished the Greeks not only from foreigners but from the Pelasgian, or pre-Greek, inhabitants of the land. In the modern Greek language, Greece is still "Hellas"; and the Hellene is both the ancient and the quintessential modern Greek.

These names were accounted for in legend by an eponym, Hellen, son of Deucalion. Hellen's sons or grandsons gave their names in turn to the Aeolians, Dorians, Ionians, and Achaeans, the four branches of the Hellenes. This legend supports Homer by placing Hellen in Thessaly. Although Hellen was said to have divided most of Greece among his children, the many sequels to the story make it evident that these lands were hard won by his supposed descendants over a period of many centuries.

Hellespont. The narrow strait (now called the Dardanelles) dividing the Thracian Chersonese from Asia Minor. The Hellespont was named for Helle, daughter of Athamas, who fell into it from the back of the golden-fleeced ram that was carrying her and Phrixus, her brother, through the air to Colchis. Both sides of the Hellespont were inhabited by tribes speaking Thraco-Phrygian dialects, and there were close alliances among them at the time of the Trojan War.

Hemera. Day, and the goddess of day. Hemera, who was born, together with Aether, from Erebus (Darkness) and Nyx (Night), regularly emerged from Tartarus as Nyx entered it, and returned as Nyx was leaving. Since Eos (Dawn) was thought of as accompanying the Sun as well as heralding his rising, she tended to usurp the functions of Hemera and was often identified with her. [Hesiod, *Theogony*, 124–125, 746–757; Pausanias 1.3.1.]

Henna or **Enna.** A city in central Sicily. Henna, one of the more widely agreed upon of the possible sites of Hades' abduction of Persephone, was an ancient cult center of Demeter and her daughter.

Hephaestus. A god of fire and metalworking. Hephaestus, whom the Romans identified with their fire-god Vulcan (also called Mulciber), was a son of Zeus and Hera, or of Hera alone. According to the latter view, Hera bore Hephaestus parthenogenetically because she was engaged in a quarrel with her husband. The child was lame, however, and Hera threw him out of heaven in disgust. He fell into the sea or the river Oceanus. There Thetis and the Oceanid Eurynome saved and cared for him in a sea cave, unknown to Hera and the other gods. Annoyed at his mother for her unmaternal behavior, Hephaestus, who had become a master artisan, sent her a gift, a splendid golden throne. When she sat on it, she found herself bound fast. (Some say that Hephaestus gave sandals of gold to the other gods and goddesses, but to Hera a pair made of adamant—which, when she sat down, somehow upended her in an ignominious fashion.) The gods pleaded with the errant artisan to forgive his mother and return to Olympus, but he refused. Finally Dionysus, whom Hephaestus unwarily trusted, made him drunk and brought him up to Olympus, where he released Hera.

According to an alternative story of Hephaestus' fall from heaven, he was flung out by Zeus because he came to his mother's rescue when Zeus was punishing her for having opposed him. Hephaestus fell for an entire day and landed on the island of Lemnos. He was cared for there by the Sintians, an ancient Lemnian tribe, but remained forever lame. Lemnos was thereafter his favorite land. Some say that Hephaestus set up his smithy there; others claim that it was under Mount Aetna, in Sicily. The earliest accounts, however, place it in heaven. There the smith used pellets of hot metal to kill the Giant Mimas during the war between gods and Giants. He was also called on by Zeus to fasten Prometheus to a cliff in the Caucasus Range.

But Hephaestus was far more than a mere blacksmith. He was a divine artisan of infinite ingenuity and equal artistic gifts. He built palaces for all the Olympian gods and turned out innumerable objects, such as the armor of Achilles, that were notable for their beauty and intricate workmanship. Most remarkable of his creations was PANDORA, the first female known to man. Perhaps an even more delicate task than molding Pandora was that of delivering Athena from Zeus's head by splitting it with an ax.

Hephaestus married either Aglaea, the youngest of the Graces, or Aphrodite. This latter union was punctuated by Aphrodite's numerous affairs with other gods and with mortals. In the most notorious of these, the goddess' long dalliance with Ares, Hephaestus emerged triumphant. Told by Helius of his wife's infidelity, he hung an invisible net over the bed that he shared with his wife, then pretended to leave on one of his frequent trips to Lemnos. Ares promptly visited Aphrodite and the guilty pair were trapped in the net. Hephaestus then called in the other gods to witness their embarrassment, held naked and helpless by the net. Having enjoyed this revenge, Hephaestus reluctantly accepted reparations from Ares at the insistence of Poseidon, who went bond for the payment.

Hephaestus himself was not wholly unmoved by female beauty other than his wife's. He once pursued the goddess Athena on the Athenian acropolis. Wishing to remain virginal, she fought him off and his semen spilled onto the ground. From it grew Erichthonius, the half-serpent progenitor of Athenian kings. Hephaestus was also the father, by the wife of Lernus, of the Argonaut Palaemon, who inherited his father's lameness. Other sons were the Epidaurian outlaw Periphetes, who was also lame, and Ardalus, who may have invented the flute. In the battle of the gods during the Trojan War, Hephaestus was pitted against the river Scamander, which he temporarily dried up with a great flame in order to rescue Achilles from drowning.

Most scholars agree that Hephaestus was originally an Asian god. Although he was one of the Olympians by Homer's time, he does not figure in many Greek myths, beyond receiving credit for numberless works of art. As a god of fire he often personified fire itself. His frequent association with volcanos has persuaded many scholars that he was originally connected specifically with gaseous fires that emanated from the earth in volcanic regions. One of the chief seats of his cult was the island of Lemnos, which contains a once-active volcano.

Both versions of Hephaestus' fall from heaven are found in Homer's *Iliad* [1.571–608, 18.368–617], as is the story of his forging of Achilles' armor and his battle with Scamander [20.73–74, 21.328–382]; his revenge on Ares and Aphrodite is the subject of the Phaeacian bard Demodocus' song in the *Odyssey* [8.266–366]. See also Hesiod's *Theogony* [570–572, 927–929, 945–946], Aeschylus' *Prometheus Bound* [1–81, 365–369], Apollonius Rhodius [1.202–205, 1.850–860], Apollodorus [1.3.5–6, 1.4.3–4, 1.6.2, 3.14.6, 3. 16.1], Pausanias [1.20.3, 2.31.3, 8.53.5], and Hyginus [*Fabulae*, 166, and *Poetica Astronomica*, 2.12–13, 2.15, 2.34]. References to Hephaestus' works in metals and other materials are found throughout Greek and Roman literature.

Hera. A goddess of marriage and childbirth, and queen of heaven.

A. Hera, whom the Romans identified with their goddess Juno, was a daughter of Cronus and Rhea. Several Greek regions claimed to be her birthplace, notably Samos, Argos, Euboea, and Stymphalus. Hera, together with her sisters, Demeter and Hestia, and her brothers Poseidon and Hades, was swallowed as an infant by Cronus, but later was vomited up. During the ensuing war between gods and Titans she was cared for by Oceanus and Tethys. Some say, however, that Hera was reared by the Seasons, or by the three daughters of the Argive river-god Asterion, or by the Arcadian Temenus, son of Pelasgus.

Zeus, after affairs with six other goddesses, courted his sister Hera, without the knowledge of their parents. Some say that he took the form of a cuckoo and seduced her when she sheltered him from the rain. She bore three children—Ares, Hebe, and Eileithyia—but the marriage was anything but harmonious. When Zeus produced a daughter, Athena, without aid from his wife or any other woman (unless it was his first wife Metis, whom he had swallowed), Hera was furious and bore a son, Hephaestus, by herself. He turned out to be lame and sickly, so his mother threw him out of heaven in disgust. He fell on the island of Lemnos and grew up to be a famous artisan. Angry at the treatment that he had received from Hera, Hephaestus devised a throne for her as a gift. Hera unsuspectingly sat in it and was held fast. Hephaestus was welcomed back to heaven, but only Dionysus could persuade him to release Hera.

According to another version of Hera's anger over Athena's birth, she retaliated by bearing the monster Typhaon, who became her husband's most dangerous adversary. (More commonly, Ge is said to have given birth to the monster and he is often called TYPHÖEUS.) Hera once joined Poseidon and Athena in binding Zeus, for some unexplained reason, and Thetis had to call up Briareüs from Tartarus to release him. On a later occasion, when Hera went too far in persecuting Heracles, who was her husband's son by Alcmene, Zeus hung her from heaven by the wrists, with anvils tied to her ankles.

In spite of her exalted rank as Zeus's wife, Hera's chastity was not immune to attack. During the battle of the gods with the Giants, Zeus led Porphyrion to attempt to rape her before blasting him into Tartarus with a thunderbolt. The Giant Ephialtes also had the temerity to woo Hera before he was killed by Artemis. Ixion, a mortal whom Zeus had invited to Olympus, grew so proud that he dared to court Hera. At Zeus's orders she substituted an image of herself made of cloud. Ixion lay with it and Zeus punished him by binding him forever to a wheel. A similar story was told of Endymion.

Hera and Poseidon vied for recognition as patron deity of Argos and the surrounding region. The judgment was finally left to three local river-gods: Inachus, Asterion, and Cephisus. They decided in favor of Hera and were rewarded by Poseidon with the drying up of their springs. The god also flooded the land, but Hera persuaded him to relent and the waters receded.

B. Much of Hera's time was spent in persecuting her husband's innumerable mistresses and their children. Although, according to Hesiod, Zeus lay with LETO before his marriage to Hera, Hera hated the Titaness and swore that no land under the sun should give her a resting place. Only through the intervention of Poseidon was Leto able to find a haven where she might bear her children by Zeus. Even then Hera tried to prevent her daughter Eileithyia, the goddess of childbirth, from attending Leto, but the other goddesses bribed Eileithyia, and Apollo and Artemis were born.

When Zeus seduced Hera's Argive priestess Io and changed her into a heifer, the goddess first set a guard on her, then sent a gadfly to drive her, half mad, through most of the world. Io at last found rest in Egypt and bore Zeus's child, Epaphus. Hera at once sent the Curetes to steal the infant and, some say, later caused Epaphus to be killed while hunting. She changed CALLISTO, another of Zeus's loves, into a bear and induced Artemis to kill her. Because Zeus lay with AEGINA, Hera caused the deaths of nearly all the people of the island that had been renamed for her.

The best known of Hera's victims, however, were two mortals who became gods. On learning that Zeus was carrying on an affair with Cadmus' daughter Semele, she tricked the girl into bringing about her own death by asking to see Zeus in his full majesty. Although Zeus saved their child, DIONYSUS, Hera not only persecuted the young god as long as she dared but brought exile, madness, or death on many of those who aided him. Even more relentless was Hera's pursuit of HERACLES, Zeus's son by Alcmene. According to some traditions, Zeus tricked Hera into giving Heracles suck while she slept. The Milky Way was caused by the spilled milk when she woke to discover the trick. Angrier than ever, Hera deprived Heracles of his birthright and tried to cause his death even in his crib. Failing in this, she pursued him throughout his life, causing him endless hardships and destructive madness. Some claim that the goddess reared the Nemean lion, the Hydra, and the Earthborn monsters of Bear Mountain to be Heracles' enemies. When he was finally taken up to heaven, Hera was reconciled to him and even consented to his marriage to her daughter Hebe, but she did not neglect to punish PHILOCTETES for granting Heracles' dying request that he set a torch to his pyre.

A legend told at Plataea had it that Hera once left Zeus for her birthplace in Euboea, presumably in anger at his infidelities. Unable to persuade her to return, he consulted Cithaeron, the clever king of Plataea. Following his advice, Zeus made a statue of a woman, veiled it, and drove it in a wagon to Mount Cithaeron, after giving out that he was about to marry Plataea, daughter of Asopus. Hera heard of the impending match and sped to the scene. Snatching the image from the cart, she discovered the trick and was reconciled to her husband.

Hera was a loyal friend to the ARGONAUTS and they could not have completed their goal without her frequent aid. Some attribute her kindness to her approval of Jason's courtesy in carrying her across a river beside which, disguised as a crone, she sat testing the behavior of men. Her desertion of the young man as soon as he returned to Greece would seem to support an opposing explanation: that she had merely used Jason as a means of getting MEDEA to Iolcus so that she might dispose of Pelias. This king had, as a young man, defiled the goddess' altar by killing his cruel stepmother, Sidero, before it. Moreover, he had steadfastly refused to honor Hera because she had shown favor to Sidero. Throughout his long reign at Iolcus, Hera had sought a way to destroy him, and Medea performed this service for her.

C. Like other goddesses, Hera was jealous of her honors and her beauty, and it did not require the gross impiety of a Pelias to incur her enmity. She sent Orion's wife Side to Hades for rivaling her beauty. Some say that the madness of the daughters of PROËTUS was caused by Hera, who was angry at them for not showing sufficient reverence for a statue of her. She transformed the queen of the Pygmies into a crane and Laomedon's daughter Antigone into a stork, because both had offended her in some way. According to some accounts, the seer Teiresias was blinded by the goddess for siding with Zeus when called in to arbitrate an argument the two were having. Hera later sent the Sphinx to ravage Thebes because the Theban king Laïus remained unpunished for his abduction of Chrysippus.

Because PARIS [B] awarded the golden apple to Aphrodite in a beauty contest, the defeated contestants, Hera and Athena, became implacable enemies of the Trojans in the ensuing war. Hera went further, according to Stesichorus: she arranged to have Hermes steal away to Egypt the true Helen of Sparta and substitute a phantom for Paris to carry off to Troy. During the Trojan War, Hera fought fiercely for the Greeks, more than once risking dire punishment from her husband, who had forbidden the gods to intervene in the conflict. Her most successful stratagem was to lure Zeus to lie with her on the top of Mount Gargarus while Poseidon roused the Greek forces against the Trojans.

D. As a goddess of women, Hera shared all their concerns. She was worshiped in the Arcadian region of Stymphalus in three forms: as Girl, Bride, and Old Woman. In both Greece and Rome she often functioned as a guardian of childbirth in place of her daughter Eileithyia, or the Roman Lucina. She occasionally assumed the guise of an old woman. Most often, however, she was worshiped as Hera Teleia (Full-Grown), the goddess of marriage. (At Temenium, in Argos, she was privileged to renew her virginity every year by bathing in the spring Canathus.) Many scholars believe that Hera was originally, like so many other pre-Hellenic goddesses, a patroness of the fertility of the earth. There are strong indications that she governed the lives of cattle and flocks, and she was sometimes connected in cult with crops and flowers.

It seems certain that Hera was originally an Argive goddess, as she is called by Homer. She had many other cult centers, the most important of which were perhaps the islands of Samos and Euboea.

E. Hera figures significantly throughout two epics—Homer's *Iliad* and the *Argonautica* of Apollonius Rhodius. She is ever present as a malign influence in the stories of Heracles and the young Dionysus, but these do not appear in extended form in any extant poetic work. References to the goddess abound. Among the more important of these are the following: Hesiod, *Theogony*, 326–332, 453–506, 921–934; *Great Eoiae* 11; *Homeric Hymn to Apollo* 3.95–101, 3.305–354; *Cypria* 1, 4; Aeschylus, *Prometheus Bound*, 590–601, and *Suppliants*, 291–309; Pindar, *Pythian Odes*, 2.21–41, and *Nemean Odes*, 1.37–40; Apollodorus 1.4.3, 1.6.2, 1.7.4, 1.8.2, 1.9.8, 1.9.16, 1.9.28, 2.1.3–4, 2.2.2, 2.4.8, 2.4.12, 2.5.9–10, 2.7.7, 3.4.3, 3.5.1, 3.5.8, "Epitome" 3.2–4, 6.29; Ovid, *Metamorphoses*, 1.601–746, 2.466–533, 3.255–338, 3.362–369, 4.416–562, 6.90–97, 7.517–613, 9.280–323, 14.829–851; Hyginus, *Fabulae*, 5, 13, 22, 52, 102, 150, and *Poetica Astronomica*, 2.3, 2.16, 2.23, 2.42–43; Pausanias 1.18.5, 1.20.3, 2.13.3, 2.15.4–5, 2.17.1–17, 2.38.2–3, 8.22.2, 9.2.7–9.3.8.

Heracles. The son of Zeus and Alcmene, called Hercules by the Romans.

A. Heracles' mother was married to Amphitryon, son of Perseus' son Alcaeüs. When Amphitryon killed his father-in-law, Electryon, king of Tiryns, he was exiled by Electryon's brother, Sthenelus. Alcmene fled with her husband to Thebes, where they were welcomed by King Creon. She refused, however, to lie with her husband until he had avenged the murder of her brothers by Taphian pirates, which had occurred some time earlier. Amphitryon successfully led an expedition against the Taphian Islands. On the night before his return, Zeus disguised himself as Amphitryon and shared Alcmene's bed. The next day the real Amphitryon was chagrined at the rather perfunctory reception that he met with in his home and bed. Alcmene was equally surprised when she was regaled with the same tales of her husband's exploits that she had heard the night before. The seer Teiresias cleared up the mystery and Amphitryon was convinced that Alcmene's abandonment of virginity had been innocent, if premature. He waited patiently to see whether his wife would bear a god's children or his own.

The goddess Hera was equally interested in this outcome, but far less patient. She had long suffered from her husband's philandering, and her implacable hostility toward the sons that Zeus had fathered on mortal women was notorious. Her feelings were hardly soothed when, nine months after his visit to Alcmene, Zeus boasted before the other gods on Olympus that on that day a son would be born of his lineage who would rule over all the land about him. Hera, pretending not to believe her husband, made him swear that it would be as he had declared. Zeus had no sooner made his unwary vow than Hera sent Eileithyia, the goddess of childbirth, to delay the hour of Alcmene's delivery at Thebes. She herself saw to it that a son was born immediately at Tiryns to the wife of Sthenelus, who had usurped the throne that should have belonged to Amphitryon. As a grandson of Zeus's son Perseus, this boy, Eurystheus, was guaranteed by Zeus's vow the rule of Tiryns and Mycenae. Zeus was furious at Hera, but could not revoke his oath.

Alcmene, meanwhile, might have died in childbirth if one of her attendants, Galanthis, had not found a way to trick Eileithyia. The goddess was sitting outside Alcmene's bedroom with legs and fingers tightly crossed as a charm to hold back the delivery. Galanthis rushed from the room crying out joyfully that the child was born. The startled goddess, forgetting the charm, leaped up. In that moment Alcmene was delivered. Eileithyia, furious at having been tricked, changed Galanthis into a weasel. Alcmene gave birth to twin sons, whom she and Amphitryon named Alcaeüs, or Heracles, and Iphicles. According to Diodorus Siculus [4.9.1–4.10.1], Alcmene exposed the baby Alcaeüs for fear of Hera's anger. Athena found him and persuaded the unsuspecting Hera to suckle him. Hera did so until he bit her. Athena then returned him to Alcmene and persuaded her to rear her own child. Other versions of this incident claim that Zeus put the baby to the sleeping Hera's breast. When she awoke, the spilled milk became the Milky Way.

Amphitryon suspected that one of the boys was his son, the other the god's, but he could not tell which was which. It was not long before the question was answered for him in a spectacular manner. Hera, foiled in her attempts to prevent the birth of her husband's son, determined to dispose of the infant. She therefore sent two snakes to the crib where the brothers, no more than eight or ten months old, lay sleeping. Iphicles screamed in terror, but Alcaeüs grabbed the snakes by the throat and strangled them. Amphitryon was no longer in doubt as to which child was the god's. According to some writers, it was Amphitryon himself who had placed the snakes in the crib in order to settle once and for all his own doubts. [Homer, *Iliad,* 19.96–133; Ovid, *Metamorphoses,* 9.280–323.]

B. Alcaeüs was at some point renamed Heracles, or, according to many accounts, bore that name from birth. His reputation must have spread when he was still very young. Although Amphitryon taught his stepson to drive the chariot, several other famous men contributed to his education. The wily thief Autolycus taught him to wrestle and Eurytus, the archer king of Oechalia, taught him the use of bow and arrows. Castor is said to have trained the youth in fencing, but Heracles seems to have relied very little on the use of the sword in later days. He is even less well known for his lyre playing, perhaps because his lessons on this instrument ended in disaster. He was taught as a child by Linus, a brother of Orpheus, who was residing at Thebes. When the teacher struck his pupil for some unrecorded offense, Heracles broke the lyre over Linus' head and killed him on the spot. He was acquitted of a charge of murder when he argued self-defense. Nevertheless Amphitryon took the precaution to send Heracles away to his cattle farm in the country.

By the age of seventeen Heracles was at least six feet tall and was so expert with both bow and spear that he never missed his mark. He also had profited from Autolycus' lessons and could rely on craft in wrestling as well as on his own prodigious strength. Apollodorus claims that the young man's first adventure was to pursue a lion which had been roaming Mount Cithaeron and eating the flocks of both Amphitryon and Thespius, king of Thespiae.

This king's interest in the prowess of his young neighbor extended beyond Heracles' talent for the hunt. He entertained the youth for fifty nights before bringing up the subject of the lion. Each night he sent another of his fifty daughters to Heracles' bed—unless, as some insist, he sent all fifty in one night. According to at least one writer, Heracles, perhaps a little befuddled by the king's wine, was unaware of the traffic in his bedroom and imagined that he was indebted to only one daughter as his partner in the night's marathon. Pausanias records with disbelief the tradition that one of Thespius' daughters refused to sleep with the guest and was condemned by him to remain forever a virgin priestess in his temple. The writer points out that Heracles had no temple and that, at least so early in his career, he had no expectation of having one. He adds, somewhat less convincingly, that Heracles was too modest to conceive of such a punishment.

After his eventful stay at the palace of Thespius, Heracles went to Mount

Cithaeron, killed the lion, and thereafter wore its skin as a cloak. Credit for destroying the Cithaeronian lion is usually given, however, to Alcathoüs, and Heracles' well-known garment is thought to have been first worn by the lion of Nemea, a far more formidable beast than the one that lived on Cithaeron. [Apollodorus 2.4.9–10; Pausanias 9.27.6–7, 9.29.9.]

C. While returning from Mount Cithaeron, Heracles met heralds on their way to Thebes to collect the annual tribute exacted of that city by Erginus, king of the Minyan city of Orchomenus. Heracles cut off their ears and noses, hung them around their necks, and sent them thus back to Orchomenus as "tribute." Enraged, Erginus advanced on Thebes with his Minyan army. Creon, whose Thebans had been deprived of their armor long before by the Orchomenians, felt that any attempt at defense was hopeless and even offered to give up Heracles to Erginus. Heracles, however, roused the young men of Thebes to resistance. They put on the rusting armor that their ancestors had dedicated in the temples and went out to meet the invading force. Catching the attackers in a narrow pass, they routed them and chased them back to their city. Heracles was not content with this success. He slipped into Orchomenus at night, burned the palace, and took the city. Whether he killed Erginus or merely subdued him is disputed, but from this time on, Orchomenus had to pay double tribute to Thebes.

The chronology of the events that followed Heracles' triumphs in the Minyan war is confused, perhaps through unsuccessful attempts to establish plausible relationships of cause and effect among traditions that were originally unconnected. Heracles married Creon's daughter Megara, and many writers have assumed that the king gave her to him as a reward for his services in the Minyan war. Other writers have said, however, that Heracles returned from this war to find that Creon had been murdered and his throne usurped by a Euboean, Lycus, who was on the point of executing Heracles' wife Megara and their children. Still other writers say that these events occurred much later, when Heracles returned from Hades. All accounts agree that he killed Lycus and saved the city. Accounts agree, too, on the tragic aftermath: struck with a sudden fit of madness through the unrelenting hostility of Hera, Heracles killed his children, two children of his nephew Iolaüs, and perhaps Megara as well.

Returning to his senses, Heracles discovered to his horror what he had done. He exiled himself from Thebes and was purified of the murders by King Thespius. Some say that it was Nausithoüs and Macris who purified him on the Phaeacian island of Drepane, and that while he was there he lay with the naïad Melite, who bore him Hyllus. After this he went to Delphi to ask the advice of the oracle. The Pythia (who some say was the first to call Alcaeüs Heracles) told him that, in punishment for his crime, he must voluntarily go to Tiryns and perform whatever ten labors King Eurystheus would demand of him. (Many writers say that twelve labors were imposed, rather than ten.) If he succeeded in these tasks he would achieve immortality. To serve any man was hard enough for Heracles. To serve Eurystheus, a weakling who occupied the throne which would have been Heracles' own if Hera had not deceived Zeus, was doubly humiliating. Nevertheless Heracles agreed to perform the labors. These labors are described below in the order given by Apollodorus, who has the most connected account of them. [Apollodorus 2.4.11–12; Diodorus Siculus 4.10.2–4.11.2; Euripides, *Heracles*; Hyginus, *Fabulae*, 31–32.]

D. The first labor that Eurystheus imposed upon his new vassal was to kill the *Nemean lion*. This was no ordinary lion. It was either one of the monstrous offspring of Orthus and Echidna, or of Typhon, or else it had been suckled by the moon-goddess. On his way to Nemea, Heracles spent a night at Cleonae in the hut of a day laborer named Molorchus. Molorchus, who had evidently never encountered such a formidable man as Heracles, offered to sacrifice to him. Heracles told him to wait for thirty days. If by this time he had not returned, Molorchus might sacrifice to him as a hero. If he did return, the sacrifice should be offered to Zeus the Savior.

Heracles then proceeded to the two-mouthed cave that was the lion's lair. He had no trouble in finding the beast or, since his aim was infallible, in shooting it; but, when his arrow bounced harmlessly off the lion's pelt, he realized that it was invulnerable to weapons. He therefore blocked up one end of the cave and strode in, unarmed, at the other mouth. Meeting the animal face to face, he strangled it with his bare hands. On the thirtieth day of his waiting period Molorchus looked up from his preparations for a hero-sacrifice and saw Hercules approaching with the dead lion slung over his shoulder. Dutifully he switched to the more elaborate rites due a god.

Heracles went on to Tiryns. When Eurystheus saw him coming he was terrified. Hiding in a bronze storage jar set in the earth, he sent word that Heracles was henceforth to display his trophies outside the city gates. Moreover, all future orders would be given to Heracles by the herald Copreus rather than by Eurystheus himself. Since Eurystheus did not want the lion, Heracles skinned it and dressed himself in its pelt, with the scalp serving as a sort of hood. The lion was immortalized, perhaps by Hera, by being made a constellation.

The second labor that Eurystheus demanded of Heracles was a far harder one: killing the *Hydra*. This hideous, many-headed creature, half-sister of the Nemean lion through either its father, Typhon, or its mother, Echidna, had been nourished, some say, by Hera herself, out of hatred for Heracles. It lived near the spring Amymone, at Lerna, in company with its devoted friend, a large crab. With his usual boldness Heracles advanced to the Hydra's lair, to drive it into the open with a flight of burning arrows. It emerged, its monstrous body surmounted by nine or more heads. When Heracles grabbed it by one of its necks, it immediately wound itself about one of his feet. He began hacking away at its heads with his sword. Soon he found that the middle head was invulnerable to his blows and that the others shared an even more disturbing characteristic: whenever he lopped one head from its neck, two other heads grew in its place. To make matters worse, the crab now sallied from the swamp and began biting Heracles' foot.

Heracles would not admit defeat, but he realized that even he could not cope with this enemy alone. He bellowed for help to Iolaüs, Iphicles' son, who had become Heracles' charioteer and friend. Iolaüs brought burning brands and, as soon as Heracles cut off one of the Hydra's heads, he cauterized the wound. In this way the two slowly disposed of all of the monster except its immortal head. Heracles severed this from the body and buried it beneath a stone beside the road that led from Lerna to Elaeüs. He then ripped open the Hydra's body and dipped his arrows in its gall. This deadly poison was in future years to destroy dozens of Heracles' enemies—and finally Heracles himself. As for the crab, Hera immortalized it in a constellation. Heracles returned triumphant to Tiryns, but Eurystheus refused to admit this as one of the ten labors, for Heracles had been unable to kill the Hydra alone. [Apollodorus 2.5.1–2; Hesiod, *Theogony*, 313–318; Hyginus, *Fabulae*, 30, and *Poetica Astronomica*, 2.23–24.]

E. The third labor that Eurystheus exacted of Heracles was the capture alive of the *Cerynitian hind*. This golden-horned deer (which some call a stag, others a doe) was sacred to Artemis. It roamed the region about Oenoë, in Argolis. In order to take it alive, Heracles pursued it for an entire year and finally ran it down in Arcadia beside the river Ladon, after crossing Mount Artemisius. Some say that he caught it in nets, others that he crept upon it while it slept. As he was carrying the deer on his shoulder through Arcadia, he met Artemis and Apollo. The angry goddess would have taken her deer from him, but Heracles appeased her by laying the blame on Eurystheus. She permitted him to carry the unharmed beast to Tiryns.

Eurystheus immediately sent Heracles back to Arcadia with orders to capture alive the *Erymanthian boar* as his fourth labor. This huge beast ranged over Mount Erymanthus and ravaged the country about Psophis. On his way past Mount Pholoë, Heracles stopped with the Centaur Pholus, a son of Seilenus by an ash-nymph. This hospitable creature brought out wine to serve his guest, but his fellow Centaurs smelled it and, going mad, tried to steal it. Some say in their defense that the wine belonged communally to all the Centaurs and that Pholus should have asked their permission before offering it to his private guests; but Centaurs were notoriously unable to hold their drink. They had, in fact, been driven to the Peloponnesus from their native Magnesia after drunkenly disgracing themselves at the wedding feast of Peirithoüs and Hippodameia. Heracles now drove most of the Centaurs back to their new home on Mount Malea, but Eurytion took refuge on Mount Pholoë and Nessus escaped to the river Evenus, in Aetolia, where Heracles was to meet him again. Other Centaurs fled to Eleusis and Poseidon hid them in a mountain there.

Pholus lived just long enough to regret his guest's assistance. While examining one of Heracles' arrows after the battle, he accidentally dropped it on his foot and soon died from the Hydra's venom. According to some stories, Cheiron met the same fate, though other versions say that Heracles accidentally shot him. In either case, Heracles applied medicines prescribed by the Centaur to the wound, but they did not help. In terrible pain, Cheiron wanted to die, but could not because he was immortal. Some say that Prometheus took on the Centaur's burden of immortality, and Cheiron went happily down to Hades. Either Cheiron or Pholus was immortalized as the constellation Centaurus.

Heracles now was able to proceed with the hunt. He trapped the boar in deep snow on Mount Erymanthus and brought it back alive to the terrified Eurystheus, who again took refuge in his jar.

During this labor Heracles had heard that Jason was gathering the bravest men of Greece at Iolcus in order to make the dangerous journey to Colchis to fetch the golden fleece. Heracles could not bear to be left out, so he postponed his next labor and set out for Iolcus. The ARGONAUTS [A–F] wanted to make him captain but Heracles deferrred to Jason. Just what part Heracles played in this voyage is much disputed. Some say that he got no farther than Aphetae, on the Gulf of Pagasae, because the *Argo*'s magical speaking beam complained that the ship could not bear his weight. Others claim that he went all the way to Colchis, or even that he led the expedition.

The best-known version of the events is that told in the *Argonautica* of Apollonius Rhodius. Heracles had killed King Theiodamas during his war with the Dryopes (which most writers place much later in his career). Noting the great beauty of his victim's little son, Hylas, he had reared the boy to be his squire and lover. Now nearly grown to manhood, Hylas accompanied his master on the *Argo*. Early in the outward voyage the ship landed in Mysia. Heracles went into the woods to cut himself a new oar and sent his squire to draw water. The nymphs of the spring fell in love with the boy and pulled him down into the water. Hearing his cry but unable to find him, Hylas' fellow Argonaut Polyphemus called Heracles. Heracles went roaming through the woods, wild with rage and grief, calling for his young friend. The other Argonauts sailed without him and Polyphemus, at the insistence of Zetes and Calaïs.

At last Heracles had to return to his labors. First, however, he made the Mysians vow never to give up the search for Hylas. For many centuries thereafter the citizens of Cius, the city founded in this region by Polyphemus, wandered about in an annual rite, calling for Hylas. As for Zetes and Calaïs, Heracles met them later on the island of Tenos and killed them for their part in his abandonment. He put up stones over their graves, one of which swayed in the breath of the dead men's father, Boreas, the North Wind. [Apollodorus 1.9.19, 2.5.4, 3.15.2; Hyginus, *Poetica Astronomica*, 2.38.]

F. Eurystheus, perhaps angry at Heracles' temporary defection, gave him as his fifth labor the most humiliating assignment of his career: to clean the dung from the *Augeian stables*. Augeias, king of Elis, owned vast herds of cattle. Their dung had by now been deposited so thickly on his land that it was no longer tillable. Heracles agreed to undertake the task of removing it in a single day, but, not mentioning to Augeias that he was required to do it in any event, he demanded as payment one tenth of the cattle. Heracles evidently did not trust the reluctant king, for he made Augeias' son Phyleus witness the bargain. He then proceeded to break through the walls of the corral and, diverting the rivers Alpheius and Peneius, flushed the area with their waters. (The literal-minded traveler Pausanias insists that the river must in fact have been the Menius, the only one that is near enough to Elis to have served Heracles' purpose.)

As Heracles had anticipated, Augeias refused to honor his contract, claiming, correctly enough, that it had been the laborer's duty to perform the work without pay. The king also denied that he had promised pay and, when Phyleus remonstrated with him, exiled his son. Phyleus went to Dulichium. Doubtless threatening revenge, Heracles left Elis. For some reason he stopped at Olenus, in Achaea, where he was entertained by King Dexamenus. He repaid his host by killing the Centaur Eurytion, who was about to marry Dexamenus' daughter Mnesimache against her will. On his return to Tiryns, Heracles found himself doubly repaid for his overcleverness in charging Augeias for this labor. Not only had he been cheated of his wages, but Eurystheus refused to count the labor among the ten, on the grounds that Heracles had undertaken it for hire.

For his sixth labor Heracles returned a third time to Arcadia in order to chase away the *Stymphalian birds*. Some say that these birds ate men, others confuse them with the feather-shooting birds that the Argonauts encountered on the Island of Ares. Apollodorus says that they were ordinary birds that had taken refuge on Lake Stymphalus to avoid wolves. In any event, there were so many of them that they had become a nuisance. Heracles either made himself a rattle or borrowed from Athena a pair of brass castanets made by Hephaestus. He clashed these on a mountain near the lake. When the birds flew up in fright, he shot great numbers of them and scared the others away.

Eurystheus demanded that Heracles capture and bring back the *Cretan bull* as his seventh labor. Until now, the tasks he had assigned had all been performed in the Peloponnesus. The envious king may have hoped that expeditions into foreign territories would prove more dangerous, or he may merely have hoped to gain more time between the disturbing appearances of his seemingly invincible vassal at the city gates. Whatever his reason, Eurystheus from now on sent Heracles as far as possible from Tiryns. It is not agreed whether King Minos aided Heracles in capturing the Cretan bull. He would have had ample reason to wish to, for the bull, which had fathered the Minotaur on Queen Pasiphaë, must have been an embarrassment to him. Heracles brought the bull back to Tiryns, showed it to Eurystheus, and freed it. After wandering about the Peloponnesus, it reached Marathon, near Athens, where it created havoc. King AEGEUS [B] sent Androgeus to capture it, with fatal results. Theseus was later successful in the task and sacrificed the bull at Athens. [Apollodorus 2.5.5–7; Pausanias 1.27.9–10, 5.1.9–5.2.2, 8.22.4.]

G. For an eighth labor Eurystheus sent Heracles to Thrace to fetch the *mares of Diomedes*. Diomedes, a savage king of the Bistones, owned four mares, which he fed on human flesh. According to Euripides' *Alcestis*, Heracles passed through Thessaly on his way to Thrace and was entertained by Admetus, king of Pherae. The king was in mourning, but, in order that his guest's pleasure should not be lessened, pretended that the dead person was a stranger in his house. After carousing awhile, Heracles learned that it was actually Admetus' wife Alcestis who had died. Heracles, embarrassed at his own seeming callousness, rushed to the queen's tomb, ambushed Thanatos (Death) as he was carrying her off, and took her from him by main force. Other accounts say that he went down to the Underworld and fought Hades for her.

After returning Alcestis to her grateful husband, Heracles went on his way to Thrace. Some writers say that he sailed there with a small force of volunteers. He overpowered Diomedes' grooms and drove the mares down to the sea. When the Bistones came in pursuit, Heracles was forced to leave the mares in the care of his young lover Abderus while he defended himself. He killed Diomedes and routed the enemy, but returned to the shore to find that the mares had eaten most of Abderus. He buried what remained of the young man and founded the city of Abdera on his grave. According to Diodorus Siculus [4.15.3–4], who does not mention Abderus, Heracles calmed the voracious mares by feeding their master to them. In all versions of the story, he brought the beasts to Tiryns and showed them to Eurystheus. He then freed them. They were later eaten by wild animals on Mount Olympus, to which they had perhaps wandered on their way back to Thrace.

Eurystheus, to please his daughter Admete, required Heracles for his ninth labor to fetch *Hippolyte's belt*. Hippolyte, daughter of Ares and Otrera, was queen of the Amazons, a warlike tribe of women who lived on the Thermodon River, on the southern shore of the Black Sea. These women were formidable enemies. Heracles therefore chose a boatload of sturdy companions to take with him on this venture. Among them were Theseus and (some say) Telamon. On their way they stopped at the island of Paros, which was ruled by sons of Minos. The Parians killed two of the crew. Heracles besieged the island until the people begged him to take hostages. He chose Alcaeüs and Sthenelus, young sons of Androgeus. After this the voyage was uneventful until the ship reached Mysia. There Heracles and his companions were entertained by Lycus, king of the Mariandyni. They repaid the king's hospitality by aiding him in his perennial border war with the Bebryces. Heracles killed Mygdon, brother of the notorious King Amycus, and gave much Bebrycian territory to Lycus, who named it Heracleia.

Sailing on, Heracles and his friends reached the Amazon capital of Themiscyra. According to Apollodorus, they were met by the queen herself. She boarded their ship for a parley with Heracles and, after some discussion, promised him the belt. Hera, chagrined that one of Heracles' labors should be accomplished with so little danger, posed as an Amazon and aroused the others with the report that Heracles was kidnaping their queen. The women charged the ship. Heracles, believing that Hippolyte had betrayed him, killed her and took the belt. According to another version of the story, Hippolyte's sister Antiope fell in love with Theseus and betrayed the Amazons to the Greeks. Whether this is true, Theseus took Antiope back to Athens with him.

On the homeward voyage the victorious company stopped at Troy. King Laomedon appealed to Heracles for help. Apollo and Poseidon, with the help of the mortal Aeacus, had built the city walls for Laomedon, but the king had refused to pay them their wages. The sea-god had punished him by sending a sea-monster to ravage the land. An oracle had told Laomedon that this threat, and the plague sent at the same time by Apollo, would end only if he offered his daughter Hesione to the monster. He had therefore chained her to a rock beside the sea to await the monster's coming. Heracles promised to save Hesione in return for the girl and the handsome mares that Zeus had given the king when he carried off the king's son Ganymede. Laomedon agreed to the bargain and Heracles waited for the monster to appear. When it did, a fierce fight ensued, during which Heracles occasionally took refuge on a wall that the Trojans, aided by Athena, had hastily heaped up for this purpose. He finally killed the monster and came to Laomedon to claim his reward. Now that Hesione was safe, the king refused to pay. Heracles did not have a force of sufficient size to make war on Troy, so he sailed away, threatening vengeance at some future date.

On his way home Heracles and his company were entertained by Poltys, king of the Thracian town of Aenus. For some reason Heracles shot his host's brother, Sarpedon, on the beach as they were embarking. Next the adventurers took the large island of Thasus, off the Thracian coast, and turned it over to their Parian hostages, the sons of Androgeus. When the Greek ship reached Torone, on the peninsula of Sithonia, Heracles was challenged to a wrestling match by Polygonus and Telegonus, sons of Proteus. He killed them both. No further events are recorded in the homeward voyage, at the end of which Heracles delivered Hippolyte's belt to Eurystheus. [Apollodorus 2.5.8–9; Homer, *Iliad*, 20.144–148; Hyginus, *Fabulae*, 30–31; Ovid, *Metamorphoses*, 194–217.]

H. As a tenth labor Eurystheus demanded that Heracles bring back to him the *cattle of Geryon*, king of Erytheia or Erythrea, now called Cadiz. Geryon, son of Callirrhoë and Chrysaor, had three heads, or else the body of three men from the waist down. His cattle were guarded by a herdsman named Eurytion, aided by Orthus, a two-headed hound born of Typhon and Echidna.

For some reason, Heracles set out by way of Libya, killing many wild beasts on his way. Reaching the Strait of Gibraltar, he set up pillars on both the African and European sides to show future travelers how far he had come. These monuments, still occasionally called the Pillars of Hercules, are the promontories Calpe (now the Rock of Gibraltar) and Abyla (now the Jebel Musa, at Ceuta, Morocco). Some say, however, that Heracles built these barriers in order to bar sea-monsters from the Mediterranean Sea, or, on the other hand, that the capes were originally joined and Heracles either wrenched them apart or dug a channel between them to provide access to the open sea beyond.

Heracles, wearied by the sun's heat, dared to draw his bow at Helius. The sun-god admired his boldness and lent him his enormous golden cup for a boat. In this craft Heracles sailed north along the Atlantic coast of Spain to Erytheia. He waited on Mount Abas until Orthus rushed at him. Heracles killed the animal with his club and gave the same treatment to his master, Eurytion, when he followed. He would have gone off with the cattle without troubling Geryon, but Menoetes, who was pasturing Hades' cattle in the same region, told the king what had happened. Geryon came rushing after the thief. Heracles turned on him at the river Anthemus and shot him dead. He then sailed to nearby Tartessus, returned the boat to Helius, and headed eastward on foot.

Passing through Abderia, in southern Spain, Heracles soon came to Liguria, the region about what is now Marseilles. There he was attacked by Ialebion and Dercynus, sons of Pos, who tried to steal the cattle. Heracles killed them, but was then attacked by a large force of Ligurians. After a fierce battle, he fell to his knees wounded and would almost surely have been killed if Zeus had not caused a shower of stones to fall. Still on his knees, Heracles pelted his enemies with these stones until they retreated. The stones still litter the plains west of Marseilles.

While Heracles, proceeding down the Italian peninsula, rested on the future site of Rome, some of his cattle were stolen by the giant Cacus. Cacus dragged them by the tails to the cave where he lived and Heracles was unable to follow their trail. As he was passing the cave with his lowing herd, one of the hidden cows lowed in answer. Cacus barricaded himself in his cave, but Heracles tore it open and killed the giant. The people of the region gratefully honored Heracles as a hero for disposing of the notorious and dangerous thief.

(According to a strange story told by Herodotus [4.8–10], Heracles somehow wandered on his homeward journey as far as the land north of the Black Sea, where he came to a region called merely Forest. While he slept, some mares that he had with him disappeared. He awoke and in searching for the horses came upon a cave. In it lived a woman whose body was that of a snake from the waist down. She readily admitted that she had the mares, but refused to give them up unless Heracles lay with her. He consented, but she delayed him in the country, of which she was queen, until he had given her three sons. As she finally gave up the horses, she asked what she should do with the boys when they grew up. Heracles gave her one of his two bows and told her that the son who could draw it should become king in her land, but the other two should be sent away. When the three boys reached manhood, only the youngest, Scythes, could draw the bow. He became the king and eponym of the Scythians. His brothers, Agathyrsus and Gelonus, were exiled, but gave their names to other powerful tribes.)

Heracles continued southward, but when he arrived at Rhegium, at the southern tip of the Italian peninsula, the finest bull of Geryon's herd broke away and swam across the channel to Sicily. Heracles left the rest of the herd in Hephaestus' keeping and followed the bull as it ran the length of the island. It reached the region of Eryx, at the western end, where King ERYX mingled it with his own herd. Heracles found the bull there and demanded its return. Eryx, a famous wrestler or boxer, was so sure of his own strength that he wagered his kingdom against Heracles' herd. Heracles killed him either in boxing or, after winning three matches, in wrestling. He could not remain to take possession of the land. Many centuries later, however, a Greek force under Dorieus tried, unsuccessfully, to wrest the land from its inhabitants, claiming it as descendants of Heracles.

The eleventh labor imposed on Heracles by Eurystheus was to bring to the king the *apples of the Hesperides*. (Many accounts call this the final labor, saying that it followed the capture of Cerberus.) These golden fruit, which Ge had once given as a wedding present to Hera, grew in a grove somewhere at the ends of the earth. There they were tended by nymphs, the Hesperides, with the aid of a hundred-headed snake named Ladon. Heracles did not know where to find the sacred grove, so he visited certain nymphs, daughters of Zeus and Themis, who lived on the Eridanus River. They told him where to find the old sea-god Nereus asleep. Heracles captured Nereus and held him tightly in spite of the many transformations that the god underwent. Finally Nereus returned to his normal form and told his captor where to find the garden. This information was evidently not passed on to ancient writers, for they have recorded many locations: beyond the river Oceanus or the north wind, or somewhere in the farthest reaches of Libya near the mountains where the Titan Atlas supported the sky on his shoulders. All of these places were in the far west, where one might expect the Hesperides (Daughters of Evening) to live.

On his way Heracles had several adventures, which will be related here in an order that allows for slightly more geographical plausibility than does the account of Apollodorus. At some point—perhaps it was on his way back from the Eridanus—Heracles found himself in the Caucasus Mountains. There he shot and killed the eagle that had for so long made its daily meal of the liver of the bound Prometheus. He then freed the Titan from his bonds (commemorating them by thereafter wearing a wreath of olive about his head). By some accounts, Heracles then arranged that Prometheus become immortal in place of

Cheiron the Centaur. Some say that Prometheus repaid Heracles by advising him to send Atlas for the apples instead of going for them himself.

Passing through Arabia, Heracles killed King Emathion, a son of Tithonus. In Egypt he came to the city of King Busiris, a son of Poseidon by Lysianassa, daughter of Io's son, Epaphus. This ruler had once called in a foreign seer when his land was struck by famine. The seer said that he must sacrifice a foreigner each year to Zeus if he wished the city to become and remain free of famine. Busiris demonstrated his faith in this advice by sacrificing the seer as the first victim. He had killed strangers to the land ever since. Heracles allowed himself to be dressed for the sacrifice and dragged to the altar. There he broke his bonds and killed both the king and his son, Amphidamas.

Moving westward through Libya, he encountered King Antaeüs, a son of Ge (Earth), who made a practice of forcing strangers to wrestle with him and killing them either in the course of the match or afterward, when they were exhausted. Heracles was able to throw Antaeüs several times, but noticed that whenever he struck the ground he seemed to gather renewed strength. Realizing that his foe's strength was coming from contact with his mother, Earth, he lifted him into the air and crushed him to death in a great bear hug.

Moving constantly westward, Heracles came at last to the spot where Atlas stood, holding the sky on his shoulders. Heracles offered to relieve him of the weight temporarily if he would fetch the apples from the nearby garden. The Titan was more than happy to oblige. When he returned in a little while, however, it became apparent that he had no intention of resuming the tiresome burden. He offered instead to take the apples to Eurystheus himself. With the sky on his back Heracles found himself helpless to escape from his predicament through boldness or main strength and was forced to resort to his wits. He pretended to be willing to agree to Atlas' proposal, but he begged the Titan to hold the sky just long enough to allow him to place a pad on his head. The gullible giant laid down the apples and took back the sky. Once free of it, Heracles picked up the prize and strode away eastward.

According to some accounts, Heracles himself stole the apples from the garden, after killing Ladon. (Some say that the constellation of the Kneeler shows Heracles fighting either the snake or the Ligurians.) Shortly thereafter his former companions the ARGONAUTS [R] were saved from dying of thirst in the Libyan Desert when the bereaved Hesperides took pity on them and showed them a spring that Heracles, with a petulant kick, had caused to gush forth beneath a rock. Heracles meanwhile took the apples to Eurystheus at Tiryns without further interruptions. Eurystheus quickly returned them to Heracles, who as quickly turned them over to Athena, presumably by dedicating them at her shrine. Athena gave them back to their original guardians, the Hesperides, for it was not proper that the sacred fruit should remain in anyone else's keeping. [Apollodorus 2.5.11; Hyginus, *Fabulae*, 30–31, and *Poetica Astronomica*, 2.3, 2.6; Hesiod, *Theogony*, 523–531; Diodorus Siculus 4.26.2–4.27.5.]

I. Eurystheus now demanded that Heracles bring up *Cerberus* from Hades as his final labor (though some say that this task preceded that of fetching the golden apples). Cerberus, a hound with three or fifty heads and a snake's tail, was one of the many monstrous offspring of Typhon and Echidna, and brother of the Hydra, the hound Orthus, and the Nemean lion. He acted as the watchdog at the gates of Hades. In preparation for this, the most difficult of all his trials, Heracles went to Eleusis in order to be initiated into the Eleusinian mysteries. First he had to be purified, by Eumolpus, of his murder of the Centaurs; then, since foreigners could not be initiated, he observed the formality of adoption by Pylius. Finally he was inducted into the ranks of the initiates, either by Eumolpus or by Musaeüs, son of Orpheus.

Heracles now proceeded to Taenarum and, guided by Hermes and perhaps by Athena as well, descended to the Underworld. When he entered the gates, the shades of the dead fled from him, except for those of Meleager and the Gorgon Medusa. He drew his sword against the Gorgon, but Hermes told him that it was only a phantom. Near the gates he saw Theseus and Peirithoüs, who had been bound to the chairs of forgetfulness by Hades when they attempted to abduct Persephone. They held out their arms imploringly. Heracles wrenched Theseus loose, but when he tried to do the same for Peirithoüs the earth quaked and he was afraid to persist. (Some say, however, that Hades released Theseus at Heracles' request.) He rolled away the stone which Demeter had laid on Ascalaphus, who had informed on Persephone when she ate the pomegranate seeds. Taking pity on the thirsty shades, Heracles killed one of Hades' cattle so that they might drink the blood. Hades' cowherd, Menoetes or Menoetius, rushed to defend his charges, but Heracles wrestled with him and cracked his ribs. He would have killed him if Persephone had not begged him to stop.

Heracles now demanded of Hades that he be permitted to carry off Cerberus. Some say that the god agreed, if Heracles could do so without the use of weapons. Others claim that Heracles fought with Hades and wounded him so severely that the god had to flee to Olympus to be treated by Paeëon, the gods' physician. (Uncertainty over the meaning of a word in Homer's account of this event in the *Iliad* has led many to believe that it happened later, during Heracles' war with Pylus.) In either case, Heracles went off dragging the hellhound, and emerged into daylight at one or another of the many entrances to Hades. He took Cerberus to Eurystheus, who told Heracles, from a safe distance, to take him back again. Heracles dutifully did so. [Apollodorus 2.5.12; Homer, *Iliad*, 5.395–402, and *Odyssey*, 11.601–625.]

J. Having at last completed the twelve labors, Heracles was now due the immortality that the Pythia had predicted would be his reward. While he remained on earth, however, he was subject to all the pain and hardships to which mortals are heir. Hera, in her undying enmity toward her husband's son, saw to it that these trials should be greater than those any ordinary man could bear.

Heracles did not return to Thebes, but instead gave his wife, Megara, to Iolaüs and set out to find a new wife for himself. He claimed as his reason for this act that, since his children by Megara had died (by his own hand), the marriage was obviously an unlucky one.

Hearing that Eurytus, king of Oechalia, was offering his daughter, Iole, as a prize for anyone who could prove himself a better archer than himself and his sons, Heracles set out to try his skill against them. The location of Oechalia was much disputed among ancient writers, who placed it in regions as far apart as Messenia, in the western Peloponnesus, and Euboea, off the eastern coast of Boeotia. Wherever it may have been, Heracles came to Oechalia and defeated Eurytus, who had long before been his own teacher in the use of bow and arrow. Eurytus, recalling Heracles' murder of his own children in a fit of madness, refused to give his daughter to him, in spite of the pleas of his elder son Iphitus that he honor his pledge.

Heracles left Oechalia, vowing vengeance. Some say that he drove some of Eurytus' mares (or cattle) with him, others that Autolycus was the thief. In either case Eurytus suspected Heracles. Iphitus refused to believe in his guilt. He found Heracles near Pherae (where some say he had just saved Alcestis) and invited him to accompany him in his search for the missing mares. Heracles entertained Iphitus at Tiryns, where he was now living, then flung Iphitus from the roof of his house, or from the walls of Tiryns. Those who consider Heracles innocent of the theft explain that Hera had once again driven him mad. Others believe that the act was deliberate.

Whichever was the case, Heracles was punished with a terrible disease. He asked Neleus, king of Pylus, to purify him of the murder, but Neleus, an ally of Eurytus, refused. Deïphobus, son of Hippolytus or Hippocoön, agreed and Heracles was purified at Amyclae, but the disease did not leave him. He therefore went to Delphi to ask advice of the oracle. Xenocleia, who was then the Pythia, refused to speak to him. Heracles not only stole her tripod but threatened to destroy Delphi and set up his own oracle. When Apollo tried to prevent him, Heracles fought with him until Zeus flung a thunderbolt between them. The Pythia now said that Heracles would be cured only if he permitted himself to be sold into slavery for three years and gave the price to the sons of Iphitus. Heracles regretfully agreed.

He was sold to Omphale, daughter of Iardanes and queen of Lydia, who had succeeded her late husband, Tmolus, as ruler. While acting as her servant, Heracles performed many feats of boldness and strength. He captured the wily Cercopes at Ephesus and killed with his own hoe Syleus of Aulis, together with his daughter, Xenodice. It had been Syleus' custom to force passersby to till his vineyard. Heracles razed the city of Itoni, whose people had long harried Omphale's land. Finally he killed a great snake that had been ravaging both crops and men near the river Sagaris, an event that is commemorated in the constellation Ophiuchus, the Serpent-Holder.

Certain Roman authors claimed that during his stay in Lydia Heracles wore effeminate dress and occupied his time with music and even with spinning in order to please Omphale. Whether this was true, Omphale was so grateful to her unusual slave that she freed him. Some add that she married him and bore a son, Lamus. Heracles had another son, Cleodaeüs, by a slave girl. At either the beginning or the end of his period of servitude Heracles was restored to health, as the oracle had predicted. On his return voyage to Greece he found the corpse of Icarus, which had washed ashore on the island of Doliche. He buried the body and renamed the island Icaria. [Apollodorus 2.6.1–3; Homer, *Odyssey*, 21.22–38; Diodorus Siculus 4.31.1–8; Pausanias 10.13.8, 10.29.7.]

K. Free once again to follow his own bent, Heracles set out to avenge himself on various kings who had insulted him at one time or another. Perhaps because he found himself in Asia Minor, he is said by some to have chosen to begin with Laomedon, who had refused to pay the reward that he had promised Heracles for rescuing his daughter Hesione (see G, above). First he returned to Greece to recruit a navy. It did not take long to find enough volunteers to sail against Troy with eighteen fifty-oared ships. Telamon, king of Salamis, was Heracles' chief lieutenant on this expedition. On reaching the coast near Troy, Heracles advanced on the city, leaving Oïcles, an Argive, to guard the ships. The Trojans managed to outflank the Greeks and reach the shore. They killed Oïcles and would have burned the ships if the Greeks had not returned to the attack.

The Trojans were driven inside their gates, and the Greeks might have had to settle in for a long and costly siege of the strong-walled city if Telamon had not managed to breach the wall. This success nearly cost him his life—not by Trojan arms but at the hands of his own general. Heracles felt insulted that his lieutenant had been the first to enter Troy. Telamon must have been well acquainted with Heracles' character. Seeing him advancing with drawn sword, the shrewd Salaminian diligently began to gather stones into a heap. Heracles demanded to know what he was doing. "I am building an altar to Heracles, the Glorious Victor," Telamon said. His vanity flattered, Heracles forgot his anger. Together the two entered the city.

Heracles killed Laomedon and all his sons but Podarces, who, according to some accounts, had sided with the Greeks against his unscrupulous father. He seized Hesione, Laomedon's daughter, and the mares (both having been part of the pay that Laomedon had withheld) and took many captives. He allowed Hesione to choose one of these captives to be freed. She chose her surviving brother, Podarces. Heracles consented, provided that she pay a token ransom for him. At this she gave up her veil. Podarces, who remained behind and became king of Troy, was thereafter called Priam, from *priamai*, a form of the verb "to buy." Heracles then gave Hesione to Telamon as his concubine. She later bore him a son, Teucer. Heracles, apparently still overcome with gratitude for Telamon's flattery, prayed to his father, Zeus, to send his friend a worthy son. An eagle, Zeus's bird, appeared and the two men knew that the god had heard. In due course Telamon's wife, Eëriboea, bore a son and Telamon named him Ajax (Aias), for the eagle (*aietos*).

This new success of Heracles' so enraged Hera that she sent violent northerly winds against the Greek vessels and drove them the length of the coast of Asia Minor to the island of Cos. In doing so, the goddess overreached herself. Zeus was so angry at her incessant persecution of his son that he hung her by the wrists from the heights of Olympus, with anvils attached to her feet. The Coans (who were also called Meropes, in honor of an early king, Merops) thought that the Greeks were pirates and tried to drive them away with stones. The Greeks took the city by night. Heracles killed King Eurypylus, a son of Pos by Astypalaea. He was wounded by Chalcodon, but Zeus snatched him away in time to save him from death.

The gods had good reason to preserve Heracles' life. They were engaged at the moment in a battle with the Giants. An oracle had declared that these formidable enemies could not be defeated without a mortal's help, and Heracles was clearly the only mortal qualified to undertake such a task. As soon as he had razed Cos, Athena appeared and conducted him to the volcanic plains of Phlegra, where the battle was raging. Fighting side by side with the gods, Heracles shot the Giant Ephialtes in the right eye, while Apollo shot him in the left. Single-handedly Heracles shot Alcyoneus and dragged him to Pallene, the peninsula that juts from Chalcidice, where he died. Having thus given aid to the gods, he returned to his own affairs. [Apollodorus 1.6.1–2, 2.6.4–2.7.1; Homer, *Iliad*, 14.249–262, 20.144–148; Pindar, *Nemean Odes*, 1.67–69, 4.22–30, and *Isthmian Odes*, 6.27–54; Ovid, *Metamorphoses*, 11.194–217; Diodorus Siculus 4.49.3–7.]

L. After the interruptions at Cos and Phlegra, Heracles continued his campaign of vengeance on his enemies. He had killed Laomedon for refusing to pay a promised fee; he now sought out another king who had treated him similarly, Augeias, king of Elis (see F, above). Raising an army in Arcadia, he marched against Elis. The expedition was a disastrous failure. Augeias had powerful generals in Amarynceus and in the Moliones, sons of Actor who may have been Siamese twins. Heracles' army was defeated, partly perhaps because of an illness that Heracles suffered. Heracles returned to Tiryns, only to be exiled by Eurystheus on the pretext that he was plotting to overthrow the government. He made his home for a time at Pheneüs, in northern Arcadia.

On recovering his health, Heracles waited until the Isthmian games were about to be celebrated. He hid by the road through Cleonae and shot the Moliones, who were on their way as the Eleian ambassadors to the games. Without the support of these two allies, the aged Augeias was unable to resist a second invasion by Heracles and his Arcadians. Some say that Heracles killed Augeias, others that he merely deposed him. In either event he called Augeias' son Phyleus home from exile and placed him on the throne of Elis. While he was in this region Heracles celebrated the Olympic games and established various shrines at Olympus, including one for his great-grandfather Pelops. Although he is often credited with founding the Olympic games, this honor really belongs to a much earlier Heracles, the Idaean Dactyl.

Heracles had not forgiven Neleus, king of Pylus, for his refusal to purify him after his murder of Iphitus. He therefore marched on Pylus and killed Neleus and eleven of his sons. One of these, Periclymenus, had the power to change his shape. Heracles shot him while he was in the form of an eagle. Nestor, the youngest of Neleus' sons, survived this invasion because he was living in Gerenia at the time. (According to many accounts, the Pylians were aided in their war with Heracles by Hades, but this statement may result from a misreading of Homer.)

Heracles now turned his attention to Neleus' allies—Hippocoön, king of Sparta, and his sons. Hippocoön had usurped the rule after driving out his brother Tyndareüs. He had doubly offended Heracles: he had, like Neleus, refused to purify him after the murder of Iphitus, and his twelve sons had murdered Heracles' young cousin Oeonus for throwing a stone at their dog. Heracles sought help from Cepheus, king of Tegea, in Arcadia, before attacking powerful Sparta. Cepheus was reluctant to go because he feared that during his absence other enemies might take Tegea. Heracles presented Cepheus' daughter Sterope with a lock of hair of the Gorgon Medusa, given him by Athena. (Some say that the king received it directly from the goddess.) He assured her that, if the city were besieged, she need only hold up the lock three times on the city wall, averting her own eyes, and the enemies would be routed. While carrying on these negotiations, Heracles seduced Cepheus' sister, Auge, who bore a son, Telephus.

Cepheus finally consented to accompany Heracles. Tegea remained safe, as Heracles had promised, but Cepheus and his sons were killed. Heracles' half-brother, Iphicles, was also killed in the fierce fighting at Sparta, but Heracles ultimately avenged his friends and relatives by killing Hippocoön and all his sons. He was wounded in the engagement, but cured by Asclepius. Recalling Tyndareüs from his haven in Aetolia, he restored him to power. [Apollodorus 2.7.2–4; Pausanias 2.15.1, 2.18.7, 3.15.3–6, 5.8.3–4; *Catalogues of Women* 10–11.]

M. Having conquered his enemies in the Peloponnesus, Heracles now left Arcadia and went to live with King Oeneus in Calydon. He fell in love with the king's daughter Deïaneira, but had a rival in Acheloüs, the Aetolian river-god. The two wrestled for the girl and Heracles broke off one of the god's horns. Some say that Heracles presented the horn to the Hesperides or to some unidentified nymphs, and they filled it with fruits and called it the Cornucopia. Others claim, however, that Acheloüs begged his horn back and gave Heracles in its place the horn of Amaltheia, who, either a nymph or a goat, had been Zeus's nurse. Hyginus [*Fabulae* 31, 33] claimed that Deïaneira was Dexamenus' daughter and that Heracles killed the Centaur Eurytion when he tried to carry her off, but Hyginus seems to have confused Deïaneira with Mnesimache (see F, above).

Heracles married Deïaneira and repaid her father by leading the Calydonians against their northern enemies the Thesprotians. He took the Thesprotian city of Ephyra and seduced Astyoche, daughter of King Phylas. She bore a son, Tlepolemus. While in Ephyra, Heracles sent directions to king Thespius about the fifty sons he had fathered in his youth on Thespius' fifty daughters. A number of them were to go with Iolaüs to found a colony in Sardinia. (This voyage, however, must have been undertaken considerably later, for Iolaüs remained on Greek soil for some time after Heracles' death.) While in Thesprotia, Heracles took a fancy to the white poplar tree and introduced it to the Peloponnesus.

Heracles returned to Calydon and would have settled there except for an unfortunate accident. During a banquet he was served with wine, or with water for washing, by Oeneus' cupbearer and relative, Eunomus or Cyathus, son of Architeles. Something that the boy did annoyed Heracles, who gave him a rap with his knuckles. The boy dropped dead. Oeneus forgave his son-in-law, since the killing was accidental, but Heracles felt that he should observe the law that murderers, intentional or otherwise, be exiled. He therefore moved on once more, heading for Trachis with his new wife. (For some reason, the Phlians claimed that Eunomus' death occurred in their city, where Oeneus was visiting.)

Not long after leaving Calydon, Heracles and Deïaneira came to the river Evenus. The Centaur Nessus, driven from Arcadia long before by Heracles, had established a profitable trade here ferrying travelers across the river. The rascally Centaur was impudent enough to claim that he had received the franchise from the gods as a reward for his virtue. Heracles needed no ferry for himself but hired Nessus' services for his new bride. As he was striding breast-deep through the water he heard Deïaneira cry out for help. He pushed his way to the far shore and shot Nessus as he was in the act of raping his beautiful passenger.

Dying, Nessus pretended to the naive Deïaneira to be remorseful. He told her to take his bloody tunic, or else to collect his spilled blood and semen and smear them on Heracles' tunic, where they would act as a love charm. Deïaneira, knowing that her husband had already taken one concubine in the short time since their marriage, thought it quite likely that she might need such a charm one day. Unaware that the treacherous Centaur's blood had been poisoned by the deadly venom of the Hydra on Heracles' arrow, she followed Nessus' directions and saved the potion for future use.

Heracles and Deïaneira continued on their way to Trachis, in the neighborhood of Mount Oeta. In this region of Doris, north of Mount Parnassus, Heracles formed a number of alliances, which, however, are confusing to trace in surviving accounts. He drove the Dryopes from Doris. This task was undertaken to aid either the Malian king Ceÿx, who had welcomed him to Trachis; or Aegimius, king of the Dorians of Hestiaeotis; or perhaps both. In this war he killed Laogoras, a Dryopian king. He then advanced against Aegimius' neighbor enemies the Lapiths, who were ruled by Coronus, son of Caeneus. He killed Coronus and routed the Lapiths, but refused to accept the land that Aegimius had promised him as a reward.

Proceeding, for some reason, northward to Itonus, in Phthiotis, Heracles was challenged to single combat by Cycnus, son of Ares and Pelopia. Cycnus, a formidable foe in his own right, was aided by his father. Athena undertook to advise Heracles. He killed Cycnus and wounded the god, but followed Athena's counsel in not pursuing him. Some say, however, that he fought Ares until Zeus flung a thunderbolt between them. Another account places this battle on the river Echedorus in Macedonia, to which Heracles had come in his search for the garden of the Hesperides. At Ormenium, not far from Itonus, Heracles' way was barred by King Amyntor. Heracles killed him and went on his way. [Apollodorus 2.7.5–2.7.7; Herodotus 8.43; *Shield of Heracles* 57–480; Diodorus Siculus 4.34.1–4.37.4.]

N. Heracles now began his final adventure. He had never forgiven Eurytus, king of Oechalia, for refusing to give him Iole, the promised prize in the archery contest that he had won. Leaving Deïaneira in Trachis, he raised an army of Malians, Locrians, and Arcadians and advanced on Oechalia. Eurytus and his surviving sons fought bravely, killing Ceÿx' son Hippasus and Licymnius' sons Argius and Melas, but Heracles killed them at last. Triumphantly he took Iole as his concubine. Coming to Cape Cenaeüm, in northwestern Euboea, he built an altar to his father, Zeus. He wished to observe the rites of sacrifice with all propriety, so he sent his herald Lichas to Trachis to fetch from Deïaneira a fresh tunic. Some say that he sent Iole as well, along with other captive women. Deïaneira, learning of her husband's new young concubine, feared that he would discard her as he had earlier discarded Megara. She remembered Nessus' supposed love charm and smeared it on the tunic, or else sent Nessus' tunic. Lichas took it to his master, who put it on.

At once the Hydra's venom, which Heracles had used to destroy so many enemies, began to do its work, eroding his skin. He tore off the tunic, but the flesh came away with it. In agony Heracles picked up the innocent Lichas, whirled him about by his heels, and flung him into the sea, where his body, turned to stone, still bears his name. The dying Heracles returned to Trachis, where Deïaneira, learning of the horror that she had unknowingly worked, killed herself.

Accompanied by Hyllus, the eldest son by Deïaneira (or the nymph Melite), Heracles climbed to the top of Mount Oeta. Hyllus, at his father's command, built a pyre, but when Heracles had climbed upon it, neither his son nor any of the mourners could bring himself to set it afire. Finally Poeas, passing by with his flocks, or else his son, Philoctetes, consented to light the pyre. In gratitude Heracles gave him his bow and arrows. The flames rose to burn away what was mortal in Heracles. As they were dying out, a cloud enveloped the pyre and lightning struck. When the cloud had passed, the mourners could find no remains of the dead hero.

Heracles had at last achieved the immortality that he had won with his twelve labors. He ascended to Olympus, where Hera became reconciled to him and even, some say, adopted him. He married her daughter, Hebe, and lived forever among the gods. He was also to be seen among the stars. When Iolaüs, then an old man, was trying to defend Heracles' children against Eurystheus, Heracles persuaded Hebe (Youth) to renew Iolaüs' youth, and, as two stars, he and Hebe rode into battle with the now vigorous leader. Later Heracles appeared to PHILOCTETES and commanded him to give up his hatred of the Greeks and go to the Trojan War, where he would kill Paris with Heracles' bow.

O. The stories of Heracles, his twelve labors, and many other exploits were well known to the ancients. Euripides' play *Heracles* depicts the murder of his wife and children in his first fit of madness. Sophocles' *Women of Trachis* portrays Deïaneira's innocent betrayal and Heracles' death. Heracles appears also at the end of Sophocles' *Philoctetes*. The fullest account of his career is that of Apollodorus [2.4.8–2.7.7]. Diodorus Siculus also tells the story at length [4.9.1–4.39.4], but his version often attempts to give rational explanations of the events which obscure the original myths. Hyginus' account [*Fabulae* 29–36] is both sketchy and confused, but contains some interesting details. References to Heracles in other Classical sources are innumerable.

Heracles the Dactyl. The leader of the Idaean Dactyls. Heracles was a son of Zeus who is said to have lived at a very early period. He wandered through the known world punishing injustice and killing savage animals. Coming to Elis with four brothers, he founded the Olympic games. The nature of his exploits resembles that of the labors of the later and more famous Heracles. It is not certain to what degree this fact caused or resulted from the frequent confusion between the two. [Diodorus Siculus 5.76.1–2; Pausanias 5.7.6–9.]

Heraclids or **Heracleidae.** Descendants of HERACLES.

A. Though born in Thebes, Heracles regarded himself as Argive and would have inherited the throne of Mycenae or Tiryns if Hera had not arranged that his cousin Eurystheus be born first. After Heracles' death Eurystheus feared that the hero's children might one day exact vengeance for his lifelong persecution of their father. Because Eurystheus, as king of Mycenae and Tiryns, was the most powerful of Greek rulers, no other city was willing to risk his wrath by offering refuge to Heracles' children. Ceÿx, king of Trachis, who had cared for them while their father lived, now suggested that they go to Athens, where Theseus might be persuaded to protect them.

Led by Iolaüs, Heracles' nephew and charioteer, they went as suppliants to the Altar of Mercy in Athens, or to Marathon, where Theseus, or his son Demophon, agreed to help them. When Eurystheus demanded their surrender, the Athenian king refused and met Eurystheus' forces in battle at Marathon. An oracle had warned that the Athenians would be defeated unless a highborn young woman were sacrificed. Heracles' daughter Macaria volunteered to be the victim and the Athenians routed the invaders and killed Eurystheus' sons. Either Iolaüs or Heracles' son Hyllus pursued Eurystheus as far as the Sceironian Rocks on the Isthmus of Corinth and there killed or captured him. According to some accounts, Eurystheus' body was buried on the spot, but his head was brought to Heracles' mother, Alcmene, who pricked out his eyes with weaving pins. Euripides claims, in *Children of Heracles*, that Eurystheus was brought alive before Alcmene and that she condemned him to death, although the Athenians protested that killing a prisoner of war was an impious act. Eurystheus predicted to the Athenians that his body would protect the city from attack, particularly from the descendants of Heracles. He was buried between Athens and Marathon, or else his head was buried at Tricorythus, his body at Gargettus, both of which towns were strategic points on the approaches to Athens.

B. The Heraclids, now under Hyllus, captured many cities in the Peloponnesus, but a year later a plague broke out which an oracle blamed on this premature invasion. Hyllus withdrew his forces, but, encouraged by the Delphic oracle's prophecy that the Heraclids would succeed in "the third crop," he made a second attempt three years later to win the Peloponnesus. The Peloponnesian armies under Atreus (who, with his brother, Thyestes, had succeeded to Eurystheus' throne) met the Heraclids on the isthmus. Hyllus suggested that the issue be settled by a duel between himself and some Argive champion, promising that if he lost there would be no more Heraclid invasions for half a century. Echemus, king of Arcadia, accepted the challenge and killed Hyllus, who was buried at Megara. The Heraclids withdrew once again (except for Licymnius and Tlepolemus, who were allowed to settle in Argos). Later Hyllus' grandson Aristomachus was killed in an abortive raid, but apart from this mishap the Heraclids honored Hyllus' promise.

Either fifty or one hundred years after the death of Heracles, the sons of Aristomachus—Temenus, Cresphontes, and Aristodemus—again asked the Delphic oracle when the Heraclids might conquer the Peloponnesus. They were given the same answer as before: "In the third crop." When Temenus pointed out that following this advice had caused the death of his great-grandfather, the oracle replied that it had been Hyllus' fault for not understanding that "the third crop" meant the third generation. Moreover, when the oracle had directed them to advance via "the narrows," it had meant not the isthmus, as Hyllus had assumed, but the wide Gulf of Corinth. Whatever the sons of Aristomachus might have thought of this explanation, they decided that they should try again to win Heracles' homeland. Accordingly they outfitted a fleet at Naupactus, on the northern shore of the gulf.

This attempt was no more successful than those of Hyllus and Aristomachus. Aristodemus was killed by lightning at Naupactus, the fleet was destroyed in a storm, and a plague decimated the army. When Temenus demanded a further explanation from the oracle, he was told that his forces were being punished for the murder of a soothsayer whom they had taken for a spy. The oracle added mysteriously that the Heraclids should be guided by "a three-eyed one." Temenus exiled Hippotes, the seer's killer, for ten years and, on meeting a man riding a one-eyed horse, engaged him as guide for the expedition, promising him the kingship of Elis as his reward.

C. For a last time the Heraclids set out to conquer the Peloponnesus. Their leaders were the two surviving sons of Aristomachus and their dead brother's sons, Procles and Eurysthenes, who were to divide Aristodemus' share of the lands between them. They sailed across the Gulf of Corinth to Molycrium or to Rhium. From there the easiest route to the southern Peloponnesus lay through Elis, but Oxylus, their guide, shrewdly suspected that if the Heraclids saw this fertile land they might regret their promise to give it to him. He therefore led the army by a less attractive route through mountainous Arcadia. Arriving in Argolis, the Heraclids attacked Argos, defeating King Tisamenus, son of Orestes. Tisamenus was killed either in this battle or later in Achaea, where he and his fleeing Argives were attempting to settle.

The Heraclid leaders now drew lots for kingship of the three chief regions that they wished to rule: Argos, Sparta, and Messenia. There are two versions of this story. In both, Cresphontes won Messenia by trickery, Argos fell to Temenus, and Sparta went to the sons of Aristodemus. These young twins hated each other so fervently that they founded two separate ruling houses in Sparta. They were, nevertheless, more fortunate than their uncles, who did not live to enjoy their new kingdoms for long. Temenus was deposed, and perhaps killed, by his own sons because he showed preference over them for his son-in-law, Deïphontes. Deïphontes withdrew to Epidaurus and became its king.

Cresphontes was accepted as ruler in Messenia, from which he exiled the principal descendants of Neleus. Perhaps in order to break the power of the old Messenian nobility, he favored the common people in his rulings. For this he was overthrown and killed by two of his sons and Polyphontes. He was later avenged by his third son, Aepytus, who established a just and peaceable rule that was to last for several generations. The Heraclids honored their promise to Oxylus by offering him Elis, but they seem to have left him to find his own way of conquering it. The king, Dius, was unwilling to yield the throne to the invader, who was supported by only a small band of Aetolians, but he agreed to Oxylus' suggestion that they settle the matter by a single combat. The Aetolian champion won. Like Aepytus, Oxylus proved a just and clever ruler, and brought considerable prosperity to Elis.

D. The Greeks of Classical times referred to the invasion of the Peloponnesus as the "return of the Heraclids," and associated it with the Dorian invasion which Thucydides [1.12.3] placed eighty years after the fall of Troy. The Dorians justified their seizure of Pylus and Sparta by claiming that Heracles, after wresting these cities from Neleus and Hippocoön, respectively, had merely left them in trust to Nestor and Tyndareüs. As for Argos, Heracles' claim to it as a descendant of Perseus was stronger than that of Tisamenus, who was descended from the Eleian interloper Pelops. Pausanias' account suggests that, in fact, the final return was met with no very great resistance, except perhaps in Argos, and that the Heraclid-Dorian rulers, particularly in Messenia and Elis, were shrewd enough to honor the religion and customs of their Achaean predecessors and to give due deference to their nobility. On the other hand, it is evident that Pausanias' informants favored the Dorian view of history.

Central though it was as an event in Greek legendary history, the return of the Heraclids is the subject of no surviving work of literary importance. Though Euripides' tragedy *Children of Heracles* chronicles the defeat of Eurystheus, the heroes are less the Heraclids themselves than their Athenian protectors. [Apollodorus 2.8; Pausanias 2.18.7–2.19.2, 3.1.5–9.]

Heraean games. An athletic festival for women held every four years at Olympia. According to legend, the Heraean games were inaugurated by Hippodameia to honor Hera for helping her to win Pelops as her husband. Chloris is said to have won the first event. In Classical times, at least, the contestants ran races with hair unbound and one shoulder bared. The youngest girls ran first, followed by two other groups in order of increasing age. As at the Olympic games, held in the same stadium, the winners were rewarded with crowns of wild olive. They also received a portion of a cow sacrificed to Hera. The Heraean games are thought to have been older than the Olympic games. The earliest building on the site of the temple of Hera, which in its latest form antedates the other buildings at Olympia, probably dated from about 1000 B.C.

Hercules. The modern name of a constellation called by the ancients the Kneeler (Engonasin). The kneeling man represented in this group of stars has been variously identified. He is Hercules fighting the Ligurians or killing Ladon, the snake that guarded the Hesperides' garden. He is Theseus lifting the stone that hid his father's sword. He is Prometheus bound to his crag, or he may be Ixion shackled to his wheel. He is Orpheus being killed by the Thracian women, or perhaps he is another bard, Thamyris, being blinded by the Muses. [Hyginus, *Poetica Astronomica*, 2.6.]

Hercules. See HERACLES.

herm or **herma.** See HERMES [C].

Hermaphroditus. A son of Hermes and Aphrodite. Hermaphroditus, who was also called Atlantiades or Atlantius, after his ancestor Atlas, was reared by naïad nymphs of Lycian Mount Ida. At the age of fifteen the youth, who was one of the most beautiful boys in the world, left his nurses and journeyed to Caria. Not far from Halicarnassus he was noticed by Salmacis, the nymph of a spring that bears her name. She fell madly in love with him, but Hermaphroditus, being inexperienced in such matters, was embarrassed by her advances. She bided her time until she saw him bathing in her spring. Leaping into it, she clung to his body and prayed to the gods that they might never be separated. The bodies of the youth and the nymph fused into one. Hermaphroditus, horrified at the change in himself, prayed to his parents that all other men who bathed in the spring of Salmacis should similarly become half-men. The hermaphrodite, with the bodily proportions of a woman but a man's genitals, became a popular subject in art in late Classical times. [Ovid, *Metamorphoses*, 4.285–388.]

Hermes. The herald and messenger of the gods and guide of travelers, identified by the Romans with Mercury.

A. Zeus fell in love with Maia, a daughter of Atlas and Pleïone. Maia was a shy nymph who lived in a cave on Mount Cyllene, in Arcadia. Zeus often visited her there at night, while Hera was asleep. One day, just at dawn, Maia bore a son. The lad turned out to be remarkably precocious. At noon of his first day on earth he stepped outside of the cave and encountered a tortoise. He killed it, and then and there invented the lyre, using the tortoise's shell for a sounding board and sheep gut for the seven strings.

By evening Hermes tired of the music that he had taught himself and yearned for adventure. Slipping out of the cave, he went to Pieria, where the gods pastured their cattle. He drove fifty of them, belonging to Apollo, to the river Alpheius, confusing the trail by making them straggle through sandy places and by driving them backward. Further, he obscured his own footprints by wearing sandals of brushwood. While passing through Onchestus, in Boeotia, or near Maenalus, in Arcadia, he was observed by an old man named Battus. He bribed Battus to say nothing of what he had seen, but he did not trust him even so. Returning in disguise, he pretended to be seeking the cattle and bribed Battus to tell him where to find them. The old man did so without hesitation. Hermes punished him for his double-dealing by turning him to stone.

On arriving at the Alpheius, Hermes made a fire with firesticks, which he invented for the occasion, and sacrificed two cows to the twelve gods, eating none of the meat himself. He burned the hooves and heads to destroy the evidence and threw his sandals into the Alpheius. At last, when the night was almost over, Hermes returned to the cave. Slipping through the keyhole, he put on his swaddling clothes and lay down in his cradle. Maia, undeceived by her son's tricks, warned him that the gods would be angry with him, but he was unrepentant.

Apollo meanwhile had discovered the theft and came in pursuit of the cattle. Some say that Battus had not been petrified and that he told Apollo that he had seen a small boy driving the beasts. Apollo learned the whereabouts of Hermes from an omen and headed straight for Cyllene. When he came to Maia's cave he searched it, to no avail. He then turned on the baby that was curled up in its cradle trying to look innocent. The god threatened the child with the dismal fate of ruling over other babies in Hades if he did not confess the theft. Hermes pretended ignorance and even swore by his father's head that he not only had not seen Apollo's cows but did not know what cows were, except by hearsay. Apollo refused to believe the wily infant, so the two gods agreed to refer the case to Zeus. Again Hermes denied everything. Zeus was amused at his son's audacity, but ordered him to give up the cattle. Hermes readily agreed.

Apollo, still unappeased, followed the child to the hiding place. There Hermes picked up the lyre that he had thrown down and carelessly began to play it. Enchanted by the music, Apollo forgot his annoyance and made a bargain. He promised that he would give Hermes, in return for the lyre, not only the cows but the office of divine keeper of herds. He also offered to turn over to the younger god the art of divining by pebbles, which was in the keeping of the Thriae, nymphs of Mount Parnassus. Hermes agreed, and received, as a badge of his new office, a shepherd's staff.

B. When Hermes grew up, his father appointed him herald of the Olympian gods and guide to mortal travelers. The symbol of this office was his caduceus (*kerykeion*), or herald's wand. On one occasion Hermes is said to have laid this wand between two fighting snakes. They made peace and permanently twined themselves about the caduceus. The task of guiding men did not end with their deaths. It was Hermes' duty to lead the souls of the dead down to Hades and, on rare occasions, back again.

The young god often aided his fellow gods. During the war between the gods and Giants he killed the Giant Hippolytus, while wearing the cap of darkness. Later, when the monster Typhöeus cut off Zeus's sinews and hid them in a cave in Cilicia, Hermes and Aegipan stole them and restored them to Zeus. On another occasion, however, he hid from Typhöeus in Egypt disguised as an ibis. When the young giants Otus and Ephialtes bound Ares, Hermes released him. He also proved of invaluable aid to Zeus in that god's amours. He killed Argus Panoptes, the monster herdsman set by Hera to guard Zeus's mistress Io. (This act is generally said to account for Hermes' familiar epithet Argeïphontes, interpreted as "Argus-Slayer.") He also rescued the infant Dionysus from the flames that had destroyed Semele.

That Hermes had more than a few affairs of his own is attested by his sons. Many accounts record that Hermes fathered the god Pan on Penelope or a daughter of Dryops, in Arcadia. Myrtilus, Oenomaüs' charioteer, was Hermes' son by Clytië. Polymele, daughter of Phylas, bore Eudorus by him, and the Argonauts Erytus and Echion were his sons by Antineira, daughter of Menetes. Aethalides, herald of the Argonauts, was also Hermes' son.

Hermes fell in love with Catreus' daughter Apemosyne on the island of Rhodes, but discovered to his chagrin that she could run faster than he. He caught her when she slipped and fell on fresh hides that he had placed in her path. No child resulted from this union, however. When the girl's brother, Althaemenes, discovered that Apemosyne was pregnant, he kicked her to death. The god was the father, by Danaüs' daughter Phylodameia, of Pharis, the founder of Pharae. Abderus, the eponym of Abdera, was also his son.

The god seduced Herse, one of Erechtheus' daughters, after, in some accounts, turning her envious sister Agraulus to stone in order to gain access to Herse's bedroom. The offspring of this union was Cephalus. Equally well known among Hermes' children was the thief Autolycus, whose mother was Daedalion's daughter Chione. Philammon, born to her at the same time, was a son of Apollo, who had seduced her on the same day as Hermes. Some say that Hermes found Perseus very attractive, and that this was the reason for the generous assistance that he offered the young man in his expedition against Medusa.

Hermes' greatest passion, however, was reserved for the goddess Aphrodite, who did not return it. Zeus, taking pity on his herald, who had so often aided him in his own amorous adventures, sent his eagle to steal one of Aphrodite's sandals as she bathed in the river Acheloüs. The bird delivered it to Hermes at the Egyptian city of Amythaonia. Aphrodite was unable to recover the lost slipper until she consented to gratify Hermes' desires. (Some, however, say that her lover was not the god but a man named Anaplades.) Hermaphroditus, who bore both his parents' names, was born as a result of this union.

Hermes' principal occupation, aside from guiding the ghosts of the dead to Hades, was to serve Zeus as a herald and factotum. He accompanied the god on his rare visits to earth incognito, such as his appearances at the home of Hyreius, king of Thrace, and at that of Baucis and Philemon. On formal occasions, like the famous contest of Hera, Athena, and Aphrodite before Paris, Hermes acted as herald at Zeus's bidding. Although most of Hermes' appearances on earth were on errands for Zeus, he was kindly disposed toward human beings, particularly on their travels, and was often called Hermes the Helper. He showed this disposition especially clearly in the aid that he gave to Priam in the Greek camp and to Odysseus on Circe's island. Examples of the god's activities as herald of Zeus are innumerable.

C. Hermes' basic function as helper of travelers, human and divine, is believed to have arisen, along with his name, from his origin as god of the stone-heap (*herma* or *hermaion*). Such heaps of stones were erected as markers along paths, often with a larger, pillarlike stone set up in the center of each pile. Hermes' role as guide of souls (Psychopompos) was an extension of his fundamental function. He never quite outgrew his humble beginning, for, although he was often represented in art as a handsome young man wearing winged sandals and a petasos, or traveler's broad-brimmed hat, his most usual

HERMIONE

image was no more than a head on a square pillar that was adorned with a man's genitals. These civilized versions of the ancient, rural herm were found in courtyards of houses, on street corners, and in marketplaces. As a patron of merchants, thieves, and rogues—among whom the Greeks evidently found it hard to distinguish—Hermes was easily urbanized. He was the god of athletic contests and games in general, and invented the knucklebones. Credited by some ancient writers with the development of astronomy, Hermes had a planet of his own: Mercury, called Stilbon by the Greeks.

D. The chief source of the elaborate tale of Hermes' birth and his theft of Apollo's cattle is the delightful *Homeric Hymn to Hermes* [4]. This story was dramatized, with minor changes, by Sophocles in his satyr play *Searching Satyrs,* but only a part of the play is extant. Hermes appears as a character in Aeschylus' *Prometheus Bound* and (without speaking) in his *Eumenides*; in Euripides' *Ion*; and in several Greek and Roman comedies. References to the god in Classical works are too numerous to cite, except for a few of the more detailed ones. These include the following: Homer, *Iliad,* 24.334–469, 24.679–694, and *Odyssey,* 5.28–148, 10.275–308, 24.1–10; *Great Eoiae* 16; *Homeric Hymn to Demeter* 2.334–384; Ovid, *Metamorphoses,* 2.685–835, 8.618–724, 11.303–317; Hyginus, *Fabulae,* 195, and *Poetica Astronomica,* 2.7, 2.16, 2.42; Apollodorus 1.6.2–3, 2.1.3, 2.4.2–3, 3.2.1, 3.4.3, 3.10.2.

Hermione. The daughter of Menelaüs and Helen. Hermione was often said to be Helen's only child, but some say that she bore Nicostratus as well. Hermione was only nine years old when Helen abandoned her to go with Paris to Troy. Later, according to Euripides' *Orestes,* she was held hostage by Orestes for his safety. Through double-dealing or a misunderstanding, Hermione was promised as a bride to both Orestes and Neoptolemus. Some say that Neoptolemus, to whom Menelaüs pledged her at Troy, took her from Orestes on his return from the war. Others claim that Neoptolemus was her first husband. In either case, Orestes married her after Neoptolemus' death, which he may have caused.

Hermione had no children by Neoptolemus. According to Euripides' *Andromache,* she blamed this on spells cast on her by Andromache, her husband's concubine won at Troy. Aided by her father, Hermione would have had both Andromache and Molossus, her son by Neoptolemus, put to death if old Peleus, Neoptolemus' grandfather, had not intervened. Fearing her husband's vengeance, she fled with Orestes to Sparta. After Neoptolemus' death at Delphi she bore Tisamenus by Orestes. This boy succeeded his father as king of Sparta. [Homer, *Odyssey,* 4.5–14.]

hero. A dead man thought to possess special powers. Persons who had demonstrated extraordinary prowess, shrewdness, prophetic powers, or other remarkable traits were believed by the Greeks to be able after their deaths to bring either blessings or harm to the living. Dead kings, bards, seers, and revered heads of families were honored with "hero-sacrifices," which were distinguished from the sacrifices offered to deities. The advice of such personages might be sought after death as it had been in life, and many heroes were thought to have oracular powers. For example, the tomb of Trophonius, the clever architect and thief, became a famous oracular shrine.

Hero-sacrifices were scrupulously carried out, for dead men were likely to be independent, and their benevolence even to their own states or families could not necessarily be relied upon. After the death of Talthybius, for example, the famous herald was more loyal to the interests of his former profession than to the welfare of his homeland. When the Spartans killed some Persian heralds, Talthybius' ghost visited dire punishment upon them. Heroes were believed to confer benefits even on former enemies on occasion, as in the case of Eurystheus, who claimed that his burial at Athens would protect his captors, the Athenians, against future invasions [Euripides, *Children of Heracles*, 1026–1044]. Creon wished to kill the aged Oedipus in order to gain similar advantage from his burial at a boundary of Thebes [Sophocles, *Oedipus at Colonus*, 784–788]. Women as well as men might receive hero-sacrifices, as did Messene, eponym of Messenia.

Herodotus. A Greek historian of the fifth century B.C. Herodotus' only surviving work is a lengthy history, *The Persian Wars*. This book ranges far afield, dealing with a variety of matters that interested its widely traveled author. It is a useful source of information on myths, particularly those connected with Asia Minor.

Herse. A daughter of Cecrops and Agraulus. Herse and her sister, also named Agraulus, betrayed Athena's trust by spying on ERICHTHONIUS. Later Herse was loved by Hermes and, though the envious Agraulus tried to bar the god from her chamber, she bore him a son, Cephalus. [Apollodorus 3.14.2, 3.14.6; Pausanias 1.18.2–3; Ovid, *Metamorphoses*, 2.552–562, 2.708–832.]

Hesiod. A Greek poet of the late eighth century B.C. Almost nothing is known of Hesiod's life except that he was a poor farmer in the Boeotian village of Ascra, at least until he won fame as a poet. Although in the Classical period many works were attributed to Hesiod, only two, *Works and Days* and the *Theogony*, are now generally thought to be his, and some scholars believe that the latter dates from a later period. *Works and Days* contains little mythology except the stories of Prometheus and Pandora and an account of the five ages of men. The *Theogony* recounts the creation of the world, the succession of the ruling deities from Uranus to Zeus, and the wars of the Olympian gods against the Titans and Typhöeus, together with genealogies of the gods and various monsters. The *Theogony* is the most connected extant account of the earliest ages of the universe. Both of Hesiod's works are available in a volume of the Loeb Classical Library.

Hesione. A daughter of Laomedon, king of Troy. When Poseidon sent a sea-monster against Troy, an oracle told Laomedon that he must sacrifice Hesione to it. Some say that he sacrificed a Trojan girl to it periodically, and in time the lot fell to Hesione. In either case, HERACLES [G, K] saved her by killing the monster when she was already chained to a rock by the shore. Laomedon refused to pay Heracles' stipulated price, which included Hesione. Heracles left Troy, but returned later with a large force. He took the city and gave Hesione to his ally, Telamon. He permitted Hesione to save one prisoner of war. She spoke for her brother Podarces and ransomed him with her veil. Thereafter he was called Priam, from *priamai* ("to buy"). Hesione bore a son, Teucer, by Telamon. [Apollodorus 2.5.9, 2.6.4.]

Hespereia or **Hesperia.** A Greek poetic name for Italy. According to Homer, Hespereia was the home of the Phaeacians before they were expelled by the Cyclopes. This imaginary western land (the name means "Land of Evening") was later identified with Italy.

Hesperides. Nymphs who guarded the golden apples. The parentage of the nymphs called Hesperides has been much disputed, as has the whereabouts of their famous garden. They have been called daughters of Nyx (Night), Erebus (Darkness), Phorcys and Ceto, Atlas and Hesperis, and Zeus and Themis. There were three, four, or seven Hesperides, and among the names given them are Aegle, Erytheia, Hestia, Arethusa, Hespere, Hesperusa, and Hespereia. Their pleasure was singing, their duty to guard a grove of trees that produced golden apples.

These apples had been given by Ge to Hera as a wedding present and Hera had asked the nymphs to keep them for her. The trees were planted at some far western corner of the earth—where one might expect to find the Hesperides (Daughters of Evening) dwelling: beyond the river Oceanus, or in the Hyperborean land, or somewhere in western Libya near the mountains of Atlas. The nymphs were aided in their vigil by the immortal snake Ladon, an offspring of Typhon and Echidna that had a hundred heads. The golden apples were eventually stolen by HERACLES [H]—or by Atlas, acting for Heracles—and taken to Eurystheus, but were returned by Athena to the garden because the sacred fruit were not to remain long anywhere else. In the theft of the apples Heracles killed Ladon. Shortly afterward the nymphs, who had temporarily transformed themselves into trees, showed the stranded ARGONAUTS [R] a spring that Heracles had created in the desert. [Apollodorus 2.5.11; Hyginus, *Fabulae*, 30, and *Poetica Astronomica* 2.3.]

Hestia. The hearth, and the goddess of the hearth. Hestia, whom the Romans called Vesta, was the eldest child of Cronus and Rhea. She was the guardian of the hearth and its fire, and therefore the patroness of household activities in general. By extension, she came to be regarded as the guardian of the home, the family, and the community—the larger family. Vesta was worshiped in even so large a state as Rome as mother of the city. At festivals she was invoked first of all the gods. She had, and needed, few shrines, for the hearth of every home and the public hearth of every city were sacred to her.

Hestia had refused marriage with either Poseidon or Apollo, vowing to remain a virgin. Her priestesses at Rome (the Vestal virgins) and elsewhere were unmarried, as were the young girls whose duty it was in most households to tend the hearthfire. [Hesiod, *Theogony*, 453–506; *Homeric Hymn to Aphrodite* 5.21–32; *Homeric Hymns to Hestia* 24, 33; Vergil, *Georgics*, 1408; Pausanias 5.14.4.]

Hicetaon. A Trojan elder. Hicetaon, a son of Laomedon and Strymo, or Leucippe, or Placia, was one of Priam's brothers. He was the father of Melanippus, who was killed in the Trojan War. [Homer, *Iliad*, 3.146–151, 20.236–239, 15.576.]

Hiläeira. A daughter of Leucippus. Hiläeira and her sister Phoebe were betrothed to their uncles Lynceus and Idas, but the Dioscuri abducted and married them.

Hippalcimus or **Hippalmus.** An Argonaut. Hippalcimus was a son of Itonus, son of Boeotus, the eponym of Boeotia. His son Peneleüs led the Boeotian forces to the Trojan War. Hyginus [*Fabulae* 14] calls Hippalcimus a son of Pelops and Hippodameia and says that they came from Pisa, but this is contrary to the usual tradition. [Diodorus Siculus 4.67.7.]

Hippasus. A son of Ceÿx. Hippasus was killed fighting with HERACLES [N] against Eurytus, king of Oechalia.

Hippocoön. A king of Sparta. Hippocoön was a son of Oebalus and the naïad Bateia. He expelled his brother Tyndareüs, the rightful king, from Sparta and usurped the rule. He and his twelve sons later refused, as did their Messenian ally, Neleus, to purify Heracles after his murder of Iphitus. (Some say, however, that his son Deïphobus consented to perform the rite.) They further offended Heracles by killing Oeonus, son of Heracles' uncle Licymnius, for throwing a stone at their dog. Heracles avenged himself by killing Hippocoön and all his sons, after which he restored Tyndareüs to power. [Apollodorus 2.7.3, 3.10.4–5; Pausanias 2.18.7, 3.15.3–6.]

Hippocrene. A spring on Mount Helicon created by PEGASUS with a stamp of his hoof to please the Muses. A similar origin was claimed for another Hippocrene at Troezen.

Hippodamas. An early Aetolian king. According to Ovid [*Metamorphoses* 590–610], Hippodamas, not Aeolus, was the father of Perimele, but the more circumstantial account by Apollodorus [1.7.3–1.7.10] makes him her son by the river-god Acheloüs. He became the father, by an unnamed wife, of Euryte, who married Porthaon and bore Oeneus and five other children.

Hippodameia. A daughter of Oenomaüs, king of Pisa. Oenomaüs killed all of Hippodameia's suitors until PELOPS overthrew and killed him. She bore many children, including Atreus, Thyestes, and Pittheus. Because of her part in murdering Pelops' illegitimate son, Chrysippus, she either killed herself or fled to Midea. Her bones were later returned to Pisa.

Hippodameia. See PEIRITHOÜS.

Hippolochus. A son of Bellerophon and Philonoë. His son Glaucus led the Lycian army at Troy. [Homer, *Iliad*, 6.196.]

Hippolyte (1). An Amazon queen. HERACLES [G] was sent by Eurystheus to Themiscyra to bring back Hippolyte's belt as his ninth labor. Meeting him on board his ship, the queen promised to give him the belt without conflict, but Hera aroused the queen's followers and in the ensuing battle Heracles killed Hippolyte and took the belt. Hippolyte is often confused with her sister ANTIOPE (2) and was said, by Euripides and others, to have been Theseus' wife, the mother of Hippolytus. [Apollodorus 2.5.9.]

Hippolyte (2). A daughter of Cretheus. Hippolyte married Acastus, king of Iolcus, but fell in love with Peleus. Some writers say that Acastus' wife was Astydameia.

Hippolytus (1). The son of Theseus and his mistress the Amazon queen Antiope, or Hippolyte. When THESEUS [G], king of Athens, was about to marry Phaedra, daughter of Minos, he sent Hippolytus to Troezen, intending that he should eventually succeed to the rule of that city, where Pittheus, Theseus' aged grandfather, was king. Later Theseus was himself exiled for a year from Athens and went with his wife to Troezen. Phaedra fell in love with Hippolytus, but he, a follower of the chaste goddess Artemis, spurned her love. She hanged herself, leaving a note for her husband which accused Hippolytus of having raped her. Theseus not only banished his son but called down on his head one of three curses that Poseidon had once granted him. A bull raging out of the sea frightened Hippolytus' horses and he was dragged to his death. Too late, Theseus learned the truth from Artemis.

According to some writers, Hippolytus was revived by Asclepius. Refusing to forgive his father, he went to Aricia, in Italy, where he became king and instituted rites in honor of Artemis (Diana). He was later honored there as the minor deity Virbius. At Troezen girls cut off their hair before marrying and dedicated it to Hippolytus. He also had a hero shrine at Sparta. The Troezenians declared that Hippolytus was transported to the sky as the constellation Auriga, the Charioteer.

Hippolytus is the principal character in two extant plays, Euripides' *Hippolytus* and Seneca's *Phaedra*. See also Apollodorus "Epitome" 1.18–19; Hyginus, *Fabulae*, 47; Pausanias 1.22.1–3, 2.27.4, 2.32.1–4; Ovid, *Metamorphoses*, 15.497–546; Vergil, *Aeneïd*, 7.761–782.

Hippolytus (2). One of the GIANTS. In the war between gods and Giants, Hermes borrowed Hades' cap of darkness and killed Hippolytus while invisible. [Apollodorus 1.6.1.]

Hippomedon. One of the SEVEN AGAINST THEBES. Hippomedon's parentage is in doubt; he was the son of Adrastus' father, Talaüs, or his brother Aristomachus, or his sister Metidice. He had a son, Polydorus, by Evanippe, and lived at Mycenae or Lerna. He was killed at Thebes by Ismarus.

Hippomenes. A son of Megareus, king of Onchestus. The same exploits are attributed to Hippomenes as to Melanion. (See ATALANTA, B, C.)

Hipponome. See ALCAEÜS (1).

Hipponoüs. See BELLEROPHON [A]; CAPANEUS; PERIBOEA (2).

Hippostratus. See PERIBOEA (2).

Hippothoë. A daughter of Mestor and Lysidice. Hippothoë was carried off to the Taphian Islands by Poseidon, by whom she had a son, Taphius, eponym of Taphos. [Apollodorus 2.4.5.]

Hippothoön or **Hippothoüs.** See ALOPE.

Homer. The poet of the *Iliad* and the *Odyssey*. Virtually nothing is known of Homer except that he was a Greek living in Ionia, probably in the eighth century B.C. Some modern scholars believe that the *Iliad* and the *Odyssey* are not from the same author or even the same period. These two poems are, in any case, the oldest sources of Greek mythology extant. The *Iliad* deals with the events of a short period near the end of the Trojan War, the *Odyssey* with the voyages and return to Ithaca of Odysseus; but both poems allude to many persons and events outside their immediate scope.

Homeric Hymns. Hymns to various gods, once ascribed to Homer. The longest of these hymns, those addressed to Dionysus, Demeter, Apollo, Hermes, and Aphrodite, are principal sources of the myths of these gods. The hymns are published in the volume of Hesiod's works in the Loeb Classical Library.

Horae. The SEASONS. Although this word can be literally translated as "Hours," it originally denoted the seasons of the year.

Horatius, Publius. A legendary Roman champion. In the reign of Tullus Hostilius, the third king of Rome, the city was at war with Alba Longa. It was agreed that the victory should be decided by combat between groups of three champions from each side. Of the six fighters, Horatius alone survived. Returning in triumph to the city, he was met by his sister, who had been betrothed to one of the Alban champions. She recognized his armor among her brother's spoils and wailed in grief. Horatius killed her on the spot, on the grounds that she was unpatriotic. He was sentenced to death, but appealed to the people and was exonerated. [Livy 1.24.1–1.26.14.]

Hours. See HORAE; SEASONS.

Hundred-handed or **Hecatoncheires.** Three giants, each with fifty heads and one hundred arms. The Hundred-handed, named Briareüs (or Obriareüs, or Aegaeon), Gyes, and Cottus, were the most terrible of all the children of Uranus (Sky) and Ge (Earth). Their father, envious of their strength, hid them within their mother, Earth. Racked with pain, Ge induced their brother the Titan Cronus to castrate Uranus. Cronus, however, kept the Hundred-handed imprisoned in Tartarus, together with their brothers the Cyclopes. Ge then induced Cronus' son Zeus to release both in order that they might aid him in his war with the Titans. When they had served his purpose, Zeus, too, returned them to Tartarus, making them guardians of the Titans now imprisoned there. Later Thetis brought Briareüs to Zeus's assistance when he was troubled by a mutiny of some of the other gods, after which the giant returned to Tartarus.

Like other monstrous offspring of Ge and Uranus, such as the Cyclopes, the Giants, and Typhöeus, the Hundred-handed have been thought to be personifications or spirits of violent natural phenomena such as volcanic eruptions. This explanation would account for the fact that the Hundred-handed, although they occasionally emerged aboveground in connection with some violent conflict, spent most of their days beneath the surface of the earth. [Hesiod, *Theogony*, 147–160, 617–735; Apollodorus 1.1.1–2, 1.1.4–5, 1.2.1.]

Hyacinth. A son of Amyclas, king of Sparta, and Diomede, or of Pierus, son of Magnes, and the Muse Cleio. A beautiful youth, Hyacinth was loved by the bard Thamyris, the first man to love another man. Apollo, too, fell in love with Hyacinth, but one day killed him accidentally with a cast of the discus. (Late writers attributed this accident to the jealousy of Zephyrus, the West Wind, yet a third lover of the boy.) From the blood of the dying youth sprang a flower that bore on its petals the syllables of lament *ai ai!* Apollo decreed that Hyacinth be honored every year in the festival of the Hyacinthia at his tomb at Amyclae. [Ovid, *Metamorphoses*, 10.162–219; Apollodorus 1.3.3; Pausanias 4.19.3–5.]

Hyacinth, daughters of. Daughters of a Spartan immigrant to Athens. When, in answer to Minos' prayers, the gods caused a severe plague to fall on Athens, the citizens sacrificed the three daughters of Hyacinth on the grave of the Cyclops Geraestus, but to no avail. Some writers mention only one daughter, Antheïs, and say that Hyacinth voluntarily sacrificed her. [Apollodorus 3.15.8; Hyginus, *Fabulae*, 238.]

Hyades. Nymphs commemorated in the constellation the Hyades. The Hyades were daughters of Oceanus and Tethys, or of Atlas by Pleïone or the Oceanid Aethra. The name of these nymphs, whom the Romans called Suculae, was derived from that of their brother, Hyas, or from *hyein* ("to rain"), or merely from the Greek letter *ypsilon*. Hyas, who is not otherwise known, may have been invented solely to explain his sisters' name. He is said to have been killed by a boar or a lion. Those of his sisters who took his name died of grief and were placed among the stars by Zeus. The remaining sisters of this large family died in turn from mourning the Hyades. They became the Pleiades. The names of the Hyades were variously given, and their number ranged from two to seven in differing accounts. Several writers claimed that they came from Dodona, where they had perhaps reared Zeus, and that they were originally called Dodonidae. More frequently they were said to have been the nurses of Dionysus on Mount Nysa. This god later persuaded Medea to rejuvenate the Hyades and finally immortalized them in the stars. [Hyginus, *Fabulae*, 182, and *Poetica Astronomica*, 2.21; Apollodorus 3.4.3.]

Hyantes. An ancient Boeotian tribe. The Hyantes were driven from the region of Thebes by the invading Phoenicians led by Cadmus. They settled northeast of Boeotian Orchomenus and founded the city of Hyampolis. In one form or another the name of the Hyantes was occasionally used by poets for the region of Thebes. [Pausanias 9.5.1.]

Hydra. A monster, offspring of Typhon and Echidna. The Hydra had many heads to begin with and grew two more whenever one was lopped off. HERACLES [D] killed it with the aid of Iolaüs as one of his labors. He poisoned his arrows with its gall. This poison later caused Heracles' death. Both the Hydra and its helpful friend the crab were placed among the stars by Hera. Some writers, however, identify the constellation as an ordinary water snake. (See CRAB.)

Hyettus. The eponym of Hyettus, a Boeotian village. Hyettus, an Argive, killed Molurus, son of Arisbas, for seducing his wife, thus becoming the first man to punish another for adultery. Fleeing Argos, he came to Orchomenus, ruler of the Boeotian city that bore his name. Hyettus was welcomed and given the land on which he built his village. [*Great Eoiae* 7; Pausanias 9.36.6–8.]

Hygieia. A daughter of Asclepius. Hygieia has no myth, being merely an abstraction. As an offspring of the god of healing, she personified health.

Hyginus. A Roman mythographer. Almost nothing is known of Hyginus except that his *Fabulae*, a confused and disorderly anthology of briefly told myths, was written sometime before the year A.D. 207, as was, probably, his *Poetica Astronomica*. Apparently based on a late Greek source, *Fabulae* retells, sketchily and inaccurately, many well-known Greek myths. Some of its short, numbered sections are mere lists: men who killed their relatives, those suckled by animals, those who returned from the Underworld with the permission of the Fates, and the like. Nevertheless Hyginus' two works contain many details or alternative versions of myth not found elsewhere. Book 2 of his *Poetica Astronomica* recounts the myths that gave their names to forty-three constellations. Translations of both works are found in Mary Grant's *The Myths of Hyginus* (1960).

Hylas. A son of Theiodamas, king of the Dryopes, and the nymph Menodice. Attracted by Hylas' youthful beauty, Heracles kidnaped the boy, after killing his father. He made Hylas his squire and lover and took him with him on the voyage of the ARGONAUTS [F]. The nymph of the spring Pegae, near Cius in Mysia, fell in love with Hylas as he was drawing water. She pulled him into the depths, where he drowned, or else lived a watery life as the nymph's consort. Enraged at Hylas' disappearance, Heracles looked everywhere for him, then left orders with the Cians that they should never cease searching for the boy. For centuries thereafter the Cians annually wandered about the countryside crying Hylas' name. [Apollonius Rhodius 1.1207–1357.]

Hylleans. A people who lived somewhere along the eastern coast of the Adriatic Sea. The Hylleans were named for their king, Hyllus, a son of Heracles, who had led them from Phaeacia to their new land. They were hospitable to the ARGONAUTS [P], who stayed with them briefly on their homeward journey. Apollonius Rhodius [4.522–551] mentions that the Argonauts had stopped at some earlier time among these people—an episode that may have appeared in his earlier and much longer version of the *Argonautica*, now lost. This visit must have taken place during the Argonauts' flight from the Colchians, so the land is likely to have been conceived of as lying on the northeastern part of the coast, not far from the mouth of the imaginary river by which the Argonauts sailed from the Danube into the Adriatic.

Hyllus. The eldest son of Heracles and Deïaneira. When Heracles knew that he was about to die, he directed Hyllus, then still a boy, to marry his concubine Iole when he came of age. As a young man Hyllus took part in the war that the Athenians waged against the Argives to protect Heracles' children. Either he or Iolaüs killed or captured Eurystheus, king of Mycenae, who had long persecuted Heracles and his family. Hyllus married Iole, who may have become the mother of his son Cleodaeüs. Through misunderstanding of an oracle, Hyllus led the HERACLIDS in an abortive attempt to reclaim his father's right to the rule of Mycenae. He was killed in single combat by Echemus.

According to a completely different tradition recorded by Apollonius Rhodius [4.537–551], Hyllus was Heracles' son by the water-nymph Melite, whom Heracles met on a visit to Drepane, the island of the Phaeacians. When Hyllus grew to manhood he wished to found a city of his own. King Nausithoüs helped him to recruit a band of Phaeacians, with whom he settled somewhere on the northeastern Adriatic coast. He was killed there during a cattle raid by the Mentores after giving his name to the HYLLEANS. [Euripides, *Children of Heracles*; Apollodorus 2.7.7–2.8.2; Pausanias 1.4.2, 1.4.10, 3.15.10, 4.2.1, 8.5.1.]

Hymen or **Hymenaeüs.** A patron deity of marriage. Hymen, who is mentioned only in the works of late Classical writers, was a mythical embodiment of the "hymeneal" songs customarily sung at weddings. Various fanciful tales were invented to account for his connection with marriage, but he had no genuine myths.

Hyperboreans. A legendary race. Apollo was believed by the Greeks to spend the three months of winter among the Hyperboreans. Herodotus reported that these people periodically sent unnamed offerings wrapped in straw to the god's shrine at Delos, but no Greek of historical times had seen the Hyperboreans themselves. Because two pairs of female envoys whom the Hyperboreans had sent to Delos in early times had not returned, they dispatched their offerings by messengers from neighboring states, including the land of the Issedones. The name Hyperboreioi, which the Greeks took to mean "Beyond the North Wind," and certain details of their very sketchy legend have led many scholars to locate this people in northern Europe. Philologists no longer accept the Greek interpretation of the name, however, and Herodotus' account tends to place the Issedones deep in Asia. Since the Hyperboreans, according to the historian's source, lived beyond the Issedones, the one-eyed Arimaspians, and the gold-guarding griffins, their home is pushed far into the east, and into the mists of legend as well.

To Greek poets, such as Pindar, the Hyperboreans were a semidivine people who lived a thousand years of Elysian existence, free from care or labor. Whatever historical reality they may have had, writers hardly distinguished them from the legendary Phaeacians or the ghostly dwellers in the Islands of the Blessed. [Herodotus 4.13, 4.32–36; Pindar, *Olympian Odes*, 3.16, and *Pythian Odes*, 10.39–45.]

Hypereia. The first home of the Phaeacians; also, a city of Argolis. The Phaeacians, under Nausithoüs, were driven from Hypereia by their neighbors the Cyclopes. Hypereia was regarded by many Roman writers as an early name of Italy. The Argive city, named for Hyperes, was combined by Pittheus with neighboring Antheia and renamed Troezen.

Hyperenor. See SPARTI.

Hyperion. A Titan and sun-god. Hyperion, a son of Ge and Uranus, married his sister Titan Theia (sometimes called Euryphaëssa), who bore Eos (Dawn), HELIUS (Sun), and Selene (Moon). Hyperion was himself a personification of the sun and was often identified with his son, whom Homer regularly referred to as Helius Hyperion. [Hesiod, *Theogony*, 134, 371–374; *Homeric Hymn to Helius* 31.]

Hypermnestra (1). The eldest daughter of DANAÜS. When her father ordered his daughters to kill their newly wed husbands, the sons of Aegyptus, Hypermnestra helped her husband, Lynceus, to flee. Danaüs punished her, but was later reconciled with her and Lynceus, by whom she bore a son, Abas. Hypermnestra and Lynceus were buried in a single tomb at Argos. [Apollodorus 2.1.5–2.2.1.]

Hypermnestra (2). A daughter of Thestius. She was said by some to have been the mother of Amphiaraüs by Oïcles.

Hypnos. Sleep, and the god of sleep. Hypnos, who was called Somnus by the Romans, was a son of Nyx (Night) and brother of Thanatos (Death). He was little more than an abstraction except in Homer's *Iliad* [14.230–360, 16.671–683], where he appears as a rather comic figure. Hera, meeting him on the island of Lemnos, asked him to put Zeus to sleep so that the gods who favored the Greeks in the Trojan War could come to their aid. At first Hypnos refused, reminding Hera that the last time he had helped her in such a way Zeus had nearly pitched him out of heaven. Hera, however, bribed Hypnos by elaborately vowing that he should have one of the Graces, Pasithea, as his bride. Agreeing, not without misgivings, Hypnos flew away and perched, in the form of a bird called a chalcis, atop a fir tree on Mount Ida. Hera visited

Zeus there and lulled him by lying with him, after which Hypnos put him to sleep. Later Hypnos and Thanatos, at Apollo's command, carried the corpse of Sarpedon to his home in Lydia.

Hypseus. An early Thessalian king. Hypseus was the son of the river-god Peneius and Creüsa, a naïad daughter of Ge. He was the father of Cyrene, Themisto, and Astyagyïa. [Pindar, *Pythian Odes*, 9.12–18; Apollodorus 1.9.2; Diodorus Siculus 4.69.1–3.]

Hypsipyle. A queen of Lemnos. When the women of Lemnos killed all the men on the island, Hypsipyle saved her father, King Thoas, by hiding him and then either putting him onto a boat or setting him adrift in a chest, which reached the island of Oenoë. The ARGONAUTS [C] came to Lemnos and were entertained by the women. Hypsipyle bore two sons by Jason, Euneüs and either Nebrophonus or Deïpylus. Later her subjects learned that she had saved Thoas. Some say that they sold her into slavery, others that, in escaping from the women, she was captured by pirates, who sold her. She was bought by Lycurgus or Lycus, king of Nemea, as a nurse for his son, Opheltes. While she was showing a spring to the SEVEN AGAINST THEBES [C], the child was killed by a snake, but the Seven interceded for her with the king. Hyginus records that Hypsipyle gave her life for her father, but the event to which he alludes is not known. [Apollonius Rhodius 1.609–909; Apollodorus 1.9.17, 3.6.4; Hyginus, *Fabulae*, 15, 254; Homer, *Iliad*, 7.469.]

Hyria. An ancient and once-powerful Boeotian city. Hyria, named for its wealthy king Hyrieus, was the home also of his sons Lycus and Nycteus, who usurped the rule of Thebes. According to one version of Orion's birth, the giant hunter grew up from the soil at Hyria. It was there, too, that Trophonius and Agamedes built the famous treasury for Hyrieus.

Hyrieus. A son of Poseidon and Alcyone, daughter of Atlas. Hyrieus was the king and eponym of Hyria in Boeotia (unless it was named for Hyrië, a local nymph). According to some accounts, he, rather than Chthonius, was the father, by the nymph Clonia, of Nycteus and Lycus. Some call him also the father of Orion. Hyrieus had a treasury built by TROPHONIUS and Agamedes and successfully set a trap for mysterious robbers, who turned out to be the builders. [Apollodorus 3.10.1; Pausanias 9.37.5–7.]

Hyrmina. A daughter of Epeius by Anaxiroë, daughter of Coronus. By Phorbas, Hyrmina was the mother of Actor, and perhaps of Augeias and Tiphys. Actor named an Eleian city for her. [Pausanias 5.1.5, 5.1.11.]

Hyrtacus. A king of Arisbe, in the Troad. Hyrtacus, an ally of the Trojans, married Arisbe, daughter of Merops, after Priam divorced her. Hyrtacus' son Asius led the Arisbean force at Troy. Another son, Nisus, sailed with Aeneas. [Apollodorus "Epitome" 3.35; Vergil, *Aeneïd*, 9.406.]

I

Iacchus. An obscure deity honored at the Eleusinian mysteries together with Demeter and Persephone. Iacchus is sometimes called Demeter's son, sometimes her husband, sometimes a son of Persephone identical with Zagreus. He was also often identified with Dionysus (perhaps only because of the resemblance between the names Iacchus and Bacchus), but was occasionally said to be Dionysus' son. A youth or child, Iacchus may have been a minor agricultural deity who was absorbed into the cult of Demeter, especially at Eleusis. Some scholars believe, however, that the "god" came into being as a personification of the cry "*Iacche!*" uttered during certain Eleusinian processions.

Ialmenus. A son of Ares and Astyoche. Ialmenus and his brother, ASCALAPHUS (2), were co-kings of Minyan Orchomenus. Both were Argonauts and suitors of Helen. Together they led thirty ships to the Trojan War. [Homer, *Iliad*, 2.511–516; Apollodorus 1.9.16, 3.10.8.]

Iambe. See DEMETER [C].

Iamus. See EVADNE (3).

Iapetus. A Titan. A son of Ge and Uranus, Iapetus was the father, by the Oceanid Clymene or Asia, of Atlas, Menoetius, Prometheus, and Epimetheus. When Zeus overthrew Cronus and the other Titans, Iapetus was confined with them in Tartarus. [Hesiod, *Theogony*, 132–136, 507–514; Homer, *Iliad*, 8.478–481; Apollodorus 1.2.3.]

Iarbas. A king of Gaetulia, in northern Africa. According to Vergil's account in the *Aeneïd* [4.196–236], Iarbas, a son of Hammon and a Garamantian nymph, sold the site of Carthage to DIDO and later courted her. His prayers to Jupiter led to Aeneas' desertion of the queen and, indirectly, to her death.

Iasion. A son of Zeus and Electra, daughter of Atlas. Iasion came from Samothrace to attend the wedding in Thebes of Cadmus and Harmonia (whom some writers call Iasion's sister). Demeter became infatuated with Iasion and lay with him in a thrice-plowed field. Homer [*Odyssey* 5.125–128] claims that Zeus killed him for this insult to a goddess. Demeter bore their son, Plutus, a minor deity of agricultural wealth, at Tripolus, in Crete. Many writers deny that Iasion was killed. Ovid [*Metamorphoses* 9.421] speaks of Demeter's regretting his graying hairs. Hyginus [*Poetica Astronomica*, 2.4, 2.22, and *Fabu-*

lae, 250] says that he was killed by his team of horses and elevated to the stars, together with Triptolemus, as the constellation Gemini. Hyginus mentions a second son of Iasion and Demeter, Philomelus, who was made the constellation Boötes by his mother for inventing the wagon. Diodorus Siculus [5.48.3–5.49.5] goes further, claiming that Iasion, after perfecting the rites of the Samothracian mysteries, married the Phrygian goddess Cybele, who bore him Corybas. After this he was elevated to Olympus.

Iasus (1). A king of Argos. A son of Argus Panoptes and Ismene, daughter of Asopus, or of Triopas, Iasus was said by some to have been the father of Io.

Iasus (2). A son of Lycurgus, king of Arcadia. Iasus was said by some to have been the father of Atalanta by Clymene, daughter of Minyas. Wanting only sons, he exposed her, but she was suckled by a bear and rescued by hunters. As an adult she was reunited with her father. He may have devised, at her request, the footrace that repeatedly preserved her virginity. [Apollodorus 3.9.2.]

Icaria. An island in the Aegean Sea, west of Samos. After Icarus plunged to his death in the Icarian Sea, his body washed ashore on the island of Doliche. Heracles found and buried it there and renamed the island Icaria. It was from Icaria that Dionysus was kidnaped by pirates, and the island was the scene of Melanippe's adventures.

Icarius (1). A son of Perieres and Gorgophone or of Oebalus and the naïad Bateia. Icarius is said by some to have helped his brother Hippocoön to expel another brother, TYNDAREÜS, from Sparta. Others claim that Icarius and Tyndareüs were expelled together, but later restored to power by Heracles. By the naïad Periboea, Icarius had two daughters, Penelope and Iphthime, and five sons, among them Perileüs or Perilaüs, who may have been Orestes' accuser at his trial on the Areopagus. When Odysseus came to Sparta to woo Penelope, Tyndareüs spoke for him to Icarius. Some say, however, that Icarius awarded her to Odysseus as the winner of a footrace that Icarius held for her suitors. In any case, Icarius tried his best to persuade Odysseus to settle in Sparta. When Odysseus refused, Icarius followed his chariot, begging Penelope to stay. At last Odysseus told her to go with him willingly or return with her father. Penelope silently veiled her face, and Icarius knew by this gesture that she wished to go with her husband. Letting her go, Icarius erected on the spot an image of Modesty. [Homer, *Odyssey*, 2.132–133, 4.797; Apollodorus 3.10.4–6, 3.10.9; Pausanias 3.20.10–11.]

Icarius (2). An Athenian. Because Icarius and his daughter, Erigone, welcomed Dionysus, the god taught Icarius the culture of the vine. Icarius loaded a wagon with wineskins, called his faithful dog, Maera, and set off to spread the word. The first persons that he met were some shepherds. He gave them some of the wine, which, from inexperience, they drank unwatered. Rousing much later from a drunken stupor, they thought that the stranger had tried to poison them. They beat Icarius to death with clubs, flung his body into a well or buried it under a tree, and ran away. Erigone looked everywhere for her father and was finally led to him by Maera, who howled over his grave. Distracted with grief, she hanged herself from the tree that grew over the grave. The dog also committed suicide, by jumping into a well.

Dionysus, angered that the deaths of his devoted followers had gone unavenged, sent a madness on Athenian girls that caused them to hang themselves from trees. The Athenians learned the cause of this phenomenon from an oracle, found and punished the murderers, and instituted rites in honor of Icarius and his daughter that were held during the grape harvest. During this "swinging festival" girls swung from trees on swings, in imitation of Erigone. Dionysus further honored the two by placing Icarius in the sky as the constellation Boötes, Erigone as Virgo, and Maera as the dog star.

The island of Ceüs was plagued with drought during the scorching heat that accompanies the rising of the dog star. On the advice of Apollo, the Cean king Aristaeüs appeased the ghost of Icarius with sacrifices. Zeus sent the etesian winds to bring relief from the drought. Presumably the drought resulted from the fact that, in this version, the murderers of Icarius had taken up residence in Ceüs. [Hyginus, *Fabulae*, 130, and *Poetica Astronomica*, 2.4.]

Icarus. The son of DAEDALUS [A]. When Icarus and his father were escaping from a Cretan prison on wings made of wax and feathers, the young man ignored Daedalus' warning not to fly too near the sun. The wax melted and Icarus fell into the sea south of Samos, which is named Icarian, for him. The body washed ashore on the island since called Icaria, and was later buried by Heracles.

Icelos. See SOMNUS.

Ida. A nymph of the Cretan Mount Ida. Ida, a daughter of Melisseus, helped her sister, Adrasteia, to nurse the infant Zeus on the milk of the goat Amaltheia. [Apollodorus 1.1.6–7.]

Ida, Mount. The name of two famous mountain ranges, one in west central Crete, the other southeast of Troy. The Cretan cave in which the infant Zeus was reared by his nurses was first said to be on Mount Dicte, but the scene was later said to have been on Ida. The Asian range called Ida (now Kazdagi) was the site of Dardania, which antedated Ilium as the chief city of the Troad. Many events of the Trojan War, beginning with the fateful judgment of Paris, took place on the slopes of this mountain.

Idaea (1). The second wife of PHINEUS (1). Idaea bore two sons, Thynius and Mariandynus. Her lying accusations against her stepsons led her husband to imprison and torture them. They were rescued by the Argonauts. Idaea was sent home to her father, the Scythian king Dardanus, who condemned her to death.

Idaea (2). A nymph of Mount Ida, near Troy. Teucer, the indigenous king of the region of Troy, was called a son of Idaea and Scamander, god of a local river. Teucer's daughter, Bateia, and the immigrant Dardanus were forebears of the Trojan royal line. [Apollodorus 3.21.1.]

Idaeüs. The herald of the Trojan forces during the Trojan War. Idaeüs drove the mulecart in which Priam went secretly to appeal to Achilles for Hector's body. [Homer, *Iliad*, 7.273–286, 24.324.]

Idas and **Lynceus.** Sons of Aphareus, king of Messenia, and Arene. Idas was inseparable from his younger brother, Lynceus. Idas was the stronger and bolder of the two, but Lynceus was gifted with vision so sharp that he could see even what was hidden in the earth. Together the brothers distinguished themselves both during the CALYDONIAN BOAR HUNT and with the ARGONAUTS, though Idas' vain boasting caused considerable trouble in the *Argo*. This same insolence led Idas to carry off Marpessa, daughter of Evenus, even though he knew that Apollo was wooing her. According to Apollodorus, Idas was aided in this venture with the loan of a winged chariot from Poseidon (who, some say, was Idas' true father). Failing in the pursuit of Idas, Evenus drowned himself in the Lycormas River, which was thereafter called the Evenus. Apollo was less easily outdistanced. He caught up with Idas in Messenia and fought him for Marpessa, until Zeus parted the two and left the choice to the girl. Marpessa chose Idas for her husband because she feared that Apollo might one day desert her. By Marpessa, Idas became the father of Cleopatra, who married Meleager.

Idas invaded Teuthrania, in Mysia, while Teuthras was king, but was repulsed by Telephus and Parthenopaeüs. Sometime after this, Idas and Lynceus came into conflict with Castor and Polydeuces, who had been their companions on both the boar hunt and the Argonautic expedition. This feud, which resulted in the deaths of both pairs of brothers, is described in the story of the DIOSCURI. [Apollodorus 1.7.8–9, 3.10.3; Hyginus, *Fabulae*, 100.]

Idmon. An Argonaut. Idmon, a seer, was a son of Cyrene and Apollo, though his reputed father was Abas. Apollo taught him the arts of prophecy, augury, and the divining of omens from burnt offerings. Idmon came from Argos to join the crew of the *Argo*, even though he knew that he would not survive the adventure. He was killed by a boar when the Argonauts stopped among the Mariandyni, on the southern shore of the Black Sea. His companions mourned him for three days and planted a wild olive tree on his barrow. Much later the colonizers of Heracleia were ordered by Apollo to build their city around this tree and to honor Idmon as their protector. [Apollonius Rhodius 1.139–145, 1.435–449, 2.815–850.]

Idomeneus. A king of Crete. Idomeneus was a son of Deucalion and grandson of Minos. He led a Cretan force of eighty ships to the Trojan War. Although he was older than most of the Greek leaders, he distinguished himself in the fighting. He returned safely to Crete, but found that his wife, Meda, instigated by NAUPLIUS (1), had lain with an ambitious Cretan named Leucus.

This ruthless man, after killing the queen and her daughter, had usurped the rule of Crete by seizing control of ten cities. He drove out the returning king and Idomeneus sailed to Italy, where he and his followers settled the Sallentine Plain, on the "heel" of Italy. [Homer, *Iliad*, 2.645–652, 13.210–519; Apollodorus "Epitome" 6.10–11; Vergil, *Aeneïd*, 3.400–401.]

Idyia. See EIDYIA.

Iliad. See HOMER.

Ilione. The eldest daughter of Priam and Hecuba. Ilione married Polymestor, king of the Thracian Chersonese, and reared her young brother POLYDORUS (2) together with her own son, Deïpylus. [Hyginus, *Fabulae*, 109.]

Ilissus or **Ilisus River.** A stream near Athens. It was from the banks of this river that Boreas carried off Erechtheus' daughter Oreithyia.

Ilium. See TROY.

Illyria. A large region of the Adriatic coast north of Epeirus. Illyria, which is now northern Albania and part of southern Yugoslavia, was looked upon by the Greeks as a barbarian land. Cadmus, his wife Harmonia, and their daughter Agave all went there after the murder of Cadmus' successor, Agave's son Pentheus. Many of the Thebans driven from their city by the Epigoni also emigrated to Illyria.

Ilus (1). The elder son of Dardanus, king of Dardania, and Bateia, daughter of Teucer. Ilus died childless and his brother Erichthonius succeeded to the rule. It may be that, in mentioning this Ilus, Homer was referring to an alternative tradition about Ilus the eponym of Ilium, whom he elsewhere called a son of Tros. [Homer, *Iliad*, 11.166, 11.372; Apollodorus 3.12.1–2.]

Ilus (2). A king of Troy and eponym of Ilium. Ilus was a son of Tros, the eponym of Troy, and Callirrhoë, daughter of the river-god Scamander. He emigrated from Dardania (where his brother Assaracus presumably ruled) to Phrygia. Games were being held there and, upon winning a wrestling match, Ilus was awarded the prize of fifty youths and as many young women. Obeying an oracle, the Phrygian king also gave him a dappled cow, with orders to found a city where it lay down. The cow led Ilus to a hill sacred to the Phrygian goddess Ate. There he built a city and called it Ilium, for himself, peopling it with the prize he had won. He prayed to Zeus for a sign of his favor, whereupon the PALLADIUM dropped from the sky in front of his tent. Ilus built a temple for this sacred object and Troy (Ilium) was said to have been invulnerable as long as the Palladium remained in the city. Ilus married Eurydice, daughter of Adrastus, and she bore Laomedon and Themiste. Themiste married Capys, son of Ilus' brother Assaracus, whose Dardanian descendants later were allies of the Trojans. Ilus is said to have driven either Pelops or his father Tantalus from the region of Mount Sipylus. At his death Ilus was succeeded by Laomedon. [Homer, *Iliad*, 20.231–236; Apollodorus 3.12.2–3; Pausanias 2.22.3.]

Ilus (3). A king of Thesprotian Ephyra. A son of Mermerus, Ilus was descended from Medea and had inherited the family's art of making poisons. Nevertheless he was a pious man and refused to sell arrow poison to the young Odysseus, when he came to Ephyra to buy it from him. [Homer, *Odyssey*, 1.259–263.]

Ilva. See ELBA.

Inachus. The chief river of Argos, often personified as a god, a son of the Titans Oceanus and Tethys. When Hera and Poseidon were wrangling over possession of Argolis, Zeus referred the question to Inachus and two other rivers, the Cephissus and the Asterion. They decided in favor of Hera, and Poseidon dried them up, so that they flow only after rains. Poseidon also flooded Argolis for a time.

Some say that Inachus was not a god but the first king of Argos, who named the river for himself and who was the first to worship Hera. Inachus married the ash-nymph Melia, also a child of Oceanus, and she bore him two sons, Phoroneus and Aegialeus, and a daughter, Io. Melia may also have been the mother of his daughter Mycene. (Hyginus names the mother of Phoroneus and Io as Argia.) It is as the father of Io [A] that Inachus is best known, though some writers claim that Io was the daughter of his descendant Iasus. When Io told Inachus of seductive dreams that Zeus had sent her, he exiled her in obedience to the oracles of Delphi and Dodona. She was transformed into a heifer and Inachus did not recognize her until she wrote her sad tale in the dust with her hoof. After this, according to Ovid, he wept in his cave, his tears presumably forming the river. [Apollodorus 2.1.1, 2.1.4, 2.15.5, 2.16.4; Aeschylus, *Prometheus Bound*, 589–655; Pausanias, 2.15.4–5, 2.22.4; Ovid, *Metamorphoses*, 1.583, 1.640 ff; Hyginus, *Fabulae*, 143, 145.]

Ino. A daughter of Cadmus, king of Thebes, and Harmonia. Ino, Agave, and Autonoë spread the rumor that their sister Semele was lying when she said that Zeus was the father of her unborn child. After Semele's death and the infant Dionysus' second birth from Zeus's thigh, Hermes persuaded Ino, who had married ATHAMAS, king of Orchomenus, to rear the child as a girl in order to deceive Hera. Later Ino, suffering the divine madness of the bacchants, helped Agave to tear in pieces her son Pentheus, king of Thebes. Ino was envious of Phrixus and Helle, the children of Athamas' first wife, Nephele, and would have succeeded in destroying them by a plot if they had not been saved by a golden ram. Later Hera drove her and Athamas mad and they killed their own children. Athamas shot Learchus, mistaking him for a deer, and Ino, after boiling the younger boy, Melicertes, leaped with him into the Saronic Gulf from the Molurian Rocks on the Isthmus of Corinth.

Ino did not die, but, like her sister Semele, became a minor deity. As Leucothea (White Goddess), she lived with the Nereïds. Together with Melicertes, who was now called Palaemon, she often came to the aid of sailors in distress. It was she who saved Odysseus from death in the sea by lending him her veil to buoy him up until he could swim ashore on the island of Phaeacia.

Leucothea was worshiped on the isthmus and in many parts of the Peloponnesus. The Romans knew her as Mater Matuta. [Homer, *Odyssey*, 5.333–353, 5.458–462.]

Io. A daughter of Inachus, the Argive river-god, and Melia, or of Iasus or Piren.

A. Io was destined to become, by Zeus, the ancestress of three great Greek dynasties: those of Argos, Thebes, and Crete. A priestess of Hera, the patroness of Argos, she attracted the attention of Zeus, who had already seduced Io's niece, Niobe. Night after night the god whispered to Io in dreams, begging her to come to him in the meadows of the river Lerna, where her father pastured his flocks. Io told Inachus of her dreams and he sent messengers to inquire their meaning of the oracles at Dodona and Delphi. After many quibbling responses he received a clear reply: he must exile his daughter forever or he and his people would suffer destruction from a thunderbolt, the weapon of Zeus. The sorrowful father obeyed the oracle and drove Io from home.

What happened next is disputed. Some say that Hera, aware of Zeus's designs, changed Io into a cow to protect her and thwart Zeus. According to a more usual account, Zeus was observed by his jealous wife as he overtook the fleeing girl and changed Io into a cow to hide his embarrassment. He then swore to Hera that he had not touched Io. (From that day the gods were necessarily tolerant of evasion in lovers' vows.) Undeceived, Hera begged her husband to make her a gift of the lovely white cow, and he could not refuse without inviting more searching inquiries. Whether he now took a bull's form and had his pleasure with Io, or waited until her long wanderings were over is uncertain.

Zeus sent Hermes to steal the heifer-maiden, but Hera set the many-eyed Argus Panoptes to guard her. He tied her to an olive tree in the groves at Mycenae and watched her day and night. Even Hermes, the god of thieves, could not at first get near, for some of Argus' eyes were always wide awake. He solved this problem (according to Ovid) by disguising himself as a goatherd and lulled Argus to sleep with stories and tunes on his pipe. The wily god then drew his sword and cut off Argus' head—a deed that won him the epithet "Argus-Killer" (Argeïphontes).

B. Hera quickly found another way to foil her husband's schemes. She sent a gadfly to sting the cow and drive her far from Argolis. Thus Io, stung by the gadfly and haunted by the ghost of Argus, began her wanderings. Various writers have described her route differently, but with equal disregard for geography. She is said to have passed Dodona, where Zeus's talking oaks greeted her as the god's mate-to-be, and to have crossed the Straits of Maeotis, which were renamed for her the Bosporus (Cow's Ford). In time she came to the rocky crag to which Prometheus was chained. The Titan foretold her tortuous route and she ran on until, near the Egyptian city of Canobus or Memphis, she sank down exhausted. There Zeus came to her beside the Nile and begot a child.

In due time, restored to human form, Io bore a son, whom she named Epaphus (for the god's "touch"). At the request of the ever-vengeful Hera, the Curetes kidnaped the child, but they were killed by Zeus for the deed. The distracted mother learned that her child had been taken to Syria. There she found him, cared for and nursed by the queen of Byblus. Returning with him to Egypt, Io married King Telegonus and instituted the worship of Demeter. It was said by many that the Egyptians worshiped both Demeter and Io under the name of Isis.

The many passing references to the myth of Io by Greek writers show that it was well known, although two plays of Aeschylus are the only extant works that make extensive use of the legend. In repeated references in the first half of *Suppliant Women*, the daughters of Danaüs claim to be Argives through descent from Io. In *Prometheus Bound* [561–886], Io herself tells her story to Prometheus. Apollodorus [2.1.3] also recounts the legend.

Iobates. A king of Lycia. Iobates married his daughter Stheneboea (or Anteia) to PROËTUS [A] and restored him to power in Argos. Later, at Proëtus' request, he tried to dispose of BELLEROPHON [A, C], but relented and gave him his daughter Philonoë.

Iolaüs. A son of Iphicles and Automedusa, daughter of Alcathoüs. Iolaüs became the charioteer and faithful companion of his uncle, Heracles, assisting him with many of his labors. He played so large a part in killing the Hydra (see HERACLES, D) that Eurystheus refused to accept this labor as the work of Heracles alone. Iolaüs is mentioned among those who hunted the Calydonian boar. When Heracles had completed his labors, he is said by some writers to have turned over his wife Megara to Iolaüs. Iolaüs tried valiantly to save the children of Heracles from persecution at the hands of Eurystheus. There is a tradition that, in the final battle with Eurystheus' Argive forces, Iolaüs prayed to Zeus and Hebe to be made young again so that he might protect his dead master's family. Some say that the deified Heracles asked his wife, Hebe, the goddess of youth, to perform the miracle. He and Hebe appeared as two stars that hovered over the yoke of Iolaüs' chariot. Rejuvenated, at least for the moment, the old man killed Eurystheus and beheaded him.

According to another tradition, Iolaüs led Thespian and Athenian settlers, among them many of Heracles' sons by the daughters of Thespius, to colonize Sardinia. Iolaüs was worshiped there as late as the second century A.D. He seems to have been one of the principal heroes of Thebes, and as such was frequently lauded by the Theban poet Pindar. He appears as a leading character in Euripides' drama *The Children of Heracles*. [Apollodorus 2.4.11, 2.5.2, 2.6.1; Ovid, *Metamorphoses*, 9.397–401; Pindar, *Pythian Odes*, 9.78–83; Pausanias 5.8.3–4, 7.2.2, 10.17.5.]

Iolcus. A Thessalian city (now Volos) at the head of the Gulf of Pagasae.

Iolcus was founded and first ruled by Cretheus, one of the sons of Aeolus. Cretheus' son Aeson, the rightful heir, was deprived of the throne by his half-brother Pelias, who ruled Iolcus for many years. The city was taken by the Argonauts under Jason (Aeson's son), after Medea had tricked Pelias' daughters into killing him, but Jason either turned the city over to Pelias' son, Acastus, a fellow Argonaut, or was expelled by him. Later another Argonaut, Peleus, came to Iolcus. When he spurned the advances of Acastus' wife, she accused him to her husband of trying to violate her. Acastus tried unsuccessfully to bring about Peleus' death. Peleus, with the aid of Jason and the Dioscuri, destroyed Iolcus and turned it over to the Haemones. Acastus may have survived, for, much later, he or his sons expelled the aged Peleus from Phthia. Little more, however, was heard of Iolcus.

Iole. A daughter of Eurytus, king of Oechalia. Eurytus promised Iole as a prize to anyone who could beat him in a contest of archery, but refused to honor this vow when defeated by Heracles. Some years later Heracles killed Eurytus and made Iole his concubine. The discovery of this fact led Heracles' wife, Deïaneira, to send him the poisoned robe that caused his death. Iole appears as a nonspeaking character in Sophocles' tragedy *Women of Trachis*. [Apollodorus 2.6.1, 2.7.7.]

Ion. The eponym of the Ionians. Ion was a son of Creüsa, daughter of Erechtheus, king of Athens, by either Xuthus or Apollo. There were two versions of Ion's paternity, representing differing traditions about the origin of the Ionians. According to one, the Thessalian Xuthus, expelled from Athens, emigrated to Aegialus, the coastal region of the northern Peloponnesus, where he died. One of his sons, Achaeüs, went to Thessaly; the other, Ion, remained in Aegialus and gathered allies about him, with the intention of seizing power in the land. Selinus, king of the original Pelasgian inhabitants, anticipated Ion's plan and forestalled it by marrying Ion to his daughter, Helice, and making him his heir. On Selinus' death, Ion became king and renamed the Aegialians Ionians. Later, however, he was called to his mother's homeland to lead the Athenians in their war with Eleusis. Dying in battle, he was buried at Potami. Many generations later the Ionians were driven from Ionia by Achaeans from Argolis and were welcomed to Attica because of Ion's connections there.

According to the second tradition, found in Euripides' play *Ion*, Xuthus had been made king of Athens on the death of Erechtheus, but he and Creüsa had no children. Creüsa had, in fact, secretly borne a son by Apollo, but had exposed it in the cave under the Acropolis where the god had violated her. Unknown to Creüsa, Apollo had arranged to have Hermes transport the child secretly to Delphi and leave it on the steps of Apollo's temple. It was taken in by the Pythia and dedicated to the god. The boy grew up serving about the temple, ignorant of his parentage. When he reached young manhood, Xuthus and Creüsa suddenly appeared at Delphi, having journeyed there to consult the oracle about their childlessness. Xuthus was overjoyed to be told by the oracle that the first person whom he would meet on leaving the temple would be his son. The first he met was none other than Ion. Both assumed that Ion was the result of some youthful indiscretion of Xuthus' and, mutually content with the god's command, agreed to break the news tactfully to Creüsa. Before they could do so, an old servant and some meddling women not only told Creüsa of Xuthus' plan but encouraged her suspicion that her husband was planning to supplant Erechtheus' descendants on the throne of Athens with an alien line.

Creüsa and the old servant plotted to kill the usurper, Ion, by giving him a drink poisoned with a drop of Gorgon's blood that Athena had given Creüsa's ancestor Erichthonius. The plot almost succeeded, but Apollo again rescued his son. At the feast laid by Xuthus in honor of his newfound child, Ion was about to drink the poison during the libations when he heard a servant speak a word of bad omen. The pious young man insisted that the ritual begin again, and he and the guests poured their wine onto the ground. To their horror, a dove that pecked at the wine spilled by Ion died at once in agony. The conspiracy was discovered and Creüsa would have been executed on the spot had not the aged Pythia brought forth the trinkets found in the basket with the baby Ion many years before. Creüsa now realized that Ion was, in fact, *her* son rather than her husband's. Athena appeared in time to prevent Creüsa's execution and advised mother and son not to disillusion Xuthus about his fatherhood. In any case, the goddess predicted, Xuthus would soon have sons of his own by Creüsa: Dorus and Achaeüs. Ion's sons, Geleon, Aegicores, Argades, and Hoples, would give their names to the four tribes of Athens. [Pausanias 2.14.2, 7.1.2–5.]

Ionia. A coastal region of Asia Minor. Ionia included parts of Caria, in the south; major coastal cities of Lydia, as far north as Phocaea; and the islands of Samos and Chios. The cities of this region were traditionally founded or conquered by the Ionians. Although under foreign domination much of the time, Ionia was for extended periods an important center of Greek culture.

Ionians. A Hellenic, or Greek-speaking, people. The traditional eponym of the Ionians was Ion, a son of the Thessalian Xuthus and an Athenian mother. Ion was reared in Aegialus, in the northern Peloponnesus, and seized the rule there from the Pelasgian inhabitants, renaming them Ionians. He was later killed in battle in his mother's homeland of Attica. The Ionians remained in the Peloponnesus until the time of the Dorian invasion, when they were driven out by ACHAEAN refugees from Argos. They fled to Attica, where they were welcomed by the Athenian king Melanthus, himself a refugee from the Dorians in Messenia. Many of the Ionians settled permanently in Attica, but, after two generations, large numbers emigrated to the Cyclades or—led by the sons of Codrus, son of Melanthus—to Asia Minor. Together with emigrants from several other Greek regions, they founded or conquered twelve cities in the land later called Ionia, driving out the native Carians in the southern areas. Here they were conquered first by Lydia, then by Persia. Philip of Macedonia later liberated them from Persian rule.

The most prevalent opinion among modern scholars is that the peoples whom Herodotus and later Classical writers called Ionian were the first of three great waves of Hellenic migration from the north into the Greek area, where they conquered indigenous PELASGIAN inhabitants. The fact that the part of the Mediterranean Sea between Greece and Italy was very early known as the Ionian Sea, together with the firm tradition that the Ionians lived in AEGIALUS, suggests that they occupied much or all of the Peloponnesus. They must have been driven almost entirely from the peninsula, for in historical times only an obscure, Dorianized group of Ionians was thought to live there. There is no reason to doubt the general accuracy of the tradition of their emigration under pressure from the Achaeans, the second wave of Hellenic migration into Greece. In Classical times the Ionians were found in Attica, in most of the Cyclades, and in Ionia. They spoke a dialect that was recognizably distinct from the dialects now called Aeolic, Doric, and Arcado-Cypriot. The Attic dialect was a form of the Ionian.

Ionian Sea. The sea that lies between southern Italy and Sicily on the west and Greece, from Epeirus to the Peloponnesus, on the east. The name of this sea tends to confirm the tradition that the Peloponnesus was once occupied by Ionians, although they were gone from the peninsula by historical times.

Iphianassa (1). A daughter of Proëtus and Stheneboea. Cured of madness by MELAMPUS [C], Iphianassa married his brother, Bias.

Iphianassa (2). A daughter of Agamemnon and Clytemnestra, according to Homer. Iphianassa is generally identified with IPHIGENEIA, but the epic *Cypria* differentiated between them.

Iphicles or **Iphiclus.** The son of Alcmene and Amphitryon. Iphicles was the twin and half-brother of Heracles. When two snakes entered the babies' crib Iphicles was terrified, but Heracles strangled them. Amphitryon thus knew that Iphicles was *his* son, whereas Heracles was a son of Zeus. Iphicles married Automedusa, daughter of Alcathoüs, king of Megara, and they had a son, Iolaüs. Later Iphicles married the younger daughter of Creon. At some point he took part in the Calydonian boar hunt. According to the *Shield of Heracles* [87–94], Iphicles left Thebes and went to his parents' city of Tiryns, where he served Heracles' enemy Eurystheus, to his own regret. This story, otherwise unknown, seems contradicted by the tradition that Iphicles died fighting with his brother against the sons of Hippocoön or against the Eleians. In the latter version, the dying man was carried to the city of Pheneüs, in Arcadia. He was buried there and afterward worshiped as a hero. [Apollodorus 2.4.8, 2.4.11–12, 2.7.3; Pausanias 8.14.9–10.]

Iphiclus. The son of Phylacus, king of Phylace, and Clymene, daughter of Minyas. Iphiclus was famous as a runner. He could run so quickly over the tops of growing grain that the stalks did not bend beneath his weight. Impotent as a youth, he was cured by MELAMPUS [B] and became the father of Protesilaüs and Podarces. Apollonius Rhodius named him among the Argonauts, who were led by Jason, son of Iphiclus' sister Alcimede.

Iphigeneia. The eldest daughter of Agamemnon and Clytemnestra. The poet Stesichorus and others alleged that Iphigeneia was really the daughter borne to Theseus by the captive Helen, who, when freed, gave the baby to her married sister, Clytemnestra. This story was not, however, generally accepted. AGAMEMNON [B] was forced to sacrifice his daughter at Aulis to appease the anger of Artemis. The goddess substituted a deer for the girl on the altar, but it is not clear from the many versions of this event whether the witnesses were aware that Iphigeneia had not been sacrificed. Accounts disagree, too, on what happened to her next. Hesiod is said to have stated that she became the goddess Hecate. The usual story is that Artemis transported her miraculously to the land of the Taurians to become her priestess there.

The barbaric Taurians sacrificed all strangers to Artemis. It became Iphigeneia's duty to prepare the victims for death. Many years later her brother, ORESTES [C], and his companion, Pylades, came to the Taurians' land to steal the wooden statue of Artemis, in the hope of curing Orestes of his madness. In his *Iphigeneia among the Taurians,* Euripides relates the circumstances of the reunion of brother and sister and their escape with the statue. After a stop at the island of Zminthe, where they were threatened, then aided, by Chryses, they reached Attica. Hyginus [*Fabulae* 122] says that they went to Delphi. Their sister Electra believed for some reason that Iphigeneia was a Taurian woman who had killed Orestes. She was about to avenge him by blinding Iphigeneia when Orestes appeared in the nick of time and told her the true story.

Iphigeneia was worshiped in at least one Greek city. Herodotus [4.103] reported that in his day the Taurians still offered human sacrifices to a virgin goddess who they said was Agamemnon's daughter. Most scholars believe that Iphigeneia was, in fact, a form of Artemis.

Iphimedeia. A daughter of Triops. Iphimedeia married Triops' brother Alöeus, but fell in love with Poseidon. She used to walk by the sea and pour its waters into her lap. The god came to her and she bore two giant sons, Otus and Ephialtes, who were called the Aloadae, after their supposed father. She also had a daughter, Pancratis, by her husband. The two women, while reveling as bacchants, were carried off by Thracian pirates to Strongyle (Naxos). Otus and Ephialtes took the island and rescued them. [Apollodorus 1.7.4; Diodorus Siculus 5.50.6–5.51.2.]

Iphis (1). A king of Argos, and a son of Alector. It was Iphis who advised Polyneices to bribe Eriphyle with Harmonia's necklace. He was the father of Eteoclus and of Evadne, who married Capaneus. When both son and son-in-law died in the war with Thebes, Iphis left the kingdom to Capaneus' son,

Sthenelus. He appears in Euripides' *The Suppliants*. [Apollodorus 3.6.2–3; 3.7.1.]

Iphis (2). The daughter of Ligdus and Telethusa. Ligdus, a poor man of Phaestus, in Crete, told his pregnant wife that she should have a son, for he would be unable to support a daughter and would have to kill one if born. Before the child was delivered, the goddess Isis (the Egyptian name of Io, according to the Greeks) appeared to Telethusa, her faithful votary, and promised to help her. In spite of this promise, Telethusa bore a daughter. In desperation the mother dressed her as a boy, named her Iphis, and somehow managed to maintain this deception for thirteen years. At that time the father betrothed the supposed youth to Ianthe, a girl of Phaestus. Telethusa, after exhausting all pretexts for delaying the marriage, prayed to Isis. In the nick of time Iphis was transformed into a boy. [Ovid, *Metamorphoses*, 9.666–797.]

Iphis (3). A Cypriot youth. Iphis loved Anaxarete so desperately that, when she not only spurned him but mocked his pleas, he hanged himself from her doorpost. While watching his funeral procession, the stony-hearted girl was transformed entirely to stone. This punishment was doubtless visited on her by the Cypriot goddess Aphrodite. [Ovid, *Metamorphoses*, 14.698–761.]

Iphitus (1). A son of Eurytus, king of Oechalia. When his father refused to honor his promise of his daughter, Iole, to HERACLES [J], who had defeated Eurytus and his sons in archery, Iphitus sided with Heracles. Later, according to some accounts, he refused to believe that Heracles had stolen Eurytus' mares and asked Heracles to help him find them. Others say that he came to Heracles to demand the return of the mares. In any event, Heracles flung him to his death from the walls of Tiryns, either treacherously or in a fit of madness. For this crime he was cursed with a terrible disease, which was cured only when he permitted himself to be sold into slavery. According to Homer, Iphitus and Odysseus met during the search for the mares at Pheneüs, in Arcadia, and became fast friends. Iphitus gave Odysseus his father's bow. [Homer, *Odyssey*, 21.22–38; Apollodorus 2.6.1–3; Diodorus Siculus 4.31.1–5.]

Iphitus (2). A son of Naubolus, king of Phocis. When Jason went to Delphi to consult the oracle about his prospects of bringing home the golden fleece, Iphitus not only entertained him at his own house but returned with him to Iolcus to join the Argonauts. Iphitus was the father of Schedius and Epistrophus, who led the Phocian forces to the Trojan War. Hyginus [*Fabulae* 14] offers the alternative possibility that Iphitus' father was Hippasus, from Pellene, in Peloponnesian Achaea. [Homer, *Iliad*, 2.517–518; Apollonius Rhodius 1.207–210.]

Irene. A latinized spelling of Eirene. (See SEASONS.)

Iris. The rainbow, and a messenger of the gods. Iris was a daughter of the Titan Thaumas and the Oceanid Electra. In Homer's epics, Iris carries messages for Zeus, but in later writings that work is generally performed by Hermes, while Iris acts for Hera. She appears in Euripides' *Heracles* and in

Aristophanes' comedy *The Birds*. In Apollonius Rhodius' *Argonautica*, she averts violence between Zetes and Càlaïs and her sisters the Harpies. Other references to her in Classical writings are innumerable.

Irus. An Ithacan beggar. Irus, who had been christened Arnaeüs, begged regularly of the suitors of Penelope. When ODYSSEUS [L] came home disguised as an aged beggar, the much younger Irus threatened him. In the resulting boxing match, arranged by the suitors, Irus was felled by Odysseus with one blow and disgraced. [Homer, *Odyssey*, 18.1–116.]

Isander. A son of Bellerophon and Philonoë. Isander was killed fighting the Solymi. [Homer, *Iliad*, 6.196.]

Ischys. See ASCLEPIUS.

Islands of the Blessed. See ELYSIUM.

Ismarus. An old name of Maroneia, in southern Thrace. Ismarus, capital of the Ciconians, was sacked by Odysseus at the beginning of his long voyage home from Troy.

Ismene. A daughter of Oedipus by Jocasta or Euryganeia. Like her sister, Antigone, Ismene is known almost exclusively from Greek tragedy. In Sophocles' *Oedipus at Colonus*, she brings to her father and sister warning of Creon's malevolent intentions. In the same playwright's *Antigone*, she is at first afraid to take part in the illegal burial of Polyneices, but later offers to die with her sister for the deed. In Aeschylus' *Seven Against Thebes*, the sisters together chant a dirge over the bodies of their brothers, Eteocles and Polyneices.

Issedones. See HYPERBOREANS.

Ister. See DANUBE.

Isus. See ANTIPHUS.

Italus. The eponym of the Italians. Hyginus [*Fabulae* 127] called Italus a son of Telegonus and Penelope. Vergil [*Aeneïd* 1.533–534] identified him as a king of the Oenotrians. Thucydides [6.1] believed him a king of the Sicels, an Italian tribe that later invaded Sicily. There were many other conflicting traditions regarding Italus.

Ithaca. An island between Cephallenia and the mainland of Acarnania. Ithaca is one of the most famous sites in all mythology, almost exclusively because it was the homeland of Odysseus in Homer's *Odyssey*. No other legends are attached to the island, and it is not even certain that modern Ithaca is the island that was earliest identified with Odysseus' kingdom.

Itoni. A Lydian tribe. The Itoni had long harried the land of Omphale, queen of Lydia, when Heracles subdued them and razed their city. [Diodorus Siculus 4.31.7.]

Itys or **Itylos.** See TEREUS.

Iülus. The son of Aeneas and Creüsa. Iülus, who was as often called Ascanius, was originally named Ilus. He fought bravely with his father against the forces of Turnus. Later he founded the city of Alba Longa and gave his name to the Julian line of Roman emperors.

Ixion. A Thessalian king. Ixion was the son of Antion and Perimela, daughter of Amythaon. He married Dia, daughter of Eioneus, but did not produce the bride-price that he had promised. When Eioneus took his mares as security, Ixion swore to pay him in full if he would come to collect the price. The unsuspecting father-in-law did so and was flung into a fiery pit. Because this first murder, or first murder of kin, was so horrifying a deed, Ixion could find neither man nor god to purify him of it. Finally Zeus undertook to do so, and even invited Ixion to Olympus. (It should perhaps be mentioned that, according to Homer [*Iliad* 14.317–318], Zeus was in love with Ixion's wife.)

The shameless man repaid this honor by trying to seduce Hera. The goddess told her husband. Zeus, apparently incredulous, shaped a cloud in his wife's likeness and put it in Ixion's bed. Delighted, Ixion made the most of his opportunity and was caught in the act. Zeus punished him by chaining him to a winged and fiery wheel, which revolved forever in the sky or (according to later Classical writers) in the Underworld. The cloud gave birth to the first of the centaurs, or else to a creature named Centaurus, who fathered them on Magnesian mares. Dia became the mother of Peirithoüs either by Ixion or by Zeus. [Apollodorus "Epitome" 1.20; Diodorus Siculus 4.69.3–5; Pindar, *Pythian Odes*, 2.21–48.]

J

Janus. The Roman god of doors and of beginnings. All doors and gates were sacred to Janus. So were all beginnings, which the Romans believed to be crucial to the success of any undertaking, presumably regarding them as doorways to the future. Janus' blessing was asked, therefore, on the beginning of every day, month, and year; the first month of the year was named for him. He also presided over the sowing—that is, the beginning—of the crops and over the start of virtually every other significant endeavor. The Romans probably marched to war through Janus' sacred gateway, the *Ianus geminus*, which stood in the Forum and remained open during wars. Janus was represented in art with two faces that faced in opposite directions, as do doors. He was also sometimes shown with four faces.

Jason. The leader of the Argonauts.

A. Jason was the elder son of Aeson, a grandson of Aeolus. His mother is usually said to have been either Polymede, daughter of Autolycus, or Alcimede, daughter of Phylacus and Clymene, but she has been given several other names as well. PELIAS, Aeson's half-brother, usurped the throne of Iolcus, in Thessaly, which should have fallen to Aeson as eldest son of Cretheus, the previous king. Aeson continued to live in Iolcus, but devoid of power and in danger for his life. When his wife bore a son, they pretended that the infant had died and secretly sent him to Cheiron the Centaur in order to protect him from the enmity of Pelias. Cheiron named the child Jason and reared him in his cave on the Magnesian mountain Pelion, east of Iolcus. Some say that Pelias knew of Jason's existence, but permitted him to live as a farmer in Magnesia. Although the king had been warned by the Delphic oracle that a descendant of Aeolus—a man with one sandal—would one day cause his death, he evidently believed that he need not fear a hillbred youth whose relatives either were powerless or lived far away.

When Jason reached his twenty-first year, he determined to declare his right to the Iolcan throne. He chose the occasion of the annual festival held by Pelias in honor of his father, Poseidon—a festival at which all the gods would be given their due respect except Hera, whom Pelias had scorned throughout his life. On the way to Iolcus, Jason had to cross a river usually identified as the Anaurus. At the edge of the stream he found an old woman who asked him to carry her across. Jason was in a hurry to reach the city in time for the ceremonies. Nevertheless he placed the old woman on his shoulders and waded into the swift current. In midstream he lost a sandal in the mud, but there was no time to go back for it when he had set his burden safely on the farther bank. He hurried on toward Iolcus and never saw the old woman again.

B. Jason did not know, and was never to learn, that the old woman was Hera in disguise. The goddess was testing him to play a part in an elaborate plan to destroy Pelias, in punishment for his many slights to her. For some reason Hera believed that only the sorceress MEDEA, granddaughter of Helius, the sun-god, would be clever enough to overthrow the powerful and treacherous king. But Medea lived in Colchis, at the farthest end of the Black Sea. A generation earlier Phrixus, son of Cretheus' brother Athamas, had flown there on the back of a miraculous ram and had nailed its golden fleece to a tree in the grove of Ares, where it was guarded by an unsleeping dragon. The inhabitants of this barbarian land made a practice of killing those few strangers who succeeded in making the perilous journey to their capital of Aea. No ordinary man would risk such dangers. Moreover, although the young woman had a strong claim on the throne of Corinth, where her father, Aeëtes, had once ruled, she had no reason to concern herself with the affairs of Iolcus. Hera saw the solution to both these problems in the bold and extraordinarily handsome youth Jason. After satisfying herself at the river that he was the right man to bring Medea to Iolcus, she set herself to guide all his crucial words and deeds with great care.

Some say that Pelias had invited Jason to the festival. It is more generally thought that the young man appeared alone and unheralded in Iolcus and that Pelias knew nothing of him until it was reported that a one-sandaled man had appeared in the marketplace. The king, who had long lived in fear of the oracle, leaped into his mule-drawn chariot and hurried to the public square. There he saw a tall youth wearing the rough trousers and pantherskin cloak of a Magnesian. One of his feet was bare. Pelias demanded the stranger's name. Jason not only gave it but calmly announced that he had come to claim the throne either for his father or for himself.

Exactly what happened next has been disputed, but it is clear that the wily Pelias cast about for some way of ridding himself of the dangerous visitor without stirring up trouble during the festival. To kill Jason or even to oppose him openly on this occasion would be an outrage against the laws of hospitality that Zeus himself rigorously enforced. Moreover, it is probable that the family of Aeson, whom Pelias had never dared to kill, had many supporters in the city. According to one version of the tale, Pelias hit upon a solution to his problem at once. He asked Jason what he would do if an oracle said that a certain citizen would kill him. The bold youth replied without hesitation, "I would order him to bring back the golden fleece." Seizing upon these words, the king commanded Jason to do precisely that.

According to Pindar, Jason was far from being alone in Iolcus. As soon as his uncles, Amythaon and Pheres, and their sons Melampus and Admetus heard of his arrival, they gathered about him. Jason feasted them for six days, perhaps in Aeson's house, then let them know of his intention to claim the kingdom. At once they went with him to the palace and confronted Pelias. Jason demanded for himself the throne and scepter that had rightly belonged to his father, but offered to let the king keep the herds and fields that he had seized. Pelias answered smoothly, inventing a story that served his purpose well. The Delphic oracle, he said, had recently interpreted a disturbing dream of his to mean that the gods of the Underworld were angry because the ghost of Phrixus had been permitted to remain unhonored in a foreign land. The oracle had warned that the spirit must be brought home from Colchis to Thessaly, and with it the golden fleece. Pleading his own advanced age, Pelias called on Jason to undertake this quest and swore that upon his return he would turn over to him the kingdom.

In both versions of this confrontation, Jason, eager for glory, accepted Pelias' proposal. He consulted the Delphic oracle about his prospects and then invited the most adventurous young nobles of all the Greek cities to share in the quest. Argus, aided by Athena, built a ship, which was christened the *Argo*. After appropriate ceremonies Jason took leave of his father and mother, and the *Argo* sailed out of the Gulf of Pagasae into the Aegean. Pelias' own son, Acastus, was on board, but in spite of this fact the king was pleased to think that he would never again see the ship or any of its crew. Pelias did not know that Jason's rash promise had been inspired by Hera, and that in the very moment when the youth had seemed to fall into the snare that he had set, the goddess' more deadly trap had begun to close about *him*.

C. The adventures of Jason in quest of the golden fleece are related in the story of the ARGONAUTS. As leader of the expedition, the young man distinguished himself more by a smooth tongue and a way with women than by good judgment and courage in emergencies. On the many occasions when the *Argo* or its crew were in danger, they were generally saved through the prowess of the other members, the sorcery of Medea, or the intervention of a god. Hera took care that Jason should return safely in order that Medea might reach Iolcus. To this end she enlisted the aid of both Athena and Aphrodite. The latter goddess was called in to cause the Colchian sorceress to fall so deeply in love with Jason that she would even betray her father and murder her brother for his sake.

All of these things came about as Hera had planned and, after many near escapes from disaster, the *Argo* neared home. Before this, however, a rumor had got about in Iolcus that the ship had gone down with all its crew. Believing himself rid of the last dangerous pretender to his throne, Pelias finally dared to do away with Aeson. He forced the aged man to drink bull's blood, a deadly poison, and took the added precaution of killing his son Promachus, a mere boy. Aeson's wife made her way to the palace, cursed the king and his household, and killed herself with a sword. Pelias now imagined that he had circumvented the fate that the oracle had predicted and that he had nothing left to fear but the old age that was threatening his powers.

D. The Argonauts, meanwhile, had put in at a point some distance from Iolcus to consider what they should do next, for Jason was sure that Pelias had no intention of keeping his promise to relinquish the throne. With only fifty-two men at his side, Jason could not hope to take the city by force. As so often before, it was MEDEA [B] who found a solution to his problem. She killed Pelias by a trick and thus allowed the Argonauts to seize the city.

Some say that Jason, having won the throne that belonged to him by hereditary right, turned it over to Acastus and went to Corinth, where Medea had been invited to rule. Others say that Acastus and the Iolcans angrily expelled Jason for his part in the atrocious murder of Pelias and that Acastus then succeeded his father as king. Whatever the reason, Jason left the city whose rule he had tried so hard to win. He never returned, except briefly to aid Peleus in his quarrel with Acastus. According to some accounts, Jason's son Thessalus returned to Iolcus and succeeded Acastus on the throne.

E. Hera, having used Jason to achieve her revenge on Pelias, took no further interest in him. According to some accounts, he became king of Corinth by virtue of Medea's hereditary claim to the throne. It is more commonly said that Jason was welcomed to Corinth by King Creon and lived there happily with Medea for ten years. At some point he took part in the Calydonian boar hunt, but distinguished himself only by killing one of the dogs. Medea bore him two sons, Mermerus and Pheres—though some writers speak of a son and a daughter, Medeius and Eriopis, or of twin boys, Thessalus and Alcimenes, and a third son, Tisandrus. (Jason had previously had sons—Euneüs and either Nebrophonus or Deïpylus—by Hypsipyle, queen of Lemnos.) According to the epic *Naupactia*, Jason went from Iolcus to the island of Corcyra rather than to Corinth. Mermerus was killed by a lioness while hunting on the mainland opposite.

After some years in Corinth, Jason became ambitious to marry Glauce or Creüsa, daughter of King Creon, in order to win advantage for himself and his children, who had no rights as progeny of a barbarian woman. He therefore divorced MEDEA [E] and Creon exiled her. She took a terrible vengeance on her husband by killing his new wife, the old king, and her own two children by Jason, before escaping to Athens. Some say that Jason was killed at the same time, but this story is not generally accepted. In any case, these events were the beginning of the end for Jason. Just how that end came is disputed. According to some writers, Jason, overcome with grief and disgrace, committed suicide. The most usual version is the most ironic: seated in despair under the rotting hulk of the *Argo*, in which he had won his brief glory, Jason was killed by a beam that fell from the wreckage.

F. The principal events of Jason's story are related in three Classical works: Pindar's fourth Pythian Ode deals with the quarrel with Pelias; the *Argonautica* of Apollonius Rhodius is the most detailed source for the voyage of the Argonauts; and Euripides' drama *Medea* tells of the tragedy in Corinth. Apollodorus [1.9.16–28, 3.13.7] made a good summary of Jason's career. Ovid [*Metamorphoses* 7.1–397] and Diodorus Siculus [4.40.1–3, 4.50.1–4.53.2] describe in considerable detail Medea's help to Jason in Colchis and Iolcus. Hyginus also relates many of the events in his *Fabulae* [12–14, 24–25].

Jocasta or **Epicasta**. A daughter of Menoeceus. Jocasta, whom Homer and some other writers call Epicasta, married LAÏUS when he returned from Pelops' court to become king of Thebes. When a son was born to them, they exposed it because Laïus had been warned by an oracle that a son by Jocasta would kill him. The child, saved by shepherds, grew to manhood in Corinth and did kill his father, neither knowing the other. This young man, OEDIPUS, had been warned by the Delphic oracle that he would kill his father and marry his mother. To avoid his supposed parents in Corinth, he came to Thebes; defeated the Sphinx, who was ravaging the land; and was rewarded with Jocasta's hand by her brother, Creon. She bore him two sons, Eteocles and Polyneices, and two daughters, Antigone and Ismene, though some writers claim that these were Oedipus' children by Euryganeia, daughter of Hyperphas. In Sophocles' tragedy *Oedipus the King*, Jocasta commits suicide on learning that she has married her son. In Euripides' *Phoenician Women*, she is still alive during the war of the Seven against Thebes and kills herself over the bodies of her sons by Oedipus, who have just battled to the death. Homer [*Odyssey* 11.271–280] implies that Oedipus' troubles after the discovery of his guilt were caused by the Erinyes of Jocasta.

judgment of Paris. See GOLDEN APPLE.

Juno. A Roman goddess of marriage and the wife of Jupiter. Like the Greek goddess HERA, with whom the Romans early identified Juno, she was the patroness of women and governed all their concerns from birth to death. As goddess of childbirth she was called Juno Lucina—though Lucina was sometimes regarded as a separate goddess with functions similar to those of the Greek Eileithyia, Hera's daughter. As Juno Moneta, the goddess also governed finances, and the Roman mint was located in her temple on the Capitoline Hill. Juno's name is the feminine counterpart of Jupiter (Heavenly Father).

Jupiter or **Juppiter**. The chief god of the Romans, identified by them with ZEUS. The name Jupiter was less an appellation than a title, being a contraction of two words meaning "Heavenly Father." Jupiter was a sky-god who had control of the weather and whose weapon was the thunderbolt. His nature and functions were very similar to those of Zeus, and most of his myths were borrowed from the Greek god. Jupiter's cult and his general character were, however, well established in Italy before the Greek religion became influential there. Juno (whose name is a feminine form of "Jupiter") was always regarded as his wife, whereas Hera probably antedated her husband, Zeus, in Greece.

Juventas. The Roman goddess of youth. An ancient goddess, Juventas was identified with the Greek goddess HEBE, whose name also meant "Youth."

K

Ker. A female death-spirit. Keres, often represented as fanged and taloned women, resembled Erinyes, both in their appearance and in their function, which was to claim and carry off the bodies of the dead to Hades. They personified, however, only the inevitability of death and generally lacked the retributive duties of the Erinyes. Occasionally, in either the singular or the plural, they are identified with the FATES as bringers of death. They were said by Hesiod to be daughters of Nyx (Night) and sisters of Moros (Doom), Thanatos (Death), Hypnos (Sleep), and other abstractions. They were invoked by Medea during her incantation that caused the death of Talos. [Homer, *Iliad*, 18.535–538; Hesiod, *Theogony*, 211–212, 217–222, and *Works and Days*, 92; *Shield of Heracles* 156–158, 248–263; Aeschylus, *Seven Against Thebes*, 1060–1063; Apollonius Rhodius 4.1665–1670; Pausanias 5.19.6.]

Kerkyra. See CORCYRA.

kerykeion. See CADUCEUS.

Kneeler, The. See HERCULES.

Kore. A title of PERSEPHONE. The Underworld goddess was worshiped at Eleusis as Kore (Maid), daughter of Zeus and Demeter, who, in her annual return to the upper world from Hades, symbolized the yearly growth of the crops.

Ktesios. An epithet (He of the Storeroom) of Zeus. Ktesios was an ancient spirit who guarded storerooms. Sacred symbolic objects representing him were placed with solemn ceremony in a jar in every storeroom. This primitive cult of an unpersonified fertility-spirit (localized at Phlya, in Attica) was assimilated to the worship of Zeus.

L

Labdacus. A king of Thebes. Labdacus was the only child of Cadmus' son, King Polydorus, and Nycteïs, daughter of Nycteus. Polydorus died when Labdacus was still an infant and left Nycteus to rule as regent. This office was entrusted by Nycteus to his brother, Lycus. On reaching adulthood Labdacus reigned briefly, but died young, after losing a short war waged over boundaries with the Athenian king Pandion. Apollodorus [3.5.5] claims that he was, like Pentheus, torn apart by women for opposing Dionysus. Lycus again became regent, ruling in place of Labdacus' young son, Laïus. [Pausanias 2.6.2, 9.5.4–5.]

Labyrinth. A mazelike building at Cnossus, in Crete. The Labyrinth was built by DAEDALUS as a prison for the Minotaur. Theseus found his way in and out with the aid of Ariadne, but Daedalus was later imprisoned in the building with his son, Icarus.

Lacedaemon. A king and eponym of Lacedaemon (Sparta). A son of Zeus and Taÿgete, Lacedaemon married Sparta, daughter of the Laconian king Eurotas, from whom he inherited the kingdom. Lacedaemon renamed the region for himself and founded what was to become its principal city, calling it after his wife. Sparta bore a son, Amyclas, and a daughter, Eurydice, who married Acrisius. [Pausanias 3.1.2; Apollodorus 3.10.3.]

Lachesis. See FATES.

Laconia. The southernmost part of the Peloponnesus. Laconia has little mythical history apart from that of its principal city, Sparta, or Lacedaemon. Although Laconia was one of the largest of the ancient Greek regions, it had no other major cities, with the exception of Amyclae. Cape Taenarum, at the tip of one of Laconia's two southern peninsulas, was celebrated as an entrance to the Underworld; Cape Malea, the tip of the other peninsula, was a notorious hazard to ships. The Laconian island of Cythera, lying off Malea, was a chief cult center of Aphrodite.

Ladon. A hundred-headed snake. Ladon, an immortal offspring of Typhon (Typhöeus) and Echidna, helped the Hesperides guard the apples in their garden. In spite of his immortality he was killed by HERACLES [H].

Ladon River. A river of western Arcadia. The Ladon, noted for its beauty, was the scene of one of Daphne's adventures and of Heracles' capture of the

Cerynitian hind. The nymph Syrinx was transformed into a reed beside its banks so that she might avoid Pan's pursuit.

Laelaps. An infallible hound. Zeus is said by some writers to have given Laelaps to Europa as a watchdog, decreeing that it should catch whatever it pursued. Europa's son Minos gave it to Procris, one of his numerous mistresses. Procris gave it to her husband, Cephalus, who in turn lent it to Amphitryon in his hunt for the Teumessian vixen. This fox had been destined by Hera never to be caught. Faced with this seemingly insoluble problem, Zeus turned both animals to stone.

Laërtes. A king of Ithaca. Laërtes, the only son of Arceisius, or of Cephalus and Procris, is said to have been an Argonaut. He conquered the city of Nericus, on the mainland, and presumably was responsible for Ithaca's dominance over the surrounding areas. Laërtes married Anticleia, daughter of Autolycus, and she bore him one son, Odysseus. According to many writers, however, Anticleia was pregnant by Sisyphus when she married Laërtes. During Odysseus' twenty-year absence from Ithaca, Laërtes was too old and feeble to protect his daughter-in-law, Penelope, from the unwelcome advances of her many suitors. It was his shroud that she pretended to be weaving in order to postpone a decision. But Laërtes lived to see the suitors destroyed by Odysseus and Telemachus, and himself killed Eupeithes.

Laërtes appears in many of the Ithacan scenes of Homer's *Odyssey*. See also Hyginus [*Fabulae* 201], Ovid [*Metamorphoses* 13.143–145], and Apollodorus [1.9.16].

Laestrygonians or **Laestrygones.** Cannibal giants. The Laestrygonians lived in a city called Telepylus, which had been founded by Lamus, a son of Poseidon. Odysseus' ships entered the quiet harbor of Telepylus and he sent scouts ashore. King Antiphates' daughter led them to her father, who promptly ate one. The others warned Odysseus in time for his ship to escape, but the other ships of his fleet were crushed with huge stones by the giants, who speared the survivors like fish and ate them. [Homer, *Odyssey*, 10.80–132.]

Laïus. A king of Thebes. When Laïus' father, Labdacus, died, Laïus was only a child. Lycus ruled as regent, as he had during Labdacus' childhood. When Amphion and Zethus were preparing to usurp the throne, the Thebans who wished to safeguard the line of Cadmus spirited Laïus away. The boy found refuge at the court of Pelops, king of Pisa, in the Peloponnesus, though this famous ruler was a brother-in-law of Amphion. Laïus grew to young manhood in Pisa and became infatuated with Chrysippus, the king's beautiful illegitimate son. While teaching him to drive a chariot, perhaps during the Nemean games, Laïus kidnaped the youth and carried him to Thebes, where the deaths of Amphion and Zethus had left the throne vacant. Laïus was duly awarded the kingdom. What happened to Chrysippus is variously related. Some say that Pelops recovered him by force of arms; others that Atreus and

Thyestes, Pelops' legitimate sons, killed the boy at the instigation of their mother, Hippodameia; still others that he killed himself from shame.

Laïus married Jocasta or Epicasta, daughter of Menoeceus, a leading descendant of the Sparti. When they remained childless, he went to Delphi, hoping to learn of a cure. Instead he received a warning: he must have no child by his wife, for if he did, that child would kill him. Laïus observed the injunction for a time, but one night, drunk on wine, he lay with Jocasta, and in due course she bore a son. Laïus pierced its feet with some sharp instrument and gave it to his shepherds to expose on Mount Cithaeron. Many years later the king learned of omens which indicated that his predicted fate would soon catch up with him. He set out for Delphi, hoping that the oracle would tell him what lay in store for him. Riding in his chariot with one or more servants, he encountered at that point known as the Cleft Way, where a second road led off to Daulis, a lone young man on foot. This stranger would not defer to the king, even though Laïus' attendants ordered him to give way. Laïus either struck him with his goad or grazed his foot with one of the chariot wheels. Enraged, the young man dragged him from the chariot and killed him with a stick. Turning on the attendants, he killed all but one, who escaped. Laïus died unaware that he had met the fate threatened so long ago by the oracle: the stranger was his own son, OEDIPUS. Laïus' body was discovered by Damasistratus, king of Plataea, who buried him, together with his servants, where he had met his death.

Ancient writers differed as to the cause of the tragedies that beset Laïus and his descendants for three generations. Some attributed these troubles to the young man's offense against the laws of hospitality in carrying off Chrysippus. Others believed that Laïus' guilt lay in ignoring the oracle's command that he have no children by his wife. Still others found a separate cause for each misfortune. [Apollodorus 3.5.5; Pausanias 9.5.5–9, 9.26.2–4; Hyginus, *Fabulae*, 85. Sources for the story of Laïus and his son will be found under OEDIPUS.]

Lampetië. See HELIUS [C].

Lampus. A Trojan elder. Lampus, a son of Laomedon and Strymo, or Placia, or Leucippe, was one of Priam's brothers. His son Dolops was killed in the Trojan War. [Homer, *Iliad*, 3.146–151, 15.525–526, 20.236–238; Apollodorus 3.12.3.]

Lamus. See LAESTRYGONIANS.

Laocoön (1). A Trojan priest of Thymbraean Apollo or Poseidon. When the Trojans were arguing whether to destroy the WOODEN HORSE left behind by the Greeks or to take it inside their walls, Laocoön warned them that there were Greeks hidden in the horse. He flung his spear at the image. Later, as he was sacrificing to Poseidon, two sea-serpents appeared and killed his two sons. When he tried to defend the boys, he too was killed. The snakes are usually said to have been sent by Apollo to punish Laocoön for having married and had children against the god's will. At the time, however, most of the Trojans believed that some god had avenged the priest's insult to the horse, and their decision to drag it into the city was confirmed. Aeneas and his followers, on the other hand, were so disturbed by this omen that they left Troy for their homes in Dardania and may thus have escaped destruction when the city fell. [Vergil, *Aeneïd*, 2.40–56, 2.199–231; Hyginus, *Fabulae*, 135.]

Laocoön (2). An Argonaut. Laocoön, a son of Oeneus, king of Calydon, by a serving woman, was sent when no longer young to guard his young half-brother Meleager on the voyage of the Argonauts. Hyginus [*Fabulae* 14] calls him a son of Oeneus' brother Porthaon. [Apollonius Rhodius 1.190–194.]

Laodamas. A king of Thebes. The young Laodamas succeeded his father, Eteocles, on the throne, but Creon served as regent for several years. Laodamas led the Thebans in their war with the Epigoni and killed Aegialeus. Some say that he was himself killed by Alcmeon, others that he led the Thebans, after their defeat, in their flight to Illyria. [Apollodorus 3.7.3; Pausanias 9.5.13.]

Laodameia (1). A daughter of Acastus, king of Iolcus. Laodameia married Protesilaüs, king of Phylace. He was killed at Troy, and Laodameia grieved so profoundly that Hermes consented to bring her husband back from Hades for a space of three hours. When he went back to the dead, Laodameia killed herself. According to another version of the story, she consoled herself with a bronze image of Protesilaüs, which she secreted in her bedroom. A servant one day saw her kissing it and reported to her father that she had a lover. On learning the truth, Acastus burned the statue, but Laodameia leaped onto the pyre. According to the lost epic *Cypria* [17], Protesilaüs' wife was Polydora, daughter of Meleager. [Apollodorus "Epitome" 3.30; Hyginus, *Fabulae*, 103–104.]

Laodameia (2). A daughter of Bellerophon and Philonoë. The mother by Zeus of Sarpedon, Laodameia was killed by Artemis. [Homer, *Iliad*, 6.196, 6.205.]

Laodice (1). A daughter of Priam and Hecuba. Laodice, the loveliest of Priam's daughters, married Antenor's son Helicaön or the Mysian king Telephus. After Troy's fall she disappeared into a chasm in full view of everyone. [Homer, *Iliad*, 3.121–124; Apollodorus "Epitome" 5.23; Hyginus, *Fabulae*, 101.]

Laodice (2). A daughter of Agamemnon and Clytemnestra, according to Homer. She may have been identified with Electra, whom Homer does not mention.

Laomedon. A king of Troy. Laomedon was a son of Ilus and Eurydice, daughter of Adrastus. Apollo and Poseidon undertook to build a wall around Troy for him, either to test his reputation for untrustworthiness or because they were required to work for hire for a year as punishment for rebelling against Zeus. Laomedon not only refused their wages when the wall was finished but threatened to cut off their ears or to sell them, bound hand and foot, into slavery. Apollo and Poseidon punished this breach of contract by sending, respectively, a plague and a sea-monster to ravage Laomedon's land.

On the advice of an oracle, Laomedon chained his daughter Hesione to a rock as an offering to the monster. Some say that many girls were sacrificed to the monster and eventually the lot fell to Hesione. She would have died too had not HERACLES [G] stopped at Troy, either on his way home from the Amazon campaign or on the outward voyage of the *Argo*. He offered to save Hesione if Laomedon would give him the mares that Zeus had paid the king (or his grandfather Tros) for Ganymede. According to some accounts, Hesione herself was to be part of the wages. Laomedon kept his bargain no better with Heracles than he had with the gods. Heracles sailed away empty-handed, swearing vengeance.

This vengeance had to await the completion of his labors, but in due course he returned to Troy with a sizable force, which included Telamon, king of Salamis. Laomedon's men fought fiercely and almost destroyed the Greek ships, but were eventually driven back into the city. After a siege Telamon breached the wall and the Greeks entered the city. Heracles killed Laomedon, gave Hesione to Telamon, and left Laomedon's son Priam to rule Troy. By a wife who is variously named, Laomedon had had several other children: Tithonus, Clytius, Hicetaon, Lampus, Cilla, and Astyoche. He also had a son, Bucolion, by the nymph Calybe. [Homer, *Iliad*, 5.638–651, 6.23–25, 20.236–238, 21.441–457; Apollodorus 2.5.9, 2.6.4, "Epitome" 3.24; Hyginus, *Fabulae*, 89.]

Laonome. See ALCAEÜS (1).

Laphystius, Mount. A Boeotian mountain, west of Lake Copaïs. On Mount Laphystius, Athamas was preparing to sacrifice his son Phrixus when the ram with the golden fleece carried off Phrixus and his sister Helle. This sacrifice was probably connected with the evidently primitive cult of Laphystian Zeus, which had its center on the mountain.

Lapithes or **Lapithus.** The eponym of the Lapiths. Lapithes, a Thessalian king, was a son of Apollo and Stilbe. Diodorus Siculus [4.69.1–2] makes him a brother of Centaurus, who is usually said to be his descendant. Lapithes married Orsinome, daughter of Eurynomus, and she bore him two sons, Phorbas and Periphas.

Lapiths or **Lapithae.** A tribe of northern Thessaly. The Lapiths traced their ancestry in differing stories to Ixion or to Lapithes, an obscure son of Apollo and Stilbe. They are famous for their battle with the Centaurs, another Thessalian tribe who were also descended from Ixion. Ixion's son, Peirithoüs, the Lapith king, led his people in the fighting, which broke out at his wedding. With the help of his Athenian friend Theseus and of Caeneus, an invulnerable Lapith leader, Peirithoüs drove the Centaurs from Thessaly. After Peirithoüs' failure to return from a visit to Hades, the Lapiths fought a border war with the Dorians. The Dorians, under Aegimius, were outnumbered but had the help of Heracles, leading an army of Arcadians. Coronus, the Lapith leader, was killed, and the Lapiths were driven from Doris. They were still strong enough after this reverse to send forty ships to the Trojan War under Polypoetes and Leonteus—sons, respectively, of Peirithoüs and Coronus. Like many other Greek generals at Troy, these two did not return to their homeland but settled elsewhere. The Lapiths seem thereafter to have lost their identity as a tribe—if, indeed, they were ever more than legendary.

Larentia or **Acca Larentia.** An obscure Roman goddess. Larentia's original functions are unknown, though she had an annual festival, the Larentalia. In Classical times, rationalizing writers converted her into a mortal woman, or two women. She was said by some to have been the wife of Faustulus, the shepherd who reared Romulus and Remus. Some writers indeed claimed that she was the "she-wolf" that suckled the children—*lupa* being as well a colloquial term for a prostitute.

Her profession in this version of the tale connects her also with a very different story. The keeper of Hercules' temple at Rome once invited the god to a contest with dice, the loser to give the winner a present. When the god won, the temple servant locked in the sanctuary, along with a sumptuous dinner, Larentia, the most beautiful prostitute in Rome. The god, after taking his fill, advised Larentia to court the next man she met. She did so and became the wife of a wealthy Etruscan, who bequeathed to her all his money. This money Larentia left in turn to the Roman people. [Plutarch, *Parallel Lives*, "Romulus," 4.3–5.5; Livy 1.4.7.]

lares or **lases.** Roman household-gods. Each Roman home had its lar, who was honored together with the family's PENATES and Vesta, goddess of the hearth. As an extension of the king's family, the state, too, had a lar—or lares, when these guardian spirits came to be regarded as multiple. Other lares were patrons of the principal crossroads of the city and of the adjacent neighborhoods. There are two main theories as to the origin of the lares: they were spirits of the founding ancestors of a family, or they were fertility-spirits who, by watching over the fields, brought each family prosperity. A family lar was often represented as a youth bearing a drinking horn and cup, familiar symbols of fertility.

Larisa or **Larissa.** The name of two Thessalian cities and of the citadel of Argos. According to Pausanias, all three were named for a daughter of Pelasgus. One Larisa was the site of Perseus' accidental killing of Acrisius.

Latins. A group of Italic tribes inhabiting Latium. The Latins who lived in the area immediately south of the Tiber River in the days prior to and during the founding and expansion of Rome were later referred to as the Ancient Latins. A considerable part of the population of Rome in imperial times was Latin.

Latinus. A king of Latium, a large area extending southward from Rome. Latinus, a son of Faunus and Marica, a Laurentine nymph, was a great-grandson of Saturn. According to Vergil's *Aeneïd*, in which he is a principal character, he would have welcomed Aeneas, with the Trojans, to Latium and offered him the hand of his daughter, Lavinia, oracles having warned that she should marry a foreigner. Latinus' wife, Amata, however, favored the suit of the Rutulian king Turnus. When war ensued with the Trojans, the aged Latinus abdicated. Some other Roman traditions have it that Latinus fought the Trojans and was killed. Lavinia finally married Aeneas and Latinus thus became an ancestor of the Romans, giving his name to their language. In Hesiod's *Theogony* [1011–1016], Latinus was identified as a son of Odysseus and Circe; Hyginus [*Fabulae* 127] made him Circe's son by Telemachus.

Latium. A region of ancient Italy extending mainly southward from Rome. According to the artificial genealogy set forth in Vergil's *Aeneïd*, it was ruled first by Saturn, then by his descendants Picus, Faunus, and Latinus. Latinus' daughter Lavinia married the Trojan Aeneas and their line ruled much of this area, first from Alba Longa, later from Rome.

Latona. The Roman name of LETO.

Laurentum. The land ruled by King Latinus, south of Rome. Laurentum was renamed Lavinium by Aeneas.

Lavinium. A city south of Rome. Lavinium was founded by Aeneas and named for his wife Lavinia, daughter of King Latinus. It seems to have absorbed the older city of Laurentum.

Learchus. See ATHAMAS [A, C, D].

Leda. A daughter of the Aetolian king Thestius. When Tyndareüs was driven from the Spartan throne in his youth, he took refuge in Aetolia. There he married Leda. She bore Helen, Clytemnestra, the Dioscuri (Castor and Polydeuces), Timandra, Philonoë, and Phoebe. Zeus was said to have been the true father of one or more of these children, usually of Helen and Polydeuces. Helen was hatched from an egg after Zeus had visited Leda as a swan. There are, however, many variations in the accounts of Leda's childbearing, including one in which the goddess Nemesis, not Leda, produced the egg.

Leiriope. See NARCISSUS.

Leïtus. A Boeotian leader. Leïtus' father is variously called Alector, Alectryon, Electryon, or Lacritus; his mother was Cleobule. An Argonaut in his youth, Leïtus became a suitor of Helen and later, together with Peneleüs, led fifty Boeotian ships to the Trojan War. Although wounded by Hector, he survived the war—the only Boeotian leader to do so—and brought the bones of Arcesilaüs home with him. [Homer, *Iliad*, 2.494, 6.35–36, 17.601–606; Apollodorus 1.9.16, 3.10.8; Pausanias 9.4.3, 9.29.3.]

Lelegians or **Leleges.** A division of the earliest inhabitants of Greece, distinct from the Pelasgians and closely related to the CARIANS. According to Herodotus, the Lelegians lived in the Aegean islands and were a powerful force during Minoan domination of the Mediterranean Sea. Later they were driven to the mainland of Asia Minor, where they became known as Carians. Pausanias identified two apparently unrelated groups of Lelegians, both of which took their name from mythical personages named Lelex. One Lelex was autochthonous in Laconia, which was first called Lelegia. The other, a descendant of the Argive princess Io, emigrated to Megara and became king. (This event occurred twelve generations after the arrival there of Car, eponym of the Carians.) Homer listed Lelegians, together with Carians and Pelasgians, among the allies of Troy, saying that they came from the city of Pedasus, on the Satnïöeis River. Other writers referred to the presence of Lelegians in Samos, Thrace, and northern Greece, It is impossible to say who the Lelegians were, but the tradition of their close relationship with the Carians suggests that they were of Asiatic origin and spoke a non-Indo-European language.

Lelex (1). The autochthonous ancestor of the Spartans and eponym of the Lelegians. Lelex was said to be the father of Myles, Polycaon, and Therapne, and, by the naïad Cleocharia, of Eurotas. [Apollodorus 3.10.3; Pausanias 3.1.1, 3.19.9, 3.20.2.]

Lelex (2). A king of Megara. Lelex, a son of Poseidon and Libya, was said by the Megarians to have come to their city from Egypt in the twelfth generation after its founding by the Argive Car. He was the father of Cleson. This Lelex was doubtless an eponym of the Lelegians, as Car was of the Carians. [Pausanias 1.39.6, 1.44.3.]

Lemnos. An island in the northern Aegean Sea. When Hephaestus was flung out of heaven, he fell on Lemnos, where the Sintians (an ancient people of whom nothing else is known) cared for him. He was later reinstated on Mount Olympus, but never forgot Lemnos, which became his chief cult center. The Lemnians also claimed close connections with Dionysus, saying that he brought Ariadne there after their marriage. One of the four sons that she bore him was Thoas, who became king of the island. During his reign a series of events initiated by Aphrodite led the Lemnian women to kill all the males on the island. Only Thoas escaped, thanks to his daughter's loyalty. Discovering that a life without men did not promise well for the island's future, the women welcomed the Argonauts when they stopped at Lemnos on their outward voyage. Among the new generation that resulted from this timely visit was Euneüs, who was king at the time of the Trojan War. During much of that war Philoctetes remained stranded alone on Lemnos, but the assumption in this myth that the island was unpeopled at the time is not supported by the other myths. Lemnos, together with several other islands of the northern Aegean, was a center of the obscure but important cult of the Cabeiri.

Lenaeüs. An epithet (He of the Winepress) of Dionysus [H].

Leo (The Lion). A constellation. This group of stars is generally said to represent the Nemean lion, killed by Heracles. [Hyginus, *Poetica Astronomica*, 2.24.]

Leodocus. An Argonaut. Leodocus, a son of Bias and Pero, sailed in the *Argo* with his brothers Talaüs and Areius, but none of the three won great fame on this adventure. [Apollonius Rhodius 1.118–121.]

Leonteus. A son of Coronus. Together with Peirithoüs' son of Polypoetes, Leonteus led forty shiploads of Lapith forces to the Trojan War. They distinguished themselves particularly in repulsing the Trojan advance on the Greek ships. After the war they joined a group that marched overland to Colophon, near Ephesus. [Homer, *Iliad*, 2.738–747, 12.126–195; Apollodorus "Epitome" 6.2.]

Lepus (The Hare). A constellation. The hare was generally said to have been placed in the sky by Hermes in honor of its fleetfootedness. Although this starry animal seems to be running from Orion, some ancient commentators felt that hare hunting was too ignominious a pursuit for the mighty hunter and insisted that Orion was actually following the Bull. Others claimed that the Hare found himself in the sky in celebration not of his swiftness but of his equally impressive powers of producing offspring, a phenomenon noted by Aristotle.

This remarkable fecundity was particularly observed on the island of Leros, where it caused an ecological dilemma. A prominent citizen of the island imported a pregnant hare. The other islanders, pleased with the furry creature, procured hares of their own and began to raise them. It did not take long for them to discover the animals' propensities, but by that time it was too late to avoid the plague that followed. The hares, when their masters stopped feeding them, began to eat the crops, and before long the hungry islanders realized that they were engaged in a life-and-death struggle with the beasts. In desperation they organized a tremendous hare hunt. To judge from Hyginus' meager description [*Fabulae* 2.33] of the event, the beleaguered human population of Leros deployed itself in a phalanx the width of the island, then moved slowly forward, beating the undergrowth. Inch by inch, foot by foot, the hares were driven into the sea, where they drowned by the thousands.

According to Hyginus, the citizens of Leros commemorated their hare-raising ordeal by placing a hare in the stars. Since mortals do not possess such divine powers, however, it seems likely that the islanders had been aided in their extremity by some deity, perhaps Artemis, who saw fit to memorialize the episode in the sky.

Lerna. A town south of Argos on the shore of the Gulf of Argolis. The swampy rivers in the region of Lerna supplied Argos with water, thanks to Poseidon's graciousness to Danaüs' daughter Amymone in return for her favors. They were also the haunt of the monster Hydra, which Heracles killed. The supposedly bottomless Alcyonian Lake, in this same region, was claimed by the Argives to be an entrance to Hades.

Lesbos. A large island off the western coast of Asia Minor. Lesbos, in spite of its size and its distinction as a cultural center in the seventh century B.C., was the scene of few mythological events. The story that Orpheus' head and lyre washed up on the island's shore and were duly honored may be an attempt to account for its later reputation as a home of lyric poets, most notably Sappho.

Lethe. An Underworld river. The dead who descended to Hades drank the waters of Lethe (Forgetfulness) and forgot their former lives. Actual streams named Lethe were found in Spain and in Boeotia, at the site of Trophonius' oracle.

Leto. A daughter of the Titans Coeüs and Phoebe. Leto (or Latona, as the Romans called her) may in ancient times have been a powerful goddess of Oriental origin. She was known to the Greeks, however, mainly as the mother of Apollo and Artemis. One of the earliest loves of Zeus, she became pregnant by him. She wandered through many lands seeking a place to give birth, but none of them would let her rest. According to the *Homeric Hymn to Apollo* [3], they were afraid to become the birthplace of so great a god as Apollo. The more usual and plausible explanation of their reluctance was their fear of offending Hera, who hated Leto even though her affair with Zeus had occurred before his marriage to Hera. Hera had already caused the dragon Python to pursue Leto as she passed through the region of Panopeus or Delphi.

There are many versions of Leto's final travail. When Python threatened her, Zeus ordered Boreas, the North Wind, to carry her to Poseidon. Some say that Hera had decreed that no land under the sun should receive her. The sea-god therefore took her to the island of Ortygia and covered it with his waves so that it would no longer fall under Hera's ban. There Leto gave birth to Apollo and Artemis while clinging to an olive tree. (Ortygia had grown out of the sea where Leto's sister, Asteria, had plunged into the waves in the form of a quail (*ortyx*) while escaping the advances of Zeus.) Some say that only Artemis was born there and that she precociously aided her mother in giving birth to her brother, Apollo, on the nearby island of Delos. More usually it is said that both children were born on Delos—then called Ortygia or Asteria—while Leto clung to a palm tree beside a lake. All the goddesses but Hera and Eileithyia, goddess of childbirth, attended her. They sent Iris to persuade Eileithyia to come, too, even though Hera was keeping her close at hand in order to prevent her aiding the delivery. Eileithyia came and, after nine days of labor, Leto bore Apollo. Themis fed him on nectar and ambrosia.

Leto's troubles were not yet over. Apparently still pursued by Hera's anger, she fled to Lycia. When the peasants there would not let her drink from a well, she changed them into frogs. Later, near Delphi, she was chased by the Euboean giant Tityus, who tried to rape her. Leto called on her children to save her and they, or Apollo alone, killed the monster. Tityus was further punished in Hades. Apollo and Artemis were always quick to rescue their mother from danger, or merely from insults. (At the age of four days Apollo had killed Python for its attempt to violate Leto.) When NIOBE (2) boasted that she was greater than Leto, Apollo and Artemis punished her by killing her many children except for Meliboea, who prayed to Leto and was forgiven.

Leto saved her son when he was threatened by Zeus with imprisonment in Tartarus for killing the Cyclopes. She prevailed on her former lover to commute the sentence to a year's bondage to a mortal. Leto often hunted with her daughter. The two persuaded Zeus to make their former hunting companion Orion a constellation at his death. Leto, like her children, took the side of the Trojans in the Trojan War. She and Artemis healed the wounds of Aeneas during one of the battles.

The most detailed account of Leto's troubles during her pregnancy is in the *Homeric Hymn to Apollo* [3]. Other versions of the events in her myth are found in Hesiod [*Theogony* 404–410, 918–920], Homer [*Iliad*, 5.447–448, and *Odyssey*, 11.576–581], Ovid [*Metamorphoses* 6.157–381], Apollodorus [1.4.1, 3.10.4], Hyginus [*Fabulae* 53, 55, 140], and the *Astronomy* [4].

Leucippus (1). A son of Perieres and Gorgophone. Though Leucippus and his brother, Aphareus, ruled Messenia jointly after Perieres' death, Leucippus is known mainly as the father of Arsinoë, who may have been the mother of Asclepius, and of Phoebe and Hilaeira, who were abducted by the Dioscuri.

Leucippus (2). A son of Oenomaüs. Leucippus dressed as a girl to win the friendship of DAPHNE. When her companions stripped him to make him swim with them, they discovered his ruse and killed him.

Leucon. See ATHAMAS [D, E].

Leucothea. See INO.

Leucothoë. See HELIUS [B].

Leucus. A Cretan usurper. During the absence of King Idomeneus at the Trojan War, Leucus seduced his wife, Meda, then killed her and her daughter, though they took refuge at a shrine. He seized power in ten cities and, on the king's return, drove him from Crete. [Apollodorus "Epitome" 6.9–10.]

Liber. An ancient Roman god of fertility. Liber, often called Father Liber, was generally worshiped together with Ceres and Libera, who were identified, respectively, with Demeter and Persephone. Iacchus, the obscure companion of the latter goddesses at Eleusis, is likely to have been equated with Liber. Perhaps for this reason Liber came to be identified with Bacchus (Dionysus), who was often confused by the Greeks with Iacchus. Originally Liber and Libera may have been Italian fertility-deities who came, in time, to be associated with Ceres when she was connected with the widespread cult of Demeter.

Libera. An ancient Roman fertility-goddess. Libera, originally the wife of LIBER, came to be identified with the Greek Persephone and worshiped together with Ceres (Demeter).

Libya. The goddess and eponym of the land of Libya. Libya was the daughter of Epaphus and Memphis. By Poseidon she had twin sons, Belus and

Agenor, and also Lelex, who became king of Megara. Apollonius Rhodius, however, calls her the wife of the sea-god Triton [4.1742]. [Apollodorus 2.1.4; Pausanias 1.44.3.]

Libya. All of northern Africa west of Egypt. This enormous area, far larger than Libya is today, was said in various myths to extend as far west as the Atlas Mountains in present-day Morocco. It included Lake Tritonis, the home of Triton and scene of an adventure of the Argonauts. The Gorgons were located in Libya by some writers. It was the home too of the Lotus-eaters and the giant Antaeüs. The garden of the Hesperides was in Libya, not far from where Atlas stood holding up the sky. The principal cities of Libya were Carthage, founded by the Phoenician queen Dido, and Cyrene, which was colonized by Battus. Cyrene was the birthplace of Aristaeüs.

Lichas. Heracles' herald. Lichas had the unfortunate duty of taking the fatal tunic to HERACLES [N]. When the Hydra poison that had been innocently spread upon it began to take effect, Heracles flung Lichas from Cape Cenaeüm, in northwestern Euboea. His body became the sea-swept rock that bears his name. [Apollodorus 2.7.7; Hyginus, *Fabulae*, 36.]

Licymnius. A son of Electryon, king of Tiryns and Mycenae, by a Phrygian servant, Midea. When all Electryon's sons by his wife, Anaxo, were killed by Taphian cattle raiders, Licymnius was too young to take part in the fighting. Electryon was killed soon afterward by Amphitryon, and Licymnius went with his half-sister Alcmene and Amphitryon to Thebes, where he grew to manhood and married Perimede, daughter of Amphitryon (or possibly of Creon). She bore three sons, Oeonus, Argeius, and Melas. Licymnius and his sons were valued supporters of their cousin Heracles, Alcmene's son. Argeius and Melas were killed in Heracles' campaign against Oechalia. When Oeonus was killed by the sons of Hippocoön for throwing a stone at their dog, Heracles killed them. In his old age Licymnius participated in an abortive Heraclid invasion of Argos, where he was killed, either accidentally or in anger, by Tlepolemus, one of Heracles' sons. [Apollodorus 2.4.5–6, 2.7.7, 2.8.2; Pausanias 3.15.4.]

Liguria. The coastal area of northwestern Italy and southern France, roughly between present-day Genoa and Marseilles. Cycnus, an early musician king of Liguria, was changed into a swan while grieving over the death of his friend Phaëthon. Heracles, on his way home from Spain with the cattle of Geryon, was attacked and severely wounded by the Ligurians. He would have been killed had not a timely shower of stones from heaven provided him with enough ammunition to rout his enemies.

Lilybaeüm. A city (now Marsala) of western Sicily. When Butes tried to swim from the *Argo* to the Sirens' island, Aphrodite rescued him and transported him to Lilybaeüm, her chief cult center in Sicily.

Lindus. An ancient city on the island of Rhodes. The eponym of Lindus was a grandson of Helius and Rhode. Two of the earliest immigrants to Greek lands, Cadmus and Danaüs, stopped at Lindus. Danaüs is credited with having dedicated Athena's famous shrine there. (The personage worshiped at this shrine is believed actually to have been an ancient local goddess who came to be identified with Athena.) The Lindians had the reputation of being among the most able sailors in the Mediterranean Sea.

Linus. A poet-musician whose death was widely mourned. The earliest mention of Linus, by Homer [*Iliad* 18.569–572], says nothing of a person but merely refers to a dirge, traditionally sung at harvest time. Pausanias claims that this tradition of mourning songs had spread as far as Egypt, where the dirge was for Maneros, a local god. When a legendary Linus is first heard of, in a fragment attributed to Hesiod, he is called a son of the Muse Urania. Later writers, who make him a famous musician and poet, all call him a son of Apollo or of a Muse, but hardly two can be found who agree entirely on his parentage. He is a son of Apollo, or Amphimarus, or Oeagrus by Urania, or Calliope, or Aethusa, or Psamathe.

Faced with so many traditions, Pausanias tried to distinguish three separate persons named Linus. The first was a son of Psamathe, daughter of King Crotopus of Argos, by Apollo. Psamathe exposed the infant in fear of her father's anger, and Linus was eaten by Crotopus' dogs. When Apollo sent a plague on Argos as a result, the people ritually mourned the child's death. The other two personages identified by Pausanias were both Theban musicians. The earlier, a son of Urania and Amphimarus, son of Poseidon, was killed by the envious Apollo because of his skill in music. The later Linus, a son of Ismenius, taught lyre playing to the young Heracles. When the teacher struck his pupil during a lesson, the boy killed him. Other writers combine these Theban traditions, making Linus a son of Oeagrus and Calliope, and brother of Orpheus. He taught Thamyris and Orpheus to play the lyre, but found Heracles a recalcitrant pupil.

It is generally believed that the figure of Linus the musician grew up as an explanation of the ancient song sung to the word *ailinon* (possibly from the Phoenician *ai lanu,* "woe to us") as a lament for the harvested crops or dying vegetation. As such, it is comparable to the mourning for other young fertility-divinities cut off in their prime, such as Adonis, whose name Sappho is said to have coupled with that of Linus in her hymns to him. [Pausanias 1.43.7, 2.29.8, 9.29.6–9; Apollodorus 1.3.2, 2.4.9; Diodorus Siculus 3.67.1–2.]

Lion, The. See Leo.

Little Iliad. See Epic Cycle.

Livy. A Roman historian who lived during the reign of Augustus. Livy (Titus Livius) wrote a long history of Rome, of which considerable fragments survive. The earlier parts are a chief source for the mythical period of Rome's "history" prior to the expulsion of the Tarquins.

Locris. The name of two regions of ancient Greece. Opuntian Locris was on the mainland side of the Euboean Sea; Ozolian Locris on the north shore of the western part of the Gulf of Corinth. Opuntian Locris was the more prominent in mythological events, most of which were connected with its principal city, Opus. Its best-known hero, Ajax, was, however, a native of Naryx. The other Locris is likely to have been the one that sent a force with Amphitryon to attack the Taphians, but few other tales are told about it.

Lotis. A nymph who gave her name to a tree. Pursued by Priapus, Lotis was transformed (presumably in answer to prayers to some deity) into a tree. Her story, briefly mentioned by Ovid [*Metamorphoses* 9.346–348], must have included a provision for the tree's protection, for Dryope, when she plucked the flowers of the lotus tree, was herself transformed into a similar tree.

Lotus-eaters or **Lotophagi.** A tribe living on the Libyan coast. Driven before a north wind from Cape Malea, ODYSSEUS [D] came with his ships to the home of the vegetarian Lotus-eaters. When his scouts tasted the fruit of the lotus, they forgot everything else and had to be dragged back to the ship by force. Herodotus [4.177] and Pliny [*Natural History* 5.28] both wrote of the fruit and its devotees. [Homer, *Odyssey*, 9.82–104.]

Loxias. A title of Apollo. This epithet (Interpreter) referred to the god's prophetic knowledge of the will of Zeus.

Lua. A very obscure Roman goddess. Lua may have been originally regarded as the wife of Saturn, but her worship had declined by Classical times.

Lucifer. The Roman name for the morning star. He was called EOSPHORUS by the Greeks.

Lucina. A Roman goddess of childbirth. Lucina was a rather specialized goddess comparable to the Greek Eileithyia. Juno and Diana, themselves goddesses of childbirth, tended to usurp Lucina's functions. Her name was often attached as a surname to theirs—especially to Juno's.

Lucretia. The wife of Lucius Tarquinius Collatinus. During a Roman war against Ardea, Collatinus, Sextus Tarquinius, and others decided over their drink to test the virtue of their wives. They rode to Rome, then to Collatia, where, everyone agreed, Lucretia proved herself the most seemly of the wives. Her virtue, however, aroused the resentment of Sextus as her beauty excited his lust. A few nights later he again rode to Collatia and raped her at sword's point. The distraught woman told the story to her husband and father, made them vow to avenge her, then killed herself. The vow, which was taken as well by Lucius Junius Brutus, a friend of Lucretia's husband, led to the death of Sextus and the overthrow of his tyrannical father, Lucius Tarquinius Superbus, thus ending the kingship at Rome. [Livy 1.57.6–1.60.4.]

Lusi. An ancient Arcadian town in the foothills of the Aroanian Mountains. In Pausanias' day (second century A.D.) not even ruins remained of Lusi. It was remembered, however, as the place where Melampus had cured Proëtus' daughters of madness after luring them down out of the mountains.

Lyaeüs. An epithet (He Who Frees) of DIONYSUS [H].

Lycaon (1). A king of Arcadia. Lycaon was the son of Pelasgus by Cyllene or Meliboea. He succeeded his father on the throne and had, by many wives, fifty sons and a daughter, Callisto. Some say that Lycaon was a good man who was the first to worship Hermes in Arcadia; others call him a savage ruler. In either case, he suffered the same fate, punished for his sons' impiety if not his own. Disturbed by the wickedness in Arcadia, Zeus visited the land in disguise. Lycaon or his sons, deciding to test whether the stranger was god or mortal, fed him the flesh of a child or of a Molossian captive mixed with a stew. Zeus overturned the table, destroyed all the sons but Nyctimus with a thunderbolt, and turned Lycaon into a wolf. It may have been because of his disgust at the Arcadians' display of human savagery that Zeus nearly destroyed the race with a flood.

Pausanias [8.2.1–8.3.6] tells a different version of the tale. According to him, Lycaon was a pious, though primitive, man. He founded the ancient city of Lycosura on Mount Lycaeüs and established the worship of Lycaean Zeus, but his sacrifice of a child was unacceptable to the god and Zeus made Lycaon a wolf. Thereafter, at every sacrifice to Lycaean Zeus, a man was transformed into a wolf, but returned to human form at the end of eight or nine years if he had abstained from tasting human flesh. Still different is the motivation ascribed to Lycaon in the *Astronomy* [3], where he is said to have served up Callisto's son Arcas to his father, Zeus, in revenge for the god's seduction of his daughter. [Apollodorus 3.8.1–2; Ovid, *Metamorphoses*, 1.196–261.]

Lycaon (2). A son of Priam and Laothoë, daughter of Altes. While the young Lycaon was cutting fig shoots to make rims for his chariot during the Trojan War, Achilles captured him and sold him as a slave to Euneüs, king of Lemnos. Eëtion of Imbros, a guest-friend of Lycaon or his family, ransomed the youth and sent him to Arisbe, from which town he made his way to nearby Troy. Twelve days later, while escaping unarmed from the flooding river Scamander, he met Achilles again and was ruthlessly killed, in spite of his pleas for mercy. [Homer, *Iliad*, 21.34–135.]

Lycaon. See PANDARUS.

Lycia. A region on the southern coast of Asia Minor east of Caria. According to Herodotus, this land was originally occupied by the Milyans, or Solymi, and was called Milyan. Its people were subdued, at least temporarily, by Cretans who arrived under the leadership of Sarpedon, an exiled brother of Minos. The Cretans called themselves Termilae. The name of the area was again changed with the arrival of Lycus, exiled from Athens by his brother Aegeus. Lycus and the colonists whom he brought with him evidently conquered the area, for the people were thereafter called Lycians. The local customs, however, remained essentially Carian and Cretan rather than Greek. It was to Iobates, a Lycian king, that Proëtus sent Bellerophon to be disposed of. Bellerophon helped Iobates to fight off perennial attacks of the Solymi and killed the monster Chimaera. Instead of killing Bellerophon, Iobates made him his son-in-law, and the young man founded a line of Lycian kings, including Glaucus, who fought in the Trojan War against the Greeks.

The Titaness Leto is identified by many scholars with the Lycian goddess Lada; and Lyceius, a common epithet of her son, Apollo, may well mean "Lycian."

Lycomedes. The king of the Aegean island of Scyrus. When Theseus was exiled from Athens, he went to Scyrus, where he had inherited estates from his grandfather Scyrius. Lycomedes treated Theseus with courtesy, but privately feared that the famous king who had lost his country might induce the Scyrians to offer him theirs. Some say that Lycomedes was in league with Menestheus, who had led the Athenians to banish Theseus. For whatever reason, it is generally agreed that Lycomedes treacherously murdered his guest by pushing him over a cliff.

Some years after this event, the sea-goddess Thetis brought her son Achilles to Lycomedes and asked him to rear the child as a girl in his palace. She vainly hoped that Achilles might thus elude death in the Trojan War. Shortly after Achilles had left with the Greeks for Troy, Lycomedes' daughter Deïdameia gave birth to a son by Achilles. Lycomedes named him Pyrrhus. (He was later called Neoptolemus.) When Pyrrhus was still young, Odysseus and Phoenix came to Scyrus and induced him also to go with them to Troy. Nothing further is recorded of Lycomedes. [Plutarch, *Parallel Lives*, "Theseus," 35; Apollodorus 3.13.8, "Epitome" 1.24, 5.11; Pausanias 1.17.6, 10.-26.4.]

Lycormas River. An Aetolian river. After Evenus' suicide by drowning, the river was renamed for him.

Lycosura. A city in southern Arcadia. Lycosura was founded by Lycaon, king of Arcadia. Pausanias believed that this city, scarcely inhabited in his day, was the world's oldest.

Lycurgus (1). A king of the Edonians, of Thrace. Lycurgus was a son of Dryas. When Dionysus came to Thrace with his nurses or maenads, Lycurgus drove them away with an oxgoad. Some say that he imprisoned the god's followers. Dionysus, and perhaps his nurses as well, took refuge with Thetis and the other Nereïds in the sea.

Accounts of Lycurgus' punishment vary. According to Homer [*Iliad* 6.130–140], he was blinded by Zeus and did not live long thereafter. Later versions recount that, after drinking wine, he tried to rape his mother. Upon discovering what he had done, he began slashing at the grapevines, believing that wine was bad medicine. Dionysus drove him mad and he cut off his own feet, thinking them vines, or else hacked his son Dryas to death under the same delusion. The latter crime brought famine on Thrace. The Edonians, learning from an oracle that the drought would not end while Lycurgus lived, bound him and flung him to man-eating horses on Mount Pangaeüs. In another variation of the story, he killed both his wife and his son, and Dionysus threw him to his panthers on Mount Rhodope. Others say that he killed himself in his madness. Lycurgus was the first of many kings who were sorely punished for their opposition to Dionysus. [Apollodorus 3.5.1; Hyginus, *Fabulae*, 132, 192, 242, and *Poetica Astronomica*, 2.21.]

Lycurgus (2). A king of Arcadia. The eldest son of Aleüs, Lycurgus inherited from him the rule of Arcadia and of Tegea, which Aleüs had made his capital city. When his brothers, Cepheus and Amphidamas, sailed with the Argonauts, Lycurgus remained behind to govern for Aleüs, who was already old. In his place he sent his son Ancaeüs, one of his children by Cleophyle or Eurynome. Of his other sons, Epochus died young and Amphidamas and Iasus were better known for their offspring than for their own exploits. Pausanias [8.4.10–8.5.1] mentions only the first two of these sons and says that, since Ancaeüs was killed by the Calydonian boar, Lycurgus outlived both and reigned until a great age, leaving the throne to his nephew Echemus. [Apollodorus 3.9.1–2.]

Lycurgus (3) or **Lycus**. A son of Pheres. Migrating to Argolis from Thessaly, Lycurgus became king of Nemea and married Eurydice or Amphithea. She bore him a son, OPHELTES, who was killed by a snake.

Lycus (1). A king of Thebes. Lycus and Nycteus were sons of Chthonius, one of the Sparti; or of Hyrieus and the nymph Clonia; or of Poseidon by the Pleiad Celaeno. Expelled from Euboea for the murder of Phlegyas, king of Boeotian Orchomenus, they settled in Hyria. Later they went to Thebes, where they were granted citizenship through their friendship with King Pentheus. Pentheus' successor, Polydorus, married Nycteus' daughter Nycteïs and, dying young, made his father-in-law regent for his young son, Labdacus. Nycteus, however, either died of a wound or killed himself from shame over the behavior of his daughter Antiope, who, when pregnant by Zeus, had run away to Sicyon and married King Epopeus. Before his death Nycteus named Lycus regent in his stead and made him promise to punish Epopeus and Antiope. According to several writers, however, Lycus did not acquire the throne by legal means, but, having been given command of the armies by the Thebans, seized full power. In either case, Lycus marched against Sicyon. Some say that he subdued the city, killed Epopeus, and captured Antiope. Others claim that Epopeus died of a wound inflicted earlier by Nycteus and that his successor, Lamedon, turned Antiope over to Lycus in order to avoid war.

Lycus brought his errant niece back to Thebes. On the way she gave birth to twins at Eleutherae, on Mount Cithaeron, but Lycus gave the boys to shepherds to be exposed. Lycus (whom some writers call Antiope's father or husband) gave the girl to his wife, Dirce, for punishment. This woman, who may have suspected Antiope of having had improper relations with Lycus, imprisoned her and cruelly mistreated her. After many years the pisoner excaped and found her sons, Amphion and Zethus, safe and grown to manhood. They avenged her by killing Lycus and Dirce. Hyginus claims that Hermes forbade the twins to kill Lycus, but made him give up the throne to them. Lycus' son, also named Lycus, apparently escaped to Euboea, but later returned and, like his father, seized the Theban throne. [Apollodorus 3.5.5, 3.10.1; Pausanias 2.6.2–4, 9.5.5–6; Hyginus, *Fabulae*, 7–8.]

Lycus (2). A king of Thebes. A son of Poseidon or a Euboean descendant of the earlier Theban king Lycus, Lycus usurped the power at Thebes after murdering the aged Creon, who was ruling as regent for Laodamas, son of Eteocles. Lycus cruelly treated the family of the absent Heracles, Creon's son-in-law, but was killed by Heracles upon his unexpected return. Laodamas apparently succeeded to the throne. Lycus appears in Euripides' tragedy *Heracles*. [Hyginus, *Fabulae*, 32.]

Lycus (3). A king of the Mariandyni. Lycus succeeded his father, Dascylus, on the throne. One or the other had been aided by Heracles against the tribes that surrounded his country, and the Mariandyni had gained considerable territory. Lycus, after Heracles' departure, lost much of this land to the savage Bebrycian king Amycus. Amycus was killed by Polydeuces and the AR-GONAUTS [G] routed the Bebryces. In gratitude Lycus entertained them royally when they reached his territory, and sent his son, Dascylus, with them in the *Argo*. [Apollonius Rhodius 2.138–142, 2.752–850; Apollodorus 1.9.23, 2.5.9.]

Lycus (4). A son of Pandion and Pylia. Lycus and his three brothers drove from Athens the son of Metion, who had deposed their father, and divided the kingdom equally among themselves. Aegeus, however, assumed full power. Lycus may have been implicated in the rebellion of his brother Pallas against Aegeus, for Aegeus drove him from Athens. According to one tradition, he took refuge in Messenia with Aphareus. He introduced or amplified the rites of Demeter at Andania and also became one of the few living men to utter oracles. Another tradition has it that Lycus fled from Athens to the land of the Termilae, in Asia Minor, where he joined the Cretan exile Sarpedon. The people there came to be known as the Lycians, because of Lycus. The Lyceum at Athens is also said to have been named for him. [Apollodorus 3.15.5–6; Herodotus 1.173; Pausanias 4.1.6–9, 4.2.6, 10.12.11.]

Lydia. A region of western Asia Minor lying between Caria, on the south, and Mysia, on the north. Lydia was an ancient name for this land (the eponym being a mythical Lydus, son of Attis), though Herodotus says that the Lydians were earlier called the Meiones or Maeones. During the reigns of Alyattes and Croesus, in the sixth and seventh centuries B.C., Lydia came to occupy most of Asia Minor, but in the period that gave rise to most of the Greek myths it was concentrated more about the central coastal area on the Aegean Sea. Pelops and Niobe, though often called Phrygians, emigrated to Greece from the Lydian region of Mount Sipylus, northeast of Smyrna. Tmolus, eponym of a mountain range south of Sardis, was the father of Omphale, the Lydian queen whom Heracles served. Arachne was changed into a spider in her native Colophon, an Ionian coastal city south of Smyrna. Lydians from the region of Tmolus (whom Homer called Maeones) fought in the Trojan War but did not distinguish themselves.

Lynceus. A son of Aegyptus. When DANAÜS' [B, C] daughters killed Lynceus' brothers, his bride, Hypermnestra, helped him to escape. Later reconciled to his father-in-law, he succeeded him on the throne of Argos and was succeeded in turn by Abas, his son by Hypermnestra. [Apollodorus 2.1.5–2.2.1.]

Lynceus. See IDAS.

Lyra (The Lyre). A constellation. The Lyre commemorated in the sky was the one used by Orpheus. [Hyginus, *Poetica Astronomica*, 2.7.]

Lyrceia. See DANAÜS [B].

Lyrnessus. A city near Troy. Aeneas fled to Lyrnessus when Achilles drove him from Mount Ida. Achilles later sacked the city, killing Mynes and Epistrophus, sons of King Evenus. Lyrnessus was the home of Briseïs, Achilles' concubine.

Lyrus. A son of Anchises and Aphrodite. Lyrus, a brother of Aeneas, died childless. He is mentioned only by Apollodorus [3.12.2].

Lysianassa. See BUSIRIS; TALAÜS.

Lysimache. See TALAÜS.

Lysippe. A daughter of Proëtus and Stheneboea. Cured of madness by MELAMPUS [C], Lysippe married him and had three sons: Abas, Mantius, and Antiphates.

M

Macareus or **Macar.** A son of Aeolus. Macareus killed himself after committing incest with his sister Canace. [Hyginus, *Fabulae*, 242.]

Macaria. See HERACLIDS [A].

Machaon. A son of Asclepius. Machaon was one of the suitors of Helen. With his brother, Podaleirius, he later led thirty ships to Troy from Tricca, Ithome, and Oechalia—cities that were in either Messenia or western Thessaly. Both brothers served as physicians to the Greeks during the siege, having learned the art from their father. (According to the lost poem *Sack of Ilium*, by Arctinus of Miletus, they learned medicine, surprisingly, from Poseidon.) One or the other healed Philoctetes of his terrible wound. Machaon was killed by Eurypylus or Penthesileia. His bones were taken to the Messenian town of Gerenia by Nestor and buried there. His sons Nicomachus and Gorgasus carried on the tradition of healing. [Homer, *Iliad*, 2.729–733; Pausanias 3.26.9–10.]

Macris. A daughter of Aristaeüs. When Hermes saved the unborn Dionysus from the flames that destroyed his mother, he took him, according to one tradition, to Euboea. There Macris (whose mother may have been the child's aunt, Autonoë) gave Dionysus honey to eat. Hera punished her by driving her from Euboea. Macris took refuge on the island of Drepane or Scherië, then or later the home of the Phaeacians. She lived in a cave and brought wealth to the island. For her sake Demeter taught the Titans, who evidently lived on Drepane at the time, to reap corn. Macris was still living in the days of Nausithoüs, the Phaeacian king, and may have helped him in purifying Heracles after his murder of his children. Her cave remained sacred to her until it was renamed for Medea. [Apollonius Rhodius 4.539–541, 4.988–990, 4.1131–1140.]

Maeander. A river, now called Menderes, that flows westward into the Aegean Sea north of the ancient Carian city of Miletus. The river-god Maeander was the father of Samia, who married Ancaeüs, king of the island that was named Samos in her honor. The tortuous course of the river was the origin of the word "meander."

maenads. Female votaries of Dionysus. Wherever DIONYSUS [C] traveled, he was followed by a train of satyrs and maenads. The maenads were often joined in their orgiastic rites by local women, to the distress of their husbands and fathers. Dancing maenads, dressed in skins and carrying thyrsi, were often represented in Greek art.

Maeon. A Theban warrior. A son of Creon's son Haemon, Maeon was sent by Eteocles with Polyphontes and fifty men to ambush Tydeus. Tydeus killed all but Maeon, whom he spared in obedience to divine portents. Pausanias claims that Maeon buried Tydeus at Thebes. [Homer, *Iliad*, 4.391–398.]

Maeotis, Strait of and **Lake of.** See BOSPORUS.

Magnes. The eponym of the Magnesians. Magnes was a son of Zeus and Thyia, or of Aeolus and Enarete, or of Argus, son of Phrixus, and Perimele, daughter of Admetus. He was the father by a naïad of Polydectes and Dictys, who colonized Seriphus. He is also said to have been the father of Hymenaeüs, whom Apollo loved, and Eioneus, one of Hippodameia's suitors killed by her father, Oenomaüs. [*Catalogues of Women* 3; *Great Eoiae* 16; Apollodorus 1.7.3, 1.9.6.]

Magnesia. The rugged coastal area of Thessaly. Magnesia was named for Magnes, whose parentage was variously reported. It was the home of the Centaurs. Cheiron, their king, lived on Mount Pelion, in central Magnesia, where he reared many famous Greek leaders. The region is particularly associated with the youth of Jason and his conflict with Pelias, king of Iolcus, a city on the border of Magnesia.

Maia. The eldest daughter of Atlas and the Oceanid Pleïone. One of the PLEIADES, Maia was shy and lived quietly in a cave on Mount Cyllene, in Arcadia. Her retiring ways did not shield her from the eye of Zeus. He fell in love with her and used to visit her in her cave at night, while Hera was asleep. Maia bore him a son, whom she named HERMES [A]. This precocious child was not yet out of swaddling clothes when he stole Apollo's cattle and hid them in his mother's cave. The angry god tracked the herd to the cave. Maia showed him the seemingly innocent baby, but the god was not deceived. Some time later Maia came to Zeus's aid when Hera caused the death of another of his mistresses, Callisto. Hermes, on Zeus's orders, saved Callisto's baby, Arcas, and brought him to Maia to rear. [*Homeric Hymn to Hermes* 4.1–16; Sophocles, *Searching Satyrs;* Apollodorus 3.8.2, 3.10.1–2.]

Malea, Cape. One of two Laconian capes that are the southernmost extensions of the Peloponnesus. This rugged cape was presumably the mountain said to be the last haven of the Centaurs after they were driven from their Thessalian home by the Lapiths. It was also said by some to be the homeland of Seilenus. Cape Malea was notorious as a danger to sailors.

Malis. The extreme southern part of Thessaly, extending westward from the Gulf of Malis to Mount Oeta. Malis was known as the home of Poeas and of his son, Philoctetes, who led the Malians to the Trojan War but was abandoned by the Greeks at Lemnos. Trachis, the principal Malian city, was ruled by King Ceÿx, with whom Heracles left his family at the time of his death.

manes or **di manes.** Roman spirits of the dead. The manes were thought to inhabit the Underworld, from which they occasionally emerged to be propitiated by the living. Among them were the *di parentes*, or ancestral ghosts, who were annually appeased by each family through certain rites and sent back safely beneath the ground for another year.

Mantius. See MELAMPUS [C].

Manto. The daughter of Teiresias, a Theban seer. At Thebes, Manto, who some say was the equal of her father in prophecy, was a priestess of Ismenian Apollo. When Thebes fell to the Epigoni, Manto was dedicated, as "the fairest of the spoils," to Apollo at Delphi. Diodorus Siculus, who calls her Daphne, says [4.66.5–6] that she became famous for her poetry and that Homer borrowed some of his best lines from her. After a time Manto and other Theban prisoners at Delphi were directed by Apollo to found a colony in Asia Minor, near the site of the city later called Colophon. There Manto married Rhacius, a Cretan or Mycenaean, and bore him a son, Mopsus, who also became a seer. While at Delphi, Manto is said to have had two children, Amphilochus and Tisiphone, by Alcmeon, who gave them to Creon, king of Corinth, to rear. [Apollodorus 3.7.4, 3.7.7; *Thebaïd* 3; Pausanias 7.3.1–2.]

Marathon. The eponym of the town of Marathon. Marathon is said to have been the son of Epopeus, king of Asopia and Ephyraea. He emigrated to Attica to escape his father's lawless rule and settled in the valley later named for him. On the death of Epopeus, Marathon returned to his homeland just long enough to divide it between his sons, Sicyon and Corinthus, who renamed Asopia and Ephyraea, respectively, for themselves. (Some, however, call Sicyon a son of Erechtheus or Pelops.) Marathon was honored as a hero in his adopted city. [Pausanias 2.1.1.]

Marathon. A town in eastern Attica. Marathon was said by the Corinthians to have been named for a son of Epopeus, king of Sicyon. When the Cretan bull was ravaging Attica, it lived near Marathon, where it was finally captured by Theseus. Later the family of Heracles took refuge at Marathon from the Mycenaean tyrant Eurystheus and were defended by Theseus' son Demophon. Marathon gained undying fame as the scene of the decisive defeat of the Persians by the Athenians. The god Pan is said to have come to the Greeks' aid in the battle.

Marathonian bull. See CRETAN BULL.

Mariandynians or **Mariandyni.** A tribe inhabiting a part of the southern coast of the Black Sea. The Mariandynians' neighbors to the east were the Paphlagonians, to the west the Mysians, Phrygians, and Bithynians. Their king, Dascylus, was aided by Heracles in conquering these enemies; later, in the reign of Dascylus' son, Lycus, the Argonauts killed Amycus, king of the Bebryces, of Mysia, the chief foe of the Mariandynians. In early Classical times the tribe became vassals of the Persians.

Marmara or **Marmora, Sea of.** The sea lying between Asia Minor and Thrace. The Sea of Marmara is entered from the Aegean Sea via the Hellespont and is accessible from the Black Sea through the Bosporus. In Roman times it was known as the Propontis. The southern shores of this sea, a part of Mysia, were the scene of several of the Argonauts' adventures.

Marmax. The first of the many suitors of Hippodameia. Oenomaüs killed Marmax and his mares. [Pausanias 6.21.7.]

Maron. A priest of Apollo at Ismarus. When ODYSSEUS [D] sailed from Troy, he sacked this Ciconian city in southern Thrace, but spared Maron, son of Euanthes, and his wife. In gratitude Maron gave him many presents, including a large store of good wine, which later came in handy in the cave of Polyphemus. Maron was the eponym of Maroneia, a later name of Ismarus, where he may have been a local demigod of wine. [Homer, *Odyssey*, 9.196–211; Euripides, *Cyclops*, 141–143.]

Marpessa. A daughter of Evenus. Marpessa was wooed by Apollo, but Idas carried her off. Apollo pursued them, and the divine and mortal lovers were about to fight over her when Zeus parted them. Allowed to choose between them, the practical-minded young woman chose Idas, fearing that Apollo would leave her when she grew old. She bore a daughter, Cleopatra, who married Meleager. According to Pausanias [4.2.7], Marpessa committed suicide after Idas' death. [Apollodorus 1.7.8–9.]

Mars. A Roman god of agriculture and war. Mars's name was a contraction of Mavors, and took the form of Mamers in some dialects. A principal god of the Romans, Mars presided over their military activities as well as their farming and was thus early identified with the Greek war-god ARES. As Ares was Hera's son by Zeus, Mars was a son of Juno, though born parthenogenetically. As a war-god, Mars was often called Gradivus; his surname as an agricultural deity was Silvanus. He is said by some to have had a wife, a minor goddess named Nerio. Mars's attendant bird, the woodpecker PICUS, had prophetic powers.

Mars was the father of Romulus and Remus, twin founders of Rome, by the Vestal virgin Rea Silvia (who was also called Ilia), daughter of Numitor, king of Alba. When the usurping king, Amulius, disposed of their mother and threw the children into the Tiber, Mars saw to it that they survived, with the help of his sacred animals, Picus and a she-wolf. Mars is said to have loved Minerva (Athena) and to have employed the old goddess Anna Perenna to speak for him. After long delays Anna reported that Minerva had consented. Mars went to claim his demurely veiled bride, only to discover beneath the veil the crone Anna herself. (Some scholars suspect that this tale, at least as told of Mars, was an invention of Ovid's.)

Marsyas. A Phrygian satyr. Athena, after discarding the double flute because playing it distorted her face, laid a curse on anyone who picked it up. It was found by the satyr Marsyas, who learned to play it. Proud of the virtuosity that he developed, he challenged Apollo to a musical contest. The god accepted, with the provision that the winner might do whatever he liked with the loser. Apollo won—though less through musical superiority than by the trick of playing with his lyre turned upside down, a feat that Marsyas could not match with his flute. Apollo hung the satyr from a pine tree and flayed him. He left the skin on the tree, at Celaenae, in Phrygia, and gave the flayed corpse to Marsyas' pupil (or father) Olympus. The satyr's blood, or else the tears of his many friends among the woodland deities, formed the river Marsyas.

The flute floated down this river into the Maeander, then reappeared in the Asopus, near Sicyon. A shepherd found it and dedicated it to Apollo. The god hated flute music for a long time after the contest. At last an Argive musician named Sacadas reconciled him to it and the god even permitted a melody, known as the Pythian flute tune, to be played at Delphi. In spite of Marsyas' ignoble end, he remained a hero in his own land. Much later the Phrygians claimed that he appeared during their war with the Gauls, bringing both his music and the waters of his river to their aid. [Hyginus, *Fabulae*, 165, 191; Ovid, *Metamorphoses*, 6.382–400; Apollodorus 1.4.2; Herodotus 7.26; Pausanias 1.24.1, 2.7.9, 2.22.8–9, 10.30.9.]

Mastusius. A nobleman of Elaeüs, on the Thracian Chersonese. Demophon, king of Elaeüs, learned from an oracle that a plague which was troubling his city could be averted only if he annually sacrificed a girl from a noble family. He carried out this command, but found an excuse to exempt his own daughters from drawing lots. One year, when Mastusius' daughter was to be included in the drawing, Mastusius refused to allow it unless the king's daughters took the same risk. Demophon immediately had Mastusius' daughter sacrificed without the formality of the drawing. The father pretended to accept this act of cruelty. Later he invited the king and his daughters to a solemn sacrifice that he was about to hold. Unable to come for the beginning of the ceremony (as Mastusius had doubtless known), Demophon sent his daughters ahead of him. Mastusius murdered them and, when the king arrived, served him a bowl of wine mixed with their blood. When Demophon learned the truth, he had Mastusius and the bowl thrown into the harbor. A promontory at this point was named Mastusia, and the harbor was called "the Bowl." The bowl was also placed in the stars as the constellation Crater, as a caution against evil deeds.

This tale was learned by Hyginus [*Poetica Astronomica* 2.40] from a work by Phylarchus, an Athenian historian of the second century B.C.

Mecionice. See EUPHEMUS.

Mecisteus. One of the SEVEN AGAINST THEBES. Mecisteus was a son of Talaüs and Lysimache. Homer says that he won the contests at Oedipus' funeral games over all the Thebans. He was later killed at Thebes by Melanippus. His son Euryalus or Eurypylus was one of the Epigoni. [Homer, *Iliad*, 2.565; Pausanias 1.38.7, 9.18.1.]

Meda. See IDOMENEUS.

Medea or **Medeia.** A Colchian sorceress.

A. Medea was a daughter of Aeëtes, king of Colchis, and Eidyia, the youngest of the Oceanides, or Hecate, daughter of Perses. A beautiful young woman, Medea was a priestess of the Underworld goddess Hecate. Like her aunt Circe, Aeëtes' sister, she was acquainted with the properties of magical herbs and, with her witch's lore, could work miracles for both good and evil.

It was these powers that brought Medea to Greece. The goddess Hera had conceived an implacable hatred of Pelias, king of Iolcus, who had refused to honor her with sacrifices. Apparently unable to bring the powerful king to heel by herself, Hera devised an elaborate scheme for getting Medea to Greece solely to destroy him. To this end the goddess arranged the expedition of the ARGONAUTS to Colchis, ostensibly for the purpose of fetching the golden fleece on Pelias' orders. When they reached Colchis, Hera, with the help of Aphrodite, caused Medea to fall hopelessly in love with Jason, the handsome leader of the Argonauts and son of Aeson, who had been overthrown by Pelias. The young woman helped him, with her sorcery, to perform the seemingly impossible feats that her father imposed on him. Further, on receiving a promise of marriage, she lulled to sleep the dragon guardian of the fleece so that Jason might steal it, and then left Colchis with the Greeks. Driven by her infatuation for Jason, she committed a final outrage against her people. She lured her own brother, Apsyrtus, to a lonely island where Jason might kill him, then, according to some versions of the tale, helped to toss the pieces of his dismembered body into the sea from the *Argo*, in order to delay pursuit while the Colchians rescued the pieces for burial.

On the homeward voyage Jason and Medea were purified of murder by Circe. They were hastily married in a cave on the Phaeacians' island of Drepane in order to prevent Medea's Colchian pursuers from returning her to her father. The site of this event was afterward known as Medea's Cave. Much later in the voyage Medea used her sorcery to destroy the bronze giant Talus, who was preventing the Argonauts from landing on the island of Crete. Not long thereafter the *Argo* reached Iolcus. The Argonauts were sure that the treacherous Pelias would not fulfill his promise to hand over the kingdom when Jason appeared with the fleece, and they were not strong enough to take it by force. As usual in moments of stress, Jason turned to his wife for help.

B. Medea had no trouble in thinking of a way to conquer Iolcus without a battle, thus fulfilling Hera's purposes. Accounts differ as to the Argonauts' precise strategy, but Medea's role in the plot is clear. Some say that the Argonauts went openly to Iolcus, delivered the fleece to the king, then sailed away to the Isthmus of Corinth to dedicate the *Argo* to Poseidon. On their return to Iolcus, Medea pretended to the daughters of Pelias that she had quarreled with Jason, and thus won their confidence. Others claim that Jason's father, Aeson, was still alive and that Jason, moved by his father's feebleness, asked his wife to take some years off his own life and give them to his father. This

Medea indignantly refused to do, but she consented to carry out the elaborate and secret rite required to restore Aeson's youth. After scouring the country-side at night for strange herbs, she slit the old man's throat, drained his body of blood, and filled his veins with the brew that she had concocted. Aeson arose a young and vigorous man. This miracle so impressed the king's daughters that they asked Medea to repeat the process on their father.

According to yet another version of these events, the Argonauts did not make their return known, but hid themselves near the city. Medea, a young and beautiful woman, transformed her appearance into that of an old crone by applying certain ointments to her skin and hair. She made a rough statue of Artemis out of wood, then hobbled alone to the city gates. Bearing the statue before her, she declared that she was a priestess of Hyperborean Artemis, sent by the goddess to bring good fortune to Iolcus by restoring the king to youth. The old woman's prophetic babbling struck the citizens with wonder and fear, especially when, closeting herself alone in a room, she removed the ointments and reemerged as a young woman. Pelias was so overawed and so fearful of approaching age that he consented to submit to the magical treatment which she promised to administer.

On the fate of Pelias all accounts agree. When Medea explained to his daughters that they must prepare their father for his rejuvenation by chopping him into bits and stewing them in a pot, they refused. Medea had anticipated this reluctance and was prepared for it. After readying her concoction in a large cauldron, she cut up an old ram and dropped the pieces into the brew. A moment later she lifted from the pot the image of a lamb, which seemed to the awestruck daughters to frisk about as though full of life. All of Pelias' daughters except the pious Alcestis were convinced by this demonstration and agreed to do as much for their father. Following the sorceress' directions, they either beat the king to death or killed him with swords, then chopped him up and threw the pieces into the pot. To their horror, Pelias failed to reemerge alive, much less rejuvenated. At a signal from Medea, the Argonauts then entered the city and captured the citadel, with little opposition from the demoralized Iolcan soldiers.

C. Jason either resigned his claim to the throne to Pelias' son, Acastus, or else Acastus drove Jason and Medea from the city. According to one account, it was again Medea's resources that saved the day for the couple. Aeëtes had long before been king of Corinth. He had left the throne to Bunus on emigrating to Colchis, but Bunus' last successor, Corinthus, had died childless. The Corinthians therefore offered the throne to Medea. The more usual story has it, however, that Jason was welcomed to Corinth by Creon, the king, because of the fame he had won as leader of the Argonauts. He and Medea lived together happily enough for ten years and she bore him two sons, Mermerus and Pheres. (Some accounts mention three sons—Thessalus, Alcimenes, and

Tisandrus—or a son and daughter, Medus, who is usually called Aegeus' son, and Eriopis.)

The story of Medea and Jason in Corinth is a grim one, best known from Euripides' play that bears Medea's name. Although Jason was accepted by the Corinthians, the presence of the barbarian sorceress Medea was less welcome. The people and even the king himself were afraid of what this powerful, dangerous woman might do, for she had proved that she would stop at nothing to gain her ends. Thus far her purposes had coincided with those of her husband, but now she was beginning to be an embarrassment to him. Finally Creon offered Jason the hand of his daughter, Glauce, or Creüsa. By Greek law Jason's sons by a foreigner were not citizens, so he could not expect to bequeath his own position to Mermerus or Pheres. He therefore determined to divorce Medea and marry Glauce. (Pausanias [2.3.11] explains the quarrel between husband and wife differently, saying that Jason left Corinth and returned to Iolcus because of Medea's habit of hiding their children at birth in Hera's shrine in the vain hope of making them immortal.)

Threatened with banishment as well as divorce, Medea reminded Jason that all the exploits for which he was famous would never have been accomplished without her help. The fact that this accusation was undeniable did not induce Jason to admit its justice. He retorted that Medea should consider herself well repaid by his having introduced her to the glories of Greek civilization. Enraged, the proud woman determined on a terrible vengeance. She pretended to submit to Jason's wishes, but sent her sons to the palace bearing a poisoned robe as a wedding gift for Glauce. When the delighted princess put it on, it burst into flame and, though she leaped into a well to quench the fire, she died in agony. Her father, coming to her aid, was consumed as well. The Corinthians stormed Medea's house, but she escaped in a chariot drawn by winged dragons, a gift from her grandfather Helius.

According to some writers, Mermerus and Pheres, though they took refuge at Hera's altar, were stoned to death by the enraged Corinthians, who were later punished by their ghosts. Others say that Medea herself killed her sons, as a final act of revenge on their father, and that she took with her their bodies so that Jason could not have even the small comfort of giving them burial.

D. Some say that Medea fled for protection to Heracles at Thebes and cured him of the madness that had caused him to kill his children. Heracles, however, was unable to delay his labors long enough to offer her any help, so she went to Athens. According to the more usual story, Medea fled directly from Corinth to Athens. Aegeus, the king of that city, had recently passed through Corinth on his way to Troezen from Delphi. Medea, who was already contemplating her savage deed, had taken the precaution to extract a vow from Aegeus to offer her protection if she came to Athens. She had managed this by promising to use her arts to give the aging king the children that he had so far been denied. By the time she arrived in Athens, Aegeus had already conceived a son, Theseus, by Aethra, in Troezen, but he was not aware of this fact. Eager to continue his line, he married Medea, who bore him a son, Medus. Later Theseus, grown to young manhood, appeared at Aegeus' court at his mother's urging, but neither father nor son knew that they were related.

Medea, no doubt fearing that Medus would lose his claim to the throne, persuaded the king that the newcomer was intending to kill him. Aegeus sent the youth out to fetch the dangerous bull of Marathon, which had already killed Minos' son Androgeus. When Theseus succeeded in the task, Medea induced her husband to give him a cup of wine that she had poisoned with aconite. As the youth accepted the cup, he showed Aegeus certain tokens given him by his mother. By these Aegeus recognized his son and struck the cup from his hand. The king exiled Medea and his son by her, either because of her enmity to Theseus or because a priestess of Artemis had warned him that she could not perform her sacred rites so long as this criminal remained in the city.

E. Medea and Medus headed for Colchis, where Aeëtes had been deposed and, according to some accounts, killed by his brother Perses. On their way they stopped at Absoros, where (in this version of the tale) Medea had buried her brother. The city was overrun with snakes and the townspeople begged Medea to help them. Through her sorcery she confined the snakes in Apsyrtus' tomb. Ever afterward, if one ventured outside the tomb, it died. Medea sent Medus, of whose existence Perses was aware, ahead of her to Colchis. The young man was immediately seized by Perses, who had been warned by an oracle that a descendant of Aeëtes would kill him. Medus pretended to be Hippotes, a son of Creon, but was imprisoned nonetheless. As a result the Colchian crops failed. Medea now arrived, impersonating a priestess of Artemis. Hearing, and believing, that the son of her old enemy Creon was there, she claimed—unaware that it was so—that he was actually Medus, who had come to kill Perses. She promised that, as a priestess, she could end the plague if they would give her the prisoner to kill as a part of her rites. Perses agreed. When Medea found that her intended victim was indeed Medus, she gave him a sword and told him to kill Perses. He did so, thus avenging Aeëtes, and claimed the throne either for himself or for his grandfather, if Aeëtes was still alive. Many say, however, that Medea herself killed Perses. Later Medus conquered the land to the east and named it Media, for himself, or else Medea went there and gave it this name in her own honor.

Nothing is known of Medea's death, if indeed she died at all. According to one tradition, she became the consort of Achilles in the Elysian Fields. Some say that she was worshiped as a goddess, but there is disagreement about the truth of this claim.

F. The story of Medea's adventure with the Argonauts is told most fully in the *Argonautica* of Apollonius Rhodius. Pindar tells a part of the tale in his fourth Pythian Ode. Euripides' tragedy *Medea* deals with the end of Medea's stay in Corinth. Hyginus relates some of her adventures in his *Fabulae* [21–27] and has the only full account of the romantic events on her return to Colchis. In Ovid's *Metamorphoses* [7.1–424], the author tells in picturesque detail of Medea's rejuvenation of Aeson and her murder of Pelias. Diodorus Siculus [4.50–52] also gives a colorful account of Pelias' end. (This is only a part of a longer discussion of Medea's story, but the rest of Diodorus' version is little relied on in the above summary because of his habit of inventing "rational" explanations of the myths that are as preposterous as the originals. Hecate, for example, turns out to have been not a goddess but Medea's mother, the bloodthirsty wife and niece of Aeëtes, who taught the virtues of poisons to her daughters, Circe and Medea.) Pausanias [2.3.6–8, 2.3.10–11, 2.12.1, 8.9.1–3] adds several interesting details to Medea's story.

Medon (1). A bastard son of O'ileus, king of Locris, and Rhene. Medon was exiled after killing a relative of O'ileus' wife, Eriopis. He fled to Phylace and later accompanied Podarces to the Trojan War. When Philoctetes was wounded, Medon took command of his forces. He was killed by Aeneas. [Homer, *Iliad*, 2.726–728, 13.693–700, 15.332–336.]

Medon (2). Odysseus' herald in Ithaca. Although Medon was forced to serve Penelope's suitors, he remained loyal to ODYSSEUS [N] and was spared by him on his return.

Medon (3). The last king of Athens. Medon, who was lame, succeeded his father, Codrus. His many brothers emigrated and settled in Ionia. A reduction of Medon's powers by the Athenians was the first of a series of limitations on the monarchy that led to its conversion to an archonship.

Medus or **Medeius.** A son of Medea by Aegeus or Jason. Hesiod and the poet Cinaethon claimed that Jason was Medus' father, and Hesiod [*Theogony* 1000–1002] adds that Cheiron reared the boy. Most accounts, however, make Medus the offspring of Medea's marriage to Aegeus, king of Athens. After her attempt to murder Theseus, presumably in the interest of Medus' succession to the throne, she and her son were driven from Athens. They went eventually to Colchis, where Medea's father, Aeëtes, had been driven from the throne by his brother, Perses. For the events of their stay in Colchis, where Medus killed Perses and won the throne, see MEDEA [E]. From Colchis, Medus went to Asia, where he conquered much territory and named the Medes for himself. [Hyginus, *Fabulae*, 27.]

Medusa. One of the three snaky-haired monsters known as the GORGONS. Medusa, unlike her sisters, Stheno and Euryale, was not immortal. In late versions of the myth, she is said to have once been a beautiful maiden. Pursued by many suitors, she would have none of them, until Poseidon lay with her in a flowery field. She incurred the enmity of Athena, either because the goddess envied her beauty or because Medusa had yielded to Poseidon in Athena's shrine. In any case, the goddess turned Medusa's lovely hair into serpents and made her face so hideous that a glimpse of it would turn men to stone. Not content with this, Athena helped PERSEUS to behead Medusa, and he later gave her the head to wear in the center of her aegis. Some writers say that Athena guided his hand, or even killed Medusa herself, flaying her in order to use her skin for an AEGIS. The drops of blood that fell from Medusa's severed head into the Libyan Desert were transformed into snakes, one of which later killed Mopsus, the Argonautic seer. In his play *Ion*, Euripides says that Athena gave two drops of the Gorgon's blood to Erichthonius, king of Athens; one drop cured disease, the other was a deadly poison. The goddess also cut off a lock of Medusa's hair and gave it, concealed in an urn, to Heracles. He later gave it to Sterope, daughter of King Cepheus of Tegea, explaining that she could repel an enemy host merely by holding it up before them. From Medusa's neck sprang the warrior Chrysaor and the winged horse Pegasus, her children by Poseidon. [Hesiod, *Theogony*, 270–283.]

Megaera. See ERINYES.

Megapenthes (1). A king of Argos. A son of Proëtus and Stheneboea, Megapenthes succeeded his father on the throne of Tiryns, but traded it with PERSEUS [E, F] for the rule of Argos. According to some writers, he later killed Perseus, who had killed Proëtus. Hyginus says that Abas killed Megapenthes to avenge his father, Lynceus, but the incident that gave rise to his enmity is nowhere recorded.

Megapenthes (2). A son of Menelaüs by a slave woman, Pieris or Tereïs. Menelaüs married Megapenthes to Alector's daughter. After their father's death, Megapenthes and his brother, Nicostratus, were said by the Rhodians to have driven Helen from Sparta. However, their claims to the throne were passed over in favor of those of Orestes. [Homer, *Odyssey*, 4.10–12; Pausanias 2.18.-6, 3.19.9.]

Megara. A daughter of Creon, ruler of Thebes, and Eniocha. Creon gave Megara to HERACLES [C] for his bride as a reward for defeating the Minyans. Later, in a fit of madness, Heracles killed his children by Megara and perhaps their mother as well. It was for this act that he was condemned to perform his twelve labors.

Megara. The principal city on the Isthmus of Corinth and capital of Megaris. According to the Megarians, at least after their domination by the Dorians, Megara was founded by Car, a son of the Argive king Phoroneus. The city was named for the shrines (*megara*) that he built for Demeter. Twelve generations later Lelex, son of Poseidon and Libya, came from Egypt and took over the rule. His son, Cleson, was succeeded in turn by Cleson's son, Pylas. Pandion, the exiled king of Athens, married Pylas' daughter, Pylia. When Pylas was banished for a murder, Pandion became king. Pylas went to Messenia, where he founded the city of Pylus.

Pandion adopted Aegeus, son of Scyrius, and later had three sons of his own. One of these, Nisus, became king on the death of Pandion, but Pylas' son

Sceiron disputed his claim. Aeacus, the pious king of Aegina, was called in as arbiter and decided that Nisus should be king, Sceiron warlord. During Nisus' reign Megara was besieged by Minos, king of Crete, and overthrown through the treachery of Nisus' daughter Scylla. According to the Megarians, who preferred to ignore this defeat, Nisus was succeeded by Megareus, a son of Poseidon, who married Nisus' daughter Iphinoë. This Megareus had come from Onchestus in Boeotia to aid Nisus in the Cretan war. The Boeotians claimed that the city was formerly called Nisa and was renamed at this point for Megareus after his death in battle. (Another possible eponym of Megara was Megarus, a son of Zeus and a Sithnid nymph, who was saved from Deucalion's Flood by swimming to Mount Gerania.) The Megarians preferred to say that Megareus lived and was succeeded in due course by Alcathoüs, a son of Pelops. Megareus awarded Alcathoüs the kingdom and his daughter's hand in marriage in return for having slain the Cithaeronian lion, which had killed one of Megareus' sons, Euippus. Alcathoüs' daughter, Periboea, married Telamon, the son of Aeacus, and eventually their son Ajax inherited the throne.

Megareus. A son of Poseidon by Oenope, or of Onchestus, Aegeus, Hippomenes, or Apollo. Megareus was the father of Timalcus, Euippus, Hippomenes, and Euaechme. A king of Onchestus in Boeotia, he went to Megara to aid Nisus in his war with Minos, king of Crete, but was killed in battle. The Megarians claimed, however, that he married Nisus' daughter Iphinoë and became king. His own sons having been killed, he gave the kingdom at his death to Alcathoüs, a son of Pelops, for killing the Cithaeronian lion. [Apollodorus 3.15.8; Pausanias 1.39.5, 1.41.3–5.]

Megaris. The eastern part of the Isthmus of Corinth, dominated by Megara.

Meges. A king of Dulichium. Meges, son of Phyleus, was one of Helen's suitors. He later led forty ships from Dulichium and the Echinadian Islands to Troy. On his way home he and Prothoüs, a Magnesian, were drowned in a shipwreck on the coast of Euboea. Aristotle wrote an epitaph for the two. [Homer, *Iliad*, 2.625–629; Apollodorus "Epitome" 6.15a.]

Meilichios. An epithet (He Who Is Easily Placated) of Zeus. "Meilichios" or "the Meilichians" was originally the title under which a minor chthonian deity or deities were worshiped, in the form of a snake, in the region of Athens. The cult was assimilated to that of Zeus, but the form of worship remained unchanged, with rites of placation totally unlike the rituals due the Olympian sky-god Zeus.

Melampodes. A northern African tribe. The Melampodes were conquered by Aegyptus, who named their land Egypt, for himself.

Melampodia. A lost poem about the seer Melampus. The surviving fragments of this poem give interesting details of the lives of Teiresias and Calchas. These fragments are available in the volume on Hesiod (to whom the poem was once attributed) in the Loeb Classical Library.

Melampus. One of the greatest, and perhaps the first, of Greek seers.

A. An Aeolid from Thessaly, Melampus migrated with his parents, Amythaon and Idomene, to Messene, in the western Peloponnesus. He and his brother, Bias, prospered for a time in Pylus, but Melampus went to stay in a rural section with King Polyphantes. When a snake bit Polyphantes' servants, the king killed it, but Melampus rescued and reared its young. One night he awoke in terror to find the snakes licking his ears. He soon discovered that, as a result, he could understand the language of birds and animals. With the aid of their knowledge of the future, and the personal interest of Apollo, whom he met one day beside the river Alpheius, Melampus became a seer.

B. The young man was devoted to his brother. Bias fell in love with Pero, the beautiful daughter of Neleus, king of Pylus. When Neleus demanded as a bride-price the cattle owned by Phylacus, king of Phylace, in Thessaly, Bias turned to Melampus for help in the difficult task of stealing the beasts, which were guarded by a dangerous, unsleeping dog. The seer divined that this venture would succeed, but would cost him a year of imprisonment. Nevertheless he undertook it for his brother's sake and, going to Phylace, was captured in the cattle yard and locked into a small cell in Phylacus' barn. There he remained for a year, as he had predicted. At the end of this period Melampus overheard a conversation between two woodworms in the roof over his head. One of them boasted that he had nearly finished gnawing through the main roofbeam. Melampus shouted for his keeper, who moved him to another cell just as the roof collapsed. (Some say that it was Phylacus' own roof that fell.)

The king, greatly impressed when he heard of Melampus' powers, sent to consult him on a problem of his own. Phylacus had a grown son, Iphiclus, by Clymene, daughter of Minyas. This youth was so fleet that he could race the wind, running over the heads of wheat and asphodel without crushing them. But the fame that his prowess won him was of little comfort to Iphiclus, for he was sexually impotent. When Melampus heard of this disability, he promised to effect a cure in return for the cattle. Phylacus consented. Melampus sacrificed two bulls and invited the birds to the feast. The last to come was an aged vulture. He recalled that as a child Iphiclus had been frightened by his father, who was coming toward him with a knife, bloody from gelding rams. Phylacus, seeing the boy run away, had struck the knife deep into a sacred oak or wild pear tree and hurried after him to comfort him. Melampus now found the knife, which had been hidden by the bark that grew around it. He directed Phylacus to make a potion of the rust on the blade and give it to his son for ten consecutive days. The king followed this prescription and Iphiclus, completely cured, became in due course the father of Podarces and Protesilaüs.

Melampus now returned to Pylus, driving Phylacus' cattle and further enriched by a reputation as a seer, which created a demand for his services. Homer says that Neleus had confiscated Melampus' considerable property in his absence and that Melampus somehow avenged himself on the Pylian king. It is certain that Neleus could no longer refuse his daughter's hand to Bias. They were married and Pero bore a son, Talaüs, and, according to various versions, several other children.

C. Some time later Melampus, now the most famous of Greek seers, was urgently requested by King Proëtus to come to Tiryns and cure his three daughters of madness. (Some writers claim that this happened much later, in the reign of Anaxagoras.) Melampus consented, but demanded a third or a half of the kingdom as his fee. Proëtus indignantly refused, whereupon the sickness spread to other Argive women. They lost their hair, their skin became leprous, and, imagining themselves to be cows, they roamed wildly through mountains and desert. (Some attribute this affliction to the anger of Dionysus, whose rites they had refused to honor, or that of Hera, whose temple they had somehow desecrated.)

Proëtus and the Argive men hurriedly accepted Melampus' terms, but, now that he had the upper hand, the seer demanded another third of the kingdom for Bias. When this was promised him, Melampus, together with Bias and a corps of Argive youths, drove the women from the mountains down to Lusi or to Sicyon. During this ordeal Iphinoë died, but Iphianassa and Lysippe and the other Argive women were cured by the seer through the use of herbs and rites of purification. Melampus then threw the herbs into a river. The poet Ovid claims that the waters were thereafter a cure for drunkenness; the prosaic Pausanias reports merely that they stank.

Melampus and Bias duly received their shares of the kingdom and, moreover, married Lysippe and Iphianassa, Pero having died. Melampus and Lysippe had three sons: Abas, Mantius, and Antiphates. Several of Bias' grandchildren were prominent in the war of the Seven against Thebes, as was Melampus' great-grandson Amphiaraüs—one of several prominent seers among his descendants. Pindar cryptically states that Melampus himself gave up his powers of divination when he became a king in Argos. Herodotus [2.49] claimed that Melampus taught many of the rites of Dionysus to the Greeks, having learned them from Cadmus. [Apollodorus 1.9.11–13, 2.2.2; Homer, *Odyssey*, 15.223–242; *Catalogues of Women*, 18.]

Melaneus. A ruler in Messenia. Melaneus, who was called a son of Apollo because of his skill at archery, was welcomed to Messenia by Perieres and given a city (now Carnasium) which he called Oechalia, after his wife. His son Eurytus became a hero in Messenia. [Pausanias 4.2.2.]

Melanion. A son of Amphidamas. Melanion defeated ATALANTA [B, C] in a footrace and won her as his bride, but both were changed into lions as punishment for a sacrilege. Melanion may have been the father, by Atalanta, of Parthenopaeüs. His adventures are often attributed to Hippomenes.

Melanippe. A daughter of Aeolus or some other king. Melanippe was seduced by Poseidon and bore two sons, Aeolus and Boeotus. Her father blinded and imprisoned her and had the babies exposed for wild beasts to eat. Instead a cow suckled them and the cowherds reared them. Meanwhile Metapontus, king of Icaria, threatened to banish his wife, Theano, if she did not give him children. She asked some shepherds to find her a child and they sent her the foundlings, which she pretended were hers. Not long afterward she bore by Metapontus two sons of her own.

As the four boys grew to manhood, it became clear that the king favored the elder pair. Jealous for her own sons, Theano told them the origin of their supposed brothers and gave them orders to kill the foundlings. When the two pairs of brothers fought, however, Poseidon came to the rescue of his sons. Theano, on learning that her own sons had been killed in the fray, committed suicide. Aeolus and Boeotus once more took refuge with the cowherds. Poseidon appeared to them, claimed them as his sons, and told them to rescue their mother. They dutifully rescued Melanippe, after killing her cruel father, and Poseidon restored her sight. They took her home to Icaria and told Metapontus the whole story. He solved the dilemma by marrying Melanippe and adopting the boys whom he had always imagined were his sons. The young men founded towns on the Propontis which they called Boeotia and Aeolia.

This tale, known mainly from Hyginus [*Fabulae* 186], is thought to have been derived by him in large part from *Melanippe Bound*, a lost play by Euripides.

Melanippe. See ANTIOPE (2).

Melanippus. A Theban champion in the war with Argos. A son of Astacus, Melanippus killed two of the SEVEN AGAINST THEBES [D], Mecisteus and Tydeus. He was killed either by Amphiaraüs or by the dying Tydeus, who ate his brains. [Apollodorus 3.6.8.]

Melanippus. See COMAETHO.

Melantheus or **Melanthius.** The chief goatherd of Odysseus. When, in Odysseus' absence, Penelope was plagued by suitors, some of the household servants, such as Melantheus' father, Dolius, remained loyal to Odysseus. Melantheus, however, betrayed his master's interests by attaching himself to the suitors. When Odysseus returned to Ithaca, disguised as a beggar, Melantheus was insolent toward him, as was his sister, Melantho. Even after his master revealed his identity, Melantheus brought weapons to the suitors. He was trapped in the storeroom by Eumaeüs and Philoetius, and bound and hung from a rafter. Later he was dragged, still living, to the courtyard, mutilated for his treachery, and left to die. [Homer, *Odyssey*, 17.204–255, 20.172–184, 22.135–200, 22.474–477.]

Melantho. A maidservant of Penelope. Melantho, daughter of Odysseus' faithful servant Dolius, proved as treacherous to Odysseus during his absence as did her brother Melantheus. She became the mistress of Eurymachus, one of Penelope's suitors. When Odysseus returned to his palace disguised as an old beggar, she twice insolently taunted him. She was presumably hanged as one of the twelve servants to be punished for having attached themselves to the suitors. [Homer, *Odyssey*, 18.320–342, 19.65–95, 22.424–473.]

Melanthus. A king of Athens. Melanthus, a descendant of Neleus, was driven from his native Messenia by the Dorians. Together with many other Messenians, he migrated to Attica, where he drove Thymoetes, a descendant of Theseus, from the Athenian throne and made himself king. During his reign he welcomed Ionian settlers, whom the Achaeans had driven from Aegialus. Melanthus was succeeded by his son, Codrus, who had married an Athenian. [Herodotus 5.65; Pausanias 2.18.8–9, 7.1.9.]

Melas. A son of Porthaon and Euryte. Melas was a brother of Oeneus, king of Calydon. According to some writers, his eight sons were killed by Tydeus for plotting against Oeneus, and it was for this crime that Tydeus was banished. [Apollodorus 1.7.10, 1.8.5.]

Melas. See ARGEIUS; ARGUS (3).

Meleager. A son of Oeneus, king of Calydon, and Althaea, daughter of Thestius. Immediately after the birth of the infant Meleager, the three Fates appeared in the mother's room. Clotho and Lachesis predicted that the child would be noble and brave, but Atropos, pointing to a stick burning in the fireplace, added that he would die the moment the brand was consumed. Althaea leaped from her bed, put out the flames, and hid the stick somewhere in the palace. Very early Meleager began to show that the first two Fates had seen the future clearly. He joined the Argonauts while still so young that his father felt it wise to send along an uncle, Laocoön, to keep an eye on him—though the boy was already second only to Heracles in prowess. Meleager did not particularly distinguish himself on the voyage, unless, as Diodorus Siculus [4.48.4] claims, he killed the Argonauts' chief enemy, Aeëtes, king of Colchis.

Not long after his return to Calydon, the young man married Cleopatra, daughter of Idas and Marpessa. She bore a daughter, Polydora. At about this time Artemis avenged herself on Oeneus, who had once forgotten to sacrifice to her, by sending a giant boar to Calydon. The beast destroyed the Calydonian crops and many men as well. Oeneus called on the bravest young men from the Greek cities to join his son in an attempt to capture the boar. This CALYDONIAN BOAR HUNT attracted many of Meleager's former companions among the Argonauts. His uncles, the sons of Thestius, were there too. So was Atalanta, the Arcadian huntress, and Meleager fell in love with her. (Some say that the son, Parthenopaeüs, whom she bore after Meleager's death was his son, not her husband's.) It was Meleager who killed the boar and was awarded the skin as a prize.

There are two very different versions of what happened next. According to Homer [*Iliad* 9.543–599], a quarrel broke out over the prize between the Calydonians and their traditionally hostile neighbors, the Curetes, who had taken part in the hunt. In the war that ensued, the Calydonian forces repulsed the enemy as long as Meleager led them. But when Meleager killed some of Thestius' sons, his mother's brothers, Althaea cursed him. Angry at this, the young man refused to fight further. The Curetes stormed the walls of Calydon, but Meleager ignored the appeals of his mother and father. Finally Cleopatra begged him to forget his anger for the sake of the city. Meleager relented and repelled the charge at the head of the Calydonian forces. All writers but Homer who follow this version add that Meleager died in the fighting. This happened either because his mother's curse (perhaps renewed when he killed her remaining brothers) aroused the Erinyes against him or because Apollo fought on the side of the Curetes.

A second version of Meleager's death was more popular with writers such as Ovid, who told it in great detail in his *Metamorphoses* [8.268–546]. By this account, Meleager gave the boarskin to Atalanta. Thestius' sons took it from her and Meleager killed them. Althaea, beside herself with rage at her son's murder of her brothers, remembered the brand that the Fates had said was the key to Meleager's life. She took it from its hiding place and flung it into the fire. Meleager died in agony. Althaea killed herself from remorse; Cleopatra did the same from grief. Meleager's sisters and the other women of the palace mourned him bitterly until Artemis, in a final act of revenge on Oeneus' house, turned them to guinea fowl (*meleagrides*). [Apollodorus 1.8.2–3; Hyginus, *Fabulae*, 171–174; Aeschylus, *The Libation Bearers*, 602–611.]

meliae. Nymphs of the manna ash trees. The meliae, together with the Giants and the Erinyes, sprang from the blood of the castrated Uranus. One melia (whom some call a daughter of Oceanus) married her brother Inachus, the Argive river-god, and bore him two sons, Phoroneus and Aegialeus, and a daughter, Io. She may also have been the mother of Inachus' daughter Mycene. (Some call the mother of Phoroneus and Io Argia.) Another melia bore the Bebrycian king Amycus by Poseidon. [Hesiod, *Theogony*, 182–187; Apollodorus 2.1.1; Apollonius Rhodius 2.1–4.]

Meliboea. See CHLORIS.

Melicertes. A son of Athamas and INO. Ino, driven mad by Hera, leaped into the sea with Melicertes in her arms. Some say that she had first boiled the child in a cauldron. Melicertes' body, carried ashore by a dolphin on the Isthmus of Corinth, was found and buried by his uncle Sisyphus, king of Corinth, who instituted the Isthmian games in the child's honor. Like his mother, Melicertes became a sea-deity. Renamed Palaemon, he came to the aid of sailors together with his mother, who was now called Leucothea. The Romans called him Portunus. It has often been suggested that Melicertes was the Greek form of Melkarth, a Canaanite deity.

Melpomene. One of the nine MUSES. Melpomene, a daughter of Zeus and Mnemosyne, was said by some writers to be the mother, by the river-god Acheloüs, of the Sirens. [Apollodorus 1.3.1–4, "Epitome" 7.18.]

Membliarus. A colonizer of Thera. Membliarus, a son of Poeciles, sailed with his relative Cadmus, who was sent from Tyre in search of his kidnaped sister, Europa. When they reached the island of Calliste, north of Crete, Cadmus left Membliarus there with a party of Phoenicians to colonize the island. Membliarus and his descendants ruled on Calliste for eight generations, after which Cadmus' descendant Theras arrived from Sparta and was made king, renaming the island Thera. [Herodotus 4.147; Pausanias 3.1.7–8.]

Memnon. A king of the Ethiopians. Memnon was the handsome son of the goddess Eos and Tithonus, Priam's brother. He led a large army to the aid of Troy in the Trojan War. Some say that Memnon had conquered all of Egypt and Persia as far east as Susa, from which he marched westward to Troy. There he killed Nestor's son Antilochus and was himself killed by Achilles. His mother begged Zeus to show Memnon some special honor. Accordingly the smoke from his funeral pyre formed itself into birds, some of which killed each other over the flames. Flocks of these birds, called *memnonides*, returned annually to sprinkle water on his grave after wetting their wings in the Aesepus River. The dew was said to be the tears shed by Eos, the dawn-goddess, for her son. The famous statue of the pharaoh Amenophis, near the Egyptian Thebes, was called by the Greeks the Colossus of Memnon, partly through confusion of names, partly because the statue made unaccountable sounds at dawn. [Hesiod, *Theogony*, 984–985; Ovid, *Metamorphoses*, 13.576–622; Pausanias 1.42.3, 10.31.5–7.]

Memphis. A daughter of the god Nile. Memphis married Epaphus and bore a daughter, Libya. Epaphus founded the city named for his wife. [Apollodorus 2.1.4.]

Memphis. A city of lower Egypt. Memphis was one of the most important Egyptian cities up to the time of Alexander's conquest of Egypt. According to Greek tradition, it was founded by Epaphus, a son of Io by Zeus, and named for his wife. Ptah, the chief deity of Memphis, was identified by the Greeks with Hephaestus. Daedalus, the Athenian or Cretan artisan-hero, was also said to have been honored there.

Menelaüs. A king of Sparta.

A. Menelaüs and Agamemnon, often called the Atreidae, were sons of Atreus and Aërope, or, according to some versions, of Atreus' son Pleisthenes and Cleolla. During Atreus' long feud with his brother, Thyestes, he sent his sons for safekeeping first to Polypheides, king of Sicyon, then to Oeneus, king of Aetolia. When they were grown, after Atreus' death, Tyndareüs, king of Sparta, brought them back to Mycenae and they drove Thyestes from the kingdom. Agamemnon inherited his father's throne at Mycenae and used his enormous wealth and influence to win Tyndareüs' daughter HELEN for his brother. Helen bore Menelaüs a daughter, Hermione, and, according to some accounts, a son, Nicostratus. Menelaüs also had two other sons: Xenodamus, by the nymph Cnossia, and Megapenthes, either by Tereïs or by Pieris, an Aetolian slave girl. The aged Tyndareüs ceded the rule of Sparta to Menelaüs.

About ten years after his marriage Menelaüs entertained a handsome visitor named Paris, who came from the Phrygian city of Troy. Nine days passed, and Menelaüs was called away to Crete to participate in funeral ceremonies for King Catreus, his mother's father. He returned in due course to find that Paris had gone off with Helen and a considerable part of the palace treasure. Although Menelaüs may have suspected that his wife was not a wholly unwilling captive, he immediately consulted with his brother as to how he might get Helen, and the treasure, back. They recalled that Tyndareüs had forced all his daughter's suitors to vow to protect the interests of whichever husband she might choose. They now sent messengers to remind these suitors—who included most of the princes of Greek cities—of their obligation. As a result, Menelaüs soon found himself on his way to Troy as a part of a large Greek force led by his brother.

B. Menelaüs and Odysseus went first to the city of Troy to demand the return of Helen and the treasure. They were refused, and a war began that lasted ten years. Menelaüs proved himself a brave if not particularly distinguished leader. Toward the end of the war he met Paris in single combat and would have killed the Trojan if Paris' patron, the goddess Aphrodite, had not saved him. At the end of the war Menelaüs found Helen in the house of Paris' brother Deïphobus, who had married her after Paris' death. Instead of killing her, as he had intended, Menelaüs merely took her to his ships in disgrace.

The voyage home proved a near-catastrophe. Menelaüs lost all but five of his fifty ships. After being driven by storms to Crete, Libya, Phoenicia, and Cyprus, he was finally stranded in Egypt. There he captured the prophetic sea-god PROTEUS (1) and forced him to predict his fate. On his way home, according to Herodotus [2.118–119], Menelaüs sacrificed two Egyptian children and was pursued by the Egyptians as far as Libya, where they lost his trail.

An entirely different version of these events has it that Helen was not taken to Troy by Paris, but was spirited away to Egypt by Hermes, while Paris carried home a cloud-phantom that he believed to be the Spartan queen. Helen was cared for by PROTEUS (2), king of Egypt, until his death. Proteus' son, Theoclymenus, tried to force Helen to marry him, but Menelaüs reached Egypt in the nick of time to save his wife and take her back to Sparta.

In both versions, Menelaüs, unlike his brother Agamemnon, was able to reassume the rule of his homeland with no opposition. At his death he and his wife achieved immortality in the Islands of the Blessed by virtue of his being a son-in-law of Zeus. The tombs of the pair were at Therapne, near Sparta.

C. Menelaüs is a principal figure in Homer's *Iliad* and in Book 4 of his *Odyssey*. He also plays important roles in five plays by Euripides. *Helen* tells the romantic tale of his finding his true wife in Egypt, where she had been throughout the Trojan War while a phantom was inspiring the bloodbath at Troy. In the other plays, Menelaüs is a far from heroic character. He helps to force his brother to sacrifice his daughter Iphigeneia in *Iphigeneia in Aulis*. In *Trojan Women*, he is easily duped by his seductive wife. He is cruel and treacherous in *Andromache*. In *Orestes*, he weakly refuses to aid his brother's son and daughter, who are being tried for the murder of their mother. Sophocles, too, portrays Menelaüs, in his *Ajax*, as heartless, denying burial to the suicide Ajax. Many events in Menelaüs' life are related by Apollodorus [3.10.8–3.11.2, "Epitome" 2.15–3.12, 3.28, 5.21, 6.29]. Other details appear in Hyginus' *Fabulae* [123], Vergil's *Aeneïd* [6.509–532], and Pausanias' *Description of Greece* [3.19.9, 10.26.7–8].

Menestheus. A king of Athens. According to Plutarch, Menestheus, a son of Peteüs and descendant of Erechtheus, was the first demagogue. While Theseus, king of Athens, was detained in Hades, Menestheus stirred up the people against him. He played on the resentment that the nobles bore Theseus for democratizing the government and pointed, with considerable justice, to the king's irresponsibility in bringing down upon the state the enmity of Sparta by kidnaping the child Helen, daughter of King Tyndareüs. Some claim that Menestheus induced Helen's brothers, Castor and Polydeuces, to invade Attica in order to recover their sister. In any case, they did so. When Menestheus induced the Athenians not to resist, the brothers placed him on the throne and withdrew. Theseus' sons, Demophon and Acamas, fled to King Elephenor in Euboea. When Theseus returned, Menestheus expelled him, or else he met with such opposition from Menestheus' supporters that he left the city forever. Some believe that Menestheus was implicated in King Lycomedes' murder of Theseus on the island of Scyrus.

Menestheus now possessed undisputed power, for Theseus' sons were young and weak. He became one of Helen's suitors and is said to have offered the richest gifts. Later he led an Athenian force of fifty ships to the Trojan War, where he distinguished himself less by personal prowess than by his ability to deploy troops efficiently. He was one of the leaders hidden in the wooden horse. Some say that Menestheus died at Troy, others that he went from there to the island of Melos, where he became king—the former ruler, Polyanax, having died. Theseus' son Demophon, who, with his brother Acamas, was also at Troy, recovered the power in Athens. [Homer, *Iliad*, 2.546–556, 12.331–378; Plutarch, *Parallel Lives*, "Theseus," 32.1–35.5; Apollodorus "Epitome" 1.23–24, 6.15b.]

Menestratus. A Thespian youth. When a dragon began to ravage the Boeotian city of Thespiae, Zeus said that the people could protect themselves only by offering one of their youths to the monster each year. This custom continued until the year in which a young man named Cleostratus was chosen by lot to be the victim. This youth had a lover named Menestratus, who could not bear to see him killed. Secretly Menestratus dressed himself in armor covered with spikes and offered himself to the dragon. As he had anticipated, the dragon demanded no more tributes and his beloved was saved. The Thespians dedicated a statue to Zeus Savior, though just what credit the god had earned is not apparent from the story. [Pausanias 9.26.7–8.]

Menodice. A nymph, daughter of Orion. Menodice was the mother of Hylas by Theiodamas, king of the Dryopes. [Hyginus, *Fabulae*, 14.]

Menoeceus (1). A Theban noble descended from the Sparti. Menoeceus was the father of Creon and of Jocasta, or Epicasta, who married Laïus and Oedipus. He is also said by some to have been the father of Hipponome, the mother, by Alcaeüs, of Amphitryon and Anaxo. [Apollodorus 2.4.5, 3.5.7–8.]

Menoeceus (2). A son of Creon, king of Thebes, and Eurydice. In the midst of the war of the Seven against Thebes, the seer Teiresias told Creon that Ares, still resenting Cadmus' killing of his sacred dragon, demanded the death of a man who was descended through both parents from the Sparti and who had never lain with a woman. The only person left in Thebes who answered this description was Menoeceus. Creon refused to sacrifice his son, but Menoeceus, knowing that the city would fall if Ares' conditions were not met, leaped from the walls of the citadel. Menoeceus is a character in Euripides' *Phoenician Women*.

Menoetes. The herdsman of Hades. Menoetes, son of Ceuthonymus, tended Hades' cattle on the island of Erytheia, where he vainly warned Geryon of the approach of Heracles. Later, apparently having driven his herds to the Underworld—or, perhaps, having been killed by Heracles—he encountered this enemy a second time. He challenged Heracles to wrestle, but had his ribs broken and was saved only by the pleas of Persephone. [Apollodorus 2.5.10, 2.5.12.]

Menoetius (1). A son of Actor and Aegina. Menoetius went from Opus to sail with the Argonauts. He married Sthenele, daughter of Acastus (or Periopis, daughter of Pheres; or Polymele, daughter of Peleus) and they had one son, Patroclus. When the boy killed Clitonymus, son of Amphidamas, in an argument over a game of dice, Menoetius fled Opus with his son and took refuge at the court of his fellow Argonaut Peleus, in Phthia. There Patroclus became the squire and lover of Peleus' son, Achilles. When Achilles left for the Trojan War, Menoetius sent Patroclus with him. Contrary to the usual tradition, the *Catalogues of Women* [61] calls Menoetius a brother of Peleus. [Homer, *Iliad*, 11.762–790, 23.82–90; Apollodorus 1.9.16, 3.13.8.]

Menoetius (2). A son of the Titan Iapetus and the Oceanid Clymene or Asia. Menoetius was blasted into Tartarus by Zeus with a thunderbolt, together with those of his brother Titans who fought against the gods. [Hesiod, *Theogony*, 507–516; Apollodorus 1.2.3.]

Mentes. A Taphian chief. Mentes' father, Anchialus, was a friend of Odysseus' father, Laërtes. Mentes, or Athena disguised as Mentes, helped to rouse young Telemachus to action in his father's absence, urging him to seek news of Odysseus from Menelaüs and Nestor. [Homer, *Odyssey*, 1.104–318.]

Mentor. An Ithacan noble. Odysseus left Mentor in charge of his household when he went off to the Trojan War. Mentor, or Athena in his likeness, did much to rouse Telemachus to action and, later, to bring peace between Odysseus and the Ithacans. He appears in many passages in Homer's *Odyssey*.

Mercury. The Roman god of merchants. Mercury was early identified by the Romans with the Greek god HERMES. The planet that bears his name was assigned to him as patron of astronomy.

Meriones. The second-in-command of the Cretan forces at the Trojan War. Meriones was a son of King Idomeneus' half-brother, Molus. An able fighting man, Meriones, together with Menelaüs, rescued the corpse of Patroclus and distinguished himself on many other occasions. Second only to Teucer as an archer, he won the contest of bowmen at Patroclus' funeral games. [Homer, *Iliad*, 23.859–883.]

Mermerus (1). The elder son of Medea and JASON [F, G]. Although the lost epic *Naupactia* related that Mermerus was killed by a lioness while hunting on the mainland opposite Corcyra, the usual story is that he and his brother Pheres were victims of the quarrel between their parents. Some say that Medea, escaping Corinth after her murder of its king and his daughter, Glauce, left the children clinging to Hera's altar. The enraged townspeople tore them from it and stoned them to death because they had, albeit innocently, carried the poisoned robe to Glauce. For this outrage the children's ghosts punished the Corinthians by causing their babies to die. When the Delphic oracle explained the cause of the deaths, the Corinthians set up a statue of Terror and instituted a yearly sacrifice in the children's honor in the hope of appeasing them. At this festival Corinthian children cut their hair and wore black clothes. This custom continued until the destruction of Corinth by Rome. [Pausanias 2.3.6–7, 3.8.9.]

Mermerus (2). A king of Thesprotian Ephyra. Mermerus' father, Pheres, a son of Jason and Medea, passed on to him the expertise in the making of poisons that he had learned from Medea. Mermerus taught it in turn to his son Ilus.

Merope. A daughter of Atlas and the Oceanid Pleïone. One of the PLEIADES, Merope married Sisyphus and bore Glaucus. Some claim that Merope's star is the dim one of the seven: she is blushing at having married a mortal while all her sisters had affairs with gods. [Apollodorus 1.9.3; Hyginus, *Poetica Astronomica*, 2.21.]

Merope. See AEPYTUS; OEDIPUS [A]; ORION.

Merops. A king of Percote, on the Asian side of the Hellespont. Merops was a seer as well as king. His daughter Cleite married Cyzicus and killed herself in grief at his death. Her sister, Arisbe, became Priam's first wife and bore him a son, but Priam, wishing to remarry, gave her to Hyrtacus. Merops tried vainly to prevent his sons, Adrastus and Amphius, from going to the Trojan War. They were killed there by Diomedes. Merops taught Aesacus to interpret dreams. [Homer, *Iliad*, 2.828–834; Apollodorus 3.12.5; Apollonius Rhodius 1.974–977.]

Messene. The eponym of Messenia. A daughter of Triopas, king of Argos, Messene married Polycaon, who had been exiled from Sparta by his brother, Myles. Determined that her husband should have title and property, Messene made Polycaon raise a force of Spartans and Argives, which they jointly led westward into the southwestern Peloponnesus. Polycaon and Messene became the first rulers of this land, which they called Messenia. They founded as their capital the city later called Andania. It was Messene who first worshiped Demeter and Kore in Messenia, the rites having been shown her by Caucon. In Pausanias' day Messene had the distinction of being perhaps the only woman to be honored with a hero's rites. [Pausanias 3.1.1–3.2.2, 4.3.9, 4.31.11.]

Messene. In Classical times, the principal city of Messenia. Andania may also have been called Messene at the time of its founding. In myth, the land of Messenia is often called Messene, though the later city of that name seems to have had no great importance in the mythological period.

Messenia. A region in the southwestern Peloponnesus. Messenia was settled by Polycaon, a Spartan, and his Argive wife, Messene. After leading there colonists from both their cities, they established as their capital the city later known as Andania, but which they may have called Messene. Nothing is known of their descendants, though Pausanias estimated that they ruled for five generations. The royal house having apparently died out, the Messenians invited the Thessalian Perieres, a son of Aeolus, to become their king. After Perieres' death his sons, Aphareus and Leucippus, ruled jointly. Aphareus founded a new capital, which he named Arene for his sister-wife. He welcomed his cousin Neleus, exiled from Thessaly, to Messenia, giving him the coastal area about Pylus. When Aphareus died childless—his sons, Idas and Lynceus, having been killed in a fight with the Dioscuri—Neleus became king of Messenia, with his capital at Pylus. He brought the land to great prosperity, which continued throughout the three-generation rule of Nestor and that of his sons Thrasymedes and Peisistratus. A part of Messenia east of the Messenian Gulf was independently ruled by Asclepius and later by his sons, Machaon and Podaleirius, who led thirty ships from that region to Troy.

The Heraclid invader Cresphontes expelled the grandsons of Nestor from Messenia and made himself king, with his capital at Stenyclerus. The Messenian refugees fled to Attica, where they expelled the king and placed Melanthus on the throne. Later Cresphontes was murdered by the usurper Polyphontes, but was avenged by his son Aepytus, who began a period of peaceful and prosperous rule that lasted through several generations of his descendants.

Messina, Strait of. The strait separating Sicily from Italy. The northern entrance of this strait was traditionally the home of Scylla, who lived on the Italian shore, and the site of Charybdis, the whirlpool that menaced ships on the Sicilian side.

Mestor. A son of Perseus and Andromeda. By Lysidice, daughter of Pelops, Mestor was the father of Hippothoë, the mother of Taphius by Poseidon. [Apollodorus 2.4.5.]

Mestra. The daughter of ERYSICHTHON (2). Because of her power of metamorphosis, given her by her erstwhile lover, Poseidon, Mestra was able to aid her father in his long torment. This same talent of hers may have induced Ovid [*Metamorphoses* 8.738–878] to say that she married Autolycus, since the famous thief had similar powers.

Metamorphoses. See OVID.

Metaneira. The wife of Celeüs, king of Eleusis. Metaneira bore several daughters and a son, Demophoön. DEMETER, employed as Demophoön's nurse, nightly placed him in a fire in order to immortalize him. Metaneira's cries on discovering this habit caused the goddess to abandon the project. [*Homeric Hymn to Demeter* 2.]

Metapontus. See MELANIPPE.

metempsychosis. The belief that the souls of the dead are reborn in the bodies of other men or animals. The transmigration of souls was a teaching of the Orphics and of Pythagoras, as it was of many later philosophers, notably Plato. Pindar wrote in one poem [*Olympian Odes* 2.68–77] that those who had thrice lived blameless lives went to live forever in Elysium. The doctrine of metempsychosis offered Vergil [*Aeneïd* 6.703–751] a plausible excuse to relate the hero of his epic to the future history of Rome and to pay a prudent compliment to Augustus, the ruler whose favor he was courting. Greek mythology, except for the more or less artificial Orphic myths, shows little evidence of a belief in reincarnation.

Metiadusa. See CECROPS (2).

Metion. A son of Erechtheus, king of Athens, and Praxithea. On the death of Erechtheus, his son-in-law Xuthus was asked to choose a successor from among the dead man's sons. He chose Cecrops, the eldest. Metion and Pandorus, angry at being passed over, exiled Xuthus. It is not recorded whether they were the cause of Cecrops' eventual emigration to Euboea, but Metion's sons rebelled against Pandion, Cecrops' son and successor, and drove him from Athens. They were in turn expelled by Pandion's sons. Asius is said to have claimed that Metion was the father of Sicyon. [Apollodorus 3.15.1, 3.15.5–6.]

Metis (1). A daughter of Oceanus and Tethys. When Zeus grew to maturity, he persuaded Metis to give his father, Cronus, an emetic. She did so and Cronus vomited up Zeus's brothers and sisters, whom he had swallowed. After deposing the elder deity, Zeus married Metis, though she took various shapes to avoid lying with him. Zeus's grandparents Ge and Uranus warned him that Metis, after she had borne the daughter now in her womb, was fated to give birth to a son who would be stronger than his father. Zeus forestalled this disaster by swallowing Metis. When she was delivered of the girl, Zeus ordered either Hephaestus or Prometheus to split open his head with an ax. Out sprang Athena, in full armor. Metis, whose name means "Wisdom" or "Cunning," remained forever inside her husband, who thus automatically enjoyed the advantage of her shrewd advice. Although in Hesiod's account Metis seems little more than an abstraction, her shape-changing ability suggests that she may once have been a sea-goddess. [Hesiod, *Theogony*, 358, 886–900, 924–929; Apollodorus 1.2.1, 1.3.6.]

Metis (2). A wife of Tereus. Aeschylus [*The Suppliants* 60–62] calls Tereus' wife "Metis the nightingale." Presumably Metis is merely another name for Procne.

Midas. A king of the Mygdonians of Phrygia. Midas, a son of King Gordius by Cybele, founded the city of Ancyra (Ankara). He is said to have been the discoverer of both black and white lead, but he is best known for his connections with another metal: gold. While Dionysus was on his expedition to India with his train, old Seilenus wandered away and was captured by Phrygian peasants, who took him to the king. Some say that Midas caught him by mixing wine with the water in a spring, presumably in the hope of profiting from his prophetic powers. In either case, the king entertained Seilenus graciously and then gave him a guide to lead him back to Dionysus and his company. Dionysus was so grateful to Midas that he offered to grant any boon that he asked. Midas, who was fond of luxury, asked that all he touched might turn to gold. Reluctantly the god consented. Midas was at first delighted with the results, but he soon discovered that when he tried to eat, the food turned to metal. Before long the ravenously hungry king was begging Dionysus to take back his miraculous gift. The god could not do that, but he advised Midas to wash in the river Pactolus. The king did so and his "golden touch" was transferred to the river, which forever after had gold-bearing sands.

Midas worshiped Pan as well as Dionysus. That woodland-god one day engaged in a musical contest with Apollo, with old King Tmolus as judge. Tmolus prudently awarded the prize to Apollo for his lyre playing, but the rash Midas let it be known that he thought Pan the better musician. Apollo rewarded him by changing his ears to those of an ass. (Some say that Midas raised his objection at Apollo's contest with Marsyas instead of Pan.)

Midas was acutely embarrassed. He wore a Phrygian cap pulled down over his ears, removing it only long enough to have his hair cut now and then. His barber, no doubt threatened with dire penalties if he revealed what he saw, was unusually discreet. In time, however, the strain of keeping the secret became too great for him. He dug a hole in a deserted meadow, whispered his extraordinary news into it, and filled it up again. All went well until the following spring, when reeds grew up on the spot. Passersby were astonished to hear them murmuring, "Midas has ass's ears"—and the king's secret was out.

Historically, Midas was one dynastic title of a succession of Phrygian kings who ruled in the valley of the Sangarius River; it alternated with the name

Gordius. Some of these kings, ruling in Gordium, achieved considerable fame because of their wealth. One Midas sent rich offerings to Delphi. The Phrygians are believed to have entered Asia Minor from Europe. They may well have brought the name Midas with them from Macedonia, for the fertile valley that surrounds the ancient capital, Aegae (later Edessa), was known as the Gardens of Midas, and the story of the king's capture of Seilenus is sometimes located there. As for Midas' wealth, it seems to have been accidentally passed on to King Croesus of Lydia. That famous monarch found his rich supply of gold in the river Pactolus, near his capital of Sardis, where Midas had washed away his golden touch. [Ovid, *Metamorphoses*, 11.90–193; Hyginus, *Fabulae*, 191, 274; Herodotus 1.14, 8.138; Pausanias 1.4.5.]

Midea. A city in Argolis, northeast of Argos and Tiryns. Midea was fortified by Perseus, along with Mycenae and Tiryns. Later Atreus, Thyestes, and their mother, Hippodameia, took refuge there when exiled from Pisa by Pelops. At the invitation of Sthenelus, king of Mycenae—of which city Midea seems to have been a vassal—the brothers accepted the joint rule of Midea. Upon the death of Sthenelus' son Eurystheus, they were invited to rule Mycenae. Midea, the Phrygian concubine of Electryon and mother of Licymnius, was perhaps regarded as the city's eponym.

Miletus. The eponym of the Asian and Cretan cities of Miletus. Miletus was a son of Apollo by Deione or Acacallis or Areia. The three sons of Zeus and Europa—Minos, Rhadamanthys, and Sarpedon—were rivals for Miletus' love. He preferred Sarpedon, and Minos drove the lovers from Crete. They fled to the Asian coast, but separately, Sarpedon going to Lycia, Miletus to Caria. Miletus, with his followers, captured a town called Anactoria, on the Maeander River, and renamed it Miletus. By the nymph Cyaneë he had a daughter, Byblis, and a son, Caunis, presumably the eponyms of Byblus and Caunus, respectively in Phoenicia and Caria. Some writers say that the three Cretan brothers competed over Atymnius rather than Miletus. [Apollodorus 3.1.2; Ovid, *Metamorphoses*, 9.441–453; Pausanias 7.2.4–11.]

Milky Way. This familiar celestial phenomenon, now known to be our galaxy viewed from the somewhat peripheral position of the earth, was called *galaxias kyklos* ("milky circle") by the Greeks. This name, and the characteristic that it described, were accounted for by variations on a myth in which Hera was tricked into nursing Heracles (or, in some versions, Hermes). On discovering that she was suckling a hated rival's child, she had torn her breast from his mouth, allowing her milk to squirt across the sky. Or the infant Heracles, unable to hold all the fruitful goddess' milk in his mouth, had spewed some of it out. Or, when Rhea offered a swaddled stone to Cronus to swallow, instead of the infant Zeus, he made her first offer it milk, which of course spilled. Ovid [*Metamorphoses* 1.168–171] saw the Milky Way poetically as the main highway of heaven, along which the gods moved on their way to Jupiter's palace. [Hyginus, *Poetica Astronomica*, 2.43.]

Mimas. One of the GIANTS. In the war between gods and Giants, Mimas' death is variously reported: Hephaestus killed him with missiles of red-hot metal, or Ares killed him at Phlegra, or Zeus killed him with thunderbolts. [Apollodorus 1.6.2; Apollonius Rhodius 3.1225–1227; Euripides, *Ion*, 212–214.]

Minerva. A Roman goddess regularly identified with ATHENA. Minerva was the patroness of the arts and crafts and therefore of the intelligence and skill required in their practice. These qualities were extended to the skills of war. Her functions were so similar to those of Athena that the two goddesses were readily equated, but Minerva was an important deity in her own right.

Minos. A king of Crete.

A. Some Classical writers, no doubt struck by the fact that Minos appears in mythology to have been almost perpetually the king of Crete, claimed that there were two kings of that name. The first was one of three sons of Zeus and Europa, the second his grandson. Minos was generally regarded, however, as one ruler. His mother, Europa, was married by her lover, Zeus, to Asterius, king of Crete. Since Asterius had no children, he adopted Minos and his brothers, Rhadamanthys and Sarpedon. When Asterius died, the brothers began quarreling, either over the kingdom or over their love for a handsome boy, Miletus (or, by some accounts, Atymnius). When this boy expressed a preference for Sarpedon, Minos drove both of them from Crete. Miletus founded the city named for him in Caria, on the Asian mainland, and Sarpedon settled in Lycia, to the north. Rhadamanthys fled Crete for Boeotia, though some say that he had first established a code of law in Crete.

Minos still had rivals for the rule. Claiming that the throne was his by right of divine birth, he declared that Poseidon would do anything that he asked. He then prayed to the god to send him a bull, which he promised to sacrifice. A handsome bull immediately emerged from the sea. The rival claimants were silenced forever; but Minos could not bring himself to sacrifice so beautiful an animal and killed another in its place.

Poseidon had his revenge for this insult. Minos had married Pasiphaë, daughter of Helius and Perseïs, and she had borne him many children: Catreus, Deucalion, Glaucus, Androgeüs, Acacallis, Xenodice, Ariadne, and Phaedra. Now the god made her fall in love with the bull. With the help of the artisan DAEDALUS [A], who had come to Crete in exile from Athens, she was able to gratify her passion. The result was a monstrous offspring, the Minotaur (Bull of Minos), a man with the head of a bull. Minos hired Daedalus to build the Labyrinth, a mazelike prison, and hid the Minotaur at its center.

Meanwhile Minos was making himself master of the seas and the most respected monarch in the civilized world. The laws that he established in Crete were said to have been given him by his father, Zeus, with whom he was on friendly terms. Minos' sons by the nymph Paria were ruling in Paria. Androgeüs lived in Athens, where he had grown up. He won all the honors at the

Panathenaic games, but was killed shortly afterward—probably at the instigation of Aegeus, king of Athens, who feared his influence. Minos made war on Athens, but was unable to take the city. He prayed to the gods, and they sent a plague on Attica.

Minos took the city of Megara, on the Isthmus of Corinth. His success there resulted from the treachery of Scylla, daughter of King Nisus, who cut from her father's head the immortal lock of hair on which the safety of the city depended. Although, according to Aeschylus [*The Libation Bearers* 612–622], Minos had bribed Scylla to do this deed, he repudiated her as soon as it was done and drowned her, either accidentally or on purpose. Athens, by now desperate as a result of the plague, sent messengers to Delphi to inquire how it might be lifted. The oracle told them that Minos must be given whatever he asked in restitution for the death of Androgeüs. Minos demanded that the Athenians send him every ninth year seven youths and seven girls, to be fed to the Minotaur. Aegeus had no recourse but to comply with this requirement.

B. Minos was as amorous as he was kingly, both traits having perhaps been inherited from his father. For nine months he pursued Britomartis, daughter of Zeus and Carme. She escaped him at last by leaping into the sea, and became the goddess Dictynna. Minos had so many affairs that Pasiphaë grew angry and bewitched her husband, so that he impregnated his mistresses with poisonous vermin. Nevertheless he bribed Procris, the wife of Cephalus, to lie with him during her stay in Crete. She gave him a dose of "Circe's root" as a precaution, and afterward carried off as her prize Laelaps, a famous hound that Zeus had given Europa as a watchdog.

Minos had some difficulty with his daughters' love affairs as well as his own. Acacallis bore children by Apollo, and perhaps by Hermes also. Minos banished her to Libya. Ariadne's ill-fated love caused the king more serious problems. When the third group of Athenian youths and girls were delivered for the Minotaur, Aegeus' son Theseus was among them. Ariadne fell in love with him, helped him to escape from the Labyrinth after he had killed the Minotaur, and fled with him in his ship. Some say that Minos forgave his daughter, and even Theseus.

He did not, however, forgive Daedalus, who had assisted them. He imprisoned the artisan, with his son, Icarus, in the Labyrinth, but the two flew away on wings that Daedalus had constructed. Minos followed and finally tracked the famous artisan to the court of Cocalus at Camicus, in Sicily. Some say that Cocalus refused to give up Daedalus and that Minos was killed in the ensuing battle. Others say that Cocalus' daughters treacherously killed Minos in the bath as he prepared for a banquet. In any case, Deucalion succeeded to the rule in Crete and Minos, together with his brother Rhadamanthys, became a judge of the dead in Hades.

According to the Athenians, who hated Crete, Minos was a cruel monarch. All other traditions, however, depict him as a great and just king who was universally admired. Homer's statement [*Odyssey* 19.178–181] that Minos ruled at Cnossus for nine years, makes it likely, in view of the usual tradition of his long reign, that Minos was a title borne by an entire dynasty of kings who ruled in Cnossus and whose influence, carried by their navies, spread far and wide during the Minoan era that has been named for them. References to Minos among Greek writers, beginning with Homer, are innumerable. The most connected single source for his story is Apollodorus [3.1.1–4, 3.15.1, 3.15.7–8, "Epitome" 1.12–15]. Other sources include Hyginus [*Fabulae*, 41–42, 44, 136, 198, and *Poetica Astronomica*, 2.5, 2.14] and Diodorus Siculus [4.60.2–4.62.1].

Minotaur. A Cretan monster, named, but seldom called, Asterius. The Minotaur (Bull of Minos) was the offspring of PASIPHAË and a bull. Pasiphaë's husband, Minos, king of Crete, had a mazelike prison built which he called the Labyrinth, and kept the Minotaur in the center of it. He fed it young Athenians until THESEUS [D, E] killed it.

Minyans. Ancient inhabitants of the region of northern Boeotia centering at Orchomenus. To judge from the confused accounts of the ancestry of the Minyans, this race seems to have been, like the Pelasgians, part of a widespread but vague tradition. They were generally thought to be descended from one or another of the sons of Aeolus, most of whom migrated from Thessaly to other Greek regions. The Minyans dominated northern Boeotia for generations from their principal capital of Orchomenus, which was noted for its wealth. In spite of a disastrous defeat by Thebans, led by Heracles, their prosperity lasted through the Trojan War, a generation later. After the Trojan War, however, Orchomenian power rapidly dwindled. Even before this time many Orchomenians had migrated to the Asiatic coast. The rulers of Miletus claimed descent from them.

The Argonauts were frequently referred to as Minyans. Apollonius Rhodius' explanation of this fact was that most of the company were descended from Minyas, but the surviving rolls indicate that this is far from true. Jason alone was descended from Minyas, and only one Argonaut, Erginus, may have come from Orchomenus. Only if the term "Minyan" is given the very broad (and unlikely) sense of "Aeolid" can it be applied with any justice to the *Argo*'s crew. Herodotus and other historians nevertheless accept the tradition and call the Argonauts' descendants on Lemnos Minyans. These people, when driven from their city of Minyae by Pelasgians, migrated to Sparta. Having made themselves unwelcome there, they moved farther west to Triphylia, in southern Elis. A group of them sailed from Sparta to Thera with Theras, and their descendants were prominent among the founders of Cyrene, in northern Africa.

Minyas. The eponym of the MINYANS. Like most eponyms, Minyas is a vague personage. His father was Poseidon, Aeolus, or Chryses, a king of Boeotian Orchomenus. He has been called both the father and the son of Orchomenus. The two facts about him that are more or less agreed upon are that he was the father of Clymene and that he was so rich that he became the first man to build a treasury. This treasury was, in Pausanias' view, as remarkable a structure as the pyramids. Although Minyas was presumably the father of the three ladies of Orchomenus, generally referred to merely as "the daughters of Minyas," who scorned to honor the rites of Dionysus, Minyas himself plays no part in the story. [*Catalogues of Women* 84; Pausanias 9.36.4–5; Apollonius Rhodius 1.229–233, 3.1093–1095.]

Mistress. See DESPOINA.

Mnemosyne. A Titaness. Mnemosyne (Memory), a daughter of Ge and Uranus, lay with Zeus for nine nights in Pieria and gave birth to the Muses. In spite of her place among the Titans, Mnemosyne seems to be no more than an abstraction: the arts, personified by the Muses, are children of Memory. Before the invention of writing, this metaphor would have been particularly apt. [Hesiod, *Theogony*, 135.]

Moerae. See FATES.

Moirai. See FATES.

Moliones or **Molionides.** Eurytus and Cteatus, twin sons of Actor or Poseidon and Molione. According to several late writers, the Moliones were Siamese twins, or else had two heads and four arms and legs attached to a single body. To Homer, they were merely twins, and most of their feats of strength and valor would seem to indicate a normal form. As mere boys they fought in a siege of Pylus. Nestor, a stripling himself at the time, later boasted that he would have killed them if Poseidon had not hidden them in a mist. The Moliones took part in the Calydonian boar hunt. They married Theronice and Theraephone, twin daughters of Dexamenus, king of Olenus. Theronice and Cteatus had a son, Amphimachus; Theraephone and Eurytus also had a son, Thalpius.

When the Moliones' uncle Augeias, king of Elis, was preparing for war with Heracles, he offered them a share in the government in order to win their aid. They fought boldly against Heracles and his Tirynthian army, killing his ally Dameon, son of Phlius, and mortally wounding Heracles' half-brother, Iphicles. Too sick at the time to fight, Heracles was forced to make peace. Not long afterward, however, he treacherously killed the twins from ambush at Cleonae as they were on their way to the Isthmian games during a sacred truce. Their tomb was shown at Cleonae for generations. Their sons distinguished themselves in the Trojan War. [Homer, *Iliad*, 11.706–752, 23.638–642; Pindar, *Olympian Odes*, 10.26–34; Apollodorus 2.7.2; Pausanias 5.3.3.]

Molossus. The eponym of the Molossians. Molossus was a son of Neoptolemus by Andromache. He gave his name to one of the tribes of Epeirus in the region ruled by his father and later by his guardian, Helenus. Molossus appears as a child in Euripides' tragedy *Andromache*. [Pausanias 1.11.1–2.]

moly. A magical herb. ODYSSEUS [F] used moly as an antidote to Circe's charms.

moon. SELENE was the Greek moon-goddess, Luna the Roman. Late Classical writers identify ARTEMIS and HECATE to some degree with the moon, but it is not certain how ancient this connection is. Pasiphaë was a name for the moon-goddess in a temple that she shared with Helius at Thalamae, in Laconia.

Mopsus (1). A warrior seer from Thessaly. Mopsus was a son of Ampycus and Chloris. He distinguished himself as a man of action both during the Calydonian boar hunt and in the battle that broke out between the Lapiths and the Centaurs at Peirithoüs' wedding. His greatest adventure was to sail with the Argonauts, though on this voyage he won fame more for his prophetic powers than for physical prowess. On several occasions he gave sound advice to Jason after reading the future in the flight of birds, an art that he had learned from Apollo and from his own father. While the Argonauts were in Libya, Mopsus was killed by a snake. [Apollonius Rhodius 1.1080–1106, 4.1502–1536; Hyginus, *Fabulae*, 14, 128.]

Mopsus (2). A seer of Colophon, in Asia Minor. After the fall of Thebes to the Epigoni, the prisoners, among them Teiresias' daughter, Manto, were dedicated by their captors to Apollo at Delphi. Later they emigrated to Clarus, in Caria. There they found Cretans under Rhacius in command of newly captured coastal areas, though Carians still held the inland region. The Cretans at first captured the Thebans but soon decided to welcome them as allies. Rhacius married Manto, and she bore a son, Mopsus. (Some claim, however, that Apollo was the father.)

On reaching manhood, Mopsus succeeded in expelling the Carians entirely from the country. He came to be known, however, at least as much for his powers of divination as for his generalship. Mopsus' ignominious defeat of CALCHAS in a contest of prophecy at Colophon led to that seer's death from sheer embarrassment. Mopsus then joined forces with AMPHILOCHUS (2), another son of Manto, who had come with Calchas from Troy. Together they founded the city of Mallus, in Cilicia. Later they quarreled and killed each other, but they nevertheless shared a highly regarded oracle for more than a thousand years thereafter. [Pausanias 7.3.1–2; Apollodorus "Epitome" 6.2–4, 6.19.]

morning star. This planet, when it rose as the morning star, was called EOSPHORUS (Dawn-Bearer) by the Greeks, Lucifer (Light-Bearer) by the Romans.

Morpheus. See SOMNUS.

Mossynoeci. A tribe inhabiting an eastern part of the southern coast of the Black Sea. According to Apollonius Rhodius [2.1015–1029], the Mossynoeci engaged publicly in sexual promiscuity. They lived in wooden huts, called *mossynes*, in the mountains. The king dispensed justice from the highest of the huts. If he made a mistake, however, he was imprisoned for a day without food. The Mossynoeci were mentioned by Herodotus among those who paid tribute to the Persian king Darius and fought in his army.

mother-goddess. A very ancient type of deity widely worshiped in the Mediterranean area. Mother-goddesses presided over the fertility of both plant and animal life. The Phrygian goddess CYBELE was the purest example of this type known to the Greeks in the Classical era, although mother-goddesses were probably worshiped by pre-Hellenic inhabitants of Greece. Strong elements of the type were also to be found in Aphrodite, Demeter, Artemis, and other divinities worshiped by the Hellenic Greeks. Cybele and other goddesses who were regularly worshiped on mountaintops are often called "mountain-mothers."

Mother-goddesses, as symbols of fertility, were interested solely in the production of offspring and therefore in the act of procreation that led to it. Unlike goddesses of marriage, such as Hera, they were little concerned with matrimonial formalities. Generally, therefore, they had young consorts rather than husbands. These consorts—Aphrodite's lover Adonis, for example, or Cybele's Attis—often died after a short period of amorous bliss, to be duly mourned by the respective goddesses and their worshipers. They then rose again—divine counterparts of the returning vegetation that resulted from their unions with the goddesses. The rites of Aphrodite and several other goddesses of her type were celebrated in some regions with ritual prostitution in the temples.

Mother of the Gods. See CYBELE.

mountain-mother. See MOTHER-GODDESS.

Mulciber. A euphemistic title of VULCAN that perhaps meant "He of the Gentle Touch."

Muses. Goddesses who inspired those who were proficient in the arts.

A. The nine Muses were said to be daughters of Zeus and Mnemosyne (Memory). Their origin as mythological figures is obscure and they were little worshiped, though often invoked. They may owe their prominence largely to poets, who identified them as the sources of their inspiration. In the days before the invention of writing, all knowledge was dependent on memory for its preservation, as is music today to those who do not read it. The Muses, then, were in part patronesses of memory, and the bards in particular had reason to honor them. According to Pausanias, the boy giants Otus and Ephialtes (who, unlikely as it seems, were the first to locate the Muses on Mount Helicon) knew only three. Appropriately enough they called them Melete (Attention or Practice), Mneme (Memory), and Aoede (Song).

The earliest story about the Muses tells of their contest at Dorium, in Messenia, with the bard THAMYRIS, who had boasted of his singing. When they won, they blinded Thamyris and took away his memory. They also blinded the Phaeacian bard Demodocus, but gave him "minstrelsy" in place of sight. Blindness would have unfitted an early Greek for most pursuits, but it would of necessity have sharpened his memory.

Pierus, son of Magnes, a Macedonian, is said to have learned from Thracian oracles that the Muses were actually nine in number. This Pierus was, presumably, the eponym of Pieria, near Mount Olympus, which rivaled Helicon as the Muses' traditional haunt. Pierus called his nine daughters by Euippe, a Paeonian woman, "children of the Muses." Growing proud, the Pierides dared to challenge the Muses to a contest of song, with the nymphs as judges. Calliope appeared for the Muses and, of course, won, whereupon the victors changed the Pierides into chattering magpies. The Sirens, urged on for some reason by Hera, also challenged the Muses to a concert. As punishment, the Muses plucked off the Sirens' feathers and made crowns of them. The Muses may themselves have had wings, for, when the Thracian king Pyreneus lured them into his house and tried to rape them, they flew away.

B. The nine Muses were named Cleio, Euterpe, Thaleia, Melpomene, Terpsichore, Erato, Polyhymnia (or Polymnia), Urania, and Calliope. Some late Classical writers attempted to assign specific arts, such as epic poetry, lyre playing, or astronomy, to individual Muses, but, since this notion was entirely artificial, no two authors could agree on the assignments. Certain of the Muses did have adventures of their own, however. Cleio, for example, bore a son, Hyacinth, by Pierus. By Pierus' son Oeagrus, a Thracian king, or by Apollo, Calliope became the mother of Orpheus and Linus. She, or Euterpe, bore the Thracian king Rhesus by the river-god Strymon. Melpomene was the mother of the Sirens. (All these offspring, except for Hyacinth, were connected with oracles.) Thaleia was said to be the mother, by Apollo, of the Corybantes. The Muses as a group taught the riddle to the Sphinx. As heavenly musicians, they are said to have sung for the gods and, on special occasions such as the wedding of Cadmus and Harmonia or the funeral of Achilles, for mortals as well. [Homer, *Iliad*, 2.594–600, and *Odyssey*, 8.63–64, 8.479–481, 24.60–61; Hesiod, *Theogony*, 36–115; Ovid, *Metamorphoses*, 5.273–340, 5.662–678; Apollodorus 1.3.1–4, 3.5.8; Pausanias 9.24.3, 9.29.1–6.]

Myagro. An Arcadian hero. Myagro, whose name means "Fly-Catcher," was honored in the town of Alipherus for his services in chasing away flies, in return for receiving the first prayers at the festival of Athena. [Pausanias 8.26.7.]

Mycenae. A major city in Argolis. According to one tradition, Mycenae was founded by Perseus, but another tradition—that the city was named for Mycene, a daughter of the ancient river-god Inachus—suggests that Perseus may merely have fortified an existing city, as he did at Midea. The Homeric stories of the Trojan War, supported by archaeological evidence, indicate that for a considerable time Mycenae dominated all of Argolis. The myths of the region suggest that this dominance began in Perseus' day and continued until the death of Agamemnon. The tradition is obscured, however, by the fact that the name ARGOS was often used interchangeably with Mycenae.

Mycene. A daughter of Inachus. All that is known of Mycene is that she married Arestor and that the city of Mycenae may have been named for her, unless Perseus named it. [Pausanias 2.16.4.]

Mygdon. The king and eponym of the Mygdonians, a Mysian or Phrygian tribe. The Mygdonians were neighbors and traditional enemies of the Mariandynians, who lived on the southern shore of the Black Sea. Heracles was an ally of the Mariandynians and killed Mygdon in a war between the two tribes. Although the Mygdonians lost territory to the Mariandynians, they later regained much of it. Mygdon's brother Amycus, king of the Bebryces, who lived on the coast of the Sea of Marmara, was killed by the Argonauts somewhat later. Priam, king of Troy, fought in his youth with the Mygdonians and the Phrygian king Otreus against the Amazons. At that time the Mygdonians lived on the Sangarius River. Mygdon's son Coroebus led a Mysian force to the Trojan War and hoped to marry Cassandra, but he was killed. Midas was called by some a Mygdonian king, but he is associated with so many places on the fringes of the Greek world that this information does little to locate the Mygdonians. [Homer, *Iliad*, 184–189; Apollodorus 2.5.9; Pausanias 10.27.1.]

Myles. A king of Laconia. The elder son of Lelex, Myles (Mill-Man) invented the mill. He left the kingdom to his son, Eurotas. [Pausanias 3.1.1, 3.20.2.]

Myrmidons. Inhabitants of Phthia. Late Classical writers, fascinated by the resemblance between the name of this people and the word *myrmex* ("ant"), invented several contradictory explanations for it. The best known was the story that Aeacus, alone on the island of Aegina, prayed to his father, Zeus, to give him companions. Zeus obligingly transformed the island's ants into people. According to this tradition, the Myrmidons later migrated to the Thessalian region of Phthia with Aeacus' son Peleus. In view of the fact that most migrations within Greece seem to have been westward and southward from Thessaly rather than the reverse, the Aeginetan story may be relatively late. A rival tradition is that the first Myrmidon was a contemporary and son-in-law of Aeolus, the early Thessalian king whose children migrated far and wide through the Greek lands. Myrmidon and Peisidice were the parents of Antiphus and Actor. The Myrmidons are perhaps best known as the soldiers whom Peleus' son, Achilles, led to Troy.

Myrrha or **Smyrna.** A daughter of CINYRAS, king of Paphos, in Cyprus, and Cenchreïs, or of Theias, king of Assyria. Either because Cenchreïs boasted that her daughter was more beautiful than Aphrodite or because Myrrha herself did not honor the goddess properly, Aphrodite punished the girl with an incestuous infatuation with her father. Aided by her nurse, Myrrha arranged to sleep with him for twelve nights while he was intoxicated or else believed her, in the dark, to be a concubine whom he was enjoying during an absence of his wife. Myrrha became pregnant. When her father discovered what had happened, he pursued her with a sword. She prayed to the gods to make her invisible and they changed her into a myrrh tree. Her tears became the precious gum of this tree. Cinyras killed himself in shame over the incestuous union. After nine months the tree split open and an infant boy, Adonis, was revealed inside. [Apollodorus 3.14.4; Ovid, *Metamorphoses*, 10.519–559; Hyginus, *Fabulae*, 58.]

Myrtilus. A son of Hermes and charioteer of Oenomaüs, king of Pisa. Bribed by PELOPS [B, C], Myrtilus caused his master's death and was cursed by him. Pelops killed Myrtilus, who, in dying, cursed him in turn. This curse may have been responsible for the bloody events in the lives of Pelops' descendants. Some claim that Hermes placed his son in the sky as the constellation Auriga, the Charioteer.

Myrto. A Euboean woman for whom the Myrtoan Sea, between the Cyclades and the Peloponnesus, was said by some to have been named. [Pausanias 8.14.12.]

Mysia. The northwestern part of Asia Minor, north of Lydia and west of Phrygia. Mysia was never a political entity, but it was a fairly well defined region that included many cities near the coast, from Cyzicus, on the Sea of Marmara, southward to Pergamon and beyond. Although the Troad was a part of this geographical area, it was generally spoken of as separate from Mysia. Many Mysian cities were allied with Troy in the Trojan War. Among the best known of the many mythological events that occurred in Mysia are the adventures of the Argonauts among the Bebryces and the Dolopians and of Telephus in Teuthrania.

N

naïad. See NYMPH.

Narcissus. The son of the nymph Leiriope by the river-god Cephissus. When Leiriope asked the then little-known seer Teiresias if her newborn son would live a long life, he replied, "If he never know himself." This seemingly meaningless remark did little to advance the diviner's reputation at the time, but sixteen years later it made him famous. The child in question, Narcissus, had grown up to be a ravishingly beautiful youth. He was courted by many lovers of both sexes, but scorned all of them in his pride. Among these adoring lovers was the nymph Echo. Her attempts to win his attention were considerably hampered by her inability to initiate a conversation, Hera having earlier punished her garrulity by dooming her forever to repeat the last words of others' speeches. She wasted away to a mere voice, unnoticed by Narcissus.

A young man whom the youth had similarly spurned at last prayed that Narcissus should himself love unrequitedly. Nemesis heard him and arranged that Narcissus should stop to drink at a certain spring on the heights of Mount Helicon. Glancing into the water, the boy saw there his own reflection and instantly fell in love with it. Since he could not embrace the image in the pool, he lay beside it, unable to tear himself away, until he died, either of the same love that had caused Echo to fade away or of simple starvation. His body was transformed into the flower that bears his name. [Ovid, *Metamorphoses*, 3.339–510.]

Nasamon. The eponym of the Nasamonians, a Libyan tribe. Nasamon was a son of the Cretan Amphithemis and the nymph of Lake Tritonis. [Apollonius Rhodius 4.1489–1501.]

Nasamonians. A Libyan tribe of the region south of Cyrene. Herodotus speaks of the Nasamonians in several passages. Their supposed eponym, Nasamon, was of Cretan descent.

Naupactus. A city of Ozolian Locris on the strait at the entrance to the Gulf of Corinth. Naupactus was the port from which the Heraclids and their Dorian allies embarked on their successful invasion of the Peloponnesus.

Nauplia. A seaport (now called Nauplion) near the head of the Gulf of Argolis. Nauplia was the home port of Nauplius, who founded the city. From there he traveled to many parts of Greece, Crete, and Asia Minor, engaging in commerce that included slave trading and a bit of piracy.

Nauplius (1). A son of Poseidon by Amymone, daughter of Danaüs. Nauplius founded and named the city of Nauplia, across the Gulf of Argolis from his native city of Argos. He became a famous navigator and was apparently a prototype of the merchant captain, who often dealt in slaves. When Heracles seduced Auge, her father, King Aleüs of Tegea, in Arcadia, asked Nauplius to drown the girl or to sell her in a foreign land. Nauplius sold her to Teuthras, king of Teuthrania (Pergamon). Later the Cretan king Catreus asked Nauplius to sell abroad his daughters Aërope and Clymene, having been told by an oracle that one of his children would kill him. Nauplius sold Aërope to Atreus or Pleisthenes, but married Clymene himself. She bore Palamedes, Oeax, and Nausimedon. (Some say that Nauplius' wife was named Philyra or Hesione.)

When Palamedes was stoned to death by the Greeks at Troy as a result of Odysseus' treachery, Nauplius sailed there and demanded satisfaction. Receiving none, he found an effective means of revenge. Sailing from one Greek city to another, he somehow induced the wives of three of the Greek leaders—Agamemnon, Idomeneus, and Diomedes—to cuckold their husbands. Not content with this, Nauplius waited until the returning Greek ships were caught in a storm off the Euboean cape of Caphareus, then lighted a great fire there. Deluded by the false beacon, many of the Greek captains made for land and were wrecked, with great loss of life. Nauplius killed those sailors who reached the shore alive. He is said to have died in a similar way, but no details of his death have survived.

Apollodorus tried to explain the fact that Nauplius was born many generations before the Trojan War with the statement that he had a long life. The Argonaut Nauplius would be more plausible as "Nauplius the Wrecker" than his ancestor, but no Classical writer seems to have identified him thus. [Apollodorus 2.1.5, 2.7.4, 3.2.2, "Epitome" 6.7–11; Euripides, *Helen*, 1126–1131; Hyginus, *Fabulae*, 116.]

Nauplius (2). An Argonaut. Nauplius, an Argive, was a son of Clytoneüs and a descendant of the navigator Nauplius. He also was an expert seaman and offered to become steersman of the *Argo* after the death of Tiphys. Because he was presumably still living during the Trojan War, this Nauplius seems likely to have been the notorious wrecker of ships and marriages, but that distinction is usually accorded to his ancestor. [Apollonius Rhodius 1.133–135, 2.896–897.]

Nausicaä. The daughter of Alcinoüs, king of the Phaeacians, and Arete. The shipwrecked Odysseus begged assistance of Nausicaä as she was washing clothes near the seashore with her attendants. She told him how he might win the help of her parents. Alcinoüs offered her hand in marriage to Odysseus, who refused it out of loyalty to his wife. [Homer, *Odyssey*, 6.15–320, 8.457–468.]

Nausithoüs. A king of the Phaeacians. Nausithoüs was a son of Poseidon and Periboea, daughter of the Giant Eurymedon. He ruled the peace-loving

Phaeacians in Hypereia. They were so harassed by their neighbors the Cyclopes that Nausithoüs led them far away to the island of Scherië, or Drepane, usually identified with Corcyra (Corfu), which was sacred to Macris, a nurse of Dionysus. Nausithoüs had two sons, Alcinoüs and Rhexenor. When Heracles came to the island after murdering his children, Nausithoüs purified him. Heracles had a son, Hyllus, by a local water-nymph, Melite. When the boy grew up he wished to found his own city and Nausithoüs aided him. At Nausithoüs' death he was succeeded by Alcinoüs. [Homer, *Odyssey*, 6.1–11, 7.56–63; Apollonius Rhodius 4.539–550.]

Naxos. An island in the Cyclades. This island, originally called Strongyle, was renamed Dia. Later it was conquered by Carians, whose king gave it his own name, Naxos. Naxos' grandson was ruling when Theseus abandoned Ariadne on the island. She was found there by Dionysus, who married her. Naxos, famous for its wine, was a center of this god's worship. It was also the scene of the deaths of Otus and Ephialtes.

Neaera. A nymph. Neaera was the mother, by HELIUS [C], of Lampetië and Phaëthusa.

Neaera. See ALEÜS; EVADNE (1).

Neleus. A king of Pylus. Neleus and his brother, Pelias, were children of Salmoneus' daughter Tyro by Poseidon. About to marry Cretheus, king of Iolcus, Tyro exposed the infants. They were found and reared by horseherders. Learning their true identity, they pursued their stepmother, Sidero, who had mistreated Tyro, and Pelias killed her. Later Pelias quarreled with Neleus and drove him out of Iolcus. Neleus took refuge in Messenia, where his cousin Aphareus was ruling. Aphareus gave him most of the coastal lands, including the city of Pylus. Neleus expelled Pylas, that city's founder, and made it his capital. He prospered there and became one of the most powerful rulers of Greek cities.

Neleus married the beautiful Chloris, daughter of Amphion. She bore him a daughter, Pero, and twelve sons, though Homer mentions only three: Nestor, Chromius, and Periclymenus. Pero was sought after by many men, but Neleus insisted that her husband-to-be bring her the cattle of Iphiclus from Phylace, in Thessaly. This bride-price discouraged all the suitors except Bias, son of Neleus' half-brother Amythaon. Bias' brother, the seer Melampus, brought back the cattle after a year of hardship in Phylace and bought Pero for Bias. Neleus thus lost both his daughter and Melampus' property, which he had seized during the seer's absence.

When Heracles killed Iphitus, he came to Neleus to be purified of the murder, but Neleus refused because of his friendship for Iphitus' father, Eurytus. Later Heracles conquered Pylus and killed Neleus, his wife, and eleven of their sons—even though, according to tradition, they were aided by Hades. Nestor, in Gerenia at the time, escaped his brothers' fate and inherited the throne. According to Homer, Neleus survived Heracles' attack and later waged a successful war with the Eleians. He is said by the Corinthians to have traveled to Corinth in the days of King Sisyphus and to have died there of disease. He was buried near the isthmus in a grave so secret that Sisyphus would not reveal its location even to Nestor. [Homer, *Odyssey*, 11.281–291, 15.228–238; Pausanias 4.2.5–4.3.1, 4.36.1–3; Apollodorus 1.9.8–9, 2.6.2, 2.7.3.]

Nemea. A city in northern Argolis. When the army of the Seven against Thebes passed through Nemea, they witnessed the strange death of Opheltes, the infant son of King Lycurgus, and instituted the Nemean games in the child's honor. The Nemean lion roamed the region about this city until it was killed by Heracles.

Nemean games. Athletic contests held at Nemea, in Argolis. The Nemean games, which were held every five years, were said to have been instituted by Adrastus in honor of OPHELTES. Victors received crowns of parsley or celery.

Nemean lion. A monster, offspring of Echidna and Orthus or of Typhon. This beast was suckled by the moon-goddess, Selene, or nursed by Hera. HERACLES [D] killed the lion as the first of his labors and thereafter wore its pelt. Hera immortalized it as a constellation.

Nemesis. A goddess of retribution for evil deeds or undeserved good fortune. Nemesis is generally, in the view of Greek and Roman writers, a personification of the resentment aroused in men—and, therefore, supposedly in the gods—by other men who commit crimes with apparent impunity, or who have inordinate good fortune. Nemesis was occasionally worshiped as two Nemeses, both of whom, like the single goddess, were said to be daughters of Nyx (Night). In one myth, Nemesis is more than an abstraction, though the tale may also have some allegorical significance. According to the lost epic *Cypria* [8] and several later works, Zeus fell in love with Nemesis, but she took various forms in order to escape his attentions. At last she became a goose and Zeus, in the form of a swan, raped her.

In a variation of this tale, Zeus and Aphrodite plotted Nemesis' downfall. Aphrodite, in the form of an eagle, pretended to chase the swan Zeus. He took refuge in the lap of Nemesis (who retained her human form in this story). The goddess, apparently overcome with compassion, did not chase the bird away but, instead, went obligingly to sleep. In both versions, Nemesis in due course laid an egg. This egg was taken, either by a shepherd or by Hermes, to Leda, wife of the Spartan king Tyndareüs. Leda hatched the egg and reared the chick as her own. No ugly duckling, the girl was named Helen. Zeus placed both the swan and the eagle in the stars to celebrate his triumph. [Hesiod, *Theogony*, 223–224; Apollodorus 3.10.7; Hyginus, *Poetica Astronomica*, 2.8; Pausanias 1.33.2–8, 7.4.2–3.]

Neoptolemus or **Pyrrhus.** The son of Achilles by Deïdameia.

A. Achilles was reared at the court of Lycomedes, king of the Aegean island of Scyrus, because of the fears of his mother, Thetis, that he would fight at Troy. Although dressed as a girl, he had an affair with Lycomedes' daughter, Deïdameia, who bore a son. The child was named Pyrrhus. After Achilles' death at Troy the Greeks learned from Helenus, the captured Trojan seer, that Troy was not fated to be taken unless three events occurred: the bones of Pelops must be brought to Troy; and both Philoctetes, who owned the bow and arrows of Heracles, and the son of Achilles must fight on the Greek side. The Eleians willingly sent the bones of their hero, and Pyrrhus joined Odysseus and Phoenix when they came to Scyrus to take him to Troy. It is said to have been old Phoenix, Achilles' tutor, who renamed Pyrrhus Neoptolemus (Young Soldier) because either Achilles or the youth himself had joined the war at so early an age. Odysseus turned over to the young man Achilles' armor, which had earlier been awarded to him.

Persuading PHILOCTETES to fight beside the Greeks was less easy to accomplish, for he had been abandoned, severely wounded, on the island of Lemnos ten years earlier. Most accounts say that Odysseus and Diomedes brought him to Troy, but according to Sophocles' tragedy *Philoctetes*, Neoptolemus was Odysseus' companion on this venture. The young man refused to aid Odysseus in his cruel plot to force Philoctetes back to the war and even promised to take the suffering man to his Greek homeland. Fortunately the deified Heracles appeared and ordered Philoctetes to Troy.

At Troy, Neoptolemus proved to be as bold and ruthless a fighter as his famous father. He killed the Mysian prince Eurypylus, Cassandra's Phrygian suitor Coroebus, and many Trojans, including Antenor. He was one of the Greeks hidden in the wooden horse. It was Neoptolemus who killed Priam at the altar of Zeus of the Courtyard, or else dragged him first to the palace gate. When Achilles' ghost demanded the blood of Priam's daughter Polyxena, Neoptolemus sacrificed her on his father's grave. Some say that it was he, not Odysseus, who killed Hector's little son, Astyanax, flinging him from the city walls. Andromache, Hector's widow, was awarded to Neoptolemus as a concubine. According to the *Little Iliad* [14], he also made a slave of Aeneas, but this account differs from the common tradition.

B. The events of Neoptolemus' life after he left Troy are told by many writers, but seldom twice in the same way. Homer recorded that he reached home safely, without having received even a wound at Troy. Some say that Thetis saved him from the storms that destroyed many Greek ships by persuading him to wait two days before sailing, and two more on the nearby island of Tenedos. Others claim that the goddess warned him to travel home by land. There is much dispute as to whether he returned to his father's homeland of Phthia or went, by sea or land, to Epeirus, on the Adriatic coast. There is a strong tradition that Neoptolemus conquered Epeirus and ruled there for some years, having his capital at Ephyra. The captured Trojan seer Helenus, who had advised him to come to this part of the world, sailed with him and founded the port of Buthrotum.

One legend has it that, when Odysseus was accused of murder by the families of Penelope's dead suitors, Neoptolemus was called upon to arbitrate. Because he hoped to add to his own dominions the island of Cephallenia (which Odysseus controlled as well as Ithaca), he ruled that his former companion be exiled. After a few years in Epeirus, Neoptolemus left for Phthia in order to marry Hermione, daughter of Menelaüs and Helen. He left Andromache to Helenus, who became guardian of their three sons: Molossus, Pielus, and Pergamus. At Neoptolemus' death in Phthia, Helenus received all or a part of his kingdom. The people of the region were renamed Molossians, for Molossus. Pergamus migrated with his mother to Mysia, where he killed Areius, king of Teuthrania, and renamed the city Pergamon. Neoptolemus' descendants ruled Epeirus for many generations, down to Olympias, the mother of Alexander the Great.

C. A quite different story tells of Neoptolemus' marriage and death in Phthia. Hermione was married to her cousin Orestes. She had been betrothed to him by her father, Menelaüs, or else her mother's father, Tyndareüs, had married them during the Trojan War. At Troy, Menelaüs, eager to win the support of Neoptolemus, upon which victory depended, promised him Hermione's hand. Some time after the Spartan and Phthian leaders had both returned home, Neoptolemus claimed his promised bride. Unwilling to go back on his word, Menelaüs agreed. He took Hermione away from Orestes, who had gone mad after killing his mother, Clytemnestra. Neoptolemus, while in Sparta to demand Hermione, treated her husband insolently and won his undying enmity.

Neoptolemus committed a far rasher act in going to Delphi and demanding redress from Apollo, who had guided Paris' hand when he killed Achilles at Troy. Some say that he even stole the votive offerings and set fire to the god's temple. The horrified Delphians killed him for this outrage. According to Euripides' tragedy Andromache, however, Neoptolemus was quite innocent of such sacrilege, having in fact gone to Delphi in order to atone for an earlier insult to the god. Orestes, hating the Phthian for his own reasons and urged on by Hermione, who feared her new huband's anger at her cruel treatment of Andromache, conspired with some Delphians to spread a rumor of the visitor's evil intentions. Neoptolemus was mercilessly cut down at the altar of Apollo, as he had once cut down the aged Priam at the altar of Zeus. Such instances of poetic justice came to be known as "the punishment of Neoptolemus." Some say that the victim's bones were scattered through the territory of Ambracia, in Epeirus, but he is usually said to have been buried in the temple precinct where he was killed. For generations thereafter the Delphians treated his grave with contempt. Then, during an attack by Gauls, three terrible figures miraculously appeared and frightened the superstitious invaders away. One of the apparitions was said to be the ghost of Neoptolemus. Thereafter his grave was annually paid the honors due a hero.

D. Neoptolemus is an important character in Sophocles' Philoctetes and in

Euripides' *Andromache*, though in the latter play he physically appears only as a corpse at the end. Among innumerable references to his exploits are the following: Apollodorus "Epitome" 5.10–11, 6.5, 6.12–14, 7.40; Homer, *Odyssey*, 3.188–189, 4.5–9, 11.492–493, 11.504–540; Vergil, *Aeneïd*, 2.453–558, 3.294–334; Pindar, *Nemean Odes*, 6.34–49; Hyginus, *Fabulae*, 123.

Nephele. The first wife of ATHAMAS, king of Boeotian Orchomenus. Nephele and Athamas had a son and a daughter, Phrixus and Helle. Athamas took a second wife, Ino, who plotted against Phrixus. When, as a result, the boy was about to be sacrificed by his father, Nephele brought a miraculous ram, which Hermes had given her, and the two children flew away on the ram's back.

Neptune. The chief Roman sea-god. Since the Romans were not in early times a seafaring people, Neptune was a water-deity of little importance. He remained so until his identification with the Greek god POSEIDON, through which Neptune acquired a multiplicity of myths. His cult, however, remained minimal.

Nereïds. Sea-nymphs. The fifty Nereïds were daughters of the sea-god Nereus and Doris, a daughter of Oceanus and Tethys. They were listed by name, differently, by Homer [*Iliad* 18.37–53], Hesiod [*Theogony* 1003–1007], and Apollodorus [1.2.7]. Only three of the Nereïds, THETIS, PSAMATHE, and Galatea (see POLYPHEMUS, 1), have significant myths of their own. Thetis often appears as their unofficial leader. For example, she directed their efforts to aid Dionysus when he was pursued into the sea by Lycurgus and to conduct the *Argo* through dangerous waters. In general, the Nereïds seem to have been amiable nymphs, though their complaint to Poseidon that Cassiopeia had boasted of being more beautiful than they resulted in the god's sending a sea-monster to ravage the land of Cepheus. [Apollonius Rhodius 4.930–964; Apollodorus 1.9.25, 2.4.3, 3.5.1.]

Nereus. An ancient sea-god. Nereus, a son of Pontus (Sea) and Ge (Earth), may have had considerable importance before Poseidon became the ruling sea-god. He is referred to by both Homer and Hesiod as the Old Man. Hesiod explains that this is because he is kind and just. He was the father, by the Oceanid Doris, of the fifty sea-nymphs the Nereïds. Like other sea-deities, such as Thetis and Proteus (the second of whom he is sometimes confused with), Nereus had prophetic powers and also the ability to change his shape. Heracles, led to his home by the Nymphs, captured him sleeping. Though Nereus took many forms, Heracles bound him and refused to release him until he revealed the whereabouts of the garden of the Hesperides. [Hesiod, *Theogony*, 233–264; Apollodorus 2.5.11.]

Nerio. See MARS.

Nessus. A Centaur. Driven from Arcadia by HERACLES [E, M], Nessus found himself a trade as a ferryman on the Aetolian river Evenus, and even claimed that the gods had set him up in business because of his sterling char-

acter. Much later he had an opportunity to ferry Deïaneira, Heracles' Calydonian bride, across the river while Heracles struggled through it alone. He
tried to rape the girl, but Heracles shot him. Dying, he persuaded the naive
Deïaneira to make a love charm of his blood and semen, knowing that the
blood contained Hydra venom from the arrow that had wounded him. This
potion later caused Heracles' death. [Apollodorus 2.5.4, 2.7.6–7.]

Nestor. A king of Pylus. Nestor was one of twelve sons of Neleus, king of
Pylus, and Chloris, daughter of Amphion. When Heracles sacked Pylus and
killed Nestor's brothers, Nestor was in Gerenia, where some say that he was
brought up. As a youth, he distinguished himself by his valor on a cattle raid
into Elis. Nevertheless, when the Eleians attacked Pylus, Neleus took away his
son's horses to prevent him from entering the battle, fearing that his inexperience would prove fatal. Nestor ventured out on foot, killed one of the Eleian
leaders (King Augeias' son Mulius), and leaped into his chariot. During the
battle he killed or wounded more than one hundred men. At the funeral games
held at Buprasium, in Elis, for Amarynceus, Nestor won over skilled opponents
in boxing, wrestling, throwing the spear, and the footrace. He was one of the
hunters of the Calydonian boar, but barely escaped the beast by vaulting on
his spear into a tree.

Nestor married Eurydice, daughter of Clymenus, or Anaxibia, daughter of
Crateius; she bore him seven sons and two daughters. After Neleus' death in
Nestor's youth, Nestor succeeded to the rule of the prosperous city of Pylus
and held the throne for three generations. In his old age he led ninety ships to
the Trojan War, accompanied by his sons Antilochus and Thrasymedes. Pindar
says [*Pythian Odes* 6.28–42] that Antilochus died in rescuing his father
from a savage attack by Memnon. Nestor's sage, if somewhat sententious,
advice was esteemed by the other Greek leaders. He was one of the few
generals to enjoy a safe homeward voyage and to regain his throne unop-
posed. Later he played host to Telemachus, who came in search of news
of his father, Odysseus. Some say that Nestor's daughter Polycaste bore a
child, Persepolis, to the youth. Her brother Peisistratus accompanied Telemachus to Menelaüs' palace at Sparta.

Nestor figures prominently throughout Homer's *Iliad* and in Book 3 of the
Odyssey. According to *The Contest of Homer and Hesiod* [569], Homer may
have been Polycaste's son. [Herodotus 5.65; *Catalogues of Women* 11–12;
Apollodorus 1.9.9, 2.7.3; Ovid, *Metamorphoses*, 8.365–369.]

Nicippe. See STHENELUS (1).

Nicostratus. A son of Menelaüs. Nicostratus' mother was either Helen or a
slave woman. With his brother, Megapenthes, he was said by some to have
driven Helen from Sparta after his father's death. The brothers' claims to the
throne were passed over by the Spartans in favor of those of Orestes. [Pausa-
nias 2.18.6, 3.19.9.]

night. See NYX.

Nike. The goddess of victory. Nike, though called a daughter of Pallas and Styx, was more a symbol than a mythological character. Like her brothers, Cratus (Strength), Bia (Force), and Zelus (Emulation), she was a constant companion—that is, an attribute—of Zeus. [Hesiod, *Theogony*, 383–388.]

Niobe (1). A daughter of Phoroneus and the nymph Teledice or Cinna. The first mortal woman to be loved by Zeus, Niobe bore him Argus and, according to some writers, Pelasgus. [Apollodorus 2.1.1; Hyginus, *Fabulae*, 145.]

Niobe (2). A daughter of Tantalus, king of Lydia. Niobe married Amphion, co-king of Thebes, and bore him many children, of whom she was inordinately proud. Most writers say that the couple had either six or seven sons and a like number of daughters, but variations in these numbers are also recorded. Niobe boasted of having more and better children than Leto. This goddess called on her children, Apollo and Artemis, to avenge the insult. They did so by killing the rash woman's children, or all but two of them. Overwhelmed with grief, Niobe could not stop weeping. She went to her home in Lydia and was turned to stone on Mount Sipylus, where she went on weeping. [Homer, *Iliad*, 24.605–617; Ovid, *Metamorphoses*, 6.146–312; Hyginus, *Fabulae*, 9, 11; Pausanias 1.21.3.]

Nisus. A king of Megara. Nisus was a son of Ares, or of Deïon, or, according to most accounts, of Pandion, the exiled king of Athens who became king of Megara. Nisus succeeded to the rule of Megara and, with his brothers Pallas and Lycus, aided his half-brother, Aegeus, to regain the kingship of Athens, lost by their father. Nisus' rule of Megara was disputed by Sceiron, son of Pandion's predecessor on the Megarian throne. Aeacus, called in to arbitrate, decided in favor of Nisus, but gave the ministry of war to Sceiron. Nisus had three daughters: Eurynome, who married Glaucus, king of Corinth, and bore a son, Bellerophon, by Poseidon; Iphinoë, who married Megareus; and Scylla, who betrayed her father for love during a war with Crete.

Minos, the powerful Cretan king, attacked Megara, either because Nisus had granted haven to Polyeidus, a seer who was fleeing Minos, or because Minos wanted to conquer Athens, ruled by Nisus' brother and ally. Nisus might have been able to defend the city if Scylla had not fallen in love with Minos, or been bribed by him with a gold necklace made in Crete. Knowing that her father's life depended on his keeping his red hair, or a single purple lock in the middle of his head, Scylla cut it off while the king slept. When she went to Minos, expecting gratitude, he drowned her in disgust, or she drowned herself when Minos rejected her. In either case, she was transformed into a *ciris*, Nisus into an osprey, or sea eagle. (It is not known what kind of bird the *ciris* was, but it is agreed that the osprey was its natural enemy.) According to the Megarians, who did not admit that their city was conquered by the Cretans, Nisus was succeeded by his son-in-law Megareus. On the other hand, Megareus' fellow Boeotians say that he died in the war with Minos and that the city, formerly called Nisa, for Nisus, was renamed Megara. The city's port kept the name Nisaea. [Aeschylus, *The Libation Bearers*, 612–622; Vergil, *Ciris*, and *Georgics*, 1.404–414; Ovid, *Metamorphoses*, 8.1–151; Apollodorus 3.15.5–8; Pausanias 1.19.4, 1.39.4–6; *Catalogues of Women* 7.]

Nostoi. See EPIC CYCLE.

Notus. The south wind. Although Notus is said to have been a son of Eos and Astraeüs, and a brother of Boreas and Zephyrus, the south wind was seldom personified as the north and west winds often were.

Numa Pompilius. The second king of Rome. Numa, a son of Pompon and son-in-law of Titus Tatius, Romulus' co-king, won a reputation for great piety and wisdom as king of the Sabine city of Cures. After the mysterious death of Romulus and a brief interregnum, the Romans invited Numa to rule Rome. He reluctantly agreed. During the forty-three years of his reign, he brought peace, law, order, and strict religious observances to a city that had thitherto been hardly more than a vast armed camp. Although many writers later attributed Numa's wisdom to the teachings of Pythagoras—a sage who, in fact, lived some generations later than Numa—he himself gave the credit to the nymph Egeria. After Numa's wife Tatia died, Egeria often appeared to him in wooded places and gave him the benefit of both her wisdom and her embraces. Many Roman laws and religious rites were said in historical times to have been instituted by Numa.

One of the quainter tales about Numa concerns his attempt to find a charm to ward off the dangers of thunder and lightning. Numa caught the satyrlike demigods Picus and Faunus by mixing honey and wine in the spring where they drank, then tied them fast, ignoring their changes of shape. They either gave Numa the charm themselves or invoked the storm-god Jupiter in person. In the latter version of the story, Jupiter angrily told Numa that the charm would require a head. "Of garlic?" Numa asked innocently. "Human," the god replied. "Hair?" Numa quickly added. "No," Jupiter thundered, "of living . . ." "Sprats," Numa interrupted. Jupiter was so amused at the king's shrewd maneuvers to save his subjects' lives that he consented to give them a charm that did not require human sacrifice. It was used for centuries thereafter. [Plutarch, *Parallel Lives*, "Numa"; Livy 1.18.1–1.21.5.]

Numitor. A king of Alba Longa. Deposed by his brother, Amulius, Numitor was restored to power by ROMULUS AND REMUS [A], the twin sons of his daughter, Rea Silvia.

Nycteus. A king of Thebes. Nycteus and Lycus were sons of Chthonius, one of the Sparti, or of Hyrieus by the nymph Clonia, or of Poseidon by the Pleiad Celaeno. Although Chthonius was a Theban ally of Cadmus, his sons, for some unrecorded reason, grew up in Euboea. Because they killed Phlegyas, king of Orchomenus, they had to flee from Euboea. They settled first in Hyria, but later went to Thebes, where, through their friendship with King Pentheus, they were granted citizenship. Polydorus, Pentheus' successor and son of Cadmus, married Nycteus' daughter Nycteïs, who bore him Labdacus. Dying while the child was still young, the king made Nycteus regent, to rule during Labdacus' childhood.

Nycteus, however, was having trouble with Antiope, his daughter by Polyxo. This girl's beauty had attracted the roving eye of Zeus and he had lain with her in the guise of a satyr. When Antiope became noticeably pregnant, she fled Thebes and took refuge in Sicyon, where she married King Epopeus. Nycteus killed himself from shame, after making his brother regent in his place and enjoining him to punish both Epopeus and Antiope. According to another version of the story, Epopeus had seduced Antiope and carried her off from her father's palace. Nycteus marched against Sicyon, but was wounded and came back to Thebes to die. [Apollodorus 3.5.5, 3.10.1; Pausanias 2.6.1–3; Hyginus, *Fabulae*, 157.]

Nyctimene. A daughter of Epopeus, king of Lesbos. When her father raped her, Nyctimene hid in the woods for shame. Athena pitied her and made her an owl, which does not appear in the daylight. [Ovid, *Metamorphoses*, 2.589–595; Hyginus, *Fabulae*, 204.]

Nyctimus. A king of Arcadia. Either the eldest or the youngest son of Lycaon, Nyctimus was saved from the fate of his forty-nine brothers, who were destroyed by Zeus, by the intervention of Ge. Presumably, however, he was killed in the flood subsequently sent by Zeus. [Apollodorus 3.8.1–2.]

nymph. One of a class of minor female divinities. A nymph was a *daimon* residing in a particular place, object, or natural phenomenon. The oreads were mountain-nymphs; naïads were nymphs of springs, lakes, and brooks; Nereïds were sea-nymphs. Dryads, hamadryads, and meliae were tree-spirits, the first two belonging originally to oak trees (though "dryad" came to signify any tree-nymph), the last to ash trees. The Oceanids, too, were nymphs, of whom relatively few had any apparent connection with the sea. Several Oceanids and Nereïds, notably Thetis and Dione, may have been ancient goddesses who had been reduced to a lesser rank. Most nymphs were confined to their own mountains, springs, groves, or even individual trees. Tales set in particular places, such as that of the aggressive love of a water-nymph for Hylas, reflect the most typical view of the localized nature of these beings. The youth, beauty, and amorous qualities ascribed to most nymphs made their love affairs favorite subjects for poets, and in their works the term "nymph" is often hardly distinguishable from "young woman"—which is, in fact, what it means.

Nysa. The mountain on which Dionysus was reared by nymphs. Nysa was variously located, from Ethiopia or Libya to India or Thrace. It may never have been anything but a mythical place, perhaps intended to explain the god's obscure name.

Nyx. Night, and the goddess of night. Nyx, whom the Romans called Nox, is a scarcely personified abstraction. She was born, together with Erebus (Darkness), Ge (Earth), Tartarus, and Eros (Love), out of Chaos. By Erebus she bore Aether (Upper Air) and Hemera (Day). Alone she spawned a large and generally unpleasant brood that included Moros (Doom), Thanatos (Death), Hypnos (Sleep), the Fates, and Nemesis. She lived in Tartarus, from which she issued each day just as Hemera was returning. Her only other recorded act was to save her son Hypnos when Zeus was about to throw him out of heaven. [Hesiod, *Theogony*, 123–125, 211–225, 744–766; Homer, *Iliad*, 14.256–261.]

O

Obriareüs. See BRIAREÜS.

Oceanids or **Oceanides.** Daughters of Oceanus and Tethys. The sons of Oceanus, the river that surrounds the earth, were, appropriately enough, river-gods. His three thousand daughters, however, seem not to have been confined to any one function. Some, notably Amphitrite and Doris, lived in the sea, like their mother. Styx, the eldest, was that rare thing a female river-deity. Metis, whose name means wisdom or craft, is said to have changed her shape, as did many sea-deities. To Hesiod, however, she was an allegorical abstraction who married Zeus, gave birth to Athena, a goddess of wisdom and craft, and was swallowed by her husband, who thus incorporated the qualities that she personified. Calypso was an island nymph, Europa and Asia gave their names to areas of land, Urania presumably had heavenly connections. The Oceanids, together with their brothers and Apollo, were guardians of youths.

The Oceanids and their Titan father appear prominently in Aeschylus' *Prometheus Bound.* Prometheus, too, had a Titan father (Iapetus) and his mother was an Oceanid, Clymene or Asia. They and he both belonged to an older order of deities that was displaced with the rise of Zeus and his fellow Olympians. The Oceanids are identified and some are named by Hesiod [*Theogony* 346–366] and Apollodorus [1.2.2].

Oceanus or **Ocean.** The river Oceanus and its god. Oceanus, the river, was believed to issue from the Underworld and flow in a circular stream about the earth, which was conceived of as flat. Helius (Sun) and Eos (Dawn) lived near its banks in the east and daily disappeared into the river in the west, Helius riding its current home each night in a golden cup. The garden of the Hesperides (Daughters of Evening) was located near it in the west, as was Hades, when it was not thought of as underground. ODYSSEUS [G] entered Hades by crossing Oceanus.

The god of this river was a Titan, a son of Ge (Earth) and Uranus (Sky). He married his sister Titan Tethys and became by her the father of all the river-gods and of the three thousand OCEANIDS. Some call him also the father of Triptolemus. Oceanus apparently did not join his brother Titans in opposing the usurper Zeus, whose power he feared. He took no part in the Olympian assemblies, but, as the source of all seas, rivers, wells, and even cooling winds, he was revered by the gods. Homer called him, without explanation, the progenitor of all the gods. Oceanus and Tethys reared Hera, taking her from her mother, their sister Titan Rhea, for safekeeping in the tense times after the overthrow of the Titans.

Oceanus appears, as do his daughters, in Aeschylus' *Prometheus Bound*, in which he sympathizes with the hero (a son of his brother Iapetus and one of his daughters, Asia or Clymene), but counsels prudence. He also appears in Homer [*Iliad*, 14.200–210, 20.7, 21.193–199, and *Odyssey*, 4.567–568], Hesiod [*Theogony* 133, 337–370, 787–791], Apollodorus [1.5.2], Ovid [*Metamorphoses* 13.949–955], and Pausanias [1.33.3–5, 9.10.5–6]. References to the river Oceanus are innumerable.

Ocnus. One of the damned in Hades. Ocnus' punishment offered comic relief among the torments of the condemned souls. He continually plaited a rope of straw, which was eaten by his she-ass as quickly as he could finish it. Pausanias [10.29.1–2] quoted a solemn explanation of Ocnus' fate that he had heard on his travels: Ocnus had been a hard-working man whose extravagant wife had immediately spent the money that he earned. Why Ocnus should have been punished in death as well as in life was not part of the explanation.

Odius. A Greek herald at the Trojan War. Odius and Eurybates, another herald, accompanied the embassy sent by Agamemnon to appease Achilles. [Homer, *Iliad*, 9.160.]

Odysseus, Ulysses, or **Ulixes.** A king of Ithaca.

A. Odysseus was the only son of Laërtes, king of Ithaca, and his wife, Anticleia, daughter of Autolycus. It was rumored, however, at least among Odysseus' many enemies, that Anticleia had been seduced by Sisyphus and that Odysseus inherited his devious traits from that rogue, as well as from his grandfather, a famous thief. When the boy was newly born, Autolycus visited him in Ithaca and was asked by the nurse, Eurycleia, to name the child. The old man, who was evidently in a wry mood, chose the name Odysseus, saying that it was in honor of the odium that so many men had borne him during his long, rascally life. Then Autolycus went home to Parnassus, promising gifts if the boy were sent to visit him when he reached manhood. Odysseus kept the appointment and received the presents. He also received a deep gash in his thigh from a boar's tusk while hunting with Autolycus' sons and bore the scar all his life.

When Odysseus was still a youth, Messenian raiders stole three hundred sheep from Ithaca, and their shepherds with them. Laërtes and the Ithacan elders sent Odysseus to Messene to demand their return. It is not known how this mission turned out, although the Arcadians say that Odysseus found some lost mares in the town of Pheneüs. While staying at the house of Ortilochus, Odysseus met Iphitus, the eldest son of Eurytus, the late king of Oechalia. Iphitus had come in search of some stolen mares. The two young men became friends and Iphitus gave Odysseus the great bow that had belonged to Eurytus, a famous archer. Odysseus valued this bow so highly that he would never use it in the field, but kept it safe at home. He journeyed to Ephyra, in Thesprotia, to get arrow poison from Ilus, Medea's grandson, who was expert in poisons. Ilus would not provide it, believing for some reason that the gods would disapprove. Odysseus managed to get poison anyway from Anchialus, king of the nearby island of Taphos.

Like most young princes of his day, Odysseus was a suitor of Helen, daughter of Tyndareüs, king of Sparta. Knowing the young lady's character, he was sure that she would choose the wealthy Menelaüs, so he wasted no gifts on her. Instead, he made a bargain with Tyndareüs. The Spartan king was concerned that violence would break out once one of the suitors was chosen. Odysseus promised to solve this problem if Tyndareüs would influence his brother Icarius to give his daughter Penelope to Odysseus. Tyndareüs agreed to this bargain. Odysseus then advised him to demand that the suitors all take a vow to defend Helen's chosen husband against any harm that might come to him as a result of the marriage. When the suitors, including Odysseus himself, had taken the vow, Tyndareüs fulfilled his part of the bargain with Odysseus by recommending him highly to Icarius as a son-in-law. According to some writers, however, Icarius held a footrace, with Penelope as the prize, and Odysseus won it.

Icarius agreed to the match, but tried to persuade Odysseus to remain in Lacedaemonia. Failing in that, he urged his daughter to stay with him, even after her marriage. It is said that, even while Odysseus was driving away in his chariot with his bride, Icarius followed, begging her not to go. Odysseus grew impatient and demanded that Penelope decide once and for all. At this she covered her face with her veil, signifying that she would go with her husband. Icarius had to content himself with building a shrine to Modesty on the spot where this incident occurred. [Hyginus, *Fabulae*, 201; Homer, *Odyssey*, 1.255–264, 19.392–466, 21.9–41; Apollodorus 3.10.8–9; Pausanias 3.12.1, 3.20.10–11.]

B. Odysseus' shrewd advice solved Tyndareüs' dilemma, but it soon created one for Odysseus. Not very long after Menelaüs married Helen, she was abducted by the Trojan prince Paris. Menelaüs turned for help to his powerful brother, Agamemnon, king of Mycenae. Agamemnon, in turn, sent ambassadors, including Menelaüs and the clever Palamedes, son of Nauplius, to remind all Helen's former suitors that they had vowed to defend her chosen husband against any threat to their marriage. Odysseus had got wind of this plan. When the visitors arrived they found him in the fields. Wearing the headgear of a madman, he was sowing salt with a horse and an ox yoked to his plow. Palamedes suspected that Odysseus was pretending to be mad in order to evade his duty to help Menelaüs. As a test, he snatched up Odysseus' infant son, Telemachus, and laid him in front of the plow, at the same time challenging the father to give up his pretense. Odysseus at once turned aside his team, thereby betraying his sanity. (Some writers say that Palamedes threatened the child with his sword, but the result was the same.) Although Odysseus went reluctantly to war, Agamemnon later acknowledged that he had proved the most loyal of all the commander-in-chief's associates. Nevertheless, Odysseus never forgave the man who had forced him to leave Ithaca.

No doubt because Odysseus was himself so adept at tricks and ruses, he easily saw through the pretenses of others. When the Greek leaders had decided to declare war on Troy, they were eager to enlist the services of ACHILLES [A], the son of the famous Peleus, king of Phthia. Achilles, however, was hardly more than a boy, and his mother, the goddess Thetis, dared not let him go to Troy, for she knew that he was fated to die there. Achilles was therefore sent to the Aegean island of Scyrus, where King Lycomedes dressed him as a girl and hid him among his daughters. Odysseus had a martial trumpet blown at Lycomedes' palace and noted the difference in Achilles' reaction from that of the girls. Achilles then readily agreed to go to Troy.

Odysseus himself led twelve shiploads of men from Ithaca and from the surrounding islands, including Cephallenia and Zacynthus. When the navy was becalmed at Aulis, the high priest Calchas declared that Agamemnon's daughter Iphigeneia must be sacrificed to appease the anger of Artemis, Agamemnon having rashly boasted that he could hunt as well as the goddess. Odysseus and Diomedes, son of Tydeus, went to Mycenae to induce the girl's mother, Clytemnestra, to send her to Aulis. Odysseus accomplished this by pretending that she was to become the bride of Achilles. After the sacrifice the fleet sailed. Philoctetes, leader of the Malian forces, was bitten by a snake during a visit to the island of Chryse. His anguish and the stench of his wound were so disturbing to the other Greeks that, at Odysseus' urging, they marooned him on the island of Lemnos.

At length the Greeks arrived at Troy. One of their first moves was to send Odysseus and Menelaüs to demand from Priam the return of Helen. The Trojans refused. In fact, they might have killed the ambassadors if Antenor had not interceded for them. This kindness they did not forget, even in the orgy of killing that followed the ultimate fall of Troy. Odysseus' loyalties did not, however, encompass those who had injured him, even among his allies. He avenged himself on PALAMEDES by a diabolical trick that led to his enemy's stoning by the Greek army. According to another story, Odysseus and Diomedes drowned Palamedes as he was fishing. [Apollodorus, "Epitome" 3.6–8, 3.22, 3.27–28; Cypria 1, 19; Hyginus, Fabulae, 95, 96, 98, 105.]

C. During the war, Odysseus, though a brave man who was not afraid to engage in dangerous undertakings, distinguished himself particularly by his shrewdness and craft and by his eloquence. As described by Homer [Iliad 3.191–224], he was short, but unusually broad of shoulder and chest. When he first grasped the speaker's staff at assemblies, he seemed stiff and stupid, but, as soon as his deep voice began to speak, this impression was dispelled and his eloquence often conquered his listeners. Only once, in fact, did this eloquence fail in its purpose: Odysseus, Ajax, and Phoenix went as an embassy from the Greeks to persuade Achilles to return to the fighting, but the aggrieved warrior refused.

Even the most dangerous of Odysseus' adventures usually called in some way upon his craft or his facility at disguise. With Diomedes, his frequent companion in these exploits, he slipped out of the Greek camp one night to spy on the Trojans. During their brief foray, the two captured the Trojan spy Dolon and learned from him the positions of the Trojan allies before killing him. They then killed the Thracian king Rhesus, together with twelve of his men, and drove Rhesus' valuable horses back to camp.

Odysseus and Ajax of Salamis saved the body of Achilles from the Trojans, Ajax carrying it while Odysseus fought off the enemy. Later the two disputed which should have Achilles' arms, each claiming greater services to the Greek cause. Odysseus' superior persuasiveness won over the Greek judges, though, according to the *Little Iliad,* it was the opinion of Trojan girls overheard discussing the two warriors that decided the outcome. Many writers claimed that Odysseus in some way unfairly influenced the vote of the other Greeks, but they did not explain how he managed this. Enraged and covered with shame, Ajax went mad and killed himself. Instead of bearing a grudge against his former adversary, Odysseus persuaded the angry Greeks to give Ajax a decent funeral.

Odysseus captured Helenus, a son of Priam who knew the oracles concerning the fall of Troy. The captive told the Greeks that before they could take Troy they must induce Achilles' son, Neoptolemus, to fight with them; bring to Troy the bow and arrows of Heracles, which they had left on Lemnos with their owner, Philoctetes; and steal from the Pergamum, the Trojan citadel, the Palladium, an ancient statue of Athena that had fallen from heaven. Odysseus played a major part in bringing about all these conditions. With Phoenix he sailed to the island of Scyrus for Neoptolemus, to whom he turned over his father's armor. He joined either Diomedes or Neoptolemus in a voyage to Lemnos to fetch Philoctetes. With Diomedes or Neoptolemus he stole into Troy at night to fetch the Palladium. Although he was effectively disguised as a beggar, he was recognized by Helen, but she aided him in the venture, perhaps sensing that she would soon be needing supporters in the Greek camp. For reasons less easy to explain, Hecuba, Priam's queen, also did not reveal Odysseus' plan, though she, too, recognized him. Odysseus and Diomedes, after killing several Trojans, escaped to the Greek camp with the Palladium.

Odysseus' most useful contribution to Troy's fall was, however, his invention of the plan involving the wooden horse, a hollow image which the deluded Trojans dragged into the city. Odysseus was commander of the Greek leaders hidden inside it. During the ensuing sack of the city, he did not forget his debt to Antenor, and, with Menelaüs, hung a panther skin on the door of the old man's house as a sign to the other Greeks that it was to be left unharmed. Not content with that, they saved two of Antenor's sons from death, Odysseus carrying one of them wounded from the field. [Apollodorus, "Epitome" 4.3–4, 5.4, 5.6, 5.8–14, 5.19, 5.21; Sophocles, *Ajax* and *Philoctetes*; Euripides, *Hecuba*, 239–250; Ovid, *Metamorphoses*, 13.1–404; *Little Iliad* 1–3, 9, 12; Hyginus, *Fabulae*, 107, 108; Pausanias 10.26.7–8; Pindar, *Nemean Odes*, 7.20–30, 8.23–27.]

D. Odysseus had little mercy on the other Trojans, or even on his fellow Greeks, if he felt that they jeopardized the welfare of the army as a whole. It was he who insisted on the murder of Hector's little son, Astyanax, believing that no male descendant of Priam should be allowed to survive. Some claim that Odysseus particularly urged the sacrifice of Priam's daughter Polyxena on Achilles' grave, though this decision is generally attributed to all the Greeks. When Ajax of Locris dragged Priam's daughter Cassandra from the image of Athena to rape her, Odysseus demanded that he be stoned in order to divert the goddess' anger from the Greeks as a whole. Ajax saved himself by clinging to the image that he had just desecrated. Odysseus' fears were later proved to be well grounded, for much of the Greek fleet was wrecked by the goddess off the Euboean promontory of Caphareus.

Although Odysseus did not incur Athena's enmity, he later earned Poseidon's implacable hatred and suffered severely for it. Few of the Greek leaders who reached home did so after surviving such strange and perilous adventures as those which befell the usually prudent Odysseus. From Troy his twelve ships sailed across the Hellespont to the Thracian Chersonese. There the Trojan queen, Hecuba, who had been awarded to Odysseus as a concubine, discovered that Polymestor, king of the Bistones, had treacherously murdered Polydorus, her only surviving son. After taking a terrible vengeance on this king, she was transformed into a hell-hound and plunged into the sea. Odysseus' ships were next driven to Ismarus, a city of the Ciconians, of Thrace. They sacked the city, sparing only a priest of Apollo—Maron, son of Euanthes—and his wife. In gratitude, Maron gave Odysseus many gifts, including a stock of fine wine. Odysseus' crew, ignoring their captain's warning, remained too long at Ismarus feasting on the spoils. The survivors had time to summon aid from neighboring tribes more warlike than the Ciconians. These attacked the Greeks and drove them off, after killing six men from each ship.

The ships were tossed about in a storm for several days, but reached Cape Malea, the southeastern tip of the Peloponnesus. They would have been safe if they had not been captured by a strong north wind that drove them before it for nine days without respite. At the end of this time they reached a strange land on the coast of Libya. Odysseus sent three men inland to reconnoiter while the others ate. The scouts did not return. Investigating, Odysseus discovered that they had come to the land of the Lotus-eaters, a peaceful, vegetarian tribe given to eating the fruit of the lotus, which robbed them of the ambition to do anything more demanding. The scouts, having themselves tasted the fruit offered them by the friendly natives, had forgotten all about their fellow crewmen and were content to remain the rest of their days living an easy life and nibbling lotus. Their captain was forced to drag them back to the ship and clamp them in irons. He then ordered the others to push off at once. [Homer, *Odyssey*, 9.39–104; Euripides, *Hecuba* and *Trojan Women*; Apollodorus, "Epitome" 7.1–3; *Sack of Ilium* 1; *Returns* 1.]

E. After several days at sea, Odysseus' ships came to the island of the CY-CLOPES, which many Classical writers identified as Sicily. These one-eyed giants were a barbarous lot, who did not cultivate the earth or practice crafts or govern their affairs in an orderly fashion. In spite of these deficiencies, they were enabled by the fertility of their land to live rather confortable lives. The sailors beached their ships at night in a quiet harbor on a small offshore island and spent several days there. On the third day Odysseus went in his flagship to explore the larger island opposite. Leaving all but twelve men on the beach, he climbed to a large cave near the sea. There was no one in it, but it contained a plentiful store of food and of lambs and kids. The sailors wanted to make off quickly with the supplies, but Odysseus, curious to know what kind of creature lived in the cave, insisted that they wait.

At dusk the gigantic owner returned, driving his flocks into the cave for the night. He pulled into place a huge stone that covered the cave's mouth. The Greeks hid, in terror of the monster, but he caught sight of them after a while. Odysseus then told the Cyclops, whose name was Polyphemus, that they were shipwrecked sailors and reminded him of the laws of hospitality ordained by the gods. Polyphemus replied that the Cyclopes recognized neither the gods nor their laws and proved it by eating two of Odysseus' men. He then went to sleep. Even if his prisoners had been able to kill him, they would not have dared to do so, for only Polyphemus was strong enough to roll away the stone door. The next morning the monster breakfasted on two more Greeks and went off with his flocks, stopping the cave's mouth once again with the stone. During the day, Odysseus devised a plan and his men waited anxiously for the giant's return.

At dusk Polyphemus came with his flocks, closed the door as before, and once again made a meal of two of Odysseus' men. Odysseus offered him a bowl of Maron's wine, which he had brought with him to the island. Polyphemus, who had never before tasted such excellent wine, was delighted and promised Odysseus a present if he would give him more. Odysseus plied him with the drink, then introduced himself as Nobody (Outis) and asked for the promised gift. "My gift," the monster replied, "will be to eat Nobody last." With that he fell into a drunken stupor and vomited up his grisly supper. Immediately Odysseus and his companions carried out his plan. Heating the point of a huge stake in the fire, they drove it into Polyphemus' single eye. The blinded giant roared for his fellow Cyclopes. They gathered about the closed door and asked who was hurting him. "Nobody is killing me," he cried.

"If nobody is harming you," his neighbors replied, "there is nothing that we can do." And they went away, after piously advising Polyphemus to pray.

Abandoned, the blind Cyclops removed the stone and sat down in the doorway, hoping to catch the Greeks as they tried to escape. Odysseus ingeniously tied together in groups of three the rams that were kept in the cave and hid one of his few remaining men under the middle ram of each group. He himself clung to the belly of the largest ram of the flock. When dawn came the giant felt the backs of the sheep before letting them leave the cave, but he did not think to feel beneath their bellies. Odysseus and his men reached safety, let go of the sheep, and drove them down to the waiting ship. As soon as the ship was a little way from shore, Odysseus began to shout taunts at the Cyclops.

Polyphemus, though blind, had lost none of his strength. By throwing huge rocks into the sea beyond the ship, he caused the waves to drive it back to the shore. The men had to row for their lives in order to escape a second time. But Odysseus made a rash and foolish mistake, ignoring the pleas of his men. Once again he taunted the blind giant, this time in his own name. When Polyphemus heard the name Odysseus he recalled the prophecy of a seer, Telemus, who had long ago foretold his blinding by a man with such a name. The monster prayed to Poseidon, his father by the sea-nymph Thoösa, to prevent Odysseus from ever reaching home, or at least to make his journey a long and lonely one and greet his return with yet more troubles in his own house. Poseidon heard the prayer of his blinded son and in that moment conceived an implacable hatred for Odysseus. [Homer, *Odyssey*, 1.68–79, 9.105–566; Euripides, *Cyclops;* Apollodorus, "Epitome" 7.3–9.]

F. From Polyphemus' island Odysseus' ships sailed to the island of Aeolia, which was ruled by King Aeolus, keeper of the winds, and which, according to most Classical writers, was one or another of the islands north of eastern Sicily that are called Aeolian to this day. There Odysseus was hospitably entertained by the friendly king, who lived a carefree existence. With his wife and their six sons and six daughters, who were married to one another, he spent most of his days in feasting. When Aeolus sent Odysseus on his way, he gave him all but one of the winds tied up in a newly made ox-hide bag. The gentle west wind was left free to waft Odysseus' ships on their homeward journey.

Thanks to Aeolus' kindliness, the ships sailed eastward for nine days and, on the tenth, came within sight of Ithaca. When he could at last see men tending their fires in his homeland, the weary captain allowed himself a peaceful sleep. His men, however, had been curious about the leather bag ever since leaving Aeolia. Suspecting that their leader had acquired some treasure that he did not intend to share with them, they opened the bag while he slept. The unfavorable winds rushed out and in a short time the ships were driven all the way back to Aeolia. Odysseus humbly asked the king's help once again, but Aeolus, realizing that the wanderer must be hated by some god or other, did not dare to help him. He drove Odysseus and all his men hastily from his island.

The next encounter of the disheartened company was even more disastrous. On the seventh day of voyaging they came to Telepylus, the city of the Laestrygonians. Most of the ships entered the quiet harbor walled in by high cliffs, but Odysseus cautiously anchored his own ship at the mouth and sent three scouts ashore. They soon encountered an enormous young woman drawing water at a spring. She introduced herself as the daughter of Antiphates, a descendant of Lamus and king of the Laestrygonians. The giantess led the visitors to her father's palace. Their admiration of her hospitable manners soon changed to horror, for Antiphates greeted them by eating one of them on the spot without ceremony. The other two escaped and managed to reach Odysseus' vessel. He quickly cut the cables and put out to sea, but the other ships, trapped in the harbor, were crushed with huge stones flung from the cliffs by the Laestrygonians. The giants speared the survivors as if they were fish and carried them home for a meal. Odysseus and the crew of his one remaining ship sailed sorrowfully on.

Before long they came to an island called Aeaea, which lies off the western coast of Italy. Many say that this island is now joined to the mainland south of Rome and is called Cape Circeo. Demoralized by their disastrous encounters with the Cyclops and the Laestrygonians, Odysseus' men did not dare to stray far from the ship for two days. At last Odysseus climbed a hill and saw, not far inland, a house in the midst of woods. He did not know that this was the home of the sorceress Circe, a daughter of the sun-god Helius and Perse, a daughter of Oceanus. Circe knew of all kinds of harmful drugs with magical properties. She was especially adept at changing men and women into beasts. Odysseus ignored the protests of his frightened companions and, dividing his crew into two groups, drew lots to see which would explore the island. Eurylochus, whom he had appointed leader of the second group, was chosen. Reluctantly he advanced into the woods with twenty-two men. Odysseus and the others waited anxiously by the ships for their return.

Not many hours passed before Eurylochus returned to the ship alone with a terrible tale to tell. He and his men had reached the house in the clearing and found it surrounded by lions and wolves. Instead of attacking the strangers, the beasts had fawned upon them. Inside the house a woman could be heard singing. When they called to her she had appeared and graciously invited them to enter. All but Eurylochus, who felt uneasy about the situation, had gone inside. (There, unseen by Eurylochus, the woman had given them wine, then touched each man with a wand. Instantly they were transformed into swine. The woman had penned them in a sty and flung them swill to eat.) Eurylochus, after waiting in vain for his comrades, had run back to the ship to report their disappearance.

Odysseus demanded that Eurylochus lead him at once to the sorceress' house, but the terrified man refused to take the path again. Odysseus went alone, for it was his duty as captain to do what he could to rescue his men. Before reaching Circe's house, he met a handsome young man, who was actually Hermes in disguise. The god warned Odysseus of Circe's tricks, telling him exactly what had happened to his men, and gave him a small plant with a white flower and a black root. He explained that the plant, which he called moly, would serve as an antidote to the sorceress' drugs. Hermes slipped away through the woods, leaving Odysseus to meet Circe alone. As the god had warned, the beautiful witch greeted him with a drugged drink. Odysseus swallowed it without hesitation, knowing that the moly would protect him from its effects. Circe touched him with her wand, but Odysseus, instead of turning into a hog, drew his sword and, as Hermes had advised him, threatened to kill her unless she swore to do him no harm. Terrified, Circe swore by the gods, an oath that even she dared not break, though she was herself a goddess of sorts.

Having failed to harm her visitor, Circe now became his mistress and his benefactress. After taking Odysseus to her bed, she readily granted his wish to see his lost companions again. She threw a drug into the pigsty that transformed them back into men, taller and handsomer than they had been before. Odysseus brought Eurylochus and the rest of the crew from the ship and Circe and her attendant nymphs made them comfortable.

They were so comfortable, in fact, that they and their captain remained there for an entire year. At the end of that time they grew restless and urged Odysseus to remember Ithaca. He reminded Circe that she had promised to send him on his way when he was ready to leave. The goddess agreed without hesitation, but told her lover that he must first visit the ghost of the Theban seer Teiresias in Hades, for only he could properly advise the wanderer how to reach his home once more. Circe gave Odysseus careful directions for the journey to the Underworld and he told his companions the frightening news of their destination. As they were preparing to leave Circe's house the youngest member of the crew, Elpenor, fell from a roof in a drunken stupor and broke his neck. Odysseus and his men were too preoccupied with the coming voyage to give their companion proper burial rites. Tearfully they set forth in their ship and Circe, by her sorcery, sent them a fair breeze to waft them on their way to the Underworld. [Homer, *Odyssey*, 10; Hyginus, *Fabulae*, 125; Apollodorus, "Epitome" 7.10–17.]

G. Odysseus' ship sailed all day, unguided, and came by night to the stream of Oceanus, which flows around the earth. There, in the land of the Cimmerians, where the sun never shines, the men disembarked. They followed Circe's instructions to the letter. At the spot where the river Acheron was joined by the Periphlegethon and the Cocytus, a branch of the Styx, they dug a pit beside a rock. Odysseus poured libations to the dead of milk and honey, of wine, and of water, then sprinkled barley meal over all. After promising the dead more sacrifices on his return to Ithaca, he sacrificed a young ram and a black ewe that Circe had given him, burning them in honor of Hades and his wife Persephone, rulers of the Underworld. As the blood of the animals poured into the trench, ghosts came swarming up, but Odysseus sat with drawn sword by the pit to prevent any from drinking till the shade of Teiresias should have his fill.

The first ghost to appear was that of Elpenor. He begged Odysseus not to leave his corpse unburied and unmourned in Aeaea. Odysseus promised to do as his former crewman asked, but would not let him drink the blood. Even when the shade of his old mother, Anticleia, appeared, he kept her from the trench, though he wept for her death, which had occurred during his long absence from Ithaca. At last the ghost of Teiresias came up, bearing a golden staff. Odysseus let him drink from the pit, then asked how he might return safely to his home. Teiresias, whose ghost was the only one in Hades to have retained its capacity for thought, then foretold what was to happen and what Odysseus must do. He warned that Poseidon would not soon forget his hatred of Odysseus for blinding his son Polyphemus, and that at best the wanderer could not expect an easy voyage home. Nevertheless, he might still reach Ithaca with his men if he would remember one thing: when they came to the island of Thrinacia, neither he nor his men must touch the herds or flocks of Helius, whose daughters pastured them there. If they were harmed, then Odysseus, if he reached home at all, would do so alone, in a foreign ship. In any case, he would find his home overrun with suitors of his wife, Penelope, and would have to dispose of them as best he could.

Teiresias then went on to speak of further adventures. Odysseus, even after making himself master once again in Ithaca, would not be able to settle down in peace. He must wander again, carrying an oar on his shoulder, until he came to a land where the people ate no salt. There, because they knew nothing of the sea, one of the natives would mistake Odysseus' oar for a winnowing fan. This would be a sign that the wanderer could at last go home. He would enjoy an easy and prosperous old age, and a gentle death would come to him out of the sea. After giving these prophecies, the ghost of Teiresias retired into the house of Hades.

When the seer had gone, Odysseus let his mother drink some of the blood, then questioned her about events in Ithaca. Anticleia assured him that Penelope still hoped for his return. Anticleia herself had died of grief, while old Laërtes, Odysseus' father, had retired from the court to live like a poor peasant. After this conversation with his mother, Odysseus saw the shades of many famous men and women, who came to the pit for their share of the blood. Among them were many of his former comrades at Troy. Agamemnon told him of his murder, at his wife's instigation, on his return to Mycenae, and advised Odysseus to approach Ithaca secretly in order to test out how things were at his court. Odysseus was able to cheer the sad ghost of Achilles with news of the exploits of his son, Neoptolemus. He could not, however, persuade Ajax to speak a word to him, for the Salaminian hero still harbored a grudge against Odysseus for winning Achilles' armor.

After this, Odysseus saw Minos, judge of the dead; the great hunter Orion; and the tortures of Tityus, Tantalus, and Sisyphus. Finally he spoke briefly with Heracles, but before he could meet any of the other great heroes, such hordes of the dead swarmed up to the trench that Odysseus retreated in sudden panic. He made his way back to the ship and sailed away with his men without further incident. [Homer, *Odyssey*, 11; Hyginus, *Fabulae*, 125.]

H. The route back from the land of the dead led past Aeaea. True to his word, Odysseus stopped to cremate Elpenor's corpse and bury the ashes. As the ghost had requested, his former comrades erected his oar as a marker in the barrow that they heaped over the grave. Circe had doubtless expected to see Odysseus again, for she had much advice left to give him about the homeward journey. She told him how to get his crew safely past the Sirens, without depriving himself of the pleasure of their seductive music. She warned him of the Wandering Rocks and of the dangers to be met in the narrow strait between Scylla and Charybdis. Finally, Circe repeated Teiresias' dire warning of the disaster that would ensue if any of Odysseus' men were to harm the herds of Helius. (Circe had reason to know personally two of the terrors of which she told, for Helius was her father and, some say, she herself had transformed Scylla, daughter of Crataeïs, from an innocent girl into a six-headed monster.) At dawn the sorceress sent Odysseus on his way once again with a favorable wind.

Before long the ship approached the Sirens' island. Following Circe's advice, Odysseus filled his crewmen's ears with melted wax and they tied him firmly to the mast. Thus he could hear the song of the two Sirens, promising to reveal to him the future if he would only stop awhile with them. Intoxicated by their lovely singing, Odysseus forgot that the bones of countless mariners lay bleaching on the island, where they had been lured by this very song. He angrily demanded that his men release him, but they, warned in advance by Odysseus himself, only tightened the ropes that bound him. Once the ship was out of range of the Sirens' song, the spell was broken. The sailors removed the wax from their ears and untied their captain.

The ship was hardly out of earshot of the Sirens when Odysseus and his crew heard the roar of the waters of the terrible whirlpool Charybdis on the western side of the northern entrance to the Strait of Messina, which separates Italy from Sicily. Odysseus had chosen this perilous route in preference to the even greater dangers of the alternative course, which led among the Wandering Rocks. He explained to his men that they must row close under the beetling cliff opposite the whirlpool. He said nothing of the terrible monster Scylla that Circe had warned him of. This creature, which bore six heads at the ends of long necks, lived in a cave high on the side of the cliff. Circe had warned

Odysseus not to attempt to fight the monster, which, in spite of all his precautions, was sure to snatch one of his men with each head. He ignored this advice and stood on the foredeck fully armed, but his determination to resist Scylla's depredations was useless. When the threat of Charybdis made him turn his eyes from scanning Scylla's cliff, the misshapen horror reached down from her cave and tore six men from their benches. Odysseus turned back only in time to see them dangling from her jaws in mid-air and screaming his name in terror. [Homer, *Odyssey*, 12.1–259; Apollonius Rhodius 4.788–832, 4.922–963; Ovid, *Metamorphoses*, 13.730–741, 13.898–14.74.]

I. Not far beyond Scylla's cliff was Thrinacia, the island where Helius (who is sometimes called Helius Hyperion) pastured his immortal cattle and sheep under the care of Phaëthusa and Lampetië, his daughters by Neaera. The sun-god owned seven herds and seven flocks, each numbering fifty head. Both Teiresias and Circe had solemnly warned Odysseus of the disasters that would ensue if he or his men harmed a single one of Helius' animals, so he told his men to row straight past the island. For the first time he met with something close to mutiny. Eurylochus reminded him that the men had rowed a perilous course almost without rest ever since leaving Aeaea. He warned that, in any case, it would be dangerous to continue sailing at night through these unknown waters. The men agreed so vociferously that Odysseus was forced to agree to their landing, but he insisted that they touch no food on the island except the plentiful provisions that Circe had given them. He felt a strong presentiment, however, that the gods had trouble in store for him.

Odysseus' fears were quickly realized. For an entire month a south wind, which would have driven them back on Scylla and Charybdis, blew without ceasing. As long as the food stores lasted, the sailors kept their promise well enough, but in time they were forced to hunt for fish and game. Odysseus went inland to pray to all the gods on Olympus in the hope that one of them would come to his aid. Worn with the strain of the voyage he fell asleep. The rebellious Eurylochus took this opportunity to urge the men to kill some of the cattle that pastured near by. They were only too ready to follow his advice. When Odysseus returned to the camp and discovered what had been done, he knew that some calamity would soon follow. He did not have long to wait. The herd-girl Lampetië quickly reported the theft to her father. Helius hurried to Olympus and demanded that the other gods punish the culprits, even threatening to shine among the dead in Hades if they refused. For six days Odysseus' men feasted on the stolen meat, but on the seventh the wind died down and they set sail once again. No sooner were they out of sight of land than Zeus sent a violent storm that tore the ship apart and flung the last of Odysseus' fellow sailors to their deaths in the sea.

Only Odysseus himself survived. By lashing the broken keel and mast together in a kind of raft, he managed to stay afloat. Through the night a south wind drove him northward and, just at dawn, brought him to the edge of the swirling waters of Charybdis. As the raft upended, Odysseus was flung into the air and managed to cling like a bat to a branch of a great fig tree that overhung the whirlpool. He hung there until, late in the day, Charybdis spewed up the mast and keel. Odysseus dropped into the water beside them, pulled himself astride them, and rowed away as fast as he could with only his hands for oars. When he was far enough from the whirlpool he rested. The makeshift raft drifted aimlessly for nine days, at the end of which it washed ashore on a strange island. [Homer, *Odyssey*, 12.127–141, 12.260–448.]

J. This island was Ogygia. It was ruled by the goddess Calypso, who lived there alone with her attendant nymphs much as did Circe on her island of Aeaea. Unlike Circe, Calypso had no evil designs on Odysseus beyond persuading him to stay with her forever in the cave that was her home. She offered to make him immortal and ageless if he would consent, but Odysseus, in spite of the delights of Calypso's lovely island and of her bed, dreamed of rocky Ithaca and his mortal wife, Penelope. He spent his days sitting by the shore and staring longingly out to sea. He might, indeed, have died there had not Athena, who had long admired Odysseus' courage and quick wit, taken up his cause on Olympus. Waiting for a time when his implacable enemy, Poseidon, was far away in Ethiopia, she reminded Zeus that Odysseus had suffered unduly long, in spite of the many sacrifices that he had made to Zeus on the plains of Troy. Zeus agreed that it was high time that the gods give the weary wanderer a helping hand. Athena went down to Ithaca to aid Odysseus' son, Telemachus, in dealing with the problems that had arisen at home, while Zeus sent Hermes to command Calypso to let Odysseus leave Ogygia.

Calypso reluctantly consented when she heard this order, and she told Odysseus of her intentions. Always wary, he made her swear that she was not plotting to harm him. He built a boat with the tools that she lent him and Calypso stocked it with provisions. After a last night with her, Odysseus set out once more on the high seas, borne along by a breeze that Calypso caused to spring up. Some say that he left behind on the island two sons, Nausinoüs and Nausithoüs. Hyginus [*Fabulae* 127] listed Latinus, too, as Odysseus' son by Calypso, but this seems to be an error.

Odysseus sailed for seventeen days until he came in sight of the mountainous Phaeacian island of Scherië. Then Poseidon, who had returned to Olympus, discovered his enemy's good fortune and immediately shattered his little boat with a storm. Odysseus might have died if the sea goddess Leucothea (who had once herself been the mortal Ino) had not come to his aid. She directed him to strip off his heavy clothes, abandon the remains of his boat, and trust to his own strength as a swimmer. She gave him her veil to preserve him from harm and disappeared into the sea.

Odysseus, fearing that the apparition might have been sent by some malevolent god, determined to cling as long as he could to the wreckage of his boat. Poseidon quickly showed him his folly by threatening him with a great wave. Stretching the veil under his chest as a life-preserver, Odysseus plunged into the sea. It buoyed him up, as Leucothea had promised, but he was almost wholly at the mercy of winds and waves. Poseidon scornfully left him to his fate, but Athena sent a north wind to drive him once more toward Scherië. After two days Odysseus saw the coastline close at hand. At first he was nearly dashed to pieces against the rocky shore, but at last he managed to find a haven at a river's mouth and dragged himself ashore. After flinging the veil back into the water, as Leucothea had directed, he crawled into a thicket and fell asleep on a bed of leaves. [Homer, *Odyssey*, 1.11–95, 1.48–50, 1.84–87, 5.28–493, 7.244–269.]

K. Athena, after busying herself on Odysseus' behalf in Ithaca, had come to Scherië to help him get ashore safely. Now she arranged that Nausicaä, daughter of Alcinoüs, king of the Phaeacians, should decide to do the family washing. This was evidently not an everyday event, since the goddess felt it necessary to persuade the girl by suggesting, in a dream, that a clean wardrobe was a prerequisite to marriage. A wagon was needed to carry all the dirty linen to the river's mouth some distance from the city. Nausicaä and her servant girls made a picnic of the occasion and played ball while the clothes were drying. Odysseus was wakened by their cries and crawled out of his thicket to beg for Nausicaä's help. His plight and his flattery won her sympathy at once. After giving him clothing and food, she led him to the city and instructed him to approach her mother as a suppliant. This approach worked well, and Alcinoüs and his nobles quickly agreed to convey Odysseus home to Ithaca the next day. Alcinoüs added, however, that he would be more than content to have the stranger remain among the Phaeacians as his son-in-law.

The next day Odysseus' sailing was postponed in favor of games and other entertainment, such as the singing of the blind bard Demodocus. During the evening feast Odysseus at last revealed his identity and recounted his adventures, to the astonishment of the Phaeacians. After another day spent in preparations for the voyage, he set foot on board the Phaeacian ship. No sooner had the sailors pushed off from shore than Odysseus fell asleep. So rapid was the magic ship that, by the time that the morning star arose, it was entering the harbor of Ithaca. The kindly sailors deposited Odysseus, still sleeping, on the shore; piled the many treasures that the Phaeacians had given him near by; and set out for home. As they were in sight of their own harbor, Poseidon, cheated of his chance to persecute Odysseus further, punished the rescuers by turning the ship to stone. The Phaeacians, watching from the shore, reported the event to Alcinoüs, who recalled Nausithoüs' prophecy that Poseidon would one day pay back the Phaeacians for their many rescues of shipwrecked sailors. He would not only wreck one of their ships, but would throw up a mountain range about their city to cut it off from its harbors. Alcinoüs led his people in sacrifices to the sea-god in the hope of appeasing him. Whether the sacrifices served their purpose is not recorded. [Homer, *Odyssey*, 6.1–13, 6.187.]

L. On waking, Odysseus at first thought that the Phaeacians had abandoned him in some strange place, but Athena appeared to him and pointed out the familiar sights of his homeland. She told him that his household was overrun with rapacious lords from Ithaca and the nearby islands who were courting the faithful Penelope in the hope of gaining control of Odysseus' wealth in herds and flocks. The goddess warned that these suitors would surely kill the rightful king if he were suddenly to reappear alone. To protect Odysseus against this danger, she aged him in appearance and dressed him in rags. After telling him that she had sent Telemachus to seek word of his father from Nestor and Menelaüs, she left Odysseus to his own devices, which were never in short supply.

Odysseus now went to the hut of Eumaeüs, his chief swineherd, who was one of the few servants to remain completely loyal to his master's interests, even though he believed Odysseus dead. The old man entertained the supposed stranger courteously. Odysseus did not reveal himself, though he made a vain attempt to convince Eumaeüs that his master would soon return. He learned from the swineherd that his father, the former king, Laërtes, had retired entirely from the palace and lived alone in a rude hut, not only from hatred of the suitors, who had invaded the palace, but from grief at the loss of his son and his beloved wife, Anticleia.

While Odysseus was staying with Eumaeüs, Telemachus returned from his visit to Menelaüs and stopped, on Athena's advice, at Eumaeüs' hut. Odysseus seemed as much a stranger to him as he had to Eumaeüs. Telemachus promised to send him food and clothing, but did not invite him to the palace for fear that the suitors would mistreat him. The youth did not believe himself strong enough yet to defend a guest against grown men. When Telemachus sent Eumaeüs to tell Penelope of his return, Odysseus made himself known to his son. After a tearful reunion they plotted how they would dispose of the suitors. Odysseus told Telemachus to return to the palace. He would follow in his beggar's disguise. At a signal from him, Telemachus was quietly to remove all the weapons from the banquet hall, where the suitors spent most of their time. Telemachus left for home, and Odysseus and Eumaeüs followed later. They were met on the way and insulted by the chief goatherd, Melantheus, who had taken up with the suitors to advance his own interests. Controlling himself with difficulty, Odysseus postponed the pleasure of punishing Melantheus' insolent disloyalty.

As Odysseus and Eumaeüs reached the palace, Odysseus' hound Argus, now too weak to stir from the dung heap on which he lay, wagged his tail with joy at recognizing his master, then died of old age. Eumaeüs went into the palace; then Odysseus entered the hall and found the suitors banqueting as usual on the best of his livestock. At Telemachus' suggestion, he begged food of them and received it from all but the arrogant Antinoüs, who flung a stool at him. Odysseus had to bear this outrage, but, when a cowardly but much younger beggar named Irus tried to impress the suitors by threatening the rival "beggar," Odysseus boxed with him and felled him with one bone-crushing blow. The suitors treated him thereafter with greater respect.

Penelope announced that, since her husband had not returned from the Trojan War and her son was now approaching manhood, she would soon consider whom she would take for a second husband, as Odysseus himself had directed before he left home. She upbraided the suitors, however, for their unseemly behavior in living off Odysseus' wealth. She retired, leaving Odysseus to admire his wife's character. Melantho, one of the serving women, insulted him, having, like her brother, Melantheus, become friendly with the suitors. Eurymachus, who had made the girl his mistress, began to taunt Odysseus, and trouble might have arisen if Amphinomus, the most reasonable of the suitors, had not advised them all to go to bed. [Homer, *Odyssey*, 13.187–18.428.]

M. When the suitors were gone, Odysseus and Telemachus took the weapons that had long stood in the great hall and stored them in the cellars. Eurycleia, at Telemachus' command, locked the womenservants in their quarters. Odysseus, alone, met with Penelope, who had heard that he had news of her husband. She spoke of the stratagem with which she had held off the importunate suitors for over three years, asking them to wait for her decision until she had finished weaving a shroud for old Laërtes. She had worked at the loom by day, but raveled out the web each night until one of her servants had given away her ruse. Odysseus, pretending to be a brother of Idomeneus, king of Crete, told Penelope that he had once entertained her husband. He then added that he had learned in Thesprotia that Odysseus would soon return to Ithaca. Though Penelope did not dare to believe the guest, she bade Eurycleia take good care of him. As the old woman, who had nursed Odysseus as a child, was washing his feet, she recognized the scar that a boar's tusk had left on his thigh in his youth. Odysseus warned her to tell no one.

Penelope told her guest that she intended soon to hold a test of strength among the suitors, the winner to take her in marriage. She would, as her husband had done in the past, set up twelve axes in a row, and would ask the suitors to shoot an arrow through all of them. Odysseus urged her to hold the contest without further delay, assuring her that her husband would take part in it.

The next day at the feast, Telemachus set a small table for Odysseus near the main door of the hall. The suitors taunted the young lord, but Telemachus replied with the strength and dignity of a man. Many omens that should have warned the suitors of impending calamity passed unnoticed by them, in spite of a dire prophecy by Theoclymenus, a seer whom Telemachus had given passage on his return voyage from Pylus.

After the banquet, Penelope brought Odysseus' bow—the one that Iphitus had given him as a young man—and the twelve axes. She explained the contest and announced the prize, her own hand in marriage. Telemachus set up the iron axes one behind another, then tried unsuccessfully to string the bow. The suitors too tried, one by one, and likewise failed. While they were testing their strength Odysseus slipped from the hall, found Eumaeüs and Philoetius, and revealed his identity to them. The two loyal servants greeted him joyfully and he told them what parts they must play in the coming battle.

Odysseus returned to the hall to find that all of the suitors had failed to string the bow except for Antinoüs, who had thought of a clever excuse not to try. Odysseus now offered to make an attempt. The suitors protested furiously, but Penelope insisted that the guest be given a chance. Telemachus sent his mother to her apartment on the upper floor. When she had retired, Eumaeüs took the bow to Odysseus. At the same moment Philoetius quietly barred the door of the hall that led into the courtyard. While the suitors watched in dismay, the man whom they still took to be a beggar strung the bow and shot an arrow through all twelve axes without even rising from his stool.

Telemachus took his place by his father's side as Odysseus turned his arrows on the suitors. Odysseus first shot Antinoüs, then Eurymachus, and Telemachus killed Amphinomus with his spear. The young man ran to the storeroom for a supply of arms while Odysseus picked off the milling suitors with his remaining arrows. The treacherous Melantheus brought arms for the suitors from the storeroom, which Telemachus had left unlocked. When he made a second trip there, however, Eumaeüs and Philoetius bound him and hung him from a rafter, then went to the aid of Odysseus and his son. Athena appeared in the guise of Odysseus' old Ithacan friend Mentor and urged him on against the suitors, who now had a few shields and weapons. In spite of the fact that they were four against many, Odysseus and his companions won the terrible battle that ensued. By its end they had killed every one of the suitors, sparing only Phemius, the minstrel, and Medon, the herald, who had served the suitors against their will. Odysseus ruled once more in his own home, though it was peopled with corpses. [Homer, *Iliad*, 19.1–22.389.]

N. Odysseus allowed none of the household to exult over the dead, but he punished those of his own servants who had aided the suitors. The twelve women who had been their mistresses were forced to carry out the bodies and clean the blood-spattered hall, after which Telemachus hanged them. Melantheus was released only to be mutilated for his insolence and treachery. Odysseus, before consenting to wash the blood from his own body, fumigated house and courtyard with burning sulphur. Eurycleia then waked her mistress from the deep sleep that Athena had brought her. At first Penelope did not believe the nurse's good news. Not, in fact, until Odysseus himself told her secrets that only the two of them knew did she allow herself to believe that her husband had returned at last.

The next morning Odysseus made himself known to his aged father on his farm. Overjoyed, Laërtes dressed himself once more in clothing suited to his dignity. Then he, with his son and grandson, sat down to discuss what to do next. By now word had reached the townspeople of the death of the suitors, many of whom had been noblemen with powerful families living either in Ithaca or the nearby islands. The Ithacan elders gathered at the place of assembly to decide how they should act toward their king, who had returned after nineteen years and killed their rebellious sons. In spite of the sensible counsel of Medon and the old seer Halitherses, the majority followed the rash urgings of Antinoüs' father, Eupeithes, and armed themselves against Odysseus. They approached the farmhouse to be greeted by Odysseus, his father and son, and the old servant Dolius, with his sons, all of whom but Melantheus had remained loyal to their master. Even the old men were fully armed. It was Laërtes who, guided by Athena, threw the first spear and killed Eupeithes, the leader of the insurgents. Odysseus and Telemachus would have killed more if Athena had not separated the warring parties with a great cry that sent the Ithacans fleeing in panic. Odysseus would have pursued them, but Zeus flung a thunderbolt to dissuade him. Athena, disguised as Mentor, the most respected leader of the Ithacans, reestablished peace between Odysseus and the townspeople.

Although Odysseus was once again confirmed as king in his own country, he had not forgotten the prophecy of Teiresias that he must endure yet more wandering before he could enjoy a peaceful old age. The story of these further adventures was recounted in the lost epic called *Telegony*. According to surviving fragments of this poem, Odysseus sailed to the mainland of Elis, where he kept his herds of cattle, and was entertained there by King Polyxenus. Returning to Ithaca, he performed certain rites that Teiresias had ordained. He then went to Thesprotia and married Queen Callidice, though Penelope still lived in Ithaca. He led the Thesprotians against the Brygi, but was defeated because Ares fought with the enemy. The Thesprotian queen died and was succeeded by Polypoetes, her son by Odysseus. Odysseus returned to Ithaca and presumably enjoyed the quiet old age that Teiresias had predicted for him.

His death was quick, if not quite so gentle as the seer had promised. While living with Circe, Odysseus had fathered at least one son, Telegonus (and perhaps Agrius and Latinus, as well). Circe, when Telegonus grew to manhood, sent him to find his father. Arriving at Ithaca without knowing it, the young man and his crew raided the island. Telemachus and his father, now aged, went out to defend their homeland. Odysseus was killed by a spear thrown by Telegonus. Because this spear had a point made of the sting of a stingray, the old man's death may be said to have come from the sea, as Teiresias had predicted. On learning the invader's identity, Odysseus' family not only forgave him but went home with him to Circe's island, where they buried Odysseus. Penelope married her stepson, Telegonus, and Telemachus married the ageless Circe.

There are many obscure traditions that either amplify or contradict Homer's account. According to some writers Penelope had a second son by Odysseus, Acusilaüs or Ptoliporthes, on his return from his wanderings. An opposing tradition denies Penelope's proverbial reputation for faithfulness. She was seduced by either Antinoüs or Amphinomus. Odysseus killed her, or else sent her home to her father, Icarius, in Sparta. She went from there to Mantineia, in Arcadia, or stopped there on her way home and bore the god Pan, having at some point lain with Hermes. The Mantineians later pointed out Penelope's tomb in their city.

According to another tale, Odysseus was brought to judgment by the families of the suitors and the case was submitted for arbitration to Neoptolemus, who ruled the offshore islands of Epeirus. Hoping to seize Cephallenia, which had been under Odysseus' control, Neoptolemus condemned him to exile, though he required the suitors' families to pay compensation to Telemachus. Some say that Odysseus emigrated to Italy, others that he went only as far as Aetolia, where his fellow-soldier Thoas ruled. He married Thoas' daughter, who bore a son, Leontophonus. Odysseus died peacefully in Aetolia in his old age. [Homer, *Odyssey*, 22.370–24.548; *Telegony* 1, 2; Apollodorus, "Epitome" 34–40; Pausanias 8.12.6.]

Odyssey. See HOMER.

Oeagrus. A Thracian king. Oeagrus, a son of Pierus, king of Pella, and the nymph Methone, is known only as the father of Orpheus and Linus by the Muse Calliope, and he is sometimes denied that honor in favor of Apollo. [*Contest of Homer and Hesiod* 315; Apollodorus 1.3.2.]

Oeax. A son of Nauplius by Clymene, Hesione, or Philyra. Like his father, Oeax seems to have been consumed with hatred of the Argives for their unjust execution of his brother Palamedes at Troy. He told Clytemnestra that her husband, Agamemnon, was bringing home a Trojan concubine. It was this news, according to Hyginus [*Fabulae* 117], that led her to plot Agamemnon's death. Later Oeax tried to persuade the Argives to banish Orestes after his murder of his mother. [Euripides, *Orestes*, 431–434.]

Oebalus. A king of Sparta. A son of Cynortas or of his son Perieres, Oebalus married Perseus' daughter, Gorgophone, after the death of her first husband, the Aeolid Perieres. She or the Naïad Bateia bore him Tyndareüs, Hippocoön, and Icarius. Gorgophone may also have been the mother of Oebalus' daughters Arene and Peirene. [Apollodorus 3.10.3–4; Pausanias 2.21.7.]

Oechalia. A Greek city of doubtful location. According to Pausanias [4.22], Oechalia was the Messenian city, later called Carnasium, which Perieres gave to Melaneus. Although Melaneus, a famous archer, had a son named Eurytus, this may not have been the archer-king of Oechalia, Eurytus, who was killed by Heracles. The city ruled by this king seems likely to have been in Euboea or western Thessaly.

Oedipodeia. See EPIC CYCLE.

Oedipus or **Oedipodes.** A king of Thebes.

A. Oedipus was the only child of Laïus, king of Thebes, and Jocasta or Epicasta. Laïus had been warned that if he had a son by Jocasta that son would kill him. He therefore pierced the infant's feet and gave him to shepherds to expose on Mount Cithaeron. Instead, the shepherds gave the infant to Merope, or Periboea, the wife of Polybus, king of Corinth or Sicyon. According to one obscure tradition the child was not exposed, but was placed in a chest and flung into the sea. Periboea found him when the chest washed up on the shore near Corinth. In either case, the childless couple brought the boy up as their own son. They named him Oedipus (Swollen Foot) for the wounds in his feet. Grown to manhood, the aggressive Oedipus was one day taunted by a drunken companion for not being a true son of mild King Polybus. For some reason this accusation troubled the young man so deeply that he made a journey to Delphi to inquire of the oracle if it were true. The Pythia, without waiting to hear his question, drove him from Apollo's shrine, saying that he would kill his father and marry his mother. In horror Oedipus turned eastward, intending never to return to Corinth, the home of the man and woman whom he supposed to be his parents.

Not far from Delphi Oedipus came to a spot known as the Cleft Way, where the road to Daulis divides from that leading to Boeotia. There he met a man in a chariot, whose charioteer demanded that the young man move aside. Oedipus refused. The charioteer urged his horses forward, so that a wheel of the car grazed Oedipus' foot. In passing, either the rider or his servant struck Oedipus on the head with his goad. Oedipus, enraged, killed the rider, the charioteer, and all but one of the retainers who, according to various versions of the story, were with them. Letting them lie where they had fallen, the young man continued on his way.

Before long Oedipus reached Thebes. He found the city in turmoil. A female monster called the Sphinx had settled herself on the walls of the citadel, or on Mount Phicium, to the north, and was eating the Thebans one by one. The last victim had been Haemon, a son of Creon, who was acting as regent for King Laïus, the king having left some time before on a trip to Delphi. Before killing her victims the Sphinx would ask them a riddle: "What is it that goes on four legs in the morning, two at midday, and three in the evening?" The Thebans had learned from an oracle that they would be free from this plague when someone answered the riddle correctly, but no such person could be found. To add to the city's troubles, Damasistratus, king of nearby Plataea, reported that he had found and buried the bodies of Laïus and his retinue on the way to Delphi. The Thebans, preoccupied with their problems with the Sphinx, had no time to seek the murderer. Indeed, Creon offered the hand of his sister Jocasta, Laïus' widow, and a share in the kingdom to any man who could save the city from the Sphinx.

Oedipus offered to undertake this task. He visited the Sphinx and gave this answer to her riddle: "Man, who crawls in infancy, walks upright in his prime, and leans on a cane in old age." The monster, chagrined that someone had at last penetrated her secret, flung herself to her death from the walls of the citadel. Oedipus was greeted as a hero and made king of Thebes. Shortly after this, a lone survivor of Laïus' retinue made his way back to Thebes. Finding Oedipus reigning, he announced that the king had been killed by several highwaymen and asked to be assigned to duties as a shepherd far from the city. The citizens, rejoicing in their new king, forgot Laïus and his unhappy fate. Jocasta had by her new young husband two sons, Eteocles and Polyneices, and two daughters, Antigone and Ismene. Some say, however, that these were Oedipus' children by Euryganeia, daughter of Hyperphas.

B. Although, according to some accounts, Oedipus shared the rule equally with Jocasta and Creon, who were descended through Pentheus from both Cadmus and the Sparti, the fame of having saved the city was all his own. How his reputation, and the arrogance with which he enjoyed it, were shattered in a moment is one of the most famous of Greek myths and the subject of one of the most celebrated of all tragic dramas, Sophocles' *Oedipus the King*. The details of the story, several of which have been recounted above, are best known from this play. According to Sophocles, when Oedipus had reigned for perhaps two decades, Thebes was visited with a great plague. The king sent Creon to Delphi to inquire the cause and learned that the disaster had occurred because the murderer of Laïus was living unpunished in the city. Oedipus at once opened an investigation. The aged seer Teiresias was consulted, and both the survivor of Laïus' company and the shepherd who had given Laïus' infant son to Polybus gave their testimony. When the king and his wife discovered the truth—that Oedipus had killed his father, Laïus, and married his mother, exactly as the oracle had predicted—Jocasta hanged herself and Oedipus jabbed out his eyes with one of her brooches.

What happened to Oedipus after his downfall is uncertain, for there are widely varying versions of his subsequent life. The best known is again that of Sophocles, who says in his *Oedipus at Colonus* that the king was exiled by Creon for fear that his presence would continue to pollute the city. He wandered for many years as a outcast, accompanied only by his faithful daughter Antigone. Before leaving Thebes he had cursed his two sons because they did nothing to oppose his banishment. Euripides, in his *Phoenician Women*, claims that Oedipus was imprisoned by his sons in the hope that his disgrace would be forgotten and not affect their fortunes. He was not banished, in this version, until after the war with Argos. Fragments of the lost epic *Thebaïd* [2, 3] indicate that Oedipus cursed his sons because they fed him a haunch of meat instead of a piece more fitting for a king, and also because of some obscure *faux pas* that they committed with the royal silver. Several lines surviving from the *Catalogues of Women* [24, 99A, 99 [2]] and three from the *Iliad* [23.678–680] suggest that Oedipus was never exiled at all, but died in battle at Thebes. To his funeral came his Argive daughter-in-law, Argeia, and two of her famous countrymen, Amphiaraüs and Mecisteus. This version is supported by Pausanias' statement [9.5.12] that Polyneices left Thebes to escape his father's curses (or perhaps involvement in the curse that clung to his father), married Argeia, and returned after Oedipus' death.

C. The tradition that Oedipus cursed his sons is widespread, though there is no hint of it in either Homer or Hesiod. Pindar attributes their deaths to the Erinyes of Laïus, who presumably wished to punish Oedipus through his sons. Oedipus' curse, if there was one, worked itself out in the strife between Eteocles and Polyneices, which ended with the brothers' deaths at each other's hands during the bloody war of the SEVEN AGAINST THEBES. In *Oedipus at Colonus*, Polyneices is said to have followed his father to the Athenian suburb of Colonus, where the old man had found a haven, and to have vainly tried to win his support, which an oracle had said would bring victory in the conflict with his brother. Creon, presumably with Eteocles' approval, tried to kidnap Oedipus and carry him back to Thebes with the intention of burying him outside the walls, where a curse on his tomb would, according to an oracle, prevent invaders from harming the city. This abduction was prevented by Theseus, king of Athens, who protected Oedipus and his daughters. Shortly thereafter, Oedipus quietly died, having prophesied that his tomb, the site of which only Theseus knew, would bring blessings on Attica.

Oedipus is the protagonist of both plays by Sophocles and of Seneca's *Oedipus*, and appears prominently at the end of *The Phoenician Women*. See also Apollodorus 3.5.7–9; Homer, *Odyssey*, 11.271–280; Hyginus, *Fabulae*, 66, 67; Aeschylus, *Seven Against Thebes*, 742–1084; and Pindar, *Olympian Odes*, 38–42.

Oeneus. A king of Calydon. Oeneus was the most famous of the sons of Porthaon (or Portheus), king of Calydon, and Euryte, daughter of Hippodamas. He married Althaea, daughter of Thestius, and she bore several sons and daughters, best known of whom were Meleager, Gorge, and Deïaneira. In his prime, Oeneus was an open-handed ruler who welcomed gods and men to his palace, usually with unfortunate results for himself. When he entertained Dionysus, he realized that the god had designs on Althaea. Out of either generosity or prudence Oeneus pretended that it was necessary for him to leave Calydon temporarily in order to conduct certain religious rituals in another city. Left alone with Dionysus, Althaea conceived Deïaneira. The god gave his host the gift of vine culture in return for his understanding hospitality.

When Deïaneira was grown, Heracles visited Oeneus. He was served at a feast by a young relative and cupbearer of the king's, Cyathus or Eunomus. Annoyed at some trifle, the guest struck the boy on the head with one finger and the lad dropped dead. (Some say that this happened in Phlius while Oeneus was visiting Heracles there.) Oeneus, with his usual impeccable hospitality, overlooked this occurrence and gave Heracles Deïaneira for his wife. Oeneus is said to have entertained Alcmeon and Bellerophon and to have given refuge to the infants Agamemnon and Menelaüs without untoward incident. It is not recorded whether Ares was ever the king's guest, but Meleager is often called the god's son by Althaea.

Oeneus killed his son Toxeus for jumping over a ditch, a crime perhaps comparable to Remus' disrespectful act of jumping over the newly built wall of Rome, for which he was killed by Romulus. The early Greek poet Asius made the seemingly improbable statement that Perimede, a daughter of Oeneus, married the Phoenician king Phoenix and became the mother of Europa and Astypalaea.

Although Oeneus seems to have been one of the most pious of men, his downfall was brought about by the enmity of a goddess. One year, as the king dutifully offered the first fruits of the harvest to the gods, he forgot Artemis. To punish him for this insult she sent a giant boar, which destroyed crops and men. Oeneus called on many of the bravest men of other cities for help. They joined Meleager in the famous CALYDONIAN BOAR HUNT and killed the monster, but a quarrel arose afterward that resulted in Meleager's death. Althaea killed herself because of the guilt she felt over her part in her son's death.

Oeneus married again. Some say that he won his new wife, Periboea, among the spoils of war when he conquered Olenus, in Achaea, where her father, Hipponoüs, ruled, or that he seduced her and that Hipponoüs sent her after him on discovering this fact. Other writers claim that Periboea had been seduced by someone else and that her father sent her to Oeneus with a request that he dispose of her. Oeneus, who had just lost both wife and son, married her instead of killing her. Periboea bore two sons, Olenias and Tydeus. According to one report, however, the mother of Tydeus was Gorge, Zeus having decreed for some reason that Oeneus should fall in love with his own daughter.

Tydeus proved to be as brave as the dead Meleager, but, while still a young man, he killed someone and was exiled from Calydon. Oeneus' envious brothers, among them Agrius, had a hand in getting Tydeus out of the country, which left the old king without support. The sons of Agrius deposed and imprisoned Oeneus and gave the rule to their father. Much later, Tydeus' son, Diomedes, came to Calydon with Alcmeon or Sthenelus, and killed some or all of Agrius' sons. He may have restored Oeneus to power, but it is generally said that he turned the government over to Andraemon, Gorge's husband, and took Oeneus with him back to Argos. According to one report Oeneus did not reach this haven, but was killed from ambush in Arcadia by Onchestus and Thersites, two sons of Agrius who had escaped Diomedes' vengeance. Others say that Oeneus died at an advanced age at Argos and that the town of Oenoë was named for him by his grandson.

Oeneus seems to have been known less for his manly prowess than as a friend of gods and great men. It has been suggested that he was a culture hero or even an Aetolian agricultural deity, since he is said to have been the first

Greek king to introduce the art of wine growing to his people, and his name may be derived from the word for wine (*oinos*). Oeneus is frequently mentioned by Homer [*Iliad* 2.641–642, 6.216–219, 9.533–583, 14.115–118]. The most detailed account of his life is that of Apollodorus [1.7.10–1.8.2, 1.8.4–6, 2.7.6, 3.7.5, "Epitome" 2.15]. Hyginus tells of him in the *Fabulae* [129, 171, 172, 175].

Oenoë. A water-nymph and eponym of the island of Oenoë, one of the Cyclades. By Thoas Oenoë became the mother of Sicinus, for whom the island was renamed.

Oenomaüs. A king of Pisa. Oenomaüs was the son of Alxion or Ares and Harpina or the Pleiad Asterope. He killed all the suitors of his daughter, Hippodameia, until he was killed by PELOPS [B–D]. Oenomaüs was also the father of Leucippus. According to Hyginus [*Fabulae* 84], his wife was Evarete, a daughter of Acrisius who is otherwise unknown. Some say, however, that Asterope was Oenomaüs' wife, rather than his mother.

Oenone. A daughter of the river Cebren. Oenone, a nymph of Mount Ida, who learned prophecy from Rhea and also knew the art of healing, married PARIS [A, C], but he abandoned her in order to sail for Sparta to win Helen. When, much later, he was mortally wounded by Philoctetes, he came to Mount Ida to ask Oenone to heal him, but she refused. She repented her decision too late to save his life and hanged herself in remorse. [Apollodorus 3.12.6.]

Oenone or **Oenopia.** See AEGINA.

Oenopion. A son of Dionysus and Ariadne. This son of the wine-god was king of the wine-growing island of Chios, which he had come to from Crete to colonize. He delayed the marriage of his daughter Merope to ORION; the frustrated giant, getting drunk, finally raped her. Oenopion blinded Orion and drove him from the island or flung him onto the beach. When the giant later returned, his sight restored, the Chians hid Oenopion underground until the avenger went away. Some say that Oenopion's underground chamber was built for him by Hephaestus.

Oenotria. An ancient Greek name for most of the southern part of Italy except the "heel."

Oeonus. A son of Licymnius. Oeonus was killed by the sons of Hippocoön for throwing a stone at their dog when it attacked him. Heracles, his cousin, avenged him by killing Hippocoön and all his sons. [Pausanias 3.15.3–6.]

Oeta, Mount. A mountain range northeast of Aetolia. King Ceÿx's city of Trachis was at the foot of Oeta. When Heracles was dying, he climbed this mountain to his funeral pyre.

Ogygia. See CALYPSO.

Ogygus or **Ogyges.** An aboriginal king in Boeotia. Ogygus ruled the Ectenes, the earliest tribe to inhabit the region of Thebes. Some call him the father of Eleusis, Aulis, and Alalcomenia, eponyms of cities in Attica and Boeotia. Ogygus may have died of plague, as did his people. Thebes was often called Ogygian by poets. [Pausanias 1.38.7, 9.4.2, 9.19.2, 9.33.5.]

Oïcles. An Arcadian king. Early writers knew nothing of Oïcles except that he was Amphiaraüs' father and a son of either Mantius or Antiphates. Later accounts added that he either was killed while guarding Heracles' ships at Troy or else ruled long in Arcadia, was visited there by his mad grandson, Alcmeon, and was buried at Megalopolis. [Homer, *Odyssey*, 15.243; Apollodorus 3.7.5.]

Oïleus. A Locrian king. Oïleus, a son of Hodoedocus and Agrianome, daughter of Perseon, was an Argonaut. Apart from that role and the fact that he was loved by Apollo, he is known only as the father of the lesser Ajax by Eriopis. He also had a bastard son, Medon, by Rhene. [Homer, *Iliad*, 2.726–728, 13.694–696; Apollonius Rhodius 1.74–76; *Catalogues of Women* 83.]

Olenus. A city of western Achaea on the Gulf of Patrae. Dexamenus, king of Olenus, entertained Heracles royally, but he married two of his daughters to Heracles' enemies the Moliones. The city was conquered by the Calydonian king Oeneus, who married Periboea, daughter of King Hipponoüs of Olenus.

Olympia. See OLYMPIC GAMES.

Olympic games. An athletic festival held every four years in Olympia, a city in Elis.

A. According to the Eleian informants of Pausanias, the institution had its origin before the human race began in footraces held by Heracles the Dactyl, who had come to Olympia from Cretan Mount Ida with his four younger brothers. This Heracles crowned the victor with wild olive, a tree that he had brought from the land of the Hyperboreans and planted at Olympia. In honor of himself and his brothers he arranged that the games be held every four years (*five*, according to the Greek custom of counting both festival years, as well as the three years between them). Some say, however, that Zeus founded the games because in Olympia he wrestled his father, Cronus, and won supremacy over the gods. The gods took part in the events. Apollo outrunning Hermes and defeating Ares in boxing.

Fifty years after Deucalion's Flood, Clymenus, a Cretan descendant of Heracles the Dactyl, ruled Olympia and held the games. He was overthrown as king by Endymion, king of Elis, who later continued the custom of the games by holding a footrace among his three sons to choose a successor to the throne. When Pelops took from Oenomaüs the throne of Pisa, he celebrated the games more elaborately than had been usual. The Aeolian Amythaon, his nephews Pelias and Neleus, and Augeias, king of Elis, also held games at Olympia, as did Heracles, son of Amphitryon, when he took Elis from Augeias. Many writers claim that it was this Heracles, rather than the Dactyl, who founded the games, marking off the boundaries of the Altis, or sacred precinct of Zeus, and traveling to the distant river Ister (Danube) to bring back the olive tree to shade the site. The Aetolian Oxylus, who became king of Elis with the return of the Heraclids, celebrated the games, but the custom was discontinued until the reign of his descendant Iphitus. Iphitus was directed by the Delphic oracle to revive the games in order to bring peace among the war-torn Greek cities.

B. Historically, the unbroken tradition of the Olympic games begins in 776 B.C., from which year the names of the victors at each festival were carefully recorded. The games had been held long before this date, and are thought to have been antedated by the HERAEAN GAMES, which took place on the same spot. The Olympic games were sacred to Olympian Zeus, whose temple was the most imposing in all of Greece. The Cronium, the hill overshadowing Olympus that was named for Zeus's father, may testify to the great age of Olympia as a cult center. It is probable that nearby Pisa controlled the Olympic games long before Elis, which lies over twenty miles away. As Eleian strength grew, a struggle for control of the games began that lasted perhaps for centuries and involved, at various times, Sparta and Arcadia, as well as Elis and Pisa. It ended with the total destruction of Pisa. Although the revival of the games did not bring about the peace that the oracle had promised Iphitus, it did have a sufficiently unifying influence to insure that, at regular intervals over a period of hundreds of years, citizens of nearly every city in the Greek world could safely travel to and from Olympia even through hostile territories, fully protected by a sacred truce.

The site and history of the Olympic games were described in detail by Pausanias, who visited Olympia about A.D. 175. The accuracy of his own observations, as they are recorded in Books 5 and 6 of his *Description of Greece,* can generally be relied upon. His historical statements are less dependable, since they reflect the biased view of the Eleians, who, by Pausanias' day, had managed the Olympic games for seven centuries.

Olympus, Mount. A mountain range in Pieria, a part of northern Thessaly near the Thermaïc Gulf (Gulf of Salonika). Nearly 10,000 feet high and snow-covered, this Mount Olympus (of the many mountains of that name in Greece and Asia Minor) was generally agreed upon as the home of the gods. Often, however, the gods were thought of as living in the sky itself. Otus and Ephialtes, when they contemplated scaling heaven, piled two other mountains on top of Olympus. This story, in which Olympus is conceived of as merely a mountain, appears in Homer's *Odyssey,* together with repeated references to Olympus as the gods' abode. This seeming confusion suggests that a primitive notion had survived as a literary convention long after more sophisticated concepts had been generally accepted. Olympus, and Pieria in general, was the particular haunt of the Muses, although the same claim was made for Mounts Helicon and Parnassus.

Omphale. A queen of Lydia. Omphale, a daughter of Iardanus, married

Tmolus, king of Lydia, whom she succeeded on the throne at his death. When HERACLES [J] permitted himself to be sold into slavery, Omphale bought him. In her service he killed or captured the Cercopes, killed the outlaw Syleus and his daughter, razed the city of the Itoni, and destroyed a great snake that was ravaging a part of Lydia. Omphale is said by some Roman writers to have made Heracles wear effeminate dress and even to spin during his servitude. After three years she freed, and perhaps married, him. She bore one son, Lamus. [Apollodorus 2.6.3; Diodorus Siculus 4.31.5–8.]

omphalos. See DELPHI.

Onca or **Onga.** A Phoenician goddess identified by the Greeks with Athena. The worship of Onca was brought to Greece by Cadmus and established at Thebes. She had a shrine there that is mentioned by Aeschylus in his *Seven Against Thebes*. [Pausanias 9.12.2.]

Onchestus. A Boeotian city on the southern shore of Lake Copaïs. According to the Boeotian version of the story of Atalanta, the suitor who won her hand was Hippomenes, son of Megareus, a king of Onchestus. This Megareus later emigrated to Megara, where he became king and evidently bequeathed his name to the city. Onchestus, an ancient city that had declined by Classical times, was noted for its grove of Poseidon. It was at a feast in this grove that a brawl occurred which led to a protracted feud between Thebes and Orchomenus and the eventual decline of the latter city.

Oncius or **Oncus.** A king of Thelpusa in Arcadia. Though a son of Apollo, he is less well known than his horse ARION, which he gave to Heracles. [Pausanias 8.25.4–10.]

Opheltes. A son of Lycurgus, king of Nemea, and Amphithea or Eurydice. According to Hyginus, Lycurgus (or Lycus) was warned by an oracle not to set Opheltes on the ground until he could walk. Therefore, Opheltes' nurse, Hypsipyle, laid him on a thick bed of parsley while she was showing the SEVEN AGAINST THEBES [C] the way to a spring. In spite of this precaution the child was killed by the snake that guarded the spring. The Seven buried the child under the name of Archemorus (Beginning of Doom), for the seer Amphiaraüs said that his death meant just that for them. Adrastus interceded for Hypsipyle with the king and founded the Nemean games in the child's honor. [Hyginus, *Fabulae*, 74.]

Ophion. An obscure ancient deity. According to Apollonius Rhodius [1.503–511], Ophion and the Oceanid Eurynome ruled Olympus from the beginning, but were defeated by Cronus and Rhea and fell into Oceanus.

Ophiuchus (The Serpent-holder). A constellation. This group of stars has been identified in many different ways. Some recognize in it Carnabon, the treacherous king who tried to kill Triptolemus. To others it is Heracles killing a Lydian snake for Omphale. Still others claim that it is Triopas, a Thessalian king who offended Demeter, or Phorbas, Triopas' son by Hiscilla. Phorbas freed Rhodes of snakes and other beasts. More usually, however, the Serpent-holder is said to be Asclepius, who is regularly represented together with a snake. [Hyginus, *Poetica Astronomica*, 2.14.]

Opis or **Upis.** A Hyperborean maiden. Opis, together with another HYPER-BOREAN woman, named Arge, came to Delos at the same time as Artemis and Apollo, and the two women were later honored in hymns by the Delians. Orion is said in some accounts to have raped Opis and been killed for the in-sult by Artemis. Most scholars believe, however, that Opis was a name of Ar-temis herself, or of a local goddess of similar functions who came to be asso-ciated with her. [Herodotus 4.33, 4.35; Apollodorus 1.4.5.]

Ops. A Roman goddess of plenty. Ops, who was identified with the Greek Rhea, was sometimes regarded as the wife of Saturn, but more often was wor-shiped together with the chthonian god Consus.

Opus. The principal city of Opuntian Locris. An ancient city, Opus claimed that Deucalion and Pyrrha had settled there after the Flood. Menoe-tius was an Opuntian prince, but he had to escape to Phthia when his young son, Patroclus, killed a playmate.

Orchomenus (1). The eponym of Boeotian Orchomenus. Orchomenus has been called both the father and the son of Minyas, eponym of the Minyans, who occupied the city of Orchomenus. He is also said to have died childless. [Pausanias 9.36.6–9.37.1.]

Orchomenus (2). The eponym of Arcadian Orchomenus. One of the im-pious sons of Lycaon, he is said to have founded Orchomenus and Methyd-rium. [Apollodorus 3.8.1; Pausanias 8.3.3.]

Orchomenus. The principal city of northern Boeotia. Orchomenus was the center of Minyan power for many generations and was famous for its wealth. Its origins are as confused with conflicting traditions as are those of the Min-yans. The two eponyms regularly connected with the area are Minyas and Or-chomenus, either of whom may have been the father of the other. According to the traditions of the second century A.D. recorded by Pausanias, the land was first called Andreïs, for its first settler, Andreus, son of the river-god Pe-neius. Andreus shared the land with Athamas, son of Aeolus, and married his granddaughter Euippe. Upon the death of their son, Eteocles, the rule fell to some Corinthian descendants of Sisyphus, another son of Aeolus. The first of these, Phlegyas, seceded from Andreïs and called his land Phlegyantis. Upon his death, his cousin Chryses succeeded to the rule. Minyas was, according to this late tradition, Chryses' son and the father of Orchomenus. Nothing is known of the deeds of any of these early rulers but Athamas, and his mythical misadventures were all in the past before he settled in this land in his old age. The legendary ancestry of the Orchomenian rulers points to a Thessalian provenance—a statement that can be made about many Greek regions.

The first Orchomenian king who seems to play a role in the mythical his-tory of Boeotia is Clymenus, and his part is to be murdered by Thebans. This was the excuse for an attack by Clymenus' son, Erginus, on Thebes, which was avenged a few years later by Heracles. Erginus' sons, Trophonius and Agamedes, are famous in their own right, but not as kings of Orchomenus. Their relatives Ascalaphus and Ialmenus were the next rulers and led a force to Troy. In this period their city was still known, as it had always been, for its wealth, but it seems to have been on the decline. Its power appears to have been destroyed by the growing influence of Thebes. The legends, sketchy as they are, suggest that this turbulent city to the south was for many generations envious of Orchomenus and tried to dominate it. The Minyan capital, for all its wealth, was not distinguished by military might. Either for commercial reasons or because of the insecure strategical position of Orchomenus, its inhabitants at various times migrated to parts of Ionia, particularly to Teos and Miletus.

Orchomenus. An Arcadian city. Like most Arcadian towns, Orchomenus claimed as its eponymous founder a son of Lycaon. The city seems to have had no mythical history of interest. In historical times it sent contingents of soldiers against the Persians at both Thermopylae and Plataea.

Orcus. A Roman name for Pluto or HADES and for his realm.

oread. See NYMPH.

Oreithyia. A daughter of Erechtheus and Praxithea. While dancing by the Ilissus River, Oreithyia was carried off by Boreas, the north wind, to Sarpedon's Rock, in Thrace. There he raped her and she bore him two daughters, Chione and Cleopatra, and two sons, Zetes and Calaïs, who were winged. [Apollonius Rhodius 1.211–223, Apollodorus 3.15.2–3.]

Oresteium. An Arcadian city. Founded by Orestheus, this city was named Oresthasium. After Orestes died there, it was renamed Oresteium.

Orestes. A son of AGAMEMNON and Clytemnestra.

A. When his father was murdered by his mother and her lover, Aegisthus, the child Orestes was sent away for safety to Phocis by his sister Electra or by an old retainer. There he was reared by the old king, Strophius, who had married Agamemnon's sister, Anaxibia or Astyoche. Orestes and Strophius' son, Pylades, became loyal friends, and Pylades accompanied Orestes in nearly all his subsequent adventures. Eight years after his escape from Argos, Orestes, now a young man, went to Delphi to ask of the oracle what it was his duty to do about his father's murderers, who were prospering in Agamemnon's palace. Apollo commanded him to kill them both. With many misgivings, Orestes journeyed to Argos with Pylades and there made himself known to Electra, whom Aegisthus had married to a commoner or otherwise humiliated. The ensuing events have been variously dramatized—by Aeschylus in his *Libation Bearers*, and by Sophocles and Euripides in their plays named for Electra. The crucial acts are universally agreed upon: Orestes, urged on and perhaps aided by his sister and Pylades, killed Clytemnestra and her lover.

B. In spite of its divine sanction, this deed led the Erinyes of Orestes' mother to drive him mad. Moreover, he was brought to trial by Clytemnestra's father, Tyndareüs, or some other of her relatives. Out of hatred for Agamemnon, Oeax urged Orestes' banishment. Euripides says in his *Orestes* that both brother and sister were condemned to death by the Argives. To avenge themselves on their uncle Menelaüs for his refusal to help them, they tried to kill his wife, Helen, but were prevented when she was transported to heaven. They then held her daughter, Hermione, hostage until Menelaüs, at Apollo's command, persuaded the Mycenaeans to banish Orestes for a year, then permit him to return to his father's throne in Mycenae. Many of these events are not recorded elsewhere, however, and some are contradicted in other plays by the same playwright.

The more usual story is that Orestes wandered to Delphi, seeking help for his madness from the god who had commanded the deed that caused it. Apollo sent him to Athens, where, as recounted by Aeschylus in his *Eumenides*, he was tried on the Areopagus by a jury of Athenians. Athena cast the deciding vote for acquittal. Although appeased to some degree, the Erinyes did not cease their persecution of Orestes. Apollo promised him that he would regain his sanity if he stole the wooden statue of Artemis that had fallen from heaven in the land of the Taurians and brought it to Attica.

C. The barbaric Taurians, a Scythian tribe that occupied the southern Crimea, regularly sacrificed to Artemis all strangers found in their land. Despite the obvious danger this practice posed, the loyal Pylades, who had recently married Electra, left his bride to sail with her brother. The two young men safely completed the difficult voyage, but they had scarcely set foot on Taurian soil before they were captured and dragged to the temple to be sacrificed. To their astonishment, the priestess of Artemis turned out to be Orestes' eldest sister, Iphigeneia. Iphigeneia arranged the escape of the prisoners and herself, together with the statue, by telling Thoas, the Taurian king, that the statue had been contaminated by the presence of a matricide and that she must cleanse both it and the prisoners in the sea with secret rites. While the credulous Taurians hid themselves in their houses to avoid the taint, the three sailed away, with Athena's help, in Orestes' ship.

Hyginus [*Fabulae* 121] says that the ship went first to Apollo's island of Zminthe, where old Chryses was his priest. Chryses' daughter, Chryseïs, had been for a time Agamemnon's prisoner (see TROJAN WAR) and had borne by him a son, whom she named for her father. Chryses would have returned the fugitives to King Thoas, but, on learning their identity, he became their ally. The younger Chryses went with Orestes to the Taurian land, where they killed Thoas—an act for which no reason is given. Other accounts say nothing of these events, but report that the statue was set up at Halae, in Attica, or at Sparta, in the famous temple of Artemis Orthia, or elsewhere, and that Iphigeneia became a priestess at Delphi or at Artemis' shrine at Brauron in Attica.

On his return, Orestes became king of Mycenae. He seized Argos when its throne became vacant at the death of Cylarabes, and also conquered much of Arcadia. As a descendant of Tyndareüs, he succeeded to the throne of Sparta when Menelaüs died. Thus Orestes became the most powerful monarch in the Peloponnesus.

D. There are many unrelated traditions about Orestes' further adventures. The most widespread of these concerns Hermione. Before leaving for Troy, Menelaüs had promised his daughter to Orestes, then only a boy. Shortly before Troy fell, however, Menelaüs betrothed her to his fellow general Neoptolemus, the son of Achilles. (Ancient writers explained away Menelaüs' duplicity in a variety of ingenious ways; some said, for example, that it was Tyndareüs who betrothed his granddaughter to Orestes during Menelaüs' absence.) Menelaüs kept his word to Neoptolemus, who thereby incurred the fatal enmity of Orestes. When Neoptolemus went to Delphi to demand recompense from Apollo for his father's death at Troy, Orestes either killed him or arranged to have him killed. Pausanias [2.29.9] says that Pylades aided Orestes in this act and suggests that he was motivated not only by friendship but by a desire to avenge his own great-grandfather Phocus by killing a descendant of Phocus' half-brother and murderer, Peleus. Some claim, however, that the Delphians killed Neoptolemus for rifling their shrines. In any case, once Hermione's husband was out of the way, Orestes married her and she bore him a son, Tisamenus, who eventually succeeded his father as king of Sparta and Argos.

Hyginus [*Fabulae* 122] says that on hearing a false report that Orestes had been sacrificed by the Taurians, Aletes, son of Aegisthus and Clytemnestra, seized the Mycenaean throne. On his return, Orestes killed Aletes and would have killed his sister, Erigone, as well, if Artemis had not carried her off to Attica to be her priestess. Others say that Orestes had a son, Penthilus, by Erigone.

Many local traditions about Orestes were recorded by Pausanias and others. The Troezenians claimed that Orestes was purified of matricide on a sacred stone in their marketplace by nine men, who used water from the nearby spring called Hippocrene. In the Arcadian city of Megalopolis it was said that Orestes was beset there by black Erinyes until, in his frenzy, he bit off one of his fingers. Instantly the Erinyes appeared white and his madness left him. The Laconians insisted that Orestes' madness was cured as he sat on a stone at Gythium. Oresthasium, in Arcadia, was thought to be the scene of Orestes' death from the bite of a snake. After this event the city was known as Oresteium.

E. The Argives and Spartans later claimed Orestes as one of their great kings and said that he was succeeded on the throne by Tisamenus. Herodotus [1.67] records a tale about the discovery of Orestes' bones. The Spartans had for many years tried unsuccessfully to capture the powerful Arcadian city of Tegea. On inquiring of the Delphic oracle how this might be done, they were told to bring the hero's remains to Sparta. The whereabouts of these remains was unknown, however, so the Spartans went again to Delphi. This time they were told that Orestes was buried at Tegea in a place where two winds blew under strong restraint, where blow met with blow and woe was laid upon woe. This information seemed hardly more helpful than the first, but a shrewd Spartan dignitary named Lichas figured out its meaning more or less by chance. One day, during a period of ostensible peace between the two cities, he went into a forge at Tegea and saw a smith beating out hot iron on an anvil, while a pair of bellows blew the flames. The smith remarked that recently, while digging a well in his yard, he had come upon a coffin ten feet long. After making sure that the box contained a skeleton of similar proportions, he had piously reburied it. Lichas interpreted the "winds" of the oracle as the bellows, the blows and counterblows as hammer and anvil, and "woe" as the iron, which, as the material of weapons, had brought woe to mankind. He was sure that he had found Orestes' bones. By deception he persuaded the smith to lease him the yard, dug up the coffin, and took it to Sparta. Thereafter that city won all its contests with Tegea.

Orestes, the last major figure of Greek mythology, was only briefly mentioned by Homer and Hesiod as the avenger of Agamemnon on Aegisthus. He is a principal character in Aeschylus' *Libation Bearers* and *Eumenides*, in Sophocles' *Electra*, and in four of Euripides' plays: *Electra, Orestes, Iphigeneia Among the Taurians*, and *Andromache*. His adventures are also described by Apollodorus ["Epitome" 6.14 and 6.24–28] and in the *Fabulae* [117–123] of Hyginus.

Oresthasium. See ORESTEIUM.

Orion. A giant hunter. According to the earliest accounts, Orion was the son of Euryale, daughter of Minos, by Poseidon. A tale known only from later writings accounts very differently for his birth. Hyrieus, king of Thrace or of Boeotian Hyria, hospitably entertained Zeus, Poseidon, and Hermes. When they offered to grant any boon he desired, he asked for children. They demanded the hide of a bull that he had sacrificed to them. Hyrieus produced it and the gods urinated on it and buried it. After nine months a child grew up from this spot. He continued to grow until he reached giant proportions. Hyrieus named him Urion, after the unusual circumstances of his birth, but later his name was happily corrupted to Orion.

Orion married Side, but she was soon sent down to Hades for boasting that she was more beautiful than Hera. Orion then went to the island of Chios and wooed Merope, daughter of King Oenopion. Some say that he raped her; others qualify this accusation by explaining that he merely anticipated, while drunk, the pleasures of their marriage, which the king had long kept postponing. In any case Oenopion blinded him while he slept for his presumption and drove him from the island or flung him onto the beach. Orion, whose father, Poseidon, had given him the power to walk on the waves or wade through the sea, now made his way northward to Lemnos, where Hephaestus had a smithy. Out of pity, Hephaestus gave Orion his servant Cedalion to be his guide, or else Orion simply snatched the boy from the smithy. The giant lifted Cedalion to his shoulders and ordered him to guide him toward the east. In time they reached the land where the sun rose and Orion was cured of his blindness by Helius. He then hurried back to Chios to take his revenge on Oenopion. The king was saved by his subjects, who hid him in an underground chamber which, some say, Hephaestus had created at Poseidon's request. Unable to find his enemy, Orion gave up his vengeance and went off to Crete on a hunting expedition.

In Crete, Orion hunted happily with Artemis, perhaps in company with her mother, Leto. There are several accounts of Orion's relations with Artemis. She shot him for challenging her to a game of quoits, or for trying to rape her or the Hyperborean maiden Opis at Delos, or for lying with Eos. The poet Istrus claimed, on the other hand, that Artemis so enjoyed her companionship with Orion that she considered marrying him. Apollo, jealous of his sister's honor, resorted to a trick. While Orion was swimming far out in the sea, Apollo caught sight of his head in the water. Pointing out the almost unrecognizable black object to Artemis, the god wagered that she could not hit it with an arrow. She could, of course, and did. Horrified when Orion's corpse floated ashore, she placed him in the sky as the constellation Orion to commemorate their friendship. A more usual explanation of Orion's death was, however, that he boasted to Artemis that he could kill all the animals on earth. In anger and alarm, Ge sent a great scorpion, which stung him to death. Artemis and Leto asked Zeus to place him in the stars. He did so, but placed the scorpion there as well.

Orion's story is one of the few Classical myths that seem to have been shaped in part in order to account for the observed movements of the stars. Like all hunters, Orion is accompanied by a dog, the constellation Canis Major. A hare (Lepus) flees before him. Some Classical writers preferred not to notice this fact, feeling that it was ignominious to represent the giant hunter chasing rabbits. They claimed that it was the Bull (Taurus) that he was following. A bear (Arctos) watches Orion suspiciously and a scorpion (Scorpio) follows him at a distance.

Some say that the hunter is pursuing not only wild game, but Atlas' daughters the Pleiades as well. They explain that, while passing through Boeotia, Orion saw and chased the maidens' mother, Pleïone (not recognizing her as his great-grandmother). After they had run for seven years, Zeus placed the weary daughters in the stars, where Orion still pursues them. What happened to Pleïone is unclear.

The myth of Orion, though widely known, never assumed a canonical form as the result of being treated by a major poet. It survives in a great many variant forms, especially among late and obscure Classical writers. Among the principal sources are the following: Homer, *Odyssey*, 5.121–124, 11.572–575;

Astronomy 4, 5; Apollodorus 1.4.3.–5; Hyginus, *Fabulae,* 195, and *Poetica Astronomica,* 2.21, 2.26, 2.33–34.

Ormenium. A city at the foot of Mount Pelion, in Magnesia. Ormenium was known as the city of King Amyntor. Amyntor's son, Phoenix, left Ormenium to become king of the Dolopians. Amyntor was later killed by Heracles.

Orneus. A son of Erechtheus, king of Athens. Menestheus, son of Orneus' son Peteüs, became king of Athens after expelling Theseus.

Ornytus. King of Phocis. Ornytus was the father of Naubolus, also a Phocian king. He may have been the same figure as Ornytion, a son of Sisyphus, king of Corinth. Both were connected with Phocis. Ornytion was said by Pausanias to be the father of Phocus (2), one of two eponyms of Phocis, and Naubolus was said by some to be the son of Phocus (1), the other eponym. Ornytion also had a son, Thoas. [Pausanias 2.4.3, 10.33.12.]

Orpheus. A Thracian minstrel. Orpheus was the son of a Thracian king, Oeagrus, or of Apollo, and the Muse Calliope. Some say that Apollo taught him to play the lyre. He became so adept at music that his playing and singing charmed wild animals and caused stones and trees to follow him when he wished. Orpheus joined the Argonauts and often kept peace among the unruly crew with his playing. He introduced them to the Samothracian mysteries on the outward voyage and, on the return trip, saved them from the Sirens by drowning out their seductive songs with the twanging of his lyre. Orpheus married a Naïad nymph, Eurydice. Shortly after their marriage, she was chased by the amorous Aristaeüs and, in her eagerness to escape him, stepped on a snake and was bitten. Orpheus mourned her death, then determined to bring her back from Hades. Descending into the Underworld by way of the entrance at Taenarum, he sang and played so movingly that the spirits came in hordes to listen, the damned forgot their labors for a moment, and even the cold hearts of Hades and Persephone were melted. They granted Orpheus' plea that he be allowed to take Eurydice back with him, provided that he promise not to look at her until they reached home. Orpheus led his wife up to the entrance of the Underworld, then, overcome with fear that she might not be following, turned to look. Eurydice instantly faded away to become once again only a shade. When Orpheus tried to reenter Hades, his way was inexorably barred.

Orpheus returned to Thrace and soon met his own death there, torn to pieces by Ciconian women raging as maenads on a mountain. The reason for their enmity is variously explained: they were inflamed by Dionysus because Orpheus had not properly honored that god, or had preferred the worship of Helius; they were angry because he remained faithful to Eurydice's memory by abjuring love altogether, or by becoming the first man to love boys; or each of the women wanted him for herself and they tore him apart in the resulting squabble. The Muses gathered the scattered pieces of Orpheus' body and buried them at his home in Pieria, except for his head. This, and perhaps the lyre as well, floated down the river Hebrus and across the sea to Lesbos, where the people kindly buried them. Orpheus rewarded the Lesbians by making them adept at music. Many say that the Muses immortalized the lyre by placing it in the sky as the constellation Lyra.

Orpheus came to be credited with the invention of mysteries and the authorship of many poems and mystical books. His cult, Orphism, became prominent about the sixth century B.C. It strongly influenced Pythagorean philosophy. A part of Orpheus' myth is closely associated with the worship of Dionysus, but did not necessarily originate in it. [Apollodorus 1.3.2; Apollonius Rhodius, *Argonautica*; Ovid, *Metamorphoses*, 10.1–85, 11.1–84; Vergil, *Georgics*, 4.453–527; Hyginus, *Poetica Astronomica*, 2.7.]

Orphism. A Greek cult first mentioned in surviving literature in the sixth century B.C. According to an Orphic myth, the evil Titans killed and ate Zagreus, son of Zeus and Persephone. Zeus blasted the Titans with his thunderbolt. From their ashes grew men, who thus incorporated a large portion of Titanic wickedness and a trace element of divinity. It was the mission of men who subscribed to Orphic beliefs to rid themselves of the evil parts of their natures, leaving only the divine part. As might be expected, this effort entailed a long, slow process of self-purgation that required more than one lifetime to accomplish. For those who managed to lead blameless lives, Hades became a kind of purgatory where the soul was purified before entering another body. After living three consecutive lives of resolute virtue, the Orphic believer could expect to be released from the "wheel of birth" by Persephone and allowed to spend eternity in Elysium.

The Orphic cult was said to have been founded by ORPHEUS. It involved various mysteries that were apparently somewhat similar to those of Dionysus. It is likely that they included a symbolic reenactment of the death of Zagreus, especially since Orpheus, too, was torn to pieces in his myth. The Orphic creation myth is too imperfectly known to be told here, and, in any case, it seems to have been largely an artificial construction, although it may have incorporated elements of ancient cult and myth. Orphism seems to have strongly influenced the teachings of Pythagoras and of some later philosophers.

Orthus or **Orthrus.** A two-headed dog. Orthus was an offspring of Typhon and Echidna. With his master, Eurytion, he guarded Geryon's cattle in Erytheia until HERACLES [H] killed them both and stole the cattle. [Apollodorus 2.5.10.]

Ortygia. The original name of the island of Delos, or else of a nearby island created when Asteria fell into the sea as a quail (*ortyx*).

Ortygia. A small Sicilian island that forms a part of the city of Syracuse. The river-god Alpheius, pursuing his beloved nymph Arethusa, flowed under the sea from his native Elis to Ortygia, where he reappeared.

Ossa, Mount. A mountain in northern Magnesia. Ossa was one of three mountains that Otus and Ephialtes piled up when they attempted to storm heaven.

Otreus. A Phrygian king. In Priam's youth, the Trojan king fought with Otreus, who ruled much of Phrygia, and Mygdon, another Phrygian king, against the Amazons at the river Sangarius. When Aphrodite appeared to Anchises she pretended to be a daughter of Otreus. [Homer, *Iliad*, 184–189; *Homeric Hymn to Aphrodite* 5.111–112.]

Otus and **Ephialtes.** Twin giants. While married to Alöeus, Iphimedeia, daughter of Triops, fell in love with Poseidon and poured seawater into her lap until she conceived. Her twin sons grew so rapidly that, by the age of nine, they were about fifty feet tall. They were also badly out of hand. Apparently from sheer pride in their strength, they piled Mount Ossa on Mount Olympus and then Mount Pelion on Ossa and showed every intention of storming heaven. As a preliminary move they captured the war-god, Ares, bound him, and stuffed him into a brazen jar. After thirteen months, the boys' stepmother, Eëriboea, betrayed them to Hermes, who rescued the half-dead Ares. Meanwhile, Otus and Ephialtes were threatening to keep moving mountains until they made the sea into land and the land into sea.

When the brash pair dared to woo Artemis and Hera, respectively, the gods began to take their behavior seriously. Apollo shot them down, or else sent a deer between them so that, in striking at it with their spears, they killed each other. Some say that Artemis herself took the form of the deer. Although the twins' death occurred on the island of Naxos, their bodies were buried at Anthedon, in Boeotia. They were said to have founded the city of Ascra, at the foot of Mount Helicon. Surprisingly, they were also credited with being the first to worship the Muses, at least on this mountain. They recognized only three Muses, instead of the later nine. Otus and Ephialtes were punished in Hades by being bound with snakes to a pillar, back to back. On the pillar sat a screech-owl. [Homer, *Iliad*, 5.385–391, and *Odyssey*, 11.305–320; Apollodorus 1.7.4; Hyginus, *Fabulae*, 28; Pausanias 9.22.6, 9.29.1–2.]

Ovid. A Roman poet who lived during the reign of Augustus. Ovid (Publius Ovidius Naso) was the author of many works, but perhaps the best known is the *Metamorphoses*, a long narrative poem concerned with myths in which the characters changed their forms. Ovid colored his stories with a great number of picturesque details, often inventing incidents and characters and occasionally, perhaps, whole myths. Nevertheless, the *Metamorphoses* is an important source of Greek and Roman mythology.

Oxylus. A king of Elis. A son of Andraemon or of Haemon, Oxylus was banished for a year from his native Aetolia for killing, perhaps accidentally, his brother Thermius or a man named Alcidocus. He took refuge in Elis. On his way home to Aetolia, he met near Naupactus the sons of Aristomachus, leaders of the Heraclids. They engaged him as guide during their invasion of the Peloponnesus, promising him the rule of Elis. Oxylus, who was distantly related to the Heraclids, consented, but led them through Arcadia, fearing that they would regret their generosity if they once saw fertile Elis.

His mission accomplished, Oxylus led a band of Aetolian colonists into Elis, where they met with resistance from King Dius. Oxylus persuaded Dius to let the rule be decided by a single combat between an Aetolian slinger, Pyraechmes, and an Eleian archer, Degmenus. Pyraechmes won and Oxylus became king. Instead of tyrannizing the land, he merely introduced Aetolian colonists. He continued the observance of local religious customs and, on the advice of an oracle, sought out a descendant of the famous Eleian king Pelops —Agorius, great-grandson of Orestes—to share the throne. Oxylus increased the city's prosperity by inducing farmers from neighboring areas to live inside the city. [Apollodorus 2.8.3; Pausanias 5.3.5–5.4.5.]

P

Pactolus River. A tributary of the Hermus River in Lydia. After the Phrygian king Midas bathed away his golden touch in the Pactolus, the sands of the riverbed contained gold. This gold (or electrum) was a traditional source of the fabulous wealth of Croesus, the Lydian king whose capital, Sardis, stood near the Pactolus.

Paeëon or **Paean.** The healing god. Nothing is said of this resident of Olympus except that he quickly healed Hades and Ares of wounds. After Homer and Hesiod, the name became an epithet of other gods—Asclepius, Apollo, or, metaphorically, Thanatos (Death). The first was a divine physician, the last the bringer of final solace; Apollo had both functions. The name Paean (as it came to be commonly spelled) was ultimately transferred from Apollo himself to a hymn sung in the god's honor or as a battle anthem. [Homer, *Iliad*, 5.388–402, 5.899–904; Hesiod, *Fragments*, 2; Apollonius Rhodius 4.1508–1517.]

Paeon. The eponym of Paeonia. A son of Endymion, king of Elis, Paeon lost to his brother Epeius a footrace held by their father to determine the succession to the throne. Exiling himself as far as possible from Elis, Paeon settled north of Macedonia in a land that he named Paeonia. [Pausanias 5.1.4–5.]

Paeonia. A region now in Yugoslavia, between Albania and Bulgaria. Paeonia was founded and named by Paeon, one of the sons of Endymion, king of Elis.

Pagasae. A town at the head of the Thessalian gulf that bears its name. Pagasae seems to have been a port for nearby Iolcus.

Palaechthon. The father of Pelasgus, king of Argos. According to Aeschylus [*Suppliants* 250–251], Palaechton (Old Earth) was born from the earth, as his son was often said to be.

Palaemon or **Palaemonius.** An Argonaut. Palaemon was reputed to be the son of Lernus or Aetolus, both of Calydon, but his true father was Hephaestus, which may have accounted for his lameness. [Apollonius Rhodius 1.202–206.]

Palaemon. See MELICERTES.

Palamedes. A son of NAUPLIUS (1) by CLYMENE (2), daughter of Catreus; by Philyra; or by Hesione. Palamedes was credited by the Greeks with having invented certain letters of the alphabet, dice, and many other useful devices. He was as clever as Odysseus and won the Ithacan's undying hatred by foiling him in the ruse by which he hoped to avoid going to the Trojan War. Palamedes and other envoys from Agamemnon went to Ithaca to enlist Odysseus' support. They found the king wearing a madman's headgear and plowing with a horse and an ox yoked together. Palamedes placed Odysseus' infant son, Telemachus, in front of the plow, or else threatened him with a sword. Odysseus saved the child and thus gave himself away.

At Troy, Odysseus avenged himself on Palamedes by means of an elaborate plot. He pretended to Agamemnon that he had been warned in a dream that the Greek encampment should be moved for one day. When the commander-in-chief had followed his advice, Odysseus buried a large amount of gold where Palamedes' tent had stood. He also wrote a letter, forging the signature of Priam, the Trojan king, and gave it to a Phrygian captive to be delivered to Priam. He then sent a soldier to kill the Phrygian near the Greek camp. The Greek forces, returning that evening from battle, found the Phrygian's body with the letter on it. The letter was taken to Agamemnon. It promised Palamedes a sum in gold if he would betray the Greeks. The innocent man protested that he knew nothing of the letter, but the exact amount of gold mentioned was found where Odysseus had buried it. Convinced of Palamedes' guilt, Agamemnon turned him over to the soldiers, who stoned him to death. Some say that Agamemnon and Diomedes envied and hated Palamedes as much as Odysseus and were involved in the plot. Others claim that Odysseus and Diomedes murdered him while he was fishing.

Nauplius came to Troy to demand some kind of payment for the death of his son, but the Greek leaders turned him away. He avenged himself by inducing several of the leaders' wives to betray them with lovers. Also in revenge, Palamedes' brother Oeax later tried to have Agamemnon's son Orestes killed by the Argives. According to Vergil's *Aeneïd* [2.77–79], the Greek spy Sinon won Trojan confidence by pretending to have earned Odysseus' hatred by speaking out against his treatment of Palamedes. [Hyginus, *Fabulae*, 95, 105, 116; *Cypria* 1, 19; Apollodorus 2.1.5, "Epitome" 3.7–8 and 6.8–9; Ovid, *Metamorphoses*, 13.34–62, 13.308–312.]

Pales. A Roman divinity of flocks and of shepherds. Although Pales was a deity of some prominence among the Romans, it is not certain whether he was male or female.

Palinurus. The steersman of Aeneas' flagship. Palinurus was washed overboard and drowned off the coast of Italy. When AENEAS [B] visited the Underworld, he met Palinurus' ghost and promised him a proper burial. He kept the promise. Capo Palinuro, on the western coast of southern Italy, bears the unfortunate sailor's name to this day.

Palladium. A sacred object preserved at Troy. According to the early mythographer Pherecydes, *palladia* were objects, not made by human hands, which fell from heaven. Other traditions, most of which appear late in Classical writings, regard the Trojan Palladium as a small wooden statue (*xoanon*) of the Phrygian Athena worshiped by the Trojans. Apollodorus described it as three cubits (about four and a half feet) in height. The feet were joined together, and one hand flourished a spear while the other held a distaff and spindle. The same author gave its origin as follows: After her birth from the head of Zeus, the child Athena was reared by the god Triton together with his own daughter, Pallas. The two girls used to practice warlike arts together, but one of their friendly bouts took a serious turn when they lost their tempers. Seeing Pallas about to strike his daughter, Zeus interposed the AEGIS. The startled girl looked away and was struck down by Athena.

The goddess, grief-stricken, made a small image of her dead friend, with its breast wrapped in the aegis, and set it up to be honored next to the image of Zeus himself. Apparently she took it with her to Olympus, for Zeus flung it from heaven when Atlas' daughter Electra clung to it in a vain attempt to avoid his embraces. The Palladium landed before the tent of Ilus, who, having founded the city of Ilium (Troy), had just prayed to Zeus for a sign. Ilus built a temple for it. According to another account, Zeus gave the image to Ilus' great-grandfather Dardanus, the Samothracian founder of Dardania. In either case the image had a place of honor in the Pergamum, the citadel of Troy, where it was carefully guarded.

Near the end of the TROJAN WAR [C] the captured Trojan seer Helenus told the Greeks that Troy would never fall while the Palladium remained within its walls. Odysseus and Diomedes therefore made their way at night into the city and, with the help of Helen, stole the image. After the war, the Greeks claimed to have taken the Palladium with them, but they could not agree on which city received it. The Argives said that Diomedes brought it home with him to Argos. The Athenians, however, said that Diomedes' ships had taken refuge at night in the port of Phalerum, near Athens, which they did not recognize as friendly territory. King Demophon of Athens, thinking the ships were filled with hostile strangers, attacked them, killed several Argives, and carried off the Palladium. It was set up in the city and gave its name to one of the Athenian law courts. The Romans, on the other hand, claimed that the Palladium remained at Troy (the Greeks having stolen only a copy that was kept on public display) until the city's fall. Aeneas rescued it and took it with him to Italy, where it was later displayed in the temple of Vesta in Rome. [Apollodorus 3.12.3, "Epitome" 5.10–13; *Sack of Ilium* 2; Ovid, *Metamorphoses*, 13.337–349; Pausanias 1.28.8–9, 2.23.5.]

Pallantids. See PALLAS (1).

Pallas (1). A son of Pandion and Pylia. Pallas and his brothers Nisus and Lycus aided their eldest brother, Aegeus (actually their half-brother), to drive from Athens the Metionids, who had exiled their father, Pandion. The kingdom was supposedly divided equally among the four, but Aegeus ruled. Nisus became king of Megara. Pallas, and probably Lycus, rebelled against Aegeus. Lycus was exiled, but Pallas, with his fifty sons, the Pallantids, continued their opposition to the king until they were killed by Aegeus' son, THESEUS [G].

Pallas (2). A Titan. Pallas was a son of the Titans Crius and Eurybia. He married the Oceanid Styx and became the father of a family of abstractions—Nike (Victory), Cratus (Strength), Bia (Violence), and Zelus (Emulation)—all of whom were attributes of Zeus. This may also be the Pallas who is called the father of Selene in the *Homeric Hymn to Hermes* [4.99–100], though he is there said to be a son of Megamedes. Some regarded him as the eponym of Achaean Pellene. [Hesiod, *Theogony*, 375–377, 383–388; Apollodorus 1.2.2–4; Pausanias 7.26.12.]

Pallas (3). One of the GIANTS. In the war between gods and Giants, Athena killed Pallas, flayed him, and used his tough skin as a shield. This improbable tale was perhaps advanced to explain both the goddess' most often used epithet, Pallas (see PALLAS, 4), and her use of the aegis, which was made of skin. This Pallas may have been regarded as the eponym of the peninsula of Pallene, though that region is generally associated with another Giant, Alcyoneus. [Apollodorus 1.6.2.]

Pallas (4). The most commonly used epithet for Athena. Pallas may be an early Greek word for girl. An attempt to explain this title may lie behind the tales of Athena's accidental killing of Pallas, a girl companion (see PALLADIUM), and her defeat of one of the Giants of the same name, whose skin she thereafter wore as armor. Some scholars have suggested that Pallas may have been the name of the Hellenic goddess with whom the invading Greeks equated the goddess Athena, whom they found firmly intrenched in Attica.

Pallas. See EVANDER; PALLADIUM.

Pallene. The westernmost of three peninsulas jutting into the Aegean Sea from Chalcidice. Pallene was the home of the Giant Alcyoneus, who was battled there by Heracles in the war between gods and Giants. According to Vergil, the sea-god Proteus lived part of the time in Pallene.

Pamphylus. See AEGIMIUS.

Pan. An Arcadian shepherd-god. Pan was a son of Hermes by Penelope or by the daughter of Dryops, of Zeus and Hybris, or of various other parents. In the second version, his goat legs and horns so frightened his mother when he was born that she ran away, but Hermes proudly took the baby to Olympus and showed it off to the other gods. Pan lived in the mountains, where he danced and sang with the nymphs and played his pipes. This instrument, the *syrinx* or Pan pipes, resulted from one of the god's many amorous forays. While hunting near Nonacris he had come upon a beautiful nymph named Syrinx. He approached her, but she fled, wanting to remain a virgin huntress. Unable to cross the Ladon River, she begged the local nymphs to transform her into marsh reeds. They did so, and Pan had to content himself with fastening several lengths of the reeds together with wax and producing a new instrument. He became so proud of his virtuosity on the pipes that he spoke slightingly of Apollo's prowess on the lyre. This rash remark led to a contest, judged by Tmolus, in which Pan was defeated.

Pan once lured Selene into the Arcadian woods by showing, and presumably promising, her a beautiful white fleece. According to Pindar [*Fragments* 95], Pan was a favorite companion of the Mother of the Gods and the Graces. It was he who discovered Demeter's hiding place in a cave near Phigalia and told Zeus, who sent the Fates to persuade her to return to Olympus. One day, when a famous Athenian runner named Philippides or Pheidippides was crossing Mount Parthenius, Pan appeared to him and demanded to know why the Athenians did not honor him, since he had befriended them in the past and would do so again. Philippides reported this conversation to the Athenians. Pan came to their aid at Marathon shortly thereafter. The Athenians gratefully established a shrine to the god under the Acropolis and honored him with sacrifices and torch races. Pan's customary method of overcoming an enemy force was to infect it, by means of a shout, with a sudden, unreasoning terror, or "panic," a word derived from the god's name. He is said to have used this weapon effectively against the Titans during their war against the gods.

These exploits of Pan took place either in his native Arcadia or in heaven. (The single exception, his contest with Apollo, may have grown out of confusion with a similar contest between Apollo and the Panlike Phrygian demigod Marsyas.) Two other stories, taking place in Egypt and Asia, are told of AEGI-PAN (Goat-Pan), who may originally have been a quite different character from the Arcadian god, though they were often identified with one another.

Because Pan was adopted late into the official pantheon, he was counted, along with Dionysus and Heracles, as one of the youngest of the gods. Undoubtedly, however, he was an ancient Arcadian god of shepherds and their flocks. His name (though Classical authors often derived it from a word meaning "all") meant "He Who Feeds." His association with Hermes may have been early, since that god (or possibly a local god who was assimilated into Hermes' cult) had also long been connected with Arcadia. The patrician Penelope of the *Iliad* is so far removed from the milieu of the rather uncouth mountain god Pan that her identification as his mother may have been due to confusion with another Penelope, possibly the "daughter of Dryops" who is Pan's mother in the *Homeric Hymn to Pan* [19]. Obvious resemblances between Pan and the Satyrs, the Seileni, and Priapus led to his being occasionally found in their company. He was sometimes multiplied into Panes.

Pan came to be a favorite figure with pastoral poets, but myths concerned with him are relatively few. Some of them are to be found in Herodotus [2.145, 6.105–106], Ovid [*Metamorphoses* 1.689–712, 11.146–179, 14.-635–641], Vergil [*Georgics* 3.391–393], Apollodorus [1.4.1, "Epitome" 7.38], and Pausanias [1.28.4, 8.36.8, 8.42.2–3, 8.54.6–7, 10.23.7].

Pancratis. A daughter of Alöeus and Iphimedeia. Pancratis and her mother were carried off by Thracian pirates to Strongyle (Naxos), where two of the pirate leaders killed each other over the beautiful girl. Agassamenus, the king, married Pancratis. Not long afterward her half-brothers, Otus and Ephialtes, avenged her and Iphimedeia by taking the island, but Pancratis died. [Diodorus Siculus 5.50.6–5.51.2.]

Pandareüs. A king of Miletus, in Crete. Pandareüs is mentioned by Homer, but his story is known only from late Classical commentators. He stole a golden dog from a shrine of Zeus. Presumably for this offense, he and his wife were killed by the gods. Aphrodite took pity on their daughters and brought them up, but when she left them to go to Olympus to arrange marriages for them, the Harpies carried them off and turned them over to the Erinyes. Before this unhappy event, one of the daughters, Aëdon, had married Zethus, the co-king of Thebes, and had borne a son, Itylos. She accidentally killed him and, because of her profound grief, was changed into a nightingale, which forever cries his name. Zethus' wife is often said to have been Thebe. [Homer, *Odyssey*, 19.518–523, 20.66–77; Pausanias 10.30.1–2.]

Pandarus. The leader of the forces of Zeleia, in Lycia, at the Trojan War. Pandarus' father, King Lycaon of Zeleia, tried to persuade him to take a chariot and horses, but, fearing that the horses would not have enough to eat, he chose to go on foot, as a bowman. Next to Paris, Pandarus was the best of the Trojan archers. It was he who, urged on by Athena (who was acting under Zeus's orders), broke a truce by shooting at Menelaüs. Later he rode with Aeneas in an attempt to kill Diomedes, but was himself killed by that Greek leader. [Homer, *Iliad*, 4.85–140, 5.166–296.]

Pandion (1). A king of Athens. Pandion was the son of Erichthonius and the naïad Praxithea. He married Zeuxippe, his mother's sister, and they had four children: Procne, Philomela, and twin sons, Erechtheus and Butes. (Erechtheus, however, is often called earthborn.) During a war over boundaries with the Theban king Labdacus, Pandion called on the Thracian Tereus for aid and gave him the hand of Procne. Demeter and Dionysus were said to have come to Attica during Pandion's reign. At his death he bequeathed the rule to Erechtheus and the priesthoods of Athena and of Poseidon Erechtheus to Butes. [Apollodorus 3.14.6–3.15.1.]

Pandion (2). A king of Athens. Pandion, the son of Cecrops and Metiadusa, daughter of Eupalamus, succeeded his father in ruling Athens, but was soon deposed by the mutinous sons of his uncle Metion. Pandion fled to Megara, where he married Pylia, daughter of King Pylas. This king killed his uncle Bias shortly thereafter and had to flee, leaving Pandion to succeed to the rule. Pylia bore Nisus, Aegeus, Pallas, and Lycus. Aegeus was thought to be a son of Scyrius, but Pandion acknowledged him as his own son. Pandion died at Megara and was succeeded by Nisus. His other sons returned to Athens and drove out the sons of Metion.

This Pandion is said by many scholars to have been (like his father) no more than a name invented to fill a gap in the mythical history of Athens. This view is supported by the fact that Pausanias [1.5.2–4] identifies him as the father of Procne and Philomela, who are usually called daughters of Erichthonius' son Pandion. [Apollodorus 3.15.5–6.]

Pandora (1). The first woman. When PROMETHEUS improved the lot of men by various tricks on the gods, Zeus avenged himself on the human race by inventing women. Hephaestus made her, the other gods gave her a variety of wicked traits, and Hermes took her to Epimetheus, who foolishly accepted her as his bride. Pandora, whose name means "all gifts," brought with her as dowry a jar filled with all sorts of evils, which she released on earth, keeping only hope inside. This, at any rate, is the story told by Hesiod [*Theogony*, 570–612, and *Works and Days*, 47–105], who took a dim view of the female sex.

Pandora (2). A daughter of Deucalion. By Zeus Pandora was the mother of Graecus, eponym of the Greeks. [*Catalogues of Women* 2.]

Pandorus. See ERECHTHEUS.

Pandrosus. A daughter of Cecrops and Agraulus (1). Unlike her sisters, Agraulus and Herse, Pandrosus was faithful to her promise to Athena not to spy on ERICHTHONIUS. She was honored on the Acropolis with an enclosure adjacent to the Erechtheüm in which Athena planted her olive tree. [Apollodorus 3.14.2, 3.14.6; Pausanias 1.18.2.]

Pangaeüs, Mount. A mountain in western Thrace. Lycurgus was torn to pieces by horses on Mount Pangaeüs when his mistreatment of Dionysus and his followers brought famine on his land.

Panopeus. The eponym of the Phocian village of Panopeus. When Panopeus' father, Phocus, was murdered in Aegina, his sons emigrated to Phocis. Panopeus took part in the Calydonian boar hunt and was an ally of Amphitryon in his raid on the Teleboans. Panopeus' daughter, Aegle, married Theseus; his son, Epeius, built the wooden horse at Troy. [Pausanias 2.29.4; Apollodorus 2.4.7.]

Panthoüs. A Trojan elder. Panthoüs, a son of Othrys, was a priest of Apollo. He was the father, by his wife, Phrontis, of Polydamas, Euphorbus, and Hyperenor. [Homer, *Iliad*, 3.146, 14.454–455, 17.9–81; Vergil, *Aeneïd*, 2.318–336, 2.429–430.]

Paphos. A city of Cyprus. The founding of Paphos is attributed to several mythical personages. The city was the chief center of the worship of Aphrodite on Cyprus.

Paraebius. A loyal vassal of Phineus. Paraebius lived a hard life and grew steadily poorer however hard he worked. He came for advice to Phineus, the seer-king of Thynia, and was told that his father had long before chopped down a tree, ignoring the pleas of the Hamadryad who lived in it. The dying nymph had cursed him and his family. Paraebius made sacrifices to appease the nymph and began to prosper. He remained forever grateful to Phineus and took care of him when the old man was plagued by the Harpies. [Apollonius Rhodius 2.456–489.]

Parcae. See FATES.

parentes or **di parentes.** See MANES.

Paris. The second son of Priam and Hecuba; also called Alexander or Alexandrus.

A. Hecuba's first child by Priam, king of Troy, was Hector. When she was about to bear a second, she had a disturbing nightmare in which she gave birth either to a firebrand, which set fire to the city, or to a hundred-handed monster, who razed it. Priam called on Aesacus, his prophetic son by Arisbe, to explain the portent. (Some say that the seer consulted was either a sibyl named Herophile or Priam's daughter Cassandra, who, in that case, must have been older than Paris.) The soothsayer warned that the child to be born would be the destruction of Troy and recommended that he be killed. Priam therefore gave the infant at birth to Agelaüs, one of his shepherds, to expose on Mount Ida. Agelaüs followed his instructions, but, on returning to the spot after five days, he discovered the baby still alive. It had been suckled by a she-bear. The shepherd could not bring himself to kill the child, so he took it to his farm and reared it as his own. The child grew to be a strong and incredibly handsome youth. His bravery in defending the flocks he tended from robbers and wild animals won him the name Alexander (Defender of Men).

One day servants of King Priam appeared and started to drive away Paris' finest bull. They explained that the king was about to hold funeral games in honor of a long-dead son and the bull was to be offered as the prize. Since Paris could not refuse the king's command, he followed the men in the hope of winning the bull back. The young shepherd entered the games against many noble contenders, including the king's sons, and won every contest. Priam's sons were furious that a commoner should surpass them at the kind of sports in which highborn young men excel. One of them, Deïphobus, drew his sword, and Paris was forced to take refuge at the altar of Zeus of the Courtyard. Fortunately his prophetic sister Cassandra recognized that the stranger was their own brother. Priam and Hecuba welcomed Paris into the family. The young man married the nymph Oenone, daughter of the river-god Cebren, and settled down to the pleasant life of a handsome prince of a wealthy city.

B. Paris did not reckon with the ways of the gods, and his parents seemed to have forgotten the warnings of the seer that this youth was born for the destruction of his city. At this moment in Phthia, across the Aegean Sea, the gods were attending the wedding of the mortal Peleus and the goddess Thetis. One goddess, Eris (Strife), who had not been invited, avenged herself by throwing a GOLDEN APPLE into the midst of the guests. When it was found to bear the inscription "For the fairest," three goddesses immediately claimed it: Hera, Athena, and Aphrodite. Zeus, wishing to avoid trouble, commanded the goddesses to present themselves to Paris, the world's handsomest man, and let him decide which was the loveliest. The young man was keeping his flocks on Mount Ida when Hermes appeared (and some say Apollo as well) leading the three goddesses. Hermes explained the situation.

The idea of relying on the judge's unbiased opinion seems not to have occurred to anyone, for the contestants immediately began to offer bribes to the judge. Hera promised to make Paris ruler of the world if he would award her the apple. Athena vowed that he would always be victorious in war if he chose her. Aphrodite, as goddess of love, had less imposing gifts at her disposal, but what she had to offer was well suited to Paris' temperament: the love of the most beautiful woman in the world. This was Helen, daughter of Tyndareüs, the former king of Sparta, who had had most of the young princes of Greece as her suitors before she chose Menelaüs for his money. Paris hesitated hardly a moment before ruling that Aphrodite was the loveliest of the goddesses.

When Paris went home to the palace and announced that he was sailing for Sparta to bring back the wife of Menelaüs, his family were considerably disturbed, particularly his brother and sister Helenus and Cassandra, both seers, and his wife, Oenone, who had been taught the art of prophecy by Zeus's mother, Rhea. These three predicted a terrible doom for both Paris and Troy if he carried out his rash plan. The young man paid no attention. When his wife saw that she could not persuade him, she told him to return to her on Mount Ida if he should ever be hurt, for only she would be able to heal him. Paris sailed for Sparta.

C. On his arrival in the Lacedaemonian capital, Paris was first entertained by the famous Dioscuri, Helen's brothers, and then by her husband, who was now king of Sparta. After nine days Menelaüs had to sail for Crete to preside at the funeral of his grandfather Catreus, but he hospitably told Helen to take care of the guest. During his absence Aphrodite proved as good as her word. She saw to it that the Spartan queen should fall madly in love with the handsome visitor. Before Menelaüs could return, the lovers sailed away, taking with them a good supply of the palace treasure. Some say that Hera, guardian of marriages, sent a great storm that drove the ship far off course to the port of Sidon, in Phoenicia. Paris captured the city, stayed for a time, and also stopped briefly in Cyprus in order to elude Spartan pursuit. Others claim that the entire journey to Troy, aided by favorable winds, took only a miraculous three days, perhaps due to the intervention of Aphrodite. A yet stranger version of the voyage has it that Helen never reached Troy at all. Hera, still angry at Paris for not awarding her the beauty prize, gave him a phantom Helen made of cloud. The true Helen remained in Egypt, while Greeks and Trojans waged a long war over the phantom.

The leaders of the principal Greek cities, many of whom had once been Helen's suitors, now gathered together a great navy and sailed for Troy to recover the supposedly kidnaped queen. Many Trojans, after ten years of fighting, would gladly have given Helen back to Menelaüs. Paris, however, refused, though he was willing to return the treasure, and Priam supported him. In the actual fighting Paris' record was unimpressive. At the insistence of Hector he met Menelaüs in single combat, but Aphrodite spirited him away to save his life. He confined himself for the most part to archery and occasionally wounded a Greek. Near the end of the war he killed Achilles, the archer-god Apollo having guided his hand on the bow. Some say, however, that Paris and Deïphobus treacherously killed Achilles when he came to the palace to sue for the hand of their sister Polyxena.

Some time later Paris was himself mortally wounded by an arrow from the bow of Philoctetes. He recalled the words of his abandoned wife, Oenone, and had himself carried to Mount Ida. Oenone refused to heal him and he returned to die at Troy. Regretting her anger Oenone hurried after him with healing drugs, but arrived too late. She hanged herself from remorse. Paris' body is said by some to have been mutilated by Menelaüs, but recovered and buried by the Trojans.

Paris appears in only one extant Greek play, Euripides' *Rhesus*, and there only briefly and insignificantly. He is, however, frequently referred to in other literary works. He appears prominently in Homer's *Iliad* [3.15–382, 3.46–58, 6.312–364, 6.503–529, 7.347–364, 11.368–383, 22.355–360]. The most connected account of his exploits is given by Apollodorus [3.12.5–6, "Epitome" 3.1–5, 5.8]. The story of his birth, his later recognition, and his judgment of the goddesses is told in Euripides' *Trojan Women* [920–932], *Andromache* [274–308], and *Helen* [22–30], and in Hyginus' *Fabulae* [91, 92, 110]. See also *Little Iliad* 1 and *Cypria* 1, 9, 10.

Parnassus, Mount. A mountain in Phocis. Parnassus is particularly famous for the fact that Delphi, the site of an ancient oracle, clings to its steep face. It was regarded as a favorite place of both Apollo and the Muses. Deucalion's boat ran aground on Parnassus when the Flood subsided.

Parthaon. See PORTHAON.

Parthenius, Mount. A mountain in eastern Arcadia. As children, both Parthenopaeüs and Telephus, the sons respectively of Atalanta and Auge, were exposed on this mountain. Pan appeared to the Athenian Philippides as the runner was crossing Parthenius.

Parthenopaeüs. One of the SEVEN AGAINST THEBES. Although the *Thebaïd* [7] calls him a son of Talaüs, the handsome Arcadian youth Parthenopaeüs is generally said to have been a son of Atalanta by Melanion, Meleager, or the god Ares. According to Hyginus, he was exposed after birth on Mount Parthenius by his mother so that she might still be thought a virgin. Telephus, Auge's son by Heracles, was exposed near by and the two children, rescued by shepherds, became close friends. Parthenopaeüs accompanied Telephus to Teuthrania and helped him to defeat Idas' attack on that kingdom. Parthenopaeüs was the father of Promachus, one of the Epigoni, or of Tlesimenes by a Mysian nymph, Clymene. He was killed at Thebes by Periclymenus, Asphodicus, or Amphidicus. [Hyginus, *Fabulae*, 70, 71, 99.]

Pasiphaë. A daughter of Helius and Perseïs. Pasiphaë married Minos, king of Crete, and became the mother of Catreus, Androgeüs, Deucalion, Glaucus, Acacallis, Xenodice, Ariadne, and Phaedra. When her husband offended Poseidon by failing to sacrifice to him a handsome bull, the god caused Pasiphaë to fall in love with the beast. DAEDALUS [A] made her a hollow wooden cow, inside which she was able to satisfy her passion. As a result, she gave birth to the Minotaur, a bull-headed man, which Minos imprisoned in the Labyrinth. Later Pasiphaë grew annoyed at her husband's many amours and, true sister of Circe that she was, bewitched him, causing him to impregnate his unfortunate paramours with poisonous vermin. Pasiphaë was worshiped as a moon goddess at Thalamae, in Laconia, and, like her daughter Ariadne, may have been regarded as divine in Crete, as well. [Apollodorus 3.1.2–4, 3.15.1; Pausanias 3.26.1.]

Patrae. A large seaport of Achaea on the Gulf of Patrae. The original ruler of the region was the earthborn Eumelus, who learned from Triptolemus to grow corn and founded the towns of Aroë and Antheia. Patrae (on the site of the modern city of Patras) was founded by Patreus, a Spartan who came to the area with the Achaeans. Patrae included Aroë within its walls, but the nearby old towns of Antheia and Mesatis were depopulated. [Pausanias 7.18.2–5.]

Patrae, Gulf of. The gulf separating the northwestern Peloponnesus from the mainland to the north.

Patreus. The founder and eponym of PATRAE, in Achaea. Patreus and his father Preugenes, Spartan descendants of Lacedaemon, shared with Tisamenus in the Achaean invasion of Ionia.

Patroclus. The son of Menoetius. Patroclus' mother is variously said to have been Sthenele, daughter of Acastus; Periopis, daughter of Pheres; Polymele, daughter of Peleus; or Philomela, which is perhaps merely a variant name for Polymele. As a boy, Patroclus accidentally killed Clitonymus, son of Amphidamas, in a quarrel during a game of dice. He and his father, forced to flee their home in Opus, were welcomed by Peleus, king of Phthia, who purified the boy of murder. Patroclus was made the squire of Peleus' young son, Achilles, and in time became his lover. When Achilles, still a youth, went to the Trojan War, Menoetius sent Patroclus with the hot-headed prince as an adviser. Patroclus fought bravely, but withdrew from the war along with Achilles until he saw the Trojans attacking the Greek ships. He then asked and received permission to go into battle wearing Achilles' armor. Patroclus caused a great rout of the Trojans, who at first mistook him for Achilles. He killed the Lycian king Sarpedon and three times led the Greeks up to the walls of Troy, but was at last wounded by Euphorbus and killed by Hector. A fight raged for hours over his naked corpse before the Greeks were able to rescue it. Achilles refused to bury the body (which Thetis embalmed with ambrosia) or to eat until he had avenged himself on the Trojans. At the funeral he killed twelve Trojan men on the grave. The bones were buried, later to be mixed with Achilles' own. Some say that Patroclus and Achilles, immortalized, lived together with other heroes of the Trojan War on the White Island in the Black Sea. [Homer, *Iliad*, 11.599–848, 15.390–404, 16.1–18.355, 19.23–39, 23.-62–107; Apollodorus 3.13.8; Pausanias 3.19.13, 3.24.10; Hyginus, *Fabulae*, 97.]

Pausanias. A Greek travelogue writer. Pausanias, who was probably a Lydian Greek, visited parts of Greece in the second half of the second century A.D. and wrote a long account of his travels, known as the *Description of Greece*. In the ten books of this work he described Attica, Boeotia, Phocis, Locris, and the entire Peloponnesus. Pausanias took pains to deal with the mythological associations of the sites that he visited, so his work is an important source of information on both myth and cult. It is available in a good translation by W. H. S. Jones in the Loeb Classical Library. James G. Frazer also translated the work, which, with copious notes, fills six volumes.

Pegasus. A winged horse. Pegasus and the warrior Chrysaor sprang from the neck of Medusa, who was pregnant by Poseidon when Perseus cut off her head. Hesiod thought that he was named for the springs (*pegai*) of Oceanus. A favorite of the Muses, he created the spring Hippocrene on Mount Helicon, and another of that name at Troezen, with a stamp of his hoof. He was tamed by BELLEROPHON [B, C] or broken by Athena or Poseidon. Pegasus carried Bellerophon during his famous exploits, but, when his master tried to ride him to heaven, the horse, stung by a gadfly sent by Zeus, threw him to earth. Pegasus continued to Olympus, where he carried thunderbolts for Zeus. [Hesiod, *Theogony*, 280, 325; Pindar, *Olympian Odes*, 13.63–92.]

Peirithoüs. A king of the Lapiths. Peirithoüs was a son of Dia by Ixion, Zeus, or Aepytus. He succeeded Ixion as king of the Lapiths in the region of Larisa, in Thessaly. The Centaurs, who lived in neighboring Magnesia, demanded a share of the kingdom, since they, too, were offspring of Ixion. Peirithoüs refused and, with his Lapiths, went to war against the Centaurs. A peaceful settlement, on some unrecorded grounds, was eventually reached. At some point Peirithoüs became a bosom companion of Theseus, the young king of Athens. They hunted the Calydonian boar together and Peirithoüs helped Theseus to carry off the Amazon Antiope. Later he married Hippodameia, daughter of Butes. He invited the Centaurs to the wedding, and they, unused to drinking wine, became violent. Eurytion or Eurytus, one of their leaders, tried to carry off the bride; his companions followed his example with the young Lapith women who were her attendants. A tremendous battle ensued in which the Lapiths, aided by Theseus, killed many Centaurs and drove the others from the region, though at considerable loss to their own numbers.

Hippodameia bore Peirithoüs a son, Polypoetes, who fought in the Trojan

War. It is otherwise not clear what happened to her, but Peirithoüs and Theseus made a vow that they would both marry daughters of Zeus. Theseus decided on the twelve-year-old Helen and Peirithoüs helped him to kidnap her
from her father's palace in Sparta. Peirithoüs, who had always tended to scoff
at the gods, made a far rasher choice: Persephone, queen of the Underworld.
Together with his friend, he went down to Hades through the entrance at
Taenarum and announced his intentions to Hades, Persephone's husband.
Hades blandly invited the interlopers to sit down. Unsuspecting, they sat on
the chairs of forgetfulness, stone seats to which they were bound with chains
or snakes or to which their naked flesh grew fast. There they remained and,
according to some accounts, were tortured for their presumption by the
Erinyes. In time Heracles came to Hades to fetch Cerberus. He either persuaded Hades to grant the companions their freedom or else grasped Theseus'
hand and tore him loose from his chair. When Heracles tried to do as much
for Peirithoüs, however, the ground quaked and he was afraid to persist. Peirithoüs remained a perpetual prisoner in the Underworld. [Apollodorus 1.8.2,
2.5.12, "Epitome" 1.21–24; Homer, *Iliad*, 14.317–318; Pausanias 1.2.1, 3.18.-
15, 10.29.9–10; Ovid, *Metamorphoses*, 12.210–535; Hyginus, *Fabulae*, 33,
79.]

Peisidice. A daughter of the Thessalian king Aeolus. Peisidice married Myrmidon and bore him Antiphus and Actor. [Apollodorus 1.7.3.]

Pelasgians. A name given by most Classical writers to the supposed aboriginal inhabitants of Greek lands. The Pelasgians were variously located in
many parts of Greece. The Dorians insisted that the IONIANS of Attica were
Pelasgians, and the Athenians themselves claimed to be autochthonous. Pelasgus, eponym of the Pelasgians, was said to have been an early king of Argos,
Arcadia, or Thessaly. Other regions said to have been originally Pelasgian
were Dodona, in Epeirus, and several parts of the northern Aegean area, including both sides of the Hellespont. Homer listed an apparently Thracian
group of Pelasgians as allies of the Trojans and mentioned other Pelasgians
from Crete. Later the name Pelasgians came to be applied to all pre-Greek inhabitants of Greece. The fact that all the early references to specific Pelasgian
groups located them in northern Greece suggests that they entered Greece
from the north, but it does nothing to identify them or to indicate what their
relationship, if any, was to the pre-Hellenic inhabitants who had Anatolian or
Cretan connections, as many of them almost certainly had.

Pelasgus. The eponym of the Pelasgians, the aboriginal inhabitants of
Greece. The Pelasgians are said to have occupied several regions of Greece
and the legends about Pelasgus vary accordingly. He was claimed as king by
the Arcadians, the Argives, and the Thessalians. Among the many parents who
were ascribed to him in various localities were Zeus and Niobe. The Arcadians, who had the fullest traditions of his exploits, called him autochthonous.
They said that during his rule he invented huts and sheepskin coats and

weaned the aborigines from their diet of grasses, leaves, and roots by teaching them to eat acorns. By the nymph Cyllene or the Oceanid Meliboea, Pelasgus became the father of Lycaon. Aeschylus followed one of the Argive traditions in his *Suppliant Women* by making Pelasgus a king of Argos who welcomes Danaüs and his daughters on their arrival and defends them against Aegyptus. [Apollodorus 2.1.1, 3.8.1; Pausanias 8.1.4, 8.2.1.]

Peleus. A king of Phthia, in Thessaly.

A. Peleus was a son of Aeacus, king of Aegina, and Endeïs. He and his brother, Telamon, plotted to kill their half-brother, Phocus, either because he excelled them in sports or merely to please their mother. One brother or the other murdered Phocus with a stone quoit during a contest, and together they hid his body. Aeacus learned of the crime and banished both. Telamon settled in the nearby island of Salamis, but Peleus wandered with his followers and flocks as far as Phthia. There King Eurytion, or his father, Actor, purified him of murder and gave him his daughter, Antigone, in marriage, along with one third of his land. Antigone bore a daughter, Polydora. According to Ovid [*Metamorphoses* 11.266–288, 11.346–409], Peleus went from Aegina to Trachis, where Ceÿx, king of Oeta, entertained him. Psamathe, Phocus' sea-nymph mother, sent a wolf to destroy Peleus' flocks. The fugitive tried vainly to appease her with prayers and sacrifice. Finally, Psamathe's sister Thetis, who later married Peleus, interceded for him and Psamathe turned the wolf to stone.

Telamon rejoined his brother on the voyage of the Argonauts and again at the Calydonian boar hunt. This last adventure ended badly, for Peleus accidentally killed his father-in-law, Eurytion, and did not dare return to Phthia. He wandered to Iolcus, where he was welcomed and purified by King Acastus, who had been one of Peleus' fellow Argonauts. Peleus might have remained there had not Acastus' wife, Astydameia or Hippolyte, fallen in love with him. When Peleus repulsed her she sent word to Antigone that Peleus was about to marry Acastus' daughter, Sterope. Antigone killed herself from grief.

Not content with this revenge, Astydameia told her husband that Peleus had violated her. Because it would have been an impious act to kill a man whom he had purified, Acastus plotted an indirect means of accomplishing the same end. He took Peleus hunting on Mount Pelion, a region where wild tribes of centaurs roamed. In order to tire his guest, Acastus proposed a contest to see who could kill the most game in a single day. Peleus saved himself the trouble of carrying his kills back to camp by cutting out their tongues and keeping them in his pouch. When he returned at the appointed hour, his opponents laughed to see him apparently empty-handed. Peleus calmly emptied the pouch and proved that he had killed more game than any other contestant.

The hunters now lay down to rest. When Peleus was asleep, Acastus took his guest's sword, made for him by Hephaestus or Daedalus, and hid it under a heap of cow dung. Then he and his Iolcan retainers stole away, leaving Peleus unarmed where hostile centaurs would be sure to find him. The centaurs did, in fact, appear, and would have killed Peleus had not their king, the wise Cheiron, saved him. Cheiron also found the sword and gave it back to Peleus. Some tell the improbable tale that Peleus went alone to Iolcus, killed Acastus, and destroyed the city. The more plausible version has it that Peleus delayed his vengeance until he was joined in the venture by his fellow Argonauts Jason and the Dioscuri. He then killed Astydameia, cut her body in half and marched his army between the pieces, and turned over Iolcus to the Haemonians.

B. Peleus now returned to Phthia, where he became king. (He had perhaps been exiled for only one year, a standard punishment for murderers.) He now received an honor reserved for few mortals: marriage to a goddess. Not long before, Zeus had fallen in love with the beautiful sea-nymph Thetis. Through loyalty to Hera, who had reared her, Thetis had fled from his advances, or else Zeus had been warned that the nymph was fated to bear a child who would be greater than his father and so restrained himself. For one reason or the other, Zeus and Hera decided to marry off Thetis at once—and to a mortal. Apparently they did not expect Thetis to be elated at this news, for they did not mention it to her. Through either Cheiron or Proteus, the Old Man of the Sea, they let Peleus know that, if he would seek out Thetis while she was sleeping in her favorite sea-cave on the Magnesian coast, and would hold her fast regardless of the forms she assumed, he would have her for a wife. Peleus took this advice. Thetis, captured in her sleep, became successively fire, water, a lioness, and a tree, but finally succumbed to Peleus' persistence and consented to become his wife.

The gods, no doubt relieved that a goddess of Thetis' disturbing destiny was safely betrothed, came in person to the wedding, which was held on Mount Pelion. They brought a number of splendid gifts, among them a jeweled crown for Thetis and the immortal horses Xanthus and Balius for Peleus. Only once before had the gods attended a wedding, that of Cadmus and Harmonia. In view of an unfortunate event that occurred on the present occasion, it is hardly surprising that the gods never again honored a mortal in such a fashion. Zeus had invited all the gods except Eris, the goddess of discord, whom no one liked. Eris came anyway, bearing a golden apple inscribed "For the Fairest." The divine rivalries that were provoked by this sly device would lead, after the famous judgment of Paris, to the Trojan War, in which would be killed, among many other young Greeks, Achilles, the son of the happy couple whose marriage was being celebrated.

Fortunately Peleus and Thetis did not know what fate held in store. For a considerable time they lived happily in Phthia. Thetis, however, was not pleased at the prospect of bearing a merely mortal child. According to the lost poem *Aegimius* [3], she bore several and dipped them at birth into a pot of boiling water to see whether they had inherited their father's mortality. They had. After losing several children this way, Peleus took a stand when Achilles was born and refused to agree to further experiments.

The more familiar story is that Thetis placed the infant Achilles, her only child, in the fire at night and anointed him with ambrosia by day, hoping by these means to make him immortal. (Another account claims that she dipped the baby in the river Styx, thus immortalizing every part of his body except the heel by which she held him.) Peleus, happening upon his wife placing his son on the coals, gave an indignant cry. Thetis was so enraged that she left her husband forever and returned to the sea. She occasionally showed a friendly interest in his affairs, however, and helped him out of difficult situations. As for the child, Peleus gave him to his old benefactor Cheiron to rear.

C. Peleus, perhaps recalling his own wanderings in exile, welcomed more than one suppliant in similar straits. The most important of these was Phoenix, son of Amyntor, king of Ormenium, who fled his homeland after severe quarrels with his father. Peleus made him king of the Dolopians and, according to one story, induced Cheiron to restore the exile's vision, Amyntor having blinded him. According to Homer, Phoenix was principally responsible for Achilles' education. Epeigeus, king of Budeum, was similarly welcomed after being exiled because of a murder. Somewhat later, the boy Patroclus came with his father, Menoetius, from Opus, having killed a playmate in a game of dice. When Achilles returned from Cheiron's period of tutelage, Patroclus became his squire and lover.

The last years of Peleus were saddened by the fate of his son. Thetis, who was, according to some accounts, still married to Peleus, knew that Achilles would die if he went to the Trojan War. She therefore sent him to the court of Lycomedes, king of the island of Scyrus, where he was reared in the disguise of a girl. When warriors were being recruited for the coming expedition, Odysseus discovered the youth by a trick and won his promise to fight. Peleus had the unhappy fortune to outlive his son. As an old man he was driven from Phthia by the sons of Acastus, who thus avenged Acastus' death and Peleus' destruction of Iolcus. According to Euripides' *Andromache*, Peleus remained at Phthia but turned over the rule to his grandson Neoptolemus. During the young king's absence, the old man protected his concubine, Andromache, from the plots of his wife, Hermione, and her father, Menelaüs. In the end he was invited by Thetis to join her in the depths of the sea and share her immortality.

Although Peleus appears as a character in extant works only in *Andromache* and, briefly, in the *Argonautica* of Apollonius Rhodius, he is mentioned in innumerable works. Apollodorus gives the most connected account of his career [3.12.6–3.13.8, "Epitome" 6.1]. His wedding is described in Euripides' *Iphigeneia in Aulis* [700–707, 1036–1047]. Homer [*Iliad* 9.432–484, 18.-

570–576] speaks of his kindness to Phoenix and Epeigeus. Pausanias details the murder of Phocus [2.29.2–10].

Pelias. A king of Iolcus. Pelias was one of the two sons of Poseidon and TYRO, daughter of Salmoneus. Pelias and his twin, Neleus, were exposed by their mother in a field. There they were found by horse herders, one of whose mares had trampled Pelias' face, leaving a livid mark (*pelios*). It was this mark that gave the child his name. When they grew to manhood, the brothers discovered their mother; their identity was confirmed when she recognized the basket in which she had exposed them. They learned that Tyro had long been abused by her stepmother, Sidero. Enraged, they pursued this woman to the precinct of Hera, and there Pelias killed her, even though she clung to the altars for sanctuary. Not content with this outrage to Hera, Pelias ignored the honors due the goddess throughout his long life—an impiety which brought down upon him a terrible, if belated, punishment.

Pelias' violent nature and his lust for power led him to persecute both Neleus and their half-brother Aeson. Either before or after the twins' birth, Tyro had married her uncle Cretheus, king of Iolcus, the most powerful city in Thessaly. The eldest of the sons she bore him was Aeson. As Cretheus' legitimate child, Aeson should have inherited the throne. Pelias prevented this, apparently through intimidation, though it was many years before he dared to kill Aeson. Aeson's brothers were not strong enough to oppose Pelias; Amythaon migrated to Messenia, Pheres founded the city Pherae near Iolcus. When Neleus put in a claim to the throne, Pelias turned on his twin and drove him out of the country. Neleus and his followers went to Messenia and carved out a kingdom for themselves at Pylus. The undisputed rule of Iolcus now belonged to Pelias.

Aeson's wife bore a son, but it was mourned as dead at birth, so Pelias felt no alarm. He married either Anaxibia, daughter of Bias, or Phylomache, daughter of Amphion, and she bore him a son and several daughters. These daughters are variously named by different writers; only one, Alcestis, became well known in her own right. The boy was named Acastus.

Setting about to dominate Thessaly, Pelias became one of the most powerful Greek kings of his day, but his pleasure in this position was shattered by a prediction of the Delphic oracle that an Aeolid wearing one sandal would one day bring about his death. This oracle was fulfilled when JASON came to Iolcus wearing one sandal and demanded the throne. He revealed that he was Aeson's son, who had not died but had been reared secretly by Cheiron the Centaur. Pelias tricked the young man into setting out on a voyage to Colchis to fetch the golden fleece—a journey that Pelias believed would be Jason's last. In his absence Pelias killed Jason's father and brother Promachus, a mere boy; Aeson's wife committed suicide. Jason returned, however, bringing with him MEDEA, a Colchian sorceress. This event was part of the plan that Hera had concocted to destroy her enemy Pelias. Medea quickly carried out the goddess' revenge by persuading the king's daughters to kill their father in the expectation that she would restore his youth. Instead she turned the city over to Jason and the Argonauts. Jason in turn either voluntarily gave the throne to Acastus or was driven out of the city by Pelias' son and the Iolcans. Though Pelias' impiety brought him at last to a terrible death, he had enjoyed a long and prosperous rule. His son and successor, Acastus, celebrated funeral games in Pelias' honor that were among the most famous ever held.

Pelias was mentioned by Homer in both the *Iliad* [2.714–715] and the *Odyssey* [11.254–257]. The story of his early life is most fully told by Apollodorus [1.9.8–10, 1.9.15–16]. Sources for the rest of his career are found under the entries for JASON and ADMETUS.

Pelion, Mount. A mountain in central Magnesia. Cheiron, the wise Centaur, reared several of the young princes of Greek cities in his cave on this mountain. Pelion was the scene of Acastus' unsuccessful attempt to cause the death of Peleus. In the plan of Otus and Ephialtes to scale heaven, Pelion was the topmost of their pile of three mountains.

Pella. A city in Macedonia. Pierus was king of Pella and learned the lore of the Muses there and in Thrace before emigrating to Pieria, in the region of Mount Olympus. Pella was later made the capital of Macedonia by Philip II.

Pelopia. A daughter of Thyestes and mother by him of Aegisthus. See ATREUS [C].

Pelops. A king of Pisa.

A. A son of TANTALUS (1) by either Dione or a Pleiad, Pelops was cut up by his father and served to the gods in a stew as a test of their omniscience. All of them saw through this trick at once except Demeter, who ate a piece of the child's shoulder. The gods quickly restored him to life, and Demeter gave him a new shoulder of ivory. The youth was now so beautiful that Poseidon carried him off to Olympus. Later, however, Pelops was sent back to earth because of his father's crimes. Pausanias claims that Pelops was driven from his homeland of Lydia by the army of Ilus—presumably the king of that name who founded Ilium.

B. Having heard of the beauty of Hippodameia, the daughter of Oenomaüs, king of Pisa, Pelops determined to win her, and with her the land of Elis, which would be her dowry. Oenomaüs either was in love with his daughter or had been warned by an oracle that he would die by the hand of the man who married her. He therefore arranged a hazardous test for her suitors. Each had to take up Hippodameia in his chariot and make for the distant Isthmus of Corinth. Oenomaüs, wearing full armor given him by Ares, followed with his swift horses. If he overtook the suitor he killed him and nailed his head over the door of his palace. So far the king had disposed of twelve or thirteen rivals for his daughter's hand.

Before setting out for Pisa, Pelops prayed for help to his patron, Poseidon.

The god gladly gave him a golden chariot drawn by winged steeds. When he reached Pisa, Pelops was nevertheless disconcerted at the sight of his predecessors' heads arrayed over Oenomaüs' door. Prudently he struck up an acquaintance with the king's charioteer, Myrtilus, a son of Hermes. Myrtilus, he found, was in love with Hippodameia, and greedy as well. When Pelops offered him half the kingdom and a night in Hippodameia's bed, the charioteer agreed to betray his master. (Some say that it was Hippodameia herself who bribed him, having fallen in love with Pelops.) Before the race Myrtilus either deliberately neglected to insert the bronze linchpins in the wheels of Oenomaüs' chariot or else substituted pins of wax. As Pelops galloped away with Hippodameia beside him, the king leaped into his own chariot to pursue this new rival with his usual deadly intent. Before he had gone far, a wheel fell from the axle and Oenomaüs, entangled in the reins, was dragged to his death (although some writers say that Pelops turned around and killed the helpless king). Dying, Oenomaüs cursed Myrtilus for his treachery and prayed that he might die by the hand of the man he had befriended.

C. As the husband of Hippodameia, Pelops inherited the throne of Pisa. It is said, however, that before accepting the rule he subdued most of the rest of the peninsula and named the entire region Peloponnesus (The Island of Pelops) for himself. Unable to conquer Arcadia, he pretended friendship with its king, Stymphalus, treacherously murdered him, and scattered his limbs abroad. This deed brought a famine on the land that was ended only by the prayers of the pious king Aeacus. Pelops also became king of Elis and thus dominated much of the Peloponnesus.

For all his power, Pelops did not rest easily on the throne because of a deed he had committed after winning Hippodameia. Myrtilus had not failed to remind him of his promises. Pelops, who no longer needed the charioteer's help, had no intention of keeping them. He invited Myrtilus to ride with him and as they were passing over the sea Pelops pushed him in. Because the large sea south of Attica was sometimes called the Sea of Myrto, many believe that Pelops must have flung Myrtilus into the water there from his winged chariot. The practical-minded traveler Pausanias preferred to believe the more reasonable story of the inhabitants of Arcadian Pheneüs, that Myrtilus was pushed from a boat near the harbor of Elis. Wherever the deed was done, Myrtilus, as he fell, invoked a curse on the descendants of Pelops.

The new king lived in fear of this curse. He journeyed as far as the river Oceanus at the ends of the earth to be purified by Hephaestus of the deed. Anticipating the anger of Myrtilus' father, Hermes, Pelops instituted the worship of Hermes in the Peloponnesus. At Olympia, which was under Eleian jurisdiction, he raised a mound in Myrtilus' honor beside the racecourse, and some writers said that it was the charioteer's ghost who repeatedly scared the horses there during the Olympic games, just as Oenomaüs' horses had been frightened by Myrtilus' destruction of the chariot (see TARAXIPPUS). Yet none

457

The Principal Descendants of Pelops

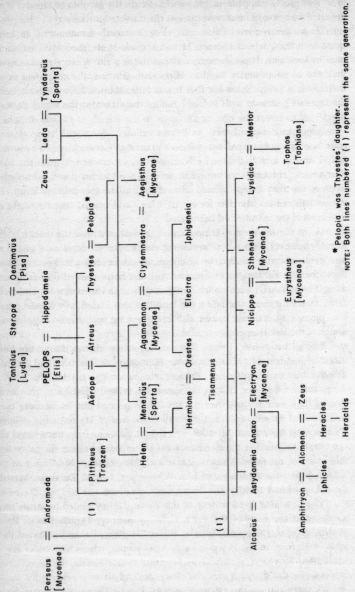

Tantalus [Lydia]

Perseus = Andromeda [Mycenae]

Sterope = Oenomaüs [Pisa]

Zeus = Leda = Tyndareüs [Sparta]

Pittheus [Troezen]

PELOPS = Hippodameia [Elis]

Aërope = Atreus

Thyestes = Pelopia*

Aegisthus [Mycenae]

Helen = Menelaüs [Sparta]

Agamemnon = Clytemnestra [Mycenae]

Hermione

Electra

Iphigeneia

Orestes

Tisamenus

Astydameia = Alcaeüs

Anaxo = Electryon [Mycenae]

Zeus = Alcmene

Nicippe

Sthenelus [Mycenae]

Eurystheus [Mycenae]

Lysidice = Mestor

Taphos [Taphians]

Amphitryon =

Iphicles

Heracles

Heraclids

* Pelopia was Thyestes' daughter.

NOTE: Both lines numbered (1) represent the same generation.

of Pelops' acts of appeasement could prevent the terrible working out of the curse in the house of his son ATREUS to the third generation.

D. At the request of his wife, Pelops raised a monument to her vanquished suitors, whom Oenomaüs had shoveled into the earth without ceremony. Pausanias shrewdly suggests that the monument served also as an advertisement to posterity of the number of prominent young men who had failed before Pelops succeeded. Hippodameia instituted the Heraean games at Olympia in gratitude to Hera for having brought about the marriage with Pelops.

Pelops and Hippodameia were said in later generations to have been the parents of many heroes, among them the eponyms of Epidaurus, Sicyon, Troezen, Cleonae, and the Eleian city of Letrini. Pelops was also called by some the father of the Isthmian bandit Sceiron, of the Megarian king Alcathoüs, and of Copreus, Eurystheus' herald. One of Pelops' shrewdest political moves was to marry several of his daughters to the sons of Perseus, which led in time to the ascendancy in Argolis of the house of Atreus. By Alcaeüs, Astydameia was the mother of Amphitryon and of Alcmene's mother, Anaxo; Lysidice bore Taphius, eponym of Taphos, to Mestor; Nicippe married Sthenelus and was the mother of Eurystheus, king of Mycenae, who was thus a Pelopid as well as a Perseïd ruler. Perhaps the most powerful of Pelops' children by Hippodameia were Pittheus, who became king of Troezen, and the brother-enemies Atreus and Thyestes. Pelops also had an illegitimate son, Chrysippus, whom Hippodameia hated. After the abduction of Chrysippus by the banished Theban LAÏUS, who loved him, Hippodameia is said to have persuaded Atreus and Thyestes to kill their half-brother, though others deny this. Pelops must have believed it, for Hippodameia either killed herself or took refuge with her guilty sons, who were then ruling Midea.

E. Nothing is recorded of Pelops' death. After it, however, he was one of the most revered of Greek heroes. His shrine at Olympia, said to have been established by his great-grandson Heracles, was known far and wide. During the Trojan War, the seer Helenus predicted that Troy would not fall to the Greeks until, among other magical objects, a bone of Pelops was brought there from Elis. For this cause the Eleians parted with his shoulder blade. As it was being returned after the ensuing victory, the bone was lost off Euboea. Years later a fisherman named Dardamenus brought it up in his net and, on the advice of the Delphic oracle, gave it back to the Eleians. They gratefully made him and his descendants guardians of the bone in perpetuity. [Apollodorus, "Epitome" 2.3–10; Pindar, *Olympian Odes*, 1; Pausanias 5.13.1–7; and many other references.]

Pelops. See AGAMEMNON [C].

Pelorus. See SPARTI.

penates or **di penates.** Roman gods of the storeroom. In early Roman times the storeroom (*penus*) was located at the center of the house. The gods that guarded it, together with Vesta, the goddess of the hearth, were regarded as the protectors of the welfare of the household. They were therefore honored by each family at meals and on special occasions. Since the state was conceived of as an extension of the king's household, the penates were also publicly honored as the *penates publici*. See also LARES.

Peneius. A Thessalian river and its god. Like most river-gods, Peneius was a son of Oceanus and Tethys. He was the father by the nymph Creüsa, a daughter of Ge, of three daughters—Cyrene, Daphne, and Stilbe—and one son, Hypseus. The Peneius flowed eastward through the Vale of Tempe, which was renowned for its beauty.

Peneleüs. A Boeotian leader. Peneleüs was the son of Hipalcimus and Asterope, of whom nothing else is known. In his youth, he and his cousin Leïtus sailed with the Argonauts. Because both had been suitors of Helen, they were obliged to aid Menelaüs, and together Peneleüs and Leïtus led a contingent of fifty Boeotian ships to the Trojan War. Peneleüs commanded the Theban troops because Tisamenus, son of Thersander, was too young for this post. Fierce in battle, Peneleüs killed two Trojan leaders but was himself killed by Eurypylus. [Homer, *Iliad*, 2.494, 14.486–507, 16.335–341; Pausanias 9.5.14–15; Apollodorus 1.9.16, 3.10.8.]

Penelope. The wife of ODYSSEUS. Penelope was the daughter of Icarius, a Spartan king, and her name became synonymous with fidelity to a husband. After marrying Odysseus, she went with him to Ithaca in spite of the urging of her father that she remain with him in Sparta. She had a son, Telemachus, by Odysseus. When her husband did not return from the Trojan War, her palace was filled with unwanted suitors, who lived off Odysseus' wealth. For three years she avoided their pleas by pretending to weave a shroud for her father-in-law, Laërtes, but when they eventually learned that she was raveling it out at night, they forced her to finish it. Just as both she and Telemachus, who was reaching manhood, began to think that she would have to choose one of the suitors, Odysseus returned secretly and killed them all. Penelope was reunited with him and bore a second son, Acusilaüs or Ptoliporthes. When Odysseus, as an old man, was killed unintentionally by Telegonus, his son by Circe, Telegonus took Penelope and Telemachus to Aeaea, Circe's home, where they buried Odysseus. Telegonus then married Penelope, and Telemachus married Circe. According to some accounts, Penelope had a son by Telegonus, Italus, eponym of Italy. Circe made her and Telemachus immortal.

The Mantineians of Arcadia tell a very different story of Penelope's last years. They claim that Odysseus, finding that his wife had been unfaithful with either Antinoüs or Amphinomus, divorced her. Penelope went home to Sparta, and thence to Mantineia, where she gave birth to the god Pan, having lain at some point with Hermes. She died and was buried in Arcadia. This local tradition was, however, completely opposed to the accepted view of Penelope's character.

Penelope appears prominently in the Ithacan books of Homer's *Odyssey*. See also Pausanias 3.20.10–11, 8.12.6; *Telegony* 1, 2; Apollodorus, "Epitome" 7.31–39; Hyginus, *Fabulae*, 126, 127.

Penthesileia. An Amazon queen. A daughter of Ares and Otrere, Penthesileia accidentally killed her ally Hippolyte (or Melanippe or Glauce), another Amazon queen. She came to Priam at Troy and was purified by him of the bloodshed, perhaps in return for her promise to aid him in the Trojan War. She became one of the most valuable of the Trojan allies, killing many Greeks, including, according to some reports, Machaon. Achilles killed her, but fell in love with her corpse. When Thersites jeered at his infatuation, Achilles killed him with a single blow. [Apollodorus, "Epitome" 5.1–2; *Aethiopis* 1.]

Pentheus. A king of Thebes. In his old age, Cadmus abdicated the throne of Cadmeia (later Thebes) in favor of Pentheus, the son of his daughter Agave and Echion, foremost of the Sparti. Pentheus, an arrogant young man, not only refused to honor the god Dionysus, son of his aunt Semele, but forbade the women of Cadmeia to join in the frenzied rites of the bacchants who roamed with the god. This injunction had no effect whatever. Pentheus' mother and his aunts, Ino and Autonoë, rushed to Mount Cithaeron with the bacchants, and even Cadmus and the old seer Teiresias were converted to Dionysus' rites. Pentheus retaliated by imprisoning the bacchants, but the prisoners' chains fell off and the jail doors were mysteriously opened. When the king tried to spy on the bacchants' revels, Dionysus had a terrible revenge. Agave and her sisters, seeing Pentheus hiding in a tree, imagined in their madness that he was a wild beast. They pulled him down and tore him to bits. For this deed they were exiled from Thebes. Pentheus was succeeded by his uncle, Polydorus.

Pentheus' story is the subject of Euripides' tragedy *The Bacchants*, with which all other sources substantially agree.

Penthilus. An illegitimate son of Orestes and Erigone. Penthilus was the father of Echelas and Damasias. Agorius, Damasias' son, was invited by Oxylus to share the throne of Elis.

Perdix. An Athenian inventor. Perdix, who is also called Talus or Calus, was the son of Daedalus' sister, also named Perdix. He was apprenticed to his uncle, the most ingenious craftsman of his day. The young man, inspired by his observations of a fish spine or the jawbone of a snake, invented the saw. He is sometimes also credited with the invention of the compass and the potter's wheel. Daedalus grew envious of his nephew and flung him off the Acropolis. Athena changed Perdix into a partridge (*perdix*). [Apollodorus 3.15.8; Ovid, *Metamorphoses*, 8.236–259.]

Pereus. See ALEÜS.

Pergamon or **Pergamum.** An important city of ancient Mysia, now called Bergama. Pergamon, formerly called TEUTHRANIA, was conquered and renamed by Pergamus, a son of Neoptolemus and Andromache.

Pergamus. The youngest son of Neoptolemus and Andromache. Since his elder brothers inherited his father's kingdom, Pergamus left Epeirus with his mother and migrated to Mysia. There he conquered Teuthrania, killing King Areius, and renamed the city Pergamum. [Pausanias 1.11.2.]

Periboea (1). The wife of Polybus, a king of Corinth or Sicyon. Periboea, who is often called Merope, was the foster mother of OEDIPUS [A].

Periboea (2). A daughter of Hipponoüs, king of Olenus. There are three conflicting versions of Periboea's marriage to Oeneus, king of Calydon. According to one, Oeneus took her as a prize of war, after sacking Olenus. Another version relates that he seduced her and her father sent her to him. The third version has it that Hipponoüs, learning that his daughter was pregnant by Amarynceus' son (or descendant) Hippostratus, sent her to Oeneus with orders to kill her, but the king, who had recently lost his wife and son, married her instead. Periboea was the mother of Olenias and probably of Tydeus. [Apollodorus 1.8.4–5.]

Periclymene. A daughter of Minyas. Periclymene was the mother of Admetus and three other children by Pheres, king and eponym of Pherae. She may be the same as Clymene.

Periclymenus (1). A Theban champion in the war with the Seven. A son of Poseidon, Periclymenus killed Parthenopaeüs and would have killed Amphiaraüs as well, had Zeus not intervened. (See SEVEN AGAINST THEBES, D.) [Apollodorus 3.6.8.]

Periclymenus (2). One of the twelve sons of Neleus, king of Pylus. Periclymenus was one of the Argonauts. He was granted by his grandfather Poseidon the power to change his shape at will in battle. When Heracles attacked Pylus, Periclymenus fought him in many forms. At last he became an eagle and tore at Heracles' face, but Heracles, acting on Athena's advice, shot him down with an arrow. [*Catalogues of Women* 10; Ovid, *Metamorphoses*, 12.556–572.]

Perieres. A king of Messenia. Some claim that Perieres was a son of the Spartan king Cynortas, but he is generally called a son of Aeolus and Enarete. At the death of Polycaon, the Messenians called on Perieres to take the throne in their capital of Andania. He married Perseus' daughter, Gorgophone, and they had two sons, Aphareus and Leucippus. Perieres was the father also of Borus, Halirrhothius, and Pisus, founder of Pisa. Although some say that this Aeolid Perieres was also the father of Tyndareüs and Icarius, they are more often called sons of Gorgophone by her second husband, Oebalus, who was the son of a second Perieres, son of Cynortas. The genealogy of Perieres, Oebalus, and their sons is, however, almost hopelessly confused, perhaps because it was later invented to justify conflicting claims to the thrones of Sparta and Messenia. [Apollodorus 1.9.5, 3.10.4; Pausanias 2.21.7, 4.2.2–4.]

Perigune. A daughter of Sinis, the Isthmian outlaw. After THESEUS [B] killed her father, Perigune bore him a son, Melanippus, ancestor of the Ioxids of Caria.

Perimede. A daughter of Oeneus. According to the early Greek poet Asius, Perimede married Phoenix, king of Phoenicia, and became by him the mother of Europa and Astypalaea. [Pausanias 7.4.1.]

Perimele or **Perimede.** A daughter of Aeolus and Enarete. Perimele was seduced by Acheloüs, the Aetolian river-god, and bore two sons, Hippodamas and Orestes. On learning of this, her father flung her into the sea at the outer edge of the Strophades. As a result of Acheloüs' prayers to Poseidon, she became an island. Perimele was an ancestor of the royal house of Calydon. [Ovid, *Metamorphoses*, 8.590–610; Apollodorus 1.7.3, 1.7.10.]

Periopis. A daughter of Pheres, king of Pherae. According to one account she was the mother by Menoetius of Patroclus. [Apollodorus 3.13.8.]

Periphas. A Thessalian king. Periphas, a son of Lapithes and Orsinome, ruled in the region of the river Peneius. His wife, Astyagÿia, daughter of Hypseus, bore him eight sons, the eldest of whom, Antion, became the father of Ixion. [Diodorus Siculus 4.69.2–3.]

Periphetes. A lame Epidaurian outlaw. A son of Hephaestus and Anticleia, or of Poseidon, Periphetes was killed by THESEUS [B]. He was called Corynetes for the bronze or iron club that he carried.

Pero. A daughter of Neleus, king of Pylus, and Chloris. Pero was courted by all the young men of Messene, but BIAS won her, with the aid of his brother MELAMPUS [B]. Pero and Bias had Talaüs and several other children.

Perse or **Perseïs.** A daughter of Oceanus and Tethys. Perse was one of the innumerable daughters of these ancient gods. Together with their brothers, the river-gods, Perse and her sisters were patrons of youths. To Helius Perse bore Circe, Pasiphaë, Aeëtes, and, presumably, Aeëtes' rather obscure brother, Perses. [Homer, *Odyssey*, 10.135–139; Hesiod, *Theogony*, 346–356, 956–957; Apollodorus 1.9.1.]

Persephone. A goddess of the Underworld. Persephone was the only child of Zeus and Demeter. Carried off by Hades, who had her father's consent, she lived with him a third of the year, but spent the rest with her mother. (For this part of her story, see DEMETER.) Her return to earth, and the consequent sprouting of the crops in spring, after the seed had remained in the ground all winter, was celebrated in many rites shared by mother and daughter, notably the Eleusinian mysteries and the Thesmophoria. In these rituals, Persephone's name was not spoken, except, perhaps, at the secret ceremonies reserved for initiates. She was referred to simply as Kore (Maiden). The Romans called her Proserpina.

In the story of her abduction and the trick by which Hades forced her to spend a part of each year with him, Persephone was the unwilling victim torn from her mother. But although she was said to spend a half or two thirds of each year on earth, there are no myths concerned with her stay there. Apart from the tales of her rape and the rites celebrating her return to earth, she always appeared in myths as the dread goddess of the Underworld. Some accounts, indeed, called her a daughter of Zeus and Styx, the goddess of the Underworld river of the same name, which would suggest that her home had always been in Hades. Persephone, even more than Hades himself, seems to have controlled the activities of the spirits of the dead. Occasionally she sent them to the upper world, and she returned at least one dead woman—Alcestis —to life. On the other hand, she is said to have taken a woman named Ethemea to Hades alive after Artemis had shot her. (This story is too sketchy, however, to be interpreted.) Persephone was often invoked in curses. Orestes and Electra, for example, prayed to Ge (Earth) to send up their father, Agamemnon, to watch them kill his murderer, Aegisthus, and asked Persephone to give them victory.

There is an ironic echo of Persephone's life on earth in the tale of her quarrel with Aphrodite over Adonis, who, like herself, was a spirit of the dying and reviving vegetation. Aphrodite placed the infant in a chest and gave him to Persephone for safekeeping in Hades. Persephone peeked inside and, on discovering how handsome the boy was, refused to give him up when Aphrodite came for him. Aphrodite took her case to Zeus, who decreed that Adonis should spend a third of his life with Persephone in the Underworld, a third with Aphrodite, and a third by himself.

Peirithoüs rashly undertook to carry Persephone back to the land of the living as his own bride. Hades, however, quickly trapped him and his companion Theseus in the Chairs of Forgetfulness. Theseus was later rescued by Heracles, but Peirithoüs, the chief culprit, remained forever in Hades.

Although the two sides of Persephone's character seem contradictory today (and may result in part from a fusion of different myths), they did not appear so to the early Greeks. The seeds of the crops on which their lives depended were, like their dead, buried in the earth, but they came up again each spring. It was natural enough to give credit for this miracle to the gods (and even to the spirits of dead heroes) who lived beneath the earth. The name of Persephone's half-brother, Plutus, and the epithet of her husband, Pluto, mean "wealth"—the wealth of the grain and other crops that they yearly sent up from below.

For sources, see the citations in the entry on DEMETER; see also Homer, *Iliad*, 9.457, 9.568, and *Odyssey*, 10.492–495, 10.510, 11.213–218, 11.225–227, 11.632–635; Hesiod, *Theogony*, 767–774, 908–911.

Perses (1). The eldest son of Perseus and Andromeda. Born at the Ethiopian court of his grandfather Cepheus, Perses remained there when his parents left and eventually inherited the throne. He was said to be the ancestor of the Persian kings. [Apollodorus 2.4.5.]

Perses (2). A king of Colchis. A son of Helius and Perse, Perses was the brother of Aeëtes, Circe, and Pasiphaë. According to some writers he was king of the Taurians. At some time after the raid of the Argonauts on Colchis, Perses deposed Aeëtes and made himself king of that city. He was warned by an oracle that one of his brother's descendants would kill him. Aeëtes' daughter Medea or her son Medus did so. Medea restored Aeëtes to power, or else Medus claimed the throne. [Apollodorus 1.9.28; Hyginus, *Fabulae*, 27.]

Perses (3). A son of the Titans Crius and Eurybia. Perses was the father of Hecate by Asteria. [Hesiod, *Theogony*, 375–377, 409–411.]

Perseus. A king of Mycenae and Tiryns.

A. Perseus' mother, Danaë, bore him in a brazen cell in which her father, ACRISIUS, king of Argos, had imprisoned her on learning from an oracle that a son of Danaë would kill him. Although Danaë claimed that Perseus was a son of Zeus, who had visited her as a shower of gold, Acrisius set mother and child adrift in a chest. Zeus saw to it that the chest floated safely across the sea to the island of Seriphus, where it was found by a kindly fisherman, Dictys. Dictys took the castaways into his home and Perseus, to whom his mother had given the added name of Eurymedon, grew to manhood there. One day King Polydectes, Dictys' lustful brother, saw Danaë and wanted to marry her, but she was unwilling and the king did not dare to oppose Perseus, who defended his mother's decision. He therefore falsely announced that he intended to sue for the hand of Hippodameia, daughter of the Pisan king Oenomaüs, and required all his subjects to contribute horses toward the bride-gift. Perseus, who owned no horses, rashly promised to bring anything else that the king might ask, even to the head of the Gorgon Medusa. Polydectes eagerly accepted this offer, knowing that no man had ever returned alive from an encounter with the Gorgons.

B. Perseus was now faced with a nearly impossible task. The Gorgons were an invincible foe for an ordinary mortal: on foot he could not get near them; to escape after a battle would be impossible, for they would follow on golden wings. To kill Medusa one would need to attack invisibly and then flee faster than her sisters could fly. Moreover, anyone who glimpsed a Gorgon's face would instantly be turned to stone. But Perseus had the help of Athena, who had her own reasons for hating Medusa. She appeared to him and explained how to proceed against the Gorgons.

Following Athena's directions Perseus traveled to the Libyan mountain on which Atlas stood. There, in a cave, he found the Graeae, two hags who had been gray-haired from birth. They shared a single eye and a single tooth between them. Knowing that, as sisters of the Gorgons, they would not willingly aid him, Perseus snatched the eye as one passed it to the other. Thus he was able to force them to tell him what no one else knew, the whereabouts of the nymphs who kept certain weapons that Athena had spoken of. Once he had this information, Perseus either returned the eye or flung it into Lake Tritonis and went off to find the nymphs.

The nymphs readily gave Perseus what he asked for: a large wallet or pouch that he slung over his shoulder; a pair of winged sandals, which enabled him to fly; and the cap of darkness, which made him invisible as soon as he placed it on his head. Hermes appeared and gave Perseus the last weapon, a sword or sickle of adamant. (Some writers claim that it was Hermes who lent Perseus the cap and sandals, his own, because he found the youth attractive.) Perseus kept his own bronze shield. Fully equipped, he flew off to find the Gorgons.

Their lair was surrounded with the petrified forms of men and animals that had looked at the Gorgons' faces. Perseus avoided this danger by keeping his eyes on the highly polished surface of his shield, in which the scene was clearly but safely reflected. Invisible, he soon found the Gorgons, hideous monsters with hands of brass and wings of gold; huge tongues lolled from their mouths between swine's tusks, and their heads were entwined with snakes. Perseus waited until they were asleep; then, avoiding the two immortal Gorgons, Stheno and Euryale, he crept toward Medusa. Watching her in his shield, he cut off her head with a single blow of the sickle, stuffed it into the wallet, and flew off. The other Gorgons rose into the air, but, unable to pursue an invisible attacker, they returned to mourn their sister.

C. Ovid claims that, as Perseus was flying away with Medusa's head, he stopped for the night in the land of the Hesperides, ruled by the Titan Atlas. When Atlas learned that Perseus was a son of Zeus, he tried to eject him forcibly from his land, for the all-knowing goddess Themis had warned him that a son of Zeus would one day steal his most precious possession, the golden apples of the Hesperides. Perseus was angered at this rudeness, but he was no match for the giant's strength. He therefore snatched Medusa's head from the wallet and held it up. Atlas was transformed into a mountain, which grew until its peak was lost in the clouds. It is known today as Mount Atlas. This tale is self-contradictory, however, for Atlas was alive generations later when Heracles, another son of Zeus, made Themis' prophecy come true.

Instead of returning directly to Seriphus, Perseus flew eastward over Egypt, stopping in Chemmis to visit the home of his ancestors Danaüs and Lynceus. As a result, the people of Chemmis were, in Herodotus' day, the only Egyptians to worship Perseus.

D. The youth came next to the land of King Cepheus, called Ethiopia, which was on a seacoast, or was an Ethiopian colony at Joppa, on the coast of Syria. Cepheus, like Perseus himself, was descended from Danaüs' father, Belus. His wife Cassiopeia was so vain that she had boasted of being more beautiful than the Nereïds. Insulted, the sea-nymphs had complained either to Poseidon or to the horned Libyan god Ammon, who sent a sea-monster to ravage the land. Cepheus learned from Ammon's famous oracle that only the sacrifice of his daughter, Andromeda, would save his people, and the Ethiopians forced him to chain the girl naked to a rocky cliff as an offering to the monster.

It was at this point that Perseus flew by. Glimpsing the tiny figure far below, he made a hasty landing. The grieving parents told him the story, as the sea-monster was approaching through the waves. Pausing only long enough to strike a bargain with Cepheus—the girl's hand in marriage and a kingdom in return for her rescue—Perseus leaped into the air and dived on the monster. After a violent but brief battle, he killed it and quickly released Andromeda. (The people of Joppa later claimed that the spring in which Perseus washed the blood from his hands ran red ever afterward.) Cepheus held a great banquet in Perseus' honor, but the young man soon learned that, in his eagerness to save his daughter, the king had failed to mention that he had already promised Andromeda's hand to his brother, Phineus. When Phineus came to the banquet to claim his bride, Cepheus slipped out the door, leaving Perseus to defend himself in the great battle that ensued. Perseus and the few Ethiopians who sided with him were greatly outnumbered. Shouting to his allies to shield their eyes, he tore Medusa's head from its pouch and held it high. At once his enemies were turned to stone.

Perseus remained in Cepheus' land for nearly a year, and Andromeda bore him a son, Perses. The girl loyally resisted her parents' efforts to persuade her to stay with them and returned to Seriphus with Perseus. They left Perses to inherit the throne, for Cepheus had no children. Herodotus says that it was from Perses that the Persians took their name. When Cepheus and Cassiopeia died, Poseidon placed them, together with the sea-monster, in the sky as constellations. This is a doubtful honor for the vain queen. Poseidon arranged it that during much of the year Cassiopeia seems to be lying on her back with her feet in the air.

E. At last Perseus returned to Seriphus. He found that, as soon as he seemed safely out of the way, King Polydectes had openly pursued Danaë. Some say that he had forced her to marry him, others that she and the loyal Dictys had taken refuge at the altars of the gods, where the king dared not harm them. Perseus left Andromeda with his mother and Dictys and went directly to the palace, where the king was banqueting with his friends. Announcing to the unbelieving company that he had brought the promised bride-gift, he held up the severed head. Polydectes and all his court were turned to stone.

Having no further use for the weapons, Perseus gave them to Hermes, who returned them to the nymphs. The youth gave Medusa's head to Athena in gratitude, and the goddess placed it in the center of her aegis. Perseus then left Dictys on the throne of Seriphus and sailed with his wife and mother to his native Argos. In spite of the cruel treatment that he and Danaë had received from Acrisius, Perseus bore his grandfather no ill-will. Acrisius, however, had heard of Perseus' exploits and feared that he was returning to seek revenge. He fled to the town of Larisa, but Perseus followed him there, leaving Danaë and Andromeda in Argos. When he arrived, King Teutamides was holding funeral games in honor of his father. Perseus, proud of his skill at discus-throwing (a sport that some say he invented), took part. During the game the wind blew the discus astray, or else Acrisius stepped into its path. The discus struck him on either the head or the foot, and the fate that the king had tried so hard to circumvent overtook him: he died at the hand of his daughter's son.

Perseus buried his grandfather either in the sanctuary of Athena at Argos or outside the city. Ovid claims that Acrisius had been driven from his capital by his brother, Proëtus, and that Perseus avenged his grandfather by turning Proëtus to stone. Hyginus' account of the events of Perseus' life is unusual. He records that Polydectes was a benevolent king who married Danaë and had Perseus brought up in the temple of Athena. When Perseus was grown, Acrisius learned of his whereabouts and pursued him to Seriphus, but Polydectes interceded for Perseus, and Acrisius was satisfied when his grandson vowed never to harm him. The result was the same, however: while Acrisius was detained on Seriphus by a storm, Polydectes died, and it was at his funeral games that Perseus accidentally killed Acrisius. As in Ovid's version, Perseus petrified Proëtus to avenge Acrisius, but Proëtus' only son, Megapenthes, later avenged his father by killing Perseus.

F. According to the usual account, Perseus was ashamed to inherit the throne of Argos from the man whom he had killed, so he traded the kingdom for Proëtus' city of Tiryns, which Megapenthes now ruled. He settled down there with Andromeda and ruled for many years, establishing as well the city of Mycenae and fortifying Midea, both near by. Andromeda bore him a daughter, Gorgophone, and five sons besides Perses: Alcaeüs, Mestor, Electryon, Sthenelus, and Heleius. Several of these children had famous descendants, though the rule of the Perseïd dynasty in Argos ended with the death of Eurystheus, Perseus' grandson.

Little more is known of Perseus himself, except that he fought against the Women of the Sea, a strange band from the Aegean Islands who came to Argos with Dionysus. A truce must have been reached, for the Argives built a sanctuary to the god, whom they called "Cretan" Dionysus. They claimed, in fact, that Dionysus buried his wife, Ariadne, in Argos. Whatever may have been his end, Perseus was remembered as one of the greatest Argive heroes. Athena arranged that Perseus and Andromeda were placed at their deaths among the stars, where they rejoined Cepheus, Cassiopeia, and the sea-monster.

As early as Homer's day the legend of Perseus was one of the most widely known Greek myths. Aeschylus wrote a tetralogy about Perseus' career, and Sophocles and Euripides each wrote at least one play on some aspect of it, but almost nothing remains of these works. Ovid recounted in his highly romanticized fashion the parts of the story that appealed to him, but a consecutive account of the events of Perseus' life can be found only in the *Library*, by the mythographer Apollodorus. [Apollodorus 2.4; Ovid, *Metamorphoses*, 4.5; Hyginus, *Fabulae*, 63, 64, 244.]

Pessinus. A city in the interior of Anatolia on the slopes of Mount Dindymus. Pessinus was associated with the strange story of Cybele and Attis. Cybele was called Agdistis in this region after Agdus, a rocky outcropping of Dindymus.

Petelia. A city north of Crotona, in southern Italy. Petelia and nearby Crimissa were traditionally founded by Philoctetes, who emigrated to Italy after the Trojan War.

Peteüs. See MENESTHEUS.

Phaea. See CROMMYONIAN SOW.

Phaeacians. A seafaring people who lived on the island of Scherië. Scherië, also called Drepane, was identified in classical times with Corcyra (Corfu), though Homer's description clearly suggested that the Phaeacians lived at some far end of the sea. They were led there by their king Nausithoüs, a son of Poseidon by Periboea, after being driven from their home in Hypereia by their aggressive neighbors the Cyclopes. There may have been an alternative tradition that the Phaeacians were autochthonous to the island, born of the blood of Uranus when the sickle with which he was castrated was buried on Drepane (Sickle). They were loved by the gods, who often appeared in person among them at their sacrifices. The skill of the men as sailors was fabulous, and the women were equally clever at the domestic arts. Because of the gods' esteem, the Phaeacians feared no enemies.

Nausithoüs had two sons, Rhexenor and Alcinoüs. Rhexenor was killed by Apollo when still a bridegroom. His posthumous daughter, Arete, married her uncle, Alcinoüs, who succeeded Nausithoüs as king. Alcinoüs was much influenced by his wise wife. It was she who persuaded him to aid the Argonauts when they were caught at Drepane by the Colchians, and later she won his help for the shipwrecked Odysseus, who was found at the seashore by their daughter, Nausicaä. The Phaeacians had so long been hospitable to mariners in distress that they had incurred the anger of Poseidon. An oracle reported that the god had sworn one day to cut off the city from its two harbors if the inhabitants did not change their ways. When they risked this fate once more to carry Odysseus home in one of their swift ships, Poseidon turned the ship to stone as it neared port on its homeward voyage. Homer leaves the Phaeacians trying to fend off a worse fate with sacrifices. It is not known what happened, but the Phaeacians are not encountered in the few myths dealing with men of times later than Odysseus' day. Much of the *Odyssey* is set among the Phaeacians, as is a long episode of the *Argonautica* of Apollonius Rhodius.

Phaedra. A daughter of Minos, king of Crete, and Pasiphaë. Phaedra married THESEUS [G] and bore two sons, Demophon and Acamas. Her unrequited love for Theseus' son Hippolytus brought about his death and her own suicide.

Phaënon. A beautiful youth created by Prometheus. When Prometheus was molding men out of clay, it was his practice to present the finished products to Zeus for his approval. Phaënon, however, turned out to be far more handsome than any of the others. Prometheus, perhaps knowing the god's fondness for beautiful boys, neglected to send Phaënon for the usual inspection. Eros reported the oversight to Zeus, who promptly sent Hermes to fetch the boy. Hermes persuaded him of the advantages of immortality and carried him off to heaven, where he became the planet Phaënon, later called Jupiter. Some say, however, that he actually became the planet now called Saturn, although others call this planet Phaëthon. [Hyginus, *Poetica Astronomica*, 2.42.]

Phaëthon (1). The son of Helius and Clymene, daughter of Oceanus. According to Ovid's elaborate account in the *Metamorphoses* [1.750–2.380], Phaëthon's mother was married to the Egyptian king Merops. Clymene told her son, however, that his father was not Merops but the sun-god. (Ovid calls him Apollo, this god having by Ovid's day taken over for many writers the functions of the ancient sun-god Helius.) One day Phaëthon's companion Epaphus, Io's son by Zeus, ridiculed his friend's story of his parentage. Stung to the quick, Phaëthon rushed to his mother and questioned her. Clymene told him to ask the sun-god himself, if he doubted her. Phaëthon journeyed through Ethiopia and India to the god's fabulous palace in the east, where the sun daily rises. There the god welcomed his son and promised, as proof of his paternity, to grant him any boon he might ask. The youth rashly demanded permission to drive the sun-chariot through the sky for one day. The sun-god repented his promise, but, unable to dissuade his son from this dangerous undertaking, regretfully consented.

Phaëthon set out boldly. Once in the sky, however, he was filled with panic. The four horses, sensing an unsure hand on the reins, first shot upward, scorching a great scar—the Milky Way—across the sky, then plunged downward until the earth was ablaze from the sun's heat. The men of equatorial countries were scorched black, and the springs and streams dried up. In order to save the world from destruction, Zeus killed Phaëthon with a thunderbolt. The youth's flaming body fell into the legendary Eridanus river. Phaëthon's sisters, the Heliades, who had yoked the sun's horses to the chariot, stood on the banks of the river and wept ceaselessly for their brother until they were changed into poplars. Thereafter, their tears fell as drops of precious amber onto the sands of the Eridanus. The musician Cycnus, Phaëthon's relative and the king of Liguria, left his people and mourned his friend among the poplars. He, too, was transformed, becoming a swan. Ever afterward, swans about to die were known to sing sad songs.

Hyginus [*Fabulae* 152A, 154] said that Phaëthon took the chariot without his father's consent. He claimed, moreover, that Zeus used the necessity of quenching the flaming earth as an excuse to loose the rivers and destroy all mankind in Deucalion's Flood. According to the writer now identified as the "Pseudo-Eratosthenes," the planet usually named Saturn was also called Phaëthon [Hyginus, *Poetica Astronomica*, 2.42]. Apollonius Rhodius [4.597–611] wrote that when the Argonauts sailed up the Eridanus, they found that the lake into which Phaëthon's body had fallen still gave off noxious steam that killed even the birds that tried to fly over it.

Phaëthon (2). A son of Eos by either Cephalus or Tithonus. Phaëthon was carried off as a boy by Aphrodite, who made him the guardian of her shrine, which was apparently somewhere in Syria. He became the father of Astynoüs and was an ancestor of Adonis. [Hesiod, *Theogony*, 986–991; Apollodorus 3.14.3; Pausanias 1.3.1.]

Phaëthon (3). An epithet for APSYRTUS. This name (Shining One) was given him because he outshone all other Colchian youths. As a grandson of Helius, the sun-god, Apsyrtus was a nephew of the Phaëthon who fell from the sun-chariot. [Apollonius Rhodius 3.245–246.]

Phaëthusa. See HELIUS [C].

Phalces. A son of Temenus. With his brothers, Phalces deposed his father as king of Argos. Kidnaping his sister Hyrnetho, wife of Deïphontes, he accidentally killed her. At the head of a Dorian army, he conquered Sicyon, but shared the throne with the reigning king, Lacestades. Phalces' son Rhegnidas captured Phlius for the Dorians and made himself king, exiling Hippasus. [Pausanias 2.13.1.]

Phalerus. An Argonaut. Phalerus, an Athenian for whom the local port of Phalerum was said to be named, was a son of Alcon. [Apollonius Rhodius 1.95–100.]

Phantasos. See SOMNUS.

Phanus. An Argonaut. Phanus and his brothers Staphylus and Oenopion were sons of Dionysus and Ariadne. [Apollodorus 1.9.16.]

Phasis River. A river, now the Rion, flowing through Colchis to the Black Sea. The Colchian adventures of the Argonauts took place on or near the Phasis.

Phegeus. A king and eponym of Phegia, in Arcadia. Before Phegeus' reign his city was known as Erymanthus. Phegeus purified ALCMEON of murder and gave him his daughter, Arsinoë or Alphesiboea, for his wife. Later, on learning that Alcmeon had tricked him in order to recover the gifts he had given Arsinoë, whom Alcmeon had deserted, the king ordered his sons to kill him. In turn, Alcmeon's sons by Callirrhoë avenged their father by killing Phegeus, his wife, and his sons.

Phegia. An early name of the Arcadian city of Psophis. At first called Erymanthus, the city was renamed by Phegeus after himself. It later was named once more.

Phemius. A minstrel in Odysseus' household. A son of Terpes, Phemius was a trusted retainer of Odysseus. He was forced to serve Penelope's suitors during his master's absence, but Odysseus spared his life on his return.

Pheneüs. A city in northeastern Arcadia. Heracles lived in Pheneüs while recovering his health after his first war with Elis. His brother, Iphicles, died there and was worshiped as a hero. For obscure reasons, the city also claimed to be the burial place of the Euboean king Chalcodon.

Pherae. A Thessalian city west of Iolcus. Pherae was founded by Pheres, who was succeeded on the throne by his son Admetus. The city was the scene of Alcestis' famous sacrifice of her life for her husband's.

Pheres (1). The founder and first king of Pherae, in Thessaly. Pheres was one of the three sons of Cretheus, king of Iolcus, and Tyro. He and Amythaon left the city when Aeson, the eldest brother, was deprived of the throne after Cretheus' death by the usurper Pelias, their half-brother. Amythaon went to Messenia, but Pheres founded Pherae, not far from Iolcus. He married Periclymene, daughter of Minyas. When Aeson's son Jason appeared twenty years later, his uncles and their sons hurried to Iolcus to support him in confronting Pelias. Jason undertook to lead the voyage of the Argonauts to Colchis, and Pheres' eldest son, Admetus, sailed with him. Pheres also had a younger son, Lycurgus, and two daughters, Idomene and Periopis. Pheres abdicated in favor of Admetus when his son was still young. When, however, Admetus was faced with death unless someone would die for him, Pheres, though already an old man, refused to volunteer. He appears in Euripides' play *Alcestis*. [Apollodorus 1.9.11, 1.9.14; Pindar, *Pythian Odes*, 4.125.]

Pheres (2). A son of Jason and Medea. Pheres is generally said to have been killed as a child by his mother, together with his brother MERMERUS (1). On the other hand, he is also said to have been the father of the Mermerus who became king of Thesprotian Ephyra.

Phicium, Mount. A mountain just southeast of Lake Copaïs. Phicium was the home of the Sphinx until she was destroyed by Oedipus.

Philammon. A mythical poet and cithera player. Philammon was said to have been a son of Apollo and Leuconoë or Chione, who bore Autolycus to Hermes on the same day. Philammon seduced the nymph Argiope, but refused to take her into his house. She bore his child, Thamyris, in Thrace. Philammon died while leading an Argive force against Phlegyan attackers of Delphi, where he had much to do with the worship in song of his father. He was the second poet to win the prize regularly awarded at Delphi; Thamyris was the third. Classical writers attributed certain ancient metrical verse forms to Philammon, but there was considerable disagreement over which forms they were. [Pausanias 4.33.3, 9.36.2.]

Philemon. See BAUCIS.

Philoctetes. The son of Poeas, king of the Malians, and Demonassa. Philoctetes, who may have been an Argonaut, lighted Heracles' funeral pyre and received his bow and arrows as a reward. (Some say that Poeas did this, and left the prize to his son.) Philoctetes was one of Helen's suitors. When the Greeks sailed for Troy, he led seven shiploads of men from his capital of Meliboea and nearby towns. On the island of Tenedos or Chryse he was bitten by a snake while sacrificing to Athena, Apollo, or the nymph Chryse. This snake may have been the guardian of Chryse's shrine, or it may have been sent by Hera, who resented Philoctetes' service in lighting Heracles' pyre, the act which had finally made him immortal. Philoctetes' wound not only would not heal, but grew so odorous and painful that his companions could stand neither his agonized cries nor the stench of the sore. Agamemnon ordered that he be marooned on a deserted coast of the island of Lemnos. His companions left him while he slept and the ships sailed without him, Medon taking charge of the Malian contingent.

During the following ten years, while the Trojan War was raging, Philoctetes lived alone on Lemnos, barely able to keep himself from starving by shooting birds with Heracles' famous bow and arrows. The noxious wound grew no better and Philoctetes, racked with pain, cursed his former companions and particularly Odysseus, whose advice to Agamemnon he blamed for his abandonment. In the last year of the war either the Greek seer Calchas or the captured Trojan seer Helenus foretold that Troy would fall when Achilles' son and Philoctetes were both brought to Troy to fight with the Greeks. The Greeks had little trouble in persuading Neoptolemus to join them, but they were certain that Philoctetes would refuse. Nevertheless, they sent Odysseus, together with Diomedes or Neoptolemus, to Lemnos. According to Sophocles' tragedy *Philoctetes*, Odysseus used Neoptolemus, whom Philoctetes had no reason to hate, as a lure. The young man promised to take the crippled castaway home to Greece, and Philoctetes trustingly lent him his bow. To Odysseus' disgust, Neoptolemus regretted his own deceit and determined to keep his promise to Philoctetes, whatever the cost. Fortunately Heracles, now a god, appeared and ordered Philoctetes to go to Troy. He foretold that he would be healed and would kill Paris. Bowing to this divine intervention, Philoctetes consented.

At Troy Philoctetes was at last healed by Machaon, Podaleirius, or their semidivine father, Asclepius. According to Homer [*Odyssey* 3.190], Philoctetes returned safely to his home after the war, but other accounts say that he sailed to the eastern coast of Italy and founded the towns of Crimissa and Petelia, north of Crotona. He built a shrine to Apollo Alaius (the Wanderer) and at last dedicated there the bow and arrows. [Homer, *Iliad*, 2.716–728; Apollodorus, "Epitome" 3.14, 3.27, 5.8, 6.15b; Hyginus, *Fabulae*, 102; Vergil, *Aeneïd*, 3.401–402.]

Philoetius. ODYSSEUS' [M, N] cowherd in Ithaca. Philoetius remained loyal to his master's interests and joined Eumaeüs in aiding him in the battle which ensued upon his return to Ithaca. [Homer, *Odyssey*, 20.185–239, 21.188–244, 21.388–393, 22.170–202.]

Philomela. See TEREUS.

Philomelus. A son of Iasion and Demeter. Philomelus did not get along well with his rich brother, Plutus. Buying two oxen with his little store of money and becoming a farmer, he made up in ingenuity what he lacked in wealth. He invented the wagon, a device which so pleased his mother that, at Philomelus' death, she placed him in the sky as the constellation Boötes. His son Parias founded Parion, in Mysia. [Hyginus, *Poetica Astronomica*, 2.4.]

Philonoë. A daughter of Iobates, king of Lycia. She married BELLEROPHON [C] and bore him two sons, Isander and Hippolochus, and a daughter, Laodameia.

Philonome. See TENES.

Philyra. A daughter of Oceanus and Tethys. While Cronus was looking for his infant son Zeus, whom his wife Rhea had hidden, he came upon Philyra and lay with her on the island in the Black Sea that took her name. He did so in the form of a stallion in order to deceive Rhea. When the Titaness surprised them, Philyra fled her home in shame and bore their child in the mountains of Pelasgia. On seeing the monster that she had spawned, she was doubly ashamed: her son had the body of a horse from the waist down. Philyra asked and received from Zeus the boon of becoming a linden tree. Thus she was not on hand to see her son, Cheiron, become king of the Centaurs and one of the wisest beings on earth. [Hesiod, *Theogony*, 1001–1002; Apollonius Rhodius 2.1231–1241; Hyginus, *Fabulae*, 138.]

Phineus (1). A blind soothsayer-king of Salmydessus, in Thrace. The events of Phineus' life are recounted in a great variety of ways. He is said to have been a son of Agenor, king of Tyre, which would make him a brother of Cadmus and Europa; of Agenor's son Phoenix and an unidentified Cassiopeia; or of Poseidon. Many different causes are suggested for his blindness. Some say that Zeus punished Phineus for revealing the future to mortals. Others claim that Boreas and the ARGONAUTS [H] put out his eyes because he had done the same to his own sons, who were Boreas' grandsons. In these two versions of the story, Phineus was further punished by having his food snatched away by the Harpies. Still other writers say that Poseidon blinded Phineus for telling Phrixus how to reach Colchis or Phrixus' sons how to reach Greece.

A part of Phineus' story concerns his two marriages. The first was to Cleopatra, daughter of Boreas and Oreithyia. She bore him two sons, who are variously named. When they were grown, Phineus took a second wife, Idaea, daughter of Dardanus, king of the Scythians. Infatuated with this woman, he believed her tale that his sons had violated her. In his rage he put out their eyes or tortured them in other ways. According to this version Phineus was punished with death or blindness by Boreas and the Argonauts. The Argonauts rescued Phineus' sons, but dissuaded them from killing their stepmother. Instead, they sent her home to her father, who condemned her to death.

The second part of Phineus' story, however, contradicts the first. In this version Phineus was already blind and was being harried by the Harpies when the Argonauts arrived in his land of Thynia. Zetes and Calaïs, Cleopatra's winged brothers, saved him by driving away the Harpies. In gratitude, Phineus told the Argonauts how they might sail safely through the Clashing Rocks.

Additional or different information about Phineus was given in the *Great Eoiae* [14] and the *Catalogues of Women* [39], but it is too fragmentary to be clear. According to these fragments, Phineus had two sons, Thynius and Mariandynus (presumably eponyms of Thynia and the Mariandyni); he was blinded either because he showed Phrixus the way to Colchis or because he preferred long life to sight; and the Harpies snatched away not only Phineus' food, but the king himself, and carried him to the land of the Scythians. [Apollodorus 3.15.3; Diodorus Siculus 4.43.3–4.44.7; Apollonius Rhodius 2.178–489; *Catalogues of Women* 20.]

Phineus (2). A brother of Cepheus, king of Ethiopia. Apollodorus says that Euripides called Phineus and Cepheus sons of Belus. Phineus, who had been betrothed to his niece Andromeda, attacked PERSEUS [D] and was killed. [Apollodorus 2.1.4, 2.4.3; Ovid, *Metamorphoses*, 5.12–235.]

Phlegethon or **Pyriphlegethon.** An Underworld river. Phlegethon was a river of flames that formed one of the boundaries of Hades.

Phlegra. The scene of the war between the Giants and the gods. Phlegra was identified by late writers with a volcanic region near Naples, but it may have originally been thought of as near Chalcidice.

Phlegyans. A warlike tribe from Thessaly or Boeotia. Precisely where the Phlegyans came from is not clear, but they (or their eponym, Phlegyas) were said to have made savage raids as far away as Delphi, where they destroyed Apollo's shrine and defeated an Argive troop of picked men under Philammon. According to Pausanias [9.36.1–4], the Phlegyans came to Andreïs (Orchomenus) and renamed it Phlegyantis.

Phlegyantis. A name for the region about Boeotian Orchomenus. Originally called Andreïs, it was renamed by King Phlegyas.

Phlegyas. The eponym of the Phlegyans. Phlegyas was a son of Ares by Dotis or Chryse. He inherited his father's warlike nature and led his people in such violent deeds that, according to Vergil [*Aeneïd* 6.618–620], he was eternally punished in Hades. Phlegyas received the rule of Andreïs (later called Orchomenus) on the death of the childless king Eteocles. He renamed the region Phlegyantis. His daughter, Coronis, became the mother of Asclepius by Apollo. This event occurred in Epidaurus, where Phlegyas had gone (or so the Epidaurians believed) on a spying expedition. Phlegyas died in battle, killed by the Theban kings Nycteus and Lycus. Phlegyas is sometimes called a Lapith king. [Pausanias 9.36.1–4; Apollodorus 3.5.5; Pindar, *Olympian Odes*, 3.8.]

Phliasia. The region lying between Arcadia and Sicyonia. The principal city of Phliasia was Phlius.

Phlius. The capital city of Phliasia, inland from Sicyon. Phlius was said to have been founded in the days of Prometheus by an autochthon, Aras, for whom the land was called Arantia. His children, Aoris and Araethyrea, were good at both warfare and the hunt; when his sister died, Aoris renamed the land for her. The next king of Araethyrea whose name is remembered was Phlias. He was a son of Dionysus or of Ceisus, the Heraclid. Phlias married Chthonophyle, daughter of Sicyon, and she bore him a son, Androdamas. Araethyrea, which at some point was renamed Phliasia for Phlias, was one of the lands listed by Homer as under the sway of Agamemnon, king of Mycenae. Two generations after the return of the Heraclids, Rhegnidas, son of Phalces and grandson of Temenus, was accepted by the Phliasians as their king. Those who objected migrated to Samos, led by Hippasus. Thereafter Phlius was a Dorian city. It probably remained under the domination of Argos, as it had been in Agamemnon's time.

Phlogius. See AUTOLYCUS (2).

Phobetor. See SOMNUS.

Phobus. A son of Ares and Aphrodite. Phobus (Panic) and his brother Deimus (Fear) were constant companions of their father and often drove his chariot into battle. They figure in myth merely as personifications of two emotions commonly felt in war. [Homer, *Iliad*, 13.298–300; Hesiod, *Theogony*, 933–936.]

Phocis. The region bordering the Gulf of Corinth west of Boeotia. Phocis had two eponyms named Phocus, one Corinthian, the other Aeginetan. The principal city of Phocis was Delphi, and much of the area is dominated by Mount Parnassus.

Phocus (1). A son of Aeacus by Psamathe, a Nereïd. Phocus grew up at his father's court in Aegina. Aeacus' wife, Endeïs, hated her rival's son and, to please her, her sons Telamon and Peleus killed him. Some say that they were also jealous of Phocus' athletic prowess. Aeacus exiled both of them. Phocus had three sons: Panopeus, Crisus, and Naubolus, who emigrated to Phocis. Phocus himself is said to have gone there for a time before returning to his death in Aegina. There was great confusion among writers over the roles that this Phocus and the Phocus who was the son of Poseidon or Ornytion played in the settlement of Phocis. It is probable either that their stories represent rival traditions about the ancestors of the Phocian hero and eponym, Phocus, or that there was also an Aeginetan hero of the name who originally had no connection with Phocis. [Hesiod, *Theogony*, 1003–1005; Apollodorus 3.12.6; Pausanias 2.29.2–10, 10.30.4, 10.33.12.]

Phocus (2). A son of Poseidon or of Ornytion, son of Sisyphus. According to Pausanias, this Phocus migrated to the region of Parnassus from Corinth and named the land for himself. A generation later the sons of the Aeginetan Phocus settled there and extended the name Phocis to a much larger area. (This tale may represent rival traditions about a single Phocus or confusion of an Aeginetan hero with a Phocian.) Ornytion's son is said to have cured Antiope of her madness and married her. They were buried in a single grave at Tithorea. [Pausanias 2.4.3, 9.17.5–6, 10.1.1.]

Phocus (3). An Argonaut. Hyginus [*Fabulae* 14] calls Phocus, who is otherwise unknown, a son of Caeneus and brother of Priasus, another Argonaut.

Phoebe. A Titaness. Phoebe, a daughter of Uranus and Ge, became the mother, by her brother Coeüs, of Leto and Asteria. [Hesiod, *Theogony*, 404–410.]

Phoebe. See HILÄEIRA.

Phoebus. A title of Apollo. This epithet (The Bright One) was often prefixed to the god's name. It may have played a part in the tendency to identify Apollo with the sun, although that had not originally been one of his spheres of influence.

Phoenicia. A coastal area of the Near East north of Palestine. The principal cities of Phoenicia familiar to the Greeks were Tyre, Sidon, and Byblus. In mythical history, Tyre (or Sidon, which was often confused with Tyre in myths) was the birthplace of Cadmus, who founded Thebes; of Europa, mother of the Cretan king Minos; of Dido, the founder of Carthage; and of the eponyms of Cilicia, Thasus, and Phoenicia itself. The Phoenicians, a branch of the Canaanites, were famous as the most skilled and venturesome merchant sailors of the Mediterranean Sea. Several myths traditionally located in Egypt might be plausibly relocated in Phoenicia.

Phoenix (1). The eponym of Phoenicia. Phoenix was one of the sons of Agenor, king of Tyre or Sidon, by Telephassa or Argiope. His brothers were Cadmus, Cilix, Thasus, and Phineus. When their sister, Europa, was kidnaped, the brothers were sent to find her or face exile. Phoenix cannot have gone very far, since the land where he settled and to which he gave his name is the very land in which Agenor is said to have ruled. The issue is further complicated by the fact that Phoenix was sometimes called the father, rather than the brother, of Europa by Perimede and of Phineus by an unknown Cassiopeia. Some say that he married Alphesiboea and became by her the father of Adonis. [Apollodorus 3.1.1; *Catalogues of Women* 19, 20; Pausanias 7.4.1.]

Phoenix (2). A king of the Dolopians. Phoenix was the son of Amyntor, king of Ormenium, at the foot of Mount Pelion. His mother persuaded Phoenix to seduce her husband's concubine, of whom she was jealous. Amyntor cursed him, asking the Erinyes to deny him children. Phoenix contemplated killing his father but instead decided to flee. He escaped, even though his relatives imprisoned him in the hope of inducing him to remain. According to a different version of the story, Amyntor blinded his son, not realizing that the charge of seduction was false. Phoenix' sight was restored by the Centaur Cheiron at the request of Peleus, king of Phthia, who befriended Phoenix in both versions. Peleus made him king of the Dolopians.

While still young, Phoenix took part in the Calydonian boar hunt. Peleus placed Phoenix in charge of his young son Achilles, whose earlier training had been in the hands of Cheiron. As an old man Phoenix accompanied Achilles to the Trojan War, after having gone to Scyrus to persuade the boy to fight. He did not desert the other Greeks when Achilles, having quarreled with Agamemnon, withdrew from the fighting. He joined the fruitless embassy of Ajax and Odysseus to plead with Achilles to relent. When it failed, he remained with Achilles. At the end of the war he set out for Greece with Achilles' son, Neoptolemus, but died on the journey. [Homer, *Iliad*, 9.168–661, 16.196, 17.553–566; Apollodorus 3.13.8, "Epitome" 4.3, 6.12; Sophocles, *Philoctetes*, 343–347.]

Pholoë. A mountain in eastern Elis near the border of Arcadia. Pholoë was named for the Centaur Pholus, who lived there after the expulsion of the Centaurs from Magnesia.

Pholus. A Centaur, eponym of Mount Pholoë in eastern Elis. When HERACLES [E] passed by Mount Pholoë on his fourth labor, Pholus brought out wine to entertain his guest, but his less civilized fellow Centaurs tried to steal it. Heracles drove them away. After the battle Pholus accidentally dropped one of Heracles' poisoned arrows on his foot and died. Some say that Pholus, rather than Cheiron, is represented in the constellation Centaurus.

Phorbas (1). A Thessalian king. A son of Lapithes and Orsinome or of Triopas and Hiscilla, Phorbas, like his brother Periphas, ruled a part of the Peneius River valley. Later he emigrated to Olenus, in Elis, at the request of King Alector, who was engaged in a struggle with Pelops, king of Pisa. Some say that he was the father by Hyrmina, daughter of Epeius, of Augeias, Actor, and Tiphys. According to a different tradition, Phorbas migrated to Rhodes at the request of the Rhodians and rid the island of snakes. He remained there and was honored as a hero after his death. According to some writers, Phorbas was immortalized in the constellation Ophiuchus (Serpent-holder). [Diodorus Siculus 4.69.2–3, 5.58.4–5; Pausanias 5.1.11.]

Phorbas (2). A king in Argolis. Phorbas was a son of Argus and father of Triopas. [Pausanias 2.16.1.]

Phorcys. An ancient sea-god. Phorcys, a son of Pontus (Sea) and Ge (Earth), may at one time have had considerable prominence as a deity, at least in some localities such as Ithaca, where the harbor was named for him. In extant myths, however, he is known mainly for his monstrous progeny by his sister, the sea-monster Ceto. These included the Gorgons, the Graeae, Echidna, and Ladon, the snake that guarded the Hesperides' garden. He is also said by some to have fathered the monster Scylla by either Crataeïs or Hecate, and the nymph Thoösa, mother of Polyphemus, by an unnamed woman. [Hesiod, *Theogony*, 237–336; Homer, *Odyssey*, 1.71–73, 13.96; Apollonius Rhodius 4.828–829.]

Phoronea. The earliest name of ARGOS, said to have been founded by Phoroneus.

Phoroneus. A son of Inachus, the Argive river-god, and Melia or Argia. According to Argive tradition, Phoroneus was first king of the area and the first man to gather scattered peoples together into a city, Phoronea, later called Argos. He is said to have received the kingship as a reward either for being the first to sacrifice to Hera or for making her armor. The Argives claimed that it was Phoroneus, not Prometheus, who discovered the use of fire. By the nymph Teledice (Cinna) he had a son, Apis, and a daughter, Niobe. His wife, Cerdo, may have been the mother of his other son, Car, who became king of Megara. [Apollodorus 2.1.1; Pausanias 2.15.5, 2.16.1, 2.19.5, 2.21.1, 2.22.2; Hyginus, *Fabulae*, 143, 145.]

Phrixus. The son of ATHAMAS and Nephele. By a plot, Athamas' second wife, Ino, forced him to agree to sacrifice Phrixus. When the boy was about to die, a miraculous ram with a golden fleece appeared and carried him and his sister Helle off through the air. The ram flew over the strait now known as the Hellespont, and Helle fell off, but Phrixus safely reached Aea, capital of Colchis, a land at the eastern end of the Black Sea. At the ram's bidding, Phrixus sacrificed it and hung its fleece on an oak in the grove sacred to Ares. Some say, however, that the remarkable beast himself presented Phrixus with his fleece and then flew off to become the constellation Aries. The paleness of this cluster of stars is due to the ram's generous sacrifice of his bright fleece. King Aeëtes welcomed Phrixus to Colchis and eventually gave him his daughter Chalciope or Iophossa as his bride. She bore him four sons—Argus, Phrontis, Melas, and Cytissorus; some writers mention a fifth, Presbon. Phrixus, according to this account, lived to a prosperous old age in Colchis. Hyginus [*Fabulae* 3] says, however, that Aeëtes killed Phrixus, having learned from an oracle that he would die at the hand of a foreigner. Phrixus' sons escaped from Aea with the Argonauts, who took with them the golden fleece. [Apollonius Rhodius 1.256–259, 2.1141–1156, 3.190–191, 3.333–339, 3.584–588; Apollodorus 1.9.1; Hyginus, *Poetica Astronomica*, 2.20; *Catalogues of Women* 39; *Great Eoiae* 14, 15.]

Phrygia. A large area of Asia Minor differing in extent in different periods. Phrygia at its peak included much of the interior of Anatolia, with outlets to the Black and Aegean seas. The Phrygians, a people speaking an Indo-European language, came into Asia Minor from Europe through Thrace. They established themselves in the central Anatolian plateau, particularly in the upper valley of the Sangarius River. Their chief cities in this region were Gordium, Pessinus, and Ancyra (now Ankara). Their kings for many generations were named either Gordius or Midas. Priam was an ally of the Phrygian king Mygdon and found his wife Hecuba in Phrygia. Partly because of the shifting boundaries of Phrygia, the name tends to be confused in Greek myths with

Mysia and Lydia, parts of which lands were originally Phrygian. Cybele was the great goddess of the Phrygians, although her cult may have been indigenous to the region that they invaded.

Phthia. The principal city of Phthiotis, or Achaea, in southern Thessaly. Phthia was the adopted home of Peleus and the scene of many myths involving that hero.

Phthiotis. A part of southern Thessaly, also called Achaea. The principal city of this region was Phthia.

Phylace. A city west of the Gulf of Pagasae, in Thessaly. Phylace was ruled by Phylacus, who named the city for himself. He was succeeded by his son Iphiclus and grandson Protesilaüs, under the latter of whom Phylace and its neighboring cities sent forty ships to Troy.

Phylacus. A king and the eponym of Phylace. A son of Deïon, king of Phocis, and Diomede, Phylacus married Clymene, daughter of Minyas, who bore him Iphiclus and Alcimede, Jason's mother. Phylacus is best known for the incident of MELAMPUS' [B] cure of Iphiclus' impotence, for which the king paid a herd of cattle.

Phylas. A king of Ephyra, in Thesprotia. In a war with the Calydonians, Phylas was killed by HERACLES [M], who seduced his daughter Astyoche. She became the mother of Tlepolemus.

Phyleus. A king of Dulichium. The eldest son of Augeias, Phyleus was driven from 'Elis by his father for protesting his treatment of Heracles. He went to Dulichium. Heracles later placed him on the throne of Elis, but Phyleus soon returned to Dulichium, letting the aged Augeias leave the throne to his younger son, Agasthenes. Tyndareüs' daughter Timandra is said to have deserted her husband, Echemus, for Phyleus. Phyleus' son Meges led the Dulichian forces to Troy. [Apollodorus 2.5.5; Pausanias 5.1.10, 5.3.1, 5.3.3; *Catalogues of Women* 67.]

Phyllis. See ACAMAS.

Phylomache. A daughter of Amphion. According to one account, Phylomache married Pelias, king of Iolcus, and bore Acastus and several daughters, the eldest of whom was Alcestis. Other accounts call Pelias' wife Anaxibia, daughter of Bias.

Picus. A Roman woodland demigod. Picus was a woodpecker, a bird sacred to Mars that was thought to have prophetic powers. Some Roman mythographers explained that he had once been a man, a son of Saturn and Venilia, daughter of Janus. He was betrothed to the nymph Canens, but the sorceress Circe fell in love with him. When he ignored her advances she lured him into the forest and transformed him into a woodpecker. Canens wasted away from grief. Picus was fitted into the mythical genealogy of Rome's founders as the father of Faunus, another woodland spirit, and grandfather of Latinus, king of Latium. [Ovid, *Metamorphoses*, 14.310–434; Vergil, *Aeneïd*, 7.48–49, 7.187–191.]

Pieria. A region about Mount Olympus, in northern Thessaly. Pieria, presumably named for King Pierus, a Macedonian, was one of the three chief haunts of the Muses, the others being Mount Parnassus and the Boeotian mountain Helicon.

Pierides. The daughters of PIERUS, the eponym of Pieria. The MUSES, too, were called Pierides because of their association with PIERIA.

Pierus. A king of Pella, in Macedonia. A son of Magnes, Pierus was presumably the eponym of Pieria, a region around Mount Olympus. He was also connected with Thrace, where he is said to have learned from an oracle that there were nine Muses, and with Thespiae, in Boeotia, to which he introduced the worship of the Muses. He was closely associated with the Muses. By one of them, Cleio, he became the father of Hyacinth. Oeagrus, his son by the nymph Methone, was the father by Calliope of Orpheus and Linus. (Some say that Orpheus was the son of Pierus' daughter Telete, and others that Pierus was a son, rather than a grandfather, of Linus.)

By his Paeonian wife Euippe, Pierus had nine daughters, whom he called "children of the Muses." These girls, the Pierides, became so expert at singing that in time, inflated with pride, they challenged their foster mothers to a contest with the nymphs as judges. Inevitably, the Muses won. They punished the Pierides for their presumption by transforming them into chattering magpies. The Muses themselves were also sometimes called Pierides because of their association with Pieria. [*Contest of Homer and Hesiod* 314; Ovid, *Metamorphoses*, 5.302–304; Apollodorus 1.3.3; Pausanias 7.29.3–4, 9.30.4.]

Pillars of Hercules or **Pillars of Heracles.** The promontories of Calpe (Gibraltar) and Abyla (Jebel Musa, at Ceuta, Morocco). HERACLES [H] set these "pillars" up in order to show how far west he had traveled or else to narrow the Strait of Gibraltar. Another version says that the capes were originally joined and that Heracles pulled the "pillars" apart to allow a passage between them.

Pindar. A Greek lyric poet. Pindar was born in Boeotia in either 518 or 522 B.C. and is said to have lived to the age of eighty. His extant works are mainly epinician odes written in honor of winners of athletic events in the Olympic, Pythian, Nemean, or Isthmian games, though a few short works and fragments in other forms survive. It was Pindar's custom to allude frequently, though briefly, to mythical events in his poems. These allusions are among the earliest and most valuable sources of Greek mythology.

Pisa. A city near the Arcadian border of Elis. Pisa was the capital of a region known as Pisatis, or merely Pisa. The city was founded by Pisus, son of Perieres, the Thessalian king of Messenia; thus, as with the city of Elis, the origins of Pisa can be traced to colonization from Thessaly. The first Pisan king of prominence was Oenomaüs, who made a practice of killing the suitors of his daughter, Hippodameia, if they could not beat him in a chariot race. Oenomaüs was overthrown and killed by the Phrygian immigrant Pelops, who was to master much of the Peloponnesus. According to Pausanias' informants from Elis, Pisa had been under Eleian rule until Pelops made it independent. Their testimony must be doubted, however, for it was Elis that destroyed Pisa after a long and bitter feud over control of the highly profitable Olympic games. It is therefore likely that Pisa was in charge of the festival at nearby Olympia for a long time before Elis, twenty miles away, grew powerful and challenged this control. Some hint of a Pisan connection with the festival of Olympian Zeus may be found in the tradition that Heracles would have destroyed Pisa in his war with Elis had not the Delphic oracle warned that Pisa was dear to Zeus. Ironically, the great temple of Zeus at Olympia is said to have been built by the Eleians with the spoils they took in the sack of Pisa and allied cities. Pisa was probably razed in the sixth century B.C.

Pisatis. The region between Arcadia and Elis. Pisatis was often called Pisa, the name of its principal city. It was absorbed into Elis in the sixth century B.C.

Pisces (The Fishes). A constellation. The two fish shown in this group of stars are Aphrodite and Eros, who leaped into the Euphrates River and became fish in order to escape the monster Typhon. [Hyginus, *Poetica Astronomica*, 2.30.]

Pittheus. A king of Troezen. Pittheus was a son of Pelops and Hippodameia. During the period when Pelops and his sons and daughters were extending their sway from Elis over much of the Peloponnesus, Pittheus and his brother Troezen settled in the towns of Hypereia and Antheia, in southeastern Argolis, and shared the rule with Aëtius, their king. Pittheus, apparently, really held the power. After Troezen's death he combined the two towns into a city, which he named for his brother. Aëtius is not heard of again.

Pittheus was known less for his prowess in war than for his knowledge and his eloquence. Bellerophon, a Corinthian prince, briefly courted Pittheus' daughter Aethra but was banished from Corinth and fled to Tiryns before the marriage could take place. Later Pittheus correctly interpreted an oracle given to Aegeus, king of Athens, and, keeping the meaning secret, induced Aegeus to lie with Aethra. She bore a son, Theseus [A], but whether his father was Aegeus or Poseidon was never certain. Theseus spent the first sixteen years of his life at his grandfather's court and no doubt much of his good sense was owed to the example and tutoring of Pittheus. Much later Theseus sent Hippolytus, his son by Antiope, to Troezen with a view to his eventually succeeding Pittheus on the throne. Hippolytus, however, died as a result of his father's curse during Theseus' year of exile in Troezen.

As late as the second century A.D. the Troezenians showed visitors the seats from which Pittheus and two fellow judges dispensed justice. Pittheus was also purported to be the author of a treatise on rhetoric. [Pausanias 1.22.2, 2.30.8–9.]

Pityocamptes. See Sinis.

Plataea. A city on the border between Attica and Boeotia. Plataea may have adopted a democratic form of government earlier than most Greek cities, for in Pausanias' day (second century A.D.) it had no traditions of early rulers. Its only myths concerned certain eponyms: King Cithaeron, for whom was named the mountain range on which the city lies; Asopus, the god of the river in the valley to the northeast; Plataea, daughter of the river-god. Although the Plataeans were known for their courage, the city's small size, its location on the main route southward from Thebes, and the distance of the fields from the city walls made them vulnerable to attack. Partly, perhaps, because of their friendly relations with Athens, they were in constant danger from Thebes, their neighbor to the north. Plataea was the site of a great battle in the Persian Wars, in which the inhabitants particularly distinguished themselves.

Pleiades. The seven daughters of Atlas and Pleïone, a daughter of Oceanus and Tethys. All but one of the Pleiades, Merope, had affairs with the gods. By Zeus, Electra was the mother of Dardanus and Iasion, Taÿgete of Lacedaemon, and Maia of Hermes. Poseidon fathered Lycus, and perhaps Nycteus, on Celaeno, and Hyrieus, Hyperenor, and Aethusa on Alcyone. Asterope (Sterope) bore Oenomaüs to Ares, unless, as some say, she was Oenomaüs' wife. Merope had a son, Glaucus, by the mortal Sisyphus. There are two principal accounts of why the sisters found their way into the sky. According to one, Zeus placed them there because they had died of grief over the death of their sisters, the Hyades—who had died of grief over their brother, Hyas. According to the other version, Zeus elevated them to save them from the lusty giant Orion, who had pursued them and Pleïone, their mother, for seven years. If this is the correct reason, it was a futile gesture, for the giant hunter was also transported to the stars, and perpetually chases the sisters across the sky at night.

One of the seven stars is so dim as to be scarcely visible. This is either Merope, blushing in shame at having married a mere mortal, or Electra, hiding her face in mourning for the death of her son Dardanus and the destruction of his city, Troy. [Apollodorus 3.10.1–3; Hyginus, *Fabulae*, 192, and *Poetica Astronomica*, 2.21.]

Pleïone. See PLEIADES.

Pleisthenes. A son of Atreus and Aërope. Hesiod and Aeschylus say that Pleisthenes was the father of Agamemnon, Menelaüs, and Anaxibia by Cleolla, daughter of Dias, although the two brothers are usually said to be sons of ATREUS [A, B]. The conflicting versions seem to have confused ancient writers. Apollodorus gives both paternities in different parts of his narrative [3.2.1–2, "Epitome" 2.10.]

Pleuron. The eponym of an Aetolian city of the same name. Pleuron, one of the two sons of Aetolus and Pronoë, married Xanthippe, daughter of Dorus. He became the father of four children, one of whom, Agenor, was a grandfather of Oeneus. [Apollodorus 1.7.7.]

Pleuron. A principal city of Aetolia. Pleuron was founded by a son of Aetolus, who named it for himself.

Plotae. See STROPHADES.

Plutarch. A Greek writer of the first and second centuries A.D. Plutarch's best-known work, his *Parallel Lives*, contrasts the careers of pairs of Greek and Roman personages. The lives of Theseus, Romulus, and Numa are good sources of the myths surrounding these figures and others of their time.

Pluto. A euphemistic name for HADES. Pluto, an epithet referring to the wealth (*ploutos*) of the Underworld god, presumably as a spirit of the earth's fertility, was used in preference to his name. The Romans borrowed the title from the Greeks but also translated it to Dives, which they contracted to Dis.

Plutus. A god of wealth. Plutus was born to Demeter, the corn-goddess, at Tripolus in Crete, after she lay with Iasion in a thrice-plowed field. He seems clearly to have originally represented the wealth that the earth brings forth under cultivation. As such, he was commonly represented in art as a boy bearing a cornucopia. Although he had a shrine at Eleusis, he seems to have had no cult of importance. He evidently remained more an abstraction than an individualized god.

Plutus is a main character in Aristophanes' comedy that bears his name. He claims in the play [87–92] to have been blinded by Zeus in order to insure that he would distribute wealth indiscriminately, rather than favor the good and deserving. [Hesiod, *Theogony*, 969–974; Diodorus Siculus 5.77.1–2.]

Po. See ERIDANUS.

Podaleirius. A son of Asclepius. Like his brother, Machaon, Podaleirius was a suitor of Helen, and with his brother he later led thirty ships to Troy, where they served as physician-soldiers. Some say that, after Machaon's death, Podaleirius cured Philoctetes of his wound. The Delphic oracle told him to settle where he would not be harmed if the sky fell. He chose the Carian Chersonese, which is ringed with mountains. [Apollodorus "Epitome" 5.8, 6.18.]

Podarces. The younger son of Iphiclus, king of Phylace. When his elder brother, Protesilaüs, was killed in the Trojan War, Podarces assumed command of the force that had come in forty ships from the Phylacian territories. According to Apollodorus [1.9.12], Podarces was Iphiclus' firstborn son. [Homer, *Iliad*, 2.694–710.]

Poeas. A Malian king. Poeas, a son of Thaumacus, was listed in some accounts as an Argonaut and credited with shooting Talus, the brazen giant of Crete, in his vulnerable heel. He married Demonassa, who bore Philoctetes. When Heracles ascended his pyre on Mount Oeta he could persuade no one to light it. Poeas, who passed that way in search of his sheep, consented to set the torch to the pyre and was rewarded by Heracles with his famous bow and arrows. These Poeas bequeathed to Philoctetes. In many accounts, however, it was Philoctetes himself who lighted the pyre. [Apollodorus 1.9.16, 1.9.26, 2.7.7.]

Pollux. The Latin form of Polydeuces. See DIOSCURI.

Polybotes. One of the GIANTS. In the war between the gods and the Giants, Poseidon chased Polybotes through the sea to the island of Cos, and crushed him under Cape Nisyrum or Cape Chelone. [Apollodorus 1.6.2; Pausanias 1.2.4.]

Polybus (1). A king of Corinth. Polybus and his wife, Merope, or Periboea, were the foster parents of OEDIPUS [A]. It may be this same Polybus whom Pausanias [2.6.6] calls a king of Sicyon. [Sophocles, *Oedipus the King*, 774–775, 939–972; Apollodorus 3.5.7.]

Polybus (2). A king of Sicyon. A son of Hermes and Chthonophyle, daughter of Sicyon, Polybus inherited his grandfather's throne and enjoyed a long reign. He married his daughter Lysianassa to Talaüs, an Argive king. A generation later, Adrastus, foremost of the sons of this union, was driven from the throne of Argos by Amphiaraüs and took refuge in Sicyon. Polybus left his throne to Adrastus at his death. [Herodotus 5.6.7; Pausanias 2.6.6.]

Polycaon. The first king of Messenia. The younger son of the first Spartan king, Lelex, Polycaon was exiled by his brother, Myles. He married the ambitious Argive princess MESSENE, and with her colonized the land which they named Messenia in her honor.

Polydamas or **Poulydamas.** A son of Panthoüs. Polydamas was one of the better Trojan warriors and a friend and companion of Hector, who was born on the same night. His best contribution to the Trojan cause was his prudent advice, which the bold Hector, to his own regret, too often dismissed. When the enraged Achilles rejoined the fighting after Patroclus' death, Polydamas advised Hector to let the Trojans retreat within their walls. Hector refused and realized his mistake too late. His feeling of guilt over the rout that resulted from his stubbornness caused him to fight Achilles alone and meet his death. [Homer, *Iliad*, 12.60–90, 12.195–250, 14.449–463, 18.249–315, 22.98–103.]

Polydamna. See HELEN [E].

Polydectes. A king of Seriphus. Polydectes and Dictys were sons of Magnes, son of Aeolus, and a naïad. The brothers colonized the island of Seriphus, where Polydectes became king. Finding Danaë in Dictys' home, Polydectes sent her son PERSEUS [A, E] to fetch the head of Medusa and then either forced Danaë to marry him or drove her and Dictys to find sanctuary at the altars of the gods, where he dared not harm them. Perseus returned with the Gorgon's head and turned Polydectes and all his court to stone. In Hyginus' unique version of the myth, Polydectes was a kindly king who married Danaë and reconciled Perseus with his cruel grandfather, Acrisius. [Apollodorus, 1.9.6, 2.4.1–4; Hyginus, *Fabulae*, 63; Ovid, *Metamorphoses*, 5.242–249.]

Polydeuces. See DIOSCURI.

Polydora. A daughter of Peleus and Antigone, daughter of Eurytion. Polydora married Borus, son of Perieres, but had a son, Menesthius, by the river-god Spercheiüs. [Homer, *Iliad*, 16.175–178; Apollodorus 3.13.1.]

Polydorus (1). A king of Thebes. Polydorus was the only son of Cadmus and Harmonia. He married Nycteïs, daughter of Nycteus, and she bore a son, Labdacus. Pausanias [9.5.3–4] says that Polydorus received the throne on his father's abdication, but it is more usually recorded that the brief rule of Pentheus, Polydorus' nephew, intervened. Polydorus died when Labdacus was only a child and left Nycteus ruling as regent. [Apollodorus 3.5.5.]

Polydorus (2). A son of Priam and Hecuba or Laothoë. According to Homer [*Iliad* 20.407–418, 21.84–88], Polydorus was the youngest and favorite son of Priam and Laothoë, a daughter of the Lelegian king Altes. Priam would not let him fight in the Trojan War, but the boy was killed by Achilles as he ran among the warriors. Another well-known tradition, in which Hecuba is Polydorus' mother, has it that, when his parents realized that the war with the Greeks might end disastrously, they sent him across the Hellespont to their ally Polymestor, king of the Bistones of the Thracian Chersonese, with the request that he keep safe both the child and a shipment of gold that was sent with him. Later the king saw that the war was going against the Trojans and murdered his guest for the gold. After the war Hecuba came to Thrace as Odysseus' slave and found Polydorus' body. She avenged him by blinding the treacherous Polymestor and killing his two sons. Later Aeneas and his Trojan survivors stopped at the Chersonese with some thought of settling there. Gathering cornel and myrtle boughs from an unmarked grave-mound, they saw that they were bleeding. The voice of Polydorus called out from the grave. The Trojans hastily sacrificed to the dead and left Thrace forever.

In a later version of the story, known only to Roman writers, Polydorus was sent to live with his eldest sister, Ilione, who was married to Polymestor. Knowing how precious the boy was to her parents, she reared him with her own son, Deïpylus, in order that she might give the latter to them if anything happened to Polydorus. When Troy fell and the Greeks wanted to exterminate Priam's line, they offered Polymestor a huge reward and the hand of Agamemnon's daughter Electra if he would kill Polydorus. The king went to the palace to do so, but, unable to tell one boy from the other, killed Deïpylus by mistake. Later Polydorus, who thought himself a Thracian, went for some reason to Delphi. The oracle told him that his city was burned, his father murdered, and his mother a slave. Hurrying home to Thrace he found his supposed family as he had left them. When he asked Ilione why the oracle had lied she told him the whole story. At her instigation he blinded and killed Polymestor.

Polydorus appears as a ghost in Euripides' tragedy *Hecuba*, which tells of his mother's vengeance. See also Ovid, *Metamorphoses*, 13.429–438, 13.536–575; Vergil, *Aeneïd*, 3.19–68; Hyginus, *Fabulae*, 109.

Polydorus (3). A son of Hippomedon. Pausanias [2.20.5] lists Polydorus among the EPIGONI.

Polyeidus or **Polyidus**. An Argive seer. Polyeidus was a son of Coeranus and descendant of Melampus. His advice helped BELLEROPHON [B] to tame Pegasus. He was at the Cretan court of Minos when the king's son Glaucus vanished while chasing a mouse. The Delphic oracle told Minos that a strange event had occurred in Crete and the man who could find the aptest simile for it would also find Glaucus. Minos learned that a calf had recently been born which was changing daily from white to red to black. Polyeidus compared this phenomenon to the stages of the ripening mulberry and Minos ordered him to find Glaucus. The seer saw an owl (*glaux*) sitting on a wine cellar, pestered by bees. Reading this omen, he found the child drowned in a large jar of honey.

Minos shut Polyeidus into a tomb with Glaucus' body and commanded him to revive the child. Soon a snake made for the corpse. Polyeidus killed it and was surprised to see a second snake appear with a herb with which it restored its mate to life. The seer promptly used some of the herb on Glaucus, and the boy revived. Minos would not let Polyeidus leave Crete until he had taught Glaucus his seer's art. As his ship was about to sail, however, Polyeidus made Glaucus spit into his mouth, and the child forgot all that he had learned. The seer went to Megara, where he purified Alcathoüs, who had killed his own son Callipolis. Minos, angered at Megara for sheltering Polyeidus from pursuit, invaded the land.

Polyeidus' son or grandson Euchenor died in the Trojan War, as his father had predicted. [Hyginus, *Fabulae*, 136; Pausanias 1.43.5; Pindar, *Olympian Odes*, 13.73–82; Homer, *Iliad*, 13.663–672.]

Polygonus and **Telegonus**. Sons of Proteus. This pair lived at Torone, on the peninsula of Sithonia. When Heracles stopped there on his homeward voyage from Troy, they challenged him to wrestle and were killed in the match. [Apollodorus 2.5.9.]

Polyhymnia. See Muses.

Polymede. A daughter of Autolycus. Those accounts that say that Polymede was Aeson's wife tell the same story of her deeds that others ascribe to Alcimede.

Polymestor or **Polymnestor**. See Polydorus (2).

Polymnia. See Muses.

Polyneices. A son of Oedipus by either Jocasta or Euryganeia. Polyneices and his brother Eteocles were cursed by Oedipus because of some act of disrespect toward him after his downfall as king of Thebes. Some say that they went so far as to imprison their father in the hope that the Thebans would forget him and the disgrace he brought upon them; others say that they did nothing to prevent Creon from exiling him. According to most accounts, the brothers agreed to rule Thebes in alternate years, but Eteocles refused to relinquish the throne at the end of his term. Banished, Polyneices spent a short while as a guest of Theseus at Athens, then went to Argos, where King Adrastus married him to his daughter Argeia. In another version of these events, Polyneices left Thebes while Oedipus still reigned in order to avoid his curse. He married Argeia and returned with her to Thebes for his father's funeral. Later he quarreled with Eteocles and fled a second time to Argos.

In either case, Adrastus raised an army and led it to Thebes in support of his son-in-law's claim to the throne [see SEVEN AGAINST THEBES]. Polyneices helped to silence the strong opposition of Amphiaraüs to this campaign by bribing the Argive seer's wife, Eriphyle, with the necklace of his ancestor Harmonia. According to Sophocles' *Oedipus at Colonus*, Polyneices tried vainly to win the support of his aged father, who had taken refuge in Attica. The ensuing war ended in the rout of the Argive forces.

Oedipus' curse was fulfilled when Polyneices and Eteocles killed one another in single combat. Creon, who took over the rule at Eteocles' death, decreed that Polyneices' body should remain unburied, but Polyneices' sister Antigone (perhaps with the aid of his wife, Argeia) defied the order at the cost of her own life. The EPICONI, sons of the seven Argive champions, together with Polyneices' son Thersander, avenged their fathers a generation later by destroying Thebes. In addition to Thersander, Pausanias names Adrastus and Timeas as sons of Polyneices.

Polyneices appears as a character in *Oedipus at Colonus* and in Euripides' *Phoenician Women*, and is discussed at length in Sophocles' *Antigone* and Aeschylus' *Seven Against Thebes*. See also Apollodorus 3.5.8–3.7.2; *Thebaïd* 2, 3; Hyginus, *Fabulae*, 68–71.

Polypemon. See PROCRUSTES.

Polypheides. A seer. A son of Mantius and grandson of Melampus, Polypheides was a leading diviner of his day, second only to his cousin Amphiaraüs. Quarreling with his father, he left Argolis for Hyperesia. His son Theoclymenus, also a seer, appears in the *Odyssey* [15.249–256].

Polyphemus (1). A Cyclops. Polyphemus, son of Poseidon by the sea-nymph Thoösa, daughter of Phorcys, lived on the island of Sicily with the other Cyclopes, a barbarous tribe of one-eyed giants who kept flocks but did not till the soil. He fell in love with the beautiful sea-nymph Galatea, daughter of Nereus and Doris, but she detested his ugly form and habits as much as she adored handsome Acis, young son of Faunus and the nymph Symaethis. Telemus, a seer who had come to live among the Cyclopes, warned Polyphemus that he was fated to lose his one eye at the hands of a man named ODYSSEUS [E]. "I've already lost it to another," the lovesick giant moaned, and paid no attention. One day, finding Galatea sleeping with her young lover, Polyphemus crushed Acis with a great rock torn from the side of Mount Aetna. He gained little by this move, for Galatea hated him more than ever, and Acis, at her prayer, was transformed into a river-god.

Many years later Polyphemus drove his flocks home to his cave one night and found thirteen puny strangers eating his cheeses. He ate a couple of the interlopers in return and penned the others in his cave for a day or two, during the course of which he ate four more. The leader of the strangers, who called himself Nobody, claimed that they were shipwrecked Greek sailors and offered his captor a bowl of the wine that he had brought with him. Polyphemus got drunk and fell into a stupor. He awoke in agony to find that the villains had driven a stake into his one eye. Taking advantage of his blindness they made for their ships, and their leader taunted him, saying that his real name was Odysseus. Too late the wounded giant remembered Telemus' prophecy. The huge rocks that he flung at the Greek ship did no harm, but his prayers to his father, Poseidon, were effectual enough to keep Odysseus from his home for ten years. [Homer, *Odyssey*, 1.68–75, 9.105–566; Ovid, *Metamorphoses*, 13.738–897; Euripides, *Cyclops*.]

Polyphemus (2). An Argonaut. Polyphemus, son of Eilatus and Hippea, daughter of Antippus, was a Lapith from Larisa, in Thessaly. In his youth he fought against the Centaurs and was one of the brave warriors of earlier time mentioned by Nestor in one of his monologues at Troy. He sailed with the ARGONAUTS [F] when no longer young and was abandoned by them in Mysia together with Heracles. Remaining there, he founded the city of Cius and later died in the land of the Chalybes.

Polyphontes. A Theban warrior. A son of Autophonus, Polyphontes was killed leading, with MAEON, the ambush of Tydeus. [Homer, *Iliad*, 4.391–398.]

Polyphontes. See AEPYTUS.

Polypoetes. A son of Peirithoüs and Hippodameia, daughter of Butes. Polypoetes was conceived on the day that his father led the Lapiths in their famous battle with the Centaurs. A formidable warrior, Polypoetes, with his inseparable companion, Leonteus, son of Coronus, led forty ships to the Trojan War, where they temporarily repulsed the Trojan attack on the Greek wall. After the war the two traveled overland to Colophon, near Ephesus. [Homer, *Iliad*, 2.738–747, 12.126–195, 23.836–849; Apollodorus "Epitome" 6.2.]

Polyxeinus (1). A king of Elis. The Taphian pirates who stole Electryon's cattle left them in Polyxeinus' care, but he permitted Amphitryon to ransom them. [Apollodorus 2.4.6.]

Polyxeinus (2). A son of Agasthenes, king of Elis. This Polyxeinus, who may be the same as a king of Elis bearing that name, led some of the Eleian forces to Troy. [Homer, *Iliad*, 2.615–624.]

Polyxena. A daughter of Priam and Hecuba. After Troy's fall Achilles' ghost demanded that Polyxena be sacrificed on his grave. The Greeks agreed, and Neoptolemus performed the rite. According to some late Classical writers Achilles fell in love with Polyxena. When he went to her home to interview her parents, Paris and Deïphobus killed him. His ghost demanded Polyxena's life in order that they might be united after death.

Polyxena appears prominently in Euripides' tragedy *The Trojan Women.* See also Hyginus, *Fabulae*, 110.

Polyxo. See ARGONAUTS [C]; HELEN [F].

Pomona. A Roman goddess of fruit trees. According to Ovid [*Metamorphoses* 14.623–771], the Latin nymph Pomona scorned the love of Vertumnus, but, in the guise of an old woman, he pleaded his cause so eloquently that she relented. Other Roman poets invented other lovers for her, but it is unlikely that any of these tales had any connection with her actual worship.

Pontus. A personification of the sea. Pontus, who was perhaps never more than an abstraction, was said to have been born, along with Uranus (Sky) and Ourea (Hills), from Ge (Earth). He lay with his mother and fathered the ancient sea-gods Nereus and Phorcys, and also Eurybia, Thaumas, and the sea-monster Ceto. [Hesiod, *Theogony*, 131–132, 233–239.]

Porphyrion. One of the GIANTS. Porphyrion and Alcyoneus were the strongest of the Giants. In the battle between Giants and gods, Porphyrion fought Hera and Heracles. Zeus, for some unexplained reason, filled him with lust for Hera, then struck him with a thunderbolt when he tried to rape her. Heracles killed him with his arrows. Pindar called Porphyrion king of the Giants. [Apollodorus 1.6.1–2; Pindar, *Pythian Odes*, 8.12–17.]

Porthaon, Portheus, or **Parthaon.** A king of Calydon. Porthaon, son of Agenor and Epicasta, is known only for his children. Euryte, daughter of Hippodamas, married him and bore Oeneus, who succeeded to the rule, and Agrius, Melas, Alcathoüs, and other children, who are variously named. Porthaon also had a son, Laocoön, by a servingwoman. [Homer, *Iliad*, 14.115–118; Apollodorus 1.7.7, 1.7.10; Apollonius Rhodius 1.190–193.]

Poseidon or **Poseidaon.** A god of the sea, of earthquakes, and of horses.

A. Poseidon, whom the Romans identified with their god Neptune, was borne by Rhea to her husband, Cronus. According to an Arcadian legend, Rhea, knowing her husband's habit of swallowing his children, laid the baby among the lambs of a flock grazing near Mantineia and gave Cronus a foal instead. Cronus, who had occasionally taken the form of a horse himself, was not unduly surprised at this unconventional offspring and ate it without comment. Thus, Rhea saved Poseidon, as well as Zeus, from the fate of their brother and sisters. A Rhodian version of Poseidon's infancy has it that Rhea gave him to the Telchines and the Oceanid Capheira to rear on the island of Rhodes. By far the more usual story is, however, that Poseidon, like Hades, Hestia, Hera, and Demeter, was swallowed by his father and later rescued by Metis, who gave Cronus an emetic. Led by Zeus, the children then defeated their father and his fellow Titans and confined them forever in Tartarus behind bronze gates made by Poseidon.

After this the three brothers drew lots to divide the rule of the universe. Zeus received heaven, Hades the Underworld, Poseidon the sea. The earth and Olympus belonged jointly to the three, but Zeus was acknowledged as king. Poseidon sometimes chafed under this domination and once joined with Hera and Athena to overthrow Zeus. They managed to bind him, but Thetis called up Briareüs, leader of the Hundred-handed, from the Underworld to release the captive.

Although all the Olympian gods shared the rule of the earth, they vied among themselves to be recognized as patron deities of particular regions. Poseidon was embroiled in more of these contests than any other Olympian. He contested the patronage of Corinth with Helius, the sun-Titan. When the two referred the question to Briareüs for arbitration, Helius received the heights of the Acrocorinth, Poseidon the Isthmus. Poseidon quarreled vehemently with Hera over Argos and its environs. This time the judgment was left to three Argive river-gods—Inachus, Cephisus, and Asterion. When they decided in favor of Hera, Poseidon angrily dried up these rivers and flooded Argos as well. Zeus decided an argument between Poseidon and Athena over Troezen by decreeing that they should share its patronage.

Best known of these many disputes was that between Poseidon and Athena for the patronage of Attica. There are differing views on the identities of the judges; they may have been the other Olympian gods, Zeus alone, or any of several kings of Attica. In order to advertise his benefits to the region, Poseidon created with a blow of his trident a spring of seawater on the Athenian Acropolis, leaving the mark of his trident for all to see. (Some late Roman poets claim that Poseidon's gift to Attica was the horse.) Athena caused an olive tree to grow near by. The arbiters adjudged the goddess' gift to be the more useful, and she became the patroness of Athens. In a rage, Poseidon flooded the plain of Attica. The Athenians prudently continued to honor Poseidon, as well as Athena, on their Acropolis.

B. When Poseidon was not on Olympus, he spent most of his time in the sea. He owned a watery palace at Aegae, on the northern coast of the Peloponnesus, and drove a two-horse chariot through the waves. His wife, Amphitrite, was a daughter of Oceanus. It is said that, when Poseidon first courted her, she fled, for some reason, to the Titan Atlas. She was found by Delphin (apparently a minor dolphin deity), who persuaded her to marry the sea-god. Poseidon rewarded the marriage broker by placing him among the stars as the constellation Dolphin. Amphitrite bore the sea-god Triton and two daughters —Rhode, eponym of Rhodes, and Benthesicyme. Poseidon's relations with several other (and possibly older) sea-gods, Nereus, Phorcys, and Proteus, were presumably harmonious, since they are scarcely mentioned.

Although the river-gods were sons of Oceanus and Tethys (except for the Sicyonian Asopus, whom some call a son of Poseidon by Pero or Calusa), Poseidon seems to have ruled fresh as well as salt waters, particularly those that sprang from the earth. He partly made up for his harsh treatment of Argos by a kindness to Amymone, daughter of Danaüs. After he had lain with her, he created with his trident the springs that are the source of the three-forked river Lerna. Amymone later gave birth to Nauplius. When Cercyon killed his own daughter, Alope, for bearing the child Hippothoüs (or Hippothoön) by the god, Poseidon caused a spring to flow from her body. Poseidon took the form of the river Enipeus to seduce Salmoneus' daughter Tyro, who bore him Pelias and Neleus. According to Herodotus, Poseidon created the river Peneius with an earthquake. Much later, he destroyed the city of Helice in the same way, and he contemplated hemming in the Phaeacian city on the island of Scherië by throwing up mountains about it. Earthquakes in general were attributed to the god, and one of his most frequently used epithets was Earth-shaker (Enosichthon).

Poseidon was also a god of horses. In Vergil's fancy, he brought forth the first horse from rock in the same manner that he created springs, with a blow of his trident. When Demeter was wandering through Arcadia in search of her daughter, Persephone, Poseidon lustfully pursued her. She changed herself into a mare in order to avoid him, but the god became a stallion and mounted her. According to one Arcadian legend, Demeter bore a daughter, Despoina, a goddess comparable to Persephone. A better-known version of the match claims that the offspring was the horse Arion. Demeter was worshiped in parts of Arcadia in a horse-headed form, and her seducer was known as Horse Poseidon. Poseidon seduced Medusa, then a lovely girl, in a temple of Athena. Athena, enraged, transformed her into a Gorgon. When Perseus later cut off the Gorgon's head, out sprang the offspring of her union with Poseidon, Chrysaor and the winged horse Pegasus. This fabulous creature was later captured and tamed by Bellerophon, a son of Poseidon by Eurynome, the wife of Glaucus, king of Corinth, who was himself famous for his horses. It was Poseidon who gave to Peleus as a wedding gift Xanthus and Balius, the immortal horses which Peleus' son Achilles inherited. The god was evidently a friend of the Centaurs, for when Heracles was warring with them, Poseidon hid them inside a mountain at Eleusis.

Like other sea-deities, Poseidon had the power of changing his shape. He seems to have used it mainly in his numerous seductions. Besides raping Demeter in the form of a horse, he is said to have visited Medusa as a bird, Theophane as a ram, Canace as a bull, and Melantho as a dolphin. Theophane, whom he made a ewe to hide her from less welcome suitors, gave birth to the ram of the famous golden fleece. The god granted this shape-changing facility to at least two mortals, Mestra, daughter of Erysichthon, and Periclymenus, Poseidon's own grandson. After seducing the Lapith girl Caenis, he granted her request that she might become a man, Caeneus.

C. Although Poseidon took Demeter by force, he was generally more circumspect in dealing with goddesses. He and Apollo regretfully respected the wish of the demure goddess Hestia to remain a virgin. Poseidon and Zeus vied for the favors of Thetis, chief of the Nereïds. When, however, they learned from Themis that Thetis' son was fated to surpass his father, both retired from the field and hastily arranged for Thetis to marry the mortal Peleus.

Poseidon's son Antaeüs, the Libyan giant whom Heracles killed, was said by some to have been fathered on Ge. The early Greek poet Musaeüs claimed that in ancient times Poseidon shared the Delphic oracles with this earth-goddess, giving his replies through a personage named Pyrcon. Ge turned over her interest in the oracle to Themis, who in turn gave it to Apollo. Poseidon resigned his share in return for the island of Calaureia, off the coast of Troezen. He retained certain connections with Delphi, however, the mother by Zeus of the Pythia Herophile having been his daughter Lamia. Parnassus, eponym of the mountain to which Delphi clings, was also a child of the god, by the nymph Cleodora, though the supposed father was Cleodora's husband, Cleopompus. Phocus, the eponym of Phocis and the reputed son of Ornytion, was also said in some accounts to be Poseidon's son.

The inhabitants of Libya are said to have claimed that Poseidon was the father of Athena by Tritonis, goddess of the Libyan lake. This story was, of course, denied by the Greeks. They agreed, however, that the god had connections in that region, having fathered Belus, Agenor, and Lelex on Libya, daughter of Epaphus and Memphis, and Busiris on Lysianassa. Poseidon had children by two of the Pleiades, daughters of Atlas: Alcyone bore him Aethusa, Hyrieus, Hyperenor, Hyperes, and Anthus; Celaeno was the mother of a Lycus who was sent by his father to the Islands of the Blessed. According to Hyginus, this was the Lycus who, with his brother, Nycteus, is usually called the son of Hyreius or of Chthonius, one of the Sown-men of Thebes.

Poseidon had innumerable children by nymphs and mortal women. Several of his sons were of giant stature. Besides Antaeüs, there were Otus and Ephialtes, children of Iphimedeia, the wife of Alöeus; and the Cyclops Polyphemus, son of the Nereïd Thoösa. Orion was said by some to be Poseidon's son by Euryale. The god, in any case, gave him the power to walk through the sea. The monstrous Eleian brothers called the Moliones were offspring of the seagod by Molione. Many of Poseidon's sons with normal bodies had savage natures and were notorious for their treatment of strangers. Among these were Busiris; the Bebrycian king Amycus, son of a Melian nymph; Cercyon, king of Eleusis; and the Isthmian bandit Sceiron, who was, however, sometimes called a son of Pelops. Many of the local rulers killed by Heracles on his travels were sons of Poseidon. Perhaps the best known of these (in addition to Antaeüs and Busiris) was the Sicilian king Eryx, though he is said by some to have been Aphrodite's son by the Argonaut Butes, another of Poseidon's sons.

Poseidon was, appropriately enough, the father of several of the Argonauts, though he did nothing to aid them on their journey. Euphemus was his son by Tityus' daughter Europa, the Samian Ancaeüs by Astypalaea (who also bore a son named Eurypylus), and the Miletian Erginus by an unnamed mother. According to a somewhat obscure tradition, Poseidon was the father of the seer Phineus, but blinded him for showing the Argonauts the way to Colchis. Canace, a daughter of Aeolus, bore five sons to the sea-god: Hopleus, Nireus, Epopeus, Alöeus and Triops. The last two were respectively the husband and father of Iphimedeia, mother of the Aloadae. Poseidon fathered Eumolpus on Chione, but she threw the infant into the sea. The father rescued it and carried it to his daughter Benthesicyme in Egypt. Cycnus, king of Colonae, in

Troas, was a son of the sea-god. Poseidon made him invulnerable to weapons, though Achilles managed to kill him by other means. Some say that Poseidon hated Achilles for this act and induced Apollo to kill him. Halirrhothius, whom Ares killed; Taphius, the Teleboan king; and other personages too numerous to mention were said to be children of Poseidon.

D. The most famous of the god's mortal sons was undoubtedly Theseus. The god lay with Pittheus' daughter Aethra on the Troezenian island of Sphaeria on the same night that Aegeus, king of Athens, visited her there. Theseus claimed the throne of Athens through Aegeus, but, when it suited his purposes, he also claimed the god as his father. The best known of these occasions was his dispute with Minos. The Cretan king threw a ring into the sea, scornfully remarking that if Theseus' boast was true he should be able to recover the ring. Theseus dived after it and Poseidon not only saw to it that he found the ring but arranged that he bring back also a jeweled crown from the palace of Amphitrite.

The god had reason to hate Minos. In order to establish his claim to the Cretan throne, that king had long before prayed to Poseidon to send up a bull from the sea, vowing to sacrifice it immediately. The god had complied, but Minos had not kept his promise. Poseidon had punished him by making Pasiphaë, Minos' queen, fall in love with the bull. This same bull was later captured by Heracles as one of his labors. Poseidon sent a bull from the sea on another occasion, at the request of Theseus, to cause the death of Theseus' son Hippolytus.

In addition to his many mistresses, Poseidon had one or two male favorites. The young PELOPS [A, B] was so handsome that the god took him to Olympus for a while to be his lover. He gave him the winged chariot that enabled him to defeat Oenomaüs and dispose of Myrtilus. He later presented a similar gift to Idas, who used it to abduct the daughter of Evenus. Some explain this latter show of generosity with the claim that Idas was Poseidon's son.

Poseidon strongly supported the Greek forces in the Trojan War, partly because he held a grudge against the city of Troy on account of his treatment by Laomedon, Priam's father. Poseidon and Apollo, having apparently heard rumors of the king's impiety, appeared to him as mortals and offered to build the city walls. They were hired, and accomplished the task with the aid of the mortal Aeacus, but Laomedon refused to pay them the promised wages. Poseidon sent a sea-monster to ravage the coast, and Laomedon's daughter, Hesione, would have been sacrificed to it if Heracles had not saved her. (On an earlier occasion Poseidon had similarly punished Cepheus and Cassiopeia for an affront to the Nereïds, but Perseus had rescued their daughter, Andromeda.)

In spite of Poseidon's support of the Greeks, he agreed to punish them after the Trojan War for the affront of the Locrian Ajax to Athena. He sent disastrous storms upon the fleet, destroying much of it, and killed Ajax by splitting the rock to which he clung.

Poseidon's anger against Odysseus for killing Polyphemus was nearly implacable. The wanderer would never have reached Ithaca if the other gods had not aided him during Poseidon's absence in Ethiopia. The god severely punished the Phaeacians for helping Odysseus. He was finally appeased by sacrifices that Odysseus made in Thesprotia after he had defeated his wife's suitors. Though a violent god, Poseidon could occasionally be moved to pity. He rescued Aeneas from death because of his piety. At the request of Aphrodite, he made Ino and Melicertes sea-deities at their death, under the names of Leucothea and Palaemon. He also gave the Dioscuri the power to aid sailors in distress.

E. Poseidon was worshiped throughout the Greek lands. This worship was extended to Rome, where the god was equated with a hitherto unimportant god of water named Neptune. Poseidon was the patron deity of a number of islands, having strong connections with Crete, Chios, Cos, Delos, and Black Corcyra, among others. He was also the dominant deity of many seaports and of the entire Isthmus of Corinth. For less obvious reasons, he had cult centers at Delphi and throughout northern Boeotia. He was also prominently worshiped in Attica long before Athens became a great sea power. Many scholars believe that two famous early kings of Athens, Erechtheus and Aegeus, were in fact local forms of Poseidon.

The god's origins are not completely clear, but there is considerable agreement among scholars that his Greek name means Consort of Da. Da probably was a pre-Hellenic name for an earth-goddess; it is also found in the name of Demeter (Mother Da). An earth mother's consort who fertilized her with water was a common type of god in the Mediterranean region long before the Hellenes arrived. It is not unlikely that one or more of these gods merged with a deity whom the Greeks brought with them. The Hellenic god would originally have had no connection with the sea, for the Hellenes were an inland people who did not even have a word for the sea. Presumably, however, he had one or more of the other functions of the local god or gods, which permitted him to absorb the pre-Hellenic cults and gradually to extend his power to include the sea.

In art Poseidon was generally shown as a powerfully built man in the prime of life. He is scarcely distinguishable in appearance from Zeus, except by his trident, a three-pronged fish-spear.

F. Poseidon figures prominently throughout Homer's *Iliad* and in his *Odyssey* [1.19–26, 1.68–79, 5.282–381, 13.125–187], and appears in person, together with Athena, at the beginning of Euripides' tragedy *The Trojan Women*. Among the innumerable other references to the god are the following: Hesiod, *Theogony*, 278–281, 453–506, 732–733; *Catalogues of Women* 7, 9, 10, 13, 72; *Homeric Hymn to Aphrodite* 5.22–25; *Homeric Hymn to Poseidon* 22; Apollodorus 1.4.3–5, 1.6.2, 1.7.4, 1.9.8, 1.9.20–21, 2.1.4–5, 2.4.2–3, 2.4.5, 2.5.4–5, 2.5.7, 2.5.9–11, 2.7.1–2, 3.1.3, 3.10.1, 3.13.5,

3.14.1–2, 3.15.4–6; Herodotus 7.129; Apollonius Rhodius 1.179–189, 4.566–571; Hyginus, *Fabulae*, 89, 140, 166, 169, 169A, 186, 187–188, and *Poetica Astronomica*, 2.5, 2.17, 2.20, 2.22; Ovid, *Metamorphoses*, 4.531–542, 2.547–595, 4.790–803, 6.115–120, 8.848–854, 12.580–596; Pindar, *Olympian Odes*, 1.25–88, and *Isthmian Odes*, 8.30–45; Pausanias 2.1.6, 2.15.5, 8.8.2, 8.25.5–8, 8.42.1–2; 10.5.6; Vergil, *Georgics*, 1.12–14, and *Aeneïd*, 1.124–156, 5.779–826.

Potniae. A town between Thebes and Plataea. Potniae was perhaps best known for its well, the waters of which drove mares mad. Since Glaucus, king of Corinth, pastured his man-eating mares at Potniae, his legend may have been connected with the reputation of the water.

Praxithea, Prasithea, or **Pasithea.** See ERECHTHEUS; ERICHTHONIUS (1).

Priam. A king of Troy. Christened Podarces, this son of Laomedon by Strymo, Placia, or Leucippe was named Priam from the word *priamai* ("to buy") when ransomed from Heracles by his sister Hesione. He succeeded his father as king of the wealthy city of Troy. He married Arisbe, daughter of Merops, king of Percote, and had a son, Aesacus. Later he gave Arisbe to his ally Hyrtacus and married Hecuba, daughter of Dymas, of Cisseus, or of the river Sangarius by Metope. It may be that he had met Hecuba while fighting beside the Mygdonians against the Amazons on the banks of the Sangarius. She bore him a son, Hector. When she was about to give birth to a second child, she dreamed that she had borne a firebrand that burned Troy. Priam took the advice of Aesacus, who had diviner's powers, and exposed the infant at birth.

Hecuba bore many other children, including Helenus, Deïphobus, Polydorus, Cassandra, and Polyxena. Troïlus may have been her son by Apollo instead of by Priam. By other women Priam had innumerable children. Many years after the exposure of Hecuba's second son, Paris, he appeared at court and was recognized by Cassandra as the child whom they had presumed dead. Unfortunately for the city, the parents forgot Aesacus' warning and welcomed him into the family. Not long afterward, while on a trip to Sparta, Paris abducted the willing Helen, wife of his host, King Menelaüs, and brought her to Troy. The TROJAN WAR was the result.

Priam would have prudently returned Helen and the Spartan gold that had been stolen with her to Odysseus and Menelaüs when they came to demand it, but his sons prevailed on him to refuse. After ten years of war a second embassy was sent by the Greeks with the same result. Hector, leader of the Trojan forces, was killed by Achilles, who refused to give up the body for burial. Priam went in a mule cart to the Greek camp to plead with him, and Achilles finally permitted the aged man to ransom the corpse. After Achilles' death at Paris' hands, his son Neoptolemus came to Troy and finally led the Greeks to victory. Priam, who had lost most of his sons in the long war, was himself murdered by Neoptolemus, though he clung to the altar of Zeus Herceius in the courtyard of his palace. [Homer, *Iliad*, 3.146–313, 7.345–379, 22.408–430, 24; Apollodorus 2.6.4, 3.12.5, "Epitome" 5.1, 5.21.]

Priapus. A Phrygian god of fertility. Priapus, who did not come to be recognized in the Greek states until the time of Macedonian domination, was said to be a son of Aphrodite by Dionysus, Hermes, or some other god. He was represented as an ugly, satyrlike man with enormous genitals. Priapus has hardly any place in mythology. Hyginus [*Poetica Astronomica* 2.23] mentions in passing the tale of an argument that the god got into with an ass to which Dionysus had given a human voice. The full story is only hinted at, but it may be guessed that Priapus and the ass, a beast noted for erotic prowess, were debating the relative sizes of the physical appendages of which they were most proud. The boasting led to a contest in which the god came off the worse. Enraged at this ignominious defeat, Priapus beat the ass to death with a stick. Dionysus immortalized the ass by placing him in heaven as one of the two stars called the Asses.

Priapus was a god of gardens, bees, goats, and sheep. Though he never achieved great importance in Greece or Rome, he was widely worshiped in Asia Minor. At Lampsacus, on the Hellespont, he was honored above all other gods. [Hyginus, *Fabulae*, 160; Pausanias 9.31.2.]

Priasus. An Argonaut. Hyginus [*Fabulae* 14] calls Priasus, who is not otherwise known, a son of Caeneus and brother of Phocus, another Argonaut.

Procles. One of the Heraclids, son of Aristodemus and Argeia, daughter of Autesion. Procles and his twin brother, Eurysthenes, became wards of Theras, their mother's brother, at their father's early death. When their paternal uncles, Temenus and Cresphontes, invaded the Peloponnesus, the brothers shared equally with them in the conquered land. Partly because of Cresphontes' trickery in the drawing of lots, Procles and Eurysthenes received Sparta. The twins hated each other so violently that they founded separate ruling houses in the city. [Pausanias 3.1.5–6, 3.1.8–9.]

Procne. See TEREUS.

Procris. A daughter of Erechtheus. Procris married Cephalus, son of Deïon. According to most accounts she was a faithful wife whose husband betrayed her with the goddess Eos. Apollodorus [3.15.1] represents her rather differently. Bribed with a gold crown, she allowed herself to be seduced by someone named Pteleon. She fled to Crete, fearing her husband's anger, and was immediately propositioned by Minos. The king had a disease that had proved fatal to his many mistresses, but he was rich. He offered Procris the infallible hound Laelaps and a straight-flying javelin in return for her favors. Hesitating only a moment, she produced a drug that cured Minos' affliction, and she duly received the prizes for the price that he had asked. The anger of Minos' wife, Pasiphaë, now seemed more ominous than that of Cephalus, so Procris returned to Athens. She gave her husband, an ardent hunter, the dog and the spear, and they were reconciled. After some further marital problems involving Eos, Procris fell victim to her own gift. She spied on Cephalus from a thicket while he was hunting. Thinking her an animal, he flung the infallible spear and killed her.

According to Hyginus [*Fabulae* 189], Procris was faithful, and the hound and spear were gifts from Artemis, who advised Procris to disguise herself as a boy and go hunting with her husband. She did so, and defeated him in a contest. He offered to buy the supposed youth's hound and spear, even at the cost of a share of his kingdom. The young man refused, but said that she would give them freely if Cephalus would lie with him. Cephalus, delighted at so easy a bargain, took the handsome lad to his room. When they undressed he recognized his wife and they were reconciled. Nevertheless, Procris was still suspicious of Eos, and her life ended as in the other versions of her story.

Procrustes. A scoundrel who lived at Erineus, near Eleusis. Although his real name was either Damastes or Polypemon, Procrustes (Stretcher) was better known by his nickname, which he earned from his habits as a host. Procrustes lived in a house by the side of the road that led from Eleusis to Athens and invited travelers to spend the night with him. If they did not exactly fit into his bed, he would either stretch them or lop off their extremities until they did. THESEUS [B] avenged many a departed guest by treating Procrustes to the same form of hospitality.

Procyon. See CANIS MAJOR.

Proëtus. A king of Tiryns.

A. Proëtus and ACRISIUS were twin sons of Abas, king of Argos, and Aglaea. They began quarreling before they left the womb and did not stop until they had torn the kingdom of Argos into two parts. Abas bequeathed the kingdom to the brothers jointly, but they were soon at war over it. Some attribute this feud to Proëtus' seduction of Acrisius' daughter, Danaë, though Danaë herself named Zeus as the guilty one. In any case, Acrisius managed to drive Proëtus from the country. The exile took refuge in Lycia at the court of Iobates (or Amphianax) and married his daughter, whom Homer names Anteia but others call Stheneboea. Iobates championed his son-in-law's cause by sending a Lycian army with him to attack Argos. The brothers met in single combat at Epidaurus and battled to a draw. (It is said that this was the first time that shields were used.) Seeing that they were equally matched, they agreed to divide the kingdom. Acrisius retained Argos; Proëtus made his capital at the city of Tiryns, which the Cyclopes fortified for him with walls of great blocks of stone.

Stheneboea bore three daughters—Lysippe, Iphinoë, and Iphianassa—and a son, Megapenthes. When young BELLEROPHON [A], son of Glaucus, king of Ephyra, came to visit Tiryns, Stheneboea found him attractive, but he spurned her advances. Furious, she told Proëtus that Bellerophon had made the advances. Proëtus sent the young man to Iobates with a sealed letter asking him to kill Bellerophon. When Stheneboea later learned that far from being killed, the youth had married her sister Philonoë, she killed herself from sheer frustration.

B. Either before or after this event, Proëtus suffered a more serious misfortune—the madness of his daughters. He called in the Messenian seer ME-LAMPUS [C], who offered to cure the women in return for a third or a half of Proëtus' kingdom. Proëtus was reluctant to pay so high a price, but was forced to agree when the madness struck the other Argive women as well. Now the greedy seer demanded another third of the kingdom for his brother, Bias. The daughters were cured, except for Iphinoë, who died, but Proëtus lost most of the land that he had wrested from Acrisius. Some claim, however, that the madness of the Argive women and the resulting bargain occurred much later, in the reign of Anaxagoras. Ovid says that Proëtus managed to drive Acrisius from the Argive throne, but PERSEUS [E] avenged his grandfather by turning Proëtus to stone with the head of Medusa. Hyginus adds that Megapenthes avenged Proëtus in turn by killing Perseus. [Apollodorus 2.2.1–2.4.1.]

Promachus (1). A son of Parthenopaeüs. One of the EPIGONI, Promachus must have been killed at Thebes, for Pausanias [9.19.2] reports that he was buried near by at Teumessus.

Promachus (2). A son of Aeson by either Alcimede or Polymede, and younger brother of Jason. While still a boy, Promachus was killed by Pelias.

Prometheus. A Titan.

A. Prometheus (Forethought) was a son of the Titan Iapetus by Iapetus' sister Themis or by Clymene or Asia, both of whom were Oceanids. Prometheus or Hephaestus is said to have delivered Athena from Zeus's head by splitting it with an ax. Prometheus is best known, however, as the principal champion before the gods of the race of men, whom he is said by some to have molded out of clay. He was accustomed to submitting his creations to Zeus for inspection, but noting the extraordinary beauty of one of them and knowing the god's fondness for handsome boys, he neglected to send this lad. Zeus heard of the boy, whose name was Phaënon, and had him carried off to heaven, where he became the planet now called Jupiter. Those who did not believe that Prometheus made men from clay said that he was their progenitor in the more conventional fashion. By a personage named Pronoea, he was the father of Deucalion; his brother, Epimetheus, was the father by Pandora of Pyrrha. The two children married each other, and, when all or most other members of the human race died in a flood, they produced more by following Prometheus' advice and tossing stones over their shoulders. Thus, in one way or another, the race owes its existence to the Titan.

It is also indebted to him for the rudiments of civilization. Zeus did not think highly of human beings. He and the other gods demanded constant sacrifices from men, who had a hard enough time finding food even for themselves. Prometheus, to his own misfortune, found several ingenious ways to better the lot of his creatures. He persuaded Zeus to allow them to sacrifice only a part of the animals that they slaughtered, instead of the whole beasts, as had formerly been required. An argument ensued as to which part should belong to the gods. The crafty Titan hid the best part of the flesh in an ox-hide or stomach and wrapped the bones and entrails attractively in rich-looking fat, then offered the god his choice. Deceived, Zeus chose the inferior part. The daily fare of men was greatly improved by Prometheus' cunning, but Zeus did not forgive him for the trick.

Men were still poorly off, for they were unable to keep warm or cook their food, fire being reserved for the gods. Prometheus determined on a dangerous course in order to benefit mankind. Stealing fire from heaven, he hid it in a stalk of fennel and carried it secretly down to earth. Zeus, enraged at the Titan's temerity, ordered Hephaestus to nail him to a cliff in the Caucasus Mountains and sent an eagle each day to peck out his liver, which grew again each night. Zeus saw to it, moreover, that men would not profit for long from the more comfortable conditions of their lives. He commanded Hephaestus to fashion a beautiful and evil creature to be a plague to Prometheus' men: woman. The other gods gave her gifts, such as craft, deceitfulness, and a generally vile nature. Hermes then presented the woman—who was ironically named Pandora (All Gifts)—to Prometheus' gullible brother, Epimetheus (Afterthought). Although Epimetheus had often been warned by Prometheus never to accept gifts from a god, he married the woman. She had brought with her as a dowry a jar of further gifts: all the evils that beset men. Pandora opened the jar soon after her arrival and released the swarm of troubles, keeping back only one gift—hope.

B. Prometheus' benevolences toward men were thus effectively nullified. As for the Titan himself, he hung on his rocky crag for thirty thousand years. What brought his sufferings to an end at last is disputed. The agent, it is agreed, was Heracles, who shot the eagle and broke Prometheus' bonds. Some say that Zeus permitted this to happen in order to add to the glory of his famous son. Others claim that Prometheus, who had prophetic powers, possessed a secret that Zeus desperately wished to know. This secret was often said to have been that Thetis, whom Zeus was pursuing, was fated to bear a son who would be greater than his father. Prometheus used this knowledge (which he had got from Themis) to bargain successfully with Zeus for his freedom. As a gesture of gratitude to Heracles, who was on his way at the time to find the apples of the Hesperides, Prometheus advised him not to try to pluck them himself, but to send their owner, Atlas, who was Prometheus' brother. It is said that when the Centaur Cheiron was in great torment from a poisoned arrow wound in his foot he wished to die, but could not because he was immortal. Prometheus, though he was at the time in equally terrible pain, consented to take on the Centaur's immortality, and Cheiron gratefully died. This story is not quite plausible, however, for Prometheus, a Titan, must have been immortal in his own right. Some say that he appears in the sky, still bound to his crag, in the constellation of the Kneeler, but this group of stars has been identified in a great variety of ways. Prometheus was remembered on earth with torch races commemorating his theft of fire.

Prometheus is the protagonist of *Prometheus Bound*, the only extant play of a trilogy on the Titan by Aeschylus. See also Hesiod [*Theogony*, 507–616, and *Works and Days*, 47–105], Apollodorus [1.2.3, 1.3.6, 1.7.1–2, 2.5.4, 2.5.11, 3.13.5], Hyginus [*Fabulae*, 54, 144, and *Poetica Astronomica*, 2.6, 2.15, 2.42], and Pausanias [1.30.2, 2.19.5, 2.19.8].

Pronax. A son of Talaüs and Lysimache. Pronax was a brother of Adrastus and the father of Lycurgus and Amphithea. [Apollodorus 1.19.13.]

Pronoë. See AETOLUS.

Pronoüs. See ALCMEON.

Propontis. See Sea of MARMARA.

Proserpina. The Roman name of PERSEPHONE.

Protesilaüs. A son of Iphiclus, king of Phylace, and Diomedeia. Protesilaüs married Laodameia, daughter of Acastus, king of Iolcus, or Polydora, daughter of Meleager. Shortly after the wedding he left for the Trojan War in command of forty ships from Phylace and neighboring cities. An oracle warned the Greeks that the first man to touch Trojan soil would be the first to die. When they were met by a Trojan force commanded by Hector and Cycnus, most of the Greeks hesitated to land, but Protesilaüs leaped ashore. He killed several Trojans before being cut down by Hector or some other Trojan. His younger brother, Podarces, took his place at the head of the Phylacian contingent. Protesilaüs was buried across the Hellespont on the Thracian Chersonese and was honored as a hero in a rich shrine at Elaeüs, near Sestus. LAODAMEIA grieved so immoderately that Protesilaüs was permitted to return briefly from Hades to comfort her, after which time she killed herself.

Generations later, the Persians under Xerxes conquered the Chersonese, and a greedy official named Artaÿctes was made governor of Sestus. Wishing to plunder Protesilaüs' temple, a deed that Xerxes would not normally have permitted, Artaÿctes told his king a false story. On the grounds that he wished to teach the Greeks a lesson, he asked to be given the house of a certain Greek who, he said, had died invading Persian territory with an army. Xerxes agreed. Artaÿctes thereupon took for himself the treasures in the temple of Protesilaüs, who had centuries before invaded an Asian land that was now claimed by Persia. Not content with this, he sowed the sacred precinct with grain and lay with women inside the temple. The hero punished the Persian for this desecration through an Athenian army which captured Sestus, together with its governor and his son. According to the Greeks of this region, the man who guarded the prisoners was startled while preparing a meal of dried fish to see the fish leaping in the pan. Artaÿctes realized that this was an omen that Protesilaüs, though his body was as dead and dry as the fish, still had the power to avenge insults. The terrified Persian promised to pay back the money that he had

stolen from the temple and to give a similar amount to his captors as ransom
for himself and his son. Unmoved, the Athenian general, Xanthippus, had Artaÿctes nailed to a cross and his son stoned to death before his eyes. [Homer,
Iliad, 2.695–710; Herodotus 7.33, 9.116–120; *Cypria* 17.]

Proteus (1). A minor sea-deity. Proteus, who, like Nereus, was often called
the Old Man of the Sea, was Poseidon's sealherd. (Some say that Poseidon was
his father, but Proteus may well have been a more ancient god of the sea.)
When MENELAÜS [B] was stranded on the Egyptian island of Pharos on his
way home from the Trojan War, a beautiful nymph named Eidothea took pity
on him and explained how he might force her prophetic father, Proteus, to reveal to him what he must do to reach Sparta again. Menelaüs followed her advice. Disguised as seals, he and three companions waited for Proteus to
emerge from the sea at noon to count his flock of seals and rest with them in a
sea-cave. As soon as the old man was asleep, they bound him and would not
let him go even though he transformed himself successively into a lion, a
snake, a leopard, a boar, water, and a tree. Proteus finally reassumed his own
form and consented to give Menelaüs the information he needed.

This tale from Homer's *Odyssey* [4.363–570] inspired a similar story
about Proteus in Vergil's *Georgics* [4.386–529]. Here, ARISTAEÜS captured
the sea-god to learn why his bees had died and what he must do to remedy
the situation. Vergil removed Proteus from Egypt, placing him on the island of
Carpathus and calling him a native of Thessaly and Pallene. Vergil even preserved the realistic touch that Homer gave the tale: the seals had such an over-
powering stench that Proteus' captors had to be anointed with ambrosia before
they could approach.

It seems evident that the old sea-god Proteus is the same as the benevolent Egyptian king of that name, presumably having been demoted from
divinity by some literal-minded writers.

Proteus (2). A king of Egypt. Proteus succeeded Pharos as king. He mar-
ried the Nereïd Psamathe, formerly Aeacus' mistress, and had by her a son,
Theoclymenus, and a daughter, Eido, who later came to be called Theonoë.
Because of Proteus' reputation as a respecter of family ties, Hermes brought
HELEN [G] to him for safekeeping during the Trojan War. According to
Euripides, Proteus died while she was in Egypt. Theoclymenus buried his
father at the palace gate, where he might greet him on entering and leaving.
He showed less piety in observing his duty to Helen and tried to force her to
marry him. Only her own cleverness and the timely arrival of Menelaüs saved
her. Herodotus records the Egyptian claim that Helen reached Egypt not with
Hermes, but with Paris. On learning of her abduction, Proteus kept her with
him and drove Paris away in disgrace. After the Trojan War, he gave her
back to Menelaüs. He was succeeded on the throne by Rhampsinitus.

Because the story that Helen did not go to Troy is said to have originated
with the poet Stesichorus, many scholars believe that King Proteus came into

existence through confusion with Proteus the Old Man of the Sea, who also lived on the island of Pharos, had a daughter named Eidothea, and was said by Homer [*Odyssey* 4.351–570] to have counseled Menelaüs on his homeward journey with Helen. [Euripides, *Helen*, 4–11, 44–48, 1165–1168; Herodotus 2.112–118, 121.]

Protogeneia. A daughter of Deucalion and Pyrrha. By Zeus or Aeolus, Protogeneia became the mother of Endymion.

Psamathe or **Psamatheïs.** A Nereïd. Psamathe bore a son, Phocus, to Aeacus, king of Aegina. The young man was killed by his half-brothers, Peleus and Telamon. Psamathe sent a wolf to ravage the flocks of Peleus in Phthia or Trachis, but was persuaded by her sister Thetis to turn the animal to stone. Psamathe later married Proteus, king of Egypt, and bore two children, Theoclymenus and Eido (Theonoë). [Ovid, *Metamorphoses*, 11.346–406; Euripides, *Helen*, 4.13.]

Psophis. A city in northwestern Arcadia. Psophis was originally named Erymanthus for a descendant of Lycaon who gave his name also to a nearby mountain and to the river that rises on its slopes and flows past Psophis. King Phegeus renamed the town Phegia. The person after whom it was finally called Psophis has been variously called a grandson or granddaughter of Erymanthus or the daughter of Eryx, king of Sicania, whom Heracles seduced and deserted. It was here that the sons of Phegeus murdered Alcmeon for his infidelity to their sister. He was buried at Psophis in a grove of cypresses called "maidens," which are sacred to him. The natives excused their failure to participate in the Trojan War on the grounds that they were unacceptable to the Argive leaders of the Greek forces, nearly all of whom were related to Alcmeon.

Psyche. A beautiful daughter of an unidentified king. Psyche's loveliness became so famous that everywhere people stopped worshiping at the shrines of Venus (Aphrodite). Annoyed, the goddess called on her son Cupid (Eros) to avenge her by making Psyche fall in love with some wretch without rank or reputation. Psyche, meanwhile, was regretting the beauty that made eligible males worship her instead of courting her, and her father was beginning to fear the anger of the gods at his daughter's fame. Apollo's oracle at Miletus did nothing to encourage him, but issued a command that Psyche must prepare to wed, on a lonely mountain top, an evil spirit feared even by the gods. Psyche sadly but bravely let herself be led by the sorrowing citizens to a craggy hilltop, where they left her and returned to hide themselves in their homes. Instead of encountering a demon, Psyche found herself carried by a gentle west wind to a flowery wood within which she came to a fairylike castle. She wandered inside, where, amid rich surroundings, she received the most royal service at invisible hands. After a splendid banquet Psyche repaired to a bedroom and undressed for the night.

When darkness came she was at first frightened, then soothed, by a man's voice that told her in gentle whispers that he was her husband. When he lay with her in the darkness she felt no fear, but only pleasure. Before dawn Psyche's unseen husband left the palace, but he came again the next night and the next. On the fourth night, however, Psyche's husband urgently warned her that her sisters were seeking her and that she must not see them. The following day Psyche suddenly felt terribly lonely. That night she pleaded with her husband so disconsolately that he promised to let the west wind waft her sisters to the palace for a day's visit. He warned her most solemnly that she must not let them induce her to try to discover his identity, for this would bring disaster on her.

Psyche's sisters were overjoyed to find her safe until she showed them the evidences of her extraordinary good fortune. Then, though the openhearted girl showered them with presents, they were consumed with envy and at once began to plot her destruction. That night Psyche's husband told her that she would bear a divine child if she remembered her promise never to look on his face. If she disobeyed, the child would be mortal. Still, Psyche could not believe her invisible husband's admonitions about her sisters and insisted on seeing them again. This time she forgot the imaginary description that she had given them before of her husband and made up a quite different one, since she was reluctant to admit that she had no idea what he was really like. The sisters quickly suspected the truth and on their next visit terrified Psyche with the tale that she had married a serpent who would eat her when she was far gone in pregnancy. They convinced the naïve girl that her only hope was to hide a lamp and a knife by her bed and kill her monstrous husband while he slept.

Somehow Psyche found the strength to carry out a part of her sisters' malicious advice, but when she held the lamp over the bed she saw not a monster but the indescribably beautiful body of the winged Cupid. At once she was overcome with love for her divine husband, but her disobedience did not go unpunished. A drop of hot oil from the lamp fell on Cupid's shoulder. The god, who had disobeyed his mother's commands for love of the foolish girl, saw that he had been betrayed and flew away, leaving Psyche inconsolable.

On learning that Psyche's husband had been the god of love, and that he had deserted her, the triumphant sisters hurried, one by one, to the crag where Psyche had first been left. Each called upon Cupid to welcome a more worthy bride and leaped confidently from the cliff. No west wind appeared to carry them to the enchanted palace. The sisters met sudden and ignominious deaths in the valley below.

Psyche, meanwhile, was desperate with grief and remorse. She prayed at the shrines of Juno and Ceres, but heavenly protocol prevented them from offending Venus by aiding her. The love goddess, furious that her son had not only failed to punish the girl whom she hated, but had actually got her with child, upbraided Cupid unmercifully, then set out to find Psyche. Psyche could not escape and had to submit to the most violent mistreatment from the goddess.

Venus first set her to sorting a roomful of assorted grains, commanding that she finish the task by nightfall. Psyche could not possibly have done so had not a colony of sympathetic ants come to her aid, neatly arranging the grains in piles by kind. Unappeased, Venus demanded that Psyche bring her a hank of wool from a flock of man-killing sheep. The poor girl was ready to die, but a talking reed dissuaded her from suicide and told her how to get the wool in safety. Following this advice, Psyche waited until the sheep lay down to sleep in the cool afternoon. She then easily gathered tufts of their wool that had clung to briar bushes in the grove.

Still Venus was unsatisfied. She now demanded that Psyche bring her a jarful of water from the deadly river Styx where it burst from the side of a precipice of Mount Aroanius in northern Arcadia. The utter impossibility of this task did not trouble the miserable Psyche, for she had determined to die. Before she could make any attempt on her life, however, her plight was detected by Jupiter's eagle. This bird owed a debt to Cupid, who had once helped him carry Ganymede up to heaven. He at once swooped down, snatched the jar, and, after filling it with Stygian water, returned it to Psyche.

The implacable Venus only issued a further order to her victim: to bring back from Hades in a box a day's supply of Proserpina's beauty ointment. Realizing that she was now being sent directly to her death, Psyche climbed a tower and prepared to jump from its top. To her surprise, the tower spoke to her, issuing elaborate directions as to how she might safely carry out this seemingly fatal task. Psyche followed these directions to the letter. Making her way to Taenarum, on the southern coast of the Peloponnesus, she entered its famous doorway to the Underworld bearing two obols in her mouth and two honey cakes in her hand. She ignored a lame man who asked her for rope to tie a load on the back of his lame ass. She let Charon take one of the coins from her mouth as fare across the Styx in his boat and refused the request of a floating corpse to be helped aboard the ferry. On the far shore, moreover, she turned her back on three women who asked her aid in weaving a piece of cloth, for the talkative tower had explained that all these plausible pleas for help were merely tricks by which Venus hoped to make her drop the honey cakes.

Psyche now made use of the first of the cakes, tossing it to the three-headed watchdog Cerberus so that she might pass into Proserpina's palace. There, as the tower had directed, she refused the Underworld queen's offer of a sumptuous meal in a comfortable chair. Sitting on the ground and accepting only bread, she delivered Venus' request. Proserpina filled the box and gave it to her readily enough. Psyche returned to Taenarum after giving up the last cake and coin as needed. Only when she was back in the upper world did Psyche forget the wise advice of the tower. Giving way to curiosity and the desire to make herself beautiful in the hope of winning back her lost husband, she opened the box that Proserpina had given her. Out stole a deathlike sleep that instantly overcame the unfortunate girl.

Cupid, meanwhile, had recovered from his burn but not from his love for Psyche. He sped through the air to her rescue, wafted the sleep back into the box with his wings, and awakened Psyche. While she went to deliver the box, Cupid flew away to beg Jupiter's approval of their marriage. The supreme god indulgently agreed. Making Psyche immortal, he married her to Cupid. In due course she bore a lovely daughter who was named Volupta (Pleasure).

The tale of Cupid and Psyche is known only from *The Golden Ass* of Lucius Apuleius [4.28–6.26].

Pterelaüs. A king of the Taphians. Pterelaüs was a son of Taphius, eponym of the Taphian islands, off the coast of Acarnania, and of Taphos, one of those islands. Pterelaüs was descended from Perseus' son Mestor, whose daughter, Hippothoë, had borne Taphius to Poseidon. The sea-god, to please his son, implanted a golden hair in the head of Pterelaüs, explaining that he would not die as long as the hair remained there. Pterelaüs sent his six sons to Tiryns to steal the cattle that belonged to King Electryon, on the pretext that the kingdom had actually belonged to Electryon's brother Mestor, their ancestor. Electryon's sons died defending the cattle, and only one of Pterelaüs' sons survived the encounter. The Taphians, however, sailed away with the cattle, which they left with Polyxenus, king of Elis. Amphitryon, Electryon's son-in-law, ransomed the cattle and later set out on an expedition against the Taphians, at the head of a large force. Pterelaüs' city would not have fallen as long as he possessed the golden hair, but his daughter, Comaetho, falling in love with Amphitryon, pulled it out. Pterelaüs died, and Amphitryon took Taphos. He executed Comaetho for her treacherous deed. [Apollodorus 2.4.5–7.]

Ptoüs. A son of Athamas and Themisto. Mount Ptoüs, in Boeotia, was named for this young man, of whom nothing else is known.

Pygmalion. A king of Cyprus. According to Apollodorus [3.14.3], Pygmalion was a Cypriot king whose daughter, Metharme, married Cinyras, an immigrant from Cilicia. Ovid added a romantic variation. Pygmalion, finding no mortal woman worthy of his love, carved a statue in ivory of his ideal mate and promptly fell in love with it. In answer to his prayer, Aphrodite brought the image to life, and Pygmalion married her. She bore a daughter, Paphos, eponym of the city that Paphos' son Cinyras later founded. The name Galatea was applied to the statue-woman only in modern times. [Ovid, *Metamorphoses*, 10.243–297.]

Pygmalion. See DIDO.

Pylades. A son of Strophius, king of Phocis. According to some writers, Pylades' mother was Agamemnon's sister, Anaxibia or Astyoche. Reared with his cousin ORESTES, he became his faithful companion, assisting him in his vengeance on Clytemnestra, his attempted murder of Helen, his trip to the land of the Taurians, and his murder of Neoptolemus. Pylades married Orestes' sister Electra, who bore him two sons, Medon and Strophius. He appears in all the plays dealing with Orestes' adventures, except for *Andromache*.

Pylas, Pylus, or **Pylon.** A king and eponym of the Messenian and Eleian cities named Pylus. Pylas, a son of Cleson, was originally king of Megara. He welcomed Pandion, son of Cecrops, when he was exiled from Athens and gave him his daughter Pylia for his wife. Later Pylas himself was exiled for killing Bias, his father's brother. Leaving the kingdom to Pandion, Pylas went to Messenia with his Lelegian followers and founded the city of Pylus. He was later driven out by Neleus and went to Elis, where he founded another Pylus. The shadowiness of this character is evidenced by the fact that in three references to him Pausanias spells his name three ways. [Apollodorus 3.15.5; Pausanias 4.36.1, 6.22.5–6.]

Pylus. The name of two cities in the Peloponnesus. The first Pylus was a coastal city in Messenia. It was said to have been founded by Pylas, the exiled king of Megara, who colonized it with his Leleges. When Neleus came to Messenia, he was welcomed by his uncle Aphareus, who ruled in Arene. Neleus settled in Pylus, driving out the Leleges, whereupon Pylas emigrated to Elis and founded a second city of the same name. After Aphareus' death, the center of Messenian government apparently shifted to Pylus. Pylus became a prosperous city under Neleus and grew more so during the three-generation rule of his son Nestor, who had escaped the sack of the city by Heracles in Neleus' old age. With the return of the Heraclids, Cresphontes drove out Neleus' descendants and ruled Messenia from Stenyclerus.

The history of the Eleian Pylus is vague. In the "Catalogue of Ships" [*Iliad* 2.591–602], Homer mentions Pylus among the cities that sent troops to Troy under the leadership of Nestor. Homer believed that the Alpheius River, the principal river in Elis, flowed through the land of the Pylians, but this may have been no more than hazy geography, for the other known cities listed in the same passage were certainly in Messenia, and Nestor is identified with Messenia in all other ancient sources. Although the Eleians showed Pausanias ruins of "Pylus" at the junction of the Ladon and the Peneius rivers, this was a long way from the Alpheius, and it was not a seaport, as Nestor's Pylus unmistakably is in Book 3 of the *Odyssey*. There is, moreover, no other mention of Pylus in Pausanias' record of the legendary history of Elis. There may have been an Eleian Pylus, but it is unlikely to have been Nestor's capital.

Pyramus and **Thisbe.** Young Assyrian lovers. Pyramus and Thisbe grew up in adjoining houses and fell in love, but were not allowed by their families to marry one another. After long nights of whispering through a chink in the wall between their houses, they determined to meet at night at the tomb of King Ninus. Thisbe arrived first, but was frightened away by a lioness, which then mauled with its bloody jaws the cloak that Thisbe had dropped. Pyramus, on finding the cloak, thought himself responsible for his loved one's death and killed himself with his sword. His blood changed the blooms and fruit of the mulberry tree beneath which he fell from their former white to purple. Thisbe returned, and, discovering Pyramus' body, killed herself with the same sword. The ashes of the unfortunate pair were buried in the same urn by their parents. [Ovid, *Metamorphoses*, 4.55–166.]

Pyriphlegethon. See PHLEGETHON.

Pyrrha. A daughter of Epimetheus and Pandora. Pyrrha, the first mortal-born woman, married her cousin DEUCALION and survived the Flood with him. They had five children: Hellen, Amphictyon, Protogeneia, Pandora, and Thyia.

Pyrrhus. See NEOPTOLEMUS.

Pythia. See DELPHI.

Pytho. See DELPHI; PYTHON.

Python. A monstrous snake, or dragon, that lived at Delphi. In the earliest extant account, this dragon was female and was not named. When Hera bore the monster Typhöeus, she gave him to the dragoness to rear. APOLLO [A] came to Delphi to establish his oracle there and killed the snake, which was ravaging the land. Later accounts specify that it was the guardian of the already existing oracle of Ge or Themis, which Apollo usurped or was given. Some say that Apollo buried the monster and established the Pythian games in its honor. Others claim that the place was named Pytho from a word meaning "to rot," because the carcass was left beside the sacred spring to decay. The snake itself (regarded in most later accounts as male) came to be called Python, and Apollo's prophetess was called the Pythia. Although killing dragons is a common enough activity of heroes, some scholars have suggested that the story of Apollo and Python arose in part out of a historical event in which invaders took over the important oracle of an earth-goddess at Delphi. The struggle between god and snake figured importantly in various rituals performed at Delphic festivals of Apollo.

Q

Quirinus. The name under which Romulus was worshiped after his deification. Quirinus was an ancient Roman god of a warlike nature who came to be identified with the hero Romulus. He was sometimes worshiped together with Bellona.

R

races of man. According to Hesiod [*Works and Days* 109–201], the gods created five races of men, who lived in successive periods often called the five ages of man. The first, a golden race, lived under Cronus' rule. Free of care in their lives, they died peacefully and, as spirits, became guardians of mortals. After this "golden age" a silver race was created, but it was vastly inferior to its predecessors, being so childish and so heedless of the honors due the gods that the Olympians destroyed it. A brazen race followed, but was so dedicated to warfare that it soon annihilated itself. After this came a race of "demigods," living in what is now called the "heroic age" and which is celebrated in most Greek myths. Many of these demigods died fighting in the war of the Seven against Thebes or at Troy; the rest were granted a carefree existence in the Islands of the Blessed, ruled by Cronus after his deposition from Olympus. The subsequent iron race—our own—is a nearly total disaster, going from bad to worse as all codes of decency are flouted. This race will be destroyed by Zeus when babies are born already old. Hesiod did not venture to predict whether the gods would replace the iron race or entirely abandon mortals as not worth the trouble of creation.

Ram, The. See ARIES.

raven. See CROW.

Rea Silvia. The daughter of Numitor, king of Alba Longa. Rea Silvia's uncle Amulius deposed her father and appointed her a Vestal Virgin to prevent her from bearing rightful heirs to the throne. She was seduced by Mars, however, and bore twin sons, Romulus and Remus, who in time overthrew Amulius.

reincarnation. See METEMPSYCHOSIS.

Remus. See ROMULUS AND REMUS.

Returns, The. The homeward voyages of the Greek leaders from the Trojan War. The name "Returns" (*Nostoi*) was given to these events by Hegias (or Hagias) of Troezen as the title of his epic poem on the subject (see EPIC CYCLE). After the fall of Troy, Menelaüs wished to sail at once for home, but Agamemnon argued that the Greeks should first try to appease with sacrifices Athena's anger over the rape of Cassandra at her altar. The Greek forces were divided. Menelaüs, Nestor, Diomedes, Philoctetes, Idomeneus, and Achilles' Myrmidons sailed without delay; the others remained at Troy with

Agamemnon. Of the first group, all reached home quickly and safely except Menelaüs, who wandered the seas for seven years before arriving in Sparta.

Agamemnon, who enjoyed a safe voyage only to be murdered in his bath or at dinner on his arrival, was only one of the returning leaders to have been played false by their wives at the instigation of Nauplius, who thus avenged the murder of his son Palamedes at Troy. Diomedes and Idomeneus also found that their wives had been unfaithful. Many other Greeks suffered even more severely from Nauplius' vengeance. A large number of those ships that were not destroyed off the coast of Euboea in a storm were driven on the rocky promontory of Caphareus, lured by false beacon-fires lighted by Nauplius, who killed the few sailors that reached land alive. Ajax, whose desecration of Athena's temple had caused her or Zeus to send the storm, made it to a rock in safety, only to have Poseidon split the rock with his trident to punish Ajax for a foolish boast.

Teucer reached his home in Salamis, but was exiled by his father, Telamon, without being permitted to land. Both Idomeneus and Diomedes were eventually banished from their homelands and settled in Italy. Philoctetes also later went to Italy.

Neoptolemus journeyed overland to Thrace, where he met Odysseus in the city of Maroneia. Phoenix, who was traveling with Neoptolemus, died before reaching home. Neoptolemus went either to Phthia or Epeirus and reigned for a time, but was later killed by Delphians either at the instigation of his enemy Orestes or because he had attacked Apollo's Delphic shrine. Odysseus' homeward voyage took ten years. Many of the lesser leaders at Troy did not make any attempt to go home, or else settled elsewhere after being thwarted on their way by various disasters. They are credited with colonizing lands from Asia Minor to the Spanish islands.

Apart from Homer's *Odyssey*, the most connected account of the Returns is given by Apollodorus ["Epitome" 6–7]. Apollodorus' account seems to have been based on the *Odyssey* and the *Returns*, of which poem a brief summary by Proclus survives. Four extant Greek dramas also deal with events in the lives of the Greek leaders after the Trojan War: Aeschylus' *Agamemnon* and Euripides' *Hecuba, Andromache,* and *Helen.* Menelaüs appears also in Euripides' *Orestes.*

Rhadamanthys or **Rhadamanthus.** A Cretan lawgiver. Rhadamanthys was a son of Zeus and Europa. He and his brothers, Minos and Sarpedon, were rivals for the love of a handsome youth, Miletus or Atymnius. The young man expressed a preference for Sarpedon, whereupon Minos drove his brothers from Crete and seized the throne. Rhadamanthys, according to some accounts, took refuge in Ocaleae, in Boeotia, and married Alcmene after the death of her husband Amphitryon. Other accounts claim that Rhadamanthys established a code of laws in Crete and that Minos gave him rule over certain Aegean islands because he feared his growing popularity. Some say that Rhadamanthys ruled much of Asia Minor as well. His sons Erythrus and Gortys gave their names to Erythraea, in Lydia, and Gortyn, in Crete. Because Rhadamanthys loved justice on earth, he, like his brother Minos, was made a judge of the dead in Hades. According to Homer [*Odyssey* 4.561–569] he ruled in Elysium. [Apollodorus 2.4.1, 3.1.1–2; Diodorus Siculus 579.1–2.]

Rhamnusia. A title of Nemesis. The goddess was so called because her chief cult center was at Rhamnus, a town on the northeastern coast of Attica.

Rhampsinitus. See PROTEUS (2).

Rhea or **Rheia.** A Titaness. Rhea, whom the Romans identified with their goddess Ops, married her brother CRONUS. He overthrew their father, Uranus, and reigned over the other Titans, but was warned by his parents that he was destined to be overthrown in turn by one of his children. In order to prevent this, Cronus ate his children one by one as they were born to Rhea. Rhea, or her mother, Ge, hid her youngest baby, Zeus, in Crete and gave Cronus in his place a stone wrapped in swaddling clothes. Some say that she had earlier hidden Poseidon among lambs and given her husband a foal to eat instead, claiming that she had just borne it. The Arcadians insisted that many of these events took place in their land, not in Crete. They added that Rhea called on Hopladamus and his giants (who are not otherwise known) to protect her if need be from Cronus. When Zeus grew to manhood, his first wife, Metis, gave Cronus an emetic so that he vomited up his children. They joined Zeus in deposing Cronus and certain of his fellow Titans. During the conflict Rhea sent Hera to Oceanus and Tethys for safekeeping. Rhea was often identified by the Greeks with the Phrygian goddess CYBELE, the Mother of the Gods. In this role she is said to have taught Dionysus many of his rites. The Curetes who helped protect the infant Zeus in Crete are confused with the Phrygian Corybantes, who were companions of Cybele. [Hesiod, *Theogony*, 135, 453–506; Homer, *Iliad*, 14.201–204; Apollodorus 1.1.3–1.2.1, 3.5.1, 3.12.6; Hyginus, *Fabulae*, 139; Pausanias 8.8.2–3, 8.36.2–3.]

Rhesus. A Thracian ally of the Trojans. Rhesus was a son of Eioneus, or of the river-god Strymon and one of the Muses. According to the latter version, the Muse was impregnated by the river as she waded in it. Later, ashamed at having borne the child, she threw it into the river. Strymon turned it over to the water-nymphs to bring up. On reaching manhood Rhesus became a king in Thrace. In Euripides' play *Rhesus*, Hector states that Rhesus owed his power in Thrace to the Trojans, who had conquered several Thracian tribes and made them Rhesus' vassals. Rhesus arrived in Troy with a large Thracian force to aid the Trojans in the last year of the war. He reached Troy at night and camped at some distance from the main camp. By chance the Trojan spy Dolon was caught that same night by Diomedes and Odysseus. In the hope of saving his own life he told his captors of Rhesus and his valuable horses. The two Greeks, after murdering their informant, stole into Rhesus' camp, killed the king and twelve of his men while they slept, and drove off the horses.

After his death Rhesus became a kind of oracular spirit, inhabiting caves in the region of the Thracian silver mines, but the reference to this fate in *Rhesus* [970–973] is vague.

Rhesus appears only briefly in the play that bears his name. His death is recounted by Homer [*Iliad* 10.432–514].

Rhexenor. A son of Nausithoüs, king of the Phaeacians. For some unexplained reason, Apollo killed Rhexenor when he was still a bridegroom. His daughter, Arete, married his brother Alcinoüs, who became king of the Phaeacians.

Rhine River. A river that rises in Switzerland and flows north and west to empty into the North Sea near Rotterdam. Apollonius Rhodius speaks in the *Argonautica* of a river that leads northward to the ocean through the "Hercynian land," an ancient name for the mountainous southern part of Germany. Although he does not give the river a name, he seems to have the Rhine in mind. The Argonauts took this route by mistake until stopped by Hera and redirected southward via the Rhône.

Rhode or **Rhodos.** A daughter of Poseidon and Amphitrite, or of some other divine couple. Rhode was the nymph and eponym of Rhodes. By Helius, the island's patron god, she bore seven sons, one of whom was the father of the eponyms of the chief cities of Rhodes. [Apollodorus 1.4.5; Pindar, *Olympian Odes*, 7.71–76.]

Rhodes. A large island off the southwestern tip of Asia Minor. Rhodes was sacred to the sun-god, Helius, who had claimed it as it rose from the sea. He named it for his wife Rhode, the nymph of the island. They had seven children, one of whom fathered the eponyms of the three principal cities (besides the city of Rhodes): Cameirus, Lindus, and Ialysus. Some say, however, that Heracles' son Tlepolemus founded these cities and ruled Rhodes. Althaemenes, son of the Cretan king Catreus, settled in Rhodes. According to a Rhodian tradition, Helen of Sparta was murdered there by Tlepolemus' widow in order to avenge her husband's death at Troy.

Rhodope, Mount. A mountain range in Thrace, now on the border between Bulgaria and Greece. It was on Mount Rhodope that Dionysus, in some traditions, threw the Edonian king Lycurgus to his panthers.

Rhône (Rhodanus) River. A river which, rising in Switzerland, flows through southern France to enter the Mediterranean sea at Marseilles. According to Apollonius Rhodius, the Argonauts sailed up the legendary Eridanus river (which Apollonius thought to be the Po) from the Adriatic sea, then down the Rhône, after briefly taking a wrong route northward by a third river that seems to have been the Rhine. Some ancient writers appear to have been aware that all three of these rivers had their headwaters in Switzerland, but they did not know that formidable alpine barriers prevented any possibility of portages from one source to another.

Rome. A city on the Tiber River, in Italy. The Dardanian leader Aeneas escaped from burning Troy with his followers and emigrated to Italy. Landing at the mouth of the Tiber, he conquered a group of local tribes led by Turnus, a Rutulian from Ardea, or by Latinus, king of Laurentum and eponym of all Latium. Aeneas established himself as a king in this region, married Latinus' daughter, Lavinia, and named the city that he founded at or near Laurentum Lavinium. Aeneas agreed that, though the Trojans would rule and their lares and penates brought from Troy be honored, they would give up the name of Trojans and adopt the local language. After Aeneas' death and a period during which Lavinia ruled as regent, Ascanius (Iülus), Aeneas' son by Creüsa or Lavinia, came of age and assumed the rule.

Lavinium prospered and after thirty years grew so crowded that Ascanius founded a new city farther inland. He called it Alba Longa. Twelve generations of kings descended from Ascanius ruled in this city. The thirteenth, Numitor, was deposed by his brother, Amulius. The tyrannical usurper apparently did not dare to kill Numitor, but he disposed of his sons and appointed his daughter, Rea Silvia, a Vestal Virgin so that she would not produce offspring. She was, however, seduced by the god Mars and bore twin sons. Amulius had the children exposed, but they miraculously survived and, on growing to manhood, killed Amulius and restored their grandfather to the throne.

The twin brothers, whose names were Romulus and Remus, determined to found a new city of their own, having gathered about them during their youth a considerable following of shepherds. A quarrel broke out between the brothers before the city could be built, and Remus was killed. Romulus became king of the new city and named it Rome, after himself. (It should be added, however, that Plutarch lists eight other possible eponyms of the city.)

Rome soon became so powerful that it was envied and feared throughout the region. It was, however, a city of men without women, and many of the men were fugitives from other cities. When the Romans' attempts to win wives from other cities by normal means failed, Romulus resorted to forcible abduction of the daughters of the Sabines, a powerful tribe from the mountains east of Rome. This act led to a war that ended only when the Romans' new wives intervened. The Romans and a large group of Sabines combined as a single political unit, with the rule centered at Rome and shared by Romulus and the Sabine king, Titus Tatius. Titus was soon killed in a private quarrel and Romulus again reigned alone. The Sabines remained a force in the government, however, and seem to have been ancestors of the patricians of the Rome of historical times.

Romulus conquered two or three other cities before his sudden and mysterious death. He was said to have been snatched up to heaven and was thereafter worshiped as the god Quirinus, though a rumor persisted that he had actually been murdered by the senators. A new king, Numa Pompilius, was chosen from the Sabine city of Cures. Numa brought a reign of law and peace to a city that thitherto had known little but warlike pursuits. He was credited with establishing many of the legal and religious practices that survived into historical times. Numa reigned for forty-three years and was succeeded by Tullus Hostilius, a warlike man who scorned Numa's peaceful accomplishments. He conquered Alba Longa and forced its citizens to move to Rome, where they doubled the city's population. Tullus also undertook a successful war against the hostile Sabine tribes to the east of Rome. Toward the end of his reign, a plague struck Rome and the king fell prey to a superstitious dread that led to his death by lightning at rites in honor of Jupiter Elicius.

Tullus was succeeded by Ancus Marcius, a grandson of Numa, who tried to combine the best characteristics of his three predecessors. He extended the dominion of Rome southward into Latium and westward to the sea, where he founded the port of Ostia at the mouth of the Tiber. Ancus was succeeded at his death by Lucius Tarquinius Priscus, an Etruscan born of a Greek father. This able man ruled for thirty-eight years, during which he conducted yet another war against the Sabines, subdued the last cities of the Ancient Latins, and busied himself with public works in the city of Rome. Because of certain portents, Tarquinius reared with great honor Servius Tullius, whose mother was a Latin captive, if not a slave. When Tarquinius made the young man his son-in-law, the sons of Ancus Marcius feared that they would lose all chance at the succession—though it was not in any case hereditary—and arranged Tarquinius' assassination. The quick thinking of his widow, Tanaquil, insured the succession to Servius. During Servius' forty-four years on the throne he made momentous constitutional changes, most of which improved the lot of the common people. These acts earned him the enmity of the patricians, however, and the ruthless Lucius Tarquinius Superbus, Servius' son-in-law and son of the former king, finally had Servius assassinated.

Tarquinius now declared himself king and held the throne for twenty-five years through sheer force. At the end of that time he was overthrown in a rebellion led by Lucius Junius Brutus. The immediate cause of the uprising was the brutal rape of Lucretia by Tarquinius' son Sextus, but the Romans, wearied by long years of tyranny, took the opportunity to expel the Etruscan Tarquins and to end the institution of kingship forever. Rome became a republic and, except for periods of dictatorship, continued to be ruled by the senate and various elected officials down to the dictatorship of Julius Caesar.

Romulus and Remus. Twin sons of Mars by Rea Silvia or, in some accounts, by Ilia.

A. Rea Silvia had been appointed a Vestal Virgin by her uncle Amulius. Having killed her brothers, he hoped thus to prevent her having heirs who might endanger his hold on the throne of Alba Longa, from which he had driven her father, Numitor. When she bore twin boys, claiming that the god Mars was their father, Amulius flung her into prison and had the babies exposed in a basket on the Tiber River. The basket floated to the shore, where the babies were suckled by a she-wolf and fed by a woodpecker, both of which creatures were sacred to the children's father, the god Mars. Faustulus, Amulius' chief shepherd, found them and took them home for his wife Larentia (often called Acca Larentia) to rear. The boys, named Romulus and Remus, grew up to be remarkably strong and bold, unafraid of either wild animals or the robbers who often troubled the region. They soon came to be recognized as leaders by a large band of shepherds.

One day the youths were ambushed by robbers. Remus was captured, haled before Amulius on a false charge of raiding Numitor's flocks, and turned over to Numitor for punishment. Numitor was impressed with the young man and began to suspect that Remus and his brother might be his supposedly dead grandsons. Faustulus, meanwhile, had decided to confide the same suspicion to Romulus. Numitor and his grandsons plotted to regain Numitor's throne. With the aid of the youths' loyal company of shepherds, they attacked the palace and killed the tyrannical usurper Amulius.

Numitor once again ruled in Alba Longa, but his ambitious grandsons yearned to found a city of their own. Each had his own followers, however, and each wanted to name the city when it was built. The brothers agreed to leave the decision to the gods. The details of the contest that ensued are variously told. According to one of the commoner versions, the brothers vowed to let the outcome depend on which of them should first see a flight of vultures. Remus, standing on the Aventine Hill, near the Tiber, soon spied six of the birds. Almost imediately afterward, Romulus sighted twelve. Each claimed victory. In the brawl that broke out between their rival bands, Remus was killed. According to another story, Romulus or one of his men killed Remus for the insult of jumping over the wall of the city that Romulus had just laid out. Whatever happened, Romulus was left alone to found a city. He named this city Rome after himself.

B. Rome prospered greatly because of the many men who came to live within her walls. Romulus knew that the city would not outlast the generation without women, but the surrounding cities, fearing and envying Rome and scornful because many of its citizens were outlaws and fugitives who had found sanctuary there, refused to allow their daughters to marry Romans. Romulus held a great festival and lured to the city many families of the Sabines and other tribes; the Romans then attacked the men and took their daughters by force. When the injured fathers and brothers later returned in force to recover their daughters and sisters, the women unexpectedly persuaded them to forgive their new husbands. Romulus took this opportunity to suggest combining the Romans and Sabines into a single group, with the central power at Rome. Titus Tatius, the Sabine king, shared the rule with Romulus. When, however, his co-king was later murdered by a Laurentian mob, it was observed that Romulus made no move to avenge him.

Romulus extended the boundaries of Rome along the Tiber, taking advantage of local wars against the growing state to excuse his moves. Thus he made Rome the strongest city on the lower Tiber, which even the powerful Etruscans to the north did not dare to attack. Although a superb soldier and highly popular with the common people, Romulus was less successful in dealing with the patricians, who doubtless resented his blunt assumption of full authority. During a muster of troops on the Campus Martius, after he had ruled for thirty-seven years, he was enveloped in clouds by a sudden storm. When the storm died down, as suddenly as it had risen, Romulus had vanished. The senators who had been nearest the king declared that he had been carried up to heaven. This story was enthusiastically accepted by the soldiers and it was agreed that Romulus, a son of Mars, had himself become a god. He was thereafter worshiped under the name Quirinus, as a god of warlike characteristics. Nevertheless, there remained a rumor, never entirely silenced, that Romulus had in fact been torn to pieces by the senators. [Livy 1.3.10–1.16.8; Plutarch, *Parallel Lives,* "Romulus."]

Rutulians or **Rutuli**. A tribe living in Latium. The Rutulians, led by Turnus, had their capital at Ardea, which was said to have been founded by Danaë. They led the other Latin tribes against AENEAS [B, C] and the Trojans.

S

Sabazius. A Thracian god similar in type to Dionysus and sometimes identified with him.

Sabines. A group of tribes living in the mountains east of Rome. After the abduction of their women by the Romans, the Sabines attacked the city, but the women intervened. Romulus, the Roman king, suggested that the Sabines and Romans combine as one tribe, with their center at Rome. He shared the rule of Rome with the Sabine king, Titus Tatius, until that ruler was killed by Laurentians. Romulus' successor, the wise king Numa Pompilius, was a Sabine from Cures. The Sabines had close connections with the patrician class in later Rome. At the time when Greek ancestry was seen as a mark of distinction, they claimed to have originally come to Italy from Sparta. They appear to have been ancestors of the warlike Samnites, who defied the later Romans from the mountains of southern Italy.

Sack of Troy, The, or **The Sack of Ilium.** See Epic Cycle.

Sagitta (The Arrow). A constellation. This group of stars represents either the arrow with which Heracles shot the eagle that was torturing Prometheus or the one with which Apollo killed the Cyclopes. [Hyginus, *Poetica Astronomica*, 2.15.]

Sagittarius (The Archer). A constellation. The personage represented in this star-group is said to be Crotus, son of Pan by Eupheme, the Muses' nurse. Crotus was a favorite of the Muses, who asked Zeus to immortalize him in the sky. [Hyginus, *Poetica Astronomica*, 2.27.]

Salamis. An island off the coast of Attica in the Saronic Gulf, named for the mother of Cychreus, its first king. When Telamon was exiled from Aegina, he was welcomed to Salamis by Cychreus and succeeded to the throne at his death. Although Telamon's son Teucer was innocent of the death at Troy of his half-brother Ajax, Telamon banished him from Salamis, and he emigrated to Cyprus, where he founded a city named Salamis.

Salmacis. See Hermaphroditus.

Salmoneus. A king of Salmonia, in Elis. One of the sons of Aeolus, Salmoneus emigrated to Elis and founded a city, Salmonia. He married Alcidice, daughter of Aleüs, who bore him a beautiful daughter, Tyro. After his first wife's death, he married Sidero. Seduced by Poseidon, Tyro bore two sons, Pelias and Neleus. Salmoneus refused to believe Tyro's story of their paternity, and he and her stepmother mistreated her. Salmoneus was notorious for his impious arrogance and either called himself Zeus or boasted that he was greater than the god. In order to prove this claim, he drove his four-horse chariot through the city with dried hides and bronze kettles dragging behind it to imitate thunder, while he flung torches into the air to simulate lightning. Zeus disposed of his would-be rival by destroying him and his entire city with a thunderbolt. According to Hyginus [*Fabulae* 60], Salmoneus and his brother Sisyphus hated one another. Sisyphus, on the advice of the Delphic oracle, seduced Tyro in order to bring about his brother's death, but the end of this story has been lost. Vergil claimed that Salmoneus was condemned to some further punishment in Hades. [Apollodorus 1.9.7–8; Diodorus Siculus 4.6.8, 6.6.4–6.7.3; Vergil, *Aeneïd*, 6.585–594.]

Salmoxis or **Zalmoxis**. A Thracian god. Although the evidence is slender, Salmoxis, a god of the Getae of Thrace, is thought to have been similar in character to Dionysus. It was believed by his worshipers that they achieved immortality, going to the god at death. Every four years they sent a messenger to the god. Choosing a man by lot, they flung him into the air so that he fell on the points of three spears held upright. If the messenger died, it was taken as proof that Salmoxis would take a favorable view of the petitions that the worshipers had confided to the messenger in advance. If he lived, this proved that he had comported himself badly in life and was, therefore, unworthy of the god. He was roundly berated for his shortcomings, and another messenger was chosen for the honor of sacrifice. Salmoxis was also known as Gebelzeïzis. [Herodotus 4.93–95.]

Salmydessus. A Thracian city on the Black Sea, west of the Bosporus. Although Salmydessus was well known in Classical times for the profitable business that its inhabitants carried on in plundering ships wrecked on their harborless coast, the references to the city or region in works based on mythology misplace it. In his geographically impossible account of Io's wanderings, Prometheus [Aeschylus, *Prometheus Bound*, 725–727] places it near Themiscyra, on the coast of Asia Minor where the Thermodon empties into the Black Sea. Those who make Salmydessus the capital of Phineus place it on the Thracian shore of the Bosporus not far from its northern end.

Samos. An Aegean island off the western coast of Asia Minor. Samos was one of the principal cult centers of the goddess Hera. Its eponym was Samia, a daughter of the river-god Maeander. Samia's Lelegian husband, Ancaeüs, became king of the island. Samian settlers on the island of Dardania in the northern Aegean were said to have given it its new name of Samothrace. Samos also had close connections with the Libyan port of Cyrene.

Samothrace. An island in the northern Aegean Sea. Samothrace was said to have been given its name by colonists from the island of Samos. Presumably the second part of the name recognized the presence of Thracians in the population. It was the homeland of Dardanus, founder of the Dardania in the

Troad, and the island, too, was originally called Dardania. Samothrace was also the home of Demeter's lover Iasion and, according to some writers, of Harmonia, the daughter of Ares and Aphrodite and wife of Cadmus. An obscure group of gods or *daimones* called Cabeiri were worshiped in the so-called Samothracian mysteries, which, in the Classical period, were second in popularity only to the Eleusinian mysteries among mystery cults.

Samothracian mysteries. See CABEIRI.

Sangarius. A river flowing westward, then northward, through Asia Minor to the Black Sea; also, its god. The upper valleys of the Sangarius (now the Sakarya) were the center of Phrygian culture, its principal cities being Pessinus, Gordium, and Ancyra. Various kings named Midas and Gordius ruled this area, which was the center of Cybele's worship. The Sangarius valley was the homeland of Priam's wife Hecuba, who was called by some a daughter of the river-god Sangarius. King Otreus and the Mygdonians also came from this region.

Sardinia. A large island west of Italy. Aristaeüs and Iolaüs are both said to have planted colonies in Sardinia. The great craftsman Daedalus was credited with certain monuments on the island.

Sardis or **Sardes.** The principal city of Lydia. Sardis, on the Pactolus River, east of Smyrna, was the capital of the famous Lydian king Croesus, who ruled much of Asia Minor until his defeat by the Persians.

Saronic Gulf. The body of water that separates Attica from the Peloponnesus. The islands of Aegina and Salamis are in this gulf, and the cities of Athens, Corinth, Megara, Epidaurus, and Troezen had ports on it. Its eponym was an obscure king and hero of Troezen named Saron, who drowned in the gulf.

Sarpedon (1). A son of Zeus by Europa or Laodameia, daughter of Bellerophon. Together with his brothers, Minos and Rhadamanthys, Sarpedon was reared by Asterius, the childless king of Crete who had married Europa. In their youth the three brothers fell in love with the handsome youth Miletus, or perhaps with Atymnius, the son of Zeus and Cassiopeia. He indicated a preference for Sarpedon, whereupon Minos drove both of his brothers from Crete. Sarpedon fled to southern Asia Minor and became an ally of Europa's brother Cilix, eponym of Cilicia, in his war with the Solymi, who occupied the territory then known as Milyan. On defeating the Solymi, Sarpedon, with his Cretan followers, who were called Termilae, ruled this land. In time Lycus, a son of Pandion, was exiled from Athens by his brother Aegeus and fled to Milyan, where he shared the rule with Sarpedon. The Termilae eventually became known as Lycians, after Lycus. Sarpedon bequeathed his kingdom to his son, Evander, who married Bellerophon's daughter, Deïdameia. They became the parents of Sarpedon, who led the Lycian forces to the Trojan War. The two Sarpedons were, however, often thought by Classical writers to have been the same man. Apollodorus explained the chronological difficulties with the statement that Zeus permitted Sarpedon to live for three generations. [Apollodorus 3.1.1–2, "Epitome" 3.35, 4.6.]

Sarpedon (2). The leader of the Lycian forces in the Trojan War. Sarpedon was regarded as the son of Bellerophon's daughter Deïdameia and Evander, king of Lycia and son of Sarpedon by Laodameia, another daughter of Bellerophon. His true father, however, was Zeus. He was, in fact, identified by most early Classical writers with his grandfather Sarpedon, Zeus's son by Europa. Sarpedon was the most powerful warrior among the Trojan allies. He was foremost in the assault on the Greek wall. Zeus, knowing that Sarpedon, his favorite son, was fated to die, wanted to save him but was rebuked by Hera. When Sarpedon was killed by Patroclus, Zeus honored him by causing bloody rain to fall. A violent struggle for the body ensued, but Zeus commanded Apollo to rescue it and prepare it for burial. Hypnos (Sleep) and Thanatos (Death) then carried it home to Lycia. [Homer, *Iliad*, 5.470–492, 5.627–698, 12.290–416, 16.419–683.]

Saturn. An ancient Roman god of fertility, especially of agriculture. Saturn, although worshiped as a god, was in many accounts converted into an early king of Latium who, in introducing the agricultural arts to Italy, had brought with them civilization. His reign was regarded as having been a golden age. According to Vergil, he was the father of Picus and an ancestor of Latinus. Saturn was identified by the Romans with the Greek Cronus, but what little myth was originally attached to the Roman god seems to have had none of the violence attributed to Cronus. The association of the two gods caused Saturn to be worshiped together with the agricultural goddess Ops (who was early identified with Rhea, Cronus' wife), but his original cult partner had been the obscure goddess Lua. Saturn was worshiped in a winter festival called the Saturnalia and gave his name to a day of the week, Saturday. [Vergil, *Aeneïd*, 7.48–49, 8.319–327.]

satyrs. Woodland spirits in the form of men with some animal characteristics. Satyrs were usually represented in art as vigorous, often young, men with horses' tails, pointed ears or small horns, and sometimes with goats' legs. They were often shown with erect or oversized genitals. The Romans identified the satyrs with their native woodland spirits, the fauns. Satyrs and their elder counterparts, the seileni (see SEILENUS), were a regular part of Dionysus' train, along with his maenads. Although satyrs often appear in mythology, they are never individualized to a significant degree. When they are not reveling with Dionysus, they are pursuing nymphs through the woods.

Satyrs were spirits of the uncontrolled fertility of the woods and unplowed fields. Associated with Dionysus, they seem also to have been the semidivine counterparts of his male human worshipers, as the Curetes were probably worshipers of the Cretan Zeus and the Corybantes of Cybele. Satyrs made up the choruses of the satyr plays, comedies on mythological themes.

Sauromatians or **Sauromatae.** A barbarian tribe living east of the Sea of Azov on the northern shores of the Black Sea. According to Herodotus, the Sauromatians were descended from Amazons and Scythian men who intermarried. The Argonauts offered to fight the Sauromatians for Aeëtes, king of Colchis, but he declined, although the tribe had long been his enemy. The Sauromatians are believed by many scholars to have been identical with the Sarmatians, a tribe which largely replaced the Scythians in the area north of the Black Sea.

Scamander or **Scamandrus.** A Trojan river (now called Menderes) and its god. Like most river gods, Scamander (whom the Olympian gods called Xanthus) was a son of Oceanus and Tethys. He was the father by the nymph Idaea of Teucer, the first king of the region of Troy; of Callirrhoë, wife of Tros; and of Strymo, wife of Laomedon. Understandably sympathetic to the Trojans when the gods took sides in the Trojan War, Scamander was opposed by Hephaestus. He became enraged when Achilles filled his waters with Trojan corpses after the death of Patroclus. Scamander flooded the plain and Achilles would have drowned, in spite of the moral support of Athena and Poseidon, had not Hera sent Hephaestus to his rescue. The fire-god dried up Scamander's stream with a great flame, and the river-god gave up the fight. [Homer, *Iliad*, 20.73–74, 21.120–382; Hesiod, *Theogony*, 345; Apollodorus 3.12.1–3.]

Scamandrius. See ASTYANAX.

Sceiron or **Sciron** (1). An Isthmian outlaw. A son of Pelops or Poseidon, Sceiron robbed travelers passing the Sceironian Rocks; then, forcing them to wash his feet, he kicked them over the cliff into the sea, where they were eaten by a sea turtle. Sceiron was killed by Theseus. According to Plutarch [*Parallel Lives*, "Theseus"] the Megarians considered this Sceiron not to have been an outlaw at all, but identified him with the Megarian warlord named Sceiron.

Sceiron or **Sciron** (2). A warlord of Megara. Sceiron was a son of Pylas, king of Megara. On being exiled from Megara, Pylas gave the rule to his son-in-law Pandion, who left it to his son Nisus. Sceiron disputed Nisus' succession but agreed to accept arbitration by Aeacus, king of Aegina. Aeacus decided that Nisus should be king, Sceiron the military leader. Sceiron not only accepted this decision, but married his daughter, Endeïs, to Aeacus, by whom she became the mother of Telamon and Peleus. The Megarians did not distinguish between this Sceiron and the Isthmian outlaw named Sceiron. [Pausanias 1.39.6.]

Sceironian Rocks. A cliff on the Saronic coast of the Isthmus of Corinth. This cliff takes its name from the Isthmian bandit Sceiron, who used to push his victims over its edge until Theseus ended his career with the same trick. According to some versions of the story of the Heraclids, Eurystheus was killed at the Sceironian Rocks while fleeing after his defeat by the Athenians.

Schedius. A son of Iphitus, king of Phocis. With his brother Epistrophus, Schedius led forty ships from Phocis to the Trojan War, where he was killed by Hector. [Homer, *Iliad*, 2.517–526, 17.304–311.]

Scherië. The island home of the Phaeacians. Homer gives no location for this island, to which the Phaeacians had been led by their king Nausithoüs. Apollonius Rhodius, who called the island Drepane, seems to have identified it with Corcyra (Corfu), as did most late Classical writers.

Schoeneus. A king of some part of Boeotia. Schoeneus, a son of Athamas and Themisto, is chiefly known as the father of Atalanta, a distinction that many writers ascribe to the Arcadian Iasus instead. Pausanias [8.35.10] says that the Arcadian city of Schoenus was named for Schoeneus, an immigrant from Boeotia, and he mentions that Atalanta's racecourse was near by. These details perhaps resulted from an attempt by the Arcadians to keep Atalanta an Arcadian heroine by incorporating into her legend some of the strong rival claims of the Boeotians. There was, however, a city named Schoeneus in Boeotia, as well. (See ATALANTA, A.)

Scorpio (The Scorpion). A constellation. These stars represent the scorpion that killed Orion. [Hyginus, *Poetica Astronomica*, 2.26.]

Scylla. A monster who devoured sailors passing through the Strait of Messina. Scylla was once a beautiful virgin of variously recorded parentage: her mother has been identified as Crataeïs, Echidna, Hecate, or Lamia; her father as Phorcys, Typhon, Triton, or the unknown Trienus. Scorning the advances of her many suitors she spent most of her days with the sea-nymphs. The sea-god Glaucus fell in love with her, and Circe, out of envy, transformed her into a monster with a woman's head and six dogs for legs, or else with six heads on long necks. The monster found a lair on the promontory named for her Scyllaeüm, opposite the whirlpool Charybdis, and leaned out to snatch seamen from their boats as they traversed the narrow strait that divides Sicily from the mainland. The Argonauts passed safely with the help of Thetis, but Scylla later caught and ate six of Odysseus' crew. Shortly after this disaster the monster was turned into a rock. [Ovid, *Metamorphoses*, 13.730–741, 13.898–14.74; Homer, *Odyssey*, 12.73–126, 12.222–259.]

Scylla. See NISUS.

Scyllaeüm. An Italian town (now Scilla) opposite Sicily at the northern end of the Strait of Messina. A cliff near Scyllaeüm was the reputed home of the monster Scylla, which preyed on sailors passing through the strait.

Scyrius. The eponym of the Aegean island of Scyrus. Aegeus was said by many writers to have been a son of Scyrius and to have been merely adopted by Pandion, the exiled king of Athens.

Scyrus. An Aegean island northeast of Euboea. Scyrus was named for Scyrius, said by some to be the true father of Aegeus. Aegeus' son Theseus was murdered there by King Lycomedes, who feared the loss of his throne to the exiled Athenian. Later Lycomedes reared both Achilles and his son Neoptolemus on the island. Some say, however, that Scyrus was merely one of the islands conquered by Achilles.

Scythians. Barbarian tribes living to the north and northeast of the Black Sea. Greek accounts of the Scythians (including a long one by Herodotus) are confused and contradictory, but the tribes seem to have been invaders from northern Asia who conquered inhabitants of the Black Sea region of Iranian origin. They were in turn supplanted by the Sauromatians. Although the Greeks of Classical times were well aware of the existence of the Scythians, they appear little in mythology. Phineus, king of Salmydessus, was married to Idaea, a daughter of a Scythian king named Dardanus. Triptolemus visited the Scythians, but their king Lyncus tried to kill him out of fear that Triptolemus, who had given the Scythians the boon of grain, would become too popular.

Sea-monster, The. See Cetus.

Seasons or **Horae.** Three daughters of Zeus and Themis. The Seasons were originally personifications of seasons of the year: spring, summer, and winter. Presumably because of their connection with the normal order of Nature, they, like their mother, came to have ethical connotations and were identified as Eirene (Peace), Eunomia (Order), and Dike (Justice). The Seasons had little mythology. Like the Graces, they were often depicted as companions of Aphrodite and sometimes of Hera, whom they were said in some accounts to have reared.

Seilenus or **Silenus.** An elderly, satyrlike companion of Dionysus. Seileni, often spoken of in the plural, were hardly distinguishable from SATYRS except that they were older, wiser, and drunker. They were also expert at music and were given to prophecy when captured. It was no doubt in the hope of gleaning some useful knowledge that Midas, king of Phrygia, captured a seilenus by mixing wine in a spring and entertained him, before restoring him to Dionysus' company. Seilenus (in the singular) is said to have been the father by an ash-nymph of the Centaur Pholus. Like his friend and foster-son Dionysus, Seilenus was brought up on Mount Nysa, or, according to a different account, on Mount Malea in Laconia. Seilenus was the chief comic character of the satyr plays. Cowardly, he boasted of his prowess, such as the time that he fearlessly sank a spear into the shield of Enceladus while fighting side by side with the gods against the Giants. [Euripides, *Cyclops;* Sophocles, *Searching Satyrs;* Apollodorus 2.5.4; Vergil, *Eclogues,* 6; Ovid, *Metamorphoses,* 11.89–101; Pausanias 3.25.2–3.]

Seirenes. See SIRENS.

Selemnus. A river near Patrae, in Achaea. Selemnus was originally a youth who loved the sea-nymph Argyra. She dallied with him for a time, but soon tired of him and came to him no more. When he died of heartbreak, Aphrodite transformed him into a river. Selemnus went right on yearning for Argyra, so the goddess granted him the gift of forgetfulness. Thereafter, the lovesick who bathed in his waters were sure of being cured. [Pausanias 7.23.1–3.]

Selene. The moon, and the goddess of the moon. Selene, whom the Romans called Luna, was a daughter of the Titans Hyperion and either Theia or Euryphaëssa, and sister of Helius (Sun) and Eos (Dawn). She bore a daughter, Pandia, to Zeus and is said to have been seduced by Pan with the gift of a beautiful fleece. The only myth of any consequence told of Selene concerns her love for the handsome young Endymion, king of Elis. She offered to grant him any boon he wished. Endymion, perhaps vain of his beauty, chose to sleep forever without aging. He could not, however, have been young when he started, for Selene is said to have had fifty daughters by him. Late Classical writers tended to forget Selene (Luna) and associated Artemis (Diana) and Hecate with the moon. [Hesiod, *Theogony*, 371–374; *Homeric Hymn to Selene* 32; Vergil, *Georgics*, 3.391–393; Apollodorus 1.7.5; Pausanias 5.1.4.]

Selinus. A king of Aegialus. Learning that Ion, an immigrant from Attica, was planning to seize his throne, Selinus saved it by marrying his daughter, Helice, to Ion and making him his heir.

Semele. A daughter of Cadmus, king of Thebes, and Harmonia. Semele was loved by Zeus and conceived a child by him. The jealous Hera learned of this affair and, disguising herself as Semele's nurse, Beroë, advised the young woman to demand of her lover that he appear to her as he did to his wife on Olympus. Zeus tried to dissuade her but, having vowed to grant whatever wish she expressed, could not refuse. He appeared as the storm god and Semele was consumed by lightning. The six-months-old child was snatched from her womb by Hermes and sewed into Zeus's thigh, from which, in due course, it was born. After Semele's death her envious sisters, Autonoë, Ino, and Agave, spread a rumor that her lover had been mortal and that her fate had been Zeus's punishment for her presumptuous lie. For this insult to Semele, the sisters were severely afflicted by Zeus or by Semele's child, the god Dionysus. At the end of his wanderings, Dionysus descended into Hades and brought his mother up to Olympus under the name Thyone.

According to certain Orphic myths, Dionysus was originally the child of Zeus and Persephone. He was dismembered and eaten by the Titans, but Zeus saved his torn heart and served it to Semele in a drink, by which she became pregnant. At the time of her destruction by a thunderbolt, a log is said to have fallen from heaven at Thebes. King Polydorus, Semele's brother, decorated it with bronze, and it was honored as Dionysus Cadmus. At the Laconian coastal town of Brasiae there was a tradition, found nowhere else, that Cadmus punished his daughter for bearing an illegitimate son by locking mother and child into a chest and flinging them into the sea. When the chest came ashore at Brasiae, Semele was dead, but her son was alive and was nursed in a cave there by his aunt Ino.

Semele was identified by the Greeks with the mother of the Egyptian god Osiris. She was probably closely related to the Phrygian earth-goddess Zemelo. [Apollodorus 3.4.4; Hyginus, *Fabulae*, 167, 179; Pausanias 9.2.3.]

Semnai Theai or **Semnai.** Goddesses worshiped at Athens. The Semnai Theai (Venerable Goddesses), sometimes referred to merely as Semnai, were worshiped in a cave on the Areopagus, at Athens. Aeschylus [*Eumenides*] and later writers identified the Semnai and the Eumenides with the Erinyes. These goddesses, of whom there seem to have been originally two and later three, were probably typical of many chthonian goddesses (see CHTHONIAN DEITIES) of fertility who were worshiped in different localities under a variety of titles. It is uncertain that they had the retributive functions of the Erinyes.

Seriphus. An island in the western Cyclades. It was said to have been colonized by Polydectes and Dictys, sons of Magnes, one of the sons of Aeolus. It is known in myth almost solely as the site of certain adventures of Perseus.

Serpent, The. See DRACO.

Serpent-holder, The. See OPHIUCHUS.

Servius Tullius. The sixth king of Rome. Accounts of the youth of this king vary greatly. According to several of them, he was the son of a captive Latin woman, who may have been a slave of Tanaquil, the wife of Lucius Tarquinius Priscus. Some say that when Servius was a child flames played around his head during his sleep. Tanaquil recognized this omen of future greatness and persuaded her husband to rear the child with honor even above that which he showed his own children. Others claim that a slave of Tanaquil's named Ocrisia saw in a fireplace at the palace a giant phallus. Tanaquil dressed the woman as a bride and left her alone with this divine manifestation. In due course, Ocrisia bore the child Servius, whom the royal couple reared with honor.

According to a different and strong tradition, Servius was an Etruscan. When he grew to manhood, Tarquinius gave him his daughter in marriage. The two sons of Ancus Marcius, Tarquinius' predecessor, feared that they would lose any chance to acquire the throne and arranged the assassination of the king. The shrewd Tanaquil, however, pretended that her husband had been merely injured and announced that Servius would rule as his regent until Tarquinius was well. This move allowed Servius to apprehend the murderers, whose confessions drove the sons of Ancus into exile. Servius became king.

Servius' prompt suppression of a rebellion of the Etruscans of Veii consolidated his position. Far more notable than his military exploits, however, were the sweeping changes that he made in the constitution of Rome in order to give greater power to the plebeians. Throughout his reign of forty-four years, Servius was popular with the common people, but in spite of his consistently fair dealings with the patricians they never ceased to resent him. Their hatred at last combined with treachery within his own family to bring about his death. Hoping to win the friendship of the two sons of Tarquinius, who had been passed over in Servius' favor, the king had married them to his two daughters, both of whom were named Tullia. Aruns was a mild man; his brother, Lucius, seethed with ambition. Lucius' wife, on the other hand, was gentle, whereas her sister, Aruns' wife, outdid even Lucius in the violence of her ambition. It was she who suggested a plot by which each disposed of his own spouse, after which Lucius and the savage Tullia were married. Tullia would not let her husband rest until he plotted, together with many of the disaffected patricians, the death of the aged king. Lucius one day seated himself on the throne and summoned the senators before him. When Servius entered the hall to protest, the usurper declared himself king and flung Servius down the steps of the senate house. The old man staggered toward his home, only to be murdered in the street by Lucius' men. Shortly afterward, Tullia, returning home in her chariot, drove triumphantly over her father's body. [Livy 1.39.1–1.48.9.]

Sestus. A city on the Thracian coast of the Hellespont. Sestus was an ally of Troy in the Trojan War and later figured in a legend concerning the ghost of the Greek hero Protesilaüs. It is best known, however, as the home of Hero in the Hellenistic romance of Hero and Leander.

Seven against Thebes. Argive champions who besieged Thebes.

A. When ADRASTUS (1), son of Talaüs, was king of Argos, he was awakened one night by two young men quarreling over a couch on the porch of his palace. He separated them and learned that one was POLYNEICES, son of Oedipus, from Thebes, and the other TYDEUS, son of Oeneus, from Calydon. Instead of rebuking the brawlers, the king promptly married them to his daughters, Argeia and Deïpyle, for, noticing that Polyneices wore on his shield the device of a lion and Tydeus that of a boar, he recalled that an oracle had told him long ago that he should yoke his daughters to a lion and a boar. The double marriage pleased the young men, for both had come to Argos to secure armed assistance in recovering their kingdoms. Tydeus had been banished from his for murder. Polyneices and his brother, Eteocles, had agreed to rule Thebes in alternate years after the deposition of OEDIPUS, but, cursed by their father with the fate of dying by each other's hands, they had soon quarreled, and Eteocles had refused to relinquish the throne at the end of his term.

B. Adrastus promised to help Polyneices first. It was not difficult for him to raise an army, for the principal chieftains of Argolis included his brother Mecisteus, his nephew Capaneus, his brother-in-law Amphiaraüs, and his nephew or cousin Hippomedon. Capaneus' brother-in-law, Eteoclus, and the Arcadian chieftain Parthenopaeüs joined their ranks, and Tydeus offered to go if the champions would next help him in Calydon. The only obstacle to the expedition was Amphiaraüs. The greatest seer of his day, he had divined that the campaign was doomed to failure and its leaders, all but Adrastus, to death.

Old Iphis, Eteoclus' father, now told Polyneices that he should win the support of Amphiaraüs' wife, Eriphyle, who was Adrastus' sister. In an old quarrel, her husband and brother had agreed thenceforth to let her decide any differences between them. Eriphyle, Iphis added, might not be above accepting a bribe. In his escape from Thebes, Polyneices had brought with him the famous necklace and robe given by the gods to his ancestress HARMONIA. Polyneices offered Eriphyle the necklace in return for her help. Iphis was right. Privately accepting the necklace, Eriphyle demanded that her husband march against Thebes. Amphiaraüs had no choice, but before leaving he made his young sons, ALCMEON and Amphilochus, promise to avenge his coming death first on the Thebans, then on their mother.

C. The seven champions, under the leadership of Adrastus, left for Thebes with their followers. (Those who count the foreigners, Polyneices and Tydeus, among the Seven do not mention Mecisteus or Eteoclus.) Polyneices and Tydeus both left behind sons, Thersander and Diomedes, respectively, as did the other leaders. At Nemea the army stopped for water. There they encountered a nursemaid who was caring for Opheltes, the infant son of King Lycurgus or Lycus and his wife, Eurydice. The nurse—who turned out to be Hypsipyle, the former queen of Lemnos—laid the child in a bed of parsley and showed the strangers the way to a spring. Returning, they found the child dead, coiled about by a snake. They killed the snake and, when Amphiaraüs said that the child's death foreshadowed their own fate, buried the babe under the name Archemorus (Beginner of Doom). They then held games in his honor, in which Adrastus drove his fabulous horse Arion to victory in the chariot race. These games were the origin of the Nemean games, in which the victors were crowned with parsley.

The army proceeded on its way, crossing the Isthmus and reaching the range called Mount Cithaeron, which overlooked the Asopus valley and the walled city of Thebes. Tydeus was sent ahead to demand that Eteocles surrender. He lent force to his threats by challenging the Thebans to single combat or to feats of strength and then defeating all comers. Eteocles, however, was not intimidated, and ordered a company of fifty men under Maeon and Polyphontes to ambush the boastful Tydeus. Tydeus killed them all, except for Maeon, whom he sent back to Thebes with the tale.

Sophocles claims that Polyneices had meanwhile sought out his father, Oedipus, who had taken refuge at Colonus, near Athens. Polyneices tried to win the blind old man's support for his campaign, for an oracle had said that the side favored by Oedipus would win. Oedipus answered only with scorn and vituperation, and Polyneices, recalling his father's curse, returned to Cithaeron sure of his own impending death.

D. The Seven now marched with their troops against Thebes. The Thebans had taken refuge behind their great walls. Adrastus assigned one of the champions to each of the seven gates, and Eteocles set his best men to their defense, keeping for himself the gate that Polyneices threatened. The famous seer Teiresias declared that the city would be saved if Menoeceus, son of Eteocles' uncle, Creon, were to sacrifice himself. This the youth willingly did.

The order of events during the battle is confused. The boastful Capaneus began to scale the walls, shouting that not Zeus himself could prevent him from burning the city. He was promptly struck from the ladder by the offended god's thunderbolt. Mecisteus and Eteoclus were killed by Theban champions. A great stone crushed the skull of the handsome Parthenopaeüs. Tydeus, mortally wounded in the belly, still managed to give a death wound to his slayer, Melanippus. It is said that the war-goddess Athena, who admired Tydeus' bravery, begged her father, Zeus, for medicine that would make Tydeus immortal. Amphiaraüs divined her intention and, hating Tydeus for past taunts of cowardice, saw a way to circumvent it. Cutting off the head of Melanippus (whom some say Amphiaraüs, not Tydeus, had killed), he handed it to Tydeus. As he had foreseen, the wounded man was swallowing the brains when Athena arrived with the medicine. The goddess, disgusted at this barbarity, spilled the medicine on the ground, and Tydeus died a mortal's death.

Shortly after this, Amphiaraüs met his own strange fate. Pursued by the Theban Periclymenus, he fled toward Chalcis with his charioteer, Baton or Elato. Zeus, seeing the Theban about to hurl his spear at the seer's back, spared Amphiaraüs this indignity. He split the earth with a thunderbolt, and Amphiaraüs and his chariot were swallowed up. His oracular shrine at the site of this event became famous in Greek lands.

Polyneices and Eteocles, whose quarrel had started the war, met in single combat. Euripides claims that their mother, Jocasta, was still alive and tried to part them, but they would not listen. They fought, and their father's curse was fulfilled: each fell dead on the other's sword. As Amphiaraüs had foretold, of all the Argive champions only Adrastus, carried from the field by his divine horse Arion, escaped with his life.

E. With Eteocles dead, the kingship of Thebes fell to his uncle, Creon. Contrary to custom, Creon refused to let Adrastus and the surviving Argives bury their dead. In defiance of this decree, Polyneices was given last rites by his sister ANTIGONE, who was defended by her betrothed, Creon's son Haemon. Both died for the deed. Adrastus and some of the widows and children of the dead went as suppliants either to the Altar of Mercy at Athens or to Demeter's shrine at Eleusis. Theseus, king of Athens, sent an army to Thebes and forced the Thebans to give up the bodies. The common soldiers were buried at Eleutherae, on the borders of Attica; the dead champions at Eleusis. Capaneus' wife, Evadne, is said to have burned herself in grief on his pyre, although some accounts insist that Capaneus was buried. Maeon may, in fact, have buried Tydeus at Thebes, presumably in gratitude at having been spared after the unsuccessful ambush. [Apollodorus 3.6–7; Aeschylus, *Seven Against Thebes*; Sophocles, *Oedipus at Colonus*, 1254–1447, and *Antigone*; Euripides, *The Phoenician Women* and *The Suppliants*.]

Shield of Heracles, The. A poem about the battle of Heracles and Cycnus. The author of this fairly early poem, once ascribed to Hesiod, is unknown. The poem, most of which is given over to a description of the shield, deals with little but its central subject. It is available in the volume of Hesiod's works in the Loeb Classical Library.

sibyl. A prophetess. The original sibyl was a woman named Sibylla who lived near Troy and, under the inspiration of Apollo, gave riddling predictions in a manner similar to that of the Pythia at Delphi. Sibylla's utterances gained such a reputation that her name became a term for all prophetesses. The Roman writer Varro compiled a list of ten sibyls on three continents. Perhaps the most famous of these was the Cumaean Sibyl, who acted as Aeneas' guide to the Underworld and, during her thousand years of life, wrote down the oracles contained in the Sibylline Books that were preserved in the Roman temple of Capitoline Jupiter, to be consulted in national emergencies. This sibyl did not underrate the value of her talents. When the Etruscan Tarquinius Superbus refused to pay the price that she demanded for the nine volumes of her collected works, she burned three of them, then three more. Tarquin finally capitulated and had to pay the full original price for the three remaining books. Many of the sibyls were said to have been inspired by Apollo, their manic babbling giving evidence of a surprisingly Dionysiac side of the god's nature.

Sicels or **Siculi.** Italic tribes who gave their name to Sicily. According to Thucydides, Italus was their king. They may have been reputed to be slave traders, for Homer [*Odyssey* 20.376–383] relates that the suitors of Penelope suggested selling to them Odysseus and Theoclymenus.

Sicily. The large island southwest of the tip of Italy. Sicily was early supposed by writers to be the "Thrinacia" mentioned by Homer as the pastureland of Helius' cattle. It was also identified as the home of Polyphemus. Scylla and Charybdis were said to be located at the northern end of the Strait of Messina, which divides Sicily from Italy. The frightening activity of Mount Aetna was explained by the claim that either Typhoeus or the giant Enceladus had been trapped under it, or the entire island, by Zeus or Athena. Later writers, including Vergil, made Aetna the smithy where Hephaestus supervised the Cyclopes as they forged Zeus's thunderbolts. The city of Henna was one of several places cited as the scene of Hades' abduction of Persephone. Demeter and Persephone were worshiped there, and Aphrodite was the patron goddess of Eryx, a large region in western Sicily, which was also the site of incidents in the lives of Heracles and Aeneas.

Sicyon. The eponym of Sicyon and Sicyonia. Sicyon is variously called a son of either Pelops or Marathon or a son or grandson of Erechtheus. [*Catalogues of Women* 73; Pausanias 2.1.1, 2.6.5–6.]

Sicyon. A city on the Peloponnesian coast of the Gulf of Corinth near the Isthmus. Sicyon and its surrounding region of Sicyonia were originally named Asopia, for the Asopus River that flowed through them, or Aegialeia, for Aegialeus, whom the Sicyonians called autochthonous (see AEGIALUS). The Argives claimed, however, that Aegialeus was a son of their own first king, Inachus. The first important figure in the Sicyonians' version of their royal genealogy [Pausanias 2.5.6–2.7.1] was Apis, who gave his name for a time to the entire southern Peloponnesus. Nine generations later, Apis' descendant Corax died childless, and Epopeus, a Thessalian, took the throne.

Epopeus, whose lawlessness drove his own son, Marathon, to emigrate to Attica, carried off Antiope from Thebes, or else she took refuge with him. Her father, King Nycteus, pursued with an army, but both he and Epopeus were mortally wounded. This was said to be the first time that Sicyon had engaged in war. Epopeus' successor, Lamedon, younger brother of Corax, averted further trouble by giving up Antiope to Nycteus' brother, Lycus, who had come with another army to take her. Later, however, Lamedon became involved in a war with Argos. While living in Attica, he had married a daughter of Clytius. He later gave his daughter Zeuxippe in marriage to an Athenian, Sicyon, a son or grandson of Erechtheus, and thus won Sicyon as an ally in his Argive war. On Lamedon's death, his son-in-law became king and gave his own name to Aegialeia.

Sicyon's daughter, Chthonophyle, bore Polybus to Hermes, but married a son of Dionysus named Phlias, by whom she had Androdamas. Polybus succeeded Sicyon as king and ruled for many years. He married his daughter, Lysianassa, to Talaüs, a king in Argolis, and later welcomed their son Adrastus when he was exiled from Argos. Adrastus became king on Polybus' death, but later returned to Argos. The Sicyonians then invited Ianiscus, a descendant of Clytius, from Attica, to rule them. He was succeeded by Phaestus, a son of Heracles, but this king emigrated to Crete on the advice of an oracle. The next king was Zeuxippus, who was called a son of Apollo and the nymph Syllis, but who was probably descended from Zeuxippe. Hippolytus, Phaestus' grandson, was next on the throne. During Hippolytus' reign, Agamemnon made the Sicyonians vassals of Mycenae. During the reign of Hippolytus' son, Lacestades, the Heraclid Phalces conquered the city but accepted Lacestades as co-king, since he too was a Heraclid. Thereafter Sicyon remained a Dorian province of Argos.

According to another version of the origins of Sicyon, Sicyonia (then Asopia) and the neighboring land of Ephyraea were under the patronage of Helius, who gave them to his sons Alöeus and Aeëtes, respectively. Epopeus, Alöeus' son, annexed Ephyraea on the death of Bunus, Aeëtes' successor, but Epopeus' son, Marathon, redivided the land between his own sons, Sicyon and Corinthus, who renamed the provinces for themselves.

Sicyonia. The region on the coast of the Peloponnesus at the eastern end of the Gulf of Corinth. Sicyonia was originally called Aegialeia or Asopia. Its principal city was Sicyon.

Side. The first wife of Orion. While married to Orion, Side offended Hera by either rivaling her in beauty or claiming to, and was sent down to Hades. [Apollodorus 1.4.3.]

Sidon. An important coastal city of Phoenicia. Greek writers on mythology tended to use Sidon interchangeably with Tyre as the scene of myths common to this region, such as the abduction of Europa. Paris and Helen were said to have visited Sidon on their way to Troy, and Teucer was befriended by the Sidonian king.

Silenus. See SEILENUS.

Silvanus. A Roman god of agriculture and of woods. Silvanus was often identified with Mars as a god of fields and farming. He had some of the characteristics of Pan and, as a god of flocks, was worshiped by shepherds. He was often represented as an amiable old man. Although his name suggests that his role as a woodland-god was originally paramount, it became less important with the spread of agriculture.

Simöeis. A Trojan river (now called Dombrek), and its god. A son of Oceanus and Tethys, Simöeis was the father of two daughters, Astyoche and Hieromneme, who married, respectively, Erichthonius, king of Dardania, and Assaracus. [Hesiod, *Theogony*, 342; Apollodorus 3.12.2.]

Sinis or **Sinnis.** An Isthmian outlaw. Sinis, a son of Polypemon and Sylea, was called Pityocamptes (Pinebender) for his habit of tying his victims' limbs to bent pine trees, which on the rebound either flung them to their deaths or tore them apart. He was killed in the same way by THESEUS [B]. Sinis' daughter, Perigune, bore a son, Melanippus, to Theseus.

Sinon. A young Greek spy, related to Odysseus. Sinon let himself be captured by the Trojans in order to tell them a false tale about the purpose of the WOODEN HORSE and thus induce them to take it inside their walls. He is also said to have lighted a beacon on Achilles' tomb to guide the Greek fleet back to Troy. Other versions suggest that the Greeks showed the beacon as a signal for Sinon to open the wooden horse, which had been dragged into Troy. [Vergil, *Aeneïd*, 2.57–198, 2.254–259; Apollodorus "Epitome" 5.15–19.]

Sinope. The eponym of an Assyrian city on the Black Sea. Some say that Zeus took Asopus' daughter Sinope there and begged for her love, promising to grant her dearest wish. "I wish to remain a virgin," she replied. By repeated use of this clever answer she managed to remain one for life, in spite of the ardent advances of Apollo and the river-god Halys, as well as Zeus. Diodorus Siculus [4.72.2] claimed that it was Apollo who carried Sinope away and that she became by him the mother of Syrus, eponym of the Syrians. [Apollonius Rhodius 2.946–954.]

Sintians or **Sinties.** Aboriginal inhabitants of the island of Lemnos. When Hephaestus was flung out of heaven and fell on Lemnos, he was kindly cared for by the Sintians. These people are known only from Homer's brief reference to them in the *Iliad* [1.594].

Sipylus, Mount. A mountain east of Smyrna, now known as Manisa Dag. The region of Sipylus was the home of Tantalus and his children, Pelops and Niobe, both of whom emigrated to Greece. Niobe returned to Sipylus after the death of the many children she had borne to Amphion and, because of her inconsolable weeping, was transformed into a rocky formation on the mountain-side down which streams flow.

Sirens or **Seirenes.** Bird-women who lured sailors with their songs. Homer did not describe the Sirens, name them, or give their lineage. Many later writers identified them as daughters of the river-god Acheloüs by either Melpomene or Terpsichore, both Muses, and said that they were winged women with bird feet or else birds with women's heads and voices. Several writers explain their form with the tale that they had been attendants of Persephone and were either transformed by Demeter as a punishment for not aiding Persephone against Hades' abduction, or else given wings by the gods to assist them in their search for the lost maiden. Homer mentioned only two Sirens, but most later writers spoke of three. They lived on an island called Anthemoëssa, near the Italian coast. When ships drew near, they sang so sweetly that the sailors forgot their native lands and, deprived of their wills, wasted away on the Sirens' island, which grew white with bleaching bones. According to Apollodorus, the talented Sirens boasted not only a vocal trio, but a small instrumental ensemble, two accompanying the third on lyre and flute.

The *Argo* passed the Sirens' island safely because Orpheus drowned out their song by twanging on his lyre. One Argonaut, Butes, heard some of their song nonetheless and plunged into the sea to swim to their island but was saved in the nick of time by Aphrodite. Later, Odysseus sailed by the island without mishap, thanks to a trick taught him by the sorceress Circe. He filled the ears of his crew with wax, then had them tie him securely to the mast. Thus he was able to hear the seductive song in safety. The Sirens sang of their power to foretell the future. According to late Classical writers, they were fated to die when any sailor who heard their song passed by unharmed. After Odysseus had done so, they flung themselves into the sea and died. Some say that the Sirens were once induced by Hera to enter into competition with the Muses. The Muses won and made crowns for themselves out of Siren feathers. [Homer, *Odyssey*, 12.39–54, 12.158–200; Apollonius Rhodius 4.891–921; Apollodorus 1.3.4, "Epitome" 7.18–19; Hyginus, *Fabulae*, 14, 125, 141; Ovid, *Metamorphoses*, 5.552–563; Pausanias 9.34.3.]

Sirius. See CANIS MAJOR.

Sisyphus. A king of Ephyra (Corinth). Sisyphus, a son of Aeolus, king of Thessaly, and Enarete, received the throne of Ephyra from Medea, or else he founded the city himself. He became noted for his cunning. When the notorious thief Autolycus repeatedly stole Sisyphus' cattle undetected, Sisyphus not only recovered them by marking their hooves, but avenged himself by seducing Autolycus' daughter, Anticleia. Her son Odysseus was said, at least by his enemies, to have been born of her union with Sisyphus, rather than that with her husband, Laërtes. Sisyphus married the Pleiad Merope, who bore him Glaucus, Ornytion, Thersander, and Almus.

According to Hyginus, Sisyphus and his brother Salmoneus bore each other a deadly hatred. Sisyphus asked the Delphic oracle how he could kill his enemy and was told to have children by Salmoneus' daughter, Tyro. She bore Sisyphus two sons, but killed them both upon learning of the oracle. This deed caused Sisyphus to commit an unspecified impious act for which he was assigned punishment in Hades: he had to spend eternity in a futile attempt to push an enormous boulder to the top of a steep hill; nearing the top, the stone was fated always to roll down again. Other reasons were given for this punishment. The most usual was that Sisyphus had informed the river-god Asopus that it was Zeus who had carried off his daughter Aegina. Some add that Sisyphus turned informer for profit, demanding that Asopus create a spring on top of the Acrocorinth, which had previously had no water.

During his reign in Corinth, Sisyphus discovered the corpse of his nephew Melicertes, brought ashore by a dolphin on the Isthmus of Corinth. Sisyphus buried the child there and established the Isthmian games in his honor. Later the king himself was buried on the Isthmus in a secret grave, as Neleus had been before him. [Apollodorus 1.9.3; Hyginus, *Fabulae*, 60, 201; Pausanias 2.1.3, 2.5.1.]

Sleep. See HYPNOS; SOMNUS.

Smintheus. An epithet of APOLLO [E] as mouse-god. This aspect of Apollo's character seems to have been celebrated widely in Asia Minor and certain islands off the coast.

Smyrna. See MYRRHA.

Solymi. A warlike Lycian tribe. Herodotus believed that the Solymi had occupied Lycia (then Milyan) before Sarpedon and his Cretan followers invaded the land. Bellerophon later defeated them, but, still later, his son Isander was killed while fighting them. [Homer, *Iliad*, 6.184, 6.203; Herodotus 1.173.]

Somnus. A Roman god of sleep. Somnus is identified with the Greek HYPNOS and, like him, is little more than an abstraction. According to Ovid [*Metamorphoses* 11.592–677], Somnus had a thousand sons. The three whose specialties were identified by the poet were Morpheus, who appears in dreams in human form; Icelos (called Phobetor by men), who takes beast forms; and Phantasos, who appears as inanimate objects. These figures are literary, not mythical, concepts, however.

Sophocles (c. 497–c. 406 B.C.). A Greek tragic dramatist. Three of Sophocles' seven surviving dramas deal with the tragic fates of Oedipus and his daughter Antigone. The others are concerned with the deaths of Ajax and Heracles, the sufferings of Philoctetes on Lemnos, and the murder of Clytemnestra and Aegisthus.

Sown-men. See SPARTI.

Sparta. The principal city of Laconia. Sparta, which was often called Lacedaemon, was for centuries the dominant power of the southernmost region of the Peloponnesus. It was separated from Messenia on the west by the imposing Taÿgetus range of mountains; to the north were Arcadia and Argos; to the east and south were the sea.

According to Spartan traditions recorded by Pausanias and others, the first king of this region was the earth-born Lelex, eponym of the Leleges. By the Naïad Cleocharia, he was the father of Myles and Polycaon. Polycaon emigrated to the land that he named Messenia, after his wife Messene, establishing the first of many mythological connections between early Messenia and Lacedaemon. Myles, or perhaps Lelex, fathered Eurotas, who, like the Argive Inachus, was either the god of a local river or a king who gave his name to it. Eurotas had two daughters, Sparta and Tiasa. Tiasa gave her name to another river; Sparta married Lacedaemon, a son of Zeus and the Pleiad Taÿgete.

Inheriting the land from his father-in-law, Lacedaemon named it for himself and called the city that he founded after his wife. Sparta bore two children, Amyclas and Eurydice. Eurydice married Acrisius and was the grandmother of Perseus. Amyclas succeeded his father as king of Lacedaemon, but he seems to have ruled principally from Amyclae, a city which he founded near Sparta. The genealogies of the next two generations are confused. According to one of the more usual versions, Amyclas' grandson Oebalus became the second husband of Perseus' daughter, Gorgophone, who bore him Tyndareüs, Hippocoön, and Icarius.

Tyndareüs was driven from Sparta by Hippocoön, but was restored to the throne by Heracles, who killed Hippocoön. Tyndareüs married Leda, a daughter of the Aetolian king Thestius, who had entertained him during his exile. To Tyndareüs or to Zeus Leda bore the Dioscuri, Helen, Clytemnestra, Timandra, and Phylonoë. Tyndareüs married Clytemnestra and Helen to Agamemnon and Menelaüs, the brothers who ruled Mycenae, and Timandra to Echemus, king of Arcadia. All three of these women played their husbands false, but the succession in their respective kingdoms was not affected. When the Dioscuri were killed, Tyndareüs turned over the rule of Sparta to Menelaüs, who was succeeded by Orestes, his son-in-law and nephew. It may have been during the reign of Orestes' son Tisamenus that the Heraclidae returned to the Peloponnesus and made Sparta one of their chief strongholds. Orestes was the last significant mythological figure to rule Sparta.

Sparti or **Sown-men.** Men born in Thebes from dragon's teeth. On the advice of Athena, CADMUS [A] sowed some of the teeth of Ares' sacred snake, which he had killed. Armed men sprang up from the furrows. Cadmus flung a stone among them and they began fighting one another. The five survivors—Echion, Udaeüs, Chthonius, Hyperenor, and Pelorus—made peace and accepted Cadmus as king. Echion married Cadmus' daughter Agave. Their son, Pentheus, succeeded Cadmus on the throne, but was killed by his mother in a fit of madness. The leading houses of Thebes claimed descent from the Sparti, who may have been regarded as representing the native peoples of southern

Boeotia who were conquered by Phoenician invaders under Cadmus but remained prominent in the government.

Another crop of Sown-men, planted by Jason at Colchis, grew from the remaining teeth of the same dragon, which Athena had given to Aeëtes, the Colchian king. None of these armed men survived the battle among themselves. (See ARGONAUTS, N.)

Spercheius. A river of southern Thessaly, and its god. This river-god was said by Homer to be the father of Menesthius by Peleus' daughter Polydora.

Sphaeria. A small island in the Saronic Gulf near Troezen. Sphaeria was named for Sphaerus, reputedly Pelops' charioteer, who was buried there and worshiped as a hero. There Aethra, daughter of Pittheus, king of Troezen, lay with Aegeus and Poseidon in one night. She later gave birth to Theseus. The island was renamed Hiera (Sacred).

Sphaerus. Pelops' charioteer. Sphaerus was buried on an island called Sphaeria, near Troezen. Aethra renamed it Hiera, or Sacred Island. The Olympians called Sphaerus Cillas. [Pausanias 2.33.1, 5.10.7.]

Sphinx. A female monster, daughter of Echidna by Orthus or Typhon. The Sphinx, sent by Hera, Hades, or some other god, flew to Mount Phicium, north of Thebes, during the regency of Creon, after the death of Laïus. From this vantage point she would apparently fly to the walls of the citadel, and there ask a riddle of young Theban men. When the youths could not determine the answer, as was invariably the case, she would eat them. The last to suffer this fate was Creon's beautiful son Haemon. Creon thereupon offered the kingdom and the hand of his sister Jocasta, Laïus' widow, to anyone who could answer the riddle, for an oracle had predicted that the Sphinx would cease to bother the Thebans when her secret was disclosed. A young traveler named OEDIPUS [A] found the answer. The monster was so mortified that she flung herself from the citadel and, apparently refusing to use her wings, destroyed herself. This success brought Oedipus great fame and honor, in addition to the promised rewards.

Pausanias [9.27.2–4] offers two ingenious, though irrelevant, explanations of the Sphinx: she was a lady bandit with headquarters on Mount Phicium; or she was a natural daughter of Laïus, who, having learned a secret from her doting father, used it to advance her claim to the throne against the claims of her (also illegitimate) brothers, and disposed of them one by one when they could not guess the secret. [Euripides, *The Phoenician Women*, 45–49, 806–811, 1019–1042, 1504; Apollodorus 3.5.8; Hesiod, *Theogony*, 326–329.]

Sporades. A group of islands off the southwestern coast of Asia Minor. The Sporades, the largest of which is Rhodes, include the Dodecanese Islands and others. Another group of islands, northeast of Euboea, are called the Northern Sporades.

Staphylus. An Argonaut. Staphylus and Oenopion were sons of Ariadne by either Dionysus or Theseus. Since Staphylus' name means "a bunch of grapes" and Oenopion's suggests wine (*oinos*), the god seems the stronger contender for the boys' paternity. A third brother, Phanus, sailed with Staphylus in the *Argo*. [Apollodorus 1.9.16, "Epitome" 1.9.]

Stenyclerus. An island city in Messenia. The Heraclid invader Cresphontes made Stenyclerus his capital in place of Pylus.

Sterope. See ACASTUS; ASTEROPE; CEPHEUS (2).

Stheneboea. The wife of PROËTUS. Failing to seduce BELLEROPHON [A, C], Stheneboea tried to bring about his death. He married her sister instead, and Stheneboea committed suicide. Euripides claimed, however, that Bellerophon killed her. Homer called her Anteia.

Sthenelus (1). A son of Perseus and Andromeda. Sthenelus married Nicippe, daughter of Pelops, who bore him Eurystheus, Alcyone, and Medusa. When his brother Electryon, king of Mycenae, was killed by his son-in-law, Amphitryon, Sthenelus seized the throne for himself, banishing Amphitryon. No doubt to secure his interests further, he invited his brothers-in-law Atreus and Thyestes to rule Midea, but in doing so he left all Argos open to rule by the sons of Pelops after the death of Eurystheus. [Apollodorus 2.4.5–6]

Sthenelus (2). The son of Capaneus and Evadne. Sthenelus marched with the Epigoni and later, after the death of both Adrastus and Aegialeus, he may have received the Argive throne, for he was descended from Proëtus. Nevertheless, he seems to have been dominated by Diomedes, for he later acted as Diomedes' charioteer when, with Helen's other disappointed suitors, they went to Troy. There Sthenelus was one of the soldiers in the wooden horse. Sthenelus' son Cylarabes became king of Argos after the death of Cyanippus. Another son, Cometes, seduced Diomedes' wife, Aegialeia, at the instigation of Nauplius. [Homer, *Iliad, passim;* Pausanias 2.18.5, 2.22.8–9, 2.24.3–4, 2.30.10; Apollodorus, 3.7.2, 3.10.8, "Epitome" 6.9; Hyginus, *Fabulae*, 175.]

Sthenelus (3). A son of Actor. Sthenelus accompanied Heracles in his campaign against the Amazons, but was killed and buried at the mouth of the river Callichorus, on the Black Sea. His ghost later appeared to the Argonauts, who sacrificed to him as a hero. [Apollonius Rhodius 2.911–929.]

Sthenelus. See ALCAEÜS (2).

Stilbe. A daughter of the river-god Peneius and the Naïad Creüsa. Stilbe was said by Diodorus Siculus [4.69.1] to have borne Lapithes and Centaurus to Apollo.

Stoëchades. Islands visited by the Argonauts. The Stoëchades, now called the Îles d'Hyères, lie off the Mediterranean coast of France east of Toulon.

Strongyle. The name of two islands, now called Naxos and Stromboli, respectively. Naxos is one of the Cyclades; Stromboli is a volcanic island in the Lipari, or Aeolian, islands, north of Sicily.

Strophades. A group of small islands off the coast of Acarnania in the Ionian Sea. These islands were said originally to have been called the Floating

Islands (Plotae) until Zetes and Calaïs, having overtaken the Harpies there, turned back. Thereafter the islands were called Strophades, or "Islands of Turning." They were equally well known as the Echinadian Islands or Echinades. The islands called Strophades today are far to the south of the ancient ones, unless Apollodorus was wrong to identify the Harpies' islands with the Echinades, in which case the present Strophades may have been the original ones.

Strophius. A king of Phocis. Strophius, the son of Crisus, was an ally of Agamemnon, and perhaps the husband of his sister, Anaxibia or Astyoche, who bore Strophius' son Pylades. Strophius reared ORESTES [A] at his court to save him from Clytemnestra and Aegisthus. When Pylades later helped Orestes to kill his mother, Strophius banished his son. Pylades' son by Electra was named for his grandfather. [Pausanias 29.4; Euripides, *Iphigeneia Among the Taurians*, 915–921.]

Strymon. A large river in western Thrace, and its god. The Edonians, whose king Lycurgus persecuted Dionysus and was punished by him, lived on its banks. The god of this river was the father of the Thracian king Rhesus by either Calliope or Euterpe. Evadne, wife of Argus, the ancient king and eponym of Argos, was the daughter of Strymon and Neaera, but this Strymon seems unlikely to have been the Thracian river-god.

Stymphalian birds. Birds that infested Lake Stymphalus, in northeastern Arcadia. These birds, which may have been man-eaters, were driven from the lake by HERACLES [F] as his sixth labor. He used bronze castanets or a rattle to frighten them into flight, then shot many on the wing.

Stymphalus. A king of Arcadia. A son of Elatus and Laodice, Stymphalus founded, or at least named for himself, a city in northern Arcadia. Pelops, when he was conquering much of the Peloponnesus, found himself unable to make much headway in Arcadia. He therefore pretended friendship with Stymphalus and treacherously murdered him, scattering his limbs. Most of the lands of Greece grew barren as a result of this heinous crime, and their fertility was at last restored only by the prayers of the pious king Aeacus. Stymphalus' sons, Agamedes and Gortys, achieved no particular renown, but descendants of Agamedes ruled Arcadia for many generations. Stymphalus also had a daughter, Parthenope. [Apollodorus 3.12.6; Pausanias 8.4.4–7.]

Stymphalus. A city in northeastern Arcadia. Stymphalus was named for a son of Elatus. It claimed to be the first home of Hera and was one of her cult centers. Lake Stymphalus, near the town, was rid of its overpopulation of birds by Heracles.

Styx. The chief river of Hades, and its goddess. Styx, like most river-deities, was an offspring of Oceanus and Tethys. She married Pallas, a Titan, and bore Zelus, Nike, Cratus, and Bia, personifications respectively of zeal or rivalry, victory, strength, and force. Styx was said by some to have been the mother by Zeus of Persephone, though this distinction is usually attributed to Demeter. Styx also bore the monster Echidna to an unidentified personage named Peiras. When the gods were warring with the Titans, Styx was the first of the uncommitted minor deities to bring her children to Zeus's aid, in spite of the fact that their father was a Titan. Zeus gratefully honored her by decreeing that her children should always remain with him and that the most inviolable oath that the gods could take should be by the waters of Styx. Thereafter, whenever a god wished to swear a solemn oath, Iris fetched a jug of water from the Styx and the god poured it out while taking the oath. If he broke his vow, he would lie a full year in a coma, after which he would recover but be ostracized by the other gods for nine years more.

Styx lived in a silver-pillared cave in Hades. The river, a branch of Oceanus, flowed out of or fell from a rock. Another river of Hades, the Cocytus, was a branch of the Styx, as was the river Titaressus, a tributary of the Thessalian river Peneius. According to Vergil [Aeneïd 6.439], the Styx flowed nine times around the borders of Hades. Those who wished to enter were ferried across the river by Charon. There was a tiny stream called Styx that flowed over a rock near the Arcadian village of Nonacris, near Pheneüs. Like the Underworld river with which it was identified, this Styx had a dire reputation. Its water was not only fatal to life, but it also broke all vessels that tried to contain it and corroded all materials except the hooves of horses. There was even a rumor that Alexander the Great was poisoned with water from this stream. The story does not explain how the water was conveyed from Arcadia to Alexander, who died in Babylon. [Homer, Iliad, 2.751–755, and Odyssey, 10.513–515; Hesiod, Theogony, 360–363, 383–403, 775–806.]

Suculae. The Roman name for the HYADES.

sun. The god of the sun was HELIUS, one of the Titans. His father, the Titan Hyperion, was also associated with the sun and his name is often substituted for that of Helius, or joined with it (as in Homer) as Helius Hyperion. In late Classical times, Phoebus APOLLO, in his capacity as a god of light, took over Helius' functions. In the Metamorphoses, Ovid makes Phoebus Apollo the sun-god in the Phaëthon story, though elsewhere he recounts stories of Helius. Sol was the Roman name for the sun-god.

Swan, The. See CYGNUS.

Sychaeüs. See DIDO.

Syleus. A Lydian outlaw. Syleus, who owned a vineyard near a highway, was accustomed to forcing passersby to till it for him. While in the service of Omphale, Heracles killed Syleus with the outlaw's own hoe, and also his daughter, Xenodice. Syleus is said to have been a native of Aulis. [Apollodorus 2.6.3; Diodorus Siculus 4.31.7.]

Symplegades. See CLASHING ROCKS.

Syria. A name given to an ill-defined and constantly changing area extending from the entire length of the eastern coast of the Mediterranean Sea eastward to the Euphrates River, or beyond. It included Phoenicia and was the scene of the many myths laid in the cities of Tyre, Sidon, and Byblus. Syria was, however, only vaguely known to the Greeks of early times. Certain myths laid in Egypt or Ethiopia seem properly to belong to Syria. Syria also served as a convenient name for all little-known eastern lands (as did Ethiopia) and was therefore called the home of Eos, the dawn-goddess. The Syrian Goddess, often identified with Aphrodite, was one of many names for the type of mother-goddess who was prominently worshiped throughout this region.

Syrinx. A nymph of Nonacris, in Arcadia. Unlike her sister nymphs, Syrinx chose to live the life of a virgin huntress. Pan saw her one day and pursued her. She ran to the river Ladon, where, unable to cross, she prayed to the water-nymphs to transform her. When Pan caught up with her he found only a clump of sadly murmuring marsh reeds. He uprooted some, cut them to different lengths, and fastened them together with wax, thus producing the first "Pan pipes," or syrinx. [Ovid, *Metamorphoses*, 1.689–712.]

Syrtis Major and **Syrtis Minor.** Gulfs at either end of the Libyan Sea. The great rectangular extension of the southern Mediterranean Sea that is called the Libyan Sea contains a smaller bay at either corner. The larger, less well defined of these, at the eastern end, is Syrtis Major, now called the Gulf of Sidra. The western bay, now the Gulf of Gabès, is Syrtis Minor. Though small, it extends inland almost to Lake Tritonis, now Chott Djerid, Tunisia. The Argonauts were carried inland in this region by high seas and trapped for a time in the lake.

T

Taenarum. The more westerly of two rugged capes that form the southern extremities of the Peloponnesus. Taenarum claimed one of the best-known entrances to Hades. According to one tradition, Arion was carried ashore by a dolphin at Taenarum.

Taking of Oechalia, The. A lost epic poem. This poem dealt with Heracles' capture of Eurytus' city, his abduction of Iole, and possibly his death, an aftermath of these events. The surviving fragments are published in the volume of Hesiod's works in the Loeb Classical Library.

Talaüs. A son of BIAS and Pero. Talaüs sailed with the Argonauts and later succeeded to his father's Argolid kingdom. By Lysimache, daughter of Melampus' son Abas (or Lysianassa, daughter of Polybus, king of Sicyon; or Eurynome, daughter of Iphitus) he was the father of Adrastus, Mecisteus, Pronax, Aristomachus, and Eriphyle, and possibly of Hippomedon, Parthenopaeüs, Astynome, and Metidice as well. Three or four of these children were among the Seven who fought at Thebes; Eriphyle abetted them.

Talthybius. The chief herald of the Greek forces in the Trojan War. Talthybius' fate, at least in surviving Classical literature, seems to have been forever to perform disagreeable duties that he did not quite approve of. In Homer's *Iliad* [1.318–348], he and his fellow herald Eurybates are sent by Agamemnon to take Briseïs from Achilles. In Euripides' tragedy *Trojan Women,* he has to take Cassandra into slavery and snatch the child Astyanax from his mother to be murdered. In the same playwright's *Hecuba,* he tells Hecuba that her daughter Polyxena has been sacrificed by the Greeks. Earlier he is said to have gone with Odysseus to bring Iphigeneia to Aulis, knowing that she was to be sacrificed there. A less painful errand was a journey to Cyprus with Odysseus to enlist the aid of King Cinyras. Talthybius returned after the war to Sparta. He died and was buried there, although the city of Aegium, in Achaea, also claimed to possess his tomb.

After his death Talthybius seems to have placed loyalty to his profession above the welfare of his country. His ghost was so outraged when his fellow Spartans, disregarding the traditional inviolability of heralds, killed two heralds of the Persian king Darius that he prevented Spartan diviners from securing any good omens. At last two prominent Spartans, Sperthias and Bulis, volunteered to go to Darius and offer themselves to be killed in atonement for the murder of the heralds. Darius sent them home unharmed, unwilling to emulate the earlier barbarity of the Spartans. Talthybius seemed to have been appeased, but later Aneristus and Nicolas, sons of the Spartan volunteers, were captured while on an embassy to Thrace and killed by the Athenians. Thus the Spartans were repaid in coin. The Athenians did not go unscathed, however. Talthybius caused great misfortunes to the household of their general Miltiades because Darius' heralds to Athens had also been received with indignities. [Herodotus 7.134–137; Pausanias 3.12.7, 7.24.1.]

Talus. A brazen giant who guarded Crete. Talus was said by some writers to have been the last survivor of the bronze race (see RACES OF MAN). Talus was given by Zeus to Europa to guard her island of Crete. According to others, Talus was one of the ingenious constructions of the divine artisan Hephaestus, who gave the robot to King Minos. Still others claimed that Talus was only a bronze bull. In the two stories that survive about him, Talus was a giant who marched around Crete three times a day and kept off intruders by pelting their ships with huge rocks. His bronze body was kept alive by an ichor contained in a single vein. This vein, closed at its end in one ankle with either a bronze nail or a thin layer of skin, was the giant's one vulnerable spot.

The ARGONAUTS [S] encountered Talus on their way home from Libya. Medea overcame him by one of three means: she maddened him with drugs; or, having won his confidence with a promise of immortality, she drew out the nail in his ankle; or she worked on him with the evil eye and the power of suggestion until he accidentally grazed his ankle against a rock and himself opened his vein. According to an entirely different version of the story, Talus was killed by the Argonaut Poeas, who shot him in the ankle with an arrow. [Apollonius Rhodius 4.1639–1693; Apollodorus 1.9.26.]

Talus. See PERDIX.

Tanagra. A town east of Thebes. The coast near Tanagra was the scene of Dionysus' battle with a triton, or of the capture of one of these sea-monsters by the townsmen.

Tanaïs River. The Greek name of the Don, which flows southward into the Sea of Azov. According to some of the more extravagant early conjectures about the homeward voyage of the Argonauts, they escaped from the Black Sea by sailing up the Tanaïs.

Tanaquil. The wife of Lucius TARQUINIUS PRISCUS, the fifth king of Rome. Tanaquil, a highborn and ambitious Etruscan woman, urged her husband to move from Tarquinia to Rome in order to advance his fortunes. Her training in the Etruscan art of augury often aided her husband in his affairs. At his death her strong-mindedness and quick thinking assured the throne to their son-in-law, Servius Tullius, in accordance with her husband's wishes.

Tantalus (1). A king of Sipylus, in Lydia. Tantalus was a son of Zeus and Pluto, daughter of Cronus. By Dione or a Pleiad he was the father of Pelops, Niobe, and Broteas. Although his punishment in Hades was known to everyone, there were many versions of his crime. All versions agreed that Tantalus proved unworthy of the extraordinary favor that the gods showed him. They invited him to dine with them in Olympus, and Zeus himself confided in him, but he stole their nectar and ambrosia and told their secrets to mortals. Worse still, according to another story, he played a gruesome trick in order to test their wisdom. Inviting the gods to a feast, he cut up Pelops and served him in a stew. The gods saw through the trick at once, except for Demeter, who ate a piece of Pelops' shoulder. The gods quickly restored Pelops to life, but consigned Tantalus to an everlasting torture in Hades. There he stood up to his chin in water, but whenever he bent to slake his burning thirst, the pool dried up. Boughs of fruit hung above his head, but when he raised his arms to pluck them, the wind blew them out of his reach. A stone, moreover, was suspended over him and threatened at any moment to fall and crush him. The ghost of Tantalus appears at the beginning of Seneca's tragedy *Thyestes*. [Homer, *Odyssey*, 11.582–592; Hyginus, *Fabulae*, 82–83.]

Tantalus (2). A son of Thyestes or Broteas. Although Hyginus [*Fabulae* 88] says that Tantalus was one of Thyestes' children killed by ATREUS [B], he is generally said to have grown to manhood and married Clytemnestra. Agamemnon killed both Tantalus and his child and took Clytemnestra for himself. [Euripides, *Iphigenia in Aulis*, 1150–1152.]

Taphians. The inhabitants of the Taphian Islands and Cephallenia, off the coast of Acarnania. Through their eponym, Taphius, the Taphians were descended from the god Poseidon and the ruling houses of both Argos and Elis. For some reason, they were originally called Teleboans. The Taphians seem to have made their living largely by piracy. The sons of Taphius' son Pterelaüs raided Mycenae and killed nearly all the sons of King Electryon. Later a company of Thebans, Mycenaeans, Phocians, and Locrians led by Amphitryon defeated them, thanks to the treachery of Pterelaüs' daughter, Comaetho. Amphitryon turned Cephallenia over to his exiled Athenian ally Cephalus, and the other islands to Electryon's brother Heleius. Anchialus and his son Mentes, later rulers of the Taphian Islands, were friends of Laërtes and Odysseus, who ruled neighboring Ithaca and perhaps Cephallenia as well. In Laërtes' day, at least, the Taphians were still pirates.

Taphius. The king and eponym of Taphos and the Taphian Islands. Poseidon carried off Hippothoë, daughter of Perseus' son Mestor by Pelops' daughter Lysidice, and lay with her on an island near Leucas, off Acarnania. She bore Taphius, who grew up to rule not only the island of his birth, which he named Taphos, but the surrounding islands. His son, Pterelaüs, succeeded him.

Taphos. One of the Taphian Islands. Named for Taphius, it was the seat of his government, which controlled all the islands of the group.

Taraxippus. A round altar near a dangerous spot on the racecourse at Olympia; also, the ghost that haunted it. During chariot races in the Olympic games, horses were unaccountably thrown into a panic upon approaching this altar. Disastrous results so often ensued that contestants offered sacrifices to propitiate Taraxippus (Horse-Scarer) before the races. The altar was generally thought to mark a tomb, the occupant of which haunted the track. Whose ghost was to be blamed was much argued. It was variously said to be that of a famous Eleian horseman, Olenius; of one Dameon, an ally of Heracles who had been killed by Cteatus in the war against Elis and buried with his horse; of Myrtilus, haunting an empty mound raised in his honor by his murderer, Pelops; or of Alcathoüs, son of Porthaon, the second of a long line of Hippodameia's suitors who were killed by her father, Oenomaüs. Some claimed that Taraxippus was not a ghost at all, but some unnamed object got from Amphion by Pelops, who buried it and frightened Oenomaüs' horses in their fatal race. Pausanias believed that the name Taraxippus did not originate with the accidents at Olympia, but was an epithet of Poseidon as god of horses.

Tarpeia. A Vestal virgin. Tarpeia, whose father was the commander of the Roman citadel during the reign of Romulus, accepted a bribe from the Sabine king Titus Tatius to let his men enter the citadel. Some say that she had demanded and been promised "what the soldiers wear on their left arms." Tarpeia meant by this their gold bracelets. Instead of giving her these, however, the Sabines crushed her under their shields, which they also wore on their left arms.

Tarquinius Priscus, Lucius. The fifth king of Rome. Tarquinius, whose real name was Lucumo, was a son of Demaratus, an exiled Corinthian who had taken up residence in the Etruscan city of Tarquinia and married a local woman. Lucumo, too, married an Etruscan, Tanaquil, a woman of great ambition. Knowing that her husband, as the son of an exiled foreigner, could never advance in Tarquinia in spite of the wealth that he had amassed there, she persuaded him to emigrate to Rome. There he took his new name and, by shrewd exploitation of his wealth and his friendships, became an intimate of the king, Ancus Marcius. When Ancus died, Tarquinius successfully won popular election as king and cemented his strength by raising a hundred Romans friendly to his cause to senatorial rank. During his long reign Tarquinius defeated the Sabines and annexed all the towns of the Ancient Latins. He had ruled for thirty-eight years when he was murdered by assassins hired by the sons of Ancus Marcius, who resented the honors that he had bestowed on his son-in-law, Servius Tullius. [Livy 1.35.1–1.41.7.]

Tarquinius, Sextus. A son of Lucius Tarquinius Superbus, the last king of Rome. The king wished to overcome the people of Gabii without having to resort to force. Sextus went to that city and, pretending to be a fugitive from his own father's tyranny, insinuated himself into the trust of the people. He gradually undermined the positions of the leading citizens and was able in time to turn Gabii over to his father without a battle. Later his cruel rape of LUCRETIA set in motion a rebellion against his father. Sextus fled to Gabii, where he was murdered by some of those whom he had earlier betrayed. [Livy 1.53.4–1.54.10, 1.57.6–1.63.3.]

Tarquinius Superbus, Lucius. The seventh and last king of Rome. An ambitious and violent man, Tarquinius was urged by his even more violent wife, Tullia, to kill her father, SERVIUS TULLIUS, and to usurp his throne. Tarquinius, although his father had reigned before Servius, had no legal claim to the rule, which was not hereditary. Moreover, in gaining it he brutally killed a noble king who had long held the affection of most of his people. Tarquinius was forced, therefore, to govern by fear and force of arms. He began by refusing burial to the old king. Surrounding himself with a bodyguard, he proceeded to rule without consulting the senate or the people, employing treachery as well as force in his dealings with both enemies and allies. In this way, for example, he conquered the city of Gabii without a single battle. During his twenty-five years of rule he carried out important public works, including the building of the temple of Jupiter on the Capitoline Hill and the Cloaca Maxima, the great sewer that served much of Rome. At last, the rape of Lucretia by his son Sextus gave some of the patricians, led by his relative Lucius Junius Brutus, an excuse to lead a rebellion against him. Tarquinius, who had long gloried in his nickname Superbus (the Proud), was driven from the city. With his exile the kingship at Rome was ended forever. [Livy 1.46.1–1.60.4.]

Tartarus. A dark region beneath the earth, and the personification of that region. Tartarus was said to be as far beneath Hades, or beneath the surface of the earth, as heaven was above it. An anvil would fall for nine days to reach it. The roots of earth and sea grew above it. Surrounded by a bronze fence with iron gates, Tartarus was the prison of Cronus and the other Titans who had warred with the gods. They were guarded there by the Hundred-handed. The vague figure who personified this sunless and terrible place is said to have issued from Chaos, together with Ge (Earth) and Eros (Love). By his sister he was the father of the monsters Typhöeus and Echidna. [Homer, *Iliad*, 8.13–16; Hesiod, *Theogony*, 119, 713–735, 820–822; Apollodorus 1.6.3, 2.1.2.]

Tartessus. An ancient city near Gades (modern Cadiz). After stealing Geryon's cattle, Heracles returned Helius' golden boat to the god at Tartessus.

Tatius, Titus. A king of the Sabines. Tatius led his people against Rome to avenge the treacherous abduction of their daughters by the Romans. The daughters separated their Roman husbands from the attacking Sabines, and Romulus, the Roman king, agreed to share the rule of the combined Roman and Sabine peoples with Tatius. Tatius was, however, soon killed in a quarrel with the Laurentians. (See ROMULUS AND REMUS.)

Taurians. The inhabitants of the Tauric Chersonese, the peninsula on the northern coast of the Black Sea now known as the Crimea. The Taurians were ruled at one time by Perses, who overthrew his brother Aeëtes, king of Colchis, but was killed by Medus, son of Medea. A later Taurian king was Thoas, during whose reign Iphigeneia was carried to his land by Artemis to be her priestess there. The barbaric Taurians sacrificed strangers, but Orestes managed to carry off Artemis' famous statue and Iphigeneia, who was his sister. The incident was the subject of Euripides' romantic play *Iphigeneia among the Taurians*.

Taurus. A Cretan noble. Taurus was the chief captain of Minos' navy. Minos hated him for his arrogance and his too-familiar ways with the queen, Pasiphaë, but Taurus regularly won the prizes for prowess at the annual games, and Minos did not dare oppose him openly. When Theseus defeated Taurus, Minos was so delighted that, according to the historian Philochorus, he remitted the tribute he had formerly required Athens to pay Crete. [Plutarch, *Parallel Lives*, "Theseus."]

Taurus (The Bull). A constellation. The bull was placed among the stars to commemorate the form that Zeus took when he carried Europa off to Crete and when he coupled with the heifer Io. [Hyginus, *Poetica Astronomica*, 2.21.]

Taÿgete. A daughter of Atlas and the Oceanid Pleïone. One of the Pleiades, Taÿgete was the nymph of Mount Taÿgetus, the range of mountains west of Sparta. Zeus fell in love with her and, although Artemis temporarily transformed her into a doe, he managed to father on her Lacedaemon, eponym of the Lacedaemonians. In honor of Artemis' efforts on her behalf, Taÿgete inscribed the golden horns of a doe with the goddess' name. This beautiful beast is said to have been the Cerynitian hind, which Heracles captured as his third labor. [Apollodorus 3.10.1, 3.10.3; Pindar, *Olympian Odes*, 3.28–30.]

Taÿgetus, Mount. A range of mountains that divides Messenia from Laconia. Taÿgetus was named for its resident nymph, the Pleiad Taÿgete.

Tecmessa. A daughter of Teleutas, a Phrygian king. Ajax made Tecmessa his concubine when he raided her father's city. She bore Ajax a son, Eurysaces. She appears in Sophocles' tragedy *Ajax*.

Tectamus. A king of Crete. Tectamus, a son of Dorus, married a daughter of Cretheus and sailed for Crete with a force of Aeolians and Pelasgians. They colonized the island and Tectamus became king. He was succeeded by his son Asterius, foster father of Minos. [Diodorus Siculus 4.60.2.]

Tegea. A city of southeastern Arcadia. Tegea was the principal city of Arcadia at least as early as the reign of Aleüs, a grandson of Arcas, the eponym of Arcadia. Heracles seduced Aleüs' daughter Auge, who bore Telephus. Aleüs' sons Cepheus and Amphidamas, together with their nephew Ancaeüs, joined the Argonautic expedition, while their brother, Lycurgus, ruled Tegea for his aged father. Cepheus and Ancaeüs later fought the Calydonian boar, which killed Ancaeüs. Cepheus was persuaded by Heracles to join his ill-fated campaign against the Eleian king Augeias. He was killed, as were all his sons but Echemus, who inherited the throne of Tegea on the death of Lycurgus. Ancaeüs' son Agapenor succeeded Echemus. He led the Arcadian troops to the Trojan War, but did not return, sailing instead to Cyprus, where he is said by some writers to have founded the city of Paphos. Tegea remained an important city in Classical times, when it was often in conflict with Sparta. The present town of Piali occupies its site.

Teiresias. A Theban seer. Teiresias was the son of the nymph Chariclo and Everes, a descendant of Udaeüs, one of the Sparti. During his youth he came upon two snakes coupling on the Arcadian mountain Cyllene or, more probably, on Mount Cithaeron, near Thebes. He either struck them with his staff or else killed the female. Immediately he found himself transformed into a woman. Seven or eight years later, coming upon the same snakes, or another pair, engaged in the same activity, Teiresias trampled or struck them again, or killed the male snake—and returned at once to his masculine form. Not long thereafter, while Zeus and Hera were disputing whether man or woman takes the greater pleasure from the act of sex, it occurred to them to call in Teiresias as an impartial arbiter, since he was the only man on earth who could answer the question from firsthand knowledge. The young man said that women experienced nine or ten times more satisfaction. This reply infuriated Hera, who blinded Teiresias on the spot. Zeus, on the other hand, rewarded him with the gift of prophecy and gave him long life as well.

Other causes have been occasionally cited for the seer's blindness. Callimachus, in his poem *The Baths of Pallas,* said that Teiresias had accidentally caught sight of Athena bathing and had automatically been struck blind. Because Chariclo was Athena's favorite nymph, the goddess gave her son, in place of his sight, second sight, long life, and the unique boon of keeping his intelligence in Hades after death. (Homer says, however, that this last was Persephone's gift.) According to Apollodorus, Athena washed Teiresias' ears, so that he could understand the language of birds, and gave him a staff of cornel wood with which he might walk as easily as if he had sight. A less colorful reason offered for the seer's blindness was that he had revealed too many of the gods' secrets to men.

Teiresias lived through at least seven generations. He joined the aging Cadmus in the revels of Dionysus, after vainly warning the brash young king Pentheus not to oppose the god. He first gained a reputation as a prophet through an obscure remark that later was thought to have foretold the fate of Narcissus. He is said, without further explanation, to have given victory to the Athenians in their war with Eleusis in the days of Erechtheus. It was Teiresias, too, who explained to the puzzled Amphitryon what had been going on between his wife and Zeus.

But the seer did not reach the heights of his fame until the days of Oedipus. Teiresias revealed that the proud king was the killer of his father and had committed incest. During the Argive invasion of Thebes he warned Creon that the city would fall if Ares were not appeased with the blood of Creon's son Menoeceus. Later he warned this king of the disaster that would result from his impiety in refusing burial to Polyneices' corpse. When the Epigoni launched a second invasion a generation later, Teiresias predicted the city's fall and induced King Laodamas to lead many of the Thebans to safety by night. Leaving with them, the seer died on drinking from the spring called Telphusa, near Haliartus. According to another account, Teiresias died at the same spot while being taken, with his daughter Manto (or Daphne) and other Theban prisoners of the Argives, to Delphi. Manto later migrated to Colophon, in Ionia; according to a fragment of the lost epic *The Returns*, it was there that Teiresias died and was buried by Calchas, Leontes, and Polypoetes, who went there overland from Troy for the purpose. Even after death the great seer uttered his prophecies in Hades. He gave sound advice to ODYSSEUS [G] on how to reach Ithaca during his long homeward voyage after the Trojan War, and on the precautions that he should take on the journey.

Teiresias is an important character in two plays of Sophocles, *Oedipus the King* and *Antigone*, and two of Euripides, *The Bacchants* and the *Phoenician Women*. His early adventures are well summarized by Apollodorus [2.4.8, 3.6.7, 3.7.3–4] and Ovid [*Metamorphoses* 3.322–350]. Odysseus' raising of Teiresias' ghost for a final prophecy is described by Homer [*Odyssey* 10.488–495, 11.90–151]. See also *Melampodia* [2–3], Hyginus' *Fabulae* [75], and Pausanias' *Description of Greece* [7.3.1, 9.11.3, 9.33.1–2].

Telamon. A king of Salamis. Telamon was a son of Aeacus, king of Aegina, and Endeïs. He and his brother, Peleus, killed their half-brother Phocus, either to please their mother or because he excelled them in sports. Although they hid the body, Aeacus learned of their deed and banished them from Aegina. Peleus emigrated to Phthia, in Thessaly, but Telamon went only as far as the nearby island of Salamis, offshore from Eleusis. King Cychreus welcomed him there; married him to his daughter, Glauce; and, dying childless, left the rule to him. (According to the early mythographer Pherecydes, Telamon was not the husband but the son of Glauce and of an Actaeüs who is otherwise unknown. A Salaminian by birth, he was a friend, rather than a brother, of Peleus.) Glauce apparently died, for Telamon married Eëriboea, or Periboea, daughter of Alcathoüs.

Like his brother, Telamon sailed with the Argonauts and took part in the Calydonian boar hunt. His most distinctive adventure, however, was to storm the walls of Troy side by side with his friend Heracles. The pair did this because King Laomedon had refused to pay them the stipulated fee for rescuing his daughter Hesione from a sea-serpent. Telamon was the first to enter Troy, and Heracles nearly killed him for this insult to his pride. He relented, however, and not only gave Hesione to Telamon as a prize but prayed to his father, Zeus, to give Telamon a brave son. Zeus's bird, the eagle, appeared in token of the god's consent. When Eëriboea bore a son, Telamon followed Heracles' directions and named him Ajax (Aias) for the eagle (*aietos*). Hesione also bore a brave son, Teucer. Some say that Telamon accompanied Heracles, or his nephew Iolaüs, in his war against the Amazons. The Eleians claimed that

Telamon was killed fighting with Heracles against Elis. It is generally said that Telamon was still king of Salamis at the end of the Trojan War and exiled Teucer for his part in Ajax' death. [Apollodorus 2.6.4, 3.12.6–7; Euripides, *Helen*, 87–94; Hyginus, *Fabulae*, 89; Pindar, *Isthmian Odes*, 6.26–54, and *Nemean Odes*, 3.36–39; Pausanias 8.15.6–7.]

Telchines. Rhodian sorcerers. All references to the Telchines are found in works by late Classical authors, and they are vague and confused. It is not unlikely, however, that local legends of the Telchines in Rhodes were ancient. According to Diodorus, Siculus [5.55–56], the Telchines, sons of Thalatta (Sea), were the first inhabitants of Rhodes. Together with an Oceanid named Capheira, they nursed the infant Poseidon at the request of his mother, Rhea, presumably to protect him from the cannibalistic habits of his father, Cronus. Their sister Halia (Sea-Woman) later bore six sons and a daughter, Rhode, to the sea-god. The Telchines were able to bring rain, hail, or snow by means of their sorcery, and could change their shapes. They invented several useful arts, including the making of statues of the gods. With their knowledge of weather, the Telchines divined the coming of Deucalion's Flood and fled to Asia Minor. Ovid [*Metamorphoses* 7.365–367] says, however, that Zeus drowned the Telchines in the sea because of the havoc they were causing with their gift of the evil eye.

Teleboans. An ancient name of the TAPHIANS.

Teledice. A nymph. Teledice bore Apis and Niobe to Phoroneus, king of Argos. (Hyginus names their mother Cinna.) [Apollodorus 2.1.1.]

Telegonus (1). The son of Odysseus and Circe. Telegonus was born during the year that Odysseus spent on Circe's island of Aeaea. On growing to manhood, he was sent by his mother in search of his father, who had long since returned to Ithaca. Telegonus and his crew did not know the island when they came to it and, being hungry, raided it for food. The aged Odysseus went out to defend his property and was killed by Telegonus with a spear tipped with the sting of a stingray. On learning whom he had killed, Telegonus brought Odysseus' body, together with Penelope and Telemachus, home to Aeaea, where they buried Odysseus. Telegonus then married Penelope, while Circe married Telemachus. Some say that Italus, eponym of Italy, was the son of Telegonus and Penelope. [*Telegony* 1–2; Apollodorus "Epitome" 7.36–37; Hyginus, *Fabulae*, 127.]

Telegonus (2). A king of Egypt. Io married Telegonus and remained with him in Egypt. [Apollodorus 2.1.3.]

Telegonus. See POLYGONUS.

Telegony. See EPIC CYCLE.

Telemachus. The son of Odysseus and Penelope. Telemachus was only an infant when ODYSSEUS [B, L–N] went off to the Trojan War. While he was growing up, his mother was besieged by suitors, who were sure that Odysseus would never return to Ithaca. Telemachus was too young and weak to eject them and make himself master of his own house. Athena, taking the form first of a Taphian visitor, Mentes, and later of Mentor, the Ithacan noble whom Odysseus had left in charge of his household, instilled manly spirit into the youth. He visited Nestor at Pylus and Menelaüs at Sparta in a vain hope of getting news of his father. On his way home, Athena helped him to avoid an ambush laid at sea by the suitors.

On reaching Ithaca, Telemachus found that Odysseus had secretly returned from his wanderings. Now a mature and courageous young man, Telemachus acquitted himself well in the tense days that followed, fighting beside his father in the final battle that destroyed the suitors. Telemachus presumably ruled Ithaca during Odysseus' subsequent wanderings. Odysseus was shot unknowingly by Telegonus, his son by Circe. On learning whom he had killed, Telegonus took Telemachus and Penelope home to his mother's island of Aeaea, where they buried Odysseus. He then married Penelope. Circe married Telemachus and made him and his mother immortal.

Telemachus is a principal character in the Ithacan books of Homer's *Odyssey*. [See also *Telegony* 1–2.]

Telephassa. The wife of Agenor, king of Tyre or Sidon. (Some writers call Agenor's wife Argiope.) Telephassa bore her husband a daughter, Europa, and five sons, Cadmus, Phoenix, Cilix, Thasus, and Phineus. When Agenor sent the sons away to find the kidnaped Europa or else be exiled, Telephassa went with them. She settled with Cadmus in Thrace, where she died. [Apollodorus 3.1.1, 3.4.1.]

Telephus. The son of Auge, daughter of Aleüs, king of Tegea, by Heracles. Telephus was exposed on the Arcadian mountain Parthenius when Aleüs learned that his daughter had been seduced, and AUGE was sold into slavery. Suckled by a doe (*elaphos*), for which he was named, and reared by shepherds, the young man consulted an oracle and was told to travel to Mysia if he wished to find his mother. On arriving there, according to one tale, he aided Teuthras, king of Teuthrania, in defending his kingdom against the Messenian invader Idas, and was rewarded with the kingdom and the hand of the king's adopted daughter, whom in the nick of time he discovered to be Auge. Other accounts say that he was adopted by Teuthras and succeeded him. Telephus found a bride in Astyoche or Laodice, daughter of Priam, who bore him a son, Eurypylus.

When the Greek fleet was on its way to the Trojan War, it came by mistake to the shores of Mysia. Telephus and his followers beat off the attack, killing Thersander, but Telephus was wounded in the thigh by Achilles. The wound refused to heal, and Telephus consulted Apollo's oracle. He was told that only the wounder could be his physician. In a beggar's rags Telephus sought out Achilles at Agamemnon's palace in Argos, where the Greek leaders were preparing another expedition. Clytemnestra, sympathizing with the suppliant but evidently having little confidence in her husband's compassion, advised Telephus to threaten the life of the infant prince Orestes. Telephus snatched the child from his cradle and demanded to be healed. This precaution turned out to be unnecessary, for the Greeks had received an oracle to the effect that they could not take Troy without Telephus' leadership. Achilles was willing to heal his victim, but protested that he knew nothing of medicine. Odysseus explained that Achilles' spear, not its owner, had inflicted the wound and could therefore heal it. Achilles scraped rust from the spearhead into the wound, and Telephus was soon well. He was now in a dilemma, however, for he had promised to give aid to the Greeks in attacking his father-in-law's city. He solved the moral problem by consenting to guide them to Troy, but not to take part in the fighting. His son Eurypylus later fought on the side of the Trojans. Telephus returned to Teuthrania and later died there. He was honored as a hero there in Classical times, even though the city had been conquered by the Epeirot Pergamus and renamed for him. [Apollodorus 2.7.4, 3.9.1, "Epitome" 3.17–20; Hyginus, *Fabulae*, 99–101.]

Tellus or **Terra.** The earth, and the Roman goddess of the earth, comparable to the Greek GE. Tellus was often associated in worship with Pluto and the manes. Like many other chthonian deities, Tellus was connected both with the fruitfulness of the earth and with its function as the abode of the dead.

Telphusa, Tilphusa, or **Tilphussa.** A spring near Haliartus, in Boeotia, and the nymph of the spring. This spring was the site of a very ancient oracle. When Apollo was first looking for a likely place to establish his own oracular shrine, he came to this spring. On learning his intentions, Telphusa suggested that he go to Delphi instead, for she evidently feared that Apollo would interfere with her business. The god of prophecy, momentarily taken in by her plausible advice, followed it. Later, however, he returned and punished her for her duplicity by hiding the spring under great rocks. Much later Teiresias, a seer inspired by Apollo, died when he drank Telphusa's waters. No reason is given for his death, but it may well have been due to Telphusa's envy.

Temenus (1). One of the HERACLIDS, a son of Aristomachus. Temenus' father and his great-grandfather Hyllus had both died in attempted invasions of the Peloponnesus that had been inspired by the Delphic oracle's promise to Hyllus that they would conquer that region in "the third crop." Temenus went to Delphi and upbraided the oracle, but was told that "the third generation" had been meant. After a disastrous false start, Temenus, his brother Cresphontes, and two of their nephews sailed from Naupactus for the Peloponnesus and won all encounters. Drawing lots with his relatives for the conquered lands, Temenus won Argos and became king. Because he made Deïphontes, the husband of his daughter Hyrnetho, his chief adviser in preference to his sons, they overthrew and perhaps killed him. Ceïsus, the eldest, seized the throne. [Apollodorus 2.8.2–5; Pausanias 2.19.1.]

Temenus (2). A son of Pelasgus. All that is known of Temenus is the local tradition in the Arcadian city of Stymphalus that he reared Hera. He is said to have built three shrines to celebrate different aspects of the goddess' nature: one as Maiden, while she was still a girl; a second as Bride, after her marriage to Zeus; and a last as Widow, when she returned to Stymphalus after one of her quarrels with her husband. [Pausanias 8.22.2.]

Temenus. See ALCMEON.

Tempe. A Thessalian valley (now called Tembi) through which the Peneius River flows. This valley was the home of Aristaeüs, and it was there that he inadvertently caused the death of Orpheus' bride, Eurydice. The Vale of Tempe was known as one of the most beautiful regions in all the Greek lands.

Tenedos. A small island off the coast of the Troad. Tenedos was settled and named by Tenes, who was later killed there during a raid by Achilles. The Greek fleet waited at Tenedos before returning to Troy by night to enter after the Trojans had taken in the wooden horse.

Tenes or **Tennes.** The founder and eponym of Tenedos. Tenes was the son of Cycnus, king of Colonae, near Troy, and Procleia, daughter of Laomedon or Clytius. (Some say that Apollo was the real father.) After Procleia's death Cycnus married Philonome, daughter of Tragasus or Cragasus. This woman fell in love with Tenes and, failing to seduce him, accused him of rape. A flute player named Eumolpus bore false witness to her story. Enraged, Cycnus locked Tenes (and, for some unexplained reason, his sister, Hemithea) in a chest and flung it into the sea. It floated only as far as the nearby island of Leucophrys, where it washed ashore. Brother and sister escaped and Tenes settled the island, renaming it Tenedos for himself. Eventually Cycnus learned of his wife's treachery. He buried her alive and had Eumolpus stoned, then sailed for Tenedos, hoping to be reconciled with his son. Tenes, however, cut the hawsers that Cycnus flung ashore and would not let him land.

When the Greeks came to attack Troy and Achilles was ravaging nearby cities, his mother, Thetis, warned him not to harm Tenes, for Apollo would avenge his son. Ignoring her advice, or else unaware of Tenes' identity, Achilles killed him while the young king was trying to ward off with stones the Greek landing. [Apollodorus "Epitome" 3.23–26; Pausanias 10.14.1–4.]

Tenos. An island in the Cyclades. Zetes and Calaïs were killed there by Heracles, who set up over their grave a large rock that swayed in the north wind.

Tereus. A Daulian or Thracian king. Tereus came to Athens from either Daulis, in Phocis, or some part of Thrace in order to help King Pandion in his boundary dispute with Labdacus, king of Thebes. He was rewarded with the hand of Pandion's daughter Procne, who bore him a son, Itys or Itylos. Tereus soon fell in love with Procne's sister, Philomela. Sending Procne to some retreat in the country, he persuaded Philomela that her sister was dead and thus succeeded in seducing her. He then cut out her tongue in order to prevent her from revealing his act when she found that Procne was still living. Philomela managed to weave the sad story into a robe in characters that Procne could read and sent it to her sister. Procne, aided by Philomela, took a terrible vengeance on her husband. Cutting up their son, she served him to Tereus at a feast. On learning too late what he had eaten, Tereus pursued the sisters with drawn sword. As they ran, Procne and Philomela were changed into a nightingale and a swallow (or vice versa), Tereus into a hoopoe. [Ovid, *Metamorphoses*, 6.424–674; Apollodorus 3.14.8.]

Termilae. See LYCIA.

Terpsichore. One of the nine Muses. Terpsichore was a daughter of Zeus and Mnemosyne. Either she or her sister Melpomene was the mother, by the river-god Acheloüs, of the Sirens. [Apollonius Rhodius 4.895–896.]

Terra. See TELLUS.

Tethys. A Titaness. Tethys, a daughter of Ge (Earth) and Uranus (Sky), married her brother Oceanus and became the mother of most of the world's river-gods and their three thousand sisters, the Oceanids. During the war between the gods and the Titans, Tethys and her husband took their niece Hera for safekeeping to their home at the ends of the earth. Out of loyalty to her foster daughter, Tethys refused to let the constellation the Great Bear (Callisto) set in the river Oceanus, because Callisto had been Zeus's concubine. When Aesacus leaped into the sea, Tethys made him a diver bird. These tales, almost the only ones that are told of Tethys, suggest that she was an ancient goddess of the sea. [Homer, *Iliad*, 14.201–204; Hesiod, *Theogony*, 337–370; Ovid, *Metamorphoses*, 11.784–795; Hyginus, *Fabulae*, 177, and *Poetica Astronomica*, 2.1.]

Teucer (1). The first king of the Troad. According to Greek writers, Teucer was an indigenous king, a son of the god of the Scamander River and Idaea, a nymph of Mount Ida. The Roman tradition made him an immigrant from Crete. He married his daughter, Bateia, to Dardanus, when he arrived from Samothrace. Dardanus succeeded Teucer in the rule and changed the name of the people from Teucrians to Dardanians. [Apollodorus 3.12.1; Vergil, *Aeneïd*, 3.107–199.]

Teucer (2). The son of Telamon by Hesione, daughter of Laomedon. Teucer, the best archer with the Greek forces in the Trojan War, often fought side by side with his half-brother, the Salaminian Ajax, darting out from behind his great shield to shoot an arrow, then ducking back into its shelter. In this fashion he disposed of many Trojan soldiers. He would have shot even Hector had not Zeus broken his bowstring. When Ajax killed himself and was at first denied burial by Agamemnon, Teucer returned from an expedition in Mysia just in time to defy the commander. Odysseus' intervention saved Teucer from a possibly fatal conflict with the other Greeks. On Teucer's return to Salamis, his old father, Telamon, refused to allow him to land, believing him guilty of either complicity or cowardice in the Greek's treatment of Ajax. Exiled, Teucer was told by Apollo's oracle that he should found a new Salamis on the island of Cyprus. He was welcomed there by King Cinyras, who gave him one of his daughters in marriage. Some say that Belus, king of Sidon, gave Cyprus to Teucer after conquering it. The kings of Cyprus down to Evagoras claimed descent from Teucer.

Teucer appears in Sophocles' tragedy *Ajax* and in Euripides' romantic drama *Helen*. See also Homer, *Iliad*, 8.266–334, 12.370–403, 13.169–185, 15.437–483, 23.859–883; Vergil, *Aeneïd*, 1.619–622; Pausanias 1.3.2, 1.28.11, 2.29.4, 8.15.6–7.

Teumessus. A town near Thebes on the road to Chalcis. Teumessus was the home of a fox that ravaged Thebes as a result of some god's anger. When about to be caught by Laelaps, the infallible hound owned by Procris, the fox was turned to stone, together with the hound. (See AMPHITRYON, A.)

Teuthrania. An ancient kingdom on the Caïcus River near the Mysian coast. Teuthrania was named for its founder, Teuthras. When the country was invaded by Greeks under Idas, Teuthras was aided in successful resistance by the Arcadians Telephus and Parthenopaeüs. He adopted Telephus and left the throne to him. The Greek forces on their way to Troy attacked Mysia in error. In order to recover from a resulting wound, Telephus helped them find Troy, but, as a son-in-law of King Priam, refused to join them. His son, Eurypylus, distinguished himself fighting with the Trojans near the end of the war, but was killed by Neoptolemus. Much later Neoptolemus' son Pergamus sailed from Epeirus and conquered Teuthrania, killing Areius, who was then reigning. Pergamus renamed the city Pergamon.

Teuthras. A king and eponym of Teuthrania, in Mysia. Teuthras bought the pregnant Auge from the slave trader Nauplius, who had received her from her father, the Arcadian king Aleüs. Teuthras married Auge and, much later, adopted Telephus, her son by Heracles, who aided him in a successful war with Idas. At Teuthras' death Telephus inherited the throne. [Apollodorus 2.7.4, 3.9.1; Pausanias 8.4.8–9.]

Thalamae. A town in western Laconia. When expelled from Sparta as a young man, Tyndareüs took refuge with Aphareus in Thalamae, which was then a part of Messenia. The town had an unusual shrine to the moon-goddess, who was worshiped there under the name of Pasiphaë.

Thaleia. One of the nine Muses. A daughter of Zeus and Mnemosyne, Thaleia is said by some to have borne the Corybantes to Apollo. [Apollodorus 1.3.1, 1.3.4.]

Thalpius. A son of Eurytus, one of the Moliones, and of Theraephone. Thalpius and his cousin Amphimachus led some of the Eleian forces to Troy. Both had been suitors of Helen. [Homer, *Iliad*, 2.615–624.]

Thamyris. A mythical bard. Thamyris was the son of the poet Philammon by the nymph Argiope. When his father repudiated his pregnant mother, she went from Parnassus to Thrace, and the child was born there. Thamyris fell in love with Hyacinth before Apollo did; he was said to have been the first man to love a person of his own sex. Like his father, Thamyris won the prize for singing at Delphi. He became so famous as a bard that he dared to challenge the Muses to a contest at Dorium, in Messenia. The Muses won the competition and were allowed by the terms of the contest to deprive the loser of anything they wished. They took away Thamyris' sight and his poetic gift as well. According to the lost epic the *Minyad*, he was further punished in Hades for his impudence. [Homer, *Iliad*, 2.594–600; Apollodorus 1.3.3; Pausanias 4.33.3, 4.33.7.]

Thanatos. Death, and the personification of death. Thanatos was born of Nyx (Night). He and his brother Hypnos (Sleep) lived together in Tartarus, hated even by the gods. On the orders of Zeus, they bore the body of Sarpedon to Lycia. The functions that one might suppose to belong to Thanatos were often performed by the Keres or the Erinyes, who carried certain dead persons to Hades. Thanatos appears in Euripides' *Alcestis* to carry off the heroine from her tomb. Heracles wrestles with him, however, and brings her back to life. [Homer, *Iliad*, 16.453–455, 16.672–673, 16.682–683; Hesiod, *Theogony*, 211–212, 758–766.]

Thasus. The eponym of Thasus, the northernmost large island in the Aegean Sea. Thasus was a son of Agenor, Cilix, or Poseidon. In search of Europa, he sailed with Cadmus from Phoenicia and founded a colony on the island to which he gave his name. [Apollodorus 3.1.1.]

Thaumas. A son of Pontus (Sea) and Ge (Earth). Except that three or four of Thaumas' brothers and sisters were ancient sea-deities, nothing can be judged of his functions. He was the father, by the Oceanid Electra, of Iris and the Harpies. [Hesiod, *Theogony*, 232–239, 265–269.]

Theano. See MELANIPPE.

Thebaïd. See EPIC CYCLE.

Thebes. A principal city of southern Boeotia. Thebes lies in the fertile valley north of the Cithaeron Range and southeast of Lake Copaïs. The river Asopus, just south of the city, drains this valley. Today Thebes (Thebai) is little more than a village. The archaeological remains that have been uncovered there, unlike those of Mycenae, Tiryns, and many other Greek cities, give relatively scant evidence of the power that the city possessed from the Mycenaean era well into Classical times.

According to legend, the aboriginal inhabitants of southern Boeotia were the Ectenes. They were ruled by King Ogygus, in whose honor poets often called Thebes "Ogygian." The Ectenes, destroyed by plague, were replaced by two tribes, the Hyantes and the Aonians. These were subdued by Canaanite or Phoenician invaders, led by Cadmus. The Hyantes fled northward, but the Aonians sued for peace and were allowed to remain. They continued to live in hill towns, while the newcomers built cities. The epithet "Aonian" was frequently applied to Thebes in later days. Many aspects of the story of the Sparti, or Sown-men, "planted" by Cadmus suggest that they may represent a tribe dominant in the area at the time of the Cadmeian invasion. They seem to have shared the government with the conquerors throughout the reign of the dynasty founded by Cadmus, and, even in the Classical era, the principal families of Thebes claimed descent from the "dragon's teeth."

Cadmus was one of the sons of the Phoenician king Agenor, who founded settlements in Asia Minor, the Aegean Islands, and the Greek mainland. Acting on the advice of the Delphic oracle, Cadmus followed a cow all the way from Phocis to southern Boeotia and founded his city where she lay down. This happened to be on top of a hill overlooking the Asopus Valley. After killing a dragon sacred to Ares and sowing its teeth, Cadmus allied himself with the Sparti, who sprang up in the field. He was punished for killing the dragon by having to serve Ares for eight years, after which he received the god's daughter Harmonia as his wife, and also the kingdom. He built a citadel on the hill and named his city Cadmeia. After a long reign he abdicated in favor of his grandson Pentheus, whose father was one of the Sparti. Pentheus was destroyed by Dionysus, another of Cadmus' grandsons, and Cadmus' son, Polydorus, took the throne.

During Pentheus' brief reign a third force had gained a foothold in the Cadmeian government with the admittance to citizenship of two Euboean brothers, Nycteus and Lycus. On dying, Polydorus, who had married Nycteus' daughter Nycteïs, left his father-in-law to reign as regent for Polydorus' young son Labdacus. Nycteus died and left the regency to Lycus, or else Lycus seized it.

Labdacus reigned briefly but died young, and Lycus continued as regent, this time for Labdacus' infant son, Laïus. After twenty years on the throne Lycus was overthrown by Amphion and Zethus, sons of Nycteus' erring daughter Antiope, who had been cruelly treated by Lycus' wife. Supporters of the line of Cadmus hastily sent Laïus to the court of Pisa, where Pelops, though he was Amphion's brother-in-law, welcomed the boy. Amphion and Zethus reigned jointly, walling in the thriving town that had grown up at the foot of the hill. These walls were famous for their seven gates. The brothers renamed the extended city Thebes, in honor of Zethus' wife, Thebe, but the citadel on the hill continued to be called Cadmeia. Amphion and Zethus died as the result of family tragedies, and Laïus, now a young man, hurried home from the Peloponnesus.

Laïus married Jocasta, daughter of Menoeceus, a prominent descendant of the Sparti. Against the advice of the Delphic oracle, the king had a son by Jocasta. Although Laïus had the infant exposed, he grew up in Corinth under the name of Oedipus. Later he killed Laïus in a quarrel, neither knowing who the other was. Jocasta's brother Creon ruled for a time as regent but offered both the throne and his sister's hand to anyone who could destroy the Sphinx, a monster that was devouring all the young men of Thebes. Oedipus succeeded in doing so and received the promised rewards. Jocasta bore him two sons and two daughters. When, after many years, Oedipus discovered that he

The House of Cadmus

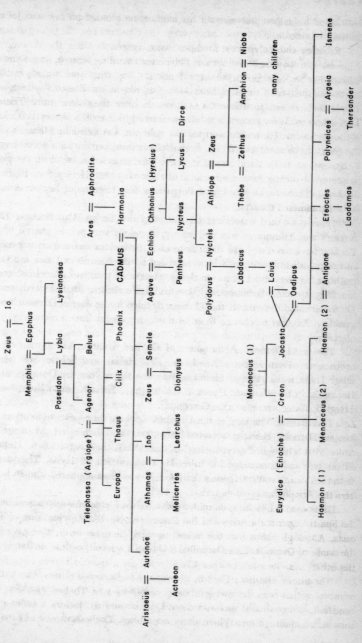

```
Zeus ══ Io

Memphis ══ Epaphus

                    Poseidon ══ Lybia     Belus
                                          Agenor ══ Telephassa (Argiope)

Memphis ══ Lybia     Lysianassa

Europa     Thasus     Cilix     Phoenix     CADMUS ══ Harmonia     Ares ══ Aphrodite

                     Zeus ══ Semele                              Chthonius (Hyrieus)
Athamas ══ Ino                                                   Nycteus     Lycus
                     Dionysus          Agave ══ Echion                   Nycteis ══ Polydorus    Antiope ══ Zeus
Aristaeus ══ Autonoe                                             Pentheus            Labdacus         Thebe     Zethus
              Learchus                                                                               Amphion ══ Niobe
     Actaeon        Melicertes                                            Laius ══ Jocasta                  many children
                                                                              Oedipus ══ Jocasta
                                    Creon ══ Eurydice (Enioche)        Menoeceus (1)
                                    Menoeceus (2)                      Antigone ══ Haemon (2)
                                    Haemon (1)                         Eteocles  Polyneices ══ Argeia     Ismene
                                                                       Laodamas   Thersander
```

had killed his father and married his mother, he blinded himself and Jocasta committed suicide.

Eteocles and Polyneices, Oedipus' sons, agreed to share the throne, but Eteocles soon banished his brother. Polyneices raised an army in Argos and attacked Thebes (see SEVEN AGAINST THEBES). The army was routed, but the brothers killed each other. Creon, acting as regent for Eteocles' young son, Laodamas, refused to allow the Argives to bury their dead until Theseus forced him to do so. Later Creon was murdered by Lycus, a descendant of the Euboean Lycus. He briefly usurped the rule but was killed by Heracles. The Epigoni, the sons of the fallen Argive champions, organized a second campaign against Thebes and seized the city. Laodamas led some of his people in a nocturnal escape from Cadmeia. This company settled in either Illyria or Hestiaea. Thebes was razed, and Polyneices' son Thersander became king of what remained of the city.

Thersander died bravely at the outset of the Trojan War. Because Thersander's son Tisamenus was still young, Peneleüs was put in charge of the Theban forces at Troy. He died there also. Tisamenus enjoyed an uneventful rule, but his son, Autesion, was so hounded by the Erinyes of Laïus and Oedipus that, on the advice of an oracle, he emigrated to Dorus. Peneleüs' grandson Damasichthon became king. Because of the rivalries that seemed inevitably to surround the throne, the Thebans decided in the time of Damasichthon's grandson Xanthus to change their form of government from a monarchy to an oligarchy.

Theia. A Titaness. A daughter of Ge and Uranus, Theia married her brother, the Titan Hyperion, and bore Eos, Helius, and Selene. She (or another Theia, a daughter of Memnon) was also the mother, by Oceanus, of the Cercopes. In the *Homeric Hymn to Helius* [31], Theia is called Euryphaëssa. [Hesiod, *Theogony*, 371–374; *Cercopes*.]

Theiodamas. The king of the Dryopes. Looking for an excuse to attack the lawless Dryopes, Heracles accosted Theiodamas and demanded one of the two bulls with which he was plowing a field. When the king refused, Heracles killed him and conquered his tribe. He then carried off Hylas, Theiodamas' beautiful young son by Orion's daughter Menodice, and reared him to be his squire. [Apollonius Rhodius 1.1211–1220.]

Thelpusa. A city in western Aracadia. When Demeter was pursued by Poseidon, she became a mare and hid among the herds of Oncius, king of Thelpusa. Poseidon became a stallion and mounted her. Demeter later gave birth to the horse Arion and to Despoina (Mistress), a local goddess similar to Persephone.

Themis. A Titaness. Themis, a daughter of Uranus and Ge, was, like her mother, with whom she was sometimes identified, an early earth-goddess. Her function was gradually specialized until she became a goddess of order in the communal affairs of men, particularly assemblies. The second wife of Zeus, she bore him several children who personified aspects of order in the universe: the Seasons (Horae)—Eunomia (Order), Dike (Justice), Eirene (Peace)—and the Fates (Moerae). It was Themis' duty to call the gods to assembly on Olympus, and she was the first to receive the cup at their feasts. Like other earth-goddesses, Themis knew the future. She was the second deity, after her mother, to hold the oracle at Delphi. She later relinquished it to Apollo, either directly or through her sister Titaness Phoebe. Some say that Apollo took it by force, after killing Python, its guardian snake.

According to some writers, Themis was the mother, by her brother Iapetus, of Prometheus. It was from her that he gained his knowledge of future events, such as the fate of Io. Themis told Deucalion how to repeople the earth by throwing behind him "his mother's bones." She warned Atlas at Delphi that a son of Zeus would one day steal the golden apples from his garden, which the Hesperides tended. The most significant of her predictions, however, was her warning to Zeus (which may have been relayed through Prometheus) that a son born to Thetis would prove greater than his father. On learning this, Zeus (and Poseidon as well) gave up his pursuit of the Nereïd and hastily married her to a mortal. [Homer, *Iliad*, 15.87–95, 20.4–6, and *Odyssey*, 2.68–69; Hesiod, *Theogony*, 132–135, 901–906; Aeschylus, *Eumenides*, 2–8, and *Prometheus Bound*, 18, 211–215, 873–874; Apollodorus 1.4.1, 3.13.5; Ovid, *Metamorphoses*, 1.320–321, 1.377–394, 4.643–645.]

Themiscyra. A city (now called Termeh) at the mouth of the Thermodon River on the southern coast of the Black Sea. Themiscyra, the principal city of the Amazons, was avoided by the Argonauts on their way to Colchis, but was raided by Heracles and Theseus.

Themiste. A daughter of Ilus, king of Troy, and Eurydice, daughter of Adrastus. Themiste, sister of Laomedon, married Capys and bore Anchises. [Apollodorus 3.12.2.]

Themisto. A daughter of Hypseus. Themisto was the second or third wife of ATHAMAS [D] and mother of his sons Leucon, Erythrius, Schoeneus, and Ptoüs—or, in various other versions of the myth, of Presbon, Sphincius, and Orchomenus. Themisto killed herself after inadvertently killing the last two of these sons in an attempt to dispose of the sons of Ino, another of Athamas' wives.

Theoclymenus. A seer. Theoclymenus, a son of the famous diviner Polypheidus, begged passage with Telemachus from Pylus to Ithaca in order to escape the consequences of having killed an Argive relative. He warned Penelope's suitors that a terrible doom awaited them, but they only laughed at his prophecy. [Homer, *Odyssey*, 15.222–281, 20.350–370.]

Theoclymenus. See PROTEUS (2).

Theogony. See HESIOD.

Theonoë. See PROTEUS (2).

Theophane. A daughter of Bisaltes. A beautiful girl, Theophane had many suitors, but Poseidon carried her off to the island of Crumissa or Crinissa. The determined suitors found out where she was hidden and sailed for the island. Poseidon foiled them by changing Theophane into a ewe and the islanders into cattle. Arriving at Crumissa, the suitors found no people but plenty of well-fed cattle, which they began to kill for food. When Poseidon saw that the innocent islanders were being slaughtered, he changed the suitors into wolves. This act hardly improved the situation for the victims, but it seems to have gratified the god. He next turned himself into a ram and lay with Theophane. The only result of these wholesale transformations, apart from an island full of animals, was a remarkable baby ram, to which the ewe Theophane gave birth in due course. This ram, which could both speak and fly, eventually saved the life of Phrixus and became the constellation Aries. Its golden fleece was the object of the Argonauts' quest. [Hyginus, *Fabulae*, 188.]

Thera. A volcanic island north of Crete (today often called Santorin). Thera was said by some writers to have grown from a clod of Libyan earth given by Triton to the Argonaut Euphemus, who threw it into the sea in obedience to a dream. As the sea-god promised, Euphemus' Minyan descendants from Lemnos, after a sojourn in Sparta, helped to colonize the island. Another story, which was to some degree combined with the Minyan version, emphasized the role of Theras, the island's eponym, a Theban who had gone to Sparta with the Heraclids. Theras' ancestor Cadmus had stopped at the island, then called Calliste, during his search for Europa, and had left his kinsman Membliarus there, with some other Tyrians, to colonize it. Eight generations later Theras led a group of Spartans, together with some Minyan refugees in Sparta, to found a new colony. Membliarus' descendants offered the throne to Theras, who renamed the island for himself. Later Battus, a Theraean descended through seventeen generations from Euphemus, reluctantly led a group of his countrymen to found, after many vicissitudes, the city of Cyrene on the coast of North Africa, thereby carrying out the implied intent of Triton.

The island of Thera, historically settled, at the latest, in Minoan times, was destroyed by a volcanic explosion of fantastic proportions, perhaps about 1400 B.C. It was later resettled, though little was left but a craggy rim of the crater, two thousand feet deep, which the sea had half filled. Disastrous earthquakes have continued up to the present day on the still-occupied island. Recent soundings in the Mediterranean Sea have brought up ash from an explosion much earlier than that of 1400 and vastly more powerful. This violent geological history has given rise to speculations that the more recent cataclysm may have caused the earthquakes thought to have contributed to the downfall of the Minoan stronghold of Knossos, and that the earlier may have been the cause of the event known to mythology as Deucalion's Flood. Some archaeologists have advanced the theory that Thera was the island of ATLANTIS, long believed to be mythical.

Theras. A Spartan ruler, and the eponym of Thera. Theras was the son of Autesion, a Theban king who had joined the Heraclids and Dorians when they were about to invade the Peloponnesus. Theras' sister, Argeia, married the Heraclid leader Aristodemus and bore him twin sons, Procles and Eurysthenes. When her husband was killed on the eve of the invasion, Theras became his nephews' guardian and stoutly defended their rights to a third of the territory conquered by the Heraclids. He claimed Messenia for them, but Cresphontes won it through trickery while drawing lots. They received instead the throne of Sparta. Theras ruled as regent for some years. When the twins came of age and became co-kings, Theras found it difficult to play a subordinate role. His chances for advancement were hampered by the fact that he was neither Dorian nor Heraclid. He determined therefore to emigrate to the island of Calliste, north of Crete. Theras' distant ancestor Cadmus, coming upon this island during his search for his sister, Europa, had left his kinsman Membliarus to settle Calliste with some other Phoenicians. Theras hoped that this man's descendants might welcome him and a party of his Spartan supporters.

While Theras was making his plans, there was trouble in Sparta with a group of Minyan refugees who had settled there. These Minyans were descended from the children born to the women of Lemnos after a visit from the ARGONAUTS [C]. They had been driven from the island by the Pelasgians or Tyrrhenians and had taken refuge at Sparta, camping on Mount Taÿgetus until the Spartans permitted them to settle in the land. The Minyans repudiated their Lemnian wives and married Spartan women. In time, however, they (or perhaps their descendants) grew so arrogant in their behavior that the Spartans imprisoned them. They would have killed them in prison, but the Minyans' Spartan wives visited their husbands and gave them women's clothes, in which they were able to escape to Mount Taÿgetus. Theras, possibly because he had been unable to recruit enough Spartans for his expedition, received permission from the Spartans to take some of the Minyans with him. The rest escaped westward into Triphylia, a region between Elis and Messenia, from which they drove the Caucones and the Paroreiates.

In his preparations for departure Theras had the joint support of his nephews. Since the twin kings had never before been known to agree on anything, it may be guessed that it suited the interests of both to get their disgruntled uncle out of Sparta. Theras was thus able to fit out three ships of thirty oars and to fill them with would-be colonists. Much to his disappointment, his son refused to join them. This refusal gained the young man the name of Oeolycus (Sheep-Wolf), for his father warned that, alone in Sparta, he would be a sheep among wolves. Theras and his colonists met with the welcome that he had hoped for on Calliste. The descendants of Membliarus relinquished the throne to Theras, eight generations after his ancestor Cadmus had landed there. Theras renamed the island Thera, for himself.

His Minyan companions had reason to be welcomed as well, for, according to one story at least, Calliste had grown from a clod thrown into the sea by the Argonaut Euphemus, ancestor of some of their own company. (Generations later Battus, a direct descendant of Euphemus, would lead a group of Theraeans to found the Libyan city of Cyrene near where Euphemus had first received the magical clod from the sea-god Triton.) Theras' colony thrived, but his children's children died, in Sparta as well as in Thera. Their parents learned from an oracle that they, like Theras' father, Autesion, were being persecuted by the Erinyes of their ancestors Laïus and Oedipus. They erected shrines to these avenging spirits and the curse was lifted. [Herodotus 4.145–149; Pausanias 3.1.7–8, 4.3.4, 7.2.2.]

Thermodon River. A small river that emptied into the Black Sea some distance to the east of the Halys River. At its mouth was the Amazonian city of Themiscyra (now called Termeh).

Thersander (1). The son of Polyneices and Argeia. By bribing Eriphyle with Harmonia's robe as his father had done with her necklace, Thersander persuaded her to urge ALCMEON to lead the EPIGONI against Thebes. The city was razed and Thersander became king. The bravest of the Greeks in their mistaken attack on Mysia, Thersander was killed by Telephus. He was succeeded on the throne by Tisamenus, his son by Demonassa, daughter of Amphiaraüs. [Apollodorus 3.7.2; Pausanias 9.5.14–15.]

Thersander (2). A son of Sisyphus. Thersander seems never to have occupied a throne, but his sons, Coronus and Haliartus, were adopted by their uncle Athamas, king of Boeotian Orchomenus, and gave their names to the cities of Coroneia and Haliartus. [Pausanias 2.4.3, 9.34.7, 9.36.1.]

Thersites. A Greek soldier in the Trojan War. Thersites was described by Homer [*Iliad* 2.211–277] as bowlegged, lame in one foot, and stooped, with a misshapen head and a scant beard. Though a soldier of no consequence, he was given to reviling the Greek leaders, particularly Achilles and Odysseus, to make the crowd laugh. He railed at Agamemnon for taking Briseïs from Achilles, and advised the soldiery to go home instead of remaining at Troy to make Agamemnon rich. Odysseus beat and threatened him. Later Thersites ridiculed Achilles for falling in love with the Amazon queen Penthesileia after killing her. Achilles killed him on the spot. This murder led to a dispute among the Greeks, and Achilles had to sail to Lesbos and sacrifice to Apollo, Artemis, and Leto before being purified by Odysseus. [Apollodorus "Epitome" 5.1.]

Theseus. A king of Athens.

A. AEGEUS, king of Athens, went to Delphi to ask advice about his childlessness. On his return journey, he stopped at the court of the wise king Pittheus, at Troezen, because he did not understand the answer that he had received from the oracle: that he should not loosen the foot (spout) of the wineskin until he reached Athens. Pittheus grasped the meaning at once, but, instead of enlightening Aegeus, he made him drunk and arranged to have him lie with his daughter Aethra. The next day Aegeus left a sword and a pair of sandals beneath a heavy stone and instructed Aethra that, if she bore a son who one day proved strong enough to move the stone, she should send him with the tokens to Aegeus at Athens. Aegeus went on his way, unaware that in the same night the sea-god Poseidon had lain with Aethra.

In due course a son was born to Aethra, and she named him Theseus. By the age of sixteen the boy was extraordinarily strong, and clever as well, as might be expected of a youth whose great-grandfather was Pelops, whose grandfather was Pittheus, and whose father was either a king or a god. Even as a boy he had demonstrated this happy fusion of traits by converting the sport of wrestling from a mere test of strength to an art requiring quickness of wit and skill. Pittheus let it be understood that Theseus was a son of Poseidon, as indeed Theseus seems to have believed himself to be. Nevertheless, when Aethra showed the youth Aegeus' tokens and he lifted the stone with ease, Pittheus agreed that he should go to Athens. The old king and his daughter tried to persuade Theseus to make the short journey across the Saronic Gulf, but the young man insisted on taking the perilous land route that led across the Isthmus of Corinth. Some say that he chose this route precisely because it was known to be beset by savage outlaws. From childhood Theseus had listened with admiration and envy to tales of the labors of Heracles. Now he was determined to emulate him and make an enviable name for himself. [Plutarch, *Parallel Lives*, "Theseus"; Apollodorus 3.15.6–7, 3.16.1.]

B. Theseus was not long in finding the adventure he sought. He had gone no farther than Epidaurus when he was accosted by Periphetes. This crippled son of Hephaestus and Anticleia was called Corynetes (Clubman) because he habitually carried a club of bronze, with which he delighted in cracking the skulls of passersby. Theseus would doubtless have been no match for this brute, or for any of the others whom he encountered on his way, in a sheer trial of strength, but he was lithe, quick, shrewd, and fearless. Somehow he managed to seize Periphetes' club. Without it the Clubman was helpless and Theseus quickly killed him. Taking a fancy to the club, more perhaps as a trophy than as a weapon, he took it with him.

On reaching the isthmus, Theseus met the robber Sinis. This man was called Pityocamptes (Pine-Bender) because of the manner in which he disposed of unwary travelers. According to one version, he would force a passerby to bend a pine tree to the ground. The powerful Sinis would help with this task, then suddenly let go of the tree. On its rebound the victim would be flung into the air and dashed to pieces. Another version describes a more terrible death: Sinis would tie a man's legs to a bent pine, his arms to another; when he released the trees the victim would be torn apart. Theseus overcame Sinis and treated him to the fate that he had so liberally dealt to others. The young man discovered, however, that Sinis had a beautiful daughter, Perigune. Fleeing in terror from her father's killer, the girl hid in a thicket of shrubs and asparagus thorn and vowed never to destroy them if they would shelter her now. They did so well enough, but when the handsome young Theseus begged her to come out and promised not to hurt her she forgot her fears. Some time later she bore a son, Melanippus, but Theseus later gave her as a bride to Deïoneus. Even though Perigune's grandson Ioxus emigrated far away to Caria, he and his descendants remembered her vow never to burn shrubs.

Theseus next went out of his way to hunt the wild sow or boar that was ravaging Crommyon. This sow, an offspring of Echidna and Typhon that was called Phaea, for the woman who had bred her, was an extremely dangerous beast, but Theseus killed her with no great trouble.

Returning to his journey along the isthmus, he came to the Sceironian Rocks. These cliffs were named for Sceiron, a robber who lived at their top. It was his peculiar custom to force his victims to wash his feet, then suddenly to kick them over the precipice, at the foot of which a giant sea turtle waited to feed on them. Theseus, apparently pretending to wash Sceiron's feet, grasped him by the legs and flung him headfirst over the brink.

The young man met with no further adventures on the isthmus, but, on coming to Eleusis, he was stopped by King Cercyon. This ruler forced all passersby to wrestle with him, killing them either during the match or afterward. The skills that Theseus had learned and his quickness proved superior to Cercyon's brute strength. It was the Eleusinian who died. Much later Theseus gave the rule of Eleusis to Hippothoön, Cercyon's grandson.

Near to Eleusis was the town of Erineüs, on the Cephissus River. Here a scoundrel named Damastes or Polypemon lived by the side of the road and used to invite travelers to spend the night with him. Once the weary guests had retired, their kindly host would insure their comfort by seeing to it that they exactly fitted his bed. If they were too long, he cut off the part that hung over the bed. If they were too short, he stretched their limbs with weights. Most of Damastes' guests must have been on the short side, for he had acquired the nickname of Procrustes (Stretcher). Theseus offered his host the same hospitality that the Stretcher had so long dispensed to guests.

Near by, the young man encountered some descendants of Phytalus, who, instead of trying to rob or murder him, gave him a warm welcome. At a shrine of Zeus Meilichius they observed rites to purify Theseus of the killings that he had committed during his journey. After being graciously entertained by them, Theseus went on his way and, at long last, reached Athens. [Plutarch, *Parallel Lives*, "Theseus"; Apollodorus 3.16.1–"Epitome" 1.4; Hyginus, *Fabulae*, 38.]

C. Theseus made his way to the Acropolis, where Aegeus' palace stood. He was wearing not the short Athenian tunic but an ankle-length robe that, to Athenian eyes, appeared feminine. As he passed the temple of Apollo Delphinius, workmen on the roof jeered at the stranger, pretending to think that he was a girl. By way of answer Theseus loosed two oxen hitched to a cart near by and flung them, one by one, higher than the roof. He heard no more ridicule as he proceeded toward the palace.

When Aegeus and the other Athenians learned that this was the young man who had cleared the notorious isthmus road of outlaws, they welcomed him eagerly, for his reputation had preceded him. Aegeus invited him to a banquet. Observing the rules of hospitality, he made no attempt to learn anything of the guest's descent or his homeland until he had been duly entertained. Theseus kept silent for the same reasons. Courtesy, as it turned out, almost caused his death.

Shortly after the journey from Delphi during which Aegeus had lain with Aethra, the Colchian sorceress Medea had flown into Athens in her chariot drawn by winged dragons. She had reminded the king that, during his recent stay in Corinth, he had promised her a refuge if she would help him to beget the children that he so much desired. Aegeus had proved as good as his word, and so had Medea. She had had a child by him, a boy whom she named Medus. Now, seventeen years later, it was Medea who realized at once the identity of the noble youth who had suddenly presented himself at the palace. She saw him, moreover, as an enemy who would snatch the royal succession at Athens from her own son. Knowing that Aegeus was suspicious and fearful because of the constant threat to his rule posed by his rebellious brother Pallas and Pallas' fifty sons, Medea did not have much trouble in persuading the aging king to regard Theseus as a potential enemy.

Aegeus remembered the wild bull that had been ravaging the region around Marathon ever since Heracles had brought it from Crete two decades earlier. Aegeus had then disposed of his enemy Androgeus, son of Minos, by sending him out to kill the bull. He now tried the same trick again. Theseus, still eager for adventure, went out against the bull. Instead of getting himself killed, he brought the bull back captive and gave it to Aegeus to sacrifice. (Some say, however, that this event occurred somewhat later.) Medea was not discouraged for long. Mixing deadly aconite in a cup of wine, she induced Aegeus to offer it to Theseus at a feast. Before the guest could drink it, however, Aegeus caught sight of the sword hanging at Theseus' belt. He recognized it instantly as the sword that he had long ago left under the stone at Troezen. Striking the cup from Theseus' hand, the king embraced him, welcoming him as his son, and exiled Medea for her treachery. [Plutarch, *Parallel Lives*, "Theseus"; Apollodorus "Epitome" 1.5–6; Pausanias 1.19.1.]

D. The Athenians as a whole rejoiced in Aegeus' public acknowledgment of his son, but Pallas and his sons, who had expected to seize the power at Aegeus' death, broke into open rebellion. Theseus, learning of their plans from an informer, Leos, killed many of the mutinous forces and forced Pallas and his sons to flee. But soon a worse problem threatened the peace of Athens. Not long before Theseus' birth, the city had been attacked by Minos, king of Crete. Aegeus' people, left helpless by plague, had followed the advice of the Delphic oracle and granted to the victorious Minos the tribute that he demanded: seven youths and seven girls to be sent to Crete once every nine years as food for the Minotaur. This monster, which bore a bull's head on a man's body, was kept by Minos in the Labyrinth, a mazelike prison from which no one, once inside, could ever find his way out. The time was now approaching when the third tribute of young Athenians must be paid. These young people were to be chosen by lot.

There are several versions as to the part that Theseus played when the fateful day arrived. Some say that the lot fell on him to be one of the seven youths, others that Minos himself came to choose the victims and picked Theseus for his beauty and strength. The most popular version among the Athenians was that Theseus volunteered to be one of the fourteen, in spite of his father's pleas. Aegeus, clinging to the faint hope that his son might succeed in his plan to kill the Minotaur and thus end the tribute forever, arranged with the captain of the ship that would bear Theseus to Crete that its somber black sail should be changed to a white or scarlet sail if Theseus were returning alive.

Theseus sailed for Crete. The stories of the adventures that befell him there are many, and often contradictory. Those who say that Minos carried the victims in his own ship add that on the voyage the Cretan king became enamored of Eëriboea or Periboea, the young daughter of Alcathoüs, king of Megara. Theseus defended the girl, who was related to him, from Minos' advances. The king was enraged by frustration, and the argument rapidly degenerated to the point where the adversaries cast doubt on each other's paternity. To prove that he was the son of Zeus, Minos prayed to his father to prove it. He was answered with thunder and lightning. Stripping the signet ring from his finger and flinging it into the sea, he dared Theseus to prove that his father was Poseidon, as the young man had claimed, by recovering the ring. Theseus dived into the water without hesitation. At once a swarm of dolphins appeared and led him to the home of the Nereïds in the depths of the sea. There the sea-nymphs gave him the ring and, in addition, Thetis presented him with the jeweled crown that Aphrodite had given her at her marriage to Peleus. Some say, however, that the crown was a gift from Amphitrite, Poseidon's wife. Returning to the ship, Theseus gave the ring to its owner but kept the crown for himself.

According to the fourth-century Athenian historian Philochorus, Minos had long been annoyed by the successes of his chief captain, a boorish but powerful Cretan named Taurus. Minos suspected him of being too familiar with the queen, Pasiphaë, but Taurus' habit of carrying off all the prizes at the annual games had made him so popular with the public that Minos dared not oppose him openly. Theseus asked to participate in these games, which were held shortly after his arrival on the island. When he defeated and disgraced Taurus in the contests, the king was so pleased that he voluntarily ended the requirement of the Athenian tribute. This version of the remission of the tribute is not, however, the usual one. [Plutarch, *Parallel Lives*, "Theseus"; Hyginus, *Poetica Astronomica*, 2.5.]

E. All versions of Theseus' adventures in Crete agree that, at these games or elsewhere, Minos' daughter Ariadne saw Theseus for the first time and fell in love with him. Knowing that even if he were able to kill the Minotaur, he would never find his way out of the Labyrinth, she went for help to Daedalus, who had designed the maze. Perhaps the fact that the great artisan was himself Athenian, though in exile, led him to risk his own safety to help Theseus. Whatever the reason, although he could not himself have found his way out of the Labyrinth unaided, he told Ariadne how she could save the young man. Ariadne gave Theseus a large ball of thread, together with Daedalus' directions. Theseus attached one end of the thread at the entrance and carefully unwound it as he made his way toward the innermost part of the maze. There he found the Minotaur, the monstrous offspring of Queen Pasiphaë and a bull. He killed it by beating it with his fists and followed the thread back to the entrance.

What happened next is disputed. Apparently Theseus and his young companions fought their way to the Athenian ship. Either Taurus or Asterius, Minos' son, was killed in the conflict. Some say that the Cretans were unable to pursue the escaping vessel because Theseus had bored holes below the waterline in the Cretan ships. In any case, the Minotaur's intended victims sailed safely away from Crete and set their course for Athens.

Theseus took Ariadne with him, as he had promised earlier, but she was not destined to reached Greece with her lover. Why they became separated is unclear, for the event has been described in many different ways. It is generally agreed that they parted on the island of Dia, later called Naxos. The earliest account, given by Homer [*Odyssey* 11.321–325], says that Artemis killed Ariadne because of some news brought her by Dionysus. Other versions say that Dionysus kidnaped the girl or took her from Theseus by force of arms, or that she married Oenarus, a Dian priest of the god. Still others claim that Theseus' ship was carried as far as Cyprus, where the pregnant Ariadne was left to rest. Theseus and his ships were swept away from the island by a sudden storm and the poor young woman died of grief. The most usual tale is the bluntest: Theseus deserted the girl who had given up everything to save his life. He did this either because he was embarrassed to take her to Athens, or because he had fallen in love with another woman, Aegle, daughter of Panopeus. Although some say that Ariadne hanged herself from grief, it is most often said that shortly after her abandonment Dionysus came to Dia and married her. It is disputed whether Oenopion and Staphylus were her sons by Dionysus or by Theseus, but their names, connecting them with wine or grapes, make the god seem the more likely father. (See ARIADNE.)

Theseus sailed on toward Greece, stopping only at the sacred island of

Delos. To commemorate this visit the Delians thereafter danced the so-called Crane, the intricate patterns of which dance imitated the windings of the Labyrinth. On the last lap of his homeward voyage, Theseus was so preoccupied with grief at the loss of Ariadne, or with joy at his own return, that he forgot his father's request that he change the black sail for a white or red one. Old Aegeus, watching the sea from a cliff, or from the parapet of the Acropolis near the shrine of Athena Nike, saw the black-sailed ship approaching the harbor. Certain that his son and the heir to his throne was dead, he leaped to his own death. Theseus landed at the Athenian port of Phalerum, to be greeted with both joy and sorrow. [Plutarch, *Parallel Lives*, "Theseus"; Apollodorus "Epitome" 1.8–10; Hyginus, *Fabulae*, 43; Pausanias 2.31.1, 10.29.4; *Catalogues of Women* 76.]

F. On his return from Crete, Theseus set about to accomplish the most significant work of his entire life—or one that was attributed to him, at least, by Athenians of a later age. The region about Athens had always been divided into many independent demes, or townships. Although these demes were dominated to a degree by the superior power of Athens, the lack of central control led to many differences and made concerted action difficult. Theseus had long dreamed of uniting the demes into a single Athenian commonwealth. Now that his Cretan adventure had brought him to the peak of his popularity as the savior of Athens, he used his political strength to persuade or force the townships to subordinate themselves to the authority of the commonwealth. He proved his own good faith by relinquishing to that authority some of his own rights as king.

Going further, Theseus strengthened the dominance of Athens over its former enemy Eleusis by granting the kingship of that city to Hippothoön, a grandson of Cercyon, whom Theseus had killed during his famous journey from Troezen to Athens. Hippothoön was officially recognized as the founder and eponym of one of the ten Athenian tribes. Next Theseus incorporated into the Athenian federation the city of Megara, which had been ruled by his uncle Nisus until its fall in the war with Crete. This move brought the territory of Attica to the borders of Corinth, at the western end of the isthmus. Theseus reinstituted the Isthmian games, founded by the early Corinthian king Sisyphus and formerly celebrated privately at night in honor of Melicertes. Theseus rededicated them to his father, Poseidon. Eager for more challenging adventures, Theseus joined, according to some accounts, the voyage of the Argonauts, and also the Calydonian boar hunt, but he did not distinguish himself on either venture. He met with more success when he accompanied Heracles in his campaign against the Amazons, or else fitted out an expedition of his own, with the aid of his friend Peirithoüs, the young Lapith king. The Amazons had their capital at Themiscyra, on the southern shore of the Black Sea. Just what happened there is not certain, for there are many versions of the battle. Some say that Antiope the Amazon queen, fell in love with Theseus and betrayed the city to him; others that he carried her off by force. In either case, he sailed home to Athens with an Amazon leader, whose named was Antiope, Hippolyte, or Melanippe. The Amazons came to Athens in pursuit and encamped in the city itself, but they were defeated in a fierce battle and a great part of their force was killed. Hippolyte, who, according to one version, was the sister of Antiope and leader of the punitive force, escaped to Megara but died of grief and was buried there. Theseus' captive died too, but not until after she had borne a son, Hippolytus. [Plutarch, *Parallel Lives*, "Theseus"; Apollodorus "Epitome" 1.16; Pausanias 1.2.1, 1.41.7.]

G. According to some writers, Theseus had deserted Ariadne for love of Aegle, whom he married. He is also said to have married Hippe, which may be another name for Hippolyte. Whatever may have happened to these two marriages, or to a number of even more obscure ones alluded to by various authors, it is known that Theseus formally arranged with Minos' son and successor, Deucalion, to marry his sister Phaedra. Deucalion apparently made no objection to Theseus' earlier abandonment of Ariadne, who was also his sister. The new match was no doubt a political one, for it was understood that Phaedra's sons, if any, were to succeed to the rule of Athens. Theseus quietly sent Hippolytus to Troezen, making arrangements that he should succeed the aged Pittheus as king. Phaedra bore two sons, Demophon and Acamas.

Now that the succession seemed to bar Pallas and his sons forever from the rule of Athens, they made a last, desperate bid for power but were defeated and killed by Theseus. Some say that Theseus was acquitted on the grounds of justifiable homicide, but the more accepted version of the outcome is that he was banished for one year from Athens. He chose to spend this period at Troezen, where his grandfather still ruled. Theseus evidently believed that Phaedra would not object to the presence of his son by a concubine so long as the young man did not stand in the way of her own sons' advancement. If Theseus had guessed at Phaedra's true feelings, he would have been far more deeply concerned. The queen had briefly seen Hippolytus once when he visited Attica in order to be initiated into the mysteries at Eleusis. She had fallen in love with him at first sight and had so yearned to see more of him that she had built a shrine to Aphrodite, on a corner of the Acropolis from which Troezen could be dimly seen across the Saronic Gulf on a clear day.

When Phaedra arrived in Troezen, she discovered that Hippolytus was a chaste youth, devoted to hunting and the worship of the virgin goddess Artemis. He scorned the rites of Aphrodite and paid no attention to any woman, least of all his stepmother. Phaedra's nurse, seeing her mistress wasting away from her hopeless love, secretly told Hippolytus of the queen's feelings toward him. The pious young man was outraged but honored the vow of silence that the nurse had first persuaded him to take. Phaedra, driven to near-madness, killed herself, dying with a sealed letter in her hand. Theseus returned from a trip to Delphi, learned of the suicide, and read the letter. In it the queen declared that she had taken her life from shame after being raped by Hippolytus. (According to some accounts, Phaedra herself declared her love to Hippolytus, accused him to Theseus, and killed herself after his death.) Theseus refused to believe his son's protestations of innocence and banished him instantly. Recalling that Poseidon had once given him three curses to use as he wished, Theseus called on the god to kill his son. As Hippolytus rode along the shore in his chariot, a bull rushed up out of the sea and so frightened the horses that they capsized the chariot and dragged Hippolytus, entangled in the reins, to his death. Too late Theseus learned from Artemis that his son had been innocent and that the entire tragedy had been engineered by Aphrodite, who was offended by Hippolytus' slights. [Euripides, *Hippolytus;* Apollodorus "Epitome" 1.18–19; Hyginus, *Fabulae,* 47.]

H. At some point in his career, Theseus had struck up a close friendship with Peirithoüs, son of the notorious Lapith king Ixion. One story has it that Peirithoüs had heard so many tales of Theseus' exploits that he determined to test the truth of his reputation for courage. He therefore stole a herd of cattle at Marathon and, when Theseus came in pursuit, returned to confront him. Instead of fighting, the two were so taken with each other's bearing that they swore eternal friendship. At Peirithoüs' invitation Theseus attended the Lapith's wedding to Hippodameia and assisted him in his battle with the Centaurs. This misfortune occurred when, getting drunk during the festivities, the Centaurs tried to carry off the Lapith women, including the bride.

Peirithoüs, who had inherited some of his father's impious rashness, seems to have had an unfortunate influence on his now middle-aged friend, for Theseus' customary common sense deserted him during the last years of his life and the two enterprises that the pair carried out together turned out disastrously for both. They decided first that they would kidnap Helen, a daughter of Zeus who had been adopted by Tyndareüs, king of Sparta. Some say that Theseus wanted to be related to the Dioscuri, Helen's brothers; others claim that he and Peirithoüs had vowed that they would both marry daughters of Zeus and that they would aid each other in fulfilling this ambition.

They met with little difficulty in carrying off Helen, who was only ten or twelve years old at the time. Theseus took her to the town of Aphidnae, in Attica, and left her in the charge of his mother, Aethra, while he went off to keep his part of the compact by helping Peirithoüs to win a bride. During their absence the Dioscuri, with a force of Spartans and Arcadians, took Aphidnae and perhaps sacked Athens as well. They not only rescued their sister but carried off Aethra to be her nurse. Some say that Helen later bore a child, Iphigeneia, by Theseus. Helen's sister Clytemnestra (who is usually called Iphigeneia's mother by Agamemnon) adopted the infant because of Helen's youth.

Theseus knew nothing of these events. Of the many daughters of Zeus that Peirithoüs might have chosen to abduct, he had hit upon the most unlikely and dangerous bride: Persephone, queen of Hades. Theseus, bound by vows to aid his friend in this suicidal scheme, went with him down into the Underworld, through the entrance at Taenarum. Hades listened blandly while Peirithoüs explained their purpose, then waved them to a seat and called for refreshment. The guests sat down on stone chairs—and discovered that they could not get up again. Some say that they were bound fast with chains or with serpents, others that their flesh grew fast to the stone, others that they had unknowingly sat on the seat of Lethe (Forgetfulness) and, presumably, had lost all recollection of why they had come. Theseus might have remained there forever (and did, according to Homer and Vergil) had not Heracles come down to Hades to fetch Cerberus for Eurystheus. Seeing Theseus and Peirithoüs seated on their chairs, he tore Theseus loose, but when he tried to do as much for his companion, the earth quaked and Heracles dared not continue. Although some say that Peirithoüs, too, was saved, it is generally agreed that he had to remain in Hades, while Theseus accompanied Heracles back to the world of the living.

Some Classical writers, evidently embarrassed by supernatural events in the story of a king whom they regarded as otherwise solidly historical, denied that Theseus went to the Underworld at all. He went merely, they claimed, to the land of the Molossians, in Epeirus. The king of this land was named Aidoneus or Pluto (both names for Hades) and had a wife named Persephone and a daughter named Kore. He also had a fierce dog called Cerberus and forced all his daughter's suitors to fight it. When he found that Theseus and Peirithoüs were planning to dispense with this obstacle by simply carrying off Persephone, he imprisoned Theseus and flung Peirithoüs to the dog. It was from this predicament that Heracles saved Theseus by persuading Aidoneus to release him. [Plutarch, *Parallel Lives*, "Theseus"; Apollodorus "Epitome" 1.21–24; Homer, *Odyssey*, 11.631; Vergil, *Aeneïd*, 6.617–618; Pausanias 1.17.2–6, 1.41.3–5, 2.22.6–7; Ovid, *Metamorphoses*, 12.210–535.]

I. Theseus returned at last to Athens. There he discovered that the Athenians, who had suffered a disastrous war as a result of his capture of Helen, no longer wanted him for their king. This change of heart was in part the consequence of the demagoguery of Menestheus, son of Peteüs. This Menestheus was a direct descendant of the great Athenian king Erechtheus. Theseus could not make such a claim, since his father, Aegeus, had only been adopted into Erechtheus' line. Menestheus played successfully on the smoldering resentment of the demes that Theseus had joined, sometimes by force, in the Athenian commonwealth. When the Spartans, led by the Dioscuri, marched against Athens to recover Helen, Menestheus persuaded the Athenians to welcome them. Once the Dioscuri had found their sister at Aphidnae, they did not trouble Athens, in most accounts, beyond placing Menestheus on the throne.

This was the situation that Theseus encountered on his return. Although he still had many supporters in Athens, he found the people generally unruly and hostile. His attempts to restore his former power were resisted on every side. At last Theseus secretly sent his sons Demophon and Acamas to his ally Elephenor, in Euboea, and himself took leave of Athens for the last time, after pronouncing a solemn curse on the city. Some say that he sailed for Crete, hoping to be welcomed by his brother-in-law Deucalion, but was carried off course by storms and forced to land at Scyrus. Others say, more plausibly, that he headed directly for this island, where Aegeus' father, Scyrius, had once ruled. Theseus asked the present king, Lycomedes, for the property that had belonged to Aegeus, and perhaps also requested his assistance against the Athenians. Lycomedes seemingly welcomed him, but he was actually envious of Theseus' fame and disturbed by the honor that his people showed toward the great visitor. It is possible, also, that Menestheus used his influence to turn the king against Theseus. One evening, while Theseus was walking by the edge of a cliff, his foot slipped and he plunged to the rocks below. This, at any rate, is the story that was given out. It was commonly believed that Theseus was pushed to his death by Lycomedes himself.

Menestheus ruled Athens while Theseus' sons were growing up as private citizens in Euboea. They accompanied Elephenor to the Trojan War and were able to rescue their aged grandmother Aethra. Menestheus, who led the Athenian forces to Troy, was killed in the fighting and Demophon returned to Athens, where he was accepted as king. Although the ship in which the young Theseus had sailed for Crete to fight the Minotaur had been preserved, the Athenians gave little thought to Theseus' memory for many generations. Then, during the Persian Wars, the Athenian soldiers became persuaded that the ghost of Theseus had led them to victory at Marathon. After the wars Theseus' bones were brought home in triumph to Athens, and thereafter the city honored him almost as a god.

J. Theseus was remembered, particularly in the works of the Athenian playwrights, as a champion of justice and defender of the oppressed. In Sophocles' tragedy *Oedipus at Colonus,* he protects OEDIPUS [C] and his daughters from Creon when that ruler tries to carry the old man by force to Thebes. In Euripides' *The Suppliants,* he forces Creon to give up the Argive dead for burial after the war of the SEVEN AGAINST THEBES [E]. In the same playwright's *Heracles,* Theseus pays his debt to Heracles by befriending him after he has murdered his wife and children in a fit of madness. After Heracles' death either Theseus or his son Demophon [as in Euripides' *Children of Heracles*] supports Heracles' family against the tyrant Eurystheus. The story of Theseus is told at length by Plutarch in his *Parallel Lives* and more briefly by Apollodorus [3.15–"Epitome" 1].

Thespiae. A Boeotian city west of Thebes. Thespiae was named for its king Thespius. This ruler entertained Heracles long enough for his fifty daughters to conceive children by him. Many of the sons born of these unions later joined Iolaüs in colonizing Sardinia. At some point the city was ravaged by a dragon but was saved by the self-sacrifice of Menestratus. Thespiae was known as a center of the worship of Eros and of the Muses.

Thespius. A king and eponym of Thespiae, west of Thebes. At Thespius' request, HERACLES [B, C] killed the Cithaeronian lion. While entertaining his remarkable guest, the shrewd king arranged to have Heracles spend a night with each of his fifty daughters. Later Thespius purified Heracles of the murder of his Theban wife, Megara, and their children.

Thesprotia. A region of southern Epeirus. The chief city of Thesprotia, Ephyra, was raided by Heracles during the reign of Phylas. Astyoche, the king's daughter, bore a son, Tlepolemus, by the invader. Neoptolemus became king of Ephyra after the Trojan War and made the captive Trojan prince Helenus king of Buthrotum. Odysseus went to Thesprotia when he was exiled from Ithaca for having murdered Penelope's suitors. He married Queen Callidice and fought an unsuccessful war against her enemies the Brygeians. The land was presumably named for Thesprotus.

Thesprotus. The eponym, presumably, of Thesprotia, a region in southern Epeirus. Pelopia was living in the household of Thesprotus when her father, Thyestes, raped her, or shortly thereafter when her uncle, ATREUS [C] married her. Thesprotus seems to have been connected in some way with Sicyon as well as Thesprotia, but, as is the case with most eponyms, his role in myth is as artificial as it is obscure. He may have been the Thesprotus listed among the fifty sons of Lycaon, king of Arcadia.

Thessalus. A son of Jason and Medea. Escaping the murder that befell his brother (see MEDEA, C), Thessalus went to Iolcus, where he succeeded Acastus on the throne and gave his name to the Thessalians. [Diodorus Siculus 4.55.]

Thessaly. The most northeasterly region of the Greek peninsula, extending northward from eastern Aetolia and Phocis to the ill-defined borders of Macedonia. The Greeks seem to have believed that Thessaly was a principal early home of the Hellenes, a belief supported by archaeological discoveries. The Aeolians, Achaeans, and Ionians were traced back to eponyms of the house of Aeolus and his brother (or son) Xuthus, both of whom reigned in Thessaly. Dorus, a third brother, lived in Phocis, but the Dorians could boast little early mythological history, whereas sons of Aeolus and Xuthus settled in nearly every Greek region and founded ruling houses. The earliest great city of Thessaly was Iolcus; Larisa and Phthia also achieved prominence. Much of Thessaly remained relatively wild, however, and was known as much for its unruly tribes of Lapiths and Centaurs as for its cities. The eponym of Thessaly was, according to one report, Thessalus, a son of Jason and Medea.

Thestius. A son of Ares and Demonice, or of Agenor, Demonice's father, and Epicaste. Thestius is known only for his children by Eurythemis, Leucippe, or some other woman. These children include Leda, Althaea, Hypermnestra, and two or more sons, who are variously named by different authors.

Thestius ruled some Aetolian city; it was perhaps Pleuron, since he was descended from that city's eponym. Tyndareüs, when exiled from Sparta, came to Thestius' court, aided him in wars with some unnamed neighbors, and married his daughter Leda. Thestius' sons were killed by their nephew MELEAGER in a quarrel after the Calydonian boar hunt. [Apollodorus 1.7.7, 1.7.10, 1.8.2–3, 3.10.5; Pausanias 3.13.8.]

Thetis. A daughter of Nereus and Doris. Though only a minor sea-goddess, Thetis played important roles in many myths. Poseidon, Hera, and Athena once rebelled against Zeus and would have bound him had not Thetis called up the hundred-handed giant Briareüs from Tartarus to rescue him. Later Zeus and Poseidon were attacted by the beautiful Nereïd and would have forced their attentions upon her. According to one version of this intrigue, the virtuous Thetis refused the advances of Zeus out of loyalty to Hera, who had reared her. Zeus angrily forced her to marry a mortal. A better-known version has it that Themis or Prometheus warned Zeus that any son of Thetis would surpass his father, or, more specifically, that if Zeus had a son by Thetis, he would one day rule in Olympus. The brother gods retired as suitors and quickly arranged to marry her to a mortal.

The chosen man was Peleus, who was considered the worthiest man of his time. Some say, however, that he had to win her by force. On Cheiron's advice, he captured her in her favorite grotto on the Magnesian coast. Like many other deities of the sea, Thetis could change her shape, but Peleus held her through several alarming transformations and finally won her. The wedding was a brilliant affair, attended by gods and mortals. It was marred by the incident of the GOLDEN APPLE, but the most serious consequences of this incident did not emerge until much later. The marriage, however, was short-lived. The goddess understandably wished her children to be immortal, as she was. She therefore held her son, ACHILLES [A–C], in the fire to burn away his mortal part. (According to a much later tale, she held him by one heel and dipped him into the river Styx.) Peleus, seeing his wife lay their son in the hearthfire, cried out in dismay. Thetis was so offended that she deserted both husband and child and went back to live in the sea. Some claim that she had already burned up several children before Peleus took a stand.

Thetis did not abandon her family entirely. When Peleus sailed with the Argonauts, she helped them to guide the *Argo* past the Wandering Rocks. She also persuaded her sister Psamathe to forget her enmity toward Peleus, which was causing him great hardship. Thetis went to greater lengths to help her son. Since, like many sea-deities, she had the gift of prophecy, she knew that Achilles was fated to die if he went to Troy. She therefore took him as a boy to the court of Lycomedes, on the island of Scyrus, and persuaded the king to rear him as a girl. Odysseus saw through this disguise, and Achilles sailed with the Greeks against Troy.

When Agamemnon forced Achilles to give up his concubine Briseïs, the young man withdrew from the war and complained to his mother. Thetis reminded Zeus that she had helped him eons earlier and persuaded him to give the Trojans victory until the other Greeks would be forced to beg Achilles to rejoin them. Zeus consented and events worked out as Thetis wished, with great suffering in both armies. Thetis gave her son a set of armor that Hephaestus made specially for him. (The artisan-god also owed her a favor, for Thetis and her sister Nereïds had cared for him in their home in the sea after Hera threw him out of Olympus.) Not long afterward she performed a sadder task, bringing a golden urn for Achilles' ashes after his death at the hands of Paris and Apollo. [Homer, *Iliad*, 1.348–430, 1.493–533, 18.35–19.39, 24.-74–140, and *Odyssey*, 24.15–97; *Catalogues of Women* 57; *Aegimius* 2; *Homeric Hymn to Apollo* 3.319–320; Pindar, *Isthmian Odes*, 8.26–47; Apollonius Rhodius 4.757–881, 4.930–967; Apollodorus 1.3.5, 3.5.1, 3.13.6, 3.13.8, "Epitome" 3.26, 6.6, 6.12; Ovid, *Metamorphoses*, 11.217–265, 11.400–401; Hyginus, *Fabulae*, 54, 92, 96, and *Poetica Astronomica*, 2.15, 2.21.]

Thisbe. See PYRAMUS.

Thoas (1). A king of the Taurians. Thoas ruled the barbaric tribe among whom Iphigeneia became a priestess of Artemis. Her brother ORESTES [C] stole away the goddess' statue and later returned to kill the king, assisted by Chryses, son of Agamemnon's concubine Chryeïs. Hyginus believed this Thoas to be the same as Lemnian Thoas. Thoas is a character in Euripides' play *Iphigeneia among the Taurians*. See also Hyginus [*Fabulae* 15, 120–121].

Thoas (2). A king of Lemnos. A son of Dionysus and Ariadne, Thoas ruled Lemnos at the time when the women killed all the males on the island. His daughter, Hypsipyle, secretly hid him and aided him in escaping, either by putting him on a boat for the land of the Taurians or by setting him adrift in a chest. According to the latter account, the chest reached the island of Oenoë, in the southern Cyclades. There it was found by fishermen. Rescued, Thoas had by the water-nymph Oenoë a son, after whom the island was renamed Sicinus. Some say, however, that Thoas was discovered by the Lemnian women and killed. Hyginus confuses this Thoas with Thoas the king of the Taurians. [Apollonius Rhodius 1.620–626; Apollodorus 1.9.17; Hyginus, *Fabulae*, 15, 254.]

Thoas (3). A king of Aetolia. Thoas, son of Andraemon by Gorge, was descended from Oeneus. He led forty shiploads of Aetolians to the Trojan War, where he proved himself both a good fighter and a good speaker. He was one of the few Greek leaders to return home almost unscathed. He had a son, Haemon, and an unnamed daughter, whom he gave in marriage to Odysseus when the old adventurer came to Aetolia at the end of his life. A son, Leontophonus, was born of this marriage. Haemon's son Oxylus was the shrewd fellow who guided the Heraclids through the Peloponnesus and maneuvered himself onto the throne of Elis. [Homer, *Iliad*, 2.638–644, 4.527–532, 7.162–169,

13.214–238, 15.281–300; Apollodorus "Epitome" 3.12, 7.40; Pausanias 5.3.6.]

Thoas. See AGRIUS (2).

Thon or **Thonis.** The warden of the mouth of the Nile, serving under King Proteus. On learning from some of Paris' sailors of his abduction of Helen, Thon reported this information to Proteus and was ordered to seize Paris. Thon's wife, Polydamna, taught Helen the properties of healing herbs. [Herodotus 2.113–115; Homer, *Odyssey*, 4.227–230.]

Thoösa. See POLYPHEMUS (1).

Thrace. An ill-defined region lying between the Black and Aegean seas to the east of Macedonia. Thrace was considered by the Greeks a cold and barbaric land. It was the home of Boreas, the North Wind, and of other gods some of whom were worshiped with cruel or licentious rites. The Greeks nevertheless adopted the worship of one of these gods, Dionysus, together with his orgiastic rituals. Ares, too, may have had a Thracian origin. Myths connected with Thrace tend to include barbarous episodes, often involving mutilation. Lycurgus and Diomedes were both fed to or otherwise destroyed by animals for their cruel treatment of others. Polymestor killed a young guest entrusted to his care and had his eyes gouged out. Tereus cut out his mistress' tongue and was later tricked into eating his own offspring in a stew. Similarly, Demophon later ate his daughters when they were served up by Mastusius. Not all Thracian kings were bloodthirsty, however. Eumolpus, a founder of Demeter's rites, came from Thrace, as did Rhesus, a gallant if none too bright ally of Troy in the Trojan War.

Thracian Chersonese. A narrow peninsula (now the Gallipoli Peninsula) extending southwestward from Thrace between the Hellespont and the Thracian Sea. Situated on this shore of the Hellespont were Sestus and other towns allied with the Trojans in their war with the Greeks. Near the tip was Elaeüs, the site of the shrine of the Greek hero Protesilaüs.

Thrasymedes. A son of Nestor by either Anaxibia, daughter of Crateius, or Eurydice, daughter of Clymenus. Thrasymedes accompanied his father to the Trojan War, where he often fought side by side with his brother Antilochus. He appears occasionally in Homer's *Iliad* and is shown after his return to Pylus in Book 3 of the *Odyssey*. His son Sillus survived him.

Thriae or **Thriai.** Three ancient and obscure prophetesses of Mount Parnassus. Most of the few Classical writers who mention these nymphs agree that they were among the earliest diviners and that they pursued their art with the aid of pebbles, which were themselves called *thriai*. Some scholars believe that the three-winged, honey-eating virgin prophetesses mentioned in the *Homeric Hymn to Hermes* [4.552–568] were the Thriae. If so, Apollo gave over to Hermes the patronage of these nymphs, which may mean merely that Hermes became the god of pebble divination, among his many other activities.

Thrinacia or **Thrinacië.** The island where Helius, the sun-god, pastured his cattle and sheep. Thrinacia was often identified in Classical times with Sicily, which was regarded by many writers (for example, Euripides, in his satyr play *Cyclops*) as the home of Polyphemus and the other Cyclopes. The Roman name for Thrinacia was Trinacria.

Thronia. A daughter of Belus and Anchinoë. To her husband, Hermaon, she bore Arabus, for whom, presumably, Arabia is named. [*Catalogues of Women* 15.]

Thyestes. A son of Pelops. With his brother Atreus, Thyestes killed their half-brother Chrysippus and fled Pisa. Later he engaged in a long and deadly feud with ATREUS. He gave his name to a tragedy by Seneca.

Thyia. A daughter of Deucalion and Pyrrha. According to the *Catalogues of Women* [3], Thyia was the mother by Zeus of Magnes and Macedon, but Magnes is usually called a son of Aeolus and Enarete.

Thyiad. A MAENAD or bacchant.

Thymbraeüs. An epithet of Apollo. At the time of the Trojan War, one of the principal centers of Apollo's worship was at Thymbre, a town in the Troad. The god was often referred to as Thymbraean Apollo.

Thynia. The land ruled by the blind soothsayer-king Phineus. In his *Argonautica*, Apollonius Rhodius placed Thynia in Thrace opposite Bithynia and called Phineus' capital Salmydessus. Herodotus [1.28] mentioned the Thynians as one of the peoples ruled by Croesus, but did not specify their location.

Thyone. The deified mother of Dionysus. Semele, daughter of Cadmus and Harmonia, was killed by a thunderbolt before the birth of her son, the god Dionysus. Dionysus, after growing to manhood and accomplishing many triumphant journeys on earth, descended into Hades and took his mother up to heaven under her new name. [*Homeric Hymn to Dionysus* 2.]

thyrsus. A pole twined with ivy or grapevine and tipped with a pine cone. The thyrsus was carried by maenads and satyrs in their revels in honor of Dionysus.

Tiasa. See EUROTAS.

Tibareni. A tribe inhabiting an eastern part of the southern coast of the Black Sea. According to Apollonius Rhodius [2.1009–1014], when a woman of the Tibareni was in labor, her husband took to his bed and had to be cared for by the women with food and childbed baths. The tribe was mentioned by Herodotus among those who paid tribute to the Persian king Darius and fought in his army.

Tiber River. The Italian river that flows past Rome. The river Alba was said to have been renamed Tiber for Tiberinus, an early Alban king who drowned in it.

Tilphusa or **Tilphussa.** See TELPHUSA.

Timandra. A daughter of Tyndareüs and Leda. Timandra married Echemus, king of Arcadia, and bore his son Laodocus, but she fell in love with Phyleus, king of Dulichium, and, like her sisters Clytemnestra and Helen, deserted her husband. [*Catalogues of Women* 65, 67.]

Timeas. A son of Polyneices and Argeia. Timeas is listed by Pausanias [2.20.5] as one of the EPIGONI.

Tiphys. A steersman of the *Argo*. Tiphys, a Boeotian, was a son of Hagnias or of Phorbas and Hyrmina. He directed the launching of the *Argo* and piloted it safely through many dangers, including the Clashing Rocks, before dying among the Mariandyni. He was succeeded as pilot by Ancaeüs, king of Samos. [Apollonius Rhodius 1.105–110, 1.400–401, 2.851–863; Hyginus, *Fabulae*, 14, 18.]

Tiresias. See TEIRESIAS.

Tiryns. An ancient city of Argolis, east of Argos. Tiryns was no doubt believed to have been founded by Argus' son Tiryns, but it first gained prominence some generations later when it was occupied by Proëtus, a refugee from the enmity of his brother Acrisius, who ruled in nearby Argos. Proëtus induced the Cyclopes to fortify the city for him. He later gave up a half or two thirds of his kingdom to the Messenian brothers Melampus and Bias in payment for Melampus' services in curing his daughters of madness. At Proëtus' death the throne fell to Perseus, Acrisius' grandson, but Perseus seems to have ruled mainly from Mycenae. The rule of Tiryns and Mycenae should have fallen three generations later to Heracles, a grandson of Perseus' son Electryon, who had inherited Mycenae from Perseus. Hera intervened, however, to arrange for Eurystheus, a grandson of Perseus, to win the rule. The position of Tiryns during Eurystheus' reign is ambiguous. Heracles, though usually away from Argolis on his ceaseless travels, seems to have occupied the Tirynthian palace from time to time. It was there that he killed Iphitus in a fit of madness. By the time of the Trojan War, the descendants of Perseus had lost control of Argolis. Argos and Tiryns, now in the hands of descendants of Melampus and Bias, were dominated in turn by Mycenae, which was ruled by a grandson of Pelops. Tiryns never again became a significant power.

Tisamenus (1). A king of Sparta and Argos. A son of Orestes by Hermione, or possibly by Erigone, Tisamenus inherited from his father the thrones of both Argos and Sparta. He was overthrown by the returning Heraclids and, if he was not killed in this encounter, led a band of refugees to the northern Peloponnesus. The Ionian rulers refused to let them settle there peaceably, fearing that Tisamenus would make himself king. Although the newcomers (later called Achaeans to differentiate them from the Dorians who supported the Heraclids) won the ensuing struggle, Tisamenus was killed and buried at Helice. Much later his bones were returned to Sparta on the command of the Delphic oracle. [Pausanias 7.1.7–8.]

Tisamenus (2). A king of Thebes. Tisamenus, the son of Thersander and Demonassa, daughter of Amphiaraüs, ascended the throne on the death of Peneleüs, who had acted as regent at Thersander's death. Tisamenus enjoyed a quiet reign and left the rule to his son, Autesion. [Pausanias 9.5.15.]

Tisiphone. A daughter of Alcmeon and Manto. Tisiphone and her brother Amphilochus were given by their father into the care of Creon, king of Corinth. Creon's wife, growing jealous of the girl's beauty, sold her as a slave, but she was bought by Alcmeon. [Apollodorus 3.7.7.]

Tisiphone. See ERINYES.

Titan. See HELIUS.

Titans. The firstborn children of Uranus and Ge. The Titans, according to the *Theogony* [132–138] of Hesiod, were Oceanus, god of the river of that name; Hyperion, a sun-god; Themis and Rhea, both earth-goddesses; Tethys, who was perhaps a sea-goddess; Mnemosyne, a personification of memory; and Coeüs, Crius, Theia, and Phoebe, whose specific functions are less clear. The youngest Titan was CRONUS, the boldest and wiliest of the lot. Ge persuaded him to rebel against his father. Alone, or with the aid of the other Titans, he castrated Uranus and usurped the rule of Olympus. He was in turn overthrown, together with those among his brothers and nephews who supported him, by his son Zeus. Zeus was aided by his brothers and by the CYCLOPES and the HUNDRED-HANDED, half-brothers of Cronus. After a ten-year war, these Titans were thrown into Tartarus and imprisoned there forever under the guard of the Hundred-handed.

Cronus, according to an alternative tradition, ruled after his fall in the Islands of the Blessed. His reign in heaven had, in fact, been a golden age in which mortals were as fortunate as gods. Atlas, one of the second generation of Titans, was condemned, because of his part in the war with the gods, to support the sky on his shoulders for eternity. Oceanus; Hyperion's son, Helius, the sun-god; and the Titanesses had taken no part in the conflict and they continued to perform their functions under the rule of Zeus, though Rhea, Phoebe, Theia, and Mnemosyne faded into the background. Oceanus, his wife Tethys, and Themis were particularly revered by the Olympians. A very different view of the Titans is expressed in the Orphic myth of Zagreus (see DIONYSUS, A), in which they appear as the cause of Dionysus' sufferings.

It is generally accepted that the Titans (except for Mnemosyne, who is merely an abstraction) were very ancient deities, connected in some way with the powers of nature. Beyond this there is little agreement. [Homer, *Iliad*, 14.277–279; Hesiod, *Theogony*, 207–210, 617–735, 389–396, 807–814; Aeschylus, *Prometheus Bound*, 201–223; Hyginus, *Fabulae*, 150; Pausanias 7.18.4, 8.37.5.]

Tithonus. A son of Laomedon by Strymo, Placia, or Leucippe, and brother of Priam. Tithonus, a handsome youth, was snatched from his father's palace by Eos, the amorous goddess of the dawn. She carried him to Ethiopia, Syria, the banks of the river Oceanus, or wherever it was in the far east that she lived, and made him her lover. She bore him Memnon and Emathion, who became kings, respectively, of Ethiopia and Arabia. Some say that PHAËTHON (2) was also their son. The goddess asked Zeus to make Tithonus immortal, but being somewhat scatterbrained, she did not think to request that he be made ageless as well. In due course her mortal consort's hair began to turn gray. Eos quickly lost interest in him. When he became too feeble to move, she put him in a room alone and shut the brazen doors on him, so that she would no longer have to listen to his endless babbling. According to a legend with a happier ending, Eos turned her old lover into a grasshopper, an insect that sloughs off old age with its skin. It pleased Homer and Vergil to speak of the dawn as Eos (or Aurora) rising from Tithonus' couch, even though by the poets' day she must long since have found another lover.

According to Apollodorus [3.14.3], Eos had a son Tithonus by Cephalus. This seems likely to be an error, for not even a goddess is likely to name a child by her lover after a former lover. [*Homeric Hymn to Aphrodite* 5.218–238; Homer, *Iliad*, 20.236–237; Euripides, *The Trojan Women*, 853–858; Hesiod, *Theogony*, 984–985.]

Tithorea. A Phocian city north of Mount Parnassus. Tithorea was regarded as one of the oldest cities in Phocis. According to Pausanias, the name was originally that of the entire district, but it eventually came to be applied to its principal city, which had earlier been called Neon. Tithorea was said to have been named for a Dryad. The town claimed the tomb of Antiope and Phocus, son of Ornytion and an eponym of Phocis. After suffering years of hardship through the enmity of mortals and gods, Antiope had found a refuge at Phocus' court and had married him. Much later, whenever the sun was in the constellation Taurus, the Tithoreans tried to steal earth from the tomb of Amphion and Zethus at Thebes to throw it on that of Antiope and Phocus, having learned from an oracle that their crops would thus prosper at the expense of those of Thebes.

Tityus. A Euboean giant. After Zeus seduced Elare, daughter of Orchomenus, he hid her in the earth to protect her from the vengeance of Hera. Ge (Earth) is therefore often called the nurse, or even the mother, of Elare's child, Tityus. Tityus grew to enormous size. He became the father by some unnamed woman of the Europa who bore Euphemus to Poseidon. For unrecorded reasons, Rhadamanthys once traveled to Euboea in a Phoenician ship to visit Tityus. The giant is primarily known for his attempt, perhaps at Hera's instigation, to rape Leto as she was going to Delphi through the Phocian village of Panopeus. For this offense he was not merely shot by Apollo and Artemis, but was eternally punished in Hades. There he was stretched helpless on the ground—his body covering nine acres—while two vultures or snakes ate his heart or liver, which grew again with each new cycle of the moon. Tityus' immense tomb was shown in Classical times at Panopeus. [Homer, *Odyssey*, 7.321–324, 11.576–581; Pindar, *Pythian Odes*, 4.46; Apollodorus 1.4.1; Ovid, *Metamorphoses*, 4.457–458; Hyginus, *Fabulae*, 55; Pausanias 10.4.5–6.]

Tlepolemus. A king of Rhodes. The son of Heracles by Astydameia, daughter of Amyntor, or by Astyoche, daughter of King Phylas of Ephyra, Tlepolemus killed his uncle Licymnius with an olive-wood club. Although this may have happened accidentally when the old man came between him and a servant whom he was beating, Tlepolemus was forced by Heracles' other descendants to leave Argos with his wife, Polyxo, and several shiploads of followers. They settled on the island of Rhodes, where they founded the cities of Lindus, Cameirus, and Ialysus. Tlepolemus led nine ships to Troy, where he was killed by Sarpedon. [Homer, *Iliad*, 2.653–670, 5.627–669.]

Tlesimenes. A son of Parthenopaeüs and Clymene, a Mysian nymph. Hyginus [*Fabulae* 71] lists Tlesimenes among the EPIGONI.

Toxeus. A son of Oeneus and Althaea. Oeneus killed Toxeus for the obscure crime of jumping over a ditch. Ovid [*Metamorphoses* 8.437–440] gives this name to one of Althaea's brothers. [Apollodorus 1.8.1–2.]

Trachis. The principal city of Trachinia, the region of southwestern Thessaly in which rose Mount Oeta. Trachis was the capital of King Ceÿx, who provided a home for the wife and children of Heracles during the last wanderings of that hero.

transmigration of souls. See METEMPSYCHOSIS.

Tricca. A city of western Thessaly, now called Trikkala. Tricca was the home of King Deïmachus, whose three sons sailed with Heracles against the Amazons. If this was the Deïmachus whose daughter Enarete married Aeolus, he must have survived for many generations. The forces of Tricca, Ithome, and Oechalia were led to the Trojan War by the two sons of the god Asclepius, who had a considerable cult center at Tricca. It is possible, however, that these were three Messenian, rather than Thessalian, cities.

Trinacria. See THRINACIA.

Triopas or **Triops.** A king of Argos, Thessaly, or Rhodes. It is likely that there were originally several mythical kings of this name, but Greek and Roman writers confused their legends so thoroughly that it is simpler to deal with them together. The Argive Triopas was called a son of Phorbas, son of Argus. His children were Pelasgus, Agenor, Iasus, and Messene. The Thessalian king, a son of Poseidon by Aeolus' daughter Canace, had a son named Phorbas by Myrmidon's daughter Hiscilla. Other children were Iphimedeia and Erysichthon. The story of Erysichthon's terrible punishment by Demeter is told of Triopas by Hyginus [*Poetica Astronomica* 2.14], who adds that he was also plagued by a snake and that his fate was commemorated by the goddess in the constellation Ophiuchus (Serpent-holder). Hyginus also records a Rhodian claim that this same constellation represented Triopas' son Phorbas, who went to Rhodes and rid the island of snakes. According to Diodorus Siculus [5.56], a Rhodian Triopas was one of the seven sons of Helius by Rhode, the nymph of the island. Since Rhodes is not far from the Carian city of Cnidus, it may have been this last Triops who founded that city and named part of it Triopion. Then again, the Cnidian may have been yet another Triopas. [Apollodorus 1.7.4, Pausanias 2.16.1, 10.11.1.]

Triphylia. A district of southern Elis. When expelled from Sparta, many of the Minyans who had come there from Lemnos moved on to Triphylia, where they settled.

Triptolemus. An Eleusinian prince. In the *Homeric Hymn to Demeter* [2], Triptolemus is mentioned merely as one of several leaders at Eleusis to whom Demeter taught her rites. Elsewhere he is said to be a son of Celeüs, king of Eleusis, and his wife, Metaneira; of Eleusis, the city's eponymous hero; of Oceanus and Ge; or of various other, more obscure figures. Demeter gave Triptolemus a chariot drawn by winged dragons and a stock of wheat, which he either sowed from the sky or taught others to sow. Late Classical authors told varying tales of his adventures. In Achaea, where he taught the culture of corn to King Eumelus, the king's son Antheias was killed while trying to drive Triptolemus' chariot. In Scythia, King Lyncus tried to kill Triptolemus out of envy of the visitor who was giving his people the boon of grain. Demeter (Ceres) quickly transformed the king into a lynx, and Triptolemus returned to Greece.

When Triptolemus, who had invented the wheel in order to speed his journey, visited the land of the Getae, in Thrace, King Carnabon welcomed him, then treacherously imprisoned him, killing one of his two dragons to prevent his escape. Demeter quickly sent a spare dragon and punished Carnabon with a life so painful that he killed himself. Presumably as a warning to others, the goddess placed Carnabon, holding the first snake, in the sky as the constellation Ophiuchus (Serpent-holder). Some say that the constellation Gemini is Triptolemus and Demeter's lover Iasion. [Apollodorus 1.5.2; Hyginus, *Poetica Astronomica*, 2.14, 2.22; Ovid, *Metamorphoses*, 5.646–661; Pausanias 1.14.1–3, 7.18.2–3, 8.4.1.]

Trito. See TRITOGENEIA.

Tritogeneia. A title of ATHENA, sometimes translated as "Lady of Trito." The original meaning of this word having been lost, the Greeks interpreted it as meaning "Born by Trito." They then identified Trito as the Libyan lake Tritonis, a stream in Arcadia, or various other bodies of water.

Triton. A minor sea-god. Triton, a son of Poseidon and Amphitrite, was said by Ovid [*Metamorphoses* 1.330–347] to calm the seas and rivers by blowing through a conch-shell horn. When the ARGONAUTS [R] were stranded in Lake Tritonis, in Libya, Triton appeared to them and directed them to the sea. He also gave them a clod of earth, which not only formed the island of Thera but much later was interpreted by the Greeks as an invitation to colonize Libya. Triton seems to have degenerated into a sea-monster in Pausanias' account, which speaks of Tritons in the plural. The women of Tanagra, in Boeotia, were attacked by one while observing a rite of Dionysus. They appealed to the god, who defeated the Triton in a fight. In a more prosaic tale from the same region, Tritons used to attack Tanagran cattle, and even boats, until the men set out bowls of wine. A Triton was caught in a drunken stupor and beheaded, after which, apparently, the depredations ceased. A Triton that Pausanias saw at Rome had hair on its head like that of marsh frogs; the rest of the body was finely scaled, like that of a shark. The beast had a man's nose, gills, a wide mouth with animal teeth, a dolphin's tail, and hands with fingers and fingernails. The eyes of this remarkable beast, Pausanias adds, seemed to be blue. [Hesiod, *Theogony*, 930–933; Apollonius Rhodius 4.1550–1622, 4.1741–1754; Herodotus 4.179; Pausanias 8.2.7, 9.20.4–9.21.1.]

Tritonis. A large lake in western Libya, now called Chott Djerid. Tritonis was the site of one of the Argonauts' adventures and was often connected with the sea-god Triton. See also TRITOGENEIA.

Trivia. An epithet of Hecate, meaning "She of Three Ways." Hecate was commonly worshiped at crossroads. The title Trivia, which derives from this practice, was also applied to Diana (Artemis), who came to be identified, particularly by the Romans, with Hecate.

Troad. A region of Asia Minor near the southern entrance of the Hellespont. This area took its name from its dominant city, TROY (Ilium).

Troezen. The eponym of the Argolic city. Troezen, a son of Pelops and Hippodameia, shared the rule of the towns of Hypereia and Antheia with Pittheus, his brother, and Aëtius, the former king. At Troezen's death, Pittheus combined the towns into a single city and named it for his brother.

Troezen. A city of southeastern Argolis, on the Saronic Gulf. According to Pausanias, the Troezenians said that their first king was Orus, who called the land Oraea. Althepus, a son of Poseidon, married Orus' daughter Leïs and succeeded to the rule, renaming the land Althepia. During his reign, Poseidon and Athena each laid claim to the region, as they did to Athens, but were commanded by Zeus to share it. Althepus was succeeded by Saron. This king drowned in the gulf, which was thereafter called Saronic. From Saron down to Hyperes and Anthas, there is a gap in the royal genealogies. Anthas' son, Aëtius, was reigning when Pelops' sons Troezen and Pittheus came to the region. The brothers may have conquered the territory, for, although the three men theoretically divided the rule equally, Aëtius had little real power.

Upon Troezen's death, Pittheus combined the towns of Hypereia and Antheia into a city, which he named for his brother. Later, descendants of Aëtius and Troezen founded colonies in Caria and Attica, respectively, and Pittheus' faction was apparently left with the sole power in Troezen. Pittheus, famous for his wisdom and eloquence, enjoyed a very long reign, outliving his great-grandson Hippolytus, who had been groomed to succeed him. Perhaps it was after Pittheus' death that Troezen, like most cities of the Argolis, fell under the dominance of Argos, which was ruled by descendants of Pittheus' brothers

Atreus and Thyestes. Diomedes led the forces of this entire region, except Mycenae, to the Trojan War. Later, along with Argos, Troezen was invaded by the Heraclids and Dorians and remained thereafter a Dorian city.

Troïlus. A son of Hecuba by either Priam or Apollo. Troïlus was ambushed and killed by Achilles during the Trojan War. Little more is known of him to Classical writers, although he played an important role in medieval tales of Troy and was immortalized by both Chaucer and Shakespeare. [Homer, *Iliad*, 24.257; Vergil, *Aeneïd*, 1.474–478; Apollodorus 3.12.5, "Epitome" 3.32.]

Trojan horse. See WOODEN HORSE.

Trojan War. A war waged by an alliance of Greek cities against the Phrygian city of Troy.

A. The origins of the Trojan War are usually traced to the GOLDEN APPLE thrown by the angry goddess Eris during the wedding of Peleus and Thetis. Dissension immediately broke out among three of the divine guests, Hera, Athena, and Aphrodite, as to which deserved the apple as a beauty prize. Zeus directed Hermes to refer the argument for arbitration to PARIS [B], a Trojan prince who was considered to be the world's most handsome man. This young man decided in favor of Aphrodite when she offered him as a bribe the love of Zeus's daughter Helen, the world's most beautiful woman. Ignoring the warnings of the Trojan seers Helenus and Cassandra, his brother and sister, Paris sailed for Sparta, where Helen's husband Menelaüs (or Tyndareüs, her foster father), ruled. There he was entertained by the king and by Helen's brothers, the Dioscuri. He repaid their hospitality by carrying off the willing Helen and a good deal of the palace treasure as well.

Before her marriage Helen had had most of the eligible princes of the Greek cities as her suitors. To avoid trouble, Tyndareüs had made them swear to accept the girl's decision and, moreover, to defend the interests of her chosen husband. Now that Helen was stolen, Menelaüs, supported by his more powerful brother, Agamemnon, king of Mycenae, reminded his former rivals of their vow and demanded that they join him in a punitive expedition to recover his wife. Many of the former suitors tried by various ruses to avoid their duty. Odysseus pretended to be mad, but was tricked by Palamedes into giving himself away. Odysseus then uncovered Achilles' disguise by another trick, after which the youth volunteered to join the Greek force. Having been too young to sue for Helen's hand, Achilles was not bound by duty to aid the others, but the seer Calchas had declared when the boy was only nine years old that Troy could not be taken without him.

Echepolus, a rich Sicyonian, bought his way out of the obligation with the gift of a fine mare to Agamemnon. The most ingenious draft-evader, however, was Cinyras, king of Paphos, in Cyprus. When Menelaüs, Odysseus, and Talthybius, the Greek herald, called on him, he generously sent a present of breastplates to Agamemnon and promised fifty ships for the Greek navy. In due course he kept his promise—but forty-nine of the fifty ships were toy boats filled with toy soldiers. Made of clay, Cinyras' fleet dissolved soon after its launching.

The squadrons sent by the participating cities assembled in the harbor of Aulis, a Boeotian town on the strait separating Euboea from the mainland. There Calchas interpreted an omen to mean that the Greeks would fight at Troy for nine years and take the city in the tenth. Calchas also declared that the unfavorable winds that kept the fleet from sailing were due to the anger of Artemis over a careless boast made by Agamemnon. The only remedy, said the seer, was to sacrifice the commander-in-chief's eldest daughter, Iphigeneia. Under pressure from the other leaders, Agamemnon consented and an embassy composed of Odysseus, Diomedes, and Talthybius brought the girl from Argos on the pretext of marrying her to Achilles. She was duly offered to the goddess, who, according to some accounts, substituted a deer as the sacrificial victim and transported Iphigeneia to the barbarian land of the Taurians to serve as her priestess there.

B. The Greeks, at last able to sail, discovered that they did not know the way to Troy. They landed by mistake in Mysia and lost some of their men to a force led by Telephus, king of Teuthrania (Pergamon), although Achilles wounded the defender. Discouraged, the Greeks returned home. A guide to Troy was unexpectedly found in Telephus, who followed them to Argos, having learned from an oracle that only the inflictor of his wound could heal it. Achilles did so and Telephus, in return, agreed to show the Greeks the way to Troy, though, as a son-in-law of Priam, the Trojan king, he refused to take part in the war. With Telephus' aid the Greeks reached Troy without further trouble, except for the loss of Philoctetes. This great archer, who owned the bow and arrows of Heracles, had been bitten by a snake and abandoned by his companions on the island of Lemnos because of the terrible stench of his wound.

The Greek force had also stopped at Delos, where it was entertained by ANIUS and his miraculous daughters, who could produce oil, corn, and wine without effort. Agamemnon carried these girls off to provision his troops. They escaped from Troy, but were soon retaken. Praying to Dionysus, they were transformed into white doves.

Before actually landing at Troy, the Greeks sent Menelaüs, the chiefly aggrieved party, and Odysseus, the most eloquent of their number, as an embassy to Priam. They demanded the return of Helen and the treasure that had disappeared with her. The older and wiser Trojans, including Priam himself, would have agreed in order to avoid a long war, but the war party prevailed. The ambassadors might have even been killed had not Antenor, the Dardanian elder who had received the two as guests, risen strongly to their defense. Odysseus and Menelaüs returned to the ships with the news that war was inevitable, and the Greeks prepared to land. None of them was eager to lead, for before arriving at Troy they had been warned that the first to set foot on Trojan soil would be the first to die. Protesilaüs, leader of the Phylacians, defied fate and, after killing several Trojans, was himself killed. After him the other Greeks landed, and Achilles killed the famous Cycnus, king of Colonae, whose father, Poseidon, had made him invulnerable to weapons.

The Greeks evidently found that they could not expect to destroy the strong and wealthy walled city of Troy as long as it could count on supplies and other aid from the many nearby cities that were under its dominance. They therefore set about destroying these vassals and allies one by one. This operation seems to have been mainly under the command of Achilles, who was later credited with conquering twelve cities by sea, eleven by land. During these raids, which occupied nine years of the war, many cities that were closely bound to Troy were ruthlessly sacked. Among them was Hypoplacian Thebes, where King Eëtion and all his sons—the father and brothers of Andromache, wife of the Trojans' chief warlord, Hector—were all killed in one day. The Dardanians of Mount Ida, who had a strong claim to the Trojan throne, were harassed, and Aeneas, their principal leader, was driven to nearby Lyrnessus. This city was destroyed in turn. When Achilles sacked the island of Tenedos, he killed King Tenes against the advice of his sea-goddess mother, Thetis, and thus incurred the enmity of Tenes' father, Apollo.

C. Through these piratical raids on the surrounding country, the Greeks not only imperiled the economy of Troy, but supplied themselves with food to support the Greek army and the plunder needed to satisfy the greed of the leaders. They also helped to keep up the general morale by furnishing the leaders, and perhaps the rank and file as well, with women. Agamemnon, for example, took Chryseïs as his concubine from the island of Chryse; Achilles abducted Briseïs from Lyrnessus. Chryseïs' father, a priest of Apollo Smintheus, persuaded the god to send a pestilence on the Greeks. Agamemnon, forced by the other leaders to give Chryseïs back, angrily took Briseïs for himself in recompense. Achilles, his pride affronted, withdrew from the war, with disastrous results for the Greeks. Only the death of Achilles' squire and lover, Patroclus, persuaded him to relent. In a fury of vengeance he killed dozens of Trojans, including Hector. He desecrated the great Trojan leader's body and refused to give it up for burial until Hector's father, King Priam, came alone to the Greek camp to plead with him. Achilles finally allowed the old man to ransom the corpse.

The Amazon queen Penthesileia joined the Trojans and killed many Greeks before being killed by Achilles, who then fell in love with her corpse. Memnon, an Ethiopian or Assyrian king, also came to the aid of Troy with a large force and was killed by Achilles. Achilles was himself shot to death by Paris, aided by Apollo. Helenus, a Trojan seer, was captured by Odysseus and revealed the oracles concerning his city: Troy would fall only if Achilles' son fought with the Greeks, if the bow and arrows of Heracles were used against the Trojans, if the remains of the famous Eleian hero Pelops were brought to Troy, and if the ancient statue of Athena, the Palladium, were stolen from the Trojan citadel. Odysseus, Talthybius, and Achilles' old tutor, Phoenix, had no difficulty in persuading Neoptolemus to leave his home on the island of Scyrus and fight at Troy in his famous father's armor. Philoctetes was understandably reluctant to join the men who had deserted him and to use his bow and arrows against the Trojans, but he was finally persuaded. The Eleians were happy to send a shoulder blade of Pelops to the aid of the other Greeks. Philoctetes, quickly healed by the Greek physician Machaon or his brother, Podaleirius, killed Paris with an arrow. Odysseus and Diomedes slipped into Troy by night and, perhaps aided by Helen, brought the Palladium to the Greek camp. Neoptolemus proved almost as bold as his father.

D. But Troy still did not fall. Although most of its strongest defenders were dead, the walls remained impenetrable. It was a trick of the cunning Odysseus that finally opened the gates to the invaders. At his suggestion, and with Athena's aid, the artisan Epeius constructed an enormous wooden image of a horse. A number of the boldest Greeks, under Odysseus' command, hid inside, and the others sailed away, leaving behind a spy, Sinon. When the puzzled Trojans came out to view the deserted Greek camp they found the strange horse on the plain and Sinon near by with his arms bound. Pretending to be enraged at his fellow Greeks, Sinon told the Trojans an elaborate tale that convinced them that the horse would bring luck to Troy. In spite of the warnings of their prophets Cassandra and Laocoön, the Trojans dragged the horse inside the city, even though they had to breach the walls to do so.

That night, while the Trojans slept, worn out with reveling, Sinon released the Greeks in the horse and showed a beacon on the walls. The Greek navy, which had gone only as far as the offshore island of Tenedos, quickly returned, and the Greeks took the city in a terrible battle by night. Priam was slaughtered as he clung to an altar of Zeus, and Cassandra was raped before the image of Athena. Of the Trojan men, only Aeneas escaped alive. The Greeks sacrificed Priam's daughter Polyxena on Achilles' grave and flung Hector's young son, Astyanax, from the walls. Menelaüs' determination to kill his unfaithful wife dissolved when the beautiful and still seductive woman pleaded with him. Troy was destroyed forever, but the war proved almost as destructive for the Greeks. Only a few of them reached their homes safely, and many of those only after years of wandering. The adventures of the homeward voyages are summarized under the entry RETURNS and detailed in the entries on individual leaders.

The most famous account of the Trojan War, Homer's *Iliad*, covers only a period of a few days near the end of the conflict. An excellent summary of the main events is found in Apollodorus ["Epitome" 3–5]. Of extant Greek tragedies, only three deal directly with incidents of the war or its immediate after-math: Sophocles' *Ajax* and Euripides' *Rhesus* and his *Trojan Women*. A description of the fall of Troy is found at the beginning of Vergil's *Aeneïd*.

Trophonius. An Orchomenian architect. Trophonius and Agamedes were sons of the aged Erginus, king of Boeotian Orchomenus, though it came to be believed that Trophonius' father was Apollo. Although the brothers would one day inherit the rule of Orchomenus, they seem to have earned their living as architects. They are credited with many buildings, including Alcmene's bridal chamber, at Thebes; the first shrine of Poseidon, at Mantineia; and Apollo's temple at Delphi, which the god himself laid out. Their most ingenious work, however, was the treasury of Hyrieus, king of Hyria, near Orchomenus. This building was safe from the cleverest of thieves—except the architects, who had inserted in the walls a movable stone, the secret of which was known only to themselves. Hyrieus was astonished to discover that his treasury was being regularly robbed, though its doors remained tightly sealed. Unknown to the brothers he hid some kind of trap in the room where his gold was kept. Agamedes was caught in this trap the next time that he entered the building. Trophonius, finding that he could not extricate him, began to fear that Agamedes might, under torture, reveal his brother's guilt as well as his own. Trophonius solved this problem by cutting off Agamedes' head and carrying it away, leaving only an unrecognizable corpse for the king to discover in the morning. Unfortunately, this precaution did not help Trophonius. As he was traveling past Lebadeia, the earth suddenly opened and swallowed him.

At some later time, the Boeotians, having suffered from a prolonged drought, sent envoys from several towns to question the oracle at Delphi. They were told to ask the advice of the oracle of Trophonius at their own city of Lebadeia. Surprised, they retraced their steps as far as this not very important town, but found no one who had heard of the oracle. At that point, Saön, one of the envoys, was inspired to follow a swarm of bees. The bees disappeared into the ground and Saön went with them. He found a cave, in which he was taught by Trophonius himself the steps necessary to receive an answer from his oracle. Pausanias, who himself consulted this oracle in the second century A.D., described the elaborate ritual that preceded and followed the descent into the cave. Of the actual replies to the applicant's questions he said merely that some learn the truth by sight, others by hearing. In the process, it seems, the petitioners were literally paralyzed with fright, though they later recovered. Trophonius' oracle enjoyed a reputation for accuracy second only to that of Apollo's oracle at Delphi. It was said by Herodotus [1.46, 8.133–134] to have been consulted by the Persian general Mardonius and the Lydian king Croesus. [Pausanias 8.10.2, 9.11.1, 9.37.4–7, 9.39.1–9.40.2.]

Tros. The king and eponym of Troy. Tros was the son of Erichthonius, king of Dardania, and Astyoche, daughter of the river-god Simöeis. He married Callirrhoë, daughter of the river-god Scamander, and she bore Ilus, Assaracus, Ganymede, and a daughter, Cleopatra. Tros is best known as the father of the beautiful youth Ganymede, who was carried off by Zeus to be cup-bearer to the gods. Tros grieved so over the disappearance of his son that Zeus gave him some handsome horses and sent Hermes to tell him of Ganymede's good fortune. [Homer, *Iliad*, 5.265–267, 20.230–233; *Homeric Hymn to Aphrodite* 5.202–218; Apollodorus 3.12.2.]

Troy. A Phrygian city, also called Ilium, near the southern entrance to the Hellespont. The mythical history of Troy, confused though it is, suggests that the people whom Classical writers called Trojans were a group of tribes which, by the time of the Trojan War, had joined in a somewhat uneasy federation to share, for defensive purposes, a great walled city. The myths offer only occasional hints as to how this situation came about. The indigenous people of the Troad, the region dominated by Troy, were the Teucrians, named for their king Teucer. This Teucer was a son of the river-god Scamander and Idaea, a nymph of Mount Ida, although Roman tradition makes him an immigrant from Crete. During Teucer's rule, Dardanus, a son of Zeus and Atlas' daughter Electra, came to the mainland from his birthplace on the island of Samothrace. (The Romans, however, claimed that Dardanus came to Samothrace from Italy.) Dardanus married Teucer's daughter, Bateia, and founded a city on the slope of Mount Ida that he called Dardania. At the death of Teucer, Dardanus succeeded to the rule of the entire region, and renamed the people Dardanians. Dardanus' son Erichthonius gained great wealth and married Astyoche, a daughter of the river-god Simöeis. Their son, Tros, gave his name to the people, who came to be called Trojans, and to the region they inhabited, the Troad.

During the next generation, a division seems to have occurred in the ruling family. By Callirrhoë, a daughter of Scamander, Tros had three sons. One of these, Ganymede (whom some call a son of the later king Laomedon), was carried off by Zeus. Assaracus seems to have remained to rule Dardania, while Ilus went off to another part of Phrygia. There he married a king's daughter and acquired as a dowry fifty young men and as many young women. It was presumably at this time that Ilus drove Pelops, or his father, Tantalus, from the region of Mount Sipylus. Ilus' father-in-law, obeying an oracle, gave him a cow and commanded him to found a city where it first lay down to rest. Like Cadmus, another Asiatic prince, Ilus dutifully followed the cow. It led him northward until it came, by a curious chance, to Ilus' homeland, the Troad. There, on the hill of Phrygian Ate that rises from the broad plain between Mount Ida and the sea, it rested. Ilus built a city that he called Ilium, after himself. The citadel he called the Pergamum, a word similar in meaning to acropolis.

When, for some reason, Ilus asked Zeus for a sign, the Palladium dropped from heaven before his tent. This object was thereafter closely guarded on the Pergamum, for it was believed that if it were taken the city would fall. Ilus

The Ruling Houses of Troy and Dardania

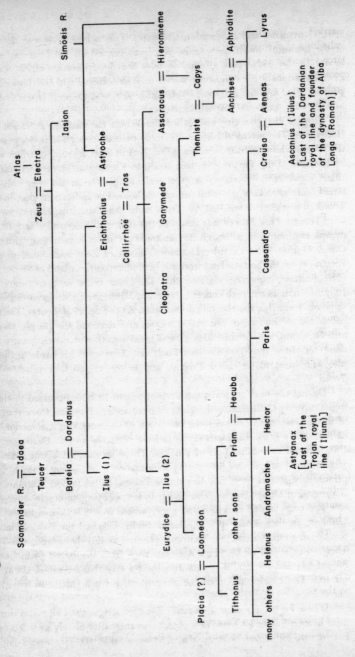

married his daughter, Themiste, to Assaracus' son, Capys. If any history is imbedded in this part of the Trojan myth, it may be that an invading Lydian force settled in the Troad. Its leaders confirmed their right to rule with a convenient sign from heaven, intermarried with the local ruling family, and even pretended to be descended from the native people's eponym, Dardanus.

Ilus' wife bore, besides Themiste, a son, Laomedon, who succeeded his father to the rule of Ilium. Laomedon was a powerful king who, with the aid of Poseidon and Apollo, built the outer walls of Ilium. It was during his reign, however, that the country was first troubled with raids by Greek pirates. Laomedon and all but one of his sons were killed by a force under Heracles, whose excuse was that the king had refused to honor a bargain over Heracles' rescue of his daughter Hesione. The Greeks sailed away, leaving Laomedon's youngest son, Podarces, in control.

Podarces, who took the name of Priam, seems to have had no trouble in maintaining the dominance that Ilium had apparently established from the first over the older city of Dardania. Moreover, he extended his dominion over many smaller cities. He first married Arisbe, daughter of Merops, king of the town of Percote, on the Hellespont. Later, he took another wife, Hecuba, from the region of the Sangarius River, east of the Bosporus. Priam's son Hector married Andromache, daughter of Eëtion, king of Hypoplacian Thebes. Although this city is often said to have been on the slopes of Mount Placus, in Cilicia, it was more likely a small city in or near the Troad.

Priam was the most famous and powerful of all the Trojan kings, but he lived to see the utter destruction of Troy by Greek invaders. Agamemnon, king of Mycenae, led a great Greek force against the supposedly impregnable city of Ilium. He used as an excuse the abduction of Helen, wife of the Spartan king Menelaüs, by Priam's son Paris. Over a period of ten years, the Greeks gradually subdued Troy's allies and decimated the ranks of the Trojans, in spite of the generalship of Hector, Priam's eldest son. Troy finally fell, however, less to force of arms than through the trick of the wooden horse, in which the Greeks gained access to the city. Nearly all the Trojan men were put to the sword, including Hector's infant son. Two Dardanians were spared, Antenor for favors to the Greeks, Aeneas for his piety. Aeneas, descended from Assaracus, led his small band of men from Troy to find a new home in Italy, where the Romans later claimed him as their ancestor.

The ruined city discovered by Heinrich Schliemann near the village of Hissarlik, in Turkey, is generally, though not universally, believed to be the remains of Ilium. The stratum of these ruins that archaeologists assign to Priam's city belongs to one of the last of many cities that were destroyed and rebuilt on the site. The myth of Troy is evidently far less violent and confused than its history.

Tullia. See SERVIUS TULLIUS.

Tullus Hostilius. The third king of Rome. Tullus scorned the peaceful and pious ways of his predecessor, Numa Pompilius, and emulated the warlike temper of Romulus. He conquered and destroyed Alba Longa, the city of Romulus' birth, and successfully fought the powerful Sabines. He showed great cruelty in some of his dealings, notably in having Mettius Fufetius, the Alban leader, torn apart by horses. Toward the end of his thirty-two-year reign, Tullus, faced with alarming portents in the Alban Mountains, a plague in Rome, and his own wasting illness, lost his courage and resorted to a superstitious observance of religious rites. In imitating Numa's propitiatory rites to Jupiter Elicius, he succeeded only in drawing the god's lightning down on his own head. [Livy 1.22.1–1.31.8.]

Turnus. A king of the Rutulians. Turnus, a son of Daunus and Venilia, claimed descent from Perseus' mother, Danaë. He courted Lavinia, daughter of Latinus, king of Latium, with her mother's encouragement. Latinus, because of certain oracles, offered his daughter instead to AENEAS [B, C], on his arrival in Italy. Turnus fought a war against the Trojan and was killed by him in single combat. [Vergil, *Aeneid*, Books 7–12.]

Twins, The. See GEMINI.

Tyche. A goddess of fortune. Tyche had no myth beyond being called one of the Fates or a daughter of Zeus. She was widely worshiped, however, often as a local guardian of the luck of a city.

Tydeus. A Calydonian warrior with the SEVEN AGAINST THEBES. A son of Oeneus, king of Calydon, by his second wife, Periboea, or by Gorge, his daughter, Tydeus was banished by his uncle Agrius for killing another uncle or his own brother or eight cousins. He went to Argos in search of help and married King Adrastus' daughter Deïpyle. Adrastus agreed to give Tydeus aid in recovering the throne of Calydon, but decided to help Polyneices to recover the Theban throne first. Tydeus joined the Argive expedition against Thebes and won great acclaim on a lone embassy to that city. In the ensuing siege, he was mortally wounded by Melanippus, but killed him in turn. A favorite of Athena, Tydeus would have been made immortal if he had not shocked the goddess by eating Melanippus' brains. Diomedes, Tydeus' son by Deïpyle, was one of the Epigoni and a hero of the Trojan War. [Homer, *Iliad*, 4.376–398; Apollodorus 1.8.4–5, 3.6.1–8.]

Tyndareüs. A king of Sparta.

A. Although the main events of Tyndareüs' life were well known, the details were disputed. It is not certain whether his father was Perieres or Oebalus or whether his mother was Perseus' daughter, Gorgophone, or a Naïad, Bateia. Aphareus and Leucippus, Icarius and Hippocoön, may all have been his brothers, but the first two are often called his half-brothers. Early in his life Tyndareüs was expelled from Sparta by Hippocoön and his twelve sons, perhaps with Icarius' aid. He may have taken refuge in nearby Pellana, or at Thalamae, then a part of Messenia, which land was ruled by Aphareus. Or it may be that Tyndareüs and Icarius, exiled together, fled to King Thestius in

Aetolia. According to this version, the brothers supported Thestius in some of his wars with his neighbors, and Thestius gave Tyndareüs the hand of Leda, his daughter by Eurythemis. Wherever Tyndareüs may have gone in exile, he was eventually restored to the Spartan throne by Heracles, who, pursuing a quarrel of his own, had killed Hippocoön and all his sons. Several generations after Tyndareüs, the descendants of Heracles conquered Sparta, claiming that Heracles had merely given the throne to Tyndareüs in trust for his own sons.

Leda had several children in Tyndareüs' house, but how many were born to her husband is a matter of doubt. Clytemnestra, Timandra, and Phylonoë were almost certainly Tyndareüs' offspring. Homer says that Leda's sons—the Dioscuri, Castor and Polydeuces—were Tyndareüs' children, but most later writers claimed that one or both were sons of Zeus. Nearly everyone agrees that Helen was the daughter not of Tyndareüs, but of Zeus; many claim that she was not Leda's daughter either. Perhaps the most usual story is that, in one night, Leda bore Castor and Clytemnestra to Tyndareüs, Polydeuces and Helen to Zeus.

B. Tyndareüs may have helped to restore Atreus' sons, Agamemnon and Menelaüs, to the throne of Mycenae, which their uncle, Thyestes, had usurped. Earlier Tyndareüs had married Clytemnestra to Thyestes' son Tantalus. Agamemnon killed both Tantalus and his infant son, and Tyndareüs promptly married the widow to her husband's murderer. Timandra married Echemus, king of Arcadia. Phylonoë apparently died young and was, for some reason, immortalized by Artemis.

Finding a husband for Helen proved to be more of a problem. This was not for any lack of suitors, even though she had had a child by Theseus, according to some reports. Nearly all the eligible young princes of Greece wanted to marry Helen, who was famous for her extraordinary beauty. These suitors (whose names were listed variously by Apollodorus [3.10.8], Hyginus [*Fabulae* 81], and the author of the *Catalogues of Women* [68], among others) were a headstrong company, and Tyndareüs feared that there would be trouble once he made his choice. He asked Odysseus' advice, offering to support Odysseus' suit for Penelope with her father, Icarius. Following Odysseus' counsel, he made the suitors take an oath, standing on pieces of a horse, as was the custom on particularly solemn occasions. By this oath, which was later to result in the Trojan War, each was bound to abide by Tyndareüs' decision and, moreover, to punish anyone who tried to take Helen by force or harm the chosen husband. Tyndareüs then gave his daughter to Menelaüs, who had brought the finest gifts. Hyginus [*Fabulae* 78] says that, even after the oath was taken, Tyndareüs was fearful and left the choice to Helen.

While sacrificing to the gods, Tyndareüs had once forgotten Aphrodite. The goddess punished him by making three of his four daughters unfaithful to their husbands. Timandra deserted Echemus for Phyleus, son of Augeias; Helen went off to Troy with Paris while Menelaüs was attending his grandfather's funeral in Crete; Clytemnestra and her lover, Aegisthus, murdered her husband, Agamemnon, on his return from Troy. When Orestes avenged his father on her, some say that it was Tyndareüs who brought against him the charge of matricide, either on the Areopagus at Athens or in Argos, as indicated in Euripides' *Orestes*. When Tyndareüs' two sons were killed in battle with Idas and Lynceus, he ceded the kingdom to Menelaüs. The epic poet Panyassis said that Tyndareüs was one of those mortals raised from the dead by Asclepius, but if this happened nothing more is known of it. [Apollodorus 3.10.4–9; Pausanias 3.1.4–5; *Catalogues of Women* 67–68; Hyginus, *Fabulae*, 77, 80.]

Typhöeus, Typhon, or **Typhaon.** A monster. After the defeat of Ge's children the Titans (or some say the Giants) by the gods, she bore Typhöeus to Tartarus in a Cilician cave. The horrible creature had a hundred burning snake heads and spoke with the voices of men and animals. He undertook to overthrow the gods and rule the universe. According to Hesiod [*Theogony* 820–880], Zeus fought him with lightning until even the Titans imprisoned in the depths of Tartarus trembled. At last the god prevailed. He crushed Typhöeus' smoking body with a mountain, then flung it into Tartarus, where it became the source of all harmful winds.

Apollodorus [1.6.3, 2.3.1, 2.5.1, 2.5.10–11, 3.5.8, "Epitome" 1.1] gives a more complicated account of the career of the monster, whom he calls Typhon. He accuses him of having fathered a foul brood of other monsters on Echidna: the Chimaera, the Nemean lion, Orthus, Ladon, the Sphinx, Prometheus' eagle, and Phaea, the Crommyonian sow. When the gods spied Typhon heading for Olympus, they fled in a body to Egypt, where they disguised themselves in various animal forms. Zeus held his ground, fighting the monster with thunderbolts and a sickle until he drove him as far as Mount Casius, in Syria. There they wrestled. Typhon got hold of the sickle and cut out the sinews of Zeus's hands and feet. Carrying the helpless god through the sea to Cilicia, he hid him in the Corycian Cave. The sinews he secreted under a bearskin and set the dragon Delphyne to guard them. Hermes and Aegipan somehow stole the sinews and refitted them to Zeus's hands and feet.

The god returned to Olympus for a new supply of thunderbolts, then rushed into the fray once again. Pelting Typhon with lightning from a chariot drawn by winged horses, he drove him to Mount Nysa. There the Fates persuaded the monster that a diet of mortal food would give him strength. Instead it weakened him, and he retreated to Mount Haemus, in Thrace. He was still strong enough to hurl a few mountains at Olympus, but Zeus parried them with thunderbolts, causing them to rebound upon Typhon. The monster's blood spurted over the mountain, giving it its name. Typhon fled through the sea to Sicily, but Zeus crushed him there under Mount Aetna, or else threw the entire island on him, with the mountain on his head. Even today the mountain gives off fiery blasts from the thunderbolts or from the monster's breath. (A similar story is told, however, of Enceladus, one of the Giants who fought the gods.)

According to one tradition, which distinguishes between Typhöeus and a similar monster named Typhaon, the latter was borne parthenogenetically by Hera, who was jealous because Zeus had borne Athena alone, and her own attempt to match this feat had resulted only in the crippled Hephaestus. Hera gave the monster to Python to rear. The unsleeping dragon that guarded the golden fleece was said to have been borne by Ge on being fertilized by the blood of Typhaon when he, like Typhöeus, was killed by Zeus.

Typhöeus, along with several other giants of Greek mythology, is generally believed to have been a personification of terrifying natural phenomena, particularly volcanoes. There were many volcanoes on the fringes of the Greek world, and the early explosions on the island of Thera, north of Crete, are known to have been of cataclysmic proportions. The transformation of the gods in Egypt no doubt resulted from a misguided attempt on the part of Greek mythographers to account for the animal forms of certain Egyptian deities whom they customarily identified with Greek gods. Typhon was the Egyptian Set, the implacable enemy of Osiris. [Pindar, *Pythian Odes*, 1.15–28, 8.16; Ovid, *Metamorphoses*, 5.321–331, 5.346–378.]

Tyre. A principal Phoenician city. Tyre was usually said to have been the home of Cadmus and Europa and their brothers, and of Dido. These honors were sometimes accorded to Sidon, however, for Greek writers seemed unable to distinguish clearly between these great Phoenician ports.

Tyro. A daughter of Salmoneus and Alcidice. Tyro, a beautiful girl, was reared by her uncle Cretheus, king of Iolcus, who later married her. She fell in love with the river Enipeus and used to spend many hours on its banks. Poseidon took advantage of her infatuation by seducing her in the form of the river. Tyro bore twin sons secretly and exposed them in a field. Some say that Salmoneus, on learning of the births, refused to believe his daughter's version of the children's paternity and mistreated her, as did her stepmother, Sidero, whom Salmoneus had married upon the death of Alcidice. In any case, the boys were found and reared by horse herders, who named them Pelias and Neleus. Meanwhile, Tyro married Cretheus and bore him three sons—Aeson, Pheres, and Amythaon. When Pelias and Neleus grew to manhood they discovered their mother. Pelias killed Sidero for her injuries to Tyro. [Homer, *Odyssey*, 11.235–259; Apollodorus 1.9.8–11.]

Tyrrhenians or **Tyrsenians.** The people later known as Etruscans. According to Herodotus [1.94], the Tyrrhenians were Lydians driven from their homeland by prolonged famine. They took their name from a son of the Lydian king Atys, Tyrsenus, who led them to a new home among the Ombrici of northern and central Italy. The true origin of the Etruscans is unknown, but archaeological evidence points to oriental connections, and Asia Minor is not an unlikely homeland for them.

U

Udaeüs. One of the Sparti. Udaeüs, one of the five survivors of the Sownmen born of the dragon's teeth sown by Cadmus [A], was an ancestor of Teiresias.

Ulysses or **Ulixes.** See Odysseus.

Underworld. See Hades.

Upis. See Opis.

Urania. One of the nine Muses. Urania, a daughter of Zeus and Mnemosyne, was said by some to be the mother of Linus by Amphimarus, a son of Poseidon. [Hesiod, *Theogony*, 78; Pausanias 9.29.6.]

Uranus. The sky and the god of the sky. Uranus was the first son of Ge (Earth), who had been born of Chaos. He married her and she bore him the Hundred-handed, the Cyclopes, and the Titans. When Uranus imprisoned his children (or all but the Titans) within the body of earth, Ge roused her children against their father and gave Cronus, the youngest and wiliest, a sickle. Uranus came at evening to lie upon Ge, but Cronus castrated him and flung the severed parts into the sea. From the foam that formed about them Aphrodite grew; the blood that fell upon the earth spawned the Erinyes, the Giants, and the Meliae.

Uranus was a personification of the sky, which seemed to rest upon the earth. If he was ever worshiped, however, no trace of his cult remains. His story was told in the *Theogony* [126–210], attributed to Hesiod.

Ursa Major (The Great Bear); Ursa Minor (The Lesser Bear). Constellations in the northern sky. The Great Bear, called Arctos by the Greeks and Ursa Major by the Romans, was commonly said to have been the Arcadian nymph Callisto, who had been transformed into a bear. This constellation is followed through the sky by Arctophylax, the Bear Keeper, who had been Callisto's son, Arcas. The sea-goddess Tethys will not allow Ursa Major to set in the ocean because of the enmity that her foster-daughter Hera bore Callisto. Another legend identified the Great and Lesser Bears as Helice and Cynosura, nurses of Zeus in Crete, but no significant myths seem to have been attached to Ursa Minor. The Great Bear was often called the Wagon (Plaustrum), and Arctophylax was called the Wagon-driver (Boötes). The driver represents either Icarius—in which case Virgo is his daughter, Erigone, and Canis Minor is his dog Maera—or Philomelus. These, at least, are the explanations given by Hyginus [*Poetica Astronomica* 2.1–2.2, 2.4], but he admits that there were many others.

V

Veii. An Etruscan city north of Rome. The Veientes warred with Rome at intervals throughout the early centuries of the new city's existence.

Venus. A Roman goddess of the fertility of gardens. Originally a minor deity, Venus was identified with the Greek APHRODITE and became important in Roman cult as the grandmother of Aeneas' son Iülus (Ascanius), who was claimed as ancestor of the emperors of the Julian line.

Vergil. A Roman poet who lived during the reign of Augustus. Vergil (Publius Vergilius Maro) is best known as the author of the epic *Aeneïd,* which narrates the adventures of the Trojan Aeneas and his followers from their escape from the sack of Troy to their defeat of the Latins near the future site of Rome. This work contains a good deal of artificial mythology, since it was intended to glorify Rome and the Julian family by connecting them with the great events of the past. Vergil's short poem *Ciris* tells the story of Scylla, daughter of Nisus. His *Georgics* and *Eclogues* contain frequent, though usually brief, references to myths.

Vertumnus or **Vortumnus.** A Roman god of fertility, particularly as evidenced in the changes in vegetation from season to season. According to a tale that was perhaps invented by Ovid, Vertumnus, who was able to change his shape at will, took the form of an old woman and pleaded his suit so eloquently in the third person that he won the love of the fruit-goddess Pomona.

Vesta. The Roman goddess of the hearth. Vesta's functions were almost identical with those of HESTIA.

Vestal virgins. See HESTIA.

Vesuvius, Mount. A volcano near Naples. The Phlegraean Plain near Vesuvius was claimed by many writers as the scene of the battle between the gods and the Giants, though early versions of the myth are likely to have placed this event farther east, perhaps in Thrace.

Virbius. A minor Italian god. Virbius seems to have been a consort of the ancient Latin goddess Diana. When Diana was identified with the Greek Artemis, Virbius was equated with Hippolytus. It was explained that he had been revived by Asclepius after his death and transported to Aricia, a center of Diana's worship near Rome. [Ovid, *Metamorphoses,* 15.490–546; Vergil, *Aeneïd,* 7.761–782.]

Virgo (The Virgin). A constellation. There was little agreement among Classical writers as to who this virgin might have been. Ancient suggestions include Dike (Justice); Tyche (Fortune); Erigone, the daughter of Aegisthus and

Clytemnestra; and Parthenos, a baby daughter of Apollo by Chrysothemis. Inexplicably, she has also been called Demeter, in spite of the well-known fact that the goddess bore Persephone, Plutos, Philomelus, and the horse Arion. [Hyginus, *Poetica Astronomica*, 2.25.]

Volscians or Volsci. An Italic tribe living to the southeast of the site on which Rome was later built. The Volscians, led by their queen, Camilla, were allies of the Latins against Aeneas and his Trojan colonists.

Vortumnus. See VERTUMNUS.

Vulcan. A Roman god of fire. Vulcan was an ancient god of fire in its uncontrolled manifestations, such as the volcanoes that perpetuate his name. Like Vesta, goddess of the beneficent hearth fire, Vulcan was worshiped at Rome from early times. However, it was only when he came to be identified with the sophisticated Greek artisan-god Hephaestus that Vulcan won a reputation as a god of smiths and other workmen who used fire for the good of mankind. Even then his newly acquired character played little part in his cult. That cult is not well known, but it was probably largely concerned with averting the dangerous wrath of the fire-god.

W

Wagon. See URSA MAJOR.

Wandering Rocks (Planctae). Moving rocks that destroyed vessels which tried to pass among them. Odysseus encountered these rocks near the Sirens' island, somewhere north of Sicily. Rather than sail among them, he chose an alternate route that led him between Scylla and Charybdis, identified with the Straits of Messina. The Argonauts, on the other hand, passed through these straits on their southward journey before coming, somewhere near Mount Aetna, to the Wandering Rocks, which they passed through safely with the aid of the Nereïds. To add to the confusion, some ancient writers did not distinguish between these rocks and the Clashing Rocks, which Apollonius Rhodius clearly places at the northern end of the Bosporus.

War of the Titans, The. A lost epic poem. The surviving fragments of this poem are published in the volume of Hesiod's works in the Loeb Classical Library.

Water-carrier, The. See AQUARIUS.

Whale, The. See CETUS.

White Island. An island in the Black Sea near the mouths of the Danube. This island was long reputed to be one of the Islands of the Blessed (see ELYSIUM), where several Greek heroes of the Trojan War lived in eternal bliss.

Winegrowers. See ANIUS.

Women of the Sea. Followers of Dionysus. The Haliae (Women of the Sea) came to Argos from the Aegean islands to support Cretan Dionysus in his war with Perseus. Perseus defeated them, put the majority to the sword, and buried them in a common grave, except for the maenad Choreia, whom he buried separately because of her high rank. Dionysus was later reconciled with the Argives, and he buried his wife, Ariadne, in a temple which they dedicated to him. This myth may have been confined to Argos, for it is related only by Pausanias, who learned it from the Argives. [Pausanias, 2.20.4, 2.22.1, 2.23.4.]

wooden horse. A large statue in which Greeks entered Troy undetected. Although the Greeks forces had fought the Trojans for ten years and had met the four conditions revealed by Helenus as necessary before Troy could be taken, the city remained impregnable. At last Odysseus or Epeius devised an elaborate plan by which the Trojans might be tricked into opening their gates. Epeius, son of Panopeus, was an ingenious artisan. He cut timbers on Mount Ida and constructed, with the aid of Athena, an enormous image of a horse. The hollow interior of this statue was large enough to contain a considerable number of men. A group of Greek leaders, under Odysseus' command, hid themselves inside the horse. The rest of the Greeks broke camp and sailed away, leaving the horse on the shore. They went only as far as the offshore island of Tenedos, where they remained to await the fall of darkness.

Finding that their enemies had apparently given up the long struggle, the Trojans poured from the city to gloat over the abandoned Greek fortifications. They were astonished and puzzled by the horse, but heartened by the inscription that they found on it: "For their return home the Greeks dedicate this thank offering to Athena." A heated argument broke out over what should be done with this strange but impressive object. The most suspicious Trojans wanted to break into it, light a fire under it, or push it over a cliff. Those who were either more optimistic or more religiously inclined wanted to drag the horse inside the city walls, in the hope that a votive offering to Athena would bring them luck. The prophetess Cassandra warned that there were spies lurking inside the horse. As usual, she was not believed, even though Laocoön, a priest of Apollo, echoed her warning and flung his spear at the horse. For some time the fate of the Greeks hidden inside the statue hung in the balance.

According to Vergil's detailed account in the *Aeneïd* [2.13–267], Odysseus had anticipated this conflict of opinion and had prepared to influence it to the advantage of the Greeks. A brave young relative of his, Sinon, allowed himself to be left behind by the Greeks, with arms bound and clothing tattered. Sinon was quickly captured by Dardanian shepherds and dragged before King Priam for questioning. The young man told an elaborately false but convincing story. He had won the enmity of Odysseus, he said, by speaking out against that leader's treacherous murder of Palamedes, Sinon's general. Odysseus had plotted with Calchas, the Greek seer, who had thereupon interpreted a supposed oracle from Apollo to mean that Sinon must be sacrificed to the gods to insure a safe homeward voyage for the Greeks. Sinon had managed to escape and the Greeks had sailed away.

The Trojans, convinced that Sinon hated the Greeks as much as they did, eagerly asked him the meaning of the wooden horse, precisely as Odysseus had expected. The young spy explained that the Greeks had incurred the anger of Athena by stealing her sacred image, the Palladium, from the Trojan citadel. In the Greek camp its eyes had flashed fire and the goddess herself had momentarily appeared. Calchas had declared that the Greeks must sail for home, after first building a wooden horse in an attempt to appease Athena. They had purposely made it too large to be squeezed through the Trojan gates, for Calchas had warned that, if it were taken to the citadel, the Trojans would invade Greek cities. If, on the other hand, the Trojans were to harm the statue, the goddess' anger would be turned against them and Troy would be destroyed.

The Trojans believed this false tale. Their belief was strengthened by an event that occurred as Sinon ended his story. LAOCOÖN was sacrificing to Poseidon by the shore when two great snakes were seen swimming through the sea from Tenedos. Coming onto the land, they snatched and ate Laocoön's two young sons. When the priest tried to protect the boys, the snakes killed him too. The snakes had been sent by Apollo to punish his priest for some insult. To the Trojans, however, it seemed that Laocoön had been punished by Athena for throwing his spear at the wooden horse. They hesitated no longer, but broke through the walls of their own city in their eagerness to bring the horse to their citadel, the Pergamum. There it remained while the Trojans feasted to honor the goddess and celebrate the end of the war.

A few Trojans remained suspicious, however. Deïphobus, who had married Helen after the death of his brother Paris, took his wife to the horse and walked around it with her. Helen called out the names of the leading Greeks, imitating the voices of their wives. Anticlus, one of the Greeks in the horse, was deceived by the trick and would have called out if Odysseus had not covered his mouth forcibly with his hand. The silence apparently satisfied Deïphobus that the horse was empty. After a few hours of carousing, the unsuspecting Trojans fell asleep, while the horse, filled with enemy soldiers, remained in the heart of their city.

Meanwhile, the Greek fleet had sailed by moonlight back to Troy. Some say that Sinon had slipped out of the city and lighted a beacon on Achilles' burial mound by the shore. Others claim that the Greeks signaled their return with a beacon, and Sinon, inside the city, made his way to the horse, opened the door in its side, and released the occupants. Echion, son of Portheus, tried to leap to the ground and was killed. The others let themselves down by a rope onto the walls of the citadel. They quickly opened the city gates and let in their fellow Greeks, who had silently stolen up from the ships. The sleeping Trojans, taken unawares, were quickly defeated.

Many Classical writers tried to find a rational explanation for the legend of the wooden horse, which was at least as old as Homer. Pausanias [1.23.8], for example, believed that the "horse" was some kind of war engine for breaking through the city walls. Others, perhaps noting that in most accounts the horse towered over the walls, believed that it was a form of scaling ladder. Although Vergil's story of the event is the most detailed, parts of the legend are told by Homer [*Odyssey* 4.271–289, 8.492–520]. Apollodorus summarized the story ["Epitome" 5.14–21]. Hyginus apparently follows Vergil's account [*Fabulae* 108].

Works and Days. See HESIOD.

X

Xanthippe. See PLEURON.

Xanthus and **Balius.** The immortal horses of Achilles. These two remarkable beasts were offspring of the Harpy Podarge by Zephyrus, the west wind, who impregnated her as she was grazing by the river Oceanus. The gods gave the horses to Peleus upon his marriage to Thetis. Seeing them later weeping over the death in battle of Patroclus, Zeus regretted causing them suffering through association with human beings, the most miserable of all creatures. Hera gave Xanthus the power of speech in order to warn Achilles of his impending death, but the Erinyes quickly took away his voice again, no doubt to prevent him from giving away more of the immortals' secrets to human beings. No harm was done in this case, since Achilles had more than once heard the same prophecy from his mother, Thetis. [Homer, *Iliad*, 16.145–154, 17.426–458, 19.392–424.]

Xanthus River. See SCAMANDER.

Xuthus. A king of Athens. Xuthus, Dorus, and Aeolus were sons of Hellen and the nymph Orseïs, though Euripides [*Ion* 63] calls Xuthus a son of Aeolus. Although Hellen awarded him the Peloponnesus as his kingdom, he never enjoyed this patrimony. He ruled in Iolcus for a time but was soon expelled by his brothers for allegedly appropriating property that belonged jointly to the three. Xuthus went to Athens, where he hired himself out as a leader of mercenary troops in the war against Chalcodon, in Euboea. He acquitted himself so well that Erechtheus, the Athenian king, gave him his daughter Creüsa as his bride. According to Euripides, Xuthus succeeded to the throne on the death of Erechtheus. Creüsa bore him Achaeüs and Ion. (Euripides calls Ion a son of Apollo and claims that Dorus was Xuthus' son, instead of his brother.) Diomede, who married Xuthus' nephew Deïon, was also Xuthus' child, though perhaps not by Creüsa.

Pausanias claims that Xuthus did not rule Athens but, at the death of Erechtheus, was asked as a disinterested party to choose a successor from among the king's sons. He chose Cecrops, the eldest, and was banished for his pains by Cecrops' brothers. With Achaeüs and Ion he settled in Aegialus, in the northern Peloponnesus, where he died. Two branches of the Hellenes were later named for his sons, the Ionians and the Achaeans.

Xuthus is an important character in Euripides' *Ion*, which deals with the melodramatic events surrounding the discovery that Ion is in fact a son of Creüsa by Apollo. Xuthus, however, remains happy in the belief that he is the young man's father—a belief that all writers but Euripides seem to have shared. [Apollodorus 1.7.3; Pausanias 7.1.2–3.]

Z

Zacynthus. A large island off the coast of Elis. Zacynthus was one of the islands near Ithaca that sent forces to the Trojan War under Odysseus' leadership.

Zagreus. An obscure god often identified with Dionysus [A]. Although Zagreus is known only in connection with the partly artificial mythology of the cult of Orphism, his story may contain elements of genuine but otherwise forgotten myths.

Zalmoxis. See Salmoxis.

Zelus. A son of the Titan Pallas and Styx. Zelus (Emulation), together with his brothers Cratus (Force) and Bia (Violence) and his sister Nike (Victory), was a constant companion of Zeus. [Hesiod, *Theogony*, 383–388.]

Zemelo. See Semele.

Zephyrus or **Zephyr.** The west wind and god of the west wind. Zephyrus, like his brother Boreas, was often personified and played some part in myth. He was a son of Eos and Astraeüs. He impregnated the Harpy Podarge by the river Oceanus, and she gave birth to two immortal horses, Xanthus and Balius. Zephyrus was said by some to have caused the death of Hyacinth through jealousy of the youth's love for Apollo. [Hesiod, *Theogony*, 378–380; Homer, *Iliad*, 16.148–151; Pausanias 1.37.2, 3.19.5.]

Zetes and **Calaïs.** Twin sons of Boreas, the north wind, and Oreithyia, a daughter of Erechtheus. Zetes and Calaïs, who were called the Boreades, wore wings, which sprouted either from their backs or from their heads and feet. These wings, some say, grew when down began to appear on the youths' cheeks, but others imply that their father presented them to the boys as equipment for their journey in the *Argo*. Either their wings or their hair is said to have been purple, perhaps because that is a color of storm clouds. The Boreades' only recorded adventure occurred during their voyage with the Argonauts [H]. Finding their aged brother-in-law, the Thracian king Phineus, beset by Harpies, they chased these vile, birdlike monsters through the sky. According to one story the Harpies managed to keep ahead of their pursuers, but fell dead of exhaustion. In this version, Zetes and Calaïs died too, as they were fated to do if they once failed to overtake their prey. In a more widely accepted tale, they pursued the Harpies to the Strophades Islands. There Hermes or Iris ordered them to spare the exhausted monsters, promising that they would no longer trouble Phineus.

The victorious brothers did not live long after the voyage ended. Heracles, learning that it was they who had persuaded the other Argonauts to abandon him in Mysia, killed them on the island of Tenos as they were returning home from Pelias' funeral games. One or both of the two columns that he erected over their graves there moved when the north wind, their father, blew upon them. [Apollonius Rhodius 1.211–223, 2.234–434; Apollodorus 1.9.21; Ovid, *Metamorphoses*, 6.711–721.]

Zethus. See AMPHION (1).

Zeus. The ruler of the Olympian gods, identified by the Romans with Jupiter.

A. Zeus was said by Homer to be the eldest of the sons of CRONUS and Rhea. Most later writers accepted the view of Hesiod that he was the youngest, born after his father had swallowed his brothers, Poseidon and Hades, and his sisters, Hestia, Demeter, and Hera. Rhea or her mother, Ge, tricked Cronus by giving him, instead of the baby Zeus, a stone wrapped in swaddling clothes, which Cronus swallowed. Quickly discovering his mistake, Cronus looked everywhere for Zeus, but Rhea had hidden him in a cave on Mount Dicte, in Crete, and the Curetes danced about clashing their spears and shields so that Cronus would not hear the baby's cries. Nymphs of Crete and the goat, or nymph, named Amaltheia provided him with nourishment. (These are the general outlines of a story that has numerous variations.)

On growing up, Zeus persuaded the clever Oceanid Metis to administer an emetic to his father. Cronus vomited up his other children, who joined Zeus in a struggle with Cronus and the other Titans for control of Olympus. On the advice of Ge, Zeus released the Cyclopes and the Hundred-handed from Tartarus, where Cronus had imprisoned them. After a ten-year war, Zeus and his allies won out and confined the male Titans, or most of them, in Tartarus, with the Hundred-handed as their guards. The Cyclopes were retained as Zeus's armorers, providing him with his invariable weapon, the thunderbolt.

According to some accounts, the three victorious brothers cast lots for the rule of the universe. Zeus received the sky, Poseidon the sea, Hades the Underworld, with all three having equal rights on earth and Olympus. In fact, however, Zeus was acknowledged as the chief of the gods, and many accounts have it that his brothers and sisters, grateful for their freedom, asked Zeus to be their supreme ruler.

Zeus accepted this honor with alacrity, but he was not allowed to enjoy it in peace for long. Ge (Earth) had been at odds with two generations of sky-gods—her husband, Uranus, and their son Cronus—and she was not quick to come to terms with her grandson Zeus. She gave birth to a race of GIANTS, who soon attacked heaven. The gods, including by now several of Zeus's children, destroyed these monsters after prolonged warfare. Ge, undaunted, bore the most frightening monster of all, Typhöeus. This terrible creature sent the gods fleeing to Egypt, where they hid in various animal forms, leaving Zeus to dispose of TYPHÖEUS. Some say that even Zeus hid for a time in the guise of a ram. According to one tale, the monster cut off and hid the sinews of Zeus's hands and feet, and he would have been permanently incapacitated if Hermes and Aegipan had not rescued and refitted the missing parts. Zeus finally beat down Typhöeus with thunderbolts and flung Sicily on top of him.

After Zeus had succeeded in destroying the Titans, the Giants, and Typhöeus, he was no longer troubled by invaders from the earth, except for the minor annoyance of the boisterous child-giants OTUS AND EPHIALTES. He was beset, however, with at least one domestic revolt in heaven. For unexplained reasons, his wife, Hera, his brother Poseidon, and his daughter Athena rebelled against his authority. They would have bound him if the Oceanid Thetis had not called up BRIAREÜS from Tartarus to dissuade them.

B. Upon being established as ruler of the gods, after the defeat of the Titans, Zeus had begun a series of liaisons with female divinities. The first of these (according to Hesiod) was with Metis. When the Oceanid became pregnant, Ge warned Zeus that, if Metis were to bear a second child, it would be a son who would rule heaven. Zeus emulated his father and swallowed Metis. In due course he had to be delivered of Metis' first child. He called in Prometheus or Hephaestus, who neatly split open Zeus's head with an axe. Out leaped Athena, fully armed.

By the Titaness Themis, an all-wise earth-goddess, Zeus became father of the Seasons—Eunomia (Order), Dike (Justice), and Eirene (Peace)—and the Fates. The Oceanid Eurynome bore him the Graces. By his sister Demeter, he became the father of Persephone; by Mnemosyne (Memory), of the nine Muses. The Titaness Leto gave birth by Zeus to Apollo and Artemis. According to Homer, Aphrodite was Zeus's daughter by Dione. Only after these temporary matches (according to Hesiod) did Zeus enter into a permanent marriage with his sister Hera. She bore Ares, Eileithyia, and Hebe. Hephaestus may also have been her child by Zeus, but in most accounts the artisan-god was conceived by Hera alone as a protest against her husband's independence in producing Athena from his own body.

Zeus's relations with his wife were far from tranquil. Hera's temper was not notably peaceable under any circumstances, and Zeus provided it with more than ample provocation by his incessant seductions of goddesses, nymphs, and mortal women. Hera generally retaliated with relentless persecutions of his mistresses and their offspring. Somehow the shy, retiring Pleiad Maia seems to have escaped Hera's harshness when she gave birth to HERMES [A] in Arcadia. On the other hand, LETO, though a goddess in her own right, suffered the severest hardships through Hera's enmity before she gave birth to Apollo and Artemis. Hera brought about the death of Dionysus' mother SEMELE and nearly prevented Alcmene from bearing HERACLES [A]. Not content with this, she persecuted their children until finally forced to accept them in heaven as fellow divinities. Her cruelty to Heracles was so severe that Zeus, in exasperation, went so far as to hang his wife from heaven for a time with anvils tied to her feet. Zeus and Poseidon vied for the love of Thetis until they learned from Themis or Prometheus that any son that the Oceanid bore was destined to overthrow his father. Both gods withdrew their claims and quickly married Thetis to a mortal, Peleus. Some say, however, that Thetis resisted Zeus's advances out of loyalty to Hera.

C. Zeus's other love affairs were too numerous to record in full. The first mortal whom he seduced was the Argive Niobe, who bore him Argus. Better known among his mistresses was Niobe's aunt Io. After long wanderings forced on her by Hera's jealousy, Io gave birth in Egypt to Epaphus. Zeus took the form of a bull to carry off EUROPA from her Tyrian home to Crete, where she gave birth to three distinguished sons—Minos, Rhadamanthys, and Sarpedon. Zeus became a shower of gold in order to gain entrance to the cell of Danaë, daughter of ACRISIUS, and fathered Perseus by her. In the form of a swan, he seduced either LEDA or NEMESIS, who bore Helen and Polydeuces. Some say that Zeus was the father also of Polydeuces' brother Castor. Two other famous brothers, AMPHION and Zethus, were sons of Zeus by Antiope.

The Pleiades Electra and Taÿgete were seduced by Zeus. The first bore him Dardanus, the second Lacedaemon. Some say that Zeus was the father by the Oceanid Eurynome of the Sicyonian river-god Asopus. Later he abducted Asopus' daughter Aegina and fathered by her Aeacus, who became king of the island that was renamed for her. When Sisyphus told Aegina's father what had happened, Zeus first drove back Asopus, who was pursuing him, then consigned Sisyphus to eternal punishment in Hades. Hera jealously destroyed the inhabitants of Aegina, but Zeus repeopled the island for his son's sake by transforming ants into men. Zeus seduced CALLISTO in Arcadia, then turned her into a bear to hide his deed from Hera. He was no more successful in this objective than when he had made Io a cow. Hera arranged to have Artemis shoot the bear. Zeus managed to save the unborn child, Arcas, and gave him to Maia to rear. He consoled himself for the loss of his mistress by making the bear a constellation.

Zeus was not unaware of the charms of boys. He carried off the Trojan lad GANYMEDE to be his cupbearer, repaying his father for the loss with some splendid horses or perhaps a golden vine. Similarly, he transported the beautiful boy PHAËNON to the stars.

According to the Plataeans, Hera once grew so furious with Zeus, presumably because of his infidelities, that she left Olympus and went home to Euboea. On the advice of the king of Plataea, Zeus let it be known that he was taking a bride and went so far as to dress a wooden image in veils and drive it in a wagon to the top of Mount Cithaeron as if for a wedding. Hera learned of the impending event and hurried to Cithaeron to prevent it. When she discovered the ruse, she was amused, and the divine couple were reconciled for the moment.

D. In spite of his arduous pursuit of mistresses, Zeus found time to rule the universe. His special function was to send rain to fertilize the earth, but he also governed the affairs of gods and men. As with other gods, his justice often consisted in punishing mortals for arrogating to themselves divine prerogatives. He severely punished Salmoneus, Ceÿx, and Alcyone for pretending to be gods; Tantalus and Phineus for giving away divine secrets; Ixion for trespassing on the hospitality of the gods. When Apollo's son Asclepius raised a mortal from the dead, Zeus killed the god of healing with a thunderbolt. Furious, Apollo killed the Cyclopes. Zeus would have hurled his son down to Tartarus if Leto had not interceded for him. Zeus relented and merely forced Apollo to work for a year for a mortal.

Zeus did not entertain a high opinion of the human race. He long withheld from them the barest necessities of life, and cruelly punished PROMETHEUS for his attempts to ease men's lot. He made an attempt to destroy the human race utterly with a great flood, but Prometheus foiled this design by warning his son Deucalion to build a boat. Zeus claimed that he wished to destroy the race for its impiety, which had been demonstrated to him through the plot of LYCAON (1) or his sons to serve the god human flesh to eat. (It was, however, to Zeus himself that Phrixus was to be sacrificed on Mount Laphystius.) According to Ovid, Zeus used the fire started by the wild ride of Phaëthon in the sun-chariot as a pretext for drowning the earth and all its inhabitants. Some say that his real reason for wishing to destroy the race was his distress over the gods' tendency to have children by them—a tendency of which no god had better reason than Zeus to be alarmed.

In spite of his unfriendly feelings toward men, the ruler of Olympus was often their most reliable protector. When the sole survivors of the Flood, Deucalion and Pyrrha, proved themselves pious, Zeus aided them in repeopling the earth. (Some say that Themis showed them how this might be accomplished, but there is no evidence that Zeus opposed her.) The king of the gods was a strong supporter of the rights and prerogatives of human kings, but he also severely punished offenses against suppliants and guests. He dispensed even-handed justice in several disputes between fellow deities, as in the quarrels between Poseidon and Athena over the patronage of Attica and Troezen and in Aphrodite's fight with Persephone over Adonis. More remarkably, Zeus dealt impartially in arguments between gods and men, not only in the case of Apollo and Heracles, both of whom were his sons, but also in the battle between the same god and Idas over Marpessa. In the latter instance, he allowed the girl to make the decision, even though she chose the mortal Idas. Zeus's Olympian detachment deserted him momentarily when, somewhat later, the life of his son Polydeuces was endangered by this same Idas. He killed Idas on the spot.

E. Zeus was at once the most complex god of the Olympian pantheon and, in his essential fidelity to his original nature, one of the simplest. Zeus began and forever remained a god of the sky and all its phenomena. He was equally manifest in the bright depths of the cloudless sky (his name being derived from an Indo-European root meaning "to shine") and in the awesome spectacle of the thunderstorm. He was "the Cloud-gatherer" whose ever-handy weapon was the thunderbolt. Not surprisingly, this imposing figure was looked upon by his worshipers as the all-powerful ruler and father of gods and men. Such was the nature of the chief god that the invading Hellenes are believed to have brought with them from their earlier home, wherever that may have been.

The invaders found nothing comparable to this all-powerful male deity in the Minoan civilization of the Mediterranean area. They did find well established the worship of a different kind of god, seemingly as far removed as possible from Zeus. The principal myth of this god concerned his babyhood and young manhood and, perhaps, his death. His name or his many local names have disappeared (unless one of them was ZAGREUS). Nevertheless, his importance can hardly be doubted, since the Hellenes felt the need of identifying him with their own mighty Zeus, even though the indigenous divinity was worshiped in orgiastic rites comparable to those of Dionysus and seemingly quite inappropriate to the storm god.

The myth of this young god, often called for convenience the Cretan Zeus, was incorporated into that of the Hellenic god as the story of his infancy. The Cretan god's manifestation as a bull survived in the episode of Zeus's abduction of Europa to Crete. The Cretan Zeus's connection with the fertility of the earth was almost lost as his cult was absorbed into that of the Hellenic sky-god, although the latter, as a rain-god, may well have had similar functions at some period before the Hellenes took up the life of nomadic warriors.

It is likely that vestiges of a concept of Zeus as a sky-god married to an earth-goddess survived in the tales of his unions with various local earth-goddesses, such as Semele and Demeter. There is considerable evidence to suggest that Hera, too, was originally an earth-goddess. Some scholars have suspected that the original consort of the Hellenic Zeus was Dione, whose name is the feminine form of Zeus (who is Dios in the genitive), as Juno is of Jupiter. The pre-Hellenic Hera was, however, so well established in several Greek areas that, instead of being supplanted by Dione, she gradually pushed the new-comer far into the background. In the process, Hera lost much of her character as an earth-goddess, a function which probably did not have a compelling significance for the nomadic Hellenes.

Many local gods and *daimones* besides the Cretan god were absorbed by the all-powerful figure of Zeus, including such primitive spirits as KTESIOS and MEILICHIOS. This multiplicity of function ultimately helped to make Zeus so broad and universal a conception that he became a symbol of divinity meaningful even to those with tendencies toward monotheism.

F. Zeus appears so constantly in Greek literature that any attempt at citing extensive sources for his myths would be of little value. Most of these sources can be found in the entries for the personages associated with him in various tales. The best picture of the relatively pure Hellenic view of the god is found in Homer's *Iliad*. A strong admixture of pre-Hellenic, and even Oriental, elements first appears in Hesiod's *Theogony*, which details the god's childhood and rise to power. Zeus does not appear in any extant Classical play except Plautus' comedy *Amphitryon*, but Prometheus' rebellion against the god's seemingly tyrannical use of his absolute power is the subject of Aeschylus' tragedy *Prometheus Bound*. Many of Zeus's love affairs were related by Ovid in his *Metamorphoses*. Apollodorus is an excellent source of the myths of Zeus.

Zeuxippe. The wife of Pandion, king of Athens. Zeuxippe, a Naïad sister of Praxithea, married her nephew Pandion and became the mother of Procne and Philomela, and twin sons, Erechtheus and Butes. [Apollodorus 3.14.8.]

Zminthe. An island of uncertain location. Zminthe, which may be the island usually called Chryse, was the home of the priest Chryses and his children, at least after the Trojan War. Orestes and Iphigeneia, landing there during their flight from the Taurians, would have been returned to the cruel Thoas by Chryses' grandson if he had not learned in time that they, like himself, were children of Agamemnon.

Pronouncing Index

This index offers pronunciations based on patterns of English as it is most widely spoken by persons of some education. These pronunciations frequently differ from those prescribed by some Classicists because the latter seem too often unrelated to ordinary habits of English speech for practical purposes.

The first word of each entry is the commonly known English form of the name, as it appears in an entry title in the text. (Only names important enough to have text entries of their own are included.) For Greek words, this form is generally a latinized spelling of the original (e.g., Antaeüs), though occasionally anglicization has changed it further (Teucer). One or two pronunciations of this word follow it in parentheses.

The word that appears after the parentheses is usually a direct transliteration into English of a Greek name, with the original accent indicated (Antai'os). No attempt is made to indicate the Greek pronunciation beyond the primary stress. The stress mark is placed according to English custom rather than Greek; that is, it does not necessarily fall on a vowel. When the English word differs from the Greek in neither spelling nor accent, the transliteration of the Greek is omitted. If the stress is the same and the only difference is in the last few letters of an unstressed syllable, only these final letters of the Greek form are shown. They should be substituted for the same number of letters in the English form. In the case of Roman names, they too are shown in their original spellings when their anglicized forms are different.

The indications of pronunciation used here are extremely simplified. The signs are confined to the usual ones for long (e.g., ā) and short (ă) vowels and to the schwa (ə), which represents the nondescript sound of *a* in "adore," the second *e* in "enemy," or the *u* in "sinus." Unmarked sounds include *ar*, as in "car"; *au*, as in "taut"; *er*, as in "her"; *oi*, as in "coin"; and *oo*, as in "boot."

Abantes (ə·băn′tēz) Ab′antes
Abas (ăb′əs)
Abdera (ăb·dē′rə)
Abderus (ăb′də·rəs) -os
Absyrtus (ăb·ser′təs) Ab′syrtos
Abydus (ə·bī′dəs) -os
Acacallis (ăk·ə·kăl′əs) Akakal′lis
Acalle (ə·kăl′ē) Akal′le
Acamas (ăk′ə·məs) Ak′amas
Acarnan (ə·kar′nən) Akarnan′

Acarnania (ăk·er·nā′nĭ·ə) Akarnani′a
Acastus (ə·kăs′təs) Ak′astos
Acca Larentia (ăk′ə lə·rĕn′shĭ·ə)
Acestes (ə·sĕs′tēz) Akes′tes
Achaea (ə·kē′ə) Achai′a
Achaeans (ə·kē′ənz) Achai′oi
Achaeüs (ə·kē′əs) Achai′os
Achates (ə·kā′tēz)
Acheloüs (ăk·ə·lō′əs) Achelo′os
Acheron (ăk′ə·rŏn) Ache′ron

Achilles (ə·kĭl'ēz) Achilleus'
Acis (ā'sĭs) A'kis
Acoetes (ə·sē'tēz)
Acrisius (ə·krĭs'ĭ·əs) Akris'ios
acropolis (ə·krŏp'ə·lĭs) akrop'olis
Actaea (ăk·tē'ə) Aktai'a
Actaeon (ăk·tē'ŏn) Aktai'on
Actaeüs (ăk·tē'əs) Aktai'os
Acte (ăk'tē) Ak'te
Actor (ăk'ter) Ak'tor
Admetus (ăd·mē'təs) Ad'metos
Adonis (ə·dŏn'əs)
Adrasteia (ăd·răs·tē'ə) Adras'teia
Adrastus (ə·drăs'təs) Ad'rastos
Aea (ē'ə) Ai'a
Aeacus (ē'ə·kəs) Ai'akos
Aeaea (ē·ē'ə) Aiai'a
Aeëtes (ē·ē'tēz) Aie'tes
Aegae (ē'jē) Aigai'
Aegaeon (ē·jē'ŏn) Aigai'on
Aegeus (ē'jūs, ē'jē·əs) Aigeus'
Aegialeia (ē·jē·ə·lē'ə) Aigial'eia
Aegialeus (ē·jē'ə·lūs) Aigialeus'
Aegialus (ē·jē'ə·ləs) Aigi'alos
Aegimius (ē·jĭm'ĭ·əs) Aigim'ios
Aegina (ē·jī'nə) Ai'gina
Aegipan (ē'jē·păn) Aigi'pan
aegis (ē'jəs) aigis'
Aegisthus (ē·jĭs'thəs) Ai'gisthos
Aegium (ē'jĭ·əm) Ai'gion
Aegle (ē'glē) Ai'gle
Aegyptus (ē·jĭp'təs) Ai'gyptos
Aeneas (ē·nē'əs) Ainei'as
Aeneïd (ē·nē'ĭd)
Aeolia (ē·ō'lĭ·ə) Aioli'a
Aeolus (ē'ə·ləs) Ai'olos
Aepytus (ē'pĭ·təs) Ai'pytos
Aërope (ā·ĕr'ə·pē) Aëro'pe
Aesacus (ē'sə·kəs) Ai'sakos
Aeschylus (ĕs'kə·ləs) Ais'chylos
Aesculapius (ĕs·kū·lā'pĭ·əs)
Aeson (ē'sŏn) Ai'son
Aethalia (ē·thāl'ĭ·ə) Aithali'a
Aethalides (ē·thăl'ə·dēz) Aithali'des
Aether (ē'ther) Aither'
Aethiopis (ē·thē·ō'pĭs) Aithio'pis

Aëthlius (ā·ĕth'lĭ·əs) Aëth'lios
Aethra (ē'thrə) Ai'thra
Aetna (ĕt'nə)
Aetolia (ē·tō'lĭ·ə) Aitoli'a
Aetolus (ē·tō'ləs) Aitolos'
Agamedes (ăg·ə·mē'dēz)
Agamemnon (ăg·ə·mĕm'nŏn)
Agapenor (ăg·ə·pē'nŏr)
Agasthenes (ə·găs'thə·nēz) Agasthen'es
Agave (ə·gā'vē)
Agdistis (ăg·dĭs'tĭs) Ag'distis
Agenor (ə·jē'nŏr)
Aglaea (ə·glē'ə) Aglai'a
Aglaurus (ə·glau'rəs) Ag'lauros
Agraulus (ə·grau'ləs) Ag'raulos
Agrius (ăg'rĭ·əs) -os
Agyïeus (ə·jĭ'ĭ·ūs) Agyïeus'
Aïdoneus (ī·dō'nūs) Aidoneus'
Ajax (ā'jăks) Ai'as
Alalcomenae (ăl·ăl·kŏm'ə·nē)
    Alalkom'enai
Alba Longa (ăl'bə lŏng'gə)
Albula (ăl'bū·lə)
Albunea (ăl·bū'nĭ·ə)
Alcaeüs (ăl·sē'əs) Alkai'os
Alcathoüs (ăl·kăth'ō·əs) Alkatho'os
Alcestis (ăl·sĕs'tĭs) Alkes'tis
Alcidice (ăl·sĭd'ə·sē) Alkidi'ke
Alcimede (ăl·sĭm'ə·dē) Alkime'de
Alcinoüs (ăl·sĭn'ō·əs) Alkin'oös
Alcippe (ăl·sĭp'ē) Alkip'pe
Alcmene (ălk·mē'nē) Alkme'ne
Alcmeon (ălk·mē'ŏn) Alkme'on,
    Alkmai'on
Alcyone (ăl·sī'ə·nē) Alkyo'ne
Alcyoneus (ăl·sī'ə·nūs) Alkyoneus'
Alcyonian (ăl·sē·ō'nĭ·ən)
Alecto, Allecto (ə·lĕk'tō) Alekto',
    Allekto'
Alector (ə·lĕk'tŏr) Alek'tor
Aletes (ə·lē'tēz)
Aleüs (ăl'ĭ·əs) Aleos'
Alexandrus (ăl·ĕk·zăn'drəs) Alex'andros
Almus (ăl'məs) -os
Aloadae (ə·lō'ə·dē) Aloa'dai
Alöeus (ə·lō'ūs) Alöeus'

Alope (ăl'ō·pē) Alo'pe
Alpheius (ăl·fē'əs) Alpheios'
Alphesiboea (ăl·fĕs·ĭ·bē'ə) Alphesi'boia
Althaea (ăl·thē'ə) Althai'a
Althaemenes (ăl·thē'mə·nēz)
    Althaimen'es
Amarynceus (ăm·ə·rĭn'sūs) Amarynkeus'
Amata (ə·mä'tə)
Amazons (ăm'ə·zŏnz) Amazo'nes
Ambracia (ăm·brā'shĭ·ə) Ambraki'a
Amisodarus (ăm·ĭ·sŏ'də·rəs) -os
Amor (ā'mŏr)
Amphianax (ăm·fī'ə·năks) Amphian'ax
Amphiaraüs (ăm·fī·ə·rā'əs) Amphia'raos
Amphictyon (ăm·fĭk'tĭ·ŏn) Amphiktyon'
Amphidamas (ăm·fĭd'ə·məs)
    Amphida'mas
Amphilochus (ăm·fĭl'ə·kəs) Amphilo'chos
Amphimachus (ăm·fĭm'ə·kəs) -os
Amphinomus (ăm·fĭn'ə·məs) -os
Amphion (ăm·fī'ŏn)
Amphithea (ăm·fĭth'ĭ·ə) Amphithe'a
Amphithemis (ăm·fĭth'ə·mĭs)
Amphitrite (ăm·fĭ·trī'tē)
Amphitryon (ăm·fĭt'rĭ·ŏn) Amphitry'on
Amphoterus (ăm·fŏt'ə·rəs) -os
Ampycus (ăm'pĭ·kəs) -kos
Ampyx (ăm'pĭks)
Amulius (ə·mū'lĭ·əs)
Amyclae (ə·mī'klē) -klai
Amyclas (ə·mī'kləs) -klas
Amycus (ăm'ĭ·kəs) -kos
Amymone (ăm·ĭ·mō'nē)
Amyntor (ə·mĭn'tŏr)
Amythaon (ăm·ĭ·thā'ŏn)
Anactoria (ăn·ăk·tŏ'rĭ·ə) Anaktori'a
Anaphe (ăn'ə·fē) Ana'phe
Anatolia (ăn·ə·tŏ'lĭ·ə) Anatoli'a
Anaurus (ə·nau'rəs) An'auros
Anaxagoras (ăn·ăk·săg'ə·rəs) Anaxago'ras
Anaxibia (ăn·ăk·sĭb'ĭ·ə) Anaxibi'a
Anaxo (ə·năk'sō) Anaxo'
Ancaeüs (ăn·sē'əs) Ankai'os
Anchialus (ăn·kī'ə·ləs) -os
Anchises (ăn·kī'sēz)
Ancus Marcius (ăng'kəs mar'shəs)

Ancyra (ăn·sī'rə) An'kyra
Andania (ăn·dā'nĭ·ə) Andani'a
Andraemon (ăn·drē'mŏn) Andrai'mon
Andreïs (ăn·drē'ĭs)
Andreus (ăn'drūs) Andreus'
Androgeüs (ăn·drŏ'jī·əs) Andro'geos
Androgeus (ăn·drŏ'jūs) Androgeus'
Andromache (ăn·drŏm'ə·kē)
    Androma'che
Andromeda (ăn·drŏm'ə·də) Androme'de
Anius (ā'nĭ·əs) -os
Antaeüs (ăn·tē'əs) Antai'os
Anteia (ăn·tē'ə) An'teia
Antenor (ăn·tē'nŏr)
Anthedon (ăn'thə·dŏn) Anthedon'
Anthemoëssa (ăn·thĭ·mō·ĕs'ə)
    Anthemo'essa
Anticleia (ăn·tĭ·klē'ə) Antik'leia
Antigone (ăn·tĭg'ə·nē) Antigo'ne
Antilochus (ăn·tĭl'ə·kəs) -os
Antimachus (ăn·tĭm'ə·kəs) -os
Antinoüs (ăn·tĭn'ō·əs) -os
Antion (ăn·tī'ŏn)
Antiope (ăn·tī'ə·pē) Antio'pe
Antiphates (ăn·tĭf'ə·tēz) Antipha'tes
Antiphus (ăn'tĭ·fəs) -os
Aones (ā·ō'nēz)
Apemosyne (ăp·ə·mŏs'ĭ·nē) Apemosy'ne
Aphaea (ə·fē'ə) Aphai'a
Aphareus (ăf'ər·ūs) Aphareus'
Aphidnae (ə·fĭd'nē) Aph'idnai
Aphrodite (ăf·rō·dī'tē)
Apia (ā'pĭ·ə) Api'a
Apis (ā'pĭs)
Apollo (ə·pŏl'ō) Apol'lon
Apollodorus (ə·pŏl·ə·dō'rəs) Apollod'oros
Apollonius Rhodius (ăp·ə·lō'nĭ·əs
    rō'dĭ·əs) -os -os
Apsyrtides (ăp·ser'tĭ·dēz) Apsyrti'des
Apsyrtus (ăp·ser'təs) Ap'syrtos
Apulia (ə·pū'lĭ·ə)
Aquarius (ə·kwĕr'ĭ·əs)
Aquila (ăk'wĭ·lə)
Aquilo (ăk'wĭ·lō)
Arabus (ĕr'ə·bəs) -os
Arachne (ə·răk'nē)

Araethyrea (ĕr·ē·thī′rĭ·ə) Araithyre′a

Arantia (ə·răn′shĭ·ə) Aranti′a

Aras (ā′rəs) Aras′

Arcadia (ar·kā′dĭ·ə) Arkadi′a

Arcas (ar′kəs) Arkas′

Arceisius (ar·sē′zĭ·əs) Arkei′sios

Arcesilaüs (ar·sĕs·ə·lā′əs) Arkesil′aos

Archemorus (ar·kə·mō′rəs) Archem′oros

Arctophylax (ark·tō·fī′läks) Arktophy′lax

Arctos (ark′tŏs) Ark′tos

Ardea (ar′dē·ə)

Areius (ə·rē′əs) -os

Arene (ə·rē′nē)

Areopagus (ĕr·ē·ŏp′ə·gəs) Areiop′agos

Ares (ā′rēz, ĕr′ēz)

Arete (ə·rē′tē)

Arethusa (ĕr·ə·thū′zə) Areth′ousa

Argeia (ar·jē′ə)

Argeius (ar·jē′əs) -os

Argives (ar′jīvz, ar′gīvz) Arge′ioi

Argolis (ar′gə·lĭs)

Argonautica (ar·gə·nau′tĭ·kə)

Argonauts (ar′gə·nautz) Argonau′tai

Argos (ar′gŏs)

Argus (ar′gəs) -os

Argyripa (ar·jĭr′ĭ·pə)

Ariadne (ĕr·ĭ·ăd′nē)

Aricia (ə·rĭsh′ĭ·ə)

Aries (ā′rĭ·ēz, ĕr′ĭ·ēz)

Arimaspi (ĕr·ĭ·măs′pī) -oi

Arion (ə·rī′ən)

Arisbe (ə·rĭz′bē)

Aristaeüs (ĕr·ĭs·tē′əs) Aristai′os

Aristeas (ĕr·ĭs·tē′əs)

Aristodemus (ə·rĭs·tō·dē′məs)
  Aristod′emos

Aristomachus (ĕr·ĭs·tŏm′ə·kəs) -os

Arsinoë (ar·sĭn′ō·ē) Arsino′e

Artemis (ar′tə·mĭs)

Ascalabus (ăs·kăl′ə·bəs) Askal′abos

Ascalaphus (ăs·kăl′ə·fəs) Askal′aphos

Ascanius (ăs·kā′nĭ·əs)

Asclepius (ăs·klē′pĭ·əs) Askle′pios

Asia (ā′zhə) Asi′a

Asius (ā′zĭ·əs) -os

Asopia (ə·sō′pĭ·ə) Asopi′a

Asopus (ə·sō′pəs) Asopos′

asphodel (ăs′fə·dĕl)

Assaracus (ə·sĕr′ə·kəs) -kos

Astacus (ăs′tə·kəs) -kos

Asteria (ăs·tĭr′ĭ·ə) Asteri′e

Asterion (ăs·tĭr′ĭ·ŏn) Asteri′on

Asterius (ăs·tĭr′ĭ·əs) -os

Asterope (ăs·tĕr′ə·pē) Astero′pe

Astraeüs (ăs·trē′əs) Astrai′os

Astyagyïa (ăs·tĭ·ə·jī′ĭ·ə)

Astyanax (ăs·tī′ə·năks) Astyan′ax

Astydameia (ăs·tĭ·də·mē′ə) Astyda′meia

Astypalaea (ăs·tĭ·pə·lē′ə) Astypalai′a

Atalanta (ăt·ə·lăn′tə) Atalan′te

Atalante (ăt·ə·lăn′tē)

Athamania (ăth·ə·mā′nĭ·ə) Athamani′a

Athamantia (ăth·ə·măn′shĭ·ə)
  Athamanti′a

Athamas (ăth′ə·məs) Atha′mas

Athena (ə·thē′nə)

Athene (ə·thē′nē)

Athens (ăth′nz) Athe′nai

Atlas (ăt′ləs)

Atreidae (ə·trī′dē) -ai

Atreus (ā′trūs, ā′trē·əs) Atreus′

Atropos (ăt′rō·pŏs)

Attica (ăt′ĭ·kə) Attike′

Attis, Atys (ăt′ĭs)

Atymnius (ə·tĭm′nĭ·əs) -os

Auge (au′jē)

Augeias, Augeas (au·jē′əs)

Aulis (au′lĭs)

Auriga (au′rĭ·gə)

Aurora (ə·rō′rə)

Ausonia (au·sō′nĭ·ə) Ausoni′a

Autesion (au·tē′sĭ·ŏn) Autesi′on

autochthon (au·tŏk′thŏn)

Autolycus (au·tŏl′ĭ·kəs) -kos

Automedon (au·tŏm′ĭ·dŏn) Automed′on

Autonoë (au·tŏn′ō·ē) Autono′e

Aventinus (ăv·ən·tī′nəs)

Avernus (ə·ver′nəs)

Axion (ăk′sē·ŏn) Axi′on

Azania (ə·zā′nĭ·ə) Azani′a

Bacchus (băk'əs) Bak'chos
Balius (bā'lǐ·əs) -os
Bateia (bā'tǐ·ə)
Baton (bā'tŏn)
Battus (băt'əs) -os
Baucis (bau'sǐs) -kis
Bebryces (bĕb'rǐ·sēz) -kes
Bellerophon (bĕ·lĕr'ə·fŏn) Bellerophon'
Bellerophontes (bĕ·lĕr·ə·fŏn'tēz)
Bellona (bĕ·lō'nə)
Belus (bĕ'ləs) -os
Benthesicyme (bĕn·thə·sǐ·kǐ'mē)
    Benthesiky'me
Beroë (bĕ·rō'ē)
Bia (bī'ə)
Bias (bī'əs)
Bistones (bǐs·tō'nēz) Bis'tones
Bithynia (bǐ·thǐn'ǐ·ə) Bithyni'a
Boeotia (bē·ō'shǐ·ə) Boioti'a
Bona Dea (bō'nə dē'ə)
Boötes (bō·ō'tēz)
Boreades (bō·rē'ə·dēz) Borea'dai
Boreas (bō'rē·əs) Bore'as
Borus (bō'rəs) -os
Bosporus (bŏs'pə·rəs) -os
Brasiae (brăs'ǐ·ē) Brasiai'
Brauron (brau'rŏn) Brauron'
Briareüs (brǐ·ĕr'ǐ·əs) -os
Briseïs (brǐ·sē'is)
Britomartis (brǐt·ō·mar'tǐs) Britom'artis
Bromios (brō'mǐ·ŏs)
Broteas (brō'tǐ·əs) Brote'as
Brygeian (brǐ·jē'ən)
Brygi (brī'jī) -oi
Bunus (bū'nəs) Bou'nos
Busiris (bū·sī'rǐs) Bou'siris
Butes (bū'tēz) Bou'tes
Buthrotum (bū·thrō'təm) Bouthro'ton
Byblis (bǐb'lǐs) Byblis'
Byblus (bǐb'ləs) -os

Cabeiri (kə·bī'rī) Kab'eiroi
Cacus (kā'kəs)
Cadmeia (kăd·mē'ə) Kadmei'a
Cadmus (kăd'məs) Kad'mos

caduceus (kə·dū'sǐ·əs)
Caeculus (sē'kū·ləs)
Caeneus (sē'nūs) Kaineus'
Caenis (sē'nǐs) Kai'nis
Calaïs (kăl'ā·ǐs) Kalaïs'
Calaureia (kə·lau'rǐ·ə) Kalaurei'a
Calchas (kăl'kəs) Kal'chas
Callidice (kə·lǐd'ǐ·sē) Kallidi'ke
Calliope (kə·lī'ə·pē) Kallio'pe,
    Kallio'peia
Callirrhoë, Callirhoë (kə·lǐr'ō·ē)
    Kallirrho'e, Kallirho'e
Calliste (kə·lǐs'tē) Kallis'te
Callisto (kə·lǐs'tō) Kallisto'
Calyce (kăl'ǐ·sē) Kaly'ke
Calydon (kăl'ǐ·dŏn) Kalydon'
Calypso (kə·lǐp'sō) Kalypso'
Cameirus (kə·mī'rəs) Kam'eiros
Camenae (kə·mē'nē)
Camilla (kə·mǐl'ə)
Canace (kăn'ə·sē) Kana'ke
Canens (kăn'ĕnz)
Canicula (kə·nǐk'ū·lə)
Canis (kā'nǐs)
Canobus (kə·nō'bəs)
Canopus (kə·nō'pəs)
Canthus (kăn'thəs) Kan'thos
Capaneus (kăp'ə·nūs) Kapaneus'
Caphareus (kə·fĕr'ūs) Kaphareus'
Caphaurus (kə·fau'rəs) Kaph'auros
Capra (kăp'rə)
Capricorn (kăp'rǐ·kŏrn) Capricor'nus
Capys (kăp'ǐs) Kap'ys
Car (kar) Kar
Caria (kĕr'ǐ·ə) Kari'a
Carme (kar'mē) Kar'me
Carmenta (kar·mĕn'tə)
Carmentis (kar·mĕn'tǐs)
Carnabon (kar'nə·bŏn)
Carpathus (kar'pə·thəs) Kar'pathos
Carthage (kar'thǐj) Cartha'go
Cassandra (kə·săn'drə) Kassan'dra
Cassiopeia (kăs·ǐ·ō·pē'ə) Kassio'peia
Castor (kăs'ter) Kas'tor
Catamitus (kăt·ə·mī'təs)

Catreus (kăt′rūs) Katreus′

Caunus (kau′nəs) Kau′nos

Cebren (sē′brən) Kebren′

Cebriones (sə·brī′ə·nēz) Kebrio′nes

Cecropia (sē·krō′pĭ·ə) Kekropi′a

Cecrops (sē′krŏps) Kek′rops

Cedalion (sə·dā′lĭ·ŏn) Kedali′on

Ceisus (sē′səs) Kei′sos

Celaeno (sē·lē′nō) Kelaino′

Celeüs (sē′lĭ·əs) Keleos′

Centaur (sĕn′taur) Ken′tauros

Centaurus (sĕn·tau′rəs) Ken′tauros

Cephalion (sə·fā′lĭ·ŏn) Kephali′on

Cephallenia (sĕf·ə·lē′nĭ·ə) Kephalleni′a

Cephalus (sĕf′ə·ləs) Keph′alos

Cepheus (sē′fūs) Kepheus′

Cephissus (sə·fĭs′əs) Kephissos′

Cephisus (sə·fī′səs) Kephissos′

Ceraunian (sə·rau′nĭ·ən)

Cerberus (ser′bə·rəs) Ker′beros

Cercopes (ser·kō′pēz) Ker′kopes

Cerdo (ser′dō) Kerdo′

Ceres (sēr′ēz, sĭr′ēz)

Cerynitian (sĕr·ĭ·nĭsh′ĭ·ən)

Cestrinus (sĕs·trī′nəs) Kestri′nos

Ceto (sē′tō) Keto′

Cetus (sē′təs)

Ceüs (sē′əs) Ke′os

Ceÿx (sē′ĭks) Ke′yx

Chalciope (kăl·kī′ō·pē) Chalkio′pe

Chalcodon (kăl·kō′dŏn) Chalkodon′

Chalybes (kăl′ĭ·bēz)

Chaos (kā′ŏs)

Charon (kĕr′ŏn)

Charybdis (kə·rĭb′dĭs) Char′ybdis

Cheiron (kī′rŏn)

Chimaera (kĭ·mē′rə) Chimai′ra

Chione (kī′ō·nē) Chio′ne

Chios (kī′ŏs)

Chloris (klō′rĭs) Chloris′

Chrysaor (krĭ·sā′ŏr)

Chryse (krī′sē)

Chryseïs (krī·sē′ĭs)

Chryses (krī′sēz)

Chrysippus (krī·sĭp′əs) Chrys′ippos

Chrysothemis (krī·sŏth′ĭ·mĭs)

Chthon (thŏn)

chthonian (thō′nĭ·ən)

Chthonius (thō′nĭ·əs) -os

Chthonophyle (thō·nŏ·fī′lē)

Cicones (sĭ·kō′nēz) Kik′ones

Cilicia (sĭ·lĭsh′ĭ·ə) Kiliki′a

Cilix (sĭl′ĭks) Kil′ix

Cinyras (sĭn′ĭ·rəs) Kiny′ras

Circe (ser′sē) Kir′ke

Cithaeron (sĭ·thē′rŏn) Kithairon′

Cius (sī′əs) Ki′os

Cleio (klē′ō) Kleio′

Cleite (klī′tē) Klei′te

Cleitus (klī′təs) Klei′tos

Cleodaeüs (klē·ŏd′ĭ·əs) Kleod′aios

Cleopatra (klē·ō·pā′trə) Kleopa′tra

Clotho (klō′thō) Klotho′

Clymene (klĭm′ə·nē) Klyme′ne

Clymenus (klĭm′ə·nəs) Klym′enos

Clytemnestra (klī·təm·nĕs′trə)
    Klytaimnes′tra, Klytaimes′tra

Clytië (klī′tĭ·ē) Klyti′e

Clytius (klī′tĭ·əs) Klyt′ios

Cnossus (nŏs′əs) Knos′sos

Cocalus (kō′kə·ləs) Ko′kalos

Cocytus (kə·sī′təs) Kokytos

Codrus (kŏd′rəs) Kod′ros

Coeüs (sē′əs) Koi′os

Colchis (kŏl′kĭs) Kolchis′

Collatinus (kŏl·ə·tī′nəs)

Comaetho (kō·mē′thō) Komaitho′

Consus (kŏn′səs)

Copreus (kŏp′rūs) Kopreus

Corcyra (kŏr·sī′rə) Ker′kyra

cordax (kŏr′dăks) kor′dax

Core (kō′rē) Ko′re

Coresus (kŏr′ə·səs) Kor′esos

Corinth (kŏr′ĭnth) Kor′inthos

Corinthus (kə·rĭn′thəs) Kor′inthos

Coroebus (kō·rē′bəs) Kor′oibos

Corona Borealis (kə·rō′nə bō·rē·ăl′ĭs)

Coronis (kə·rō′nĭs) Koronis′

Coronus (kə·rō′nəs) Koronos′

Corvus (kŏr′vəs)

Corybantes (kŏr·ĭ·băn′tēz) Kory′bantes
Corynetes (kŏr·ĭ·nē′tēz) Koryn′etes
Cos (kŏs) Kos
Cottus (kŏt′əs) Kot′tos
Cranaüs (krə·nā′əs) Kranaos′
Crataeïs (krə·tē′ĭs) Krataiïs′
Crataïs (krə·tī′ĭs) Krataiïs′
Crater (krā′ter)
Cratus (krā′təs) Kra′tos
Creon (krē′ŏn) Kre′on
Cresphontes (krĕs·fŏn′tēz) Kresphon′tes
Crete (krē′tē) Kre′te
Cretheus (krē′thūs) Kretheus′
Creüsa (krē·ū′sə) Kre′ousa
Crissus (krĭs′əs) Kris′sos
Crisus (krī′səs) Kri′sos
Crius (krī′əs) Kri′os
Crommyonian (krŏm·ĭ·ō′nĭ·ən)
Cronian (krō′nĭ·ən)
Cronus (krō′nəs) Kro′nos
Cteatus (ktē′ə·təs) Kte′atos
Cupid (kū′pĭd) Cu′pido
Cures (kū′rēz)
Curetes (kū·rē′tēz) Koure′tes
Cyanean (sī·ā′nĭ·ən)
Cybebe (sĭ·bē′bē) ⟂ybe′be
Cybele (sĭb′ĭ·lē) Kybe′le
Cychreus (sĭk′rūs) Kychreus′
Cyclopes (sī·klō′pēz) Kyk′lopes
Cycnus (sĭk′nəs) Kyk′nos
Cygnus (sĭg′nəs)
Cyllene (sĭ·lē′nē) Kylle′ne
Cynortas (sī·nŏr′təs) Kynor′tas
Cynortes (sī·nŏr′tēz) Kynor′tes
Cynthia (sĭn′thĭ·ə) Kynthi′a
Cyparissus (sī·pĕr′ĭ·səs) Kypar′issos
Cypria (sĭp′rē·ə) Kyp′ria
Cypris (sĭp′rĭs) Kypris′
Cyprus (sī′prəs) Ky′pros
Cypselus (sĭp′sə·ləs) Kyp′selos
Cyrene (sī·rē′nē) Kyre′ne
Cythera (sĭ·thē′rə) Kythe′ra
Cytisorus (sī·tĭs′ə·rəs) Kytis′oros
Cytissorus (sī·tĭs′ə·rəs) Kytis′soros
Cyzicus (sĭz′ĭ·kəs) Kyz′ikos

Dactyls (dăk′tĭlz) Dak′tyloi
Daedalion (dē·dā′lĭ·ŏn) Daidali′on
Daedalus (dĕd′ə·ləs) Dai′dalos
daemon (dē′mŏn) dai′mon
daimon (dī′mŏn)
Damastes (də·măs′tēz)
Danaë (dăn′ā·ē) Dana′ë
Danaïdes (də·nā′ĭ·dēz) Danai′des
Danaüs (dăn′ā·əs) Danaos′
Daphne (dăf′nē)
Dardania (dar·dā′nĭ·ə) Dardani′a
Dardanus (dar′də·nəs) -os
Dascylus (dăs′kĭ·ləs) Das′kylos
Deïaneira (dē·ə·nī′rə) Deïan′eira
Deïmachus (dē·ĭm′ə·kəs) -os
Deimus (dē′məs) -os
Deïon (dē·ē′ŏn)
Deïphobus (dē·ĭf′ə·bəs) -os
Deïphontes (dē·ĭ·fŏn′tēz)
Deïpyle (dē·ĭp′ĭ·lē) Deipy′le
Delia (dē′lĭ·ə) Deli′a
Delos (dē′lŏs)
Delphi (dĕl′fī) Delphoi′
Delphinius (dĕl·fĭn′ĭ·əs) -os
Delphinus (dĕl·fī′nəs)
Delphyne (dĕl·fī′nē)
Demeter (dē·mē′ter)
Demodice (dē·mŏd′ĭ·sē) Demodi′ke
Demodoce (dē·mŏd′ə·kē) Demodo′ke
Demonassa (dē·mō·năs′ə) Demon′assa
Demonice (dē·mŏn′ĭ·sē) Demoni′ke
Demophon (dĕm′ō·fŏn) Demophon′
Demophoön (dē·mŏf′ō·ŏn) Demopho′on
Dendrites (dĕn·drī′tēz)
Deo (dē′ō) Deo′
Despoina (dĕs·poi′nə) Des′poina
Deucalion (dū·kā′lĭ·ən) Deukali′on
Dexamenus (dĕk·săm′ə·nəs) Dexamenos′
Dia (dī′ə)
Diana (dī·ăn′ə)
Dicte (dĭk′tē) Dik′te
Dictynna (dĭk·tĭn′ə) Dik′tynna
Dictys (dĭk′tĭs) Dik′tys
Dido (dī′dō)
Dike (dī′kē)

Dindymene (dĭn·dĭ·mē′nē)
Dindymus (dĭn′dĭ·məs)
Diodorus Siculus (dī·ə·dō′rəs sĭk′ū·ləs)
   Diod′oros Sik′ylos
Diomedes (dī·ō·mē′dēz)
Dione (dī·ō′nē)
Dionysus (dī·ō·nī′səs) Dion′ysos
Diores (dī·ō′rēz)
Dioscuri (dī·əs·kū′rī) Dioskou′roi
Dirce (der′sē) -ke
Dis (dĭs)
Dius (dī′əs) -os
Dodona (dō·dō′nə)
Doliche (dō·lĭ′kē)
Doliones (dō·lē·ō′nēz)
Dolius (dō′lĭ·əs) Doli′os
Dolon (dō′lŏn)
Doris (dō′rĭs, dōr′ĭs)
Dorus (dō′rəs) -os
Doso (dō′sō) Doso′
Draco (drā′kō)
Drepane (drə·pā′nē)
dryad (drī′ăd) dry′as
Dryas (drī′əs)
Dryope (drī′ə·pē) Dryo′pe
Dryopes (drī·ō′pēz)

Echemus (ĕk′ə·məs) -os
Echetus (ĕk′ə·təs) -os
Echidna (ē·kĭd′nə) Ech′idna
Echinades (ē·kī′nə·dēz) Echina′des
Echinadian (ĕk·ĭ·nā′dĭ·ən)
Echion (ē·kī′ŏn)
Echo (ĕk′ō) Echo′
Ectenes (ĕk′tə·nēz) Ek′tenes
Edoni (ē·dō′nī) Edonoi′
Edonians (ē·dō′nĭ·ənz)
Eëriboea (ē·ĕr·ĭ·bē′ə) Eëri′boia
Eëtion (ē·ēt′ĭ·ŏn) Eëti′on
Egeria (ē·jĭr′ĭ·ə)
Egypt (ē′jĭpt) Ai′gyptos
Eidothea (ē·dō′thĭ·ə) Eidothe′a
Eidyia (ī·dī·ī′ə)
Eileithyia (ī·lī·thī′yə) Eilei′thyia
Eioneus (ē·ō′nūs) Eioneus′
Eirene (ī·rē′nē)

Elatus (ĕl′ə·təs) -os
Elba (ĕl′bə)
Electra (ē·lĕk′trə) Elek′tra
Electryon (ē·lĕk′trĭ·ŏn) Elektry′on
Eleius (ē·lē′əs) -os
Elephenor (ĕl·ə·fē′nŏr)
Eleusinus (ĕl·ū·sī′nəs) Eleu′sinos
Eleusis (ē·lū′sĭs) Eleusis′
Eleutherae (ē·lū′thə·rē) Eleutherai′
Elicius (ē·lĭsh′ĭ·əs)
Elis (ē′lĭs)
Elissa (ē·lĭs′sə)
Elpenor (ĕl·pē′nŏr)
Elysium (ē·lĭz′ĭ·əm, ē·lĭzh′ĭ·əm) Elys′ion
Enceladus (ĕn·sĕl′ə·dəs) Enkel′ados
Endeïs (ĕn·dē′ĭs) Endeïs′
Endymion (ĕn·dĭm′ĭ·ŏn) Endymi′on
Enna (ĕn′ə)
Enyalius (ĕn·ĭ·ā′lĭ·əs) -os
Enyo (ē·nī′ō) Enyo′
Eoiae (ē·oi′ē) Ehoi′ai
Eos (ē′ŏs) Eos′, E′os
Eosphorus (ē·ŏs′fə·rəs) -os
Epaphus (ĕp′ə·fəs) -os
Epeirus (ĕp′ī·rəs) -os
Epeius (ē·pē′əs) Epeios′
Ephialtes (ĕf·ĭ·ăl′tēz)
Ephyra (ĕf′ĭ·rə) Ephy′re
Ephyre (ĕf′ĭ·rē) Ephy′re
Epicaste (ĕp·ĭ·kăs′tē) Epikas′te
Epidaurus (ĕp·ĭ·dau′rəs) Epi′dauros
Epigoni (ē·pĭg′ō·nī) -oi
Epimetheus (ĕp·ĭ·mē′thūs)
eponym (ĕp′ə·nĭm)
Epopeus (ē·pō′pūs) Epopeus′
Erato (ĕr′ə·tō) Erato′
Erebus (ĕr′ə·bəs) -os
Erechtheus (ē·rĕk′thūs) Erechtheus′
Erginus (ĕr·jī′nəs) -os
Eribotes (ĕr·ĭ·bō′tēz)
Erichthonius (ĕr·ĭk·thō′nĭ·əs) -os
Eridanus (ē·rĭd′ə·nəs) Eridanos′
Erigone (ē·rĭg′ə·nē) Erigo′ne
Erinyes (ē·rĭn′ĭ·ēz) Eriny′es
Eriopis (ĕr·ĭ·ō′pĭs)
Eriphyle (ĕr·ĭ·fī′lē)

Eris (ē′rĭs, er′ĭs)

Eros (ē′rŏs, er′ŏs)

Erymanthian (ĕr·ĭ·măn′thĭ·ən)

Erymanthus (ĕr·ĭ·măn′thəs) Ery′manthos

Erysichthon (ĕr·ĭ·sĭk′thŏn)

Erytheia (ĕr·ĭ·thē′ə) Ery′theia

Erythras (ē·rē′thrəs)

Erythrius (ē·rĭth′rĭ·əs) -os

Erytus (ĕr′ĭ·təs) -os

Eryx (ĕr′ĭks)

Etearchus (ē·tē·ar′kəs) Ete′archos

Eteocles (ē·tē′ō·klēz) Eteokles′

Eteoclus (ē·tē′ō·kləs) -os

etesian (ē·tē′zhĭ·ən)

Ethiopia (ē·thĭ·ō′pĭ·ə) Aithiopi′a

Etna (ĕt′nə)

Etruscans (ē·trŭs′kənz)

Euboea (ū·bē′ə) Eu′boia

Euchenor (ū·kē′nŏr)

Euippe (ū·ĭp′pē)

Eumaeüs (ū·mē′əs) Eu′maios

Eumelus (ū·mē′ləs) Eu′melos

Eumenides (ū·mĕn′ĭ·dēz) Eumeni′des

Eumolpus (ū·mŏl′pəs) Eu′molpos

Euneüs (ū′nĭ·əs) Eu′neos

Eunomia (ū·nō′mĭ·ə) Eunomi′a

Eunomus (ū′nə·məs) -os

Eupeithes (ū·pī′thēz)

Euphemus (ū′fə·məs) -os

Euripides (ū·rĭp′ĭ·dēz)

Euripus (ū·rī′pəs) Eu′ripos

Europa (ū·rō′pə) -pe

Eurotas (ū·rō′təs)

Euryalus (ū·rī′ə·ləs) -os

Eurybates (ū·rĭ·bā′tēz)

Eurybia (ū·rĭb′ĭ·ə) Eurybi′e

Eurycleia (ū·rĭ·klē′ə, ū·rĭ·klī′ə)
    Euryklei′a

Eurycyda (ū·rĭ·sī′də) Euryky′de

Eurydamas (ū·rĭd′ə·məs) Euryda′mas

Eurydice (ū·rĭd′ĭ·sē) Eurydi′ke

Euryganeia (ū·rĭ·gə·nē′ə) Euryga′neia

Eurygyes (ū·rĭ·jī′ēz)

Eurylochus (ū·rĭl′ə·kəs) -os

Eurymachus (ū·rĭm′ə·kəs) -os

Eurymede (ū·rĭ·mē′dē)

Eurynome (ū·rĭn′ə·mē) Euryno′me

Euryphaëssa (ū·rĭ·fā·ĕs′ə) Eurypha′essa

Eurypylus (ū·rĭp′ĭ·ləs) -os

Eurysaces (ū·rĭ·sā′sēz) -kes

Eurysthenes (ū·rĭs′thə·nēz) Eurysthen′es

Eurystheus (ū·rĭs′thūs) Eurystheus′

Euryte (ū·rī′tē)

Eurytion (ū·rĭt′ĭ·ŏn) Euryti′on

Eurytus (ū′rĭ·təs) -os

Euterpe (ū·ter′pē)

Euthymus (ū·thī′məs) Eu′thymos

Euxine (ūk′sĭn, ūk′sīn)

Evadne (ē·văd′nē)

Evander (ē·văn′der) Eu′andros

Evenus (ē·vē′nəs) Eu′enos

Fauna (fau′nə)

Fauni (fau′nī)

Faunus (fau′nəs)

Faustulus (faus′tū·ləs)

Flora (flō′rə)

Fortuna (fŏr·tū′nə)

Gabii (gā′bĭ·ī)

Gaea (jē′ə) Gai′a

Gaia (gā′ə, gī′ə)

Galanthis (gə·lăn′thĭs) Galanthis′

Galatea (găl·ə·tē′ə) Gala′teia

Ganymede (găn·ĭ·mē′dē)

Ganymedes (găn·ĭ·mē′dēz)

Ge (jē, gā)

Gebeleïzis (jĕb·ĕl·ē′ĭ·zĭs)

Gegeneës (gā·gĕ·nē′ēz)

Gelanor (jĕ·lā′nŏr)

Gemini (jĕm′ĭ·nī)

Gerenia (jə·rē′nĭ·ə) Gereni′a

Geryon (jē·rī′ŏn, gĕr′ē·ŏn) Geryon′

Geryones (jə·rī′ō·nēz)

Giants (jī′ənts) Gi′gantes

Glauce (glau′sē) -ke

Glaucus (glau′kəs) -kos

Gorge (gŏr′jē)

Gorgons (gŏr′gənz) Gorgo′nes

Gorgophone (gŏr·gŏf′ə·nē) Gorgopho′ne

Graces (grā′səz) Gra′tiae

Gradivus (grə·dī′vəs)

Graeae (grē′ē) Grai′ai
Guneus (gū′nūs) Gouneus′
Gyes (jī′ēz)

Hades (hā′dēz) Ai′des, Hai′des
Haemon (hē′mŏn) Hai′mon
Haemus (hē′məs) Hai′mos
Haliartus (hăl·ĭ·ar′təs) Hali′artos
Halirrhothius (hăl·ĭ·rō′thĭ·əs) -os
Halitherses (hăl·ĭ·ther′sēz)
Halys (hā′lĭs)
hamadryad (hăm′ə·drī′ăd) hamadry′as
Harmonia (har·mŏ′nĭ·ə) Harmoni′a
Harpies (har′pēz) Har′pyai
Harpina (har·pī′nə) Har′pina
Hebe (hē′bē)
Hebrus (hē′brəs) -os
Hecabe (hĕk′ə·bē) Heka′be
Hecate (hĕk′ə·tē) Heka′te
Hecatoncheires (hĕk·ə·tŏn·kī′rēz)
    Hekaton′cheires
Hector (hĕk′ter) Hek′tor
Hecuba (hĕk′ū·bə) Heka′be
Heleius (hē·lē′əs) Hel′eios
Helen (hĕl′ən) Hele′ne
Helenus (hĕl′ə·nəs) -os
Heliades (hē·lī′ə·dēz) Helia′dai,
    Helia′des
Helicaon (hĕl·ĭ·kā′ŏn) Helika′on
Helice (hĕl′ĭ·sē) Heli′ke
Helicon (hĕl′ĭ·kŏn) Helikon′
Helius (hē′lĭ·əs) -os
Helle (hĕl′ē)
Hellen (hĕl′ən)
Hellenes (hĕl′ēnz)
Hellespont (hĕl′əs·pŏnt) Helles′pontos
Hemera (hē′mer·ə) Hemer′a
Henna (hĕn′ə, ĕn′ə)
Hephaestus (hē·fĕs′təs) He′phaistos
Hera (hē′rə) He′ra, He′re
Heracleidae (hĕr·ə·klī′dē) Heraklei′dai
Heracles (hĕr′ə·klēz) Herakles′
Heraclids (hĕr′ə·klĭdz)
Heraean (hē·rē′ən)
Hercules (her′kū·lēz)
herma (her′mə)

Hermaphroditus (her·măf·rō·dī′təs)
    Hermaphrod′itos
Hermes (her′mēz) Hermes′, Hermei′as
Hermione (her·mī′ō·nē) Hermio′ne
Herodotus (hə·rŏd′ə·təs) -os
Herse (her′sē)
Hesiod (hē′sĭ·əd, hĕs′ĭ·əd) Hesi′odos
Hesione (hē·sī′ō·nē) Hesio′ne
Hespereia (hĕs·pĭr′ĭ·ə) Hesperei′a
Hesperia (hĕs·pĭr′ĭ·ə) Hesperei′a
Hesperides (hĕs·pĕr′ĭ·dēz) Hesperi′des
Hestia (hĕs′tĭ·ə) Hesti′a
Hicetaon (hĭ·kĕt′ā·ŏn) Hiketa′on
Hiläeira (hĭl·ā·ē′rə) Hila′eira
Hippalcimus (hĭ·păl′sĭ·məs)
    Hippal′kimos
Hippalmus (hĭ·păl′məs) Hip′palmos
Hippasus (hĭp′ə·səs) -os
Hippocoön (hĭ·pŏk′ō·ŏn) Hippoko′on
Hippocrene (hĭp·ō·krē′nē) Hippokre′ne
Hippodamas (hĭ·pŏd′ə·məs)
    Hippoda′mas
Hippodameia (hĭp·ə·də·mī′ə)
    Hippoda′meia
Hippolochus (hĭ·pŏl′ə·kəs) -os
Hippolyte (hĭ·pŏl′ĭ·tē) Hippoly′te
Hippolytus (hĭ·pŏl′ĭ·təs) -os
Hippomedon (hĭ·pŏm′ə·dŏn)
    Hippomed′on
Hippomenes (hĭ·pŏm′ə·nēz)
    Hippomen′es
Hipponome (hĭ·pŏn′ə·mē) Hippono′me
Hipponoüs (hĭ·pŏn′ō·əs) -os
Hippostratus (hĭ·pŏs′trə·təs) -os
Hippothoë (hĭ·pŏth′ō·ē) Hippotho′e
Hippothoön (hĭ·pŏth′ō·ŏn)
Hippothoüs (hĭ·pŏth′ō·əs) -os
Homer (hō′mer) Ho′meros
Horae (hō′rē) Ho′rai
Horatius (hō·rā′shəs)
Hyacinth (hī′ə·sĭnth) Hyak′inthos
Hyades (hī′ə·dēz) Hya′des
Hyantes (hī·ăn′tēz) Hy′antes
Hydra (hī′drə)
Hyettus (hī·ĕt′əs) Hy′ettos
Hygieia (hĭ·jē′ə)

Hyginus (hĭ·jī′nəs)

Hylas (hī′ləs)

Hylleans (hĭ·lē′ənz)

Hyllus (hĭl′əs) -os

Hymen (hī′mən)

Hymenaeüs (hī·mə·nē′əs) Hymen′aios

Hyperboreans (hī·per·bō′rĭ·ənz)
　　Hyperbo′reioi

Hypereia (hī·pĭr′ĭ·ə) Hyperei′a

Hyperenor (hī·per·ē′nôr)

Hyperion (hī·pĭr′ĭ·ən) Hyperi′on

Hypermnestra (hī·perm·nĕs′trə)

Hypnos (hĭp′nŏs)

Hypseus (hĭp′sūs) Hypseus′

Hypsipyle (hĭp·sĭp′ĭ·lē)

Hyria (hī·rē′ə) Hyri′e

Hyrieus (hī′rĭ·ūs) Hyrieus′

Hyrmina (her·mī′nə)

Hyrtacus (her′tə·kəs) -kos

Iacchus (ĭ·ăk′əs) I′akchos

Ialmenus (ĭ·ăl′mə·nəs) -os

Iambe (ĭ·ăm′bē)

Iamus (ĭ′ə·məs) -os

Iapetus (ĭ·ăp′ə·təs) Iapetos′

Iarbas (ĭ·ar′bəs)

Iasion (ĭ·ā′sĭ·ŏn) Iasi′on

Iasus (ĭ′ə·səs) -os

Icaria (ĭ·kĕr′ĭ·ə) Ikari′a

Icarius (ĭ·kĕr′ĭ·əs) Ikar′ios

Icarus (ĭk′ə·rəs) Ik′aros

Icelos (ĭ′sə·lŏs)

Ida (ī′də) I′de

Idaea (ĭ·dē′ə) Idai′a

Idaeüs (ĭ·dē′əs) Idai′os

Idas (ī′dəs)

Idmon (ĭd′mŏn)

Idomeneus (ĭ·dŏm′ə·nūs) Idomeneus′

Idyia (ĭ·dĭ·ī′ə)

Iliad (ĭl′ĭ·ăd) Ili′ados

Ilione (ĭl·ē·ō′nē) Ili′one

Ilissus (ĭ·lĭs′əs) Ilissos′

Ilisus (ĭ·lĭs′əs) Ilisos′

Ilium (ĭl′ĭ·əm) Il′ion

Illyria (ĭ·lĭr′ĭ·ə) Illyris′

Ilus (ī′ləs) -os

Ilva (ĭl′və)

Inachus (ĭn′ə·kəs) -os

Ino (ī′nō) Ino′

Io (ī′ō) Io′

Iobates (ĭ·ŏb′ə·tēz) Ioba′tes

Iolaüs (ī·ō·lā′əs) Iol′aos

Iolcus (ī·ŏl′kəs) Iolkos′

Iole (ī′ə·lē) Io′le

Ion (ī′ŏn)

Ionia (ī·ō′nĭ·ə) Ioni′a

Iphianassa (ĭf·ĭ·ə·năs′ə) Iphian′assa

Iphicles (ĭf′ĭ·klēz) Iphikles′

Iphiclus (ĭf′ĭ·kləs) Iphiklos′

Iphigeneia (ĭf·ĭ·jə·nī′ə) Iphige′neia

Iphimedeia (ĭf·ĭ·mə·dē′ə) Iphime′deia

Iphis (ĭf′ĭs)

Iphitus (ĭf′ĭ·təs) -os

Irene (ī·rē′nē) Eire′ne

Iris (ī′rĭs)

Irus (ī′rəs) -os

Isander (ī·săn′der) Is′andros

Ischys (ĭs′kĭs)

Ismarus (ĭs·mĕr′əs) Is′maros

Ismene (ĭs·mē′nē)

Issedones (ĭs·ə·dō′nēz)

Ister (ĭs′ter) Is′tros

Isus (ī′səs) I′sos

Italus (ī′tə·ləs) Italos′

Ithaca (ĭth′ə·kə) Itha′ke

Itoni (ĭ·tō′nī) It′onoi

Itylos (ĭt′ĭ·lŏs)

Itys (ĭt′ĭs)

Iülus (ū′ləs)

Ixion (ĭk·zī′ŏn)

Janus (jā′nəs) Ia′nus

Jason (jā′sən) Ia′son

Jocasta (jō·kăs′tə) Iokas′te

Juno (joo′nō) Iu′no

Jupiter (joo′pĭ·ter) Iu′piter, Iup′piter

Juventas (joo·vĕn′təs) Iuven′tas

Ker (ker)

Kerkyra (kĕr′kĭ·rə)

kerykeion (kē·rĭ·kī′ŏn)

Kore (kō′rē)
Ktesios (ktē′sĭ·ŏs)

Labdacus (lăb′də·kəs) -kos
Labyrinth (lăb′ə·rĭnth) Labyr′inthos
Lacedaemon (lăs·ə·dē′mŏn) Lakedai′mon
Lachesis (lăk′ə·sĭs)
Laconia (lə·kō′nĭ·ə) Lakoni′a
Ladon (lā′dŏn)
Laelaps (lē′lăps) Lai′laps
Laërtes (lā·er′tēz)
Laestrygones (lēs·trĭ·gō′nēz)
    Laistrygo′nes
Laïus (lā′ĭ·əs, lā′əs) La′ïos
Lampetië (lăm·pē′shĭ·ē) Lampeti′e
Lampus (lăm′pəs) -os
Lamus (lā′məs) -os
Laocoön (lā·ŏk′ō·ŏn) Laok′oön
Laodamas (lā·ŏd′ə·məs) Laoda′mas
Laodameia (lā·ō·də·mē′ə) Laoda′meia
Laodice (lā·ŏd′ĭ·sə) Laodi′ke
Laomedon (lā·ŏm′ə·dŏn) Laomed′on
Laonome (lā·ŏn′ō·mē) Laono′me
Laphystius (lə·fĭs′tĭ·əs) -os
Lapithae (lăp′ĭ·thē) Lapi′thai
Lapithes (lăp′ĭ·thēz) Lapi′thes
Lapiths (lăp′ĭthz) Lapi′thai
Lapithus (lăp′ĭ·thəs) Lapi′thos
lares (lā′rēz)
Larisa (lə·rĭs′ə) La′risa
Larissa (lə·rĭs′ə) La′rissa
lases (lā′sēz)
Latinus (lə·tī′nəs)
Latium (lā′shĭ·əm)
Latona (lə·tō′nə)
Laurentum (lau·rēn′təm)
Lavinium (lə·vĭn′ĭ·əm)
Learchus (lē·ar′kəs) Le′archos
Leda (lē′də)
Leiriope (lē·rī′ō·pē) Leirio′pe
Leïtus (lē′ĭ·təs) -os
Leleges (lē·lē′jēz) Lel′eges
Lelex (lē′lĕks)
Lemnos (lĕm′nŏs)
Lenaeüs (lə·nē′əs) Lenai′os
Leo (lē′ō)

Leodocus (lē·ŏd′ə·kəs) -kos
Leonteus (lē·ŏn′tūs) Leonteus′
Lepus (lē′pəs)
Lerna (ler′nə) Ler′ne
Lesbos (lĕz′bŏs)
Lethe (lē′thē)
Leto (lē′tō) Leto′
Leucippus (lū·sĭp′əs) Leu′kippos
Leucon (lū′kŏn) -kon
Leucothea (lū·kŏth′ĭ·ə) Leukothe′a
Leucothoë (lū·kŏth′ō·ē) Leukotho′e
Leucus (lū′kəs) -kos
Liber (lī′ber)
Libera (lī′ber·ə)
Libya (lĭb′ĭ·ə) Liby′e
Lichas (lī′kəs)
Licymnius (lī·sĭm′nĭ·əs) Likym′nios
Liguria (lī·gū′rĭ·ə)
Lilybaeüm (lĭl·ĭ·bē′əm) Lilybai′on
Lindus (lĭn′dəs) -os
Linus (lī′nəs) -os
Livy (lĭv′ē) Liv′ius
Locris (lŏk′rĭs) Lokris′
Lotis (lō′tĭs)
Lotophagi (lo·tŏf′ə·jī) Lotopha′goi
Loxias (lŏk′sĭ·əs) Loxi′as
Lua (lū′ə)
Lucifer (lū′sĭ·fer)
Lucina (lū·sī′nə)
Lucretia (lū·krē′shə)
Lusi (lū′sī) Lou′soi
Lyaeüs (lī·ē′əs) Lyai′os
Lycaon (lī·kā′ŏn) Lyka′on
Lycia (lĭsh′ĭ·ə) Lyki′a
Lycomedes (lī·kō·mē′dēz) Lykome′des
Lycormas (lī·kŏr′məs) Lykor′mas
Lycosura (lī·kō·sū′rə) Lykos′oura
Lycurgus (lī·ker′gəs) Lykour′gos
Lycus (lī′kəs) Ly′kos
Lydia (lĭd′ĭ·ə) Lydi′a
Lynceus (lĭn′sūs, lĭn′sĭ·əs) Lynkeus′
Lyra (lī′rə)
Lyrceia (lĭr·sē′ə) Lyrkei′a
Lyrnessus (ler·nĕs′əs) Lyrnessos′
Lyrus (lī′rəs) -os
Lysianassa (lĭs′ĭ·ə·năs′ə) Lysian′assa

Lysimache (lĭ·sĭm′ə·kē) Lysima′che
Lysippe (lĭ·sĭp′ē)

Macar (mə·kar′) Makar′
Macareus (măk′ər·ūs) Makareus′
Macaria (mə·kĕr′ĭ·ə) Makari′a
Machaon (mə·kā′ŏn)
Macris (măk′rĭs) Makris′
Maeander (mē·ăn′der) Mai′andros
maenads (mē′nădz) maina′des
Maeon (mē′ŏn) Mai′on
Maeotis (mē·ō′tĭs) Maio′tis
Magnes (măg′nēz)
Magnesia (măg·nē′zhĭ·ə) Magnesi′a
Maia (mī′ə)
Malea (mə·lē′ə) Male′a, Malei′a
Malis (mā′lĭs)
manes (mā′nēz)
Mantius (măn′shĭ·əs) -os
Manto (măn′tō) Manto′
Marathon (mĕr′ə·thŏn) Marathon′
Mariandyni (mĕr·ĭ·ăn·dī′nī)
    Mariandynoi′
Marmara (mar′mə·rə)
Marmax (mar′măks)
Marmora (mar′mə·rə)
Maron (mā′rŏn)
Marpessa (mar·pĕs′ə) Mar′pessa
Mars (marz)
Marsyas (mar′sĭ·əs) Marsy′as
Mastusius (măs·tū′zhĭ·əs)
Mecionice (mē·sē·ŏn′ĭ·sē) Mekioni′ke
Mecisteus (mē·sĭs′tūs) Mekisteus′
Meda (mē′də)
Medea, Medeia (mē·dē′ə) Me′deia
Medeius (mē·dē′əs) -os
Medon (mē′dŏn)
Medus (mē′dəs) -os
Medusa (mə·dū′sə) Med′ousa
Megaera (mə·jē′rə) Meg′aira
Megapenthes (mĕg·ə·pĕn′thēz)
Megara (mĕg′ə·rə) Mega′ra
Megareus (mĕg′ə·rūs) Megareus′
Megaris (mĕg′ə·rĭs) Megaris′
Meges (mē′jēz)
Meilichios (mē·lĭk′ĭ·ŏs)

Melampodes (mə·lăm′pə·dēz)
    Melampo′des
Melampodia (mĕl·əm·pō′dĭ·ə) -eia
Melampus (mə·lăm′pəs) Melam′pous
Melaneus (mĕl′ə·nūs) Melaneus′
Melanion (mə·lā′nĭ·ŏn) Melani′on
Melanippe (mĕl·ə·nĭp′ē)
Melanippus (mĕl·ə·nĭp′əs) Melan′ippos
Melantheus (mə·lăn′thūs) Melantheus′
Melanthius (mə·lăn′thĭ·əs) -os
Melantho (mə·lăn′thō) Melantho′
Melanthus (mə·lăn′thəs) -os
Melas (mē′ləs)
Meleager (mĕl·ē·ā′jer) Mele′agros
meliae (mē′lĭ·ē) meli′ai
Meliboea (mĕl·ĭ·bē′ə) Meli′boia
Melicertes (mĕl·ĭ·ser′tēz) Meliker′tes
Melpomene (mĕl·pŏm′ĭ·nē) Melpomen′e
Membliarus (mĕm·blĭ′ə·rəs) -os
Memnon (mĕm′nŏn)
Memphis (mĕm′fĭs)
Menelaüs (mĕn·ə·lā′əs) Menel′aos
Menestheus (mə·nĕs′thūs) Menestheus′
Menestratus (mə·nĕs′trə·təs) -os
Menodice (mə·nŏd′ĭ·sē) Menodi′ke
Menoeceus (mə·nē′sūs) Menoikeus′
Menoetes (mə·nē′tēz) Menoi′tes
Menoetius (mə·nē′shĭ·əs) Menoi′tios
Mentes (mĕn′tēz)
Mentor (mĕn′tŏr)
Mercury (mer′kū·rē) Mercu′rius
Meriones (mə·rī′ō·nēz) Merio′nes
Mermerus (mer′mə·rəs) -os
Merope (mĕr′ō·pē) Mero′pe
Merops (mĕr′ŏps)
Messene (mə·sē′nē)
Messenia (mə·sē′nĭ·ə) Messeni′a
Messina (mə·sē′nə)
Mestor (mĕs′ter)
Mestra (mĕs′trə)
Metaneira (mĕt·ə·nē′rə) Metan′eira
Metapontus (mĕt·ə·pŏn′təs)
Metiadusa (mĕt·ĭ·ə·dū′sə) Metia′dousa
Metion (mē′tĭ·ŏn) Meti′on
Metis (mē′tĭs)
Midas (mī′dəs)

Midea (mĭd′ĭ·ə)
Miletus (mī·lē′təs) Mil′etos
Mimas (mī′məs)
Minerva (mĭ·ner′və)
Minos (mī′nŏs)
Minotaur (mĭn′ə·taur) Mino′tauros
Minyans (mĭn′ĭ·ənz) Miny′ai
Minyas (mĭn′ĭ·əs) Miny′as
Mnemosyne (nē·mŏz′ĭ·nē) Mnemosy′ne
Moerae (mē′rē)
Moi′rai (moi′rī)
Moliones (mō·lī′ō·nēz)
Molionides (mō·lĭ·ŏn′ĭ·dēz)
Molossus (mō·lŏs′əs) Molossos′
moly (mō′lē)
Mopsus (mŏp′səs) -os
Morpheus (môr′fūs, môr′fĭ·əs) Morpheus′
Mossynoeci (mŏs·ĭ·nē′sī) Mossyn′oikoi
Mulciber (mŭl′sĭ·ber)
Muses (mū′zəz) Mou′sai
Myagro (mĭ·ăg′rō)
Mycenae (mī·sē′nē) Myke′nai
Mycene (mī·sē′nē) Myke′ne
Mygdon (mĭg′dŏn) Mygdon′
Myles (mī′lēz)
Myrmidon (mer′mĭ·dŏn) Myrmidon′
Myrrha (mĭr′ə)
Myrtilus (mer′tĭ·ləs) Myrti′los
Myrto (mer′tō) Myrto′
Mysia (mĭsh′ĭ·ə) Mysi′a

naïad (nī′ăd, nā′ăd) naïas′
Narcissus (nar·sĭs′əs) Nar′kissos
Nasamon (năs′ə·mŏn) Nasa′mon
Naupactus (nau·păk′təs) Nau′paktos
Nauplia (nau′plĭ·ə) Naupli′a
Nauplius (nau′plĭ·əs) -os
Nausicaä (nau·sĭk′ā·ə) Nausica′a
Nausithoüs (nau·sĭth′ō·əs) -os
Naxos (năk′sŏs)
Neaera (nē·ē′rə) Ne′aira
Neleus (nē′lūs, nē′lĭ·əs) Neleus′
Nemea (nē′mĭ·ə, nē·mē′ə) Neme′a
Nemesis (nĕm′ə·sĭs)
Neoptolemus (nē·ŏp·tŏl′ə·məs) -os
Nephele (nĕf′ə·lē) Nephel′e

Neptune (nĕp′tūn) Neptu′nus
Nereïds (nē′rĭ·ĭds) Nereï′des
Nereus (nēr′ūs, nē′rĭ·əs) Nereus′
Nerio (nē′rĭ·ō)
Nessus (nĕs′əs) -os
Nestor (nĕs′tŏr)
Nicippe (nī·sĭp′ē) Nikip′pe
Nicostratus (nī·kŏs′trə·təs) Nikos′tratos
Nike (nī′kē)
Niobe (nī′ə·bē) Nio′be
Nisus (nī′səs) -os
Nostoi (nŏs′toi)
Notus (nō′təs) -os
Numa Pompilius (nū′mə pŏm·pĭl′ĭ·əs)
Numitor (nū′mĭ·tŏr)
Nycteus (nĭk′tūs) Nykteus′
Nyctimene (nĭk·tĭm′ĭ·nē) Nyktime′ne
Nyctimus (nĭk′tĭ·məs) Nyk′timos
nymph (nĭmf) nym′pha
Nysa (nī′sə)
Nyx (nĭks)

Obriareüs (ō·brī·ĕr′ĭ·əs) -os
Oceanides (ō·sē·ăn′ĭ·dēz) Okeani′des
Oceanids (ō·sē′ə·nĭdz) Okeani′des
Oceanus (ō·sē′ə·nəs) Oke′anos
Ocnus (ŏk′nəs) Ok′nos
Odius (ō′dĭ·əs) Odi′os
Odysseus (ō·dĭs′ūs, ō·dĭs′ĭ·əs) Odysseus′
Odyssey (ŏd′ĭ·sē) Odyssei′a
Oeagrus (ē′ə·grəs) Oi′agros
Oeax (ē′ăks) Oi′ax
Oebalus (ē′bə·ləs) Oi′balos
Oechalia (ē·kăl′ĭ·ə) Oichali′a
Oedipodeia (ē·dĭ·pō·dē′ə) Oidipodei′a
Oedipodes (ē·dĭp′ə·dēz) Oidipo′des
Oedipus (ĕd′ĭ·pəs, ē′dĭ·pəs) Oidi′pous
Oeneus (ē′nūs) Oineus′
Oenoë (ē·nō′ē) Oino′e
Oenomaüs (ē·nŏm′ā·əs) Oinom′aos
Oenone (ē·nō′nē) Oino′ne
Oenopia (ē·nō′pĭ·ə) Oinopi′a
Oenopion (ē·nō′pĭ·ŏn) Oinopi′on
Oenotria (ē·nō′trĭ·ə) Oinotri′a
Oeonus (ē·ō′nəs) Oionos′
Oeta (ē′tə) Oi′te

Ogyges (ō·gī′jēz)
Ogygia (ō·gī′jĭ·ə) Ogygi′a
Ogygus (ō·gī′gəs) -os
Oïcles (ō′ē·klēz) Oï′kles
Oïleus (ō′ē·lūs) Oïleus′
Olenus (ō·lē′nəs) Ol′enos
Olympia (ō·lĭm′pĭ·ə) Olympi′a
Olympus (ō·lĭm′pəs) O′lympos
Omphale (ŏm′fə·lē) Ompha′le
omphalos (ŏm′fə·lŏs) omphalos′
Onca (ŏng′kə) On′ka
Onchestus (ŏn·kĕs′təs) Onchestos′
Oncius (ŏn′sĭ·əs) On′kios
Oncus (ŏng′kəs) On′kos
Onga (ŏng′gə) On′ga
Opheltes (ō·fĕl′tēz)
Ophion (ō·fī′ŏn)
Ophiuchus (ŏf·ĭ·ū′kəs)
Opis (ō′pĭs)
Ops (ŏps)
Opus (ō′pəs) Opous′
Orchomenus (or·kŏm′ə·nəs) -os
Orcus (ŏr′kəs)
oread (ō′rĭ·ăd) o′reas
Oreithyia (ō·rī·thī′ə) Orei′thyia
Oresteium (ō·rĕs·tē′əm) -on
Orestes (ō·rĕs′tēz)
Oresthasium (ō·rĕs·thā′zĭ·əm) -on
Orion (ō·rī′ən)
Ormenium (ŏr·mē′nĭ·əm) -on
Orneus (ŏr′nūs) Orneus′
Ornytus (ŏr′nĭ·təs) -os
Orpheus (ŏr′fūs, ŏr′fĭ·əs) Orpheus′
Orthrus (ŏr′thrəs) -os
Orthus (ŏr′thəs) -os
Ortygia (ŏr·tĭj′ĭ·ə) Ortygi′a
Ossa (ŏs′ə)
Otreus (ō′trūs) Otreus′
Otus (ō′təs) -os
Ovid (ŏv′ĭd) Ovid′ius
Oxylus (ŏk′sĭ·ləs) -os

Pactolus (păk·tō′ləs) -os
Paean (pē′ăn) Pai′an
Paeëon (pē·ē′ŏn) Paie′on
Paeon (pē′ŏn) Pai′on

Paeonia (pē·ō′nĭ·ə) Paioni′a
Pagasae (pə·găs′ē) Pagasai′
Palaechthon (pə·lĕk′thŏn) Palaich′thon
Palaemon (pə·lē′mŏn) Palai′mon
Palamedes (păl·ə·mē′dēz)
Pales (pā′lēz)
Palinurus (păl·ĭ·nū′rəs)
Palladium (pə·lā′dĭ·əm) -on
Pallantids (pə·lăn′tĭdz) Pallanti′dai
Pallas (păl′əs)
Pallene (pə·lē′nē)
Pamphylus (păm′fĭ·ləs) -os
Pancratis (păn′krə·tĭs) Pankra′tis
Pandareüs (păn·dĕr′ī·əs) -os
Pandarus (păn′də·rəs) -os
Pandion (păn·dī′ŏn)
Pandora (păn·dō′rə)
Pandorus (păn·dō′rəs) Pan′doros
Pandrosus (păn′drə·səs) -os
Pangaeus (păn·jē′əs) Pangai′os
Panopeus (păn·ō′pūs) Panopeus′
Panoptes (păn·ŏp′tēz)
Panthoüs (păn·thō·əs) Pan′thoös
Paphos (pā′fŏs)
Paraebius (pə·rē′bĭ·əs) Parai′bios
Parcae (par′sē)
parentes (pə·rĕn′tēz)
Paris (pĕr′ĭs)
Parnassus (par·năs′əs) Parnassos′
Parthaon (par·thā′ŏn)
Parthenius (par·thē′nĭ·əs) -os
Parthenopaeüs (par·thə·nō·pē′əs)
    Parthenopai′os
Pasiphaë (pə·sĭf′ā·ē) Pasipha′e
Pasithea (pə·sĭth′ī·ə) Pasithe′a
Patrae (păt′re) Pat′rai
Patreus (păt′rūs) Patreus′
Patroclus (păt′rə·kləs) -klos
Pausanias (pau·sā′nĭ·əs)
Pegasus (pĕg′ə·səs) -os
Peirithoüs (pī·rĭth′ō·əs) -os
Peisidice (pī·sĭd′ī·sē) Pisidi′ke
Pelasgians (pə·lăz′jĭ·ənz) Pelasgoi′
Pelasgus (pə·lăz′gəs) Pelasgos′
Peleus (pē′lūs, pē′lĭ·əs) Peleus′
Pelias (pē′lĭ·əs) Peli′as

Pelion (pē'lĭ·ŏn)

Pella (pĕl'ə)

Pelopia (pē·lō'pĭ·ə) Pelopi'a

Pelops (pē'lŏps)

Pelorus (pē·lō'rəs) Pel'oros

penates (pə·nā'tēz)

Peneius (pē·nē'əs) Peneios'

Peneleüs (pə·nĕl'ĭ·əs) -os

Penelope (pə·nĕl'ə·pē) Penelo'pe

Penthesileia (pĕn·thə·sĭ·lē'ə)
    Penthesil'eia

Pentheus (pĕn'thūs) Pentheus'

Penthilus (pĕn'thə·ləs) -os

Perdix (pẽr'dĭks)

Pereus (pēr'ūs) Pereus'

Pergamon (per'gə·mŏn)

Pergamum (per'gə·məm) Per'gamon

Pergamus (per'gə·məs) -os

Periboea (pĕr·ĭ·bē'ə) Peri'boia

Periclymene (pĕr·ĭ·klī·mē'nē)
    Periklyme'ne

Periclymenus (pĕr·ĭ·klĭm'ə·nəs)
    Periklym'enos

Perieres (pĕr·ĭ·ē'rēz)

Perigune (pĕr·ĭ·gū'nē) Perigou'ne

Perimede (pĕr·ĭ·mē'dē)

Perimele (pĕr·ĭ·mē'lē)

Periopis (pĕr·ĭ·ō'pĭs)

Periphas (pĕr'ĭ·făs) Peri'phas

Periphetes (pĕr·ĭ·fē'tēz)

Pero (pē'rō) Pero'

Perse (per'sē)

Perseïs (per·sē'ĭs) Perseïs'

Persephone (per·sĕf'ə·nē) Persepho'ne

Perses (per'sēz)

Perseus (per'sūs, per'sĭ·əs) Perseus'

Pessinus (pĕ·sī'nəs) -os

Petelia (pē·tē'lĭ·ə)

Peteüs (pĕt'ĭ·əs) Peteos'

Phaea (fē'ə) Phai'a

Phaeacians (fē·ā'shĭ·ənz) Phai'akes

Phaedra (fē'drə) Phai'dra

Phaënon (fā'ə·nŏn) Phaën'on

Phaëthon (fā'ə·thŏn) Phaëthon'

Phaëthusa (fā·ə·thū'sə) Phaëth'ousa

Phalces (făl'sēz) -kes

Phalerus (fə·lē'rəs) Phal'eros

Phantasos (făn'tə·sŏs)

Phanus (fā'nəs) -os

Phasis (fā'sĭs)

Phegeus (fē'jūs) Phegeus'

Phegia (fē'jĭ·ə) Phegi'a

Phemius (fē'mĭ·əs) -os

Pheneüs (fē'nĭ·əs) Pheneos'

Pherae (fē'rē) Pherai'

Pheres (fēr'ēz)

Phicium (fĭsh'ĭ·əm) Phik'ion

Philammon (fĭl·ăm'ŏn)

Philemon (fĭl·ē'mŏn)

Philoctetes (fĭl·ŏk·tē'tēz)

Philoetius (fĭl·ē'shĭ·əs) Philoi'tios

Philomela (fĭl·ō·mē'lə)

Philomelus (fĭl·ō·mĕl'əs) Philom'elos

Philonoë (fĭl·ŏn'ō·ē) Philono'e

Philonome (fĭl·ŏn'ō·mē) Philono'me

Philyra (fĭl'ĭ·rə) Phily'ra

Phineus (fī'nūs, fĭn'ĭ·əs) Phineus'

Phlegethon (flĕg'ə·thŏn) Phlege'thon

Phlegra (flĕg'rə)

Phlegyans (flĕg'ĭ·ənz) Phlegy'ai

Phlegyantis (flĕg·ĭ·ăn'tĭs) Phlegyantis'

Phlegyas (flĕg'ĭ·əs) Phlegy'as

Phlias (flē'əs)

Phliasia (flē·ā'zhə) Phliasi'a

Phlius (flē'əs) -os

Phlogius (flō'jĭ·əs) Phlogi'os

Phobetor (fō'bə·tŏr)

Phobus (fō'bəs) -os

Phocis (fō'sĭs) Phokis'

Phocus (fō'kəs) -os

Phoebe (fē'bē) Phoi'be

Phoebus (fē'bəs) Phoi'bos

Phoenicia (fə·nĭsh'ə, fə·nĭsh'ĭ·ə)
    Phoiniki'a

Phoenix (fē'nĭks) Phoi'nix

Pholoë (fō·lō'ē)

Pholus (fō'ləs) -os

Phorbas (fŏr'bəs)

Phorcys (fŏr'sĭs) Phor'kys

Phoronea (fō·rō'nĭ·ə) Phorone'a

Phoroneus (fō·rō'nūs) Phoroneus'

Phrixus (frĭk'səs) -os

Phrygia (frĭj'ĭ·ə) Phrygi'a
Phthia (thĭ'ə)
Phthiotis (thĭ·ŏ'tĭs)
Phylace (fī·lā'sē) -ke
Phylacus (fĭ'lə·kəs) -kos
Phylas (fī'ləs)
Phyleus (fī'lūs) Phyleus'
Phyllis (fĭl'ĭs) Phyllis'
Phylomache (fī·lŏm'ə·kē) Phyloma'che
Picus (pī'kəs) -kos
Pieria (pī·ĭr'ĭ·ə) Pieri'a
Pierides (pī·ĕr'ĭ·dēz) Pieri'des
Pierus (pī'ə·rəs) -os
Pindar (pĭn'der) Pin'daros
Pisa (pī'sə)
Pisatis (pī·sā'tĭs) Pisatis
Pisces (pĭs'ēz)
Pittheus (pĭth'ūs) Pittheus'
Pityocamptes (pĭt·ĭ·ō·kămp'tēz)
    Pityokamp'tes
Plataea (plə·tē'ə) Platai'a
Pleiades (plē'ə·dēz, plī'ə·dēz) Pleia'des
Pleïone (plī·ō'nē)
Pleisthenes (plĭs'thə·nēz) Pleisthen'es
Pleuron (plū'rŏn) Pleuron'
Plotae (plō'tē) Plotai'
Plutarch (ploo'tark) Plou'tarchos
Pluto (ploo'tō) Plou'ton
Plutus (ploo'təs) Plou'tos
Podaleirius (pō·də·līr'ĭ·əs) -os
Podarces (pō·dar'sēz) -kes
Poeas (pē'əs) Poi'as
Pollux (pŏl'əks)
Polybotes (pŏl·ĭ·bō'tēz)
Polybus (pŏl'ĭ·bəs) -os
Polycaon (pŏl·ĭ·kā'ŏn) Polyka'on
Polydamas (pə·lĭd'ə·məs) Polyda'mas
Polydamna (pŏl·ĭ·dăm'nə) Poly'damna
Polydectes (pŏl·ĭ·dĕk'tēz) Polydek'tes
Polydeuces (pŏl·ĭ·dū'sēz) -kes
Polydora (pŏl·ĭ·dō'rə)
Polydorus (pŏl·ĭ·dō'rəs) Poly'doros
Polyeidus (pŏl·ĭ·ī'dəs) Poly'eidos
Polygonus (pə·lĭg'ə·nəs) -os
Polyhymnia (pŏl·ĭ·hĭm'nĭ·ə) Polyhymni'a
Polyidus (pŏl·ĭ·ī'dəs) -os

Polymede (pŏl·ĭ·mē'dē)
Polymestor (pŏl·ĭ·mĕs'ter)
Polymnestor (pŏl·ĭm·nĕs'ter)
Polymnia (pō·lĭm'nĭ·ə) Polymni'a
Polyneices (pŏl·ĭ·nī'sēz) -kes
Polypemon (pŏl·ĭ·pē'mŏn)
Polypheides (pŏl·ĭ·fī'dēz)
Polyphemus (pŏl·ĭ·fē'məs) Polyph'emos
Polyphontes (pŏl·ĭ·fŏn'tēz)
Polypoetes (pŏl·ĭ·pē'tēz) Polypoites
Polyxeinus (pō·lĭk'sə·nəs) -os
Polyxena (pō·lĭk'sə·nə) Polyxe'ne
Polyxo (pō·lĭk'sō) Polyxo'
Pomona (pə·mō'nə)
Pontus (pŏn'təs) -os
Porphyrion (pŏr·fĭr'ĭ·ŏn) Porphyri'on
Porthaon (pŏr·thā'ŏn)
Portheus (pŏr'thūs) Portheus'
Poseidaon (pō·sī·dā'ŏn)
Poseidon (pə·sī'dŏn)
Potniae (pŏt'nĭ·ē) Potniai'
Poulydamas (poo·lĭd'ə·məs) Poulyda'mas
Prasithea (prə·sĭth'ĭ·ə) Prasithe'a
Praxithea (prăk·sĭth'ĭ·ə) Praxithe'a
Priam (prī'əm) Pri'amos
Priapus (prī·ā'pəs) Pri'apos
Priasus (prī·ā'səs) Pri'asos
Procles (prŏk'lēz) Prokles'
Procne (prŏk'nē) Prok'ne
Procris (prŏk'rĭs) Prokris'
Procrustes (prō·krŭs'tēz) Prokrous'tes
Procyon (prō'sĭ·ŏn) Proky'on
Proëtus (prō·ē'təs) Proï'tos
Promachus (prŏm'ə·kəs) -os
Prometheus (prō·mē'thūs, prō·mē'thĭ·əs)
    Prometheus'
Pronax (prō'năks)
Pronoë (prŏn'ō·ē) Prono'e
Pronoüs (prŏn'ō·əs) -os
Propontis (prō·pŏn'tĭs)
Proserpina (prō·ser'pĭ·nə)
Protesilaüs (prō·tĕs·ĭ·lā'əs)
    Protesil'aos
Proteus (prō'tūs, prō'tĭ·əs) Proteus'
Protogeneia (prō·tō·jə·nē'ə)
    Protogen'eia

627

Psamathe (săm'ǝ·thē) Psama'the
Psamatheïs (săm·ǝ·thē'ĭs)
Psophis (psō'fĭs) Psophis'
Psyche (sī'kē) Psyche'
Pterelaüs (tĕr·ǝ·lā'ǝs) Pterel'aos
Ptoüs (tō'ǝs) -os
Pygmalion (pĭg·mā'lĭ·ŏn) Pygmali'on
Pylades (pĭl'ǝ·dēz) Pyla'des
Pylas (pī'lǝs)
Pylon (pī'lŏn)
Pylus (pī'lǝs) -os
Pyramus (pĭr'ǝ·mǝs) -os
Pyriphlegethon (pī·rĭ·flĕg'ǝ·thŏn)
    Pyriphlege'thon
Pyrrha (pĭr'ǝ)
Pyrrhus (pĭr'ǝs) -os
Pythia (pĭth'ĭ·ǝ) Pythi'a
Pytho (pī'thō) Pytho'
Python (pī'thŏn)

Quirinus (kwĭ·rī'nǝs)

Rea Silvia (rē'ǝ sĭl'vĭ·ǝ)
Remus (rē'mǝs)
Rhadamanthus (răd·ǝ·măn'thǝs)
    Rhada'manthos
Rhadamanthys (răd·ǝ·măn'thĭs)
    Rhada'manthys
Rhamnusia (răm·nū'zhĭ'ǝ) Rhamnusi'a
Rhampsinitus (rămp·sĭ·nī'tǝs)
    Rhampsin'itos
Rhea (rē'ǝ)
Rheia (rē'ǝ)
Rhesus (rē'sǝs) -os
Rhexenor (rĕk·sē'nŏr)
Rhode (rō'dē)
Rhodes (rōdz) Rho'dos
Rhodope (rŏd'ō·pē) Rhodo'pe
Rhodos (rō'dŏs)
Rome (rōm) Ro'ma
Romulus (rŏm'ū·lǝs)
Rutuli (roo·tū'lĭ)

Sabazius (sǝ·bā'zĭ·ǝs) -os
Sabines (sā'bīnz, săb'īnz) Sa'bini
Sagitta (sǝ·jĭt'ǝ)

Sagittarius (să·jĭ·tĕr'ĭ·ǝs)
Salamis (săl'ǝ·mĭs) Salamis'
Salmacis (săl'mǝ·sĭs) Salmakis'
Salmoneus (săl·mō'nūs, săl·mō'nĭ·ǝs)
    Salmoneus'
Salmoxis (săl·mŏk'sĭs) Salmoxis'
Salmydessus (săl·mĭ·dĕs'ǝs) Salmydessos'
Samos (sā'mŏs)
Samothrace (săm'ō·thrās) Samothra'ke
Sangarius (săng·gĕr'ĭ·ǝs) -os
Sardes (sar'dēz)
Sardinia (sar·dĭn'ĭ·ǝ)
Sardis (sar'dĭs)
Saronic (sǝ·rŏn'ĭk)
Sarpedon (sar·pē'dŏn) Sarpedon'
Saturn (săt'ern) Satur'nus
satyrs (săt'erz, sā'terz) sat'yroi
Sauromatae (sau·rō·mā'tē) -ai
Sauromatians (sau·rō·mā'shĭ·ǝnz)
Scamander (skǝ·măn'dĕr) Skam'andros
Scamandrius (skǝ·măn'drĭ·ǝs)
    Skaman'drios
Sceiron (skī'rŏn) Skei'ron
Schedius (skĕd'ĭ·ǝs) Schedi'os
Scherië (skĕr'ĭ·ē) Scheri'e
Schoeneus (skē'nūs) Schoineus'
Sciron (skī'rŏn) Skei'ron
Scorpio (skŏr'pĭ·ō)
Scylla (sĭl'ǝ) Skyl'la
Scyllaeüm (sĭ·lē'ǝm) Skyl'laion
Scyrius (skĭr'ĭ·ǝs) Sky'rios
Scyrus (skī'rǝs) Sky'ros
Scythians (sĭth'ĭ·ǝnz) Sky'thai
Seilenus (sī·lē'nǝs) Seilenos'
Seirenes (sī·rē'nēz)
Selemnus (sĕl'ǝm·nǝs) -os
Selene (sē·lē'nē)
Selinus (sē·lī'nǝs) Selinous'
Semele (sĕm'ǝ·lē) Semel'e
Semnae (sĕm'nē) -nai
Semnai Theai (sĕm'nī thē'ī)
Seriphus (sǝ·rī'fǝs) Ser'iphos
Servius Tullius (ser'vĭ·ǝs tŭl'ĭ·ǝs)
Sestus (sĕs'tǝs) -os
Sicels (sĭs'ĕlz) Sikeloi'
Sicily (sĭs'ĭ·lē) Sikeli'a, Sicil'ia

Siculi (sĭk'ū·lī)
Sicyon (sĭsh'ĭ·ŏn) Sikyon'
Sicyonia (sĭsh·ĭ·ō'nĭ·ə) Sikyoni'a
Side (sī'dē)
Sidon (sī'dn)
Silenus (sī·lē'nəs) Seilenos'
Silvanus (sĭl·vā'nəs)
Simöeis (sĭm'ō·ēs) Simo'eis
Sinis (sī'nĭs)
Sinnis (sĭn'ĭs)
Sinon (sī'nŏn)
Sinope (sĭ·nō'pē)
Sintians (sĭn'shĭ·ənz) Sin'ties
Sintiës (sĭn'tĭ·ēz)
Sipylus (sĭp'ĭ·ləs) -os
Sirens (sī'rənz) Seire'nes
Sirius (sĭr'ĭ·əs) Sei'rios
Sisyphus (sĭs'ĭ·fəs) -os
Smintheus (smĭn'thūs, smĭn'thĭ·əs)
    Smintheus'
Smyrna (smer'nə)
Solymi (sō'lĭ·mī) -moi
Somnus (sŏm'nəs)
Sophocles (sŏf'ə·klēz) -kles
Sparta (spar'tə) Spar'te
Sparti (spar'tī) Spartoi'
Spercheius (spĕr'kĭ·əs) Spercheios'
Sphaeria (sfē'rĭ·ə) Sphairi'a
Sphaerus (sfē'rəs) Sphai'ros
Sphinx (sfĭnks)
Sporades (spŏr'ə·dēz) Spora'des
Staphylus (stăf'ĭ·ləs) -os
Stenyclerus (stĕn·ĭ·klē'rəs) Stenyk'leros
Sterope (stĕr'ō·pē) Stero'pe
Stheneboea (sthĕn·ə·bē'ə) Sthene'boia
Sthenelus (sthĕn'ə·ləs) -os
Stilbe (stĭl'bē)
Stoëchades (stō·ĕk'ə·dēz) Stoecha'des
Strongyle (strŏn'jĭ·lē) Strongy'le
Strophades (strŏf'ə·dēz) Stropha'des
Strophius (strō'fĭ·əs) -os
Strymon (strī'mŏn) Strymon'
Stymphalian (stĭm·fā'lĭ·ən)
Stymphalus (stĭm·fā'ləs) Stym'phalos
Styx (stĭks)
Suculae (sŭk'ū·lē)

Superbus (sū·per'bəs)
Sychaeüs (sī·kē'əs) Sychai'os
Syleus (sī'lūs) Syleus'
Symplegades (sĭm·plĕg'ə·dēz)
    Symplega'des
Syria (sĭr'ĭ·ə) Syri'a
Syrinx (sĭr'ĭngks)
Syrtis (ser'tĭs)

Taenarum (tē'nə·rəm) Tai'naron
Talaüs (tə·lā'əs) Tal'aos
Talthybius (tăl·thĭb'ĭ·əs) -os
Talus (tā'ləs) -os
Tanagra (tăn'ə·grə)
Tanaïs (tăn'ā·ĭs)
Tanaquil (tăn'ə·kwĭl)
Tantalus (tăn'tə·ləs) -os
Taphians (tăf'ĭ·ənz)
Taphius (tăf'ĭ·əs) -os
Taraxippus (tə·răk'sĭ·pəs) -os
Tarpeia (tar·pē'ə)
Tarquinius Priscus (tar·kwĭn'ĭ·əs
    prĭs'kəs)
Tartarus (tar'tə·rəs) -os
Tartessus (tar·tĕs'əs) Tartessos'
Tatius (tā'shəs)
Taurians (tau'rĭ·ənz) Tau'roi
Taurus (tau'rəs) -os
Taÿgete (tā·ĭj'ĭ·tē) Taÿge'te
Taÿgetus (tā·ĭj'ĭ·təs) -os
Tecmessa (tĕk·mĕs'ə) Tek'messa
Tectamus (tĕk'tə·məs) Tek'tamos
Tegea (tē'jĭ·ə) Tege'a
Teiresias (tī·rē'sĭ·əs) Teiresi'as
Telamon (tĕl'ə·mŏn) Telamon'
Telchines (tĕl·kī'nēz)
Teleboans (tĕl·ə·bo'ənz)
Teledice (tē·lĕd'ĭ·sē) Teledi'ke
Telegonus (tē·lĕg'ə·nəs) -os
Telegony (tē·lĕg'ə·nē) Telegonei'a
Telemachus (tə·lĕm'ə·kəs) -os
Telephassa (tĕl·ə·făs'ə) Teleph'assa
Telephus (tĕl'ə·fəs) -os
Tellus (tĕl'əs)
Telphusa (tĕl·fū'sə) Telphou'sa
Temenus (tĕm'ə·nəs) -os

Tempe (tĕm′pē)
Tenedos (tĕn′ə·dŏs)
Tenes (tĕn′ēz)
Tennes (tĕn′ēz)
Tenos (tē′nŏs)
Tereus (tēr′ūs, tē′rĭ·əs) Tereus′
Termilae (ter′mĭ·lē) Termi′lai
Terpsichore (terp·sĭk′ə·rē) Terpsicho′re
Terra (tĕr′ə)
Tethys (tē′thĭs) Tethys′
Teucer (tū′ser) Teu′kros
Teumessus (tū·mĕs′əs) Teumessos′
Teuthrania (tū·thrā′nĭ·ə) Teuthrani′a
Teuthras (tū′thrəs)
Thalamae (thăl′ə·mē) Thalam′ai
Thaleia (thə·lī′ə)
Thalpius (thăl′pĭ·əs) -os
Thamyris (thăm′ĭ·rĭs)
Thanatos (thăn′ə·tŏs)
Thasus (thā′səs) -os
Thaumas (thau′məs)
Theano (thē·ā′nō) Theano′
Thebaïd (thē′bā·ĭd, thē·bā′ĭd)
Thebes (thēbz) The′bai
Theia (thē′ə)
Theiodamas (thē·ŏd′ə·məs) Theioda′mas
Thelpusa (thĕl·pū′sə) Thel′pousa
Themis (thē′mĭs)
Themiscyra (thĕm·ĭs·kī′rə) Themisky′ra
Themiste (thē·mĭs′tē)
Themisto (thē·mĭs′tō) Themisto′
Theoclymenus (thē·ō·klĭm′ə·nəs)
    Theoklym′enos
Theogony (thē·ŏg′ə·nē) Theogonei′a
Theonoë (thē·ŏn′ō·ē) Theono′e
Theophane (thē·ŏf′ə·nē) Theopha′ne
Thera (thē′rə)
Theras (thē′rəs)
Thermodon (ther·mō′dŏn)
Thersander (ther·săn′der) Ther′sandros
Thersites (ther·sī′tēz)
Theseus (thē′sūs, thē′sĭ·əs) Theseus′
Thespiae (thĕs′pĭ·ē) Thespi′ai
Thespius (thĕs′pĭ·əs) -os
Thesprotia (thĕs·prō′shĭ·ə) Thesproti′a
Thesprotus (thĕs·prō′təs) Thesprotos′

Thessalus (thĕs′ə·ləs) Thessalos′
Thessaly (thĕs′ə·lē) Thessali′a
Thestius (thĕs′tĭ·əs) -os
Thetis (thē′tĭs)
Thisbe (thĭz′bē)
Thoas (thō′ăs)
Thon (thŏn)
Thonis (thō′nĭs)
Thoösa (thō′ə·sə)
Thrace (thrās) Thra′ke
Thrasymedes (thrăs·ĭ·mē′dēz)
Thriae (thrī′ē) Thri′ai
Thriai (thrī′ī)
Thrinacia (thrĭ·nā′shĭ·ə) Thrinaki′e
Thronia (thrō′nĭ·ə) Throni′a
Thyestes (thī·ĕs′tēz)
Thyia (thī·ē′ə)
thyiad (thī′ăd) thyi′as
Thymbraeüs (thĭm·brē′əs) Thymbrai′os
Thynia (thĭn′ĭ·ə) Thyni′a
Thyone (thī·ō′nē)
thyrsus (ther′səs) -os
Tiasa (tī′ə·sə)
Tibareni (tī·bə·rē′nī) Tibarenoi′
Tiber (tī′ber) Tib′eris
Tilphusa (tĭl·fū′sə) Tilphou′sa
Tilphussa (tĭl·fŭs′ə) Tilphous′sa
Timandra (tĭ·măn′drə)
Timeas (tĭ·mē′əs)
Tiphys (tĭf′ĭs)
Tiresias (tī·rē′sĭ·əs) Teiresi′as
Tiryns (tĭr′ĭnz)
Tisamenus (tī·săm′ə·nəs) Tisamenos′
Tisiphone (tĭ·sĭf′ə·nē) Tisipho′ne
Titan (tī′tən) Titan′
Tithonus (tĭ·thō′nəs) Tithonos′
Tithorea (tĭ·thō′rĭ·ə) Tithore′a
Tityus (tĭt′ĭ·əs) Tityos′
Tlepolemus (tlə·pŏl′ə·məs) -os
Tlesimenes (tlə·sĭm′ə·nēz) Tlesimen′es
Toxeus (tŏk′sūs) Toxeus′
Trachis (trā′kĭs) Trachis′
Tricca (trĭk′ə) Trik′ke
Trinacria (trĭ·năk′rĭ·ə)
Triopas (trī′ō·pəs) Trio′pas
Triops (trī′ŏps)

Triphylia (trī·fĭl'ĭ·ə) Triphyli'a
Triptolemus (trĭp·tŏl'ə·məs) -os
Trito (trī'tō) Trito'
Tritogeneia (trī·tō·jə·nī'ə) Tritogen'eia
Triton (trī'tŏn)
Tritonis (trī·tō'nĭs) Tritonis'
Trivia (trĭv'ĭ·ə) Trivi'a
Troad (trō'ăd) Tro'as
Troezen (trē'zn) Troizen'
Troïlus (troi'ləs) Troï'los
Trophonius (trō·fō'nĭ·əs) -os
Tros (trōs)
Troy (troi) Troï'a
Tullia (tŭl'ĭ·ə)
Tullus Hostilius (tŭl'əs hŏs·tĭl'ĭ·əs)
Turnus (ter'nəs)
Tyche (tī'kē) Tyche'
Tydeus (tī'dūs, tī'dĭ·əs) Tydeus'
Tyndareüs (tĭn·dĕr'ĭ·əs) -os
Typhaon (tī·fā'ōn)
Typhon (tī'fŏn) Typhon'
Typhöeus (tī·fō'ūs) Typhoeus'
Tyre (tīr) Ty'ros
Tyro (tī'rō) Tyro'
Tyrrhenia (tĭ·rē'nĭ·ə) Tyrrheni'a
Tyrsenians (tĭr·sē'nĭ·ənz)

Udaeüs (ū·dē'əs) Oudai'os
Ulixes (ū·lĭk'sēz)
Ulysses (ū·lĭs'ēz)
Upis (ū'pĭs) Ou'pis

Urania (ū·rā'nĭ·ə) Ourani'a
Uranus (ū'rə·nəs) Ouranos'

Veii (vā'ē)
Venus (vē'nəs)
Vergil (ver'jĭl)
Vertumnus (ver·tŭm'nəs)
Vesta (vĕs'tə)
Vesuvius (və·soo'vĭ·əs)
Virbius (ver'bĭ·əs)
Virgo (ver'gō)
Volsci (vŏl'sī)
Volscians (vŏl'shĭ·əns)
Vortumnus (vŏr·tŭm'nəs)
Vulcan (vŭl'kn) Volca'nus, Vulca'nus

Xanthippe (zăn·thĭp'ē)
Xanthus (zăn'thəs) -os
Xuthus (zū'thəs) Xou'thos

Zacynthus (zə·sĭn'thəs) Zak'ynthos
Zagreus (zăg'rūs, zăg'rĭ·əs) Zagreus'
Zalmoxis (zăl·mŏk'sĭs) Zal'moxis
Zelus (zē'ləs) Zelos'
Zemelo (zē·mĕl'ō)
Zephyrus (zĕf'ə·rəs) -os
Zetes (zē'tēz)
Zethus (zē'thəs) -os
Zeus (zūs, zoos)
Zeuxippe (zūk·sĭp'ē)
Zminthe (zmĭn'thē)

COLLINS
REFERENCE

COLLINS REFERENCE DICTIONARIES form a new series of paperback subject dictionaries covering a wide variety of academic and general topics, ranging from Biology to Art, and from Maths to Music. Collins Reference Dictionaries fully maintain the reputation of Collins English and bilingual dictionaries for clarity, authority, comprehensiveness and ease-of-use.

For the series, Collins have commissioned expert authors who combine a profound understanding of their subject with great skill and experience in explaining and clarifying difficult terms and concepts. A consistent style and approach is adopted throughout the series with encyclopedic-style explanations following each precise initial definition. Where appropriate, extensive use is made of worked examples, line illustrations, graphs and tables to further aid the reader.

The academic titles are primarily designed to meet the needs of undergraduates, although the dictionaries will also be of considerable value to advanced school students and to people working in related disciplines. The general titles will provide the layman with comprehensive, lively and up-to-date reference works for a wide range of subjects.

Details of some of this exciting new range of dictionaries can be found on the following pages.

COLLINS DICTIONARY OF ART AND ARTISTS

General Editor: Sir David Piper

Collins Dictionary of Art and Artists is the most up-to-date and comprehensive dictionary of art available in paperback. It covers all schools and periods of Western art – from the Ancient Greeks to the present day – in over 2,500 entries. As well as the giants of painting and sculpture, the Dictionary also includes many fascinating minor figures, and in addition there are entries on groups, movements, writers on art, materials, and techniques.

Contributed by a panel of more than 70 scholars under the General Editorship of Sir David Piper, the entries are succinct, accurate and lively, forming an authoritative guide to all the names and terms the general reader might wish to look up. Entries range in length from a few lines up to 700 words, and although they are concise they do much more than simply list facts. Artists are firmly characterized so as to give the reader a clear idea not only of their work but also of their significance in the history of art. Thousands of works of art are cited, with dates and locations, and the text is enlivened with contemporary anecdotes and quotations.

Sir David Piper is Director of the Ashmolean Museum in Oxford, and one of the most distinguished art historians and critics of his generation. His numerous publications range from the scholarly to the popular, and he has reached a wide audience as one of the presenters of the BBC television series *100 Great Paintings*.

ISBN 0 00 434358 1

COLLINS DICTIONARY OF MUSIC

Sir Jack Westrup and F. L. Harrison
Revised by Conrad Wilson

Collins Dictionary of Music is a concise third edition of the critically acclaimed *Collins Encyclopedia of Music*, and brings that work right up to date with the inclusion of entries on such figures as Jessye Norman, Michael Berkeley, Arvo Pärt, Nigel Osborne, Janet Glover, Philip Glass, Steve Reich and Nigel Kennedy. In addition, existing entries have been updated with, for example, the inclusion of composers' new works, and details of performers' recent careers.

Covering the whole field of Western music, over 6,500 articles describe composers, instruments, compositions, technical terms, performers, musical forms, periods, styles, movements, critics, musicologists, librettists, instrument makers, orchestras, and opera companies.

The essay-length articles on the major composers include a biographical outline and an assessment of their achievements, together with a list of their principal compositions. Extensive articles have also been devoted to such topics as the history of opera, ballet, film music, and music criticism. The numerous articles on musical theory and notation, carefully cross-referenced, are clarified by the use of music examples, and there is also an appendix of signs and symbols.

The late Sir Jack Westrup was Oxford Professor of Music and one of the foremost musical scholars of his day. Frank Harrison has had a distinguished teaching career, his posts having included professorships at Amsterdam, Yale and Princeton. Conrad Wilson, who also revised the second edition, is music critic of *The Scotsman*.

ISBN 0 00 434356 5

COLLINS DICTIONARY OF QUOTATIONS

Donald Fraser

"I might repeat to myself, slowly and soothingly, a list of quotations beautiful from minds profound; if I can remember any of the damn things." *Dorothy Parker.*

Very much a book for the 1980s, the coverage of the *Collins Dictionary of Quotations* ranges from Thucydides to Thatcher, from William Shakespeare to Woody Allen, taking in all the classics as well as the colourful and witty sayings of the 20th century. The wit and wisdom, pithiness and poetry of over 1,300 authors provide a total of over 8,000 quotations, all arranged alphabetically by author. The extensive index, a vitally important part of any dictionary of quotations, comprises one third of the book, and features both keywords and the phrases in which they occur.

As a reference work the Dictionary can be used to verify half-remembered quotations, or to give the source of common phrases or sayings whose origin has been forgotten. It can also be used – with the aid of the index – to suggest apposite quotations on particular subjects, or simply to provide hours of entertaining browsing.

Donald Fraser is a lecturer in English at the University of Strathclyde. He is also the co-author of *A Dictionary of Musical Quotations*.

ISBN 0 00 434350 6

COLLINS DICTIONARY OF BIOLOGY

W. G. Hale and J. P. Margham

The *Collins Dictionary of Biology* is a completely new, authoritative and comprehensive guide to the complex discipline of biology. The book is directed primarily to the needs of undergraduates and advanced school students, but will also prove an invaluable source book for anyone with an interest in this wide-ranging and fascinating subject.

The Dictionary has over 5,600 entries ranging from *abdomen* to *zymogen*. There are also 285 diagrams illustrating such features as the generalized structures of animals, genetic organization, parts of plants and animals, etc., plus numerous tables.

All the major fields within biology are covered, including anatomy, biochemistry, ecology, genetics, physiology, evolutionary theory and taxonomy. The entries have been structured to provide more than an isolated definition of the term in question. An entry such as *acquired characters* is thus set in the context of the development of evolutionary theory, while the series of genetic entries guides the reader through such concepts as the basis of *genetic code* and the industrial implications of *genetic engineering*. The Dictionary also includes brief biographies of major biologists.

Professor Hale is Dean of the Faculty of Science and Head of the Department of Biology at Liverpool Polytechnic. Dr Margham is Principal Lecturer and Course Leader for the B.Sc. Honours Applied Biology Degree at Liverpool Polytechnic.

ISBN 0 00 434351 4

COLLINS DICTIONARY OF ECONOMICS

Christopher Pass, Bryan Lowes and Leslie Davies

The *Collins Dictionary of Economics* is a completely new and definitive guide to the intricate structures and forces of the economic world. The Dictionary is addressed primarily to the requirements of undergraduates and advanced school students, but will also prove an invaluable reference book for students of the subject at a wide range of levels or for anyone studying economics as part of a broader-based course such as business studies or social science.

The Dictionary has over 1,700 entries – from *ability-to-pay principle of taxation* to *zero-sum game*. There are also over 190 diagrams, plus numerous tables. Essential mathematical and statistical terms are included, as are brief biographies of major economists.

In addition to providing clear definitions of economic terms, the Dictionary summarizes the important theoretical principles behind the science of economics, from the "invisible hand" of Smith and the class analysis of Marx to the "rigid wages" of Keynes and the free-market monetarism of Friedman.

As well as the basic definition and explanation of a particular term, the reader who requires further exposition is guided, where appropriate, through cross references to related terms and refinements of the original concept.

Dr Pass and Dr Lowes are lecturers in managerial economics at the University of Bradford's Management Centre. Dr Davies is a research assistant at the same institution.

ISBN 0 00 434353 0

COLLINS DICTIONARY OF MATHEMATICS

Ephraim Borowski and Jonathan Borwein

Containing over 4,000 entries and 400 diagrams, this is the only reference work at this level to present this coverage at an accessible price. Covering an enormous range of technical terms from both pure and applied maths, the Dictionary goes beyond basic definitions to provide helpful explanations and examples, geared to the level of student who is liable to be looking up the particular term.

At undergraduate level, the reader will find extensive information on such fields as real and complex analysis, abstract algebra, number theory, metamathematics and the foundations of mathematics, topology, vector calculus, continuum mechanics, differential equations, measure theory, and graph theory. At the advanced school level the subjects covered include set theory, matrices, trigonometry and geometry, calculus, mechanics, statistics, and logic. The biographies of major mathematicians and the discursive explanations of paradoxes also make the Dictionary interesting and informative for the browser, and help to round off what will be an ideal course companion at many levels.

Ephraim Borowski, B.Phil., is a lecturer in philosophy at Glasgow University with a particular interest in logic and the philosophy of mathematics. He is also mathematics consultant to the *Collins English Dictionary*. Dr Jonathan Borwein is a professor of mathematics at Dalhousie University, Nova Scotia.

ISBN 0 00 434347 6

COLLINS DICTIONARY OF STATISTICS

Roger Porkess

The *Collins Dictionary of Statistics* is a new and authoritative guide to a subject which has seen a marked increase in its teaching and applications in recent years, in the academic sphere and beyond.

Encyclopedic in treatment after each initial definition, its 426 entries have been selected primarily to cater for the needs of students studying mathematics for university entrance exams, at A level or similar, and for those studying statistics as a service subject in higher education such as scientists and social scientists. However, the Dictionary will also prove to be an invaluable reference guide for the informed layman with a professional interest in the subject.

A comprehensive range of concepts and terms are covered – from *abscissa* to *z-transformation* – including how various statistical measures are calculated and their tests applied. Many of the more advanced topics are dealt with at length and the text contains over 100 graphs and diagrams and numerous worked examples to aid the reader. The Dictionary also contains a useful series of appendices which include full lists of symbols and formulae used, together with the statistical tables required for the tests and techniques described within the book.

Roger Porkess is Head of Mathematics at Denstone College, Uttoxeter and is an experienced A-level examiner. He has written several textbooks, including *Mathematics: a Complete Course for First Examinations*, and the Datalog computing books.

ISBN 0 00 434354 9

COLLINS DICTIONARY OF COMPUTING

Ian R. Sinclair

Aimed primarily at those using microcomputers as a tool – whether it be at university, school or college, or in the home or office – rather than the professional computer expert, the Dictionary will also prove invaluable to anyone whose work is related in any way to computers, be they micro, mini or mainframe.

Far too many computer manuals assume that even the beginner knows the meaning of a vast array of specialized jargon, leaving the user in a state of near despair. Although not a handbook to particular machines, *Collins Dictionary of Computing* contains definitions and explanations of over 2,000 of the terms that the average user is most likely to come across, from *access* to *zero compression*. Written with a clarity and precision that will be welcomed by all computer users, the entries are augmented by nearly 100 diagrams and explanatory captions.

Comprehensive without indulging in unnecessary padding, and of course completely up-to-date, the Dictionary includes such basic terms as *BASIC*, *bit* and *binary*, as well as those strange terms that computer buffs have made peculiarly their own, such as *blow*, *bomb* and *bubble*. Fields covered range through hardware, software, programming, computer logic, data and word processing, languages, systems, and graphics, to those areas of information technology in which computers play such a vital role.

Ian Sinclair, a full-time technical author, has written numerous best-selling computer books for Collins, and is also author of the *Collins Dictionary of Electronics*.

ISBN 0 00 434349 2

COLLINS DICTIONARY OF ELECTRONICS

Ian R. Sinclair

The *Collins Dictionary of Electronics* is a completely new and up-to-date guide to the science and technology of electronics. Containing over 2,000 entries, from *aberration* to *zero error*, the Dictionary also includes over 100 diagrams, together with lists of symbols used in electronics.

The Dictionary is intended for anyone who needs a source book providing clear, helpful definitions of electronic terms, including advanced school students and those embarking on higher-education courses, as well as technicians and hobbyists. The Dictionary will also prove useful to anyone whose work or study involves the use of electronic devices – which now have become vital tools in areas as diverse as music, archaeology and medicine.

The Dictionary guides the reader through the various fields within electronics such as microprocessor technology, digital electronics, telecommunications, hi-fi, radio, and television. The emphasis throughout is on the practical application of concepts and devices, although the theoretical background is also well covered, and the reader will find entries on such topics as the *superposition theorem*, the *Biot-Savart law*, and the *permeability* and *permittivity of free space*. Where appropriate, the mathematical aspect of a topic is introduced, although this is generally avoided.

Ian R. Sinclair is a professional technical author. He has written many books on computing for Collins, including the *Collins Dictionary of Computing*.

ISBN 0 00 434345 X